STORY OF NATIONS

HOLT, RINEHART AND WINSTON INC., NEW YORK • TORONTO • LONDON • SYDNEY

STORY OF NATIONS

LESTER B. ROGERS • FAY ADAMS • WALKER BROWN

About the Authors:

LESTER B. ROGERS: Late Dean of the School of Education, University of Southern California

FAY ADAMS: Professor of Education, University of Southern California

WALKER BROWN: Late Principal of Alexander Hamilton High School, Los Angeles

Consultants:

Edwin Karpf: Teacher of Social Studies,
Bronx High School of Science, New York
Robert K. Windbiel: Teacher of Social Studies,
White Plains High School, White Plains, New York

Cover Illustration: Marvin Goldman

Photo Acknowledgements: to be found on page 787

Printed in the United States of America
ISBN: 0-03-003821-9

9012 039 987

Preface

With this revision, *Story of Nations* has passed its thirty-ninth anniversary. Through its pages generations of students have learned the fascinating story of man from his earliest appearance on earth to his life in the twentieth century.

When *Story of Nations* first appeared it introduced new concepts in the teaching of history. In the first place, it was written to hold the attention of students. The study of history ought to be an exciting adventure of discovery, and the authors tried to convey both the reality and the drama of the past. *Story of Nations* emphasized people and the roles they have played—how men have acted and interacted to create what we know as history. The value of this approach has been amply confirmed by the enthusiastic response of teachers and students.

The readability of *Story of Nations* is made possible by the book's unique organization. The story of each people is told as an entity in itself. It is not necessary to consult numerous index entries to piece together the history of a single nation. When the student begins to study a nation or region he is assured that a single theme will be adequately developed without frequent detours into confusing and irrelevant bypaths. This approach has made it possible for young readers of widely varying ability gain a rich and well-rounded understanding of history.

The present *Story of Nations* retains the best features of earlier editions. Hundreds of teachers will recognize aspects of the text as time-tested friends. There is the same organization into nations, the same emphasis on people, and the same narrative style that presents a meaningful story rather than facts and dates in unrelated succession. But it is a truism that the world has never changed so rapidly as it has in recent years—and the pace of this change continues. This *Story of Nations* reflects our rapidly changing times.

Each section of the new *Story of Nations* has been revised according to the latest scholarly research. The sections on India, Southeast Asia, Africa, and Latin America give fuller treatment to the countries of these regions. Part 23, which discusses the contemporary international scene, gives emphasis to present-day developments.

As this edition of *Story of Nations* goes to press, the most important task facing the world continues to be the attainment of peace. A sympathetic understanding of the various cultures of the world's peoples is necessary for maintaining world peace, and *Story of Nations* gives special emphasis to each nation's scientific, cultural, and artistic accomplishments. These highlights show how writers, musicians, artists, and scientists all over the world have contributed to civilization. Study of their achievements emphasizes the common bonds that unite all men.

Story of Nations deals with the events that have most significantly affected man's life on earth. To help the student, a variety of features have been included. Major sections of the text open with a "geographic setting," which relates geographic factors to the history of the people who have lived and who now live in these regions. Full page maps enable the student to visualize areas about which he is reading. In each unit a "perspective"—a brief dramatic account—sets the tone and stresses the most important aspects of the chapters to follow. At the end of each chapter "check-up" questions enable the student to test his comprehension of the text. Within the chapters appear maps, time lines, charts, and illustrations, that help to make world history a vivid, and interesting story. Each Part of *Story of Nations* concludes with a synopsis, lists of significant terms and important people, questions for discussion and review, suggestions for reports, and projects, and an annotated bibliography.

Contents

PART 5 ROME RULER OF THE ANCIENT WORLD

PART 6 JUDAISM, CHRISTIANITY, ISLAM

FORCES THAT INFLUENCED THE WESTERN WORLD

PART 7 THE MIDDLE AGES AN AGE OF FAITH

PART 8 THE RENAISSANCE AND REFORMATION

BIRTH OF THE MODERN WORLD

PART 9 GREAT BRITAIN TRIUMPH OF REPRESENTATIVE GOVERNMENT

PART 10 FRANCE SEARCH FOR LIBERTY, EQUALITY, FRATERNITY

PART 11 THE LOW COUNTRIES

HEROIC RESISTANCE TO INVADERS AND THE SEA

Special Features

MAPS

CHARTS

TIME LINES

ARCHITECTURE THROUGH THE AGES

History—It Is Your Future

You are a very vital part of this country. You will be the men and women scientists, the business people, the thinkers and doers who will make the decisions and face the problems of living in this land in the years ahead. You are the ones who in ten, fifteen, or twenty years will determine the role and the posture of the United States both at home and throughout the world. You will be faced with such challenges of leadership, direction and moral decision making that will make today's concerns seem as games children play on a rainy afternoon.

But in order to become tomorrow's leaders and decision makers, you must have knowledge of where you are and where you have been. This introduction will focus on the present: the United States in the Nineteen Seventies. Where you have been, or, more specifically, where mankind has been, will be the main thrust of the book. But ultimately you will have to determine where you are going—and perhaps where America is going.

Perhaps the greatest concern of the American people in the Nineteen Seventies is peace. Establishing peace means a chance to regain stability of purpose in the political, social, economic and moral spheres of life. It means a chance for America to concentrate on its rightful priorities: an end to poverty, a reinvigoration of the cities, full employment, the total defeat of discrimination and prejudice, the conquest of disease, the protection of our natural environment, and, most of all, the moral triumph of human dignity.

The American people entered the decade of the seventies not having known peace for many years. In 1963, this country became strenuously engaged in the third largest war in American history with more than half a million military personnel engaged, nearly fifty thousand American dead and thousands of prisoners of war and men missing in action. And all this is to say nothing of the millions of killed, maimed, or displaced Vietnamese on both sides—either those actively involved in war or innocently surrounded by the brutality of aggression.

In 1954 President Eisenhower sent military advisors to South Vietnam after the Geneva Convention of 1954 had divided Vietnam between the North and South Vietnamese governments. It was a small, but important gesture in our attempt to stamp out Communism in Southeast Asia. In the early Sixties, President Kennedy continued to add to our forces, and by the time President Johnson was at the end of his term of office in 1968 more than five hundred thousand Americans were in Vietnam. With more and more grim reports of dead, wounded and missing being recorded by the press and the media; with the obvious evidence that we were not winning the war, in effect losing in certain areas to Chinese—and Soviet—supported North Vietnamese, the realization began to grow that perhaps the war, at least this war, was too high a price to pay for the loss of so many men, for so little in return: we were not defeating North Vietnam and only containing Communism. Even President Nixon assumed before taking office in 1969 that the war should end, but on terms that were honorable both to the United States and South Vietnam. He began to wind down the military action on the ground and recall our troops so that in 1972 we had fewer than fifty thousand ground personnel in Indochina. Efforts to end the war through negotiation continued all during this period, but the results were negligible. Even in 1971 when Cambodia and Laos were attacked by South Vietnamese troops and U.S. aircraft, the war continued unabated. And even when the North Vietnamese harbor of Haiphong was mined and when American B-52 bombers and U.S. Navy planes attacked in waves, the war continued seemingly without an end in sight.

The effect of all this at home during the late sixties and early seventies were devastating. Sides were formed and battle lines drawn among the people, government officials, and even in households. "Hawks," those in favor of continued war, and "Doves," those who wanted the war ended, fought it out in Congress, through the papers, on television, and even on the streets. Peace rallies and peace marches throughout the country created a split in our society that hadn't been seen since the Civil War.

In 1970 violence spilled onto the college campuses. At Kent State University in Ohio National Guard troops fired into students protesting the war and killed four. At Jackson State College in Mississippi, state police sent a hail of bullets into a dormitory killing two students and wounding nine others. Students all over the country reacted violently, breaking, entering, and destroying property. Many colleges closed temporarily to quiet the demonstrations. Even on Wall Street in New York City, construction workers carrying placards reading "Our country—love it or leave it" clashed with peace demonstrators carrying signs stating "End the slaughter now," and though no one was killed, the poison of hatred over the war was spreading into all segments of our society, and disrupting living on all levels, and in many different ways.

Economic problems began to hurt America in the late sixties and early seventies. Though some economists could argue that a mild depression was inevitable in our economy at regular intervals regardless of the war, others felt that the war's end would divert business from war to peace and provide new opportunities. Whatever the theory, it was obvious in 1972 that five million were unemployed, wages and prices were controlled, but inflation was rampant. Ask any housewife what it had cost to put a meal on the table in 1962 and what the same meal cost in 1972. To many there was no stability in the economic picture and even if the war were to end, the prospect for immediate economic advancement was not apparent.

The downward trend in our economy brought into sharp focus the plight of the poor, most of whom were ethnic minorities. Though the average income of all Americans in 1970 was over $3,800, the average income for the ethnic poor minorities was not even $2,000. Needless to say, protests and racial riots against economic injustice and human indignity burst forth in the sixties and spread into the seventies. As inflation continued to grow, it affected all, but none more than the poor, who were forced onto welfare, lived in substandard buildings and spent lives of noisy desperation in collapsing cities. The cities became plagued by rising costs, near financial bankruptcy, the problem of crime, drugs, and the flight of people to the suburbs.

The cities are vast, sprawling complexes that contain close to 65 percent of the population. New York City alone has a metropolitan population of over 16 million, and Chicago, Los Angeles, Philadelphia and others are bulging at the seams. This concentration of sheer numbers has brought problems that seem insurmountable. Transportation, traffic, health, education, welfare, pollution, and slums are on a scale that stagger the imagination. In New York City, the largest of our urban complexes, welfare is higher than any single item on the budget, even more than education.

But the cities are also the life blood of business and industry. Even though many corporations have moved from large cities to avoid congestion and high taxes, they still depend on the cities, as do the agricultural areas, for their markets and ultimate profits. The cities are also the cultural centers of the country, thriving with creative people in the arts, sciences, advertising and the media. It may be more pleasant living in rural areas and in the suburbs, but it is the excitement of the cities that lures the young and moves the destinies of countless millions. Sincere advocates of reform place the need of the cities as the most pressing concern of this country as we move into the middle seventies. The cities seemed to capsulize nearly all the problems besetting America.

By October, 1972 there seemed to be light at the end of the tunnel. After unprecedented air assaults by American bombers during the war, which surpassed the allied total of bombs dropped on Germany in World War II, negotiations between North Vietnam and the United States began to bear fruit. A cease fire appeared at hand.

The world hoped that the war was coming to a close. Despite the political warfare that existed between President Nixon and Senator George McGovern, the Democratic nominee for the presidency in 1972, both gave indication that the end of hostilities would begin to ease the domestic situation, provided that peace in Indochina would mean a return to domestic tranquility. Differences between the two candidates were significant especially on the domestic front, but both were agreed that the war had to end.

In November, 1972, President Nixon was re-elected by a huge majority, though the Democrats retained control of Congress. He pledged to bring about not only "peace with honor" in Vietnam, but "a new era of peace" and a "prosperity without war."

But if the war was to be over, how would this affect America? What was to be the position of the United States in relation to the rest of the world? Had we won? Hardly. Had we lost? Not really. Had we stopped Communism? Yes and no. But what did the rest of the world think of us? Were we still proud because we had stopped Communism after ten years of war? Did we know we were still the most powerful nation in the world? Were we now reevaluating our total commitment to the world community of nations? What were our goals? Where did we stand?

We are great and powerful, full of the mission of wanting for all what we have done for ourselves. Basically, we want to help all who are in need, but, sometimes, all too many times, we don't know how to go about it, or don't get our priorities in the right perspective.

While providing for most, we have neglected the few; our own sense of mission toward the Indian and the Black has been all too lacking.

We fought for ideals of life, liberty and the pursuit of happiness almost two hundred years ago. They are not idle nor indifferent statements of our country's worth. But we have perhaps been led too far away at times from their true meaning as the years progressed from 1776. They may now have become clouded or slightly misplaced in the problems of the present time. It is present time, not just today, which is in a sense the culprit, that makes the world about us confused and difficult to grasp. And because the present is the only time we do live in, we sometimes tend to think of the past as unimportant.

You could find an argument for this position. How can anyone believe anything? How can history really claim a position of worth when all it does is verify our distrust for all politicans, all governments, all people in power? Who wants to study history when all it does is show one side right, the other side wrong. All it does is favor dictatorship and neglect people, or favor democracy and neglect minorities; or try to be all things to all people and end up being nothing at all. As such, history is nothing more than showing how big and great and powerful anyone is, and how all the kings, dictators, and presidents become bigger and greater and more powerful than the people who gave them their rights and their powers.

So who cares? The past is something done and best forgotten or appreciated only when we think of wonderful times. The past we don't like, especially if there are problems still unsolved. It makes us fidgety. Yet we can't escape it. We dwell on the past personally, we think about past mistakes of our own, and wonderful moments we shared with our friends, and our families. The past need not be so ridiculous, nor meaningless, nor hateful when we have the good remembrance of things past.

But what has this to do with history?

History somehow takes on the pompous, the removed, the studied plaything of the scholars. It concerns itself with great events far from our daily lives. When you stop and remember the personal past that affected you most, you realize that somehow a person or event gave you an insight not only into himself and yourself, but also into the world around you. How many times have you said, "Yes, Mother and Father, or Grandad and Grandma made me understand?" But did you ever ask yourself why these people gave you this insight? Because they were not only acting as people, but also because they lived at a particular time—a time somewhat lost to you, but a time that influenced them as much as your time is now influencing you.

Thus it is with history. History gives you a real insight into yourself and a feeling for the world around you by knowing the past as real. But history isn't a one-way street. As in life, you too have to participate, and give back what you feel about man in his time and place. But don't be overawed by great names and events that have happened in the past; if you are, history will become a parade ground and you merely the onlooker. Think of the people you will meet, great and small, as people who helped and hindered their own; think of these people with the same loves, hates, joys and concerns as you have, not as cold figures forever frozen in time as on a vase. Even John Keats, the English poet, never thought the figures on the Grecian urn as static, but forever in motion. And history, like the urn "...shall remain in midst of other woe than ours, a friend to man..."

The text that follow this introduction is not designed to be a collection of historical facts, but a pointer, a sign post toward the discovery of a historical consciousness, a beginning of your self realization. In the book itself, though it is full of facts, you will discover that the main seam that binds the Story of Nations together is the feeling and the real consciousness that man can begin to achieve understanding of himself and others, (and begin to attain peace of mind and peace between men) if he will begin to understand and to profit by the past. The past, however, is not a wonder drug or a miracle worker. It is only that reminder so we don't forget.

Artifacts and skeletal remains indicate man's story may have begun two million years ago. This 20,000 year-old skull belonged to a young girl who lived in what is now southern France.

Part 1
EARLY MAN
FORERUNNER OF CIVILIZATION

Early Man: PERSPECTIVE

Most scientists assert the earth was born at least four billion years ago. Some scientists even think that it may already have lived about a third of its life. They believe that sometime within the next few billion years, the sun may become an explosive inferno of such incredible heat that it will scorch and char the entire surface of the earth. Then all forms of life would vanish. It is small wonder that an English author once characterized the earth as "but a small parenthesis in eternity."

The story of the earth has many chapters, and the history of man forms only a brief paragraph or so toward the end of the chapter in which we live. Indeed, it is only during the last million years that we and our ancestors have walked the face of the earth. Before that, there were strange beasts and birds and swimming creatures, and before that there were no living things at all.

Story of Nations, which tells about man's part in the "small parenthesis in eternity," opens in Chapter 1 on a panorama of the infant earth as it probably looked before life appeared. You will learn how the earth may have been formed, how it has changed through the ages, and in what ways it is still changing. You will read about the first simple creatures and about the later animals that stalked the dense forests thousands of years ago. In Chapter 2 you will finally see the appearance of man on the earth. Later chapters of *Story of Nations* will chronicle man's activities since his arrival on earth.

CHAPTER 1

In the Silence of Space, the Earth Was Born

SCIENTISTS THINK THE EARTH HAS EXISTED FOR BILLIONS OF YEARS

No one knows exactly how old the earth is. Geologists, the scientists who study soil and rocks to discover the earth's story, say that it is at least four billion years old. Some form of animal life has existed for perhaps a quarter of that time, but again no one can be certain. Man's earliest ancestor probably appeared less than two million years ago. Thus man has inhabited the earth for a tiny fraction of its existence. Indeed, if for the sake of comparison we consider the age of the earth as one year, then man arrived only two hours ago and began to leave written records only ten minutes ago!

What happened during the long period before man appeared? Written records of man and his life go back less than seven thousand years. The many thousands of years before man began to do his first crude writing is called the *prehistoric* period; the comparatively brief time during which he has been recording his story is known as the *historic* period. Prehistoric events are known only dimly. The hand of time has erased many traces of what happened before man appeared on the planet. Examining scraps of evidence, however, geologists and other scientists have been able to piece together parts of the earth's story.

The earth's crust is made up of layers called strata (*stray*-tuh), which extend far down into the earth. By digging into the strata of rock, shale, sediment, and soil, geologists can tell what the earth was like when successive layers were being formed. They have learned that the earth has gone through tremendous changes since its birth billions of years ago.

THE EARTH'S SURFACE HAS UNDERGONE MANY CHANGES

As the molten earth cooled, land and seas formed. The earth probably began as a huge mass of liquid gas and flame which cooled gradually. The earth's crust started to grow firm, and the sea of air we call atmosphere surrounded the world. Great masses of land formed. Rains came and began to wash away the land and carry it toward the sea which was forming in the great hollows of the earth.

Land surfaces shifted and changed. Dry land sank beneath the surface of the sea, and sea floors rose to become dry land. Molten lava came out of the earth and formed new land. The cooling of the earth's interior forced the crust to fold and buckle, causing what we call earthquakes. The great upheavals formed high mountains and deep valleys through which rivers flowed in sharply twisting courses. When young mountains were formed they were rough and jagged, much as the Rocky Mountains are today. Gradually wind, rain, and rivers wore down the rough surfaces until they became rounded like the Appalachian Mountains, which were formed millions of years before the Rockies. The rivers, wearing away their banks, straightened out and broadened as the Mississippi has.

Erosion helped shape the earth's surface. We know that wind, rain, and running water constantly wear away the earth's surface. This wearing-down process is called *erosion*. Perhaps the most dramatic form of erosion began a little over a million years ago when great rivers of ice, or glaciers, started to move across the earth, digging valleys, and leaving trails of polished boulders, gravel, and grooved rock. Pushing southward over the earth's surface like giant carpenter's planes, glaciers have left their marks on the valleys and lakes of the British Isles, France, and Germany. Our own Great Lakes were scooped out by the mighty force of these flowing ice sheets.

During this million-year period known as the *Glacial Age*, ice covered much of North America and Europe four different times. No one is certain what caused the ice to appear and disappear. Apparently something happened to make the climate of the earth much colder. Each year the snow and ice piled higher and higher, until glaciers were hundreds of feet thick. When they began to move, either under the pull of gravity or their own pressure, they covered much of the land in the earth's Temperate Zones. Though the last great glacial advance ended about twenty-five thousand years ago, glaciers still remain on the earth. Greenland and Antarctica are largely covered by vast ice sheets called continental glaciers. Smaller glaciers, called mountain glaciers, can still be found in the Alps, the Himalayas,

Spiral Nebula. Far off in space, this whirling mass of flaming gas looks like a giant pinwheel. Scientists think the earth and the other planets may have been formed when spiral nebulae like this one cooled billions of years ago.

A Glacier. Under the pull of gravity and the weight of its own pressure, the Rhone Glacier in Switzerland inches downward from the Alps like a vast river of ice.

the Andes, the Rockies, and most other high mountain ranges.

The earth has never stopped changing. Perhaps you have visited the seashore in the summer. If you returned the next summer, you may have noticed that the contours of the beach have changed. Or you may have seen the gulleys formed in a hillside by a heavy rainfall. These are examples of the way in which the earth's surface is constantly changing. Ice is still wearing it away. Erosion by wind and water goes on all the time. Fertile lands become barren, desert regions begin to get rain, rivers change course, lakes dry up, small islands appear or disappear, and land masses rise or fall. Most of the changes occur so slowly that you do not realize they are happening, but occasionally a violent change reminds us of the continuing process. New volcanoes burst forth every few years. Earthquakes occur every day somewhere in the world. Sometimes gradually and sometimes with terrible swiftness, the earth's surface has been changing constantly during the billions of years it has existed.

Chapter Check-up

1. What is a geologist?
2. How old have geologists estimated the earth to be?
3. How long has some form of animal life existed on earth?
4. How long ago did man's earliest ancestor probably first appear?
5. What is the difference between prehistoric and historic times?
6. How far back can we trace some kind of written records of man?
7. How do we know what happened on earth before man began to keep records?
8. What is meant by the term *erosion?*
9. What was the Glacial Age?
10. What evidence is there that the earth's surface is still changing?

CHAPTER 2

The Earth Became the Home of Man

LIFE APPEARED MILLIONS OF YEARS AGO

Cells were the earliest forms of life. For the first half of its life, the earth was a shifting mass of rock, soil, and water. Its crust wrinkled into great mountains, and oceans formed as water condensed out of the cooling atmosphere. Then, in the vast silence of the lifeless planet, a miraculous event took place: life emerged.

There is of course no record of this extraordinary event, but scientists think that life first appeared as a simple one-celled organism which grew at the edges of lakes and oceans where the shallow water was warmed by the sun. From this single form, increasingly complex water plants and sea animals slowly developed. After the passage of millions of years these primitive animals began to creep from the sea onto the bank. The struggle to exist under the new conditions gradually caused them to change. To breathe air, they developed lungs; to walk, they grew legs.

The first land animals were reptiles, cold-blooded creatures covered with scales or bone as modern lizards, crocodiles, and turtles are. During the *Age of Reptiles,* huge lizard-like creatures, the dinosaurs, roamed the earth's warm marshlands. Although the largest dinosaur was nearly five times as long as an elephant, it was a peaceful, plant-eating beast. Indeed, its gentleness often made it the prey of a smaller, fiercer, meat-eating dinosaur that walked upright on its hind legs. The dinosaurs probably died out when the swamps dried up and left too little for the great beasts to eat.

Through the ages, warm-blooded birds and early forms of mammals developed. Then, shortly before the Ice Age began, the most advanced of the earth's creatures appeared: man.

Tools are clues to the story of early man. How did scientists learn when or where man first arrived on earth? They know that two of the characteristics that distinguish man from the animals are his larger brain and skull, and his ability to use tools. Archaeologists (ar-kee-*ahl*-oh-jists), men who study the remains of prehistoric man, carefully examine strata of the earth's surface. When they discover skulls with large brain cavities, or bits of bone and rock that have been used as tools, they know they have found traces of human life. As we saw in Chapter 1, geologists know when the various strata of the earth were built up. They can thus tell approximately when the men who used the tools lived. Since these remains have turned up in Europe, Asia, and Africa, and since many seem to be of approximately the same date, archaeologists conclude that early man did not have one single place of origin but appeared at about the same time in many parts of the Eastern and Western hemispheres. You will read about the known types of prehistoric man later in this chapter.

The first tool was probably a stone which an early hunter picked up to hurl at some animal. Then man learned that with his intelligence and his nimble hands he could make the stone serve his purposes better. He discovered, for example, that he could use one stone to chip a cutting edge on another. Because stone tools are more likely than any other objects to withstand the effects of time, archaeologists use the development of early man's tools to divide his story into periods. The thousands of years (*c.* 1,000,000? B.C.–*c.* 8000 B.C.) during which men used clumsy tools of chipped stone is called the *Old Stone Age.* It corresponds in time to the Ice Age. The period during which men used polished stone tools is called the *New Stone Age* (*c.* 5000–3500 B.C.). You will see, however, that these periods were also marked by far more important changes than the changing styles in tools.

PREHISTORIC ANIMALS. *Above:* In the Age of Reptiles over 100 million years ago, huge dinosaurs roamed the wild forests and marshlands of the earth. *Left:* Their immense size may be seen by comparing the skeleton with the man below it. This reconstructed dinosaur may be seen at the American Museum of Natural History in New York City.

OLD STONE AGE MEN WERE HUNTERS

Most of the remains of Old Stone Age man were crushed and destroyed by the glaciers that moved southward over Europe and Asia in four stages during the Ice Age. Only occasionally do archaeologists come across enough bones or artifacts to form a picture of the *culture,* or way of life, of Old Stone Age man.

The earliest known artifacts, fossilized bones and crude tools, were discovered in 1959 by a British anthropologist, Dr. L. S. B. Leakey, in the Olduvai Gorge in the African country of Tanzania, south of the glacier area. According to the potassium-argon dating method, which determines the age of fossils by measuring the atomic change in nearby rock samples, these bones and tools are at least 1.75 million years old.

Other fossils had been discovered in 1891 on Java, one of the main islands of Indonesia. From

EARLY MAN. Dr. L. S. B. Leakey, famed British scientist is shown examining bone fragments at Oldvai Gorge in Kenya. His findings have placed early man as far back as two and a half million years.

these remains—four skulls and some leg bones which are about 500,000 years old—scientists have described an early type of man called Java man. He was about five and a half feet tall; walked in a stooped position, and had a rather small skull.

The remains of Peking man date later than both Java man and the Olduvai fossils. Among these remains, found near Peking, China, were charred bones. These reveal that Peking man made one of the most important discoveries of early man—fire. He probably found a tree that had been set afire by a bolt of lightning and decided to bring a smoldering branch home to his cave. He soon learned that fire kept him warm, frightened away wild animals, and greatly improved the taste of meat.

Neanderthal man took important steps forward. Valuable clues to the progress of early man are revealed by Neanderthal man, whose bones were discovered in a cave in the Neander Valley in Germany. He and his relatives lived in Europe and Africa between the third and fourth glacial periods, approximately 100,000 years ago. His bone structure reveals that he had a large brain, even though his low forehead, jutting jaw, and receding chin made him look as much like an ape as a man. He was short and stooped and had powerful arms.

As the increasingly cold climate brought by the fourth glacier approached, Neanderthal man

NEANDERTHAL HUNTERS. Emerging from the mouth of their cave, these early men are preparing to hunt the game that provided them with most of the necessities of their life.

sought shelter in caves. The bones he tossed on the cave floor after dinner indicate the animals that were his food: the woolly mammoth, the rhinoceros, the Scandinavian reindeer, the fox, the wild horse, the bear, the lynx, the saber-toothed tiger, and the hare. These creatures also supplied Neanderthal man with skins for clothing and with bone for tools and jewelry. Neanderthal man's whole livelihood depended on his ability as a hunter and food gatherer.

Although he spent most of his time defending and feeding himself and his family, Neanderthal man did not think only of the present. In 1908 archaeologists found in France the skeleton of a young Neanderthal boy. The head was pillowed on a small pile of stones. A fine fist hatchet lay close to his hand, and bones of wild cattle surrounded him. These articles seem to indicate that Neanderthal man wanted to provide for life after death.

Neanderthal man gradually developed different tools for different purposes. Rounded stone fist hatchets were displaced by choppers, drills, scrapers, and spear heads. By using tools Neanderthal man was taking the first steps toward a more advanced kind of life.

Cro-Magnon man was a remarkable artist. As the fourth glacier slowly receded about 75,000 years ago, Neanderthal man gradually disappeared. No one knows exactly why his race vanished from the earth. Many archaeologists think that some Neanderthal men were already developing into so-called modern man. Modern man in Europe, known as Cro-Magnon man, was a handsome six-footer with a broad face, a high, intelligent forehead, and a square chin. He stood as straight as men now do. If he were alive today, you would not be able to distinguish him from other existing men. Cro-Magnon man took over the caves of the extinct Neanderthal man and hunted the same animals.

The most remarkable accomplishments of Cro-Magnon man were his paintings, which can still be seen on the walls of dark caves in France and northern Spain. Almost all the paintings are of animals. Archaeologists conclude that the artist created them as a form of magic rather than as decoration. Cro-Magnon man probably believed that if he painted a picture of a successful hunting expedition, showing game wounded by spears or arrows, this would somehow help to bring about the actual occurrence. In order to make his magic

AT A GLANCE—THE EARTH AND EARLY MAN

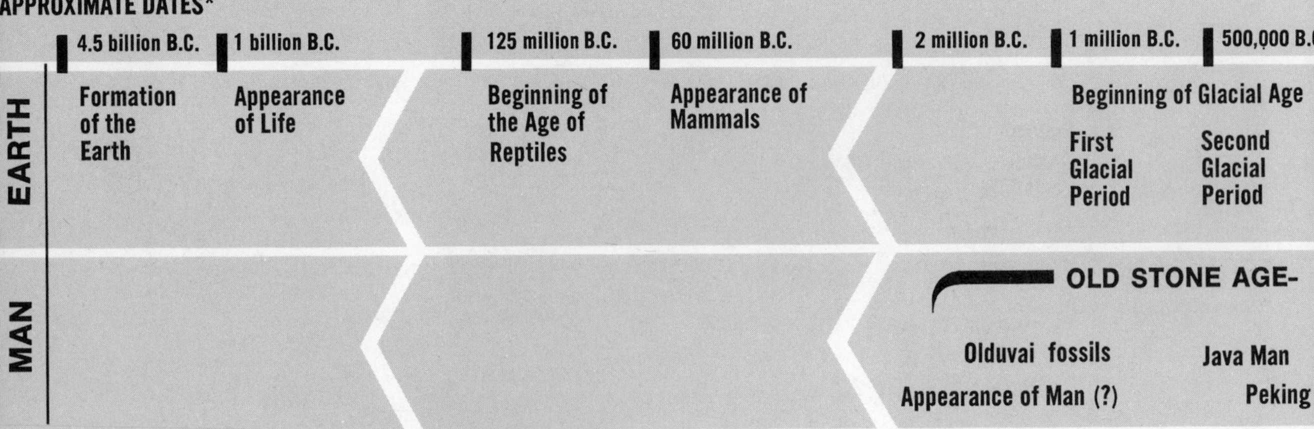

*The time scale of this chart will continue to be modified by new research.

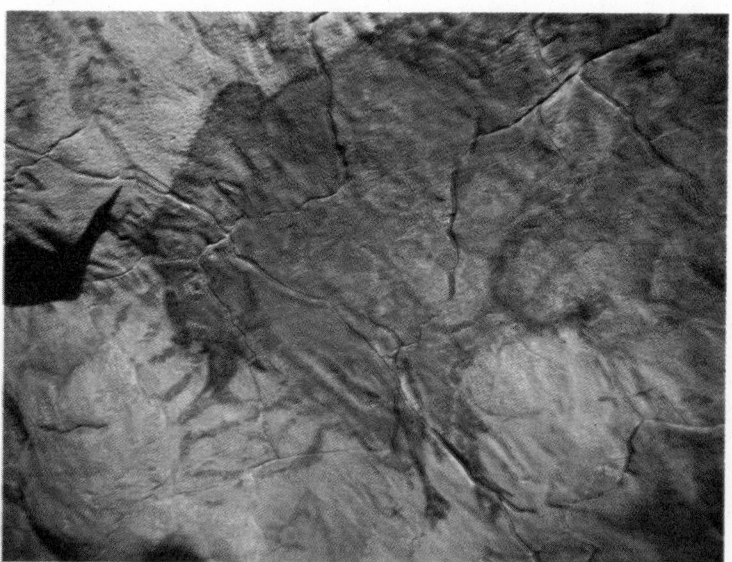

PREHISTORIC PAINTING. This painting of a bison is one of many found on the walls and roof of a cave at Altamira in northern Spain. It was painted during the Old Stone Age, probably between 30,000 and 10,000 B.C. The cave was discovered in 1868 and the paintings were first noticed in 1879.

as effective as possible, he made the drawings as lifelike as he could.

Cro-Magnon man also fashioned small stone figures of animals and humans and learned to decorate his weapons by carving designs in the handles. With bone needles, he sewed clothing out of animal hides. He learned how to light a fire by rubbing two sticks together so that he did not have to depend on a lightning-struck tree or worry about perpetually guarding the tribal fire. He probably had a larger vocabulary than Neanderthal man. Language gave him an enormous advantage over animals because he could convey all his own knowledge and experiences to succeeding generations.

Modern man is divided into three physical types. During the Old Stone Age, Neanderthal men were developing slight physical differences, perhaps as a result of the climate and other conditions of their homelands. As modern man de-

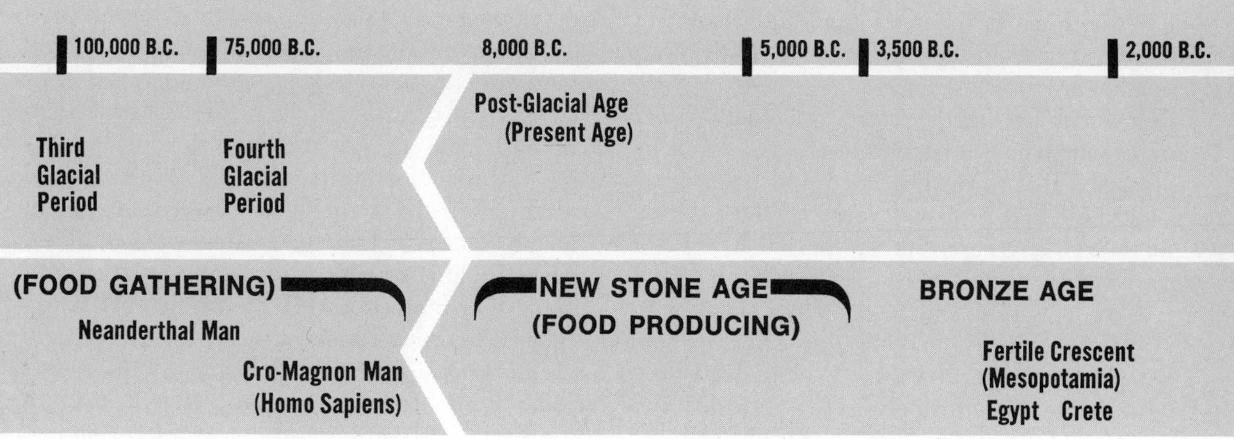

veloped, these differences became more marked. Today scientists recognize that all men belong to one great human family, or species, called *homo sapiens* ("thinking man"), which is divided into three physical types based on such characteristics as shape of the skull, type of hair, and skin color. Caucasians (kaw-*kay*-zhunz) have the least pigment in the skin, and Negroes have the most. Mongolians have yellow or red pigment.

No one is sure where the Caucasians originated. We do know, however, that in a series of migrations they moved into Europe, northern Africa, the Middle East, and India. The Negroes probably first appeared in Africa south of the Sahara Desert and in Southern Asia. From here they may have migrated to the islands of the Pacific. The Mongolians apparently developed in Central Asia and spread to Siberia, China, Japan, and Southeast Asia. No one of these groups, or *races*, remained isolated from the others. In the course of migration there was much intermarriage. The result was the development of many racial subdivisions such as the Polynesians (pahl-in-*nee*-zhunz) in the Pacific and the Dravidians in India. The United States has large numbers of the three major races: Caucasians (Europeans), Negroes (Africans), and Mongolians (Chinese, Japanese, and American Indians).

NEW STONE AGE MEN LEARNED TO PRODUCE THEIR OWN FOOD

As the fourth glacier disappeared, many areas in the Southern Hemisphere that had supported rich animal life became deserts, and areas in the north that had been buried under ice and snow became habitable. Old Stone Age men had to adjust to these climatic changes. Some of them followed the receding glacier northward into newly created forest areas where they could continue to live as hunters. Those who remained had to find a new way of obtaining food. As they became farmers and shepherds, their new life marked a revolutionary change in man's history. Farming, far more than the use of polished stone tools, marks the most important change in the transition from the Old Stone Age to the New Stone Age.

How man learned the secrets of agriculture will probably remain a mystery forever. No doubt he discovered that wild wheat, rice, and barley were good to eat, and he may have stored them during the winter. Perhaps one day he left a heap of grain where rain or flood waters soaked it. Soon it began to sprout and send up tall stalks with heads of grain. Observing this phenomenon, New Stone Age man began to plant seeds and create his own food supply. He still fished and hunted, but agriculture freed him from absolute dependence on wild plants and animals. By farming the land, he was able to live in areas where wild animals had died out. As his supply of grain increased, he was able to use some of it as fodder for his livestock.

Many of the New Stone Age men, especially those who lived in plains areas, specialized in keeping flocks of domesticated animals. They became wandering herdsmen, or nomads, and spent their lives roaming the plains in search of food for their animals. Their ceaseless quest is one reason for the many migrations of the New Stone Age.

Men learned to live in communities. The development of agriculture and the domestication of animals meant that man had changed from a food-gatherer to a food-producer and had thus taken another important step toward civilization. Because man now raised crops instead of wandering in search of game, he was able to settle in one place and build a shelter for his family. Soon men began to live together in small villages. They built low huts of woven branches plastered with mud. For protection they made fences of sharpened poles or built their huts on posts in the middle of lakes. One such village was discovered about a hundred years ago in Switzerland when the level of a lake dropped during a dry summer. On the lake bottom was a forest of wooden posts

A NEW STONE AGE VILLAGE. Some groups of New Stone Age men settled in villages such as this one, which was modeled from those discovered in Switzerland. These lake dwellers wove cloth and made furniture and pottery. They also grew grain and vegetables; earlier men had only collected and gathered food.

and heaps of rubbish that New Stone Age villagers had discarded.

Pottery and weaving marked important steps in man's development. The rubbish heaps at the bottom of lakes in Europe show that New Stone Age man knew how to make pottery and weave cloth. The development of these skills marked a great step foıward. Man had discovered that the clay under his feet and certain plants in the ground could be fashioned into dishes and cloth. Primitive baskets were made of woven reeds daubed with clay. When someone used one of these baskets as a cooking utensil, he discovered that heat hardened the clay and made it waterproof. Gradually man learned to fashion clay pots without using reeds and to harden them by baking them in an oven. Later he decorated them with paintings. Broken pieces of pottery give archaeologists valuable clues to the dates of various settlements of New Stone Age man.

New Stone Age man left mysterious monuments. Archaeologists have identified a number of unusual monuments left by men of the New Stone Age. How they were built or what purpose they served is uncertain. One of the most famous is at Stonehenge in England where a number of huge dressed stone slabs are arranged in a circle, their tops spanned by horizontal slabs. Within this outer ring other stones from a horseshoe around a flat stone that may have been an altar. The stones are aligned, their lintels leveled with great care. The axis of the Stonehenge monument is in line with sunrise at midsummer. At Carnac in France long rows of huge upright stones also seem to lead directly to the sun at certain times of the year. Archaeologists think that Stonehenge and Carnac may have been open-air observatories in which men made calculations about the sun. Many scientists believe they were also places of worship.

New Stone Age man was unaware of the scientific explanation of such natural events as the rising and the setting of the sun, thunder and lightning, and the sprouting of new grain in the spring. He probably believed such occurrences were under

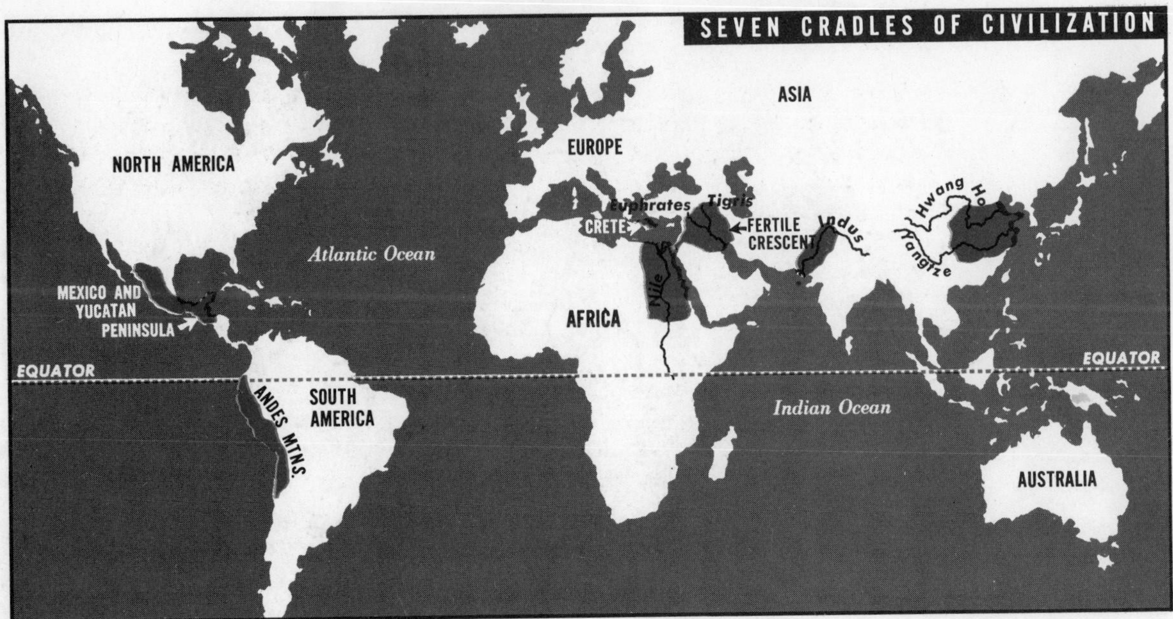

the influence of spirits or nature-gods whose favor he tried to win by offering them sacrifices.

New Stone Age man lived in seven cradles of civilization. Although evidence indicates that New Stone Age men lived in many parts of the world, their achievements were particularly advanced in seven areas or centers. These were 1) the valley of the Nile River in Egypt, 2) the valley of the Tigris and Euphrates rivers in Mesopotamia, 3) the valley of the Indus River in western India, 4) the valley of the Hwang Ho River in northern China, 5) the island of Crete in the Mediterranean Sea, 6) the Andes Mountains in South America, and 7) the Yucatan Peninsula, Mexico, and Central America. In these areas men brought agriculture, crafts, community living, language, and religion to high levels of development. They improved farming implements and learned to irrigate their fields. They made beautiful pottery and fine, brilliantly dyed cloth.

As they began to live together in villages and as life became more complex, early men appointed rulers and made laws to regulate community affairs. Religion became organized around local gods and the priests who served them. Often the priests were chosen to be the heads of the government. Gradually language became more exact and was written down. In the course of these developments, men passed from the primitive stages of savagery and barbarism and became civilized. You will read about each of the seven cradles of civilization and the men who dwelt in them in the following Parts of *Story of Nations.*

Chapter Check-up

1. What are two of the characteristics that distinguish man from the other animals?
2. How do archaeologists help us to learn more about prehistoric man?
3. How have scientists been able to suggest what early man looked like?
4. What was the main occupation or means of livelihood of Old Stone Age man?
5. What were some of the accomplishments of Neanderthal man?
6. In what ways was Cro-Magnon man more highly developed than other early men?
7. What does the term *homo sapiens* describe?
8. Why were the development of agriculture and the domestication of animals such important steps in the history of man?
9. Which areas of the world served as cradles of civilization for the development of man?
10. How or why did government develop?

Early Man: SYNOPSIS

Scientists think that the earth probably formed over four billion years ago from a mass of liquid gas and flame. As it cooled, earthquakes, volcanoes, glaciers, winds, and rains came, shaping the surface into seas and continents, mountains and valleys. The first form of life was probably a single cell from which, over millions of years, higher and higher forms of living creatures gradually developed.

Perhaps more than two million years ago, at the beginning of a period known as the Old Stone Age, man appeared. As early men began their long march toward civilization, they learned how to make tools, build fires, and construct shelters. One early type, Cro-Magnon man, was a skillful artist who drew pictures of animals on the walls of caves.

As man developed, three different racial or physical types emerged: Caucasian, Negro, and Mongolian. New Stone Age men learned the secrets of agriculture and became food producers. They began to live in communities where they made pottery and wove cloth. They apparently had a sense of religion too. These New Stone Age men were the forerunners of civilization. Their progress was especially rapid in certain favored areas of the earth, called "cradles of civilization."

Terms

Be sure that you understand clearly the meaning of each of the following:

archaeologist
dinosaur
erosion
geologist
strata
race

Glacial Age
historic
homo sapiens
culture
Age of Reptiles
Temperate Zone

New Stone Age
Old Stone Age
prehistoric
Stonehenge
cell
cradles of civilization

Questions for Discussion and Review

1. What is one theory advanced to explain the earth's beginnings?
2. How do we know that the Appalachian Mountains are much older than the Rocky Mountains?
3. What evidence is there for or against the idea that twentieth-century man may be living in an interglacial period?
4. What is historically wrong with the comic strip that shows a cave man riding a dinosaur?
5. Is our knowledge of prehistoric man based on actual evidence? Explain your answer.
6. Why is it that we know more about the appearance and habits of Cro-Magnon man than about other early men?
7. In your opinion, what was the greatest accomplishment of early man? Why?
8. What evidence is there that early man had some primitive religious beliefs?
9. Modern man belongs to the species *homo sapiens*. Into what different racial types or groups has he been classified?
10. Why is there no such thing as a pure or superior race?

Interesting Things to Do

Here are some interesting things to do. You will find that if you put your new knowledge to use it will become more firmly fixed in mind. Choose one or more of these things to do, alone or with a committee of the class. Display your completed projects or maintain them in a notebook so that you and your classmates may increasingly enjoy the rewards of the study of history.

1. Make a map of the world highlighting the spots where the bones and relics of early man were discovered. On the same map, show with colors and labels the areas which served as cradles of civilization for the development of man.
2. Prepare a written or illustrated time chart of prehistoric times. Label the approximate time periods and the names of the early men of each period.
3. Construct an illustrated time line showing the development of man and his tools from the time of earliest man to the present.
4. Duplicate the muted colors and lifelike subjects of some of the cave drawings of the Cro-Magnon artists.
5. Make a sketch or model of a volcano, showing how it functions. Label carefully to explain your work.
6. Illustrate a booklet or poster about the Age of Reptiles by drawing and labeling pictures of dinosaurs that once roamed the earth.
7. Prepare a talk, "Our Own Region in Prehistoric Times." Investigate local land formations for the geology of the earth layers, traces of the ice ages, and fossil remains of animal life. Consult your school or local librarian for sources of information.
8. Prepare a written or oral report on one of the following topics: (a) glaciers, (b) volcanoes, (c) erosion, (d) the Glacial Age.
9. Investigate and write the story of the Piltdown man to illustrate how difficult it is to be certain of the facts about early man.
10. Make a list of all the new words or phrases you learned in reading the story of early man. Show that you understand each by defining, illustrating, or using it in a sentence.

Interesting Reading about Early Man

*Baumann, Hans, *Caves of the Great Hunters*, Pantheon.

Bibby, Geoffrey, *Four Thousand Years Ago*, Knopf.

Burns, William A., *Man and His Tools*, McGraw-Hill.

Edel, May, *Story of Our Ancestors*, Little, Brown.

Evans, Eva, *All About Us*, Capitol. Deals with the effects of environment on early man.

Fisher, James, *Wonderful World*, Hanover.

Kjelgaard, J. A., *Fire-Hunter*, Holiday.

Life, *The World We Live In*, Simon and Schuster.

Moore, Ruth, *Man, Time, and Fossils*, Knopf.

Quennell, Marjorie and Charles H. B., *Everyday Life in the New Stone, Bronze and Early Iron Age*, Putnam.

———, *Everyday Life in the Old Stone Age*, Putnam.

Simak, Clifford, *Trilobite, Dinosaur, and Man*, St. Martin's Press.

*White, Anne T., *First Men in the World*, Random House.

* Indicates easy reading

Ancient Egypt was not all death and slavery. Shown here is a hunting scene with the hunters using boomerangs to stun flying birds.

Part 2
EGYPT
EARLY CIVILIZATION ON THE NILE

Chapter 3 THE NILE HAS INFLUENCED THE STORY OF EGYPT
Chapter 4 THE OLD KINGDOM SET THE PATTERN OF EGYPT
Chapter 5 TWO GREAT KINGDOMS ROSE AND FELL

ANCIENT EGYPT

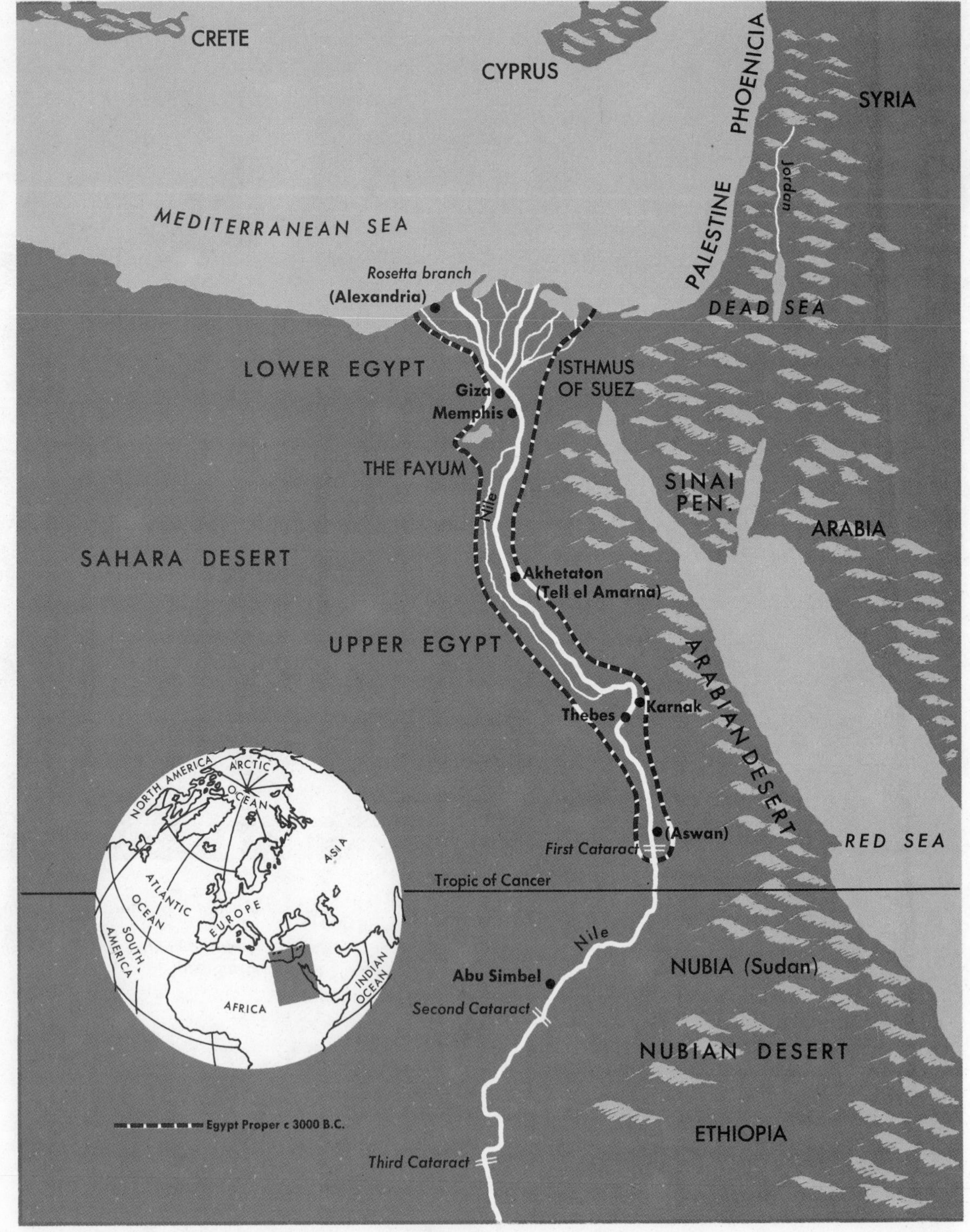
CRETE
CYPRUS
PHOENICIA
SYRIA
Jordan
PALESTINE
MEDITERRANEAN SEA
Rosetta branch
(Alexandria)
DEAD SEA
LOWER EGYPT
ISTHMUS
OF SUEZ
Giza
Memphis
THE FAYUM
SINAI
PEN.
Nile
ARABIA
SAHARA DESERT
Akhetaton
(Tell el Amarna)
UPPER EGYPT
ARABIAN DESERT
Karnak
Thebes
NORTH AMERICA
ARCTIC
OCEAN
ASIA
ATLANTIC
OCEAN
EUROPE
SOUTH
AMERICA
AFRICA
INDIAN
OCEAN
(Aswan)
First Cataract
RED SEA
Tropic of Cancer
Nile
Abu Simbel
NUBIA (Sudan)
Second Cataract
NUBIAN DESERT
Egypt Proper c 3000 B.C.
ETHIOPIA
Third Cataract

Egypt: GEOGRAPHIC SETTING

The Nile, the longest river in the world, drains Lake Victoria in central Africa and follows a northerly course to the Mediterranean Sea. During a portion of the early part of its four-thousand-mile journey to the north, it is called the White Nile, because of its milky-gray color. The clear waters of the Blue Nile, a tributary, join it at Khartoum (shown on the map on page 38).

Proceeding north (downstream) between Khartoum and Aswan, the Nile flows through six cataracts, or rapids. In the cataracts the water rushes over rocky beds between high cliffs and sometimes drops as much as two feet each mile. Beyond the northernmost, or First Cataract, the Nile has cut a narrow valley ten to thirty miles wide in the rocky, brown, desert plateau that stretches away on either side. This narrow strip of land along the river is fertile and green because it is watered by the Nile floods. Historians call this river valley Upper Egypt.

About six hundred miles farther north, beyond Memphis, the river divides into two branches (seven in ancient times), and the narrow valley widens into a steaming, marshy, triangular plain. This region, comprising about 150 miles from Memphis to the sea, is called the Delta, or Lower Egypt. Its hot, humid climate is less comfortable than that of Upper Egypt, where the air is dry.

The ancient Egyptian civilization, which we are about to study, was almost entirely confined to the Delta and the narrow valley of Upper Egypt. Eventually, Egyptians settled south of the First Cataract, but the rough waters made transportation upstream more difficult. Notice that ancient Egypt was protected by natural boundaries on all sides: the Mediterranean Sea to the north, the Libyan Desert to the west, the Nubian Desert (today the Sudan) to the south, and the Arabian Desert and Red Sea to the east. The strip of land between the Red Sea and the Mediterranean, called the Isthmus (*iss*-mus) of Suez, was Egypt's only land link with Asia.

Egypt: PERSPECTIVE

A hundred years ago men knew much less about the history of ancient Egypt than they do today. Scholars depended upon the accounts of Greek and Roman writers for their knowledge of Egyptian traditions. Occasionally, robbers would break into ancient tombs and steal their contents, but for the most part the story of ancient Egypt that lay buried beneath the sands remained hidden from men.

At the beginning of the nineteenth century historians discovered how to read ancient Egyptian hieroglyphics. Venturing into the Nile Valley, archaeologists began to dig in the ruins left by men who had lived thousands of years ago. The remarkable discoveries they made aroused great interest in ancient Egypt. Today's historians probably know more about life in ancient Egypt five thousand years ago, than they know about life in North America only five hundred years ago. What accounts for the popularity of ancient Egypt among modern historians? For one thing, Egypt's climate favors the work of archaeologists. Over the centuries, the dry heat has preserved remains of the ancient Egyptian civilization and has prevented the deterioration that in most other regions has reduced valuable relics to dust. Then too, the Egyptian custom of preserving an amazing variety of objects in their tombs has made the tombs virtual museums of Egyptian history.

But until only recently the most important reason for the interest in Egypt was that scientists regarded the region as the home of the first civilized people. Now,

although it appears that equally early civilizations also developed along other river valleys, the importance of Egypt in the puzzle of ancient man remains great. Underlying all of man's interest in ancient Egypt is his desire to know more about his forebears, to discover what kind of people lived in the world at the dawn of history, and to search for clues to their lives and their achievements. In Part 2 you will share some of the excitement of that search.

CHAPTER 3

The Nile Has Influenced the Story of Egypt

GEOGRAPHY MADE EGYPT A CRADLE OF CIVILIZATION

Egypt is the gift of the Nile. Geography and climate show their importance in Egypt more clearly than in any other ancient country. Nearly all of North Africa is desert and has a hot, dry climate. Along the banks of the Nile, however, the landscape changes dramatically into a green, fertile valley. This natural garden spot provided the setting for one of man's first great civilizations, that of the Egyptians.

Twenty-five hundred years ago, Herodotus (heh-*rod*-oh-tus), a Greek historian, was correct when he said: "All Egypt is the gift of the Nile." Since it seldom rains in the Nile Valley or in the surrounding deserts, all water, including that for drinking and bathing, comes from the river. Even the fertile soil of Egypt is a gift of the Nile, for with unfailing regularity floods have deposited a new layer of soil in the valley each year.

To most ancient Egyptians, the cause of the Nile floods was a mystery. Only a few guessed that the flooding was the result of heavy rains in the mountains of Abyssinia (ab-ih-*sin*-ee-uh), the source of the Blue Nile. Modern explorers have confirmed this belief. From June to September, melting snow and heavy rainfall turn the Blue Nile into a thundering torrent. The sudden increase in water and soil, which the Blue Nile dumps into the White Nile at Khartoum, causes the level of the river downstream to rise gradually and spill onto the flat, sunbaked fields of Egypt. The flood reaches its crest in October. Then the river level slowly drops, leaving a new layer of rich mud ready for planting. As the fields become a broad green carpet of waving grain, the Nile continues to recede until a new cycle begins in the following year.

In addition to supplying water and soil, the Nile also served ancient Egyptians as a highway linking Upper and Lower Egypt. Boats traveling north can glide easily with the current, while those going south need only to hoist a sail to take advantage of steady winds from the north.

Egypt was protected by sea and desert. Doubtless one of the reasons for the development of civilization was Egypt's natural protection from enemy invasion. The surrounding seas and deserts assured the Egyptians of peace and enabled them to devise better ways of living instead of constantly defending themselves from attackers. The Isthmus of Suez was the only easy point of entry, and, as long as Egypt was strong, she guarded that. Not until she became weakened from within did she fall prey to enemy invaders.

Men of the New Stone Age settled in the Nile Valley. Eleven thousand years ago, North Africa was covered with forests and grassy plains

THE NILE TODAY. Transportation on Egypt's great waterway has not changed much since ancient times. The prevailing winds blow south, but the river current flows north, so boats can travel easily in either direction.

through which men of the Old Stone Age wandered in search of food and shelter. During the last centuries of the Old Stone Age, the climate gradually grew hotter and drier, eventually turning the hunting grounds into the Sahara Desert. As a result, beginning about 5000 B.C., these hunters were forced to retreat eastward to the still fertile Nile Valley. There they happily discovered that geography had given them ideal conditions for a permanent home: sun, fertile soil, water, and natural protection from invasion.

During the New Stone Age, these ancestors of the Egyptians grew wheat, barley, vegetables, and flax along the banks of the Nile. The river also supplied them with waterfowl, fish, and even mud from which they made bricks to build their huts. The papyrus (puh-*pi*-rus) reeds that grew thickly along the marshes furnished these early farmers with material for rope, sandals, thatched roofs, and even light fishing boats. In the graves of these early settlers, archaeologists have found copper and polished stone tools, carved figures, pottery, and ivory combs. Thus while the continent of Europe was still an undeveloped wilderness, these ancient men in Egypt were well on their way to becoming civilized.

FISHING AND FOWLING. The waters of the Nile provided staples for the Egyptian diet. This wall painting from an Egyptian tomb shows the man on the right spearing fish while his companion hunts birds with a boomerang-like stick. The figures look flat because painters apparently did not know how to achieve three-dimensional effects.

THE NILE RIVER SHAPED EGYPTIAN CIVILIZATION

Egyptian government was born out of attempts to control the Nile floods. For nearly two thousand years the farmers along the Nile made few changes in their way of life; but as the population increased, it became necessary to raise more food. Men enlarged their fields by digging ditches to drain the marshlands and by building canals to bring the water to the nearby desert. They soon learned that by erecting dikes they could conserve some of the flood water for irrigation in the dry season. This reservoir of water enabled them to grow two or three crops a year.

Because so much digging, draining, and irrigating required a great deal of co-operative effort, farmers began to live together in villages instead of in their own fields. Leaders were needed to organize the work and to make sure that each man did his share of digging and took no more than his share of water. Gradually a few capable leaders brought several villages under their control and developed a system of government. Finally, around 4000 B.C., two powerful leaders succeeded in uniting the groups of villages into the two kingdoms of Upper and Lower Egypt.

The details of government created a need for writing. As villages were organized into kingdoms, government became more complicated, and some form of permanent records became a necessity. The tax collector, for example, had to know how much grain a farmer owed the king, and whether he paid it promptly.

To meet this need for records, the Egyptians developed a system of writing. At first they simply drew pictures of objects, such as a circle for the sun or a four-legged animal with horns for a cow. They slowly learned to use pictures to represent not only objects, but also certain sounds or syllables. Egyptian writing finally included three kinds of symbols, representing objects, syllables, and letters all mixed together. This complicated system of writing is called hieroglyphics (hy-er-oh-*glif*-iks). Later, the Egyptians developed a kind of shorthand hieroglyphics called *hieratic* writing, to meet the needs of government and business.

A NOBLE'S TOMB. In this detail from the tomb of nobleman Uzerhat, the paintings depict aspects of food preparation.

Records were written on a kind of paper. The Egyptians wrote on a paper that was made by weaving dried reeds of the papyrus plant. Instead of cutting sheets of this paper into pages and binding them like our books, the Egyptians fastened them together end to end to make strips that were sometimes a hundred feet long. These strips were rolled into scrolls and stored in jars. Egypt's dry climate has preserved many of them so well that they can still be read.

Written records are one of the foundations of civilization. They enable each generation to use and to add to the knowledge gained by its forerunners. Without some form of writing, such as that invented by the ancient Egyptians, culture might never have advanced beyond the New Stone Age.

The Rosetta Stone provided the key to Egypt's secrets. During Napoleon's campaign in Egypt in 1798–99, French soldiers digging for a fort near the Rosetta branch of the mouth of the Nile turned up an extraordinary stone which became the key to Egypt's past. This "Rosetta Stone," as it is called, is covered with inscriptions in three languages: Greek, hieroglyphics, and an unknown script which later proved to be the simplified Egyptian hieratic. Scholars from many countries tried to read the Egyptian writing on the Rosetta Stone. Twenty years after it was discovered, a French scholar, Jean Francois Champollion (shahn-paw-*lyawn*), correctly assumed that the three inscriptions were exactly the same message written in three different languages. This discovery enabled him to begin translating and interpreting the hieroglyphics on the stone and helped scholars to unlock the secrets contained in other Egyptian inscriptions. The story of ancient Egypt could now be read.

The Nile floods led to the development of geometry and the calendar. Experience with the floods brought home to the Egyptians the usefulness of developing accurate measurements of distance and time. Each year's food supply depended on how much water the flood brought to the land. One year the river might rise so high that it would wash away dikes and villages. The next year it might be so low that it would not even fill all the irrigation ditches. It was important to foresee what the Nile would do. At several points along the river the Egyptians built stone stairways called Nilometers on which they measured the level of the water each year. If the water reached a certain point by July they knew whether to build their dikes higher or to deepen their canals.

HIEROGLYPHICS. The writing in this tomb painting tells us that the lady playing checkers is: "The King's Great Wife, the Mistress of the Two Lands, Nefret-iry, beloved of Mut, justified under Osiris, the Great God." Mut was the wife of the god Amon-Re. Osiris was the god of the dead. (See Chapters 4 and 5.)

GEESE. Egyptian art was usually symmetrical, as can be seen in this painting.

Because the annual floods often washed away boundary lines, the Egyptians needed a simple and accurate way to measure land. They devised a method of marking out angles and calculating areas that enabled them to redraw the original boundary lines. Thus geometry, the science of space measurement, was born.

The ancient Egyptians also learned to measure time as well as space. They noticed that the average number of days between the peaks of the Nile flood was the same, 365, and that when the Nile reached its high-water mark, Sirius, the Dog Star, always appeared on the horizon. From observations like these, and from watching the phases of the moon, the Egyptians constructed a calendar year of 365 days which they divided into twelve months of thirty days each. The five days left over were set aside for feasting. This calendar told the Egyptians when to expect the Nile flood and when to start planting new grain in their fields.

Chapter Check-up

1. In which direction does the Nile River flow?
2. How were the Egyptians able to navigate their boats in both directions on the Nile River?
3. What was the weak point in Egypt's natural defenses against invasion?
4. What geographic conditions favored the growth of a civilization in the Nile Valley?
5. Why did Stone Age men settle in the Nile Valley?
6. What was the main occupation of the ancient Egyptians?
7. How did the earliest Egyptian writing differ from our method of writing today?
8. What is papyrus and how was it used by the ancient Egyptians?
9. Why was the development of writing such an important step in history?
10. How was the Rosetta Stone a key to our understanding of ancient Egypt?

CHAPTER 4

The Old Kingdom Set the Pattern in Egypt

RELIGION DOMINATED EGYPTIAN LIFE

Menes started Egypt on the road to three periods of greatness. In our discussion of the beginnings of Egyptian civilization, we noted that the early farmers of the Nile Valley lived in villages and were gradually united by strong leaders into the two kingdoms of Upper and Lower Egypt. For about a thousand years, Egyptian rulers fought for control of the two kingdoms. At last, probably about 3000 B.C., Menes (*mee*-neez), a strong ruler of Upper Egypt, conquered Lower Egypt. To symbolize his achievement he wore a double crown and built his capital at Memphis, midway between Upper and Lower Egypt. During his lifetime, Menes laid the foundation on which later rulers built a mighty state.

Historians have divided Egypt's history into three periods: the Old Kingdom, the Middle Kingdom, and the New Kingdom or Empire Age. Each of these periods of achievement was followed by a time of confusion and civil war. Taken as a whole, however, Egyptian civilization lasted over three thousand years, longer than any other civilization in history. Egyptian life changed very little during that time, for the Egyptians were a conservative people who preserved the ways of their ancestors. For this reason, a careful study of the government, religion, and art of the Old Kingdom will give us a fairly typical picture of ancient Egyptian life. We shall now examine life in Egypt during the period known as the Old Kingdom, approximately 2700 to 2200 B.C.

The Pharaohs of the Old Kingdom ruled with absolute power. Menes' successors strengthened their power over the Egyptian people. Gradually the people came to regard their rulers with such awe that they no longer called them by name. Instead they used the title *Pharaoh* (*fay*-ro), meaning "Great House," which referred to the royal palace near Memphis. Every subject, even the greatest noble, felt honored if he were allowed to kiss the dust at the Pharaoh's feet.

The Pharaoh was the head of the government, the commander-in-chief of the army, and, as we shall see later, the chief religious leader. He appointed his sons, brothers, and favorite nobles as assistants to help him fulfill his duties, but he was careful to tell them exactly what to do. In this way his power, unchecked by man or law, became *absolute*.

The Pharoah closely regulated the economic life of his people. He consulted daily with his officials about such matters as irrigation projects and the number of jars of wheat and bolts of linen which the Egyptian people paid as taxes. He kept a close watch on the royal copper and gold mines in the eastern deserts and sent expeditions to Nubia to trade Egyptian wheat for ivory and incense. Royal fleets brought pottery from Crete and cedar wood, which Egypt lacked, from Phoenicia (feh-*neesh*-ee-uh). These goods filled the royal storehouses to overflowing.

The power of the Egyptian Pharaohs marks the introduction of a new concept, or idea, in history, that of a large area ruled by one man rather than small areas ruled by tribal chiefs or village elders. This arrangement is the earliest form of what we call *central government*. How were the Pharaohs of the Old Kingdom able to achieve such complete control over the lives of the Egyptian people? There are two explanations. First, you will recall from our discussion of Egyptian farming that a high degree of co-operation was needed in order to carry out irrigation and flood control

THE DOUBLE CROWN. The Pharaoh, represented as the hawk-like god Horus, wears the double crown—the white crown of Upper Egypt and the red crown of Lower Egypt—that symbolized the union of the two regions.

EGYPTIAN ARCHITECTURE

The dominant theme of Ancient Egyptian architecture is death. Thus the typical structures reflective of this attitude were the tomb pyramid and the temple. The architecture, constructed from local stone, is massive, solid and solemn. One gets an overpowering feeling of awe when looking upon these receptacles of the dead, and even peasants' huts seem stifling in their gloom.

Shown here are the *Sphinx and Pyramids of Gizeh* with the pyramid of *Chephren* in the immediate background. The Sphinx has the head of the pharoah Chephren and body of a lion.

The Great Temple of Ammon at Karnak (shown here in part) is perhaps the most impressive of all Egyptian temples and took over 1200 years to complete to its present form. Many pharoahs added on to its original structure and today it would be larger than four football fields.

This Nile delta village of dried mud homes also reflects the interior darkness and gloom of the mightier structures.

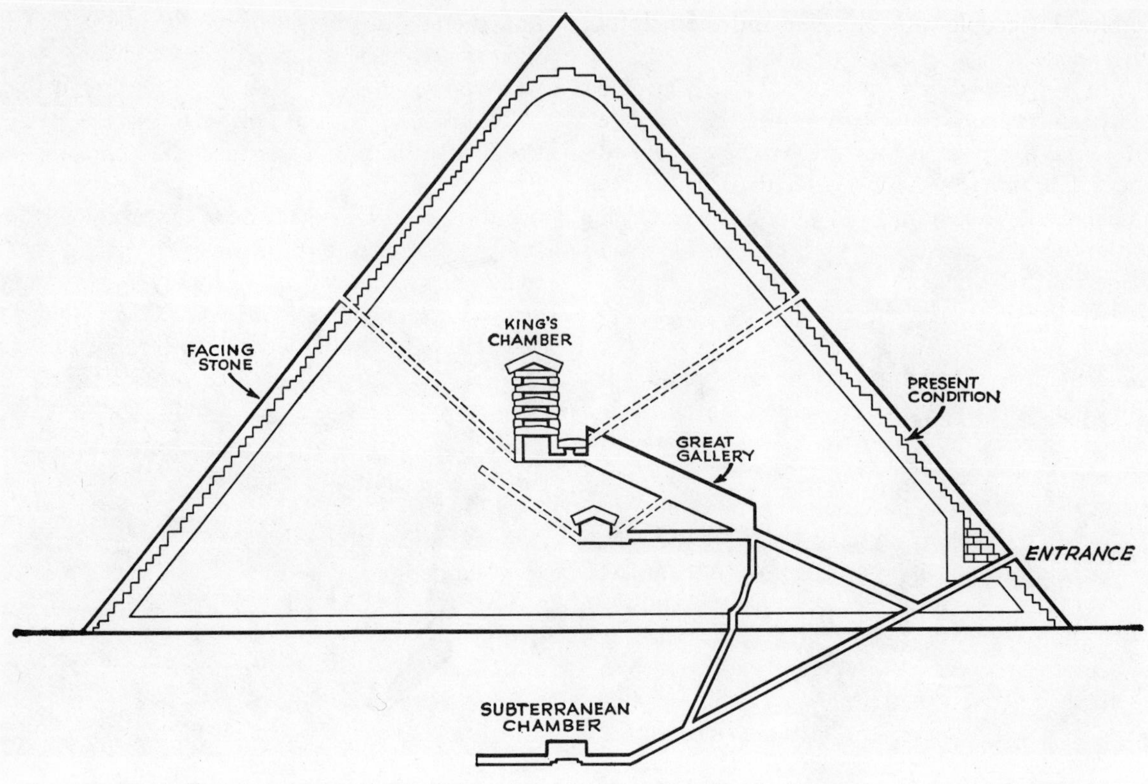

PLAN OF KHUFU'S PYRAMID. To keep the entombed Pharaoh's body safe forever, this pyramid was designed with hidden entrances and secret passageways. Nevertheless, grave robbers long ago entered it and carried away the riches it contained, such as jewels and objects of gold.

projects. These projects required leadership and direction. As the population grew, improved methods of agriculture were urgently needed. To increase efficiency, the Pharaoh gradually came to direct the labor of every man and woman. Using hoes, plows, and other tools of copper and wood, agricultural workers made Egypt into the granary of the ancient world. Wheat was used for making bread, as archaeologists know from finding loaves in tombs, and farmers also raised corn and barley and grew grapes.

The Pharaoh's power did not, however, result only from his control of agriculture. A second reason is even more important. We shall discuss that next.

The Egyptians worshiped the Pharaoh as a god. The Egyptians, a deeply religious people, believed that everything in the world could be explained by the action of some god or spirit. One of their many gods was the sun god, Amon-Re (*ah*-men *ray*), whom they believed to have been the first ruler of Egypt. According to legend, when he grew tired of earth he appointed his son, whose mother was an Egyptian woman, to rule after him. Then he returned to heaven. His son and all the succeeding Pharaohs were thus believed to be half god and half man.

Men were eager to please the Pharaoh because he could protect them not only while he was on earth, but even after he went to heaven. The Egyptians believed that the Pharaoh did not die but joined Amon-Re in the sky. There he watched over Egypt forever and persuaded the other gods, who were his kinsmen, to continue to bless his people with sunshine and the helpful Nile floods.

The Egyptians were probably the first people in history to adopt the idea of immortality, or life after death. In time they grew more concerned about life in the next world than with the affairs of the present one. Doubtless the fact that the dry climate preserved the bodies of the dead made it easy for them to think man's life continued forever. The Egyptians apparently enjoyed life so much that they did not want to see it end. Because they believed that man could not enjoy life after death unless his body were carefully preserved and provided for, their most extraordinary creations were their magnificent tombs. These tombs have become archaeologists' chief source of information about ancient Egypt.

The Egyptians believed that the joys of the next world were reserved for the Pharaoh and for a few nobles whom he specifically chose to accompany him. The ordinary man felt that he had no chance of immortality. (As you will see, this belief changed during the Middle Kingdom.) Nevertheless, he was anxious to help the Pharaoh reach heaven, where he could use his influence to insure that Egypt would continue to receive the blessings of the sun and the floods. You can see how the religious beliefs of the Egyptians explain their willingness to submit to the Pharaoh's absolute power.

The pyramids were symbols of the power of the Pharaohs. To honor their god-Pharaohs, the Egyptians of the Old Kingdom willingly carried out their ruler's orders to build magnificent stone tombs called pyramids. Generations of men have marveled at the pyramids. For over five thousand years, these huge monuments have risen above the sands to proclaim the faith of the ancient Egyptians and the power of their Pharaohs. There are more than thirty large pyramids and many small ones on the west bank of the Nile at Giza (*gee*-zuh), near Memphis. Others of varying sizes were built along the Nile as far south as Nubia, but they were much simpler in construction and furnishings. If you walked around the base of the Great Pyramid, built about 2600 B.C. by the Pharaoh Khufu (*koo*-foo), or Cheops (*kee*-ahps) as he is called in Greek, you would realize what an enormous undertaking it represents. The Greeks considered it one of the Seven Wonders of the Ancient World. Each of its four sides is as long as two city blocks and rises to a peak nearly five hundred feet above the desert. Originally the Great Pyramid was covered with smooth white

MODEL OF AN EGYPTIAN BOAT. The Egyptians filled their tombs with useful objects for use in the afterlife. This wooden model of a Theban travelling boat comes from an Eleventh Dynasty tomb (about 2000 B.C.)

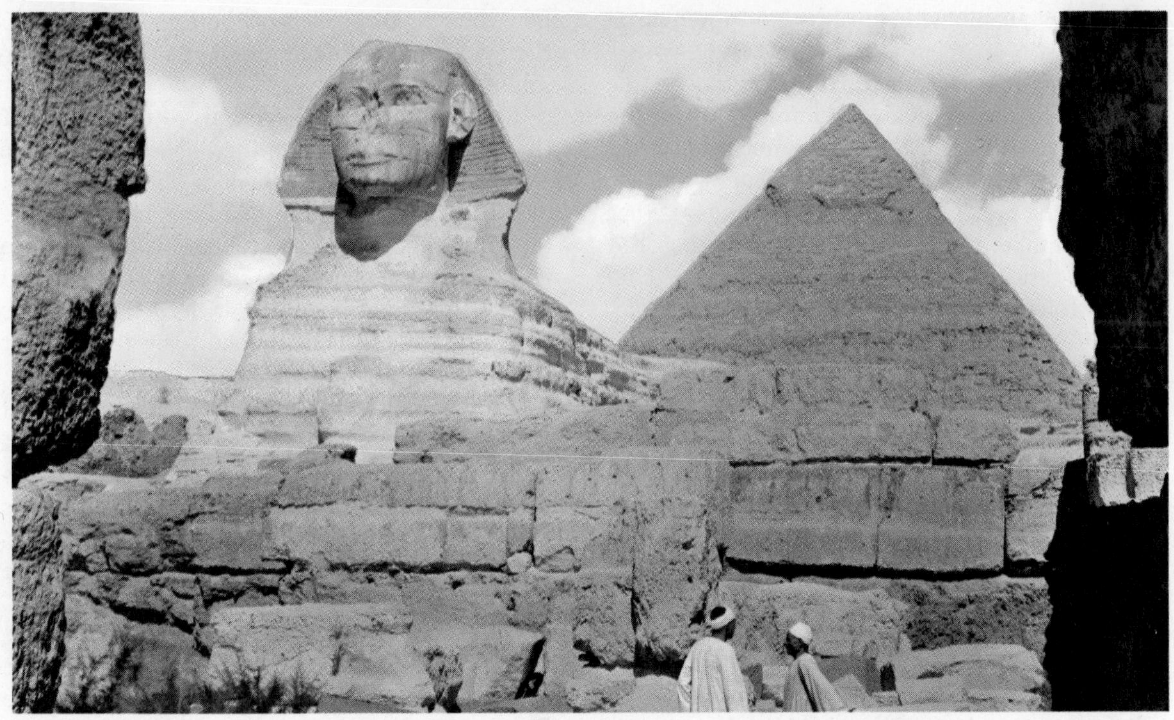

The Great Sphinx and Pyramid of Khufu at Giza. These massive structures, built during the Old Kingdom, still tower over the desert. The Greek sphinx with its lion's body and man's head is over 172 feet long and 66 feet high.

limestone, but it has long since been stripped off. Part of the limestone removed from the pyramid was used to build modern Cairo. A great deal of the stone, some of which was intricately carved and decorated, was burned to make lime for mortar, but now a law prohibits the use of any carved fragments for such a purpose. Today you can climb the step-like structure that the limestone once covered.

To raise this mighty monument and the temple attached to it, Khufu ordered 100,000 men to work in shifts for twenty years. Because there was no machinery, the task required great physical effort on the part of the labor gangs and much careful organization and engineering on the part of the royal officials. Huge limestone blocks, some weighing fifteen tons, had to be cut from the royal quarries on the east bank of the Nile and floated across the river on rafts. Then they were hauled on rollers up an earthen ramp, and fitted so closely into place that a knifeblade could not be inserted between the joints. All this difficult work was done with simple hand tools of stone, copper, and bronze. Although the Egyptians used rope, they never discovered the principle of the pulley or block and tackle. But their craftsmen turned out excellent work by using the level, the plumb bob, and the square.

The Great Pyramid is one of the outstanding accomplishments of the Old Kingdom. But Khufu could never have completed the project if he had not had absolute power over all aspects of Egyptian life. In spite of their great power, however, the Pharaohs did not force their subjects to work. Most of the pyramid builders were ordinary farmers who could not labor in the fields anyway during flood season. The Pharaohs built a city for them and fed and clothed them while they were in the royal service. The men worked willingly because they believed that by pleasing the Pharaoh they were fulfilling a religious duty and insuring Egypt's future welfare.

Religion influenced Egyptian art. Religion was so important in Egyptian life that almost all art and architecture was devoted to the gods and the god-Pharaoh. Since a pyramid was designed to be the eternal home of the Pharaoh's body, the decorations and furnishings had to be as magnificent as those in his palace on earth. The walls of the king's chamber, a room hidden deep within the pyramid, were covered with flat carvings called bas (bah)-reliefs. These brilliantly painted wall carvings depicted scenes of the Pharaoh's elaborate garden, his great hunting expeditions, and his glorious victories in battle. Some of the carvings were copies of prayers or magic charms. Craftsmen furnished the chamber with beautiful gilded chairs, beds, chests, and utensils. Stone jars, filled with food, incense, oils, and tiny clay statues representing servants, were also provided to help the Pharaoh live in comfort in the next world. His coffin was covered with sheets of gold and laid in a room below the king's chamber.

To protect the Pharaoh's body and his possessions from robbers, the passages leading to the king's chamber and to the subterranean room were blocked. The outside entrances were concealed by blocks of stone which looked exactly like the others on the surface of the pyramid. The workers who set the final stones in place were often slain to keep them from revealing the location of the entrance. In spite of these safeguards, robbers long ago found their way into many of the pyramids and carried off their treasures.

Other examples of Egyptian architecture are the huge stone temples built by the Pharaohs to honor the gods or to glorify themselves. The approach to an Egyptian temple was usually a long avenue lined with *sphinxes,* large stone lions with human or animal heads symbolizing various gods. Behind the high, sloping towers of the main gate was a courtyard, and beyond that a hall crowded with rows of massive stone columns to hold up the flat stone roof (see picture on page 20). The columns were often carved to resemble the lotus, the sacred flower of Egypt. Behind the hall was a series of small chambers, in the smallest of which the god was supposed to dwell. All of the temple walls were decorated with beautiful carvings and paintings.

The influence of religion is also revealed in Egyptian sculpture and painting. The most famous example of sculpture is the *Great Sphinx,* found near the pyramid of the Pharaoh Khafre

A COSMETIC BOX. This ivory grasshopper is actually a box for kohl, the black powder used by Egyptians to darken the eyelids. The box is opened by separating tiny wooden wings concealed under the outer wings.

A TOMB OBJECT. The Egyptians placed such objects as this blue earthenware hippopotamus in their tombs. The decorations probably represent lotus buds and suggest the Nile River surroundings of the animal.

A Tomb. This decorative entrance to a tomb shows how the Egyptians covered the walls with paintings. Scenes like this have enabled scholars to discover much about how ancient Egyptians lived.

(*kah*-fruh), brother of Khufu. To emphasize his descent from the sun god, he ordered the sphinx, which symbolized the god, to be carved with a face resembling his own. This massive monument is nearly 200 feet long.

Other outstanding examples of Egyptian sculpture were the impressive stone statues of the Pharaohs which decorated their temples. Most of these statues are dignified and formal, with massive shoulders, stiff royal headdresses and beards, and calm expressions to show their god-like qualities. In wall paintings and bas-reliefs, the Pharaoh usually appears twice as big as anyone else because he was considered so much more important. As you can see, nearly all Egyptian art and architecture was inspired by religion.

EGYPTIANS OF THE OLD KINGDOM DEVELOPED A REMARKABLE CIVILIZATION

The priests and nobles lived in luxury. Because religion was so important to the Egyptians, the priests had great power. Outside the temple they led worldly lives identical to those of other royal officials. Inside the temple, they conducted ceremonies and made sacrifices to the gods. The people provided the wine, goats, and other objects for sacrifice because they believed that the gods would not favor Egypt unless they were fed and entertained. The Pharaoh gave the priests huge grants of land to honor the gods. Neither the people nor the Pharaohs dared to criticize the vast wealth of the priests because to anger the priests was to anger the gods. The priests and the nobles steadily gained power until, as you will see, they finally brought about the collapse of the Old Kingdom.

In the meantime, Egypt's wealth made it possible for the upper classes to lead very pleasant lives. Because time on earth was brief compared to time in the next world, the nobles built their houses only of temporary, sun-dried brick rather than of the more enduring stone which they used for their tombs. Even so, such a house was a delightful place to spend one's time on earth. The rooms were spacious, airy, gaily painted, and they opened onto a green garden. Fig and palm trees shaded the surrounding walls, and a pool filled with blue lotus flowers and fish provided coolness and ease that contrasted pleasantly with the scorching, dry climate.

An Egyptian noble passed his days hunting or tending his vast estate. He spent his evenings at lavish feasts. The menu for such a feast might include four meats (duck, beef, lamb, goat), bread, onions, and finally figs, dates, pomegranates, and wine. During the meal, harp players and dancers entertained the noble and his guests.

When attending such a banquet, both the noble and his lady wore carefully pleated skirts of fine white linen, broad collars of semiprecious stones, gold bracelets, and curled, black, perfumed wigs. The women shadowed their eyelids with a black powder, called *kohl,* which made the eyes look larger and protected them from the dazzling sun. The little alabaster rouge pots, dainty glass perfume vials, and polished copper mirrors that archaeologists have found in tombs show that Egyptian women spared no pains to make themselves attractive.

The farmers led a life of toil. Most Egyptians were farmers. There were also a few craftsmen, such as bricklayers, masons, and potters. The lives of these people were very different from those of the nobles. The farmers lived in villages of mud huts near the river bank, and the craftsmen were jammed into low apartment houses along narrow alleys in the towns. The farmers shared their huts with the farm animals. Although neither a farmer nor a craftsman owned more than a stool, a box, and a few pottery jars, he was not greatly disturbed by these unpleasant conditions, because from sunup to sundown he was in the shop or field. Such a man had to work very hard to be able to feed his family after he had paid his taxes and made donations to the temple. But landlords and royal officials usually treated him fairly, and he had equal rights before the law. He derived his greatest pleasure from religious festivals which were celebrated with colorful processions and feasts.

Rich and poor alike valued family life and taught children to be courteous and respectful. Children did their share of work in the home and were trained for the lives they were destined to lead. If the parents could afford it, a boy was sent to school, but girls were prepared for domestic duties and an early marriage. Women shared the responsibilities and privileges of their husbands. Queens signed royal decrees, and noblewomen went on hunting trips and attended banquets. The respect paid to women arose partly from the fact that all land was held in the wife's name and was passed on to her eldest daughter. (But management of the land was usually left to the husband.)

MUSICIANS. An orchestra of women is playing while a youthful apprentice listens attentively.

LUXOR. Opposite Thebes which was the ancient capital of Egypt, lies Luxor and the Valley of the Kings where the Pharoahs were buried. The picture shows workers preparing a tomb.

The scribes and priests studied only practical subjects. A poor man's son was usually destined to become a farmer, but one way was open for him to rise above his family's class. If his father could afford to send him to one of the temple schools to learn hieratic writing, the boy could become a scribe, or public clerk. He would also learn arithmetic and geometry, so that he could keep accounts, measure land, and supervise the building of tombs and dams. No time was wasted on such subjects as poetry or music. Everything he studied had to be of practical value in preparing the boy for his future work. The hours were long, and Egyptian schoolmasters frequently beat their students. But if a boy could become a scribe, he was on the path to possible success as a merchant or an official in the Pharaoh's service. One ambitious father urged his son to

> . . . set to work to become a scribe, for then you shall become a leader of men . . . he who is industrious and does not neglect his books, he may become a prince . . .

The priests, who also studied for practical purposes, sought to maintain their power by acquiring knowledge that ordinary men did not possess. They commanded great respect and admiration because they seemed to understand the movements of the stars. Since the Egyptians believed that

HARVESTING. Laborers are harvesting grain while scribes keep a record of the yield. The rich soil around the Nile made Egypt the granary of the ancient world.

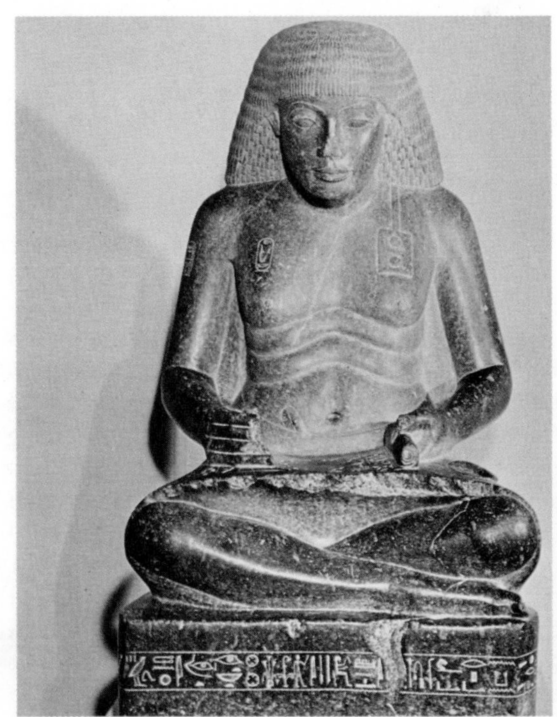

A SCRIBE. This Egyptian scribe is shown reading a papyrus scroll. In an age when few people could read or write, scribes were important members of society.

the stars influenced affairs on earth, this knowledge was considered very important. Sirius, for example, was believed to cause the Nile floods. In order to foretell the future, the priests identified the largest stars and showed their positions on maps. Their work pointed the way to future developments in astrology and astronomy.

Other priests specialized in healing the sick and skillfully setting broken bones. Modern scientists have discovered the earliest evidence of dentistry in Egyptian mummies with gold foil neatly pounded into their teeth. Indeed, we are told by an ancient writer that "it was enough for a doctor to say he had studied in Egypt to recommend him." Egyptian doctors, of course, also believed that many diseases were caused by evil spirits. Many of their cures involved the use of magic chants and charms. Neither in their study of the stars nor in their practice of medicine did the priests try to discover general laws or formulate theories like modern scientists. But they developed many practical skills in caring for and healing the sick. They even tried to foresee the future to relieve the anxiety of their patients.

Dark days followed the Old Kingdom. During the five hundred years of the Old Kingdom, Egyptians built a strong state, created magnificent monuments to its power, and established a way of life that was to last another two thousand years. Egypt did not, however, enjoy unbroken peace and prosperity. By 2200 B.C. the Pharaoh had lost control of his nobles and royal governors. The lands and power given to these men became hereditary. As strong landed families arose, the Pharaoh was unable to maintain his absolute power. Money also became a problem because his now independent lords refused to pay the high taxes necessary to build pyramids and satisfy the greedy priests. No longer was one man strong enough to protect the country from civil wars and enemy invasions. Temples were destroyed and irrigation works neglected. Famine and disease swept over the land. The glory of the Old Kingdom was at an end. Egypt was in chaos for the next two hundred years.

Chapter Check-up

1. Who was the first ruler of all Egypt?
2. What are the three great periods of ancient Egyptian history?
3. How long did the civilization of the Old Kingdom last?
4. What is the meaning of the title "Pharaoh," and to whom was it applied?
5. Why did the Egyptians worship their rulers?
6. For what reasons were Egypt's pyramids built?
7. What was the status of women in ancient Egypt?
8. How did religion influence Egyptian art and architecture?
9. In what ways did the Egyptians pioneer in the fields of medicine and dentistry?
10. What factors caused the downfall of the Old Kingdom?

Chapter 5

Two Great Kingdoms Rose and Fell

THE MIDDLE KINGDOM BROUGHT PROSPERITY AND HOPE TO THE COMMON PEOPLE

A new middle class gained wealth and privilege under the absolute rule of Amenemhet III. For two hundred years after the fall of the Old Kingdom, the nobles fought among themselves while three different families of Pharaohs tried in turn to gain authority. This period of struggle ended in 2000 B.C. when a powerful noble from the city of Thebes, Amenemhet I (ah-meh-*nem*-het), crushed all opposition, seized the throne, and reunited Egypt. The nobles, who by this time held complete control over their estates, refused to give up their local power or to pay heavy taxes. Amenemhet I finally won their support with gifts and replenished his treasury by building up foreign trade.

Amenemhet III, who succeeded to the throne in 1849 B.C., regained some of the absolute power held by Old Kingdom Pharaohs. The nobles submitted because they realized that only a strong ruler could successfully undertake great trading, mining, and irrigation projects. Amenemhet III built a canal around the First Cataract of the Nile and strengthened his control of Nubia so that his ships could meet the caravans from the Sudan (see map on page 38). He then built a canal between the Red Sea and the Nile through which, 3,500 years before the present Suez Canal was built, ships could sail from the Mediterranean to the Red Sea. The wealth that poured in from increased trade brought prosperity to merchants and craftsmen. Government revenues increased, too. This enabled Amenemhet III to undertake many new projects. One of these was a huge dam which turned a vast marshland called the Fayum (fy-*oom*) into one of Egypt's most productive regions and created a valuable reservoir for storing water from the Nile floods.

To make these improvements, Amenemhet III needed the help of more scribes and minor officials than had been necessary during the Old Kingdom. Because the nobles were untrained and unwilling to fill these positions, educated men (scribes) of low birth were appointed. It became traditional for a scribe's position to be passed on to his son. This new group of royal officials gradually came to share in the wealth and privileges that had formerly been reserved exclusively for the nobles. Thus the Middle Kingdom saw the rise of a "middle class" in Egypt.

At A Glance

Eras and Rulers of Ancient Egypt

Unification of Two Egypts (*c.* 3000 B.C.)
- Menes

Old Kingdom (2700–2200 B.C.)
- Khufu (Cheops)
- Khafre

Middle Kingdom (2100–1788 B.C.)
- Amenemhet I
- Amenemhet III

Hyksos Domination (1680–1580 B.C.)

New Kingdom, or Empire (1580–1090 B.C.)
- Ahmose I
- Hatshepsut
- Thutmose III
- Amenhotep IV (Ikhnaton)
- Ramses II
- Ramses III

Rule of the Ptolemies (323–30 B.C.)
- Cleopatra

Burial Jars. When the body of an Egyptian was mummified, the internal organs, such as heart, lungs, liver, and intestines, were carefully removed and individually preserved in four jars. These jars contained the remains of an Egyptian princess.

Every Egyptian aspired to eternal life. As the common people came to share offices and some of the wealth that had once belonged only to the Pharaoh and the nobles, they began also to seek to share the favor that they believed was granted to Pharaohs and nobles in the next world. Although Amon-Re and the departed Pharaohs were considered too important to pay attention to the prayers of ordinary men, there were lesser gods who might. These lesser gods became the favorites of the common people. Most loved was Osiris (oh-*sy*-ris), because he granted the most precious of all gifts, eternal life.

The people believed that Osiris had been cut into pieces by his wicked brother and scattered along the banks of the Nile. This destruction symbolized the dry season when nothing grew. Osiris's wife, Isis (*eye*-sis), gathered up the pieces and brought Osiris back to life. Her actions were a symbol of the earth's annual revival after the Nile floods. Instead of returning to this world, Osiris went to the underworld to become the god of the dead. The Egyptians believed that because Osiris had been restored to life, ordinary men might also find new life after death.

As you will recall, the Egyptians believed that no man could enjoy a happy future life unless his body were correctly entombed. Increasingly, the middle-class merchants, government officials, and scribes began to make the same careful preparations for their own tombs that, during the Old Kingdom, had been reserved solely for Pharaohs and nobles. These middle class tombs were not, of course, as luxurious as those of the Pharaohs, but they were the best their owners could afford. While he was still young and strong, the well-to-do Egyptian had a tomb cut into the stone cliffs west of the Nile. Then he added furniture, wall paintings of food, statues of servants, and other things which he might need after death. When he died, priests, using a process still not fully understood, soaked his body in soda, embalmed it in resin, spices, and honey, and wrapped it in strips of linen. (Bodies prepared in this way, called *mummies*, have been preserved by the dry Egyptian climate for thousands of years.) The body was then placed in a coffin that often had the owner's portrait painted on it. Mummies of cats, hawks, and other sacred animals have also been found.

A MUMMY AND THE DETAIL OF A COFFIN PAINTING. *Above:* The carefully preserved body of an infant prince is identified by the tag on its breast. *Left:* The interior of an Egyptian coffin was often as ornately decorated as the walls of many Egyptian tombs.

Egyptians thought that if the body were properly sealed in its tomb, the soul of the dead man started on a long, perilous journey by boat to the underworld. When a man's soul finally reached the palace of Osiris, he had to swear to forty-two judges in the Hall of Truth that he had never committed such sins as lying, stealing, and murder. To test his honesty, the presiding judge weighed the man's heart on a pair of scales against a feather, the symbol of truth. If he had spoken falsely, the heart was thrown to a horrible monster called "The Eater of the Dead." If he had spoken truly, his soul was admitted to the "Fields of Content," the Egyptian heaven.

The Egyptians were the first people to adopt the idea of eternal life as a reward for good conduct on earth. But they also believed in the power of magic charms, or sayings, which they bought from the priests. When painted on the tomb, the charms gave protection from evil demons and helped insure the attainment of eternal life. These charms were later collected and written down in *The Book of the Dead.* It is important to note that the Egyptians' interest in death was not the result of dissatisfaction or misery in this life. On the contrary, they thoroughly enjoyed earthly life. Their concern with life after death was simply an attempt to continue forever the joys of life on earth.

The glories of the Middle Kingdom faded with the coming of the Hyksos. In addition to restoring order to their country, the Egyptians of the Middle Kingdom made notable achievements in other areas. They are credited with developing non-religious literature during this period and were among the first people to compose love songs, folk songs, and tales of adventure.

In spite of these achievements, the Pharaohs were unable to hold the kingdom together.

This ancient papyrus shows Osiris, God of the dead seated on his throne giving and pronouncing judgment on one who has just died.

The nobles, bitterly resentful of the newly won privileges of the middle class, plunged the country into civil war. Weakened from within, Egypt was an easy prey for invading tribes called the Hyksos (*hik*-sose). About 1700 B.C. the Hyksos left their homes in Arabia and Syria and burst across the Isthmus of Suez in horse-drawn chariots. The terrified Egyptians, who had never seen a horse or chariot before, were easily conquered. The Hyksos established their capital in the Delta and forced the Pharaoh's subjects to give them part of proud Egypt's wealth as tribute. The Hyksos' conquest of Egypt brought another period of confusion and misery to the country.

DURING THE NEW KINGDOM, EGYPT RULED THE ANCIENT WORLD

Ahmose made Egypt a powerful military state. In the sixteenth century B.C., Ahmose, an able prince from Thebes, raised a powerful Egyptian army and drove out the Hyksos. His defeat of the Hyksos marked the beginning of the third period of Egyptian power, the New Kingdom or Empire Age.

Ahmose proved to be a skillful general. He realized that the scorching desert wastelands would no longer serve as a barrier to invaders with war chariots, like those in which the Hyskos rode to battle. Therefore, instead of allowing his soldiers to return to their fields, he made them push the Hyksos all the way to Syria in order to prevent any future invasions. The taste of plunder and the tribute from the defeated Syrian cities made the Egyptians greedy for more. Greed and fear of attack caused them to support a strong army, which Ahmose used to crush the nobles who rebelled against his authority. Thus, the Egyptians of the New Kingdom, for the first time in Egypt's history, created a strong military state.

Thutmose III created the Egyptian Empire. About 1500 B.C. the throne was inherited by a boy who was to become one of Egypt's greatest rulers, Thutmose (*tut*-moze) III. For the first twenty years of his reign he was pushed into the background by his strong-willed stepmother, Hatshepsut (hot-*shep*-sut). Although Hatshepsut was legally the joint heir to the throne, according to Egyptian custom no woman was actually supposed to rule. But she proved so capable that the Egyptians allowed her to claim the titles and powers of the Pharaoh. She spent large sums of money to bring rare treasures to Egypt and to build a magnificent temple where she was to be worshiped after her death.

The ambitious Thutmose III was apparently jealous of his stepmother and bitterly resented being shoved aside. As soon as he managed to overthrow her, he scratched out or covered every inscription that had been carved on monuments as a record of her achievements. He then turned his attention to bringing foreign lands under Egyptian control. The empire which he created brought Egypt to the height of her power.

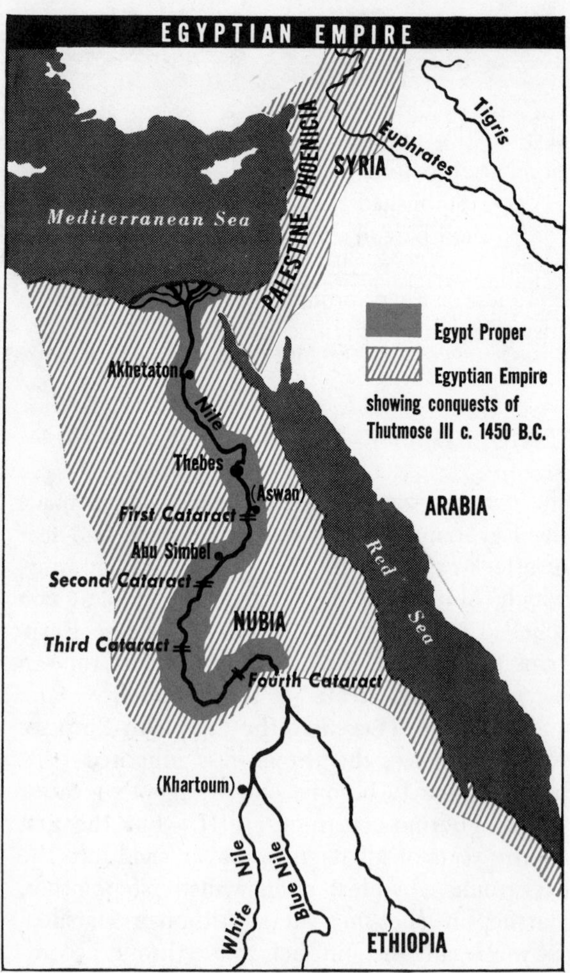

The Egyptians had learned from the Hyksos to use war chariots to protect their foot soldiers, much as a modern army uses tanks. Aided by the chariots, Thutmose's well-disciplined army easily captured the rich cities in Syria and Phoenicia. At the high point of Thutmose's seventeen campaigns, he defeated the enemy on the far side of the Euphrates and built a monument there to mark the eastern limits of the Egyptian empire.

Thutmose spent half of each year conquering new lands to the northeast of Egypt. During the other six months, he supervised the government at home, campaigned in Nubia, and built magnificent temples with the rich tribute from his subject cities. His outstanding monuments are the great temple at Karnak and four tall, granite obelisks (*ahb*-eh-lisks) covered with records of his victories. One of the obelisks stands today in New York City's Central Park.

Amenhotep IV tried to force his people to believe in one god. For seventy years after the death of Thutmose III, Egypt's conquests gave her great luxury and power. Toward the end of this period, however, the empire began to crumble. A new eastern people, the Hittites, attacked the Egyptian provinces in Syria. Unfortunately for Egypt, one of the Pharaohs who followed Thutmose III, Amenhotep IV (ah-men-*hoe*-tep), became so involved in a religious controversy that he did not even take time to answer letters from the loyal Syrians, who begged for help against the invaders. Amenhotep did not believe in the multitude of gods which his people worshiped. He believed that the one true god was Aton (*ah*-tun), god of the sun, the creator and source of all life, the god of goodness and truth, and the ruler of men's spirits. He tried to suppress the worship of Amon-Re (by this time simply called Amon). Amon's priests had gained so much wealth and power from the charms they sold and from the land they held (nearly 10 per cent of Egypt) that they were a threat to the power of the Pharaoh. Partly out of sincere belief, therefore, and partly out of desire to break the hold of the priests of Amon-Re over the people, Amenhotep sought to abandon the old gods entirely and to establish the worship of the one true god, Aton.

Ramses II. This remarkable photograph of the ancient Egyptian ruler illustrates embalming technique. Not much is known about Egyptian embalming methods but vital organs were removed and even the brain was removed through the nose!

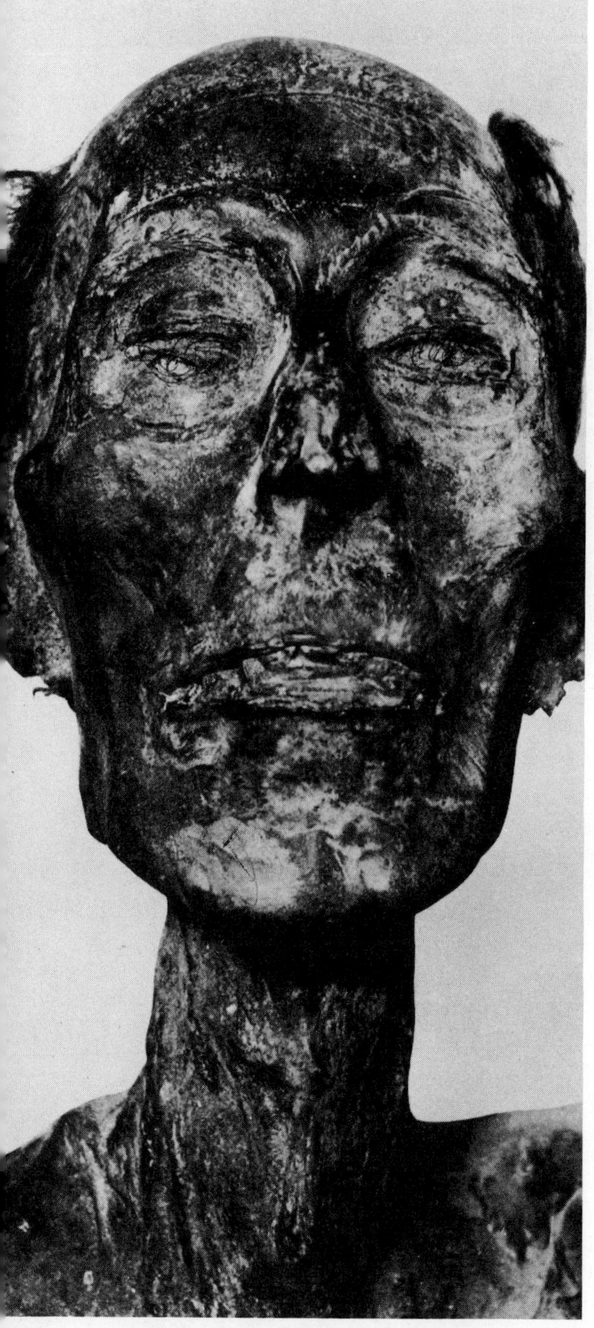

Amenhotep IV did everything in his power to show his devotion to Aton. He even changed his own name to Ikhnaton (ike-*nah*-tun), meaning "pleasing to Aton." He closed Amon's temples in Thebes and built a whole new city, Akhetaton (ah-keh-*tah*-tun), to be his capital. There, amid shady gardens, brilliant palaces, and the sunny courts of a huge temple, the Pharaoh could worship Aton in joy and peace.

Paintings and carvings never show him as a stern king or mighty warrior. Instead, they portray a gentle man who loved to have his beautiful wife, Nefertiti (nef-er-*tee*-tee), and their seven small daughters near him. Ikhnaton's hymns, many of them similar to the psalms of the Old Testament, express his love of living things and his devotion to the god who created them.

While the Pharaoh was pre-occupied with religious matters, the angry priests of Thebes and the frustrated warrior-nobles tried to weaken his government. The Hittites took advantage of Egypt's internal quarrels and conquered Syria, Palestine, and Phoenicia. When tribute from these countries stopped, Egypt suffered a financial crisis. Ikhnaton's empire faced destruction.

Ikhnaton's efforts to change the religious beliefs of his subjects also failed. The people refused to abandon their old gods who could be won over with charms, for belief in a single god who required strict ethical behavior. When Ikhnaton died, the priests forced the new thirteen-year-old Pharaoh Tutankhamen (too-*tahnk*-ah-mun) to move the capital back to Thebes and to worship the old gods. In spite of his failings, Ikhnaton is important in history. He is the first known ruler who professed a belief in the idea of one god.

Ramses II brought new glory to Egypt. The warlike Pharaohs who followed Ikhnaton regained some of the eastern territory that Egypt had lost. Ramses II spent most of his sixty-seven-year reign fighting the Hittites. Because he left so many monuments, historians know more about Ramses II than they do about most of the Pharaohs. Four statues of Ramses II, which are twelve times life size, stand in front of his temple at Abu Simbel (*ah*-boo-*sim*-bel). Unfortunately, he destroyed many of the monuments to earlier Pharaohs.

Temple at Abu Simbel. Over 3200 years ago two temples were carved out of a Nubian cliff overlooking the Nile. They glorified the god-king Ramses II and his wife Nefertari. The picture above shows the larger temple. Its entrance is guarded by four huge seated figures of Ramses II, sixty-seven feet high. The head of the second statue from the left crashed to earth in ancient times. Rising behind the Aswan High Dam, the Nile threatened to submerge these temples. The United Nations Educational Scientific and Cultural Organization (UNESCO) undertook the job of moving them to higher ground. The cliff behind the monuments was first removed, as is shown in the picture at the bottom left. The picture at the right shows how the statues were cut into sections. In the picture at left center a nineteen-ton face is lifted free. Cutting began in October 1965 and was finished in August 1966. It will take five years, and will cost $36,000,000, to completely reassemble the temples on their new site.

QUEEN NEFERTITI. The wife of Ikhnaton is represented in this painted limestone bust found at Akhetaton (modern Tel-el-Amarna). In Egyptian, "nefer" meant beautiful, a word that certainly applied to this lovely queen.

After 1200 B.C., Egypt's power faded steadily. Internal weakness once again combined with external attack to bring about Egypt's decline. The last strong Pharaoh, Ramses III, tried desperately to defeat invaders, but he ran out of money. The high wages of his mercenary soldiers, who fought for pay rather than for love of country, and his enormous gifts to the priests emptied the treasury. When the government, which could no longer afford to feed workers on state projects, began using more captured slaves, the people revolted. The rich priests and nobles then struggled for the throne, while strong invaders swept over the land. The power of the once mighty Pharaohs was destroyed forever.

Egypt was dominated by foreigners for two thousand years. In the years that followed Egypt's downfall, many people conquered the Nile Valley. About 670 B.C. Egypt was conquered by Assyria, and in 525 B.C. by the Persians. Alexander the Great, a Greek conqueror whom you will meet later, seized Egypt from the Persians in 332 B.C. and built Alexandria, a city that became a center of Greek art and learning in the ancient world. After Alexander's death, Egypt was ruled by a new line of Pharaohs descended from Ptolemy (*tahl*-eh-mee), one of his generals. The last of the Ptolemies, Cleopatra (klee-oh-*pat*-truh), tried to restore Egypt's power by winning the favor of the Roman general, Julius Caesar. When Caesar was killed, she tried to strengthen her country by joining forces with his friend, Mark Antony. This plan also failed, as you will see in Part 5 of *Story of Nations,* and Egypt became part of the Roman Empire.

About six centuries later, in 640 A.D., Egypt was conquered again, this time by the Moslems. They dominated Egypt until the nineteenth century, when the British bought control of the country from the Moslem ruler. Not until 1956, when British forces were withdrawn from the Suez Canal, was Egypt restored to full independence for the first time in two thousand years.

Chapter Check-up

1. What were some of the important accomplishments of Amenemhet III?
2. Why was Osiris an important Egyptian god?
3. What effect did the invasion of the Hyksos have on later Egyptian history?
4. What did Thutmose III contribute to Egyptian history?
5. Why do we remember Ikhnaton?
6. What lesson do we learn from Ikhnaton's failure?
7. Why do we know more about Ramses II than about most other Egyptian rulers?
8. How did Cleopatra try to restore Egypt's power?
9. Why did the Egyptian empire collapse?
10. What countries or peoples have controlled Egypt since the fall of the empire?

Egypt: SYNOPSIS

Ancient Egyptian civilization was influenced greatly by the favorable climate and location of the Egyptian homeland. The sunny, protected, ever-fertile Nile Valley gave the Egyptians a cheerful, confident outlook and a deep appreciation of the pleasures of life. Certain that their land was especially favored by the gods, they freely devoted their lives to serving the gods and god-Pharaohs. Their love of life led them to devote great energy to insuring that the joys of this world would continue in the next. Their magnificent temples and pyramids, indeed nearly all Egyptian artistic achievements, were intended to serve these two purposes: retaining divine favor and preserving earthly pleasures in the next world.

In spite of their trust in the gods and their preoccupation with life after death, the Egyptians were a very practical people. Their efforts to improve their surroundings mark important steps in the development of civilization. Their success in increasing the food supply through co-operative building of irrigation systems gave the ancient world a foretaste of the kind of large-scale projects that would be successfully undertaken in later times.

We have seen how the practical problems of land measurement, flood control, tax collection, and pyramid-building led the Egyptians to devise such useful tools as arithmetic, geometry, the calendar, and written language. Ancient Egyptians also made significant beginnings in astronomy, medicine, and dentistry. Even though their complete trust in their gods tended to keep the Egyptians from taking a questioning, scientific approach toward the knowledge they had gained, their work nevertheless provided much basic information for later peoples to draw on. As we shall see in Part 5, the Greeks in particular were indebted to the ancient Egyptians.

Important People

How did each of the following influence the story of Egypt?

Menes
Hatshepsut
Khufu
Ikhnaton
Amenemhet III
Ramses II
Thutmose III
Cleopatra

Terms

Be sure that you understand clearly the meaning of each of the following:

central government
delta
hieroglyphics
irrigation
Upper Egypt
Lower Egypt
mummy
mercenary
papyrus
Pharaoh
pyramid
hieratic writing
Rosetta Stone
scribe
sphinx
Old Kingdom
Middle Kingdom
Empire Age

Questions for Discussion and Review

1. Explain the statement "All Egypt is the gift of the Nile."
2. Why do we say that Egypt was well protected from invasion? Is she today?
3. How did farming in the Nile Valley lead to the development of Egyptian government?
4. Why did the growth of Egyptian government create a need for writing?
5. Why was Egyptian hieroglyphic writing so difficult for archaeologists to decipher?
6. What important religious ideas did the ancient Egyptians develop?
7. It is said that necessity is the mother of invention. What necessities led to the invention or development of the calendar and of geometry in ancient Egypt?
8. What are some of the accomplishments of the Egyptians of each of the three ages, (a) the Old Kingdom, (b) the Middle Kingdom, and (c) the New Kingdom?
9. What do you consider Egypt's greatest contribution to civilization? Why?
10. From what we have learned of the three periods of Egyptian history, what would you conclude are common causes for the decline of a civilization?

Interesting Things To Do

1. Prepare a map of ancient Egypt showing the location of the important cities, temples, and tombs. Use illustrations to make your map more interesting.
2. Construct an enlarged, illustrated time line of Egyptian history. Complete your work in scroll form in true Egyptian style.
3. Make a series of sketches or cartoons to illustrate Egyptian writing, art, sculpture, architecture, or clothing.
4. Prepare an illustrated travel folder urging tourists to visit Egypt to see the wonders of the ancient world.
5. Make an architect's sketch of the Great Pyramid showing the method of construction and the location of chambers and passageways.
6. Construct a model in clay, wood, or paper of an Egyptian pyramid, mummy, temple, or obelisk.
7. Prepare and present a brief talk on one of the following topics: "The History of the Calendar," "The Great Pyramid," or "The Contributions of Ancient Egypt."
8. Write a report based on additional reading about Champollion and the translation of hieroglyphics, about the Suez Canal, or about the importance of the written word today.
9. Imagine that you were a reporter with the archaeological party which opened the tomb of King "Tut." Write an article for your newspaper describing this historic and impressive occasion.
10. Start a "Who's Who in World History" series for your notebook by writing brief biographical portraits of one or more famous ancient Egyptians. Illustrate your reports if you wish to make them more interesting. Add to your "Who's Who" series as you study each of the different nations covered in this book.
11. Prepare a report on recent archaeological investigations in Egypt. By consulting an encyclopedia or other reference works, describe the location of major "finds" and tell what each discovery reveals about the history of ancient Egypt.
12. Visit a museum that has a collection of ancient Egyptian art. Take notes on the paintings and sculpture you see and describe them to the class.
13. Plan a trip to Egypt, including in your itinerary those places that would most interest you. Describe the significance of each place in Egyptian history.

Interesting Reading about Egypt

Breasted, James Henry, *Conquest of Civilization*, Harper & Row. Rich in information about the ancient world in general.

Ceram, C. W., *Gods, Graves, and Scholars*, Knopf.

Edwards, I. E. S., *The Pyramids of Egypt*, Penguin.

*Fairservis, Walter A., *Egypt, Gift of the Nile*, Macmillan.

*Gatti, Ellen and Attila, *Here is Africa*, Scribner. Story of ancient and modern Egypt.

Hartman, Gertrude, *Builders of the Old World*, Heath. Influences of geography on man's history.

*Lamprey, Louise, *Long Ago in Egypt*, Little, Brown. Egyptian life in reign of Queen Hatshepsut.

*Meadowcroft, Enid L., *Gift of the River*, Crowell Collier.

Morrison, Lucille, *The Lost Queen of Egypt*, Lippincott.

Steindorff, George, and Seele, K. C., *When Egypt Ruled the East*, University of Chicago Press. One of the best modern accounts of the Egyptian Empire. Especially strong in art and religion.

*Van Loon, H. W., *The Story of Mankind*, Garden City. Comprehensive and entertaining universal history.

*White, Anne T., *Lost Worlds: Adventures in Archeology*, Random House. Vivid account of the work of archaeologists.

*White, Jon E. M., *Everyday Life in Ancient Egypt*, Putnam.

* Indicates easy reading

In ancient Sumer (Mesopotamia) some 5000 years ago, priest-kings, like the one portrayed here, ruled over city-states in the name of an all powerful god.

Part 3
THE FERTILE CRESCENT
CRADLE OF NINE CIVILIZATIONS

FERTILE CRESCENT

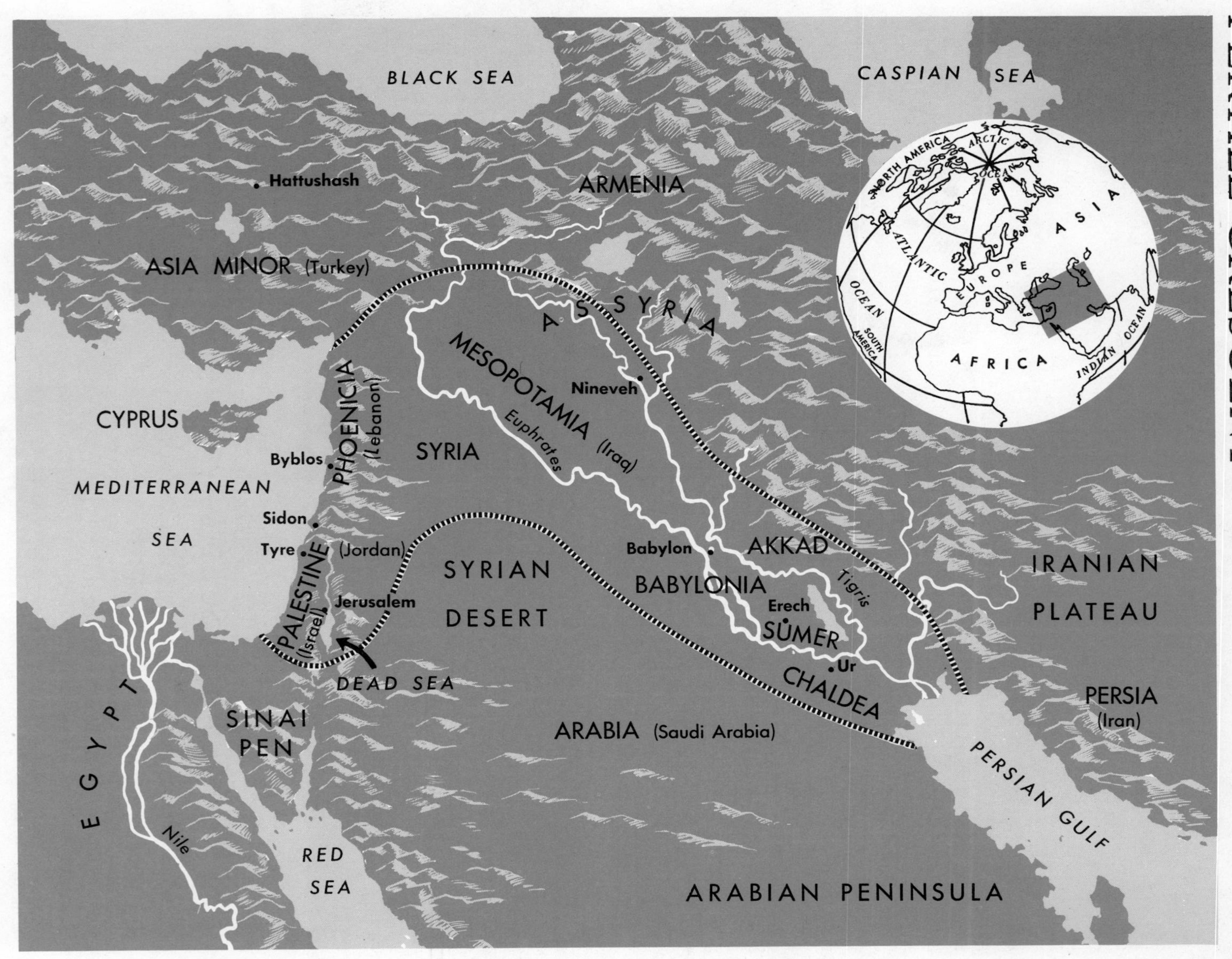

The Fertile Crescent: GEOGRAPHIC SETTING

The Middle East is a vast area that includes parts of southeastern Europe, northeastern Africa, and western Asia. In Part 2 we saw how Egyptian civilization developed in the African sector of the Middle East. We now shift our focus to the heartland of the Middle East, which in ancient times included Phoenicia, Syria, Palestine, Mesopotamia (mes-oh-poe-*tay*-mee-uh), Asia Minor, and Persia. The first four of these regions form a great curving plain that lies in an arch against the Armenian mountains. This curved (or crescent-shaped) plain was one of the few areas of the Middle East that had enough water to insure successful farming. This fact explains why it became known as the *Fertile Crescent*.

The Fertile Crescent is watered by three rivers, the Tigris, the Euphrates, and the Jordan. The two most important rivers, the Tigris and Euphrates, originate in the mountains of Armenia and flow southeast through Mesopotamia, which means "the land between the rivers," to the Persian Gulf. Ancient Mesopotamia itself was divided into four parts. The southernmost part was a marshy region similar to the Nile Delta, called the land of Sumer. Moving upstream to the northwest, we find the regions of Babylonia (bab-ih-*lo-nee*-uh), Akkad (ahk-*odd*), and the rocky highlands of Assyria (uh-*seer*-ee-uh).

The climate of the Fertile Crescent is very hot and there is little rainfall. But because Mesopotamia was watered by the Tigris and Euphrates, in ancient times it was a productive farming region. There, ancient men built a series of civilizations that rivaled the splendor of ancient Egypt.

Fertile Crescent: PERSPECTIVE

In the modern nation of Iraq, six miles from the Euphrates River, and more than a hundred miles inland from the coast of the Persian Gulf lie the remains of a vanished city. Great mounds of dirt rise like ghosts out of the sands of the Arabian desert, and there is no trace of the people that once lived there. Today the site has few visitors other than the archaeologists who travel across the desert to probe in the earth.

The ruins are all that is left of Ur, which more than five thousand years ago was a magnificent center of civilization, a crossroads of trade, and the home of famous men. Located at the junction of the Tigris and Euphrates rivers, it was also a principal seaport on the Persian Gulf. But over the centuries, the courses of the rivers have changed. Silt has been deposited by the rivers and sand has been washed ashore by the sea. As the changing face of the earth left Ur alone in the desert, her people sought new homes and her splendor faded and died.

The shifting sands over Ur are typical of the shifting history of the Fertile Crescent. The region had long been the home of early man and civilization developed even earlier here than it did in the Nile Valley. But its history is much more complex than that of Egypt. The Fertile Crescent was the setting for a series of civilizations. During the years that early Egyptian civilization flourished near the Nile, at least nine different peoples rose to power in and around the Fertile Crescent (see the chart on page 50).

Although each of the invading peoples developed its own culture, they were all strongly influenced by the first civilized people of the region, the Sumerians, with whom we begin our study of Part 3.

CHAPTER 6

The Sumerians, Akkadians, and Babylonians Developed the Earliest Civilizations in Mesopotamia

MESOPOTAMIA WAS LESS FAVORED BY GEOGRAPHY THAN EGYPT

Mesopotamia, located as it was between the Tigris and Euphrates rivers, had certain geographic advantages similar to those of Egypt. Both regions were river valleys with hot, arid climates. Periodic floods in each of the valleys kept them covered with fresh topsoil. But Mesopotamia had geographical problems that Egypt did not have to face. One problem arose from the fact that the volume of flood water in the Tigris and Euphrates depended on the unpredictable winter snowfalls in the mountains of Armenia. The floods were also influenced by landslides in the gorges of the tributary rivers and by the accumulation of silt in the river bed. As a result, the rivers sometimes changed course or overflowed unexpectedly, bringing to the valley disaster instead of benefit. The Tigris once carried off seven thousand houses in a single night. The story of the Great Flood in the Old Testament was probably based on an actual river flood in Mesopotamia.

Another problem created by geography was the absence of natural barriers to invasion. There were no impassable deserts like those surrounding Egypt to protect the Mesopotamians. Wandering tribes of shepherds in the barren Arabian Peninsula or on the dry, stony hillsides of Assyria watched jealously as the Mesopotamians irrigated their land to grow crops. One hungry tribe after another swept in from the desert or down from the hills to seize the fertile plains of Sumer. It is not surprising that the history of Mesopotamia is one of continual struggle. The ever-present threats of flood and invasion made the lives of the Mesopotamians much less secure than those of the Egyptians. As you might expect, this insecurity is reflected in the customs and beliefs of the Mesopotamian peoples.

THE SUMERIANS DEVELOPED THE EARLIEST CIVILIZATION IN MESOPOTAMIA

Sumerian villages grew into warring cities. Sometime before 5000 B.C. a people known as the Sumerians wandered down from the Iranian highlands and settled in the land that was later named for them. They became farmers like the early Egyptians, and gradually developed the beginnings of civilization. Archaeological remains indicate that they refined copper and used it in their weapons and tools. They also made pottery from sun-dried clay, built ovens to bake their bread, and perfected a means of waterproofing their houses and boats with a kind of asphalt.

The recurrent flooding of the Tigris and Euphrates created problems similar to those caused in Egypt by the Nile. To solve them, the Sumerians gradually learned to work in large, well-organized groups. Co-operation made it possible to dig irrigation canals and provide waterways between the villages. Aerial photographs of the region reveal traces of the ancient canal system, which modern engineers consider so well planned that no better system could be devised. Gradually, the villages began to grow into independent cities, each of which served as the center for a large area. The resulting unit, called a *city-state,* introduced an entirely new form of government. You will read later about the importance of the city-state in the stories of Greece and Rome.

The process of government organization stopped short, however, of uniting the Sumerians under one government. Wars often broke out between the city-states over such matters as boundaries and water rights. Occasionally, strong leaders succeeded in uniting the city-states under their rule, but none of these early Sumerian unions lasted very long. The Sumerian cities remained quarrelsome and disunited.

Sargon of Akkad created the world's first empire. While the Sumerians were busy fighting each other, nomadic tribes began to invade Mesopotamia. About 2400 B.C., one of these tribes, the Akkadians, launched a full-scale invasion of Sumer. Their great king, Sargon, brought all of the Fertile Crescent under Akkadian control, thus creating the world's first empire nearly a thousand years before the Egyptian empire of Thutmose III. Very little is known about the Akkadians. Apparently Sargon's successors lacked the skill and force necessary to hold his empire together. At any rate, the Akkadian empire was destroyed in a new wave of revolts and invasions. At last, under the leadership of the city of Ur, the Sumerians established a unified government of their own. This period of Ur's supremacy, the Golden Age of Sumer, only lasted for a hundred years.

Military necessity led to important inventions. As a result of their continual wars, the Sumerians developed military arts much earlier than the Egyptians did. Military requirements led them to invent the first wheeled war chariots. In fact, historians think the Sumerians may have been the first people to use the wheel for any purpose. Their early wheels were heavy, solid wooden disks with leather rims. Chariots drawn by a kind of wild donkey gave the Sumerian armies a great advantage over their enemies.

The Sumerians also learned, probably by chance, how to mix copper with tin to make a much stronger metal, bronze, which they used principally for weapons. Sumerian generals developed a military maneuver in which groups of armed foot soldiers, protected by an unbroken wall of shields, marched very close together. Centuries later the Greeks and Romans used the same formation in their famous phalanx (*fay*-lanks).

The temple dominated Sumerian life. Like the Egyptians, the Sumerians were strongly influenced by religion. But because Sumer did not remain united for long, the Sumerians never developed national gods. Instead, each city had its own god, who was thought to make his home in

THE WHEEL. The Sumerians were among the first peoples to use the wheel. In this battle scene from an inlaid panel, four-wheeled chariots are drawn by four wild asses. In the first line of figures, a king, taller than the rest, has descended from his chariot to inspect captives.

At A Glance

The Succession of Empires in the Fertile Crescent

Rise of Sumerian City-States (*c.* 2850–*c.* 2450 B.C.)

Akkadian Empire (*c.* 2450–*c.* 2270 B.C.)
 Sargon

Babylonian Empire (*c.* 1800–*c.* 1600 B.C.)
 Hammurabi

Hittite Empire (*c.* 1600–*c.* 1200 B.C.)

Phoenician Cities (*c.* 1200–*c.* 700 B.C.)

Hebrew Nation (*c.* 1200–586 B.C.)
 Moses
 The Hebrew Kingdom (*c.* 1000–933 B.C.)
 Saul
 David
 Solomon
 Kingdom of Israel (933–722 B.C.)
 Kingdom of Judah (933–586 B.C.)

Assyrian Empire (*c.* 900–612 B.C.)
 Ashurbanipal

Chaldean Empire (612–538 B.C.)
 Nebuchadnezzar

Persian Empire (550–331 B.C.)
 Cyrus
 Darius I
 Xerxes I

---

the temple which the people built for him. The god ruled over the city through his representative, a man who was especially chosen to be high priest, general of the army, and head of the government. The people allowed this priest-ruler to regulate their lives, because they considered obedience to him the only way to please their god. They believed that if the god became displeased, he might send a flood or an invasion.

In this way religion and government were combined under one man, as they were in Egypt. Gradually, the priest-ruler came to have almost absolute power. He was always closer to the people, however, than the Egyptian god-Pharaoh, because he was merely a representative of the god, not the god himself.

The priest-ruler had many duties. As priest, he spoke to the god on behalf of the people and offered him food three times a day. As ruler, he, like the Egyptian Pharaoh, was responsible for administering nearly all aspects of Sumerian life.

Temple priests controlled the Sumerian economy. All the land of the city presumably belonged to the god of the temple. The priests administered the land for the god and allotted a certain part for the use of each man. For this privilege, he was expected to pay a third of his crop in rent. In addition, everyone, whether priest, soldier, merchant, or farmer, had to spend a specified number of days working on the land which had been retained by the temple for its own use. In this way the temple accumulated vast stores of supplies. From these stores the priests of the temple provided tools and seed for the farmer and regularly distributed food to the people. In times of famine or on feast days, extra portions were provided. Thus all citizens served their god by serving the local temple, and in return the priests of the temple looked after the needs of the people.

The priests also directed the work of craftsmen who were employed to make articles both for use in the temple and for sale in the market place. The temple storehouses were filled with delicate woolen fabrics and rugs, fine pottery and stone bowls, gold helmets, cups, animal statues, and copper and bronze weapons. Any man was allowed to sell privately whatever extra goods or crops he could produce. But since the temple priests controlled the output of both craftsman and farmer, they also controlled trade. The priests sent caravans of grain, dates, woolens, and metalwork to Egypt, Syria, and India. The caravans brought back lumber, stone, gold, silver, copper ore, and semiprecious stones, none of which Sumer possessed. As you can see, the temple priests effectively controlled agriculture, industry, and trade in the Sumerian city-state.

The Sumerians invented arithmetic and writing. The management of the city-state's economic affairs posed problems for the Sumerian priests. Their attempts to solve them resulted in many useful ideas and inventions. For example, in order to find out just how much barley a farmer owed as rent, or how much copper ore a caravan should be instructed to obtain, the priests established standard weights and measures. To make the exchange of goods easier, they introduced money in the form of silver bars and invented fractions and decimals so that they could figure values precisely. To help trade, they established a banking system and passed laws that regulated prices and wages.

To aid in recording all these transactions, the Sumerians as early as 3000 B.C. developed what was probably the first system of writing, cuneiform (kyoo-*nee*-ih-form). Cuneiform writing is a series of small wedge-shaped marks made on a soft clay tablet with a blunt instrument called a stylus. After being inscribed, the tablet was baked in an oven to make it hard, then placed for protection in a clay envelope which had the writer's seal and a brief summary of the contents on the outside. Cuneiform was difficult to use because, like hieroglyphics, the characters stood for syllables or words instead of for letters of the alphabet.

Except for the peasants, every writer had a personal seal, which he pressed on the clay tablet instead of signing his name. The seal was a small stone cylinder on which was beautifully carved a miniature scene and the owner's name. The seals could also be used in other ways. A man who fastened the lid of a storage jar or the door of his house with a dab of clay stamped with his seal could tell, when he returned, whether anyone had disturbed his possessions.

CUNEIFORM TABLET. Sumerian writers used a stylus to make the wedge-shaped marks on wet clay. The clay tablet was either sun-dried or hardened by baking.

WARRIOR'S HELMET. This beautiful gold helmet, made in the form of a wig, protected the Sumerian warrior's ears as well as his head.

The Sumerians developed the first written code of laws. The Sumerians discovered that the complicated affairs of a city-state could not be efficiently settled by individual argument or by force, but required regulation by the government in the form of laws. Accordingly, each city's priest-ruler formulated laws and presided over courts which dealt with such matters as the rights of slaves and women, prices and wages, criminal offenses, and debt. The priest-ruler acted as judge, and scribes made records of all court proceedings.

One of the Sumerian priest-rulers drew up what was probably the first written law code. The law code set limits on the authority of the temple priests. Tax rates and fees for religious services had to be fair. The laws protected the poor by ordering the rich to pay a just price for a poor man's goods, and by making it illegal to collect taxes from widows and orphans.

In spite of its advantages, Sumerian justice had many limitations. Because it was expensive to take a case to court, the poor man was at a disad-

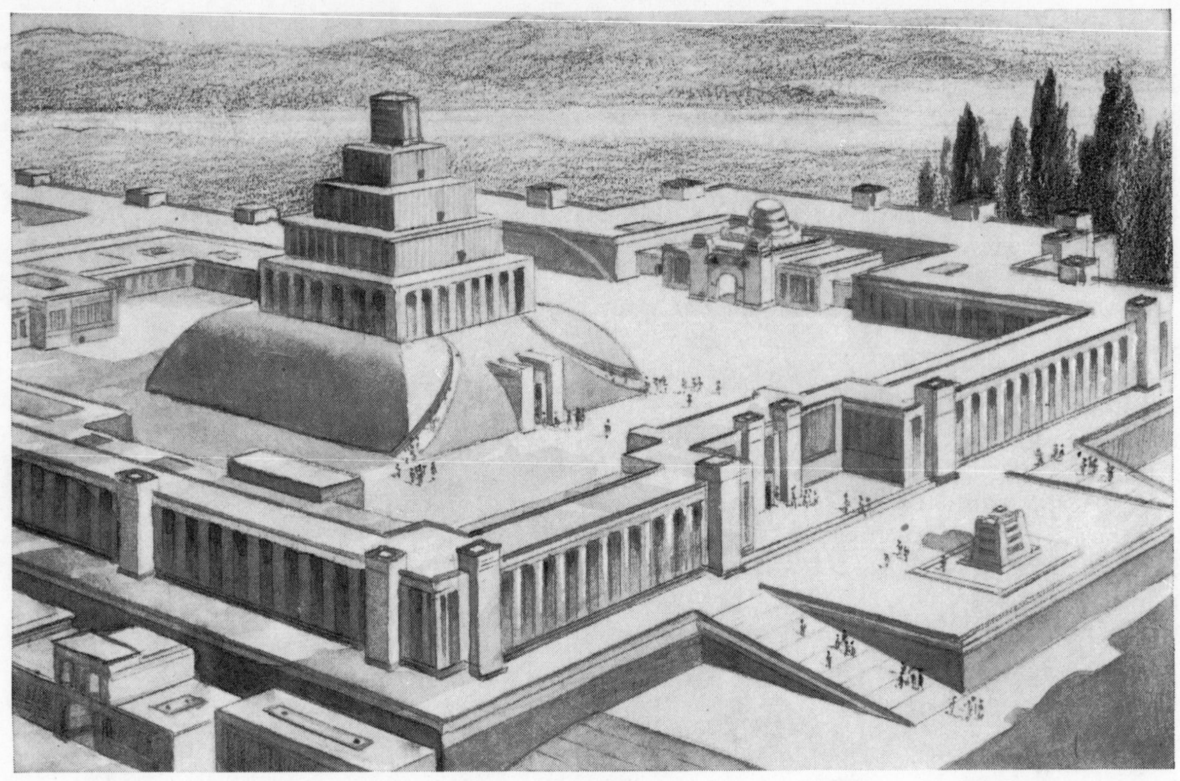

SUMERIAN TEMPLE. The Sumerian temple, or ziggurat, elevated and enclosed within massive walls, gave protection from floods and invaders. The ziggurat was covered with brightly colored enameled bricks which gleamed brilliantly in sunlight.

vantage. If the priest-ruler chose to ignore the law, there was no legal way to stop him. Many men who suffered misfortune were more inclined toward appeasing the angry gods than seeking justice in Sumerian courts. Nevertheless, the Sumerian law codes were an important step forward for early man because they introduced the idea that all men had certain rights and that the government should protect those rights.

Religion and geography influenced Sumerian architecture. A pyramid, you will remember from the story of Egypt, was the symbol of the power of the god-Pharaoh. In the same way a ziggurat (*zig*-er-aht), the tower of a Sumerian temple, symbolized the power of the local god and his priest. The Sumerians made very elaborate towers, for, like the Egyptians, they wanted to win favor with their gods.

The ziggurat, or "Mountain of God," consisted of many levels (see the illustration above). Each level was smaller than the one below it, much like those of a modern skyscraper. A great stairway or ramp led to the god's shrine at the top, where sacrifices were made. The Sumerians believed the god used the ramp to pass up and down between his two homes, the earth and the sky. Often the various levels were planted with beautiful gardens, and each level was painted a symbolic color. For example, black symbolized the underworld, and blue symbolized heaven. The ziggurat was surrounded by courts for worship, storerooms, workrooms, and school rooms. The temple also provided living quarters for the priests and women who served it.

Geography as well as religion influenced Sumerian architecture. Since the Sumerians could not obtain stone from the flat, muddy plains, they used bricks made of clay. The use of bricks created a difficult problem in making doors and windows. How could the area above the openings be supported? The Egyptians used long stone beams called lintels across the tops of doors and windows. But lintels could not be made of mud brick, so the Sumerians devised an *arch*, which made it possible to leave openings in walls that were made entirely of brick.

The Sumerians learned how to build roofs by using wooden beams to support an outer covering that was made of brick. Since even wood was scarce and expensive, temples and houses were usually divided into many small rooms whose walls then helped support the roof. The ziggurats and many other Sumerian buildings were, in fact, almost solid masses of brick.

Unfortunately, the brick buildings of Sumer did not survive. Even though every city was built on a raised mound, none escaped eventual destruction by winds, floods, and sandstorms. Whereas the stone ruins of ancient Egypt still stand, the remains of the brilliantly painted Sumerian buildings are today only heaps of earth.

Religion led the Sumerians to study the heavens. Like most primitive peoples, the Sumerians pictured the parts of nature, such as rivers and the sun, as gods. The god of storm and earth was Enlil, the god of the sky, Anu, and the god of water, Enki. Sometimes the patron gods of cities were identified with the gods of nature. Anu, for example, was also god of the city of Erech (*air*-ek).

The Sumerians believed that the gods caused floods, famines, and invasions, and even interfered in a man's private business. No Sumerian made a major decision without consulting the priests to see what the gods were going to do. The priests carefully studied the movements of the planets, which they considered to be the gods' handwriting. From the tops of the ziggurats high above the fields, they watched the brilliantly clear skies every night. If an invasion occurred when a planet was in a particular part of the sky, they expected another invasion when the planet reached the same point the following year. The priests also kept track of the motions of the moon and made a lunar calendar that told when to repair the canals, when to plant, and when to harvest.

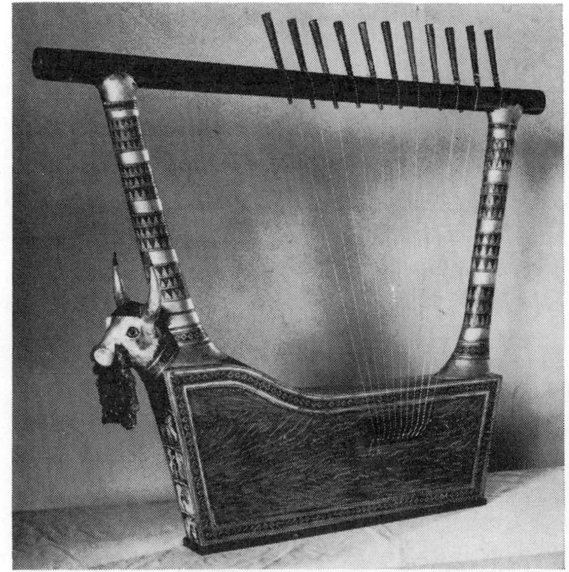

SUMERIAN LYRE. More than five thousand years ago, Sumerian musicians strummed melodies on this ornate lyre, an early ancestor of the modern harp. Patient Sumerian craftsmen carved the lyre of wood and decorated it with gold, silver, red stone, and white seashell.

To make their calculations easier, the Sumerians invented a system of numbers based on units of sixty. This system is used today to divide the day into hours and minutes and to divide a circle into degrees. The Sumerians also developed such mathematical skills as multiplication, division, and the use of square root. For difficult mathematical calculations, they devised reckoning tablets comparable to our slide rules.

Religion influenced Sumerian literature. In contrast to the Egyptians, the Sumerians cared little about life in a next world. They regarded it as a gloomy and unpleasant experience, possibly because life as they knew it in this world seemed so uncertain. In any event, they were chiefly interested in winning divine favor during their own lifetimes. Much of Sumerian literature is made up of charms, hymns, and rules for religious ceremonies to please the gods. Especially interesting are the Sumerian stories of the Creation and the Great Flood, which are very similar to the descriptions found in the Old Testament. One story tells how the gods decided to destroy all men by sending six days of rain. One man, who, like the biblical Noah, was given advance warning, built an ark and saved enough people to start life again. Archaelogists, who have dug through the layers of Mesopotamian cities built on older ruins, have found evidence that such a flood occurred.

Sumerian civilization was preserved by conquering tribes. Sumerian civilization continued to influence the Middle East long after Sumer itself had been destroyed. Beginning with the Babylonians, each new tribe that became dominant in the Fertile Crescent adopted or preserved Sumerian ways of living.

THE BABYLONIANS CONQUERED SUMER BUT PRESERVED ITS CULTURE

Hammurabi established the Babylonian Empire. If the Sumerians had been able to maintain a unified state, they might have warded off their enemies. But the rivalry between Sumerian cities was too strong. Between 2000 B.C. and 1800 B.C., Mesopotamia was again beset by invasion and warfare. About 1800 B.C. a Semitic people from Babylonia rose to power. Their king, Hammurabi (*hahm*-oo-*rah*-bee), conquered all of Mesopotamia and established a great empire whose capital was at Babylon.

The Babylonians adopted and preserved Sumer's remarkable culture. Although the temples of the Sumerian cities were supervised by Hammurabi, they remained the dominant force in the people's lives. Hammurabi made the patron god of Babylon, Marduk (*mar*-duke), the chief god of Mesopotamia and declared that he was Marduk's spokesman on earth. Thus, Hammurabi possessed both political and religious authority.

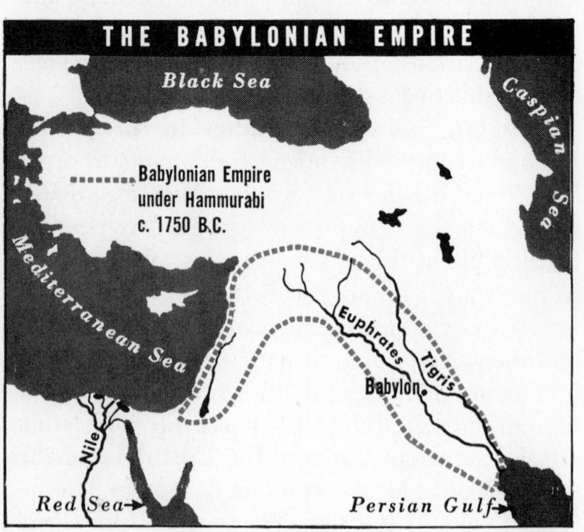

The priests of Babylonia advanced the study of the stars. The Babylonians gave the Sumerian gods new names and identified them with planets. The Sumerian goddess of love and war, Innana (ih-*nah*-nah), was called Ishtar and was thought to be the planet Venus. Enlil, god of earth and storm, was identified with Marduk and was thought to be the planet Jupiter. The Babylonians were as convinced as the Sumerians that the movements of the planets held the secret to the future. They divided the week into seven days, one for each of the five known planets, one for the sun, and one for the moon. Their calculation of the length of the year (the time it took the earth to circle the sun) came within twenty-six minutes of its actual duration. Babylonian priests invented water clocks and sundials to measure time, and they foretold eclipses of the sun and moon.

In spite of these achievements, the Babylonians were not true scientists. Like the Egyptians, they studied the heavens only to discover what the gods would do next, not to discover scientific laws. The priests considered the advice of the soothsayers just as important as the movements of the stars. Soothsayers were specially trained men who foretold the future by examining the inner organs of freshly killed animals.

Hammurabi's Code preserved and organized Sumerian laws. Hammurabi was an able ruler. He is most famous for the code of laws by which he skillfully regulated his empire. Before Hammurabi's time, each Sumerian city had its own code of laws. Hammurabi compiled all these laws in a single code that applied to all the people under his control. He had the laws inscribed on large stone slabs or pillars, so that everyone could see them. Hammurabi, who liked to be called "King of Righteousness," began his code with the words, "I am the shepherd, the savior, whose scepter is the right one, the good protecting shadow over my city...."

The most familiar part of Hammurabi's Code deals with criminal law and declares that if one man should inflict injury on another, he must suffer the same injury as a penalty. This part of the code was based on the principle of "an eye for an eye and a tooth for a tooth." All men were subject to the law, but punishment varied according to the social class of the criminal and his victim. Because priests and aristocrats belonged to the smallest and most honored class, crimes against them were considered more serious than crimes against merchants or peasants. Similarly, a crime committed by a priest or aristocrat bore a stiffer penalty than one committed by a merchant or peasant because the educated upper classes were supposed to have been taught respect for the law. The Code of Hammurabi made the state instead of the individual the dispenser of justice and helped do away with personal vengeance. It marked a major step forward in establishing government by law.

The Code covered almost every aspect of Babylonian life. Under Hammurabi's Code, every man was fixed in his class. For example, peasants could not become scribes, as they could in Egypt. The law did, however, allow slaves captured in war to accumulate property and buy their freedom. The position of women was better in Babylonia than it was in Egypt. Babylonian law permitted them to control property and engage in business. An ancient temple payroll reveals that when women replaced men at a task they received as much pay as the men. A woman was also protected by her marriage contract, but its terms depended on the value of her dowry (the wealth she brought her husband). If she had no dowry at all, she might be treated like a slave. The Code also regulated a variety of social practices. It provided, for example, that every man had to serve in the army and work on the irrigation canals, or pay a fine. But if a man's land was ravaged by floods, he was allowed to postpone paying his debts until the following year. The law also required that business agreements, wills, and other such documents had to be witnessed in order to be valid.

Although severe in its punishments, Hammurabi's Code protected the people's rights and provided for uniform justice administered by the central government. Perhaps most significantly, publication of the law implied that even the king was expected to abide by it.

Despite Hammurabi's wisdom in governing, the Babylonian Empire was unable to withstand the attacks of neighboring tribes who jealously eyed its wealth and splendor. In 1600 B.C. the Hittites captured Babylon. A short time later another invading tribe completed the destruction of its empire, temporarily ending the dominance of Mesopotamia. To follow the rise of new powers, we must now shift our attention to the western end of the Fertile Crescent.

Chapter Check-up

1. Why do historians call this land the Fertile Crescent?
2. What is the meaning of the term *Mesopotamia* and to what area is it applied?
3. What were the three important rivers which watered the Fertile Crescent?
4. In what ways did the Sumerians provide a foundation and pattern for the other civilizations of the Fertile Crescent?
5. What two dangers constantly threatened the peace and security of the Mesopotamians?
6. What were some of the important contributions or achievements of the Sumerians?
7. In what ways did religion dominate the lives of the Sumerians?
8. How was Sumerian architecture influenced by geography?
9. In what sense was Sumerian civilization not destroyed by the Babylonians?
10. What was Hammurabi's Code and how did it influence Babylonian life?
11. What was the status of Babylonian women?
12. What group conquered the Babylonians?

CHAPTER 7

The Hittites, Phoenicians, and Hebrews Rose to Power at the Western End of the Fertile Crescent

THE HITTITES TRANSMITTED BABYLONIAN CIVILIZATION

The Hittite Empire rivaled the Egyptian Empire. For years, the Hittites were a mystery to scholars. Practically nothing was known about them. Then, late in the nineteenth century, archaeologists began intensive study of the ruins of the Hittite capital, the city of Hattushash (kah-too-*shash*). They concluded that in about 2000 B.C., this warlike people of Indo-European stock moved into eastern Asia Minor, where they established a number of independent cities. Eventually these cities united under one king, and by about 1600 B.C. the Hittites were strong enough to invade the Fertile Crescent and conquer Babylon. About 1400 B.C. a great Hittite king recaptured all northern Syria from the Egyptian Pharaoh Ikhnaton, who, as you will recall, was so engrossed in matters of religion that he neglected his empire. Mysteriously, about 1200 B.C. the Hittite Empire was completely destroyed, probably by waves of invaders from the Aegean Islands that lay off the coast of Greece.

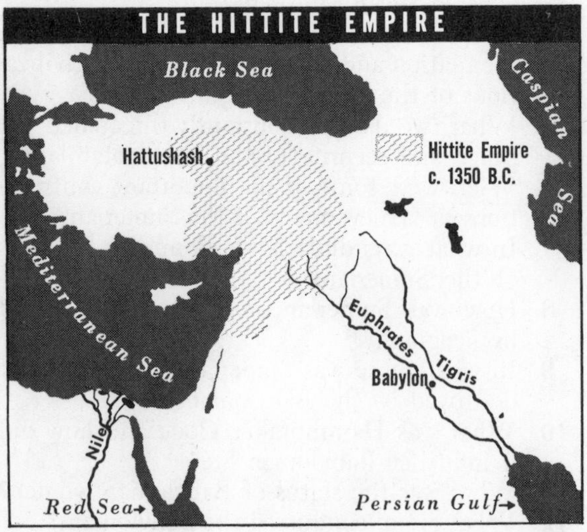

The Hittites introduced the use of iron into the ancient world. One of the Hittites' most important contributions to civilization was the use of iron. The dry hills of Asia Minor were rich in iron ore, which the Hittites learned to mine and smelt. Their iron weapons were so much stronger than weapons of bronze that every king wanted them for his army. The Hittites, who exported iron all over the Middle East, helped the ancient world progress from the *Bronze Age* into the *Iron Age*.

The Hittites regarded iron as the most important metal, but their mines also yielded copper, silver, and lead. Copper was used chiefly in trading with other peoples. Silver was made into bars and used as money. Although farming was the Hittites' chief occupation, mining and metal-working were also very important.

The Hittites were also great horsemen. They were the first people to use the horse-drawn war chariot, which both the Assyrians and the Hyksos later used in their conquests. In other respects, archaeological evidence indicates that Hittite culture was based on that of Babylon. The brick ruins and stone carvings of the palace at Hattushash are of Babylonian design. Archaeologists have found clay tablets which show that the Hittites kept cuneiform records in two languages, their own and Akkadian, the language of the Babylonians. Hittite religion and literature closely resembled those of Babylon, and Hittite laws were similar to those found in Hammurabi's Code but were less severe. Much of this Babylonian culture was passed on to other ancient peoples by the Hittites.

GEOGRAPHY DIVIDED THE WESTERN END OF THE FERTILE CRESCENT INTO SMALL STATES

In the Fertile Crescent the period between 1200 B.C. and 900 B.C. is called the *Era of Small States*. During these years no empires arose in the eastern part of the Crescent to replace the Babylonian Empire. The western end of the Crescent, which included Syria, Phoenicia, and Palestine, has always either been divided into small states or ruled by foreign emperors. In 1200 B.C. it was occupied by four Semitic tribes who had wandered in from the Arabian Desert many years earlier. The Aramaeans (ar-uh-*mee*-unz) settled in Syria, and the Phoenicians (feh-*neesh*-unz) occupied the Syrian coast. The Philistines (fih-*lis*-tinz), from whom the name "Palestine" is derived, held the fertile coastal plain south of Phoenicia. The Hebrews occupied the eastern part of Palestine, which was then called Canaan (*kay*-nun). (Today the western end of the Crescent is divided among the states of Syria, Lebanon, Israel, and Jordan.)

Several factors were responsible for the failure of the early Semitic tribes to unite into a single empire. For one thing, there was no great river like the Nile or the Euphrates to bring them together. Another factor was that they were under constant attack from invaders. In fact, their land became a kind of highway between Egypt and Mesopotamia. Because the Arabian Desert blocked the direct route, Egyptian traders and soldiers marched up the Mediterranean coast, east to the Euphrates, and downstream to Babylon. Armies from Mesopotamia followed the same path when they invaded Egypt. No wonder this area of the Crescent, the crossroads of the Middle East, was slow to develop. The destruction of the Hittite Empire in 1200 B.C. was followed, however, by a period of three hundred years during which no major power dominated the Fertile Crescent. During this time, the Semitic tribes developed flourishing, independent states.

THE PHOENICIANS CARRIED CIVILIZATION WESTWARD

Phoenician ships explored the Mediterranean world. The Aramaeans had pushed the Phoenicians into a narrow strip of coastal land which lacked enough fertile soil to support its inhabitants. Furthermore, traffic over the busy Egypt-Mesopotamia trade route made it difficult to cultivate what land there was. That same route made the Phoenician cities of Tyre, Sidon (*sy*-d'n), and Byblos (*bih*-blose), with their good harbors, natural centers of exchange. So the Phoenicians turned from agriculture to trade.

The Phoenicians had no rivals for control of the Mediterranean, because Mesopotamia had no seaports and the Egyptians were afraid to venture out into the open sea. The Phoenicians built small, sturdy wooden ships from the cedar trees which grew on the slopes of the Lebanon mountains. As Phoenician sailors became more skillful, they explored all of the Mediterranean. They even ventured out past Gibraltar into the stormy waters of the Atlantic Ocean to obtain tin from the mines of western Britain. There is some evidence that they may have sailed around Africa, a feat that was not repeated for two thousand years.

The Phoenicians were clever traders and fine craftsmen. Phoenician merchants built a thriving commerce by exporting cedar logs to Babylon and Egypt, where few trees grew. These clever Phoenician merchants soon learned that the peoples at the western end of the Mediterranean were eager to trade hides and copper for luxuries from the Middle East. In order to take advantage of this trade, the Phoenicians established many colonies throughout the Mediterranean. Two of their most famous colonies were Carthage in North Africa and Cadiz (kuh-*diz*) in Spain.

The Phoenician ships carried to Western Europe such luxuries as perfume, incense, fine

CANAANITE-PHOENICIAN-ARAMAIC	GREEK	LATIN
𐤀	A	A
𐤁	B	B
𐤂	ΓC	CG
𐤃	ΔD	D
𐤄	Ε E	E
𐤅	Ϝ Y	FVUWY
𐤆	I	Z
𐤇	H	H
𐤉	I	I J
𐤊	K	K
𐤋	Λ L	L
𐤌	M	M
𐤍	N	N
𐤎	+ Ξ	X
𐤏	O	O
𐤐	Π Γ	P
𐤑		
𐤒	Ϙ	Q
𐤓	P R	R
𐤔	Σ ϛ	S
𐤕	T	T

woolen and linen cloth, and beautiful metal work, which Phoenician traders obtained in Egypt and Mesopotamia. Some of the goods they exchanged were manufactured in their own workshops and were often copied from the work of Egyptian and Mesopotamian craftsmen. The Phoenicians were particularly famous for their delicate glassware and for a rich purple dye made from shellfish. Because the dye was so expensive that only kings could afford to wear garments colored with it, the color became known as royal purple. Thus, through trade, the Phoenicians brought backward Western Europe into contact with the more civilized Middle East.

The Phoenicians gave us the alphabet. Phoenician traders found hieroglyphics and cuneiform awkward to use in making out bills of sale. They quickly saw the advantage of Egyptian hieratic writing, in which each symbol stood for a letter instead of for a syllable. The Phoenicians borrowed the system and eventually perfected a method of writing based on an alphabet of twenty-two letters.

The alphabet, which was spread throughout the Mediterranean world by Phoenician traders, was quickly adopted because it was helpful in trade and easy to learn. It was improved by the Greeks, who added letters for vowel sounds. (The Greek influence is shown in the word *alphabet,* which comes from the Greek names for the first two letters, *alpha* and *beta.*) The alphabet passed from the Greeks to the Romans, and then to the peoples of Western Europe.

The Phoenicians founded many trade colonies around the Mediterranean. By 700 B.C. the Assyrians had subdued the Phoenician cities of Asia, but other Phoenician colonies continued to flourish. Two of them, Carthage in North Africa, and Cadiz in Spain became famous commercial centers. The Phoenician alphabet was one of ancient man's most important achievements.

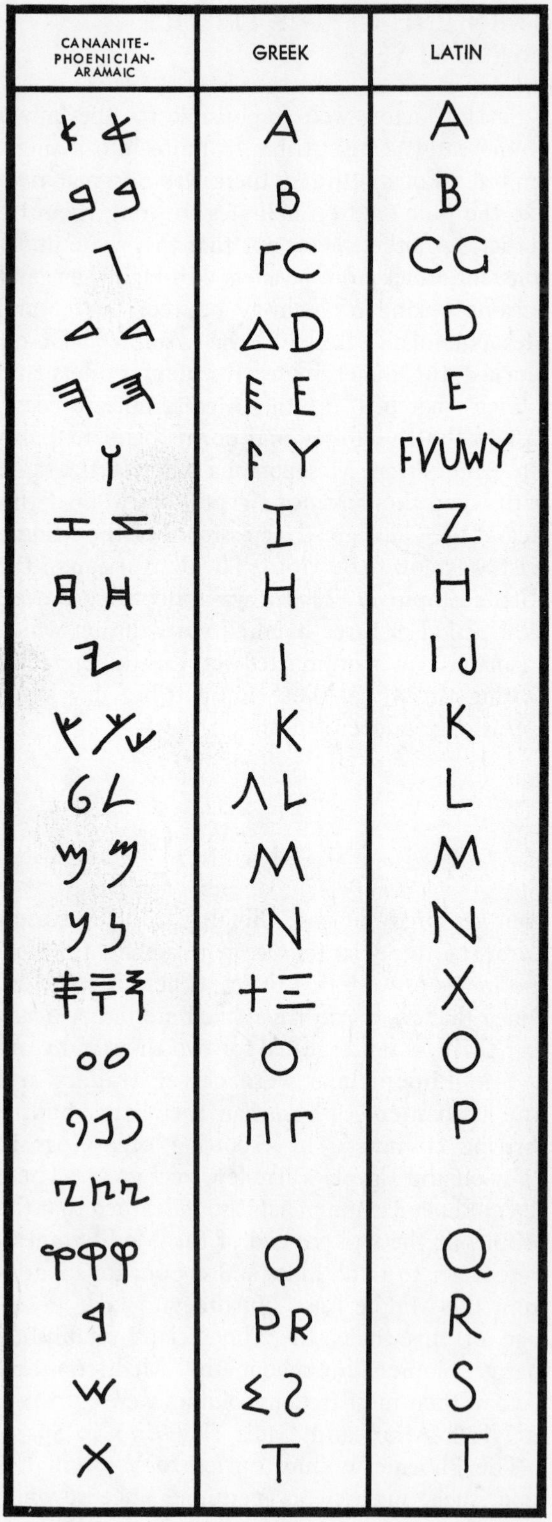

Development of the Alphabet. The alphabet that was invented long ago in the Fertile Crescent is reflected in the writing we use today. Read across to see how our alphabet developed.

THE HEBREWS FOUNDED A KINGDOM IN CANAAN

Moses led the Hebrews to the Promised Land. The Hebrews were shepherds who had wandered for centuries in the Arabian Desert seeking grass for their flocks. Sometime between 1400 B.C. and 1300 B.C. their search led many of them out of the desert into the land of Canaan in eastern Palestine. As a homeland, Canaan left much to be desired. It lacked fertile soil, natural resources, and harbors. Although winds from the Mediterranean brought plenty of rainfall in winter, it quickly drained off. In summer, the hills in the south were burned brown and covered with dust carried by the hot desert winds. Since the hills were far more suitable for grazing than for crops, most of the Hebrews continued to be shepherds. In spite of its drawbacks, however, the Hebrews found Canaan a better home than the Arabian Desert had been. The Jordan River, in the northern part of the country, created a rich, well-watered valley which seemed like a paradise to the Hebrews. They called it the "land of milk and honey."

Meanwhile, another group of Hebrew shepherds had wandered into Egypt. According to the account in the Old Testament, these tribes were captured and enslaved by the Egyptian Pharaoh Ramses II. Perhaps you are familiar with the story of how Moses, the Hebrew leader, led his people out of Egypt into the wilderness of the Sinai Peninsula, where they wandered for forty years. Finally, in about 1200 B.C., they reached Canaan, where they united with the other Hebrew tribes in the wars against the Canaanites. After the Canaanites were defeated, the Hebrews began to develop their new homeland. They built permanent houses and began to farm the land.

Civil wars among the twelve Hebrew tribes divided Canaan, and for some time the Hebrews remained weak and disunited. Each of the twelve tribes was ruled by a wise man, or judge. Eventually fear of the Philistines on the coast caused ten of the tribes to unite. They chose one strong leader, Saul, to be their king. Saul was popular and won many victories for his people, but when the tide of war began to turn in favor of the Philistines he grew despondent and took his own life.

Hebrew kings brought their people glory. The next Hebrew king was a young shepherd, David, who had been called to entertain Saul by playing the harp. In a crucial conflict with the Philistines, David, armed only with a slingshot, volunteered to fight the Philistine giant, Goliath (go-*lie*-uth). In gratitude for David's victory the

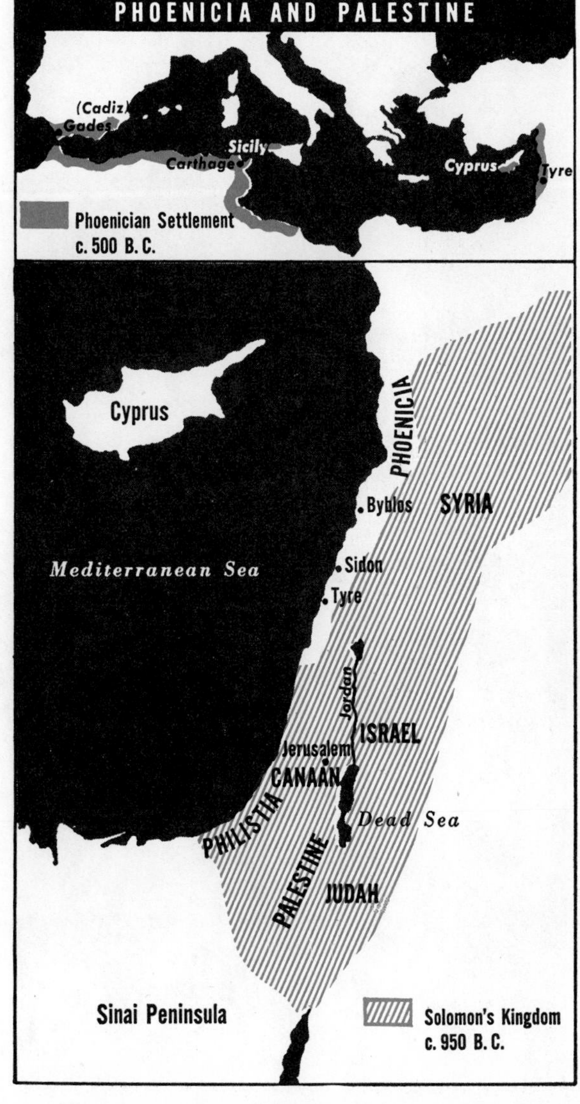

Hebrews chose him to succeed Saul as king of the Hebrews. About 1000 B.C. David united the Hebrews into a strong kingdom with Jerusalem as its capital. During the forty years of his rule, David conquered many enemy tribes and enabled the Hebrews to dominate the western end of the Fertile Crescent.

MOSES. The great leader of the Hebrew people is shown here as he was envisioned by the sixteenth-century artist Michaelangelo. In his right hand Moses holds the tablets on which are written the Ten Commandments.

During the reign of David's son Solomon, the Hebrew kingdom reached the height of its power and splendor. The Old Testament refers to Solomon as a ruler of great wisdom and describes the vast extent of his trading enterprises. Because of Palestine's location on the route between Egypt and Mesopotamia, Solomon was able to control much of the overland trade between these two points. He and the king of Tyre made a commercial alliance that provided for sharing their merchant fleets. Unfortunately, the gold, silver, and ivory that these ships brought back to Palestine did little to benefit the Hebrew people. Although Solomon built a magnificent temple in honor of the Hebrew god, he squandered most of his wealth on personal luxuries.

Solomon's projects were so expensive that he had to tax his people heavily and force many of them to work in Phoenician mines. When he died, the ten northern tribes angrily broke away and established the independent kingdom of Israel. Disunited, the Israelites were too weak to withstand the onslaught of the Assyrians, who thundered through Israel in 722 B.C. on their way to Egypt. The Assyrians captured the Israelites and forced them to march across the hot plains to Assyria, where they vanished and were never heard of again. In Hebrew tradition these Israelites became known as the Ten Lost Tribes.

The remaining two tribes in the south formed the kingdom of Judah. The people called themselves Jews, from a shortened form of "Judah." One country after another exacted tribute from the tiny kingdom. In 586 B.C. Jerusalem was destroyed by the Chaldeans, about whom you will read in the next chapter, and the Jews were marched off to captivity in Babylon. Even though they later returned to Canaan, they were unable to regain their former unity or power.

The eastern end of the Fertile Crescent regained its dominance. The three peoples we have studied in Chapter 7, the Hittites, the Phoenicians, and the Hebrews, flourished during a period when there was no strong military state in the Fertile Crescent. Thus, free from the threat of foreign domination, these tiny lands were able to make important contributions to history. We

TEMPLE OF SOLOMON. The Temple of Solomon, a vast structure of walls and towers, perhaps looked like this artistic reconstruction. It was destroyed by Nebuchadnezzar in the sixth century B.C.

have noted, for example, that the Hittites introduced the use of iron and the Phoenicians perfected the alphabet. Perhaps the greatest contribution of all came from the Hebrew peoples, who were responsible for important religious developments. We shall discuss their religious ideas in Part 6.

We now continue our study of the Fertile Crescent by turning our attention to the eastern sector of the region. For it was there, many hundreds of years ago, that three of the most remarkable of the ancient civilizations appeared. In the following chapter we shall see how each of these civilizations developed.

Chapter Check-up

1. In what way did the Hittites serve as carriers of civilization?
2. What was the most important contribution of the Hittites to the ancient world?
3. In what two ways did geography work to prevent the tribes in the western end of the Fertile Crescent from uniting to form a powerful empire?
4. How were the Phoenicians encouraged to become traders?
5. What were Phoenicia's most famous trading colonies in the Mediterranean?
6. What great contribution did the Phoenicians make to the ancient world?
7. Why did the Hebrews consider Canaan a "land of milk and honey?"
8. Who led the Hebrews out of Egypt?
9. Under which of their kings did the Hebrews reach their greatest height of wealth and power?
10. What is our best source for the history of the Hebrews?
11. What condition allowed the Hittite, Phoenician, and Hebrew cultures to flourish?

CHAPTER 8

The Assyrians, Chaldeans, and Persians Created Empires in the Middle East

THE WARLIKE ASSYRIANS DOMINATED THE MIDDLE EAST

Assyrian life was organized around the army. During the centuries after the fall of the Babylonian Empire, the Assyrians slowly gained power in the hills around the Upper Tigris. By 900 B.C., having built the strongest army in Mesopotamia, they began a series of wars against neighboring tribes. With surprising ease, they conquered the Babylonians and overran all of Mesopotamia. By 700 B.C. the Assyrian king, Sargon II, had created the greatest empire (comprising all of the Fertile Crescent and Egypt) yet seen in the ancient world.

The fierce Assyrian soldiers struck terror in the hearts of their enemies. Their reputation for cruelty made them the most hated and feared of all ancient conquerors. After winning a battle, they often reduced the defeated city to rubble and then burned their victims in great bonfires or blinded them and left them to die in the sun. Survivors, if any, were forced to move to some other city. One of the Assyrian kings, filled with pride in his savage deeds, wrote this account of a successful military campaign.

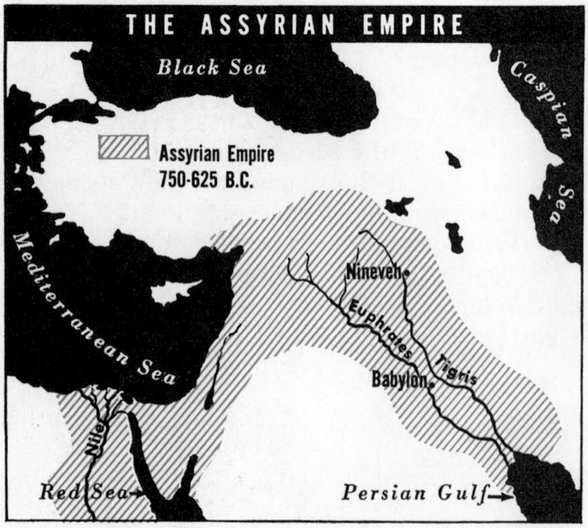

> "I shut up the king in his royal city. I raised monuments of bodies before his gates. All his villages I destroyed, desolated, and burned. I made the country a desert, I changed it into hills and mounds of debris."

You can easily see why the other peoples of the Fertile Crescent hated the Assyrians and their proud capital, Nineveh (*nin*-uh-vuh).

The Assyrians turned their empire into a mighty war machine. The army was made up of professional soldiers, who fought for the love of fighting and for the spoils of war. It included specially trained units of spies, engineers, and supply personnel. Assyrian soldiers, who had learned from the Hittites how to make iron-tipped spears and arrows, were splendidly armed and well-protected by helmets and breastplates of bronze. They used a spoked wheel on their war chariots. Because it was lighter than the solid wheel of the Sumerians, it greatly increased the speed of the Assyrian chariots. Their magnificent army enabled the Assyrians to build a mighty empire. For over a century they dominated the Fertile Crescent.

An Assyrian king established a great library. Despite their ferocity, and although they produced practically no literature of their own, the Assyrians preserved much of Babylon's culture. One of the last rulers, Ashurbanipal (ah-shoor-*bah*-nih-pahl), employed scribes to collect and copy thousands of clay tablets which he placed in a great library.

LION HUNTING. This wall carving from Ashurbanipal's palace at Nineveh shows the Assyrian king lion hunting. The lion has a fierce expression of pain on his face. In Assyrian reliefs, animals are often depicted more realistically than human figures. Note the spoked wheel on the king's chariot.

Many of these tablets have survived and are an invaluable source of information about Babylonian mathematics and literature.

In building their cities and palaces, the Assyrians followed Babylonian plans. They used stone instead of brick, however, because their country, unlike Babylon, was located on high, rocky ground. While the Assyrians are not noted for their artistic achievements or their creative abilities, they produced elaborate stone carvings in bas-relief. These carvings usually depicted Assyrian warriors in blood-chilling battle scenes or engaged in hunting, another favorite pursuit of the Assyrians.

THE CHALDEANS MADE BABYLON A CENTER OF CULTURE

The Assyrians, who for nearly two hundred years had waged war on the people of the Fertile Crescent, at last met defeat themselves. A later group of Babylonians, the Chaldeans, led a series of revolts against Assyrian rule. In 612 B.C., while other tribes were assaulting the Assyrian frontiers, the Chaldeans attacked and destroyed the Assyrian capital, Nineveh. "The lair of lions, the bloody city, the city gorged with prey," as it has been called, never rose again.

Under the rule of Nebuchadnezzar (neb-uh-kad-*nez*-er), the Chaldeans extended their control over Syria, Palestine, and Egypt. Babylon, covering an area almost equal to that of present-day Chicago, was the most magnificent city of its time. Herodotus, a Greek historian who visited Babylon in the fifth century B.C., gives us a vivid picture of it which has been confirmed by modern archaeologists. In the time of Herodotus the city was surrounded by a double row of fortified walls and a deep ditch filled with water. A long, walled avenue led up to the city and passed through the imposing Ishtar (*ish*-tar) Gate. The wall was decorated with more than a hundred life-sized yellow lions carved on a background of bright blue glazed brick. High over the roofs of the city towered a ziggurat, the famous Tower of Babel (*bay*-bel). Its seven stories were painted red, blue, orange, and other colors to symbolize celestial bodies. You probably know the biblical story of how the workmen failed to complete the Tower of Babel because they could not understand one another's language. This story reveals how many different groups of people had been brought to Babylon by trade and conquest.

Babylon was most famous for the breathtaking beauty of its "hanging gardens." Nebuchadnezzar had the gardens planted in order to please his wife, who missed the trees and flowers of her childhood home in the mountains to the north. Flowers, shrubs, and vines were planted on the high terraces and roofs of the imperial palace. A water system, hidden beneath the greenery and pumped by slaves, kept them beautiful. Viewed from the ground, the gardens seemed to be hanging in the sky. The Chaldean civilization, although brilliant, was short-lived. In less than a century, the Chaldeans were forced to surrender their splendid capital to a new wave of invaders from the Iranian highlands to the east.

THE PERSIANS CREATED A GREAT EMPIRE

Cyrus the Great led Persia to power. For many centuries the Persians had herded sheep and horses in the Iranian highlands east of Mesopotamia. About 550 B.C. a Persian leader, later known as Cyrus (*sy*-rus) the Great, quietly annexed his nearest neighbors. A few years later he led his armies to Babylon. What happened is not entirely clear, but apparently the Babylonian nobles were angry at their king and surrendered the city to Cyrus without a struggle. After capturing the city of Babylon, Cyrus rapidly extended his empire eastward to India and westward to Egypt.

Cyrus was a wise statesman. He ruled his subjects with kindness rather than oppression. When he fell in battle, his people sincerely mourned their loss. "O man, I am Cyrus, who founded the greatness of Persia and ruled Asia. Grudge me not this monument." These are the words Cyrus had engraved on his tomb. (Compare them with the cruel boast of the Assyrian king quoted on page 62).

Darius administered the Persian Empire wisely. About eight years after the death of Cyrus, Darius (duh-*ry*-us), Persia's greatest emperor, came to power. He expanded the Persian empire until it reached from the Indus River in India to Thrace in southeastern Europe (see the map below). Eventually he came into conflict with the Greeks. You will read the story of the war between Persia and Greece in Part 4.

Darius, like Cyrus, proved to be an excellent ruler as well as a great warrior. He learned, as the Assyrians and Chaldeans never had, that an empire composed of many different peoples with a variety of languages and traditions must be well supervised or fall into disunity and conflict. Instead of relying entirely on military power to hold his empire together, Darius developed an elaborate system of imperial government. He di-

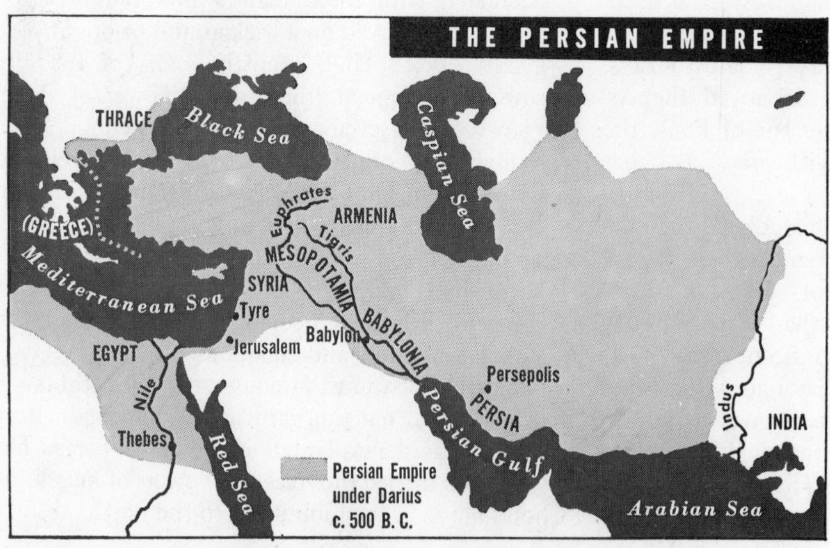

THE HANGING GARDENS OF BABYLON. Because his wife missed the mountains of her homeland, Nebuchadnezzar ordered these Hanging Gardens built for her. They were famous in antiquity. Here is an artist's conception of how they may have looked.

vided the empire into twenty-one provinces, each of which was ruled by a military governor, a civil governor, and a visiting official known as the "King's Ears and Eyes." Each of these men was expected to check on the other two and report directly to Darius, who hoped that the system would make his officials efficient and loyal.

Darius sought to keep his subject peoples content by allowing them to keep their own laws, language, religion, and, occasionally, even their local rulers. He built excellent roads and established a postal system in order to keep in close touch with every part of his empire. Thus he avoided a problem that had helped to cause the downfall of earlier empires, poor communication. Darius also encouraged trade, knowing that it would help unite his empire. For this purpose he coined money, established a wise tax policy, and rebuilt the canal that the Egyptians had dug earlier between the Nile River and the Red Sea. All these measures made the Persian Empire the largest and best organized the world had yet seen.

Zoroaster gave the Persians a new faith. The Persians borrowed much of their civilization from the Sumerians and the Greeks, but their religion was entirely their own. About 600 B.C. a teacher named Zoroaster began to preach a new faith, which differed greatly from the old Sumerian beliefs based on magic and fear. Zoroaster taught that the world was the battlefield for a continual struggle between the forces of good and the forces of evil and that men had to join one of these forces. On a final judgment day, all men would be punished or rewarded according to the choice they had made. Ahura Mazda (ah-*hoo*-ruh *mahz*-duh), the god of purity, truth, and light, was expected to preside at the final judgment. The Persians worshiped Ahura Mazda in the form of fire because to them it symbolized his qualities.

After two hundred years the Persian Empire met defeat. For two hundred years after the death of Darius, Persian rule brought peace and prosperity to the Middle East. But in Persia, as in Egypt, internal weakness combined with ex-

RUINS AT PERSEPOLIS. More than two thousand years ago this staircase echoed to the footsteps of the Persians who were ruled by Darius and his successors. Above the stairs is the great audience hall, and in the distance is the palace.

ternal attack to bring about the decline of the empire. Weak kings and mercenary soldiers became too fond of luxury and pleasure. First, the outlying provinces of the Persian Empire revolted and broke away. Then, in 331 B.C., the Persians met final defeat at the hands of Alexander the Great (see Chapter 13). When Alexander died a short time later, the empire fell to pieces.

A new Persian Empire arose about two hundred years after the birth of Christ, but it was never able to regain its former glory. Finally, in 651 A.D., Persia became part of the great Moslem Empire. You will learn more in Part 23 about the Middle East after the fall of the Persian Empire.

Chapter Check-up

1. Why did the people of the Fertile Crescent fear and hate the Assyrians?
2. Why were the Assyrians so successful in warfare?
3. How did the Assyrians add to our knowledge of civilization in the Fertile Crescent?
4. Under whose rule did Babylon become the most beautiful city of its day?
5. How did Darius make the Persian Empire the best organized the world had yet seen?
6. What important new religious idea was contributed by the Persians?
7. What were the causes of the decline and final defeat of the Persian Empire?

The Fertile Crescent: SYNOPSIS

The story of the Fertile Crescent, unlike that of Egypt, involves the rise and fall of at least nine distinct civilizations. Several important points should be noted. The first is the effect of geography on the people of this region. A comparison of Egypt and Mesopotamia shows that in one important respect they were alike. Both were river valleys where living conditions made it possible for men to take the first steps beyond the Stone Age. In both lands, men became farmers under conditions that required social co-operation. As they learned to work together, the solutions to their problems started them on the road to civilization.

But the stories of these two civilizations show strong contrasts, in which the influence of geography can again be seen. In Egypt, the floods were regular and the country was protected by natural boundaries. In Mesopotamia, different conditions existed. Floods came unexpectedly, and hostile neighbors found invasion easy. Thus, while the Egyptians developed a confident outlook and were able to concentrate on peaceful achievements, their less secure neighbors in Mesopotamia had to devote their energies to the arts of war. The uncertainty of the inhabitants of Mesopotamia is reflected in their fearful submission to their governments and their gods.

A second point to note is that because warfare was constant in the Fertile Crescent, no single people was able to remain long in power. Over and over again, cities, kingdoms, and empires rose to great heights, weakened, and collapsed under attack. For this reason, it is remarkable that the civilization, started by the Sumerians and adopted by each new conqueror, survived for nearly three thousand years.

Finally, you should remember the important contributions that the peoples of the ancient Middle East have made to modern civilization. They invented the wheel, wrote the first law code, and introduced the use of iron. They made important contributions to modern knowledge of the stars and devised a numerical system, based on units of sixty, which is still used to measure such things as circles and hours of the day. Modern man is also indebted to these ancient peoples for discovering the principle of the arch and for inventing the alphabet in which this book is printed. Without these many contributions from the peoples of the Fertile Crescent, civilization as we know it today would not have been possible.

Important People

Tell the part played in the story of the Fertile Crescent by each of the following:

Sargon of Akkad
Hammurabi
Saul
David
Solomon
Ashurbanipal
Nebuchadnezzar
Cyrus the Great
Zoroaster
Darius

Terms

Be sure that you understand clearly the meaning of each of the following:

cuneiform
city-state
Fertile Crescent
"King's Ears and Eyes"
Hammurabi's Code
Mesopotamia
priest-ruler
Sumerian law code
ziggurat

Questions for Discussion and Review

1. In what ways is the history of the Fertile Crescent different from that of Egypt?
2. Explain the statement, "The peoples of the Fertile Crescent made variations on one pattern of civilization."
3. How was nature kinder to the Egyptians than to the Mesopotamians?
4. Why is it possible today to see so much more evidence of ancient civilization in Egypt than in Mesopotamia?

5. Why is the first written law code of the Sumerians important in the story of mankind?
6. What were some of the goods which Phoenician merchant ships carried throughout the Mediterranean world?
7. Explain briefly the history of the alphabet.
8. Why is the history of the Hebrews so important to us?
9. In your opinion, what were the three greatest contributions of the Fertile Crescent civilizations? Why?
10. Why is the Fertile Crescent no longer fertile? What lesson is there here from which we can profit today?
11. What present-day countries are included in the area of the Fertile Crescent?

Interesting Things to Do

1. Draw a map of the Fertile Crescent area showing the nations which exist there today. Sketch over this map the approximate boundaries of the old Fertile Crescent and write in the names of the ancient states.
2. Make a comparative time line for Egypt and the Fertile Crescent. Using illustrations wherever possible, add events and achievements which will make your time line more meaningful and interesting.
3. Prepare a summary chart of the ancient civilizations of the Fertile Crescent. Column headings for your chart should be as follows: State, Period of Power (approximate dates), Important Rulers, and Significant Contributions to Civilization.
4. Make a series of sketches or cartoons showing: (a) the development of the wheel and the ways in which it has served mankind, or (b) the outstanding contributions of the Fertile Crescent civilizations.
5. Prepare a clay tablet with wedge-shaped marks to illustrate how cuneiform writing was done.
6. Prepare a talk entitled "Pick and Shovel Historians," telling of the work of archaeologists in uncovering the story of the Fertile Crescent in ancient times.
7. Arrange an informal debate on the subject, "*Resolved,* That the peoples of the Fertile Crescent made greater contributions to civilization than did the people of Egypt."
8. Devise an imaginary shipping list showing a Phoenician trading vessel's typical cargo.
9. Write an historical sketch, "The ABC's Go Westward," explaining how the alphabet traveled from the Fertile Crescent westward through the Mediterranean into Europe.
10. Add to your "Who's Who in World History" series by writing brief biographical reports on one or more of the important leaders of the Fertile Crescent civilizations.

Interesting Reading about the Fertile Crescent

Breasted, James Henry, *Conquest of Civilization,* Harper & Row.

Ceram, C. W., *The Secret of the Hittites,* Knopf.

Contenau, Georges, *Everyday Life in Babylon and Assyria,* St. Martin's Press.

*Fairservis, Walter A., *Mesopotamia the Civilization that Rose out of Clay,* Macmillan.

Falls, C. B., *First 3000 Years: Ancient Civilizations of the Tigris and Euphrates, and Nile River Valleys,* Viking.

*Gere, Frances K., *Boy of Babylon,* Longmans Green.

Heaton, Eric William, *Everyday Life in Old Testament Times,* Scribner.

*Hoffman, Gail, *Land and People of Israel,* Lippincott. Story of the Hebrews from Old Testament times to the present.

Ogg, Oscar, *Twenty-Six Letters,* Crowell Collier. Development of written language, written by an expert on the subject.

* Indicates easy reading

The free citizens of Greek city-states strove for mastery over mind and body. This charioteer, found at Delphi, personifies Greek confidence that man could achieve this ideal.

Part 4
GREECE
BIRTHPLACE OF DEMOCRACY

ANCIENT GREECE

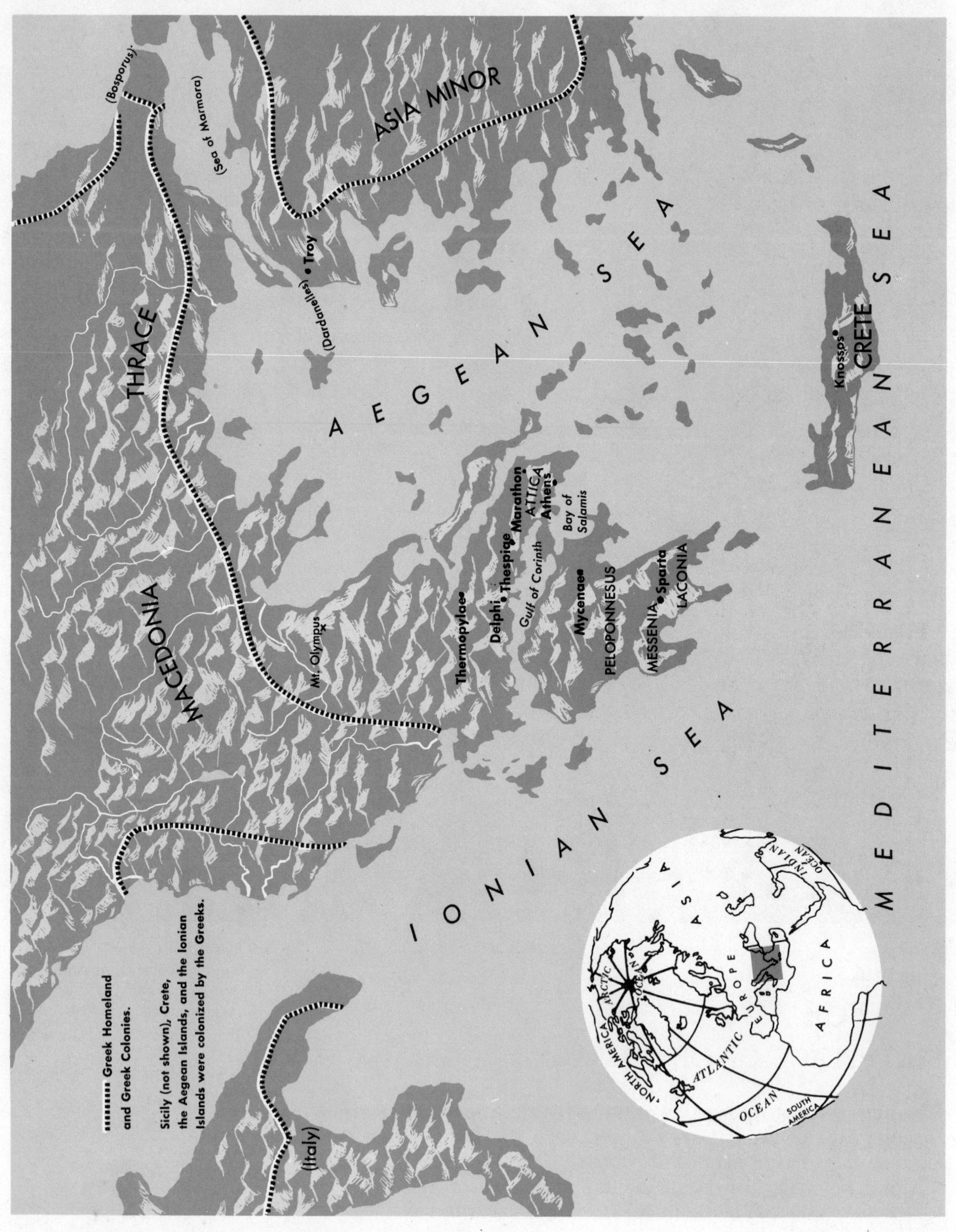

Greek Homeland and Greek Colonies.
Sicily (not shown), Crete, the Aegean Islands, and the Ionian Islands were colonized by the Greeks.
(Italy)
IONIAN SEA
MACEDONIA
THRACE
(Bosporus)
(Sea of Marmora)
ASIA MINOR
Troy
(Dardanelles)
AEGEAN SEA
Mt. Olympus
Thermopylae
Delphi
Thespiae
Marathon
ATTICA
Athens
Bay of Salamis
Gulf of Corinth
Mycenae
PELOPONNESUS
MESSENIA
Sparta
LACONIA
Knossos
CRETE
MEDITERRANEAN SEA
NORTH AMERICA
ARCTIC OCEAN
ATLANTIC
OCEAN
SOUTH AMERICA
EUROPE
ASIA
AFRICA
INDIAN OCEAN

Greece: GEOGRAPHIC SETTING

The Balkan Peninsula is a mountainous land mass protruding from Europe into the Eastern Mediterranean. Ancient Greece occupied the southern tip of this peninsula and included many of the nearby islands. Notice that southeastern Europe is separated from Asia Minor by two narrow straits, the Dardanelles (dar-dan-*elz*) and the Bosporus. Greece is bounded by seas on three sides: the Aegean (ee-*jee*-un) on the east, the Ionian (eye-*oh*-nee-un) on the west, and the Mediterranean on the south. Hundreds of islands dot the Aegean Sea. The largest and most important is Crete, which lies southeast of Greece within easy reach of Asia Minor and North Africa.

No part of Greece is more than seventy-five miles from the sea, and there are good harbors, especially on the east coast. Gulfs and bays bite deeply into the rocky coastline. The Gulf of Corinth, which nearly cuts Greece in two, lies between the two most important regions of ancient Greece, Attica and the Peloponnesus (*pel*-oh-pah-*nee*-sus). The country is divided still further by the rugged Balkan Mountains. Notice that Greece has no great rivers to form fertile valleys or to unite the people. As you study Part 4, consider carefully the many ways in which the geography of Greece has shaped the lives of the people who have inhabited this historic region.

Greece: PERSPECTIVE

For centuries, leadership in the Assembly had been firmly in the hands of aristocrats. Meeting outdoors on a sunny hillside, Athenian citizens had listened to eloquent speeches by men of high birth and great wealth. The ordinary man of Athens, having neither wealth nor a distinguished family, remained quietly in the background.

Then, in the fourth century B.C., a remarkable change took place in the Assembly, the ruling body of Athens. The dignified eloquence of the aristocratic leaders was replaced by crude accents and violent gestures, first of a simple man who tanned hides, then of another man who made lamps for a living. Eventually there was still another leader whose trade was making lyres. As the Assembly came to accept these men and their strange ways, Athens moved more and more quickly along the road to democracy. In this Part you will read about some of the important signposts along that road.

The glory of ancient Greece faded more than two thousand years ago, and today the visitor sees only crumbling ruins of temples and public buildings. But the early Greeks left behind something far more indestructible than monuments of stone and marble. They left a rich heritage of ideas in government, philosophy, art, science, and drama.

It is this heritage of ideas that historians have in mind when they say, "Ancient Greece is immortal." For Greek ideas, particularly the principles of freedom and self-government, are the cornerstone on which the free nations of the Western world have been built. As you study Part 4, notice how the lives of the Greeks who lived centuries ago continue to influence your life today.

CHAPTER 9

Greece Became the Center of a New Civilization

THE STORY OF GREECE BEGAN IN CRETE

About the same time that some men of the New Stone Age were settling in the Nile Valley, others probably crossed from North Africa to Crete and the Aegean islands. Archaeologists have discovered that these island settlers developed an advanced civilization at an early date. Evidence indicates that by 2500 B.C. the Cretans had already developed a written language and mastered such crafts as weaving, the manufacture of pottery and jewelry, and the fashioning of bronze weapons. They traded extensively with Egypt and Phoenicia and even with the undeveloped lands that later became Greece and Spain. Modern knowledge of Cretan civilization is limited by the fact that one of the languages used by the Cretans was translated only recently, while another has never been translated. But archaeological evidence indicates that by 1700 B.C. the Cretan king Minos (*my*-nahs) had brought under his control not only Crete but also the Aegean islands and the Greek Peninsula. His ships controlled the sea lanes and kept them free of invaders. Thus the sea served Crete both as an avenue of trade and a wall of protection.

In recent years, archaeologists have unearthed remarkable ruins of the ancient Cretan civilization at the royal city of Knossos (*nahs*-us) on the northern coast of Crete. Remains of the city, which may have been the capital of King Minos, show that the Cretans built palaces with many rooms, excellent plumbing, and brilliant frescoes, or scenes painted on the fresh plaster of the walls. (One of these frescoes is shown on page 75.) Rich merchants built three-story houses with large workshops where craftsmen produced delicate vases, textiles, perfume, and finely carved figurines. Archaeologists, who began digging in Crete only about sixty years ago, have unearthed enough relics to reveal a highly developed civilization.

THE ACHAEANS ADOPTED CRETAN CIVILIZATION

When the civilizations of Egypt, Mesopotamia, and Crete were well over a thousand years old, the land that was later called Greece was still a wilderness. About 2000 B.C., it was invaded by Indo-European tribes from the mountains to the north. They spoke a language called Greek, from which the land took its name. One of the most important of these Greek tribes was the Achaeans (uh-*kee*-unz), who settled in central and southern Greece. The Achaeans began to trade with Crete and eventually came under its rule. In about 1450 B.C., the Achaean city of Mycenae (my-*see*-nee) led a successful revolt against Crete and a few years later replaced Crete as the center of Aegean civilization. The Achaeans adopted Cretan achievements, much as the tribes of the Fertile Crescent had adopted the more advanced Sumerian civilization.

About 1184 B.C., the Achaeans came into conflict with the city of Troy, located on the coast of Asia Minor. The Trojans had grown rich from taxes they imposed on ships passing through the nearby Dardanelles. The Achaeans, refusing to pay tribute, led an attack that resulted in a ten-year siege of Troy. This encounter was the famous Trojan War, which the Greek poet Homer, some four hundred years later, described in his epic the *Iliad*.

KNOSSOS. These are some of the remains of the great palace at Knossos, the center of the early Cretan, or Minoan, civilization. The palace was destroyed by an earthquake sometime before 1500 B.C., but was later rebuilt.

LION GATE AT MYCENAE. The famous Achaean city was protected by a fortified hill, or acropolis, surrounded by a wall. Here Schliemann, the archaeologist who discovered Mycenae's ruins, stands at the Lion Gate.

TEMPLE AT AGRIGENTUM. Wherever the Greeks settled along the Mediterranean, they carried their arts and traditions. This temple in Sicily is one of the oldest and finest still standing.

GREECE EXPERIENCED A DARK AGE BUT RECOVERED

The Dorians invaded Greece. About 1100 B.C., a fierce Greek tribe, the Dorians, swept down from the north. In a short time they conquered the Achaeans and destroyed nearly all traces of their proud capital, Mycenae. The two hundred years following the Dorian onslaught were filled with disorder and bloodshed. This period is often called the Dark Age of Greece.

Homer's poems gave the Greeks a feeling of unity. Songs and legends about the Trojan War and the deeds of the Achaeans survived the Dark Age. Scholars believe that about 800 B.C., a blind poet named Homer wove these songs into two great epic poems, the *Iliad* and the *Odyssey* (*ahd*-ih-see). The *Iliad* describes such episodes in the siege of Troy as the hand-to-hand combat between the brave Achaean warrior Achilles (uh-*kill*-eez) and the Trojan prince Hector. Perhaps you are familiar with the Iliad's account of the huge wooden horse built by the clever Odysseus (od-*dis*-yus) to outwit the Trojans. In the *Odyssey*, Homer relates other adventures of Odysseus, including his encounter with the one-eyed giant, Cyclops, and the sorceress Circe on his way home from Troy. As wandering singers carried these epics throughout Greece and passed them on from generation to generation, the Greek tribes came to regard the Homeric heroes not just as Achaean heroes, but as Greek heroes. The Homeric legends gave the tribes a unity of tradition that helped them overcome their geographical and political division.

Greeks established colonies overseas. As Greece recovered from the Dorian invasion, the population increased rapidly. Good farm land became scarce, and many land-hungry Greeks left their home to establish colonies on the Aegean islands. By 750 B.C., colonies had also been established on the Mediterranean coast of Asia Minor and on the Italian Peninsula. The shortage of farm land caused some of the Greeks to turn to trade. The Aegean islands proved to be convenient steppingstones to the East, and Greek ships used them as way stations on their voyages to Phoenicia, Egypt, and Asia Minor.

The Greeks learned much as they came into

The Trojan Horse. According to the Homeric legend, this great wooden horse appeared before the gates of Troy after the Greek army had pretended to go away. The Trojans were curious and brought it inside the walls. At night, Greek soldiers hidden inside came out of the horse and opened the city gates to the waiting Greek army.

AJAX AND ACHILLES. During the Trojan War the two Greek heroes find a little time to pause for a game. This scene is found on an earthware vessel, or *amphora,* which was used to hold liquids.

contact with their more advanced neighbors to the east. You may recall from Chapter 7 how the Greeks adopted the Phoenician alphabet. But the brilliant Greek civilization that was soon to develop was in no sense a carbon copy of Middle Eastern or Cretan civilization. As we shall see in Chapter 10, the Greeks developed a way of life totally unlike that of any earlier people.

Chapter Check-up

1. What sea washes the eastern shore of Greece? The western shore?
2. How did the mountains of Greece influence the unity of the region's people?
3. Where was the first center of Aegean civilization? With what civilizations that you have already studied did these people have contact?
4. What geographic conditions caused the Greeks to become a trading, seafaring people?
5. Who were the Trojans? What was the cause of the Trojan War?
6. What effect did Homer's epic poems have on the various Greek tribes? What are the names of these two epic poems?
7. Why did the Greeks establish so many overseas colonies?
8. How was Greece influenced by the other civilizations of the Mediterranean world?

FRESCO AT KNOSSOS. A fresco painting in the palace at Knossos shows a girl turning somersaults on a bull while one assistant waits to catch her and the other diverts the bull. "Bull dancing" was a favorite spectacle of the sophisticated Cretans.

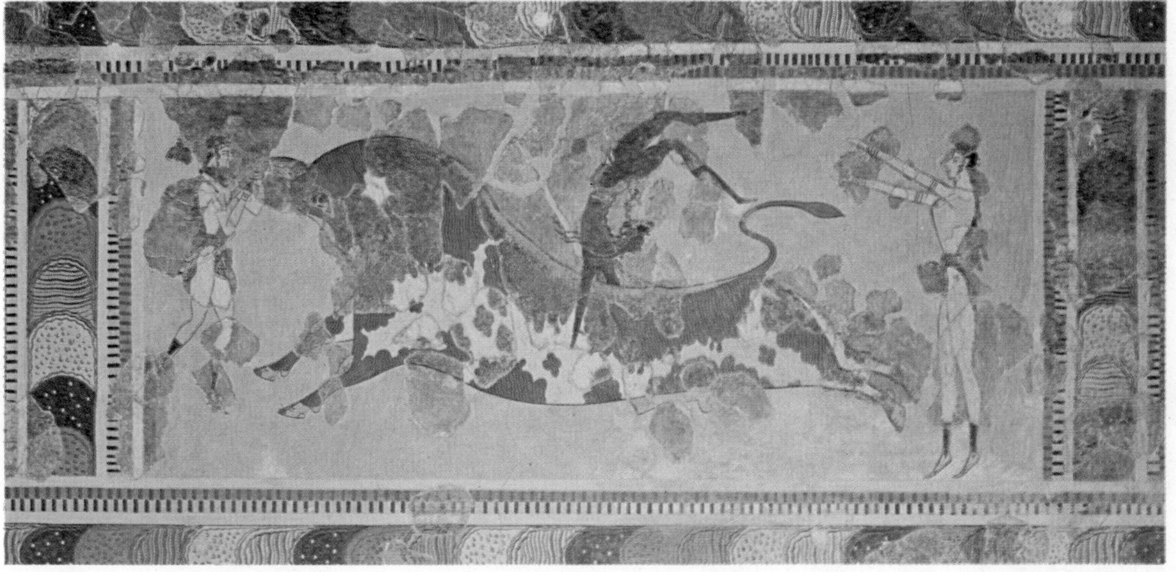

CHAPTER 10

Greek City-States Developed the Ideal of Democratic Citizenship

THREE BELIEFS DISTINGUISH THE GREEKS FROM OTHER ANCIENT PEOPLES

The Greeks were curious about the world in which they lived. They sought answers to many questions about life that had apparently never occurred to earlier people. Their curiosity resulted in the creation of a fund of knowledge and belief that greatly influenced the Western world.

Three beliefs distinguish Greek civilization from all earlier ones. Although these beliefs were held most strongly by philosophers and educated men, they influenced the outlook of all Greeks. The first is the belief that man is valuable for his own sake. Unlike the Egyptians and the peoples of the Fertile Crescent, who considered man no more than a servant of the gods, the Greeks believed that man has a duty to himself and an important purpose of his own to fulfill.

A second belief held by the early Greeks is that there are natural causes for everything that happens. The Greeks were convinced that the universe and the lives of men are governed by unchanging *natural laws.* In contrast, the ancient peoples of the Middle East believed that disasters such as famine, floods, and epidemics were caused by the whims of the gods. But the curiosity of the Greeks led them to seek more scientific explanations of such occurrences.

Finally, the Greeks believed that the natural laws that govern the universe and the lives of men could be discovered by man if he thought deeply and observed the world carefully. It is important to note, however, that the Greeks were, on the whole, more interested in discovering the natural laws than they were in making use of them. Although they believed that knowledge of natural law should be used to guide the actions of men, the Greeks did not think of applying the knowledge, as modern scientists do, to raise their standards of living or to control nature. For this reason, the knowledge accumulated by the Greeks did not result in practical invention. But it did lead them to remarkable achievements in government, art, literature, and philosophy. In the next two chapters you will learn why these achievements are important to the modern world.

THE CITY-STATE BECAME THE CENTER OF GREEK LIFE

The Greeks believed in developing the "whole man." The conviction that man is not a helpless creature controlled by the whims of the gods made the Greeks self-confident and ambitious. While other ancient peoples believed that man's only duty was to the gods, the Greeks thought that man owed much to himself. Convinced that man was capable of great achievement, they sought to develop their full mental and physical abilities. Homer clearly expressed this idea of the complete or "whole" man when he described the great warrior Odysseus as a man who could perform with equal skill as an athlete, soldier, orator, hunter, and farmer.

The ideal man was a responsible citizen of a city-state. The Greeks thought that no man could become whole, or ideal, unless he were an active member of his *polis* (*poe*-lis), or city-state.

The Acropolis. Over two thousand years ago the Acropolis is believed to have looked like this. Towering above the other buildings is the magnificent Parthenon, and to the left is the statue of Athena.

The Acropolis Today. The remains of the Parthenon can still be seen today on the Acropolis. The famous hill took its name from a Greek word meaning "high point of the city."

The Greek city-states, like those established earlier by the Sumerians, were organized as tiny independent countries. The two most important were Athens and Sparta.

At first, each of the Greek city-states was ruled by one man, who, like the Egyptian Pharaoh or the Sumerian priest-ruler, served as king, priest, judge, and army commander. But the Greeks, unlike the Egyptians and Mesopotamians, did not believe their rulers represented gods, and they would not, therefore, submit to absolute rule. Instead, they established a council of aristocrats, composed of wealthy, respected citizens who were authorized to help the king rule. Ultimately, in most of the Greek city-states, every citizen was given a voice in the government.

The Greeks believed that self-government would not work unless all citizens were free to meet in some central place, such as the *agora*, or market place, and discuss political affairs. They concluded from their knowledge of Egypt and Mesopotamia that large areas of land were probably best ruled by one man. To avoid this kind of government, they were perfectly content to keep their city-states small. The Greeks were aided in their desire to maintain small, independent states by their mountainous homeland, which was already subdivided by nature.

The city-state encouraged its citizens to develop their abilities. The Greek city-state not only gave its citizens political rights but also offered opportunities for personal self-development that were unmatched in any earlier civilization. For example, the citizen was encouraged to develop his political ability through experience in self-government. He was also encouraged to develop his physical and artistic abilities through attendance at the public gymnasium and the public theater. In exchange for these privileges, he had a solemn duty to serve in the army and share in the responsibilities of governing the city-state. The Greeks had contempt for a man who attended only to his private affairs, because he improved only a small part of himself while letting all his other abilities go to waste. Exile from the *polis* was considered a very heavy punishment, because without citizenship no man could hope to lead a happy and creative life.

Most inhabitants of a city-state were not citizens. The freedom and responsibilities we have been describing were reserved only for citizens of the Greek city-state, and citizenship was not easily attained. It was limited to male inhabitants who were property owners and whose parents had been citizens. Foreign-born persons, slaves, and women were barred from becoming citizens. Although the property and birth restrictions were later relaxed, there were never as many citizens as non-citizens in a city-state. Of the non-citizens, a majority were slaves.

Greek civilization, like all earlier civilizations, depended partly on slave labor. Slaves in Greece were of two kinds: foreigners who had been conquered in war, and debtors. At first, only a few slaves were used, and these chiefly as house servants or farm hands. Later, as trade and industry developed, they increased in number and performed many other tasks until, at one point, probably two-thirds of the population of Athens were slaves. Those who worked in the mines led miserable lives, but those who worked in the house or field were well treated. Slaves of the latter type were permitted to own property, and many could earn their freedom. The use of slaves left the wealthy Greek citizen free to devote himself to civic affairs and self-development.

ATHENS DEVELOPED A DEMOCRATIC GOVERNMENT

Early Athens was ruled by the aristocracy. Of all the city-states, Athens best expressed the Greek faith in man's ability to govern himself. The resourceful Athenians made their city-state the cultural center of the ancient world and the birthplace of democracy. The word *democracy* comes from two Greek words meaning "rule by the people."

Democratic government developed slowly in Athens. From about 1200 B.C. to 800 B.C., Athens was ruled by a king. Gradually, control of the government passed into the hands of an Aristocratic Council, headed by nine officials called *archons* (*ar*-konz). One branch of the government, the Assembly, was open to virtually all citizens who owned property, but its powers were very limited. Under this arrangement, the aristocrats governed Athens to suit their own interests and passed harsh laws affecting the less fortunate classes. One of these laws, for example, provided that a man who did not pay his debts could be sold into slavery.

Draco and Solon limited the power of the aristocracy. Before long, the farmers, merchants, and laborers began to protest the selfish rule of the aristocracy and to demand reforms. About 620 B.C., one of the Archons, Draco (*dray*-ko), was appointed to draw up a code of laws for Athens. His code, like the earlier one by Hammurabi, required that the aristocracy as well as the common people obey all laws.

Bitterness between the classes continued, however, and in 594 B.C. the city was threatened with civil war. To avert bloodshed, the Athenians turned to Solon (*so*-lahn), an aristocrat whose reputation for honesty had earned him the confidence of every class. To aid the poor, Solon made a number of economic reforms such as a repeal of the debt-slavery law and the establishment of a limit on the amount of land one man might own. He brought prosperity to Athens by encouraging the production of olive oil and the mining of silver for use in foreign trade. Under Solon's rule, Athens adopted a new constitution which empowered the Assembly, rather than the Aristocratic Council, to vote on laws and to elect government officials.

Under Cleisthenes, Athens became a democracy. After Solon's death, the movement toward democracy suffered a setback when a powerful aristocrat, Peisistratus (py-*sis*-truh-tus), illegally seized control of the government. The Greeks called such a man a *tyrant*. Peisistratus was such an able leader that the people accepted his rule. But his son, who also tried to rule as a tyrant, proved unpopular and was eventually driven from the city. Finally the poorer citizens asked another aristocrat, Cleisthenes (*klise*-thee-neez), to be their leader. He proved a wise choice, for he firmly established the principles of democracy in Athenian government. Cleisthenes declared the Assembly open to every free male Athenian, whether or not he had property. To encourage trade, he offered citizenship to foreign merchants and craftsmen who came to Athens.

Harvesting Olives. Three men and a boy are knocking olives from the trees before gathering them to make oil. In ancient times, as now, olive oil was an important source of Greek wealth.

Solon. Solon instituted many needed economic reforms, and gave the Athenians laws that protected their personal freedom.

Under the new government, the Assembly met about once a week in a natural amphitheater outside Athens. On meeting days, hundreds of citizens could be seen milling around waiting for the Assembly to be called to order. Each session opened with a prayer. Then a herald cried, "Who wishes to speak?" Those desiring to be heard mounted the platform and presented their suggestions or problems. After a subject had been thoroughly discussed, the citizens voted.

The Assembly did not, however, have the power to propose laws. That privilege was restricted to a

Council of Five Hundred, which was chosen by lot from the whole body of citizens. The Council was also responsible for the conduct of most of the routine business of government. Military and foreign affairs, however, were handled by a special board of ten generals elected by the Assembly and called the *strategi* (*strah*-tee-jee).

Because the Athenians assumed that every citizen was equally capable, all government offices except those of the *strategi* were filled by citizens chosen annually by lot. It became not only a citizen's privilege but also his sacred duty to take part in government. Since poor men could not afford to leave their work long enough to hold government offices, Athenians began to pay their officials. Eventually, everyone who attended the Assembly was paid; it was then possible for any citizen to be active in the government.

Citizens' courts maintained justice. The rights of Athenian citizens were protected by a system of public courts originally established by Solon. Cases were decided by juries made up of citizens over thirty years of age who were chosen by lot in the Assembly. The juries were very large, to prevent bribery. A typical jury might consist of 201, 501, or even 1,001 jurors, depending on the seriousness of the case. Jurymen swore to listen carefully to the arguments of both sides and to decide the case fairly. There were no judges or professional lawyers. A citizen was expected to present his own case intelligently, just as the jury was expected to weigh the facts of the case intelligently.

The jury decided by majority vote whether the accused was innocent or guilty. If found guilty, the defendant was asked to suggest his own punishment. The accuser was also asked what he thought the punishment should be. The jurors then chose the punishment they thought fairest, usually a fine or exile rather than imprisonment or death.

Athenian democracy had its limitations. If men are to govern themselves well, they must be trained. In Athens, the education of the aristocrats, about which you will read later, often produced men of great ability. But the poorer citizens, who could not afford schooling, were much less fitted to govern. They were sometimes influenced by tyrants or by *demagogues*, candidates for office who would promise anything to gain power. The fact that most officials were chosen by lot meant that not all were able men, and the rotation of offices each year meant that officials did not have time to gain experience. For this reason, the real power in the government stayed in the hands of the educated, experienced aristocrats. A further limitation on Athenian democracy resulted from citizenship restrictions, which

A Greek Boy's Music Lesson. This vase painting shows a boy being taught to play the lyre, a kind of harp.

A Victorious Youth. In this temple carving from the fifth century B.C., a young athlete is shown placing a victor's wreath on his head. The lost wreath, perhaps made of metal, had been attached by pegs.

barred a majority of male inhabitants from ever becoming citizens. But within these limitations, Athenian democracy functioned admirably.

Unlike American *representative democracy*, in which a few elected lawmakers represent all the citizens, the *pure democracy* of Athens allowed every citizen to vote directly on the laws. The Greeks never developed the principle of representative government. They would have asked, "How can men become competent citizens if they leave the responsibility for making laws to a select group?"

"The good life" was demanded of Athenian citizens. Athenian democracy created loyal and devoted citizens. Each man believed that by sharing in the government, fighting in the army, and working as farmer, sailor, or merchant, he was benefiting his city-state and himself. If he were wealthy, he was expected to make donations for the construction of public buildings and temples, or for the support of public festivals. Any citizen, even the poorest, was expected to increase his knowledge of government by regular attendance at the Assembly and the public courts. He could also improve himself by attending public games, poetry contests, or the theater. As the Greek philosopher Aristotle observed, "not life, but a good life" was expected of every citizen. To an Athenian, a good life meant a life of service to the state and self-development through training the body and the mind. This concept is clearly revealed in the oath that every Athenian youth took when he became a citizen. He promised:

> . . . never to disgrace his holy arms, never to forsake his comrade in the ranks, but to fight for the holy temples; to leave his country, not in a worse but in a better state than he found it; to obey the magistrates and the laws, and to defend them against attack . . .

SPARTA BUILT A MILITARY STATE

Sparta needed soldier-citizens. Turn back to the map on page 70. Notice again that the Gulf of Corinth nearly cuts the peninsula of Greece in two. The southernmost half of the peninsula, the Peloponnesus, was divided into several states. One of the Peloponnesian states, Laconia (luh-*ko*-nih-uh), was the homeland of Sparta. The Spartans were descendants of the fierce Dorians, who, you will remember, had earlier conquered the Achaeans. The Spartans forced the captive

A GREEK WARRIOR. This small bronze shows a Greek soldier wrapped in his cloak and wearing a Corinthian-styled helmet. It dates from about 490 B.C.

Achaeans to work on the land as *helots* (*heh*-lots), or virtual slaves. Later, the pressure of a growing population drove the Spartans to make helots of their neighbors, the Messenians (meh·*see*-nee-uns). The helots lived under such wretched conditions that they constantly threatened revolt. One such uprising, by the Messenians in 650 B.C., lasted for twenty years.

The need to control their rebellious subjects forced the Spartans to center their lives around the army and to place their government under the control of a military aristocracy. To become a well-trained and well-disciplined soldier was the sole job of the Spartan citizen.

Spartan education created an efficient army. On the day of his birth, a Spartan boy was taken to the elders of Sparta for a careful inspection. If the infant had been born weak or deformed, he was left on a mountainside to die, because the elders thought that he could never perform his strenuous duties as a citizen-soldier. If declared physically fit, he was allowed to live with his family until the age of seven. Then he left his home to live in public barracks and begin his military training. A Spartan boy was trained to become a strong and fearless soldier, able to endure hardship and suffering. Even in winter he was allowed to wear only one garment and was required to go barefoot and sleep outdoors. His chief food was a very bad-tasting black broth, but as part of his training he was taught to feed himself by stealing food from farms and gardens. If caught, he was whipped—not for stealing, but for being so clumsy as to be found out. As a boy approached manhood and service in the army, he was beaten each year in public. This abuse taught him to endure pain in silence.

Spartan youths were expected to be modest in manner and brief in speech. According to tradition, Lycurgus, a famous Spartan lawgiver, made special rules governing the behavior of Spartan boys in public.

> . . . They were to walk in silence . . . and to keep their eyes fixed upon the ground before them. And you might sooner expect a stone image to find a voice than any of those Spartan youths.

Spartans were known for their short, abrupt speech, a way of talking which is now called *laconic*, after Laconia, the state ruled by Sparta. You will see in Chapter 12 how the Spartan system of education differed from that of other city-states of ancient Greece.

Spartan girls, like their brothers, were given athletic training and taught to be fanatically loyal to the city-state. When a soldier left for battle, his mother handed him his shield, on which his body would be brought back if he were killed. The shield was so large that flight from the enemy was possible only by leaving it behind. As his mother gave her son the shield, she warned, "Come back with your shield or on it."

Sparta became a totalitarian state. Although the citizens of Sparta and Athens shared the ideal of loyal service to the state, the same goal led to a vastly different way of life for each. The Spartans assumed that service to the state required rigid control of every aspect of the lives of its citizens. Thus Sparta became a *totalitarian* state, in which the lives of the people were totally controlled by the government.

Sparta's military aristocracy toughened and disciplined the citizens and forced them to give up all the pleasures of life in order to concentrate on military training. A citizen never dared criticize the government, and he was kept isolated from the influence of other city-states. Trade was purposely discouraged by the use of heavy iron bars for money, instead of gold and silver coins like those used in the other city-states. Spartan rulers feared that trade would bring in luxuries to soften the citizens, or new ideas to weaken their faith in Spartan traditions.

GREEK WARRIOR. A painting on a dish shows an infantryman exercising. The Greeks put great stress on physical fitness.

Sparta's excessive concern with the maintenance of military efficiency, based on the need to control the helots, severely limited the Spartan way of life. While achievement in art and philosophy made Athenian civilization one of the most glorious ever known, Sparta completely ignored these fields. From the Spartan point of view, a poet or a philosopher was of little value compared to an efficient, disciplined soldier who was loyal to the state.

THE PERSIAN EMPIRE THREATENED TO ABSORB THE GREEK CITY-STATES

Athens defeated Persia at the Battle of Marathon. Although the Greek city-states frequently quarreled among themselves, they were not threatened by a foreign power until 500 B.C. In that year the Persian king Darius, whom you met in Chapter 8, extended his empire to include all of Asia Minor. When the Greek colonists in Asia Minor revolted against Persian rule, they turned to Athens for help. Despite Athenian intervention, Darius suppressed the revolt. But he was enraged by the thought that the Athenians had dared to interfere in his affairs. He promptly sent messengers to the cities of Greece demanding that they acknowledge him to be the ruler of all land and sea. Many of the Greek cities obeyed, but when Athens and Sparta refused, Darius prepared for war.

In 490 B.C., the soldiers of Darius landed on the plains of Marathon, twenty-four miles north of Athens. In alarm, Athens sent to Sparta for help, but the Spartans, who were celebrating a religious festival, delayed in sending troops. Alone and greatly outnumbered, the Athenian citizen-army won an astounding victory at Marathon.

Greek Against Persian. In this vase painting a Greek warrior attacks a Persian. Although fighting against great odds, the Greek city-states successfully resisted two Persian invasions.

Athens and Sparta met a second Persian invasion. Darius died while collecting his forces for another invasion of Greece. But his son Xerxes (*zerk*-seez) was also determined to conquer Greece, and he set about to build an enormous army and fleet. In 480 B.C., Xerxes moved his army across the Dardanelles on specially built pontoon bridges and marched into northern Greece. A short time later a Persian fleet headed across the Aegean Sea toward the Greek coast. To reach central Greece, the Persian army had to march through the narrow pass of Thermopylae (ther-*mop*-ih-lee), between the mountains and the sea.

Thermopylae was held by a small band of Greek soldiers led by the Spartan king, Leonidas. Because the pass was so narrow that only a few of the Persian soldiers could attack at once, the Greeks were able to hold back the entire Persian army for three days. Xerxes was completely baffled until a Greek traitor offered to show the Persians a secret pass across the mountains. At dawn, Persian forces surprised the Greeks from the rear. When Leonidas realized that his troops would be trapped in the pass, he gave each soldier the choice of leaving or staying. In the battle that followed, the brave Greek soldiers who remained fought until not one of them was left alive.

In the meantime, under the leadership of the Athenian statesman Themistocles (thee-*mis*-to-kleez) the Athenians had built a fleet of ships to meet the Persian attack from the sea. As the Persian army approached, the Athenians fled from the city and took shelter in their ships. They watched helplessly from the sea while the Persians burned Athens to the ground.

Only the Athenian fleet remained to prevent the Persians from completing the conquest of

Greece. Themistocles cleverly tricked the Persian fleet into entering the narrow Strait of Salamis (*sal*-uh-mis). There, the light, maneuverable Greek ships, though greatly outnumbered, proceeded to annihilate the clumsy Persian fleet. Xerxes, who had been watching the battle from a hill, left Greece at once to prevent Asia Minor from taking up arms as Athens had done. He left behind a portion of his army with orders to finish the conquest of Greece. The next year the Athenians met this remnant of the Persian army and defeated it.

This remarkable episode from Greek history illustrates how brave and resourceful men, fighting for their homeland, can triumph against overwhelming odds. The Greek victory was important to the future because it meant that the Greek ideal of democracy, rather than the Persian concept of absolute monarchy, would be passed on to the Western world.

Chapter Check-up

1. What were the three important beliefs or ideas of the Greeks which distinguished them from the other ancient peoples?
2. What standards did the Greeks set for the ideal man?
3. Why didn't the city-states of Greece unite?
4. Were all the inhabitants of the city-states citizens? Explain.
5. What were the names of the two most important city-states? How did they differ?
6. What were the limitations or weaknesses of Athenian democracy?
7. Describe the Athenian idea of good citizenship and a good life.
8. Why did Sparta make fewer contributions to civilization than did Athens?
9. What foreign empire threatened the Greek city-states in 500 B.C.?
10. Why are Marathon and Salamis proud names in Greek history?

CHAPTER 11

Peace Brought a Golden Age to Greece

ATHENS BECAME THE DOMINANT FORCE IN GREEK POLITICS AND CULTURE

The Athenians built an empire. Although the Persian forces had been driven from Greece, Xerxes still controlled the Greek cities of Asia Minor. When these cities asked for help, the Athenians combined them with a number of city-states on the mainland into the *Delian League* for mutual protection against Persia. The League worked well enough, but when danger of Persian attack passed, the Athenians refused to allow the member cities to withdraw. In fact, they transformed the League into an Athenian Empire. This strange turn of events is explained by the fact that the League had enabled Athens to gain control of commerce in the Mediterranean, with the result that she enjoyed great prosperity. Naturally the Athenians were reluctant to surrender their favored position. In the years that followed, Athens became the capital of a great commercial empire and mistress of the Aegean Sea. The wealth that flowed into Athens made possible a Golden Age, in which Athenian sculptors, dramatists and philosophers created a truly remarkable level of culture.

Pericles became the "first citizen" of Athens. The Golden Age of Athens (460–429 B.C.) is sometimes called the Age of Pericles (*per*-ihkleez), after its most important citizen. Pericles combined the talents of statesman, orator, poet, and philosopher. His fellow citizens trusted him completely and elected him chief of the *strategi* year after year. Pericles used his great power to strengthen Athenian democracy. It was he who insisted that office-holders should be paid by the state, so even the poor could take an active part in the affairs of government. He spent money for the construction of temples. He increased the size of the Athenian navy. He encouraged sculptors, architects, philosophers, and playwrights. Under Pericles' leadership, Athens became the most beautiful city of the ancient world.

GREEK ART AND LITERATURE WAS CENTERED ON MAN

You will recall that the Egyptians and Sumerians had built tombs, palaces, and statues chiefly to please and glorify the gods. The Greeks, however, placed their emphasis on man himself, and their art reveals an effort to glorify and satisfy human beings rather than gods. Because the Greeks believed that an appreciation and understanding of beauty is an essential part of man's development, Greek sculpture and architecture put great emphasis on artistic *form* rather than on great size or external decoration.

Greek sculpture described the ideal man. The preoccupation of the Greeks with artistic form is readily seen in their sculpture. Study the picture of Myron's "Discus Thrower" on the opposite page. It reflects some of the most admired elements of form: balance, dignity, and restraint. Notice that the placement of the subject's limbs in relation to his torso lends balance to the statue. In spite of his violent action, his movements and his facial expression are dignified. He is powerful, but his strength is carefully restrained.

Because the Greeks believed that the ideal man must be properly developed physically, they studied the human body very carefully. Greek sculptors often chose athletes for models because they had the most perfect bodies. The gods, too, were represented as athletic young men, as Praxiteles' (prak-*sit'l*-eez) statue of "Hermes and the Infant Dionysus" shows. Most of the figures portrayed in Greek sculpture are, like the "Discus Thrower," graceful, slim, and well-proportioned. Thus they represented an ideal. In each of their works, the Greeks sought to achieve *ideal form* rather than a lifelike imitation of individual models. Greek art of the fifth century B.C., which expresses this ideal form, is said to be *classical*. Today the term *classical* has a broader meaning and is applied to any work of art that is a perfect example of its kind.

PERICLES. This famous man, whose name is often given to the Golden Age of Greece, was the greatest statesman of Athens.

THE DISCUS THROWER. The Romans were very fond of copying Greek works of art. It is through these copies that we know of objects lost many centuries ago. This copy of a statue by Myron is an excellent example of the Greek ideal of physical perfection and grace.

Architecture in Athens set standards of excellence. The most famous examples of Greek architecture are the magnificent temples erected on a sacred hill in the center of Athens called the Acropolis (uh-*crop*-oh-liss). Most of the temples were built by Pericles to replace those destroyed by the Persians. He intended them not only to honor the gods but also to display the wealth and skill of the Athenian people.

The most important temple, the Parthenon (*par*-the-nahn), was dedicated to the patron goddess of Athens, Athena (uh-*thee*-nuh). It was designed by Ictinus (ik-*tie*-nus) and was built of white marble in the simple but stately Doric style. (You will find examples of the various styles of Greek architecture on the next page.) The Parthenon, although simple in design, was amazingly beautiful. The length of the building, the number of columns, the spaces between them, and their height were all determined mathematically. Not a stone could be changed without spoiling the perfection of the temple's proportions. In the triangular space created at each corner of the roof, figures representing legendary episodes in the life of Athena were placed. The roof was supported by columns, which surrounded the walls. High

HERMES BY PRAXITELES. Of all the works of the great Greek sculptor Praxiteles, this statue is the only known example still in existence. It depicts two gods, Hermes and the infant Dionysus.

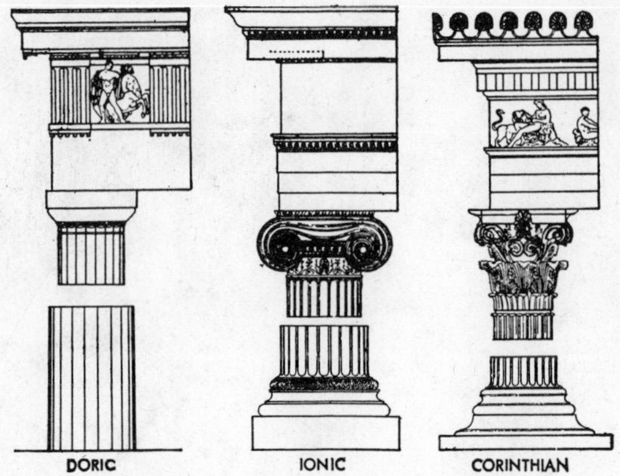

THE STYLES OF GREEK ARCHITECTURE. The three orders, or styles, of Greek architecture pictured here were developed by the Greeks nearly 2,400 years ago and are still used by architects today. From the photograph on the opposite page, can you tell what type of columns were used in the Parthenon?

up on these walls, behind the tops of the columns, a band of brilliantly painted sculpture called a *frieze* (freez) depicts a procession bringing gifts to Athena. In the dark interior of the temple was placed a huge statue of the goddess carved in ivory and gold by the great sculptor Phidias (*fid*-ee-us). Outside the Parthenon, Phidias created a gigantic similar statue in bronze that rose seventy feet into the air. As protectress of the city, Athena was armed with a shield and spear. The glint of sunlight on the gilded tip of her spear told sailors approaching Attica that they were nearing home.

Greek dramatists united myth and fate. Another of the important areas of Greek achievement was drama. The first great plays in history came from the pens of Athenian playwrights who lived in the Golden Age. Most of these plays were tragedies based on Homer's myths and legends. Since the audience already knew these stories, the playwrights sought to inspire men to moral behavior, rather than simply to repeat the details of the stories. The Greeks believed that certain laws of the universe, called *fate*, governed men's actions and would punish anyone who broke the laws. Such a man was pursued by endless misfortune; even his children and grandchildren were made to suffer for his misdeeds. The tragedy of a play which related this unhappy chain of events lay in the fact that a man was held responsible for the consequences of his acts even if it were impossible for him to foresee them. But the hero's recognition that he was nevertheless responsible and that fate was just, presented the audience with an example of noble action that won him admiration and respect.

The workings of fate were the main concern of the first great Greek dramatist, Aeschylus (*es*-kih-lus), often called the "Father of Greek Tragedy." Of his ninety plays, only seven have survived. One of the most famous, *Agememnon* (a-ge-*mem*-nahn), is the story of a Homeric hero who was too proud to turn back from the invasion of Troy when unfavorable winds, sent by an angry goddess, kept his ships in the harbor. To win the good will of the goddess so that he could proceed with the invasion, he sacrificed his greatest treasure, his daughter, at the goddess' altar. Fate punished him for his pride by causing his wife to murder him when he returned to Greece after the war.

The second famous Greek dramatist, Sophocles (*sahf*-oh-kleez), raised tragedy to a new peak of nobility and dignity. One of his greatest plays, *Antigone* (an-*tig*-oh-nee), deals with the struggle of a young woman torn between duty to her family and duty to the state. Her uncle, the king, had forbidden anyone to touch the body of a rival whom he had defeated in battle. But when Antigone recognized the slain man as her brother, she secretly sprinkled dust on his body, because the Greeks believed that a spirit wandered in this world forever if the body were left unburied. For her disobedience to the law, the king condemned Antigone to death. As it turns out, her death proves to be the last step in a long story of tragic deeds done by her family before her. Although tragic in its outcome, Antigone leaves the audience with a feeling that man is somehow better for such noble sacrifice.

The works of Euripides (yoo-*rip*-ih-deez), youngest of the three great tragedians, do not reflect such strong religious themes. Euripides was

ATHENIAN TEMPLES. The Acropolis in Athens contained some of the world's most beautiful buildings, including the two temples shown here. To the right is the Parthenon, dedicated to Athena the Virgin. It was begun in 447 B.C. and finished fifteen years later. Below is the Erechtheum (er-*ek*-thee-um), built between 421 and 407 B.C. It is named after Erechtheus, a legendary king of Athens and supposedly contained his tomb. Six draped female figures support the roof of the building's south porch.

more concerned with individual human suffering, especially that of women and slaves, than with the working of fate. In *The Trojan Women,* he tells sympathetically of the misery brought by war to the defeated queen of Troy and her daughters.

Although tragedy was the favorite dramatic form for Greek playwrights, there were some exceptions. Aristophanes (ar-is-*tof*-uh-neez), for instance, wrote very amusing and popular comedies in which he made fun of prominent Athenians, even those who headed the government.

Drama was important in Athenian life. Greek plays were presented partly to honor the gods but chiefly to teach good conduct to citizens. The plays showed how the ideal Greek should behave in difficult circumstances and demonstrated how justice always triumphed. Pericles considered this training so important to good citizenship that he decreed that all citizens who could not afford to attend should be admitted free. The theater consisted of rows of stone seats on a hillside, forming a semicircle around a stage. Very little action took place on the stage. The actors wore huge, grotesque, canvas masks. Men played all the roles because women were forbidden to act. A specially trained chorus of citizens recited parts of the play to interpret some of its events to the

Open-air Theater at Epidaurus. This great open-air theater, with its semicircular tiers of seats and round stage, could accommodate thousands of spectators. The theater is located across the Bay of Salamis from Athens.

audience. The audience, which became thoroughly absorbed in the emotions of pity and fear that the plays aroused, sometimes expressed its reactions by hissing, cheering, or throwing old vegetables at the actors.

Greece produced the first historians. History is not merely a record of what has happened in the past. It is also an interpretation of events and an explanation of how and why they happened. Many early civilizations had kept records of the past or told legends about the gods, but it was the Greeks who first inquired into the meaning, or significance, of particular events. For this reason, the Greeks are considered to be the world's first true historians.

Herodotus (hee-*rod*-oh-tus), who lived in the middle of the fifth century B.C., was regarded by the Greeks as the "Father of History." He traveled throughout the eastern Mediterranean, visiting both Egypt and the Fertile Crescent in order to learn the customs and histories of these areas. He gathered information by questioning the learned men of both civilizations. For the most part, he used only accurate and reliable accounts, but occasionally he could not resist including much that was either silly or incredible, if it made a good story. In his major work, which tells the history of the Persian Wars, he made little effort to conceal his favoritism toward Greece.

Thucydides (thyoo-*sid*-ih-deez), who was younger than Herodotus, was more careful in selecting his facts. His history is much more reliable. Thucydides claimed that his writings contained only what "I either saw myself, or learned from others of whom I made the most careful and particular inquiry." Although he had fought as an Athenian general, his writings provide an impartial account of the war between Athens and Sparta. They are also notable for the speeches in which Thucydides has prominent figures in the war express their attitudes and beliefs. Although he was a loyal Athenian, Thucydides concedes that a major cause of the conflict with Sparta was the expansion of Athens' Empire.

THE GREEKS SOUGHT WISDOM IN PHILOSOPHY

The Greeks were avid questioners. Other ancient peoples accepted the world as they found it, but the Greeks persisted in wanting to know why it was that way. They believed that, by thinking, questioning, and observing, man could discover the natural laws that governed the universe. And they believed that every intelligent citizen should share in man's quest for wisdom.

The word *philosophy* comes from two Greek words that mean "love of" and "knowledge" or "wisdom." A philosopher is a lover of wisdom and therefore a seeker of it. The Greeks began searching for wisdom long before the Age of Pericles. At first, philosophers tried to understand where the world came from and what it was made of. Today, such a study would be called "science." Gradually, however, more and more thinkers became interested in studying man rather than his physical surroundings. During the Age of Pericles, the Greeks sought to gain understanding of mankind through careful study of the works of the great dramatists. After Pericles' death, they turned to philosophy and science in their quest for the truth about man.

SOCRATES. Though he wrote nothing, Socrates' philosophy was preserved and expanded by his pupils, the most famous of whom was Plato. The death of Socrates was a sad loss to the Athenians.

Socrates urged men to use their reason. The first philosopher to discuss the problem of man in relation to other men and to the universe was Socrates (*sok*-ruh-teez). If you had lived in Athens about 400 B.C., you might have seen, strolling barefoot through the city street, a shabbily dressed, unattractive man with a flat nose and massive forehead. If you had followed him for long, however, you would have discovered that he was one of the most respected men in Athens and was frequently an honored guest at the banquet tables of the most prominent Athenians. They recognized that Socrates was an intelligent man engaged in a noble quest for wisdom and the meaning of life. He believed that just as there were laws to explain the universe, so there were principles of truth, goodness, and justice by which men could learn to know themselves and to regulate their lives. These unchanging principles exist everywhere. Man had only to use his reason to discover them. Once he knows what true justice is, he will always act justly. He will then be a wise man and a good citizen.

Socrates helped men to examine the meaning of things by asking them questions. He did not tell them what justice was, for example, but asked them what they thought it was, forcing them to organize their thinking on the subject. Socrates asked more and more questions until men began to see that they had never really thought the matter over carefully but had relied on hearsay, tradition and superstition. In the course of many such discussions with his friends, he would analyze cases in which a man was said to have acted justly. Gradually his companions began to reach a truer idea of justice. While Socrates never saw fit to define justice, he encouraged men to use their own reason as he did, in an effort to understand its true meaning.

Most Athenians, however, were strongly influenced by old habits and superstitions. They believed, for example, that it was the duty of every citizen to worship the traditional Greek gods whose temples stood on the Acropolis. They disapproved of Socrates because they thought he was not paying the gods proper respect. Furthermore, they suspected that Socrates did not believe in democracy. They were right about that. Socrates was dedicated to the welfare of Athens, but he thought that only the few citizens with the best knowledge and training should rule. Although he had nothing to do with the attempt of one of his pupils to overthrow the Athenian democracy, public opinion turned against him. He was put on trial for corrupting the morals of the young men of Athens and for not believing in the traditional gods. By a narrow margin he was condemned to death. Refusing his friends' offer of escape, he calmly drank the hemlock juice with which the Greeks executed condemned men. Socrates died because he believed that, regardless of the consequences, a citizen must obey the laws of the state, just as a philosopher must search for the truth.

Plato carried on the work of Socrates. Because Socrates wrote no books, almost all knowledge of him comes from the works of his greatest pupil, Plato. Plato put Socrates' philosophy into *dialogues*, or conversations, which clearly show Socrates' technique of discovering truth through clever questioning. Plato later wrote many dialogues in which he presented his own philosophy. He also established an Athenian school known as the Academy, where philosophy and science continued to be taught for almost nine hundred years after his death.

Like his master, Plato believed in certain principles of goodness and justice which man's reason could discover. In his most famous work, the *Republic*, Plato describes what he believes is an ideal state. It is based on justice, served by loyal citizens, and ruled by philosopher-kings.

Aristotle organized all Greek knowledge. The philosopher Aristotle (*ar*-iss-tot'l) was a member of Plato's academy for twenty years before he started his own school. Many historians consider him the most intelligent man who has ever lived. His range of interests and his wealth of learning were enormous. He collected, catalogued, and analyzed all the knowledge of his day. Aristotle's work was so effective that for nearly two thousand years he ranked as the highest authority on astronomy, biology, mathematics, physics, poetry, politics, and ethics.

Like Socrates and Plato, Aristotle believed that

PLATO'S ACADEMY. Plato taught in Athens in grounds dedicated to the Greek hero Academus. This first century Roman mosaic shows Plato seated on a stone bench surrounded by his students. He holds a stick in his right hand. Note the Acropolis at the top right.

reason should guide man. He placed special emphasis on the fact that man should maintain a careful balance between the pleasures of the body and those of the mind. Perhaps Aristotle's greatest contribution was his invention of rules for the science of reason, which is called *logic*. Logic is the method by which reason works. It teaches you how to arrange related statements that you believe to be true so as to reach a correct conclusion:

Anything that has weight and occupies space is matter.
Air has weight and occupies space.
Therefore air is matter.

True science began in Greece. The Greeks believed, as we noted earlier, that certain unchanging laws govern everything that takes place in the world. They felt that by carefully observing the world around them, they could discover these laws. This attitude, and the discoveries that it made possible, mark the Greeks as the first true scientists. Their achievements were particularly significant in medicine, biology, astronomy, geography, mathematics, and physics.

In about the middle of the fifth century B.C., the Greek physician Hippocrates (hih-*pok*-ruh-teez), who became known as the "Father of Medicine," declared that every disease results from a natural cause. You will recall that Egyptian doctors, like all early peoples, believed incorrectly that diseases are caused by evil spirits and can be cured only by charms or magic phrases. Hippocrates, however, carefully observed the symptoms of his patients and concluded that a man becomes sick, not because of evil spirits, but because some part of his body is not working properly. Dismissing charms and magic phrases as useless, he recommended surgery, drugs, diet, or rest, much as modern doctors do. Several centuries later, another Greek physician, Herophilus (hih-*rah*-fuh-lus), discovered that the blood is pumped by the heart and that the nerves affect and are affected by the brain.

Aristotle, who is known chiefly as a philosopher, combined a belief in natural law with painstaking observation of various plants and animals to take a first step along the road to modern biology.

The scientific spirit also helped the Greeks in their study of astronomy and geography. Unlike earlier peoples who had thought that the movement of stars and planets was governed by the gods, the Greeks believed that the heavenly bodies are regulated by natural law. Observation and mathematical calculation led certain Greek astronomers to state that the earth is a sphere, not a flat surface, and that the moon circles the earth. Some of them even guessed that the earth and other planets move around the sun. Long before the Age of Pericles, a Greek astronomer used this new knowledge to predict an eclipse. Several centuries later, Eratosthenes (er-uh-*tahs*-the-neez) combined astronomy with geography to calculate the length of the earth's equator and came within two hundred miles of the correct distance. He also drew a map of Asia, Africa, and Europe that was the most accurate map of the region until nearly 1500 A.D.

The outstanding Greek mathematician, Euclid (*yoo*-klid) stated in his *Elements of Geometry* principles which still serve as the basis for modern textbooks on the subject.

But of all the Greek scientists, probably the greatest was Archimedes (ar-kih-*mee*-deez), to whom modern scientists are indebted for the discovery of important principles in physics.

Archimedes was the first man to describe the importance of the lever, a simple mechanical device by which a small force can be made to move a very large load. To dramatize its power, he is reported to have boasted, "Give me a place to stand, and I will move the world." Today you are able to see the usefulness of the lever in such a device as the automobile jack, with which even a child can lift a car.

Archimedes also discovered the principle by which the specific gravity of a substance, or its weight compared with that of water, can be found. This discovery, known as Archimedes' Principle, is one of the cornerstones of modern science. According to popular belief, it first occurred to Archimedes when he observed the displacement of water as he sat in the bathtub.

Greek science was speculative, not practical. Although the Greeks are acclaimed as pioneers in

ARCHIMEDES. The great scientist was in Syracuse when the city was captured by the Romans. Caught in the middle of a problem, he was slain by a soldier who disobeyed special orders to spare him.

science, they left technology, or the practical application of scientific principles, to later generations. Men today are likely to insist that science be useful or practical. They expect it to make their lives more comfortable and secure. Although Greek scientists believed in many of the same principles that twentieth-century scientists believe in, they had far different goals.

The learned men of ancient Greece usually belonged to the upper classes. They were seldom confronted with the urgent need to solve practical problems. In fact, such routine matters as agriculture and commerce were felt to be the business of the lower classes and the slaves. Thus the aristocrats were free to attend to the more important affairs of state and to pursue the study of philosophy.

Science was of interest to the philosopher primarily because it could help him arrive at a better understanding of universal truths. He tended to consider himself first a philosopher and incidentally a scientist. So the learned men of ancient Greece sought scientific knowledge to satisfy their curiosity about man and the universe, rather than to improve their standard of living.

Chapter Check-up

1. How did Athens become the center of a rich and powerful empire?
2. What was the Golden Age of Athens?
3. How was Greek art different in purpose from that of Egypt and the Fertile Crescent?
4. What was the most important temple of Athens and where was it located?
5. Identify and describe the three styles of architecture developed by the Greeks?
6. How was drama important to the Athenians?
7. Why do we say that history was born in Greece?
8. Why did Socrates never define "justice"?
9. Why is Aristotle considered to be one of the most learned men who has ever lived?
10. What contributions were made by the Greeks in the field of science?
11. How did the ancient Greeks' attitude toward science differ from modern man's?

Chapter 12

The Daily Lives of the Greeks Reflected Their Ideals

THE GREEKS EMPHASIZED SIMPLE VIRTUES

The ancient Greeks enjoyed life. They believed, however, that their enjoyment increased if they practiced self-control and moderation in everything they did. In their daily lives they were more concerned with cultivating their appreciation of beauty and wisdom than they were with living in comfort and indulging in pleasure. One reason the Greeks were able to spend so much time on civic and artistic development is that they were so little concerned with earning money to buy luxuries.

Greek education trained the whole man. The goal of Greek education was not to train a young man to make a living but to help him develop a healthy body, a well-trained mind, and a strong character. A boy's schooling began at the age of seven, and from sunrise to sunset he worked hard. Two areas of study were designed to train the two sides of man's nature, "gymnastics for the body" and "music for the soul." Gymnastics were intended to build more than physical strength, for competition in sport required the use of the mind as well as the body. For the rest of his life a boy would spend some time every day exercising and talking with his friends in the local gymnasium. The Greek gymnasium was as much a cultural center as a place for physical training.

The study of "music" included such subjects as poetry, drama, history, science, melody, and public speaking. All of these subjects, except public speaking, were believed to be inspired by nine goddesses, who were called the Muses. Homer's epics were more widely read than the works of any other Greek writer. The Greeks considered the heroes of Homer's stories perfect examples of ideal men and his style a perfect example of poetic form. After careful training of all his capabilities, the Greek boy was prepared to take his place wherever either thought or action was needed. This pattern of education was followed all over Greece, except of course in Sparta (see page 82).

Greek houses were plain and simple. The Greeks spent much of their time outdoors, in the gymnasium or the market place. Their houses were simple and plain. Even the homes of the wealthy had little furniture or decoration. A typical Greek house was a series of small chambers grouped about an open central court. It was flat-roofed and only one or two-storied. There were

Wrestling. These boys are engaged in an exercise that the ancient Greeks considered one of the most important for the training of the body.

few if any outside windows, and the heavy solid door of the house opened directly onto the street. Very often a Greek house would have neither running water nor drainage. Meals were usually simple—barley cakes, salads, fish, olives, and wine. A banquet might feature a roast fowl or lamb.

Greek women led sheltered lives. In the Greek tradition, a man gave his best to the state while a woman gave her best to the home. Girls were usually not sent to school, but taught at home to be good housekeepers and managers. When a girl was fourteen or fifteen her parents arranged a marriage for her. Usually the size of the bride's dowry and the land owned by the bridegroom were the most important factors in the marriage arrangements.

A well-born Greek lady rarely left her house after her marriage, except to attend weddings, funerals, and the theater. She could not own any property as Egyptian and Babylonian women could, and she could not dine with her husband's friends or go hunting with him. But even though her civil and social rights were limited, within the home she was highly respected.

RELIGION INFLUENCED MANY ASPECTS OF GREEK LIFE

The Greeks worshiped many Gods. All Greeks were interested in religion and worshiped many gods. The philosophers tried to reconcile the religious myths and beliefs that the Greeks had inherited from the past with their search for the causes of things. The average Greek who believed in many gods probably did not try to reason out his beliefs. He accepted these supernatural persons with a mixture of piety and superstition.

According to Greek legend the home of the gods was Mount Olympus (oh-*lim*-pus), the highest mountain in Greece. Here the gods displayed such human emotions as jealousy, anger, and love. On occasion they even made fools of themselves. The whims and fancies of the gods were the favorite subjects of Greek myths. Natural occurrences such as storms, earthquakes, and the changing seasons were attributed to the changing moods of their gods.

The three greatest gods were Zeus, Athena, and Apollo. Zeus, the father and ruler of all the other gods, was the giver of justice, the protector of those in distress. Lightning and thunder were the signs of his anger.

Gray-eyed Athena, the goddess of wisdom and a daughter of Zeus, was especially beloved by the Greeks. They believed she had given them the precious olive tree and taught them to weave cloth. Athens was named in her honor and looked to her for protection. To all Greeks, however, Athena was a symbol of knowledge, courage, and self-control.

Apollo was the sun god who inspired the poets and musicians. Playing soft music on his lyre, he protected the flocks in the field. The Greeks believed his priests or oracles could foretell the future. The entire Greek world contributed to the construction of a temple in his honor at Delphi (*del*-fie) in Central Greece.

There were many other gods and goddesses. Hera (*hee*-ruh), wife of Zeus, protected married women and kept a watchful eye on husbands, including her own. Aphrodite (af-rah-*die*-tee) was the goddess of love and beauty. Hermes (*her*-meez), with winged feet, was messenger of the gods and protector of commerce. Sailors looked to Poseidon (poe-*sy*-d'n), lord of the sea, for help in danger. The Greeks thought that every place had its protecting spirit. There was even a god of mischief, noise, and revel, called Pan.

The Greeks paid honor to their gods in contests of skill. The Greeks regularly held great religious festivals in honor of the gods. Some festivals took the form of athletic contests; others were contests of drama, poetry, or artistic skills. Twice each year, for example, Athens held dramatic festivals in honor of the gods. It did not seem strange to the Greeks to dedicate games or plays to the gods. Any action of man, if it were well done, was pleasing to them.

TEMPLE OF ATHENA AT DELPHI. This round building was surrounded by a wreath of twenty Doric columns. Delphi, the seat of Apollo's oracle, had temples dedicated to many gods.

The best known of the athletic festivals were the Olympic games. According to tradition they were begun in 776 B.C. and were held every four years. To protect travellers who attended these games from all over Greece, the Greek city-states observed a truce while the games were held. Contests included foot races, jumping, wrestling, boxing, and hurling the javelin and the discus. A victor was a hero to all Greeks. In the games a winner's prize was simply an olive wreath. But in his home city a champion was honored with many gifts. The Olympic games continued to be held until the Roman emperor Theodosius I stopped them at the end of the fourth century A.D.

In modern times the Olympic games have been revived. The first modern games were held in Athens in 1896. Except for suspensions during World Wars I and II they have been held at four-year intervals ever since in a city selected by an international Olympic committee. Sports such as swimming, basketball, and hockey have been added to the list of events.

ATHENA IN MOURNING. A stone tablet, probably erected as a memorial to those slain in battle, shows Athena gazing with downcast eyes at a gravestone.

Signs and oracles were believed to reveal the future. From the Egyptians and Babylonians the Greeks adopted the belief that it was possible to foretell the future by interpreting certain marks found on the livers and kidneys of animals. Greek priests also studied the heavens, the flights of birds, and the movements of horses for telltale signs. These methods of predicting what will happen in the future are called *divination* (div-ih-*nay*-shun). The Greeks often used divination to decide whether to fight a battle or what course to take in the Assembly.

Many Greeks also believed that the gods had empowered certain priests with an ability to foresee the future. These priests could be found at various oracles (*or*-uh-kuls) located throughout Greece. The most famous was the Oracle of Apollo at Delphi, located in central Greece. Here a priestess sat in a cave inhaling vapor that rose out of a deep cleft in the rocks. In a semiconscious state she would mumble answers to questions put to her. Supposedly Apollo himself told her what to say. In reality, priests within the temple at Delphi prepared the answers. Because they were clever men, they avoided straightforward replies. When, for example, Athens was threatened by the Persians, the advice of the oracle was, "Safe shall the wooden walls continue for thee and thy children." Some Athenians thought the oracle intended them to take refuge on the Acropolis, which had once been surrounded by a wooden wall. Others said it meant the "wooden walls" of the Athenian ships. Fortunately, the Athenians chose the latter interpretation, because the Persians captured and burned Athens.

Fate ruled gods and men alike. Although the Greeks brought their questions to the priests or the oracles, they did not really believe that the

A GREEK GRAVESTONE. The Greeks were much less concerned with an afterlife than were the Egyptians. This grave marker shows no suggestion at all of life after death. The scene depicts a simple act of everyday life, rather than one from an imaginary world beyond. The woman is trying to decide which jewels she should wear.

gods knew all the answers. The Egyptians and Mesopotamians, you will remember, believed that their gods were all-powerful and controlled men's destinies. Greek gods, however, were thought to be very much like ordinary human beings, except that they did not grow old and die. Greek gods were no freer to do as they pleased than men were. The real ruler of both gods and men was the natural law of the universe, or fate.

We have noted that Greek dramatists, philosophers, and scientists believed that all occurrences have natural causes. Events followed each other in an order determined by natural law, as day was followed by night and wrongdoing was followed by punishment.

Because the gods were ruled by the same laws that ruled men, the Greeks did not fear the gods. Hence religion was not so much a matter of devotion as a mechanical ceremony for keeping the gods in a pleasant frame of mind so that they would grant favors. Since the head of each family sacrificed wine or meat directly to the gods in his own home, few priests were needed, and their power was limited. In truth, the Greeks learned more about the importance of moral behavior through drama and philosophy than they did through their religion.

The Greeks were concerned mainly with life on earth. The Greeks believed that after death most men went to a shadowy underworld called Hades (*hay*-deez), ruled by the god Pluto. A few heroes and men who were greatly loved by the gods were allowed to go to another part of the underworld called the Elysian (ee-*lizh*-un) Fields, where they enjoyed endless bliss. Although the Greeks paid little heed to the prospect of life after death, they strongly believed that the body needed a proper burial if the spirit were to find rest.

The vast majority of Greeks believed that the best life for a Greek citizen was one devoted to the interests of his city-state. To make his city a noble and beautiful one was far more important to him than building tombs, regretting his mistakes, or worrying about death.

Chapter Check-up

1. What was the goal of Greek education, and what subjects were taught to achieve this?
2. Why did the Greeks give so little thought to the comfort and quality of their homes?
3. How were the girls of Greece educated?
4. What was the status of Greek women?
5. What was the significance of Mount Olympus to the Greeks?
6. Who were the three leading Greek gods, and what did each represent?
7. With what forms of religious festivals did the Greeks honor their gods?
8. What part did the oracles play in Greek life?
9. The Greeks believed in fate. What did this mean to them?
10. What was the attitude of the Greeks toward their gods and their religion?

CHAPTER 13

Alexander the Great Conquered the East

THE PELOPONNESIAN WARS WEAKENED THE GREEK CITY-STATES AND BROUGHT THEIR DOWNFALL

Athens and Sparta engaged in tragic wars. By the middle of the fifth century B.C., the Athenian Empire was at the height of its power. The citizens of Athens, who had become increasingly dependent on the income from their empire, were anxious to maintain and extend their control of Mediterranean trade. Greek city-states outside the empire, however, feared that the rising power of Athens threatened their independence. Many of them allied with Sparta to form the *Peloponnesian League.* In 432 B.C., the League declared war on Athens.

For the next thirty years the "Peloponnesian Wars" raged over Greece, leaving much of it devastated. At the peak of the conflict, Athens was struck by a terrible plague which killed a third of her population, including the great leader Pericles. Eventually, Sparta starved Athens into submission.

But Sparta's victory did not put an end to conflict in Greece. In a short time, other city-states grew jealous of Sparta, rose against her, and defeated her. Neither Athens nor Sparta ever recovered from these ruinous wars, although Athens continued to be a cultural and commercial center. With its two greatest city-states powerless, Greece became easy prey for invaders.

Philip of Macedon conquered the Greeks. North of Greece lay a wild, rugged country called Macedonia (mas-eh-*doe*-nee-uh). Although the Macedonians spoke Greek, they had adopted few Greek customs and remained largely uncivilized. In the middle of the fourth century B.C., a strong and intelligent leader, Philip of Macedon, came to power. To bring peace to his quarrelsome countrymen, Philip established a powerful army and ruled the country with an iron hand. Slowly, he extended his control over Macedonia.

With a strong, unified country behind him, Philip turned his attention to his southern neighbors. Philip took careful note of the opportunity that presented itself when the Peloponnesian Wars weakened Athens and Sparta. He formulated an ambitious plan to bring all the Greeks under his rule and unite them against Persia.

At A Glance

Important Periods in Greek History

Cretan civilization (*c.* 2400–*c.* 1450 B.C.)
  Minos

Achaean Dominance (*c.* 1450–*c.* 1100 B.C.)
  Trojan War

Dorian Invasions (*c.* 1100–*c.* 900 B.C.)

Greek Colonization (*c.* 900–*c.* 600 B.C.)

Rise of Athens (*c.* 650 B.C.)
  Draco
  Solon
  Peisistratus
  Cleisthenes

Persian Wars (490–479 B.C.)
  Marathon
  Thermopylae
  Salamis

Golden Age of Athens (*c.* 460–429 B.C.)
  Pericles

Peloponnesian Wars (432–402 B.C.)

Macedonian domination (346–323 B.C.)
  Philip
  Alexander

Demosthenes (de-*mahs*-the-neez), a farsighted Athenian statesman, tried to awaken his fellow citizens to the danger from Macedonia. He delivered fiery speeches against Philip, called *philippics.* He pleaded with the Athenians to defend themselves by uniting with other city-states before Philip swallowed them up one by one. Unfortunately, Greek city-states could not overcome the bitterness and distrust that had developed among them during the Peloponnesian Wars. As the Greek states quarreled among themselves, Philip quietly made preparations for their conquest. When he attacked in 346 B.C., Athens and the few allies she gathered around her were no match for his well-trained army. Proud Athens was defeated in battle, and the other city-states, too fearful of each other to unite, quickly surrendered. Philip was master of Greece.

ALEXANDER CREATED A VAST EMPIRE

Philip's son became king. As a youth, Philip's son, Alexander, showed such extraordinary ability that his father vowed he would give the boy the best education possible. Accordingly Philip sent this letter to the famous philosopher Aristotle:

> "Be informed that I have a son, and that I am thankful to the gods not so much for his birth, as that he was born in the same age with you; for if you will undertake the charge of his education, I assure myself that he will become worthy of his father, and of the kingdom that he will inherit."

Aristotle journeyed to Macedonia to become the tutor of Alexander.

When Alexander was twenty, his father was assassinated, leaving the young man King of Macedonia. As king, Alexander was determined to win glory and to spread Greek civilization throughout the world. First he put down revolts at home; then, gathering his army, Alexander marched through Greece, demanding that the city-states give him the same promise of allegiance they had made to his father. When the city of Thebes resisted, he ruthlessly destroyed it. The terrified Greeks quickly submitted to his rule.

Alexander demonstrated military genius. Alexander inherited not only his father's kingdom,

ALEXANDER THE GREAT. This detail from a first-century Roman mosaic shows Alexander the Great at the Battle of Issus in 333 B.C. The mosaic is a copy of a painting done by a contemporary of Alexander.

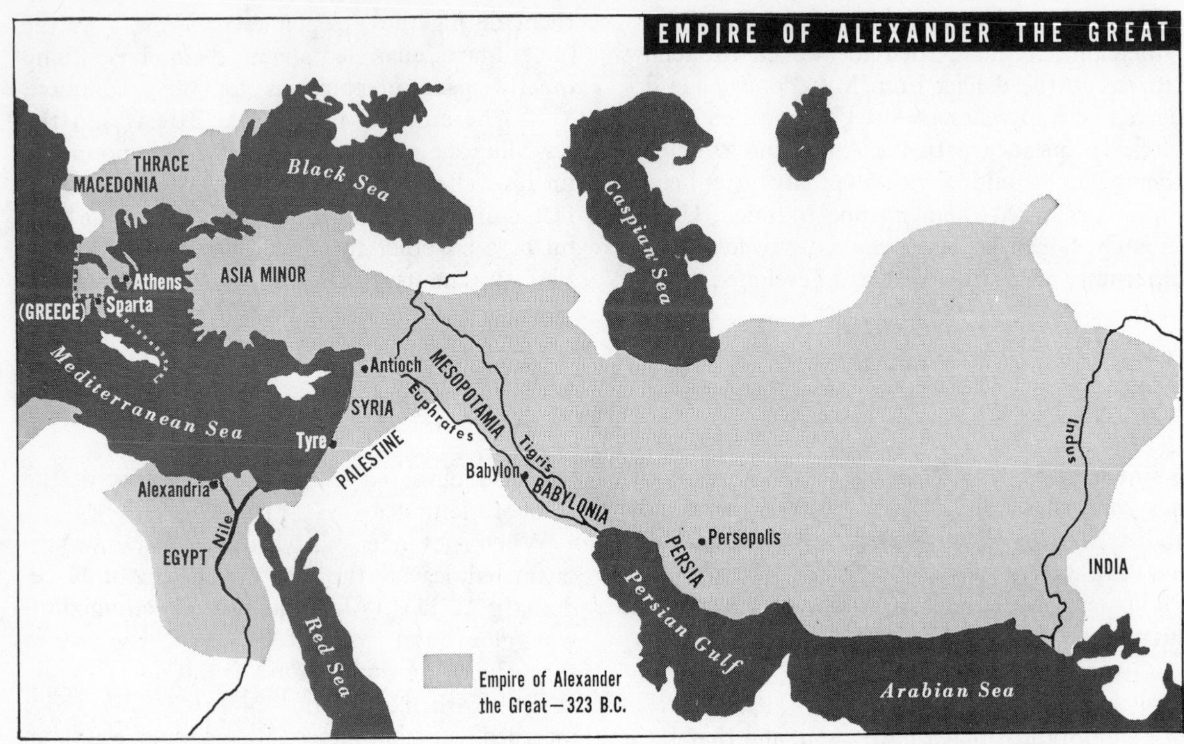

but also the war that Philip had begun with the king of Persia. In the spring of 334 B.C., Alexander crossed the Aegean Sea into Persian territory with an army of thirty thousand foot soldiers and five thousand cavalrymen. Included in his army were engineers to build siege machinery and bridges, surveyors to collect information about routes and camping grounds, and a secretarial force to maintain a careful record of his exploits. He also brought scholars whose task was to collect geographical information and to bring back specimens of plants for his friend and tutor, Aristotle.

Alexander, whom many historians consider the ablest general in history, won a brilliant victory over the Persian king in Asia Minor. Unopposed, he marched down the coast of the eastern Mediterranean, freeing Phoenicia, Palestine, and Egypt from Persian rule. Because he abolished the hated tribute that had been exacted yearly by the Persians, Alexander was welcomed everywhere. In Egypt he was joyfully received as a liberator, crowned Pharaoh, and declared a god.

Still unsatisfied, Alexander turned his army east and marched across the Euphrates and Tigris rivers into the heart of Persia. There he won another great victory over the Persians, and declared himself king of Persia by right of conquest. In less than a decade, Alexander had built the greatest empire the world had yet known.

But Alexander's ambitions were still not satisfied. Aristotle had taught him that the Asian continent ended just beyond the Indus River, where an eastern ocean began. Hoping to explore this region and add it to his empire, Alexander led his army into the east, taking with him Phoenician rowers and shipbuilders.

When Alexander crossed the eastern branches of the upper Indus, his army mutinied and refused to go further. They did not want to be explorers; they were tired and homesick. They had fought in Asia for many years and had marched more than ten thousand miles. Alexander was forced to turn back. If he could not reach the great eastern ocean, however, he was determined to explore the Arabian Sea. Accordingly, he ordered his Phoenician workmen to build a flotilla of ships on which he sailed to the mouth of the Indus. There he built a harbor, hoping to establish regular communication by sea between the Indus and the Euphrates rivers.

Alexander sent the fleet west across the Arabian Sea to the mouth of the Euphrates, while he and his troops took the overland route. His guides soon became lost in the desert, but luckily the army found its way back to the Persian Gulf.

Alexander sought to win the support of his conquered subjects. To please the Persians, who now made up the largest part of his empire, Alexander adopted Persian dress and certain Persian customs. He insisted that all who came to him on business should bow and kiss his feet as if he were divine. Kissing feet was a normal ceremony for the Persians, but the Greeks, who were not accustomed to treating any man in this fashion, refused. Alexander's Macedonian soldiers began to think their king had let success go to his head when he claimed to be a god. During a banquet, Alexander, in a fit of drunken anger, put to death several of the most popular and respected officers of his army, one of whom had saved his life in battle. Alexander grieved for the death of his friend for three days. But his soldiers were not impressed; they openly mutinied and demanded to go home. Alexander was furious. He dismissed the whole army from his service with an impassioned speech.

> "And now, as you all want to go, go, every one of you, and tell them at home that you deserted your king who had led you from victory to victory across the world and left him to the care of strangers he had conquered; and no doubt your words will win you the praise of men and the blessing of heaven. Go."

Shamed by this speech, his men called off their mutiny. But a short time later Alexander arranged to send home ten thousand of them.

Soon after this incident, Alexander, who was not yet thirty-three years old, fell ill with fever and died. He had dreamed of a great empire in which all the peoples would live together harmoniously under his rule, but he had unwisely left no plans for a successor. Without his leadership, the army fell into disorder and the empire was divided among his generals. Not until two centuries later was Alexander's empire united again, this time under the Romans.

Hellenistic culture combined Greek and eastern ways of life. Short though it was, the twelve years of Alexander's career wrought great changes in the ancient world. Wherever Alexander went, he founded cities and Greek colonies, which became centers of Greek literature, art, and philosophy. By spreading Greek culture, he hoped to create, for the first time, a single civiliza-

The Winged Victory of Samothrace. This statue, one of the finest examples of Hellenistic art, commemorated a successful naval battle. It is thought to represent Nike, the goddess of victory, as she alights on the prow of a ship.

tion that would cover the whole of the ancient world. His ambitious plan very nearly succeeded. Greek culture was carried into every land that bordered the eastern end of the Mediterranean. Two of his eastern cities became world famous centers of learning: Alexandria, in Egypt, and Antioch (*an*-tee-ahk), in Asia Minor. In time they replaced Athens as the cultural centers of the ancient world.

As Greek culture moved along the highways of trade, it became mixed with Persian learning and customs. This combination of Greek and Persian learning is called *Hellenistic culture*. Thus the Greek civilization that was spread in the Middle East was somewhat different from the civilization of Greece itself. As we shall see in Part 5, much of this Hellenistic culture greatly influenced the Romans, who were destined to be the next rulers of the ancient world.

Chapter Check-up

1. Why did the other Greek city-states rise up against Athens?
2. What was the outcome of the Peloponnesian Wars?
3. How did Philip of Macedon influence the history of Greece?
4. Who was the teacher of Alexander?
5. What was the geographic extent of Alexander's empire?
6. What caused the collapse of Alexander's empire after his death?
7. How did Alexander's conquests influence the spread of Greek culture?
8. What was Hellenistic culture?

Greece: SYNOPSIS

One of the most important skills man has ever developed is the ability to think logically. The application of logical thinking to the mysteries of nature enabled the Greeks to overcome the fear of the unknown which characterized such early peoples as the Egyptians and Mesopotamians. Gradually the ancient Greeks came to believe that events and actions could be logically explained by natural laws. The faith of the Greeks in this belief led to the development of such studies as philosophy, biology, medicine, and physics.

A second great development in the history of mankind is the idea that man is capable of governing himself and making his own decisions. In a desperate quest for security, earlier peoples had entrusted themselves to the absolute rule of kings and priests. But not the Greeks! They had enough faith in man's abilities to establish a democratic government. Thus all citizens were given a voice in public affairs and were inspired to develop their talents in a climate of freedom. Today enlightened nations assume, as the Greeks did, that men are capable of self-government and that the best government is one that is based on the will of its citizens. These nations, too, attempt to create a free society in which man can develop his fullest abilities, to the mutual benefit of his nation and himself.

Twentieth-century man's debt to the Greeks becomes even more apparent when we take a moment to examine certain words used commonly in the English language. We find that many fields of learning are still described by Greek names—a tribute to the inquiring spirit of the Greeks and their high level of achievement. Such words as *politics, democracy, history, comedy, tragedy, philosophy, physics, geometry,* and *trigonometry* illustrate this point.

In some areas Greek scholarship has never been surpassed. The thought-provoking ideas expressed by Socrates, Plato, and Aristotle continue to challenge men everywhere. The famous plays of Aeschylus, Sophocles, and Euripides continue to fascinate audiences all over the world, and Euclid's geometric principles are still part of every student's training. Greek sculpture, the writings of Greek historians, and the discoveries of Greek scientists set the standards and laid the foundations for much of our present-day achievements in these areas.

The inspiring ideas and remarkable achievements of the early Greeks constitute a precious legacy for mankind. Can you now understand why ancient Greece is hailed as "immortal"?

Terms

Be sure that you understand clearly the meaning of each of the following:

classical	philosophy	*strategi*
fresco	speculative science	pure democracy
frieze	"whole man"	representative democracy
Iliad and *Odyssey*	*polis*	totalitarian
natural law	*archons*	"ideal form"
oracle	demogogues	Hellenistic

Important People

How did each of the following influence the story of Greece?

Minos	Xerxes	Aeschylus	Herodotus
Homer	Leonidas	Aristophanes	Hippocrates
Achilles	Themistocles	Socrates	Archimedes
Draco	Pericles	Plato	Philip of Macedon
Cleisthenes	Myron	Aristotle	Alexander the Great

Questions for Discussion and Review

1. How did each of the following geographic conditions influence the development of Greek civilization? (a) Nearness to older civilizations; (b) indented coastlines and nearness to the sea; (c) mountainous terrain; (d) rocky soil.
2. How has Greek thought influenced the political and scientific life of the Western world?
3. How does the Greek ideal of good citizenship compare with our standard today?
4. In what ways was the Spartan state like that of Nazi Germany and Communist Russia?

5. Compare Sparta and Athens as to: (a) education; (b) rights of the citizen; (c) contribution to civilization.
6. Athenian democracy had its limitations. Can you suggest any ways in which our own democracy might be improved or made more complete?
7. What are the similarities and differences between the Olympic games of the Greeks and those of today?
8. Were the Greeks more advanced in philosophy or in religion? Explain.
9. What is history? How is it influenced by those who write it?
10. What were the most valuable contributions of the Greeks to modern civilization?

Interesting Things to Do

1. Prepare a map of Greece and the Mediterranean area showing the location of the important city-states, Crete, Macedonia, the islands of the Aegean, and the colonies in Asia Minor.
2. Summarize in chart form the contributions to civilization made by famous Greeks in the fields of government, art, literature, drama, philosophy, and science.
3. Sketch columns representing the three styles of Greek architecture, or collect and display a series of pictures illustrating the influence of Greek architecture in our own country.
4. Design a poster or draw a series of cartoons comparing Sparta and Athens in government, education, citizens' rights, and contributions to civilization.
5. Make a booklet or poster illustrating the religion of the Greeks. Include pictures or drawings of the gods and goddesses, and explain what each was noted for.
6. Prepare and present a talk entitled "The Olympic Games, Then and Now."
7. Hold an informal panel discussion on the achievements of the Greeks. First let each panel member discuss one area of achievement, and then let the panel decide which of the areas was most important.
8. Compile a brief dictionary of some of the important words in our language which have come to us from the Greeks. Be sure to define each word.
9. Write a poem describing some famous person or event in Greek history.
10. Continue or begin your "Who's Who in World History" series by writing one or more brief biographies of outstanding Greeks. Tell why each is important.

Interesting Reading about Greece

Asimov, Isaac, *The Greeks,* Houghton Mifflin. History of Greek civilization from the Mycenaean age to the present.

Coolidge, Olivia E., *Trojan War,* Houghton Mifflin.

*Davis, William S., *A Day in Old Athens,* Allyn & Bacon. Glimpses of life at the height of Greek civilization.

Gunther, John, *Alexander the Great,* Random House.

Hamilton, Edith, *The Greek Way,* Norton. Thought-provoking discussion of Greek art, literature, and philosophy.

Kieran, John, *Story of the Olympic Games,* Lippincott.

*Lamb, Harold, *Alexander of Macedonia,* Doubleday.

Lawrence, Isabelle, *Niko, Sculptor's Apprentice,* Viking. Account of how the Parthenon was built.

*Miller, Walter, *Greece and the Greeks,* Macmillan. Picture history of Greece.

Quennell, Marjorie and Charles H. B., *Everyday Things in Ancient Greece,* Putnam.

*Tappan, E. M., *Story of the Greek People,* Houghton Mifflin.

* Indicates easy reading

Roman civilization, law, and order followed Roman soldiers such as these all over the Mediterranean world.

Part 5
ROME
RULER OF THE ANCIENT WORLD

THE ROMAN EMPIRE

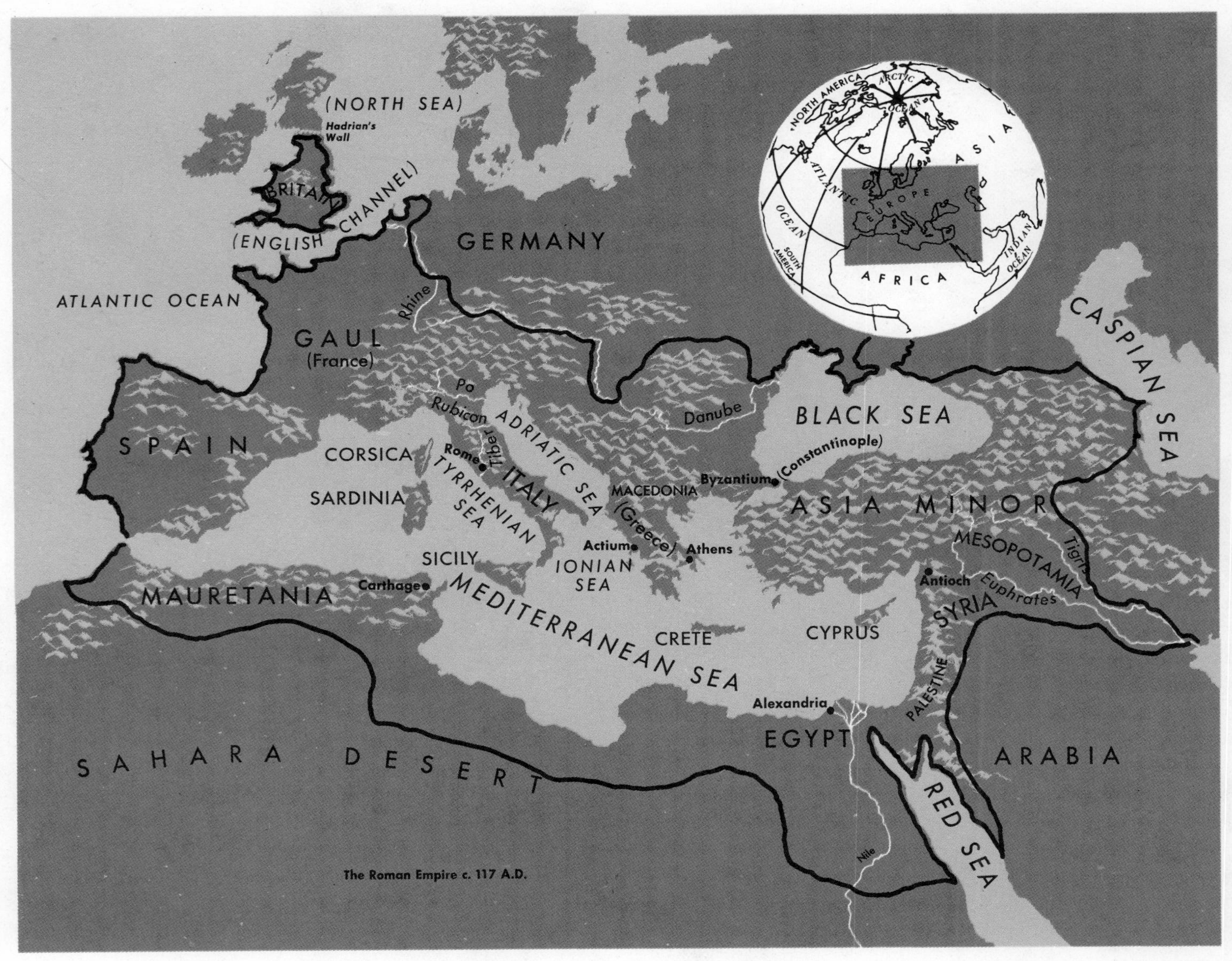

The Roman Empire c. 117 A.D.

Rome: GEOGRAPHIC SETTING

The Italian peninsula is a boot-shaped projection, seven hundred miles long, jutting southward from Europe. It is surrounded on three sides by the Adriatic, Ionian, and Tyrrhenian (tih-*ree*-nih-un) seas. In the north the Alps separate the peninsula from the rest of the continent. Three large islands lie to the southwest: Sicily, Sardinia, and Corsica. The Italian peninsula has a *Mediterranean climate,* with cool, rainy winters and hot, dry summers. The seas tend to prevent the temperature from reaching extremes in any season.

Although Italy is mountainous, the mountains do not break up the country into separate parts as they do in Greece. The Apennine (*ap*-eh-nine) Mountains begin in the north and run the length of the peninsula, almost completely occupying the eastern and southern parts of it. As a result, most of the important rivers flow westward into a broad, fertile plain along the Tyrrhenian coast. This area, with one exception in the north (the Po Valley), is the only good farm land on the peninsula. The best harbors, too, are found in the bays or river mouths along the western coast. The city of Rome was built on the Tiber River near one of Italy's natural harbors. Thus, while Greek civilization was influenced chiefly by contact with eastern lands, Rome's natural outlook was toward the west.

Rome: PERSPECTIVE

An aged Roman farmer, Lucius Quinctius Cincinnatus, was digging in his field outside Rome one day in 458 B.C. when a delegation of men from the city came hurrying to his farm. They had come to warn of hostile invaders who were threatening the walls of Rome, and to ask for help from the old man. Although nearly eighty, Cincinnatus left his field, joined a Roman legion that swiftly crushed the enemy horde, and was back at his farm in sixteen days.

So goes an early legend. Whether true or false, it suggests the patriotism and valor that made the Roman Empire into something the world had never known before and has never seen since. From Africa to Britain, from the Atlantic Ocean to the Caspian Sea, Rome at her height held sway. For over two hundred years the Empire brought to this vast area a period of order, prosperity, and peace. Rome built amphitheaters, aqueducts, and public buildings; she established a code of laws that remains a strong influence on modern legal practice; and she built roads over which people are still traveling two thousand years later.

But the seeds of the Roman Empire's decay were being planted even at the time of her greatest flowering. As wealth increased, so did the indolence of her citizens. As the boundaries of the Empire grew, so did taxes. As life became harder, discontent spread and patriotism faded. Then, from the north, barbarian tribes swept into the Empire to put to death the already dying civilization.

In this Part you will learn about some of the people and institutions that made a famous poet speak in wonder of "the grandeur that was Rome." You will also learn what forces brought an end to that grandeur.

Chapter 14

Rome Established a Republic and Won Control of the Mediterranean

PATRICIANS AND PLEBEIANS STRUGGLED FOR POWER

Italy developed in isolation from the East. The first inhabitants of the Italian peninsula were unnamed peoples who never advanced beyond the New Stone Age. About 2000 B.C., they were overrun by a primitive Indo-European tribe from the north, the Italians. The peninsula, which became known as Italy, remained for centuries a backward area.

One reason for the late development of Italy was that the Italian invaders did not find an advanced civilization there as the Achaeans had in Greece. Another factor was Italy's westward orientation. Because the important harbors and islands of Greece were on her eastern coast, contact with older, more advanced civilizations was easy. But Italy's best harbors and most fertile lands faced west, where the inhabitants were still chiefly barbarians. The early Italians had more contact with these peoples than with the civilized Greeks, Phoenicians, and Egyptians to the east.

Surprisingly, Italy's progress was hindered by the fact that she had enough good land to support her people. Unlike the Greeks and Phoenicians, whose lack of fertile soil caused them to become traders, the early Italian farmers stayed home and therefore had little opportunity to learn from foreigners. For nearly a thousand years, the Italians lived in isolation.

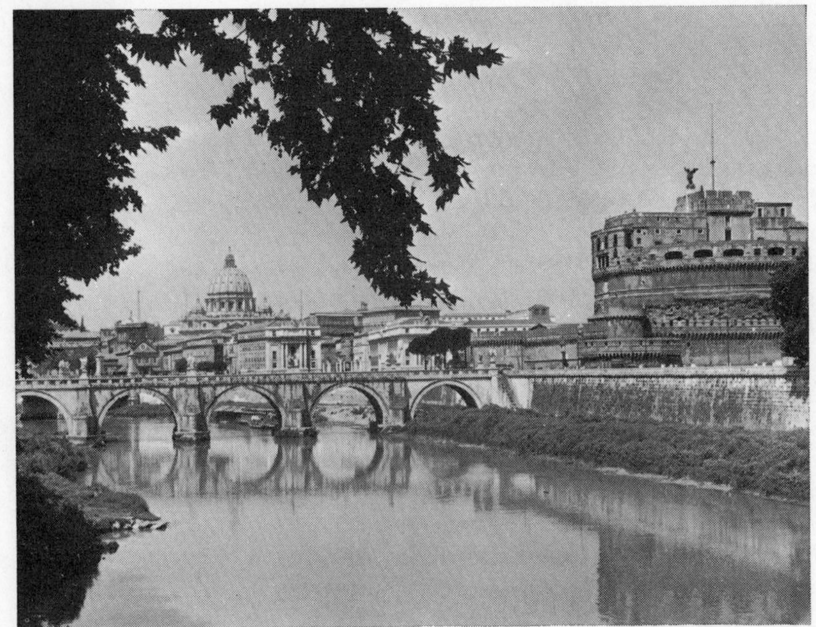

ROME. The ancient, medieval, and modern worlds all mingle together in the Eternal City. This view shows the Tiber River, the tomb of the Emperor Hadrian (the Castel Sant' Angelo) at the right, and St. Peter's in the distance.

Latin tribes settled Rome. One of the early Italian tribes, the Latins, built their villages on the low hills that overlook the Tiber River. Because the Latins could not write, no records exist of the founding of Rome in these hills. But there are many legends.

One legend tells how the hero Aeneas (uh-*nee*-us), who had escaped from the destruction of Troy, came to Italy and married a Latin princess. Hundreds of years later, their descendants, the twin brothers Romulus and Remus, were thrown into the Tiber by a wicked uncle. The twins were found and nursed by a she-wolf. When they grew up, they killed their uncle and laid the foundations of the city that was to rule the ancient world. Romulus killed Remus in a quarrel over who should name the city. Romulus became king in 753 B.C., and the city was called Rome in his honor. Whether or not the legend is true, historians agree that sometime between 800 B.C. and 700 B.C. the villages on the seven hills united to form the city of Rome.

Rome rapidly gained importance as a commercial center, largely because she was located at the point where a north-south road crossed the Tiber River. The seven hills on which the city was located made a natural stronghold from which the Romans could control traffic on the road and on the river.

Rome was first ruled by the Etruscans. About a century and a half before Rome was founded, a people from Asia Minor, the Etruscans (ee-*trus*-kunz), settled in Italy north of the Tiber. During the sixth century B.C. they moved south and conquered Rome. From their Etruscan masters, the simple Roman farmers learned to build temples and roads. But most important for the future, they learned the highly efficient Etruscan methods of warfare. In 509 B.C. the Romans succeeded in driving out their Etruscan conquerors. The Romans did not again fall prey to outsiders for nearly a thousand years.

After 509 B.C., Roman history falls into two distinct periods of approximately five hundred years each. The first is called the period of the Roman Republic (509 B.C.–31 B.C.), and the second is the period of the Roman Empire (31 B.C.–476 A.D.). We should keep in mind, however, that the transition from the Republic to the Empire was a gradual one, covering a span of nearly half a century.

Early Rome was controlled by the patricians. Roman society was divided into two distinct classes or groups. The smaller class, called *patrician*, was an hereditary nobility made up of wealthy land-owning families. The much larger class, called *plebeian*, was composed of shopkeepers, artisans, and small farmers. After Rome's Etruscan kings were expelled, the government of the city fell into the hands of the patricians. They set up a Roman Republic. In place of a king two patricians, known as *consuls*, were elected yearly by a tribal assembly of the Roman people. The consuls were aided by a *senate*, a body of some 300 patricians who were appointed for life by the consuls. The Republic was supposed to represent the interests of all the people. In practice, however, it was dominated by the patricians. Although the plebeians had their own assembly, it had little effective power in the early Republic. The senate proposed new laws and controlled revenues.

Under the existing laws, the plebeians were effectively prevented from improving their status. They could not marry into patrician families, and if they fell into debt their patrician creditors could hold them as slaves. Debt was always a threat to the plebeians because constant warfare between Rome and her neighbors frequently left their fields in ruin. Since the plebeians had no legal means of changing the unjust laws which the patricians had passed, they had to find some other way to voice their demands.

The plebeians went on strike. Throughout the period of the Republic the plebeians struggled toward political and social equality. Their one important weapon in the struggle was the fact that they were desperately needed to serve in the army.

In 494 B.C., according to legend, the plebeians marched out of Rome and threatened to set up a city for themselves. Historians are not certain of the outcome of the strike, but shortly after it ended, the plebeians won the right to elect their own officers, called *tribunes*. The tribunes were to have the special duty of protecting the plebe-

AN ETRUSCAN COFFIN. The Etruscans believed that the souls of the dead lived in their tombs. On this coffin an Etruscan and his wife recline on a couch as if attending an eternal banquet.

ians and seeing that they received justice in the law courts. Eventually the tribunes gained the right to sit outside the door of the Senate and shout, "*Veto*" (I forbid) whenever they opposed a measure. There were at least four other strikes in Rome's early history, and apparently they, too, aided the plebeians in winning concessions from the patricians.

In 449 B.C. the Senate agreed to a demand that the laws be put into writing. Up to that time Roman law was supposed to be based on ancient custom, but because the laws were unwritten no one was sure what they said. Patrician judges took advantage of this situation and often made harsh judgments against the plebeians who were brought before them in court. Finally, in response to plebeian demands, the laws were inscribed on twelve bronze tablets. This set of tablets was placed on public view in the Forum, Rome's great marketplace and center of business. From that time on, every Roman schoolboy memorized the laws found on the Twelve Tablets as part of his schooling.

Gradually the plebeians increased their privileges and rights. Debt slavery was abolished. In time, well-to-do plebeians were permitted to marry into the patrician class. The Assembly was given the right to elect minor officials and to make laws without the consent of the Senate. All offices, including the consulship, were eventually opened to plebeians, and, because all consuls went on to be senators, a few plebeians invaded the Senate itself.

Rome never became a true democracy. Although we call the Roman government a republic, its organization was very much like that of the Athenian democracy. Indeed, in ancient times *republic* and *democracy* had the same meaning. In both Athens and Rome all male citizens eventually gained the right to vote and to hold office, and they automatically became members of a legislative body. Modern democracies are too large to permit the latter practice. Instead, the citizens elect representatives to a congress or a parliament, and the representatives then make the laws. Today the term *republic* refers to "representative democracy" and the term *pure democracy* or *direct democracy* distinguishes the form of government used by the Greeks and Romans.

Despite their outward resemblance, the Roman and Athenian governments were not really alike. In Rome, the plebeian's vote was ineffective, and his right to hold office existed only in theory, since the Roman government did not pay its officials a salary. The wealthy men of Rome had still another advantage. They could win popularity with voters by furnishing free food and entertainment at political gatherings. As it turned out, even when a few plebeians were elected to the Senate, they rarely used their power to benefit the plebeian class. Instead, they identified themselves with the patricians and became just as anxious as any patrician to preserve the privilege and influence of the Senate. Thus the Roman people never had real self-government. Effective power was tightly held by a wealthy aristocracy, never by the citizenry as a whole.

ROME SUBDUED ITALY AND BECAME MISTRESS OF THE MEDITERRANEAN

Rome made allies of her conquered neighbors. Even during the struggle between the patricians and plebeians, Rome was busy fighting other cities and tribes in Italy. By 265 B.C. the Romans had defeated the Etruscans in the north and the Greek cities in southern Italy, thus gaining control of the whole Italian Peninsula.

Instead of annexing their conquests directly, the Romans sought to win the allegiance of the conquered peoples. The Romans demanded no tribute from them, and as the conquered peoples proved their loyalty they were even granted citizenship. Frequently the Romans allowed them to keep their own customs and local government. Gradually these wise policies transformed Rome's enemies into loyal allies.

Rome and Carthage fought bitterly to control the seas. Rome's victory over southern Italy left only a narrow strip of water between her territory and that of Carthage, another of the great powers of the ancient world. Carthage had been founded as a Phoenician trading post in 814 B.C. Gradually she had become the ruling power of the western Mediterranean, bringing under her control North Africa, parts of Spain, southern Gaul, and Sicily. Rome jealously eyed the rich Carthaginian trade, and Carthage, in turn, feared Roman expansion. In 264 B.C., a quarrel over control of Sicily plunged the two rivals into a series of wars which lasted for over a century. The Romans called them the Punic (*pyoo*-nik) Wars, from the Latin word for Phoenician.

Her powerful navy appeared to give Carthage the advantage in the war. The Romans, who had never been to sea, set to work copying the Carthaginian galleys and practicing rowing on the beach. But in spite of their efforts, the experienced Carthaginian sailors had no trouble defeating the hastily assembled Roman navy. The Romans, however, were more experienced in hand-to-hand fighting. To take advantage of their skill, they mounted on the prow of each of their ships a heavy plank with an iron hook at the end, which could be lowered onto an enemy ship. This device was called a *corvus*, from the Latin word for the raven, a bird with a strong beak. When an enemy ship drew near, the Romans dropped the *corvus* and swarmed aboard. In this way the Romans cleverly turned a naval battle into the kind of hand-to-hand combat at which they excelled. After twenty-three years of fighting, the Carthaginians were finally driven from Sicily. But proud Carthage had no intention of meekly accepting defeat. Her leaders began to plan revenge.

Hannibal devoted his life to restoring his country's power. The peace that followed the First Punic War was like a slumbering volcano. Rome still envied the wealth of Carthage, while Carthage burned with hatred for her conqueror. Few men in Carthage had a greater longing for revenge than a dashing young general named Hannibal. His father, Hamilcar, bitterly hated the Romans, whom he had fought in the First Punic War, and he instilled his hatred in Hannibal. When Hannibal was only nine years old, his father asked the boy to pledge that he would never be a friend to the Romans. Hannibal solemnly swore that he would follow his father's wishes—and he always did. For many years he was a powerful and dreaded enemy of Rome.

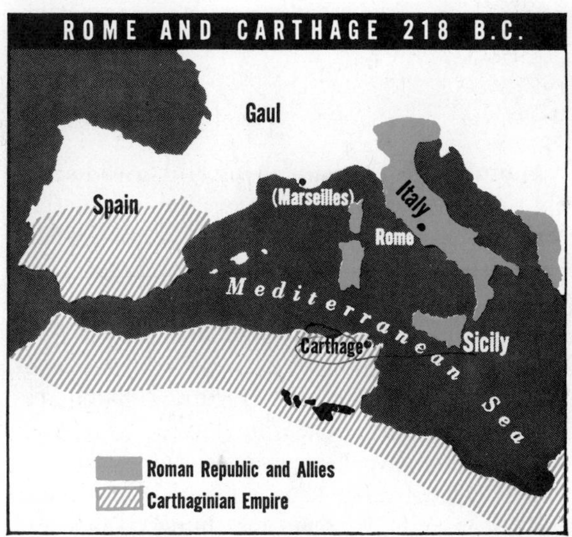

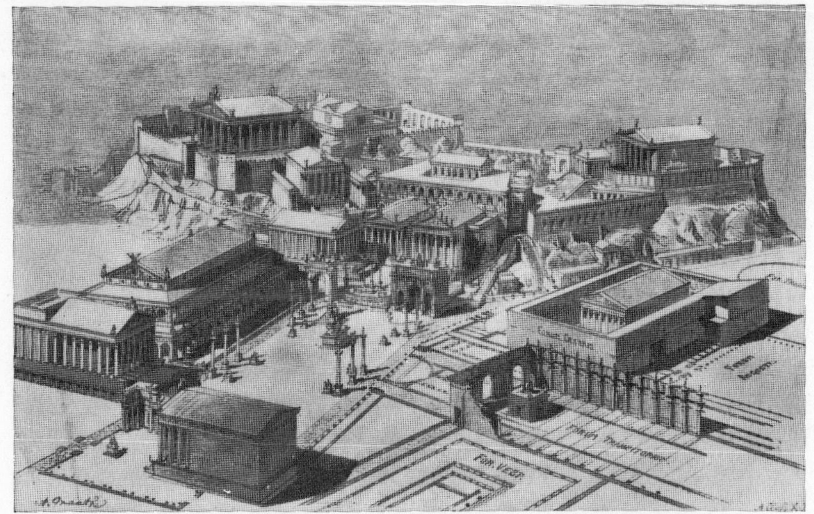

THE ANCIENT FORUM. The buildings of the Forum looked like this in the days of Rome's glory. The Forum was the focal point of the city. Here, the citizens of Rome gathered for meetings and ceremonies and to hear speeches.

THE ROMAN FORUM TODAY. Of the once-magnificent Forum, only these ruins remain. In the left foreground is the Arch of Septimus Severus, and on the right is the Palatine Hill, one of the seven hills of Rome.

Hannibal crossed the Alps and invaded Italy. The second war between Rome and Carthage broke out in Spain early in 218 B.C. There Hannibal's forces defeated the Romans. Then Hannibal planned a surprise for Rome. When spring came, he set out with his infantry, his matchless cavalry, and elephants—the tanks of ancient warfare. He marched from Spain across southern France. Then he crossed the Alps, making a mighty journey over wind-swept, icy passes, through deep snow and sudden, blinding storms. Hannibal's men were hungry, cold, and worn. Many of them died. Thundering avalanches of snow swept some over dizzy precipices. Native mountaineers hurled rocks down on them. But on they went. Only half of Hannibal's force reached the sunny valleys of northern Italy.

Yet that half seemed enough. Astonished, Rome sent her legions hurrying north to halt Hannibal, but he tricked them into destruction time after time. Rome lost battle after battle, then stubbornly rearmed to fight again. The fighting continued for fifteen years. Despite his victories, Hannibal was never able to launch a

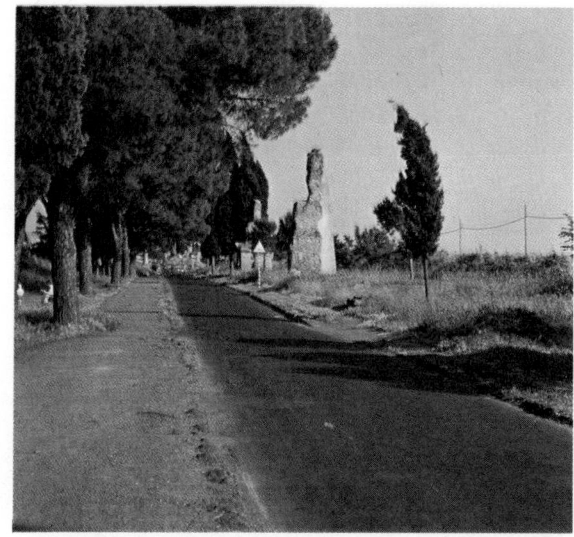

The Appian Way. Over such excellently constructed roads as this the Roman generals were able to dispatch their forces to meet any threat and to attack with speed. Roman engineers constructed the Appian Way so well that it is used even today.

successful attack at the city of Rome itself. He could not drag heavy siege machinery over the Alps, so he did not have the tools to batter down the city walls. Then, too, he had counted on getting recruits from towns and cities that Rome had conquered in Italy, but he got no help from that source. Rome's policy of rewarding loyalty with citizenship paid. Her neighbors were faithful to her. They would not join Hannibal.

Rome brought the war home to Carthage. The tide turned when a brilliant Roman general, Scipio, carried the war across the Mediterranean into Carthage. Soon Carthage sent a message to Hannibal begging him to leave Italy and return to protect his home city. Hannibal nearly wept when he received the summons, but like a true patriot he obeyed the order, leaving his campaign in Italy unfinished.

Not even Hannibal's courage and skill could save Carthage. The Romans were victorious, and Hannibal was put to flight. Rome took possession of the parts of Spain which Carthage had been ruling but was not content until Carthage itself was completely crushed. Cato, a Roman statesman who was known for his upright life, ended all his speeches in the Roman Senate with the words, "Carthage must be destroyed."

In 146 B.C. the order was given that Carthage should be completely wiped out. The Roman army ruthlessly carried out the command. The Carthaginians who were not killed during the siege of the city were slaughtered or sold into slavery. Carthage was plundered and then burned. After that, the ground on which Carthage had stood was turned under with a plow,

Hannibal Crossing the Alps. Horrified and frightened, the Roman legions were thrown into confusion by the sight of the strange monsters, the elephants. When the tide finally turned against Hannibal, he went into voluntary exile. Later, just as he was about to be delivered over to Roman officials, he poisoned himself.

and a terrible curse was laid on anyone who should ever try to rebuild the city. Thus the great Phoenician trading center of the Mediterranean passed out of existence. Rome stood as the unchallenged mistress of the western Mediterranean.

The Mediterranean became a Roman lake. Even before the destruction of Carthage, Roman armies had made conquests in many other places. In order to keep or enforce peace in the eastern Mediterranean, the Romans conquered Macedonia, Greece, and Asia Minor. Between 200 B.C. and 146 B.C. Rome took many of the lands that had made up the empire of Alexander the Great, about whom you read in the story of Greece. By 50 A.D. the little city of farmers on the Tiber had become the capital of the Mediterranean world.

Although the Romans ruled a vast empire, they strived to maintain the republican form of government that they had developed as a small city-state. As you will see in the next chapter, however, their new status brought problems that forced the Romans to alter their form of government drastically in the period that followed.

Chapter Check-up

1. Give two reasons why the people living on the Italian peninsula became civilized more slowly than did the Greeks.
2. What geographic conditions favored the growth of the city of Rome?
3. How did the plebeians gain political rights?
4. What was the Roman Forum?
5. How did the Twelve Tablets protect the rights of Roman citizens?
6. What system did Rome use to control and unite her conquered Italian neighbors?
7. Why did Rome and Carthage come to blows?
8. What was the final result of the Punic Wars?
9. What areas of the Mediterranean world did Rome control by the end of the Republic?

CHAPTER 15

The Growth of the Empire Wrought Changes in Roman Life

ROME'S CONQUESTS BROUGHT ECONOMIC CRISIS AND CIVIL WAR

The destruction of Carthage and the conquest of the Eastern Mediterranean brought neither peace nor prosperity to Rome. Indeed, for many citizens Rome's military success meant economic disaster and loss of independence. Failure to solve these problems caused civil war in Rome and resulted in the destruction of the Roman Republic.

Small farmers were driven off their land. In the early days of the Republic, Rome's citizen-soldiers were never called on to fight "overseas." They were able to cultivate and harvest their fields between campaigns. But this was not possible during the wars of the second century B.C. Thus, many soldiers returning from overseas duties found that their farms had been sold for unpaid taxes. Others found it impossible to compete with the rich landowners who had acquired large tracts of conquered land in areas such as North Africa. Their huge estates were worked by captured slaves and produced so much cheap grain that the small farmers were ruined and were forced to sell their land.

STREET MUSICIANS. Many musicians in Rome made their livelihood by playing and begging in the streets. Some were Greek or Greek-trained. This mosaic was found in the excavation of Herculaneum, a Roman resort city which was buried in the eruption of Mt. Vesuvius in 79 A.D.

In growing numbers, the once proud and independent citizen-farmers of Rome became tenant farmers or drifted into the city. But because slaves from the conquered countries made up a third of the population of Rome, there were few jobs for free men. The government, despite its democratic form, was firmly under the control of Rome's aristocracy and showed little sympathy for the plight of the poor. Lacking land, work, or a chance to improve their situation, the once loyal, responsible citizen-soldiers of Rome gradually degenerated into a restless, hungry, purposeless mob. They wandered the streets of Rome and were easily swayed by unscrupulous politicians who fed them in exchange for votes.

The Gracchus brothers attempted reform. Two patrician brothers, Tiberius and Gaius Gracchus, realized the danger of letting the small farmers become a rootless mob. When Tiberius became tribune he tried to limit the amount of land one man could hold, so that all land over that limit could be sold to the small farmers. The senators so violently opposed Tiberius' ideas that they had him murdered and forced his brother to commit suicide. Over three thousand of their followers were put to death. The stubborn refusal of the Senate to heed the plight of the poverty-stricken and unemployed touched off an era of bloodshed and violence which lasted nearly half a century.

Marius and Sulla plunged Rome into civil war. There seemed to be no political solution to the problems of the frustrated masses. It is not surprising that they turned to a military hero for leadership. The Roman general Marius won popularity with the mob by allowing the unemployed to enlist in his army and paying them for their service. He thus created a "professional" army. Up to this time, the Roman army had been open only to landowners, who served out of patriotism and in defense of their land rather than for pay. Since the new soldiers lacked land and political loyalty and depended on Marius for their pensions, they swore personal allegiance to him rather than to Rome. For a time Marius remained loyal to the Republic. But when he came into conflict with the Senate in 87 B.C., he used his army to seize control of the Roman government and killed many distinguished senators.

The Senate had a champion of its own in the Roman general Sulla, but he was busy fighting in Asia Minor at the time of Marius' revolt. When he returned, Sulla found that Marius had already been killed, but he took a bloody revenge on those who had aided Marius. With the full support of the Senate, Sulla invoked an old law which authorized dictatorial rule during an emergency. The law provided, however, that when the crisis had passed, the dictator was supposed to resign. In no case was he to hold office for more than six months. Sulla broke the law by remaining dictator for three years.

CAESAR BECAME MASTER OF ROME

Caesar's victories in Gaul made him a popular hero. For twenty uneasy years after Sulla's retirement, the Senate maintained control of the Roman government. Then, in 60 B.C., three prominent Roman leaders united to form a Triumvirate (try-*um*-vih-ret), or alliance, against the Senate. The triumvirate was composed of Pompey, a successful general; Crassus, a rich would-be politician; and Julius Caesar, an ambitious young patrician who, though related to Marius, had managed to survive the slaughter of Marius' followers. These three agreed to govern Rome by taking turns as consul. Caesar served as consul for one year. Then he had himself appointed military governor of the Roman province of Gaul. He hoped to enhance his popularity by winning a reputation as a great military leader. From 58 B.C. to 50 B.C., Caesar successfully extended Roman authority in Gaul and, in the process, built a strong and loyal army. Because he was a clever politician, Caesar sent back to Rome his vivid *Commentaries on the Gallic Wars*, which made him popular with the Roman masses and prepared the ground for his re-election as consul.

Caesar "crossed the Rubicon." The Senate resented Caesar's success, and Pompey in particular was jealous of him. (In the meantime, Crassus had been killed fighting in Asia.) When Caesar's tour of duty in Gaul ended, the Senate ordered him to disband his legions and return to Rome alone. On a momentous night in 49 B.C., Caesar reached the Rubicon River, the boundary between Gaul and Italy. If he led his troops across the river, he would be breaking a Roman law and defying the Senate. But if he went to Rome alone, he would probably be killed or imprisoned by the senators. For a moment Caesar was undecided. Then, calling out, "The die is cast," he led his legions into the water. The phrase "crossing the Rubicon" has come to mean taking a step from which there is no turning back.

Pompey had boasted that merely by stamping

CAESAR. In ancient Rome, the term *dictator* referred to a man who was appointed to rule in times of emergency. A dictator had sweeping powers, but he was held strictly accountable for his acts, and his term was limited to six months. Caesar, however, abolished all such restrictions and had himself appointed dictator for life.

THE DEATH OF CAESAR. Unwilling to believe that his friend had raised his hand against him, Caesar cried *"Et tu, Brute"* ("Even you, Brutus") and fell dead. He was slain on the Ides of March (March 15), a day which an oracle had warned would be a fateful day for him.

his foot he could create an army to fight Caesar. But when Caesar boldly crossed the Rubicon, Pompey decided that it would be easier to raise an army if he and the Senate withdrew to Greece. Caesar followed Pompey to Greece and defeated his army, forcing Pompey to flee to Egypt, where he was later killed by the Pharaoh. Caesar then crushed revolts in Syria, North Africa, and Spain, and in 45 B.C. returned triumphantly to Rome.

Caesar became dictator for life. Caesar, like Marius and Sulla, was ambitious for personal power, but, unlike them, he sought to use his power to restore order to Rome and to carry out badly needed reforms. The people allowed him to become dictator for life because they preferred the firm rule of one man to "liberty" that seemed to bring only bloodshed and civil war. From 46 B.C. to 44 B.C. Caesar used his power to carry out many of the reforms proposed by the Gracchus brothers. He relieved poverty in Rome by starting public works projects and by sending many landless veterans to the provinces to establish cities and farms there.

To keep the people in the new colonies loyal to Rome, Caesar granted them the privileges of Roman citizenship. He allowed some colonies to establish local self-government. He reformed the system of provincial taxation and appointed honest governors. Caesar enlarged the Senate and made it possible for more plebeians to become members. He also permitted some citizens from the provinces to become Senators. This action weakened the Senate and lessened the influence of the patricians in Rome's government.

One of the most lasting of Caesar's reforms was his revision of the calendar. Except for the few changes made by Pope Gregory in the sixteenth century, Caesar's calendar is the basis of the one used today throughout the Western world. (The month of July is named for Julius Caesar.)

Caesar's ambition led to his downfall. Despite the fact that Caesar had brought stability to Rome and hope to the common people, he had made many enemies. He was opposed by many senators, who resented his weakening of the Senate and who feared that he planned to make himself king. They were jealous of his great power. Caesar's trusted friend Brutus joined in a plot with the senators to assassinate the dictator. On a fateful March day in 44 B.C., as Caesar entered the Senate, the conspirators rushed at him with drawn daggers. When he saw his friend Brutus among them, he offered no resistance and was slain. (The English dramatist William Shakespeare offers a vivid fictional account of these events in his play "Julius Caesar.")

After Caesar's death, rioting and civil war broke out. The conspirators fled from the city to escape an infuriated mob which had gathered to protest the assassination. Caesar's loyal followers then gave him an elaborate funeral and proclaimed him a god. Ironically, the death of Caesar did not end one-man rule in Rome. Instead, it gave rise to a long line of absolute rulers.

THE EMPERORS OF ROME RULED THE ANCIENT WORLD

Augustus became "first citizen" of the Roman Empire. Under the terms of his will, Caesar designated his eighteen-year-old adopted son Octavian as his successor. But Mark Antony, a popular general and close friend of Caesar, also aspired to the job. Together they seized control of Rome and executed thousands of Caesar's enemies. They shared the Empire, Octavian ruling the western provinces and Antony ruling the east. Antony hoped to create an independent eastern empire which he would rule jointly with the Egyptian queen Cleopatra. On the other hand, Octavian was ambitious to unite the empire under his own rule. As a result war broke out between them and culminated in a great naval victory for Octavian at Actium in 31 B.C. After Antony was defeated at Alexandria, he and Cleopatra committed suicide to avoid the disgrace of being paraded into Rome as Octavian's captives.

After Antony's defeat, Octavian became absolute ruler of the Roman Empire. But he knew that the Roman people would accept his rule peacefully only if he concealed his power under the traditional republican form of government. Accordingly, he made no attempt to have himself crowned king. However, he quietly arranged to have the Senate appoint him to the chief government offices for life. Finally the Senate bestowed upon him the title *Augustus*, which means "honored" or "consecrated" although he personally preferred to be known as *First Citizen*. Throughout his reign (31 B.C. to 14 A.D.) Octavian, or Augustus as he became known, made a great show of increasing the prestige of the Senate. Actually he controlled Rome as completely as he could have if he had been emperor. For this reason, he is often referred to as the first Roman emperor.

Augustus brought peace, justice, and unity to the Roman world. Although his nearly half-century of rule marked the end of the Roman Republic, Augustus established the Roman Peace, a period of order and unity which the Mediterranean world had never known before.

He wisely put a stop to the expansion of Rome, contenting himself with rounding out the

---

At A Glance

Important Events in Roman History to the Empire

Early Italy
- Founding of Rome (753 B.C.)
  - Romulus and Remus
- Height of Etruscan civilization (6th century B.C.)

The Roman Republic (*c.* 500–31 B.C.)
- Rome gains control of the Italian peninsula (*c.* 265 B.C.)
- Punic Wars
  - *First Punic War* (264–241 B.C.)
    - Hamilcar
  - *Second Punic War* (218–201 B.C.)
    - Hannibal
    - Scipio
  - *Third Punic War* (149–146 B.C.)
    - Cato
- Gracchus reforms (133–123 B.C.)
- Civil war between Marius and Sulla (87–82 B.C.)
- Triumvirate of Caesar, Pompey and Crassus (60 B.C.)
- Dictatorship of Julius Caesar (49–44 B.C.)

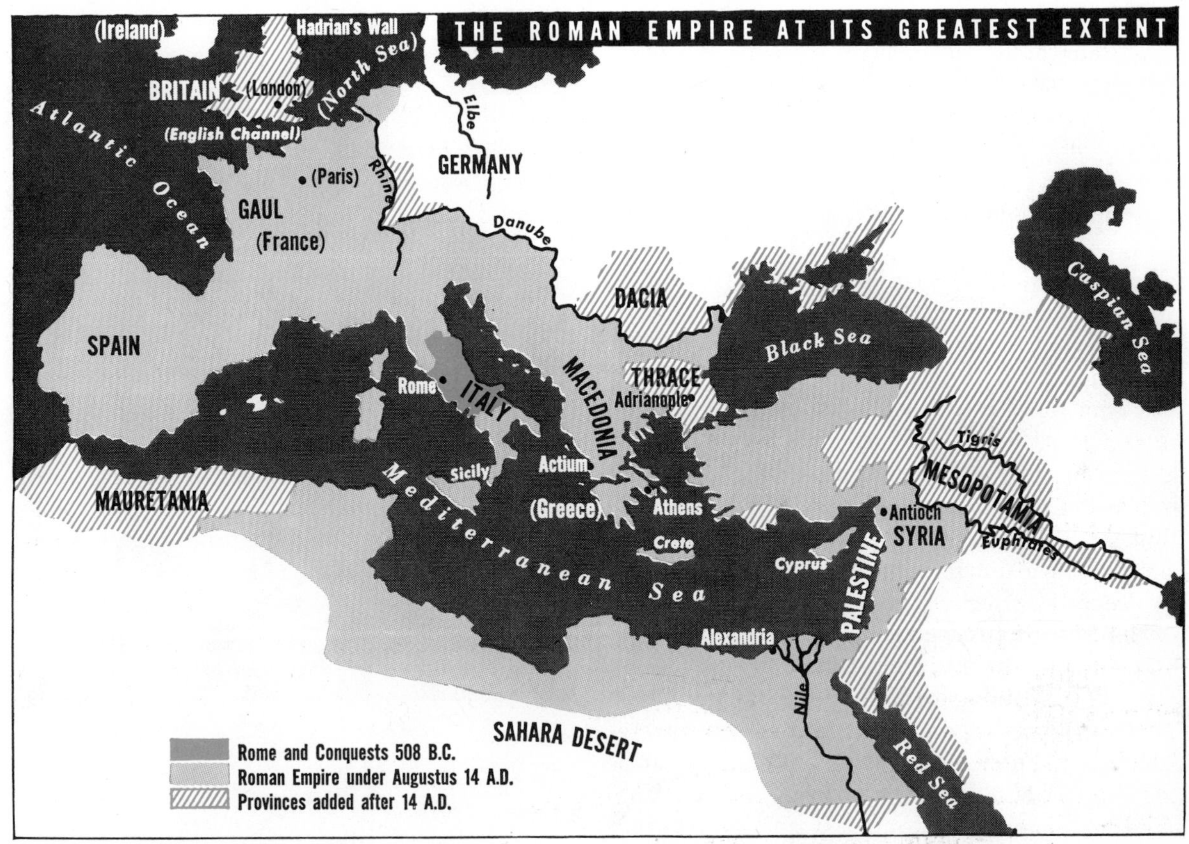

Empire until it reached defensible boundaries: the English Channel, the Rhine, and the Danube in Europe; the Euphrates in Asia; and the Sahara Desert in Africa. To protect the frontiers, he utilized not only legions composed of Roman citizens, but also auxiliary forces composed of men from the provinces. He especially fortified the frontiers on the Rhine and the Danube, where the pressure from barbarian tribes was greatest. He built roads over which Roman legions could quickly march wherever trouble arose. These measures protected the Empire from attack and encouraged the development of trade.

Augustus also made important reforms in the government. He established an imperial civil service composed of government officials, chosen largely from the middle class, who were paid a salary by the state. In their duties they were far more loyal and honest than the unsalaried aristocrats who had held power under the Republic. Augustus appointed civil servants to represent him in the outlying provinces and gave them long terms of office during which they could gain experience. Although senators continued to act as governors of the inner provinces, they were paid salaries and were carefully supervised by Augustus in order to reduce their temptation to overtax the people for personal gain.

Augustus' reign is sometimes called the "Golden Age of Rome" because of the prosperity and artistic achievement that characterized the period. When Augustus died, there was great sorrow in Rome. Temples were built in his honor, and he was worshiped along with the Roman gods. Before his death, Augustus designated his successor in order to avoid civil war such as followed the reign of Julius Caesar. Many of the rulers who followed Augustus also adopted this wise policy.

Beginning with Augustus' successor, Tiberius, all of the Roman rulers openly took the title

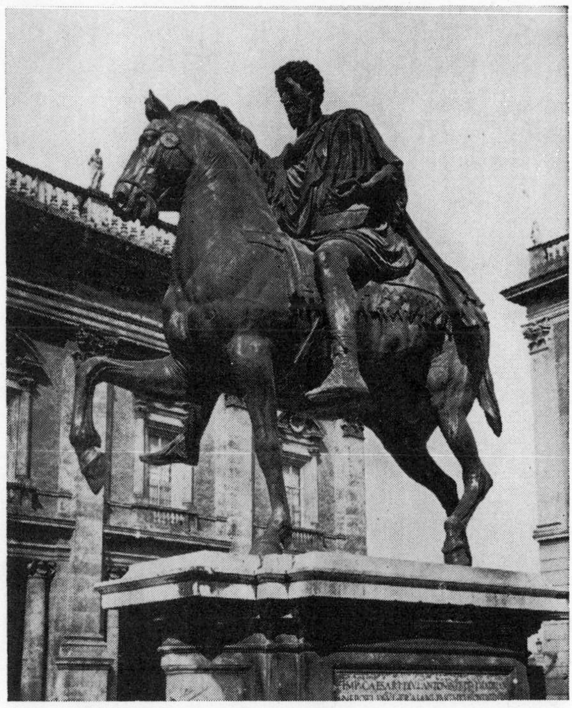

Marcus Aurelius. This splendid equestrian statue of the philosopher-king is the only one that has come down to us from the ancient world. It is known to be similar to one of the Emperor Trajan that has been lost.

of Emperor, and made no attempt to disguise their power. The fact that the Roman people tolerated this action is an indication of their approval of Augustus' methods. They felt that the best way to maintain peace and harmony within the Empire was through the absolute rule of a wise emperor. Unfortunately, not all of Augustus' successors ruled wisely or justly. Some were ruthless tyrants like Nero who emptied the treasury by staging games and gladitorial shows for the Romans. For the most part, however, the Roman empire was maintained in good order for nearly two centuries after Augustus' death.

The Empire prospered under the Five Good Emperors. The five emperors who ruled between 96 A.D. and 186 A.D. were so able and conscientious that they are known as the Five Good Emperors. Three of the five, Trajan, Hadrian, and Marcus Aurelius (aw-*reel*-yus), were outstanding. Trajan was descended from an Italian family which had moved to Spain. His election shows that even the highest government offices were eventually open to everyone in the Empire, not just to residents of Rome. Trajan was the last emperor to be a great conqueror. His victories north of the Danube made the Empire larger than it had ever been before or would be again.

Trajan's successor, Hadrian, spent much of his time visiting Roman officials in the provinces to insure their efficiency and honesty. His magnificent villa, or country house, near Rome was filled with souvenirs of his travels.

Marcus Aurelius, the last of the Five Good Emperors, regarded himself as the servant of the Roman people. Believing that war was evil, he would have much preferred to spend his life studying philosophy. But no matter how tired or sick he felt, he was constantly on the battlefield protecting Rome from invasion. A famous collection of his writings, called *Meditations,* reveals Marcus Aurelius as a man of great personal courage and selfless devotion to Rome. But as we shall see in Chapter 17, even Marcus Aurelius was unable to cope with the many serious faults that were beginning to undermine the Empire.

Chapter Check-up

1. What caused the unrest, class hatred and strife in Rome after the Punic Wars?
2. How did the Gracchus brothers try to improve the lot of small farmers?
3. What conditions brought about the end of the Roman Republic?
4. How did Caesar assure himself of continuous power in office? What were some of the reforms carried out by Caesar from 46–44 B.C.?
5. Why did the Romans accept a dictator?
6. How and why was Caesar finally removed from power?
7. Why did Augustus and the Roman Senate declare war on Antony and Cleopatra?
8. For what reasons is Augustus considered to have been one of Rome's great leaders?
9. How was the Roman Peace maintained?

CHAPTER 16

Roman Civilization Reflected the Fortunes of the Roman State

ROMAN CULTURE WAS BASED ON GREEK LEARNING AND PRACTICAL NECESSITY

The serious-minded Romans of the early Republic were more interested in the practical pursuits of farming, politics, and war, than in art, literature, and philosophy. During the Empire, when many well-educated and wealthy Romans became lavish patrons of the arts, they were likely to order statues or paintings in the Greek or Hellenistic tradition. But even though Roman artists often imitated Greek models, they put their own stamp on many of their works. Roman architects, especially, showed great originality and engineering skill in erecting aqueducts and other useful structures and monumental public buildings of great beauty. Roman artists created fine mosaics, and were skillful in their use of metals. Portrait sculpture reflected the typical Roman love of the real and the natural rather than the ideal.

Rome preserved Greek art and learning. To the credit of Rome, she seldom destroyed the civilizations of the peoples she conquered. Indeed, she often copied the best that she found in them, particularly in the case of Greek civilization, which the Romans came to admire and appreciate. As they conquered Greece and the Greek colonies, Roman generals carried off statues and columns to decorate their villas in Italy. It became so fashionable for a wealthy man to have Greek statuary in his garden that

THE PANTHEON. Originally erected in 27 B.C. and rebuilt by the Emperor Hadrian a century later, this great temple to the Roman gods is now a church and the resting place of Italian royalty. Note the obelisk of Ramses II, which was brought to Rome in antiquity from Heliopolis in Egypt.

soon many Roman workshops were manufacturing imitations of Greek art.

Wealthy Roman families imported Greek slaves to educate their children or sent their sons to school in Athens or Alexandria. Greek comedies were translated into Latin so that even the common people could enjoy them in the theaters. In the hospitals, which they built to serve their armies, the Romans put the medical discoveries of the Greeks to practical use. To a large extent, Rome preserved Greek culture for the modern world.

The Romans were skilled engineers. At first the Romans limited their creative energies to such necessary tasks as the building of bridges, roads, and aqueducts. A number of these projects were so soundly constructed that they are still in use. Later the Romans became interested in the arts. Caesar sought to make Rome equal in beauty and splendor to Athens or Alexandria, and his plans were largely carried out by the later emperors. The Romans designed their temples and halls from Greek models, but they devised a way to make them much larger. Athens had a small population, but Rome, whose population grew to over a million, needed large public buildings. Roman architects gained the necessary space by building high, vaulted ceilings which would support a roof that could cover a large area. The Pantheon (*pan*-thee-ahn), Hadrian's temple to the gods, has a dome that spans a chamber 142 feet across.

The Romans invented a kind of concrete which they employed in constructing their public buildings. Famous examples of its use are the Baths of Diocletian (dy-oh-*klee*-sh'n), which could accommodate three thousand patrons, and the Colosseum, an open-air arena that seated fifty thousand spectators. Roman concrete was usually covered with thin slabs of marble or travertine stone for decoration. Almost every emperor built a magnificent bath, temple, or theater to glorify Rome and enhance his own reputation. Ruins of many of these great projects can still be seen.

Roman literature was practical. Roman authors usually relied on Greek works both for style and information, but they adapted them to practical purposes. Cicero, one of Rome's greatest orators, delivered a number of political speeches in the Senate which are still famous. They are models of the best form of Latin composition and are read in high school and college Latin classes today. He also wrote letters which give us a glimpse of the daily life of the upper-class Romans of his day.

Julius Caesar, as you know, wrote a lively description of his military campaigns as propaganda to win popular support. Two other historians deserve recognition among Roman writers. One of these was Livy, who wrote a history of early Rome, most of which has been lost. The other was Tacitus (*tas*-ih-tus), who gives us a picture of conditions in Rome during the days of the first five emperors, and the only account that has been preserved of the customs of early German tribes, whose simple virtues he contrasted with Rome's moral decay.

Vergil, Horace, and Ovid were three of Rome's greatest poets. In his *Aeneid* (eh-*nee*-id), Vergil relates the myth of Aeneas' voyage from Troy to Italy. The *Aeneid*, which is in verse, tells the mythical story of Rome's founding by the descendants of Aeneas with the help of the gods. Vergil says that the gods intended Rome to have a magnificent destiny. His poetry is still read by Latin students. Horace is noted for his *odes* (poems intended to be sung), which have been imitated in many languages for centuries. Some of his most beautiful lyrics dealt with love, friendship, and civic virtue. Ovid, whose poetry was influenced by Greek poetry and Greek myths, has in turn influenced such English writers as Spenser, Shakespeare, and Milton. His long narrative poem, the *Metamorphoses* (met-uh-*mor*-foeseez), recounts legends about miraculous transformations of shape; he tells, for example, of how Julius Caesar turned into a star after his death. Other poetry of Ovid gives a picture of the Roman world of wealth and fashion.

Thus Roman authors not only helped to preserve and arouse interest in Greek literature but also added their contribution to the literary heritage of Western civilization. Their works are still studied by scholars and read for pleasure.

ROMAN WALL RELIEF. This well-preserved wall relief is one of the most famous pieces of sculpture that has been found in Rome. Called the Altar of Piety, it is thought to depict the poets Livy, Vergil and Horace as they watch a procession.

Latin became the language of the Western world. In the five hundred years that Rome ruled the Western world, her language was spread over all parts of the Empire. To protect their rights in the courts or to trade with the Roman merchants, people outside Rome found it desirable to know Latin. Thus the Latin language, as well as the Roman army, helped to bind Rome and her provinces into one great state. In the story of the Middle Ages, you will see how Latin became the language of the scholar, the courts, and the Church.

After the fall of Rome, many provinces again became separate nations and developed their own languages, but all of them were influenced by Latin. Some of the languages, including modern Italian, French, Romanian, Spanish, and Portuguese, are directly based upon Latin and are therefore known as *Romance* languages. (That is, they are derived from the language of the Romans.) Although English is not as closely related to Latin as the Romance languages are, almost half of its vocabulary is borrowed from Latin.

For centuries, the Romance languages were neither widely known nor precise enough for literary or scientific writing. During the Middle Ages, and long afterward, churchmen, lawyers, and scholars who wished to express complicated ideas and who wanted to be understood all over Europe continued to use Latin, the traditional literary language.

Rome gave the Western world its laws. The development of her law code best illustrates Rome's practical genius and was her greatest and most lasting contribution to the Western world. Other peoples had created vast empires, but no people were more skillful than the Romans in uniting men of widely different backgrounds.

In large measure, the successful management of the Empire was based on Rome's excellent system of law. The Twelve Tablets established a foundation for the laws, but Roman judges were permitted to interpret the old laws to meet changing conditions. As the Empire grew, foreigners trading with Roman citizens refused to recognize the traditional Roman laws that governed transactions between one citizen and another. Gradually the judges developed new laws so that both foreigner and Roman would receive just treatment. From these laws arose the *jus gen-*

JUSTINIAN. This mosaic portrait is in the Italian city of Ravenna, a western capital of the Byzantine Roman Empire.

tium, the law of nations, which provided a beginning for international law.

In addition to the Twelve Tablets and the decisions of the judges, Roman law included decrees issued by the Senate and the emperor and the laws passed by the popular assemblies. Eventually the laws became so complex that no judge could know them all. In 530 A.D., Justinian, one of the last great emperors, ordered all the laws of Rome collected and organized into a code. Justinian's Code forms the basis of the laws of most European countries today.

More important than the Code itself are the principles behind Roman law. These principles, along with English Common Law, have strongly influenced the laws of the United States. For example, the Romans believed that 1) all free men have equal rights before the law; 2) a man is presumed innocent until he is clearly proven guilty; 3) before a case is decided, the circumstances and the motive of the man must be considered; 4) there is a divinely established, eternal, unchanging law, called *natural law*, which applies to every man, regardless of his city or class. Natural law gives man what the Declaration of Independence calls "certain unalienable rights" which no man or government can take away. The Greeks, you will recall, had earlier expressed a belief in one universal law of reason for all men, but it was the Romans who gave widespread application to this idea by embodying it in a formal written code.

THE EXPANSION OF THE ROMAN EMPIRE SHAPED THE LIFE AND IDEALS OF ITS PEOPLE

Early Romans led simple lives and served their country loyally. During the early period of the Republic, all Romans, even the patricians, were loyal, hard-working farmers who led simple lives. A patrician served the Republic by taking an active part in the government, rising from one office to another until he reached the Senate. The plebeian also took a lively interest in politics, although his vote carried much less weight than a patrician's. When war came, every citizen stood ready to sacrifice himself and his possessions for the defense of his fields and his city. The plebeians served as common soldiers, the patricians as officers. Such was the patriotic zeal of the early Roman that a story is told of a patrician who killed his own son when the boy disobeyed him on the field of battle.

In many ways, the devotion of the early Romans resembled that of the Greeks. But there was one important difference in attitude. A Greek believed that service to the state was a necessary and natural part of his personal development as a "whole man." The Roman regarded such service as a necessary duty. His government did not encourage him to develop a love of beauty, or athletics, or drama, or a philosophy of life. As a result, the Roman attitude toward civic matters was limited and narrow compared to the Greek attitude. Nevertheless, the Roman citizen's intense patriotism and conscientiousness provided the foundation for Rome's greatness.

The family was the basis of early Roman life. From the earliest times, the family was one of the most important and sacred of Roman institutions. The father, who was undisputed head of the family, had complete authority over the lives and property of his children until his own death. He taught his sons the practical lessons of farming and war and demanded absolute obedience from them.

A Roman. This bust of an unknown Roman of the first century B.C. shows the disciplined, uncompromising character of the men who built the Roman Republic.

The Roman wife was highly honored and respected. Unlike the Athenian woman, she could dine with her husband and go out to the public market. Although women did not have the right to vote, Cato complained that they were openly campaigning and influencing elections during the late Republic. Most Roman women, however, spent their time spinning, weaving, and doing household chores. There were few slaves in early Rome and every member of the family had to work hard.

The Romans borrowed many of their religious ideas from the Greeks. In the days of the early Republic, Roman religion reflected the citizens' interest in farming. The Romans worshiped *lares* (*lay*-reez), minor gods who protected the fields, and *penates* (peh-*nay*-teez), gods who watched over the pantry. The most honored goddess was Vesta, protectress of the hearth. Her symbol was the glowing fire, which was allowed to go out only at the New Year and was then ceremoniously rekindled by the head of the house. Each day the entire household gathered at the hearth to worship while the father made offerings of wine and oil.

After the Romans came into contact with the Greeks, they adopted much of Greek religion. Zeus and Hera, the Greek king and queen of the gods, were renamed *Jupiter* and *Juno*. Athena became the Roman goddess *Minerva*, patroness of art and wisdom, and *Venus* replaced Aphrodite as goddess of love and beauty. Ares, the Greek god of war, was renamed *Mars*, and Poseidon, lord of the sea, became *Neptune*. The Romans adopted the Greek belief that the gods were to be bargained with rather than loved and revered. They believed that if a man made the proper offering to a god at the right time and place, the god would then listen sympathetically to his requests for divine favor.

Conquest brought luxury and splendor to the Romans, but destroyed their self-reliance. As we have seen, the wars in the East brought great wealth and many slaves into Rome, so that people of property did not have to work hard for a living. When life became a continual round of pleasure and there was little work to balance the

GREEK AND ROMAN ARCHITECTURE

Roman architecture borrowed, of course, from the Greek forms, but improved and expanded upon them. The true arch, though known by the Greeks was seldom used, but the Romans used it to great advantage in temples, aqueducts, bridges and great public buildings. The post and lintel form was basic to both cultures, but the Romans covered vast spaces with arches and domes which the Greeks did not utilize. Basically Greek architecture was simple and beautifully proportioned; Roman architecture used the same ideal, but was grander, greater in scope. As Edgar Allan Poe eulogized, it was: "The glory that was Greece, the grandeur that was Rome."

Shown here is the Greek *Temple of Ceres* in Paestum, Italy. This temple built about 510 B.C. displays the post and lintel (vertical and horizontal) technique as well as the symmetry of the Greek ideal.

The grandeur of the Romans was displayed on a superb scale when the *Coliseum* was built between 70 A.D. and 82 A.D. This showplace for gladiators and Christian martyrs is truly one of the wonders of Roman life. Only the great stadiums in the United States rival it in size, but never in splendor. It combined all the Greek beauty with the unique Roman engineering ingenuity. Even today in ruins it is a magnificent tribute to Roman art.

Roman architecture must be judged not only by its grandeur but by its utility. Nothing is more exemplary of utility than this Roman interior of a senator's house in *Herculaneum*, south of Naples. The atrium, or court, was the guests' ante-room and relaxation chamber and the pool area was for use and beauty. Romans knew how to relax and enjoy the good life.

play, the well-to-do Romans tended to become soft and dissipated.

It should be noted that these conditions were true not only in the city of Rome itself, but in many parts of the Roman Empire. Wherever large groups of people lived in communities, the middle and wealthy class lived in luxury and indolence. One reason dictators and emperors came to power is that Roman citizens became politically as well as physically lazy. They gradually allowed slaves to do all the work, and the emperors and their officials did all the governing. The poor man and the patrician alike lost interest in serving the state. Loyalty faded, and love of comfort and pleasure took the place of a serious interest in affairs of government.

The Romans built elaborate cities and luxurious houses. Wherever they went, the Romans built cities that became centers of government and culture. They usually laid out the cities according to a uniform plan. Two main streets, lined with shops and houses, intersected at right angles to make a forum in the center of the city. A narrow porch with a roof supported by columns, called a colonnade, surrounded the forum. Near the forum could be found the temples, assembly halls, public baths, and theaters for which Roman towns were famous. Even small towns in distant Britain had public baths and theaters.

The remains of Pompeii (pahm-*pay*) and Herculaneum (her-kyu-*lay*-nee-um), located on the Bay of Naples at the foot of Mount Vesuvius (veh-*soo*-vee-us), present a unique insight into Roman cities. An eruption of Vesuvius in 79 A.D. covered the cities with lava and fine ashes. The lower stories of the houses, containing many objects of interest to archaeologists, were preserved perfectly.

The houses that have been reconstructed on the site of Pompeii reflect the Roman taste for luxury and comfort. Bronze statues, Greek sculpture, inlaid couches and tables, and rich tapestries adorned the rooms. The walls were often painted with landscapes to make the rooms seem larger. Roman builders did not overlook practical details. Lead pipes carried running water into the kitchen and hot air under the floors to warm the rooms in winter.

POMPEII. We can walk along this ancient street today and see houses and shops that are amazingly preserved. Pompeii was completely buried in the eruption of Vesuvius in 79 A.D. and was forgotten until it was rediscovered in 1748.

Roman Temple. Built in the first century A.D. at Nimes, France, this Roman temple called in French the Maison Carrée ("square house") is the best-preserved in existence. While Thomas Jefferson was U. S. minister to France, he saw this temple and based his plan for the new Virginia state capitol on it.

The wealthy citizen enjoyed a life of comfort and amusement. The patricians obtained their wealth from inherited estates, government salaries, or gifts from the emperor; they were forbidden by law to engage in trade and industry. When Augustus stripped the Senate of its powers, he destroyed the chief occupation open to the patricians—politics. Those who did not choose to follow the other possible career, service in the army, were left with plenty of free time, which they filled with an unending round of banquets, games, or idle amusements. The well-to-do members of the middle class did their best to copy the patrician way of life.

The typical wealthy Roman rose as early as five o'clock to take advantage of the cool morning hours. After a light breakfast, he wrote letters and reviewed the affairs of his estate. Then he entered a large reception room where his *clients* gathered. Clients were poor relations and men of low rank who attached themselves to a wealthy citizen and earned their keep by flattering him, running his errands, and applauding his public speeches. The more clients a man had, the more important he appeared to be.

Later he strolled to the Forum, where he discussed the latest news or attended a session of the Senate or the law courts. At noon he lunched at home and then slept until sundown. When he awakened he might visit one of the public baths, walk in the adjoining gardens, or go to the gymnasium. Many of his evenings were spent at magnificent banquets in the homes of his friends, where he feasted on such delicacies as roast peacock or pomegranates brought from distant parts of the Empire.

Roman education was practical. The prosperous families bought Greek slaves to tutor their sons or sent them to private schools. Other boys attended a kind of public elementary school supported by the government. For a small fee, they were taught music, geography, history, mathematics, and passages from Greek and Roman literature. When a boy was twelve, if he did not have to help support his family, he could enter an advanced government school to learn rhetoric in preparation for a career in politics. Because the emperors allowed no criticism of themselves or their actions, a clever politician concentrated on how well he spoke, rather than on what he said.

THE GAMES. Having defeated his opponent, a gladiator turns to the crowd, which indicates by "thumbs down" that the victim must die. Before the games began, the gladiators stood before the emperor and gave him their famous traditional greeting: "We who are about to die salute you."

Girls were never sent to school. By the time she was fifteen, a girl was usually married to a man chosen by her father.

The poor were kept docile by free bread and circuses. The great mass of Rome's inhabitants were crowded into squalid, dark tenements which usually faced narrow, dirty streets. As slavery became widespread, free men were unable to find employment. As a result, it became necessary for the government to feed nearly two-thirds of the population of Rome. To keep the jobless citizens in a good humor, politicians offered them free entertainment at the Colosseum. Thus Rome's masses lost their self-reliance and became content with "bread and circuses."

The favorite amusements of the mob were thrilling chariot races and brutal hand-to-hand combat between captives. At first they fought with their fists bound with leather strips to serve as boxing gloves. Later, slaves were trained in special schools to fight with swords. The Latin word for sword is *gladius*, and the men became known as gladiators. The crowd, by pointing their thumbs up or down, told the victor whether he should spare his victim or kill him. Not satisfied with combats between gladiators, the Romans arranged fights between wild animals or between men and ferocious beasts. In later times the persecuted Christians were often sent unprotected into the arena to fight hunger-maddened beasts. In this manner the citizens celebrated a "Roman holiday." Today people use the phrase "Roman holiday" when referring to an entertainment that causes misfortune for those providing it.

Chapter Check-up

1. In what ways did the Romans help preserve Greek culture?
2. What were some of the engineering achievements of the Romans?
3. Why are the writings of Livy important to historians?
4. Who were the three great poets of Rome?
5. How did Latin become the basis for so many languages, and what are such languages called?
6. What was Rome's greatest and most lasting contribution to mankind?
7. What are the principles behind Justinian's Code, and why is the Code an important step in the history of man?
8. How did the Roman attitude toward public service compare with the Greek?
9. What aspects of their religion did the Romans borrow from the Greeks?
10. In what ways did the Roman conquests affect the lives of individual Romans?

CHAPTER 17

Internal Weakness and Barbarian Invasion Destroyed the Roman Empire in the West

THE INTERNAL PROBLEMS OF THE ROMAN EMPIRE WERE DEEPLY ROOTED

Just as the mighty empires of Egypt, Persia, and Macedonia had eventually crumbled away, Rome also began to decline. In the days when rapid communication was very difficult, all but the ablest rulers found a large empire almost impossible to control. Historians can see at least two reasons for the decline of these ancient empires. Each empire was attacked by outside forces at a time when it was already troubled by weaknesses within. A close scrutiny of the Roman Empire reveals that very serious internal problems were gnawing at its foundations long before the onslaught of the barbarian tribes.

The selection of emperors led to civil war. One of Rome's most serious political problems was that of choosing an emperor. The Romans had never passed a law of succession allowing the emperor's son to inherit his father's office. For this reason the choice of a new emperor was always open to dispute among the old emperor, the Senate, the Praetorian Guard (the emperor's private army), and the army. Gradually the Guard gained complete authority to choose the new emperor. In turn, the emperor handsomely rewarded the Guard for its support.

In the early days of the Empire, the system worked fairly well because the army usually agreed with the Guard's choice. But when Marcus Aurelius died in 186 A.D., the army legions stationed in the provinces revolted against the new emperor. The civil war that followed kept the Empire in turmoil for fifty years. Legions from the Danube, Africa, and Spain fought one another to install the emperor of their choice. In a fifty-year span, Rome had twenty-six different emperors; twenty-five of them were removed from office by assassination.

The power to make all the important decisions concerning Rome's affairs was centered in the emperors. Thus it was important that they be independent and capable men. But in the century following the death of Aurelius, they were little more than puppets of the army.

Diocletian and Constantine tried to save the Empire. In 284 A.D., Diocletian became Emperor of Rome. In order to restore stability in the Empire, he issued a decree providing for the

At A Glance

Important Men and Events of the Roman Empire

Period of the Empire (31 B.C.–476 A.D.)
- Augustus
- Nero
- Trajan
- Hadrian
- Marcus Aurelius
- Civil Wars (192–284)
- Diocletian
- Constantine

The barbarian invasions (3rd–6th century)
- Visigoths
  - Alaric
- Huns
  - Attila
- Vandals
- Fall of Rome (476)
  - Odoacer
  - Theodoric

Empire in the East (395–1453)
- Justinian

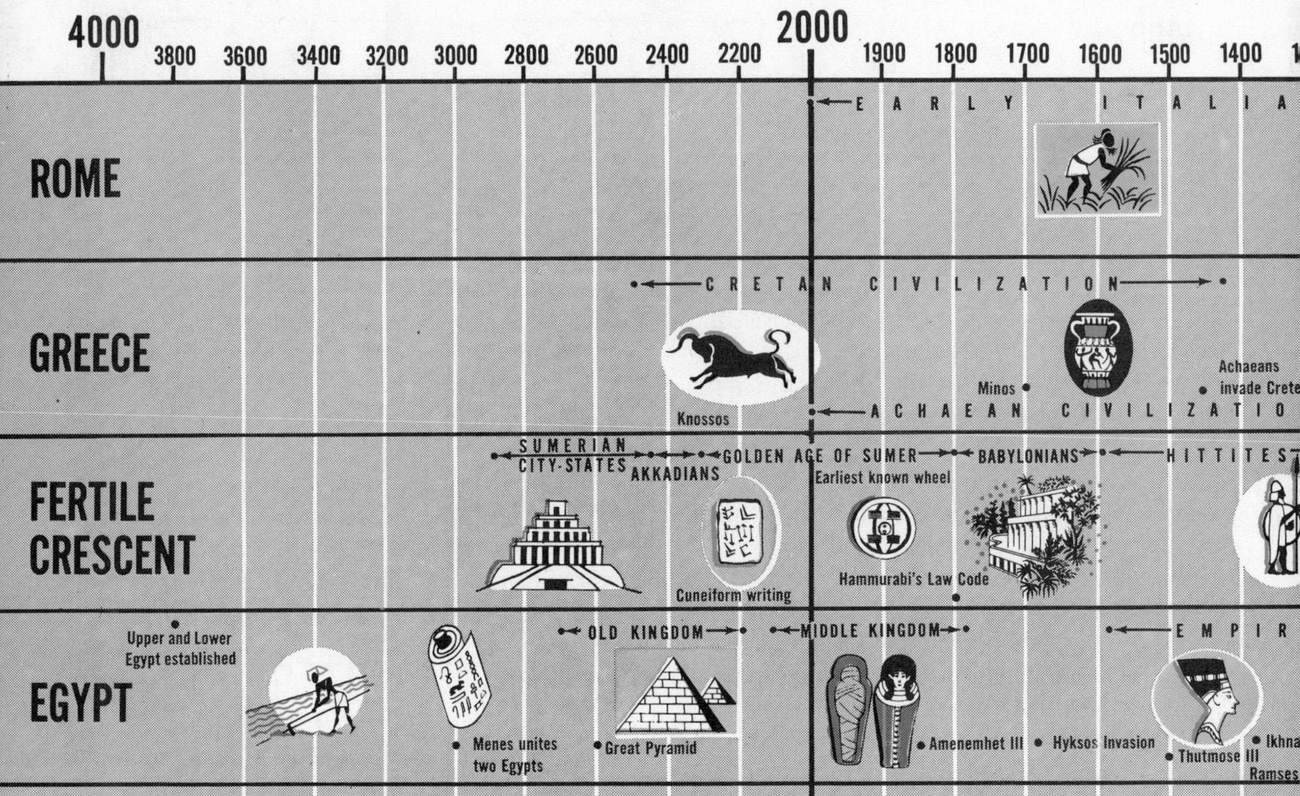

choice of his successor, and then had himself proclaimed a god. Like Alexander, he copied the ceremonies of the absolute rulers of Persia. Diocletian hoped that his crown, his magnificent purple robe, and the sight of his courtiers on hands and knees would so impress the soldiers that they would not dare to revolt.

Unfortunately, when Diocletian retired to private life, civil war broke out again. The struggle that followed was won by Constantine. When he became emperor, he moved the capital from Rome to Byzantium (bih-*zan*-shee-um), a Greek city on the European side of the Dardanelles. He extensively rebuilt the old city on the model of Rome and renamed it Constantinople—"the city of Constantine." Rome, the Eternal City, was no longer the heart of the Roman Empire. Constantine had purposely placed his new capital close to the eastern frontier in order to protect the rich cities of the East from Persian invasions. Moving the capital from the center of the Empire made it more difficult to rule the outlying western provinces. As a result, Constantine's successors found it necessary to appoint co-rulers to manage the armies in the western part. This ultimately led to the permanent division of the Empire.

The decline of the cities in the West brought economic collapse to Rome. Rome had serious economic as well as political weaknesses. One of these was the Empire's dependence on its major cities for tax revenues. When these cities were allowed to decay, the Empire itself was endangered.

Such eastern cities as Antioch and Alexandria were wealthy and strong because for centuries they had been centers of manufacturing and trade. While the new cities that Rome established in the West appeared to be prosperous, their wealth was based on the tribute exacted from conquered lands. Once expansion of the Empire stopped,

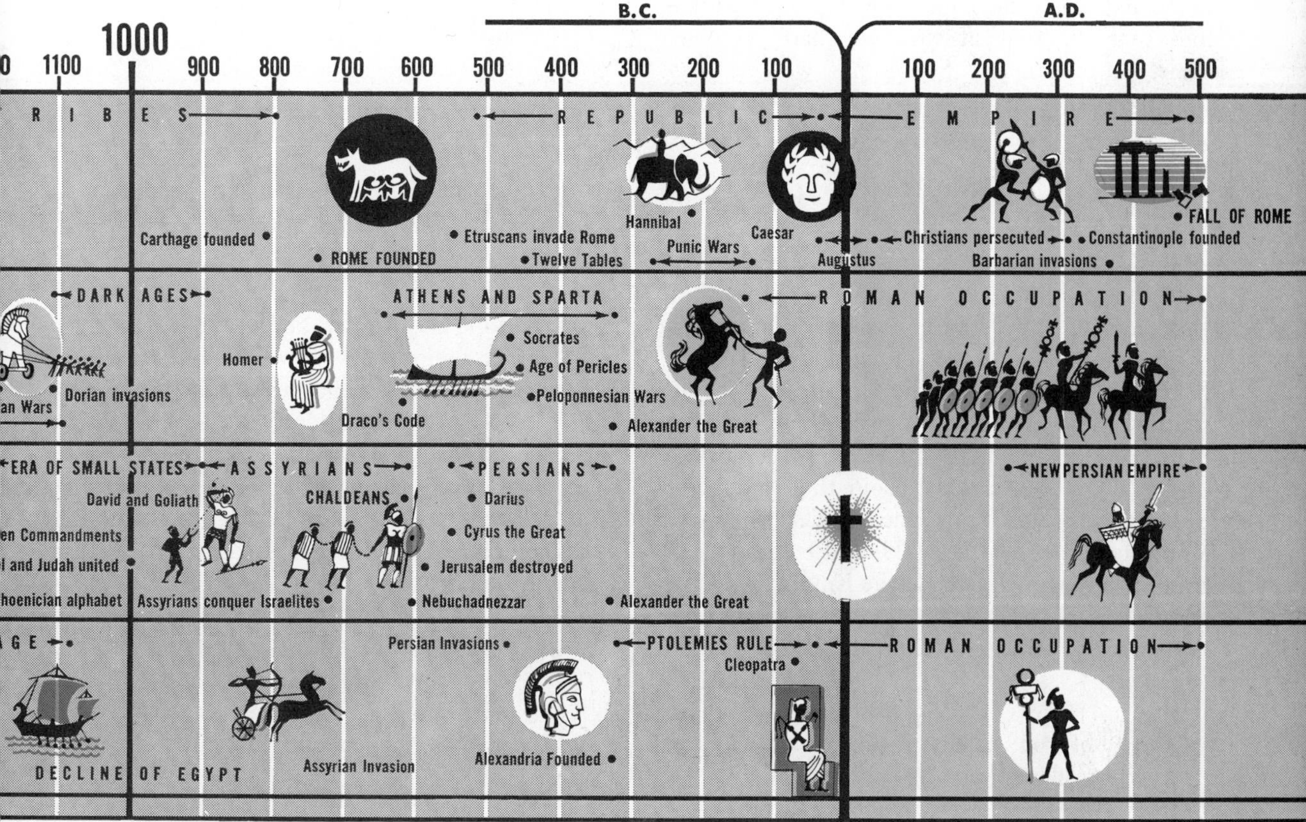

the cities could no longer rely on plunder from abroad. Their problem was intensified by the fact that the patricians considered themselves too dignified to engage in manufacturing and trade.

The patricians' decision to live in country villas completed the ruin of the western cities. The civil wars among the legions in the third century A.D. made the western cities so unsafe that the patricians withdrew to their villas in the country. Each of these isolated, self-sufficient estates could supply its needs without buying goods from the cities. As a result, the few craftsmen who had worked in the cities lost their jobs and became tenants on the villas or joined the city mobs. The western cities were doomed and with them the western part of the Empire.

High taxes further weakened the Empire. Although their income was dwindling, there was no reduction of taxes for the Romans. Maintaining the army and the luxury of the court continued to drain the treasury. As the disillusioned populace lost its zeal to defend the Empire, the government found it necessary to rely increasingly on mercenary soldiers recruited from the unemployed city mobs or the conquered peoples. Such an army proved not only unreliable, but very expensive. Thus the emperors were forced to raise the already burdensome tax even higher. Tax collection became increasingly difficult.

The population of the Roman Empire shrank. The economic depression that struck Rome in the fourth century A.D. was so serious that it brought about a marked decline in population. Romans had fewer children because they could not afford to raise large families. Disease and war further reduced the population. Soon there were not enough people to work in the fields or to manufacture needed goods. Desperate measures were taken by the emperors to combat the labor shortage. Diocletian decreed that workers could not leave the land on which they worked and that the sons of workmen had to follow their father's trade. Sometimes workers were branded to make sure they could never change occupations. Such harsh measures were no cure for the serious problems that beset the Roman government. They served only to create greater discontent and thus further weakened the Empire.

INVASIONS OF BARBARIAN TRIBES HASTENED THE DECLINE OF THE EMPIRE

In the cold forests of Germany to the north of Italy lived many barbarian tribes. During the first century A.D., the attraction of the cultivated fields and rich cities of the Empire drew them southward. For years, the well-disciplined Roman army held the barbarians in check. Many of them were persuaded to join the legions and eventually became Romanized settlers on vacant lands near the frontier. The vast majority of tribesmen remained outside the Empire, however, and continued to threaten its security. When the soldiers were withdrawn from the Rhine-Danube frontier in the third century A.D. to fight in civil wars in Italy, the Roman border was open to attack. Germanic tribes swept deep into Gaul, where they plundered and destroyed the country.

The Visigoths humiliated the Roman army at Adrianople. Like earlier emperors, Diocletian and Constantine struggled against the barbarian tide. After Constantine's death, the situation worsened. A fierce tribe from central Asia, the Huns, swept down on the Germanic tribes from the rear, driving them southward. One of these tribes, the Visigoths (West Goths), begged the

ATTILA. Leaving behind death and destruction as he swept over Europe, the "Scourge of God" finally met defeat when he encountered Theodoric at Chalons. After their leader's death, the Huns vanished from history.

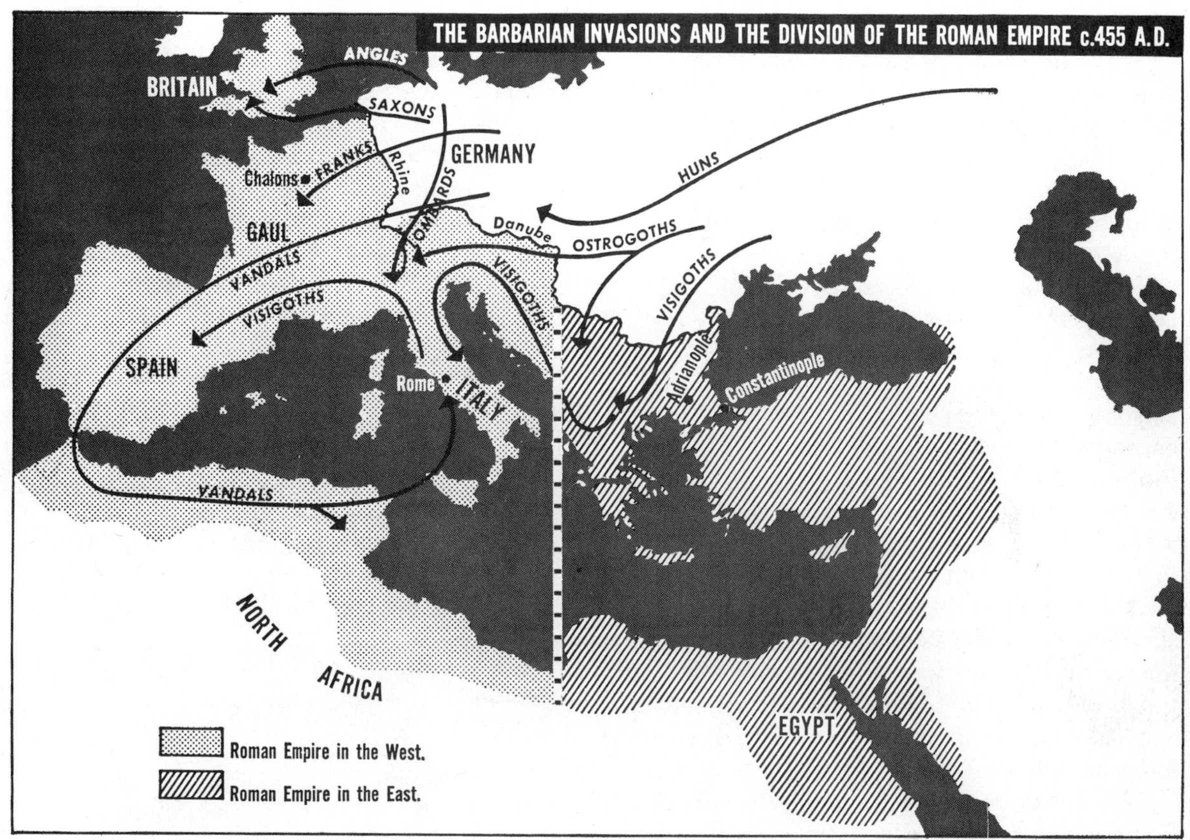

emperor to let them into Roman territory where they would be safe. When the emperor granted their request, they poured across the Danube. Unfortunately, the Roman officials who were sent to supervise their entry took advantage of them by selling them rotten food and seizing some of their children as slaves. Outraged, the Visigoths took up arms. At Adrianople (ay-dree-an-*oh*-pul) in 378 A.D., they defeated a Roman army and slew the emperor. In 395 A.D. the Empire was permanently divided into two parts, East and West. Gradually, these barbarian tribes turned westward and eventually overran the entire western part of the Empire.

Barbarians sacked Rome, and the Western Empire disintegrated. Adrianople revealed the military weakness of the West. Alaric (*al*-uh-rik), leader of the Visigoths, marched into Italy and even sacked the city of Rome itself. Shock and dismay swept through the Mediterranean world as people realized that not even the mightiest of cities could withstand the invaders. The Visigoths moved further westward and established a kingdom in Spain, but Rome was not left in peace.

Close on the heels of the Visigoths came the terrifying Huns, fierce fighters with strong, wiry physiques, who virtually lived on horseback. Their great leader, Attila (*at*-ih-luh), was called the "Scourge of God" and boasted that grass never grew where the hooves of his horses had trod. Fear of the Huns was so great that the Romans and the Germanic tribes, who had been enemies up to this point, joined forces to defeat Attila at Chalons (shah-*lawn*) in 451 A.D. A year later, the Huns threatened Rome itself. Pope Leo I rode out to Attila's camp and persuaded him to spare the city.

In 455 A.D., Attila died and the Huns ceased to play an important part in history. But that same year, a barbarian tribe called the Vandals, who had established a kingdom in North Africa, invaded Italy and sacked Rome. Because the Vandals caused so much senseless damage, they have given their tribal name to the term *vandalism*. According to one story, the Vandals smashed a beautiful mosaic floor to see whether the ducks in the design were real.

We have seen that Roman power had been in decline for many years. 476 A.D. is usually given as the date when the Empire collapsed in the West. In that year the Germanic general Odoacer (oh-doe-*ay-ser*) overthrew the last of the Roman emperors and made himself ruler of all Italy. From then on, the western part of the Empire was dominated by Germanic tribal chiefs. One of the German rulers, Theodoric (thee-*ahd*-uh-rik), king of the Ostrogoths (East Goths), established a kingdom in Italy but had difficulty controlling his restless warriors. Roads and bridges were left in disrepair and many fields were left untilled. Pirates and bandits made travel unsafe. Cities declined and trade and commerce began to disappear.

The Byzantine Empire and the Christian Church preserved civilization. Much of the achievement of the Roman Empire was preserved by its heir, the Eastern or Byzantine Empire, which continued to exist for nearly a thousand years after the "fall" of Rome. The Byzantine Empire flourished because eastern cities remained prosperous. The military power of Constantinople protected them from the barbarian attacks that had laid waste much of Western Europe.

Throughout the Middle Ages, the Byzantine Empire maintained civilization and order in the East. As you will see in Part 6, the Christian Church eventually adopted a similar responsibility in Western Europe.

Chapter Check-up

1. How did the quarrel over the succession of emperors weaken Rome?
2. What steps did Diocletian and Constantine take to try to save the Empire?
3. Why did the cities in the western part of the Empire decline?
4. Why were the Visigoths admitted into the Empire?
5. What is the significance of: (a) the battle of Adrianople and (b) the battle of Chalons?
6. What date and event marked the final end of the Empire? Why is this date chosen?
7. How were the traditions and achievements of Roman civilization preserved after the fall of the Empire?

Rome: SYNOPSIS

Rome began as a tiny city-state inhabited by sturdy, patriotic citizen-farmers living under a republican government. As the Romans expanded their control over Italy, they came into conflict with Carthage. After a long war they emerged as masters of the Mediterranean world.

Under a series of able rulers, Rome became a mighty and prosperous empire. Ironically, the growth of empire created problems which in the end were to bring about Rome's downfall. Foremost was the dependence on slave labor, which brought widespread unemployment. Citizens who had once been proud and self-reliant were reduced to a landless mob willing to follow whoever provided "bread and circuses."

The government, too, underwent a change, and the Republic became an absolute monarchy like those established in the eastern lands. The Romans became more interested in attaining efficient government than in maintaining self-government. For a time they were blessed with a series of good emperors who brought an era of peace and harmony without equal in the modern world. But when the emperors neglected internal problems and in fact became puppets of the army, Rome was doomed. By 476 A.D. the western half of the Empire had been completely overrun by barbarian tribes. The eastern half of the Empire, whose capital was at Constantinople, continued to flourish, however, until the mid-fifteenth century.

We are heavily indebted to the Romans for preserving Greek culture. As a matter of fact, much of the early Roman endeavor in art and science was merely a carbon copy of Greek achievement. Later, however, the Romans made distinctive artistic and literary achievements of their own. Three of their greatest contributions to civilization were their engineering skills, their great law code, and the Latin language. Like many other aspects of Roman culture, these three developments arose from the necessity of solving practical problems of empire management.

Although the Empire itself was destroyed, the influences of Roman civilization can be seen today in the buildings, highways, literature, language, and law of many of the countries that you will read about in Story of Nations.

Terms

Be sure that you understand clearly the meaning of each of the following:

"bread and circuses"
dictator
gladiator
Golden Age of Rome
Justinian's Code
Roman Peace
patricians
professional army
Republic
Senate
plebeians
tribunes
Twelve Tablets
"Roman Holiday"
Praetorian Guard

Important People

How has each of the following influenced the story of Rome?

Hannibal
Gracchus brothers
Marius
Sulla
Julius Caesar
Mark Antony
Augustus
Nero
Trajan
Marcus Aurelius
Livy
Vergil
Ovid
Diocletian
Constantine
Odoacer

Questions for Discussion and Review

1. What were the important steps by which Rome developed from a small city into a great empire?
2. Why is Hannibal considered to be one of the great military men of history?
3. What lessons about citizenship and democracy can Americans learn from the fall of the Roman Republic?
4. What arguments can you see for and against Caesar as an ideal ruler for Rome?

5. In what professions is a knowledge of Latin important today? Why?
6. What guiding principles of Roman law do we still follow today?
7. Which do you admire more, the Republic or the Empire? Why?
8. How did Rome bring peace to the world?
9. What conditions inside the Empire made it fairly easy for the barbarians to conquer Rome?
10. Why did the Eastern Roman Empire continue to flourish after 476 A.D.?
11. In your opinion, what were the three greatest contributions of the Romans? Why?

Interesting Things to Do

1. On a map of the Mediterranean world, show the boundaries of the Roman Empire at its greatest extent. Within these boundaries label the modern nations which have developed from land once ruled by the Romans.
2. Using outline, chart, illustrated booklet or poster, describe the contributions of the Romans in the fields of: (a) government; (b) law; (c) engineering and architecture; (d) literature, and (e) language.
3. Build a model or draw a sketch of the Colosseum, a Roman house, or an aqueduct.
4. Prepare a travel poster or pamphlet for modern Italy, featuring those things which would attract today's tourists.
5. Prepare and present a talk on one of the following topics: (a) The Colosseum; (b) Roman Aqueducts; (c) Julius Caesar; (d) Augustus.
6. Organize and present an informal debate on the topic, "*Resolved,* That the Romans made greater contributions to civilization than did the Greeks."
7. Review and then read to the class a selection from Shakespeare's "Julius Caesar." Suggested readings are the explanation by Brutus of the reasons for Caesar's assassination, or Mark Antony's oration at Caesar's funeral.
8. Imagine that you were a soldier who crossed the Alps with Hannibal's forces. Write in your diary an account of your experiences on this famous expedition.
9. Write an editorial for or against the continued use of Latin terms in the fields of law and medicine.
10. Add to, or begin, your "Who's Who in World History" series by writing one or more brief biographies of famous Romans.

Interesting Reading about Rome

Asimov, Isaac, *The Roman Republic,* Houghton Mifflin. A rapid survey of ancient Roman history.

Bulwer-Lytton, Edward R., *The Last Days of Pompeii,* Macmillan. A classic novel about the destruction of this Roman city.

*Davis, William S., *Friend of Caesar,* Macmillan. Accurate historical novel with good plot.

Duggan, Alfred Leo, *Julius Caesar,* Knopf. Vigorous and unbiased.

Foster, Genevieve, *Augustus Caesar's World,* Scribner.

*Hall, Jennie, *Buried Cities,* Macmillan.

Katz, Solomon, *The Decline of Rome and the Rise of Medieval Europe,* Cornell University Press.

National Geographic Society, *The Grandeur that Was Rome,* National Geographic Society.

Powers, Alfred, *Hannibal's Elephants,* Longmans Green.

Seredy, Kate, *White Stag,* Viking. Story of Attila the Hun.

Tappan, E. M., *Story of the Roman People,* Houghton Mifflin.

Wallace, Lew, *Ben Hur,* Dodd, Mead. A classic novel of a Jewish boy in old Rome.

* Indicates easy reading

Deliverance was central to Christianity. This 7th century mosaic depicts Noah releasing the dove of deliverance.

Part 6
JUDAISM, CHRISTIANITY, ISLAM
FORCES THAT INFLUENCED THE WESTERN WORLD

Jewish Religious Symbols. Shown in golf leaf on a fragment of Roman glass are the Shofar, or ram's horn, used in synagogue services, the Menorah, or seven branched candlestick, that represents the seven days of creation, and the Ark of the Law, containing the scrolls of the Law, or the Torah.

Mohammed with the Angel Gabriel. This fourteenth-century manuscript painting shows the Angel Gabriel visiting Mohammed. The Islamic religion accepts the Hebrew Old Testament as divinely inspired and reveres Angels as God's messengers.

Scenes from the Passion. Carved on an ivory casket from the fifth century are three scenes from the passion of Jesus. On the left, Pilate washes his hands after condemning Jesus to death. In the center, Jesus carries his cross, and on the right, Peter, warming himself before a brazier, denies to a maidservant that he knows Jesus, while a cock crows in the background.

Religion: PERSPECTIVE

Ancient peoples often said that the gods were more numerous than men. Indeed, from man's early beginnings until the civilizations of Greece and Rome, the earth and heavens were believed to be filled with a throng of deities so vast that the average man could scarcely hope to keep track of them all. Men thought that strange forces existed in rocks and trees, that gods inhabited Mount Olympus, and that clouds of spirits flitted invisibly through the atmosphere.

Western man's religious development has traveled a long road from polytheism, the belief in many gods, to monotheism, the worship of one god. Whatever his individual religious conviction, he believes for the most part that there exists only one Supreme Being. Whether he is a Jew, a Moslem, or a Christian, his spiritual world is monotheistic. Monotheism began, as you will see, with the ancient Hebrews and was adopted by the Christians and later by the Moslems. These three great faiths of the West thus hold in common a crucial belief. As you will discover in Part 6, they also share many of the same traditions and goals.

The photographs on the opposite page show Jewish, Moslem, and Christian religious symbols and traditions. You can easily see similarities between them. All three religions believe that God intervenes in men's lives and has given man a Law, a code by which to live. In the following pages you will learn about the origin and development of these three great religions, and you will see how they became guiding forces in Western civilization.

CHAPTER 18

The Hebrews Were the First People to Believe in One God

JUDAISM IS BASED ON THE TEACHINGS OF MOSES AND THE PROPHETS

Moses led his people out of Egypt. Western civilization owes much of its religious tradition to the Hebrews, whom you met earlier in the story of the Fertile Crescent. You will recall that one group of Hebrews wandered into Egypt and was enslaved by the Pharaoh. After many years, a great leader, Moses, appeared among the people to lead them from their bondage.

Perhaps you recall the biblical story of how Moses tried to persuade the Pharaoh to set the Hebrews free. When the Pharaoh refused, a series of terrible plagues came to punish the Egyptians. In one of the plagues, death took the eldest child in every Egyptian household but passed over the houses of the Hebrews. This event is the origin of the great Jewish festival of the Passover. The Pharaoh at last consented to free the Hebrews. Moses led them across a branch of the Red Sea to the Sinai Peninsula. A short time later the Pharaoh, regretting his decision to free the He-

Moses Receiving the Ten Commandments. The great Hebrew leader, standing on the top of Mount Sinai, receives the Ten Commandments from God while the Children of Israel wait below in awe and wonder. This detail is a panel from the famous doors of the baptistery of the Cathedral of Florence in Italy.

brews, sent his armies in pursuit. The Bible tells how the waters of the Red Sea closed on the Egyptians and drowned them.

Moses gave the Hebrews the Ten Commandments. Even when the Hebrews had escaped from Egypt and reached the Sinai Peninsula, many of Moses' followers were afraid and wanted to turn back. Some of them had adopted the religion of the Egyptians, and, having left Egypt, they feared that they had no gods to protect them.

The Bible relates that Moses led his followers to Mount Sinai. There he left them for forty days and forty nights while he went to the top of the mountain to pray and to receive help from God. When he returned, Moses brought with him the Ten Commandments, engraved on stone tablets. The Hebrews promised to obey the Ten Commandments and called themselves the "Chosen People" because God had given them written rules to follow.

After forty years of wandering in the desert, Moses guided his people to the edge of the "Promised Land," but he died before they gained possession of it. He had left behind him, however, one of the most important teachings in the history of religion, that of a belief in one god, or what is called *monotheism*. You will recall that an Egyptian Pharaoh also had taught that there was but one god. His people had refused to accept the idea. But among the Hebrews the belief in one god, whom they called Yahweh (Jehovah), was widely accepted and in time became the underlying principle of the Hebrew religion.

Great prophets influenced Hebrew beliefs. After the establishment of the kingdom in Pal-

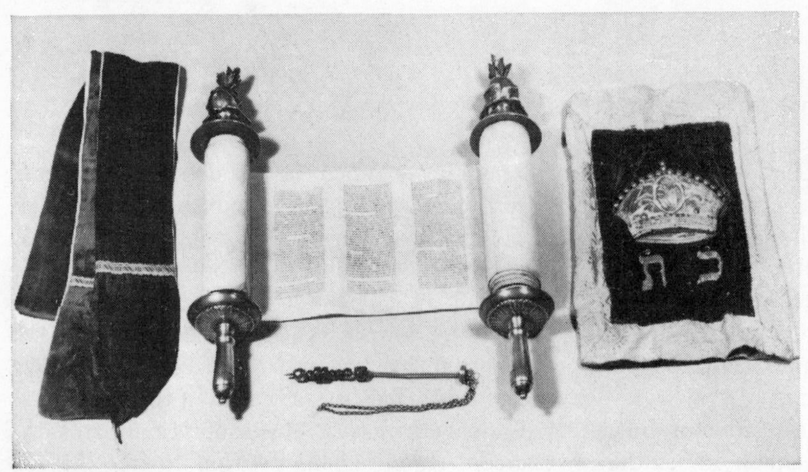

The Torah. The pointer below is used for reading the Torah because men are forbidden to touch it. The two covers protect the Torah when it is not in use.

ARK FOR THE TORAH. Behind the closed doors of the Ark, the scroll containing the Torah is kept. Above the doors are inscribed the Ten Commandments and the words: KNOW BEFORE WHOM THOU STANDEST.

estine, many of the Hebrew people began to ignore the Commandments and to abandon the teachings of Moses.

During the seventh and eighth centuries B.C., there appeared a series of great religious teachers, called prophets, who tried to lead the Hebrews back to the traditions of their ancestors. One of them, Amos, predicted that Israel would be destroyed as a result of the greed and selfishness that had come into the lives of the people. Others taught that Jehovah demanded righteous behavior rather than gifts to a temple or sacrifices on an altar. This idea is eloquently expressed in the teachings of the prophet Micah (*my*-kuh), who said: "What doth the Lord require of thee, but to do justly, and to love mercy, and to walk humbly with thy God?" Isaiah (eye-*zay*-uh), another of the great prophets, taught that Jehovah was not only the god of the Hebrews but also the god of all men. This message was a revolutionary one in the history of religion.

The Old Testament tells the story of the Hebrews. In 538 B.C. the Persian king Cyrus freed the Jews from their captivity in Babylon and allowed them to return to Palestine (see page 60). Many of them returned joyfully and began to rebuild the great temple in the city. During this period Jewish scholars began to collect and write down the traditions of their people. Their work, the Old Testament, was finally completed about 100 A.D.

The Old Testament is one of the greatest of man's literary achievements. It has become the foundation for the religious teachings of both the Jews and Christians, and it is generally accepted by them as being inspired directly by God. Most modern knowledge of the ancient Hebrews comes from the Old Testament. It shows how Hebrew religious ideas developed side by side with the history of the people, and it contains accounts of the creation of the world and the great flood. It also describes the adventures of Moses, Saul, David, and other heroes of Hebrew history and contains the writings of the great prophets. The Jews call the first five books of the Old Testament the Torah (*toe*-rah), or the Law of Moses.

THE JEWS PRESERVED THEIR UNITY THROUGH FAITH

In the first century B.C. the Romans incorporated Palestine into their Empire. On several occasions, the Jews rebelled against Roman authority. After one serious outburst in 70 A.D., the Romans destroyed the temple in Jerusalem and forbade the Jews to enter the city.

From that time on, Jews have been scattered all over the world. Until recently (see Part 23) they

THE SPOILS OF JERUSALEM. In 70 A.D. the Roman emperor Titus destroyed Jerusalem to punish the Jews. Booty and captives were taken back to Rome. In this relief from the Arch of Titus, which was erected in Rome to commemorate the emperor's victory, men are shown carrying sacred objects plundered from the Jewish temple. Many Jews migrated to Western Europe because they were not allowed to live in Jerusalem.

have not had a homeland of their own. They preserved their unity as a people not by sharing a common land but by sharing a common faith. In practicing their faith, most Jews have tried to strike a balance between the details of ritual developed by the Jewish teachers, or rabbis (*ra*-bys), and the ethical spirit of justice and love urged by the prophets. Almost all Jews share the belief that if they are faithful to Jehovah, he will send a liberator, or Messiah (meh-*sy*-uh), who will help them regain the "Promised Land."

Throughout the centuries, Jews have suffered persecution. Spain, Russia, and Germany have been particularly harsh in exiling or executing Jews. In spite of such opposition, the Jews have never lost their faith in the two ideas that have made Judaism different from all preceding religions, the belief that Jehovah is the one god for all men and the belief that he wants men to live according to certain ethical rules. These beliefs were to have great influence on the two other monotheistic religions that have shaped the Western world, Christianity and Islam.

Chapter Check-up

1. What is the Hebrew name for God?
2. What are the Ten Commandments? What was their significance to the early Hebrews?
3. How did the religion of the early Hebrews differ from the other religions of that time?
4. Describe the ways in which Moses influenced the course of the Hebrew religion.
5. How did the prophets influence the Hebrews?
6. What was Isaiah's message to the Jews?
7. Why is the Old Testament considered to be one of the great books of all times?
8. What has kept the Jews united throughout centuries of persecution and separation?
9. Explain the meaning of the following terms: monotheism; Messiah; Torah.

CHAPTER 19

Christianity Offered Man the Promise of Peace and Salvation

THE LIFE AND TEACHINGS OF JESUS PROVIDE THE FOUNDATIONS FOR CHRISTIANITY

The New Testament tells of Jesus' birth. Christianity is based on the life and teachings of one of the most important figures in history, Jesus of Nazareth. According to stories that have come down to us through the New Testament, Jesus was born in a stable in Bethlehem because his mother, Mary, could find no room in the village inn. The New Testament tells of how angels appeared before shepherds in the fields and told them of the birth, and of how a star guided wise men to the stable with gifts for the baby.

Little is known of Jesus' life for the next thirty years. He returned with his family to Nazareth, a small town in northern Palestine. There he worked as a carpenter and, like all Jewish boys, studied the writings of the Hebrew prophets. In his studies, he displayed a keen interest and aptitude for Jewish religious teachings. While on a visit to Jerusalem one day, he went to the temple to hear the rabbis who taught there. His family, missing him, searched the city. At last they found him "sitting in the midst of the doctors, both hearing them, and asking them questions. And all that heard him were astonished at his understanding and answers."

Eager crowds gathered to hear Jesus preach. When he was thirty, Jesus began to teach. He declared that God had sent him to bring a message of hope to all men, and he traveled through the countryside, teaching and healing the sick. Eager crowds followed him everywhere. According to the New Testament, Jesus sometimes worked miracles; once he fed hundreds of people with two fish and five loaves of bread. When he taught, he often used a story, or parable, to explain what he meant. The story of the good Samaritan, one of these parables, tells of a man who was robbed, wounded, and left by the side of the road. Two passers-by ignored him, but a man from the city of Samaria stopped, took the injured man to an inn, and cared for him. This parable of the good Samaritan was Jesus' way of instructing his followers to always show kindness and consideration toward their fellow men.

THE NATIVITY. In this scene by the famous fourteenth-century Italian painter Giotto, Mary is shown tending the infant Jesus while Joseph sleeps. The animals of the stables are gathered around while shepherds and angels rejoice.

Jesus chose twelve men of the hundreds who heard him to be his disciples (dih-*sy*-puls), or followers. The devoted apostles, as the twelve are called, gave up their families and possessions to follow him. These men, who traveled about teaching and preaching, helped spread the doctrines of Jesus throughout the ancient world.

Jesus urged men to serve God with love. Study of the Old Testament and a strong belief in God had given Jesus respect for the laws of Moses. Jesus proclaimed that he came to uphold Jewish law and that his God was the Jewish God of salvation. But Jesus also expressed new ideas about the way in which Jewish law should be interpreted and applied. Among other things, he said that people must go beyond the letter of the law to its spirit. He also said that in God's eyes a person's rank and wealth meant nothing. God loved all people and was pleased with any person who loved and served him in return.

The best way to serve God, Jesus explained, was to help other men and to observe the Golden Rule: "Therefore all things whatsoever ye would that men should do to you, do ye even so to them." Earlier religious teachers had also taught consideration for others, but for Jesus, love of one's fellow man was second only to love of God. He summed up man's duty to God in two brief statements: "Thou shalt love the Lord thy God with all thy heart . . ." and "Thou shalt love thy neighbor as thyself."

Jesus was arrested and condemned to death. As news of the miracles which Jesus performed spread, some people came to believe he was the Messiah who had been promised long ago by the

THE LAST SUPPER. In this psychological masterpiece by Leonardo da Vinci, Jesus is shown with the twelve disciples at the moment when he says, "One among you shall betray me." The impact of his announcement on the disciples is reflected in their electrified expressions of surprise and dismay. In executing this wall painting, Leonardo unsuccessfully experimented with new methods and materials. For this reason the painting has been deteriorating steadily.

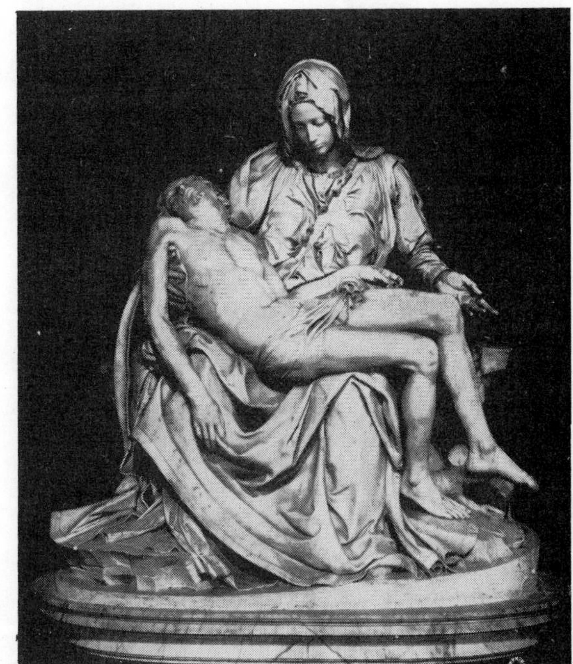

AFTER THE CRUCIFIXION. This magnificent sculpture, created by the Italian artist Michelangelo, shows Mary holding the body of Jesus after he was removed from the cross.

Hebrew prophets. They expected him to declare himself their king and lead a revolt against the Romans. When Jesus and his disciples entered Jerusalem just before the great Jewish feast of the Passover, crowds rushed to meet him. Hoping the day of national liberation was near, they filled the air with shouts of excitement and scattered palm branches before him.

Other people were displeased with this demonstration. They did not believe that Jesus was the Messiah. Furthermore, they feared he would only be the cause of fruitless riots and provoke the Romans to punish the Jewish people or send even more troops into the country. They looked for a way to discredit Jesus. One of the disciples of Jesus, called Judas, offered to betray his master for thirty pieces of silver. Jesus was quickly taken prisoner and hailed before the Roman governor, Pontius Pilate (*pahn*-shus *py*-lut), for judgment. Jesus was charged with stirring up the people, and attempting to set himself up as a king in opposition to the Romans. Pilate could find no proof of the charges, and, fearing a riot, offered to set Jesus free. The crowd that had gathered for the trial protested. Many of those present were enemies of Jesus and they began to demand his death. Pilate did not wish to anger the crowd and perhaps provoke demonstrations among the large numbers of Jewish pilgrims who were crowding into Jerusalem for the holy days. He sentenced the prisoner to death by crucifixion, or execution by being nailed to a wooden cross, and had the sentence carried out.

THE CHRISTIAN FAITH GAVE THE WORLD NEW HOPE

Belief in Christ is the cornerstone of Christianity. Jesus' Crucifixion filled his followers with despair. Some of the disciples fled Jerusalem in fear of losing their own lives, but five days later they returned, excitedly bearing the news that Jesus had appeared among them. They declared that he had risen from the dead to ascend into heaven, and that he had then returned to appear before them. The Resurrection convinced Jesus' followers that he was truly the Son of God and the Messiah. They called him *Christ,* from the Greek word for "Messiah."

The Resurrection of Jesus was interpreted by his followers to mean that any man who truly lived by the principles laid down by Jesus could also overcome death and attain eternal life. Recognition of Jesus as the Son of God and belief in his Resurrection are two of the central doctrines of Christianity.

Paul taught that Christianity was a religion for all men. The spread of the Christian religion was due largely to the efforts of a few skilled and devoted missionaries. The most important of the early missionaries was Paul (also known as

Saul), a Roman citizen from the city of Tarsus in Asia Minor. Although Paul was a Jew, he was well educated in Greek and Roman culture. At first Paul was opposed to Christianity, which he considered a false doctrine, and he took the lead in seeking to stamp it out.

According to the New Testament, Paul was on his way to suppress the Christians in Damascus, when suddenly he saw a brilliant light which seemed to him to be a vision of Christ. At the same time he heard a voice cry out, "Saul, Saul, why persecutest thou me?" Paul did not recover his sight for three days. He was so moved by his experience that he became a Christian, and instead of persecuting followers of the new religion, he devoted all his energies to converting others to it.

THE CONVERSION OF ST. PAUL. On his way to Damascus Paul is overwhelmed by a blinding light in which he hears the voice of Jesus calling to him. Because he was a Roman citizen the great apostle is known by two names. Paul was his Roman name. His Hebrew name was "Saul."

In the years immediately following Jesus' death, most Christians were converted Jews who believed that Jesus' message should be carried only to other Jews. Paul became convinced, however, that Christianity should welcome all men, including non-Jews, or Gentiles. He traveled tirelessly throughout the Roman world, establishing new Christian communities wherever he went and writing letters to guide and advise the people of these communities. His letters constitute a large portion of the New Testament.

The early Christians suffered persecution for their faith. Paul and the original apostles carried Christianity to the farthest corners of the Roman Empire. For a while the Romans tolerated the new religion, but gradually they began to look on Christians as a threat to the state.

The Christians formed a closely united group that seemed to challenge the authority of the government. They balked at paying taxes or serving in the army, and they steadfastly refused to worship Roman gods. The emperors were infuriated by what they regarded as unpatriotic and subversive behavior. Nero, you will recall, accused the Christians of setting fire to Rome, and he savagely persecuted them. The philosopher-emperor Marcus Aurelius regarded them as a threat to the state and considered it his duty to suppress them. Under Diocletian, thousands of Christians were condemned to death in battles with wild beasts that provided entertainment for the Romans. The calmness and dignity with which the Christian martyrs accepted their terrible fate inspired many pagans to become converts.

Constantine the Great became the first Christian emperor. Early in the fourth century, Constantine the Great became emperor of Rome. According to legend, Constantine, while marching to battle against a rival emperor, saw in the sky a flaming cross on which was written *In hoc signo vinces* ("In this sign you shall conquer"). Constantine ordered his soldiers to paint the initials of Jesus' name on their shields. In the ensu-

THE COLOSSEUM. Within these walls, gladiators and beasts fought for the pleasure of the mob. Whether Christians were thrown to the lions here is not certain, but today a cross stands in the arena commemorating their tremendous faith and bravery under persecution.

ing fight at the Tiber River, nine miles north of Rome Constantine won a great victory. The encounter is known as the Battle of the Milvian Bridge after a bridge which crossed the Tiber at this point.

In gratitude for his victory, Constantine issued the Edict of Milan (313 A.D.), giving Christianity equality with all other religions. He built churches in Rome and Palestine and took an active part in strengthening the Church. Constantine himself did not become a Christian until just before his death. Toward the end of the fourth century Christianity was made the official religion of the Empire, and pagan worship was outlawed.

THE EARLY CHRISTIANS DEVELOPED A CHURCH ORGANIZATION AND A DISTINCTIVE LITERATURE

The sacraments helped to give early Christians a feeling of spiritual unity. Early Christians thought of themselves as a group of men set apart from the rest of the world by their belief in Christ. They lived in daily expectation that the world would come to an end and that Christ would return to earth and establish the Kingdom of God. Thus they saw little need for establishing an organization or building special houses of Christian worship.

In time, however, they came to observe certain ceremonies, called *sacraments*, which gave them a feeling of belonging to a unique spiritual community. They believed that Jesus had established the sacraments as signs of God's love for them. Two of the most important sacraments were *baptism*, the ceremony by which a person became a Christian, and the *eucharist* (mass), through which the early Christians symbolized the Crucifixion of Jesus.

There were also five other sacraments. In *confirmation* a Christian reaffirmed his faith and received the strength necessary to be a good Christian. Through *penance* he could be forgiven his sins. In the *anointing of the sick* he was strengthened in illness and prepared for death. *Matrimony* was the sacrament in which a Christian man and woman were wed. By the sacrament of *holy orders* a Christian became a priest. Some Christians have accepted all seven of these sacraments as we have described them. Other Christians believe in only some of them.

The early Christians recognized the need for an organized church. By the second century, Christians began to realize that since the end of the world was not immediately at hand, they could conduct their worship more effectively if they were better organized. Men were needed to preach, to administer the sacraments, and to help the poor and needy. Christians had always believed that Jesus had given his apostles special authority to carry on his mission. After the apostles died, Christians began to look on those who led the Christian communities in the various cities as successors to the apostles and as recipients of their authority. Such men were called bishops.

By the end of the fourth century, the Church had many kinds of officials. They were arranged in a pyramid-shaped pattern called a hierarchy (*hy*-er-ar-kee), which was based on the pattern of the government of the Roman Empire. At the bottom of the hierarchy were deacons and other minor officials. They helped the priest, who had charge of a single church in a small area called a parish. The priests were supervised by a bishop, whose church was the largest in the city. The city and the area around it were called a diocese (*dy*-oh-sees). The bishops themselves were supervised by an archbishop, whose area of authority was called a province.

The Church officials were known collectively as the clergy; ordinary worshipers were called lay-

THE SACRAMENT OF BAPTISM. While his parents and sponsors look on, a child becomes a member of the Church. Baptism is often called *christening*, which means "making Christian." In many churches the child is also given his Christian name at the time of baptism. This scene is from a series of fifteenth-century Flemish tapestries that show the seven sacraments.

men. The duties of the clergy were to preach, to collect offerings for the Church and the poor, and, most important, to administer the sacraments. Since early Christians believed that they needed to receive the sacraments in order to be assured of entry into heaven, the clergy held great power. The bishops gained additional power by taking over many of the duties of the Roman officials during the decline of Rome.

Church councils solved questions of Christian belief. The early Christians realized that they needed an authority to answer questions about the Christian faith. Some clergymen disagreed about the exact meaning of Jesus' teachings. Others could not understand how Jesus could be both God and man at the same time. Although the bishops realized that quarrels over such questions were weakening the Church, they seldom were able to reach agreement.

The Emperor Constantine, like the bishops, wanted all Christians to be united. He called bishops from all over the empire to attend the first general council of the Church, the Council of Nicaea (ny-*see*-uh), which met in 325 A.D. The bishops decided on the basic teachings of Christianity and put them into the Nicene Creed. The creed is still used in many churches today. Later emperors followed Constantine's example by calling councils. Whatever the councils decided was to be accepted by all Christians. Anyone who did not follow the orthodox doctrine of the Church, which the councils established, was guilty of believing in false doctrine, or *heresy*.

The New Testament expressed Christian belief. The Church councils performed another important function by deciding just what documents should be included in the part of the Bible called the New Testament. Jesus himself had written nothing. Devoted Christians recorded all the facts of his life which they could discover and added all the legends that were being told about him. Church councils in the fourth century decided how much of this material was genuine. They accepted as authentic four versions of the life of Jesus, called the Gospels, and some carefully preserved copies of letters written by Paul and the disciples. This material, called the New Testament, was officially accepted by the Church for public reading and teaching. Christians believe that the teachings of Jesus in the New Testament are closely related to the principles established in the Old Testament. Most Christians regard as sacred both documents, which together make up the Bible as we know it.

ST. JEROME. The scholarly saint, who devoted his life to translating the Bible into Latin, is portrayed in this painting by the seventeenth-century Spanish artist El Greco.

Since there were virtually no original manuscripts of either the Old Testament or the New Testament, you can easily understand the great excitement created by the recent discovery of ancient religious scrolls in caves high above the Dead Sea. Scholars believe that the Dead Sea scrolls were written before and during the lifetime of Jesus. They were carefully stored in jars many centuries ago and have been preserved by the dry climate. Some of the scrolls contain the earliest known texts of Old Testament prophets. Others describe the life of a previously unknown Jewish sect living on the edge of the Dead Sea. Scholars are still disputing whether or not this sect had great influence on Jesus. In any case, the Dead Sea scrolls are adding a great deal to our knowledge of the Bible and the biblical period of history.

The Church Fathers defended their faith. Beginning in the fourth and fifth centuries the Christian Church became the object of frequent criticism both from those outside the Church and from heretics within it. Certain bishops and other churchmen, known as Church Fathers, undertook to defend the Church from its detractors. One of the most famous, St. Jerome, spent much of his life in Bethlehem translating the Bible from its original Hebrew and Greek into Latin, which the Western world could read. His version, called the Vulgate, or "common" edition of the Bible, was adopted as the official Bible of the Church in the sixteenth century. It is the oldest version of the whole Bible in existence. He is also famous for his brilliant letters, of which over a hundred still exist. They are interesting not only for their discussion of religious issues but also for their account of the times.

Another of the outstanding Church Fathers was St. Augustine, bishop of Hippo, a Roman province in North Africa. When the Visigoths sacked Rome in 410, the Romans accused the Christians of bringing on the attack by their failure to worship Roman gods. Augustine stopped writing books against heretics long enough to defend the Christians against this charge. In his book *The City of God*, he explained that Christians were concerned with eternal life in heaven and had nothing to do with what had happened to Rome at the hands of the Visigoths. As you will see in Part 7, Augustine's writings guided Christian thinking for the next thousand years.

WESTERN AND EASTERN CHRISTIANS ESTABLISHED SEPARATE CHURCHES

The Bishop of Rome claimed to be head of the Church. Although Christianity developed a highly efficient organization, there remained conflict over who should be head of the Church. The bishops of five different cities could claim approximately equal stature and importance. The five cities were Rome in the West, and Constantinople, Jerusalem, Antioch, and Alexandria in the East. Gradually Christians in the western part of the empire began to consider the Bishop of Rome more important than the other four bishops. They believed that Jesus had made his disciple Peter the head of the whole Church. ("And I say also unto thee, that thou art Peter, and upon this rock I will build my church. . . .") According to tradition, Peter was the first Bishop of Rome. Each succeeding Bishop of Rome was believed to have inherited Peter's authority. This

St. Peter. This famous statue in the cathedral bearing his name, represents St. Peter holding his traditional symbol of authority, the key to the Kingdom of Heaven. The toe of the statue has been worn smooth by the kisses of devout visitors.

The Empress Theodora. This mosaic shows the wife of Emperor Justinian with her attendants. Because she belonged to a Christian sect to which her husband was opposed, she used her great influence on the emperor to prevent him from persecuting those who did not agree with his orthodox beliefs. Theodora is an important and interesting historical figure because of the active part she took in affairs of Church and State.

belief, called the *Petrine Theory*, provided the basis for the authority of the Roman Catholic Church.

The prestige of the Bishop of Rome, or the Pope, as he is called, became even greater when the Roman Empire was divided in 395 A.D. You may recall that after the division of the empire the Roman emperors in the West grew steadily weaker. Eventually they moved the capital from Rome to the city of Ravenna because it was safer from barbarian attacks. Thus the city of Rome was left without leadership. Gradually the popes took over the duties that the emperors had previously performed. One of the ablest of the early popes, Leo the Great (440–61), persuaded Attila the Hun not to invade Rome. Leo claimed authority over the whole Christian Church and attempted to settle questions of doctrine without calling Church councils.

Gregory the Great (590–604), who wanted only to spend his life in quiet prayer, was chosen as Pope just at the time Rome needed a strong leader to defend her from the invading Lombards. Because there was no emperor, Gregory protected the city and made a treaty with the Lombards. He organized a police force and imported grain to feed the Roman population. Like Leo before him, he claimed authority over the whole Church. By serving as both religious and political leaders, Leo and Gregory helped establish the Roman Pope as the acknowledged head of the Christian Church in the western half of the empire.

The Church in the East refused to accept Rome's authority. Christians in the eastern part of the empire did not want to be controlled by the Bishop of Rome. When Pope Leo declared that Rome's authority was supreme, the Bishop of Constantinople, or the *Patriarch* (*pay*-tree-ark), as he is called, openly disagreed. From then on, the Church in the East grew further and further away from the Church in Rome. In 1054 the split was made official, and a separate Church was established in the East under the authority of the Patriarch of Constantinople. This Church became known as the Eastern (Greek) Orthodox Church.

There were several reasons for the division of the Church. For one thing, the Eastern Christians steadfastly refused to accept the Petrine Theory. By the fifth century the eastern half of the empire had grown stronger and wealthier than the western part. Naturally, the stronger of the two empires, the Eastern, was reluctant to accept the authority of the weaker.

Perhaps the chief reason for the split within the Church, however, was the fact that certain differences had developed between Christians in the two parts of the empire. The language of the Roman Church was Latin: that of the Eastern Church was Greek. The two churches also differed on questions of belief and practice. These differences eventually resulted in the permanent division of the Church. After 1438 no Pope and Patriarch even met until January, 1964, when Pope Paul VI met with the Eastern Patriarch in Jerusalem.

Christianity continued to triumph. In spite of the division within the Church, Christianity continued to spread throughout Europe. Missionaries from the Eastern Church, encouraged by the Byzantine emperor, converted the Slavic peoples of Eastern Europe and Russia. Missionaries from Rome, sent by the Pope, converted the barbarians of Western Europe. When Europeans sailed to the New World a thousand years later, they brought Christianity with them.

Almost two thousand years have passed since the birth of Jesus. (As you know, the Western world bases its calendar on the date of his birth.) There is scarcely a country in which Christian missionaries have not worked, and today it is estimated that about a third of the world's population is Christian.

Chapter Check-up

1. What are the basic teachings of Jesus?
2. Why was Jesus crucified?
3. What is the Resurrection? What is its significance in Christian belief?
4. What part did Paul play in the growth of Christianity?
5. How did Emperor Constantine influence the history of Christianity?
6. Name the seven sacraments. What is the purpose of each?
7. What important function was performed by church councils?
8. What is the New Testament?
9. What are the two churches that resulted from the split between the East and the West?
10. Why did the Eastern Church refuse to accept Rome's authority? Give three reasons.

CHAPTER 20

Mohammed's Teachings United Millions of Believers

ISLAM WAS BORN ON THE ARABIAN DESERT

Islam (or as it is sometimes referred to, Mohammedanism) is another of the world's great religions. Islam was established in Arabia by the merchant-prophet Mohammed about six hundred years after the birth of Jesus. Although the early Arabs were a backward people, their religious zeal enabled them to spread their faith with amazing speed. Within a hundred years after Mohammed's death his followers had established an empire larger than Rome's and were threatening to bring all of Europe under their control.

Mohammed lived among primitive tribesmen. When other Semitic tribes, such as the Babylonians, Phoenicians, and Hebrews, came out of the desert into the Fertile Crescent, the Arab tribes remained behind. They continued to live as nomadic herdsmen, roaming the desert in an endless search for water and grass for their flocks.

The Arabs were untouched by the main stream of civilization in the Fertile Crescent, except in a few towns along the Red Sea where caravans stopped occasionally.

Like other early peoples, the Arabs believed in many gods. Their center of worship was the town of Mecca on the western coast of the Arabian Peninsula. Here priests watched over the idols which tribesmen from all parts of the desert came to worship. A sacred stone building in the heart of Mecca, called the Kaaba (*kah*-buh), contained a large black stone which the Arabs believed had been sent from heaven. They regarded it as the holiest of objects. Every year they stopped wandering the deserts long enough to pay a visit to the Kaaba, which became as sacred to Arabs as the birthplace of Jesus became to Christians. In 570 A.D. Mohammed was born among these primitive tribesmen.

When he was twelve, Mohammed became a camel driver for one of the caravans crossing the Arabian desert between Mecca and Damascus. His travels brought him into contact with Jewish and Christian ideas. During the long, lonely journeys across the desert Mohammed pondered matters of religious belief. Once a year he retired to a cave in the mountains where he devoted himself to solitary contemplation. One day, while sleeping in the cave, the angel Gabriel came to him in a vision and inspired him to become a prophet. He was to lead his fellow men away from the worship of idols to the worship of the one true God, Allah.

Enemies forced Mohammed to flee for his life. Mohammed continued to receive revelations. Sometimes, when walking in the streets of Mecca, he fell into a trance and words poured from his mouth. His wife, his nephew, and two friends were his first converts. As more and more people became his followers, the leaders of Mecca became alarmed. They feared that if the Arab tribesmen accepted Mohammed's teachings and began to worship only Allah, they would stop making pilgrimages to Mecca to worship the idols there. The merchants and businessmen of Mecca knew that this would be a serious blow to the city's economy.

They began to plot against Mohammed. Afraid that he would be killed if he stayed in Mecca, he and a few followers fled one night to Medina, a town two hundred miles away. His escape is called the *Hegira* (heh-*jy*-rah), the Arabic word for "flight." Just as Christians consider the birth of Jesus as the beginning of a new age, so the Moslems, as the followers of Islam are called, count the year of the Hegira, 622 A.D., as the beginning of their era.

Mohammed made many converts in Medina. He called his new faith *Islam*, which means "surrender to the will of God." Soon he gained control of the government and established a powerful army, which he headed. He used his army to plunder the rich caravans headed for Mecca. During the next ten years Mohammed converted most

THE KAABA. The black structure in the foreground is the most sacred building of the Moslem world. It is the focal point for the prayers of Mohammedans everywhere.

of the tribes in the Arabian Desert and brought them under his control. He returned to Mecca in triumph and forced the priests to swear obedience to Allah. Mohammed established Mecca as the center of the Islamic faith and proclaimed the Kaaba as the chief shrine of all Moslems. As a result of this proclamation, pilgrimages to Mecca greatly increased and the prosperity of the city was assured. The people of Mecca were grateful for this and became enthusiastic Moslems.

The writings of the Koran are sacred to Moslems. Like Jesus, Mohammed left no written account of his teachings. The only record of his words is that written by his devoted followers in a book called the Koran. The Koran is as important to Moslems as the Bible is to Christians. It provides a code of laws under which they must live to win favor with Allah. The Koran, which is written in a beautiful poetic style, contains many hymns, prayers, and stories. Moslems believe it to be inspired directly by Allah, who gradually revealed its text to his prophet Mohammed.

To become a true Moslem, a man must faithfully carry out the instructions of the Koran. He must 1) recite the creed daily: "I believe that there is no god but Allah, and that Mohammed is his prophet"; 2) pray five times each day, always facing the holy city of Mecca; 3) fast for one month each year; 4) give alms to the poor; 5) make, if possible, a pilgrimage to Mecca at least once in his lifetime.

The Koran forbids the use of altars, images, and pictures of living things in Moslem temples, which are called *mosques* (mahsks). The faithful of Allah pray in the courts and squares outside the mosques. Up in the slender towers called minarets (min-uh-*rets*) go muezzins (myoo-*ez*-inz) five times every day. Their shrill voices cry out across the rooftops calling in Arabic the short creed of Mohammed. At once the crowd quiets; the people face Mecca, the holy city; they fall upon their knees and bow their heads to the ground and pray. In their desert tent homes, with their caravans, on the windswept sand wastes, no matter where a true follower of Allah may be, he spreads his prayer rug five times a day and faces Mecca to perform his devotions.

Mohammed gave his followers many other laws to guide their conduct. One of these resembles the Golden Rule: "Let no man treat his neighbor as he himself would dislike to be treated." Another limits the number of wives a man could have to four, and still others prohibit Moslems from drinking wine, gambling, or charging interest on loans. All Moslems who faithfully carry out the laws of Islam are considered equal in the sight of Allah, regardless of their country or their rank in society.

Many Moslem beliefs are similar to those of Jews and Christians. Moslems, like Christians and Jews, believe in one divine being. The Moslem Allah, the Hebrew Jehovah, and the Christian God are names for three different concepts of this one divinity. Similarities can also be seen in the prayers of the three faiths. Here is one of the most frequently used prayers from the Koran:

> . . . Praise be to God, the Lord of the worlds, the merciful, the compassionate, the ruler of the judgment day! Thee we serve and Thee we ask for aid. Guide us in the right path, the path of those to whom Thou art gracious.

You can easily see the similarity between this Moslem prayer and the following one taken from the Sixty-seventh Psalm (which is used by both Christians and Jews):

> God be merciful unto us, and bless us, and cause his face to shine upon us; . . . That Thy way may be known upon earth. . . Let the people praise Thee, O God; let all the people praise Thee.

The three religions also share the belief that all men will be rewarded or punished in the after life. Mohammed describes paradise as a pleasant garden where men rest in silken robes beside cool fountains—a delightful prospect in the after life for the Moslems, who lived in the hot, arid desert. The counterpart of the Moslems' belief in a paradise after death is found in the Christian belief in heaven and the Jewish belief in the Kingdom of God on earth.

All three religious faiths regard the Old Testament as a divinely inspired document. Many of the Old Testament leaders, such as Moses and Isaiah, are found in the Koran. Because the Moslems respected the Old Testament, they treated Jews and Christians much less harshly than they treated pagan peoples. The Moslems, however, believe that the Koran was the last revelation from Allah, and they guide their lives by it rather than by the Old Testament.

In Moslem eyes, Jesus is respected as one of the Hebrew prophets; he is not, however, accepted as the son of God. Moslems do not consider Mohammed to be divine either. They regard him as an ordinary man chosen by Allah, not to perform miracles, but to lead men to the true faith.

ISLAM SPREAD THROUGHOUT NORTH AFRICA AND THE MIDDLE EAST

By the time of Mohammed's death in 632 A.D., he had converted the entire Arabian peninsula to Islam. In the next century his followers waged a holy war that carried the faith to India, Africa, and even into Europe itself. The remarkable success of the expansion of Islam was made possible by an extraordinary combination of military skill and religious zeal.

The Moslems fought a holy war. Before the appearance of Mohammed, the restless Arabian tribes fought continually among themselves. Mohammed was able to capitalize on their natural militancy by uniting them and giving them a noble cause for which to fight. Islam taught that there should be only one faith for all men. Thus it was the sacred duty of Moslems to convert other people, particularly pagans, at the point of a sword if necessary. A soldier who died fighting for Allah would certainly be admitted to heaven. Moslem soldiers plunged into battle under the command,

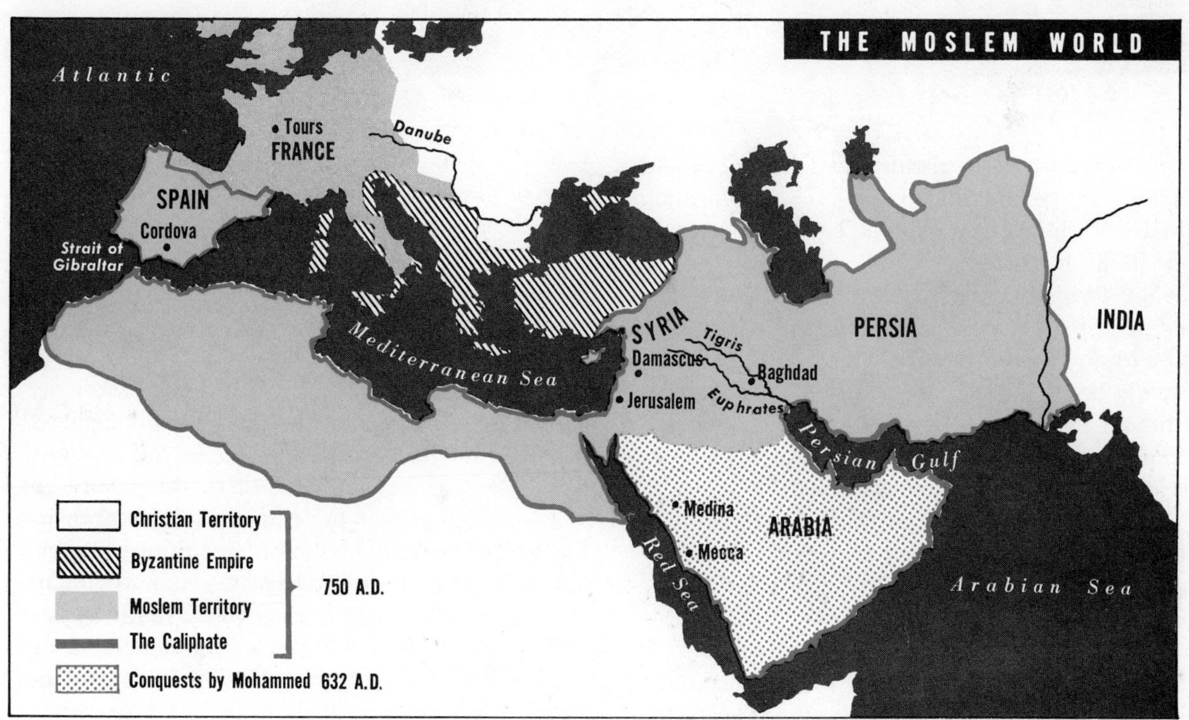

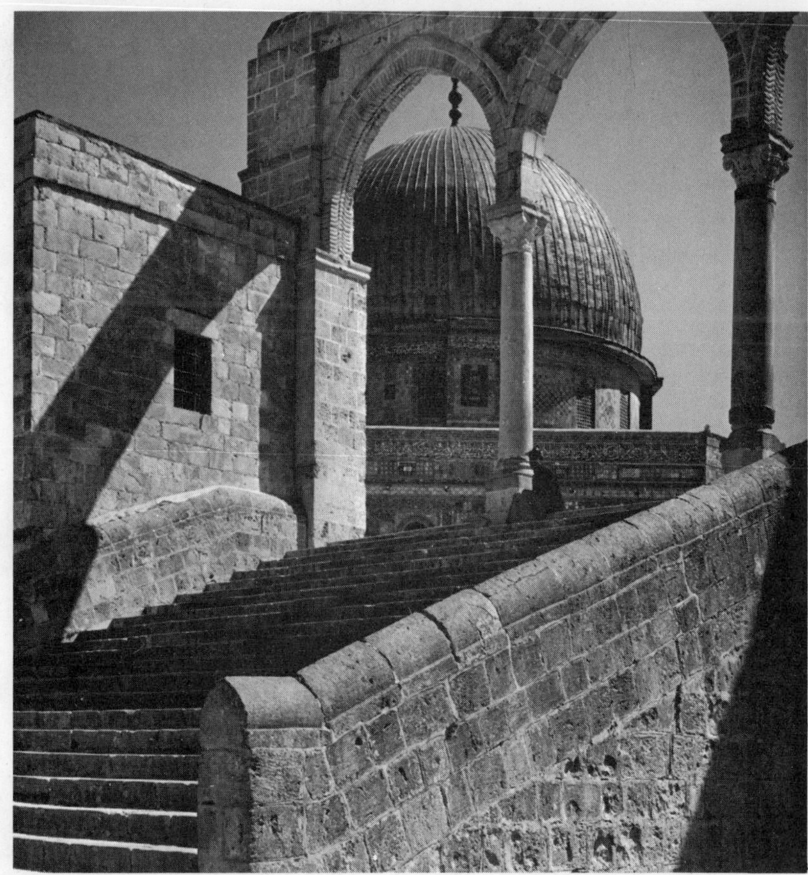

A MOSQUE. The Mosque of Omar, known as the Dome of the Rock, was completed in 691 and is the oldest Islamic building in Jerusalem. Covering the top of Mt. Moriah in the Jordanian sector of the city, it is revered as the site of Abraham's sacrifice and the journey of Mohammed into heaven.

"Victory or paradise is before you. The devil and hell-fire are behind you. Charge!" Arab armies, fired with enthusiasm and religious zeal, overcame one foe after another.

The peoples conquered by the Moslems were not required to adopt Islam, but most found it wise to do so. For one thing, non-Moslems were heavily taxed and were barred from holding government office. If a Jew or Christian wished to keep his religion, however, he was allowed to do so as long as he paid the necessary taxes.

Islam created a vast empire. By the end of the seventh century the Moslem world stretched from India to the Atlantic Ocean (see map on page 159). The Moslems of North Africa (who were called Moors) crossed the Straits of Gibraltar, conquered Spain and southern France, and threatened to overrun all of Europe. They were halted in 732 A.D. by the Frankish leader, Charles Martel, in a fierce battle near the French town of Tours. The Moors remained in Spain for the next eight centuries and developed one of the most brilliant civilizations in Europe. You will learn more about this Moorish civilization in the story of Spain.

Throughout the Middle East the Moslems adopted the customs of the more highly civilized peoples they had conquered, just as the Romans had done eight centuries earlier. Many of the Arabs moved out of their homes in the Arabian Desert and settled in the cities of the Mediterranean and the Fertile Crescent. About 670 A.D. they moved their capital from Mecca to the Syrian city of Damascus to bring it nearer the center of the empire. Later it was moved to Baghdad in Persia. The Arabs wisely kept the forms of government which their subjects had developed and generally treated the conquered peoples well.

The Moslem ruler was called a caliph (*kay*-lif), which means "successor to Mohammed." Like Mohammed, he was both the political and religious leader of the Moslems, and he held absolute power. You may have read *A Thousand and One Nights*, which paints a vivid picture of the Moslem world under one of the most famous of the caliphs, Harun al-Rashid (hah-*roon* al *rash*-id).

Moslem culture made important contributions to Western Europe. Moslem scholars absorbed much of the Greek culture that had been preserved in Egypt, Syria, and Persia. Later their translations of the Greek and Roman classics were widely used in Western Europe, as you will learn in the story of the Middle Ages. Moslem scientists went far beyond the Greeks in their development of laboratory techniques, especially in chemistry and medicine. They also advanced the study of mathematics and progressed so far in astronomy that they were able to use the stars to guide their caravans across the desert.

One of the greatest Moslem contributions to civilization was the introduction of Arabic numerals (such as 1, 2, and 3) to replace the clumsier Roman system (I, II, III). Probably the Moslems learned this method of writing numbers from the Hindus with whom they came in contact in India. It was the Moslems, however, who introduced the system to the Western world.

Moslem craftsmanship became famous throughout the Middle East and Europe. Moslem jewelry, glassware, and textiles were the finest of their day. Steel made in Damascus was in great demand for swords and armor. Mosques were noted for the beautiful glazed tiles with which they were decorated. The tiles were often painted with intricate geometric designs.

Damascus and Baghdad became great centers of trade. There, Moslem goods were exchanged for the silk and spices of the Far East. In Syria, southern Italy, and Spain, enterprising Moslem merchants sold these goods from the Far East to merchants from Western Europe. This trade brought the backward areas of the West into contact with Eastern culture.

THE KORAN. This page from the holy book of Islam is part of a fourteenth-century manuscript. The writing is Arabic.

Moslem influence remained strong even after the caliphs lost their power in the eleventh century. As you will see later in *Story of Nations*, Moslem rulers to this day continue to hold power in many areas of North Africa and the Middle East. In these areas, Islam still offers its followers a sense of unity and common destiny.

Chapter Check-up

1. Why were the Arabs almost completely untouched by the civilizations of the Fertile Crescent?
2. What are the followers of Islam called?
3. Who was the prophet of the Moslems?
4. Why did Mecca become the Holy City of the followers of Islam?
5. What is the Koran?
6. According to Allah's laws expressed in the Koran, what five things are required of every Moslem?
7. How do we account for the rapid spread of Islam?
8. What contributions have the Moslems made to the Western world?
9. How did the Moslems help to bring the West into contact with the East?
10. In what areas do Moslem rulers still hold power today?

Religion: SYNOPSIS

Judaism, Christianity, and Islam have many characteristics in common. Their most important similarity is a belief in one god. All three also emphasize ethical behavior as a means of pleasing God. They believe God will judge a man's actions and reward him accordingly, whether they visualize the reward as the Jewish Kingdom of God on earth, the Christian heaven, or the Moslem paradise. In addition, they share respect for the prophets of the Old Testament. Judaism, the oldest of the three faiths, introduced these beliefs, but Christianity and Islam have absorbed them and spread them over vast areas of the world. Their impact has been especially strong in the West and the Middle East, where there were no other great religions to rival them.

In spite of their outward similarities, each religion is distinctive. Jews take great pride in the belief that they are a chosen people who enjoy God's special favor. Their history, from the appearance of the first tribes in Canaan, contains many examples of God's watchful care for them. The idea that they are a chosen people largely explains why the Jews, unlike Christians and Moslems, do not try to convert others. The Jews feel strongly that their most important mission is to preserve and pass on to their children the precious faith they inherited from their fathers, in spite of persecution. Their great importance as a people has arisen from their religious ideas.

Many of the religious ideas of the Jews form the foundation of Christianity. Christians accept the basic principles of the Old Testament, including the teachings of the great Hebrew prophets. They believe, however, that the ideas of the Old Testament find their fullest expression in the life and teachings of Jesus. In the Christian view, Jesus was sent to earth by God to save men from sin and to allow them to share in eternal life. Because Christians believe that Jesus was divine, they call him Christ, which means "the Messiah."

Christianity began almost two thousand years ago as the faith of a small group of Jews. The Romans tolerated the new religion until the rapid growth and unity of Christian communities seemed to challenge the authority of the state. A period of suppression and persecution followed. Early in the fourth century A.D., under the Roman emperor Constantine, Christianity was finally given full equality with all other faiths in the Roman Empire. From its modest beginnings, Christianity spread widely among other peoples, until today one out of every three persons in the world is a Christian. For nearly a thousand years after the fall of Rome, the Christian Church dominated life in the Western world.

The Moslems, too, inherited many of their religious ideas from the Jews. These ideas were developed and modified by their great prophet, Mohammed. Moslems believed it was the will of Allah that Mohammed's teachings be spread as widely as possible, a mission that they carried out with great enthusiasm. The vast empire which they created lasted until the nineteenth century. Today Moslem demand for political power is an important factor in international relations. Along with their political empire, the Moslems also developed an outstanding culture. Moslem scholars preserved many aspects of Greek learning for the Western world. They also made important achievements in the fields of science and mathematics.

Important People

How has each of the following influenced the story of religion?

Moses	Constantine	Gregory the Great	Harun al-Rashid
Jesus	St. Augustine	Mohammed	Charles Martel
Paul	Peter	Micah	Isaiah

Terms

Be sure that you understand clearly the meaning of each of the following:

Allah	Hegira	Moors
apostles	heresy	Petrine Theory
caliph	Islam	Pope
Council of Nicaea	Koran	religion
Dead Sea scrolls	Messiah	sacraments
Golden Rule	monotheism	Ten Commandments

Questions for Discussion and Review

1. Why is the Old Testament important to Hebrews? Christians? Moslems?
2. Why have religions had such a great influence on the history of nations?
3. What are some of the ways in which religion influences our thought and action today?
4. In your opinion, what has been the outstanding contribution of the Hebrews?
5. Would the Jews of today best be characterized as a nation, a race, or a religion? Explain your answer.
6. Why is the Moslem world vitally important in world affairs today?
7. In what ways are the Moslem, Jewish, and Christian faiths similar? In what ways do they differ?
8. Trace the geographic steps by which Christianity traveled from the Middle East to the New World.
9. What is the close connection between Judaism and Christianity?
10. Why are the Dead Sea scrolls important?

Interesting Things to Do

1. On an outline map of the world use colors to show the geographic regions in which the various religions predominate.
2. Make a summary chart of the religions which arose in the Middle East. Head your columns as follows: (a) Country of Origin, (b) Countries or Areas Where It Is Now Prevalent, (c) Founder or Leader, (d) Basic Teachings or Beliefs.
3. Construct a circular "pie" chart showing how the world's population is divided among the various religions. Use an almanac or an encyclopedia as your reference source.
4. Imagine that you are taking a trip to the

Holy Land. Tell the class about the different places you are planning to visit and why each is important in the history of religion.

5. Make a poster which could be used to teach people to respect different religions.
6. Recount to the class one of the parables of Jesus and explain its meaning.
7. The Ten Commandments are the basis of many of our laws and social customs today. Make a copy of them for your notebook.
8. Prepare a report on the Dead Sea scrolls. Describe their importance.
9. Write a letter, story, poem, or play which deals with an incident in the life of one of the leaders of the great religions.
10. Add to or begin your "Who's Who in World History" series by writing one or more brief biographies of important leaders in the history of religion.
11. In many large cities of our nation there are local chapters of the National Conference of Christians and Jews. If there is such an organization in your community, see if it can provide speakers or films for your class.

Interesting Reading about Religion

*Bainton, Roland H., *Church of Our Fathers*, Scribner. A vivid history of Christianity.

*Browne, Lewis, *This Believing World*, Macmillan.

Burrows, Millar, *Founders of Great Religions*, Scribner.

Case, Shirley J., *Makers of Christianity*, Holt, Rinehart and Winston.

Cranston, Ruth, *World Faith*, Harper & Row.

Daniel-Rops, Henry, *The Book of Books*, Kenedy. Story of the Old Testament.

Douglas, Lloyd C., *The Robe*, Houghton Mifflin. Novel about Jesus.

Fitch, Florence M., *Allah, The God of Islam*, Lothrop, Lee & Shepard.

———, *One God; The Ways We Worship Him*, Lothrop, Lee & Shepard.

Forman, Henry James, *Truth is One*, Harper & Row. Brief, clear accounts of the world's great religions.

*Gaer, Joseph, *How the Great Religions Began*, Dodd, Mead. Ten world religions.

Hitti, Philip K., *The Arabs: A Short History*, Regnery.

Lang, Andrew, ed., *Arabian Nights*, Longmans Green. This classic gives us the flavor of the Islamic world.

Life, *The World's Great Religions*, Simon and Schuster.

Oursler, Fulton, *Greatest Story Ever Told*, Doubleday.

Sienkiewicz, Henry K., *Quo Vadis*, Little, Brown. Exciting novel of early Christians in ancient Rome.

* Indicates easy reading

In a world of unusual terrors, medieval man still found time for the pleasures of life as this tapestry from the Loire Valley, France indicates.

Part 7
THE MIDDLE AGES

AN AGE OF FAITH

MEDIEVAL EUROPE

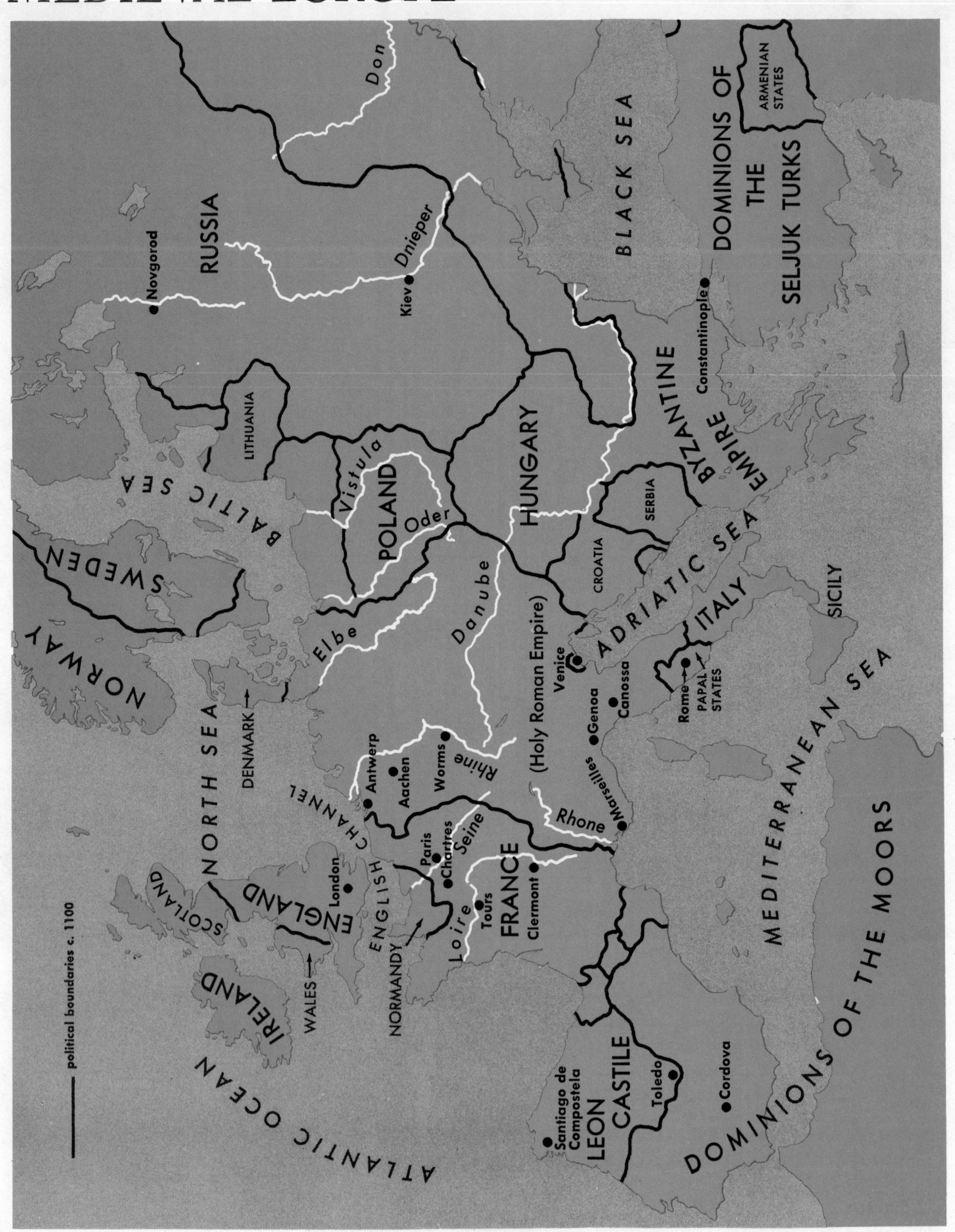

political boundaries c. 1100
RUSSIA
Novgorod
Kiev
Dnieper
Don
BLACK SEA
ARMENIAN STATES
DOMINIONS OF THE SELJUK TURKS
Constantinople
BYZANTINE EMPIRE
LITHUANIA
POLAND
Vistula
Oder
HUNGARY
SERBIA
CROATIA
ADRIATIC SEA
ITALY
SICILY
Rome
PAPAL STATES
Venice
Genoa
Canossa
Danube
Elbe
(Holy Roman Empire)
Rhine
Worms
Aachen
Antwerp
Marseilles
Rhone
BALTIC SEA
SWEDEN
NORWAY
DENMARK
NORTH SEA
ENGLISH CHANNEL
SCOTLAND
ENGLAND
London
IRELAND
WALES
NORMANDY
Paris
Chartres
Seine
Loire
Tours
FRANCE
Clermont
MEDITERRANEAN SEA
ATLANTIC OCEAN
Santiago de Compostela
LEON
CASTILE
Toledo
Cordova
DOMINIONS OF THE MOORS

The Middle Ages: GEOGRAPHIC SETTING

Beginning with the river valley civilizations of the ancient Middle East, our focus has gradually shifted west to Greece and Rome, and now in Part 7 it centers on Western Europe in the Middle Ages, the period between ancient and modern times.

A broad, fertile plain sweeps across what is today northern France, Belgium, the Netherlands, and northern Germany. This land was even more fertile in the centuries after the fall of Rome than it is now, because it was then cleared and plowed for the first time. Its crops supported a growing population; thick forests provided fuel and building material. The climate was invigorating, with cool summers and only moderately cold winters.

Western Europe is blessed with many rivers connecting the interior with the coast. These rivers became the highways of Western Europe after the Roman roads fell into disrepair. The Rhone (rone) flows south from the highlands of central France into the Mediterranean. The Loire (lwar) follows a westerly course to the Atlantic, and the Seine (sayn) flows north to the English Channel. The Rhine begins in the Alps and follows a wandering northerly course to the North Sea. From the mouths of the Seine and the Rhine it is only a short voyage to England.

The map on the opposite page shows Europe as it looked at the beginning of the twelfth century. You must remember, however, that unified nations as we know them now did not then exist. The basic unit of government and the center of medieval life was the local village manor.

For a short time the Holy Roman Empire restored order to much of Western Europe and gave it a unified government. But throughout most of the Middle Ages the Empire existed in name only. In Eastern Europe the dominant force was the Byzantine Empire, whose capital was at Constantinople.

The Middle Ages: PERSPECTIVE

It was dangerous to venture into the dense wood around the town of Gubbio, and any citizen who went forth to hunt did so at his peril. For in the wood lived a wolf of great size and ferocity. Unsatisfied by a meal of small game, the huge beast had set upon and devoured many a luckless inhabitant of Gubbio.

One day in the early thirteenth century, the people of Gubbio heard that St. Francis of Assissi was approaching their town. They hastened to warn the beloved saint not to pass by the wood, saying that the wolf would surely devour him as it had so many others. But St. Francis, a gentle, barefoot man who wore a simple brown robe, ignored their warnings and went in search of the wolf. When he encountered the animal, it rushed toward him with bared fangs. But the saint, making the sign of the Cross, said to the wolf, "Come to me, Brother Wolf. In the name of Christ, I order you not to hurt me or anyone." The wolf lay down like a lamb at the feet of Francis, placed its paw in the saint's hand, and after that lived in peace and friendship among the inhabitants of Gubbio.

In the twentieth century this story sounds, to say the least, like a highly improbable tale; but to our predecessors seven hundred years ago it had the unmistakable ring of truth. For St. Francis lived in an age of profound religious faith, characterized by the unquestioned acceptance of wondrous acts and miracles. In Part 7 you will read about that age, which is called the *medieval*, or middle period, of history

because it seems to modern historians to mark a halfway point in the study of Western man's development. Chronologically, the Middle Ages comprise the thousand years between the collapse of the Roman Empire and the beginning of modern history. The story of those years opens on a desolate European landscape scarred by the ravages of the barbarian tribes; it ends, as you will see, on a scene of prosperous towns, magnificent cathedrals, and thriving universities.

CHAPTER 21

The Church Provided a Foundation for Medieval Life

RELIGION ANSWERED THE NEEDS OF MEDIEVAL MAN

The fall of Rome created serious problems. With the decline of Roman power in the fifth century, Western Europe was divided among the Germanic peoples who had settled down in former Roman provinces. Germanic kingdoms were set up in Gaul (France), Spain, and Italy. The collapse of the old imperial civil service caused the cities of Europe to shrink in size. As urban markets disappeared, trade and commerce slowed down. No one kept up the roads or repaired the bridges. Bands of robbers often attacked travelers, and even a short journey became difficult and dangerous. Men lived in small farming villages or on landed estates called manors that supplied most of their needs.

The decline of Rome and the barbarian invasions created three basic problems for European man: 1) keeping his religious faith, 2) restoring law and order to society, and 3) making a living. To solve these problems men organized their lives around the Church, the custom or practice of Feudalism, and the self-sufficient method of farming known as the manorial system. In this part we shall examine all three of these social institutions, and show how they shaped Roman, Germanic, and Christian traditions into a new civilization. Historians have long referred to the years between the end of the classical world and the stirrings of the Renaissance roughly from 500 A.D. to 1500 A.D. as the Middle Ages. The civilization which developed during this period is known as *medieval* (med-ih-*ee*-v'l).

Medieval man lived to love and serve his God. Although medieval man found joy in the physical world, he was much more concerned with the spiritual one. His life was centered about religion and the belief that he was put on earth to please God and prepare for death. In the Middle Ages all art and learning had a religious purpose. Greek and Roman art, philosophy, and literature were often practical, or efforts to achieve beauty for their own sake. Medieval civilization grew out of a desire to glorify God.

Medieval men did not think of themselves as Frenchmen, Greeks, Germans, or Egyptians, as men do today, but saw themselves as Catholic Christians, Orthodox Eastern Christians, or Moslems. These three religions, rather than political loyalty, united each of the three civilizations that replaced the single civilization of Rome. The Roman Catholic Church gave Western Europe a common set of beliefs. Learned men in Spain or Germany understood one another because they wrote and spoke Latin, the language of the Church.

The Orthodox Eastern Church and the Greek language united the Byzantine Empire. Islam was the common faith of the Moslem world. Moslems from Spain and Moslems from Persia both spoke Arabic, the language of the Koran.

At the beginning of the Middle Ages there was little exchange of ideas between the peoples of these three civilizations. Christians who were intensely devoted to their faith feared and hated the Moslems. The Moslems for much the same reasons had little regard for the Christians.

You will recall that even Christians themselves had become divided. Differences between the Roman Catholic Church and the Orthodox Eastern Church caused doubts and suspicions which gradually widened the breach between them. Furthermore, the very languages (Latin, Arabic, and Greek) that helped to unite men within each civilization made it difficult for the people of one civilization to understand the others. We shall now study more closely the Catholic Christian civilization that developed in Western Europe.

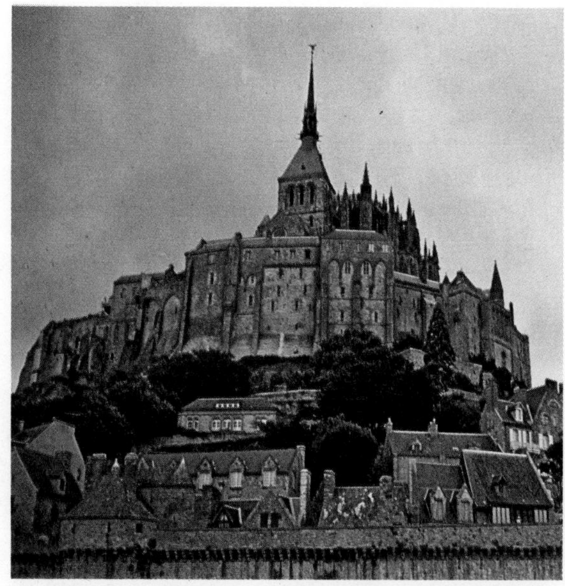

MONT ST. MICHEL. This famous abbey off the coast of Brittany in France was founded in 708 by a bishop who, according to legend, built it after receiving instructions from the Archangel Michael. It is a monument to the spirit of the Middle Ages.

The Church dominated medieval life. The Roman Catholic Church had great power over medieval man. One reason was medieval man's belief that only by taking the sacraments of the Church could he attain salvation (see page 151). Another reason was that the fall of Rome had left the Church as the only source of authority in Western Europe. Thus bishops and priests provided not only moral guidance but also practical leadership, often replacing the Roman authorities in the towns. The Church fed the poor, cared for the sick, and protected those who were trying to escape their enemies. The bishops formulated a system of church law and established church courts which dealt with any case involving the clergy, orphans, widows, or persons charged with breach of promise. Because no one else performed these services, men tended to look to the Church for order, authority, and aid.

The Church also controlled education. The first schools were established in monasteries and later in connection with the bishops' churches (cathedrals). Because no other schools existed, anyone who wished to learn went to a Church school or was taught by a parish priest. For centuries, most educated men in Europe were churchmen. Therefore, the new ideas that men developed were largely those that were approved and taught by the Church.

Another fact that explains the dominant position of the Church was that it acquired nearly a third of the land in Western Europe. You will read in the next chapter how the Church received such land in the form of gifts from devout Christians. This ownership of land made it necessary for the Church to take an active part in the politics and wars of medieval Europe.

These four factors, 1) belief that salvation depended on the sacraments, 2) a strong organization in time of need, 3) control of education, and 4) control of land, made it possible for the Church to unify Western Europe and provide the foundation for medieval civilization.

Monasteries offered men a chance to devote their lives to God. The bishops and priests who ministered directly to the people were called the *secular clergy,* from the Latin word *saecularis,* meaning "of the world." Another branch of the clergy, considered even more devout, withdrew from the world to monasteries to lead lives of prayer and self-discipline. These churchmen, whose lives were governed by strict rules, were called the *regular clergy,* from *regularis,* the Latin word for "ruled." A member of the regular clergy was known as a *monk,* from a Greek word meaning "alone." As we shall see, the monks became very important members of medieval society. Women who wished to devote their lives to the service of God entered convents and became *nuns.*

Monasteries first appeared in Egypt and Syria in the very early days of Christianity. By 500 A.D. many monasteries had been established in Western Europe. One Italian monk, St. Benedict, realized that even very devout men who lived in groups needed organization and rules. In 519 he founded a monastery at Monte Cassino (*mahn*-teh kah-*see*-no), in Italy, and drew up a code of regulations for the conduct of monks. The Benedictine Rule soon became accepted as the model for all the other monasteries of the Middle Ages.

Under the Benedictine Rule, a monk took a threefold vow of poverty, chastity, and obedience. The vow of poverty meant he could own nothing, not even the rough black or gray robe which he wore. If a prospective monk were wealthy, he had first to give away all that he owned. In the vow of chastity the monk promised never to marry, and in the vow of obedience he solemnly pledged to obey the head of the monastery, the abbot.

By serving God, monks served their fellow men. Monks served God with their hands as well as with their prayers. The Benedictine Rule required that they spend part of each day doing manual labor. Their motto was "To work is to pray." The monks cleared and plowed the land of the monastery with enthusiasm because they believed that their work honored God. Their success in draining marshes, using fertilizer, and breeding cattle, was a practical example to the neighboring landowners. Thus the monks' hard work benefited not only the monasteries, but influenced the development of agriculture all over Europe.

The monks performed another valuable service by preserving much of the learning of the past. During the troubled times of the Germanic invasions, few men had either the leisure or the desire to study. Many Roman manuscripts were lost or destroyed because few men could read them or cared about them. Gradually the learning of the ancient world was discarded or forgotten. Because the world between 500 A.D. and 900 A.D. nearly lost the great contributions of the Greeks and the Romans, these first centuries of the Middle Ages are sometimes called the *Dark Ages.*

Because printing presses and paper had not yet

A MONASTIC CELLARER. The monk who had charge of the monastery's storerooms was called the cellarer. In this illumination from a fourteenth-century manuscript, a cellarer samples the wine while he fills his pitcher.

A MONK AT WORK. With ink pots and paint bottles at hand, a medieval monk copies a manuscript. In their monasteries, monks preserved the learning of the ancient world after the fall of Rome.

been invented, books were written by hand on specially prepared animal skins called parchment. Only the monks had the time, training, and patience to produce these early books. They were interested in making each copy as fine as possible, not in turning out great numbers of copies, so they illuminated their work by painting tiny pictures and elaborate scarlet and gold decorations around the most important capital letters on a page. Most of the books were Bibles, prayer books, or hymnals; but the monks also copied a few classical authors and recorded the events of the day. Historians have learned much medieval history from these chronicles. Without the devoted labor of the monks, much of modern man's knowledge of both the ancient world and the Middle Ages would be lost.

The monks performed many other services such as conducting schools, caring for the sick and the poor, and receiving travelers. These services were especially important in a period when there were no schools, hospitals, or inns. As you can see, monasteries contributed greatly to medieval life and to our knowledge of the Middle Ages.

THE CHURCH CO-OPERATED WITH THE GOVERNMENT

The Church was chiefly concerned with timeless, spiritual things, but gradually it became involved with rulers and governments. Sometimes the Church, or the *spiritual power*, came into conflict with the government, or *temporal power* (from *temporalis*, the Latin word for "of time"). Sometimes the Church and government worked closely together. Early Christian leaders, like Augustine (see page 154), tended to ignore the temporal world because they considered the world of the spirit more important. But, as we have seen, the Church took over many of the duties of government when the Roman Empire declined. In the years between 500 A.D. and 900 A.D. the Church and the rulers of the Germanic tribes found that each could do better with the other's help. The Church and the rulers of one tribe in particular, the Franks, co-operated closely.

The Church helped the Franks build a strong kingdom. Although most of the Germanic tribes had been converted to Christianity, Church leaders in Western Europe did not think that the Germans held orthodox, or correct, beliefs. The Franks were one of the few orthodox Catholic tribes. Their leader, Clovis, believed that Christ had helped him to win an important battle. In gratitude, Clovis ordered all his people to be converted to the Catholic faith in 496. He frequently used his new faith as an excuse for conquering the other Germanic tribes and making them Catholic. Later leaders of the Franks continued Clovis' policy of alliance with the Church. You may remember that one of these Frankish leaders, Charles Martel, turned back the Moslems at the Battle of Tours in 732. After his death, his son, Pepin, declared himself king of the Franks with the support of the Pope. In return he successfully defended Rome against the invading Lombards. By 750, the Franks had the largest and strongest kingdom in Western Europe. The Frankish kingdom was brought to the height of its power by Pepin's son, Charlemagne (*shar*-leh-mayn), or Charles the Great.

Charlemagne increased Frankish power and spread Christianity. Charlemagne, a bold warrior, great leader, and devoted Christian, became king of the Franks in 768. For the forty-five years of his reign, he worked tirelessly to give his subjects good government and to make them loyal Christians.

Charlemagne. The great emperor holds the symbols of his kingship over Europe and his association with the Church. This interpretive portrait was painted about 1512 by the famous German artist Albrecht Dürer.

Charlemagne spent much of his life at war. The famous epic poem, *The Song of Roland*, tells how this great king and his nephew, Roland, valiantly tried to keep the Moors in Spain from invading Frankish territory. Charlemagne also waged war against the heathen Saxons who lived in the northern part of Germany. He tried for over thirty years to convert them to Christianity. He also fought against the Lombards who, although Christians themselves, continued their efforts to capture Rome. Charlemagne eventually conquered the Lombards and gave a large strip of their land in central Italy to the Pope. This section of Italy became known as the Papal States. Charlemagne built a great empire in Western Europe (see the map on page 174). By skillful management, he restored law and order to his domain and, for a time, brought an end to the dark days that followed the decline of Rome.

Charlemagne governed his people by issuing decrees based on reports made to him by bishops and counts (royal officials). His reliance on bishops in formulating decrees showed how much Charlemagne depended upon the Church. He consulted the Pope whenever questions arose about the orthodoxy of any religious belief. In turn, Charlemagne supported the Church by insisting that the clergy lead moral lives and that all men obey the Pope in matters of faith.

Learning, like government and religion, was a major concern of Charlemagne. In the eighth and ninth centuries, when few men could read, priests often knew barely enough Latin to stumble through the church services. Charlemagne realized that these clergymen needed to be educated in order to study Christian writings and to teach. He started schools in many churches, and he invited scholars from all over Europe to his palace

CHARLEMAGNE'S SCHOOL. The emperor frequently entered the schoolroom unexpectedly and questioned the students to see whether they had learned their lessons.

school at Aachen (*ah*-ken). The English churchman Alcuin (*al*-koo-in), the most scholarly man of his time, came at the Frankish king's request to take charge of the new schools. Charlemagne himself studied rhetoric, astronomy, and Latin under Alcuin. The scholars whom Charlemagne had brought together made copies of all the available Latin writings of the past. These men made few new contributions to learning, but without their efforts and those of the later monks, the Western world would have few of the Latin classics that exist today.

Charlemagne's coronation symbolized the unity of his people and the co-operation of Church and State. There had been no emperor in Western Europe since 476. Then on Christmas Day of the year 800, as Charlemagne knelt in prayer, the Pope solemnly placed a crown on the king's head and proclaimed him Roman emperor in the West. This coronation signified the Pope's approval of the empire Charlemagne had built and of his worthiness to rule it.

In one sense this crown symbolized the unity that Charlemagne had achieved by combining the Germanic and the Roman traditions. The fierce Germanic invaders had become so civilized and Christianized that many of Charlemagne's scholars were of Germanic descent. Romans and Germans were brought together by their common loyalty to a ruler whom they considered the successor of the Roman emperors and by their devotion to the Catholic Church. For a brief period, Western Europeans had become one people in religious faith and government.

Charlemagne's coronation also marks the height of co-operation between the spiritual and temporal powers of Europe. By defeating the Lombards, Charlemagne had helped the Pope keep his position in Rome; the Pope in return gave Church approval to Charlemagne's political power. Ironically, Charlemagne's empire later caused serious conflict between Church and State.

Chapter Check-up

1. In what ways did geography encourage the development of medieval civilization in Western Europe?
2. What happened to civilization in Western Europe after the Roman Empire collapsed?
3. What are the approximate dates of the Middle Ages?
4. What three religious civilizations replaced the single civilization of Rome?
5. In what ways did the Church dominate medieval life?
6. What four factors helped the Church to control and to unify Western Europe?
7. Why are the first few centuries of the medieval period often called the Dark Ages?
8. In what ways did the monks of the Middle Ages contribute to medieval civilization?
9. In what ways did the leadership of Charlemagne benefit Western Europe?

CHAPTER 22

Feudalism and the Manorial System Divided Europe into Two Great Classes

VIOLENCE AND CONFUSION RAGED THROUGH WESTERN EUROPE IN THE NINTH CENTURY

Charlemagne's empire collapsed. As we have seen, Charlemagne gave Western Europe more peace and order than had existed since the decline of Rome. Unfortunately, the order depended on Charlemagne's personal ability to command his subjects' loyalty. After his death in 814, his empire began to fall apart. Officials of the royal court and great landowners took advantage of Charlemagne's less able successors to break away from their control. Charlemagne's heirs could neither buy back the loyalty of the nobility nor enforce it with a paid army, because the empire had so little trade for the government to tax. Another important reason for the destruction of the empire is that shortly after Charlemagne died new waves of invaders attacked Western Europe.

Thus a combination of weakness and war destroyed Charlemagne's empire, just as it had destroyed the Roman Empire. To make matters worse, Charlemagne's sons and grandsons fought among themselves for control of the empire. Finally in 843, by the Treaty of Verdun (ver-*dun*), they divided the empire into three parts. The western part, named after the Franks, became France. The eastern part eventually became Germany. The middle strip, Lotharingia (lo-thuh-*rin*-jee-uh), ran from northern Italy to the North Sea and included present-day Alsace-Lorraine. The rivalry of later rulers of France and Germany for control of this area has caused many wars.

Three waves of invaders threatened to destroy civilization in Europe. The invaders who contributed to the collapse of Charlemagne's empire made the ninth century a period of horror and destruction. They attacked Europe on every side except the west, where the Atlantic afforded

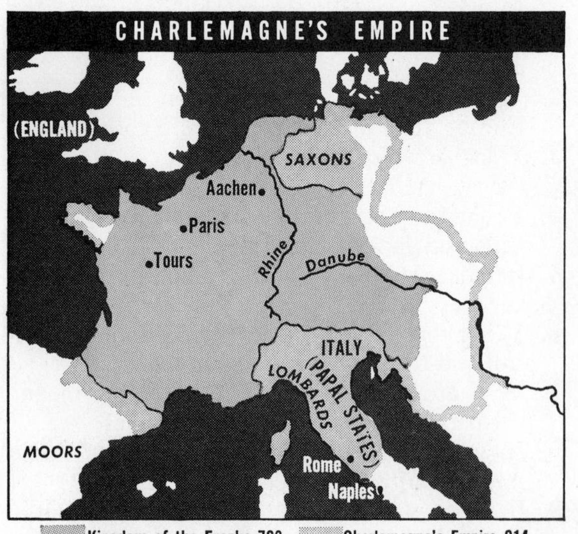

protection. Europe was just beginning to recover from the Moslem invasions when the Magyars (*mag*-yars), wild tribes of horsemen from Asia, moved into what is today Hungary and ravaged Europe from the east.

Most feared of all were the invaders who sailed down from Scandinavia in the north to raid the coasts of England and France. These fierce warriors were known variously as Norsemen, Vikings, or Danes. They anchored at islands in the mouths of the chief rivers, from which they made lightning raids on inland settlements and then escaped quickly by sea. They stole everything they could carry off and destroyed the rest. Eventually, in many parts of Europe, the Norsemen settled down and took possession of the land itself.

Even if Charlemagne's successors had not been busy fighting one another, they could not have protected their people against the invaders. The king's armies of foot soldiers, hastily called together from the fields, made slow progress over the bad roads. Usually by the time they arrived at the scene of a Viking raid, the settlement would be in smoking ruins and the raiders gone. During the ninth century, Western Europe was subjected to the same kind of ruinous warfare that had desolated Rome four centuries earlier.

A VIKING ATTACK. In one of their lightning raids, the fierce Norsemen surprise the guards of a medieval castle.

FEUDALISM BROUGHT ORDER TO MEDIEVAL SOCIETY

Vassals exchanged loyalty and military service for protection. During the early Middle Ages, when no central government existed to provide police protection for the individual, able men who owned horses and armor offered their services to the nearest large landowner. In doing so, they followed the example of earlier German tribesmen who had offered their skills and loyalty to their chieftains. Since the landowner needed help to defend his land from attack, he welcomed such men and made them his soldiers, or *knights*. In exchange for their military service he gave them protection and, at first, food and clothing. Later, as money became scarce and it became inconvenient to feed a great many men, he gave them land in exchange for their services.

Only the large landowners, however, could afford to maintain a body of hired knights. Small landowners continued to live in fear that their land would be seized and their families carried off into slavery. For this reason, they sought the protection of the nearest powerful lord and his band of knights. Gradually the wealthy lords came to an agreement with the small landowners. In exchange for the protection of the great lord, the small landowner turned over to him his land and often also agreed to do military service for him as a knight. The lord then allowed his new knight to use the land that he had once owned. The knight who held land under such an arrangement was called a *vassal* and the land which he was allowed to use was called a *fief*. Over the years it became the custom for the vassal's son and grandson to serve the lord and hold the land under the terms of the original agreement. Thus the bargain became hereditary, or binding on succeeding generations, and the vassal gradually came to look upon the land as his own.

The feudal contract was an honorable one. The ceremony of becoming a vassal was solemn and impressive. Kneeling and placing his hands between those of his lord, the vassal promised to be the lord's man and to defend him against all dangers. The lord then kissed the man and accepted him as a vassal. This part of the ceremony was called *homage* from the French word *homme*, "man." Then the vassal swore an oath of loyalty, or *fealty*, after which the lord gave his vassal a branch or lump of earth to symbolize his fief. This part of the ceremony was called *investiture*. This relationship was a personal agreement between the lord and vassal in which loyalty and military service were exchanged for protection. A vassal usually received a *feudum*, the Latin term for a fief, which gave the agreement, called *feudalism*, its name. But the fief was not always a part of the feudal bargain. The only necessary element was military service, which was promised in the act of homage. For this reason *feudalism* is strictly defined as an honorable military relationship between two men of noble birth.

Vassals had special duties. Every vassal owed his lord military service, usually forty days each year. In the absence of strong central government, each lord ruled his domain with the assistance of his vassals, who gathered at his castle several times each year to advise him and to help him decide cases in his court. Because a lord's army was made up of his vassals, he found it unwise to make decisions without their advice and consent. Thus, in the feudal system, the vassals acted as a check on the lord's power.

Swearing Fealty. A lord takes his vassal's hands between his own as the two men enter into a sacred agreement. This practice is the origin of the modern custom of shaking hands to seal a bargain.

Vassals did not pay rent for their land, but they had to make certain other payments. The vassals were required to pay the ceremonial costs for the knighting of the lord's eldest son and for the marriage of his eldest daughter, and the lord's ransom if he were captured by an enemy. A vassal's son also gave the lord a sum of money or a gift in exchange for the privilege of inheriting his father's fief. Vassals were expected to entertain the lord at their castles once each year. Such a duty was no small responsibility, because often as many as a hundred people had to be fed and housed for days or even weeks. If the vassal failed in his obligations, the lord could take back his fief. On the other hand, if the lord angered his vassals, they could refuse to fight for him, or they might even rise against him. Thus, it was to the advantage of each party to keep his share of the feudal bargain.

Feudalism hindered the growth of central government. Feudalism brought order and stability to medieval society. As a system of government, however, it often proved unwieldy, and hindered the development of modern nations.

With the decline of Rome, more and more land had fallen into the hands of lords, who, in times of great danger, turned for protection to more powerful lords and became their vassals. When Charlemagne became king of the Franks, he saw an opportunity to make this lord-vassal relationship work to his advantage, and he proceeded to make all the great lords and counts his vassals. They then were expected to bring their own vassals to serve in his army. Eventually every landowner except the king became someone's vassal.

It would be a mistake, however, to conclude that feudalism was a simple pyramid of obligations with the king on top, for the king did not directly control every vassal in his kingdom. Each vassal continued to obey only the lord to whom he had personally sworn loyalty. Nor did he feel that he owed loyalty to the king simply because his lord did. This situation divided men's political loyalties in many directions. Feudalism thus tended to delay the building of strong, unified nations in Western Europe.

The confusion of political allegiances was a result of the fact that the feudal system grew "like Topsy." It sometimes involved extremely complex relationships. On the surface it appeared to

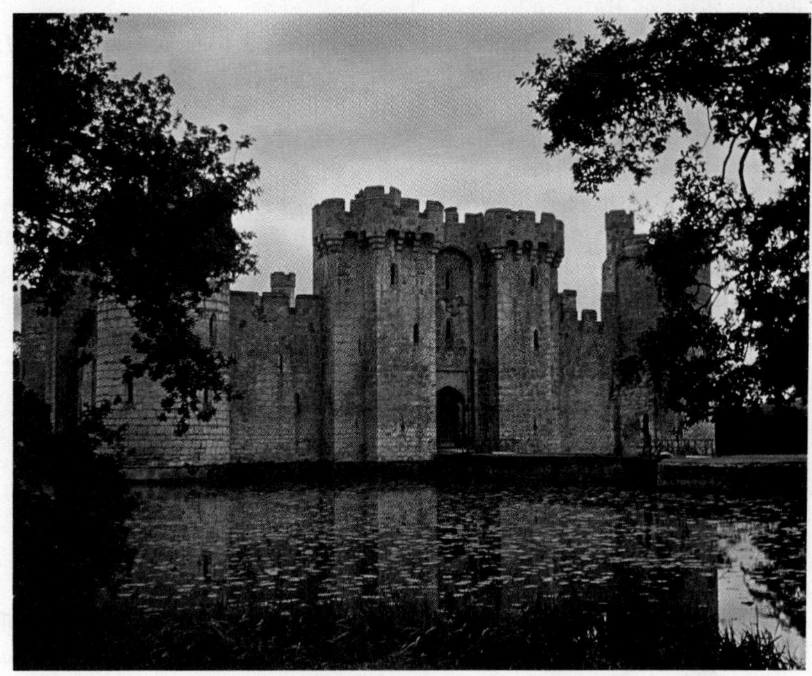

MEDIEVAL CASTLE. The medieval castle was both a fortress and a home for the lord and his household. This English castle of the later Middle Ages is surrounded by a moat. On all sides of its thick stone walls are the towers from which it was defended. In the earlier Middle Ages fortresses were often built partly or completely of heavy timber and were surrounded by dry ditches.

be a simple and honorable bargain between two men. In practice, however, many vassals owed loyalty to two, three, or more lords. The problem of divided loyalty arose if a knight inherited a second fief from a different lord. This awkward situation occurred, for example, when a knight received his wife's land as a dowry and became her father's vassal. If the knight's original lord should go to war with his father-in-law, which side would he take? He owed each man loyalty until death. Such occurrences made feudal society extremely complicated and difficult to regulate.

In spite of all its drawbacks, feudalism did restore to Europe a degree of order when society seemed headed for utter chaos. Feudal agreements linked a country's landholders and fighting men, and feudal armies were able ultimately to subdue the invading tribes. By the year 1000, the onslaught of the Magyars and the Moslems had been halted, and the fierce Norsemen had not only been contained but also converted to Christianity. Thus Western Europe settled down to several centuries of stability and order.

A castle was built for defense. The medieval nobility was made up of freeborn men who owned horses and armor and knew how to use them in battle. Frequently, a noble was the vassal of a great lord and, in turn, lord of his own vassals. Even if he had no vassals himself, he was considered the lord of his own fief; and, as we shall see, his way of life reflected the chief duty of the nobles in medieval society: waging war.

The typical lord lived in a castle and ruled his fief as if he were king. The castle was built to serve as a fort because the chief obligation of each lord was to protect his vassals and peasants. During the ninth and tenth centuries, a castle was usually a crude, wooden tower raised on a mound of earth and surrounded by a wooden wall. By the eleventh century, however, powerful lords were building the walls and central towers of stone, sometimes ten to fifteen feet thick, to withstand attack. The lord sought to build his castle in a place that would be very difficult for an enemy to attack. He might choose a rocky cliff, an island accessible only by a movable bridge, or high ground surrounded by a wide, deep ditch filled with water, called a *moat*. The water at the base of the castle wall prevented an enemy from scaling the wall and from tunneling his way beneath it.

The most important part of the castle was the central stone tower called the *keep*, which contained the living quarters of the lord and became his last stronghold in case of attack. A typical castle also included a guardroom, kitchens, storerooms, stables, and a chapel. These buildings were built around a large open courtyard where peasants from the village gathered during an enemy attack. They were careful to bring with them enough food and livestock to withstand a long siege. When the watchman atop the keep saw the enemy approaching, he rang the alarm bell. The drawbridge over the moat was raised and the heavy wooden doors were slammed shut. From the small towers that overhung the walls, bowmen shot at the more distant enemy, and other defenders prepared molten lead or boiling water to pour on the foe if he reached the castle wall.

Military necessity influenced the interior of the castle as well as the exterior. The thick stone walls made the rooms inside the castle cold, damp, and dark. The windows, designed to keep arrows out, were simply narrow slits in the wall. Most of the light came from huge fireplaces, which, until the chimney was developed in the twelfth century, not only filled the room with heat and light, but also frequently with clouds of smoke. Comfort was not the first consideration.

The main room of the castle was the great hall, where the lord held court. The great hall also served as the dining room and, in the early days at least, as the place where the inhabitants of the castle slept. Not until the thirteenth century did castles include separate withdrawing rooms and bedrooms. The cold stone floor of the great hall was covered with rushes, which served as a kind of carpeting. The walls were hung with beautiful tapestries woven by the ladies of the castle to provide color and to shut out drafts. Blazing torches cast flickering light over the shields and battle flags that hung from the ceiling and over the spears and suits of armor that were stacked in the corners of the great hall.

Religion was deeply ingrained in the medieval mind. This exquisite tapestry shows one of the Magi being directed to the Christ Child in Bethlehem by a guiding angel.

At mealtime, servants set up long tables by laying boards on trestles. Such a custom explains the origin of the word *board,* meaning food, as in "room and board." Forks, plates, and napkins were unknown. Slabs of stale bread, later replaced by wooden trenchers, served as plates. Even the lord ate with his fingers, wiping them on his clothes or on the fur of the dogs that scampered under, and sometimes over, the tables. There were often a dozen courses in a banquet, which could include soups, roasts, meat pies, sweet jellies, and spiced wines. After dinner, the lord's jester would amuse the company, or a band of dancers and acrobats would perform in payment for their meal. Occasionally a wandering minstrel would play the lute and sing songs of adventure and love.

Prospective knights were rigidly trained. A lord's household contained many people in addition to his own family. Often lords sent their sons to a neighboring castle to be educated, to keep their mothers from spoiling them at home. At the age of seven the young nobleman became a *page,* the first step in preparation for knighthood. As a page, he was taught riding, the care of arms and armor, and such virtues as humility and courtesy. At the age of fourteen or fifteen he became a *squire* and entered the second stage of his training. He learned to fight on horseback and to use the heavy weapons of a knight, such as the lance, battle axe, sword, and mace. Each squire served a knight, and it was part of a squire's duty to accompany his knight to the battlefield and to rescue him if he fell in combat.

At twenty or twenty-one a squire was ready to take his place in society as a knight. The ceremony of knighthood was one of solemn dignity. On the evening before the great event, the young squire was given a ceremonial bath of purification. Afterward, he was dressed in special garments that symbolized his new duties. Then he prayed all night in the chapel of the castle. The following morning, friends helped him put on his armor. In the presence of the assembled knights and ladies, he knelt before his lord or his father. The lord gave the young man a hard blow on the shoulder with the flat of his sword. This part of the ceremony was known as the *accolade* (ak-oh-*layd*) and was intended to remind the young man of a knight's heavy duties. As he delivered the accolade, the lord said, "In the name of God and St. Michael and St. George, I dub thee knight. Be brave and loyal."

A true knight was expected not only to be a valiant warrior, but also to fulfill the knightly ideal of *chivalry* (from the French word *chevalier*, meaning "a man who rides horseback"). The code of chivalry, which required a knight to be truthful, kind, devout, and courteous to noblemen and women, did much to soften and refine the rough medieval warrior.

A knight's chief occupation was war. A knight spent most of his time fighting or preparing to fight. Castles were equipped with exercise grounds where a knight could practice such skills as knocking an enemy off his horse and fighting on foot with swords. It required a great deal of skill to manage a horse, armor, heavy weapons, and a shield all at once. A mistake could mean disgrace, a wound, or even death.

During the early Middle Ages, a knight's armor was simply a shirt made of intertwined metal rings called chain mail. Over his metal shirt he wore a long woolen or velvet tunic. Gauntlets, heavy leather gloves with metal rings on the backs, protected his hands. His head was protected by an iron helmet with a movable visor, which a knight could lift when he wished to be recognized. The lifting of the visor is the origin of the modern custom of tipping one's hat. In the late Middle Ages, when metal workers became more skilled, armor was improved. A suit of jointed steel plate was devised to go over the chain mail; it provided far better protection than chain mail alone. These suits were so heavy that the knight had to be hoisted onto his horse with ropes and pulleys. Because armor often made it impossible to tell friend from foe, knights began to have figures such as lions, eagles, or lilies painted on their shields in order to identify themselves. These coats of arms became identified with the fame and honor of the knight's family and were handed down from father to son for generations.

By the twelfth century, strong lords and kings had enforced order in Europe to the point that life became dull for war-loving knights. To avoid boredom and to maintain their military prowess, they held mock battles. A battle between two individual knights was called a *joust*, whereas in a *tournament*, two teams of knights fought. If a lord announced that he planned to hold a tournament, perhaps in honor of the knighting of his son, the news spread quickly. Great crowds gathered for the event. Trumpets blew, and heralds cried "Come forth, knights, come forth." Then the knights, fully armed and mounted, lined up, with the colored gloves and scarves of their ladies fluttering brightly from their lances and helmets. At the signal they dashed upon the field. Victory went to the knights who successfully unhorsed their opponents. Defeated knights sometimes lost their horses and armor to the victors. Tour-

RECEIVING THE ACCOLADE. Striking his squire with a sword, the lord turns him into a knight. Englishmen are still knighted in much the same way.

naments were very popular among the feudal nobility. Although they were usually fought with blunted weapons, and both horses and men were well padded, lives were sometimes lost

A medieval noblewoman's freedom was limited. In medieval society, where skill in battle was essential in order to protect one's land, a woman was not allowed much independence. At birth she was subject to her father's wishes, and when she married, she had to obey her husband. If she lost her husband, she was placed in the keeping of her husband's lord or of her eldest son. From childhood, a girl of noble birth was trained to please her future husband and to manage his household. She learned to sing, dance, ride, and hunt so that she would make a good companion. She was taught to spin, weave, sew, embroider, and care for the sick and wounded. At fifteen, when she was considered fully grown, her parents arranged a suitable marriage for her.

A medieval nobleman married not for love but for money. A knight tried to win the lady who could bring him the most land as a dowry. After marriage, the wife had few rights. Her husband controlled her land and could beat her or starve her if he wished. There was almost no escape from an unhappy marriage, because the Church forbade divorce and there was no way for an unmarried girl of noble birth to make a living. If a girl were not happily married, she could do little but retire to a convent. But marriage had certain practical advantages for a woman. The wife shared her husband's rank, received his guests, and, if he were away, ruled the castle and the fief. Her husband's vassals owed allegiance to her, and many women successfully defended their husbands' fiefs in time of war. In spite of her lack of independence, the medieval noblewoman was a dignified, capable, and highly respected member of feudal society.

A SUIT OF ARMOR. Armor such as this gave the knight excellent protection but left him practically helpless afoot. The suit shown here belonged to a German knight of the sixteenth century.

Medieval architecture is basically massive. Whether it be a cathedral or a castle the theme is size, strength, and domination. Serfs' homes were squalid and made of the meagrest materials; only in the towns were there beginnings of decent dwellings and these were all too frequently crowded, noisy and smelly.

Religion ruled all, and therefore the greatest effort was put into churches and abbeys. A magnificence of detail and beauty made these edifices things of beauty, wonder and reverence. Castles were strong and stalwart, protecting the nobleman's preserves as well as his serfs. Only when the towns became necessary to the economy of the countryside and the nobility did architecture begin to become secular.

Shown here is an example of sublime medieval vaulting, harmony, and color in the nave of *San Francesco* in *Assisi*, Italy. This is also a monastery but showing the entire complex is the Abbey of *Maria Laach* in Germany. The abbey or monastery in Europe dates back to St. Benedict in the 6th century. Religion brought love; the castle brought order. Shown here is the *Angers Castle* in the Loire Valley France. Huge battlements defied attack and preserved the countryside. But the town eventually took over and became the center of activity for the area. This town scene from Germany is typical of middle fifteenth century dwellings.

THE MANORIAL SYSTEM PROVIDED SECURITY FOR THE PEASANT, BUT AT THE PRICE OF HIS FREEDOM

During the invasions of the ninth century, Western Europe was plunged into a search for security. We have seen how, for mutual protection, those who could fight on horseback or who owned enough land became the vassals of great landowners. Those who were too poor to make this arrangement became tenants on the great lord's estate, or manor. This method of earning a living was known as the *manorial system.*

Tenants on the manor were of two classes, peasants and serfs. Those who had been free men and had owned some land, but not enough to become vassals, were peasants. They gave their small holdings to the local lord, who let them work it for him because he could not farm and fight at the same time. Serfs were those freemen who had no land at all, or men whose fathers had been Roman slaves or tenants on Roman villas. Thus the manorial system was partly Roman in origin.

Peasants and serfs had protection but few rights. There were several important differences between peasants and serfs. Because peasants originally had land to offer the lord, they could bargain with him to determine how much rent they would pay and how much work they would do. But serfs, who had nothing to bargain with, were forced to accept whatever the lord would offer. Unlike peasants, they became bound to the soil and were unable to leave the lord's estate without his permission. Although their way of life resembled slavery, they were not technically slaves because they could not be sold apart from the land. In exchange for his protection and permission to work on the land, the serf owed many obligations to the lord. For one thing, a serf had to pay his lord a large portion of the crop as rent. In addition, he owed three days labor a week on the lord's fields, and he was also required to build bridges and repair roads. These duties were called labor dues. The serf also had to give various amounts of cheese, wood, pork, or eggs to the lord in payment for the use of the lord's pastures, woodlands, mill, and ovens. A serf paid for permission to marry someone from another manor and for the privilege of inheriting the use of his father's land. Then, if the serf still had any goods after paying dues to his lord and a tenth of his income to the Church, the lord could tax the surplus. A serf was seldom left with more than enough for survival.

If a serf or peasant had a complaint, the lord's chief official, the steward, held a hearing in court, where all matters were settled according to the custom of the manor. But if a serf were caught stealing, or beating the lord's favorite horse, he might be punished or even killed without ever appearing in court. The quality of justice varied greatly from one manor to the next.

Some lords treated their serfs with barbaric cruelty, but since a live serf was more useful than

Paying a Toll. As they pass over the bridge, these peasants are obliged to pay a toll to the gatekeeper. Such toll bridges were common in the Middle Ages.

JOUSTING. A tournament was a colorful, exciting event in the Middle Ages. In this scene a knight is about to fall from his horse as his opponent's lance knocks him off balance. A squire stands ready to help his fallen master.

a dead one, most of the lords were more humane. Probably the average serf preferred life on a manor to the risk of almost certain destruction at the hands of invaders or lawless knights.

Class lines between noble and serf hardened. The peasants and serfs, who made up 90 per cent of Western Europe's population, supplied the goods and services which kept the clergy and nobility living comfortably. Since the peasants and serfs did menial work with their hands, they were considered base and ignoble. A peasant or serf could not be expected to keep his word as, for example, a knight could. It is therefore not surprising that laws and punishments for the peasant class were different from those for the nobility. The peasant could never become a vassal. His relation to the lord of the manor was one of permanent inferiority. This distinction between the honorable military life of the lord and the humble, impoverished existence of the peasantry created a wide gulf between the nobility and the lower classes.

Farming methods were not too efficient. Transportation was poor in the Middle Ages and most often towns did not exist nearby to absorb the produce of the manor or to supply the wants of its inhabitants. As a result, the manor had to furnish almost everything its people needed. Most of the land was devoted to the raising of grain. There were also orchards and vineyards, and common lands where cattle and sheep were kept.

The fields of the manor were farmed in three sections, one for winter wheat, one for spring wheat, and one that was allowed to lie fallow, or uncultivated, to regain its fertility. The fields were divided into strips, half of which were owned by the lord and the rest by his tenants. To divide the good and poor land equally, each man had a

MEDIEVAL CALENDAR. These pages (left and right) are from the famous Book of Hours of the Duc de Berry, a great nobleman of late medieval France. The Book of Hours is an illustrated calendar, containing daily devotions, prayers, psalms, and other religious texts. *Left:* The calendar for February shows peasants gathering firewood and warming themselves by the open fire on a bitter winter day. *Right:* The March calendar shows a peasant plowing a field, as others tend grapevines on the Duc's lands.

few strips in each of the three fields. A team of oxen plowed all the strips together because few peasants could afford their own animals. Because everyone had to wait his turn for the oxen, plowing was very slow. Often birds ate much of the seed after it was sown. Because of the lack of good fertilizer an acre only yielded six to eight bushels of grain. A modern farmer can raise thirty or forty bushels an acre.

A low yield of grain sometimes came from the fact that the manor had to be more or less self-sufficient. Certain soils are more suitable for some crops than for others. For instance, a manor in northern Germany could produce much more barley on its flat, fertile fields than could a manor in the south of France, where the hilly land was better suited for vineyards. But because long distance trade was at a standstill, the German manor had to produce its own wine and the French manor had to grow its own barley. The result was often poor quality and limited quantity. Even in the best of times, some manors produced barely enough food to keep the people alive. Few farmers dared to experiment with new ideas for crops and fertilizer, because if the new methods failed, everyone would starve.

Peasants and serfs often lived in poverty and misery. Life on a medieval manor was never easy for any member of the lower class. A free peasant had a somewhat better life than a serf because he owed less labor service to the lord of the manor and could devote more time to his own fields. But all the inhabitants of a manorial village lived in small, dark cottages of one or two rooms. These huts with thatched straw roofs might be made of stone, but often they were simply made out of mud and woven branches. Windows were covered with oiled linen instead of glass. The floor was earthen, covered with straw. The hearth was in the center of the room. The smoke escaped as best it could through a hole in the roof.

Peasants and serfs owned very little furniture. Beds were often crude platforms covered with straw, in the corner of the hut. In cold weather serf families would share their living quarters with whatever cattle or sheep they might own. The smoky interior of the hut and the presence of the animals made winter-life very unpleasant.

Peasant diet was poor especially in the winter time when there was no fruit or fresh vegetables. A meal would consist of coarse dark bread, porridge, and cider or beer. The peasants rarely ate

fresh meat unless the lord of the manor gave a feast. Serfs were forbidden to hunt, and farm animals were too valuable to kill. In times of famine serfs and peasants would sometimes be forced to eat bark and roots from the manor woodlands.

Chapter Check-up

1. How did the Treaty of Verdun influence the history of Western Europe?
2. What groups invaded and plundered Western Europe during the ninth century?
3. Why were the Europeans at first unable to defend themselves against invaders?
4. What was the feudal system and why did it come into being?
5. What were some of the drawbacks of feudalism? What were its advantages?
6. How were boys of noble birth trained for knighthood?
7. What group included the greatest percentage of the population during medieval times?
8. How was the manor important in medieval life?
9. What was the status of the serf?
10. Why did the medieval manor have to be self-sufficient?

CHAPTER 23

The Church Became Involved in European Politics and Wars

THE CHURCH AND THE TEMPORAL POWERS STRUGGLED FOR POLITICAL SUPREMACY

Churchmen became vassals of feudal lords. As we have seen, the Church was originally concerned solely with spiritual matters. It became involved with temporal affairs only when it acquired land. The Pope became a temporal ruler when Charlemagne gave him the land which later became the Papal States (see page 172). During the Middle Ages, many lords gave fiefs of land to the Church in the hope of improving their chances for salvation. The abbot or bishop who

CLOISTERS. In such enclosed monastery courtyards as this, medieval monks spent many hours at prayer and meditation. In the open area of the court were herb gardens from which the ingredients of many medieval medicines were obtained.

received such a fief thereby became the vassal of the lord who gave it and, under the feudal bargain, owed him military service. Since churchmen were not supposed to fight, they granted some of their land as fiefs to lords or knights who would fight in their place. In this way, churchmen became entangled in the web of feudal obligation. They were vassals of lords, and lords of their own vassals, just as the noblemen were.

As the temporal wealth of the Church grew, so did its temporal problems. One result of acquiring land was that a bishop really had two masters, his lord and the Pope. Because the lords and kings did not want to lose control of the lands that they had given to the Church, they insisted that churchmen fulfill all the feudal obligations. They discovered that churchmen were particularly valuable vassals because their education made them capable of governing. The churchmen also made good vassals because they usually did not marry and leave sons to inherit the fief. Thus, the lord could later grant the fief to another churchman of his choice.

Suppose that a lord gave a fief to a neighboring bishop. When the bishop died, the lord wanted to be sure that the new bishop would be a trustworthy vassal. For this reason, he often gave the office to a relative or friend. If the lord needed money, he might even sell the office to the highest bidder. The practice by which the lord appointed the new bishop and presented him with the symbols of his office (his ring and staff) was called *lay investiture*. Lay investiture created a serious problem for the Church because a bishop or abbot chosen by a lord could become more loyal to him than to the Pope. Thus the Church sometimes found itself in the awkward position of not being able to control its own officials. This situation made it impossible for the Church to enforce uniform standards of conduct.

The Church began reforms. By the eleventh century, wise churchmen began to realize that the Church should be independent of the nobility. In order to achieve independence, the Church sought first to increase its prestige. It achieved this aim in several ways. One was by sponsoring certain reforms within the Church itself. For example, new monastic orders which imposed stricter rules on the monks were founded. Then Pope Gregory VII (1073–85) decreed that the clergy was no longer allowed to marry. This change was intended to remove the temptation for a priest to use Church lands to support his family. In addition, Gregory forbade *simony*, the practice of buying and selling Church offices or any other privilege of the Church.

The Church also sponsored reforms to benefit society in general. One of these, introduced about 1000 A.D., was the *Truce of God*. According to the Truce, all knights were forbidden to fight during Lent, on Christmas and Easter, and from Wednesday evening to Monday morning of each week. The nobles did not always obey the Truce, nor indeed did they adhere to many of the other reforms of the Church. But the Church had an effective weapon. It could cut men off from the Church completely, by excommunicating them. A man under ban of *excommunication* was not permitted to go to Church or receive the sacraments. No one was allowed to speak to him or give him food. If he died, he could not be buried in sacred ground, and the gates of heaven would be forever closed to him. The prospect of losing all hope of eternal salvation made the most quarrelsome knight think twice before breaking the Truce of God.

Popes and rulers struggled for the right to choose bishops. Gregory VII knew that if he hoped to free churchmen from the nobles, he would have to put an end to the practice of lay investiture. When he issued a decree forbidding the practice, however, most of the kings and nobles simply ignored the order. The German king, Henry IV, who needed loyal bishops to help him suppress the rebellious German nobles, went much further. He openly defied Gregory and even declared that the Pope had wrongfully usurped St. Peter's throne and should give it up at once. Gregory, shocked at this attitude in a Christian prince, excommunicated Henry and released all of Henry's vassals from their vows of loyalty to him.

HENRY AT CANOSSA. Standing barefoot in the snow for three days, Henry IV awaits the Pope's forgiveness. In spite of his submission to the Pope, Henry had the last word in the end.

hgeneratio

THE BOOK OF KELLS. Shown here are superb examples of the art of Illumination done by Irish monks in the eighth or ninth centuries. The intricate design of the Book of Kells embellished in gold and vari-colored inks is generally considered to be the finest example of Illumination extant. Depicted are initial letters and portraits of Christ and the Virgin Mary. The art flourished in the Middle Ages and usually displayed religious themes, but secular interests as in the Book Hours were also illustrated. The Book of Kells is on display in Trinity College, Dublin.

The German nobles quickly sided with the Pope against King Henry. The king, realizing that he had underestimated the power of the Pope, hastily decided to ask his pardon. Dressed in the humble garb of a penitent, Henry came to the Pope's palace at Canossa in the Italian Alps. For three days the proud king stood barefoot in the snow outside the Pope's gates, begging forgiveness. Finally Gregory relented, and the ban of excommunication was lifted. This incident at Canossa shows how the power of the medieval Church could be used to force even the greatest rulers of Europe to bow to its will.

But Canossa did not mark the end of the quarrel. The German nobles openly expressed disappointment that the Pope had let Henry off so lightly. Many of them transferred their support to the king. Strengthened by the nobles' support, Henry reasserted his right to appoint Church officials. In fact, a short time later he invaded Italy and drove Gregory off the papal throne. The investiture struggle was finally settled in 1122 at a council held in Worms on the Rhine. Church and State reached a compromise which provided that clergymen would elect bishops and abbots, but that the man chosen must be acceptable to the ruler or feudal lord. Thus, even though the Church had won its point, the State would still have influence over the German clergy.

In the early thirteenth century the investiture question arose again, this time in England. The quarrel resulted in a notable victory for Pope Innocent III. King John of England, like Henry in Germany, wanted to choose his own bishops. He refused to accept the Pope's choice for archbishop of Canterbury and defiantly seized Church lands in England. When Innocent excommunicated him, John, who was not very devout, ignored the ban. But then Innocent declared that John had forfeited his right to the English throne and invited the King of France to invade England. In order to save his crown, John was forced to do homage to the Pope as a vassal and to agree to accept England from him as a fief. Innocent's victory over the English king marked the high tide of the Church's temporal power.

Popes and emperors fought for power. Another aspect of the conflict between Church and State was the rivalry for political control of northern Italy. In 800, the Pope had crowned Charlemagne emperor (see Chapter 24). After Charlemagne's death, the idea of reviving the Roman Empire in the West was temporarily forgotten. In the tenth century, however, Otto the Great (936–973), king of the German states, followed Charlemagne's path of conquest to northern Italy and was crowned emperor. Otto's successors to the German throne kept the title. Once again Western Europeans looked upon the emperor as the supreme temporal power in the world. They expected him to use his sword in the service of the Pope, the supreme spiritual leader. Thus Church and State would work together for the good of Christendom. Unfortunately for the peace of Europe, the Popes, especially Innocent III, began to assert that God intended them to control the emperors. The German emperors, however, insisted that God intended them to be ruled by no one, not even the Pope. A three-hundred-year power struggle, which often flared into actual warfare, followed.

The struggle reached a crisis in 1084 when Henry IV drove Pope Gregory VII out of Rome and had himself crowned emperor by a Pope of his own choosing. Another crisis arose when the handsome, red-bearded emperor Frederick Bar-

FREDERICK BARBAROSSA. Many legends grew up about this great emperor, whose fiery red beard captured the popular imagination.

barossa (1152–90) refused to hold the Pope's horse while he mounted because the emperor thought such an act beneath his dignity. Frederick took the title Holy Roman emperor to signify that his power was equal to the Pope's, and he spent much of his time leading armies against the Pope in a contest for control of the rich cities of northern Italy. Still another crisis flared up when Holy Roman emperor Frederick II repeatedly invaded northern Italy; the Pope excommunicated him on four separate occasions. Although the Popes of this period never managed to make good their claims to political power, the strength of their efforts is a demonstration of the vigor of the medieval Church.

The Holy Roman Empire lasted a thousand years. The Holy Roman Empire had its origins in the time of Charlemagne, although it was not known by that official title until Frederick Barbarossa's reign in the twelfth century. The Empire continued for over a thousand years, until it was destroyed by Napoleon in 1806. During most of this time, the Empire included eastern France (Lotharingia), present-day Belgium and the Netherlands, and most of present-day Austria, Germany, and northern Italy (see map on page 174). But as the German emperors gradually lost their political power, the title Holy Roman emperor became little more than an honorary one. Even when the Empire exercised little real power, however, it continued to play an important part in European affairs. You will read more about the Holy Roman Empire in the stories of Italy, Germany, and Eastern Europe.

THE CHURCH SPONSORED HOLY WARS

The medieval Church, as you have seen, was only partially successful in asserting its claims to political power. In spiritual affairs, however, the Church held unquestioned sway. Its spiritual influence is demonstrated by the fact that the greatest wars of the Middle Ages were inspired and sponsored by the Church. Let us see how they came about.

Christians made pilgrimages to win the blessing of the Church. A pilgrimage was a religious journey to a sacred Christian shrine where a saint or martyr had died or where some relic, such as a saint's bones or a piece of the cross on which Jesus was crucified, was supposed to have been preserved. The pilgrim might pray there to atone for his sins, to give thanks for a blessing, or to seek a cure for illness. Most Christians sought to make one such pilgrimage during their lifetime. Although many pilgrims regarded the journey as a solemn occasion, others were more interested in seeing new lands and meeting new people. In the prologue to Chaucer's *Canterbury Tales* (see Chapter 35) you will find an excellent description of how entertaining a pilgrimage could be.

Some of the famous Christian shrines in Western Europe were at Canterbury in England, at Tours in France, at Campostella in Spain, and at Rome, the Pope's home and the city where many martyrs had died. But the most difficult and most rewarding pilgrimage of all was to Palestine, the Holy Land, where Jesus had taught and been crucified. In the eleventh century a tide of religious enthusiasm sent Christians from Western Europe to Palestine in ever-increasing numbers.

Pope Urban called an urgent council. Unfortunately for Christians, the Holy Land had been in the hands of the Moslems since the seventh century. Christians had long sorrowed over this fact but were grateful that the Moslems allowed them to make pilgrimages to Palestine. Then in the eleventh century, a fierce people from central Asia, the Turks, conquered their fellow Moslems along the Mediterranean and gained control of Jerusalem. Stories soon reached Western Europe of the Turks' enslavement of Christian pilgrims and their persecution

CHAUCER'S PILGRIMS. On the eve of the pilgrimage to Canterbury, the pilgrims gather to eat and celebrate. Journeys were difficult in the Middle Ages, and travelers usually stocked up well before setting out.

of Christian priests. The Byzantine emperor, fearing that the Turks would attack Constantinople, the last Christian stronghold in the Middle East, appealed to Pope Urban II for help. In 1095 Urban called a great council at Clermont (kler-*mone*), in southern France.

A great throng of people assembled at Clermont to hear Urban plead that they take up arms to rescue the Holy Land from the Turks. In his speech, one of the most persuasive in history, the Pope promised the crowd:

> If you are slain, you will indeed have lost your bodies, but you will have saved your souls. Do not refuse for the love of your families, for you must love God more than these. Those who live will behold the sepulcher of the Lord.

"God wills it! God wills it!" shouted the crowd. As enthusiasm for the Pope's proposal spread over the land, knights, peasants, monks, and even women, children, and cripples, eagerly sewed crosses of red cloth on the front of their robes to symbolize their intention of rescuing Palestine. Those who "took the cross" were called *crusaders,* from *crux,* the Latin word for "cross."

Peter the Hermit roused the masses. A French monk, Peter the Hermit, had visited Jerusalem before the First Crusade and had seen Christians attacked. As he knelt at the Holy Sepulcher, believed to be Jesus' tomb, he seemed to hear Jesus saying, "Peter, arise, hasten to proclaim the suffering of my people." Peter hurried home to France, and carrying a heavy wooden cross, tramped barefoot from village to village urging people to join the Crusade. He promised rich and poor alike that "He who strikes a blow to rescue the Holy Sepulcher . . . has thrown open the door of heaven for himself."

Thousands of men and women took the cross with the earnest desire to serve Christ and save their souls, but many crusaders had less noble motives. Some knights loved a good fight for any reason, and many saw in the crusades a wonderful opportunity to gain land and riches. Serfs often volunteered for the crusades to escape from

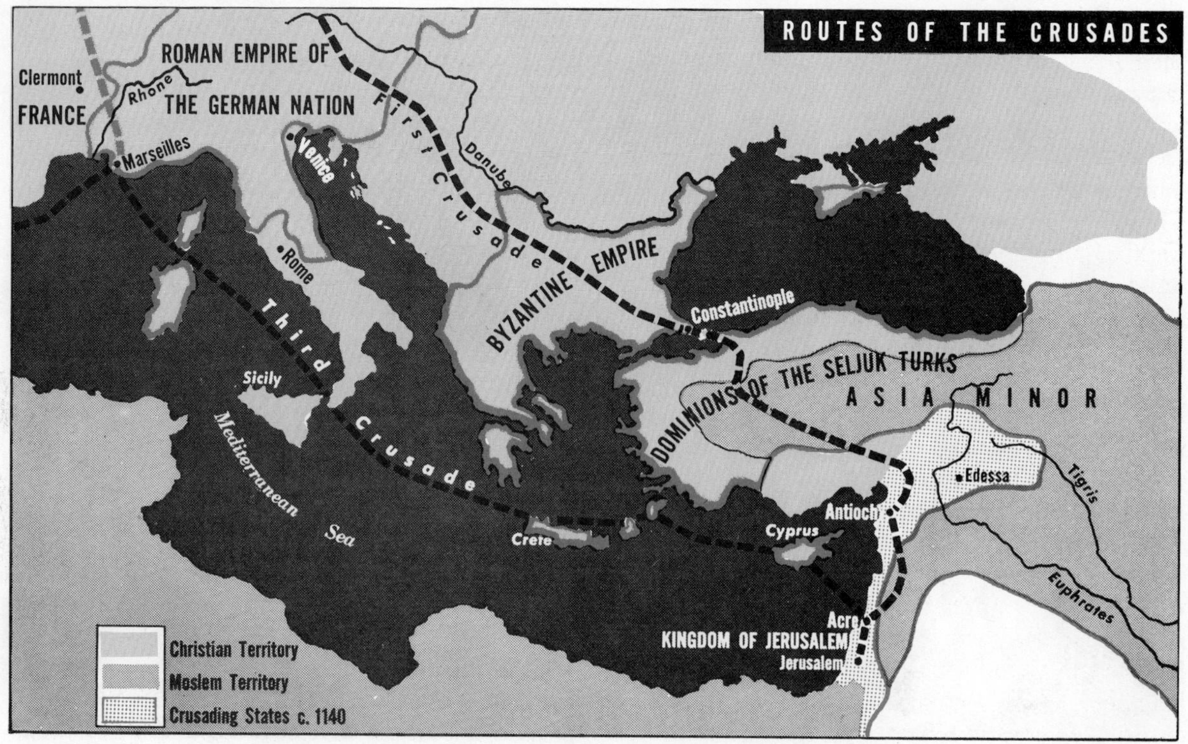

CRUSADERS. Inspired by such devout leaders as Peter the Hermit, men flocked by the hundreds to fight for the Holy Land. Their journeys helped bring about a revival of learning and trade in Europe.

their manorial obligations. Debtors became crusaders to have their debts canceled, and criminals went crusading to be forgiven for their crimes. Doubtless, Pope Urban himself saw in the crusades an opportunity to increase the power of the Church by temporarily ridding Europe of its most warlike knights and by uniting them in a holy cause. Thus, religious and worldly forces combined to produce the Crusades.

The First Crusade was successful. The First Crusade, led by some of the greatest medieval knights, left for the Holy Land in 1096. The journey was long and difficult. Some crusaders climbed over the mountains of Greece, and others took the easier route through the Danube Valley. After several skirmishes in Asia Minor, in which one Turkish army was defeated, the crusaders finally reached Jerusalem. Then began a strange procession. Led by priests, the crusaders, like the Hebrews in the biblical story of Jericho, began a barefoot march around the city, praying and chanting hymns as they walked. Probably they hoped that God would work another miracle and cause the walls of Jerusalem to tumble down, as he had those of Jericho. When, after nine days of marching, the walls were still standing, the crusaders attacked the city. After bitter fighting and a brutal slaughter of the Turks, Jerusalem was captured.

Because the knights faced tremendous problems, the success of the First Crusade is truly remarkable. Although skilled in battle, the crusaders had made no preparation for obtaining supplies or arranging communications. Thousands starved, lost their way, or died in the filthy, disease-ridden camps. As if these problems were not great enough, the leaders quarreled continually over who should give orders and who should keep which captured city.

Nonetheless, the crusaders succeeded in conquering a long, narrow belt of land along the Mediterranean coast, which they divided into four Christian states. Although the shape of the new Christian territory made defense difficult, the

Fighting the Turks. The knights of Western Europe fought bravely to wrest the Holy Land from the Turks, but they were only temporarily successful.

crusaders built castles and managed to hold it for eighty-eight years. Then, however, the Turks began to reconquer this coastal strip. Their conquest of the stronghold of Edessa (eh-*des*-uh) in 1144 roused Europe to a new effort.

Later crusades failed. The great Christian leader St. Bernard persuaded the king of France and the German emperor to lead a Second Crusade (1147–49), but this time the Christian forces were badly defeated.

Turkish pressure steadily grew stronger. Jerusalem, capital of the crusaders' kingdom, was taken in 1187 by the great Moslem leader, Saladin (*sal*-uh-din). Shocked by the loss of Jerusalem, King Philip II of France, Richard the Lionhearted of England, and the Holy Roman emperor, Frederick Barbarossa, set out with their armies for the Holy Land on the Third Crusade. When Frederick drowned while crossing a stream in Asia Minor, most of his followers returned home. Philip and Richard took the easier but more expensive route by sea. Each day they quarreled more and more bitterly. Philip stayed only long enough to help capture the port of Acre (*ah*-ker) before sailing back to France in disgust. Richard, left alone to battle the mighty Saladin, fought gallantly, but the Third Crusade ended in failure.

The Fourth Crusade (1202–04) never reached the Holy Land at all. On this crusade the knights were persuaded by Italian ship owners to attack the rich Christian city of Constantinople. Their intention was to plunder the city and use the booty to finance the Crusade. But once the plundering began, the crusading spirit was forgotten, and the would-be crusaders simply stayed in Constantinople. The failure of the Fourth Crusade reveals a changing attitude in Western Europe. New interests were pushing religion into the background; material wealth began to rival spiritual salvation in importance; and religious enthusiasm among the nobles lessened. The fact that the Turks had proved to be better warriors than the Christians had expected also dampened the knights' crusading spirit.

The Children's Crusade expressed the deep faith of the common people. Perhaps religious enthusiasm was dying among the nobles, but many of the common people still had faith in the crusades. They believed that earlier crusades failed because knights had fought for lands and riches rather than for the love of God. They were sure that with God's help the pure in heart could capture Jerusalem. In 1212 a French shepherd boy, Stephen, gathered a band of children to begin a new crusade. The French King was able to send the children back to their homes, but that same year a band of German children actually did set out for the Holy Land.

The parents of these children did not try to prevent them from going. Since the children would be in God's care, no one thought it necessary to provide adequate food, clothing, arms, or medical care. Many children died of hunger, cold, and sickness along the way. When a few of the children actually reached the Mediterranean coast they expected God to open the sea so they could safely cross. Instead, they were captured by ruthless merchants and sold into slavery.

The Children's Crusade ended in tragedy, but the idea of the crusades did not entirely disappear in the Middle Ages. Several more unsuccessful expeditions set out for the Holy Land. When the Turks recaptured Acre in 1291, the last Christian stronghold in the Middle East was lost.

The crusades were "successful failures." Although the crusades failed to regain the Holy Land, they had far-reaching results for Europe. They weakened both feudalism and the manorial system. Many knights left their fiefs to fight in the crusades, and many serfs were freed. As great nobles became involved elsewhere, the kings of Europe became more powerful. The crusades also stimulated trade between Europe and the Middle East. Ships that carried crusaders eastward returned loaded with spices and other luxuries which were soon in great demand. This rush for goods from the East, and the military failure of the crusades led ultimately to the discovery of America. The crusades also increased the use of money throughout Europe. A crusading knight could not pay all his expenses with sacks of grain. Although most of these changes were slowly taking place as Europe became more stable, the crusades hastened them. Perhaps the most significant thing is that the crusades took place at all. They indicate the religious faith and the optimism of medieval man which was to shape Western civilization.

Chapter Check-up

1. How and why did the Church become involved in the feudal system?
2. What major problem arose from the involvement of the Church in the feudal system?
3. By what strong means could the medieval Church control its members?
4. How did the medieval Church show its power over the great rulers of the Middle Ages? Give two examples.
5. What were pilgrimages and why were they made?
6. What was the chief purpose of the crusades?
7. Why can it be said the crusades were made up of many kinds of people?
8. Did the crusades accomplish their purpose? Explain.
9. How did the crusades weaken the feudal system and usher in the modern world?

CHAPTER 24

Towns and Trade Weakened the Feudal System

TOWNS DEVELOPED IN THE LATE MIDDLE AGES

Life in early medieval Europe, which was organized around the local manor village, was largely isolated from the rest of the world. This isolation was reflected in the narrow outlook and interests of medieval man. In the centuries during and following the crusades, however, the people began to awaken. They discovered new interests, new tastes, and new ways of making a living. Towns began to develop and new schools were opened. All these changes helped bring an end to the feudal system in Western Europe.

The medieval town was based on trade. Trade in Europe virtually disappeared between the years 400 and 1000, because men lacked the

COMMERCE ON A RIVER. As men hoist goods into a boat, they are protected from robbers by armed guards. Rivers were the principal means of transportation in the Middle Ages.

two necessary conditions for trade: transportation and a supply of goods to exchange. Disorder, confusion, and danger from invaders and warring knights made travel extremely difficult and helped prevent farmers from producing surpluses to offer in trade.

Conditions began to change in the eleventh century, however, when feudalism restored order to Europe. As danger from hostile attack decreased, merchants were again able to travel, and peasants could devote their full time to farming. At the same time, agriculture was stimulated by the development of a heavier and more efficient plow. Thus travel grew safer, food supplies increased, and a surplus was available for trade.

The Italian cities of Venice (*ven*-iss) and Genoa (*jen*-oh-uh), whose excellent harbors were close to the eastern Mediterranean, had traded with the Middle East even during the Dark Ages. As it emerged from its isolation, Western Europe became a ready market for the silks, velvets, spices, rare fruits, rugs, and fine metalwork from the East. As we have seen, the crusades encouraged the rebirth of trade. Italian cities willingly aided the crusaders in the hope of gaining further trade privileges in the Middle East and destroying Moslem competition. Thus the crusades increased the trade advantage held by the Italian cities.

Trade resulted in better use of resources. We have seen that in the early Middle Ages each manor tried to become self-sufficient, whether or not its soil and climate favored the growing of a variety of crops. As transportation became safer, each manor or locality was able to specialize in its best crop, because the product could be exchanged for the specialties of other places. England's climate, for instance, was unsuited for growing grapes but was excellent for grazing sheep. English farmers therefore concentrated on the raising of sheep and sent their surplus wool across the English Channel to Flanders (present-day Belgium). The people of Flanders, who lived on poor soil, became expert weavers of English wool. In turn, French farmers, aided by good soil and plenty of sun, cultivated thriving vineyards. From their grapes they made wine, which they exchanged for Flemish woolens.

Many medieval towns became famous for their specialties. Antwerp, in Flanders, was noted for fine quality woolen cloth. The Spanish town of Toledo became known for high-quality swords and armor. The French weavers of Arras (*ar*-us) produced beautiful tapestries out of wool that was imported from nearby Flanders. Notice that although these favorable conditions of geography and climate had always been present, it was not until trade made exchange of goods possible that men could fully use nature's gifts.

Geography influenced the location of trade routes. Trade routes sprang up along the easiest paths between areas that exchanged goods. Among the most important was the route between the cloth-producing cities of Flanders and the luxury-selling ports of northern Italy. Because transportation by water was easier than by land, merchants followed the Rhine. Elsewhere, they began to follow other great rivers and finally even the smaller rivers, until eventually much of Europe was linked by water trade routes.

Two main routes connected Europe with the East. The easiest route was by sea from China to the Persian Gulf, then up the Tigris or the Euphrates, and overland by caravan to Constantinople. This trip took as much as two years. The overland journey across the mountains and deserts of central Asia took even longer. Because great distances made eastern goods extremely expensive, most European traders continued to deal in such goods as wool, hides, and salt, rather than in luxury goods from the East.

The medieval fair was a center for the exchange of goods and ideas. At certain times during the year, merchants from all over Europe gathered at a convenient town to exchange their wares. Such a gathering was called a *fair*, from the Latin word *feria*, meaning "festival," because early medieval fairs were usually held on the date of a Church festival or holy day. Often a fair was sponsored by the lord who owned the town, for he reaped large profits from the fees which merchants paid to display their wares. Some of the most famous fairs were at Champagne (sham-*payn*), in northeastern France near the Rhine, and at Novgorod, on the river route between Constantinople and Scandinavia. A large fair might last several weeks, during which nobles stopped fighting and the lord promised safe conduct to every merchant. At the fair, stewards from abbeys and castles laid in a year's supply of cheese, wine, pepper, cinnamon, linen, and furs. Knights and ladies bought rare foreign luxuries, such as silken robes, fine leather, perfumes, pearls, and oils. Wide-eyed

A FAIR. Life was hard in the Middle Ages, but cares were forgotten at fair time. How many different activities can you find in this scene of a fair in the sixteenth century?

peasants came to marvel at the wonders and to buy ironware, salt, and hides. Men settled debts incurred during the year and made new loans. Money-changers traded the coins of one district for those of another. Jugglers, gypsies, and wandering minstrels entertained the crowd. Thus a fair presented a wonderful opportunity to conduct business, to meet new people, and to enjoy the merriment. You can see why a fair provided such a welcome break in the dull routine of life on the manor.

Towns grew up as centers of trade. Because towns depended on trade, they developed at convenient points such as river fords, crossroads, harbors, and river mouths. Antwerp, for example, lay at the mouth of the Rhine on the North Sea. Venice was on the Adriatic with easy access to the Mediterranean. As houses, shops, warehouses, and inns were built for the merchants, towns increased in size. Craftsmen flocked to the towns in search of more people to buy their wares and services. Peasants from the manors sold their surplus eggs, butter, and vegetables in the town.

Not every town owed its existence to trade, however. Some had survived from Roman times because they offered protection from attack. Paris, for example, was on an island in the middle of the Seine. Others had grown up in the shelter of a great monasteries or strong castles which could defend them. By the twelfth century, however, most towns, whatever their origins, were prospering and growing.

CITY AIR WAS FREE AIR

Townsmen bought charters of freedom. At first the towns were controlled by lords or bishops who owned the land on which the town stood. Many merchants and craftsmen who settled there were considered the lord's property, just as if they were still on the manor. But the restrictions of the manorial system increasingly conflicted with men's new status as city dwellers. Men who were bound to the land and owed labor dues to the lord had neither the money for travel nor the time to practice their craft. Merchants were annoyed at paying manorial rents, tolls, and taxes. Townsmen who relied on the slow-working lord's court for justice lost many cases, because an accused foreign merchant often left town before the case was decided. These grievances caused the townsmen to seek freedom from the lord's control. They wanted personal freedom from their ties to the land, economic freedom from manorial dues, and political freedom to govern themselves.

The lord was, of course, reluctant to give his subjects these freedoms, but he needed money. He had discovered that merchants would not accept grain or other goods in exchange for their wares. They demanded gold and silver coins. A crusading lord also learned quickly that bushels of wheat were not very convenient for paying travel expenses on a crusade. Therefore, the lord became willing to grant the town's request for freedom if townsmen paid their manorial dues in money instead of in grain and labor.

Many lords granted personal freedom to any townsman who paid them a bag of silver. Gradually the lord freed townsmen from all their dues in exchange for one lump sum to be paid each year. If townsmen paid an additional sum, the lord allowed them to hold their own courts and to elect a mayor and councilmen. These privileges, guaranteed by charters, did much to increase the population and prosperity of the towns. The population of free towns was also constantly increased by runaway serfs. It became the custom that if a runaway serf could live a year and a day in the city, he was declared free. Thus, city air became truly free air.

The growth of towns produced the middle class. Early medieval society, as we have seen, was divided into three traditional classes: the clergy, the nobles, and the peasants and serfs. The townsmen, or burghers, belonged to none of these classes. Their status was based on wealth acquired in trade or manufacturing. Some of

CARCASSONE. This old city in southern France was restored in the nineteenth century. Parts of the solid stone walls that surround the fortress city date back to the fifth century. The building within the walls were built in the later Middle Ages.

them grew even richer than the nobles and acquired elaborate houses, silver dishes, and fur robes. But the nobles scorned even the well-to-do burghers because they were not of noble birth and had not been trained as knights. Consequently, the prosperous burghers slowly emerged as a new middle class that not only destroyed society's old pattern of feudal and manorial customs, but also established standards of conduct and thought that set the tone for the modern world.

Life in the town was uncomfortable but exciting. The medieval town was surrounded by a high wall whose heavy gates were shut at night and guarded by soldiers. Because a wall was expensive to build and maintain, it enclosed the smallest possible area. In order to pack many people into a crowded space, the upper stories of houses were extended over the narrow streets below. No provision was made for the disposal of garbage or sewage. Often garbage was thrown from windows into the muddy gutters, where it was eaten by dogs, cats, pigs, and rats that roamed the town.

This decaying refuse and a polluted water supply were the source of many serious epidemics. The worst of them, the famous Black Death or bubonic plague, destroyed almost a third of the population of Europe in the fourteenth century. Probably rats aboard ships brought the plague from the eastern Mediterranean to Italy. It quickly spread throughout Europe. Sometimes the population of an entire village died, and in many towns there were not enough men left to bury the dead.

Town dwellers who could ignore crowds and filth and escape the dangers of plagues, fires, and thieves found the town an exciting place to live. The center of interest was the bustling marketplace where peddlers sold their wares and housewives bargained energetically with merchants. Occasionally a friar would begin to preach to the crowd. Near the square could be found the cathedral, the town hall, the larger shops, and an inn. The narrow streets were lined with craftsmen's shops: goldsmiths on one street, cloth merchants on another, butchers on a third. Tanners, who needed water for the preparation of leather, were established along the edge of the river, where fishmongers also sold their wares. Since few people could read, painted signs hung over each shop to indicate what was sold. A boar's head stood for an inn, a mortar and pestle for a drugstore. In both European and American cities today, three balls still signify a pawnshop, and a red and white striped pole indicates a barber shop.

TOWNSMEN SOUGHT SECURITY IN GUILDS

Medieval guilds regulated commerce. Townsmen reflected the medieval quest for security by organizing guilds to control trade and industry. *Merchant guilds,* which began in the eleventh century, were associations of the merchants who lived in a town or area. *Craft guilds,* which developed in the twelfth century, were composed of craftsmen who practiced a single trade, such as weaving, baking, or making shoes.

Both kinds of guilds protected members from outside competition by forbidding non-members to sell goods in the area which a guild included. For example, the shoemakers' guild of Antwerp would not allow shoemakers from Rotterdam or London to sell shoes in Antwerp. In other words, the guilds attempted to establish a monopoly, or sole control of a product, in their area. Competition within the guild was controlled by fixing prices. The "just price" was supposed to cover the cost of materials and labor, but no more because the Church taught that it was wicked to make too much profit. If necessary, guild members attacked other members who undersold the just price. The guilds, which also set standards of quality, punished members who did not adhere to standards, because the inferior goods of one tradesman damaged the reputation of the whole guild.

Craft guilds regulated wages and limited the number of workers a man could hire. Night work was forbidden because goods made in bad light were often shoddy. These restrictions and standards, while they protected the guild member and gave him security, also limited his opportunity for advancement and profit. But they helped their members in other ways. The guild treasury paid for such emergencies as medical and funeral expenses, and it gave financial support to the widows and children of guild members. The guilds built elaborate guild halls, or meeting places, for their members. On holidays the members wore their official robes and carried banners in processions honoring the guild's patron saint. Guild members elected the town government from among their numbers. In the absence of police, they formed military bands to guard the city.

A Medieval Shop. While two workmen stitch shoes, another sells a pair to a customer. Other shoes are hanging in the front of the shop to attract passers-by.

The merchants' guilds of seventy cities in northern Europe formed the Hanseatic League, which, in addition to monopolizing trade, protected the members from attack. At one point, the League even commanded warships, with which it fought pirates on the North Sea.

From apprentice to guildmaster was a long road. The craft guild provided three stages of training. At seven, a boy became an *apprentice* to a master craftsman and spent three to seven years learning his master's trade. During this time, the apprentice was required to obey his master, to keep his trade secrets, and to work faithfully. In return, the master fed, clothed, and sheltered the boy in his own home and taught him the trade. When the apprentice had served his term, he could work as a hired day laborer in a master's shop. During this stage of his training, he was known as a *journeyman*.

At first, it was usually possible for any journeyman to become a master craftsman. If the guildmasters approved a sample of his best work, called his masterpiece, they accepted him as one of them. He could then open his own shop and have his own apprentices. By the fourteenth century, however, the masters sought to retain their privileged positions by preventing virtually all journeymen but their own sons from becoming masters. As a result, many capable men were forced to remain journeymen all their lives.

In some ways, the medieval craft guild resembled a modern labor union. Both, for example, were organized for the protection of their members. But there were also important differences. For one thing, since the craft guild included masters, journeymen, and apprentices, it was an organization of employers as well as employees.

Burghers. The burghers of a city gather together to discuss their charter. City people enjoyed freedoms and privileges that were unknown to serfs and peasants on country estates.

Guild Halls. These old guild halls along the Lys River in the Belgian town of Ghent are still in use today for business and commerce.

Furthermore, the masters (or employers), rather than the employees, ran the guilds. Trade unions today are operated by and for employees only.

Did guilds help or hinder medieval trade? Guilds hindered trade and industry in several ways. They discouraged competition, kept secret their knowledge of a trade, and frowned on more efficient ways of production for fear they would throw men out of work.

On the other hand, the guilds maintained high standards of quality and provided a basis for order and government in the town. They encouraged the craftsman to take personal pride in his work and, above all, they gave him economic security.

FRIARS BROUGHT THE CHURCH CLOSER TO THE PEOPLE

After the crusades the Church began to lose its dominant position in Western Europe. With the revival of trade and commerce Europeans became more interested in wealth than in religion. Even churchmen were caught up in this desire for material goods. In the economy of the early Middle Ages money played a very limited role. The Church had even forbidden men to charge any interest on money they lent to men in distress, calling it the sin of usury. Now serious churchmen tried to protect the poor by insisting that a merchant charge no more than a just price for his goods, and by limiting the amount of interest that could be charged for the use of money.

The ability of the Church to regain a position of importance in the lives of the people was due largely to the work of two young friars, who became famous medieval saints. The first, St. Francis, was not unusually religious as a young man. He was the son of a rich cloth merchant in the town of Assissi (uh-*see*-zee) in Italy, where he led a gay life and planned to be a soldier. Then he became desperately sick. During his long recovery, he came to believe that he should devote his life to God. Francis gave away all his possessions and tried to help those in distress. He wandered barefoot throughout Italy clad in a coarse sackcloth robe tied with a rope. St. Francis became a devoted and beloved teacher. He emphasized the need for brotherhood among men and urged his listeners to live a Christlike life, as he himself sought to do. Twelve of Francis' hearers were so impressed by his cheerful nature, his sweet temper, his life of poverty, and his personal example of devotion and humility, that they became his followers. They were called the Friars Minor, from the Latin words meaning "little brother." The Franciscan order of friars won the approval of the Pope in 1215. From then on it rapidly

St. Francis of Assissi. This painting by Bondone shows the gentle saint blessing the birds and requesting their silence.

gained new members. Soon Franciscan friars could be found in every part of Europe, preaching and helping the poor and unfortunate.

St. Dominic, a Spanish priest who preached in southern France, founded the order of Preaching Friars in 1216. The Dominican friars, as they were called, particularly devoted their efforts toward bringing heretics and doubters back to the Catholic faith. St. Thomas Aquinas (uh-*kwy*-nus), the renowned medieval scholar, was a Dominican friar, having entered the order in 1244.

Both Franciscan and Dominican friars took the same vows of poverty, chastity, and obedience as monks took. But friars differed from monks by teaching and living among the people instead of remaining behind monastery walls. Their work was especially valuable because they were able to minister to the needs of townspeople, the very people whose ties with the Church were most likely to be weakened by wealth, trade, and new ideas. The Franciscans and Dominicans probably did more than any other group in the thirteenth century to bring Christianity closer to ordinary men and women.

THE DEVELOPMENT OF TOWNS LED TO REPRESENTATIVE GOVERNMENT

The use of money paved the way for modern times. In the early Middle Ages, wealth was based on ownership of goods produced directly from the land. This system was known as *land economy*. As trade developed, it depended first on direct exchange of goods. Gradually, as we have noted, merchants adopted money as a more convenient medium of exchange. Lords had to have money to buy what they needed and to pay their debts. They sold freedom to townsmen in exchange for money and allowed serfs on the manor to become free peasants and pay their manorial dues in money. The lords accepted money from their vassals in place of military service. Finally, the lords even sold some of their land to merchants for money. Thus, as money became a more important source of power than land, Western Europe shifted from a land economy to a *money economy*.

The burghers' money strengthened the power of the king. Kings gradually discovered that professional soldiers and government officials who depended on the crown for a salary were much more loyal and efficient than more or less independent vassals who inherited land. In order to find money to pay professionals, the king turned to the wealthy burghers. The burghers contributed to the king's cause because they wanted royal charters granting them trading rights and privileges of self-government.

The king often appointed burghers as his officials, or agents, because they were educated but, unlike churchmen, did not have to obey the Pope. Burghers, for their part, were eager to serve the king. The law and order that he imposed on the nobles helped trade and industry. Nobles were forced to respect the royal agent even though they regarded him as an ignoble "commoner." The more important the king was, the more important his agents were. Therefore, the townsmen were eager to help the king increase his power. They served as paid judges in the royal courts that the kings established for all freemen. By 1500, most freemen looked to the king and his agents, instead of their feudal lord, for justice and protection.

The burghers and the king were not always in agreement. Townsmen did not want to be controlled by the king any more than they wanted to be controlled by the nobles. Nor did the king willingly allow the townsmen to become independent of royal authority. In spite of their differences, the burghers and the king usually cooperated in order to limit the power of the nobles.

Towns sent representatives to bargain with the king. The king often needed more money than he received from the royal charters he had given to the towns. Because many towns were free, they could not legally be forced to pay new levies. When the king tried sending agents to the

COURT SCENE. Various scenes of medieval lawmaking are shown in this fifteenth-century manuscript. On the left, the Duke of Normandy sits in session with his nobles. In the center, two men argue over a pot, get in a fight, are arrested, and then are brought before a magistrate. At the top right, the magistrate swears witnesses.

towns to ask for gifts, the burghers often failed to co-operate. Then the king worked out a better plan. He ordered each town to send one or two men to the king's court as representatives of their fellow townsmen. The king explained to these representatives why he needed money. Confronted directly by the king, the town representatives found it difficult to refuse his request and usually promised, on behalf of their fellow citizens, to pay what the king asked.

In time, however, the representatives of the towns learned to bargain with the king and began to win concessions from him. The king eventually gave the townsmen a voice in making the laws of the country. This practice was particularly true in England, as you will discover in Part 9. By 1300, when a medieval king wanted to discuss government affairs, he invited to his court not only the great lords and high churchmen, but also representatives from the towns. Thus, in the medieval towns, we can see the beginning of *representative government*. You will see later how the principle of representative government influenced the political development of Europe.

Chapter Check-up

1. What conditions encouraged the growth of towns during the last half of the Middle Ages?
2. How did medieval fairs help to introduce new ideas and new products?
3. What new class of people developed in medieval society with the growth of towns?
4. Why were the people in the towns and cities able to bargain successfully with the lords of the manors?
5. In what ways was life in the town exciting, though uncomfortable?
6. What is the difference between a merchant guild and a craft guild? How did the guilds protect their members from competition?
7. What were the steps in the training for guild membership?
8. Who were the friars? How did their work differ from that of the monks?
9. What effect did the increasing use of money have on the feudal system?
10. Why did the burghers willingly give financial support to the king? How did this lead to the development of representative government?

CHAPTER 25

Medieval Culture Was Devoted to Serving God

Men of the early Middle Ages were concerned almost exclusively with their personal survival in a highly insecure world. They had little time for arts and learning. By the thirteenth century, however, Western Europeans were building magnificent cathedrals, establishing universities, and reviving an interest in philosophy and learning. This astonishing transformation resulted from the rise of towns in the twelfth century. Just as the wealth of Periclean Athens had made possible the glories of its Golden Age, so prosperous medieval towns provided the money and leisure necessary for the flowering of medieval culture. Although some of this new wealth was used to purchase eastern luxuries, much of it was used to build cathedrals and universities for the service of God.

CATHEDRALS WERE THE CROWNING ACHIEVEMENT OF THE MIDDLE AGES

Men contributed their labor to the cathedral as a token of faith. By the end of the eleventh century, the same religious enthusiasm that produced the crusades was also finding expression in architecture. A wave of church building spread over Europe. By the middle of the thirteenth century, even the smallest village could boast at least one church, and the larger towns had a surprising number. London alone had 120 churches within her walls. A traveler approaching a medieval town from a distance could see the church spires rising high above the slate-roofed houses crowded within the town walls.

The chief pride of the burghers of the larger towns was their cathedral, the church in which the bishop presided. Medieval cathedrals were so expensive and magnificent that they often required hundreds of years to complete. Even today they are among the most beautiful and durable buildings in Europe. Nearly every citizen, rich or poor, young or old, contributed something to the building of the cathedral. Merchants and lords frequently donated the expensive silver candlesticks, tapestries, and altarpieces. Ladies embroidered altar cloths. Craftsmen volunteered their services as stone masons or woodcarvers. Poor men, who had nothing else to give, contributed their labor. Patience, devotion, and painstaking care helped to make the medieval cathedral one of the most wonderful creations of man.

Romanesque and Gothic churches were different expressions of men's devotion. During the eleventh and early twelfth centuries, churches were built in the *Romanesque* (ro-man-*esk*) style, which was adapted, as the name implies, from Roman architecture. Romanesque churches were solid structures with square towers and thick walls. Heavy columns inside the church supported the arched stone ceiling. Windows were small and narrow, so that they would not weaken the walls. One can easily recognize a Romanesque church by looking at the tops of the windows, which look like small Roman arches. Although the interior of the church was dark, the mosaics of gold and blue glass that covered walls and ceilings glowed richly in the light from the candles on the altar. The cool dimness of a Romanesque church was a welcome relief to people who spent most of their day in the hot sun of Italy and southern France, where many Romanesque churches were built.

Gothic architecture developed from Romanesque, but with a very different effect. A Gothic church was a more delicate structure and had many windows which flooded the church with

A ROMANESQUE CHURCH. This church at Poitiers in France is an example of early Romanesque architecture, which is characterized by rounded arches, small windows, and thick walls.

sunlight. In the twelfth century, architects discovered that by using a pointed arch instead of a round one, they could enclose a wider floor space and raise the ceiling higher than was possible in a Romanesque church. Using a new engineering principle, they constructed the vaulted stone ceiling so that its weight was concentrated at only a few points instead of along the entire length of the wall. In order to support the weight at these points, architects devised a winglike bridge of stone called a flying buttress, which connected the wall with a support standing on the ground outside the church. Because the flying buttress took the weight of the roof off the walls, large portions of the walls could be replaced by huge windows. Medieval craftsmen filled these windows with hundreds of small pieces of brilliantly colored stained glass. The pieces, joined together by strips of lead, formed a picture. At the front of the cathedral, between two high bell towers, was a huge circular window shaped like an open rose. Sunlight poured through the stained glass and cast jewel-like reflections on the gray walls. The stained glass in the cathedral of Chartres (*shar*-tr') in France is one example of the breathtaking beauty which could be achieved in the Gothic cathedral. Most of the Gothic cathedrals were

A GOTHIC CATHEDRAL. Notice how the cathedral at Chartres dominates the surrounding town. It was begun during the twelfth century through the co-operative efforts of all the townspeople. Because of lack of funds, the left tower was not finished until the early sixteenth century.

GARGOYLES. Atop Notre Dame Cathedral these gargoyles seem to peer down at the city of Paris. This famous medieval cathedral was built on the site of the original fortress city. Paris has no very tall buildings, so Notre Dame even now dominates the skyline.

built in northern Europe, where the brilliance of the sunlit interiors made a pleasant contrast with the damp, cool climate. The pointed roofs were much better suited to the snow and rain of northern climates than were the flat roofs in the south. Thus, we again see geography influencing architecture. But the vertical lines of steep roofs, high slender towers, delicate columns, and pointed arches also had a symbolic purpose. Because this architecture drew the eyes of the worshiper upward, it seemed to draw his thoughts upward too.

Cathedrals were the Bibles of the people. Most people in the Middle Ages could neither read nor write. Almost no one but the clergy studied the Bible, but laymen could learn about the Bible from the cathedrals. The stained glass windows told, in pictures, the stories of Jesus, Mary, and the many saints. Hundreds of carvings on the inside and outside of cathedrals represented biblical characters. Wherever there was room, the artists tucked in scenes from everyday life. People could see carvings showing peasants in the fields and craftsmen at work. Marvelous carvings of flowers and animals reminded them that God had created the world and everything in it. Devilish and grotesque gargoyles, which served as waterspouts, glared down at worshipers to warn them against temptation and sin.

UNIVERSITIES TAUGHT MEN TO SERVE GOD THROUGH REASON

Western scholars came into contact with Moslem culture. Until the twelfth century, a young man who wanted an education had to go to a monastery. As towns developed, cathedral schools were opened. In the cathedral school, all the teachers were clergymen and nearly all the students planned to become priests. Understandably enough, the subjects were almost entirely religious. In the twelfth century, the emphasis began to shift from religion. Increased Mediterranean trade brought Western Europe into contact with Moslem civilization. Moslem scholars, you will remember from Chapter 20, had studied and translated Greek and Roman works, which had been preserved in the Byzantine Empire. Many European scholars were attracted to centers of Moslem learning in Constantinople and Spain. They translated the works of the ancient world from Arabic into Latin. The European scholars also began to read the Latin classics that had been gathering dust in monastery libraries. When these scholars returned home, they spread the new learning that they had acquired. Lecture groups, formed by these scholars, became the basis for the medieval university.

Medieval universities set the pattern for our schools of higher learning today. A visitor to the University of Paris in the twelfth century would have found no libraries, no dormitories, no laboratories, and no campus. In fact, the medieval university had little except the two essential ingredients, teachers and students. A teacher who had earned a reputation for learning, perhaps from study in Spain, would rent a room in the town and announce the subject on which he planned to lecture. He would then charge a fee for attendance. Students moved from town to town listening to the lectures of the various teachers. There were no boards of admissions to accept students formally, no degrees, and no examinations by which to measure learning.

STUDENTS. In this classroom at the University of Paris, students are being led in discussion as three proctors maintain order. Texts and seats, as portrayed here, were considered luxuries in the schools of the Middle Ages.

Gradually, the teachers in Paris united into a guild or corporation and drew up rules to protect teaching standards (*university* comes from the Latin word *universus,* meaning "combined"). By banding together, the teachers were able to prevent unqualified people from teaching. The responsibility for choosing teachers was left to the chancellor, who was the head of the university and also a high Church official. He was careful to select only scholars whose teachings would not weaken the Christian faith. Thus the Church, by maintaining general direction of the universities, continued to influence medieval education.

All students were considered to be members of the clergy, although many planned to become doctors or lawyers instead of priests. They even wore black gowns like those of the clergy. Today American college students wear the same kind of gown when they receive degrees. The tradition reminds us that all education was once under the direction of the Church.

The University of Paris, which became the model for other universities that developed in northern Europe, was divided into four schools. Boys studied logic, grammar, rhetoric, arithmetic, geometry, music, and astronomy for four years. When they completed these subjects, they received the degree of Bachelor of Arts, just as a college graduate does today. Then, if they were able, they could study for six additional years at the schools of theology, medicine, or law until they won master's degrees and earned the right to teach their specialties. Just as the journeyman laborer was required to submit his masterpiece before becoming a master craftsman, so the medieval stu-

ST. THOMAS AQUINAS. A brilliant scholar and lecturer, St. Thomas's system of thought provided a firm foundation for Catholic philosophy. He was affectionately nicknamed "the dumb ox" because he was slow in manner and quite stout.

dent had to take oral examinations to determine whether he was qualified for his degree.

Often the student went to lectures at five in the morning. With his feet wrapped in straw, he sat in the cold lecture room and took notes while the professor read aloud and made comments. The textbook was usually by Aristotle, whom medieval scholars considered the greatest of the Greek philosophers. Because books were too expensive, students had to write down or memorize everything. No student was required to work at his studies if he chose not to. Those students who found study too much effort spent their time in the wine shops singing rowdy songs in Latin or brawling with the apprentices. Students spoke Latin, the language of all their books and lectures. One interesting result is that the Left Bank of Paris, where the University stood, is still known as the Latin Quarter.

Abelard asked too many questions. Western scholars greatly admired the works of Aristotle and were fascinated by his system of logic. But Aristotle was a pagan, whose ideas sometimes differed from those of Christians. Some churchmen feared that a knowledge of Aristotle might undermine men's faith in Christianity. The Greek habit of asking questions seemed particularly dangerous, in what was seen as a conflict between reason and faith.

One scholar who had studied Aristotle's teachings seemed to justify these fears. Peter Abelard (*ab*-eh-lard) began to lecture at Paris in the twelfth century. His fame as one of the greatest teachers of the Middle Ages brought students to him from all over Europe and made Paris the capital of learning in the West. Like Socrates, Abelard taught that men should ask questions about their faith. Only when they really understood could they believe. Abelard's famous book, *Sic et Non*, which means "Yes and No," asked many questions. The answers, which he took from the writings of the Church Fathers, presented conflicting sides of religious questions. The student was left to draw his own conclusions. Although Abelard was a devout Christian, many theologians disapproved of his method. Abelard's book seemed to deny that Christianity gave men precise answers to all questions. The Church felt that to leave religious matters up to the student's choice was to risk the safety of his soul. Besides, Abelard's fellow teachers were jealous of his success. As a consequence, he was charged with heresy and driven out of Paris. Eventually he retired to a monastery. We know much of Abelard's life from his autobiographical writings.

St. Thomas Aquinas tried to combine reason and faith. A century later, St. Thomas Aquinas, the Dominican monk whom you met in Chapter 24, succeeded in combining Greek reason with Christian faith. He believed that Aristotle's logic need not threaten man's faith but should instead be used to help him better understand God. St. Thomas followed Abelard's method of asking questions, but he was careful to work out a definite answer to each question. In his books he used Aristotle's logic to examine the teachings of Christianity. The Roman Catholic Church today still uses many of these books, the most famous of which is *Summa Theologica.*

The University of Paris, where St. Thomas taught, became the center of the new philosophy that tried to combine reason and faith. This philosophy was called *scholasticism.* The scholastics began by compiling everything that had been said by ancient authorities on a particular subject, then reached conclusions by logical argument.

By the fourteenth century, many churchmen began to doubt the value of using reason to decide religious questions. The philosopher Duns Scotus was much closer to the point of view of modern science. He declared that reason could not supply proof in matters of faith; it could only tell men about the world in which they live. Scotus pointed out that even Aristotle, for all his reasoning, had died a pagan. Knowledge of God, Scotus said, must come through faith.

Chapter Check-up

1. Why did the people of the Middle Ages spend so much time, effort, and money on their cathedrals?
2. How do the Romanesque and Gothic styles of architecture differ?
3. What influence did Moslem scholars have on learning in medieval Europe?
4. How did the Church maintain control over medieval education?
5. What were some of the techniques used in teaching at the University of Paris that we might think strange today?
6. What was studied in medieval universities?
7. How have medieval universities influenced those of today?
8. Why were Abelard's methods of teaching disapproved of by many churchmen?
9. What is scholasticism?
10. How do St. Thomas Aquinas and Duns Scotus reflect differing attitudes toward reason?

The Middle Ages: SYNOPSIS

The Middle Ages bridge the great gulf between the destructive barbarian invasions of the fifth century and the dawn of modern times in the fifteenth. During those ten centuries, the bleak European wilderness underwent a remarkable transformation. By 1200, newly developed cities could boast of their prosperous industry and trade, their marvelous architectural achievement, and their reawakened interest in learning. In the process of this transformation, four distinct forces were at work. The first three, the Roman Catholic Church, feudalism, and the manorial system, restored spiritual, political, and economic security to medieval man. Later, the rise of towns and the development of trade brought him the wealth to express his faith more fully. This new wealth also increased his power to bargain with the local lord and led ultimately to the destruction of feudalism.

Unlike modern civilization, medieval civilization was almost totally inspired and directed by the Church. Medieval man believed that the next world was more important than this one. He obeyed the Church because it held the key to the most precious of all gifts, spiritual salvation. He relied on the Church not only for salvation, but for many other services, such as education, protection from injustice, and the preservation of peace and order. When churchmen became entangled in the feudal system, however, the Church and the temporal powers came into prolonged conflict. Although this conflict did not result in a complete victory for the Church, the Church remained the dominant force throughout the Middle Ages. The crusades marked the high point of the Church's influence.

The development of trade and the rise of independent towns tended to draw men's interest from spiritual to worldly affairs. Both the crusading spirit and interest in religion in general began to lessen. But the movement away from the Church was slowed by the work of two new religious orders: the Franciscan and Dominican friars. Merchant and craft guilds, by limiting competition and setting just prices, also reinforced the Church's teaching that making money at the expense of others was wrong. Much of the wealth of rich merchants and guild masters was given to the Church for cathedrals and works of charity. Even medieval scholars used their new knowledge to strengthen the Church. They believed that knowledge and artistic achievement were valuable only if they helped man to understand or glorify God. Thus the Middle Ages was truly the Age of Faith.

Feudalism and the manorial system have long since been discarded, but other developments of the Middle Ages live on today. The Roman Catholic Church, although it no longer dominates Western civilization, remains an important influence. The vast changes brought on by the rise of towns and the introduction of a money economy are still being felt. During the Middle Ages, important steps were made toward the development of representative government. You will see in later Parts of *Story of Nations* how important these changes were in helping to bring about the kind of world in which you now live.

Important People

How has each of the following influenced the story of the Middle Ages?

St. Benedict
Clovis
Charlemagne
Pope Gregory VII
Henry IV
Pope Urban II
Peter the Hermit
Stephen
Saladin
Frederick Barbarossa
Richard the Lionhearted
St. Francis
St. Thomas Aquinas
Abelard

Terms

Be sure that you understand clearly the meaning of each of the following:

Book of Hours
burgher
chivalry
crusades
Dark Ages
excommunication
feudalism
fief
friars
Gothic
guilds
Hanseatic League
Holy Roman Empire
illuminated manuscript
knight
lay investiture
manor
manorial system
medieval
regular clergy
money economy
page
representative government
Romanesque
scholasticism
spiritual power
temporal power
Truce of God
vassal
secular clergy

Questions for Discussion and Review

1. Explain how feudalism helped meet the needs of medieval times.
2. What is the difference between the feudal system and the manorial system?
3. How did each of the following act to weaken the feudal system? (a) crusades (b) growth of towns (c) wider use of money.
4. Briefly describe a typical medieval castle. Explain how it met the needs of the time.
5. How did the different regions of Europe take advantage of geography as trade increased?
6. How did the medieval guilds differ from the labor unions of today?
7. In what way did the growth of towns encourage the development of self-government?
8. Do you consider the power of the Church to be as great today as it was during medieval times? Explain your answer.
9. In what sense can the crusades be considered successful failures?
10. The medieval period was above all the Age of Faith. Explain.

Interesting Things to Do

1. Make a map of medieval Europe showing the important rivers, trade routes, and cities. Also show the Holy Roman Empire.
2. Prepare a chart or poster graphically illustrating the organization of a feudal kingdom. Be sure that your work explains the meanings of the terms *lord*, *vassal*, and *fief*.
3. Draw some medieval costumes, showing the typical clothing of nobles, clergy, and serfs.
4. Present a short recorded program of medieval folk songs and church music.
5. Report to the class on the life of one of the great religious leaders or scholars of the Middle Ages, such as St. Thomas Aquinas, St. Benedict, St. Francis, or Peter Abelard.
6. Prepare and present to the class a report on the famous Cathedral of Notre Dame.
7. Read the prologue to Chaucer's "Canterbury Tales" and write a description of a medieval pilgrimage.
8. Add to or begin your "Who's Who in World History" series by writing one or more brief biographies of important leaders of the Middle Ages.

Interesting Reading about the Middle Ages

*Augur, Helen, *Book of Fairs*, Harcourt, Brace & World.

Brooks, Polly S. and N. Z. Walworth, *The World of Walls*, Lippincott. A history of the Middle Ages.

Chaucer, Geoffrey, *Canterbury Tales*, ed. R. A. Jeliffe, Scribner. Glimpses of medieval life through Chaucer's eyes.

Davis, William S., *Life on a Medieval Barony*, Harper & Row. Rich in details of medieval life in the twelfth century.

*Gray, Elizabeth J., *Adam of the Road*, Viking.

*Hartman, Gertrude, *Medieval Days and Ways*, Macmillan. Full account of daily life.

*Hewes, Agnes D., *Boy of the Last Crusade*, Houghton Mifflin.

Hollister, Charles Warren, *Medieval Europe: A Short History*, Wiley.

Jewett, Sophie, *God's Troubadour*, Crowell Collier. Story of St. Francis.

*Lamb, Harold, *The Crusades*, Doubleday

*Mills, Dorothy, *Middle Ages*, Putnam. Good source material.

*Pyle, Howard, *Men of Iron*, Harper & Row.

Sellman, Roger R., *The Crusades*, Roy.

*Tappan, E. M., *When Knights Were Bold*, Houghton Mifflin.

Temko, Allan, *Notre Dame of Paris*, Viking.

* Indicates easy reading

Renaissance man had such confidence in his intellectual powers, he felt he could cope with any problem—human or divine—that might arise in his expanding universe.

Part 8
THE RENAISSANCE AND REFORMATION
BIRTH OF THE MODERN WORLD

RENAISSANCE EUROPE

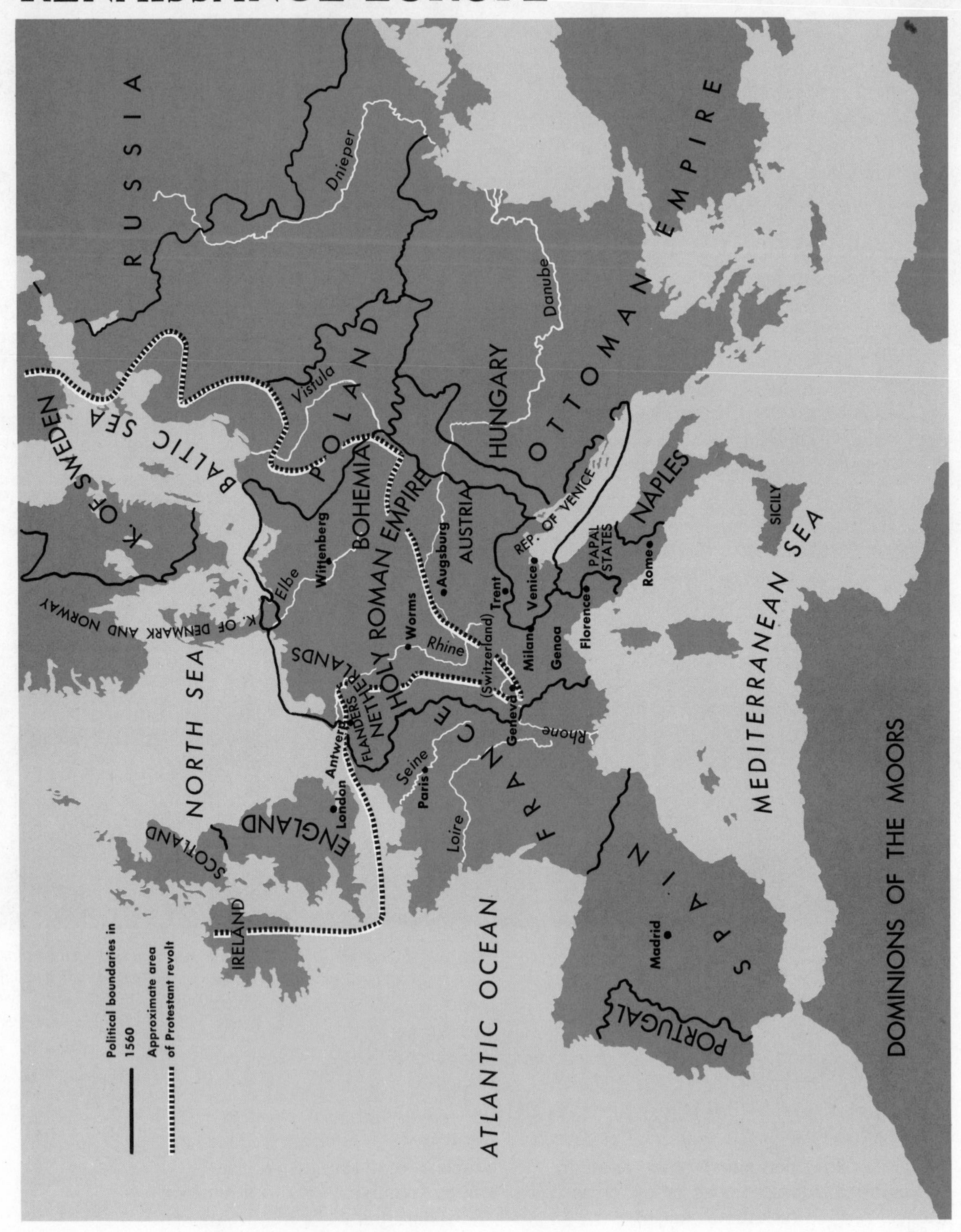

Renaissance & Reformation: GEOGRAPHIC SETTING

In Part 7 we saw how the people of Europe lived during the period of history known as the Middle Ages. We now move forward in time, but our attention remains focused on Europe. For it was here, in the twilight of the Middle Ages, that vast changes began to reshape men's lives and to mark the beginning of modern times.

The birthplace of many of these changes was the Italian Peninsula, which had earlier served as the hub of the ancient Roman Empire. The peninsula's location on the Mediterranean trade routes, midway between Western Europe and the Middle East, gave rise to great commercial cities and a rich merchant class. Such cities as Venice, Florence, and Genoa played an important part in the revival of learning that characterized the Renaissance in Western Europe.

In time, commercial rivalry and new inventions made longer voyages possible, and men began to turn their attention to the unknown lands beyond the Atlantic. As they did so, the ports of Spain, Portugal, England, and the Low Countries increased in importance and eventually became the main trading centers of Europe. Daring explorers began to chart unknown territories.

One of the most important changes that occurred at this time was in the area of religious faith. New ideas and attitudes caused many men to question traditional religious teachings. The result was a break with the Church, known as the Reformation, which began in Germany in the sixteenth century. Soon it spread throughout northern Europe. The map on the adjoining page shows the extent of the Reformation.

Renaissance & Reformation: PERSPECTIVE

Men of all ages and all nations have been fascinated by the stars, believing that somehow the heavenly bodies could provide answers to nature's mysteries. During the Middle Ages men peered endlessly into the night sky to study the positions of the sparkling pinpoints of light overhead. Then, thumbing through musty old hand-copied books, they tried to unlock the secrets of nature. These men were called astrologers, and their main purpose was to foresee the future. They never succeeded, but they kept trying because their books told them it was possible—and it never occurred to them to question their books. For centuries, they continued to read the books and look at the stars.

In the sixteenth century, as the Renaissance was spreading in Europe, men were still looking at the stars, but their purpose had undergone a remarkable change. The most advanced minds of the age no longer believed they could foresee the future by studying the position of stars. Instead, they wanted to know what the heavenly bodies were made of and why they moved the way they did. One man, Galileo, used the first crude telescope to make important new observations which caused scientists to alter their beliefs about the universe.

Renaissance man's curiosity about the heavens was paralleled by a similar desire to know more about the earth and about man's place in it. No longer content to accept the ideas they found in old books, men began to look closely at nature itself. In doing so, they challenged opinions which had been accepted for centuries. In science, geography, art, and especially in religion, the Renaissance and Reformation marked a break with the past and a rapid movement in a new direction.

CHAPTER 26

The Renaissance Brought a New Spirit to Western Europe

THE MEDIEVAL WORLD BECAME MODERN

The medieval quest for security gave way to Renaissance enthusiasm for individual freedom and worldly interests. You live in a world that is basically different from the medieval world. Today most men are no longer lords or serfs but free citizens of independent nations. Their attitude toward life has changed. They are more questioning and critical toward the things they are asked to believe. They are much less concerned about life after death, and they possess a great variety of interests and tastes that are not connected in any way with religious affairs.

Most of the changes that make the modern world so different from the medieval world took place in Europe between 1400 and 1600. This period is known as the *Renaissance* (ren-eh-*zahns*), a French word that means "rebirth." The Renaissance saw the rebirth of two important beliefs that had been lost to the world after the decline of Rome: 1) the belief that man should be free to develop his abilities and interests; and 2) the belief that man should seek the fullest enjoyment of life.

Individual self-development played little part in the medieval world where man was so desperate to achieve security that he willingly gave up his independence in exchange for it. Whether churchman, vassal, serf, or guild member, he was bound to his group and forced by circumstances to obey the Pope, his lord, or his guildmaster. During the Renaissance, however, man developed confidence in himself and became much more self-reliant. He was imbued with a spirit of enterprise and adventure. Renaissance men made fortunes at trade, went on daring voyages to discover new lands, and created works of great beauty.

Europeans acquired many new interests and tastes. They wanted to make money so they could live in comfort and luxury. The Church of the Middle Ages had stressed the joys of the spirit in contrast to worldly pleasures. While Renaissance man was still religious, he also developed many other interests and sought variety. Religious affairs became just one part of his life instead of the controlling force.

The Renaissance belief in the importance of the individual man and his earthly affairs is called *humanism.* Because the attitude toward life adopted by Renaissance man is so much like that of men today, the Renaissance is often said to mark the beginning of modern times.

Widespread use of money undermined feudalism and increased the power of kings. The Renaissance was not born overnight but was the fruit of important developments that were already taking shape in the late Middle Ages. One of these developments, the increased use of money, helped to bring an end to the feudal system and thus cleared the way for the kings and merchants who were to dominate Renaissance Europe.

As trade expanded, prices and wages rose. Craftsmen, merchants, and even peasants shared in the prosperity. The feudal lords were at a disadvantage, however, because their income depended on rents and charters which were established by custom and could not be changed. Refusing to become merchants because they believed trade dishonorable for a nobleman, they were forced to borrow money and then to sell their lands to maintain themselves.

The financial difficulties of the lords forced them to accept money in place of feudal and manorial obligations. Thus they lost control of their vassals and serfs. Meantime, the kings, supported by the rich merchants, were establishing paid armies and officials to take over the feudal tasks of providing protection and justice. The result of these changes was that great feudal barons became little more than landlords, while the power of kings steadily increased. The decline of the nobility and the rise of the monarchy played an important part in freeing Renaissance man from the feudal restrictions which had so rigidly controlled the lives of men in the Middle Ages.

Increased interest in wealth weakened the Church; strong kings challenged it. Another late medieval development that helped to produce the Renaissance was the steady decline of the Church's influence during the fourteenth century. As we have noted, Renaissance man was more and more attracted by worldly interests, and he sought to use his new-found wealth to make his earthly life more enjoyable. Even members of the clergy were influenced by the trend toward making life comfortable and pleasant. Indeed, some churchmen were accused of being more interested in such matters than they were in the performance of their churchly duties.

The appearance of strong kings toward the end of the Middle Ages also weakened the Church because these kings were able to challenge the authority of the Pope. In 1296, a French king, Philip IV, quarreled with Pope Boniface VIII about the king's right to tax the French clergy. Philip sent soldiers to capture Boniface and made him a prisoner. Later Philip forced another Pope to move the papal residence to Avignon (ah-vee-*nyawn*) in France, where it remained for the next seventy years. The prestige of the Church suffered greatly as a result of this act. Englishmen and Germans were reluctant to accept a Pope who was under the thumb of the French king.

Toward the end of the fourteenth century the Church suffered another blow to its unity and authority when two different men, one at Rome and one at Avignon, claimed to be Pope. For nearly forty years the matter remained unsettled. Finally a great council of Church officials and secular leaders assembled to decide the issue. They agreed on the selection of a new Pope, who returned the papal residence to Rome. The incident was closed, but the authority and dignity of the Church had been seriously shaken.

The Renaissance began in Italy. Although the Renaissance eventually affected all of Europe, it had its beginnings in Italy, where the people were surrounded by the remains of the glorious Roman civilization. Italy's classical heritage kept medieval ideas from taking as firm root there as they had in the North.

Italy was the birthplace of the Renaissance for still another reason. As we have seen many times in *Story of Nations*, geography plays a vital role in shaping historical events. In the case of Renaissance Italy, it was geographic location that was

The Pazzi Chapel. The Renaissance witnessed a great rebirth of interest in classical architecture. Notice the Roman arch and the Corinthian columns of this little chapel built by the wealthy Pazzi family, rivals of the Medicis in Florence.

AVIGNON. The Popes have not always lived in Rome. The building in the background is called the Palace of the Popes because they resided here during their enforced stay in France. Today this fourteenth-century palace is a museum.

the vital factor. Notice on the map on page 221 that Italy lies halfway between Western Europe and the Middle East. This position gave Italy a natural advantage in trade between the two areas, and many of its cities became great commercial centers. Italian merchants were soon numbered among the richest men in Europe. The central location of Italy also enabled it to receive a steady influx of ideas from both East and West.

Because medieval Italy had been the scene of constant struggle among Popes, emperors, and nobles, no single authority controlled the northern part of the peninsula. Italian cities such as Venice, Florence, Genoa, and Milan were free to elect their own rulers. Often they chose their leaders from among the rich merchants and bankers who, in turn, used their wealth to finance the great cultural revival of the period. Just as wealth and freedom were necessary to the flowering of genius in Athens, so riches and self-government in the Italian cities provided the soil in which Renaissance ideas flourished. Indeed, Florence produced such a brilliant Renaissance culture that it became known as the "Athens of Italy."

THE HUMANISTS FOUND NEW INSPIRATION IN CLASSICAL IDEALS

Humanism became the guiding force of the Renaissance. Humanism is an attitude toward life that centers on man and the opportunities for a full and rich life available to him here on earth. The humanist outlook shaped the thinking of all the great artists, writers, and scientists of the Renaissance. You may recall that the ancient Greeks and Romans had a similar viewpoint. They, too, centered their interests on human activities and human achievements. It is not surprising then, that the great humanists of the Renaissance carefully studied the literature and art of the Greeks and Romans in order to gain inspiration for their own works.

Dante created a masterpiece of Italian poetry. Although the great Florentine poet, Dante, did not live during the Renaissance, he is considered one of its important forerunners because his writings did so much to change the world of literature from medieval to modern. His masterpiece, *The Divine Comedy*, has a conventional medieval religious theme, but the kind of characters he created and the language he used are more typical of Renaissance literature.

The poem, written about 1300, describes Dante's imaginary trip through hell, purgatory, and heaven. Intensely religious himself, Dante wrote the poem to show men that God would reward or punish them according to their behavior on earth. In this respect he voiced the medieval opinion that man's principal duty in this world was to prepare himself for the next.

The characters Dante used show that he had a humanist's admiration for the classics. He made the Roman poet Vergil his guide through hell, and he included in his poem many other figures from classical history and mythology. Other individuals whom he encountered on his journey were Italians of his own day. He even included in hell a Pope of whom he disapproved—an act of disrespect which a medieval writer would never have considered.

Perhaps the most important feature of *The Divine Comedy* was the fact that it was written in everyday Italian rather than in Latin, the language which had always been used for religious subjects. Dante employed Italian so beautifully that men began to realize that the common people's native

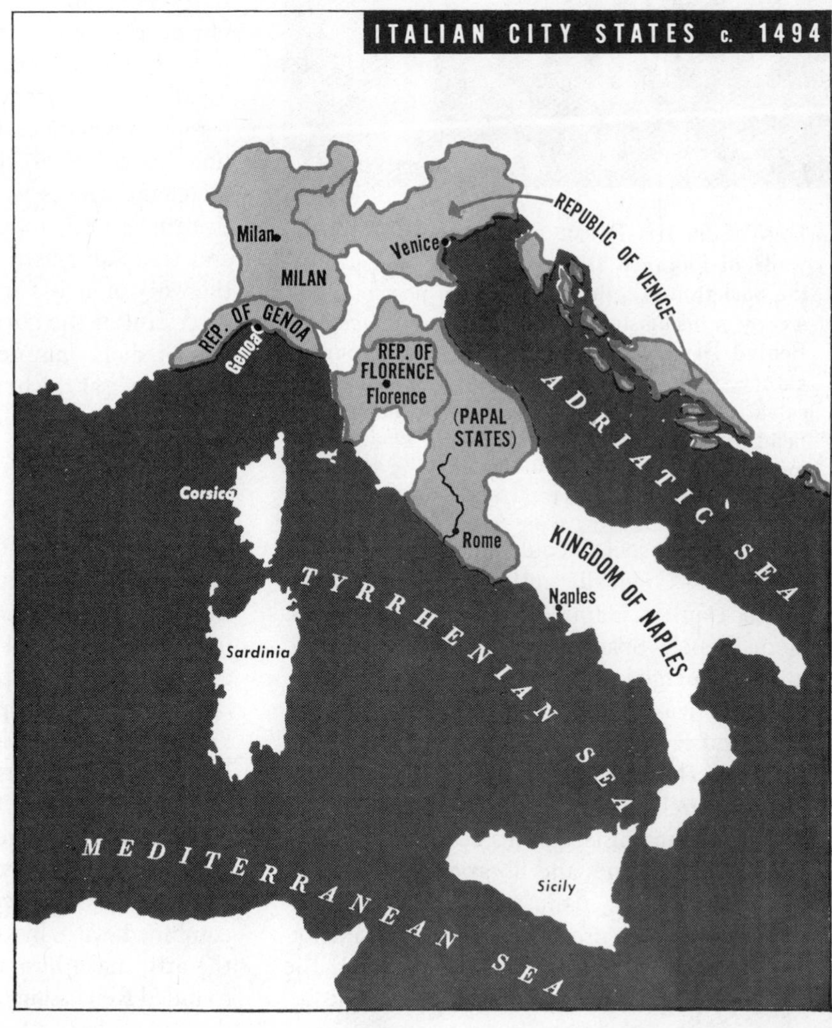

DANTE AND HIS POEM. Standing before the walls of Florence (the cathedral dome is in the background), the great Italian poet holds a copy of his masterpiece, *The Divine Comedy*. Behind Dante's right hand is the hill of purgatory, where souls are working to achieve salvation. The angel is marking on the forehead of each the number of sins for which he must atone.

tongue, the *vernacular*, could be effectively used in literature. Gradually authors all over Europe followed Dante's example. From their efforts, modern French, Spanish, and German literature eventually emerged.

Petrarch was devoted to the works of the Greeks and Romans. Because of his passionate devotion to the classics, the brilliant Florentine scholar, Petrarch, is considered the foremost of the Renaissance humanists. In his zeal Petrarch ransacked the monasteries and libraries of all Europe for Latin and Greek manuscripts, often unearthing rare literary treasures where they had lain forgotten for many centuries. Petrarch studied the Latin manuscripts until his own literary style became as polished as that of Cicero, the Roman author whom Petrarch most admired. Although he could not find anyone to teach him Greek, he cherished the Greek manuscripts as much as he did the Latin.

Petrarch's enthusiasm for classical literature captured the imagination of Italian scholars and rulers. For the next two hundred years they devoted themselves to classical rather than Christian literature. Later Renaissance writers copied the style of the Roman poets Horace and Ovid, and Renaissance philosophers diligently studied the works of Plato.

Italian merchant-princes aided the development of Renaissance culture. The Italian city-states were ruled not by hereditary kings, as the rest of Europe was, but by local businessmen who were elected to office. These elected officials were usually chosen from among a town's most prosperous merchants. Because they held their position by virtue of ability rather than birth, the merchant-princes were frequently the most effective rulers in Europe. They encouraged industry and trade and used their own wealth to finance the work of artists and scholars. One of the most successful of the governing merchant families was the Medici (*may*-dee-chee), who ruled the city of Florence at the height of its glory.

Lorenzo de' Medici, the most famous of the Renaissance princes, took a great interest in the work of humanist scholars. He supported an academy where scholars met to discuss Plato, and he hired agents to hunt out rare books and manuscripts for the library that his grandfather had started. Nor did Lorenzo himself neglect learning. He diligently studied Latin and Greek. As a pastime he composed poetry in Italian, the language of his people. He filled the gardens of his palace with classical statues, many of which he bought from farmers who accidentally unearthed them while plowing their fields. Because Lorenzo did so much to make Florence the cultural center of Renaissance Italy, he became known as "Lorenzo the Magnificent." His practical ability, combined with his enthusiasm for learning and the arts, make him a perfect example of the well-rounded Renaissance man.

THE CATHEDRAL OF FLORENCE. When Michelangelo was commissioned to build a dome for St. Peter's in Rome, he first studied this one designed by Brunelleschi. He said that a bigger dome could be built, but never one more beautiful. The equally famous bell tower was designed by the Florentine painter and architect Giotto.

The humanist ideal influenced education. The scholarly interests of Lorenzo and other princes of the day showed how medieval ideas were changing. Because a medieval man most admired knights and monks, he wanted his sons to train for these specific vocations. But the ideal man of the Renaissance was expected to perform ably in many fields. According to the description given by the Italian nobleman Castiglione (kahs-tee-*lyo*-nay) in his widely read book, *The Courtier*, a perfect gentleman should combine the attributes of warrior and scholar and should cultivate an appreciation of art, music, and poetry.

As the belief that education should create well-rounded gentlemen gained acceptance, Renaissance schools began to train boys in many different skills and branches of learning. The great humanist teachers of the day required that their pupils study the classics because they believed that knowledge of Greek and Roman literature liberated the mind from the narrowness of personal experience or prejudice. This desire to "liberate" the mind is the underlying principle of the modern liberal arts college. Today's educational ideals are closely related to those of the Renaissance.

Machiavelli wrote a "handbook" for rulers. A Florentine diplomat named Niccolo Machiavelli (mah-kyah-*vel*-lee) expressed in his book, *The Prince*, a philosophy of success that was to have great influence on modern governments. Written early in the sixteenth century, the book advised rulers not to hesitate in using cunning, cruelty and even dishonesty to gain and hold power. Nothing, said Machiavelli, must be allowed to stand in the way of building a strong, unified nation. His ideas are expressed in the slogan "Might makes right."

Machiavelli's goals were in agreement with the humanist emphasis on worldly success, but the methods he advanced were rejected by humanists who believed that a good ruler should govern according to Christian principles of justice. Machiavelli claimed to be taking a practical "scientific attitude" toward politics in an effort to learn how a successful ruler actually governed, not in how he was believed to govern. After studying Roman history and the conditions in Italy in his day, Machiavelli concluded that the most successful rulers were usually the most ruthless. For this reason, he argued, an ambitious politician should not hesitate to commit any deceitful or unjust act that would enhance his power. Many people, upon reading *The Prince,* thought that Machiavelli was a spokesman for the devil. Even today, a crafty, treacherous person is often said to be "Machiavellian."

Machiavelli himself was an honest, upright man, and a good father to his children. He was an intensely patriotic citizen of Florence. His observations of Italian politics convinced him that the only way to save his beloved city and restore Italy to its ancient glory was under a strong and ruthless leader. *The Prince* was to provide a practical plan for all this. Machiavelli felt that only a strong and clever prince could succeed in uniting the warring, independent Italian city-states, even against their will if necessary.

Machiavelli was unsuccessful in persuading the Medici rulers of Florence to accept his formula for uniting Italy. In the nineteenth and twentieth centuries, however, Machiavellian political principles became the basis of a new school of political thinking that had great impact on the world. The most enthusiastic modern advocates of Machiavelli's philosophy have been dictators like Mussolini, Hitler, and Stalin.

Machiavelli. **Coldly practical in his political thought, Machiavelli wished above all to see Italy united and free. He is often credited with having originated the art of modern politics.**

RENAISSANCE ARTISTS SAW BEAUTY IN EVERYDAY LIFE

Humanism influenced Italian artists. Because medieval painters and sculptors had believed that the soul was more important than the body, they tended to use their art to teach Christianity rather than to stress the beauty of the human form. Like the humanist scholars, Renaissance artists turned to Greek models for their inspiration. They went to the palaces of rich merchants like Lorenzo de' Medici, who had collected Greek and Roman statues. There they studied the classic masterpieces in order to improve their own work. Like the Greeks, they took an almost scientific interest in the human body, making detailed drawings of muscles and bones. They experimented with light and shade in order to make their figures look round, instead of flat as in medieval paintings. A Renaissance artist wanted to make his work of art resemble the real object as it appeared in nature.

Their interest in nature led the Renaissance artists to try to place man against a natural background. Medieval artists had usually painted flat, unrealistic backgrounds. To capture the proper effect in showing distance, Renaissance painters made use of the laws of perspective. Because they admired the beauties of nature, their landscapes included such details as clouds, trees, flowers, and even blades of grass. Italy became such a brilliant center of artistic achievement that many foreign artists went there to study. When they returned to their own countries, they brought the new ideas with them.

Leonardo da Vinci was a versatile genius. One of the most remarkable figures of history is Leonardo da Vinci (*veen*-chee), who was not only a renowned Renaissance painter but also an accomplished sculptor, architect, musician, engineer, and philosopher. His amazing versatility makes him one of the best examples of the ideal Renaissance man. Indeed, many of his ideas reveal that Leonardo was hundreds of years ahead of his time. He designed, for example, a crude airplane, a self-propelled vehicle that resembled a car, and many kinds of military machinery, such as catapults and tanks.

Leonardo is best known today, however, for his painting. His interest in science led him to fill his notebooks with careful calculations of perspective and with painstaking studies of light and shadow. He analyzed the structure of the human skeleton, of plants, and even of rocks. The knowledge he gained in this way helped to give his paintings their outstanding qualities and to make them remarkably true to life. One of his most famous paintings is "The Last Supper," which shows Jesus with his twelve disciples on the eve of his Crucifixion (see page 148.) The work, painted nearly five hundred years ago, shows such

Lorenzo de' Medici. Called Lorenzo the Magnificent, this Renaissance man was a statesman, poet, and financier. As a patron of the arts, he enabled many of the greatest artists of his time to produce the masterpieces for which we know them today.

A Self-propelled Car. Leonardo's inventive genius took many turns. This fifteenth-century vehicle was constructed from directions he left in his notebooks. Power was provided by a system of springs and gears.

THE CREATION OF ADAM. God imparts life to Adam in this fresco, which is a panel from Michelangelo's monumental epic of mankind on the ceiling of the Sistine Chapel.

skill that no painting of the same scene has ever surpassed it. Another well-known work that shows Leonardo's accomplishments as a painter is the "Mona Lisa," a portrait of a woman whose mysterious smile has been the subject of much discussion. Although it is a small painting (only about twenty by thirty inches), you can see in it Leonardo's wonderful skill in handling soft light and shadows to make figures come alive. In the background, a fantastic, rocky landscape reveals the artist's mastery of perspective and reflects his interest in the science of geology.

Michelangelo was a master sculptor and painter. Another of the great geniuses of the Italian Renaissance is Michelangelo (my-kel-*an*-jeh-lo). At thirteen he became an apprentice to a famous Florentine painter. His work won the favor of Lorenzo de' Medici, who invited him to study the Greek statues in the Medici garden.

MONA LISA. The mysterious smile on the face of Mona Lisa in this famous painting by Leonardo has puzzled and intrigued the world for generations. She has been the subject of innumerable poems and songs.

MADONNA OF THE GOLDFINCH. The Virgin Mary, the infant Jesus, and St. John holding a goldfinch are grouped against an Italian background in the favorite triangular design of the painter Raphael.

Michelangelo combined a rare ability with an intense devotion to work. These qualities are shown in his first masterpiece, the statue of David. Someone urged him to try his hand at a huge block of marble which, forty years earlier, another artist had spoiled. Michelangelo prepared sketches and wax models, and then he hammered away at the block with mallet and chisel. For two years he worked at the task. Finally there emerged from the block of stone a magnificent statue of the Hebrew hero, David. This statue won immediate acclaim and Michelangelo became one of the most popular sculptors in Italy.

His fame so much impressed Pope Julius II that he asked Michelangelo to paint the ceiling of the Sistine Chapel in the Vatican (the papal palace). Michelangelo protested that he was a sculptor, not a painter. When Julius insisted, however, the artist set to work with characteristic vigor. For the next four years, he worked day after day flat on his back on a narrow scaffold built so that he was within reach of the high ceiling. He often worked under the most cramped conditions, and frequently the unheated chapel was cold and damp. The strain on Michelangelo's eyes left his sight permanently impaired. When at last he finished, he had completed one of the world's great works of art. The paintings of the Sistine ceiling told the biblical story of the world from the Creation to the Flood. The hundreds of figures, larger than life-size, reveal Michelangelo's marvelous knowledge of human anatomy. Because he preferred sculpture to painting, he made some of the figures look as if they had been carved out of stone.

Both the "David" and the "Creation" were religious subjects, but their execution shows that Michelangelo was inspired by the work of Greek artists. The statue of David resembles that of a Greek god, and in his "Creation" Michelangelo even included some Greek figures among the Hebrew prophets on the Sistine ceiling. His statues of the Virgin and Christ were also executed in the beautiful form reminiscent of Greek sculpture. Michelangelo did not, however, simply copy the art of the ancient world. He was a powerful and original genius whose use of classical forms had a depth of feeling and a force of expression which the Greeks and Romans never had achieved.

Raphael was called the "perfect painter." Both Leonardo and Michelangelo influenced Raphael (*raf*-ay-el), another of the famous Renaissance artists. Because of the classical harmony and balance of his compositions, he was called the "perfect painter."

During the thirty-seven years of his life, Raphael finished several hundred paintings. Many of them were large frescoes on the walls of the Vatican, like "The School of Athens," a huge piece representing the philosophers, poets, and scientists of ancient Greece. His most popular works,

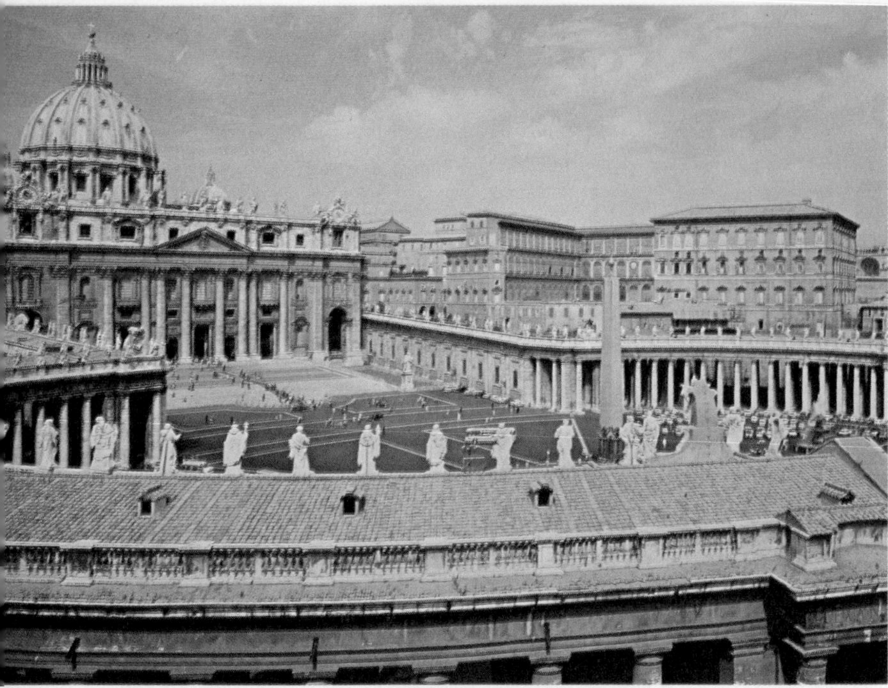

ST. PETER'S. This famous church, the largest in the world, is built on the site of a fourth-century basilica. Among the well-known architects who worked on it were Bramante, who made the original design, Michelangelo, who designed the dome, and Bernini, who designed the colonnades enclosing the piazza, or open courtyard.

however, were his graceful, polished paintings of the Madonna and Child, such as the "Sistine Madonna" and the "Madonna of the Goldfinch." The second of these famous paintings by Raphael is reproduced at the top of the preceding page.

Renaissance architecture followed classical forms. Merchant princes in the Italian cities preferred comfortable palaces to castles that were constructed to withstand siege. They hired architects to plan their palaces and churches according to classical designs. The builders of the Italian Renaissance used Greek columns, Roman arches and domes, and other features of ancient buildings which had survived the Middle Ages. Since the Gothic architecture of northern Europe (see pages 207–209) had never taken root in Italy, the classical form of Renaissance architecture marked a revival of the ancient Greek and Roman styles rather than a change of taste.

One of the finest examples of Renaissance architecture is St. Peter's Church in Rome. The massive dome, which was designed by Michelangelo, rises four hundred feet into the air and is the largest in the world. Another architect, Bramante (brah-*mahn*-tay), designed the rest of the building. The many Greek columns and classical statues suggest the architecture of a Greek or Roman temple. St. Peter's is the largest church in the world. Together with the Vatican, it covers thirteen acres. The picture at the top of this page shows St. Peter's as it looks today.

Modern musical forms developed during the Renaissance. The music of the fifteenth and sixteenth centuries also reflected the Renaissance spirit. Church leaders recognized that music was one of the matters that required change; the use of the same melodies for religious masses and for popular songs seemed sinful. A gifted young musician, Palestrina (pal-ess-*tree*-nah), composed Masses that were models of what sacred music should be. He produced hundreds of compositions. When he died, the words *Princeps Musicae* "Prince of Music" were engraved on his tombstone. Many of his compositions are still played and admired today.

The sixteenth century also saw the beginning of written instrumental music. Medieval composers had written only the words of songs, and singers made up their own accompaniment on such instruments as the lute, the viola, the oboe, or the organ. During the Renaissance, composers began to write music for voices and instruments together. The *oratorio*, a religious drama set to music, was written for several solo voices, a chorus and an orchestra. From the oratorio, the first modern operas developed.

The Renaissance spirit spread throughout Europe. During the sixteenth century, the center of trade began to shift from the Mediterranean to the Atlantic. As wealth began to flow into France, England, and the Netherlands, these countries, too, began to experience an artistic and scientific awakening. The northern Renaissance produced such great literary and artistic figures as Erasmus of Rotterdam, William Shakespeare, and the Van Eyck brothers. You will read about these and other leaders in the northern Renaissance in later chapters of *Story of Nations.*

The Renaissance spirit also inspired explorers and scientists and affected the fortunes of the Church. It is to these developments that we shall devote the remaining two chapters of Part 8.

Chapter Check-up

1. What is the meaning of the term Renaissance? Where did the Renaissance begin?
2. Why is the Renaissance often said to be the beginning of modern times?
3. How did the widespread use of money undermine feudalism and increase the power of kings?
4. What factors tended to weaken the influence of the medieval Church?
5. What contributions did Dante and Petrarch make to the Renaissance?
6. For what reasons was Lorenzo de' Medici called "the Magnificent"?
7. What was the purpose of education during the Renaissance?
8. What philosophy was expressed by Machiavelli in *The Prince?* How have his ideas influenced the modern world?
9. Describe briefly the artistic achievements of Leonardo, Michelangelo, and Raphael. Which of the three do you think was the most versatile in his talents? Why?
10. Who was the Italian "Prince of Music" and why was he so called?

Chapter 27

Discoveries in Geography and Science Widened Men's Knowledge of the World

EUROPEAN EXPLORERS CONQUERED THE OCEANS AND REACHED THE NEW WORLD

Although Europeans of the fourteenth century knew somewhat more about the world than their predecessors did, they did not venture far from familiar shores. We have seen in Chapter 26 how the Renaissance spirit opened the realm of nature and the achievements of the classical past to eager European minds. Now we shall see how that same spirit led to the conquest of the oceans and the discovery of the New World.

Commercial rivalry and new inventions turned men's eyes to the Atlantic. During the crusades, the Italian city-states had taken advantage of their nearness to eastern Mediterranean ports to gain control of trade with the Middle East. Italian merchants bought the goods carried there by the great caravans from the Far East and resold them to the merchants of Western Europe. The profits from this trade provided the wealth to finance the cultural revival in Renaissance Italy.

In 1271 two enterprising merchants from Venice, the Polo brothers, ventured all the way to China. One of the brothers brought along his son, Marco Polo, and the boy spent the next twenty years traveling about China in the service of the Great Khan. After nearly a quarter of a century the three Polos returned to Venice, dressed in rags so that robbers would not molest them. In the seams of their clothing, however, they had carefully sewn a fortune in rubies, sapphires, and diamonds. Marco's published account of his adventures with the Mongols and of the riches he had seen aroused the interest of men in other European countries. Hoping to avoid the high prices that resulted from dealing with Italian and Arab middlemen, kings and merchants pondered the possibility of establishing a direct water route to the Far East.

PRINCE HENRY THE NAVIGATOR. Prince Henry's interest and encouragement made Portugal a leading maritime nation during the Renaissance.

By the fifteenth century certain new inventions and improved equipment made such a journey possible. Italian sailors had learned from the Arabs how to make a compass by rubbing a steel needle with a magnetic stone (a lodestone). When the needle was balanced on a piece of floating cork, it swung freely and always pointed to the north. The compass made it possible for the captain of a ship to sail out of sight of land and still know in what direction he was traveling. The astrolabe was another invention which made navigation easier. This instrument, the predecessor of the modern sextant, enabled a sailor to measure his position by the stars. In northern Europe ships began to make use of the square sail, which proved so efficient that rows of oarsmen were no longer needed and the ships could be made lighter and more seaworthy.

Portugal and Spain took the lead in opening the Atlantic. Portugal's favorable location on the sea route from Venice to Flanders encouraged her to seek a share of the profitable trade which the Italians had developed. Prince Henry the Navigator, brother of the king of Portugal, was intent upon finding a direct route to the East by sailing around Africa. He established a school where men could study navigation and map-making, and he financed many expeditions. In the fifteenth century, Portuguese sailors ventured farther and farther south along the African coast. When the weather grew warmer near the equator, some of the men feared that they would be burned alive. In 1488, however, a Portuguese explorer, Dias (*dee*-ash), reached the Cape of Good Hope at the southern tip of Africa. Ten years later Vasco da Gama (*ga*-muh) rounded the Cape and succeeded in planting the flag of Portugal on the shore of India.

CHRISTOPHER COLUMBUS. A priest gives his blessing to Columbus and his men as they start off for unknown territories across the Atlantic.

While the Portuguese were investigating the African route to the East, the Spanish were hoping to outrace them to India by sailing west. The discovery of an Atlantic route was delayed, however, by fear and ignorance. Although they believed the earth to be round, Spanish navigators could only guess at its size. Most ordinary seamen believed the world was flat, and they feared falling off the edge or being dragged down by sea monsters. But in 1492 Christopher Columbus won the backing of Queen Isabella of Spain and set off to find the Indies. Instead, as you doubtless know, he discovered the New World.

Columbus' voyage inspired many other adventurers to explore the Americas, as the New World came to be called. The most remarkable voyage was made by Ferdinand Magellan (muh-*jel*-un), who also sailed under the Spanish flag. Magellan's expedition was the first to complete a voyage around the world, although Ma-

VENICE. Venetian supremacy stemmed from the city's position on the Adriatic. This view of the Grand Canal shows the Palace of the Doge, the Venetian ruler. Behind the palace can be seen the famous bell tower and the cupolas of St. Mark's. To this day the gondolas are painted black in memory of those who died in the plague.

gellan himself was killed in the Philippines. This voyage proved to the world that the earth was a sphere, and that the eastern land mass discovered by Columbus was not part of Asia but a whole new continent.

A shift in trade routes stimulated the rise of prices and the development of banking. As a result of the exploration and discoveries of the fifteenth and sixteenth centuries, the major trade routes shifted from the Mediterranean to the Atlantic. Italy, cooped up in the Mediterranean, lost the dominant position which she had held since the Middle Ages, while the ports of Spain, France, Flanders, England, and the Netherlands began to thrive. A great variety of new products began to appear in Europe: spices and silks from the East, corn, tobacco, fur, timber, and pitch from North America, coffee, gold, and silver from South America, and sugar, molasses, and indigo from the West Indies.

The gold and silver which Spanish ships brought from the mines of Mexico and Peru were to make great changes in European society. As the amount of money in circulation rapidly increased, the demand for goods rose. But the supply of goods could not increase fast enough to meet the new demand, so prices rose sharply. Merchants who made money on each shipment and kings who owned mines or controlled overseas trade grew rich. The nobles, whose income was fixed by feudal law, did not share in the new wealth, however. Thus the rapid rise of prices in the Renaissance hastened and made permanent the shift of power from the nobles to the merchants and kings.

The increased use of money and the growth of trade also led to the development of banking. Since merchants could not carry sacks of gold coins around with them, they deposited their money with banks, such as the Medici bank in Florence. Then, if a merchant happened to need money in Antwerp, he could withdraw his money from the Medici branch bank there by writing a draft or check against his account in Florence. In this way bank checks came into use and eventually were circulated as a form of money. This custom was the origin of paper money.

Capitalism helped to bring on the Commercial Revolution. Hand in hand with rising prices, the development of banking, and the shift of trade routes went the formation of a new, more productive economic system. During the Middle Ages, people rarely produced more than enough to live on. They had no extra money and gave little thought to making more. But in the fifteenth and sixteenth centuries, merchants made large profits and were anxious to increase them. Instead of hoarding money in strongboxes, they

At A Glance

Important Renaissance Explorers

EXPLORER	SPONSORING COUNTRY	AREA EXPLORED
(Prince Henry the Navigator)	Portugal	
Bartholomew Díaz	Portugal	Africa—Cape of Good Hope
Vasco da Gama	Portugal	India
Pedro Álvarez Cabral	Portugal	Brazil
Amerigo Vespucci	Portugal and Spain	South America
Christopher Columbus	Spain	Americas (1492)
Vasco Nuñez de Balboa	Spain	Pacific Ocean
Ferdinand Magellan	Spain	Circumnavigation of the globe (1519)
Hernando Cortez	Spain	Mexico
Hernando Pizarro	Spain	Peru
Ponce de León	Spain	Florida
John Cabot	England	North America
Walter Raleigh	England	Virginia
Giovanni de Verrazano	France	Hudson River and Manhattan Island
Jacques Cartier	France	St. Lawrence River and Canada
Samuel de Champlain	France	St. Lawrence River and Canada

began to invest it in order to make more money. A merchant could invest a thousand gold ducats to build a ship which, if it returned safely from the East with a rich cargo, might pay him two thousand ducats when the goods were sold.

Money which is accumulated and invested to produce more wealth is called *capital*. A system under which private individuals invest capital in the hope of making a profit is called *capitalism*. Usually one individual could not afford to finance the outfitting of a merchant vessel, so several merchants would contribute to the cost and would share the risks and profits. This arrangement, called a *joint stock company*, provided the capital necessary to finance the ventures which brought prosperity to Europe. The modern corporation had its origin in the joint stock company.

These four economic changes—the shift in trade routes, the rise of prices, the development of banking, and the growth of capitalism—made up a much larger movement called the *Commercial Revolution*. Like the development of Renaissance humanism, the Commercial Revolution marked the beginning of modern times.

THE INVENTION OF PRINTING OPENED A NEW WORLD TO MANKIND

The development of cheap paper and movable type caused a revolution in book-making. During the Middle Ages few men were aware of what was going on outside their local manors. The few who could read found hand-copied parchment books much too expensive. Two inventions appeared during the Renaissance which made it possible to produce many books quickly and at a much lower price. The first of these was paper, which was introduced into Europe by the Arabs even before the Renaissance. By the mid-fifteenth century much less costly methods of making paper had been developed.

The second invention, which was destined to revolutionize man's methods of communication, was movable type. Europeans had learned from the Chinese how to print from a wood block, but the process was slow because a new block had to

GUTENBERG AT HIS PRESS. Holding up a printed page, Gutenberg and his assistant admire their handiwork. The invention of movable type enabled ideas and knowledge to be spread quickly over the world.

be carved for each page. About 1450, a German, Johannes Gutenberg (*goo*-ten-burg), developed a new kind of printing based on movable type. Each letter was separately carved on metal and then arranged to spell words. The letters were inked and a sheet of paper pressed on them to produce a printed page. Once all the pages of a book had been set in type, the printer could make many more copies than could be made from wood blocks because metal was more durable than wood. When the printer wanted to make a new book, the same letters could be rearranged and used again.

The printed book spread new ideas throughout Europe. Soon printing presses in many cities were turning out quantities of inexpensive books and pamphlets. The first great publishing house was that of a Venetian printer, Aldus Manutius (muh-*nyoo*-shih-us), who undertook the ambitious task of printing all the Greek classics. He cast type, made ink, and printed and bound books in his own shop. The type Aldus used is called Aldine. It is said that he had it engraved after a model of Petrarch's handwriting. Printers call the Aldine style of type *italic* and use it to draw attention to important words and for other purposes. *This sentence is printed in italics.* Notice how this type seems to lean toward the right. (The other type used in this text is called Roman.)

The printing of books made them more accurate and helped to standardize grammar and spelling. But many scholars disliked the printing press because it made books available to everyone. They felt that if knowledge spread to the masses, it might give the people new ideas that would stir them up against their masters. Others believed that it was disrespectful to print holy scripture and great classical literature by "machines." None the less, printed books rapidly gained acceptance. Thus, Western man took an important step toward throwing off the shackles of illiteracy.

THE RENAISSANCE USHERED IN THE SCIENTIFIC AGE

Medieval acceptance of theology and tradition gave way to scientific questioning and observation. As we learned earlier, the Greeks were the first people to express a scientific curiosity. They looked for the natural explanations or causes of events. During the Middle Ages this questioning attitude did not, of course, entirely disappear. But medieval man was much more aware of the presence of God in the universe. He was much more likely to think of God's direct intervention in the things that happened to him. Medieval scholars rediscovered Aristotle, and followed his lead in making observations and cataloging nature. But medieval man even studied nature in order to know and understand more about God. Roger Bacon, for example, said that since God made the light, if men knew more about light they would therefore know more about God.

In the late fifteenth and early sixteenth centuries, however, a new scientific spirit began to change traditional medieval views of learning. Scholars again adopted a more questioning attitude toward the natural world, and they relied only on their own observations in seeking answers.

One of the first men to show the influences of the scientific spirit was Leonardo da Vinci. By patiently observing the flight of birds, he discovered the principles necessary to design his helicopter and parachute. Leonardo also applied his scientific knowledge to his painting, which reveals a mastery of the fundamentals of perspective and light. According to one story, in order to make his figures as lifelike as possible, he bought the bodies of criminals from the hangman so that he could make a detailed study of the structure of human muscles and bones.

Three great scientists changed man's picture of the universe. Scientific thinking about the place of the earth in the universe had long been dominated by tradition. Knowledge of astronomy was based on Aristotle's theory that the earth was the center of the universe. Medi-

NEWTON. GALILEO. DESCARTES. Newton (left) not only discovered the laws of gravitation but by his experiments with light originated the science of modern optics. Galileo (center), an astronomer, mathematician, and physicist, formulated the law of moving bodies that made possible the science of mechanics. He was also the first man to study the heavens through a telescope. Descartes (right), a great mathematician and scientist, wished to prove all things by scientific reasoning. He built up his philosophical system starting from the premise "I think, therefore I am."

eval man believed that God had set the sun and moon in motion around the earth for the purpose of providing light. In the early sixteenth century, however, a Polish astronomer named Copernicus began to question this traditional view. He believed that the arrangement of the heavens could be explained by a few simple mathematical principles, but in trying to apply them to the Aristotelian system, he discovered many conflicts. His calculations convinced him that all the planets, including the earth, revolved about the sun.

Scientists did not pay much attention to Copernicus' theory because he was unable to support it with evidence. But his work was not forgotten. In the last half of the sixteenth century, the German astronomer Kepler used observations made by his teacher to verify the Copernican theory. Kepler discovered the mathematical laws which describe the paths of the planets as they revolve around the sun.

In the early seventeenth century the great Italian scientist Galileo discovered convincing proof of the correctness of the Copernican theory. He gathered his evidence by developing a crude telescope which allowed him to make much more detailed studies of planets. His observations supported the idea that the earth was just one of many planets revolving around the sun. This concept was in conflict with the Church belief that the earth was especially created by God and, therefore, was naturally in the center of the universe. Many Christian scholars refused to accept Galileo's conclusions, and the Church not only forbade Galileo to publish his theory but eventually made him deny it. A century later, however, most learned men, including Popes, had come to accept Galileo's main conclusions.

Bacon and Descartes urged man to think for himself. At the same time Galileo was making his observations in Italy, an English courtier, Sir Francis Bacon, and a French mathematician, Rene Descartes (day-*kart*), were bringing about important changes in philosophy. Bacon urged men to stop studying the old, outworn ideas of Aristotle and to turn instead to the discovery of new knowledge. He insisted that this new knowledge could best be acquired through experiments with nature.

Descartes was even more impatient than Bacon with traditional science and philosophy. He had thoroughly studied the works of the scholastic philosophers of the Middle Ages and was disgusted with the senselessness of their concern with such trivial questions as "Can God make two hills without an intervening valley?" and "How many angels can dance on the head of a pin?" Descartes decided to abandon everything that had been thought and believed in the past. In the spirit of Copernicus and Galileo, he would accept nothing until he had proved it to be true by scientific reasoning.

Starting with nothing but his own reason, Descartes said that because he used his reason he existed. Then he deduced that God also existed. He believed, however, that reason had a far more important function than in formulating impractical theories about God. Reason, he declared, should "render ourselves the masters and possessors of nature." Descartes went on to state that the whole world is governed by certain mathematical laws which man could understand and use to his own advantage. In seeking to prove his theory, he developed the branch of mathematics known as analytic geometry.

Sir Isaac Newton was the giant of the scientific Renaissance. The ideas of Galileo, Bacon, and Descartes were summed up by the great English mathematician Sir Isaac Newton (see page 296). By means of astronomical observations and an advanced mathematics called calculus, he proved that the scientific principles discovered by Kepler and Galileo were really part of the same law, the law of universal gravitation. Newton reasoned that every planet in the universe possessed a gravitational force or "pull" whose strength depended on its mass. The balance of these forces kept the planets in their proper orbits. This unseen force of gravity also explained, said Newton, why objects thrown into the air were pulled back to the earth. His masterpiece, *Mathematical Principles of Natural Philosophy,* stated even more conclusively than Descartes had done that the universe was governed entirely by mathematical laws.

Newton's work had tremendous effect on educated men everywhere. Before this time, only a few advanced scholars had accepted the scientific view of the universe. But Newton's carefully reasoned theories seemed indisputable. In general, scientists accepted the idea that the universe was not held together by a mysterious divine will, but by mathematical laws of nature which could be comprehended through reason and observation. They began to look upon knowledge as a useful tool to give man power over nature rather than as a means of glorifying God. Thus modern science was born.

In the eighteenth century, scientists applied Newton's teachings to all branches of knowledge and even began to search for natural laws that governed human behavior. You will read later in *Story of Nations* how their efforts played an important part in such great events as the French Revolution and the Industrial Revolution. Modern developments in chemistry, physics, medicine, agriculture, business, education, and many other fields are based on the beliefs of Galileo, Bacon, Descartes, and Newton, the heralds of the Scientific Age.

Chapter Check-up

1. Why did Marco Polo's adventures stimulate interest in the East?
2. What inventions of the Renaissance period made ocean navigation safer and easier?
3. For what geographic reason did Portugal and Spain take the lead in opening the Atlantic Ocean to travel and trade?
4. Who were some of the great explorers of the fifteenth and sixteenth centuries, and for what is each noted?
5. What were some of the important trade products found in Africa and the New World?
6. What were the four main aspects of the Commercial Revolution?
7. How did the invention of printing benefit mankind?
8. How did Francis Bacon influence the scientific spirit of the Renaissance?
9. Why were people slow to accept the scientific theories of men like Copernicus and Galileo?
10. How did Descartes influence the philosophy of the Renaissance?
11. What was Newton's law of universal gravitation? How did Newton's ideas influence the thinking of other scholars?

CHAPTER 28

The Reformation Ended the Religious Unity of Western Europe

THE SPIRIT OF THE RENAISSANCE LED TO THE QUESTIONING OF CHURCH AUTHORITY

Wycliffe and Huss challenged papal rule. Throughout the Middle Ages the Roman Catholic Church had united the people of Western Europe under a single faith. Virtually everyone was born into the faith of the Church, lived under its guidance all his life, and died within its spiritual care. To most men it was unthinkable that there should be any other way to attain salvation. Nevertheless, from the days of Constantine there had always been a few men who found something objectionable in the doctrine or practice of the Church. In the late fourteenth century, criticism of the Church became more outspoken. John Wycliffe (*wik*-lif), a professor at Oxford University, declared that many of the Church doctrines did not conform with the Bible and that men should therefore reject the authority of the Pope. Wycliffe translated the Bible into English so that everyone could read it. He rejected so many of the teachings of the Church that most Englishmen were shocked and the king ordered him to be silent. The Pope summoned him to Rome to answer the charge of heresy for opposing the teachings of the Church. But he refused to answer the Pope's summons.

Wycliffe's beliefs influenced John Huss, a priest in a part of the Holy Roman Empire called Bohemia (bo-*hee*-mee-uh). He, too, began to preach against the authority of the Pope. He caused such an uprising among the Bohemians that in 1415 he was ordered to appear before a Church council. The council declared Huss a heretic, and he was

HUSS AT THE STAKE. Found guilty of heresy, Huss is led to the stake to be burned alive, the fate of many condemned heretics in the Middle Ages.

burned at the stake. The death of Huss aroused bitter resentment among the Bohemian people. You will see in the story of Eastern Europe how this incident triggered a series of tragic wars.

For the next hundred years or so the Church throughout most of Europe managed to keep its authority in religious matters. The movement away from the Church gathered strength, however, when it was joined by an increasing number of people who, for various reasons, began to question that authority. For one thing, many Christians felt that certain members of the clergy were no longer leading simple and humble lives. Renaissance popes like Julius II were criticized for spending too much time and too much Church money patronizing artists rather than attending to Church affairs. Another Church practice which was criticized had to do with the sale of *indulgences,* or forgiveness of sin.

Erasmus, prince of humanists, remained loyal to the Church but criticized certain practices. We noted earlier that Italy's humanist scholars centered their attention on man and his earthly affairs, and they tended to neglect or ignore religious matters. This was not true in northern Europe, however, where many humanist scholars tried to use the new knowledge of the Renaissance to resolve the disputes within the Church. They encouraged men to use their reason in an effort to become better Christians.

The spokesman for the northern humanist point of view was a scholarly priest, Erasmus of Rotterdam. His clear mind and careful scholarship in the classics won him the favor of statesmen, popes, and kings. Erasmus' study of the classics led him to believe that men should have tolerant, reasonable minds free from superstition and violent passions. He saw nothing wrong with the doctrines of the Church but he felt that men did not practice their religion as they should. His witty, scholarly book, *The Praise of Folly,* made fun of good-hearted but foolish men who thought that pilgrimages, prayers, and attendance at mass were enough to send them to heaven. He found fault with pious monks because they lived an unnatural life away from the world, and he sharply criticized certain bishops and Popes who saw fit to live in luxury and splendor. He ridiculed scholastic philosophers because they argued about the exact meaning of biblical passages rather than practicing Christian virtues. Erasmus urged all men to follow what he called a reasonable "Christian philosophy" that was much like the philosophy of Socrates.

ERASMUS. Called the "prince of humanists," Erasmus was the leading figure of the Northern Renaissance in the sixteenth century.

Erasmus' respect for learning and for the teachings of Jesus made him want translations of the Bible to be as accurate as it was possible to make them. When he read the original Greek version of the New Testament, he became convinced that the Vulgate Bible, which was used by the Church, had introduced many errors. In 1516 he published his own Latin translation of the original Greek work. Though he was critical of the Church, Erasmus remained steadfastly loyal to it throughout his lifetime.

The rise of national feeling weakened the Church. During the sixteenth century national feeling, or a growing sense of loyalty to one's king and country, began to stir men's emotions. The French became sensitive to the fact that their language, history, and customs differed from those of the English or Germans. When such national groups became conscious of their differences, they tended to regard the people of other nations with suspicion and distrust. In the nineteenth and twentieth centuries this national feeling took an extreme form called *nationalism* and became a political and emotional force that set nation against nation in bitter struggles for freedom, prestige, and economic advantage. But in the Renaissance period, national feeling was important largely because of its effect on the fortunes of the Church. Increasingly the peoples in each part of Europe regarded the Pope as a foreigner, and they supported their king's efforts to gain control of the Church in his own nation.

The strong kings of France and Spain had reached agreements with the Pope which limited his authority in the appointment of bishops and certain other Church matters, but German rulers had been unable to make any such agreement. As we shall see, German national opposition to the power of the Pope was to become an important factor in undermining the authority of the Church in northern Europe.

MARTIN LUTHER BEGAN THE PROTESTANT REFORMATION

Luther criticized practices of the Church. Martin Luther was the son of a German miner in a small village in Saxony. His father was ambitious that his son should become a lawyer, so the young man entered the University of Erfurt in central Germany.

While he was a student at the University, Luther made a good record in his studies, particularly in public speaking and composition. He was religious by nature, and he finally became convinced that God had called him to the service of the Church. Instead of finishing his legal training, Luther took the vows of a monk. Two years later he was ordained a priest. He spent much of his spare time studying the original Hebrew and Greek texts of the Bible.

Luther's ability as a scholar won him an appointment as a professor of religion in the University of Wittenberg. His reputation as a speaker and his outspoken religious ideas attracted wide attention and many followers. Soon he began to attack some of the practices of the Church, particularly those relating to forgiveness of sins and ways of collecting money.

According to official Church belief, if a man who committed a sin truly repented and confessed to a priest, God forgave him through the sacrament of penance administered by the priest. The man was then expected to do some penitential act to show his sincerity. Although his sin was forgiven, a sinner still had to make reparation during his life or be purified after death in a state of purgatory. Under certain conditions, if the repentant sinner went on pilgrimage, for example, or gave money to the Church's good works, he could be granted an indulgence. The Church declared that his good action had won him the forgiveness of some or all of the punishment that might be due for his sins. Many abuses crept into this practice of granting indulgences. Luther found that some clergymen (in order to raise money to build St. Peter's Church in Rome) were selling indulgences. In those days, before newspapers, people who wished to put their ideas before the public used to post bulletins in a public place for all to read. In 1517 Luther listed ninety-five statements, or theses (*thee*-seez), criticizing what he considered wrongs committed by the Church. He nailed his bulletin on the door of the church at Wittenberg. Soon his statements came to the attention of the Church authorities.

Luther broke with Rome. In spite of his attack on Church practices, Luther had no intention of breaking away from the Roman Catholic

LUTHER. In this portrait by Cranach, who has been called the painter of the Reformation, the leader of the Protestant Reformation holds in his hands the Bible that he translated into German.

Church. As time went on, however, Luther's views began to alarm Church officials. For one thing, he declared that a man could be forgiven by God without the help of the Church and the sacraments. Moreover, the sacraments were holy not because the priest gave them but because of men's faith in them. Luther also stated that no "good works," such as praying, receiving sacraments, or giving to charity, could earn salvation. A man was saved only if he had faith in God. Luther's doctrine of "salvation by faith" denied the importance of the sacraments and made it clear to his followers that man did not need the organized Church in order to reach God. Recognizing the danger of this teaching, the Pope excommunicated Luther.

One of the duties of the Holy Roman emperor was to punish heretics. Accordingly Charles V ordered Luther to appear before the imperial council, the Diet of Worms. Although Charles gave him a chance to admit that he had been wrong, Luther was convinced that his own beliefs were correct. He boldly declared to Charles and the papal representatives, "I cannot and will not recant anything, for it is neither safe nor right to go against conscience."

Religious conflict split Germany. Luther might well have been burned at the stake as John Huss had been a hundred years earlier, but conditions had changed in the Holy Roman Empire. Many German princes came to Luther's support. Some of them believed in Luther's teachings. Others, influenced by national feeling, welcomed any excuse to stop sending German money to an Italian Pope. Still others saw an opportunity to gain independence from the Catholic Emperor Charles. Because Luther had the support of many of the German princes, Charles V could do no more than declare him an outlaw. For some time Luther went into hiding in an out-of-the-way castle where he translated the Bible into German.

The princes who supported Luther took possession of Church property and turned over local churches to Lutheran clergymen. Lutheran services were not very different from Catholic masses but were conducted in German rather than in Latin. Lutheran clergymen replaced priests and were allowed to marry, as Luther himself did.

Most of the princes in southern Germany remained Catholic. They tried to stop the swing toward Lutheranism by persuading Charles to order strict enforcement of all laws against heretics (meaning Lutherans). The Lutheran princes drew up a protest against the Emperor's order. As a result of this protest, all non-Catholic Christians in Germany came to be called *Protestants.* The term was later extended to include non-Catholic Christians everywhere.

The differences between Catholic and Lutheran princes led to a long and bloody war. After nine years of fighting, both sides were exhausted. They agreed to accept the Peace of Augsburg in 1555, which provided that each prince had the right to choose either Catholicism or Lutheranism as his state's religion. The people living under his rule then had to accept his religion or move to another state.

The Peace of Augsburg also allowed the Protestant princes to keep the land they had confiscated from the Catholic Church. Possession of the land was a strong inducement to remain Protestant. Thus, in a few short years, the combination of Luther's religious fervor and German national feeling cracked the religious unity of Western Europe. As time went on, the Reformation spread and the split between Catholic and Protestant became permanent.

THE PROTESTANT REFORMATION SPREAD THROUGHOUT NORTHERN EUROPE

Henry VIII became supreme head of the Church of England. Although King Henry VIII of England, about whom you will read more in Chapter 31, opposed Luther, he soon split with the Church for reasons of his own. Like many Englishmen, Henry resented the Pope's control of religion in England. He persuaded the English Parliament to cut all ties with Rome and to declare him "the only supreme head of the Church in England." This declaration brought to England what the Peace of Augsburg had to Germany: state control of the church. The kings of Denmark and Sweden became Lutherans in the 1520's. Like Henry in England, they imposed their faith on their subjects.

Calvin believed that man's fate was decided by God. Another important leader of the Reformation was the French lawyer John Calvin, who summarized Protestant beliefs in a famous work, *Institutes of the Christian Religion*. The most striking feature of Calvin's religion was his belief in *predestination*. According to Calvin, God determined, before each man was born, whether or not he could be saved. Salvation was reserved in advance for a chosen few; the rest of mankind was hopelessly lost. Like Luther, Calvin emphasized that the chosen people owed their salvation only to God's mercy, not to their own efforts. Yet even though good works could not win salvation, they were important as a sign of divine favor, since, according to Calvin, no man could perform them without God's help. Similarly, the wicked were obviously without divine favor. This point of view encouraged Calvin's followers, particularly the Puritans in America, to lead stern, upright, God-fearing lives as proof to themselves and

LUTHER AT WORMS. Defending himself so eloquently that he acquired many supporters, Luther refused to recant when ordered to appear before the Emperor Charles V.

CALVIN. Because Calvin viewed art with suspicion, we have few portraits of the stern reformer. In Geneva he created a *theocracy*, or a state run by the church.

the world that God had chosen them to be saved.

Like Luther, Calvin also believed that the Bible was the proper guide of life, but Calvin carried his belief further than Luther had. He forbade his followers such "frivolity" as dancing, playing cards, drinking wine, and going to the theater. Calvinists were expected to spend all of every Sunday listening to sermons. These teachings were put into effect first in Geneva, Switzerland, where Calvin and his followers gained control of the government. Calvin introduced many principles of democracy into church government. Calvinist ministers were elected by the members of the church congregation, who also chose certain laymen called presbyters (*prez*-bih-ters) to control church policy. (Presbyterian and Congregational churches in America were later organized along these lines.)

THE COUNTER-REFORMATION WAS THE CATHOLIC ANSWER TO THE CHALLENGE OF THE TIMES

The Roman Catholic Church defined its position at the Council of Trent. There were many men who, like Erasmus, criticized certain practices of the Catholic Church but had no desire to break away from it. They urged the Church to correct these abuses if it had any hope of stemming the tide of Protestantism and reclaiming some of its lost members. Thus began a movement called the Counter-Reformation. Pope Paul III, who was genuinely concerned with reform, invited the bishops to the Council of Trent, where they officially clarified Catholic belief. The bishops established high standards of conduct for all members of the clergy, and declared the Pope to be head of the Church and sole interpreter of the Bible. They reaffirmed the belief that, except in rare instances, a man obtained salvation only through the sacraments. The council drew up a catechism (*kat*-eh-kizm) of these beliefs and published an Index of books which Catholics were forbidden to read. Their statement of Catholic position greatly strengthened the Church, but at the same time it ended all practical hopes of bridging the gap between the Catholic and Protestant viewpoints.

The Jesuit order of Loyola served to strengthen the Church. One day early in the sixteenth century, a young Spanish captain broke his leg in battle. During his slow recovery he passed his time in reading. It happened that the only books he had at hand were books about the lives of Jesus and the saints. He decided to give up his knightly adventures, become a soldier of Christ, and spread the teachings of the Church.

ST. IGNATIUS LOYOLA. In this engraving the founder of the Society of Jesus accepts the charter of his order from the Pope. In the scene at the right, he is depicted receiving instructions from God.

That was how the Catholic Church gained one of her most able servants, Ignatius Loyola (ig-*nay*-shus loy-*oh*-luh). Loyola spent eleven years preparing himself for the cause he wished to serve. Finally, with a group of companions, he founded the Society of Jesus.

The members took four vows. The first three, poverty, chastity, and obedience, were the same as the vows of the medieval monks. In the fourth, the members promised to obey the Pope and to undertake any missionary service, at home or abroad, that he might ask of them. Loyola and his small group hoped to go to the Holy Land, where they would live as Jesus had done and convert Moslems to Christianity. The Turkish wars prevented their departure from Rome, so they were asked by the Pope to remain there and help combat the Reformation in Europe.

Unlike the monks, who sought the quiet of the monastery, the members of the Society of Jesus mingled with the people as preachers, teachers, and missionaries. The Jesuits (*jez*-yu-its), as they came to be known, were the soldier-crusaders of the Church. They became one of the strongest forces in the Counter-Reformation. Jesuit missionaries in Europe won many Protestants back to the Roman Catholic Church. During the seventeenth century, Jesuits converted thousands of Chinese and established many missions in the New World. One of the most famous missionaries was Father Marquette (mar-*ket*), who taught Catholicism to the Indians who lived around the Great Lakes in North America. Jesuits influenced European politics by becoming advisers to kings and to high government officials. They influenced young men by founding excellent schools and colleges all over the world. Numbered among the Jesuits are many famous scholars and teachers.

Chapter Check-up

1. Why were Wycliffe and Huss considered to be heretics?
2. What Church practices began to draw criticism?
3. What was Erasmus' attitude toward the religious disputes of his day?
4. How did national feeling weaken the control of the Church?
5. How did Luther's views differ from the official, or orthodox, Church teachings?
6. For what reasons did many German princes come to Luther's support?
7. How did non-Catholic Christians come to be called Protestants?
8. How did Henry VIII of England influence the spread of the Protestant Reformation?
9. What was the Counter-Reformation? What part did Loyola play in it?

The Renaissance and Reformation: SYNOPSIS

The Renaissance brought a new spirit to Western man. He became eager to know more about the world in which he lived. His interests broadened and his intellectual curiosity deepened. He found great joy in rediscovering the brilliant achievements of ancient Greece and Rome, but he did not stop with knowledge of the past. As he gained confidence in his own abilities and powers of reason, he began to search for new ideas, new ways of living, new means of enjoying life, and new lands to conquer.

The Renaissance spirit, combined with the wealth and independence of the Italian city-states, provided the conditions necessary for the creation of such literary and artistic achievements as the masterpieces of Petrarch, Leonardo, Michelangelo, and Raphael. Not only is their work outstanding in its own right, but it was also the means by which the classic styles of Greece and Rome were passed on to the Western world.

Interest in the world about them and desire to break the hold of the Italians on the sea lanes to eastern markets led explorers to make daring voyages. The result of Columbus' expedition was the discovery of the New World. The explorations of the Renaissance also brought about the Commercial Revolution in which capitalism and banking developed. New wealth flowed into northern Europe as that area began to replace Italy as the center of trade. This development, which led to the weakening of the feudal nobility and the strengthening of the middle class, was a change of great importance to the future of Europe and America.

A reawakening of the scientific attitude inspired men like Kepler, Galileo, and Bacon to observe nature for themselves rather than to rely on the traditional teachings of Aristotle or the superstitions of the past. The correctness of their observations was established by Descartes and Newton, who declared that the universe is governed by mathematical laws which men can discover and understand. This belief is one of the foundations of modern science.

In religion, Martin Luther's criticism of the Church combined with national feeling to bring about the Protestant Reformation, which in turn spurred the Catholic Church to reform. The Protestant churches founded in the sixteenth century still hold men's loyalty, while the beliefs stated in the Council of Trent remain the foundations of the Catholic faith.

When you consider how much of your world has its roots in the Renaissance, you will agree that the Renaissance truly ushered in modern times. National feeling has gathered strength in the centuries since the Renaissance, and today nationalism is one of the dominant forces in world affairs. Since the Renaissance, history has been shaped by the creation of many new and powerful nations, each of which has had a part to play in molding the modern world. For this reason, the next thirteen Parts of *Story of Nations* are divided into the histories of nations rather than periods of time. You will read about the development and achievements of England, France, Germany, Russia, China, and many other nations. We shall go back into medieval and ancient history far enough to give you a brief outline of what happened to make each nation develop as it did.

Important People

Dante	Leonardo da Vinci	Manutius	John Huss
Petrarch	Michelangelo	Galileo	Martin Luther
Lorenzo de' Medici	Palestrina	Newton	John Calvin
Machiavelli	Gutenberg	Descartes	Ignatius Loyola

Terms

Be sure that you understand clearly the meaning of each of the following:

capitalism	humanism	predestination
Commercial Revolution	italic	Protestant
Council of Trent	Jesuits	Reformation
Counter-Reformation	Machiavellian	Renaissance
heresy	ninety-five theses	vernacular

Questions for Discussion and Review

1. How did men's points of view differ in the Middle Ages and the Renaissance?
2. How did the thinking and outlook of artists and scholars differ in the Middle Ages and the Renaissance?
3. How do the educational ideas of the Renaissance influence our schools today?
4. How did the Commercial Revolution lead to the development of capitalism?
5. What were the most important effects of the production of inexpensive books?
6. Why is the work of Renaissance scientists important in our world today?
7. How did the Lutheran and Calvinist Protestants differ in their religious beliefs?
8. In what ways did the Protestant Reformation reflect the spirit of the Renaissance?
9. In your opinion, who was the greatest man of the Renaissance? Why?
10. What is meant by the expression "spirit of the Renaissance"? How was that spirit reflected in art? Philosophy? Religion?

Interesting Things to Do

1. On a map of the world show the different routes of the voyages of the famous explorers of the Renaissance.
2. Make a chart of the achievements of the Renaissance in the fields of religion, music, art, science, and philosophy. The columns should be headed *Name of Person, Field of Work, Contributions or Achievements.*
3. Make a diagram showing how the Christian peoples have branched out from one Church into many churches because of the events of the Reformation.
4. Draw a poster showing how the Renaissance served as a connecting link or bridge between the Middle Ages and modern times.
5. Prepare and present to the class an oral report

on one of the following topics: (a) The Story of the Compass, (b) The Story of Printing, (c) The Story of Paper.

6. Make a needle compass and demonstrate its operation to the class.
7. Secure phonograph records of the religious music of the Renaissance and play selections for the class.
8. Make an illustrated booklet of the art of the Renaissance. Include prints of famous masterpieces and write briefly about each work and the artist who created it.
9. Write a poem or a story about the "Mona Lisa," about "Madonna of the Goldfinch," or about some other famous work of art by a Renaissance painter or sculptor.
10. Add to or begin your "Who's Who in World History" series by writing brief biographies of one or more of the important leaders of the Renaissance.

Interesting Reading about the Renaissance and Reformation

Armitage, Angus, *Sun, Stand Thou Still,* Schuman. Story of Copernicus.

Bainton, Roland, *Here I Stand,* Abingdon Press.

*Cottler, Joseph and Jaffe, *Heroes of Civilization,* Little, Brown. Renaissance scientists and explorers.

———, *Map Makers,* Little, Brown. Expansion of knowledge about geography.

Cottler, Joseph, *Man With Wings,* Little, Brown.

Davidson, H. M. P., *Good Christian Men,* Scribner.

Durant, Will, *The Reformation,* Simon and Schuster.

Gombrich, E. H., *Story of Art,* Oxford.

Kelley, Eric P., *At the Sign of the Golden Compass,* Macmillan.

*Kent, L. A., *He Went with Marco Polo,* Houghton Mifflin.

Life, *Picture History of Western Man,* Simon and Schuster.

Lucas, Mary S., *Vast Horizons,* Viking. Explorations and maps thirteenth to eighteenth centuries.

Mills, Dorothy, *Renaissance and Reformation Times,* Putnam.

Morison, Samuel Eliot, *Christopher Columbus, Mariner,* Mentor.

Outhwaite, Leonard, *Unrolling the Map,* Reynal.

Polo, Marco, *Travels of Marco Polo,* ed. Manuel Komroff, Julian Messner.

Reade, Charles, *The Cloister and the Hearth,* Novel about Erasmus' parents.

Reinach, Solomon, *Apollo; an Illustrated Manual of the History of Art,* Scribner.

Ripley, Elizabeth, *Michelangelo,* Oxford.

Welch, R., *Ferdinand Magellan,* Criterion.

* Indicates easy reading

The Industrial Revolution turned yeoman farmers into miners and factory workers. This Welsh miner typifies the strength of character that has made Britain a great industrial nation.

Part 9

GREAT BRITAIN

TRIUMPH OF REPRESENTATIVE GOVERNMENT

BRITISH ISLES

SHETLAND ISLANDS
ORKNEY ISLANDS
HEBRIDES
NORTH AMERICA
ARCTIC OCEAN
ATLANTIC OCEAN
ASIA
EUROPE
SOUTH AMERICA
AFRICA
INDIAN OCEAN
ATLANTIC OCEAN
SCOTLAND
Glasgow
Edinburgh
NORTH SEA
NORTHERN IRELAND
Belfast
ULSTER
ISLE OF MAN
Lancaster
York
Manchester
Liverpool
IRISH SEA
Dublin
EIRE
WALES
ENGLAND
Thames
London
Runnymede
Canterbury
Winchester
Hastings
Calais
ENGLISH CHANNEL
CHANNEL ISLANDS
NORMANDY

Great Britain: GEOGRAPHIC SETTING

The British Isles are separated from the European continent by the English Channel, whose choppy waters are only twenty miles wide at their narrowest point. The largest and most important of the several hundred islands are Great Britain and Ireland.

Great Britain is a political unit as well as a geographic one. It is small in comparison to the United States—about half the size of Texas. Great Britain is subdivided roughly according to geography into three parts: England, Scotland, and Wales. Scotland and Wales are rugged and mountainous, while England, except for the Pennine (*pen*-ine) Mountains in the north, is a rolling plain. The entire island is cut by deep, navigable rivers and notched with good harbors.

Ireland is divided into two states, the Republic of Ireland, or Eire (*ay*-reh), which has been independent since 1921, and Northern Ireland. Northern Ireland and Great Britain together make up the *United Kingdom*.

Although the British Isles are in the same latitude as Labrador in Canada, warm ocean currents from the Equator give them a temperate climate. Rainfall is heavy and dense fogs are frequent. From earliest times, England—"this precious stone set in the silver sea"—had been influenced by her isolation from the European continent and by her contact with the surrounding sea. As you study the story of Great Britain, you will see how those geographic factors have helped shape her long, exciting history.

Great Britain: PERSPECTIVE

One winter day over 350 years ago, three small ships ventured from London harbor into the icy waters of the Atlantic and trimmed their sails for a westward course. For four months the vessels, with 120 people aboard, churned through storms, snows, and freezing rains. Then spring came, and the adventurers found themselves at the mouth of a great river. Sailing upstream, they saw great oaks, pines, and cypresses entwined with grapevines equal in circumference to a man's leg. The river abounded with fish, luscious oysters, and mussels with pearls inside. Flowers blanketed the countryside, and out of the rich soil grew strawberries twice as large as those in England. Nearby, the men anchored their ships and went ashore to begin clearing the land that was to be their new home.

Those British settlers, who came to Jamestown, Virginia, in 1607, made their influence felt on the new continent and began a process that has been going on ever since. As you read about the development of Britain, you will see many ways in which it is linked to the history of the United States. For this reason, a knowledge of British history is essential to an understanding of your own land. It is also essential to an understanding of such distant parts of the world as India, Australia, Canada, Africa, and China. British political and cultural institutions have shaped the course of civilization in many lands.

In Part 9 you will discover how these institutions began and how they developed into their present form. You will also learn how this tiny island nation gained control of the seas and possession of a quarter of the earth's land surface.

CHAPTER 29

The British Are a Mixture of Many Peoples

THE CELTS GAINED CONTROL OF THE BRITISH ISLES

Far back in the past, before the fourth Glacial Age, the island of Britain was probably connected with Europe by a bridge of land across what has since become the English Channel. Over this bridge, men first reached Britain some 200,000 years ago, during the Old Stone Age. Although these early men left no written records, archeological diggings have shown that they were hunters who used stone tools and lived in the dark forests of oak. Centuries later, invaders introduced agriculture and the use of bronze tools.

Between 1000 B.C. and 400 B.C. several waves of Celtic tribesmen came to Britain from Western Europe. The Celts, who had a more advanced culture and used iron weapons and tools, gradually subdued the earlier peoples.

The Celts are the first inhabitants of Britain about whom historians have much knowledge. Archeologists have found Celtic weapons and jewelry decorated with elaborate designs, and they have even discovered primitive razors and cosmetic jars. The Celts, who worshiped in sacred groves in the depths of forests, called their priests Druids (*droo*-ids). The Druids used baskets woven of mistletoe to offer animal, and sometimes human, sacrifices to the Celtic gods.

BRITAIN BECAME A ROMAN PROVINCE

Caesar raided Britain twice. The British Isles take their name from the Celtic tribes who inhabited the southern part of what is now England at the time of Caesar's campaigns in Gaul. These peoples called themselves *Brittones* (Britons), and the Romans referred to them as *Brittani* and their island home as *Brittania.* Caesar discovered that his enemies in Gaul were receiving aid from this land which could sometimes be dimly perceived off the northwest coast of Gaul. Determined to cut off this outside help, Caesar invaded Britain in 55 B.C. The stubborn resistance of the Celts surprised the Romans. So did their appearance. Before they went into battle the Britons painted themselves blue to frighten their foe. In his writings Caesar describes these Celts as tall, blue-eyed giants with long yellow hair. Caesar was forced to leave the island. But he returned again a year later. His legions were able to force their way up the Thames (*tems*) River to a large town that stood on the site of the present city of London. There the Britons put up such a staunch defense that Caesar withdrew a second time.

Roman civilization was carried to Britain. A century after Caesar retreated from Britain, the Romans launched another invasion and secured the main part of the island as an outpost for protecting Gaul. Although they chose not to pursue the Celts into the northern mountains of Scotland, the Romans wanted to prevent them from raiding their new colonies in the south. To keep the Celts safely isolated, the Emperor Hadrian ordered a great wall built across northern England. The ruins of Hadrian's wall, which stretched from the Irish Sea to the North Sea, may be seen today.

In order to move their troops rapidly, the Romans built a network of excellent paved roads which later became modern English highways. (See the map of Roman Britain on page 252.)

Roman Ruins. Evidence of Roman rule is still found in England. This guard tower and wall are in northern England at York.

Such cities as Lancaster, Winchester, and Manchester began as army camps built along these roads by the Romans. The suffix of their names comes from *castra*, the Latin word for "camp."

The Romans built over fifty walled cities. The countryside surrounding the cities was divided into large estates known as "villas." The cities and villas became thoroughly Romanized. Luxurious homes containing spacious rooms and baths were built. Occasionally when an excavation is made in Britain today, ruins of Roman cities are found.

For nearly four centuries Britain was a Roman colony. The Romans treated the Celts harshly. But the Celts learned from the Romans many things about their language, customs, and construction methods. During the time of the Roman occupation, Christianity was brought to Britain.

ANGLES AND SAXONS INVADED BRITAIN

Britain became England. The Celts came to depend on the Roman legions to protect them from invasion. Early in the fifth century, however, the Romans withdrew from Britain, leaving the Celts on their own. Barbarian tribes from the north swarmed over Hadrian's Wall and pushed southward. Tribes of Germanic invaders, the Angles and the Saxons, crossed the Channel and raided the southeast coast of Britain in search of new land for settlement. The Celts fought desperately but were eventually forced to flee to Wales, to Ireland, or across the Channel to northwestern Gaul. This period of British history was described centuries later in the legends of King Arthur and the knights of the Round Table. King Arthur was a heroic Celtic warrior who fought valiantly against the invading tribes.

By the end of the sixth century, the Anglo-Saxons had conquered all of Britain except Wales and Scotland, whose protecting mountains proved as great an obstacle for the Anglo-Saxons as they had for the Romans. Most of the Romanized Celts took refuge there. In the southeast, the Latin language and other signs of Roman civilization completely disappeared, and even Christianity was almost entirely replaced by the religion of the pagan Anglo-Saxon conquerors. Soon that part of the island ceased to be called Britain and

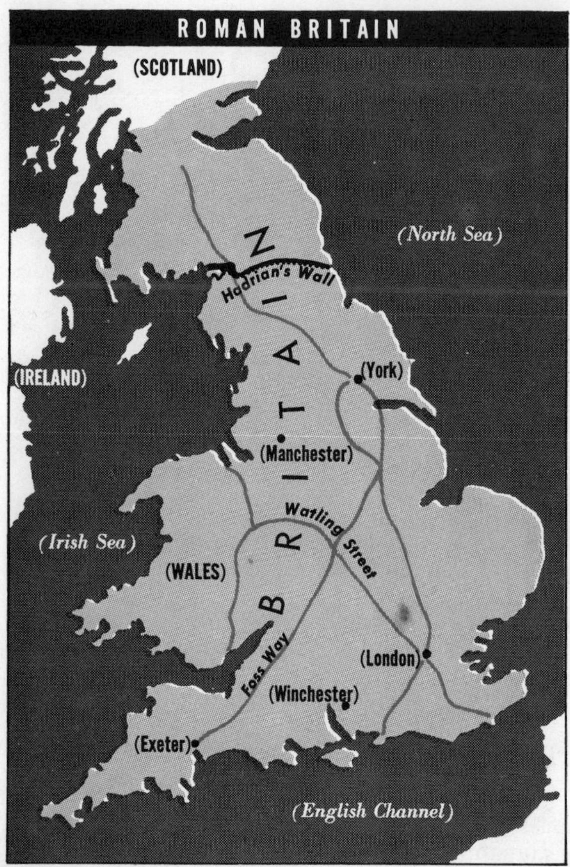

became known as Angleland, or England. Roman towns there met the same fate as Roman towns throughout Europe—desertion, ruin, and decay.

The Anglo-Saxons told marvelous stories about their great warrior ancestors. Their most famous hero was Beowulf (*bay*-oh-wolf), a Swedish prince who, according to legend, killed a terrible monster and saved the lives of a Danish king and his followers. For hundreds of years, the exploits of Beowulf were celebrated in story and song by wandering minstrels. Finally, they were written down in Anglo-Saxon, the language from which modern English developed. Today the story of Beowulf is regarded as the first epic written in the English language.

St. Patrick and St. Augustine revived Christianity in the British Isles. Early in the fifth century a great Christian missionary who had been born in Britain and trained in Gaul came to Ireland to convert the people to his faith. He was later known as St. Patrick. So successful was he that even when Christianity was almost stamped out in England by the pagan Anglo-Saxons, it continued to prevail in Ireland. During the seventh and eighth centuries Ireland became such a brilliant center of Christian culture that it was known as the "island of saints and scholars." Irish monks, who during this period were among the most learned men in Western Europe, laboriously copied Latin and Greek manuscripts and decorated them with intricate, richly colored designs. Irish missionaries established monasteries in northern England, France, and Germany. The monasteries in northern England soon produced excellent artists and scholars, the

Celtic Cross. Carved stone crosses, like this gravestone from the tenth century, are reminders of the flourishing Christian civilization of early Ireland.

most famous of whom was Alcuin of York. Alcuin, you may recall, was chosen by Charlemagne to preside over the palace schools. The learned monk instructed the children of government officials and nobility, and Charlemagne himself, in all branches of learning. Textbooks written by Alcuin were used in schools throughout Charlemagne's kingdom.

Southern England remained for many years under the domination of the pagan Anglo-Saxons. To the Christian leaders, however, all people, even pagans, were regarded as God's children. A story is told that one day Pope Gregory the Great saw some young boys from England being sold as slaves in Rome. Amazed by their fair appearance, he asked what people they were. When he heard that they were pagan Angles, he murmured, "No, not Angles, angels." In 596 Pope Gregory sent a devoted monk, later known as St. Augustine, to England to convert the pagans. St. Augustine won many new followers to the Christian faith. He established monasteries and churches and became the first Archbishop of Canterbury.

Converting the pagans was a slow task, but by the end of the seventh century nearly all of England had become Christian.

THE DANES FOUGHT FOR CONTROL OF ENGLAND

Danish invaders laid waste northeastern England. For many years England remained a disunited country. Anglo-Saxon tribes, each under its own leader, had established seven separate kingdoms. Because they quarrelled so much among themselves, the rulers of these kingdoms were unable to defend their land against a new enemy that threatened them all, a Germanic tribe from Scandinavia, the Danes. During the eighth and ninth centuries, the Danes, who were also called Norsemen or Vikings, went to sea in search of plunder as the Anglo-Saxons had done before them. Using fast ships, the Danes made lightning raids on the seacoast towns of England and northern France. Under cover of night, the ships carried the invaders far up the shallowest rivers, where they swept down on unsuspecting Anglo-Saxon villages. Churches and monasteries, with their rich altar decorations of gold and precious stones, were the Danes' favorite targets.

The Danes were awesome in appearance. Their horned helmets and the fantastic painted carvings on their ships gleamed ominously in the light of burning villages. Small wonder that the invaders struck terror in the hearts of the Anglo-Saxons! By the end of the ninth century, the Danes had conquered most of northern and eastern England. The only region still strong enough to oppose them was Wessex in the south,

KING ALFRED AND THE BUNS. According to legend, the king in disguise stopped one night at a peasant's cottage. The peasant's wife asked him to watch her buns while they baked, but the king fell asleep and the buns burned. In the scene above, the woman is roundly scolding her unknown visitor for his carelessness.

and before long they were threatening to overrun that too.

Alfred the Great prepared the way for a unified England. Alfred, the young king of Wessex, knew that his first task was to prevent the Danes from overrunning all of England. For seven years he fought to hold them back. Finally the Danes agreed to stay in the north and east, leaving Alfred free to turn his attention to strengthening his kingdom (see map on page 253). He divided the land into counties, or *shires*, and appointed military commanders to lead the men of each shire against the Danes. The stockades that he erected along the frontier and garrisoned with soldiers not only prevented the Danes from invading but also served the Anglo-Saxons as points from which to attack.

Because the Danes came by sea as well as by land, Alfred built ships to protect his coastline and thereby earned the title "Father of the British Navy." Thanks to Alfred's firm leadership in building a strong army and navy, later kings of Wessex were able to reconquer all of England and unite it into one kingdom.

Alfred was more than a good military leader; he was also a just ruler who believed that God expected kings to rule with wisdom and humility. As Alfred himself put it, his aim was "to live worthily while I was alive, and . . . to leave to those that should come after me my memory in good works." He and his council examined the traditional laws of his people and kept only those that seemed most just. His laws became the basis for all later English law.

Alfred was also a scholar. Anxious to educate his people for church and government posts, he established a palace school and invited learned men from the Continent to teach. He personally translated Latin works into Anglo-Saxon so that more people could understand them, and he encouraged a group of monks to write what was later called the *Anglo-Saxon Chronicle,* a history of England from early times. It is mainly because of the work of the monks, who added to the *Chronicle* year after year, that historians know what happened in England during the two centuries after Alfred's death in 899.

Such able men as Alfred appear only rarely in history. An excellent general, a just ruler, and a learned man, Alfred is the only English king acclaimed as "the Great."

Alfred's successors unified England and developed local government. In the years following Alfred's death, fear of the Danes made the

Anglo-Saxons forget their rivalries and look to Wessex for leadership. Thus Alfred's successors were able to reconquer the northeast and unite England under one ruler for the first time.

As the Anglo-Saxon rulers took over new territory, they followed Alfred's policy of dividing the land into shires. In addition to a military commander, each shire was assigned a *sheriff*, the official representative of the king. His duties were to keep peace, collect money from his estates, and preside over the local court of justice. The court met twice a year, usually in an open field. At these times, the sheriff heard the complaints of anyone who had a grievance. Because they were administered by royal officials, the courts enabled the Anglo-Saxon kings to see that their laws were obeyed throughout the land. The shire system is still in use in England, and the subdivision of each of our states into counties is its American counterpart.

Canute of Denmark became King of England. England had not seen the last of the Danes however. Within a century after Alfred's death, a new wave of Danish warriors invaded the land. The Anglo-Saxon king, Ethelred the Unready, tried to bribe them to go home, but bribery proved an unwise policy; it simply attracted more Danes who were eager to share his generosity. Finally, the Danish warrior Canute (kuh-*noot*) defeated the English and became king of England and later of Norway and Denmark as well.

Canute proved to be a wise ruler. He became a Christian and won the support of the clergy by his generosity to the churches. Although English laws were different from those of the Danes, Canute knew that he would only confuse and anger Englishmen if he forced them to obey Danish laws. He therefore preserved English law and the shire courts. During his reign, peace between the Anglo-Saxons and Danes finally came to England.

Canute's peaceful rule lasted about twenty years. But his sons proved to be cruel and weak rulers. In 1042 the English rebelled in anger and enthroned Edward the Confessor, the pious son of Ethelred.

Canute and the Sea. The people of his court tried to flatter King Canute by telling him his powers were so great even the waves would recede if he commanded them to. Upon hearing this, Canute directed that his chair be placed at the edge of the sea. Then he ordered the tide to stop rising. When the tide continued to rise, he turned to his courtiers and said: "Let all men know how empty and worthless is the power of kings; for there is none worthy of the name but Him whom heaven, earth, and sea obey." What does the legend of Canute and the sea tell us about the character of this great king?

THE NORMANS BROUGHT FRENCH CULTURE TO ENGLAND

William of Normandy defeated Harold at Hastings. While Alfred was fighting one wave of Danes, another group was busy plundering northern France. This latter group settled near the mouth of the Seine, in a region which became known as Normandy. Just as the Danes who mixed with the Anglo-Saxons had learned their ways, so the Normans intermarried with the French and adopted their language and customs.

When the English king, Edward the Confessor, named as his heir a distant Norman relation, William Duke of Normandy, a violent dispute arose. The Anglo-Saxon nobles had no intention of allowing a foreigner to rule England. When Edward died, they disregarded his preference and chose as their king Harold, greatest of the Anglo-Saxon lords.

William was furious when he heard the news, and he vowed that he would make good his claim to the throne. In the autumn of 1066, William gathered a large army and sailed across the Channel to southern England. Harold, who had been busy fighting Norwegian invaders in the north, turned his army about and raced to the southern coast. There he met the Norman army at Hastings in one of the most important battles in history. After a fierce struggle in which Harold was killed, the English line of defense broke and the Norman cavalry chased Harold's army from the field. William marched to London and was crowned king on Christmas Day.

The Battle of Hastings was important to the future of England. William's conquest marked a turning point for England. Six hundred years of invasion had wiped out the effects of Roman civilization and cut England off from developments on the Continent. The Battle of Hastings broke England's ties with the barbaric

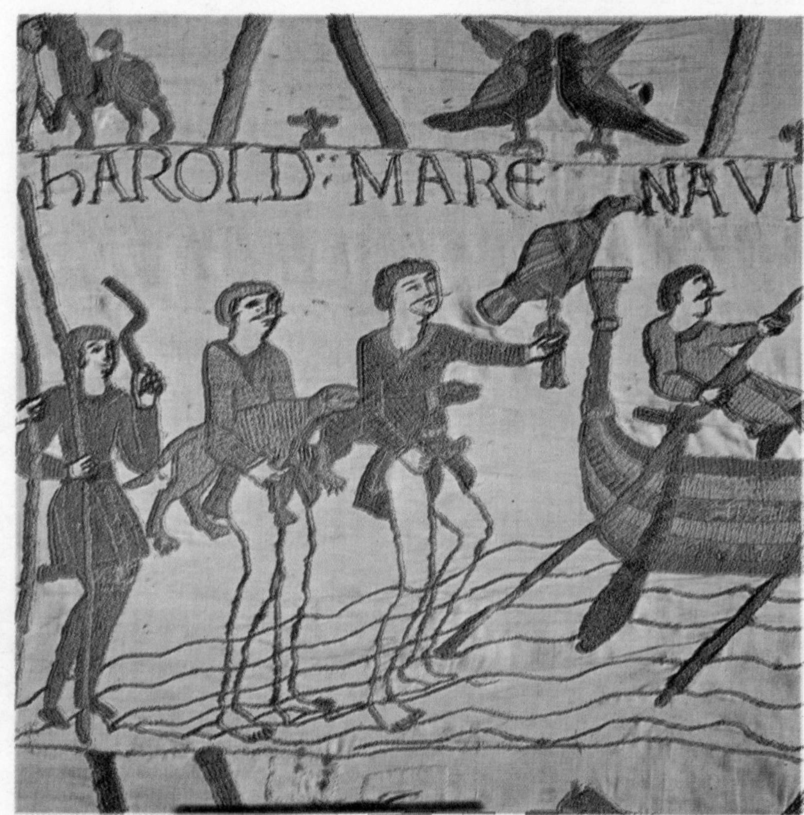

THE BAYEUX TAPESTRY. This famous tapestry which is 230 feet long, tells the story of the conquest of England by William the Conqueror of Normandy. This section depicts the Norman invaders boarding the long boats with their pet dogs and falcons apparently expecting little opposition and preparing to stay for an extended period.

north and brought her once more into contact with Western Europe. The Normans imposed the more civilized French customs and social life on the English. Many castles and cathedrals in Norman style began to dot the English countryside. Elegant French manners gradually replaced primitive Anglo-Saxon ways. The Anglo-Saxon language was enriched with new words from the Norman French. For example, the Anglo-Saxon word *lamb* was replaced by *mutton; pig* became *pork;* and *cow* and *calf* became *beef* and *veal.*

These changes came slowly because at first there was a wide gulf between the Norman conquerors and their Anglo-Saxon subjects. In the century that followed, however, the Normans gradually intermarried with the Anglo-Saxons, and the two peoples were eventually merged into one, with English as their common language.

Chapter Check-up

1. What groups populated Britain before the Romans arrived?
2. What was the purpose of Hadrian's Wall?
3. How has Britain's geographical location influenced her history as a nation?
4. What happened to Roman civilization in Britain after the Romans withdrew?
5. From what early language did modern English develop?
6. How did St. Patrick and St. Augustine influence the religious history of the British Isles?
7. In what ways did Alfred the Great contribute to the beginnings of a united England?
8. Who was the great Danish ruler of England?
9. Who were the last invaders of England?
10. What was the importance of William's conquest to the future of England?

CHAPTER 30

England Struggled for Justice and Self-Government

WILLIAM THE CONQUEROR STRENGTHENED THE POWER OF THE CROWN

During the Middle Ages, England was the scene of continual struggle between kings and nobles. The more powerful the kings became, the harder the nobles fought to maintain their own importance. While the crown emerged as the chief power in the land, the nobles, and later the common people, won rights that limited the king's power and prepared the way for self-government.

Under William the Conqueror, England experienced the strongest government it had known. William claimed all the land in England by right of conquest, and he proceeded to parcel it out as fiefs to his Norman knights and to certain English nobles. Thus he made all the great landholders, both English and Norman, dependent on him. In addition, he forced each of them to swear allegiance directly to him. He was very careful to see that the fiefs of the great lords were widely scattered. This kept the great lords separated and thus helped prevent them from plotting uprisings against his authority.

William ordered a census taken to determine how heavy a tax his landholders could pay. Into all the shires he sent royal agents who made the people take an oath that they would answer truthfully a long list of questions. Their answers went into the *Domesday Book,* an official record of social and economic conditions of the time. It told the king who held how much land, who worked on it, and what its value was. From King William's assumption of the power to force men to answer his questions under oath was developed our modern jury system (from the French word *jurée,* meaning legal inquiry or oath).

The strong central government established by William brought peace and order to England. Men were forced to recognize that the good of the whole country, as enforced by the king's will, was more important than the interests of their local village or shire. Many Englishmen resented William's attempts to strengthen the central government, but few dared to disobey him. When he died an Anglo-Saxon wrote:

> "King William was very wise and a great man . . . but severe beyond measure to those who withstood his will . . . the good order that William established is not to be forgotten; it was such that any man, whatever his rank, might travel over the kingdom with a bosomful of gold, unmolested; and no man dared kill another. . . ."

HENRY II ESTABLISHED JUSTICE IN ENGLAND

Henry suppressed the barons. After the death of the two sons who followed William to the throne, feudal warfare broke out in England. For twenty years the English barons ruled the land and nearly ruined it with constant war. Much of William's good work was undone.

But in 1154 William's great-grandson, Henry II, came to the throne, determined to restore its power. Stocky and powerfully built, he had a shock of fiery red hair and a temper to match. Henry set out to restore peace in England by subduing the barons and establishing a system of justice which would be fair and would at the same time increase the power of the crown.

The barons were his first target. To be on the safe side, Henry destroyed all the castles that might be used as centers of revolt and decreed that no lord could maintain a castle without his permission. To be doubly sure, Henry made tours of inspection over all parts of the kingdom. He rode so fast and appeared so unexpectedly that no one dared plot against him.

To strengthen his position, Henry encouraged the barons to pay him in money instead of by feudal service. He used the funds to hire mercenary soldiers whose loyalty he could count on more than that of the usual feudal army. Furthermore, he filled the chief government offices with paid officials instead of feudal lords. As you can see,

WESTMINSTER ABBEY. This church, many times rebuilt, was begun in 1050 by Edward the Confessor. Since William the Conqueror was crowned here in 1066, this church has been the traditional site of British coronations.

TRIAL BY COMBAT. Before the introduction of trial by jury, disputants often settled their differences by dueling, or trial by combat. Because the outcome was in God's hands, the victor of the duel was considered to be innocent.

Henry took great strides toward making the king independent of the barons.

Henry II introduced trial by jury. Henry found a new purpose for the jury, which William had used only to gather information for the *Domesday Book*. Henry introduced it into the shire courts as a means of peacefully settling quarrels over land. Such disputes were normally settled, under feudal law, by dueling, or trial by combat. Anxious to keep his nobles from fighting one another, Henry offered the shire courts for the settlement of such cases. The jury, a group of men who presumably knew all the facts about the case, was summoned to the court. Before the jury members stated which lord was in the right, they took an oath in which they swore to tell the truth. Under this arrangement many disputes were settled justly and without violence.

The next step in the development of the jury system was its use in determining who should be brought to trial in criminal cases. Before Henry's time many crimes went unreported, or, even worse, innocent men were sometimes brought to trial as a result of false accusation. In order to be sure that no crimes went unnoticed but that innocent people were not accused out of spite, Henry put the jury to a second use. He ordered his sheriffs to appoint twelve men from each neighborhood to report under oath any crimes that had recently been committed. This practice was the origin of the modern *grand jury*, which accuses or indicts criminals but does not determine their guilt or innocence.

Trial by jury replaced trial by ordeal. For many years, criminal cases were not heard by a jury, as were cases involving land. Instead, criminal cases were settled by "trial by ordeal." Under this system, an accused person had to perform some dangerous and painful feat, such as walking barefoot over red-hot coals. If the burns healed cleanly, people thought that God had obviously performed a miracle to protect an innocent man. There was no legal inquiry into the facts.

In 1215, about twenty-five years after the death of Henry II, the Pope forbade the use of trial by ordeal. It then became necessary to find some other method of determining a man's guilt or innocence. Gradually, English judges began to use the jury system for such determinations. They established special "petit juries" (from the French word *petite*, meaning "little") to hear evidence and pass judgment in criminal cases. The petit jury was the beginning of the modern *trial jury*. As members of juries, Englishmen gained valuable experience in weighing evidence and reaching conclusions. Such experience prepared them for the time when they would have a voice in the government of England.

Royal justice gave England its Common Law. There was not enough legal business in each shire for Henry II to appoint a judge for each one. Instead, he appointed a royal official to hear cases in a number of shires through which he traveled on a regular "circuit." The decisions of the so-called circuit judges were the beginnings of *English Common Law*. Having no patience with feudal laws or with the varying customs of different parts of the country, the circuit judges insisted upon hearing evidence and giving judgment according to certain rules. Later judges used the carefully recorded decisions of the circuit judges to establish general legal principles that became common to all England.

English Common Law resembles Roman law in many ways. Indeed, the royal justices studied Justinian's Code and were influenced by many of its principles, such as the belief that all men are equal before the law. But there were also important differences between the two systems of law. Common Law contained no royal decrees and was never written down in an orderly code; it consisted simply of legal rulings and principles that were developed in the circuit courts over a period of many years.

The jury system and Common Law were applied only by the royal justices in the king's court, however. They did not influence the conduct of the feudal courts. Fortunately, decisions of feudal courts involving land could be appealed to the king's court. In this way the king's court became the safeguard of small landholders against injustices at the hands of the feudal lords. As Englishmen began to look to the king for justice, they gradually transferred their loyalties to him at the expense of the barons.

Henry lost his struggle with the Church. Although Henry greatly enhanced the status of the king, he could not successfully challenge the power of the medieval Church. You will recall from Chapter 21 that the Church maintained its own system of courts for handling cases involving clergymen. Because Church law forbade the clergy to shed blood, penalties administered by Church courts were often much less severe than those of royal courts. Henry resented the fact that a clergyman might commit a serious crime and be released after paying only a small fine to the Church. Henry wanted Church courts to hand over clergymen found guilty of major crimes to the royal courts for punishment.

One of Henry's best friends and most loyal supporters was a royal official named Thomas à Becket. Henry thought that if he appointed him archbishop of Canterbury, Becket would see to it that the Church agreed to Henry's requests. Once he had become archbishop, however, Becket seemed to forget his friendship with Henry. As a devout churchman, he stubbornly opposed every attempt to limit the authority of the Church courts. He

HENRY II AT THE SHRINE OF THOMAS. In this print taken from a stained glass window, Henry is publicly flogged for the murder of the archbishop Thomas à Becket who had once been his close friend.

BLONDEL. King Richard's faithful minstrel hears his song answered from within the castle where Richard was held captive.

warned Henry that if he persisted in trying to run the affairs of the Church, "this friendship would soon turn to bitter hate." In a fit of rage, Henry shouted in the presence of his knights that he wished Thomas were dead.

Four of the knights took Henry seriously. They hurried to Canterbury and, slipping into the cathedral by a side door, stabbed the archbishop as he knelt in prayer. England and Europe, shocked by the frightful murder, held the King responsible. As penance for his words, Henry allowed himself to be publicly whipped by the monks at the door of the cathedral, and he did not interfere with the Church courts thereafter.

Henry's reforms survived despite his son's irresponsibility. In 1189 Henry's son, Richard the Lionhearted, inherited the throne. He regarded himself as a great warrior and was little concerned with the details of government. You will remember from Chapter 23 that Richard cut a dashing figure as the foe of Saladin and as the leader of the Third Crusade. On his way home to England, he was captured and imprisoned by his enemy, the Holy Roman emperor. According to legend, for more than a year no one knew where Richard was. His faithful minstrel, Blondel, wandered throughout Germany playing Richard's songs at every castle gate, hoping that the familiar tunes might reach the ears of his master. At last Blondel heard Richard's answering voice from a castle window. A ransom was arranged, and a few months later Richard was able to return to England.

His many travels and adventures made Richard a colorful and romantic figure, but they left England without a leader. He spent only five months of his ten-year reign in England. In the best of times it was dangerous for a king to turn his back on restless nobles and an ambitious brother. In Richard's case, matters were made worse by the fact that the country was growing resentful of the heavy taxes he imposed to finance his exploits. Yet Henry II had established the throne so securely that it survived despite his son's neglect. Richard went soldiering with a light heart, while appointed officials conducted England's internal affairs in his name.

THE MAGNA CARTA PROVIDED A FOUNDATION FOR LIBERTY

The barons forced King John to sign a charter of rights. After Richard was killed in France, his brother John became king. John was cruel, unjust, and generally unpopular. He overrode or ignored the rights of his barons. To pay for his disastrous wars in France, he taxed the barons heavily, used the courts to extort money from them, and refused to let the justices hear their complaints. If any baron objected, John attacked his castle and seized his family as hostages.

John Signing the Magna Carta. Reluctantly holding the pen, King John is forced to put his signature on one of the most important documents of English history.

His quarrels with the barons and his troubles with the Church (see page 191) were to prove his undoing. Finally, in 1215, many barons revolted and began to move a large army toward London. John met them at Runnymede on the Thames River, where he reluctantly signed a document promising to observe certain rights of the nobility and clergy. This famous document became known as the *Magna Carta* (Latin for "Great Charter"). Henceforth, John and all future kings of England were required to respect the rights listed in the Magna Carta. As you will see, it became one of the most important documents in English history.

The Magna Carta became a landmark of freedom. The barons did not intend to undermine the structure of the English government; they simply wanted the king to stop violating the rights to which they were entitled under the feudal bargain. The charter stated:

> "No freeman shall be taken . . . imprisoned . . . or exiled or in any way destroyed—except by lawful judgment of his peers (equals) or by the law of the land. To no one will we (the king) sell, to no one will we refuse or delay, right or justice."

More important than these special provisions was the implication that the king must act according to the law. In future years, statesmen were to find the Magna Carta one of their most effective weapons in their fight to limit royal authority. The principle that the king is subject to the law is the basis of the modern English constitutional monarchy. As used in the Magna Carta, the word *freeman* was intended to mean landholders; that is, knights and barons. But as more and more Englishmen became townsmen or free farmers who paid rent instead of performing services for a lord, they too came to look upon the Magna Carta as a statement of their liberties. Because of this later development, the signing of the Magna Carta is regarded by all Englishmen as a great landmark of personal liberty.

PARLIAMENT GAVE LORDS AND COMMONERS A VOICE IN THE GOVERNMENT

Although the Magna Carta protected the rights of Englishmen, it did not grant them a share in the government; that privilege was won in gradual steps during the next two hundred years. England's development of representative government is particularly significant to Americans because it strongly influenced the thinking of the men who framed this country's Constitution.

Simon de Montfort laid the foundations for representative government. The signing of the Magna Carta was only one phase in the struggle between the king and the barons. On occasion, both John and his son, Henry III (1216–72), antagonized the nobles by ignoring the charter. Henry III demanded huge sums from the barons, but he refused to take their advice or to tell them why he wanted the money. The barons resented his high-handed attempt at one-man rule. As far back as Anglo-Saxon times, the important landowners and churchmen had met with the king to discuss problems of government. The Norman kings had continued the practice by consulting with a Great Council, which was composed of the leading barons and bishops. When Henry III ignored their traditional right to advise him, the nobles, under the leadership of Simon de Montfort, the king's brother-in-law, revolted and made Henry their prisoner.

Simon called a meeting of the Great Council to which he invited not only the barons and important churchmen, but also two knights from every shire and two burgesses (townsmen) from every city. This council came to be called *Parliament*, from the French word *parler*, which means "to speak." The calling of the Parliament marked the first time townsmen had ever been admitted to a Great Council. Their presence indicated the political importance of their growing wealth. Although Simon's Parliament had no legal authority, it proved to be an important step in the development of representative government.

The House of Commons developed during the fourteenth century. Even though many of the reforms made by Simon's Parliament were

PARLIAMENT OF EDWARD I. This curious and interesting picture is probably the earliest representation of Parliament in session. The king is flanked by his advisors and the King of Scotland and Prince of Wales. Seated below him on the outside benches are the Church dignitaries and the peers. The judiciary sits on sacks of wool in the center. Just below the judiciary are the representatives of the minor knights and townsmen.

wise, most Englishmen were not ready to accept them. For one thing, the barons were jealous of Simon's power. Many of them supported Henry III's son, Edward, when he raised an army to oppose Simon. In the battle that followed, Montfort was killed and Henry III was restored to the throne. Both Henry and Edward (who came to the throne seven years later), seemed to have learned a lesson. They adopted more conciliatory policies toward the barons and, most important, they found it advisable to continue calling meetings of the Parliament.

As Parliament began to meet regularly, it became the custom for all members to sit together in one hall to hear the king's business, then to separate into small groups to discuss their replies. During the middle of the fourteenth century, the knights, who were afraid to disagree publicly with the barons, began to hold their discussions together with the townsmen. They chose a speaker who gave their collective, or common, views before the whole Parliament. Their union later became known as the *House of Commons*. The barons and churchmen later formed the *House of Lords*. Parliament is divided into these two houses today.

Parliament's strength depended on the power of the purse. Today Parliament makes the laws of England, but during the reign of Edward I it acted chiefly as a law court. It could not propose laws, and Edward did not have to consult it or heed its recommendations. Indeed, he called Parliament not to gain its advice but because he found it easier to request money from one group of men than from many individuals. Before long, however, Parliament began to insist that the king could not tax the people without Parliament's consent, and before it would give consent, it demanded certain rights. For instance, if the members of Parliament objected to a law, they could withhold their approval of tax concessions until the law was changed. Thus the "power of the purse," as it was called, became an important check on the king's authority.

The power of the purse also became the tool by which Parliament won the right to propose legislation. For many years the individual members of Parliament had the right to present private petitions to the king, which he cheerfully ignored if he so chose. But during the reign of Edward II (1307–27), the Commons as a whole began to present petitions to the king and to demand his approval of them before tax requests would be granted. When such petitions were signed by the king, they became the law of the land. Thus the exercise of the right of petition, backed by the power of the purse, enabled Parliament to acquire certain legislative, or lawmaking, powers. Over the years these powers have been steadily enlarged.

The disputes between Parliament and the English kings were not always settled in Parliament's favor, however. The rise of Britain's present system of parliamentary government was gradual but not always smooth. During the sixteenth and seventeenth centuries, a series of capable and popular monarchs succeeded in restoring much of the Crown's authority. In the next chapter you will meet two of the most successful of these rulers, Henry VIII and Elizabeth I. Their reigns mark the beginnings of modern England.

Chapter Check-up

1. How did William the Conqueror use the feudal system to gain complete control over his kingdom?
2. What was the effect of William's strong central government on England as a whole?
3. How did Henry II strengthen the throne?
4. Why was trial by jury more just than trial by ordeal?
5. How does a *trial jury* differ from a *grand jury?*
6. What is English Common Law and how did it develop?
7. Why is the Magna Carta so important in the history of England?
8. What was the Great Council? How did the convening of the Great Council lead to the development of Parliament?
9. What groups are represented in the two houses of Parliament? What are the origins of these two houses?
10. What was the main check which the early Parliament had on the power of the king?
11. How did Parliament gain the right to propose legislation?

CHAPTER 31

Tudor England Produced a National Church and a Great Queen

HENRY VIII SEPARATED THE CHURCH OF ENGLAND FROM THE ROMAN CHURCH

Royal quarrels brought prolonged warfare to England. One reason that the English kings of the fourteenth and fifteenth centuries were unable to check the rising power of Parliament was that they were preoccupied with affairs in France. Ever since the Norman Conquest in 1066, the two countries had been bitter rivals. The rivalry developed partly from the fact that the English king and many of the Norman lords living in England held estates in France. At one point, Henry II was vassal to the King of France and owned more land in France than the French king did, as you can see on the map at the right.

Henry's son, the inept King John lost most of England's French possessions. Later English kings, in an effort to regain the lands, touched off a prolonged conflict that became known as the Hundred Years War (1337–1453). At the close of the war, England had lost all her territories in France except the town of Calais (kal-*ay*), although the English monarch continued to refer to himself as "King of Great Britain, France, and Ireland" for many years. England's defeat proved to be a blessing for later English kings who were now able to build up their power at home.

No sooner had the war with France ended, however, than civil war broke out in England. The king, Henry VI of the House of Lancaster (1422–1461), went insane. Richard, Duke of York, claimed the throne. Some barons supported his family, the House of York, and some the House of Lancaster. For thirty years England was ravaged by a struggle that is called the War of the Roses. A red rose was the symbol of Lancaster; a white rose the symbol of York. In 1485 Henry Tudor, a member of the House of Lancaster, won a great victory and was crowned King Henry VII. His marriage to a princess from the York family put an end to the feuding, and his son, who became

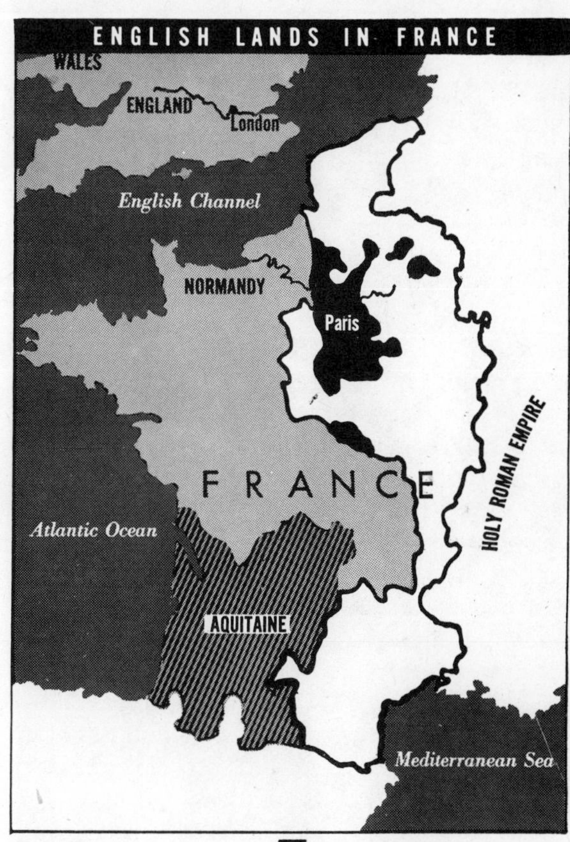

Henry VIII (1509–47), was unanimously accepted as the next ruler.

A century and a half of fighting had made Englishmen, particularly townsmen and lesser lords, weary of war. They welcomed Henry VII and Henry VIII because their reigns brought peace. The Tudors made themselves even more popular by encouraging business and by managing the royal finances so shrewdly that they seldom had to ask Parliament for taxes. About this time the cannon came into use. With this weapon the kings could make short work of castles, as ambitious or rebellious barons quickly learned. With the support of England's growing middle class, the Tudors became the strongest kings in England's history.

Henry VIII became head of the Church of England. Henry VIII showed much promise when he came to the throne in 1509 at the age of eighteen. He was a handsome, athletic, and scholarly ruler who quickly became very popular.

HENRY VIII. In a superb stone carving, measuring only 3½ x 5⅝ inches, Henry VIII, reputed in his youth to have been the handsomest man in Europe, is depicted in middle age.

The Pope was so much pleased by Henry's pamphlet attacking Luther's ideas that the young king was given the title "Defender of the Faith." (English rulers still bear that title, although the faith that they defend is that of the Church of England, not Roman Catholicism.)

Before long, however, a great dispute arose between Henry and the Pope. More than anything else, Henry wanted a son who could inherit his throne and carry on the Tudor line. In twenty years of marriage, Henry's wife, Catherine of Aragon, had given him only one child, a daughter. In the meantime, Henry had fallen in love with a charming young lady named Anne Boleyn. He asked the Pope to annul his marriage so that he could legally marry Anne. When the Pope refused, Henry arranged for the appointment of an archbishop of Canterbury, who married him to Anne and declared his previous marriage invalid. Shortly afterwards, Henry persuaded Parliament to pass a series of laws which denied the authority of the Pope to control the English church and declared Henry to be its supreme head. Under this arrangement, the Church of England kept the traditional Catholic doctrine and form of worship but the king appointed the bishops. A short time later, Henry closed the English monasteries and seized their lands. He gave much of the land to his friends or sold it to small landowners in the vicinities of the monasteries. The rest he used to build schools or kept for himself.

The English people supported Henry's break with Rome. Henry's defiance of the authority of the Pope, who of course excommunicated him, was successful because it had the support of the English people. Many earlier English rulers had also attempted to limit the power of the Roman Church. William the Conqueror had insisted on appointing his own bishops, Henry II had questioned the authority of the Church courts, and John had openly opposed the Pope on the

TOWER OF LONDON. Once a royal residence, the tower was later a prison for illustrious persons. Nearly all of Henry VIII's wives passed through its gates.

question of lay investiture. None of these earlier rulers, however, chose to deny openly the Pope's authority. The medieval Church was too strong, and the secular rulers were relatively insecure.

By the sixteenth century, however, conditions in England had changed. The rise of national feeling stimulated by the Renaissance made the English resentful of the interference of an Italian Pope in their affairs. Furthermore, the people sympathized with Henry's desire to have a son, since a son would prevent civil war over the choice of a king. Many of the nobles who shared in the distribution of the Church lands opposed a return to papal authority because they knew they would have to give up their new properties. Then, too, Henry had been careful to gain Parliament's approval of his action so that no one could complain that he had forced the Church of England on the people.

Edward was a Protestant, Mary a Catholic. Henry had six wives, but only the third gave him a son, Edward VI. During Henry's reign, the doctrine and form of worship in the church had remained virtually unchanged. But under Edward, the Church of England became much more Protestant in its beliefs, because his advisors were influenced by Lutheran ideas from the Continent. After six years Edward died, and Henry's eldest daughter, Mary, became queen. Through the years, Mary had remained loyal to the Catholic Church and to her mother, Catherine of Aragon, whom Henry had divorced. Mary did everything possible to bring the Church of England back under the authority of the Pope. She persecuted the Protestants vigorously and had so many put to death, that she was given the nickname "Bloody Mary." She might have succeeded in her undertaking if she had not made the mistake of marrying Prince Philip of Spain. Her marriage infuriated all Englishmen because Spain was England's greatest rival. Thus Mary's efforts to restore the Catholic faith failed.

UNDER ELIZABETH I ENGLAND BECAME A POWERFUL NATION

Elizabeth's compromise gave the Church of England its present form. When Henry's only surviving heir, Elizabeth I (1558–1603), came to the throne, everyone wondered which side of the religious question she would support. Wisely, she chose a middle ground. Unlike her brother and sister, she was little concerned with the details of her subjects' beliefs as long as they joined the Church of England and she controlled that church. Although she appointed her own bishops and demanded that all clergymen swear allegiance to her, she was willing to compromise on matters pertaining to the forms of worship. To make it easier for everyone to accept the English church, she instructed her Protestant bishops to make certain changes in the church services. The result was a compromise between the Roman Catholic and the Lutheran and Calvinist points of view. By making these compromises, Elizabeth won the gratitude and loyalty of most Englishmen.

The queen's clever statesmanship kept England free and Protestant. Elizabeth's solution to the religious problem satisfied her subjects, but it greatly disturbed the Catholic rulers of Europe who wanted to see the Pope's authority restored in England. They hoped that she would marry a Catholic king and make an alliance with his country. Three of her most ardent suitors were Philip II of Spain and the two brothers of the French king. All three were Roman Catholics, and a marriage to one of them would gain a strong ally for England. Elizabeth, however, regarded herself as "married to the English throne." Yet she dared not spurn their attentions openly for fear of touching off war. Instead, for many years she diplomatically allowed each to believe that she would marry him.

When the Catholic rulers finally realized that Elizabeth would remain Protestant and unmarried, they pinned their hopes on Elizabeth's beautiful cousin, Mary Queen of Scots. Mary, a Catholic, was next in line for the English throne because Elizabeth had no children. Indeed, Mary's supporters claimed that she, and not Elizabeth, was queen. In the eyes of Catholics, Elizabeth was the illegitimate daughter of Henry VIII and therefore could not inherit the throne. As a result of a Protestant uprising in Scotland, Mary fled to England. Elizabeth, who considered her cousin a grave threat to the crown, put her in prison and kept her there for the next nineteen years. During this time, England seethed with Roman Catholic plots to assassinate Elizabeth and crown Mary. While it appears that Philip was chiefly responsible for the efforts to assassinate Elizabeth, she believed that Mary was involved in the conspiracy. As a result, Mary was put on trial for treason, found guilty, and beheaded.

Mary Queen of Scots. After nineteen years of imprisonment by her cousin Elizabeth, Mary Stuart is led to her execution. Mary's personal and public life had been almost entirely tragic. Her son was to become James I, the first of the Stuart kings of England.

ELIZABETH I. Magnificently attired in the rich clothes and jewels she loved, the red-headed queen sits for her portrait. Because of her insistence on a sound fiscal policy, England experienced its Golden Age.

England defeated the Spanish Armada and emerged as a great power. Philip II was determined not only to make England Roman Catholic, but also to stop her from interfering with Spain's trade with the New World. The English were frankly envious of the gold and silver which flowed into Spain from her colonies in the New World. Daring English adventurers like Hawkins, Morgan, and Drake smuggled goods into Spanish colonies and later turned to plundering Spanish treasure ships. On one occasion Drake sailed into Cadiz, one of Spain's largest harbors, and burned the Spanish fleet stationed there. This bold stroke was carried out while England and Spain were at peace. Elizabeth claimed she was helpless to control the piracy of the English "sea dogs," but secretly she gave them her support and shared their booty. (The thrifty queen apparently enlisted the services of private adventurers in order to spare the royal navy and her treasury.)

At length Philip decided that he would invade England, restore the Roman Catholic faith, and put an end to the piracy. He sent a fleet of 130 armed ships, which he called the Invincible Armada, to crush the English. In July, 1588, the Spanish Armada sailed into the English Channel. Drake and his fellow commanders waited in their smaller, more seaworthy ships. The battle that followed lasted intermittently for more than a week. Finally the English bottled up the Spanish fleet by blocking the escape route to the south. When the Spaniards ran low on ammunition, they tried to retreat around northern Scotland, but a terrible storm destroyed many of their ships. Less than half of the mighty Armada limped back to Spain in defeat.

Englishmen rejoiced at the news that the hated Spaniards had met their match. Flushed with patriotism and national spirit, they could declare, as England's greatest poet, Shakespeare, later did, that "this England never did, nor ever shall, lie at the proud foot of a conqueror. . . ." The defeat of the Spanish Armada became a milestone in English history. From then on, Spain's power withered while England's grew. Neither England's independence nor her Protestant church was ever seriously threatened again. Because Spanish sea power was hopelessly crippled, English ships could roam the seas at will. The way was clear for England to found colonies in North America in the next century and to rise to a position of new importance in Europe.

Elizabeth had the support of her people in England's Golden Age. Englishmen look back on the reign of Elizabeth I as one of the most glorious periods in English history. The Renaissance spirit, which had been slowly moving north from Italy, had a strong impact on England in the sixteenth century. Combined with the threat of Spanish invasion, it awakened in Englishmen a new intensity of national feeling. It fired the

English with enthusiasm for increasing their knowledge of the world, and inspired such poets as Ben Jonson and William Shakespeare (about whom you will read in Chapter 35) to write some of the masterpieces of English literature.

To her subjects, Elizabeth was "Good Queen Bess," whose charm, fiery temper, and love of ostentation delighted them. They crowded the banks of the Thames to see her, dressed in one of her three thousand jeweled robes and surrounded by the French and Spanish ambassadors, glide by in her royal barge. Englishmen and foreigners alike admired her keen mind and her excellent Renaissance education.

Elizabeth worked closely with her wise minister, Lord Burghley (*ber*-lee), to encourage England's manufacturing and trade. She improved the financial system by minting standardized silver coins to replace the old ones, which had been mixed with lead. To stimulate the production of goods, Elizabeth welcomed skilled weavers from the Continent and took steps to eliminate the low wages paid to apprentices under the guild system. To encourage trade she gave charters to trading companies, permitting them to send ships to Russia, the eastern Mediterranean, and India. She knighted Drake for being the first Englishman to sail around the world. As England's power and wealth continued to grow, the Queen became more and more popular. No one, not even Parliament, could oppose her successfully.

Elizabeth ruled with the aid of a small group of advisers called the Privy Council. She purposely chose for councilors small landholders or townsmen who had no power except that which she gave them. They would, therefore, serve her well because their fortunes depended on her favor. She was careful, as her father had been, to win Parliament's consent whenever possible. She called Parliament no oftener than was absolutely necessary. When she had to ask for money, she arranged for the election of certain of her councilors to Commons so that they could present her wishes. Elizabeth was held in such respect that very few members of the Commons dared to speak on two forbidden topics: the Queen's marriage, and religion.

You can see that, although Elizabeth made a point of winning popular approval, she really wielded absolute power. But because the people were grateful for England's wealth and new-found religious harmony and because Elizabeth was tactful, they did not object to her firm rule. The spirit of the Elizabethan Age is well-expressed by one of the characters in Shakespeare's chronicle play *Richard II:*

THE ARMADA. The defeat of the Spanish fleet in 1588, England's greatest sea victory, made her mistress of the seas and assured the triumph of the Church of England.

FALCONRY. Hunting with hawks was a favorite pastime in Elizabethan England. Notice the costume of the three falconers. Well-rounded pants were the height of fashion, and the stockings were often stuffed with sawdust to make the legs appear more shapely.

. . . This scepter'd isle,
This earth of majesty, this seat of Mars,
This other Eden, demi-paradise,
This fortress built by Nature for herself
Against infection and the hand of war,
This happy breed of men, this little world,
This precious stone set in the silver sea,
Which serves it in the office of a wall
Or as a moat defensive to a house,
Against the envy of less happier lands,
This blessed plot, this earth, this realm, this
England.

Chapter Check-up

1. How did the Hundred Years War affect the history of England?
2. Why were the Tudors among England's strongest and most popular rulers?
3. Why did Henry VIII break with the Roman Catholic Church?
4. How was Henry VIII able to succeed, where others had failed, in denying the power of the Pope?
5. How did Elizabeth I solve the religious problem in England?
6. Why was the question of Elizabeth's marriage of such importance to all of Europe?
7. How did Elizabeth deal with the threat to her throne caused by Mary Queen of Scots?
8. Why did Philip II send the Spanish Armada to England?
9. Why is the defeat of the Spanish Armada a milestone in English history?
10. What were the major accomplishments of the rule of Elizabeth I?

CHAPTER 32

Parliament Gained Control of England's Government

ENGLISHMEN REVOLTED AGAINST RULE BY DIVINE RIGHT

James I claimed to rule England by divine right. Under the capable rule of the Tudors, England had risen to a high place among the nations. But when Elizabeth died in 1603, she left no heir. Her councilors had favored James VI of Scotland, son of Mary Queen of Scots and a Stuart, as her successor. Parliament accepted him because they thought that, being an outsider (from Scotland), he would be easy to control. He became James I (1603–25) of England.

James' concept of what it meant to be king brought him into conflict with Parliament. He declared that he ruled by *divine right;* that is, by the will of God. Therefore, he said, the way he ruled concerned only himself and God, not the people. (Egyptian Pharaohs, Persian kings, and Roman emperors had had similar ideas, you will remember.) As James put it, "The state of monarchy is the supremest thing on earth, for kings are not only God's lieutenants upon earth . . . but even by God himself are called gods." Needless to say, Parliament did not accept this definition of the king's status. The English were not used to being told that government was none of their business. James further alienated his subjects when he declared that their liberties were not theirs by right, as the Magna Carta said, but were a gift of the king, who could take them away at his pleasure.

James expected the House of Commons to do only as he commanded. He neglected, however, to have his councilors elected to Parliament as Elizabeth had done. Gradually the House of Commons began to oppose the king's wishes. When James demanded money and refused to explain how it would be spent, Commons refused to grant it. Finally James dissolved Parliament and raised money by borrowing from friends and by selling titles of nobility.

Recurrent religious controversy increased the friction between James and his subjects. Many Englishmen still felt that the Church of England was too much like the Roman Catholic Church. They were called Puritans, because they wanted Parliament to pass laws to "purify" the Church. By purifying, they meant that the Church service should be made simpler and that the use of altars and statues should be discontinued. When James opposed any change in the English Church, many Puritans left England. As you know, some of them came to America. Those who stayed behind openly criticized the government. On the questions of religion, taxation, and the rights of Parliament, James and his subjects continued to grow further and further apart. But there was no open split between them during James' lifetime.

Charles I's disregard of the Petition of Right led to civil war. James' son, Charles I (1625–49), stubbornly pursued his father's policies. When Parliament refused his request for funds, Charles disbanded it and tried by illegal means to force the people to pay taxes. But the serious financial troubles that arose out of his unsuccessful war against France and Spain forced him to reconvene Parliament. In 1628 the House of Commons took advantage of Charles' plight by de-

KING JAMES AND THE PURITANS. A group of Puritan lords is petitioning the king to "purify" the services of the Church of England. James did not approve. He did, however, authorize a new translation of the Bible, which is known to us as the King James Version.

manding that he sign a Petition of Right, setting forth the liberties of Englishmen. In desperation Charles agreed that:

1. No one could be taxed without the consent of Parliament.
2. No one could be imprisoned without a jury trial.
3. No one could be compelled to quarter soldiers in his home in peacetime.

When the war ended, Charles' financial problems eased, and he proceeded to ignore the Petition of Right. For eleven years he ruled England without calling Parliament into session. But in 1639 rebellion broke out in Scotland, and Charles needed money to crush the uprising. He summoned Parliament, but this time the House of Lords and the House of Commons made a united effort to limit the king's power.

Englishmen began to take sides in the struggle between a determined Parliament and a stubborn king. Most of the royal officers and large landowners, called Cavaliers (kav-uh-*leers*), supported the king. They were gentlemen of leisure who wore wide lace collars and velvet doublets and had long, flowing hair. The townsmen and small landowners, on the other hand, supported Parliament in the contest for power. These men of the middle class dressed in dark clothing and plain linen collars and wore their hair cut close to their heads. They were called Roundheads. In 1642 civil war broke out between the Roundheads and the Cavaliers. Under the Puritan leader, Oliver Cromwell, the Roundheads defeated the king and his followers. For several years Charles was held a prisoner. But Cromwell and his supporters believed that as long as Charles was alive he would be a threat to their liberties. When they gained control of Parliament in 1649, they ordered the king brought to trial as a tyrant and a traitor to England. Charles, who refused to make any plea before the court, was found guilty and sentenced to death. He accepted his execution with such courage and dignity that he later came to be regarded by many Englishmen as a martyr.

Cromwell became the ruler of England. After the execution of Charles, the House of Commons met and voted to abolish the office of king and the "useless and dangerous" House of Lords. It also declared England to be a "Commonwealth and Free State." A few years later the English people became dissatisfied with Parliament when it refused to hold new elections. Apparently the members wanted to keep their seats in Parliament and thus retain their power. Finally Cromwell and his soldiers drove the members of the House of Commons out of the halls of the Parliament building. Cromwell had the doors locked, and he pocketed the key. The government of England was then the army, with Cromwell at the head. He took the title of "Lord Protector," but today he would be regarded as a dictator.

CROMWELL IN PARLIAMENT. Declaring that Parliament was no longer representative of the English people, Cromwell dissolved it in 1653 and took the title Lord Protector.

Oliver Cromwell was a strong ruler. He was deeply religious and ruled with the conviction that he was carrying out a duty imposed on him

The Execution of Charles I. Escorted by armed soldiers, the king walks from St. James Palace to Whitehall, where he was beheaded in 1649. He accepted his fate with such dignity and nobility that Englishmen soon regretted his execution.

by God. Although he was not excessively strict in matters of conduct, other Puritan leaders sought to put an end to gambling, theater-going, and various other forms of amusement which they regarded as frivolous. Although Cromwell's authoritative rule was efficient, Englishmen grew to hate it. They longed for their traditional king and Parliament. Cromwell's son tried to carry on after his father's death, but he was forced to resign. The houses of Parliament met and invited the son of Charles I to return from exile in the Netherlands. England welcomed the restoration of Charles II (1660–85) with great rejoicing. Ever since the *Restoration*, England has had a monarchy.

The English carried out a "Bloodless Revolution" in 1688. The English people had no intention of giving up any of their hard-won rights, and Charles II knew it. Although he was no more willing to let Parliament rule than his father had been, he was cautious and tried to keep on good terms with the House of Commons. During his reign Parliament and the king had nearly equal constitutional powers. Fortunately for him, people had grown so resentful of Cromwell that Charles II was accepted as a welcome change. By skillful managing, Charles, who was an able politician, acquired a great deal of power before his death in 1685.

His brother, James II (1685–88) was neither cautious nor skillful. He refused to rule by the Constitution (which included the Magna Carta and the Petition of Right) and made no secret of the fact that he was Roman Catholic and planned to abolish the Protestant faith in England. James' appointment of Catholics to government office, and the birth of his son, which insured a Catholic succession, provoked a general rebellion. In 1688 Parliament deposed James and elected a new king and queen who it felt could be trusted. This act became known as the *Bloodless Revolution* because James fled and there was no fighting. Thus Parliament made itself the chief power in the government and settled for all time the bitter struggle for power between the English kings and the Parliament.

The Bill of Rights guaranteed the power of Parliament and the liberties of Englishmen. After successfully dethroning James, Parliament decided to ask the ruler of Holland, William of Orange, who was a grandson of Charles I, and his wife Mary, Protestant daughter of James II, to become king and queen of England, provided they would accept certain limitations on their authority. Parliament put the conditions of their reign in the form of a written document called the *Bill of Rights.* In 1689 William and Mary signed the Bill of Rights and came to the throne of England. Many ideas in the English Bill of Rights later became a part of the Constitution of the United States. Its most important safeguards against tyranny were:

1. The king must enforce all laws passed by Parliament and no other laws.
2. Neither excessive bail nor fines should be imposed, nor cruel and unusual punishments inflicted.
3. No taxes can be levied without the consent of Parliament.
4. There must be freedom of speech and debate in Parliament without fear of punishment.

English political history had reached an important milestone. When William and Mary signed the Bill of Rights in 1689, they accepted the fact that Parliament was more powerful than the crown and, in fact, that the king ruled at the pleasure of Parliament. Thus the Bill of Rights was one of the most important steps in England's long journey from the iron-handed rule of William the Conqueror to the limited, or constitutional, monarchy of present-day Britain.

POLITICAL PARTIES AND THE CABINET SYSTEM DEVELOPED IN BRITAIN

The victory of Parliament was not a clear-cut victory for democracy. It would be a mistake to think that because Parliament had proved its power over the king, England had suddenly become a democracy. Before a government can be said to be truly democratic, it must do three things:

1. It must give a large part of the adult population the right and the opportunity to vote as it sees fit. A country which allows men to vote but gives them only one choice or punishes them for the wrong choice is not a democracy.
2. It must see that those who make the laws are responsible to the voters. If laws are made which the majority does not like, there must be a way of voting the lawmakers out of office and replacing them with others.
3. It must see that those who enforce the laws are also responsible to the voters or to the *legislative* (lawmaking) assembly. A country can have the best laws in the world, but if its *executive* (law-enforcing) power is in the hands of men who ignore the laws, it is not a democracy but a dictatorship.

These three provisions make a government democratic in form, but they do not necessarily make it a just government. In order for a democracy to produce good government, its citizens must be educated, informed, and actively interested not only in their own welfare but also in that of their fellows. Furthermore, the citizens of a democracy must have such a strong faith in democratic government that they are willing to work to make it succeed. They must respect the right of every individual to believe, to speak, and to act as he pleases, so long as he does not endanger the rights of other men.

A close look at the England of 1689 reveals that it could not, even after the passage of the Bill of Rights, be considered truly democratic because Parliament was not representative of all the people. The House of Lords was not elected; its members held their seats because of noble birth or high office in the Church of England. Although the House of Commons was elected, it did not represent all segments of the population. In 1689, only men who owned land or had a certain annual income had the right to vote; the mass of the people had no voice in choosing members of Parliament. Until well into the nineteenth century, only the rich and highborn could make their voices heard effectively.

Organized political parties expressed different points of view. If every man simply spoke his own mind without ever learning to co-operate or compromise with others, Parliament or any legislative assembly would be nothing but a babble of voices; it would never reach any decisions. Every democracy has the problem of allowing free speech and at the same time reaching enough

WILLIAM AND MARY. William and Mary are jointly offered the crown of England by Parliament in 1689. Both monarchs were grandchildren of Charles I. Because they left no heirs, Mary's sister Anne reigned after William's death.

agreement in the assembly to pass laws. As long as the English Parliament had to defend its right to make laws and grant taxes, most of its members were united by their opposition to the king. But after the Restoration, when Parliament began to shape government policy, its members began to express differing opinions. Barons, merchants, churchmen, and country gentry could not agree on any one plan of action or government policy. But because of the development of political parties in Parliament in the seventeenth and eighteenth centuries, Englishmen learned how to maintain an effective government despite the many conflicts of interest.

After the Restoration, two separate groups began to form in Parliament. One, the *Tories*, believed that the king should have a great deal of power and should be advised by the House of Lords. The Tories supported Charles II and no doubt would have supported James II if he had not tried to restore Catholicism to England. Many of the Tories were descendants of the Cavaliers and shared the views of their ancestors. They were often chosen by the king to hold high office in the church or to serve at court. Because they all belonged to the Church of England, they wanted to limit appointment to government offices and membership in the House of Commons to members of that church.

Those men who believed that Parliament should be stronger than the king and that he should be guided by the House of Commons were called *Whigs*. The Whigs were merchants, businessmen, and certain great lords who feared the power of the king. Many of them were Dissenters (Protestants who did not agree with the doctrines of the Church of England). The Whigs were more democratic than the Tories in their beliefs. Eventually they favored the extension of the voting privilege to the whole middle class.

These two parties still exist in England. As you will see in the next chapter, however, they have changed their names and modified their beliefs. The Tories became the Conservative Party and the Whigs the Liberal Party. The power of the Liberal Party has steadily declined. Today most Englishmen belong to the Conservative Party or to a new party composed largely of members of the working class, the Labor Party. Since the Labor Party victory in 1945, one of these two parties has controlled the government.

Control of the British Government passed into the hands of the Cabinet and the Prime Minister. Under Queen Anne (1702–14), the last of the Stuarts, Parliament passed the Act of Union, which joined England and Scotland under one crown and one Parliament. Since that time, the two countries have been referred to as *Great Britain*. When Anne died without leaving an heir, Parliament chose as king George I (1714–27), ruler of the German state of Hanover and a Protestant descendant of James I. George was the first of a family of rulers who still occupy the British throne, although during World War I the family name was changed from Hanover to Windsor. For over two hundred years the descendants of George I have ruled England without further civil wars.

Although William and Mary had surrendered to Parliament the right to make laws, they were still the executive heads of the state. George I, however, allowed Parliament to take over the executive power as well. This remarkable development came about as the result of the strengthening of the Cabinet, a select group of advisers to the king.

At A Glance

Major Documents in English History

Magna Carta—1215
Petition of Right—1628
Bill of Rights—1689

The idea of special advisors to the king was not new. As early as the 1500's the kings of England began to turn for advice to a "Privy Council," an outgrowth of the Great Council (see page 263). But the Council in time became too large, and the kings began to rely on a small group of ministers to help them with important problems. The group was sarcastically called the "king's cabinet" because it met secretly in a small room called a cabinet. Queen Anne established an important precedent when she selected for her cabinet only members of the majority party in Parliament. Those men could then persuade the House of Commons to pass laws that she desired. Anne's practice has been retained by all of her successors.

Canvassing for Votes. The politics of eighteenth-century England were satirized by the artist William Hogarth in a series of engravings. In the center a voter is beset by agents of different candidates. Another vote-getter offers trinkets to the woman leaning out the window at the right, hoping that she will influence the voting of her menfolk in return.

ROBERT WALPOLE. As England's first prime minister, Walpole held office for twenty-one consecutive years. Who is Britain's prime minister today?

Under George I, the Cabinet became the very heart of the British government. Members of the Cabinet were (and still are) the heads of various departments of government, such as Foreign Affairs, Exchequer (treasury), War, Admiralty, and Home Affairs. These ministers were supposed to advise the king so that he could make informed decisions. But George I did not even bother to attend Cabinet meetings. As a German prince who was used to having complete control over Hanover, he could not understand the relations between Parliament and an English king. Even if he had tried to listen to his ministers, he could not have understood a word they said because he spoke no English. He therefore allowed one member, who became known as the *Prime Minister*, to speak for the entire Cabinet. The first to hold that title was Robert Walpole, who for twenty-one years was the real ruler of England. He served in Parliament for nearly a half century.

In the United States, the members of the President's Cabinet are not Congressmen, but in Britain Cabinet ministers are nearly always members of the majority party in the House of Commons. They regularly attend sessions of Parliament and take an active part in its proceedings. The Cabinet members have great influence because they decide what business shall be discussed in Parliament, what new bills shall be introduced, and how to defend the actions of the government when the minority party attacks it. Since the nineteenth century, the Cabinet has taken over most of the king's executive power. It is important to note that since the Prime Minister and the other members of the Cabinet must first be elected to Parliament, they have become more responsive to the voters' wishes than to those of the king. After each general election, the Prime Minister, who is the leader of the majority party in the House of Commons, selects the Cabinet. Today the Prime Minister, not the king or queen, is the real head of the British government.

Chapter Check-up

1. What is the belief in the divine right of kings which the Stuarts followed?
2. Why is the Petition of Right one of England's great documents?
3. What events led to the execution of Charles I?
4. How was England ruled after the death of Charles I?
5. How did Parliament make sure that William and Mary would not overreach the limits of their authority?
6. Why is the Bill of Rights a turning point in British history?
7. What two political parties and points of view became dominant in Parliament after the restoration of the kings?
8. What was the purpose of the early Cabinet?
9. Why was the position of Prime Minister first created?
10. Why is the Prime Minister, not the king, the real head of the British government?

CHAPTER 33

The Industrial Revolution Led to Sweeping Changes in English Life

CONDITIONS IN EIGHTEENTH-CENTURY ENGLAND FAVORED RAPID INDUSTRIAL CHANGE

If an Egyptian farmer of four thousand years ago had visited England in the early eighteenth century, he would have found many things familiar. At that time, most Englishmen lived on farms or in small villages and worked the land with crude tools and the aid of horses or oxen. The women spun thread with a distaff and spindle, just as the ancient Egyptians had, and wove cloth in their own homes. The world's methods of raising food and making cloth had not changed much since the days of the Pharaohs.

If, however, the same Egyptian farmer had visited England a century later, he would have been a total stranger to the country's agricultural and manufacturing methods. Great factories had begun to dot the landscape and new cities were growing up around them. Large numbers of farmers had left the fields to work in the factories, and those who stayed behind were able to produce much more food because of improved farm machinery and large-scale operation. People now wore ready-made clothing turned out by machinery rather than by hand labor. New and faster means of transportation were available, too. Because these changes came about so rapidly (approximately 1750 to 1850) this period of English history is known as the *Industrial Revolution.* It marks two important changes: 1) from making goods by hand to making them by machine; and 2) from working in the home to working in a factory away from home.

What brought about these sweeping changes? The most obvious answer is that new machines appeared in England between 1750 and 1850 which made hand labor seem very slow and inefficient. Why, you may ask, did not all European countries make use of the new machines since the scientific principles on which they were built were known to the scholars of many countries? The answer is that many factors in addition to scientific principles are necessary to bring about an Industrial Revolution. As we shall see, of all the countries of eighteenth-century Europe, England was best equipped to become the first great industrial nation.

A revolution in agriculture meant a large number of unemployed workers. One condition favoring the development of an industrial nation is a supply of cheap labor. There could be no factories in England until there were people to

RURAL COTTAGE. This cottage is typical of those that dotted the English countryside before the Industrial Revolution.

NIGHT. Eighteenth-century city life was sometimes comic and sometimes brutal but never dreary. This engraving by William Hogarth (1697–1764) shows a scene that takes place in an alley at night. At the left, a barber, who was also a dentist when necessary, shaves a customer; underneath a window children huddle for a night's rest; in the center a carriage has broken down, and in the foreground a passer-by has just been hit with a bucket of refuse.

work in them, and as long as people were farmers they needed no other jobs. During the eighteenth century, however, a revolution in agriculture changed this situation. Men discovered how to improve land and increase its yield. They planted different kinds of crops in rotation, instead of letting a third of their fields lie fallow, as they had done in the Middle Ages. They also discovered a better means of planting crops, and they developed improved breeds of cattle and sheep.

The large landowners were in the best position to take advantage of these new methods. As a result, many of the small farmers were forced to sell out and become tenants. Later, even the tenant farmers were driven off the land when the wealthy landowners found it more profitable to combine into one big field the many small separate strips which their tenants farmed. This process was known as "enclosing" the land. Having lost their land, the English farmers, like the Roman farmers of the third century, drifted to the cities. There, to keep from starving, they were willing to work in factories for pitifully small wages. The increased supply of grain and meat from the great estates made it possible to feed the growing city population which could no longer raise its own food. Because city-dwellers could not make their own clothing either, they created a new market for factory goods. As you can see, the revolution in agriculture prepared the way for the Industrial Revolution.

England had the capital to invest in new industries. An industrial nation must have capital, or money for investment in business, as well as an adequate labor supply. English merchants and bankers who had grown rich from trade had money available for investment. Thus England could afford the expense of introducing new machinery and building new plants earlier than many other nations. Moreover, a system of *free enterprise* prevailed in England, which meant that private businesses were free to compete for profit with a minimum of government interference. The hope of making a profit gave people a strong incentive to invest their savings in new industries.

New machinery increased the production of cloth. A vital role in the Industrial Revolution was played by the inventors who applied scientific principles to practical needs. The impact of their inventions was felt first in the textile industry, which had always been important in England. One of the earliest inventions, John Kay's *flying shuttle* (1733), greatly increased the speed with which cloth could be woven. But the usefulness of the flying shuttle was limited by the fact that the spinners, who were still twisting yarn with a simple spinning wheel, could not work fast enough to keep up with the weavers. This bottleneck was overcome a few years later when James Hargreaves devised a means of turning eight spindles with just one spinning wheel. He called his machine the *spinning jenny*. A barber named Richard Arkwright improved the spinning jenny by adding rollers through which the yarn was drawn into thread. His machine was called a *water frame* because its rollers were turned by a water wheel.

The yarn produced by the spinning jenny was too soft and uneven, however, and that produced by the water frame was too coarse. Samuel Crompton combined the good points of both machines with some ideas of his own to produce a spinning machine called a *mule*. An improved version of the same machine is still used today. In 1785 Edward Cartwright applied the use of water power to his *power loom*, thus enabling a weaver to produce as much as twelve men had been able to do with hand looms.

A number of other inventions also helped expand the textile industry. In 1794 an American inventor, Eli Whitney, developed the *cotton gin* ("gin" is a shortened form of "engine"), which enabled one man to pick the seeds out of as much as a thousand pounds of raw cotton in a day. A few years later a machine was developed to stamp brightly colored designs on cloth.

At A Glance

Inventors and Inventions: 1750–1850

INVENTOR	INVENTION	NATIONALITY
Hargreaves	Spinning jenny—1767	English
Arkwright	Water frame—1771	English
Watt	Steam engine—1769	Scotch
Crompton	Spinning mule—1779	English
Cartwright	Power loom—1785	English
Murdock	Gas lighting—1792	English
Whitney	Cotton gin—1793	American
Whitney	Interchangeable parts—1800	American
McAdam	Macadam roads—1800	Scotch
Fulton	Steamboat—1807	American
Stephenson	Railroad locomotive—1829	English
McCormick	Reaper—1831	American
Faraday	Electric dynamo—1832	English
Daguerre	Photography—1839	French
Morse	Telegraph—1844	American
Howe	Sewing machine—1846	American

The steam engine provided power for the new machines. James Watt, a Scottish instrument maker, made an important contribution to the Industrial Revolution when he devised an improved steam engine which could be used in place of water power to run machinery. Watt did not invent the steam engine, but when he repaired a model of one designed by Thomas Newcomen he saw that its poor construction allowed much of the steam to escape. Watt built an engine whose parts fitted so precisely that very little steam was lost. In 1790 his engine was introduced as a source of power to drive the machines in Arkwright's factory. Steam engines proved so efficient and so cheap to operate that they soon became the most important source of power in British industry.

Coal and iron helped English industries grow. Another factor that favored England in the movement toward industrialization was her

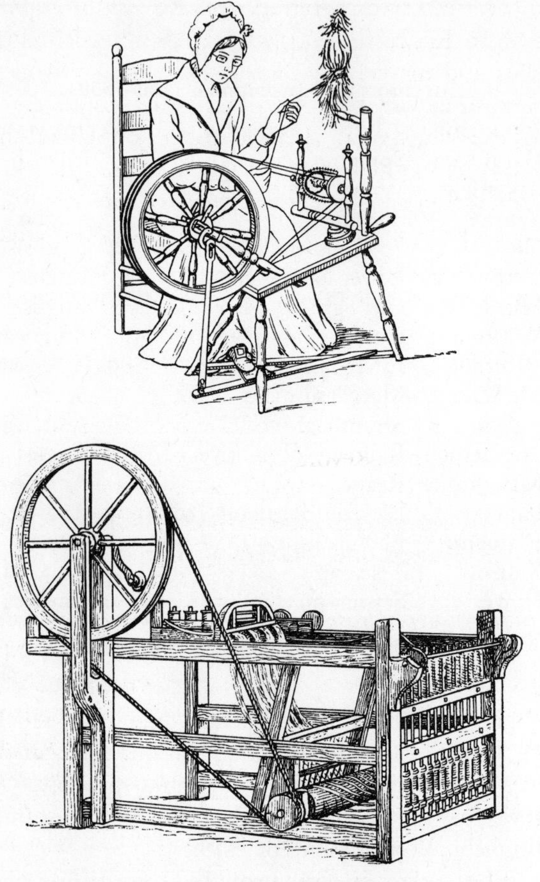

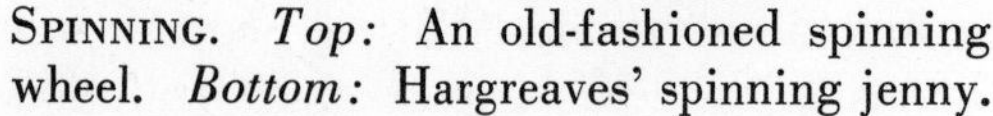

Spinning. *Top:* An old-fashioned spinning wheel. *Bottom:* Hargreaves' spinning jenny.

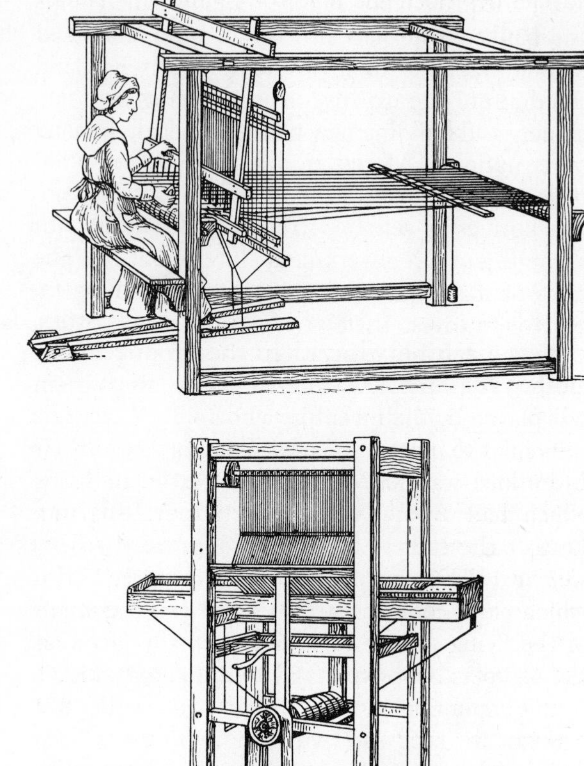

Weaving. *Top:* An old-fashioned hand loom. *Bottom:* Cartwright's power loom.

abundant deposits of coal and iron ore. These raw materials were needed to power the machinery then in use and to build new machines.

For centuries Englishmen had been smelting iron ore in a charcoal fire, but when the hardwood forests had been depleted, they had to find another fuel. Blacksmiths discovered that by blowing currents of air with bellows into a coal-burning furnace, a fire hot enough to smelt a high quality of iron could be produced. If the molten iron were stirred, or "puddled," most of the impurities could be removed. Then someone found a way to roll the hot iron into sheets. The improvement in quality and quantity made it possible to use iron and steel in the construction of machines, bridges, locomotives, and ships. As steel was made more flexible and rust-resistant, it could also be used as a skeleton, or framework, for large buildings.

Roads, canals, and railways increased the flow of trade. The success of the Industrial Revolution depended to a large extent on the development of improved means of transportation. Most English cities specialized in one manufactured product, such as cotton cloth or steel knives. Such cities could not survive unless they could ship their finished goods to other cities and countries in exchange for food, raw materials, and other articles that they could not produce. Before the Industrial Revolution, roads were bad and transportation was slow and expensive. One unhappy traveler described the roads of eighteenth-century England as follows:

> Of all the cursed roads that ever disgraced this kingdom . . . none ever equalled that from Billerica to the King's Head at Tilbury. It is for near twelve miles so narrow that a mouse cannot pass by any carriage. The ruts are of incredible depth . . .

Fortunately, in the early nineteenth century a Scottish engineer, John McAdam, invented an improved method of building roads of crushed rock, gravel, and tar. This paving material is called macadam after its inventor.

Even with improved roads, overland transportation remained slow and expensive. Finally, in 1830, George Stephenson proved that Watt's steam engine could be successfully employed to facilitate land travel. His steam-driven locomotive, the "Rocket," reached the amazing speed of twenty-nine miles per hour while pulling a long line of cars. His success marked the beginning of a revolution in land transportation. Within twenty years, networks of steel rails covered the British Isles and much of Western Europe. In America the railroads soon stretched westward, and by 1869 the Union Pacific Railroad linked the Atlantic and Pacific coasts.

Overseas transportation was also vitally important to England. English factories needed supplies and markets in Europe and the new world. English clipper ships had long sailed to all parts of the world, but they depended on uncertain winds and could not carry much cargo. In 1807 Robert Fulton, an American, used an English-built steam engine to power his boat, the Clermont, and began regular operations on the Hudson River in New York. In 1819, the first steam-driven ocean liner, the Savannah, crossed the Atlantic. By 1860 steamships were rapidly replacing sailing ships on the high seas.

Machines changed man's way of life. While the Industrial Revolution was making England the world's strongest power, it was also transforming the lives of her people. Before factories were built, spinners and weavers worked in their own cottages. They lived in scattered villages throughout England and depended upon traveling merchants to bring them wool or yarn and to buy their finished goods. Often only one merchant came to the village, and the people thus had to accept whatever price he offered. As a result, earnings were very low. There were, however, certain advantages to the system. A man took pride in the cloth he produced and, although he worked hard, he could choose his own hours.

CARRIAGE TRANSPORTATION. Travelers in the eighteenth century found transportation difficult and uncomfortable. Space was limited and quarters stuffy, as shown by the dog catching a breath of air.

SLUM DWELLINGS. Crowded and dirty, these flats were typical of factory workers' dwellings in nineteenth-century England.

He could enjoy the green countryside in his leisure time, and he could grow food to feed his family when there was no yarn to weave.

But with the introduction of machinery, conditions changed. The new machinery could produce cloth so efficiently that no hand-worker could possibly compete. Thus, the hand-worker was forced to go to work in the factory. Spinners and weavers, like the farmers whose land had been enclosed during the Agricultural Revolution, reluctantly left their villages and farms to crowd into the new factory towns.

Ugly, smoke-grimed cities spread over the countryside in northern England, where coal, iron, and water power were abundant. Row after row of cheap, dingy tenements were built to house the workers who poured in from the villages. Often several families shared a single room. Before long unsanitary living conditions and contaminated water touched off frightful epidemics in the tenement areas.

In the city a worker could not maintain a garden in his spare time, and he became entirely dependent on his factory job for a livelihood. With so many workers available, factory owners paid wages of only a few pennies per day. If a worker complained about low pay or poor working conditions, other men could easily be found to replace him. Women and children also worked in the factories, often as long as sixteen hours a day. In some cases even children only five years old got up before daylight, trudged several miles to the mill or factory, and worked until long after dark. The overseer whipped them if they were late or fell asleep.

There was little time for family life under such trying conditions. Workers sometimes fell asleep from exhaustion as soon as they came home. Children had no time for school or play, and there were no amusements. When the factories produced more than they could sell, they closed down. Then workers were laid off and many went hungry until the demand for factory goods increased and the factories opened again.

CHILDREN WORKING IN A MINE. Crouched in a mine, these young "hurriers" struggle to push a coal cart along a track. Child labor was not effectively abolished until the twentieth century.

Was the lot of the ninteenth-century factory worker worse than that of the medieval peasant? You will remember from the story of the Middle Ages that the serf on the manor was forbidden to leave the land and that he led a life of drudgery and toil. While factory workers were free men, in many ways their lives were more miserable than those of the serfs. At least the serf had the security of his land on the manor. The factory worker lived in daily fear of being replaced by a machine or being laid off if the factory closed. The serf could rely on his garden or livestock if the crop failed, but the factory worker had only his job to keep him housed and fed.

While the serf's cottage was only a sod hut, it was often better than the crowded, unsanitary tenement. Certainly a serf's work in the fields was healthier and more pleasant than work in a gloomy, damp coal mine or in an unventilated, smoky factory.

A comparison of the two ways of life must take into account the worker's morale and self-respect. The medieval peasant felt that his crop and his garden were the result of his own efforts, just as the craftsman felt pride in his skill at weaving. But the factory worker who spent his day monotonously tending a machine had no responsibility for planning or turning out a finished article and therefore had no reason for pride in his work. As you can readily see, in many ways the lot of the "free" factory worker in the nineteenth century was more unhappy than that of the serf.

PARLIAMENTARY REFORM GAVE THE WORKERS NEW STATUS IN THE VICTORIAN AGE

It might seem, to judge by the conditions of the poor, that civilization was going backward; but it was not. During the long reign of Queen Victoria (1837–1901) conditions improved steadily. The revolutions in agriculture and industry and the vast increase in trade brought such prosperity to England that eventually her people achieved a standard of living higher than that in any other country of the world. The reforms of Parliament during the Victorian Age helped the workers to share in the nation's new wealth and to gain a voice in its affairs.

The Whigs and the Tories agreed that reform was necessary. Parliament was slow to correct the evils of the Industrial Revolution. For years it did nothing because it was controlled by aristocratic landowners who were more interested in keeping their own privileges than in solving the problems of the working class. The Tories did not want the workers to have the vote because they believed that the masses were incapable of ruling themselves. They felt that England had developed a perfectly good system of government and that a whole new group of voters would only upset it. This was a *conservative* point of view, and the Tories eventually took the name *Conservative Party*.

The Whigs, who had a more *liberal* point of view, later became the *Liberal Party*. They were willing to give the vote at least to the middle class because they believed that if men were educated they could satisfactorily govern themselves. But many of the Whigs were factory owners who opposed any effort to pass laws to help the workers. They feared that such laws would deprive factory owners of their freedom to produce and sell goods at the highest possible profit. They believed that if a worker were poor and hungry, it was because he lacked ambition or industry. It did no good to pay lazy people higher wages or to give them charity. Such people would only have larger families and would therefore still be hungry. For this reason the Whigs believed that the government should not interfere in the business affairs of the nation. We call this attitude *laissez faire* (*leh-say fair*), meaning "let alone" or "hands off."

The Tories thus blocked Whig attempts to extend the vote, and the Whigs blocked Tory at-

QUEEN VICTORIA. Two aspects of the life of Victoria: *below*, as Queen—stately and dignified; *above*, as wife—domestic and solicitous with her beloved husband Prince Albert.

tempts at social reform. As a result, workers were not allowed to help make laws, and Parliament refused to act on their behalf. When the frustrated workers threatened revolt, Parliament realized that it could no longer ignore them. Both the Whig and Tory leaders agreed that reform was better than revolution.

The workers won the right to vote. Neither the Whigs nor the Tories dashed headlong into a reform program. Changes came slowly, but each party became more willing to let the other pass the reforms that it wanted.

The first of the reforms was the extension of voting rights. At the beginning of the nineteenth century the House of Commons was, as we have noted, largely controlled by rich landowners. Even the moderately wealthy middle class (composed of small businessmen and merchants) that was created during the Industrial Revolution had been barred from voting. The Reform Bill of 1832 distributed the vote more fairly but was only a small improvement. Under this act Parliament cautiously extended the privilege of voting to include factory owners, merchants, and professional men.

The Reform Bill of 1867, sponsored by Benjamin Disraeli (diz-*ray*-lee), the brilliant Jewish leader of the Conservative Party, finally gave factory workers the right to vote. Disraeli hoped that his act would win the worker's support for the Conservatives, but the Liberals were not to be outdone. Their leader, a dignified, pious Scotsman named William Gladstone, extended the vote to farm workers by the Reform Bill of 1884. The passage of these bills made practically every adult male in England eligible to vote. It was not until 1928, however, that the privilege was extended to include all women over twenty-one.

Three other reforms gave meaning to England's growing democracy. Another important step forward was taken by the passage of the Australian Ballot Act of 1870, which made voting secret and helped to eliminate bribery and intimidation. Under the Education Act of 1870, public schools were made available for everyone at a small fee.

The Parliament Bill of 1911 greatly weakened the power of the House of Lords by taking away its power to veto money bills. Today the Lords cannot veto any bills, and they can delay only those that do not deal with money. Under present law, a bill that passes the House of Commons three times becomes a law at the end of the year, whether the Lords approve or not.

The workers gained collective bargaining rights. The plight of Britain's laboring class is revealed in the kind of legislation that was passed for its relief. Two of the earliest reform bills were the Factory Act of 1833, which outlawed the employment in textile factories of children under nine years of age, and the Ten Hours Act, which limited the work day of women and children to ten hours.

Gradually living and working conditions in England improved. In 1825 a law was passed that permitted laborers to organize unions, and in 1875 collective bargaining was made legal. *Collective bargaining* is a process in which the workers elect a spokesman to talk to the employer and to bargain with him for improved pay and working conditions. Workers are in a much stronger position when they bargain collectively than when each one speaks for himself. The Trade Unions Act of 1906 aided workers by strengthening the bargaining power of the unions.

That same year the workers formed their own political party, the Labor Party, and began to elect their spokesmen to Parliament. The Labor Party grew in strength until, in 1945, it gained control of the government. In 1951, however, the Conservatives were returned to power. They won again both in the general election of 1955 and in 1959, nearly doubling their parliamentary majority in 1959. But after 1960 the voters grew dissatisfied with the Conservatives, and the Labor Party's strength again increased.

Money and manners characterized Victorian England. During the long reign of Queen Victoria (1837–1901), England enjoyed economic prosperity. The problems created by the Industrial Revolution were gradually being solved and the people began to show enthusiasm for the machine age. The newly created middle class especially shared in the prosperity brought by industrial progress. Money became the sign of success. People of wealth built huge, lavishly decorated houses and rode in splendid carriages.

WILLIAM GLADSTONE. A skillful orator and expert financier, Gladstone was prime minister four times.

BENJAMIN DISRAELI. A novelist in youth and a brilliant statesman in age, the leader of the Tories was Victoria's favorite prime minister.

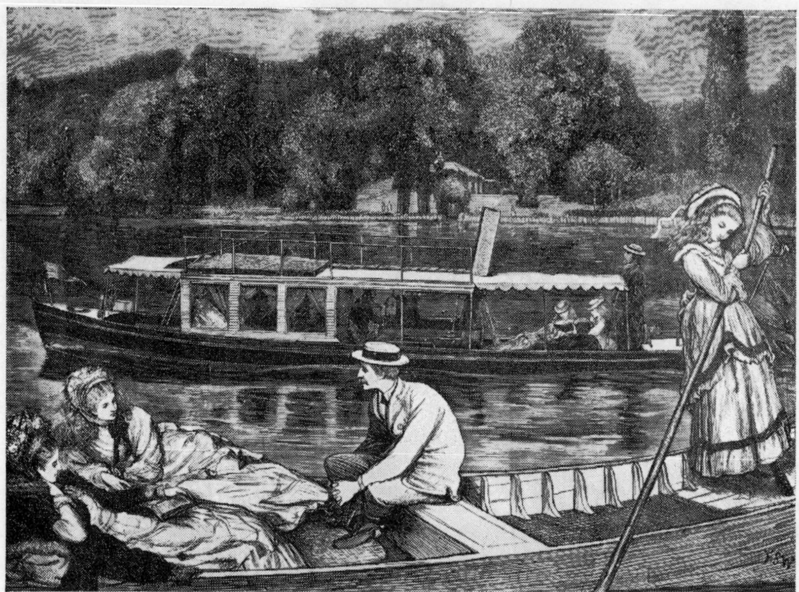

BOATING. Taking leisurely boat trips was a favorite pastime in Victorian England. Propelling the boat with a pole, as in the foreground, was known as "punting." Here a group is punting on the Thames.

Although Queen Victoria had little actual power, the people admired and respected her, and she had great influence on manners and morals of the time. She believed that proper manners were very important and she raised her nine children under strict discipline. Families all over England followed the example set by Victoria. They regarded their upright, conscientious Queen as the symbol of middle-class virtues.

During the reign of Victoria, Britain acquired colonies all over the world, and the wealth from these colonies enabled the nation to attain new heights of prosperity and power. The British people showed their unity and patriotism when, by the thousands, they flocked to the Diamond Jubilee in 1897, a great national celebration to honor the empress of a realm that now stretched around the globe.

TWO WORLD WARS HAVE UNDERMINED BRITAIN'S ECONOMY

Britain lost her foreign markets. The prestige and prosperity of Victorian England continued under the reign of Victoria's son, Edward VII (1901–10). But serious political and economic difficulties followed World War I. The last years of the reign of George V (1910–36) were marked by serious unemployment and a world-wide depression. George's son, Edward VIII, became king in 1936 but abdicated eleven months later in order to marry a woman whom Parliament would not accept as queen. He became the Duke of Windsor, and his brother was crowned George VI (1936–52).

World War II struck a disastrous blow to Britain's position as a world power. Under the inspiring leadership of the Conservative Prime Minister, Winston Churchill, Britain held out alone against Hitler for over a year. Death and destruction rained out of the skies. German submarines sank British ships faster than they could be replaced. With the help of the Allies, the war was finally won. But they had paid a terrible price in human and property losses.

The British set about with characteristic vigor to rebuild their factories and cities. Their most damaging loss was that of foreign markets. After World

War I, countries such as the United States, Germany, and Japan were no longer dependent on imported manufactured goods. Industrialized themselves, they began to compete with Great Britain for many of her former customers. This process was greatly speeded up in the period of adjustment after World War II.

Britain tries to adjust to a new role in the world. Britain's economic problems brought an election victory for the Labor Party in 1945. The new government aimed at a modified socialism which it called economic democracy. It tried to provide more jobs and a higher standard of living through government control of the basic industries (such as mining, steel, and railroads) and a vast social welfare program. This program included unemployment insurance, pensions, medical care, and housing for millions. But its expense has led to high taxes and inflation and the basic problem of an unfavorable balance of trade has remained.

The Conservative Party was returned to control of Parliament again under Churchill in 1951 and has been in power most of the time since then. They accepted and continued the basic policies of economic democracy which proved popular with the people, while trying to cut taxes and inflation. They also agreed with the Labor Party in granting independence to Britain's former colonies in Africa because of the world-wide movement against colonialism. An historic step by the present Conservative government, under Prime Minister Edward Heath, was Britain's joining of the European Common Market in 1971. This break from centuries of isolation is an attempt to improve Britain's economic position by integration in the trade of Europe. Whether this will be the answer to Britain's nagging post-war economic problems remains to be seen.

HOW WILL THE PROBLEMS OF A CONTINUING INDUSTRIAL REVOLUTION BE SOLVED?

The century between 1750 and 1850 is often called the period of the Industrial Revolution, but in reality it was just one phase in a continuing revolution which has now spread throughout much of the Western world. Since 1850, science and industry have produced many remarkable discoveries, such as the Bessemer steel process, the combustion engine, the reaper, the sewing machine, electricity, the telephone, the airplane, and atomic power.

Thanks to the revolution in industry, machines now do most of our dull and disagreeable work, and they produce so efficiently that we work shorter hours and have more time for leisure. You can appreciate the Industrial Revolution even more if you imagine what life would be like without the telephone, radio, television, automobiles, central heating, and other such conveniences.

The Industrial Revolution has made nations interdependent. While machines were making Britain the leading nation of the world in the nineteenth century, they were also making her dependent on the rest of the world. Britain must be able to sell her manufactured goods to other nations, or she cannot afford to buy from them raw materials for her factories or food for her people. The disruption of the two world wars in the twentieth century, and especially German sinking of many British ships, brought great economic suffering to Britain. Today Britain's dependence on oil from the Middle East makes her concerned over any problems in that area.

Every modern industrial nation shares this problem with Britain. The other smaller ones like Japan, Germany, Belgium, and Switzerland

THE ROYAL FAMILY. Queen Elizabeth II is shown with her family on her recent birthday. In the picture are—left to right—Prince Charles of Wales, Philip Duke of Edinburgh, Prince Andrew, Princess Anne, Prince Edward, and the Queen.

are good examples. But even large countries like the United States and Russia need foreign trade to support their modern industries. Today every nation is interdependent. That is one reason for the importance of world peace.

In her own interdependence, Britain has been closely tied with the United States and the nations of the British Commonwealth. Britain's recent entry into the European Common Market probably means turning away from these historical partners to new ones in Western Europe.

Increasing use of machine power poses many problems. One of the serious problems resulting from the machine age is technological unemployment, which is caused by the replacement of workers by machines. In addition, as we have seen, modern machines often take away the pride that comes from planning and carrying out a piece of work. The men who spend their hours mechanically tending machines or monotonously working on an assembly line derive little satisfaction from their efforts. Such work creates no sense of responsibility or personal accomplishment.

We have seen how parliamentary reforms have eliminated many of the evils of the Industrial Revolution, such as long hours, unsanitary working conditions, and economic insecurity. But many men today are deeply concerned about whether the growing power of machines will be used

At A Glance

Important Kings and Queens of England

Anglo-Saxon
- Alfred the Great (849–899?)

Norman and Angevin (1066–1399)
- William the Conqueror
- Henry II
- Richard the Lion-Hearted
- John
- Henry III
- Edward I
- Edward II
- Edward III

Lancaster (1399–1485)

Tudor (1485–1603)
- Henry VII
- Henry VIII
- Edward VI
- Mary
- Elizabeth I

Stuart (1603–1714)
- James I
- Charles I
- Charles II
- James II
- William and Mary
- Anne

Hanover (1714–present)
- George I
- Victoria
- Edward VII

(Windsor)
- George V
- Edward VIII
- George VI
- Elizabeth II

wisely. Will men create machines that will crush their human individuality? Will a nation's desire for wealth and political power lead it to use machines in a war that will destroy civilization? Will men learn instead to live in peace and make the earth a land of plenty for all men to enjoy? The answer that mankind provides to these questions may prove to be the most crucial in history.

Thus far we have watched the story of Britain unfold within her own boundaries, noting particularly the development of the institutions of self-government and the change from an agricultural to an industrial nation. In Chapter 35 we shall discover how Britain's power and influence spread far beyond the limits of the British Isles to the most distant corners of the world. But first we shall turn our attention to the achievements of the British people in the arts and sciences.

Chapter Check-up

1. What important changes characterized the Industrial Revolution?
2. What four conditions were necessary to support the Industrial Revolution in England?
3. How did practical inventors help England to become an industrial nation?
4. Explain the function of (a) the spinning jenny (b) the power loom (c) the cotton gin.
5. Describe living conditions in the factory towns of early nineteenth century England.
6. Why were coal and iron vital to England's growing industry?
7. Why was good transportation a necessary condition for the Industrial Revolution?
8. How did the various reform bills increase democracy in England?
9. Why did industrialization help England? What problems did it bring?

CHAPTER 34

British Authors, Artists, and Scientists Have Enriched the Culture of the Western World

BRITAIN HAS PRODUCED OUTSTANDING POETS AND DRAMATISTS

Mankind will long remember Britain's gifted writers of prose and poetry who have helped to make English literature one of the richest in the world. Her writers developed the basic forms of literary expression which are used today throughout the English-speaking world. Since all of the great British novelists, poets, playwrights, and essayists cannot be mentioned here, we shall discuss only a few of the most important.

Chaucer gives a lively picture of medieval life. For centuries, excellent poetry of all types has been written by English poets. The first great English poet was Geoffrey Chaucer (*chaw*-ser), who lived in the fourteenth century. His most famous work, *Canterbury Tales*, describes a group of pilgrims on their way to the shrine of St. Thomas à Becket at Canterbury. To pass the time on their journey, the travelers tell stories. These stories give a lively, entertaining picture of life in the Middle Ages and help the present-day reader to see how people lived in Chaucer's time. Chaucer describes such things as the squire's embroidered coat and the nun's careful manners so clearly that the fourteenth century is made vividly alive to us.

Chaucer was the first English poet to write in iambic pentameter, a rhythmic verse form which has been used by many later poets. Shakespeare, for example, wrote most of his play *Julius Caesar* in iambic pentameter. The language of Chaucer's poetry is Middle English, from which modern English developed. Although Middle English is somewhat difficult to read today, you can probably recognize many words. The poem begins:

"When that Aprille with his shoures soote
The droghte of Marche hath perced to the
roote, . . ."

Shakespeare created masterpieces of literature. People of every country recognize William Shakespeare as one of the greatest dramatists of all times. He was the most important of all the writers who made the reign of Elizabeth I the Golden Age of English literature. No one knows much about Shakespeare's youth or about the years he spent working at small jobs and acting in London theaters. By the time he was twenty-eight, however, he was becoming famous as a writer of plays.

Shakespeare probably had little schooling, and he never left England, but his plays would lead you to believe that he was a well-traveled scholar. Whatever his experience did not furnish him, his wonderful imagination did. The plays *Henry V* and *Julius Caesar* reveal a keen understanding of English and Roman history. In *Merchant of Venice* Shakespeare recreates Renaissance Italy with surprising accuracy.

Shakespeare's plays also reveal an insight into human nature. Whether describing Hamlet's doubt, Macbeth's ambition, or Othello's jealousy, Shakespeare captures the emotion with marvelous intensity. Here are quotations that show Shakespeare's understanding of the strength and weakness of mankind:

"Cowards die many times before their deaths;
The valiant never taste of death but once."

—*Julius Caesar*

"Neither a borrower nor a lender be;
For loan oft loses both itself and friend . . .
This above all: to thine own self be true,
And it must follow, as the night the day,
Thou canst not then be false to any man."

—*Hamlet*

"O, beware my lord of jealousy! It is the green-eyed monster which doth mock the meat it feeds on."

—*Othello*

THE GLOBE THEATER AND SHAKESPEARE. Many of Shakespeare's great plays were first produced in this theater, shown here as it appeared in 1598. The theater burned down, was rebuilt, and then was destroyed by the Puritans in 1644.

Not all of Shakespeare's plays have a serious or tragic theme, however. Read, for example, these lines from *As You Like It:*

"All the world's a stage,
And all the men and women merely players:
They have their exits and their entrances;
And one man in his time plays many parts,
His acts being seven ages. At first the infant,
Mewling and puking in the nurse's arms.
And then the whining school-boy, with his satchel
And shining morning face, creeping like a snail
Unwillingly to school. And then the lover,
Sighing like a furnace, with a woeful ballad
Made to his mistress' eyebrow. . . ."

The influence of the Renaissance on Shakespeare's writing is revealed in his emphasis on human character and in the rich and expressive language of his plays. The form of language used by Shakespeare is the same as that found in the King James Version of the Bible, which was translated during Shakespeare's lifetime. The King James Bible, one of the greatest works of English literature, found its way into every house in England and was so thoroughly read that it has influenced spoken English ever since.

Milton was the poet of the Puritans. As a poet, John Milton ranks with Shakespeare. He lived during the age of Cromwell, when religion was a burning issue, and his poetry reflects an interest in religious ideas. As a child, Milton spent so much time reading, and he later worked so hard at his government post, that he eventually went blind. Not even that misfortune, however, prevented him from writing his masterpiece, *Paradise Lost*, a long work which is considered the greatest epic poem in the English language. Written in twelve books, *Paradise Lost* tells the story of Satan's rebellion against God and the story of Adam and Eve in the Garden of Eden. Milton's purpose was to account for the evil in the world and to "justify the ways of God to men." A later poem, *Paradise Regained*, describes how Jesus overcame the temptations of Satan. Milton wrote his poetry in an unrhymed style called blank verse, which has influenced many later poets.

SHELLEY. After leaving England for Italy, where he lived the last three years of his life, Shelley was drowned at the age of thirty while sailing on the Mediterranean. His wife Mary wrote the famous horror story *Frankenstein.*

The romantic poets created a revolution in literature. At the end of the eighteenth century, a young man named William Wordsworth led a new movement in English literature. He and his friends and followers were called the romantic poets. They appealed to man's emotion rather than to his mind. The romantics tried to write their poems in simple language that everyone could understand. They often chose to write about children and humble peasants whose emotions they believed to be purer than those of "refined" ladies and gentlemen. Wordsworth expressed his feelings through descriptions of nature. His poem "I Wandered Lonely as a Cloud" is one of the best examples of English romantic poetry.

Two other young poets, Percy Bysshe Shelley and John Keats, carried forward the Romantic movement. Shelley spent his short life in passion-

OLIVER TWIST. While Oliver looks on aghast, an unsuspecting gentleman has his pockets picked. Much of Dickens' work was published first in installments.

ate revolt against his own upper middle-class family and against the British government, which he blamed for many of the evils of his day. Through his poetry Shelley tried to show men that they could rise to a better life through a spirit of love. His "Ode to the West Wind" shows the intensity of his emotions and his marvelous imagination in describing the forces of nature.

Keats was not interested in the problems of the day. He wrote his poetry as a means of giving pleasure and expressing beauty. He delighted in describing the figures on a Grecian urn or the warmth and beauty of an autumn day. Keat's "Ode to a Nightingale" is one of the finest works ever produced by a romantic poet. His masterpieces influenced young poets all over Europe.

Charles Dickens and T. S. Eliot each criticized his own time. For the last century, English writers have begun to deal with the problems of ordinary men living in a confused and troubled world. The novels of Charles Dickens provide a vivid account of the suffering of the poor during the Industrial Revolution. Two of Dickens' most famous characters are Bob Cratchit, the poverty-stricken clerk of *A Christmas Carol*, and Oliver Twist, who was compelled to make his living as a pickpocket in the London streets. Dickens' work influenced public opinion so greatly that Parliament passed laws to improve conditions for the working people. Dickens' books do not all deal with human misery. Such characters as David Copperfield, Mr. Pickwick, and Tiny Tim, were portrayed in a warm and lighthearted vein.

Thomas Stearns Eliot (1888–1965) was born in the United States but became a British subject. His poetry reveals a concern for what the pressures of life in the twentieth century are doing to men's minds and souls. His most famous poem, *The Waste Land*, is a despairing protest against the emptiness of modern life and the unhappiness of twentieth-century man. You might find the poem difficult to read, because Eliot's writing requires a wide knowledge of many types of literature. But his style has had a great influence on modern poets. His more recent writings, which are chiefly in the form of plays, suggest that solutions to the problems of mankind may be found in religion.

ENGLISH PAINTERS CAUGHT THE SPIRIT OF THEIR TIME

Gainsborough painted the English aristocracy. One of England's best painters was Thomas Gainsborough (*gaynz*-ber-oh), who lived during the late eighteenth century, when England was beginning to enjoy the fruits of the Industrial Revolution. Wealthy men of the period built large, handsome brick houses designed in classical Roman style by the famous Adam brothers (see pages 298–299) and furnished by the renowned furniture maker Thomas Chippendale. It be-

VIEW OF VENICE. In this painting of one of the world's most romantic cities, the English artist Joseph Turner, with great skill and imagination, achieved the shimmering colors and misty effects for which his work is renowned. The scene shows a view of the Grand Canal in the light of the sinking sun.

THE BLUE BOY. To disprove the contemporary theory that the color blue could not be used successfully as the dominant color in a painting, Thomas Gainsborough created one of his most celebrated works. The artist was a painter of both portraits and landscapes. Though success came slowly to Gainsborough, in his lifetime he was able to earn princely sums for his elegant portraits. His landscapes went unrecognized (as they were until recent years) and cluttered his studio. It is said that visitors to his studio could hardly get around them.

came fashionable for men of wealth to commission artists like Thomas Gainsborough to paint their portraits. Although Gainsborough preferred to paint landscapes, he eventually became one of England's best portrait painters. His most famous painting, "The Blue Boy," skillfully blends the blue of the boy's elegant satin costume with the blue sky and green foliage of the background. Some art critics say that Gainsborough painted "The Blue Boy" to disprove the statement of another popular portrait painter, Sir Joshua Reynolds, who said that large areas in a picture should always be warm colors like red or yellow.

Turner captured brilliant sunsets on canvas. Just as Wordsworth had new ideas about poetry, so Joseph Turner wanted to make great changes in painting. His originality was not appreciated in his own lifetime, but today he is valued as one of England's great painters. Turner was one of the first artists in the nineteenth century to become interested in the way in which weather conditions affect light. He wandered about Europe painting seascapes in fog and mist to determine how water in the air broke up the light of the sun into the varied colors of the rainbow. Turner was especially skilled in capturing the rich, luminous colors of the setting sun as its rays were reflected against the clouds. These characteristics of Turner's work are seen in "View of Venice," which is reproduced on the preceding page.

There is a story that one day, when Turner was boating on the Thames near London, he watched a tugboat tow an old sailing ship past him. The glorious days when the ship fought with the British navy were over. Now, surrounded by the golden light of the setting sun, she was going to her last berth. Turner was fascinated by the combined themes of the end of the day, the end of the warship, and the end of the age when men used sails instead of steam. He captured all these elements in another famous painting, "The Fighting Temeraire."

BRITISH SCIENTISTS HAVE MADE NOTABLE CONTRIBUTIONS TO MAN'S PROGRESS

Sir Isaac Newton became one of the world's foremost scientific thinkers. As you may recall, Isaac Newton was one of the outstanding figures of the Scientific Renaissance. When he was a child, his neighbors thought him rather strange because he spent so much time reading and building windmills, water clocks, and sundials. They did not recognize his genius. One day, as Newton sat in his garden, some apples fell from a nearby tree. He began to wonder whether the earth pulled the apples toward it or whether the apples pulled the earth. Then Newton became curious as to whether the apples fell any faster as they came closer to the earth.

To solve problems like these, Newton invented a new kind of mathematics called *calculus.* With calculus he could prove what he already suspected—that everything in nature acted according to certain definite, predictable laws. Newton discovered and worked out one of the most important of these laws, the *law of universal gravitation,* which says that every object in the universe attracts every other object according to the weight of the objects and the distance between them. Gravitation helps to hold the sun, the stars, and the planets in their places, and it controls the tides and the position of objects on earth. Newton proved what the ancient Greeks had suspected, that the universe is controlled by natural laws that men can discover and understand.

Faraday learned how to generate electricity. Did you ever wonder how man learned to generate electricity? Michael Faraday made the discovery that harnessed electric power. Faraday's father was a blacksmith near London. As a boy, Faraday became an apprentice to a bookbinder. He must have been more interested in reading books than in making them. He used his spare time to read many scientific books which found their way into the shop of his master. A customer noticed the

SIR WILLIAM HARVEY. The discoverer of the circulatory system is shown here explaining how the heart works as a pump.

boy's interest in science and encouraged him to attend the lectures of one of the great scientists of the day, Sir Humphrey Davy. Before long, Sir Humphrey, a renowned chemist and physicist, made Faraday his assistant. Years later, when Davy was asked what he considered his greatest discovery, he replied, "Faraday."

Once when experimenting, Faraday turned a coil of wire between the ends of a horseshoe magnet. He noticed that he had set up a current of electricity. He had discovered how to generate, or produce, electricity. Faraday's discovery makes it possible for immense power stations to produce the current to light streets and homes, to move trains, and to turn factory wheels.

Since the nineteenth century, when Faraday did his work, the world has almost left the age of steam power and entered an age of electricity. Few things have had as great an effect on our everyday lives as the discoveries of the British blacksmith's son who became a world-famous scientist.

The British have made important contributions to medicine. Modern medicine is said to have begun with the work of William Harvey, an English doctor. In the early seventeenth century Harvey discovered how blood circulates in the body. Correcting the observations of earlier doctors, he showed that the heart is a pump that moves blood throughout the body. A more recent discovery of great importance was made by a Scot, Sir Alexander Fleming. In 1928 Fleming, a professor at the University of London, noticed that germs were killed by a mold that formed on one of the bacterial cultures in his laboratory. The observation led to the discovery of penicillin. In 1945 Fleming won the Nobel Prize for his work with the new germ-killer.

Darwin's belief about the origins of living things caused bitter dispute. Charles Darwin, a quiet young man, was passionately devoted to science. When he was twenty-two, he joined a British scientific expedition that was sailing to the South Seas. In spite of seasickness, he visited dozens of islands and strange lands. He filled endless notebooks with the descriptions of toads, turtles, finches, and thistles which he found there. From his observations, Darwin developed the famous theory of evolution, which attempts to explain the way in which plants and animals have developed their present forms. He said that the forms of life were not the same at the beginning of the world as they are today, but that they devel-

ENGLISH ARCHITECTURE

English architecture from the Saxon hut to the gothic glory of Parliament's Big Ben has influenced much of the Western World, particularly the United States and Canada.

England went through a period of trial and error. English towns displayed timbered houses in the latter Middle Ages, clean appearing with leaded window frames such as these in *Warwick*. With the Renaissance, the Italianate influence conquered England and palaces sprung up on the moist soil of Britain, as this early seventeenth century country home, and also the Howard Castle of the eighteenth century.

The *Great Banquet Hall* at Whitehall by Jones and *St. Paul's* by Wren are outstanding examples of English Renaissance architecture.

Parliament by Pugin is perhaps the most outstanding example of modern day gothic medieval architecture extant. But nothing is more indicative of the architecture and the people than *Big Ben*.

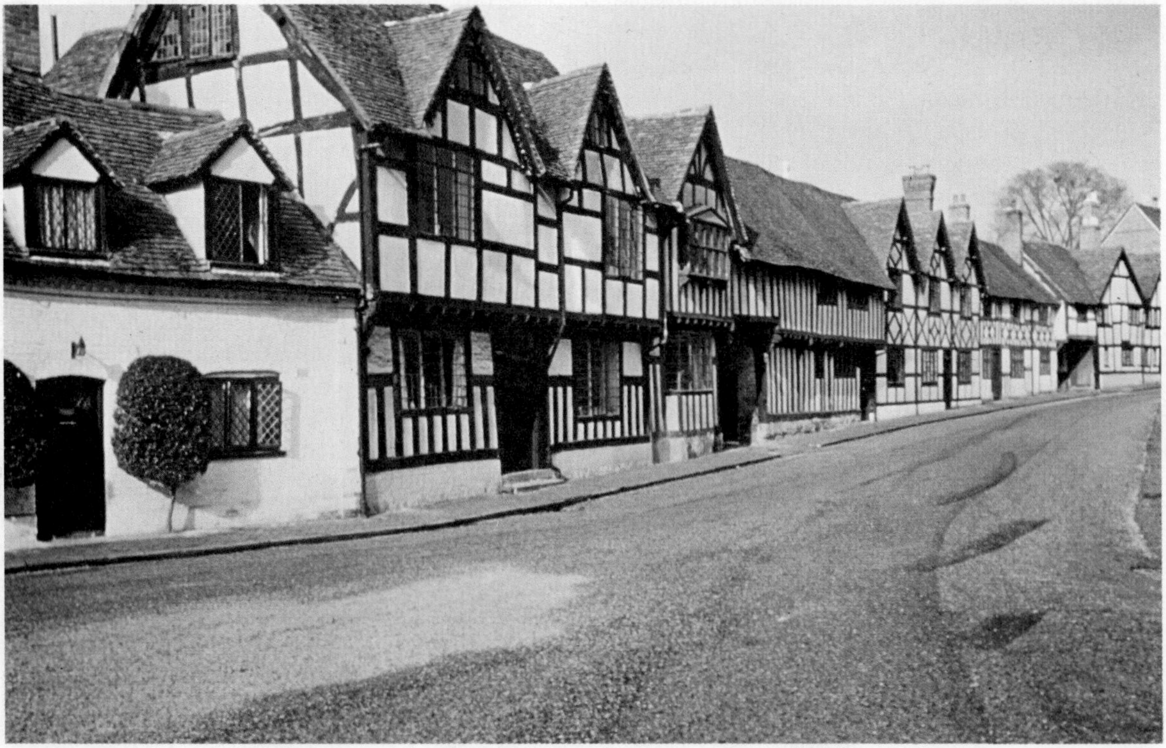

oped slowly from earlier, simpler forms in a process which took millions of years. Because conditions on the earth's surface are constantly changing, plants and animals must adjust accordingly. Those that do not, such as dinosaurs, become extinct. Thus Darwin's theory describes a process known as "survival of the fittest."

Other scientists had suggested similar theories of natural selection, but Darwin was the first to state it clearly and attempt to support it with scientific facts. When Darwin's theories were published in his famous book, *Origin of Species,* they caused great excitement and controversy. His ideas were accepted by most scientists but were violently opposed by people who believed in the literal biblical description of how the earth was created in seven days. Many people were repelled by Darwin's suggestion that man was only the highest form of animal and that strength and cleverness seemed to be more important in man's development than moral goodness and justice.

CHARLES DARWIN. A great naturalist and explorer, Darwin was a pioneer in the study of biology. His theories caused world-wide controversy.

British scientists pioneered in the development of radar. Modern scientific discoveries are usually the result of teamwork rather than individual efforts. One example of this fact is the development of a defense system for England during World War II. British scientists, under the leadership of Sir Robert Watson-Watt, worked day and night to find a way to warn Britain of enemy air attacks. They solved the problem by using high frequency radio waves, called radar. A radar set transmits radio waves which bounce back as an echo when they strike an object. An observer measures the strength of the echo and the time it takes to return. From this information he can calculate how far away an unseen object is, and in what direction it is moving. When the Germans bombed Britain in World War II, radar enabled the British to discover planes long before they reached the coast. Later, radar was used to direct the fire of antiaircraft guns and for bombing unseen targets through cloud formations. Today nearly all commercial airlines and steamship companies use radar equipment to help insure the safety of their passengers.

Chapter Check-up

1. Who was the first great English poet and for what work is he especially noted?
2. Why is Shakespeare considered one of the greatest writers of all time?
3. What was the central theme of Milton's work?
4. How did England's romantic poets differ from previous poets?
5. How did Dickens' writing help to change social conditions in England?
6. For what form of art is Gainsborough best known? In what type of subject matter was Turner most interested?
7. Why is each of the following among the great men of science? (a) Newton (b) Faraday (c) Darwin.
8. What important medical discoveries were made by (a) Harvey and (b) Fleming?

Chapter 35

Britain's Empire Became a Commonwealth

BRITAIN BECAME MISTRESS OF THE SEAS

As soon as the Tudor rulers had ended the Wars of the Roses and established peace at home, England set out on a path of exploration, trade, and conquest that resulted in the development of the greatest empire the world has ever known. Encouraged by Elizabeth I, English merchants established trading connections all over Europe and the Middle East. Soon they were also sharing in the growing American trade. Here they had a natural advantage, for the shift of trade routes from the Mediterranean to the Atlantic put England in the mainstream of traffic between the Old and New Worlds. The English seized the opportunity that geography offered them by making a determined national effort to build the finest navy in the world. Their sturdy ships, manned by daring, highly trained crewmen, outsailed and outfought all opponents.

England faced three rivals for control of the seas: Spain, the Netherlands, and France. When Elizabeth came to the throne, Spain was mistress of the seas. Then, in 1588, in one of the world's greatest naval battles, England defeated the Spanish Armada and broke the naval power of Spain (see page 269). England's newly won supremacy of the seas was soon challenged by the Dutch, who proved to be both able seamen and stubborn fighters. Ambitious Dutch merchants had established a thriving overseas trade, which provided fierce competition for England. During the quarrel between Parliament and the Stuarts, England was too busy to pay much attention to the Dutch. When Cromwell came to power, however, the rivalry between the two countries led to a war which resulted in the defeat of the Dutch. Soon after the Restoration, the English took over New Amsterdam, the chief Dutch colony in North America, and renamed it New York.

In the meantime, France was also becoming a formidable colonial power, and by the early part of the eighteenth century she controlled much of Canada and seaports in India. French expansion

Old New York. This old print shows New York as it appeared in the seventeenth century under Dutch rule. Called New Amsterdam, it was a far cry from the present metropolis.

BRITISH LAND IN NORTH AMERICA

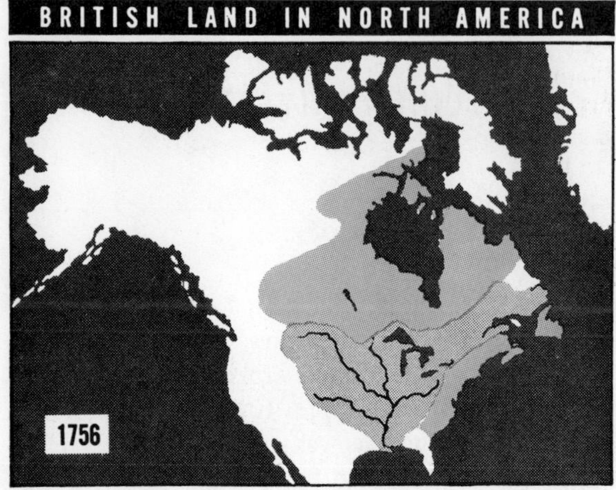

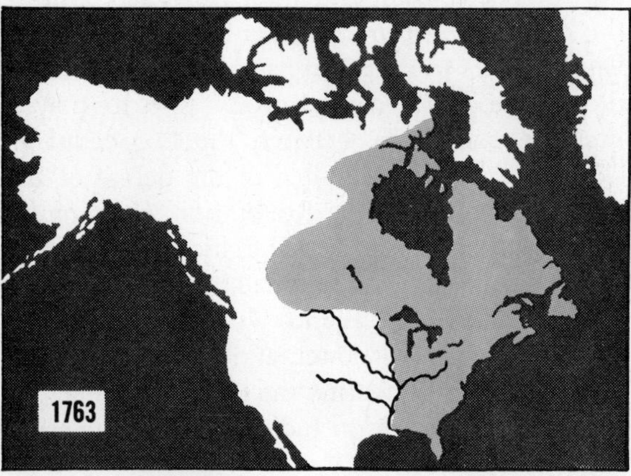

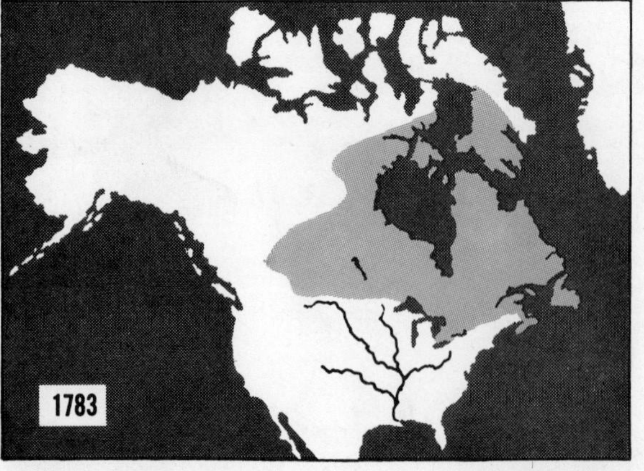

British French

in these areas brought her into conflict with Britain, and from 1689 to 1763 the two nations fought a series of wars which ranged over Europe, Asia, and North America. The phase of this conflict that was fought in North America was called the French and Indian War. As you may recall from your study of American history, this war was decided when the British general, Wolfe, made a successful surprise attack on the French fortress at Quebec. This battle marked the end of French power in North America. At about the same time, on the other side of the world, another British general, Clive, drove the French from India. Britain emerged from these wars with France as "mistress of the seas" and, also, the ruler of an enormous empire.

Belief in mercantilism caused the British to seek colonies. The violent scramble for colonies that characterized the eighteenth century arose from a belief in an economic theory called *mercantilism*. According to this doctrine, the wealth and power of a nation depend on how much gold it possesses. The power of Spain, which was based almost entirely on the gold she acquired from her American colonies, seemed to support the theory of mercantilism. The nations that were not fortunate enough to control gold mines in the New World sought to earn gold by selling products abroad. At the same time, they wanted to avoid spending gold for food and raw materials that they could not themselves produce. They believed that the establishment of colonies offered a solution by providing a source of raw materials and a ready market for the finished goods produced at home.

The mercantile system brought many benefits to the mother country at the expense of her colonies. For example, the British government passed strict laws forbidding American colonists to trade with any country except Britain or to manufacture anything which they could buy from Britain. The system was not completely successful, however, because the British were much too involved in the struggle with France to enforce these laws. American colonists continued to trade with the French West Indies, and smuggling of foreign goods was commonplace.

The American Revolution was a protest against mercantilism. Britain needed money to pay off the debt incurred during the costly war with France. After her victory in 1763, Britain decided to enforce the laws restricting colonial trade and to impose new taxes. The colonists objected violently to these actions and began to *boycott*, or refuse to buy, British goods. The colonists declared that they should not be expected to pay taxes, even though they were British subjects, because they were not represented in Parliament. When the British government attempted to enforce her mercantile policies, the colonists revolted. With the help of the French, who could not resist the opportunity to square accounts with their old enemy, the colonists won their independence.

Adam Smith urged the British to abandon mercantilism in favor of free trade. In the late eighteenth century the famous Scottish economist Adam Smith published his influential book, *Wealth of Nations*, in which he analyzed the weaknesses of mercantilism. He pointed out that if every country refused to buy manufactured goods from its neighbors, there would be no foreign trade at all. Furthermore, Smith argued, nations were better off without colonies since, in the long run, the colonies cost more to acquire and maintain than they were worth.

To replace mercantilism, Smith recommended a policy of *free trade* under which every nation would be able to trade with every other nation without restriction. This idea strongly influenced the adoption of the laissez-faire policy discussed in Chapter 33. As a result of Smith's influence and the unprofitable experience with the American colonies, Britain changed her colonial policy. To prevent another colonial revolution, Canada was granted self-government and mercantilism was abandoned in favor of a policy of free trade.

Britain established a lifeline to the East. Although the British abandoned their policy of mercantilism, they continued to acquire small colonies and naval bases to protect their merchant fleet. Turn to the map on Page 307. Notice that one of the great trade routes of the world begins

GIBRALTAR AND THE SUEZ CANAL. Gibraltar, *left*, an important British naval base, is the famous "rock" at the southernmost tip of Spain which guards the entrance to the Mediterranean. The Suez Canal, *right*, controlled by the Egyptian government since 1956, connects the Mediterranean and the Red Sea, is one of the busiest in the world. Through the canal, which is 100 miles long, passes half of the annual commerce between Europe and the Far East.

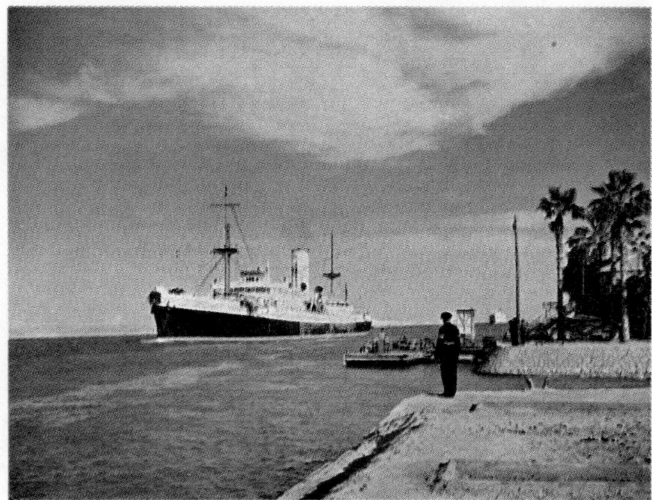

NELSON. The son of a clergyman, Nelson rose through the ranks to become an admiral. He lost his right arm and the sight of one eye in the service of his country. His brilliance in the strategy of naval warfare thwarted Napoleon's plans to invade England and complete the conquest of Europe.

in the British ports of Glasgow, Liverpool, and London, and then passes down the coast of France and Spain to the Strait of Gibraltar. Here the British have established a powerful fortress to guard the approach to the Mediterranean.

Follow the route past the naval bases on Malta and Cyprus to the Suez Canal, which controls the entrance to the Red Sea. From the Red Sea the great trade route moves into the Indian Ocean, where it winds its way to Ceylon and Calcutta, India. Then it swings down to Singapore on the Malay Peninsula, and finally northward to the island of Hong Kong off the China coast. For many years this route gave Britain safe, easy access to the profitable eastern trade which was so important to her prosperity. The British could protect their trade by stopping all traffic on the Mediterranean Sea or the Indian Ocean simply by closing Gibraltar or Suez. You can see why the route has been called Britain's lifeline to the east. When you remember how much the Industrial Revolution made Britain dependent on foreign trade, it is easy to understand why she sought to acquire key bases to control that vital route to her markets and sources of raw materials.

Under Nelson's leadership, the British navy defeated Napoleon at Trafalgar. Britain's control of the seas did not go unchallenged. In 1805 the French, under the Emperor Napoleon, combined their fleet with the conquered Spanish fleet and met the British in a great naval battle at Cape Trafalgar on the southwest corner of Spain. Just before the engagement, Admiral Nelson, the famed commander of the British fleet, gave the

TRAFALGAR. Nelson's great victory off the coast of Spain ended in his death. The Nelson Column in Trafalgar Square, London, commemorates him for the battle that saved England.

signal which has since become legendary: "England expects every man to do his duty." After a desperate fight, Britain won her most important naval victory, although Nelson was killed.

Victory at Trafalgar left Britain secure in her position as mistress of the seas. Until World War I no other country was strong enough to challenge her. British ships roamed the waters of the earth undisturbed, maintaining peace and British authority in the farthest corners of the world.

BRITAIN EXPANDED HER EMPIRE AND ADOPTED AN ENLIGHTENED COLONIAL POLICY

Imperialism led to a new wave of colonial expansion. In the years after 1815, the population of Great Britain grew steadily larger as a result of the Industrial Revolution. More and more of her subjects moved to Britain's overseas possessions. Two of her most successful Far Eastern colonies, Singapore and Hong Kong, began as small trading posts but quickly developed into great commercial centers.

Prior to 1870, the expansion of the empire was an outgrowth of Britain's commercial activity rather than the result of a campaign of conquest. Toward the end of the nineteenth century, however, a renewed interest in acquiring colonies swept over Europe. Recently created nations, such as Germany and Italy, wished to build colonial empires. The competition for new colonies, especially in Africa and the Far East, grew keen and created tensions which helped bring on World War I.

This race for colonies was the result of *imperialism,* or a desire on the part of the more advanced or industrialized countries to extend their control over weaker lands. From 1870 to 1914 the major European nations, and even the United States, shared in the general scramble for colonies. During this period England acquired many additional colonies, including Sudan, South Africa, Kenya, Afghanistan, Burma, and Shanghai.

Geography and "balance of power" explain Britain's success. By the end of the nineteenth century the Union Jack was raised over some part of every continent in the world, and it was said that the sun never set on the British empire. What were the reasons behind Britain's extraordinary success?

One answer lies in her geography. Remember that Britain was kept safe from invaders by surrounding seas so that, while nations on the Continent were building armies to defend their homelands, Britain was free to concentrate on naval power. Her navy proved to be the deciding factor in overseas expansion and trade. Then, too, as we noted earlier, the British Isles were in a strategic location on the trade routes between east and west and between Europe and the New World. Furthermore, the prosperity that came to Britain as a result of the Industrial Revolution provided her with the capital to finance the development of the Empire.

Britain's location and industrial prosperity, however, only partially account for her success. If any European nation had been able to dominate the continent of Europe, it doubtless could have challenged Britain's supremacy. Recognizing this fact, Britain deliberately adopted a policy aimed at preventing any European nation from becoming too strong. In other words, Britain tried to maintain a "balance of power" among the nations of Europe. During the eighteenth and early nineteenth centuries, when France was the greatest European power, Britain frequently aided the Germans and Austrians to check French power. Later, when Germany threatened to overrun Europe, Britain allied herself with France as a check on German power. Thus, by preventing any nation from gaining control of Europe, the British made their homeland secure and retained mastery of the seas. So successful were Britain's efforts that by 1914 she controlled a fourth of the earth's surface. The eve of World War I found the British Empire at its greatest extent.

THE CHANGING OF THE GUARD. The colorful Queen's Horse Guards are a part of the strong sense of history and tradition that governs much of British life.

The British Empire became the Commonwealth of Nations. After the loss of her American colonies, Britain adopted a more enlightened colonial policy by which she encouraged her various territories to develop self-government within the Empire. The change began in Canada where, as in the thirteen American colonies, there were many British subjects accustomed to the traditions of English parliamentary government and Common Law. In 1837 the Canadians protested against Britain's strict control of their affairs. The British very wisely headed off a full-scale revolt by sending Lord Durham, a liberal member of Parliament, to Canada to study the possibility of granting self-government. He recommended that Canada be given dominion status and that she be allowed to have her own parliament. As the "Canadian Plan" was applied to other territories, such as Australia, New Zealand, and the Union of South Africa, the British Empire became known as the Commonwealth of Nations. In 1931, under the Statute of Westminster, the dominions of the British Commonwealth were given complete control of their own affairs and were proclaimed equal in status to Great Britain herself.

After World War II, dominion status was extended to India, Pakistan, Burma, Ceylon, Ghana, and the Federation of Malaya. India and Pakistan, however, have since been granted the status of independent republics within the Commonwealth, and Burma has left the British Commonwealth entirely.

The Commonwealth of Nations today includes two kinds of territories, *independent self-governing states* (the term *dominion* is no longer used) and *dependencies.* The dependencies include *crown colonies,* such as Hong Kong and Aden; *protectorates,* such as the Bahrein Islands, the Solomons, and Bechuanaland; and *trust territories,* such as New Guinea, which are administered under United Nations supervision by either Britain or an independent Commonwealth nation.

Although the members of the Commonwealth are linked to one another by special commercial and military arrangements, their strongest bonds are pride in their common history, belief in demo-

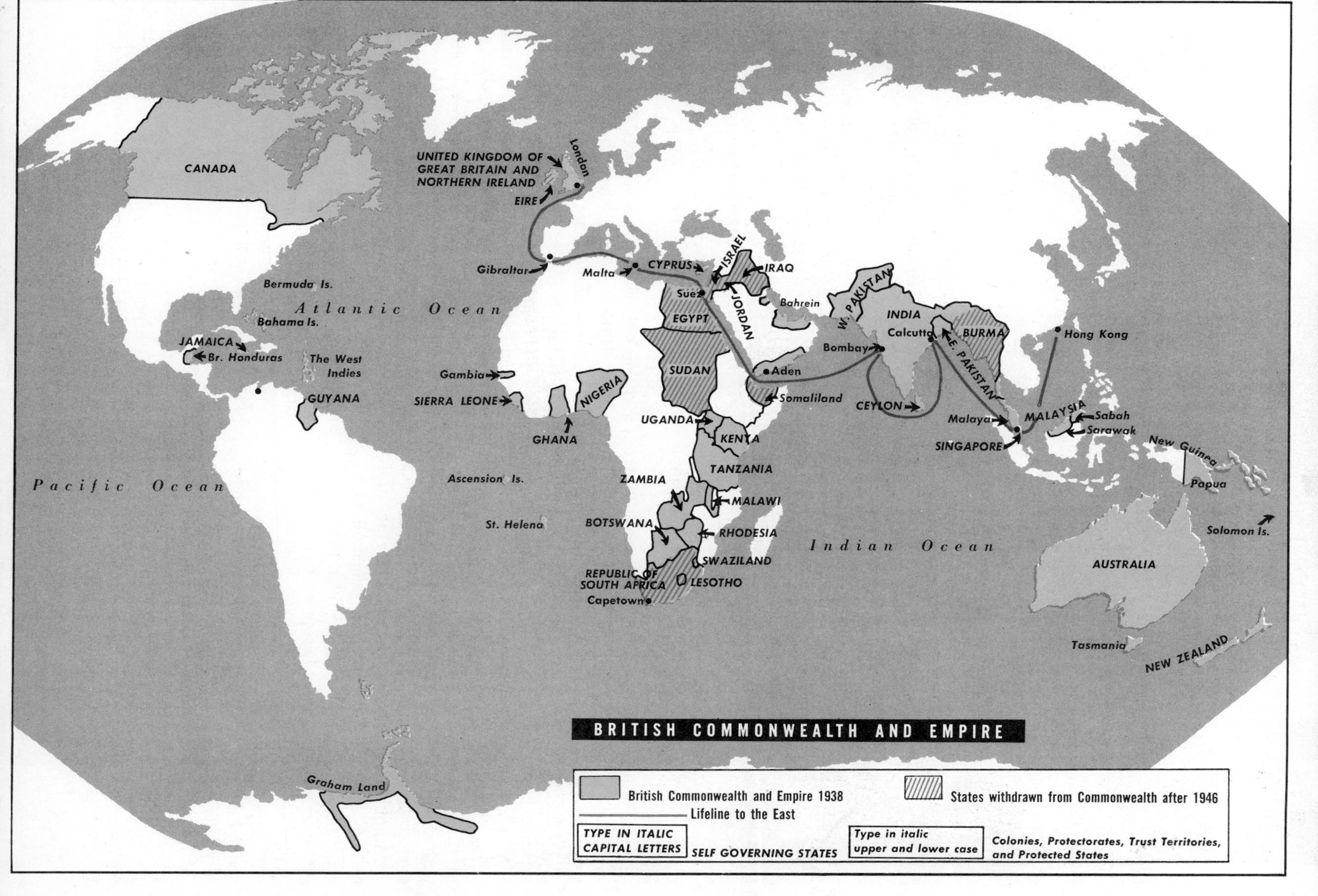
CANADA
UNITED KINGDOM OF GREAT BRITAIN AND NORTHERN IRELAND
London
EIRE
Gibraltar
Malta
CYPRUS
ISRAEL
IRAQ
Suez
JORDAN
Bahrein
EGYPT
SUDAN
Aden
Somaliland
W. PAKISTAN
INDIA
Calcutta
BURMA
E. PAKISTAN
Bombay
CEYLON
Hong Kong
Malaya
MALAYSIA
Sabah
Sarawak
SINGAPORE
New Guinea
Papua
Solomon Is.
AUSTRALIA
Tasmania
NEW ZEALAND
Bermuda Is.
Atlantic Ocean
Bahama Is.
JAMAICA
Br. Honduras
The West Indies
GUYANA
Gambia
SIERRA LEONE
NIGERIA
GHANA
UGANDA
KENYA
TANZANIA
ZAMBIA
MALAWI
BOTSWANA
RHODESIA
SWAZILAND
REPUBLIC OF SOUTH AFRICA
LESOTHO
Capetown
Ascension Is.
St. Helena
Pacific Ocean
Indian Ocean
Graham Land
BRITISH COMMONWEALTH AND EMPIRE
British Commonwealth and Empire 1938
States withdrawn from Commonwealth after 1946
Lifeline to the East
TYPE IN ITALIC CAPITAL LETTERS
SELF GOVERNING STATES
Type in italic upper and lower case
Colonies, Protectorates, Trust Territories, and Protected States

Commonwealth Prime Ministers. The prime ministers of the British Commonwealth of Nations are shown at the start of a two-week conference in London in June, 1965. A common belief in democratic government is the strongest bond between the Commonwealth nations.

cratic government, and recognition of the British monarch as head of the Commonwealth.

What is Britain's future as a world power? Britain's position of dominance in the nineteenth century depended on her control of the Empire. As historians have long observed, empires seem to experience life cycles resembling those of men. Just as a boy becomes a mature man and then grows old, so an empire passes through a period of struggle and growth, achieves strength and prosperity, and then declines. In many ways this analogy can be applied to the British Empire.

Although Britain's power began to fade after World War I, the decline has been most rapid since the 1940's. Wisely, the British granted independence to such former possessions as Ireland, Burma, and India in order to avoid violence and revolution. By doing so, however, she lost Ireland and Burma completely when they chose to withdraw from the Commonwealth. The areas vital to British security are becoming more and more difficult to control. For example, when Egypt gained her independence, she forced British troops to withdraw from the Suez Canal.

Britain no longer controls the seas or supplies the world with manufactured goods. Instead of power, she has to depend on the loyalty and support of the Commonwealth nations.

The British realized that they must gradually and peacefully grant independence to their possessions in Africa and elsewhere. Britain tried to help these developing nations establish democratic forms of government modeled on her own in preparation for the independence they demanded. Most of them have decided to remain in the Commonwealth, as independent equal partners trading freely with Britain. Although Britain will probably never regain the power she had in the nineteenth century, as long as she is spokesman for the Commonwealth she will continue to play an important role in world affairs.

It is not possible to describe here all the lands of the Commonwealth. In Part 20 you will read about the British in Africa and in Part 19 you will see how Disraeli made Victoria Empress of India. Here we will deal briefly with only four countries that have been closely connected with the development of the Commonwealth: Ireland, Canada, Australia, and New Zealand.

IRELAND WAS THE FIRST BRITISH CONQUEST AND THE MOST TROUBLESOME

Britain tried for centuries to crush patriotism in Ireland. Ireland is an island about the size of the state of Maine lying just west of Great Britain, and with a smaller population than metropolitan Philadelphia. Though recently becoming industrialized, it was long an agricultural country with most of its dairy and meat exports going to neighboring Britain. But it is a nation with its own culture, proud history, and fierce spirit of independence.

Relations between Britain and Ireland have been a tragic problem for centuries. The Irish wanted to be left alone, but the British refused to comply. Because the British were more powerful and because they feared Ireland might be used by some European enemy as a base from which to attack them, they seized control of Ireland in the first step of British imperialism. The Irish bitterly resented and gallantly resisted this takeover of their homeland. For eight hundred years, since Henry II brought Ireland under the English crown, they struggled for freedom.

Because the Irish proved so rebellious, the British treated them with harshness and contempt. English kings took away the land of the Irish farmers and gave it to English nobles who became absentee landlords. The Irish had to pay rent to these English landlords to farm land that had been their own, and they were also heavily taxed. When the people of Ireland revolted, British soldiers hunted down and killed Irish patriots and even massacred women and children in the process.

Religious differences added to the bitterness. Ireland remained Roman Catholic when England and Scotland separated from Rome during the reign of Henry VIII. But England forced the Irish Catholics to pay financial support to the Protestant Church which England established there. Many Presbyterians from Scotland settled in a part of northern Ireland called Ulster, where they established linen and other industries. The Catholics of Ulster became a displaced and discriminated against minority, which only confirmed the bitter feelings of the Irish-Catholic south toward the Scottish-Presbyterian north and its British patron.

During the 1840's a new and terrible disaster struck Ireland. Plant diseases ruined the potato crop which the Irish peasants depended on for most of their food. Famine struck the land. English landlords evicted farmers who could not pay their rent and they either starved or, if possible, came to America. About a million died of starvation and a million-and-a-half emigrated to America in a mass depopulation of Ireland within a few years. The old bitterness toward Britain was carried across the sea by these Irish-Americans and still plays a part in American politics.

Southern Ireland becomes independent. Toward the end of the nineteenth century, British Prime Minister Gladstone realized what a mistake it was to treat Ireland so harshly. Gradually laws were passed which permitted some Irish farmers to own their land. Other laws were designed to prevent discrimination against Catholics. The Irish, however, neither forgave nor forgot. They demanded that the British get out of Ireland.

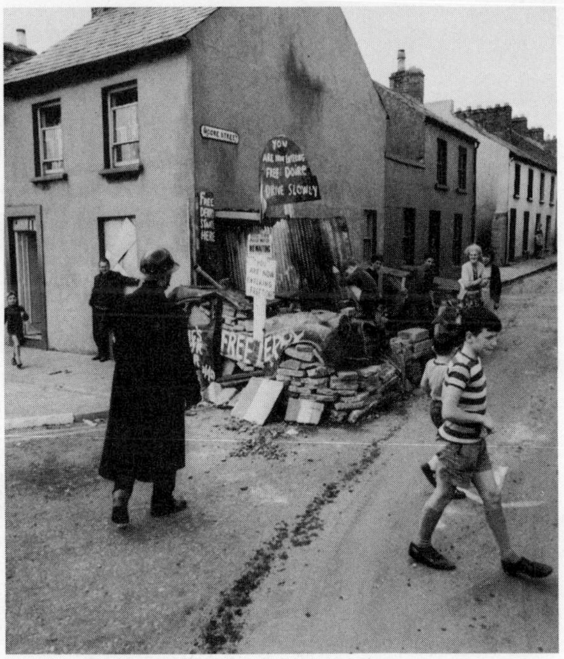

NORTHERN IRELAND. This picture in Londonderry shows a barricade that is all too typical of the conditions in plagued Northern Ireland. The Gaelic Doire on the sign means Derry.

Some Irish patriots saw Britain's World War I emergencies as an Irish opportunity. In 1916 the Irish staged a terrible uprising called the Easter Rebellion. Britain crushed the revolt and, in 1921, granted dominion status in the Commonwealth to southern Ireland, known as Eire.

This did not settle the "Irish Question." While the south had gained free dominion status the Protestants of Ulster did not want independence. They feared being outvoted by the Catholic majority and threatened civil war to remain part of Great Britain. The British solution was to partition Ireland, with the smaller northern part as a self-governing part of Britain.

The Irish Struggle goes on. While the British have accepted the loss of most of Ireland, the Irish have not been content with the British solution. In 1949 it withdrew from the Commonwealth as an independent republic. Since 1969, Catholics in Ulster, protesting against discrimination and the continued division of the island, have brought guerrilla warfare to Northern Ireland. In 1972 Northern Ireland was still in ferment. Where does Ireland go from here?

CANADA CARRIED ON BRITISH TRADITIONS IN NORTH AMERICA

Canada stretches from sea to sea. Canada, the oldest dominion in the British Commonwealth, includes all the northern half of North America except Alaska. Canada is considerably larger than the United States, but her population of about twenty-two million people is only slightly more than that of California. The eastern provinces and the Pacific coast are the most populous regions. An arctic climate in the north keeps population very sparse there.

Canada, like the United States, is a huge basin with mountain ranges on the east and west. The coasts are cut by fine harbors, many of which are open all year. Although Hudson Bay has been important for trade since the time of the earliest settlements, it is frozen eight months each year. The Great Lakes and the St. Lawrence River form part of the Canadian boundary on the south. The St. Lawrence Seaway, developed jointly by Canada and the United States, allows ships to sail from the Atlantic to ports on the Great Lakes.

Canada is rich in natural resources. Canadian mines yield gold, copper, lead, iron, and asbestos. Important deposits of uranium and oil are also being developed in the west. The wheat fields of Canada's western provinces are among the most productive in the world. Most of the newspapers you read are made from the wood pulp of Canadian forests. The country also has industries, such as steel and automobiles,

mostly financed by American companies. American tourists in great numbers visit Canada each year to enjoy the beauties of the seacoast, mountains, and wilderness, still far less polluted than in America.

New France becomes a British colony. Most Canadians speak English and have manners and customs which resemble those of Americans. British traditions are strong in the provinces of Ontario and British Columbia. But in the province of Quebec, the people speak French and their culture and customs all derive from France.

For two centuries, Canada belonged to France. The French claim to the area was based on the explorations of Jacques Cartier (kar-*tyay*) and Samuel de Champlain (sham-*playn*) in the sixteenth century. Later Jesuit priests established missions in New France (Canada) which became centers of French culture. French colonists were lured by the rich fur trade with the Indians. Unlike the English in the thirteen American colonies, they were not seeking farm lands, or self-government, or religious freedom. Also, the French government strictly controlled New France and, unlike the English king, did not allow men with political grievances to go to the New World. For all these reasons, New France had a smaller population than the English colonies from the start.

As you remember, Britain won Canada from France in 1763. Under the terms of the peace treaty, Britain promised the French Canadians that they could keep their language, customs, and religion. Because the promise was kept, French Canadians became loyal to Britain while preserving their own culture. During the American Revolution, however, large numbers of British colonists fled from the thirteen colonies to Canada because they wished to remain loyal to the British king. When they settled in Canada their British traditions clashed with those of the French and there were frequent disputes.

The Canadian provinces won self-government. The quarrels and suspicions between French and British Canadians were climaxed in the Rebellion of 1837. The uprising, led by a printer named William Lyon MacKenzie, was not nearly as large as the American Revolution, but the British had learned from that one and were alarmed. After studying the problem, they agreed to let the provinces manage their own affairs. In 1867 the four original provinces of Nova Scotia, New Brunswick, Quebec, and Ontario united under a central government and established a national capital at Ottawa. Gradually, as the population increased and railways linked east and west, new provinces were added. Canada now has ten provinces in addition to the Northwest Territories and the Yukon.

Canada charts her own course. After two centuries of political domination by the French and one by the British, Canada has been economically dominated by the United States. The richer and more powerful southern neighbor has had much control over Canadian resources and markets and a balance of trade that has worked against Canada. Also, Canada's relatively small population has held back development. Friction still exists between French-speaking and English-speaking Canadians. However, in recent years Canada under Premier Trudeau has sought her own more independent course both politically and economically. Canada was one of the first Western Hemisphere nations to have diplomatic relations with Communist China and she has found new trade partners around the world. The French-English tension has been muted by a law making both languages official. Recognizing the ecological threat posed by these industrial resources in her wilderness, Canada's conservation laws are in the forefront of the world movement. She is charting her own independent course freeing herself of outside domination, but on a firm foundation in the Commonwealth and with confidence that her frontier with the United States will remain the longest undisputed border in the world.

AUSTRALIA AND NEW ZEALAND BECAME MEMBERS OF THE BRITISH COMMONWEALTH OF NATIONS

Australia is the only continent that is also a dominion. When England acquired Australia, following the explorations of Captain James Cook along the southeast coast in 1770, it was the only time in history that one nation had peacefully gained control of an entire continent. At first it was used as a kind of huge open-air prison, as British convicts sentenced for minor offenses were shipped there. Gradually other settlers came and made sheep-raising the major occupation. Since gold was discovered in 1851, Australia has developed rapidly. Great cities, such as Melbourne and Sidney, became established along the southeastern coast. But Australia is still the least densely populated continent, with only about thirteen million people.

Australia gained dominion status as a member of the Commonwealth in 1901. Her people in six states and the desolate Northern Territory are united under a federal constitution similar to that of the United States. The Australian government makes a great effort to bring education to the sparsely populated inland areas through traveling teachers, correspondence schools, and lending libraries. Australia is making strides toward integrating descendants of the original population, the brown-skinned aborigines, into its national life. The type of ballot used in British and American elections originated in Australia as a step to further democratic practices.

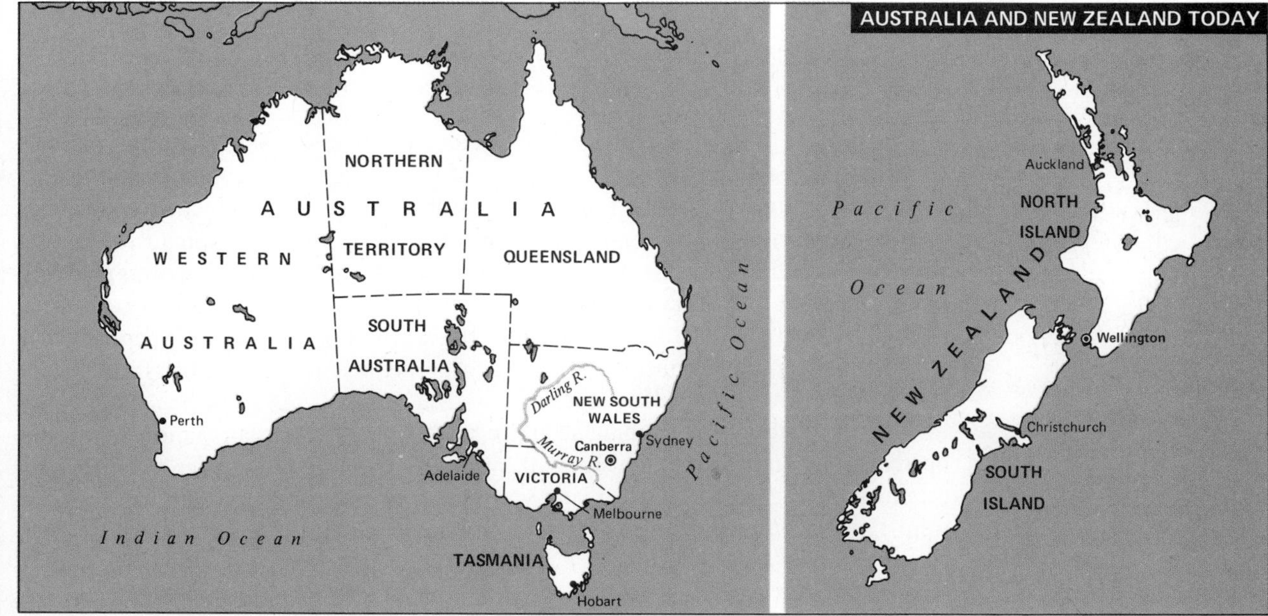

During World War II, Australia found that it had to rely more on America than Britain for protection against the Japanese threat. Since that time, although the development of Australian industry has been hindered by its small population, its mines have become leading suppliers of lead, zinc, and other minerals, based on the investment and trade, not only of Britain, but of America and Japan. Australia has become more conscious of itself and has grown closer to its ally and to its former enemy and further from its "Mother Country."

New Zealand is prosperous and progressive. New Zealand consists of two large islands and a number of smaller ones, with a total area about the size of Colorado, lying twelve hundred miles southeast of Australia. This country of broad fertile valleys and towering mountains was discovered by the Dutch explorer Abel Tasman in the seventeenth century, but became a part of Britain's empire in 1841. It gained dominion status in the Commonwealth in 1907.

New Zealand's three million inhabitants are mostly of Scottish descent with a minority of integrated Maori natives. They are prosperously engaged in meat and dairy product raising and processing. New Zealand is the world's leading exporter of dairy products.

The country is noted for its progressive government which pioneered systems of medical insurance and old age pensions, and was the first nation to give women the vote. New Zealand, like Australia, has become more aware of itself as a Pacific, rather than a Commonwealth, nation in recent years.

Chapter Check-up

1. When England was establishing her empire, who were her three great rivals?
2. How did the policy of free trade differ from that of mercantilism in British history?
3. What is Britain's "life line to the East?" How has it been weakened?
4. What was the importance of the British naval victory at Trafalgar?
5. What caused a race for colonies after 1870?
6. How did geography and the balance of power help England to build and maintain her powerful empire?
7. How do nations benefit by membership in the British Commonwealth?
8. Why is the story of Ireland a dark page in British history?
9. What are the important problems of modern Canada?
10. How have Australia and New Zealand shown themselves to be progressive countries?

Great Britain: SYNOPSIS

The story of Britain resembles that of Rome in many ways. Both nations rose from modest beginnings on the outskirts of civilization to become the centers of power and influence in their respective worlds. Roman legions penetrated forests and deserts; British battleships ranged the seas. The works of Roman poets were read in the farthest corners of the Roman Empire; the great English writers similarly helped to shape the ideas and traditions of countries thousands of miles from Britain. Latin was understood throughout the ancient world; today people whose native tongue is not English use that language for business and politics more than they use any other foreign language.

Both the British and Romans exhibited skill in political affairs, and each developed a strong and efficient government. Britain, of course, was by far the more successful in giving all classes of men a voice in their government. Thus when kings were rigidly controlling the Continent, England was ruled by the decisions of a representative Parliament.

Like the Romans, the British conquerors and colonists carried their traditions and institutions with them wherever they went. Thus we find the governments of such widely separated areas as the United States, Canada, South Africa, India, and Australia all modeled on the British system. Courts of justice in these countries are also based largely on the principles of English Common Law.

Today Britain's power is declining, but her Empire is not dissolving as the Roman Empire did when soldiers could no longer hold subject peoples in check. The British long ago wisely abandoned a colonial policy of rule by force and substituted one in which subject colonies could become free and self-governing members of a Commonwealth. Today, many former colonies are independent nations, but they remain within the Commonwealth in a spirit of friendly cooperation, united by their common British heritage and by their traditional loyalty to the British monarch.

Through the many centuries of her development, Great Britain has often demonstrated a spirit of progress that has served as a model for the other countries of the world. The wide scope of her influence testifies to the continuing strength of the country's institutions.

Important People

How has each of the following influenced the story of Great Britain?

St. Patrick	Elizabeth I	William Gladstone	John Milton
Alfred the Great	Oliver Cromwell	Queen Victoria	William Wordsworth
Canute	William and Mary	Admiral Nelson	Charles Dickens
William the Conqueror	George I	Lord Durham	T. S. Eliot
Henry II	James Watt	Eamon de Valera	Joseph Turner
King John	Edward Cartwright	William MacKenzie	Adam Smith
Simon de Montfort	George Stephenson	Geoffrey Chaucer	Michael Faraday
Henry VIII	Benjamin Disraeli	William Shakespeare	Charles Darwin

Terms

Be sure that you understand clearly the meaning of each of the following:

balance of power	Industrial Revolution	laissez-faire
British Commonwealth	Magna Carta	Conservatives
English Common Law	mercantilism	Laborites
free trade	Parliament	Cabinet
grand jury	Tories and Whigs	Bill of Rights
Celts	divine right of kings	House of Commons
shire	power of the purse	House of Lords

Questions for Discussion and Review

1. Why does an understanding of British history help us to understand our own country?
2. How did each of these geographic conditions help Britain to become a powerful nation? (a) island location, (b) climate, (c) natural resources, (d) rivers and harbors.
3. What were the groups, in order, which invaded and settled England?
4. What similarities are there between the British Magna Carta, Petition of Right, and Bill of Rights and our own Bill of Rights?
5. What are the basic conditions necessary for democratic government?
6. It took more than inventions to bring about the Industrial Revolution. Explain this statement.
7. How and why did the British Empire become the Commonwealth of Nations?
8. Why is Britain often referred to as a welfare state?
9. What are the highlights in the history of each of these countries? (a) Ireland, (b) Canada, (c) Australia, (d) New Zealand.
10. In your opinion, who was England's greatest scientist? Most talented artist? Most influential writer? Explain why.

Interesting Things to Do

1. Complete one or both of the following map projects: (a) Make a product map of Britain, showing with labels, samples, or pictures the various industrial and agricultural products of the different areas; (b) on an outline map of the world show with labels and colors the locations of the member nations of the British Commonwealth.
2. Make an illustrated time line of the story of the British people. This might be done with a series of cartoons to show important people and events.
3. Prepare a summary chart of the contributions of the British to the fields of literature, art and science. Use the following column headings: *Field, Name, Period or Date, Contribution.*
4. Make an imports-exports balance sheet showing on one half of the page the things which Britain imports or buys, and on the other half the things she exports or sells.
5. Prepare an illustrated booklet or poster showing by means of sketches or pictures the various machines and inventions which made the Industrial Revolution possible in England.
6. Organize a panel to present to the class a report on the British Commonwealth. Let

each panel member report on the geography, history, government, and economy of one of the Commonwealth nations.

7. Imagine that you are the newly arrived American ambassador to Britain and that you will soon make your first speech at a dinner given in your honor. Prepare a talk which will show your understanding of the British people, of the ideas and customs which we have in common with them, and of the many contributions which the British have made to the American way of life.

8. Write a newspaper story account of one of the following: (a) Battle of Hastings, (b) Defeat of the Spanish Armada, (c) Naval victory at Trafalgar.

9. Make a list of famous quotations from the works of William Shakespeare. Interpret or explain the meaning of each selection in your own words.

10. Add to or begin your "Who's Who in World History" series by writing brief biographies of one or more of the important leaders of British history.

Interesting Reading about Great Britain

Adams, James T., *Empire on the Seven Seas*, Scribner.

Anderson, Maxwell, *Elizabeth the Queen*, Harcourt, Brace & World.

Antony, I. W., *Raleigh and His World*, Scribner.

Bolton, Ivy M., *Son of the Land*, Messner. England of Richard II.

Burton, Elizabeth, *The Pageant of Stuart England*, Scribner.

Cheyney, Edward Potts, *Short History of England*, Ginn.

Churchill, Sir Winston, *History of the English-speaking Peoples*, Dodd, Mead.

Costain, Thomas, *The Conquerors*, Doubleday. Novel about the Norman Conquest.

———, *Magnificent Century*, Doubleday. England in the time of Henry III.

Davis, William S., *Life in Elizabethan Days*, Harper & Row.

Daugherty, James H., *Magna Carta*, Random House.

Derry, Thomas, K., *Great Britian: Its History from Earliest Times to the Present Day*, Oxford.

Furneaux, Rupert, *Invasion 1066*, Prentice-Hall.

Hartman, Gertrude, *Machines and the Men Who Made the World of Industry*, Macmillan.

Irwin, M., *Young Bess*, Harcourt, Brace & World. Elizabeth I as a young princess.

Kingsley, Charles, *Westward Ho!* Dodd, Mead. Adventures of Elizabethan sea dogs.

*Lamprey, Louise, *Building an Empire*, Stokes.

Moore, Marian, *The United Kingdom*, Nelson. Emphasis on its changing life and looks.

Quennell, Marjorie and Charles H. B., *Everyday Life in Roman Britain*, Putnam.

Shippen, Katherine B., *The Bright Design*, Viking. Story of Electricity.

*Snedeker, Caroline D., *White Isle*, Doubleday. Roman life in Britain.

Street, Alicia, *The Land of the English People*, Lippincott.

Trease, Geoffrey, *This is Your Century*, Harcourt, Brace & World. A British historian's view of the era, 1901–1964.

Trotter, R. G., *The British Commonwealth-Empire*, Holt, Rinehart and Winston.

Whitelock, Dorothy, *The Beginnings of English Society*, Penguin.

* Indicates easy reading

This French vintner represents a part of a culture that has helped civilize the western world.

Part 10
FRANCE

SEARCH FOR LIBERTY, EQUALITY, FRATERNITY

FRANCE

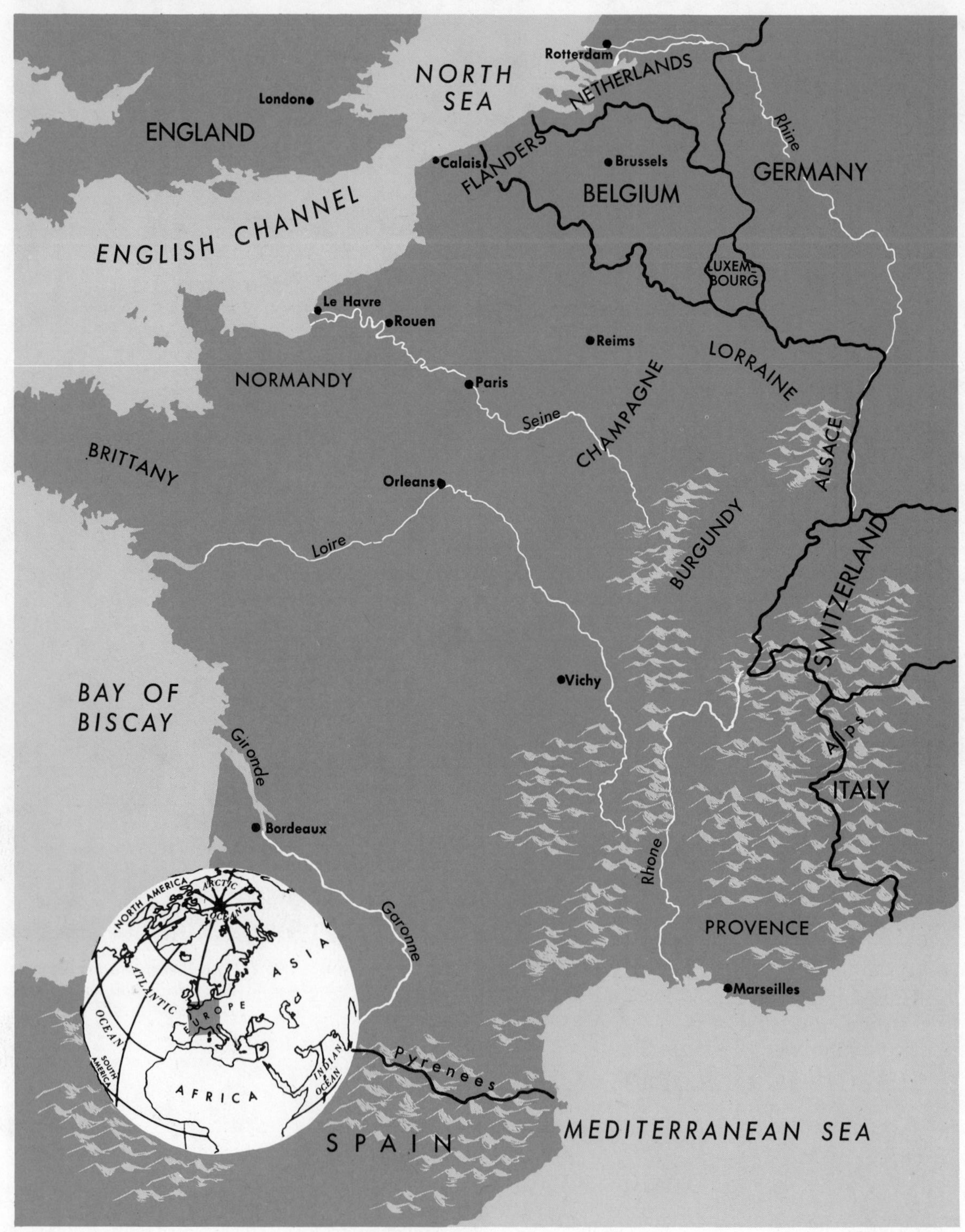

Rotterdam
NORTH SEA
NETHERLANDS
London
ENGLAND
Rhine
Calais
FLANDERS
Brussels
GERMANY
BELGIUM
ENGLISH CHANNEL
LUXEMBOURG
Le Havre
Rouen
Reims
LORRAINE
NORMANDY
Paris
CHAMPAGNE
Seine
ALSACE
BRITTANY
Orleans
BURGUNDY
Loire
SWITZERLAND
Vichy
BAY OF BISCAY
Gironde
Alps
ITALY
Bordeaux
Rhone
NORTH AMERICA
ARCTIC OCEAN
Garonne
ASIA
PROVENCE
ATLANTIC OCEAN
EUROPE
Marseilles
SOUTH AMERICA
INDIAN OCEAN
AFRICA
Pyrenees
SPAIN
MEDITERRANEAN SEA

France: GEOGRAPHIC SETTING

France is a richly varied country of deep rivers, good seaports, abundant natural resources, and mild climate. Cargo vessels sail far inland along a seven-thousand-mile network of rivers and canals, mines tap rich veins of coal and iron, and agriculture flourishes in the fertile soil of the countryside. Although France is smaller than Texas, her position at the western edge of Europe has made her important in the history of the Continent, both as a crossroads for trade and as a prize for invaders.

Notice on the map that France is roughly six-sided. On five sides, boundaries are formed by seas and mountains: the English Channel on the north, the Bay of Biscay on the west, the Pyrenees (*pihr*-uh-neez) Mountains on the southwest, the Mediterranean Sea on the south, and the Alps on the east. The weakest link in the natural chain around France is a broad plain at her northeast boundary where, as you will learn, invaders have again and again threatened the country. Locate on the map the four great rivers of France, the Seine, the Loire (lwahr), the Garonne, and the Rhone. The most important French ports, Le Havre (leh *ha*-vr'), Bordeaux (bawr-*doe*), and Marseilles (mahr-*say*), are found at or near the mouths of the rivers.

While a number of industrial towns have grown up near the mines in the northeast, agriculture remains the backbone of the French economy. In the rich soil of the great plain that stretches from the Bay of Biscay to Germany, farmers raise wheat, potatoes, apples, and sugar beets. Grapes for wine are grown in the vineyards of Burgundy, Bordeaux, and Champagne. Famous cheeses are made from the milk of cows, goats and sheep. Northern France has a mild, damp marine climate, but winds from Africa give the south the hot, dry summers and mild winters of a Mediterranean climate.

France: PERSPECTIVE

The great stone fortress towered grimly above the narrow streets and densely clustered houses of Paris. From openings high in its thick walls, men who had been imprisoned by the king stared out hopelessly at the sky. Jailed secretly and without trial, they were the victims of a monarchy whose power knew few limits. In 1789 the Bastille, as the prison was called, was almost empty. But long ago it had become a symbol of the tyranny of the French kings and their ruthless agents.

France's new middle class had been growing rapidly in the seventeenth and eighteenth centuries. Merchants, traders, and shopkeepers were gaining wealth and demanding recognition of their improved status. But the king and his nobles stubbornly continued to resist the efforts of this commercial class to gain an effective voice in the government. Middle-class discontent at high taxes and governmental inefficiency was fanned by the scathing criticism of keen and outspoken philosophers and men of letters.

When the Estates General convened in 1789, the king tried to preserve the power of the upper classes. Angry mobs formed in Paris to express its outrage at this injustice of royal authority. The hated Bastille was a natural target. On July 14, 1789, the people stormed the fortress, freed the prisoners, and finally destroyed it with cannon shots. Soon rioting spread from Paris into the surrounding country-

side. The French Revolution had begun. Within a few days, nobles all over France, fearful of danger to themselves, surrendered their age-old privileges.

The effects of the French Revolution were felt far beyond the borders of France. The great uprising signaled the beginning of widespread changes throughout the world. Feudalism was doomed and the power of kings was checked as individuals gained new rights. In Part 10 we shall see how these dramatic changes came about in France, and why the search for "Liberty, Equality, Fraternity" remains important for us today.

CHAPTER 36

France Became United Under Powerful Kings

ROMAN, FRANK, AND NORMAN INVADERS SHAPED THE STORY OF FRANCE

Romans left their mark on Gaul. For many hundreds of years before the birth of Christ the region that is now France was occupied by peoples whom we call the Celts. These same tribes had also invaded the British Isles and settled there. About a half-century before the birth of Christ the Romans overran the territories of the Celtic tribes. They founded colonies, and imposed Roman rule. For over four hundred years—until the Empire in the west began to crumble in the fifth century—the Romans controlled this region which they called Gaul.

The Roman occupation of Gaul made a permanent impression upon the inhabitants and upon their country. The Romans founded many cities and built many roads, bridges, and aqueducts. The Romans constructed so well that many of their buildings and public works still stand. Ancient Roman laws have greatly influenced the legal codes of modern France. But perhaps the greatest Roman influence on the Gauls was in the development of language. During the centuries of Roman rule the Celtic tongue spoken by the natives during Caesar's conquest gave way to the Latin language. Except for the remote western section of France that is today called Brittany, the Celtic language almost disappeared. When German tribes invaded Gaul in the fifth century A.D. Germanic words were mixed with Latin and remnants of the old Celtic languages. Out of this mixture of tongues developed modern French. In spite of the German and Celtic influence, however, the French language is chiefly based on Latin. It is therefore known as a Romance language. Even the beginning student of French who knows some Latin will recognize many similar words in the two languages. Here are some examples: father: *pater, pere;* mother: *mater, mere;* sister: *soror, soeur;* brother: *frater, frere;* man: *homo, homme.*

When Rome weakened, barbarian tribes came into Gaul. From the stories of the Romans and the English, you will remember that in the third century the Roman Empire began to weaken. Gradually the German barbarians from the north and east began coming into southern and western Europe to find new lands and homes.

Three different barbarian peoples settled in Gaul. One group known as Visigoths made their homes in the south near the Pyrenees; the Burgundians settled in the beautiful valley of the Rhone River; and the most able of all the invaders, the Franks, began to spread westward from the Rhine Valley. The Gauls, whom the Romans had helped to civilize, gradually mixed with the

Aqueduct at Nîmes. This aqueduct was built in 19 B.C. to supply water to the city of Nîmes. The massive structure, which is about six hundred feet long, shows the skill of Roman engineers and builders.

conquering German tribes and occupied the central part of the country. The French of modern times are descendants of four peoples: the Romanized Gauls and the Germanic Visigoths, Burgundians, and Franks.

A Frankish king converted his people to Christianity. It was not long before the Franks had won control of most of Gaul. By keeping in constant touch with their people in the Rhine Valley, the Franks, unlike the other invading barbarians, were continually reinforced. They avoided being cut off and absorbed by the Gallic tribes. Thus they were able to conquer the other peoples in Gaul. Gaul came to be known as France, or the land of the Franks.

An outstanding king of the Franks was Clovis. This name, which later was changed in form to Louis, is one that many kings of France have had. Clovis made his headquarters in Paris. From there he directed the conquests which made him master of almost all of what is now modern France. Clotilda, his wife, was a Christian. She was anxious to convert Clovis to her religion. According to tradition, the king clung to his Germanic gods for a long time. He did permit the queen to baptize their first-born son. When the child died within a week, Clovis was convinced his gods were better than the Christian God.

Some time later, Clovis was in a desperate battle and things were going against him. Despairing of help from his own gods, he cried out that if the queen's God would bring him victory he would be baptized. The tide of battle turned. Clovis won and kept his promise. Not only did he become a Christian, but he began to convert all his followers. Before long the Franks had become a Christian tribe.

The Frankish kings lost much of their power. When Clovis died early in the sixth century, his kingdom was divided among his sons. The first successors of Clovis continued to conquer new lands until the territory of the Franks extended far into what is now central Germany. But the later descendants of Clovis quarreled and fought with one another. Sometimes the kingdom of the Franks was united under one ruler, and sometimes it was divided among several heirs to the throne.

As a result of this situation, the Frankish king lost much of his power to strong nobles. The chief officers of the government were the *counts*, who represented the king in the various local territories into which the kingdom was divided. The territories became known as counties because the local rulers were counts. The counts began to ignore the authority of the Frankish king. At the same time the palace officials began to take the real power out of the king's hands, leaving him little more than an empty title. As the king's power was weakened, a number of the counties broke away from Frankish rule and became independent.

Pepin, backed by the Pope, became king. Finally, in the middle of the eighth century, the king's minister, Pepin (*pep*-in), grew so powerful that he was able to sweep away the old line of kings begun by Clovis. But first he came to an understanding with the Pope. The Pope agreed that Pepin should become king of France. The agreement is more important than it seems at first. The new king became, in theory at least, a representative of the Pope and the Church. As time passed, many people came to feel that obedience to the king was a kind of religious duty. Here we see the beginning of the "divine right" idea that you read about in the story of the quarrel between the English kings and Parliament. Pepin, as the new king of the Franks, strengthened his kingdom and passed it on to his famous son, Charlemagne.

Charlemagne brought order to France. You will remember from the story of feudalism how well Charlemagne ruled his domains. He established schools, encouraged the arts, and strengthened the Church. To keep the local governments of the counts firmly under his power, he sent officials into the counties. It was their job to hold courts, to hear appeals, and to see that justice was done throughout the kingdom. The officials traveled in pairs from county to county, over an assigned route, or circuit.

The people in France benefited by the peace and order Charlemagne brought to the country. But when Charlemagne died in the early years of the ninth century, his empire began to go to pieces. His successors set a bad example for the jealous dukes and counts of their realms. They began to quarrel with one another for land and power. France broke up into hundreds of small warring states. The strength and unity Charlemagne had brought to France were gone, not to return for nearly six centuries.

The Norsemen invaded France. In the last part of the ninth century, about twenty thousand Norsemen, in seven hundred ships, landed on the northern shores of France and began to take possession of the country. In a few years the Norsemen, or Normans, had become so strong in northern France that the French king, Charles the Fat (884–7), decided it would be better to make the Normans his friends. He therefore made the Norman leader, Rollo, one of his vassals and gave him rich farming lands in northern France as a fief. That land is still called Normandy. To strengthen Rollo's loyalty, Charles gave him a French princess in marriage. In 1066, another Norman leader, Duke William, crossed the Channel from Normandy and invaded England with the aid of the king of France. He became Wil-

Paris Besieged. Paris, only an island in the Seine during her early history, was a prey to many invaders. Here, Norman raiders have set part of the city ablaze but are unable to mount the strongly defended walls.

liam the Conqueror of England, about whom you read in the story of Great Britain.

During the invasions of the Norsemen one of the French nobles showed himself to be a man of great courage and action. He was Hugh Capet (*kay*-pet), Count of Paris, who controlled the land around Paris. When the nobles decided to get rid of the king who was descended from Charlemagne, they chose Capet to be king. The Church leaders approved their choice. The new line of kings that began in the tenth century ruled France for hundreds of years (see chart on page 332).

THE CAPETIAN KINGS STRENGTHENED THE FRENCH MONARCHY

Early French rulers were kings in name only. For a long while the French kings were not nearly so powerful as the English kings. You will recall how William the Conqueror strengthened the feudal system in England. He saw to it that he himself was the foremost feudal lord. In France, however, the king had no such power over the chief feudal lords. The duke of Paris, who was automatically considered king of France, was simply one of many powerful lords. Other feudal lords in various parts of France considered themselves just as important as the king. They had strong armies, many vassals, and vast amounts of land. The king was seldom able to make them obey him, even though they were his vassals. For two centuries the king of France was king in little more than name.

French kings increased their power. Beginning in the thirteenth century, the authority of the king of France became greater than that of the other lords. There were several reasons for the change. For one thing, kings stopped dividing the kingdom among all their sons. Instead, they awarded the crown and the entire kingdom to the eldest. In the line of kings which Hugh Capet began, it happened that there was always a son to take the place of the king when he died. So from the first, the Capetian kings began the custom of having the heir to the throne crowned while the old king was still alive. Thus, when the old king died, there could be no dispute over who should inherit the throne. The people became accustomed to looking up to the count of Paris as the real king of France, though he was absolute ruler only of his own domain.

During the twelfth and thirteenth centuries, the crusades provided an excellent opportunity for the French kings to strengthen their position. When the French nobles left their estates and went to the Holy Land, the king found his own army more effective in the absence of strong opposition. He gradually added the lands of many of his former vassals to the royal domain.

In the later Middle Ages, trade increased in France as it did in many other parts of Europe. Money came into circulation. The cities and towns gained greater freedom. A new middle class made up of tradesmen, bankers, and other businessmen appeared. The middle-class people were not much interested in the petty quarrels

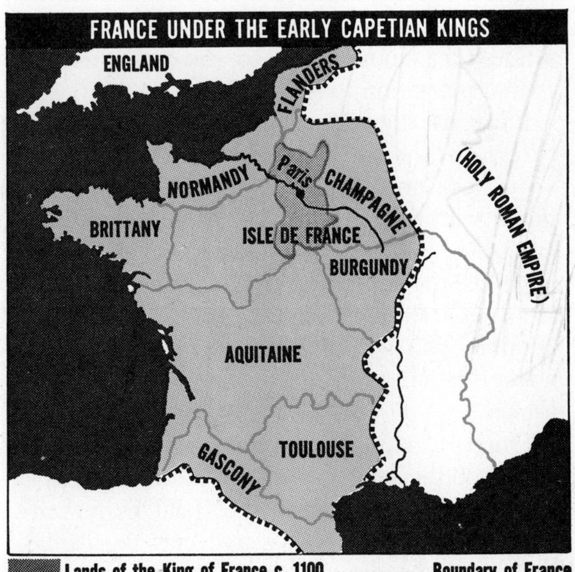

SAINTE-CHAPELLE. Built by St. Louis to shelter relics gathered on the crusades, this small chapel is a gem of thirteenth-century Gothic architecture. Its fifteen stained glass windows, which reach from floor to ceiling, make the interior glow with magnificent color.

among the great feudal lords. They wanted peace and security. They gradually came to believe that a strong national government, headed by the king, would give them the peace and order they needed to carry on their business.

The kings were also supported by the Church leaders. They knew that a strong Christian king would bring more peace to the land and offer greater protection to the Church.

Four of the Capetian kings proved able rulers. Although a few of the Capetian kings were weak and lost ground in the struggle for power with the nobles, many were able men who gradually built a strong French kingdom. To enlarge his kingdom Louis VI (the Fat), 1108–37, arranged a marriage between his eldest son, who became Louis VII, and Eleanor of Aquitaine, the heiress to a vast feudal estate in southwestern France.

Philip II (1180–1223) further strengthened the power of the king. As they became vacant, he left unfilled many offices once held by powerful feudal lords. He then created new royal offices that would be directly responsible to him.

Next Philip turned his attention to the English lands in France. Since the days of William the Conqueror the kings of England were also dukes of Normandy and thus ruled certain lands in France. When Eleanor of Aquitaine, who had been divorced from Louis VII, married the English king Henry II, her lands became part of England's territory in France. So more than half of France came under English control.

Years later, Philip took advantage of disputes among Henry and his sons over the division of Henry's lands among them. (Henry wished to arrange their inheritances during his lifetime.) In the midst of this dissension Philip began to regain the French territory held by the English. After Henry died, and while his successor Richard the Lionhearted was fighting in the Holy Land, Philip recovered most of the English lands in France. Thus, under Philip II France emerged as a major European power.

Louis IX (1226–70) was a pious, unselfish, and just ruler. He made the monarchy popular with the French people. After he was killed while leading a crusade in the Holy Land, he was declared a saint.

Philip the Fair (1285–1314) tried to strengthen the French monarchy by introducing a number of new taxes. But when he tried to tax the clergy he came into conflict with the Pope. To win the support of the people in his quarrel with the Pope, Philip met with the *Estates-General*, a kind of congress made up of representatives from the nobility, the clergy, and the townsmen. The Estates-General supported him, and Philip succeeded in getting the seat of papal authority moved to Avignon in southern France.

As you can see, the power of the French kings rose to new heights during the thirteenth century. In a few years, however, France became involved in a prolonged war with England which brought the French nation to the brink of disaster.

JOAN OF ARC INSPIRED FRANCE TO VICTORY IN THE HUNDRED YEARS' WAR

Bitter rivalry led to a century of warfare between France and England. Many disagreements led to the Hundred Years' War. The French and the English each wanted to have all the fishing rights in the English Channel and the North Sea. The two nations were trade rivals as well. Flanders was at that time the greatest manufacturing center of woolen cloth, and the weaving industry depended on the importation of English wool. When the French interfered with the Flemish wool trade, the laborers and manufacturers of Flanders united with the English against the French.

While disagreements over fisheries and the wool trade were developing between France and England, the French king, Louis X (1289–1316) died leaving only a daughter, Jeanne. His brother Philip proclaimed himself king and won the support of the nobles. In 1317 he got an assembly of notables to declare that women could not succeed to the throne, thus eliminating the claims of his niece. When Philip also died without leaving a son another brother, Charles, became king. At this time Edward III, the king of England whose mother had been a French princess decided to press his slight claim to the French throne. He hoped to win the support of some of the French nobles.

Rivalry between the French and English for territories and for trade then drove the two nations headlong into war. In history the conflict between the French and the English is known as the Hundred Years' War, but it was actually a succession of wars lasting from 1337 to 1453.

A peasant girl saved France from disaster. For a time the Hundred Years' War went very badly for the French. The king of France had recently died and the dauphin (*daw*-fin), or heir to the throne, had not yet been crowned. Furthermore, the English held the city of Reims (reemz), where the French kings had been crowned since the time of Clovis. In fact, the English had conquered all the northern part of the country and even occupied Paris. The unlucky dauphin fled south for safety. He did not have good military leaders, and he had neither the money nor the men to defeat the English. The English made good use of a fine new weapon, the long bow, by which they were able to shoot arrows through the best French armor. The French knights, who had awkward and heavy armor, were no match for the English archers. The day of the knight on horseback as the supreme weapon of war came to an end.

A LONGBOWMAN. The longbow, which made its first appearance at the Battle of Crécy in 1346, enabled the English to defeat the French and changed the methods of warfare.

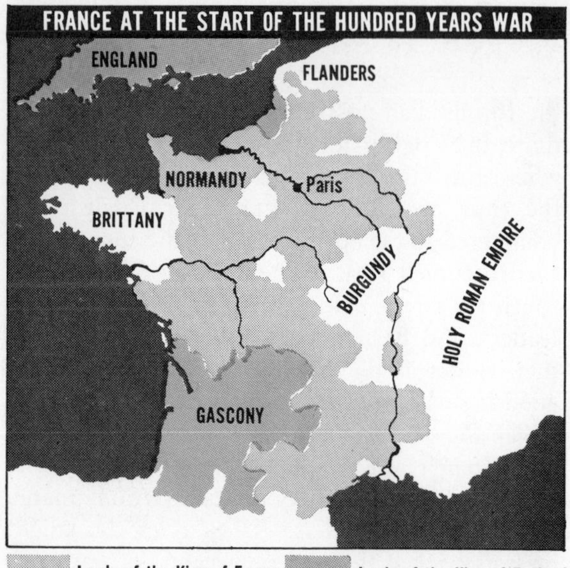

JOAN OF ARC. Guided only by "divine voices," the Maid of Orléans heeded her visions and went forth when she was sixteen to save France from the English.

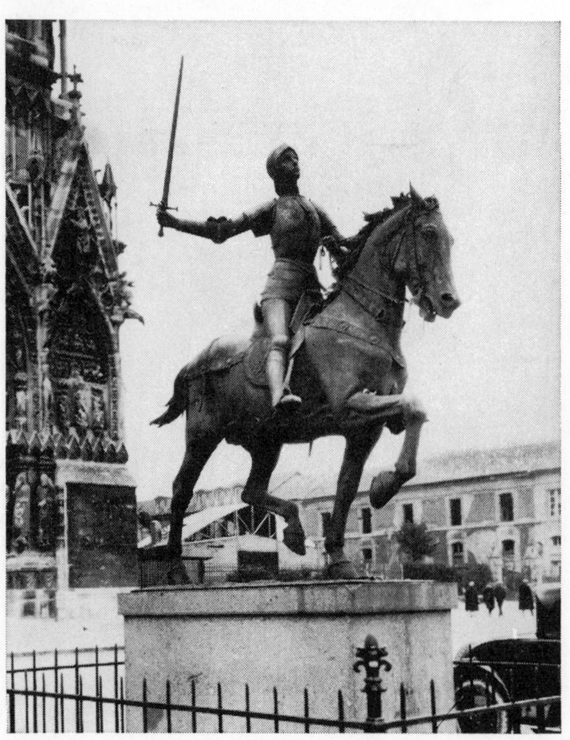

Neither a brilliant general nor a courageous king changed the course of events. It was Joan of Arc, a simple peasant girl. Though still in her teens, Joan felt sure that she could aid the cause of France. She believed that she had the power to help the French dauphin become king. Her self-confidence did not come alone from her courage and patriotism; it sprang mainly from her religious faith. Joan of Arc told of having visions in which she was commanded to help the dauphin and to save France from her enemies. In her visions she was promised the help of the saints in carrying out her great task.

Joan's faith in the visions and "voices" that advised her was very strong. After much difficulty she received permission to speak with the dauphin. She begged him to let her lead a force against the English, who were trying to capture the city of Orleans (or-lay-*an*), just south of Paris. The timid dauphin finally gave his consent.

Mounted on a horse and wearing the dress of a feudal page, Joan led the French soldiers against the English. The sight of the young French girl courageously leading an army against the invaders kindled the spirit of the French. They fought as soldiers had seldom fought before, and Orleans was saved.

The English were struck with awe. They looked upon Joan as a witch. Cities which had sided with the English threw open their gates to the Maid of Orleans. Finally, on the march northward, the French took the city of Reims. There, with Joan standing by him, the dauphin was crowned Charles VII, King of France.

Joan became a martyr. With the crowning of the king, Joan felt that her services should be at an end. But since the weak, lazy king did little to follow up the victories, Joan continued to resist the English. Within a few months she was taken prisoner by the English.

The English turned Joan over to the Church to be tried for heresy, or violating Church teachings. The trial took place in the city of Rouen (roo-*ahn*) on the River Seine. Joan was condemned to death. In the old market place of Rouen she was chained to a stake. Fuel was piled high about her and the torch applied. According to legend, one of the English soldiers who had come to rejoice at the death of an enemy was heard to cry out, "We are lost—we have burned a saint!"

Indeed, the English cause in France was lost. In the next few years the French slowly but steadily drove back the English invaders. Finally only Calais (kal-*ay*) remained in English hands. The faith of Joan of Arc still lives. In the present century, she has been officially declared a saint of the Roman Catholic Church and is the subject of much European and American literature.

THE POWER OF THE FRENCH KINGS BECAME ABSOLUTE

Representative government died out in France. During the crisis in the early part of the Hundred Years' War the Estates-General gained considerable power in the French government. Because the king needed its support so desperately, the Estates-General was able to demand the right to levy all taxes and to get a full accounting of how the money was spent. But by the end of the war, the assembly had lost all of its power. For the next three centuries it had almost no influence in government.

Why did representative government die out in France while it grew powerful in England? In England, the lesser nobility united with the commoners in Parliament to curb the king's power. But in France there was no such alliance in the Estates-General. As long as the nobles kept their feudal powers, members of the middle class felt they had to support the king. He was the only one who could keep peace and order. Later, when the nobles lost their feudal powers and became mere courtiers to the king, they too supported him. The nobles depended on him to save their privileges and protect them against the rising middle class. So, in the long run, the Estates-General failed to become an effective means of limiting the king's authority.

France became the king's toy. During the Estates-General's brief period of power, it gave the king the right to levy a permanent tax on land. Before that the king could collect only such fees as feudal custom permitted him to have. The Estates-General voted the new tax so the king could raise money in a hurry to fight off an invasion from England. In voting the tax, the Estates-General really signed its own death warrant. With the power to collect the new tax, the king did not have to ask the Estates-General for money. If he needed more money, he simply raised the tax rate and collected the money. The power of the king was thus greatly increased.

There were a number of other changing conditions that favored the growth of the king's power. At the close of the Hundred Years' War the king was the leading feudal lord, and master of all France. Gradually the king broke up the remaining powerful dukedoms in France. Because of his power to levy direct taxes, he had the money to keep up a large army. He no longer had to

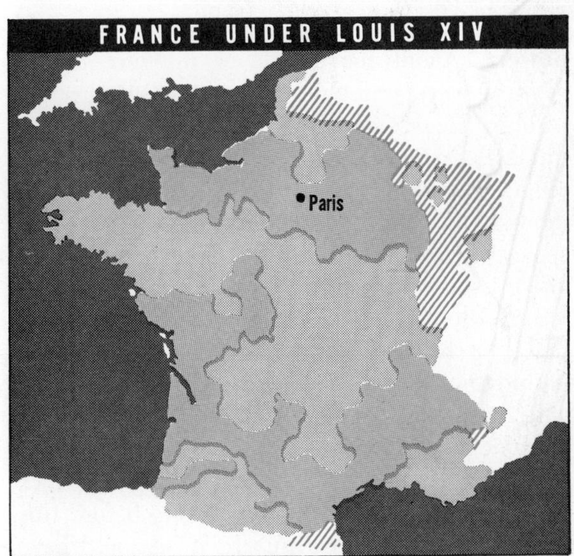

LOUIS XIV. The Sun King, attired in his robes of state, posed for this impressive portrait by Rigaud.

depend on the influence and resources of his nobles to raise an armed force.

As long as the nobles held on to their social privileges and got out of paying most of the taxes, they had little interest in restricting the king's power. If a rebellion did threaten, the king put it down promptly with his own army or bought off the rebels.

In the reign of Louis XIII, early in the seventeenth century, there was a brilliant and ruthless royal minister named Richelieu (*ree*-sheh-loo). He finished the job of making the king all-powerful by taking over the local government of all the provinces of France. He left the governors with no power except in unimportant local affairs. He cut down the power of the nobles. It was Richelieu who started the policy of getting the nobles to stay at the court. There it was easy to keep an eye on them and to stop any ideas of rebellion. Richelieu and Louis XIII died within a year of each other. Together they had completed the work of making France feared abroad and of giving the king vast new powers at home.

Louis XIV ruled with pomp and supreme power. About the middle of the seventeenth century, a five-year-old lad inherited the French throne. He was fated to become one of the most interesting kings that ever ruled any nation. His reign of seventy-two years is the longest of any monarch in European history. His rule and personality had a marked effect on his times in France and in other nations.

Like the English King James I, Louis XIV believed in his divine right to rule. Louis is reported to have said, "I am the state." The nobles, who had once spent most of their time fighting the king, were now content to live at the palace in his favor. Hugh Capet, the feudal king of France who lived some seven hundred years before this time, would have been amazed if he could have seen the pomp of Louis XIV. He would have seen the nobles handing the king his clothes when he arose in the morning and standing by respectfully when the monarch ate his meals. He would have seen the nobles listening politely to the great artists and writers Louis XIV brought to his court. True, the French king had become powerful and had unified the nation. But the extravagance and selfishness of divine-right monarchs were bound finally to lead to dissatisfaction and rebellion in France just as they had in England.

Europe followed French fashion. Louis XIV and his court became the wonder of Europe. French manners and dress were imitated in the courts of other nations. The French language became the fashionable tongue of polite society and the official language of many royal courts. Following the example of Louis XIV, the rulers of other nations began to encourage writers and artists. A few rulers even tried to copy the splendor of the French court.

Louis XIV dictated the dress and the customs of the upper classes. His wars upset the peace of Europe. His interest in art, architecture, and other fine arts made the French call his times the Grand Century. Louis XIV himself came to be known as the Grand Monarch, the Sun King.

The glory of the Sun King at Versailles shone over all Europe. Louis wanted not only to be the most important person in Christendom but also to look the part. To make himself taller and even more dignified, he wore enormous curled wigs, plumed hats, and high scarlet heels on his shoes.

As the Great Pyramid symbolized the power of the Egyptian Pharaoh, so the palace of Versailles (ver-*si*) reflected Louis' grandeur. Versailles originally was a hunting lodge a few miles outside Paris. Louis hired the best architects, painters, and gardeners in the country to turn it into a magnificent royal residence which could hold ten thousand people. It had hundreds of rooms with marble columns, polished inlaid floors, brilliant rugs and tapestries, and richly painted ceilings. The surrounding countryside was molded into formal gardens and parks dotted with classical statues and marvelous fountains. The fountains are still turned on for special occasions. Avenues through the forest spread out on all sides of the palace like the rays of the sun which Louis XIV was supposed to represent.

Versailles was more than a palace; it was a way of life. The magnificence of the palace and the strict formality of court etiquette formed a setting for the splendor of the Sun King. Louis invited the entire court to come and live at Versailles. He demanded courtly manners and elegant dress of his nobles. He could be charming, but he never allowed anyone to endanger or upset his royal dignity.

The rigid etiquette and extreme luxury of court life were not designed just to please Louis' vanity. They had the far more practical purpose of transforming rebellious feudal nobles into perfumed, powdered courtiers anxious above all to please the king. For Louis improved on Richelieu's policy by requiring his great lords to live at court all year. They were quite willing to do so because life on a manor was dull. Much more important, if they were not in constant attendance on the king, he would forget to give them the pensions and army commissions on which their income depended. In this way, Louis completed the job which French kings ever since Hugh Capet had tried to accomplish. He subjected the nobles completely to the absolute power of the king.

In order to entertain his nobles, Louis organized great festivals at Versailles. The best composers wrote music for ballets in which Louis, dressed as the sun god Apollo, danced the leading role.

VERSAILLES. In the elegant palace and the vast landscaped gardens of Versailles, Louis XIV and his court lived in pomp and luxury.

There were also balls, fireworks, and mock battles between ships on an artificial lake. Louis hired the foremost artists and dramatists, such as Racine (rah-*seen*) and Moliere (maw-*lyayr*) to add to the luster of his court.

Versailles was a dreamland for Louis XIV and the men and women of his court. But it was a nightmare of suffering and taxation for the common people. Thousands of peasants and soldiers were forced to work without pay. The extravagant king is said to have destroyed the records showing how much he spent. Probably the palace cost the people of France close to a hundred million dollars, an expense which the French economy, already weakened by a costly series of wars, could not easily bear.

The extravagance of the French court was a heavy burden on the economy, but foreign nations feared and respected the military power of France and the brilliance of the French court. France was a leading world power in the seventeenth century. She was a feared rival of the English. Her explorers and missionaries made their influence felt in the New World.

The costly grandeur of Versailles was, however, only a veneer of elegance covering the hardship and poverty of the majority of the people. The oppression they suffered and the rebellious feelings it aroused led to a bloody revolution in France that changed the course of history throughout the Western world.

Chapter Check-up

1. In what ways did the Romans influence French history?
2. What groups invaded Gaul when the Roman Empire weakened?
3. Where did France get its present name?
4. In what ways did the French kings increase their power?
5. Why were the French and English kings in continual dispute?
6. What was the mission of Joan of Arc? What was her fate?
7. Which three groups were represented in the Estates-General.
8. Why did representative government die out in France while it grew powerful in England?
9. How did Richelieu help to make the French king an absolute monarch?
10. Why was Louis XIV considered to be the cultural leader of Europe?

CHAPTER 37

The French Revolution Sought Liberty, Equality, and Fraternity for All Mankind

DISCONTENT STIRRED THE PEOPLE OF FRANCE

France was in need of reform. The grand monarch Louis XIV dazzled Europe and had the people of France at his feet. But within a century after his death the population cheered as the head of a later king, Louis XVI, fell into the executioner's basket. The story behind this drastic change in the fortunes of the kings of France is a fascinating and extremely important one for the modern world.

When Louis XV (1715–74) inherited the throne, the French people waited hopefully for the reforms they thought he would bring about.

VOLTAIRE. This famous French writer and philosopher wanted a constitutional government for France. His writings helped stir up a revolution. Voltaire sat for this bust by Houdon, the renowned sculptor, who made portraits of many of the famous people of his day (including George Washington).

The bourgeoisie, or middle class, sought a voice in the government and an end to petty restrictions on trade. The peasants, who were forced to pay over half their income in taxes and feudal dues, were reduced to poverty. But Louis disappointed both groups. He continued to waste money and devoted his time to selfish pleasures. He paid little attention to the French colonies in America. In a series of wars with the British, the French lost both their American colonies and their settlements in India. "After me, the deluge," Louis XV is supposed to have said, thereby admitting the corruption and inefficiency that characterized his government.

Voltaire ridiculed the nobility and clergy. The French nobles, however, were quite satisfied with their special privileges, such as exemption from almost all taxation. They did not want to see conditions changed. But during the eighteenth century there were a number of keen, critical Frenchmen who spoke up for the common man. The writings of the French reformers, aimed at the injustices of the times, did much to stir the people to action.

The most famous of the reformers was Voltaire. With keen mind and quick wit he heaped ridicule upon the narrow-mindedness of the nobility and the clergy. Voltaire was twice a political prisoner in the Bastille, but he was so clever that even royalty liked to listen to him. He lived for a time in England, and he was a guest at the court of Frederick the Great of Prussia. He wrote plays and novels. He contributed articles to a famous series of books, the *Encyclopedie,* in which he explained the scientific ideas of the Renaissance.

In his most famous book, *Letters on the English,* Voltaire praised England for its free speech and religious liberty and contrasted it with the persecution in France. Here are a few lines from one of Voltaire's letters. They will give you an idea of how he used words to scorn the conditions of his times:

". . . I agree with you that it is somewhat a reflection on human nature that money accomplishes everything and merit nothing. . . .

"It is sad to see . . . those who toil, in poverty, and those who produce nothing, in luxury; . . . violence in high places which engenders violence in the people: might making right not only amongst nations but amongst individuals."

The most familiar statement attributed to Voltaire is: "I do not agree with a word you say, but I will defend to the death your right to say it."

Voltaire's scathing attacks on the evils of eighteenth century France did not advise revolt. But they caused many Frenchmen to think that unless the old order changed, it would have to be swept away.

Rousseau claimed that government is based upon the consent of the governed. Another reformer whose writings stirred the French people was Jean Jacques Rousseau (roo-*so*). In *The Social Contract,* Rousseau attacked the right of kings to rule without the consent of the people they governed. "Man," he said, "is born free and yet is now everywhere in chains. One man believes himself the master of others and yet is after all more of a slave than they." The people, he claimed, had a right to decide for themselves how they were to be governed. He believed not only in the right of people to determine their own government, but also in each one's obligation to take part in government. Rousseau wrote, "As soon as any man says of the affairs of the State, 'What does it matter to me?' the State may be given up for lost."

Both Rousseau and Voltaire were writing at the middle of the eighteenth century. Their teachings influenced American leaders in their struggle for independence. Many of the ideas expressed in our Declaration of Independence can also be found in the writings of Rousseau and Voltaire.

THE PEOPLE OF FRANCE OVERTHREW THEIR MONARCH

Louis XVI aided the American Revolution but created a financial crisis in France. It was Louis XVI's misfortune to come to the throne in 1774, for it was he who was made to pay for the misrule of his predecessors. Louis was a fat, good-natured man who liked to tinker with locks. When the American colonies revolted against England in 1776, Louis XVI had an opportunity to strike back at the English. He listened willingly to the arguments of Benjamin Franklin that France should aid the Colonies. France contributed two and a half million dollars to the American cause. This aid enabled the United States to win its independence, but it helped bankrupt the French government. The expense of maintaining the court at Versailles continued to increase. Louis' wife, Marie Antoinette (an-twah-*net*), earned such a reputation for extravagance that she became known as "Madame Deficit." Louis ordered his officials to raise more and more money. When they could not raise enough money to please him, he dismissed them and appointed others.

The stage was set for revolution. By 1789 the French government was hopelessly in debt. The king's officials were no longer able to wring money from the overburdened merchants and peasants. They could not tax the nobles or the clergy. So the king was forced to call a meeting of the Estates-General, the legislative parliament, which had not met for 175 years. The meeting was held in one of the palaces at Versailles.

The Estates-General was composed of representatives of the three classes: the First Estate (clergy), the Second Estate (nobility), and the Third Estate (commoners). The Third Estate was composed of the broadest segment of society.

At A Glance

French Kings Before the Revolution

Early Rulers (486–987)
- Clovis
- Pepin the Short
- Charlemagne

Capetian Kings (987–1589)
- Hugh Capet
- Louis VI
- Philip II
- Louis IX
- Philip the Fair
- Louis X
- Charles VII

Bourbon Kings (1589–1792)
- Louis XIII
- Louis XIV
- Louis XV
- Louis XVI

THE ESTATES-GENERAL GREETS LOUIS XVI. When Frenchmen became discontented with Louis' policies, he was finally forced to call a meeting of the Estates-General. Above, Louis is arriving to open the first session in 175 years.

It included merchants, professional men, the workers of the towns and cities, and—the largest group of all—the peasants. Because the Third Estate accounted for about 96 per cent of France's population, its representation in the Estates-General was equal to the combined membership of the other two Estates. Naturally the Third Estate wanted the three groups to meet as one body and vote as individuals. In that way, the Third Estate would have a majority and would be in control. But Louis ordered the Estates to meet separately, each Estate casting a single vote. The representatives of the Third Estate refused to obey. They knew that the first two Estates would outvote them.

For six weeks the representatives of the Third Estate stubbornly held out. Then acting on the motion of one of its representatives, the Third Estate declared that the king must not levy any more taxes without its consent. This made Louis XVI so angry that he ordered his soldiers to prevent a further meeting in the palace. The members of the Third Estate, angry and aroused at the king's interference, met in an indoor tennis court in Versailles. There they declared themselves to be empowered to make laws for all of France, and they took a solemn oath not to adjourn until they had written a constitution for France. This defiant *Oath of the Tennis Court* marked the real beginning of the Revolution. Louis finally gave in and ordered the three Estates to meet together as a National Assembly. The days of divine-right monarchy in France were almost over; the power of Louis XVI was crumbling.

Meantime, political clubs of various shades of opinion had been established among the members of the Estates-General. So when all the members at last met in one body as the National Assembly, the delegates sat together according to their political views. From this seating arrangement have come the political terms used today: the left means the radicals (as the revolutionary Third Estate was considered to be), while the right means the conservatives (as the nobles certainly were). The center means the moderates, or people whose views are between the conservatives and radicals.

July 14 became "Independence Day" for France. If Louis had decided to cooperate with the National Assembly, France might have peacefully become a constitutional monarchy and the Revolution might have ended at this point. Instead, he listened to the advice of his nobles and

THE PEASANT'S BURDEN. This cartoon, printed in 1789, dramatizes the lot of the French peasant, who is forced to support the nobility and clergy while birds and rabbits nibble away at his few remaining possessions.

discharged a popular finance minister. Then he ordered troops to Versailles. The people of Paris interpreted this move as a threat to the members of the Third Estate and a sign that Louis intended to put down the Revolution by force.

Soon the people formed an angry mob and began to look for weapons. Someone suggested that there might be muskets and powder stored in the hated fortress of the Bastille, where political prisoners were kept. On July 14, 1789, the mobs stormed and took the Bastille.

When a messenger brought the news, Louis exclaimed, "This is a revolt!" "Not a revolt, Sire," replied the messenger, "but a revolution." The news frightened Louis. Turning his back on the nobles, he tried to make friends with the National Assembly. He withdrew his troops, recalled the minister of finance whom he had dismissed and drove into Paris with the tricolor—the blue, white, and red symbol of the Revolution—in his hat. The delegates to the Assembly cheered, and Paris rejoiced. Ever since that day, July 14 has been the French day of independence just as July 4 is Independence Day in the United States. The motto "Liberty, Equality, Fraternity" became the watchword of the Revolution, and in the years

THE FALL OF THE BASTILLE. This grim symbol of French absolutism was attacked by an angry mob on July 14, 1789. Its fall marked the beginning of the French Revolution.

following it became the custom in France to inscribe the words on public buildings. (A *Tale of Two Cities,* by Charles Dickens, the English novelist, gives us a vivid, though fictional, description of the days of the French Revolution.)

The "Declaration of the Rights of Man" was the death blow of the old order. The fall of the Bastille was the signal for outbursts of revolt all over the country. By burning down castles and terrorizing their landlords, peasants made it clear that the manorial system must come to an end. The nobles in the National Assembly realized that unless they gave in to the peasants, the whole country would go up in flames. In one dramatic session of the Assembly, the nobles voluntarily surrendered the feudal and manorial privileges that they had exercised for centuries. Serfdom was ended, special rights for nobles were repealed, and unfair taxes were abolished.

The old order was dead. In its place the National Assembly issued the "Declaration of the Rights of Man and the Citizen." This famous document declared in ringing tones that "men are born and remain free and equal in rights." Their rights included "liberty, property, security, and resistance to oppression." All men were guaranteed freedom of speech, press, and religion, so long as their actions did not injure someone else. All men were declared equal before the law and given the right of self-government. You can see how much the "Declaration of the Rights of Man" was like the American Declaration of Independence and how much it owed to the teachings of Voltaire and Rousseau. All over France and in most of Europe men read the "Declaration of the Rights of Man" with excitement and hope. Even today, it remains, like the Magna Carta and the Bill of Rights, one of the great documents of human freedom.

The king was condemned to death. The National Assembly was in desperate need of money to run the government, just as Louis had been. As a result, the members of the Assembly voted to have the government take over, or *nationalize,* all the land owned by the Church. It was also decided that all clergymen would be elected by the people and that their salaries would be paid by the government.

The seizing of Church property shocked Louis. Under the influence of the nobles, and in answer to his wife's pleas, he began to plot with foreign powers to put down the Revolution. But to carry out the plot he had to escape from France. He and the queen managed to get away from Paris disguised as servants. They rode in a carriage as far as the border of France without being

DEATH OF LOUIS XVI. Calling out loudly over the drum rolls, "People, I die innocent," the knife descended and Louis XVI, always a little pathetic in life, met death bravely. As the executioner holds up the king's head, there are a few cries of "Long live the Republic."

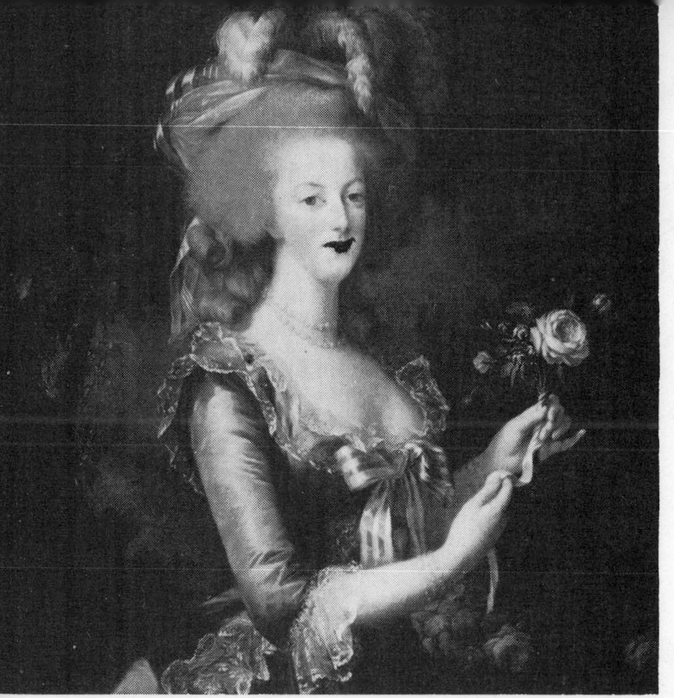

Marie Antoinette. Gay and frivolous in happy times, she met death with dignity and courage. The luckless queen was a daughter of Empress Maria Theresa of Austria.

caught. But there an alert soldier, who had never seen either of them before, recognized the king from having seen his likeness on French coins.

The French people lost all confidence in the king from that moment, although it was more than a year before he actually lost his throne. In September, 1792, the monarchy was abolished, and Louis XVI was accused of treasonous conduct and summoned for trial. He was condemned to death on the guillotine (*gill*-oh-teen), and a few months later, his wife, Marie Antoinette, was also beheaded.

France was attacked by the other nations of Europe. The Revolution in France had frightened the other kings of Europe. They feared the revolutionary ideas of Liberty, Equality, and Fraternity would spread into their own countries. For that reason they had conspired with Louis to crush the Revolution. They were shocked and dismayed at his execution, and they vowed revenge. Armies from Austria and Prussia began to march against France. The French responded with a new patriotism and quickly raised republican armies for the defense of the nation. At this time a young French army captain, Rouget de l'Isle (roo-*zheh* deh-*leel*), composed a stirring marching song for young republican volunteers as they made their way to Paris. The song, the "Marseillaise" (mar-seh-*layz*), has become the national song of France.

Under the stress of a defensive war, the leaders of the Revolution voted themselves dictatorial powers to organize resistance. At the same time, to prevent counter-revolution, they opened a Reign of Terror against all suspected of sympathizing with the king. The Terror was directed by a fanatical young lawyer, Maximilian Robespierre, who was responsible for the beheading of nearly forty thousand people, many of them innocent of disloyalty to the Revolution.

The new government was ruthless but efficient. It managed to hold off the invading armies and then took the offensive. The French revolutionists turned the tables on their enemies. They invaded the Netherlands and began to spread ideas of freedom to the rest of Europe.

Robespierre. In the end, Robespierre, a lawyer and disciple of Rousseau, was forced to give his life in the revolution for which he had fought so fanatically.

NAPOLEON USED THE REVOLUTION TO RISE TO POWER IN FRANCE

Napoleon saved the Directory from mob vengeance. The horrible Reign of Terror that had taken so many lives came to an end with the execution of Robespierre in 1794. Meantime, a convention had been elected to write a new constitution for France. When it was finished, the new constitution provided for a republican government with a legislature and an executive body called the Directory. But many people objected to provisions in the constitution which were designed to assure the re-election of those who had favored the execution of the king. They organized a rebellion and began to march against the new government.

The task of holding off the mob was entrusted to a young officer named Napoleon Bonaparte. When the rioting mob appeared, Napoleon drove them away with a volley of grapeshot from his cannon. Many were killed and the others fled. The harsh treatment of the Paris mobs taught them a lesson: violence and rioting were no longer to be tolerated. The new government had established its authority.

Under the Directory, the new government turned its attention to its foreign enemies. Great Britain and Austria were the chief enemies of the republic at this time. The Directory planned a widespread campaign against the Austrians. As a reward for his action in defending the Convention, the government made Napoleon a general. He took command of a small army. He was only supposed to carry out a minor part of the Austrian campaign. It was his job to attack the Austrians in Italy.

General Bonaparte directed his small force with such military skill that he was completely victorious. His brilliant campaign in Italy forced the Austrians to make peace with France. Napoleon also established French influence in much of northern Italy. After his first success, Napoleon met defeat in a campaign against the English in Egypt. But in spite of the setback, when he returned to Paris the people greeted Napoleon as a national hero.

The new government of France, under the Directory, had grown corrupt and inefficient, and it had lost popular support. So in the last year of the eighteenth century Napoleon overthrew the Directory and made himself First Consul of the French Republic. Already popular with the French people, he put down with a strong hand small rebellions within France. Then he turned to the French frontiers and cleared them of foreign armies.

Napoleon made himself emperor. Less than five years after he had become First Consul of the Republic, Napoleon Bonaparte stood in the famous Cathedral of Notre Dame in Paris. There he had come to be crowned emperor. Seizing the crown from the hands of the Pope, he placed

NAPOLEON. The "Little Corporal," surrounded by his officers, directs the Battle of Wagram which resulted in the defeat of Austria in 1809. Napoleon's power had already passed its peak.

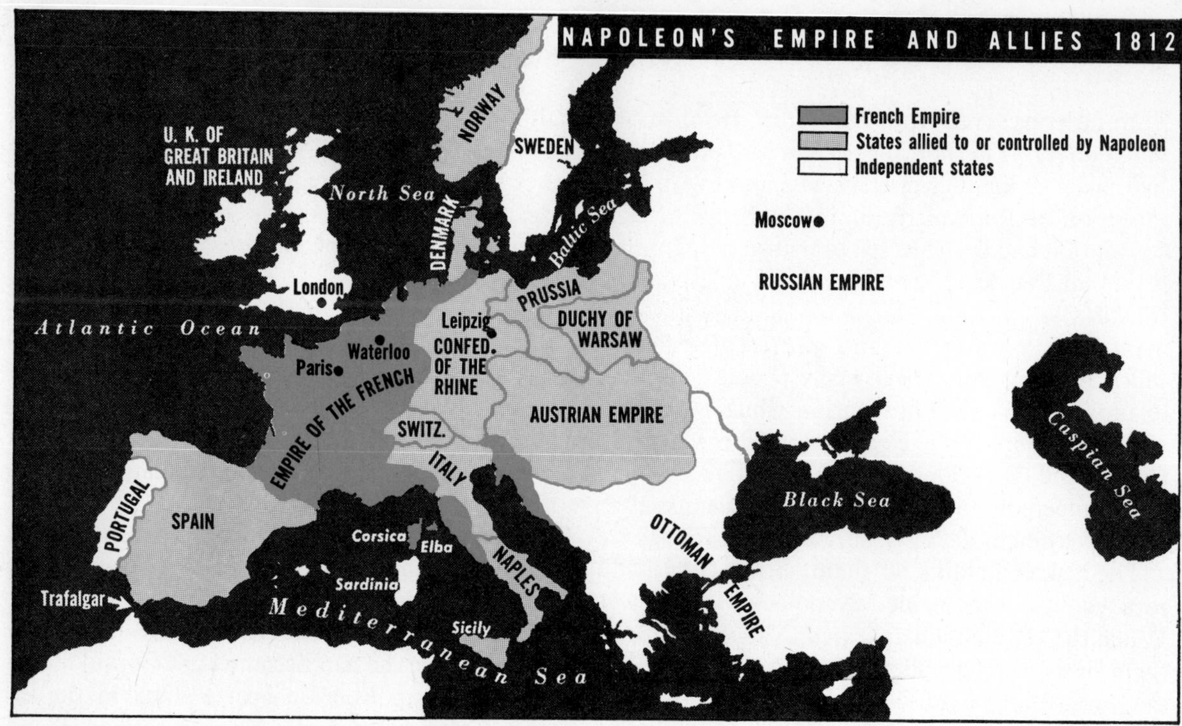

it upon his own head and became "Napoleon I, Emperor of the French." Liberty was a thing of the past. In fourteen years the French government had passed through the stages of absolute monarchy, limited monarchy, republic, rule by a Directory, and then back to the one-man rule of Napoleon. The course of the Revolution seemed to prove the truth of an old French proverb: "The more things change, the more they stay the same."

Napoleon proved to be both soldier and statesman. Napoleon Bonaparte was not a native Frenchman. He was born on the island of Corsica, which lies just off the southern coast of France in the Mediterranean. He was only five feet one inch tall. But Napoleon had matchless ability to inspire others with faith in him. He believed so thoroughly in his own superiority that he made others believe in it also, as other dictators have done. Once he said, "I am the child of destiny . . . ," and again, ". . . I began to make mistakes only when I listened to advisers."

Napoleon is most famous as a great military commander. His name was feared by all the monarchs of Europe. The rulers of other nations were eager to punish the French for revolting and for beheading their king, Louis XVI. At various times Napoleon's Grand Army had to face the combined forces of many enemy nations. But Napoleon was usually the victor. He freed France from invaders. Then he set out to conquer all those who had opposed him: Spain, Austria, many of the German states, Russia, and Great Britain. His ideal was to bring all of Europe under one emperor—himself. He planned to set up his friends and relatives as kings in the various states of his empire. Napoleon's success was with land forces. England, his greatest enemy, he could not attack successfully because of her control of the seas. In the end, Napoleon was undone by his widespread conquests, for he had conquered more territory than he could hold.

Napoleon was interested in improving the land he ruled. Like the Roman emperors, he built roads and other public works. He erected buildings and triumphal arches to remind people of his victories. The most famous of the arches is the

NAPOLEON. After crowning himself emperor in 1804, Napoleon turned to his wife, Josephine, and crowned her empress. The moment of her coronation is portrayed in this painting by Jacques Louis David, Napoleon's official court painter.

Arc de Triomphe (ark deh tree-*ahmf*), which towers 165 feet above one of the prominent squares of Paris. Today it shelters the grave of the French Unknown Soldier of World War I.

Napoleon also set legal minds to work collecting and rearranging the laws. The Code of Napoleon was the result. It became the model for legal systems in other countries of Europe and is the basis of modern French law. In the constitutions of some of our states there are traces of the Code of Napoleon, for the Louisiana Territory, sold to the United States by Napoleon, was formerly part of the French Empire.

Napoleon showed he was a statesman as well as a soldier. During the Revolution, the Church had been frequently scoffed at. Napoleon reached an agreement with the Pope. It was called the Concordat. It restored the Church to an important position in France. The Concordat lasted more than a century. Napoleon also reorganized the school system of France so that all children could get an education. Some American school systems later copied certain features of Napoleon's plan.

Napoleon met his Waterloo. The tide turned against Napoleon at last. As Hitler was to do almost a century and a half later, Napoleon made the mistake of invading Russia. His armies managed to reach Moscow. But the Russian winter, the long supply line, and the tough Russian resistance forced Napoleon to retreat from Moscow. It was one of history's most disastrous routs. The Russians gave thanks to "General Winter" and "General Mud" for his defeat.

The next year, combined armies of the nations that were allied against Napoleon defeated him in Europe. He was sent to the island of Elba, off the coast of Italy, as a prisoner. One of

Louis XVI's brothers became king of France. But Napoleon escaped from Elba to Marseilles in southern France. He made a triumphal march to Paris. When the soldiers who had been sent by the king to stop Napoleon again saw their "Little Corporal," tears came to their eyes. They begged to be forgiven, and shouted, "Vive l'Empereur!" (Long live the Emperor!) Under the spell of Napoleon's personality they were ready to fight again under the banner of the Revolution and Napoleon.

Napoleon quickly raised an army. He met the allied forces of England, Holland, and the German states at Waterloo in Belgium. There, after a hard-fought and bloody battle, he was finally defeated. His power was forever crushed, and the old line of kings once more returned to the throne of France. Napoleon threw himself on the mercy of his most bitter enemies, the English. He was exiled to the distant island of St. Helena in the South Atlantic. There he died six years later.

Napoleon I became a glowing legend. To many Frenchmen, the name of Napoleon has become more glorious with the passing years. His deeds, like those of Joan of Arc, have become a patriotic legend. Napoleon has come to stand for the ideals of the Revolution, for law and order at home, and for the power and glory of France among foreign nations.

There is, however, another side to the story. In his *Outline of History*, the English writer H. G. Wells gives us his opinion of Napoleon: "The figure he makes in history is one of almost incredible self-conceit, of vanity, greed, and cunning, of callous contempt and disregard of all who trusted him, and of a grandiose aping of Caesar, Alexander, and Charlemagne which would be purely comic if it were not caked over with human blood."

WATERLOO. The British are capturing the French artillery in this scene from the battle in which Napoleon, who had escaped from Elba, met his final defeat. He lived in British custody during his final years on the remote island of St. Helena.

Talleyrand. A bishop, courtier, and noted diplomat, Talleyrand held important posts in six different French governments, including those of the Revolution. He achieved his greatest diplomatic triumph at the Congress of Vienna, where he played his hand so skillfully that France was able to participate in the talks as an equal rather than as a conquered nation.

The Congress of Vienna tried to restore the absolute power of kings. With Napoleon out of the way, representatives of the great powers met at Vienna to rearrange the boundaries of the European nations.

The decisions made at Vienna in 1815 gave weary Europe years of peace. The conservatives came back into power everywhere. In later chapters you will read of the effect the decisions of Vienna had on the stories of other nations. As far as France was concerned, all of Napoleon's conquests were lost to her, and her boundaries were redrawn along lines that are approximately the same as her present boundaries.

The Congress of Vienna favored bringing back the old royal families. It tried to revive the absolute power of the kings over the people. It seemed as though the Third Estate in Europe had made no advance in its struggle for liberty. But that was not entirely true. In France, Napoleon had adopted many of the social gains of the Revolution. Napoleon's reforms remained in force. For example, the idea of equal opportunity for everyone remained alive in France. The people had some say in government. No king or emperor was ever again to rule France without consulting a National Assembly. Napoleon's soldiers had taken the ideas of the Revolution into many lands. Though their leader was an emperor, the soldiers did not forget the motto of the Revolution—"Liberty, Equality, Fraternity." In many countries people cherished a dream of the ideals of justice and equality.

The restoration of the old order in Europe was not fated to last for many years. While the Congress of Vienna was significant as the first attempt by an international conference to deal with the problems of Europe as a whole, it failed to suppress the rise of nationalism and overlooked the widespread social changes created by the Industrial Revolution.

Chapter Check-up

1. Who were the two great political thinkers of the Enlightenment?
2. How did the ideas brought forth by the political philosophers pave the way to revolution?
3. How did the American Revolution affect the French?
4. How did the political terms *left, right,* and *center* arise?
5. What happened on July 14, 1789, the French Independence Day?
6. Why did Louis XVI lose the confidence of the French people?
7. Who was the leader of the Reign of Terror?
8. By what steps did Napoleon become emperor of France?
9. What reforms were carried out by Napoleon?
10. What was the greatest extent of Napoleon's empire?
11. What was the purpose of the Congress of Vienna? How well did it succeed?

French architecture has always been the glory of its people, reflecting their spiritual needs and gallic spirit. No structure in Western Europe is more indicative of these qualities than *Notre Dame* in Paris.

Characteristic of the growing wealth of the aristocracy were the chateaus. *Azay-le-Rideau* built in the sixteenth century is typical of the extravagance that helped bring about the French Revolution.

Napoleon, seeking identification with classic greatness, initiated an era of Roman and Grecian design. Shown here is *Napoleon's Study*: simple, classic, but quite opulent.

Gallic innovativeness, striking and bold, is given ample expression in the work of *Le Corbusier*, twentieth century architect. The *Ronchamp* with its open air pulpit, ship-like shape, and irregular openings combine both the spiritual need and the striking originality of the French.

CHAPTER 38

France Became a Democracy but Declined as a Great Power

THE THIRD REPUBLIC BROUGHT NEW HOPE TO FRANCE

France overthrew another king and gained another emperor. The governments of Louis XVIII, who was restored by the Congress of Vienna, and his successor, Charles X, were never very popular. In 1830 Louis Philippe (fee-*leep*), the "Citizen-King," came to the throne on condition that he let the legislative assembly have all the power of government. The assembly, however, represented only the richest men in France because only they were allowed to vote. French workers in the early nineteenth century, like those in England at the same time, had no voice in the government.

During these years, the Industrial Revolution was spreading through France. In its early stages it caused as much suffering to French workers as it had to those of England (see Chapter 33). Soon the workers of France began to demand voting rights, better wages, and improved working conditions. When the government of Louis Philippe proved unsympathetic, the workers in Paris revolted. They built barricades of paving stones and old furniture across the narrow streets of Paris. From this defense they fired on the king's guard. The violence of the uprising caused this affair to be known as the Bloody June Days. When the rioting seemed to be getting out of control, the Citizen-King fled and the Second Republic was established. Louis Napoleon, a nephew of Napoleon I, was elected president. The ambitious Louis intended the presidency to be only a stepping stone to higher things. In 1852 he proclaimed the Second French Empire and asked the French to accept him as Emperor Napoleon III (1852–70). Hoping that he would restore the unity and glory that his famous uncle had brought to France, the people supported him.

Prussia humbled France and became a constant threat to her safety. Napoleon III ruled with considerable success for about eighteen years, but then he ran afoul of one of Europe's craftiest statesmen, the Prussian Chancellor Otto

NAPOLEON III. A great success during his first ten years as emperor, Napoleon III suffered exile in disgrace at the close of the Franco-Prussian War.

NINETEENTH-CENTURY FASHIONS. The artist Daumier, who first worked as a political cartoonist for newspapers, here spoofs the huge crinoline dresses of his time, which made it all but impossible for one lady to enter the cab, let alone two.

von Bismarck. Bismarck built the Prussian army to a peak of efficiency and then deliberately provoked France into war. In the Franco-Prussian War of 1870, France was defeated by Prussia in a matter of months. Napoleon III was forced into exile. Under the terms of the peace treaty France was forced to pay a huge sum of money to her conqueror and to surrender Alsace-Lorraine, a territory rich in coal and iron ore.

Bismarck used Prussia's victory to unite all the German states into a German Empire (see page 449). He added to the humiliation of France by having the German emperor crowned in the palace of the French kings at Versailles. The new Germany rapidly increased its population and built up its industry, until by 1900 Germany and not France was the strongest nation on the European continent. The bitterness aroused by the treaty of 1870 was still strong nearly a half-century later. France watched fearfully for signs of trouble with her rival across the border and dreamed of regaining Alsace-Lorraine.

The Third Republic helped France develop as a modern nation. The National Assembly, which had been elected by the people to make peace with Germany in 1870, also changed the national government. The new government was called the Third Republic. It lasted until World War II. Under the Third Republic, the two houses of the legislature elected the French president for a seven-year term, but he did not have the powers of an American president. As in Britain, the chief minister, or premier, had real control of the government. He was chosen by the lower house and held office only as long as he received its support.

But the Third Republic had a serious weakness. Many Frenchmen had opposed the Republic from the start and wished to see it fail. Highly individualistic, they broke up into dozens of small parties instead of forming two large ones as in Britain. Because no one party had enough of a majority to choose a leader, the premier had to depend on the support of several parties in order to stay in office. This arrangement is known as a *coalition* government. If an important issue arose on which the premier wished to take some strong action, he was sure to offend somebody, so the coalition would break up. Then a new coalition had to form and choose a new premier. France had fifty such changes in about as many years.

The civil service established by Napoleon I kept France on a steady keel despite shifts in the government. The Prussian defeat caused the French to reorganize and enlarge the army and navy. Under the Third Republic, the government improved roads, railways, canals, and harbors. Industry, particularly the manufacture of silk and lace, flourished. Between 1870 and 1914 France enjoyed stability and prosperity, and the Third Republic gradually won the loyalty of most of its citizens.

TWO WORLD WARS BROUGHT FRANCE TO THE BRINK OF DISASTER

The Germans invaded France in World War I. Frenchmen neither forgave nor forgot the humiliating defeat of the Franco-Prussian War and they lived in fear of Germany's growing power. They built up their army and formed alliances with Russia and Britain to offset Germany's strength. But France was still unable to stop the new German invasion of World War I. Between the years of 1914-18 German, British, French, and eventually American armies struggled for possession of northern France. The cities and factories destroyed by the war left the industrial center of the country in ruins. After the war, attempts to repair the damage were hindered by high taxes and social unrest, as well as Germany's inability to pay the heavy reparations that France had demanded in the peace treaty. The financial depression of the 1930's lead to great unemployment and a loss of foreign trade. Besides these problems, so many young Frenchmen had been killed in the war that France's population was falling far behind Germany's in the post-war years.

As long as the Third Republic government maintained prosperity it was widely supported. But when the depression brought uncertainty and unrest to France, many turned against the government. In 1936 the French, disturbed by the rise of Hitler and fascist agitation at home, elected the Popular Front government in which Radicals, Socialists, and Communists had the most strength. At first the Popular Front was able to make some reforms. But in the years just before World War II, France became so divided that she was unable to maintain a stable government and could not deal effectively with the threat of Nazi Germany. France was the only major democratic nation on the European continent, and her weakness seems to have encouraged Hitler in his plan to conquer Europe.

A French Tragedy. Nazi troops march down the Champs-Elysées after the fall of France in 1940. The Arch of Triumph, in the background, commemorates the victories of Napoleon I. Beneath it is the tomb of a French unknown soldier of World War I.

The Germans invaded France for the second time in twenty-five years. When Hitler came to power and began to rebuild the German army in the 1930's, France tried to protect herself from attack by constructing the Maginot (mah-jih-no) Line of fortifications along the eastern frontier. Not only were the French unable to build an army the size of Hitler's, but many Frenchmen feared that a large French army might provoke him to declare war. Having already suffered from two wars in less than fifty years, the French did not want to risk starting a third. At the Munich Conference in 1938, France and Britain tried to avoid trouble by letting Hitler annex part of Czechoslovakia (chek-oh-slo-vah-kee-uh), a small state east of Germany. But Hitler had no intention of keeping the promise of peace he made at Munich. Within a year he attacked Poland and started World War II.

France's weak northeast frontier was again a path for invasion. As in 1914, the Germans reached France by striking through Belgium, completely bypassing the Maginot Line. France was caught completely unprepared and with a government undecided as to what to do. After a brief struggle France surrendered. With the bitter pain of defeat, the French had to accept German occupation of two-thirds of their country. Marshal Petain (pay-tan), a World War I hero, became the head of unoccupied France in a kind of puppet government for the Germans at Vichy.

General de Gaulle led the Free French. But millions of Frenchmen refused to admit defeat. Some of them joined the Free French government which General de Gaulle (deh gol) organized in London, and fought with the allied armies. Many others stayed in France to become members of the "Resistance," a secret organization that worked constantly against the Germans. They blew up German troop trains and supply depots. They acted as spies for the Allies and sent valuable information from secret radio stations. Hundreds of Allied airmen, shot down in France, owed their lives to members of the Resistance who hid them and helped them return to England.

At A Glance

French Heads of State and Governments Since the Revolution

First Republic (1792–1804)

First Empire (1804–1815)
  Napoleon I

Bourbon Restoration (1815–1848)
  Louis XVIII
  Louis Philippe

Second Republic (1848–1851)
  Louis Napoleon

Second Empire (1852–1871)
  Napoleon III (Louis Napoleon)

Third Republic (1871–1940)

German Occupation (1940–1944)
 Vichy Government
  Henri Petain

 (Free French Government—London
  Charles de Gaulle)

Fourth Republic (1946–1958)

Fifth Republic (1958–Present)
  Charles de Gaulle

At first the United States seemed friendly to the Vichy government, which angered the Free French. But this was the American plan for preventing Petain from suspecting the Allies' plans. Suddenly, in November, 1942, British and American forces invaded France's North African colonies, taking Vichy and the Germans by surprise. That invasion and the invasion of Normandy in 1944 led to the defeat of Germany.

The Fourth Republic faced many problems. After the war, France obviously needed a strong government to replace the Third Republic, which had provided such weak leadership. But the many political parties began to quarrel again. De Gaulle was the logical choice for a leader, but he refused to accept the job of premier unless a new constitution was adopted to strengthen the powers of that office. But the National Assembly re-

President Charles De Gaulle. Leader of the Free French during World War II, and Premier of the provisional government of 1944-1946, De Gaulle was elected President of the Fifth Republic in 1958 and reelected for a second term in 1966.

fused to support the changes that de Gaulle wanted, fearing they would lead to a military dictatorship. De Gaulle completely withdrew from public life, and the various parties established a Fourth Republic based on the same division of powers as the Third. The premier still required the support of a coalition of parties to remain in office.

Meanwhile, the French people were again suffering through the disorders and hunger of a postwar period. Prices shot up, food was scarce, and riots broke out. Many Frenchmen became Communists. The French government faced many crises and leadership changed frequently from one weak government to another. In 1948 the United States helped rescue France and other European countries with financial help under the Marshall Plan (you will read about the Marshall Plan in Part 23). With this help France made steady progress in recovering from the destruction of World War II. But de Gaulle's emergence from retirement and a new government was needed in 1958 for France to meet the new problem brought on by her unsolved colonial problems. To understand this complex development it is necessary to go back briefly to the story of France's colonial empire. (See the map on page 357.)

France lost a second colonial empire. In the eighteenth century France lost her empire in North America and India to Britain in war. During the nineteenth century, however, France built a new colonial empire in Africa and Indochina second in size only to that of Britain. The fertile coastal plains of Algeria, Tunisia, and Morocco in North Africa became one of France's greatest assets. Indochina in southeast Asia provided a rich market for France.

In the years after World War II, Asia and Africa became engulfed in a great tide of nationalism. Colonial peoples in these areas began to demand their independence. As Britain quickly lost control of India, Burma, Egypt, and Sudan, and the Netherlands lost its possessions in the East Indies, France was forced to recognize the independence of Tunisia and Morocco and lost her colonies in Indochina in guerilla warfare to native Communists and nationalists.

Algeria presented a different problem, however. The country was considered a part of France and all Algerians were regarded as French citizens with representation in the French National Assembly. But the native Algerian population demanded full independence. Heavy French investment in the country and the settlement of many French colonists there seemed to prevent any French government from granting this independence. The Algerian nationalists resorted to guerilla warfare, inspired by the Indochinese success, which became a heavy drain on French resources and sharply divided French opinion.

In 1958 this divided opinion led to revolt in the French army in Algeria which soon spread to France itself. In the midst of a chaotic situation, the French National Assembly appealed to the strong man they had turned aside, Charles de Gaulle, to end the crisis, giving him full powers to run the government for six months. De Gaulle took charge forcefully. A new constitution which greatly strengthened the executive branch of the government was drawn up and overwhelmingly approved by the voters. De Gaulle was elected president of the new Fifth Republic for a seven-year term. He submitted the Algerian problem directly to the voters and the great majority voted to grant Algeria independence.

De Gaulle outlined a new role for France in world affairs. With the problem of Algeria out of the way, de Gaulle set about trying to revive France's prosperity and influence in world affairs. Without the tensions of colonial power, France increased trade with her former colonies which since 1958 have formed the French Community.

De Gaulle was reelected in 1965. He pulled away somewhat from the traditional alliance with the United States and Britain, withdrawing French military forces from the North Atlantic Treaty Organization, denying Britain membership in the European Common Market, developing a French nuclear force and establishing better relations with Russia. He was seeking to develop a new position of influence in a world otherwise dominated by the United States and the Soviet Union.

Since de Gaulle's retirement, France has followed a less colorful path. His successor, President Pompidou, was a political follower of his but has allowed Britain into the Common Market and has been more concerned with problems of inflation and the growing industrialization in what was long mainly a farming country.

Chapter Check-up

1. Why was Louis Philippe overthrown?
2. Why did the French accept Napoleon III?
3. How did the Franco-Prussian War spell a loss of power for France?
4. What were the weaknesses of the Third Republic? What helped keep France on a steady keel in spite of these weaknesses?
5. How did France suffer in World War I?
6. Why was France unable to defend herself against Hitler's armies in World War II?
7. Which of the French colonies were granted independence shortly after World War II?
8. Why did France fight to keep Algeria?
9. What has Charles de Gaulle done for France?
10. What new role in the world did France choose under de Gaulle's leadership?

CHAPTER 39

French Contributions to the Arts and Sciences Have Helped Mold Western Civilization

FROM ALL OVER THE WORLD, PARIS ATTRACTS MEN WITH CREATIVE MINDS

Since the Middle Ages, French writers, painters, musicians, and scientists have inspired and influenced the rest of the world. The center of French art and learning is Paris, the only very large city in France. Paris has neither mountains nor a harbor to provide natural splendor; her great beauty is largely man-made. The Cathedral of Notre Dame rises above the trees and roof tops on an island in the Seine. Many historic bridges span the river. On the left bank lie the formal flower beds and fountains of the Luxembourg Gardens. Not far away stands the Sorbonne (sawr-*bahn*), the oldest part of the University of Paris. Broad avenues, lined with fashionable shops and sidewalk cafes, crisscross the city. Artists gather on the hill of Montmartre (mawn-

mar-tr'), which is crowned by the white domes of the Church of the Sacré Coeur (*sah*-kray *ker*).

More important than the city's physical charms, however, is the atmosphere of Paris. The Parisian is quick to appreciate new ideas and new talent. Newspaper critics and interested crowds discuss exhibitions by young painters and sculptors and the openings of experimental plays. The French government holds exhibitions and buys paintings. It supports famous theaters, such as the *Comédie Francaise* (ko-may-*dee* frahn-*sez*) and the Opéra, and sponsors the French radio network. The network offers lectures by university professors, discussions of poetry and drama, and recent as well as classical musical compositions.

With such encouragement from the government and the public, men who have wanted freedom and sympathy in which to express their ideas have found Paris a second home. The achievements of such foreigners as the Polish composer Frederic Chopin (*show*-pan), the Polish scientist Marie Curie, the Spanish painter Pablo Picasso, the Dutch painter Vincent van Gogh, and the Belgian composer César Franck are considered French contributions to civilization. Dozens of American writers and painters, especially during the 1920's, found inspiration in France. The American novelist Ernest Hemingway, winner of the 1954 Nobel Prize for literature, is one of the most famous of this group.

FRENCH ARTISTS DISCOVERED NEW WAYS OF LOOKING AT LIFE

Millet painted French peasants, and Corot painted the French landscape. In 1814 Jean François Millet (mee-*lay*) was born in Normandy, in northwestern France. His parents were humble farmers. As a boy, Millet was interested in drawing and tried to copy the only pictures he had about him—engravings in the family Bible.

At the age of eighteen Millet went to a nearby city to study art. A few years later he went to study in Paris. Although he enrolled in one of the best art schools, he made little progress because he disliked the old-fashioned styles taught at the school. Millet soon left the art studio to work alone, supporting himself by painting signs

Sacré Coeur. A famous landmark in Paris, this striking nineteenth-century church crowns the hill of Montmartre, the city's highest elevation.

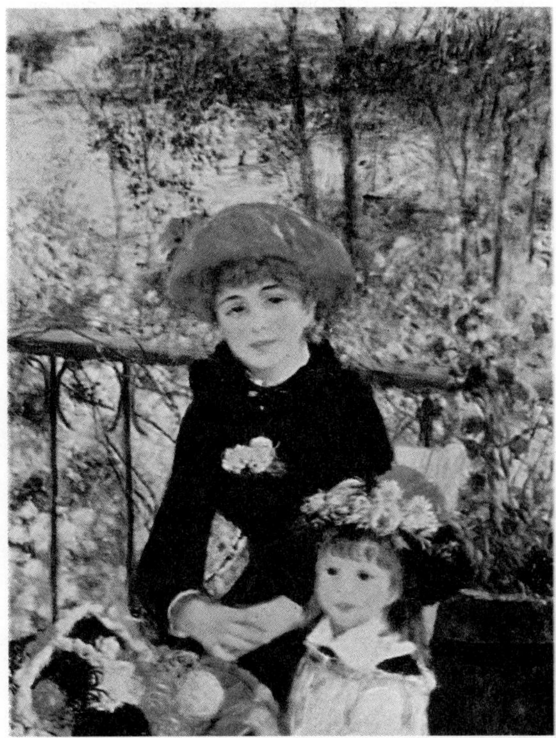

A COROT AND A RENOIR. Corot's cool hues and balanced composition and Renoir's mastery of color to express the warmth and joy of life have made their works significant in the history of painting and popular in museums. *Left:* Corot's "The Ferryman"; *right:* Renoir's "On the Terrace."

and making copies of great paintings. The artist toiled for twenty years, enduring illness and poverty, before his work was finally recognized.

Millet's favorite subjects were the peasants and farm scenes he knew from his childhood, when he had spent much of his time at work in the fields with his parents. From memory, without models or scenes before him, Millet depicted the life of the peasants on canvas. He showed them as they sowed and harvested their crops and as they stopped in their work to pay reverent thanks to God. "The Angelus" is one of Millet's best-loved pictures. The peasant and his wife stand with bowed heads as the bells of the Angelus from the distant church summon them to worship. "The Gleaners" and "The Man With the Hoe" are also fine examples of his work.

Jean Corot (kaw-*row*) lived at the same time as Millet. But instead of picturing the sturdy, simple peasants, Corot painted poetic, harmonious landscapes. Today Corot's pictures are found in museums all over the world.

The Impressionists were the first modern painters. Curiously, the discovery of photography in the nineteenth century brought about a revolution in painting. Many artists felt that there was no longer a need to "imitate" nature when a camera could do it much better. Instead of striving for photographic likenesses they developed a new form that conveyed their personal "impressions" of the world. The Impressionists, as these artists were called, were the first modern painters. They wanted particularly to show the effects of different kinds of light.

MILLET'S THE ANGELUS. Standing in silence with bowed heads, the peasant and his wife give thanks to God. Millet's greatness lies in the way he captures the underlying dignity and worth of human life in his portrayals of humble folk.

Among the greatest of the Impressionists was Auguste Renoir (reh-*nwar*). Instead of working in a studio, he painted outdoors in order to study the warm colors of sunlight playing on the flesh of his three sons and of his cook, whom he used as models. Some of his most popular paintings are of mothers with their children or of young Parisians dancing at an outdoor cafe or picnicking near a river. Another of the Impressionists, Edgar Degas (deh-*gah*), used line and light to catch the movements of ballet dancers in action. Henri de Toulouse-Lautrec (too-*looz* low-*trek*), who was strongly influenced by Degas, painted the entertainers in Montmartre cafes with a marvelous sense of their moods and expressions.

Many modern artists consider the subject of a painting less important than the artist's point of view. At the beginning of the twentieth century, certain French artists began to paint according to their individual tastes instead of according to established rules. These artists did not want to represent an actual person or object. Each painter tried to depict his subject as he alone saw it. He hoped that his work would be enjoyed primarily for its color and design.

Vincent van Gogh (kawk) was a Dutchman who did his best work in southern France. To express his emotions effectively, he distorted whatever he painted. He used thick strokes of yellow to show how he felt when he looked at the intense blaze of the sun on a wheat field or at the depressing glare of a light bulb over a billiard table.

Paul Gauguin (go-*gan*) used color not to convey emotion but to please the eye. He left his job and his family to go off to the South Seas in search of strong, exotic colors and bold shapes. Henri Matisse (mah-*tees*) also loved exciting combinations of color. He would simplify the sketch of a woman into a few graceful curved spaces filled in with brilliant scarlet, orange, and blue.

Cezanne and Picasso have influenced other artists. Paul Cezanne (say-*zahn*) has influenced almost all contemporary art. He thought that the Impressionists' emphasis on the effects of light had often blinded them to the shapes of objects. He therefore developed an original style that was characterized by a vivid use of color and an attempt to show depth by shadows and outlines. Cezanne, who had studied the great Italian Renaissance painters (see Chapter 26), tried to unite the best of Impressionism with the best in the art of the past.

Pablo Picasso, a young Spaniard who came to live in Paris shortly after 1900, carried Cezanne's theories much further. Picasso and a friend, Braque (brahk), puzzled over the problem of drawing a solid world on a flat canvas. They analyzed wine bottles, newspapers, and violins into broken cubes. Then they arranged the cubes to show both the side view and top view of the objects at once.

Picasso can paint highly emotional canvases as well as coldly scientific cubist studies. People who look at his huge black and white mural, "Guernica" (ger-*nee*-kuh), cannot help being stirred. It shows the terrifying destruction caused by the Fascist bombing of the small Spanish town of Guernica in the Spanish Civil War (1936–39). Its tortured figures convey, better than any photograph could do, the horrors of modern warfare. Today, in his studio on the Mediterranean coast, he continues to experiment with new styles. The revolution that the French started in painting still goes on.

A PICASSO PORTRAIT. In this painting of a woman seated by a window, the artist has broken the human figure into geometric shapes. We see not only her full profile but the other side of her face.

THE THINKER. The realism of the sculptor Rodin shocked the critics of his day, but he is now recognized as a great artist.

A modern Frenchman became one of the greatest sculptors. As a boy Auguste Rodin (roe-*dan*) was up at six o'clock in the morning to sketch animals. He went to drawing school from eight o'clock to noon. He carried his lunch in his pockets so he could spend the noon hour in the Louvre (*loo*-vr'), the most important museum of art in Paris. He worked as a clerk all afternoon in the shop of an ornament maker. Then he worked at his drawings until late in the evening.

Despite his efforts, however, Rodin worked for years without receiving recognition. Finally, when he was middle-aged, he submitted a statue for an exhibition in Paris. The French government bought his work. From then on his fame

THE ARC VALLEY. Paul Cezanne (1839–1906) dedicated his life to perfecting his art. In the landscape below, he avoided detail and concentrated on the basic elements in nature—the shapes and colors—that would be seen first and remembered longest by the ordinary viewer.

STREET IN TAHITI. Paul Gauguin (1848–1903), at first a banker and a "Sunday painter," left France to seek a new life on this exotic island in the South Seas. Though he did not find the ideal existence he had expected, Gauguin produced his finest paintings in this remote land.

THE TARASCON STAGECOACH. Vincent van Gogh (1853–1890) was an intense and sensitive artist whose emotions finally drove him to madness. His use of colors and his frenzied brush strokes can be seen in this example of his work. In the ten years before he took his own life, van Gogh learned and mastered the techniques of painting for which he is famous today.

grew. Rodin's critics complained that he too often emphasized the ugly features in his figures, but Rodin replied, "Nothing is ugly that has life." At the time of his death in 1917, Rodin had come to be recognized as one of the greatest sculptors in history. A well-known example of his work is "The Thinker," which stands in front of the Pantheon in Paris. There are other fine examples of his sculpture in the Metropolitan Museum of Art in New York City. The Rodin Museum in Philadelphia contains originals or replicas of almost all of Rodin's work.

FRENCH WRITERS HAVE CREATED MASTERPIECES OF IMAGINATION

Hugo and Dumas wrote stirring novels. In drama, the novel, and the short story, French authors have made lasting contributions to the world's literature. There is La Fontaine, whose fables French children know by heart. There are the masters of the short story, Daudet (doe-*deh*) and de Maupassant (moe-pah-*sahn*). Daudet's "The Last Class" and de Maupassant's "The Diamond Necklace" are stories you would especially enjoy reading.

Victor Hugo, the son of one of Napoleon's distinguished generals, was also a great novelist and poet, but he was a fiery patriot as well. When he strongly denounced Louis Napoleon and his attempt to bring back the days of the Empire, Hugo was forced to flee from France. While living in exile, he wrote *Les Miserables* (the unfortunates), one of the great novels of all time. Until he was eighty-three years old Hugo kept on writing. Some of his finest poems were written during his last years. When Hugo died, all France mourned his passing.

You may have read some of the novels of Alexandre Dumas (doo-*mah*). *The Count of Monte Cristo* is the thrilling tale of Edmond Dantes, who escaped after fourteen years from his island prison to take revenge on those who had wronged him. *The Three Musketeers* is the story of three rollicking soldier-adventurers whose motto was "all for one and one for all."

Molière and Rostand were France's greatest playwrights. Two of the most famous of all French dramatists were Jean Molière (maw-*lyair*), who lived in the seventeenth century, and Edmond Rostand (raws-*tahn*), who lived in the nineteenth. Molière is noted for his lively come-

THE THREE MUSKETEERS. In the exciting novel by Dumas, the three great friends fought together for the honor and safety of Louis XIII.

A Sidewalk Cafe. The sidewalk cafes of Paris are gathering places for intellectuals and students.

dies that dramatized the manners and weaknesses of the court and the people. Molière's plays were so popular that Louis XIV often asked him to write special ballets and entertainments for royal festivals. Today many of Molière's plays are read in high school French classes. You may already know *Le Bourgeois Gentilhomme* (the would-be gentleman). When he wrote *Le Malade Imaginaire* (the imaginary invalid), a drama of a man who only imagined he was sick, Molière himself was very ill. In fact, he died only a week after the play was first produced.

Rostand wrote two plays that gained wide popularity in the English-speaking world. Both of them have been produced frequently in this country. *L'Aiglon* (the eaglet) is the unhappy story of Napoleon's son. Early in the twentieth century the immortal French actress, Sarah Bernhardt, and the great French actor, Coquelin (kawk-*lan*), played in *L'Aiglon* in the United States. But Coquelin was even more celebrated as Cyrano in Rostand's *Cyrano de Bergerac* (*see*-rah-no duh ber-zheh-*rahk*). The play has been translated into many languages, and many famous actors have played the part of Cyrano with great enthusiasm and success.

Sartre and Camus find little hope in the modern world. France's decline in power after World War I and her sufferings during World War II caused many of her foremost writers to doubt that civilization was truly making progress. Their doubts are expressed with great force in the writings of Jean-Paul Sartre (*sar*-tr') and Albert Camus (kah-*myoo*), both of whom fought in the Resistance movement against the Germans. (Camus died, at the height of his career, in an automobile accident in 1960.) Each writes of the anxieties and the hopes of man in the modern world.

During World War II Sartre spent his free moments in a Paris cafe, where he wrote plays and books of philosophy to express his disillusionment, just as T. S. Eliot had done in England in the 1920's. One of his best-known plays, *The Flies*, shows the value of courage in the face of great difficulties.

Camus had written comparatively little, but his work is so highly regarded that he received a Nobel Prize in 1957. He is especially noted for a lucid style in which he was able to express very complicated ideas clearly. Like Sartre, Camus believed that modern men must courageously battle against their difficulties no matter how hopeless the odds may seem. The characters in his novels are often caught in impossible situations, as in his famous novel *The Plague*. Here, a doctor is faced with a terrible epidemic. Even though he cannot prevent the plague, the doctor acquires great dignity in Camus' eyes by simply doing the best he can in a hopeless situation.

In their works, both Sartre and Camus express a philosophy known as French *existentialism*. According to this philosophy, of which Sartre was the originator, men must not follow the dictates of society but must carefully choose the kind of life they wish to lead. Existentialism has many followers in France today.

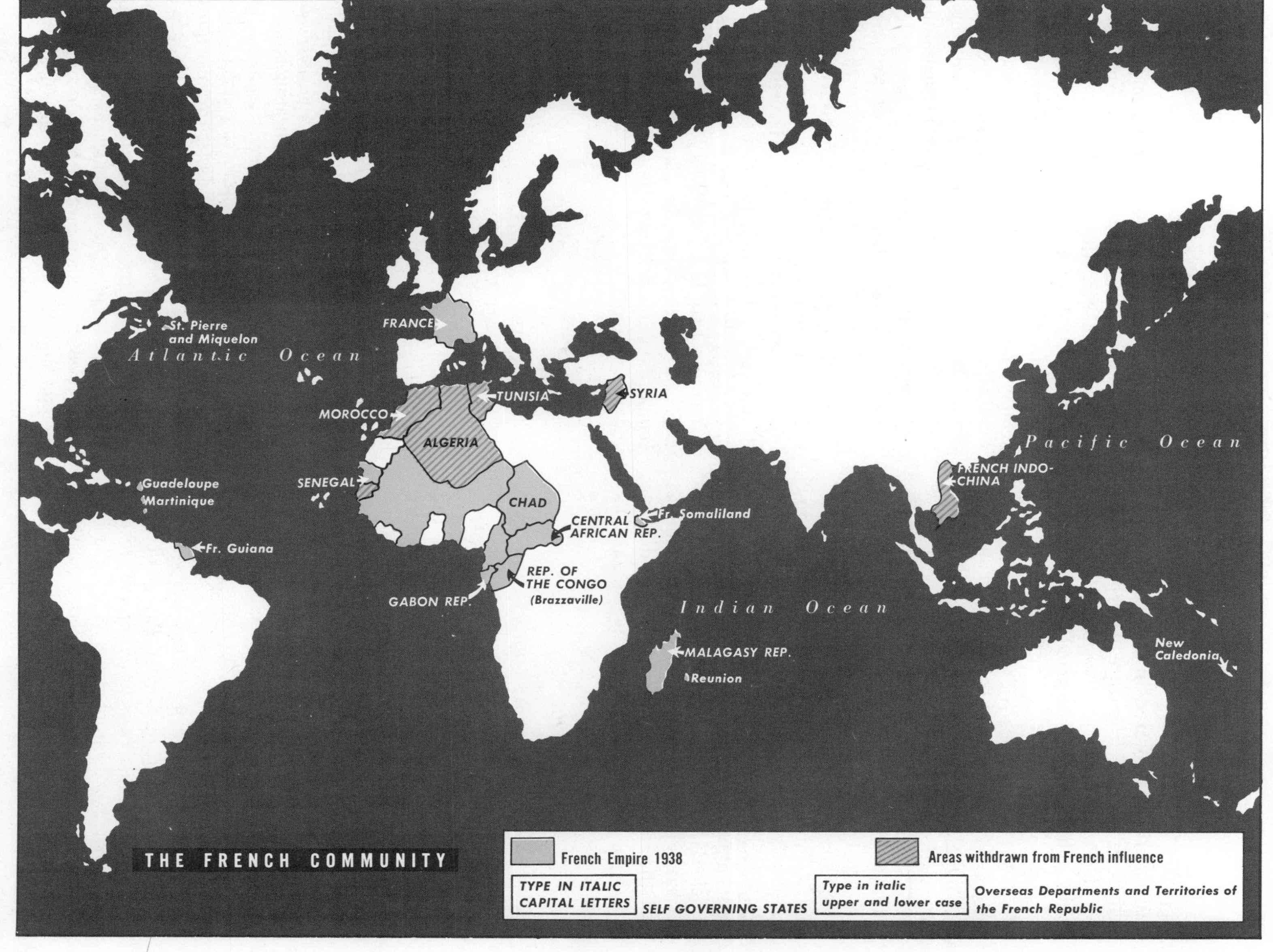

THE FRENCH COMMUNITY
St. Pierre and Miquelon
Atlantic Ocean
FRANCE
MOROCCO
ALGERIA
TUNISIA
SYRIA
SENEGAL
Guadeloupe
Martinique
Fr. Guiana
CHAD
CENTRAL AFRICAN REP.
Fr. Somaliland
REP. OF THE CONGO (Brazzaville)
GABON REP.
Indian Ocean
MALAGASY REP.
Reunion
Pacific Ocean
FRENCH INDO-CHINA
New Caledonia
French Empire 1938
Areas withdrawn from French influence
TYPE IN ITALIC CAPITAL LETTERS
SELF GOVERNING STATES
Type in italic upper and lower case
Overseas Departments and Territories of the French Republic

OPERAS AND SYMPHONIES FLOWED FROM THE PENS OF FRENCH COMPOSERS

Romanticism flowered in French music as well as in art and literature. Hector Berlioz (*ber*-lih-oze) wrote dramatic symphonies, such as *Romeo and Juliet*, which required huge orchestras and choruses. He developed new ways of using the orchestra to give more richness, variety, and volume than had existed in the restrained music of the eighteenth century. George Bizet's (bee-*zeh*) opera *Carmen*, with its violent emotions and strong Spanish flavor, is one of the best examples of romantic music. Frederic Chopin was an outstanding romantic composer. His melodious studies for the piano, which were based on the dances of his native Poland, are full of the romantic's love of sentiment and country.

Claude Debussy (deh-byoo-*see*) brought Impressionism to music, just as modern painters established it on canvas. He mixed musical tones to create images in sound, much as the painters used their colors. His music was intended to awaken the ear to unusual, vibrating effects. Debussy produced such masterpieces of imagination as "Claire de Lune" (moonlight), "La Mer" (the sea), and "L'Après Midi d'un Faun" (the afternoon of a faun). At the same time, his new theories of music led the way for modern Russian composers, such as Stravinsky and Prokofiev, who were working in France. Stravinsky's "Rite of Spring" is like much modern music in its attempt to free the listener entirely from traditional forms of melody, harmony, and rhythm.

Saint-Saëns (san-*sahns*), another modern composer, heard his own symphony performed when he was only sixteen. In addition to his symphonic and operatic works, he composed an amusing and lifelike "Carnival of Animals." He used the instruments of the orchestra to create a lively parade of elephants, kangaroos, cuckoos, swans, and lions.

You may have heard of Ravel's (rah-*vel*) "Bolero." It is one of the best known of French compositions and is frequently played at concerts and on the radio.

FRANCE HAS CONTRIBUTED FAMOUS NAMES TO MODERN SCIENCE

Pasteur discovered how to prevent the spread of many diseases. A nineteenth-century scientist named Louis Pasteur (pahs-*ter*) discovered that many diseases, including hydrophobia (rabies), are caused by tiny germs, or bacteria, which are invisible to the naked eye. He had also learned how to prevent these diseases in animals by injecting them with a serum, or antitoxin, made from the blood of an animal that was already infected with the disease. One day a terrified mother brought to Pasteur her son who had been bitten by a "mad" dog. Pasteur decided to give the boy injections in an attempt to prevent his dying of hydrophobia. When the boy miraculously recovered, Pasteur declared that "one of the great medical facts of the century" had been established. He had proved that many diseases which had been considered incurable could be successfully prevented in man by treating him with antitoxins.

Pasteur did not confine his experiments to the hydrophobia germ alone. He proved that milk and wine soured because of bacteria and that heat could kill the germs. We call this heating process pasteurization, and most milk sold commercially today is pasteurized. In France, Pasteur's discoveries saved the wine industry from serious losses and won him the gratitude of his countrymen. He also found out how to prevent anthrax and cholera, diseases which were killing off large numbers of sheep, cattle, and chickens. Pasteur's great scientific achievements, the discovery of bacteria and founding of preventive medicine, have made his name world-famous.

Pierre and Marie Curie became world-famous scientists. In an abandoned shed connected with one of the buildings at the University of Paris, two scientists set up a chemical laboratory. They were Pierre Curie and his wife, Marie Curie. Life for them was not easy. Pierre taught in the university. Marie also taught and had to care for their home and children as well. But the couple spent every moment they could find in the dusty old laboratory, where they tended their flasks and fires. Madame Curie would stand for hours, stirring a boiling mass with an iron rod. Pierre, with instruments he had constructed, made delicate tests.

The work lasted for years, but the Curies showed the spirit of true scientists. They were on the trail of a secret of nature. They had found that uranium ore was more radioactive than the uranium it contained; that is, that the ore gave off more rays of invisible, electrically charged particles than did pure uranium. Therefore, they reasoned, there must be something else in the ore. For three years they worked with great courage and patience. Finally, in 1898, they discovered that the mysterious ingredient was a new element called *radium.*

Radium is a substance that gives off penetrating rays of astonishing strength. Madame Curie found that radium gave off each hour enough heat to melt its own weight in ice, without seeming to change itself in appearance or effectiveness. It was soon found that radium rays destroyed living tissues when they came in contact with them, much as extreme heat does, but without the accompanying pain. For this reason, radium is very dangerous if one is exposed directly to it. Nevertheless, when used to destroy abnormal tissue growths like cancer, radium can be one of the most valuable tools of medicine.

As the Curies well knew from their difficult laboratory work, radium is scarce. More than five hundred tons of high-grade radium ore are neces-

LOUIS PASTEUR AND MARIE CURIE. Pasteur's discovery of germs led the way to modern preventive medicine. Madame Curie's work in physics and chemistry won her two Nobel prizes.

sary to produce one gram of radium. Its price was therefore high—nearly twenty-five thousand dollars a gram. The high price of radium, however, does not mean that its discoverers became wealthy. Listen to the words of Madame Curie:

> "There were no patents. We were working in the interests of science. Radium was not to enrich anyone. Radium is an element. It belongs to all the people."

Soon after the Curies made their discovery, Pierre was run over by a wagon in the streets of Paris and killed. Madame Curie took his place as professor at the Sorbonne and continued the research with radium. Four years later she was able to isolate the pure metal itself, and she won the Nobel Prize for her achievement. Her work has proved so important in furthering the study of the atom that she is regarded as the greatest woman scientist in history. Finally Marie Curie died a victim of poisoning by the very element she had discovered.

Chapter Check-up

1. How does the French government encourage the arts?
2. Why has Paris been a center for foreign writers, artists and composers?
3. Who are some of France's great writers? For what is each noted?
4. Who is the greatest of French sculptors, and what is the most famous of his works?
5. Who are the best known French Impressionist painters?
6. Which French artists are noted for their abstract paintings?
7. How did photography bring about a revolution in painting?
8. How are we all affected by the work of Louis Pasteur?
9. What was the great discovery of the Curies?

France: SYNOPSIS

The French forged their nation out of an ancestry that included Celts, Romans, Franks, and Normans. Beginning as the homeland of scattered barbarian tribes, France became, by the seventeenth century, a nation in which the king reigned supreme. During the long reign of Louis XIV, the country became the wonder of Europe. Other countries imitated French manners, French dress, and even the French language. The customs of the king's ornate palace at Versailles became the fashion for polite society everywhere on the Continent.

Even as "the Sun King" blazed at his most glorious, however, new ideas were developing in France. French thinkers like Voltaire and Rousseau soon spread the revolutionary argument that the rights of individual men are far more fundamental than the power of a king. The new ideas stirred men to resist tyranny and corruption. The French Revolution showed oppressed peoples everywhere that they too might achieve "liberty, equality, fraternity." France became the model for the revolutionary fever that quickly swept Europe, forcing kings to grant constitutions and to share their powers with legislative assemblies.

The French belief in the right of each man to think for himself and to act freely has had its rewards. It has made Frenchmen tolerant and sympathetic to new ideas. It has made Paris a home for writers and artists who seek recognition for their efforts to achieve something new, to create something uniquely their own. In the climate of freedom of thought, the French creative genius and love of liberty have continued to make the country great.

Ironically, many of France's contemporary problems stem from these same factors. The traditional love of liberty, which was strongly expressed in the Revolution, has made the French fiercely individualistic. Although they have adopted a parliamentary system, they have never been able to make it work as successfully as the English or the Americans have. The many shades of French political opinion have resulted in the formation of so many political parties that responsible government is difficult to achieve. Because of this individualism, governments in France have gone from crisis to crisis since the days of the Revolution. Under de Gaulle France achieved stability, but at the price of virtual one-man rule.

Relations between France and the United States have for the most part been close, and the friendship of the two countries has been important in war and peace. During the two world wars, American troops fought with French soldiers against a common enemy, and United States aid helped France recover from World War II.

Important People

How has each of the following influenced the story of France?

Clovis
Charlemagne
Hugh Capet
Joan of Arc
Richelieu
Marie Antoinette
Louis XIV
Voltaire
Jean Jacques Rousseau
Louis XVI
Maximilian Robespierre
Napoleon Bonaparte
Louis Philippe
Louis Napoleon
Charles de Gaulle
Louis Pasteur
Marie Curie
Victor Hugo
Albert Camus
Auguste Rodin
Paul Cezanne
Auguste Renoir
Claude Debussy

Terms

Be sure that you understand clearly the meaning of each of the following:

coalition
Code of Napoleon
Congress of Vienna
"Declaration of the Rights of Man"
Directory
Estates-General
Hundred Years' War
impressionism
"Marseillaise"
nationalism
Oath of the Tennis Court
pasteurized
radical
Reign of Terror
reparations
Third Estate
Versailles
Vichy government

Questions for Discussion and Review

1. How did each of the following conditions help the French to build a strong nation: (a) location in Europe; (b) mountain barriers, and other natural boundaries; (c) climate, soil, and other resources; (d) navigable rivers.
2. Why did the Estates-General fail to become as strong as Britain's Parliament?
3. What are the meanings and derivations of the terms "left," "right" and "center"?
4. What were the major steps in the rise and fall of Napoleon?

5. Summed up, would you say that the career of Napoleon hurt or helped France? Why?
6. What was the effect of the American and French revolutions on the rest of the world?
7. After reading about the French legislative body and its many political parties, what advantages do you see in the United States' two-party system?
8. Do you think de Gaulle's tendency to bypass France's legislative body and appeal directly to the people by referendum is a wise policy? What are its dangers?
9. Do you think France can maintain a stable government after de Gaulle?
10. What, in your opinion, was France's greatest contribution to the arts and sciences? Why?

Interesting Things to Do

1. Make a map of France showing the bordering lands and seas. Be sure to locate and label the important mountain ranges, rivers, and cities. Include drawings or cut-out pictures to make your map more interesting.
2. Make a chart of the contributions of the French to the fields of art, music, literature, and science. Head the columns as follows: *Name of Person, Field of Work, Contributions or Achievements.*
3. Imagine that you are working for a French travel agency and prepare a travel folder urging Americans to visit France.
4. Make an illustrated time line of the story of France. Use as many original illustrations as possible.
5. Prepare a miniature French art collection, including copies of paintings representing the different schools of art.
6. Give an oral report to the class on "One Day in Paris," telling what you would do and see.
7. Present an informal debate. *Resolved,* that de Gaulle should concentrate more on domestic problems than prestige abroad.
8. Prepare a written or oral book report on Dickens' *A Tale of Two Cities.*
9. Make a notebook copy of the first verse of the French national anthem.
10. Add to or begin your "Who's Who in World History" series by writing one or more brief biographies of important leaders in French history.

Interesting Reading About France

Bragdon, L. J., *Land of Joan of Arc,* Lippincott.
Curie, Eve, *Madame Curie,* Garden City.
Davis, Robert, *France,* Holiday House.
*Davis, William, *Whirlwind,* Macmillan. A novel about the French Revolution.
Ehrlich, Blake, *Resistance: France 1940–1945,* Little, Brown.
Gershoy, Leo, *From Despotism to Revolution, 1763–1789,* Harper & Row. Events leading to the French Revolution.
Guérard, Albert, *France: A Short History,* Norton.
*Komroff, Manuel, *Napoleon,* Messner.
Pickles, Dorothy, *France,* Oxford.
*Vance, Marguerite, *Marie Antoinette,* Dutton.

* Indicates easy reading

* Indicates easy reading

The history of the Low Countries is wedded to the sea. Many of their citizens, like this Dutch sailor, have spent their lives upon it.

Part 11
THE LOW COUNTRIES
HEROIC RESISTANCE TO INVADERS AND THE SEA

THE LOW COUNTRIES

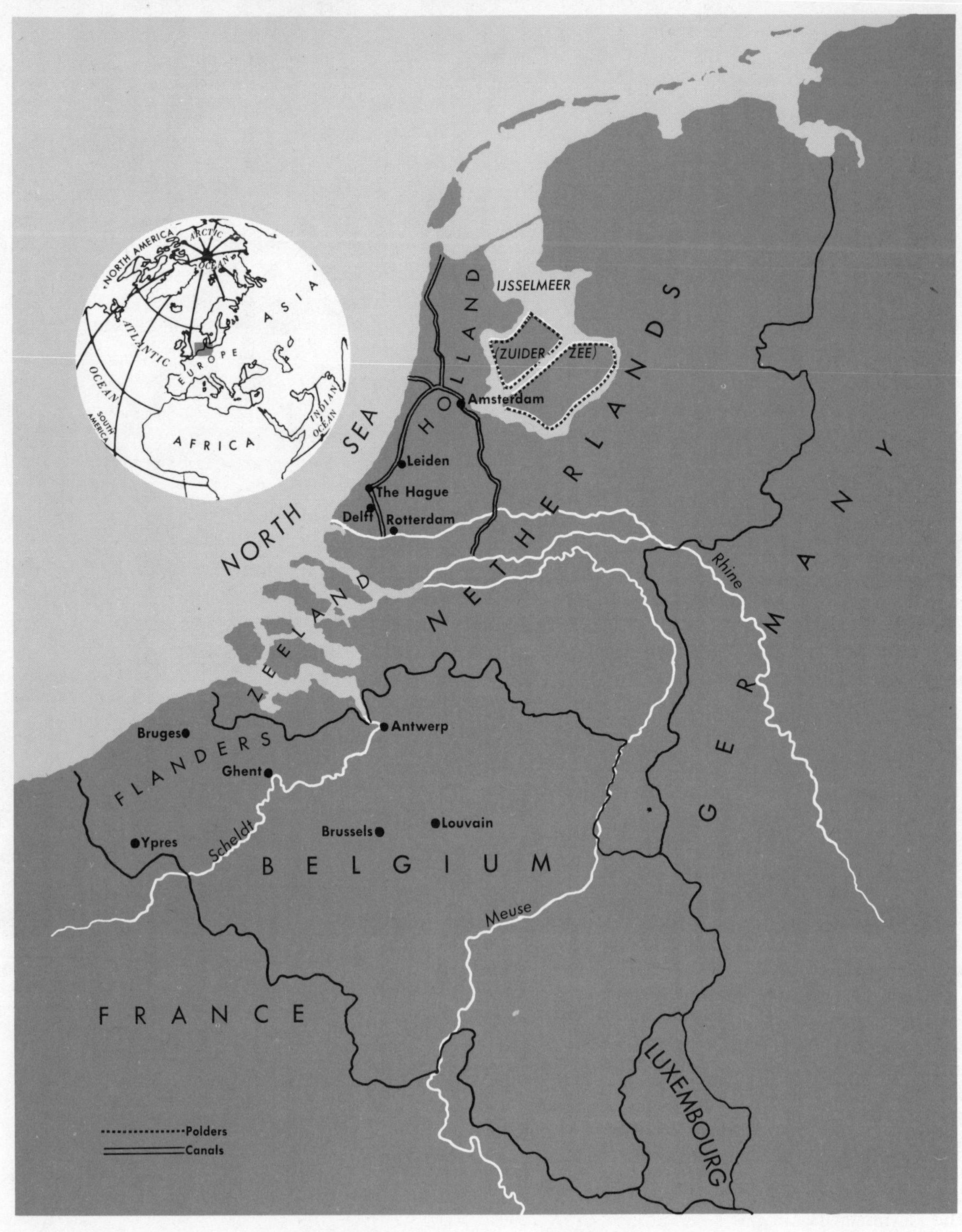

The Low Countries: GEOGRAPHIC SETTING

The Low Countries—Belgium, the Netherlands, and Luxembourg—are wedged between France, Germany, and the North Sea. This location has proved both a blessing and a curse. Since the time of the Romans, three great rivers, the Meuse, the Scheldt (skelt), and the Rhine, have carried into the Low Countries commerce and cultural influence from southern and central Europe. This has made the North Sea harbors of Antwerp, Rotterdam, and Amsterdam among the greatest in the world. On the other hand, the location of the Low Countries on the great plain of northern Europe has again and again made them a prey to invaders. So many battles have been fought there that historians have called it the "cockpit of Europe."

These countries have had to struggle not only against invading armies but also against the invading sea. Dikes, canals, and windmills have for centuries held the waters back. The Dutch have also been draining a large bay, the Zuider Zee (*zy*-der zay), adding nearly a hundred square miles of *polders,* or land reclaimed from the sea, to the Netherlands and providing a living for 200,000 farmers. "God made the sea," the Dutch say with pride. "We made the land."

Crops grow well and dairy farming flourishes in the moderate marine climate of the Low Countries. The Dutch export a great deal of butter, milk, and cheese. Near the coast the sandy soil is excellent for growing vegetables and flowers. Since the sixteenth century, when merchants brought the tulip from Constantinople, the Dutch have grown and sold millions of tulip bulbs.

Because of their location on the sea, the Lowlanders, as the inhabitants of the region are called, have turned to fishing and shipbuilding. Their fishing vessels challenge the stormy North Sea every day, and for hundreds of years the region's shipyards have been among the most important in Europe.

Rich veins of iron and large deposits of coal enable the Lowlanders to manufacture machinery and railroad equipment to sell at home and abroad. The Low Countries also produce textiles, chemicals, and firearms, and Amsterdam and Antwerp are important centers of the diamond-cutting industry.

The Low Countries: PERSPECTIVE

In 1948 a remarkable agreement, called the Benelux Customs Union, came into existence among the three nations that comprise the Low Countries. The agreement not only gave modern Belgium, the Netherlands, and Luxembourg far greater economic power than they had alone, but it also enabled them to rise above many of the age-old differences that had separated them for centuries.

The people of Belgium and Luxembourg are mostly Catholics. The Netherlands has long been considered a Protestant country, but today over forty per cent of her citizens are Catholic. Dutch is the language of the Netherlands. Flemish and French are both spoken in Belgium. And tiny Luxembourg has two official languages, French and German, and a national dialect, Letzeburgesch. Industry thrives in the southern part of the Low Countries, dairy farming and fishing in the north. The Benelux Union (whose name comes from the first letters of each country's name) has united the three nations into a single trading area. In 1957, all three Benelux countries joined with France, West Germany, and Italy to form the European Economic Community, or Common Market.

In today's divided world, unions like Benelux and the Common Market are significant, both as practical solutions to economic problems and as symbols of hope for the future. If, despite differences in religion, language, and economic makeup, various peoples can work successfully together in one part of the world, they might be able to do so in other areas. Thus, in creating Benelux, the people of the Low Countries met their problems as they have for centuries, with patience, energy, and resolve. And in doing so, they pointed the way to future co-operation among nations.

CHAPTER 40

The Peoples of the Low Countries Built Three Separate Nations

FOR CENTURIES THE LOW COUNTRIES WERE PART OF FOREIGN EMPIRES

Caesar conquered the Lowlanders and Charlemagne ruled them. Our first glimpse of the early peoples of the Low Countries comes in the writings of Caesar. While campaigning with his legions in the part of Gaul that is now northern France and Belgium, Caesar met the Belgae, a tribe whose bravery he greatly respected. In describing the various tribes, he wrote, "The fiercest of these are the Belgae." Caesar subdued the Belgae but went no farther into the Low Countries. The Romans kept the Rhine as a wall between themselves and the Franks, who occupied what is now the Netherlands.

After the barbarians defeated the Romans in the fifth century, the Franks steadily gained power in Gaul, and Charlemagne used the Low Countries as a base from which to attack the Saxons. After the break-up of his empire, (see page 174), the northern portion of the Low Countries became part of the German kingdom, and the southern part joined the French kingdom. Even today the Dutch speak a language that resembles German, while many Belgians and Luxembourgers speak French.

Bustling towns grew strong at the crossroads of great rivers. You have already read of the early cities of Italy and their exciting business activities. Cities as rich and busy as those of medieval Italy grew up in the Low Countries. Merchants from all over Europe traveled up the great rivers, the Rhine, the Meuse, and the Scheldt, and came together in the Lowlands to buy and sell their wares. The revival of trade in the eleventh and twelfth centuries brought worldwide traffic in people, goods, and money, all of which found a center in the Low Countries. In time, cities like Bruges, Ghent, and Antwerp in Flanders became highly prosperous.

Bruges took the lead in the manufacture of fine wool. Flemish weavers, known the world over, led the British in the development of the industry for which both countries are famous. Antwerp became the leading port and money market of Europe. The *bourse* (boors), or Merchant's Exchange, was a flourishing market something like the Stock Exchange in New York City today. Huge transactions took place in the great hall, and speculation was a common practice. The

THE NETHERLANDS. Throughout her history the Netherlands has had to protect herself from the sea. Windmills acted as pumps to keep water off land that had been reclaimed. Today electric pumping stations have replaced most of the windmills that once dotted the Dutch landscape.

Merchant's Exchange was later copied in England.

A new way of life and a new middle class grew up in prosperous cities like Bruges, Ghent, and Antwerp. Many of the cities were originally built around forts or castles called *burghs*. The merchants and other members of the middle class were called burghers. They became very influential in the new cities. Burghers banded together in associations, or guilds, to win freedom from the feudal lords who were still trying to rule them. A money economy was fast replacing the old order of feudal services, and since the lords, like the merchants, needed money, the guilds were often able to buy their freedom from the lords. In exchange for money the lords granted the cities charters, or written contracts to guarantee their rights. Then the burghers established their own city governments. The power of the merchant guilds and the prosperity of the middle class were evidenced in the building of great town halls and guild halls, which rivaled the medieval cathedrals in their magnificence.

Philip the Good united the Low Countries. Early in the fifteenth century Duke Philip (called Philip the Good) became the first statesman of the Low Countries. He was the powerful ruler of Burgundy, an area in east-central France opposite Switzerland. Duke Philip brought the separate provinces of the North under his control. The territories that Philip the Good acquired as Duke of Burgundy formed what was virtually an independent state between France and the various German states.

Philip established a colorful court at Brussels, where scholars, poets, and artists gathered and formed a center of civilization that rivaled even the court of the king of France. He took one of the first steps that was to lead eventually to representative government. He called representatives from the different parts of his land to meet in an Estates-General, or legislative assembly. The Estates-General, which continued as part of the government, was the first step toward political unity in the Low Countries.

Charles V ruled the Low Countries as part of the Holy Roman Empire. We have seen in the story of feudalism how land rights were held by certain lords or overlords and were handed down from father to son. By inheritance, a mere duke or a baron might accumulate holdings widespread and strong enough to rival the king, whose territory was built up in much the same way. We must remember that kings at the time were not recognized heads of organized national states. They were supreme overlords of inherited or conquered territories. In order to protect their possessions, royal families allowed their members to marry only into other royal families. Since there were not many ruling families in Europe, a number of them were soon related. A prince might inherit from one or another of his ancestors the right to rule over lands far away from the place of his birth or residence and over peoples to whom he was a stranger.

In the sixteenth century, as a result of intermarriage, the Austrian Hapsburgs dominated the royal families of Europe. Their vast territories were scattered over the whole of the Continent. Hapsburgs had married into other royal families, putting Hapsburg princes, dukes, kings, and princesses

CHARLES V. Charles, who inherited vast domains from his Spanish mother and Austrian father, found governing such an empire more and more difficult as he grew older. He finally abdicated as emperor and spent the last years of his life in a monastery.

practically everywhere. So it happened that a prince born in the Low Countries early in the sixteenth century inherited a patchwork empire from the Hapsburgs and became the most powerful ruler of the century. He was Charles I of Spain, who was also Charles V of the Holy Roman Empire and ruler of the Low Countries, Austria, the German states, Sicily, the kingdom of Spain, Naples, and great territories in the New World. As ruler of many parts of a vast empire, Charles held three titles at the same time: Grand Duke, King, and Holy Roman Emperor. Charles inherited the first two titles from his grandparents. He received the third in 1519 when he was crowned by the Pope.

Charles V wanted to restore religious unity to his empire. Charles V dreamed of achieving a peaceful union of all the peoples under his rule as the emperors of Rome had done twelve centuries earlier. To accomplish this, Charles felt that the most important thing was to keep all the people true to the Roman Catholic faith. He failed to understand the meaning of the Reformation and the determination of the thousands of Luther's followers who gave up the Roman Catholic faith. He considered himself to be a Catholic ruler of a Catholic empire. Unfortunately for him, Charles V came to power too late in history. The Protestant Reformation which Luther started was more powerful and far-reaching than Charles realized. There was very little he could personally do about it but he believed that it was "rank heresy" for anyone to deviate from the Roman Catholic Church. To him these people were rebels for whom even the death penalty was insufficient punishment. In an attempt to stem the rising tide of Protestantism, Charles issued edicts against heretics, but political considerations finally forced him to adopt compromise measures. Among other things, he continued to inflict penalties on heretics but postponed their punishments for long periods.

When Protestantism swept over the northern part of the Lowlands, suffering and death followed, as it did all over Europe in the bloody struggle over religion. Nowadays we consider religious belief to be a person's own business, so it is difficult for us to understand the storm of feeling that raged over religious questions in the sixteenth and seventeenth centuries. There was a death penalty for discussing the Bible or attending secret religious meetings. Violent loyalties divided the people according to their religious beliefs. The southern provinces held on to their Catholic faith and grew further and further away from the northern provinces. More and more northerners were converted to Luther's teachings, or to the even more radical doctrines of John Calvin. Thus the political wedge between the northern and southern provinces, which started at the death of Charlemagne, was increased by religious differences in the Lowlands.

THE NETHERLANDS FOUGHT FOR LIBERTY AND BUILT AN EMPIRE

Philip II continued the war against heresy. Several years before his death, disappointed and tired, Charles gave up trying to control his vast empire. He gave it to his relatives and retired to a monastery. He gave the Spanish and Burgundian parts of the realm to his son, Philip II (1556–98) of Spain.

Philip was even more determined than his father to crush the growing Protestantism. He said, "I would lose all my states to the Pope and a hundred lives if I had them, rather than be lord of heretics." He carried on the war against the Protestants as his father had before him. He, too, failed to understand the strength of their religious beliefs or the political freedom to which they were accustomed in their independent cities.

The people had not rebelled against Charles, for he was a native prince of the Low Countries as well as king of Spain, but they had double reason to resent Philip. He not only persecuted them, but he was a foreigner, a native of Spain, who ruled from Madrid, far away from the patriots of the Lowlands.

Finally, driven by their sufferings, some Protestants started an open rebellion. They broke into churches and destroyed sacred images and works of art. Still Philip could not realize that the uprising was a real threat to his rule. Either they would halt the rebellion, or he would "so waste their land, that neither the natives could live there, nor should any thereafter desire the place for habitation."

True to his word, Philip, in 1567, sent one of the most brutal tyrants in history, the Duke of Alva, to carry out his threats. With the support of thousands of soldiers from Spain, Alva tried to crush the spirit of the rebels. He set up a tribunal that was soon called the Council of Blood, for anyone suspected of taking part in the riots was condemned to death without mercy or justice. Thousands fled the Low Countries in fear of their lives, as other thousands were executed or deprived of their property. Alva himself boasted that he had put eight thousand people to death.

William the Silent and the "Beggars" led the Lowland provinces to freedom. As armed revolt spread right under the nose of the "Spanish fury," the patriots of the Lowlands found their George Washington in the wealthiest prince of the Lowlands, William of Orange. Although he was a fine orator and knew seven languages, he was known as William the Silent because he was a cautious and a patient man who knew when to hold his tongue.

William the Silent understood what was happening, for he had served Charles V as a youthful page and grew up to be a representative to the Council of State. When he first became leader of the newly created patriotic party, William had no more notion of fighting a war for independence than George Washington had at the beginning of our Revolutionary War. He had only two objects. The first was to rid the Lowlands of political tyranny, and the second was to bring religious freedom to his followers. William fought well with the patriots and gained the respect of all

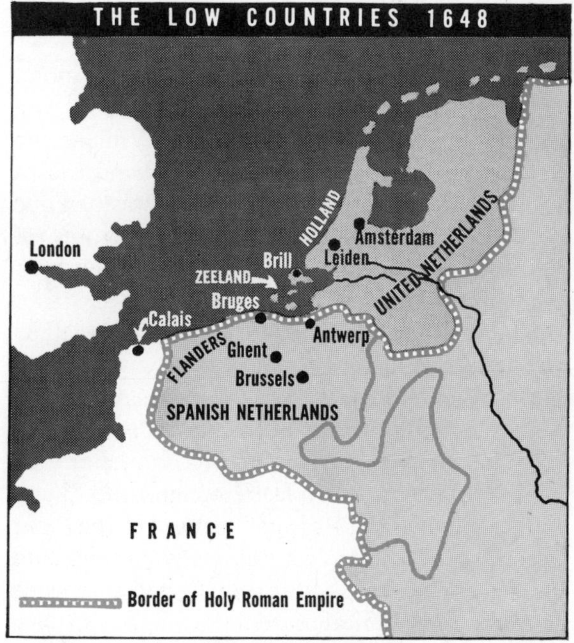

William the Silent. Born of Protestant parents, William was raised to be a Catholic at the insistence of Charles V, but later he became a Calvinist.

classes of people for his courage and wisdom. He won their affection by his tolerance and sympathy. In 1572 the troops, under William the Silent, had taken all the cities of Holland except Amsterdam. (At that time Holland was just one of the northern provinces.) The assembly of Holland met to appoint William as their governor, or *statholder*.

The ill-equipped thousands of men who rallied to support William the Silent were condescendingly called "Beggars" by the Spaniards. But before long the Beggars filled the land with fighting men who were demanding freedom, and even complete independence from foreign rule. Their cry, "Long live the Beggars!" echoed throughout the war-torn land. Not too successful in land combat, they were skillful seamen and succeeded in causing a great deal of trouble at sea for Spanish ships of war and commerce. The sea, in fact, proved the best ally of the patriots.

The most dramatic and exciting incident of the war has become a legend of Dutch daring. Spanish soldiers had kept the city of Leyden surrounded for months. The people of the city were slowly starving to death. Reduced to eating leaves from the trees and sacrificing dogs for food, they stubbornly refused to surrender. Finally William the Silent and his men came to the rescue by cutting the dikes. During the night a high tide and a strong wind swept the sea past gardens, houses, and orchards, over the twenty-two miles to the walls of the city. Boats filled with supplies and soldiers sailed over the crest of the waves to the besieged people. The surprised

Smashing the Images. Inspired by the Reformation, Dutch Protestants are shown in this drawing defiantly smashing the images on a Roman Catholic church.

Spanish soldiers fled in terror. At last the siege was lifted.

William wanted to reward the people of Leyden for their bravery in withstanding the long siege. He offered either to have Leyden freed forever from taxes, or to set up a university there. The decision was left to the people, who chose a university. William then established the University of Leyden, which still stands as a symbol of the suffering the people of Leyden endured to gain freedom of thought and belief.

The seventeen provinces temporarily united against Spain. By this time, the unsuccessful Alva had asked to be withdrawn as governor. His unpaid troops mutinied and swarmed into the rich southern provinces, where they sacked Antwerp and Ghent. Every Lowlander was enraged. Common hatred of Spain drove the seventeen provinces, some of which were Catholic and some Calvinist, to forget their differences. They joined forces under William the Silent. Philip appointed a new governor, Alexander Farnese (far-*nay*-say), Duke of Parma. Farnese, who wanted to make sure that William's dream of a united republic was thoroughly shattered, cleverly used the religious problem to split the provinces wide apart. Then the southern provinces proclaimed their loyalty to the Pope and to Spain. In 1581 the seven northern provinces, which were strongly Calvinist, declared their independence from Spain. They formed a new republic called the United Provinces of the Netherlands, but often referred to simply as Holland. (Holland was the name of the first of the provinces which William liberated.)

FEEDING THE PEOPLE OF LEYDEN. The starving inhabitants of the besieged city joyously welcome the rescuers who arrive on the waves of the flooded dikes. The University of Leyden, founded in 1575, is the oldest university in the Netherlands.

Withdrawal of the Duke of Alva. Returning to Spain to resign, the hated duke and his followers leave Amsterdam as the citizens look on with ill-concealed contempt.

Spain refused, of course, to recognize the new republic. In a desperate attempt to get back the rich territories in the north, Philip hired an assassin to murder William the Silent. Philip believed that without the guidance of William, the newly formed union would fall apart. But once again Philip underestimated the Dutch people. Shocked by William's tragic death, they fought more stubbornly than ever. For the next seventy years Spain tried unsuccessfully to reconquer the northern provinces. England and France, anxious to check Spain's power, sent ships and men to help the Dutch. In 1648, at the close of the Thirty Years War (see page 439), the powers of Europe finally recognized the Dutch Republic as an independent nation. Except for a brief period in the nineteenth century, however, the northern and southern parts of the Low Countries have remained divided.

The Netherlands built an empire and became a leading commercial center. Late in the sixteenth century, the Netherlands became a prosperous and powerful nation. The city of Amsterdam—the heart of the Dutch Empire—became a world center of banking and trade. Cargo ships and fishing vessels sailed in and out of her harbor. The tulip, fishing, and diamond industries sent merchants off to every port in the world. From 1595 to 1602, more than sixty Dutch ships sailed around the tip of South Africa to the East Indies. To protect their interests, Dutch merchants formed one of the world's first great corporations, the East India Company.

The officers of the new company were merchants, but the Dutch government raised the necessary funds to equip the company and supply it with an army and a navy to extend Dutch power in the East. Thus it was actually a government corporation. For twenty years the growing organization fought to gain the East Indies for the Dutch. Although they lost other territories to the Portuguese and then to the English, the merchant-soldiers finally brought the rich islands of the East Indies under Dutch rule. They also established important trading centers in Formosa, India, Ceylon, and Persia. The Netherlands was the only Western nation to trade with Japan.

It was the Dutch East India Company which hired an unknown sea captain, Henry Hudson, to find a northwest passage to China and the Indies. Hudson's explorations gave the Dutch their claim to territory in North America, where he gave his name to the Hudson River and Hudson Bay. Not long afterward, the Dutch organized the West India Company to develop colonies in America and to exploit the still undeveloped wealth across the Atlantic. They built the colony of New Amsterdam on territory claimed by Henry

BURGHERS. Rembrandt's famous painting, "The Syndics of the Drapers' Guild," shows the worthy burghers not entirely in the flattering light they expected when they commissioned the portrait. On close observation each of the subjects is revealed as an individual, with foibles and failings of self-satisfaction and pride.

Hudson. The West India Company sent over one-legged Peter Stuyvesant, the stern governor of old New York (then New Amsterdam). His farm, or *bourie,* was on the site known as the Bowery today.

Other settlements in New York and New Jersey soon followed. The Dutch annexed a Swedish colony in Delaware and established trading posts in the West Indies and South America. Although the British seized the Dutch possessions in North America in 1664, the Netherlands still retains one of its South American colonies, Surinam. (See map on page 400.)

In the seventeenth century the Dutch enjoyed a "Golden Age." As we noted earlier, the prosperous burghers became the controlling in-

THE AMSTERDAM EXCHANGE. This institution was the financial center of sixteenth-century Europe and the predecessor of modern stock exchanges.

fluence in the governments of the various provinces of Holland. They guided the affairs of each province with more authority than the central government had. Although the burghers were strict Calvinists themselves, they had learned a great deal from their suffering and were willing to lend a helping hand to other oppressed peoples. Persecuted Protestants and Jews discovered religious freedom and tolerance for new ideas in the Dutch Republic, and thousands fled to the welcoming provinces. The story of the Pilgrims, who left England in their search for religious freedom, is no doubt an old one to you by now. Surely all American students remember that it was the Dutch who gave hundreds of Pilgrims, or Separatists, shelter in the city of Leyden for eleven years early in the seventeenth century, before they finally set sail for America where they founded the Plymouth Colony.

Just as Protestants and Jews found a haven in the new republic, so students seeking new ideas and the freedom to express them flocked to the universities of the Low Countries. Their achievements helped make Holland the center of the Renaissance in the North. The new-found wealth of the Dutch Republic financed a great cultural revival. As you will see in Chapter 41, Dutch artists and scholars of the seventeenth century made many outstanding contributions to European civilization.

BELGIUM WON HER FREEDOM, BUT THE POWER OF THE LOW COUNTRIES DECLINED

The Dutch Republic could not compete with the rising power of England and France. Part of Holland's amazing success in becoming a great commercial power resulted from the fact that Britain and France, her most serious rivals, were too preoccupied with internal conflicts to offer much competition. By the middle of the seventeenth century, however, strong governments had been established in both France and England. These two nations began to challenge the expansion and commercial supremacy of the Dutch trading empire.

In a brief span of time the Dutch fought five wars which greatly weakened their military and naval power. The worst blow came when the armies of the French Revolution overran the Low Countries in 1795, and Napoleon annexed them to France. During the years when the Dutch were under French rule, the British seized many of their colonies and gradually replaced the Dutch as the chief carriers of the world's trade.

The southern provinces experienced similar defeats. You will remember that when the seven northern provinces declared their independence, the southern provinces of the Low Countries chose to remain loyal to Spain. For years they were governed successively by Spain, Austria, and France. The southern provinces had prospered in manufacturing and commerce too. Their trade, like the Dutch Republic's, was also ruined by competition from England and other powers.

Time Out for a Story. Wearing wooden shoes, crewmen of a canal boat trade stories as they pause in their day's work. Boats are a common sight on the many waterways that crisscross Holland.

THE CITY OF LUXEMBOURG. The City of Luxembourg is the capital of the Grand Duchy of Luxembourg, a country that covers only 999 square miles.

Both the northern and the southern provinces were crushed. The English took over some of their colonies and most of their trade. At the Congress of Vienna in 1815, foreign powers decided the fate of the provinces. France, Prussia, Austria, and England agreed to re-establish the independent Dutch country under a king. To strengthen the new kingdom as a strong buffer state between France and the German states, they tacked on the southern provinces and called the new country the Kingdom of the Netherlands.

Belgium and Luxembourg won their independence. The union proved to be a short-lived one. The Catholic Belgians, more than half of whom spoke French, sharply resented being subjects of a Calvinist, Dutch-speaking king. They had economic grievances as well. Belgium had long been an industrial state; her manufacturers wanted high tariffs to protect the home markets from foreign imports. The agricultural and commercial Dutch, on the other hand, wanted free trade. It was no wonder, then, that the Kingdom of the Netherlands lasted only fifteen years. In 1830 the southern provinces, which felt the surge of nationalism that was sweeping over all Europe, revolted and established the independent Kingdom of Belgium. After some consultation, the great powers agreed to recognize Belgium as a separate nation.

Independence from the Netherlands did not, however, solve all Belgium's problems. Small as she is, Belgium has to struggle with a population divided into two groups: the Flemish, whose language is like Dutch, and the Walloons, who speak French. The Walloons have long controlled the government, and Flemish resentment against them has sometimes threatened to lead to civil war.

Belgium, like many other European states, became the ruler of an empire. In 1885, King Leopold II (1865–1909) became the owner of a huge private estate in central Africa, the Belgian Congo. How the Congo was explored and how it became a Belgian colony and finally gained independence is a story to be told in Part 20.

Like Belgium, Luxembourg resented being subjected to a Dutch king but was too small to dream of staging a successful revolt. In 1867, the great powers recognized Luxembourg's grievances and made her an independent state. Called the Grand Duchy of Luxembourg, the tiny nation, which is only fifty-five miles long and thirty-four miles wide, has its own ruling family and legislature. Luxembourg was ruled by the Grand Duchess Charlotte from 1919 until she retired in 1964 in favor of her son, Prince Jean. This was the longest reign of any living sovereign.

The Low Countries are recovering from the devastation of two World Wars. During both wars the geography of the Low Countries laid them wide open to German armies on their way to France. In World War I the Germans respected the neutrality of the Netherlands, but they swept through Belgium and Luxembourg and entrenched themselves in those unfortunate lands. Torn by four years of struggle between the Allies and the Germans, Belgium suffered more than any other nation involved in the war.

When World War II broke out in 1940 the Low Countries put up a brave resistance, but they were soon overwhelmed by the German army. The people of the Low Countries suffered hunger and imprisonment under the German occupation. When the Allied armies freed them in 1945, they worked hard to recover.

BRUGES. One of the important towns of Belgium during the Middle Ages, Bruges was a busy port and a center of the wool industry. The many canals and the medieval atmosphere make the city a favorite tourist attraction today.

Besides much destruction from the war at home, the Dutch also lost their colonies in the East Indies. These South Pacific islands produced riches in sugar, tin, rubber, coffee, tobacco, cocoa, and spices for the Dutch investment. But the mother-country had not won the loyalty of the people there or given them a part in governing themselves. The native people who resented Dutch rule helped the Japanese to occupy the islands in World War II and rebelled at Dutch attempts to regain the islands after the war. After a costly

GHENT. This historic city is Belgium's second largest port and leading textile center. The sidewalk flower markets shown here are typical of the open-air markets found in most of the cities of Europe. The treaty which ended the War of 1812 between the United States and Great Britain was signed here.

struggle, similar to the French battles in Indochina, the Dutch were forced out. The islands today form an independent nation called Indonesia. The loss of Indonesia was a serious blow to the Dutch who have long been economically dependent on commerce. But they have found new opportunities in the European Common Market.

Belgium also suffered from World War II, but did not lose her rich Congo colony in Africa until 1960. Even since this nation, now called Zair, became independent, Belgium continues good trade relations with it and benefits from its resources of gold, tin, and copper. Belgium's government has also encouraged foreign investment that has made its capital city of Brussels one of the economic centers of the world, including being headquarters of the European Common Market. All this has given the Belgians one of the highest standards of living in Europe. Luxembourg's steel mills and well-cultivated soil have enabled her people to regain much of their former prosperity also.

Chapter Check-up

1. What nations are called the Low Countries?
2. Why have historians often called the Low Countries the "cockpit of Europe"?
3. What are polders? What is their importance in the Netherlands?
4. How did the Low Countries come to belong to Spain, and why did they rebel against Spanish rule?
5. What major problem split the provinces of the Low Countries?
6. What part did William the Silent play in the history of this region?
7. Where did the Dutch establish trading centers and colonies?
8. How and why did the Kingdom of Belgium come into being?
9. How did the Low Countries fare in World Wars I and II?
10. What was the serious economic loss suffered by the Dutch after World War II?
11. Why is Belgium such a prosperous nation today?

CHAPTER 41

The Dutch and the Belgians Have Enriched European Civilization

THE GENIUS OF THE LOW COUNTRIES REACHED ITS GREATEST HEIGHT IN PAINTING

In the sixteenth and seventeenth centuries the increased wealth of the Low Countries helped produce a great flowering of artistic achievement that is called the Northern Renaissance. Rich merchants and bankers of the day tried to add comfort and luxury to their lives. Among other things, they bought beautiful paintings to hang in their houses.

The burghers did not care for pictures of Greek gods and goddesses like those the Italians were turning out. Instead, they wanted pictures of real life—a Flemish landscape, a corner of the kitchen, or a family portrait. They also wanted their pictures to be true to life. They went to a portrait painter as people today go to a photographer. In their efforts to please the burghers, the artists of the Northern Renaissance became famous for the skill with which they painted fine portraits and realistically detailed scenes.

The van Eyck brothers and Breughel gave new inspiration to Flemish painting. The first great period of painting in the Low Countries began in the fifteenth century in Flanders where Jan van Eyck (ike) was court painter to Philip the Good. Jan and his brother Hubert developed a new kind of paint made by mixing ground pigments with oil instead of with egg and glue. With this oil paint, the brothers were able to achieve far more brilliant, long-lasting color than had been possible before. The van Eycks painted not only portraits of merchants but also religious pictures like their famous altarpiece for the Cathedral of Ghent, "The Adoration of the Lamb." They were the first to make their figures look as if they were standing in real light and air instead of against a flat wall. The van Eycks took great pains, as did other Flemish painters of the time, to paint every detail. You can count every petal on the flowers and almost stroke the fur collars worn by the fashionable Dutch merchants.

Pieter Breughel (*broy*-gel) the Elder was often called "Peasant" Breughel. This good-natured artist filled his canvases with peasants going about their daily work in the Flemish countryside. "The Wedding Dance," with its boisterous merrymakers painted in bright scarlets and greens, reveals a

ARNOLFINI AND HIS WIFE. This masterpiece by Jan van Eyck depicts a prosperous Flemish merchant and his wife. The husband's fur-trimmed robe and the furnishings in the room reflect his wealth. Van Eyck's skillful rendering of details—the brass chandelier and the mirror with its ten scenes from the life of Christ—does not detract from the couple who dominate the scene.

REMBRANDT—SELF PORTRAIT. Rembrandt used light and shadow to bring out the important emotional facets in each of his pictures. Many times he used his own face for study. This self-portrait was painted when the artist was no longer a popular portrait painter.

cheerful side of peasant life. Sometimes Breughel used his canvas to protest against the hated Spanish rule. In the "Massacre of the Innocents," Breughel depicts Spanish troops brutally destroying a Flemish village on a bitter winter day.

Rubens created masterpieces for kings. Peter Paul Rubens, probably the greatest of the Flemish painters, was a scholar and world traveler. He spent eight years in Italy, where he became strongly influenced by Venetian painters like Titian. Then, because of his ability to speak many languages, he was sent on government missions to England and Spain. He did a hundred paintings for the King of Spain and a whole series showing the life of the Queen of France.

At home in Antwerp, Rubens built a magnificent house and garden which you can still visit. Commissions poured in so fast that he had to have a studio full of apprentices to fill in the backgrounds of his huge canvases. Some of his more than two thousand paintings are portraits of his beautiful wife and children; some are of religious subjects; others, like "Venus and Adonis," are taken from mythology. All Rubens' work glows with color and moves with figures caught up in a swirl of violent action.

Hals and Vermeer caught the mood and the surroundings of their fellow citizens. The second great period of painting in the Low Countries came in the seventeenth century and centered around Amsterdam, which became very prosperous after the founding of the Dutch Republic. Franz Hals (hahlz), one of the best painters of the Dutch school, spent most of his time in the streets and taverns of Amsterdam, where he loved to study the faces of the barmaids, the singers, and the customers. His swift brush strokes show his wonderful skill at catching the expressions of the Dutch in all their moods. "The Laughing Cavalier" is a portrait of a stout, good-humored young burgher whom Hals might have met at a tavern.

Jan Vermeer (yahn ver-*mair*) worked in quite a different fashion. He lived in the town of Delft, where he devoted countless hours to painting scenes in middle-class Dutch houses. He worked with great patience to achieve almost photographic realism. He was such a painstaking craftsman that he was said to create his oil paintings one drop at a time. In his famous "Serving Girl With a Water Jug" (see page 381) Vermeer transformed a simple scene into a beautiful and polished composition. Like many Dutch painters of his day, he was a master at using soft light to pick out the differing textures of fur, brocade, pottery, glass, and wood. His paintings tell us a great deal about the life of his countrymen in the seventeenth century.

Rembrandt overshadows all the artists of the north. Rembrandt van Rijn (rin) stands in a class by himself. When he was still a young

BREUGHEL'S SUMMER. The sixteenth century artist, Pieter Breughel, painted the common people of his time at work and play. This painting, one of a series representing the seasons, shows a group of peasants resting from their heavy labor and from the heat of the noonday sun. Breughel the Elder is considered the first great modern painter.

man, the Dutch already considered him the greatest artist in the Netherlands. He grew rich on commissions from the wealthy merchants of Amsterdam who wanted to be painted in elegant costumes and flattering poses. He was not satisfied with his early work, however. He began to experiment with light and shadow in order to show strong contrasts and to emphasize what he thought were the important parts of the picture. Soon his style was so much changed that he lost his popularity. The ever-practical burghers who commissioned him to paint the "Night Watch" objected to being seen in obscure half-light, however artistic it might be.

Rembrandt was soon bankrupt. He had to sell his fine house and move to a poor quarter of the city. Having no more commissions, he painted such subjects as his housekeeper, his son Titus, and beggars whom he picked up off the street. Rembrandt continued to turn out hundreds of

THE MERRY COMPANY. Franz Hals, a popular Dutch painter of the seventeenth century, is famous for his realistic but sympathetic studies of everyday life. This scene is typically festive.

VERMEER'S "SERVING GIRL." Vermeer was a master at creating visual reality by the use of light, as can be seen in this painting of a serving girl in a sun-filled room.

paintings, etchings, and drawings until his death in 1669. "The Syndics of the Drapers Guild" and his self-portraits are fine examples of his combination of marvelous technique with a deep sympathy for human beings. These qualities make him one of the world's greatest painters.

The Dutch have produced two men who are outstanding in modern art. Van Gogh (see page 354) was born in the Netherlands, but he did his best work in southern France. Piet Mondrian studied in Paris early in the twentieth century. His works are particularly noted for their vertical and horizontal black lines which form crosses and rectangles and his use of primary colors. His work has had a powerful influence on modern architecture and design. An example of his work is shown at the top of the next page.

LOT AND HIS DAUGHTERS. Peter Paul Rubens, the most influential and successful of the seventeenth century Flemish painters, often depicted scenes from the Bible and mythology. In this famous painting, Lot and his daughters are being led by an angel from the city of Sodom, which the Lord has warned him will be destroyed for its wickedness. Rubens painted mainly for the aristocracy and great ruling families of Europe.

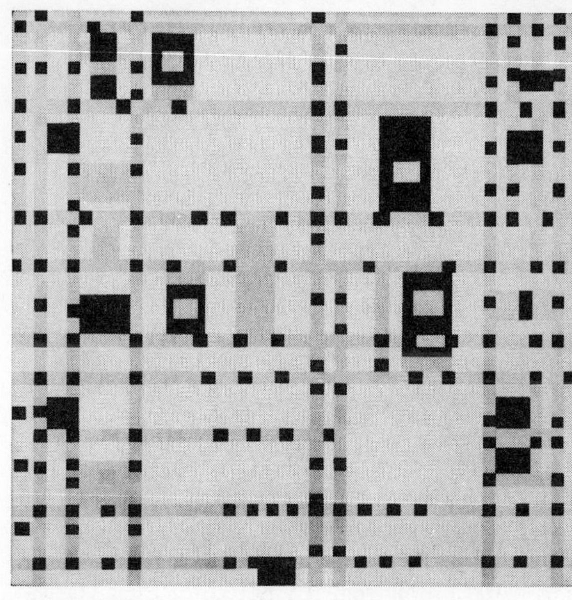

PAINTINGS BY MONDRIAN. *Left:* Composition (1925). *Above:* Broadway Boogie Woogie.

THE DUTCH MADE VALUABLE CONTRIBUTIONS TO SCIENCE AND PHILOSOPHY

Clocks and microscopes were developed by Dutch scientists. Some of the world's oldest, most respected universities are found in the Low Countries. The University of Louvain in Belgium, established in 1426, became a great cultural center which drew students from all over the world. In the following century the University of Leyden was established by William the Silent. Both universities have long been known as centers of truth and freedom. A professor at Leyden developed a device called the Leyden jar, in which static electricity can be stored. This device, which is simply a corked glass jar coated with tin foil, was a simple form of condenser. The Leyden jar is now used only in laboratory experiment, but its discovery made possible radios, X-ray machines, and other electrical instruments.

Every time you look at a clock or at your watch, you should remember that you are indebted for it to a seventeenth-century Dutch mathematician, Christian Huygens (*hoy*-genz). By combining weights, wheels, pulleys, and a swinging pendulum, he so improved the clock that it was possible to keep correct time. He also substituted the coiled spring for weights so that a clock no longer had to stand upright to run. The invention made possible the development of the pocket watch and the modern wristwatch.

Lens grinding was a flourishing industry in the Netherlands, so it was natural that the microscope and the telescope should have been invented by Dutch spectacle makers. In the seventeenth century, Antony von Leeuwenhoek (*lay*-vun-hook) developed an improved microscope which enabled him to make such important discoveries that he became one of the founders of modern biology. He gave the first complete description of red blood cells. He was also the first scientist to see protozoa and bacteria, "little beasties," as he called them in his notes.

Dutch scholars and philosophers made important contributions. The famous Dutch scholar Hugo Grotius (*grow*-shih-us) combined a wide knowledge of the classics, theology, history,

A UNIVERSITY "SWEATROOM." The entrance to this room, where students of Leyden await their examinations, reflects the humor found in students everywhere. The Italian words above the door are taken from Dante's *Inferno*. The motto reads, "Abandon all hope, you who enter here."

law, and politics. He is remembered today chiefly for his writing on law, and is known as the father of international law.

Erasmus (see Chapter 28), "prince of humanists," was born in Rotterdam, although he traveled widely throughout Europe. His attacks on superstition, intolerance, and ignorance mark him as the man who most clearly expresses for us the spirit of the Northern Renaissance.

The writings of Spinoza, a Jewish lens grinder in Amsterdam, marked a milestone in Western philosophy. He believed that everything that exists in nature is part of God and that whatever seems evil to men is really part of a divine plan. Spinoza was not very popular for his beliefs, but he was allowed to go on writing. He was only one of many men who, like the Pilgrims, would no doubt have been imprisoned had they not found freedom of thought in the Netherlands.

LEEUWENHOEK. The inventor of the microscope is shown here with one of the lenses he used to examine cloth in his work as a linen draper.

Chapter Check-up

1. What determined the kind of paintings done by the artists of the Northern Renaissance?
2. Who were the great Flemish painters?
3. Why is Rembrandt considered one of the world's greatest painters?
4. What practical contributions have been made by Dutch scientists?
5. What field of science was made possible by the development of the microscope?
6. Who are the famous philosophers of the Netherlands? For what is each noted?
7. What man most clearly expresses the spirit of the Northern Renaissance? Why?
8. What philosophical idea did Spinoza express?

The Low Countries: SYNOPSIS

The people of the Low Countries have written an inspiring chapter of world history. They have won freedom from ambitious and powerful neighbors and have triumphed over an encroaching sea. Meantime, they have created prosperous nations under democratic governments. The ideal of freedom is deeply rooted in the Low Countries.

The Low Countries first appear in history in the writings of Julius Caesar, who was impressed by the bravery of one of the tribes there, the Belgae. Centuries later, the Low Countries were used as a base by Charlemagne in his encounters with the Saxons. During the Middle Ages, the great cities of this region became bustling centers of commerce, and then, in the seventeenth century, the Netherlands became the hub of a vast empire that included important trading centers in many parts of the world.

The Lowlanders have been ravaged by war twice in the twentieth century, and their experience has taught them that they cannot protect themselves from conflict simply by declaring themselves neutral. For this reason, statesmen of the three countries have enthusiastically encouraged proposals for international co-operation. A decisive step in that direction was the formation of the Benelux Customs Union in 1948. Later the three countries joined the Common Market.

Benelux was one of the first of the moves toward European unity which took place after World War II. It represents a triumph over religious, political, economic, and linguistic differences. If unions such as Benelux and the Common Market prove effective, they may suggest the answer to the problems of other nations in the world. Perhaps someday in the future the major contribution of the Lowlands will prove to be their example of how to attain security and a better way of life through peaceful co-operation.

During the Renaissance the Low Countries were the scene of a great flowering of artistic achievement. While artists of the Italian Renaissance were creating works based on Greek models, those of the Northern Renaissance turned to scenes of everyday life. In the works of such painters as Hals and Vermeer, we get a glimpse of the way people of the seventeenth century actually lived. Another northern painter, Rembrandt, ranks among the most skilled of all time. Dutch scientists have also made important discoveries, and Dutch philosophers have been pioneers in modern thought.

Important People

How has each of the following influenced the story of the Low Countries?

Philip the Good	Henry Hudson	Jan Vermeer
Charles V	Jan van Eyck	Franz Hals
Duke of Alva	Peter Rubens	Spinoza
William the Silent	Rembrandt van Rijn	Christian Huygens
Philip II	Alexander Farnese	Piet Mondrian

Terms

Be sure that you understand clearly the meaning of each of the following:

Beggars	dike	Leyden jar
Benelux	East India Company	polders
bourse	Flemish	*statholder*
burghers	guild	Thirty Years War
Council of Blood	Holland	Walloons

Questions for Discussion and Review

1. In what way has geographic location been both a blessing and a curse to the Low Countries?
2. Show how the Zuider Zee is an example of Dutch industry, patience, and ingenuity?
3. With which of the ancient civilizations might the Dutch be compared? Why?
4. What are some of the major differences between the Belgians and the Dutch?
5. How does the history of the Low Countries show that size is not necessarily a measure of importance?
6. Why do economic wealth and cultural contributions seem to go hand in hand in a nation's history?
7. Which of the Low Countries has the greatest economic problems today? Why?
8. How does the recent history of the Low Countries suggest that in modern warfare there is no place for neutrals?
9. Why have the Low Countries supported Benelux and other proposals for economic cooperation among nations?
10. What differences have tended to divide the people of the Low Countries? What has helped bring them together?

Interesting Things to Do

1. Make a map of northern Europe showing the Low Countries and the surrounding lands and seas. Be sure to locate and label the important rivers, seaports, and cities.
2. Make a raised flour map of the Netherlands, showing how dikes are used to save the land from the seas.
3. Make a model of a windmill used to pump water off the land into the canals in Holland.
4. Organize a panel to discuss the problems of the Benelux countries. Let two panel members present the needs, problems, and proposals of each member country.
5. Give an oral report to the class about the reclamation project on the Zuider Zee.
6. Prepare a written or oral report on Rembrandt van Rijn, including copies and brief explanations of some of his famous paintings.
7. Gather as much information as you can on the Brussels World Fair of 1958. Prepare an illustrated booklet telling of the fair and some of its outstanding features.
8. Investigate one of the important industries of the Netherlands such as diamond-cutting, tulip culture, or cheese-making. Organize your information in written form or give it orally.
9. Imagine that you are traveling in the Low Countries. Write a letter to your classmates telling about the places you have visited and the interesting customs you have observed.
10. Add to or begin your "Who's Who in World History" series by writing brief biographies of one or more of the important leaders of the Low Countries.

Interesting Reading about the Low Countries

*Baker, Nina Brown, *William The Silent*, Vanguard. The Netherlands' struggle against Spanish rule.

*Barnouw, A. J., *The Land of William of Orange*, Lippincott. Geography, history, and culture of the Netherlands.

*De Jong, Dola, *Return To The Level Land*, Scribner. The struggles of a Dutch family to overcome the ravages of World War II.

De Leeuw, A. L., *Year of Promise*, Macmillan. A novel about a young American art student who studies in Holland and lives with a Dutch family.

Dumas, Alexandre, *Black Tulip*, Temple. Adventure tale of William of Orange and his struggle against Louis XIV.

Frank, Anne, *Anne Frank: Diary of a Young Girl*, Doubleday. Journal of a teen-age girl during the German occupation of the Netherlands in World War II.

Lauber, Patricia, *Battle Against the Sea*, Coward-McCann. A description of the Dutch and their endless fight to keep their land free of water with maps and illustrations of Holland.

*Loder, Dorothy, *Land and Peoples of Belgium*, Lippincott. History and everyday life of Belgium.

Peck, Anne M., *Belgium*, Harper & Row.

Wedgewood, C. V., *William the Silent*, Yale. Biography of Holland's founder of independence.

Yaukey, Grace S., *The Low Countries*, Holiday.

* Indicates easy reading

The spirit and nobility of the Spanish is typified by this cabellero during a parade in Madrid.

Part 12
SPAIN AND PORTUGAL
RISE AND FALL OF EMPIRE

THE IBERIAN PENINSULA

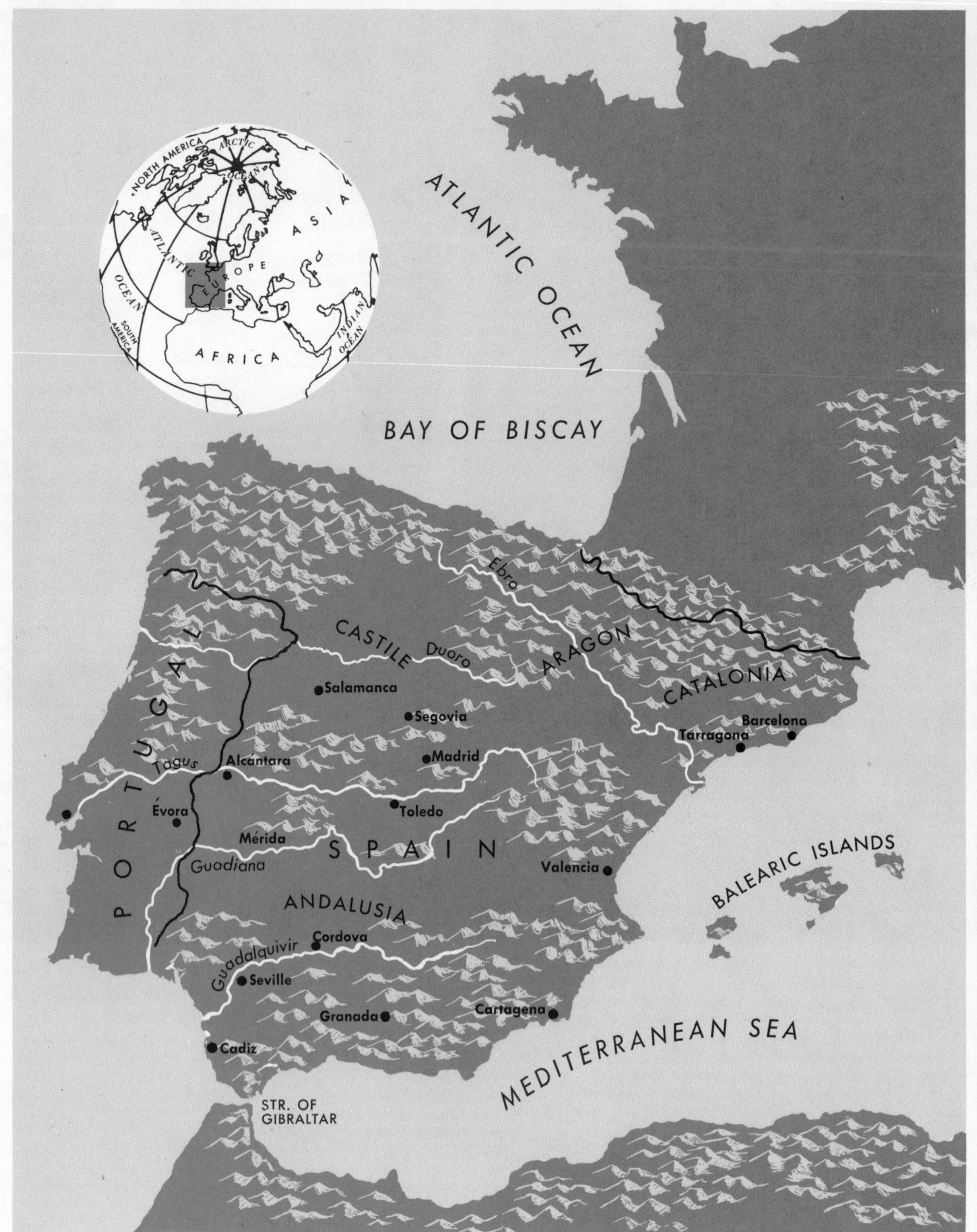

Spain and Portugal: GEOGRAPHIC SETTING

Spain and Portugal together form the Iberian Peninsula, which juts southwestward from Europe between the Atlantic Ocean and Mediterranean Sea. Spain occupies 85 per cent of the area, while Portugal occupies a narrow strip of coastline about the size of Maine.

Though it is joined to the rest of Europe, the peninsula is almost like an island. The Pyrenees Mountains, which rise up to twelve thousand feet, separate Spain from France. On all other sides, the peninsula is surrounded by water. Its most accessible neighbor is Africa, which is only eight and a half miles from Spain across the Strait of Gibraltar. Because North Africa is so near, it has had a great deal to do with the history of both Spain and Portugal.

Variations in climate and land surface divide the Iberian Peninsula itself into three principal areas. The coastal plains of the north and west, which receive ocean winds from the Bay of Biscay and the Atlantic Ocean, are mild and damp. Here, forests and farms cover the land. On the central highlands, the soil is poor except in a few fertile valleys like those of the Ebro (*ay*-bro) and Guadalquivir (gwahd'l-*kwiv*-er) rivers. The rocky southern and eastern coastlines have a mild Mediterranean climate in which oranges, grapes, and olives flourish.

The fact that Spain is divided by mountains has kept her people apart and contributed to the growth of varying customs and traditions. The mountainous terrain has also made it difficult to build roads and railways in Spain. Although most of the inhabitants of the peninsula work in agriculture, the steep hills, the bad soil, and the dry climate prevent them from raising enough to support the growing population. On about a fifth of the land it is impossible to grow anything at all. But the problems of agriculture are partially offset, at least in Spain, by the rich mineral deposits in the Pyrenees and other mountains in the north. The mines in that area yield gold, silver, lead, copper, iron, zinc, mercury, and tungsten. There is very little coal, however, and Spain has lagged far behind the rest of the European nations in developing industries.

Spain and Portugal: PERSPECTIVE

On the dock at Seville, excitement gripped the crowds as they watched the sailors cast off the lines. Amid cheers and farewells, the five sturdy ships under the able command of Ferdinand Magellan started down the Guadalquivir River, their holds bursting with food for 280 crewmen, and their bright pennants whipping in a summer wind. On board the vessels, hopes for a successful voyage ran high. The year was 1519; it was the Age of Exploration; and although the journey was clouded by the threat of disaster, it also held the promise of riches and fame.

Three years later, one of the ships limped back into the Spanish port. Its sails were tattered and its hull was thick with slime and barnacles. Of the eighteen survivors, most were sick from eating sawdust, rats, old hides, and anything else they could substitute for food. That single ship, the "Victoria," and its emaciated crew were all that remained of the gallant expedition.

Although it had been plagued by starvation, mutiny, and desertion, the voyage had been one of the most remarkable triumphs in the history of exploration. The

Spanish ships had ventured where men had never sailed before, and the eighteen remaining sailors had been the first men to sail around the world.

Magellan's perilous voyage was one of many that Spanish and Portuguese adventurers made as they pushed back the horizons of the known world. In this Part you will learn about the successes that for many years kept the two countries among the foremost powers of the globe. You will also read about the later failures that contributed to their decline and hindered their progress as modern nations.

CHAPTER 42

The Peoples of the Iberian Peninsula Formed Two Nations: Spain and Portugal

MANY PEOPLES WERE ATTRACTED TO THE IBERIAN PENINSULA

Phoenicians, Greeks, Celts, and Carthaginians colonized Iberia. Primitive men from Africa crossed the narrow Strait of Gibraltar and settled in the Iberian Peninsula during the Old Stone Age. By 15,000 B.C. Cro-Magnon man had arrived in the peninsula, probably also from Africa. Many of his tools and his wonderful cave paintings have recently been discovered. Through succeeding centuries other peoples entered the peninsula, but who they were and where they came from are mysteries.

In the tenth century B.C. the Phoenicians arrived in search of trade. They founded the city of Cadiz (*kah*-diz) and established colonies on the southern coast. The Phoenicians taught the natives to write, to mine silver and copper, and to preserve fish with salt. Under Phoenician influence, Cadiz became one of the largest and most prosperous cities in the ancient world.

Greek merchants and colonists appeared on the peninsula in the sixth century B.C. They called the natives Iberians and their land Iberia. The Greeks fought with the Phoenicians for trading rights and, like their rivals, did much to spread the civilization of the eastern Mediterranean. Many ruins of Greek temples and statues are still standing. The beautiful "Lady Elche" (*el*-chay) on page 391 was probably the work of an Iberian sculptor, but it shows Greek influence.

While the Phoenicians and Greeks were invading the peninsula from the south and east, the Celts were invading from the Pyrenees in the north. They mixed with the Iberians, especially in the north and west, where they built forts and walled cities. During the same century, Carthaginians came from Africa to help the Phoenicians in their struggle against the Greeks. The Carthaginians gradually took over Cadiz and set out to extend their power over the peninsula. They founded Barcelona and Cartagena (kar-tah-*hay*-nah), which later served as a base for Hannibal.

Roman soldiers and Germanic tribesmen conquered the peninsula. The defeat of Carthage by Rome in the Second Punic War (see page 114) brought Roman armies to Iberia. After a 150-year struggle which ended shortly before the

THE WOMAN OF ELCHE. This piece of stone sculpture, thought by some to represent the Virgin Mary, is one of the earliest examples of Iberian Art.

birth of Jesus, Rome's control over her new province was assured. The Romans called it Hispania, which later became Spain. Hispania became one of the richest as well as one of the most Romanized provinces of the Empire. The Romans imposed their language, laws, education, customs, and religion on the Iberian peoples. In turn, the province of Hispania produced a number of outstanding Latin writers and even two Roman emperors, Trajan and Hadrian.

During the six hundred years that Rome ruled in Spain she left a lasting mark. Even today there are in Spain reminders of Roman civilization: strong stone bridges arching over streams, great aqueducts bringing fresh mountain water into the cities and villages, roads so well built that they have stood for almost two thousand years.

Of particular interest is the Roman aqueduct that brings water to the city of Segovia (seh-*go*-vyah). During the Middle Ages, after the power of Rome had crumbled, the peasants in the neighborhood called the aqueduct *el diablo* (the devil). Not knowing who had built it, they decided that only the magic art of the devil was strong enough to place one massive stone on top of the other with such clever design.

A ROMAN THEATER. Many evidences of Roman rule can be seen in Spain even today. The ruins of this theater are at Mérida in southern Spain.

Both the Spanish and Portugese languages are Romance languages, derived from Latin. The fundamental laws of Spain and Portugal are based on Roman law. Like Italy, the Iberian Peninsula still has an essentially Roman culture. It was the Romans, too, who brought Spain her religion—first her pagan gods and finally Christianity. The Roman Catholic faith has been the principal religion of Spain and her colonies ever since, except during the eight hundred years of Moorish rule when Islam was dominant.

Early in the fifth century, while the Roman Empire was collapsing, Germanic tribes swept over the Pyrenees into Spain. The Vandals (see Chapter 17) settled in southern Spain in the region later called Andalusia (and-duh-*loo*-zhuh). A few years later they crossed the Strait of Gibraltar to Africa. Another German tribe, the Visigoths, arrived in the peninsula and set up a Christian kingdom that lasted for almost three centuries. The kingdom fell only with the onslaught of the Moors from North Africa.

THE MOORS BROUGHT THEIR CIVILIZATION TO SPAIN

The Moors conquered Spain and made it prosperous. At this point in the story of the Iberian Peninsula something happened in Spain which promoted culture and learning, while the other European countries were still living in the Dark Ages. To understand what occurred we must recall the story of Mohammed which you read in Part 6. At the beginning of the seventh century Mohammed gave a new faith to the Arabs who lived on the great Arabian Desert. His followers pushed across northern Africa, taking the Islamic faith with them. Less than a hundred years after Mohammed had given his new religion to the world, one band of his followers, known as the Moors, stood ready to cross the narrow Strait of Gibraltar and carry their religion and civilization into Europe.

THE IBERIAN PENINSULA c. 1200

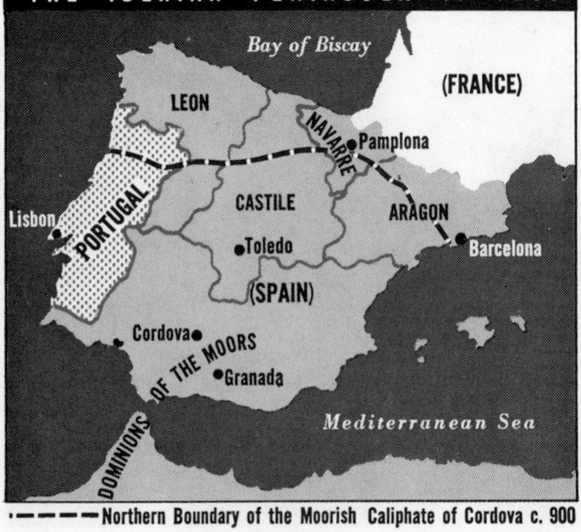

Bay of Biscay
(FRANCE)
LEON
NAVARRE
Pamplona
CASTILE
ARAGON
Lisbon
PORTUGAL
Toledo
Barcelona
(SPAIN)
Cordova
DOMINIONS OF THE MOORS
Granada
Mediterranean Sea

----- Northern Boundary of the Moorish Caliphate of Cordova c. 900

Early in the eighth century the Moors from North Africa made what we would now call an amphibious landing at Gibraltar. The Goths put up a sturdy resistance, but it was useless. Soon nearly all of Spain was overrun by the Moors. Here is a first-hand description of the Moors given by an author who sympathized with the Christian inhabitants of Spain:

> ". . . the reins of their horses were as fire, their faces black as pitch, their eyes shone like burning candles; their horses were swift as leopards and the riders fiercer than a wolf in the sheepfold at night; . . . the noble Goths were broken in an hour, quicker than tongue can tell. Oh, luckless Spain!"

On through Spain marched the victors, over the Pyrenees Mountains and into France. As you read, they were defeated there by Charles Martel at the Battle of Tours in 732, an important date in Europe's history. When the Moors found they could not push their way through France and on into Europe, they returned to settle down in Spain. There they built up a Moorish state that lasted almost eight hundred years. During the eight centuries a remarkable civilization developed in southern Spain.

THE MOSQUE AT CORDOVA. Supported by a thousand stone columns, this great structure was begun in 786 and enlarged in the tenth century when the city was the capital of the Caliphate of Cordova. It has been a Christian cathedral since the thirteenth century.

While the rest of Europe was in darkness and ignorance, Spain benefited from the learning of the Moors. When London, Paris, and other European cities were mere villages, Cordova (kawr-*doe*-vah), the capital of Spain, was a flourishing city with 200,000 houses and more than a million people. A Moorish writer says that after dark one could walk ten miles through Cordova and never pass through a street not lighted by public lamps. During the same years, if a man ventured out after dark in Paris or London, he had to take a lantern to light his way and had to wear high boots to wade through the thick mud that often covered the streets. When other Europeans were dressed in skins of animals and in coarse clothing, the Moors were wearing bright silks, cotton cloth, and fine linens. There were nine hundred bathhouses in Cordova, though plumbing was virtually unknown elsewhere in Western Europe.

The caliph built a comfortable palace. The palace of the caliph, or ruler of the Moors, was far more beautiful and comfortable than any of the castles of the medieval knights. Although rather plain outside, the interior was beautifully finished with highly polished marble. The walls were elaborately carved, and the floors were covered with colorful decorations called mosaics (moe-*zay*-iks). Mosaics are made up of small pieces of colored tile, glass, and stone, carved and fitted together to make patterns. The Moors were masters of mosaic work.

In the palace of the caliph were carved marble columns and fountains. Jets of water played from the fountains. In the winter, soft, hand-woven Persian rugs from the East were spread on the floors. Hot and cold water was piped into the bathrooms even at this early date.

Moorish civilization influenced Spain and Western Europe. Most of the learning of Greece and the ancient Near East was unknown in Europe in the Middle Ages. But the Arabs had come into contact with Greek and Persian civilization and they brought it to Spain. There were many noted scholars, both Arabic and Hebrew, in Moorish Andalusia. They helped to transmit Greek and Oriental culture to the rest of Europe.

Moorish scholars made notable contributions in philosophy, medicine, mathematics, chemistry, astronomy, and botany. They established many schools, including hundreds that were free. The rich could go to private academies and later to

THE ALHAMBRA. The intricacies of Moorish art are shown in the delicate pattern that cover the walls and ceiling of the Hall of Justice in this citadel of the Moorish kings.

universities. There were splendid libraries. In the tenth century the scholarly caliph of Cordova gathered books from all over the world. His library contained nearly a half million volumes.

Christians in northwest Spain and Western Europe marveled at Moorish learning. During the eleventh century, Christian scholars flocked to Spain to study geometry, mechanics, astronomy, philosophy, literature, and medicine—subjects which had previously been almost unknown to them. A French monk probably introduced Arabic numerals to France. The new knowledge from the Moors did much to enrich the civilization of medieval Europe.

The Moors left beautiful buildings in southern Spain, many of which have been preserved: the graceful and lovely Alhambra (al-*ham*-brah) at Granada (grah-*nah*-dah), the thousand-columned Mosque of Cordova, and the colorful palace of Alcázar (al-*kaz*-er), at Seville, to mention only a few.

Moorish life was based on agriculture and good trade. The Moors introduced rice, cotton, peaches, oranges, and lemons into Spain. They also introduced silk culture. They had fine pottery, glazed tiles, silks, brocades, velvet, ornamental leather products, and jewels. Moorish civilization had a tremendous effect not only on Spain but also on the rest of Europe.

THE CHRISTIANS RECONQUERED AND UNITED SPAIN

Christian knights drove the Moors southward. The reconquest of Spain by the Christians took a very long time. Of the several little Christian kingdoms in the North of the Iberian Peninsula, Castile finally became the most powerful. In the latter part of the eleventh century the Castilian king, Alfonso VI, extended his power over Toledo. This meant that most of the northern half of Spain was in Christian hands. His most important vassal and best warrior was the Cid (sid)—an Arabic word for lord or master—Spain's foremost national hero. The Cid was a great soldier, an excellent organizer, and a faithful servant of his sovereign. The Spanish poem *El Cid* tells the story of the Castilian hero. He conquered the great Moorish city of Valencia (vah-*len*-shi-uh). Much later, in the thirteenth century, the king of Castile conquered Seville and Cordova. Afterward the Moors were confined to a small area near the city of Granada.

In the meantime feudal warriors from all over Europe swarmed into Spain to help in the war against the Moors. One French warrior, Henry of Burgundy, received the grant of the fief of Portugal for his services. His son, Alfonso Henriques, in 1139 assumed the title of King of Portugal. Alfonso captured Lisbon. Over the years the Moors were gradually driven southward in Portugal, as they had been in Spain. Portugal remained a separate kingdom for over four hundred years. In 1580 she was taken over by her strong neighbor and remained a part of Spain until 1640.

Social conditions in the peninsula were improving. The history of kings and battles is only part of the story of any nation. The life of the people is of even more importance. And life in the Middle Ages in the Iberian Peninsula gradually improved. Spain and Portugal had relatively prosperous agriculture. They were also engaged in extensive trade and manufacturing. As in the rest of Europe, a middle class in the towns rose to prosperity and power, and the lot of the serfs improved considerably.

The kings often sided with the people and the towns against overbearing feudal nobles, and the towns acquired special charters giving them greater privileges. The Spanish kings needed the support of the middle class in the bitter struggles against the Moors. That may have been one of the reasons representatives of the towns were admitted to the national council as early as the twelfth century—earlier than either England or France had commoners in their national councils.

The great medieval University of Salamanca was founded very early in the thirteenth century. Several other universities were founded slightly later. The early Christian rulers encouraged Christian, Hebrew, and Moslem scholars, poets, and musicians. The Moors were among the best-educated peoples of Europe, and education was gradually improved. Literature flourished; poets wrote epic poems and the spirited ballads in which Spanish literature has always been extraordinarily rich. The people could see simple dramas and religious plays. Religion was an essential part of life in Spain; the government and the Church became more and more united. Religious unity made it easier to gain national political unity.

A marriage made a nation. By the middle of the fifteenth century Castile controlled most of central Spain. Soon the kingdom of Aragón (*ar*-uh-gahn) gained control over all of the eastern part of the peninsula. Then, shortly before Columbus discovered America, another very significant event occurred in Spain; the two Spanish kingdoms of Aragon and Castile were united.

In Castile a young girl, Isabella, had come to the throne. Her beauty and manner were so ap-

SEVILLE. Whitewashed buildings, bright sunlight, and narrow streets are typical of this city in southern Spain. In the distance is the tower of the Cathedral of Seville.

pealing that people thought she would make a good wife for Ferdinand, the handsome young King of Aragon. The advisers of the kingdoms did not have to arrange the match, for the two young people fell in love and were married. It was said, "Never in the annals of courtly marriage was a match so happy and so entirely blessed."

Ferdinand and Isabella proved to be able and determined rulers. Isabella, to force the nobles to recognize her leadership, once had the castles of sixty troublesome barons torn down. Ferdinand was also determined to be complete ruler of his kingdom. "When anything needs to be done," he said, "one head is better than a thousand."

Ferdinand and Isabella tried to unite Spain and to expand their territory abroad as well. Their policy was to have a tremendous effect on the rest of the world. Soon Isabella and Ferdinand became the undisputed rulers of all Spain that was not held by the Moors. Ferdinand wanted to extend his kingdom and increase his power, while Isabella hoped to spread religion through southern Spain. She was a devout Roman Catholic and felt it her duty to fight battles for the Church.

In their zeal for national unity, the Spanish monarchs revived an old institution to put down heresy, or religious beliefs opposed to those of the medieval Church. People with Jewish or Moorish blood who were suspected of not being loyal Christians were the chief victims of the Spanish Inquisition (in-kwih-*zish*'n), as the institution was called. The Inquisition was under the control of the king, who appointed its officers. Thus the Inquisition came to have as much political as religious significance.

THE DEFEAT OF THE MOORS. In 1492 the armies of Ferdinand and Isabella forced the surrender of Granada, the last stronghold of the Moors in Spain. The scene below shows the Moorish ruler riding out to surrender the city.

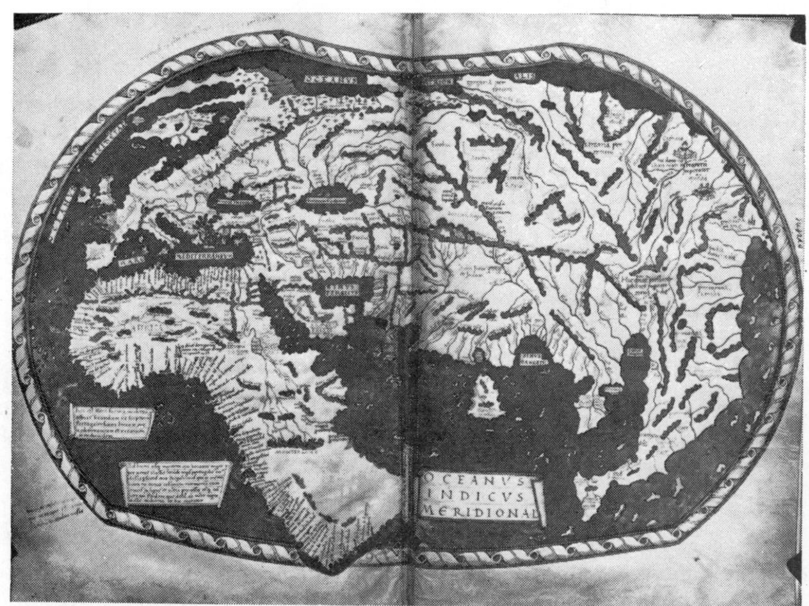

THE WORLD. In 1492 a map of the world did not show either North or South America. Even the existence of these continents was not generally known. In that same year, however, Columbus discovered this New World, and claimed it for Spain, beginning an age of exploration and European colonial expansion.

The Jews and the Moors were expelled from the peninsula. The officials of the Inquisition had no authority to try Jews and Moors who made no pretense of being Christians. The Spanish monarchs, however, believed they could not unify Spain unless all the people belonged to the Church. So in 1492 Jews who would not accept Christianity had to leave Spain. Portugal soon followed suit.

The Jews had entered Spain at a fairly early date. Many of them had become prosperous and some had reached high positions in the government. Most of the Jews were able and industrious. They were the craftsmen and businessmen of Spain. The expulsion of the Jews had much to do with the decline of prosperity in the peninsula. Science, particularly medicine, suffered a great setback, because there were many learned men among the Jews who were forced to leave Portugal.

Meanwhile the combined kingdoms of Aragon and Castile became so strong that the separate Moorish rulers had to pay yearly tribute to Ferdinand and Isabella. The king and queen sent messengers to collect the gold every year. One year, when the tribute collector arrived at Granada, the Moorish ruler told him to tell his king and queen that the mines no longer contained gold but steel. The haughty reply started a war which went on until 1492, when Granada surrendered.

The Moors were given a choice of either becoming Christians or leaving Spain. During the next hundred years nearly three million Moors left Spain for North Africa. They were driven from Portugal too. Driving out the Jews and Moors dealt a heavy blow to Spain and Portugal and retarded their development for many years.

Chapter Check-up

1. What were some of the main groups to invade and colonize or settle the Iberian Peninsula?
2. Iberia and Hispania were names given to this area by what two nations?
3. In what ways did the Romans influence the history of Spain and Portugal?
4. In what specific ways was the Moorish civilization more advanced than that of Christian Europe?
5. Who led the reconquest for the Christians?
6. How did Portugal happen to become a separate kingdom?
7. How did royal marriage help to unite Spain?
8. What was the Spanish Inquisition?
9. What adverse effects did the Inquisition have on Spain and Portugal?

CHAPTER 43

Spain and Portugal Created Great Empires but Experienced a Decline in the Modern World

SPAIN AND PORTUGAL FOUNDED WORLD EMPIRES

A united Spain discovered and explored the New World. When the Moors were conquered, all of Spain was ruled by Spaniards. The kingdom of Isabella and Ferdinand extended from the bleak northern mountains to the warm southern plains. A common purpose—the desire to drive out the Moors—had done much to unite the Spanish people. Spaniards from all parts of the peninsula had fought side by side and rejoiced together when they were victorious. With strong rulers to head the nation and with the people unified as never before, Spain was ready to take a leading place in the world.

The year 1492 marked the beginning of a new era in Spanish history. Not only was the entire Iberian Peninsula reconquered, but it was the year when Columbus, using ships Isabella had furnished, discovered the New World.

You already know that Spain took the lead in exploring the New World. Hundreds of adventurers sailed in ships that were bought by the King of Spain. Other farsighted men sent out expeditions at their own expense. Some went for gold; some to win glory; some to carry the word of God to the New World. But Spain's glory came mainly from the explorers who planted the flag of Spain in all the Americas.

From American history you remember the story of Balboa, who discovered the distant Pacific; of Cortez, who invaded Mexico; of Ponce de León (day lay-*awn*), who searched for the Fountain of Youth; of De Soto, who found the Mississippi. Spanish explorers claimed much of the New World for Spain.

During the sixteenth century quantities of gold flowed into the treasury of Spain from her colonies in America. Spain became the wealthiest nation in Europe. The nobles of Spain, enriched by plunder, ate their food from gold and silver plates. Ladies wore priceless gems and dresses of gold cloth. Wealth brought power, and everywhere the flag of Spain was feared and respected.

The Portuguese established the first overseas empire. The Portuguese started sailing to faraway places considerably earlier than the Spaniards. A guiding spirit was Prince Henry the Navigator, who encouraged explorations in Africa and South America. In the fifteenth century the Portuguese carried on the explorations that Prince Henry had started. They rediscovered and colonized Madeira (mah-*deer*-ah) and the Azores Islands. Diaz rounded the African Cape of Good Hope. In 1498 Vasco da Gama, following the same route, finally anchored in the harbor of Calicut, in western India.

During Portugal's period of discovery, the Pope gave the Portuguese king the title of "Lord of the navigation, conquest, and commerce of Ethiopia, Persia, Arabia, and India." The Portuguese also discovered Java, Siam (now Thailand), part of the China coast, and Japan. Magellan, the first man whose ships sailed around the globe, was a Portuguese, though he was in the service of Spain. In the sixteenth century Alfonso de Albuquerque (al-buh-*kur*-kee) developed Portuguese trade in India and the Indies. Through his efforts, the Portuguese for years were the most important traders in the Far East.

The Portuguese were seeking trade, so they did not go far inland in the countries they discovered. Nevertheless, they gained an extensive foreign empire, which included Brazil, discovered

Cabral. The Portuguese explorer Cabral plants his country's flag on Brazilian soil.

by Alvares Cabral. Later, Brazil became greater than the mother country, and had the largest Portuguese-speaking city in the world, Rio de Janeiro.

Portugal and Spain enjoyed a Golden Age, then rapidly declined. The Golden Age of Portugal, like that of Spain, was in the sixteenth century. Portuguese merchants gained control over the profitable Eastern carrying trade, and set up colonies in India and in the New World. But Portugal's population was too small, and she lacked too many natural resources to keep her leadership. Her trade monopoly was broken by the more powerful English and Dutch. In 1580 the king of Spain inherited the Portuguese throne and united the two countries. It was only sixty years later that Portugal regained her independence.

During the first half of the sixteenth century Spain's ruler was Charles I, who was also called Charles V of the Holy Roman Empire. The most powerful sovereign of his time, he extended Spain's political power in Europe. He inherited the Low Countries, as you read in Part 11. Sardinia, southern Italy, and Austria were ruled by him, and he conquered most of northern Italy. Because Charles V made Spain the center of his empire, all his lands except Austria became, in effect, possessions of Spain. As Emperor of the Holy Roman Empire, Charles V was also the overlord of Germany. He wanted to make himself ruler of all Christendom in the same way Roman emperors had once ruled the known world. He completely ignored the feeling of nationalism that was growing in Western Europe.

Charles also wanted to insure the complete power of one universal church in all the countries he was trying to unite. The Protestant movement, therefore, was a serious blow to his hopes and desires. He was unable to stem the growth of the Protestant faith in Germany. Discouraged, he gave up his imperial duties and retired to a monastery. His industrious son, Philip II, took over the throne of Spain. He inherited all his father's possessions except Austria and the Holy Roman Empire, which went to Charles' brother, Ferdinand.

Philip II was called by the Spaniards the "Prudent," and by his enemies, the "Devil of the South." He tried hard to pursue his father's policies but also failed.

Under Charles V, and later under his son Philip, Spain owned rich colonies in the New World and ruled most of the countries of Western Europe. But she governed poorly. Instead of helping her colonies and territories and winning their loyalty, she overtaxed the people and took their gold for herself.

The English navy and the weather defeated the Spanish Armada. The disaster that overtook the Spanish fleet in 1588 marked the beginning of Spain's decline as a sea power. In that year, as you will recall from reading the story of the English, Philip II sent a fleet of more than a hundred ships and thousands of men against England. He meant

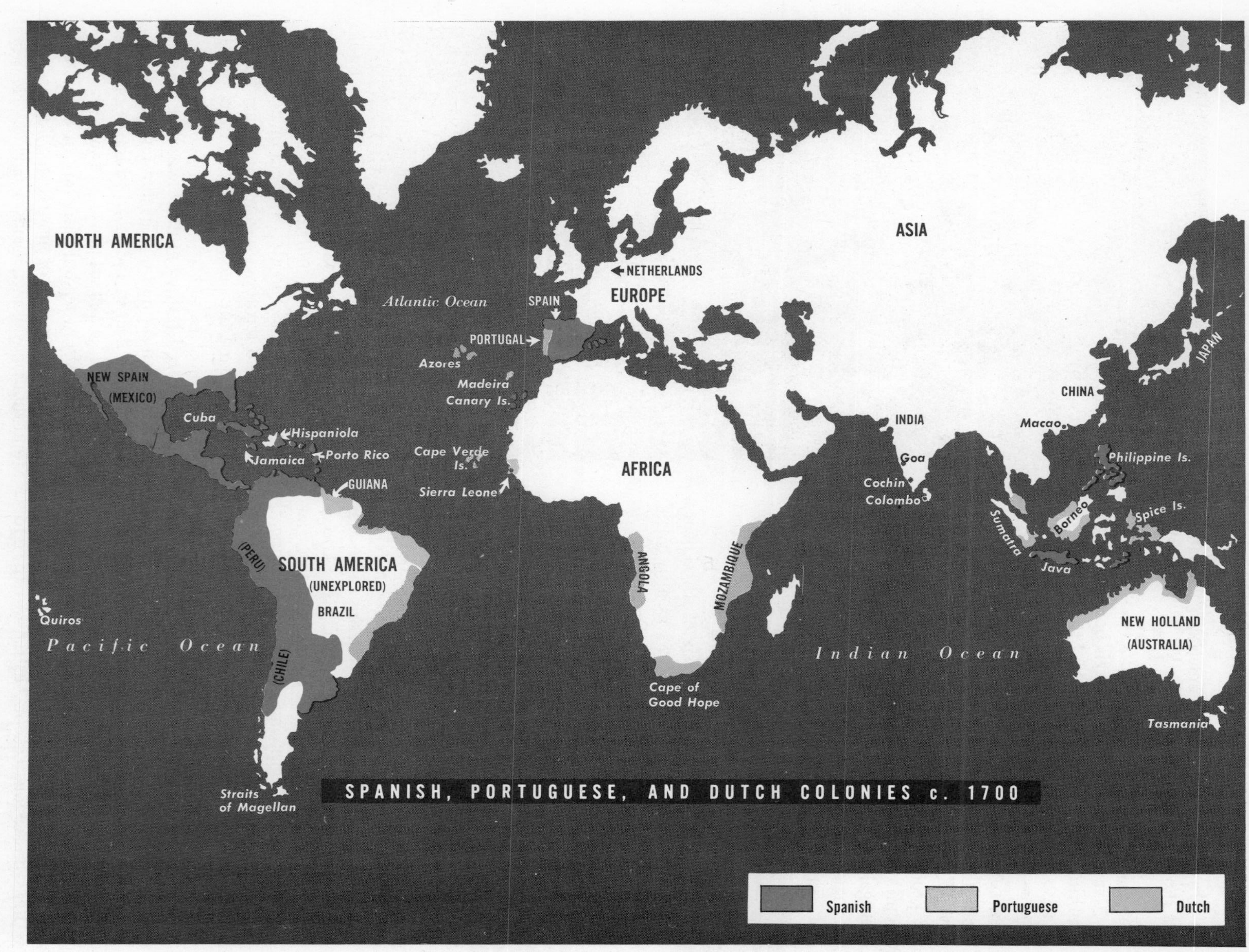

SPANISH, PORTUGUESE, AND DUTCH COLONIES c. 1700

PHILIP II. Philip, who inherited the Spanish throne from his father, Charles V, determined to uphold Roman Catholicism throughout his domain. Deeply religious, he is remembered for the great palace and monastery of the Escorial outside Madrid, whose construction he personally supervised.

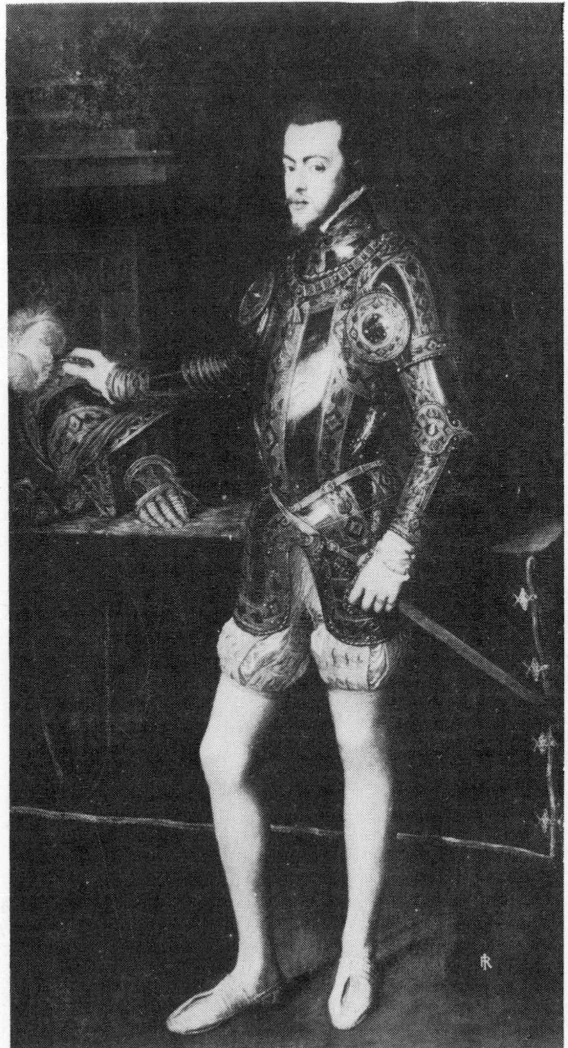

to punish her for helping the people of the Low Countries gain their independence.

The Armada got under way on July 22, 1588, and reached the southern coast of England on July 29. The English fleet slipped out of Plymouth harbor and began an attack of several days running against the Spanish galleons. The English ships were more maneuverable than the lumbering Spanish men-of-war, but their guns were not heavy enough to inflict much damage. The Armada reached the Straits of Dover and anchored off Calais, France. Here it was blockaded by the English fleet and Dutch privateers. In the nights of August 7 and 8 the English sent fire boats toward the Spanish anchorage. The Spanish captains cut their cables and the Spanish fleet drifted eastward, its defensive formation broken. Now the English ships were able to get close enough to inflict serious damage. The Armada fled northward, and was forced to return to Spain by way of the North Sea and the open Atlantic. The Spanish lacked water, food, and provisions for such a long voyage. Many ships were lost in severe storms, or wrecked along the Irish coast. Some fifty-one ships did not reach Spain.

The glory of Spain and Portugal began to fade. During the seventeenth century both Spain and Portugal began to decline. Spain lost her dominant position in Europe and the Spanish monarchy became more despotic at home. In strengthening royal power the Spanish kings revoked many of the freedoms and liberties of the towns. Charles V, for example, vigorously punished cities like Toledo, which dared to fight against him for their rights. The national assembly met less and less frequently. There was no religious liberty. Foreign nations were jealous of Spain's great power and attacked her whenever they could. The foreign wars were so expensive and taxes were so high that people lost their incentive to work. Gold and silver from America seemed to make Spain rich for a time, but the riches caused high prices and were wasted.

Spain and Portugal had laid no firm foundation for wealth in colonies or trade, or for stability at home. Wealth became concentrated in the hands of a few. Court life was extravagant and splendid, much as it was in France before the Revolution. The people became more and more wretched.

In general, Spain and Portugal doomed themselves to downfall and decay by the seventeenth century. They had followed a feudal policy at home. The Church and State in each country had combined to gain wealth and to destroy economic and religious liberties.

But liberty was on the march in the seventeenth and eighteenth centuries. The peoples of other European countries were winning many rights in government, religion, and trade. You will remember that the British during that period beheaded their "divine right" king, wrote their bill of rights, and developed their parliamentary system. The French, suffering under oppression as the Spaniards were, rose in their revolution to demand liberty, equality, and fraternity. The Netherlands threw off Spanish tyranny and developed representative government. All over the Western world the people of many countries were demanding the separation of Church and State and a lessening of royal powers.

In Spain, however, an autocratic government resisted every check on its authority. Furthermore, the Spanish peoples did not develop the vigorous national spirit that new liberty brought to the other peoples of Europe. They lost their foreign trade to England, Holland, and France. The Industrial Revolution scarcely touched life in Spain and Portugal. Both countries lost most of their influence in world affairs.

SPAIN SUFFERED REVOLUTION AND CIVIL WAR

The United States seized the last of Spain's colonies. Early in the nineteenth century many of Spain's colonies, inspired by the American and French revolutions, revolted against the mother country and declared their independence. By 1825 only Cuba, Puerto Rico, and the Philippines remained in Spain's empire.

The Cuban struggle for independence began in 1895. The American press reported sensational stories of Spanish atrocities. People in the United States sympathized with the rebels, but the American government remained neutral. In December 1897, the United States battleship Maine was sent to Havana to protect American interests. In February 1898, the Maine was blown up and sank in Havana Harbor. The cause of the explosion was unknown, but Spain was blamed. The United States declared war in April, and quickly defeated Spain's poorly equipped army and navy. In July, Spain asked for peace. By terms of the peace treaty Cuba won independence, and Puerto Rico and the Philippines were ceded to the United States.

Three powerful groups dominated Spain. In the nineteenth and twentieth centuries Spain was mainly held in the grip of three powerful groups: the large landowners, the clergy, and the army. The land was held by a small number of people: the *grandees* (Spain's high-ranking noblemen) and the wealthy landlords. The peasants did not own the land, but farmed it for the landlords, much as the serfs did in the Middle Ages. While the peasants were not bound to the land as their ancestors had been, they were held in such poverty that they seldom escaped. There were few factories, so they could not find jobs in manufacturing. They had to stay on the land whether they wanted to or not.

The large landowners of Spain were not good managers. While the people went hungry, large estates remained uncultivated. Spain's landlord-and-land problem was a tremendous one. Little was done about it under the monarchy, for the king looked to the wealthy landowners for support.

The greatest landlord in all Spain was the Church, which had become more than a religious institution. It engaged in many activities, the most important of which were publishing, banking, and government. The Church press was the best equipped and most powerful in Spain. The Church was a powerful economic, social, and political force in the life of the country. It has been said that it was stronger than any man, mightier than any grandee, and more powerful than the monarchy or the army.

A third powerful group in Spain was the army. The Spanish army was unique in many ways. Its size was strangely out of proportion to the needs of the country, and its staff of officers was completely out of proportion to the needs of the army. There was one officer for every six to ten men. For years, from two-thirds to three-fourths of the military budget went to pay officers' salaries. Only a small amount was devoted to weapons and to the pay of the men in the ranks. The Spanish army under Alfonso XIII was notoriously inefficient, poorly organized, and badly armed. Yet no other army has ever had a greater influence in the rule of a country. Its officer class resisted change and used its power to keep Spain from becoming a progressive nation.

The combined power of the wealthy landlords, a powerful Church, and the army kept Spain weak and backward. This was the state of affairs at the beginning of the twentieth century when the last Spanish king inherited the throne.

The Spanish republic failed to make democracy work. Alfonso XIII, the last king of Spain, came to the throne at the age of sixteen. He had been brought up to believe it was desirable to keep the wealthy landlords, the priests, and the military caste in their traditional roles of power. Alfonso also firmly believed in the divine right of kings.

In some ways Alfonso was effective. He realized that Spain needed more industries and better education. He wanted the country to try to catch up with her more prosperous neighbors. Under his rule some factories, mines, and other industries developed. He promoted the building of a beautiful university city on the outskirts of Madrid. He encouraged trade and friendship with the South American nations.

Yet underneath this surface progress, trouble was brewing. A series of incidents occurred that Alfonso could not handle successfully. World War I broke out, changing life in every European country. Alfonso, probably guided by a few intellectuals who warned him against military suicide, managed to keep his country out of the war. But he could not escape its consequences. During the war, Spanish industries boomed, but with peace came unemployment, hunger, and unrest. Violent strikes helped to undermine Alfonso's popularity and position. The labor movement was becoming stronger.

Alfonso desperately sought to regain popularity by trying to conquer a section of Morocco in North Africa, but the Spanish army proved hopelessly unfit for the task. Thousands of Spanish

TOLEDO. The city is shown from the opposite bank of the Tagus River, which almost surrounds it. The metalwork and jewelry of Toledo's craftsmen are famous.

KING ALFONSO AND PRIMO DE RIVERA. The king, left, is shown in 1923 with the army general whom he appointed as prime minister and dictator.

soldiers were killed, the treasury was exhausted, and most of the army and its equipment were captured. This military fiasco united all Spain against the king. To save himself, Alfonso allowed General Primo de Rivera (ree-*vay*-rah) to take over the government as dictator. Rivera, with help from the French, who wanted to protect their own colony in Morocco, saved the Moroccan situation from becoming a complete disaster. But he did nothing to solve the economic problems of Spain. The people were angry because he proclaimed military rule. After seven years he was forced to resign. The next year, 1931, the parties of the Left won the majority of seats in the national assembly. At their request, Alfonso left the country, ending the rule of the Bourbons which had begun in 1700. The assembly proclaimed the Republic of Spain.

For the first time, the new middle class and workers had a chance to influence the government. They wrote a liberal constitution which included the reforms they had wanted for so long, including the renunciation of war. But the reformers had little chance of success without the support of the landowners, the army, and the Church. The terms of the constitution made that support impossible. The landowners were opposed because their estates were being broken up and redistributed to the peasants. The army officers were opposed because the constitution made them subject to political leaders elected by the people. The Church was opposed because the State took over all Church property, although the clergy was left in charge. The State outlawed all religious orders and forbade the Church to maintain schools. The result was that the republic depended on the support of the small middle class, some hungry workers, and the mass of impoverished peasants.

The republic was doomed to failure. The parties of the Left quarreled among themselves. Their reforms were not enough to please those on the extreme left. There was a general strike in Barcelona and an uprising of the miners in the north. Churches and monasteries were burned. The parties of the Right, supported by the landowners, the army and the Church, were terrified by the ways in which the parties of the Left were using their power. In July, 1936, the army staged an uprising that quickly spread through the country. Spain was plunged into civil war.

The Spanish Civil War was a testing ground for World War II. Spain was divided into two opposing camps. Members of the parties of the Left, which supported the republic, were called Loyalists. Members of the parties of the Right, who wanted to overthrow the republic and restore the monarchy, were called Rebels or Nationalists. An army general, Francisco Franco, led the attack on the republic. Both sides committed acts of cruelty and savage violence.

The other nations of Europe looked on in horror. France and England, which were anxious at all costs that the war should not spread, persuaded twenty-five nations not to take sides. But Germany and Italy intervened when Franco asked them for help. Hitler and Mussolini saw the Spanish Civil War as an excellent chance to test new weapons and techniques of warfare. Mussolini sent over fifty thousand troops. Hitler sent several thousand trained pilots who bombed and strafed the civilian population of the Loyalist-held cities. England and France, unable or unwilling to recognize the attack upon democracy that motivated the intervention of Germany and Italy, continued to refuse aid to the Loyalists. Communists became stronger in the Republican government, and the Loyalists accepted help from the Soviet Union. The Russian government sent tanks, guns, and military advisers. This Communist support, and the growing Marxist influence, among the Royalists furnished Franco and the Nationalists with a rallying cry. It also won them the backing of some moderate elements in the Loyalist-held territory. When one of Franco's generals attacked Madrid, he boasted that he had four columns of troops marching on the city and a fifth column working for him inside the city. That boast was the origin of the term *fifth column,* which means people who secretly work in support of an enemy during war.

Franco rules Spain. After three years of bitter fighting and destruction that was to cripple Spain for years to come, the Spanish Civil War ended in victory for General Franco and the Nationalists. Franco set up a dictatorship backed by the parties of the Right. Although Spain declared neutrality in World War II, Franco openly aided Germany against Russia.

After World War II, Western Allied leaders hoped to see Franco's government replaced by a democracy. But as their fear of Soviet expansion increased, their disapproval of the strongly anti-

SPANISH CIVIL WAR. The marked anxiety of these people during an air raid on Barcelona is captured by the famed photographer, Robert Capa. The Spanish people have not forgotten the destruction and cruelty of the Civil War.

Communist Franco decreased. In return for acceptance of him and financial aid, Franco allowed construction of NATO air bases in Spain.

By a Law of Succession passed in 1947, Spain was confirmed as a kingdom, with Franco acting as head of state. He has named Prince Juan Carlos, grandson of the last king, as his successor. If he succeeds, he will be a constitutional monarch because of the 1966 constitution which also somewhat limited Franco's dictatorship.

Though Spain suffered terribly from her civil war and has been kept out of the European Common Market by the anti-Franco feelings of its members, she has begun to share in general European prosperity through a great tourist trade. But it is only a beginning and many problems remain including an unfavorable balance of trade and questions about the government after Franco.

Portugal under a loosening dictatorship. Since 1910 Portugal has been a republic. Her modern history has been much like Spain's, but with less violence. Portugal's once worldwide empire has shrunk. Brazil became independent peacefully in

FRANCO. Head of the Falange Party, Franco has been dictator of Spain since 1939. Recently he has become friendlier to the democracies.

CAETANO. Prime Minister Caetano, successor of Salazar is shown receiving Portugese troops in Angola, Portugese West Africa.

1822 and the last Indian territories were lost in 1961. The large African territories of Angola and Mozambique are left, but these present the problem of native uprisings which Portugal has tried to meet by declaring them provinces of the mother country with equal rights and by spending large sums from her poor economy on a military force there.

Portugal was inactive in the World Wars except for granting bases in the Azores to the Allies. Poverty and unemployment in the years between the wars led to the establishment of an authoritarian government under the economist Antonio de Oliveira Salazar as prime minister. Salazar stabilized the economy while ruling as a virtual dictator until his retirement in 1968. Since then his successor, Marcello Caetano, has made some steps toward liberalizing Portuguese life.

Chapter Check-up

1. Why did 1492 mark the beginning of a new era in the history of the Iberian Peninsula?
2. How did little Portugal become wealthy and powerful?
3. How did the great wealth Spain obtained from her colonies help bring about her downfall?
4. Who were Spain's leaders during that country's Golden Age?
5. How did Spain's kings weaken her economy?
6. How and to whom did Spain lose the last of her empire?
7. Which three groups have continued to dominate Spanish life?
8. In what ways was the Spanish Civil War a testing ground for World War II?
9. What Nationalist leader now rules Spain?
10. How and by whom is Portugal ruled today?

Chapter 44

The Spanish and Portuguese Developed a Colorful Literature and Art

THE MUSIC AND ARCHITECTURE OF THE IBERIAN PEOPLES IS UNIQUE

Traditional songs and dances have been preserved. The people of Spain and Portugal have expressed themselves in many forms of art. Their love of beauty shows itself in the so-called minor arts—weaving, ceramics, carving, ironwork, lace-making—as well as in architecture, painting, and literature. They have brilliantly expressed their joy of life in music and dancing.

Folk songs and dances have often been replaced elsewhere in Europe by television, movies, and radio, but in Spain these traditional forms of entertainment still survive. Andalusia is the home of the fiery dance called the Flamenco, which is performed to the clicking of castanets, small pieces of hard wood or ivory that are usually played by the dancers themselves. The Flamenco, which begins slowly and becomes progressively faster and more deliberate in tempo, is the Spanish dance most frequently seen abroad, but other districts of Spain have their distinctive dances as well.

In Spain the great holidays, called fiestas, continue to be held on the holy days of the Catholic Church. Virtually everyone closes his shop or leaves the fields to take part in the pageants and parades. Before Easter, long, solemn processions of barefoot men with lighted candles wind through

ANDRÉS SEGOVIA. The concerts and recordings of the guitarist Segovia have made his country's music familiar and appreciated throughout the world.

the streets. On gay holidays, such as Carnival before Lent, men and women deck themselves in their traditional costumes. Most women wear high combs draped with lace mantillas (man-*til*-uz), or shawls, and usually dress in black. Women in Andalusia, however, wear wide skirts in bright colors. People dance in the street to the music of the guitar, Spain's traditional instrument. Those who have heard the guitar only as a minor part of a dance band may not realize its musical capabilities as a solo instrument in Spanish music. The most renowned guitarist today is Andrés Segovia (say-*go*-vyah), whose concerts and recordings have made him popular throughout the world.

Spanish architecture reveals both Moorish and classic influence. Spain's contribution to architecture is as unique as her music and her national dances. The two characteristic features of the Spanish house are the patio, around which the house is built, and the plain walls with small windows on the front or street side. The patio, or open court, is the living room of the Spanish home. It is surrounded on three or four sides by rooms that open into it and by arcaded walls and projecting balconies. Spanish houses are designed for coolness and for protection from the hot sun.

The Alhambra, which is an ancient palace and fortress in southern Spain, is an outstanding example of Moorish architecture. The Moorish rulers of Granada built it nearly seven centuries ago. Although much of the old palace was destroyed, the parts that remain and have been restored are enough to give an idea of its grandeur. The Alhambra is a beautiful building, built about many courts, or patios. The walls are lace-like and the ceiling suggests a starlit sky. The fountains and trees in the courtyards give an impression of coolness and freshness. Pointed or horseshoe-shaped arches, often carved to look like honeycombs, frame the view from the courtyard to the rooms beyond. Such arches, when used between columns in a room, enable them to support a heavy vaulted ceiling. The walls of the Alhambra are covered with lacy geometric decorations carved in plaster or marble.

The plain white plaster walls are brilliantly contrasted with the doors and windows which are edged in red, blue, and gold tile. In the strong sun or in moonlight, the beauty of the Alhambra is overwhelming. (A picture of the Alhambra's interior is shown on page 394.)

On their return from Italy, Spanish merchants introduced the classic style of Renaissance architecture into Spain. But the Spaniards' love of rich decoration caused them to abandon the balance and restraint of the traditional classic style. They twisted the straight classic columns, cut recesses in the walls, and heaped intricately carved decorations around doors and windows. Elaborate wrought iron balconies protected the windows. The roofs were usually of slate or brightly colored tile. Spanish conquerors brought this modified classic style, called *baroque* (bah-*roke*), to the New World. In California, New Mexico, and Latin America you can see many stucco houses with red tiled roofs, wrought iron balconies, and patios in the Spanish manner.

CERVANTES AND CAMOËNS HAVE PRODUCED MASTERPIECES OF LITERATURE

Spanish literature clearly reflects the life and character of the Spanish people. It is individualistic, showing a keen sense of reality, a thirst for adventure, and the vision of an ideal. It may be grave or gay, mild or violent, like the Spaniards.

We have already read about the poem *The Cid* which recounts the bold and chivalrous acts of Spain's greatest warrior. Other early ballads, written in a direct, vigorous style, also reveal the daring and warlike character of the Spaniards. The Spanish novels of chivalry, of which the greatest is *Amadis de Gaula* (ah-mah-*dees* day *gow*-lah), are romantic adventures, much like the stories of King Arthur and the Knights of the Round Table.

If you had to pick just one book from all Spain's rich literature, your choice should certainly be the famous novel *Don Quixote* (kee-*ho*-tay). Its author, Miguel de Cervantes (ther-*vahn*-tays), was the greatest writer of Spain's Golden Age. Cervantes was a poor nobleman who fought the Moors and was imprisoned by them. His novel not only gives a wonderful picture of sixteenth-century Spain, but it also shows the author's wise and witty understanding of human nature.

The hero of his novel, Don Quixote, is a brave but foolish knight who seeks to live according to the medieval ideal of chivalry. (The word *quixotic*, which comes from the novel, means idealistic

COURT OF THE LIONS. This courtyard at Granada, Spain is named for the stone lions that encircle the fountain. It is found in the Alhambra, a palace and fortress built by the Moors between 1248 and 1354.

but impractical.) In Cervantes' story, Don Quixote is an old man, too poor to be able to afford a knight's equipment. In his search for romance and adventure, Don Quixote is forever "riding furiously in all directions" on his weary, half-starved horse, Rosinante. He is famous for attacking windmills which he mistakes for dragons. Don Quixote is a symbol of the hero and the fool in every man. His squire, Sancho Panza, a loyal, sensible fellow, does not understand his master but does his best to keep him out of trouble. Sancho represents the practical side of human nature.

Portugal, too, has her ballads and chivalrous tales. She also has a native lyric poetry and was the first section of the peninsula to produce sophisticated troubadour poems. Several thousands of them survive. The greatest masterpiece of Portuguese literature was written in the sixteenth century. It is *The Lusiads*, an epic poem about the life of the great adventurer, Vasco da Gama. The author was a sturdy soldier, Luiz de Camoëns (*kam*-oh-enz), who was exiled from court and sent to India along the route taken by da Gama. In writing *The Lusiads*, Camoëns employs a vigorous but dignified style. His famous poem captures the drama and heroic spirit that inspired Portuguese adventurers and explorers during Portugal's golden age.

Don Quixote and Sancho Panza. In this illustration from Cervantes' famous novel, Don Quixote, in search of romance and adventure, has just lost a battle with a windmill that he mistook for an enemy knight.

SPANISH ARTISTS ARE HIGHLY REGARDED

El Greco, Velásquez, and Goya were Spain's greatest painters. Painting became important in Spain in the sixteenth century, when Charles I and Philip II invited Italian artists to Spain, and Spaniards, in turn, went to study in Italy. Because only the Church and the nobility could afford works of art, Spanish artists usually painted religious subjects or portraits of important churchmen and nobles.

One of the most famous painters of Spain's Golden Age was El Greco (*grek*-oh), which means "the Greek." He was so called because he was born on the island of Crete. El Greco's religious devotion influenced all his work. His paintings are amazing in structure and balance, and they show El Greco's desire to go beyond realism into spiritual interpretation. His figures are frequently elongated, or stretched out, as if they were being swept up toward heaven. Often they are bathed in cold white light, and their large dark eyes seem to be gazing at visions of another world. El Greco used gleaming highlights and dramatic dark shadows to create a gloomy and mysterious effect. "The Assumption of the Virgin" is a good example. In "Toledo in Storm" (see page 412), even the brooding clouds of this unusual landscape seem to have a spiritual quality. El Greco's work has influenced many artists.

"The Maids of Honor." The king and queen, faintly visible in the mirror, are looking into the room where the court painter Velásquez works on a canvas.

Another of Spain's great painters is Diego Velásquez (vay-*lath*-kayth) of Seville. As official court painter during the seventeenth century, he painted many portraits of the royal family. One of Velásquez' most famous portraits is of the charming Prince Balthasar. Velasquez also painted the vain and haughty aristocracy. In these paintings the nobles are often depicted with an unreal, almost comic seriousness, as if the artist sensed the decline of the Golden Age. Velásquez was interested in the effect of color and light on his subjects. He skillfully used dashes of brilliant color contrasted with cool gray to show the thick embroidery, heavy silks, and rich velvet worn in his day.

Francisco Goya (*go*-yah) became court painter in the late eighteenth century. He painted many delicate and tender portraits of women and children. His smooth, gay colors and his charming scenes of court life made him very popular. After Napoleon's invasion of Spain, Goya's style changed. In his series of etchings known as "The Horrors of War," he used stark black and white and extremely realistic detail to show the frightful effects of war on human life.

Today many of Spain's artists live in exile. Because many painters, musicians, and writers were Loyalist sympathizers, they preferred to leave Spain rather than live under the Fascist dictatorship of Franco. Pablo Picasso, who has exerted a wide influence on modern art, is one of several important Spanish painters who live in France. He painted the mural "Guernica" (ger-*nee*-kah) to express his horror at the bombing of defenseless towns by German pilots in the Spanish Civil War. Pablo Casals (kah-*sahls*), who is considered to be

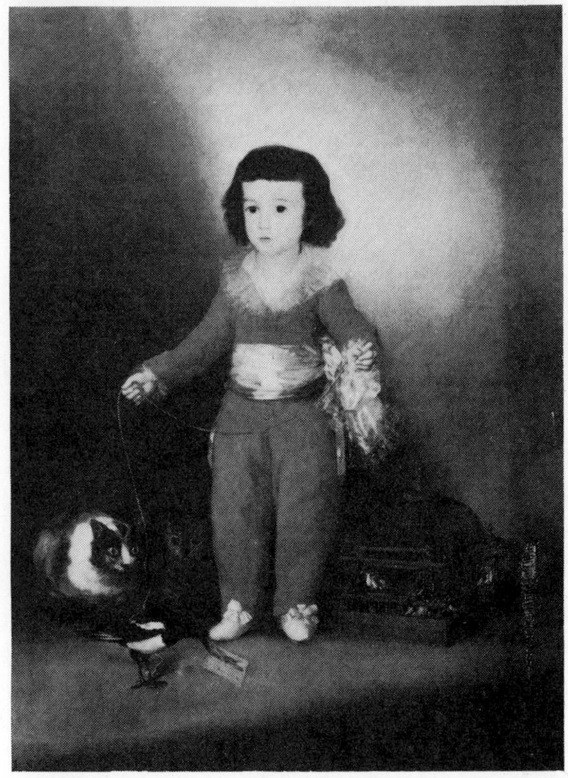

"Don Manuel." In this painting by Goya, a small child, attired in elegant clothes, plays with his pet bird while his cats look on hungrily.

"VIEW OF TOLEDO." The Spanish artist El Greco transformed this scene into an imaginative view of the city, making it a place of mystery shrouded by an ominous sky. Compare this painting with the photograph on page 403.

the world's greatest cellist, refuses to live or play in Spain as long as Franco rules. Juan Ramón Jiménez (hee-*may*-nayth), the best of modern Spanish poets and the recipient of a Nobel Prize in 1956, lived in South America until his death in 1958. His *Platero and I*, the story of a donkey and his philosophical master, is popular with children of Spain and South America. The rigid censorship of the arts in Spain has not only resulted in the loss of many of her own men of talent, but has isolated her from many of the artistic and intellectual currents of our times.

Chapter Check-up

1. For what type of singing and dancing is Spain best known today?
2. What influences are evident in Spanish architecture?
3. Who is Spain's greatest author and for what work is he famous?
4. What is considered to be the masterpiece of Portuguese literature?
5. Who were Spain's three greatest painters?
6. Why do modern Spanish artists such as Casals, Picasso, and Jimenez live and work outside of Spain?

Spain and Portugal: SYNOPSIS

Spain and Portugal struggled for many centuries to drive the Moors from the Iberian Peninsula and to unite the small Christian states into which their land was divided. When their efforts proved successful, the two countries rose to become, for a time, leading powers in Europe. They built empires in the East and in the New World, and they established a flourishing civilization at home. The character of modern Latin America is largely the result of Portuguese and Spanish colonization from the sixteenth to the nineteenth centuries.

In modern times, Spain and Portugal have faced serious political and economic problems. Though their land is poor, they remained chiefly agricultural long after their neighbors became industrialized. The reasons for their slow development are not hard to find. Both countries lack a middle class. (It is that class, you will recall, that has made England and France prosperous democratic nations.) Most of the population of Spain and Portugal is uneducated and does not understand change; the upper class does not want change. Despite recent signs of prosperity in Spain, lack of natural resources remains an obstacle in both countries.

Despite their slow development as modern peoples, however, the inhabitants of the Iberian Peninsula have made important cultural achievements. Cervantes, the author of *Don Quixote*, is one of the most admired of all authors. El Greco, Velásquez, and Goya are important figures in the history of painting. In modern times, the peninsula has been the homeland of Pablo Casals, considered to be the world's greatest cellist, and Juan Ramón Jiménez, a poet who received the Nobel Prize in 1956.

Important People

How has each of the following influenced the story of Spain and Portugal?

Cid
Alfonso VI
Isabella and Ferdinand
Prince Henry of Portugal
Charles V
General Primo de Rivera
Franco
Salazar
Miguel de Cervantes
El Greco
Pablo Picasso
Alfonso XIII
Luiz de Camoëns
Pablo Casals
Juan Jiménez

Terms

Be sure you understand clearly the meaning of each of the following:

Alhambra
baroque
Inquisition
Moors
reconquest of Spain
Fifth Column
Flamenco
caliph
Iberia
peninsula
quixotic
Armada

Questions for Discussion and Review

1. How does geography help to explain each of the following:
   (a) the poverty of the Spanish people,
   (b) the lack of Spanish industrialization,
   (c) Spain's isolation from the rest of Europe.
2. Would you say that the Moorish occupation of Spain was beneficial to that country? Why?
3. What were the causes of the decline of Spain and Portugal?
4. Why is Cervantes' *Don Quixote* considered an outstanding literary work?
5. How would you try to raise the living standards of Spain if you were in control?
6. Historically, how would you rate Spain on a scale of religious tolerance? Why?
7. Why was the Spanish Republic doomed to failure?
8. In what way do Spain and Portugal resemble medieval states?
9. Into what two main groups was Spain divided in her Civil War?
10. Why is the Spanish Civil War considered a testing ground for World War II?
11. What contributions has Spain made to American culture?
12. What two aspects of human nature do the central characters in *Don Quixote* represent?

Interesting Things to Do

1. Make a map of the Iberian Peninsula showing Spain and Portugal and the surrounding lands and seas. Be sure to locate and label the important mountain ranges, rivers, and cities.
2. On a world map, show with colors all of the territories that belonged to Spain and to Portugal at the height of their powers.
3. Make an illustrated travel folder to encourage American tourists to visit Spain.
4. Make a poster showing all the peoples and nations which had an important influence on the development of Spanish civilization.
5. Show slides or display pictures demonstrating the strong Moorish influence or the baroque in Spanish architecture.
6. Obtain and play for the class recordings of Spanish music. Include some Flamenco, some traditional bullfight music, and some classical guitar by Segovia.
7. Read aloud to the class selections from Cervantes' *Don Quixote*.
8. Organize and present a panel discussion on modern Spain, its problems and its future.
9. Imagine that you are a foreign correspondent for an American newspaper. Write an account of the Spanish Civil War.

Interesting Reading about Spain and Portugal

Colman, Elizabeth, *Portugal, Wharf of Europe*, Scribner.

Criss, Mildred, *Isabella, Young Queen of Spain*, Dodd, Mead.

Crow, John A., *Spain: The Root and the Flower*, Harper & Row.

Ellis, Havelock, *The Soul of Spain*, Houghton Mifflin.

Fitzmaurice-Kelly, J., *New History of Spanish Literature*, Oxford.

Goldston, Robert, *The Civil War in Spain*, Bobbs-Merrill. How it happened and what it has done.

*Hewes, Agnes, *Spice and the Devil's Cave*, Knopf. Adventure story about Portugal in the days of Vasco de Gama.

Kingsley, Charles, *Westward Ho!* Dodd, Mead. Novel about fifteenth-century Spanish and English competition for control of the seas.

*Loder, Dorothy, *Land and Peoples of Spain*, Lippincott. Survey of Spanish history, customs, and culture.

Thomas, Hugh, and Editors of Life, *Spain*, Time, Inc.

Williams, Jay, and Editors of Horizon Magazine, *The Spanish Armada*, Harper & Row.

* Indicates easy reading

Modern Italy was born in the nineteenth century. Many of her people still consider themselves Sicilians, Tuscans or—like this woman in the window—Genoan, rather than Italians.

Part 13
ITALY
QUEST FOR UNITY AND ANCIENT GLORY

ITALY

SWITZERLAND
AUSTRIA
HUNGARY
Alps
VENETIA
Milan
Trieste
Turin
Po
LOMBARDY
Venice
YUGOSLAVIA
Apennines
Genoa
Carrara
Pisa
Florence
Arno
Tiber
ADRIATIC SEA
ELBA
CORSICA
(France)
Rome
Apennines
Naples
SARDINIA
TYRRHENIAN SEA
SICILY
MEDITERRANEAN SEA
NORTH AMERICA
ARCTIC
OCEAN
ASIA
ATLANTIC
OCEAN
EUROPE
SOUTH AMERICA
AFRICA
INDIAN OCEAN

Italy: GEOGRAPHIC SETTING

Italy is the boot-shaped peninsula that was once the heart of the great Roman Empire. Although only about seven hundred miles from north to south, it is divided by geographical features into three distinct regions, each of which has developed along somewhat different lines.

Northern Italy, which extends from the Alps to the Apennines, is the peninsula's richest area. Wheat-growing and dairy farming flourish in the fertile soil of the Po Valley, and manufacturing prospers in such cities as Milan and Turin. Central Italy, lying between the Arno River and Rome, is composed mostly of the rocky slopes of the Apennine chain. Here grape vines and olive trees abound. Although Central Italy is less prosperous than the northern part, it has always been an intellectual and artistic center, just as Rome has been the spiritual center for the world's Roman Catholics. Southern Italy, from Rome to Sicily, is largely an agricultural region whose inhabitants frequently have had to face poverty and a low standard of living. Although in ancient times it was the most attractive and civilized part of the country, today it consists mainly of exhausted farmlands which must be heavily fertilized in order to be made productive. The government has recently created a special cabinet post to deal with the problems of southern Italy.

Long ago Rome united all Italy, but in the fourteen centuries since the fall of the Roman Empire each section of the country has tended to go its own way. Modern Italy has been a nation for little more than a hundred years. Many of her people still consider themselves Venetians, Romans, or Sicilians rather than Italians. A long tradition of independent states and the economic differences of Italy's three regions have made the country's lack of unity a serious problem.

Disunity is not, however, Italy's only problem. She is also hampered by inadequate natural resources. Large quantities of food must be imported to feed her people, and coal, iron, and petroleum must be imported to keep her industries running. To solve the problems created by these shortages, the government is now reclaiming swampy wilderness for farmland, and industries are turning to new sources of power. Natural gas has been discovered in the Po Valley, and the Italians are beginning to harness the country's abundant water power.

Italy: PERSPECTIVE

No region of its size has been as important in the history of the world as Italy. Although it is slightly smaller than New Mexico, it has twice dominated the Western world—first as a political and military power, later as a cultural leader.

The first period of greatness came to Italy during the years of the Roman Empire, about which you read in Part 5. Under such leaders as Julius Caesar and the Emperor Augustus, Rome radiated her brilliant civilization to distant corners of a vast empire. She pioneered in government, law, engineering, and architecture and brought unity and order to diverse peoples. The second flowering of her civilization came over a thousand years later, when all Europe again looked to the Italian Peninsula for leadership. As you learned in Part 8, it was in Italy that the dawn of the Renaissance signaled the end of the Middle Ages and the beginning of modern

times. The work of Italy's writers, artists, sculptors, and scientists inspired creative people of the rest of Europe.

But the country's history is by no means one of uninterrupted greatness. Until recently Italy has been divided by internal conflict and political unrest, and today she is still struggling toward a mature and stable democratic society. The results of that struggle are crucial to the political balance of Europe. In Part 13 we shall read about the great events and the new leaders who have shaped the destiny of Italy since the fall of Rome.

CHAPTER 45

The Italians Overcame Centuries of Disunity to Form a Nation

ITALY SUFFERED YEARS OF INVASION AND DIVISION

The Italians had known periods of glory. The earliest part of the story of Italy is the story of Rome. All Italians are proud of the "grandeur that was Rome." You will remember reading in Part 5 how the Roman legions brought the entire ancient world under Rome's sway. As Rome declined in the fourth and fifth centuries, however, the barbarian tribes ravaged the peninsula. Italy, like the rest of Europe passed into an era of darkness, in which feudal conflicts and constant invasion caused the Italians to lose sight of their common heritage from Rome. Not until almost a thousand years later did Italy again hold the center of the world's stage.

The Renaissance, which was centered in Italy, brought a cultural reawakening to Europe. You learned in Chapter 26 about the wealth of such cities as Venice and Florence and about the achievements of their citizens. From the fourteenth to sixteenth centuries, Renaissance Italy was the intellectual and artistic center of Europe.

Foreign soldiers and lack of trade caused the decline of the Italian city-states. Renaissance Italy was not one nation, but a collection of independent states that remained stubbornly disunited. No one, not even the Pope, was strong enough to gain supremacy. Invasion by foreign armies made the situation worse. In the early sixteenth century the kings of France struggled against the Holy Roman emperor, Charles V, and against King Philip of Spain for control of Italy. You may recall that it was at this time that Machiavelli, in his book *The Prince,* urged a strong and ruthless leader to come forward and unite Italy. But the city-states were too proud of their independence and too jealous of each other to submit to unification.

When the trade routes shifted from the Mediterranean to the Atlantic after 1500 (see Chapter 27), Italy lost its monopoly on trade with the east. Gradually the city-states lost their wealth, and then their independence. While England, France, and Spain were becoming unified nations, war and foreign domination left Italy hopelessly divided and weak. For the next three centuries the Italian city-states were controlled by foreign countries and ruled by despots who gave little thought to the welfare of their people.

BARTOLOMMEO COLLEONI. This statue in Venice honors one of the great captains of war, or "condottieri," soldiers who offered their services to the highest bidder during the conflicts that plagued the Italian city-states in the Middle Ages and Renaissance. Colleoni fought both for Milan and Venice.

Napoleon's conquest stimulated the rise of Italian nationalism. By the late eighteenth century, most of Italy was under the control of Austria. The Italians who lived under Austrian rule enjoyed nearly forty years of peace and prosperity. But you may recall that during the French Revolution, France went to war with Austria, and Napoleon seized Austria's Italian possessions.

For three reasons the presence of the French in Italy brought the day of Italian unification closer. First, for his own convenience Napoleon combined the multitude of separate states into three, thus imposing by force a unity which the Italians had been unable to achieve voluntarily. Secondly, the French soldiers brought with them the revolutionary ideas of "liberty, equality, and fraternity." These inspiring watchwords seemed to offer a promise of freedom from foreign domination. But the Italians soon learned that Napoleon had no such lofty intentions. Instead of putting into practice these ideals, he ruled as a dictator and regulated Italy's economic and political affairs to his own advantage. With good reason the Italians grew resentful of French rule. Their resentment provided the third factor in hastening Italy's unification—a common desire for a free and independent nation. Nationalistic yearnings began to awaken in the Italian people.

THREE GREAT PATRIOTS WORKED FOR THE UNIFICATION OF ITALY

After Napoleon's defeat in 1815, the Congress of Vienna sought to restore Europe to its condition prior to the French Revolution. Accordingly, Italy was again divided into small states, most of which were placed under Austrian control. The Kingdom of the Two Sicilies was created in the south and became an Austrian-dominated state. The Papal States of central Italy were restored to the Church. Only the Kingdom of Sardinia, which included the northwestern corner of Italy as well as the island of Sardinia, was placed under the rule of an independent Italian king.

Mazzini was the champion of a united, democratic Italy. The Italians, however, had not forgotten their nationalistic ideas. They were more and more determined to have a united Italy ruled by Italians. The most ardent Italian patriot was a Genoan lawyer and journalist, Giuseppe Mazzini (mat-*tsee*-nee). Mazzini believed it was God's will that the Italians should liberate themselves from foreign rule and create a united, democratic country. He taught that unification should be achieved through revolution against foreign domination, but he cautioned that unless the Italians

MAZZINI, CAVOUR, AND GARIBALDI. Mazzini, the revolutionary, Cavour, the diplomat, and Garibaldi, the fighter, were all great Italian patriots. Although they used different means, each worked to unite his country and free it from foreign rule.

were guided by a spirit of justice and unselfishness they would not be worthy of self-government.

While he was still a young man, Mazzini suffered imprisonment and exile for attempting to organize a revolt against Austrian authority. At the age of twenty-six, he organized a secret society, called Young Italy, whose purpose was to prepare Italians for revolution. Finally, in 1848, he inspired his countrymen to attempt armed revolt. The king of Sardinia tried to drive Austrian troops from the Italian province of Lombardy, but he was defeated and forced to give up his throne. Mazzini succeeded in establishing a short-lived republic in Rome, but in less than a year he was driven out and forced to flee for his life. Although he continued to work for Italian independence, Mazzini's failure in 1848 convinced Italians that they could not throw out their foreign rulers by their own efforts alone. The Italian patriots realized that they needed a powerful ally.

Cavour asked for French aid to unite Italy. The chief minister of Sardinia, Count Camillo di Cavour (kah-*voor*), shared with Mazzini the dream of a united Italy, but Cavour had different ideas about how to achieve it. Rejecting Mazzini's belief that an Italian revolution was the answer, Cavour believed that the aid of a strong foreign nation needed to be enlisted before independence could be won.

Cavour deliberately set out to win the active support of Britain and France. First, Cavour made Sardinia an industrial state and established a liberal parliamentary government. He wanted to impress England and France with the fact that Italians were not simply angry revolutionaries, but responsible and enlightened people. He also wanted to show other Italians that if they became unified under Sardinia's leadership, they would have a constitutional government. Next, Cavour sent Sardinian troops to help the English and French in a war against Russia in 1854. Although he had no particular interest in the war against Russia, he was already planning a war against Austria, and he wanted to be sure he had the sympathy of England and France. His next step was to persuade the French emperor Napoleon III to help Sardinia in the event of war with Austria. Then, by massing troops near the border of Lombardy, Cavour provoked the Austrians into declaring war. Napoleon III sent an army to Sardinia's aid. The Austrians were defeated in two battles, and they agreed to cede Lombardy to Sardinia. Despite this success, Cavour was disappointed because Napoleon III suddenly withdrew his French army. Cavour was forced to abandon his plan to drive the Austrians out of Italy entirely. Nevertheless, by 1860, all the states of northern Italy, except Venetia, had broken away from Austria and come under the rule of the Sardinian king, Victor Emmanuel II.

Garibaldi captured the Kingdom of the Two Sicilies. In the south, the Kingdom of the Two Sicilies was still dominated by Austria and under the rule of an absolute monarch who was hated by his subjects. At this pont Italy's third great patriot, Giuseppe Garibaldi (gar-ih-*bawl*-dih), took over the task of Italian unification. Garibaldi had spent his life fighting for liberty, first in South America and later with Mazzini as co-ruler of the republic in Rome. To escape the Austrian secret police, Garibaldi had fled to the United States, but he never forgot Italy. In 1860 he gathered and trained an army of a thousand men who were devoted to the cause of Italian liberty. A few months later, Garibaldi and his red-shirted followers landed in Sicily. So many Sicilians flocked to his banner that Garibaldi quickly won control of the island. Next, he crossed to the mainland and took Naples itself. The King, deserted by his own people, fled from the city, leaving Garibaldi in command of southern Italy.

Garibaldi might have chosen to become ruler of southern Italy. Instead, in the interest of Italian unification, he unselfishly resigned his powers over Sicily and Naples and acknowledged Victor Emmanuel II of Sardinia as the monarch of the new Kingdom of Italy. The people of some of the papal provinces also voted to join the new kingdom. Then, his great task accomplished, Garibaldi returned to his farm, taking only a bag of seed corn and a small handful of money.

A new Italy was born. In 1861 Victor Emmanuel II was proclaimed King of Italy. With the exception of Rome, which had been occupied by French troops ever since 1849, and Venetia, which was still under Austrian control, Italy was united. Italy gained Venetia in 1866 as a reward for helping Prussia in a war against Austria. Four years later Rome at last joined the new united Italian kingdom when Napoleon III called his troops home to fight in the Franco-Prussian War. After nearly fifteen hundred years of discord and disunity, Italy was once more united and entirely free of foreign domination.

The new Italy became a constitutional monarchy with an elected parliament, but the Italians were poorly trained for self-government. They split into many parties, whose lack of agreement made it very hard for the government to act. Furthermore, not all the people had the right to vote. The lower classes regarded the government as an agent of the rich. The people of southern Italy in general believed that the government favored the northern sector. Thus, even though the country was unified, the Italian government did not have the support of all the people.

VICTOR EMMANUEL IN ROME. The king receives the plebiscite of the people of Rome in 1870 after they voted to join the Kingdom of Italy rather than remain under the authority of the Pope.

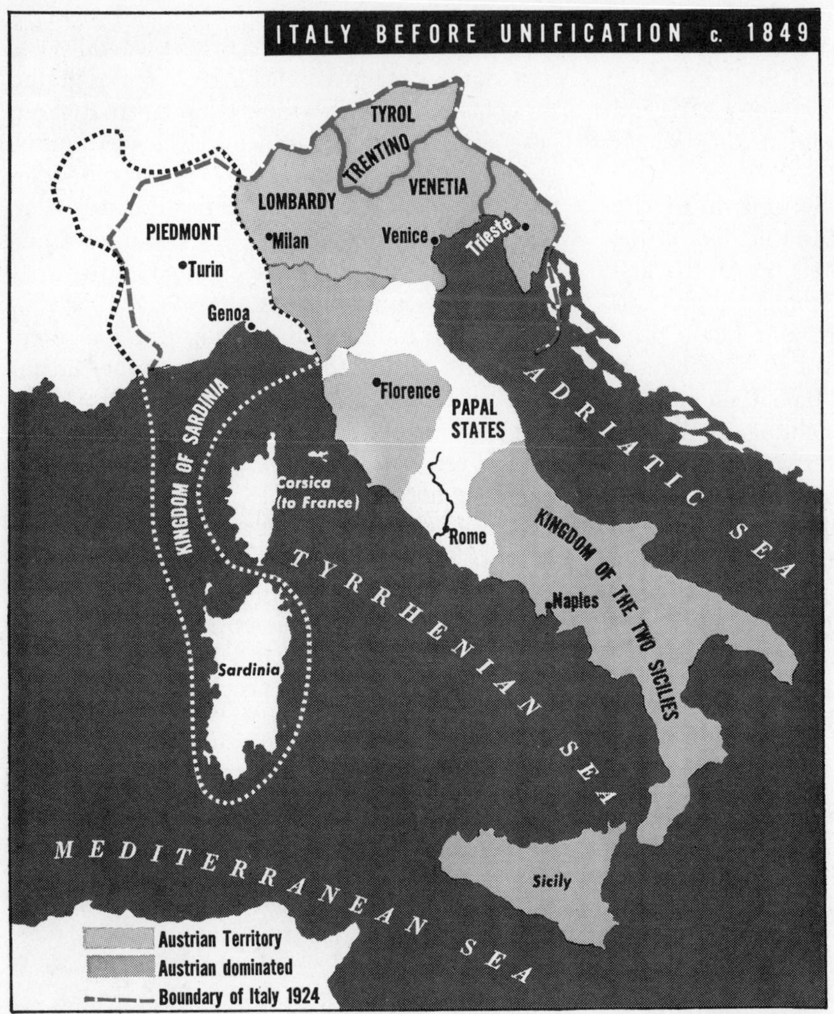

ITALY ACQUIRED A DICTATOR AND AN EMPIRE

World War I created many problems for Italy. At the outbreak of World War I in 1914, Italy had a defensive alliance with Germany and Austria-Hungary. After considerable hesitation as to which side she should join, Italy went into the war in 1915 as one of the Allied powers against Germany and Austria-Hungary. By doing so she hoped to gain certain Italian-speaking territories then under Austrian control, which were known as "unredeemed Italy."

Italy was successful in getting part of what she wanted, but the end of the war in 1918 found her in a worse economic condition than any other nation in the war except Russia. Unemployment was serious and widespread. There were not enough jobs for the returning soldiers. The ruined fields would not supply enough grain, and the government had no money to buy it abroad. Prices skyrocketed. The government was weakened by inaction and by constantly shifting political sentiments.

As conditions grew worse in Italy, socialism and communism gained many followers. Both parties thought that all the property of the country from which people made a living or produced wealth—the land, the mines, the factories, and the railroads—should belong to the State. Both parties could trace their origins back to Karl Marx, a German economist who advocated socialism in the middle of the nineteenth century. But they have become very different today, as you will learn in Part 22.

As unrest increased in Italy, industrial, agricultural, and railroad strikes broke out over the country. Some of the peasants refused to pay rent. The Socialist party dominated the port of Genoa to such an extent that no ship could be loaded or unloaded unless it was by men who belonged to the Socialist union. Radical groups seized a number of factories, and local Communist governments controlled some cities and villages.

Violence accompanied many of the strikes and changes. Rioting broke out in some of the large cities. Groups of young men of intense national feeling banded together and armed to oppose the Socialists and Communists by force. These military-political groups were known as Fascists. They took their name from the fasces (*fas*-eez), the bundle of sticks bound about an ax which was the symbol of authority in the days of ancient Rome. (The same symbol appears on some of the coins of the United States.)

Mussolini considered himself a modern Caesar. The man who organized and controlled the Fascist party was Benito Mussolini (moos-oh-*lee*-nee). He called himself the Caesar of modern Italy. He was an aggressive and ambitious man who had been a school teacher, a radical journalist, and a soldier in World War I. In his earlier days he belonged to the Socialist party. But after World War I he quarreled with the Socialists, and organized the Fascist party, which bitterly opposed both the Socialists and the Communists. Unfortunately, the Fascists were also opposed to democracy and believed in force and dictatorship. (In Part 22 you will read more about what the Fascists believed and did.)

The Fascist groups at first were composed largely of former soldiers. They claimed to be the upholders of law, order, and a strong Italy, which they promised to defend from the forces of com-

munism. But they felt that a strong Italy was impossible as long as the country was run by a weak parliamentary government. Mussolini said the Italians should be prepared to give up their individual liberties for the good of the state.

The Fascists were intensely nationalistic and had great ambitions for Italy. Soon armed conflicts broke out between the Fascist and liberal factions. Ordinary citizens began to carry guns for self-protection. Italy was on the brink of civil war.

Mussolini brought Italy under the rule of the Fascist party. The Italian government did not succeed in restoring order, and in 1922 the Fascists took control of the country by force. Led by Mussolini, about fifty thousand men marched on Rome. (Actually, the fifty thousand marched, but Mussolini took the train!) Each man wore the black shirt of the Fascists, just as the men of the great patriot, Garibaldi, had worn red shirts when they united Italy.

King Victor Emmanuel III refused to declare martial law. He wanted to avoid bloodshed. So his prime minister resigned, and the king asked Mussolini to become head of the government. Although the king kept his crown, Mussolini was the actual ruler and became one of the most powerful men in Europe. Almost at once Mussolini declared himself dictator. He abolished labor unions, forbade strikes and lockouts, and made it a crime for men to be idle. He allowed the factory owners to keep their factories, but every detail of production was supervised by the national government.

Many thoughtful Italians looked on the Fascist government with great misgiving. It is true that some acts of the Fascists appealed strongly to the Italian people. Mussolini cleared many of the slums and built public works, great buildings, and first-class roads. Foreigners traveling in Italy brought back reports of the cleanliness, order, and efficiency of the Fascist state. The young people, who had been trained in Fascist schools and youth organizations, were generally enthusiastic.

For years Italian railroads had been notoriously bad. Trains never ran on time. Mussolini made strict rules for railroad men and punished severely anyone responsible for delaying a train. Foreign travelers often came home enthusiastic about this change, because, as they exclaimed, "Mussolini has made Italian trains run on time!" However, more thoughtful people asked, "But does justice run on time?" For behind all this fine-looking front there was trouble in Italy. Courts of law became mere agents of Fascist rule. There was little personal liberty. No one dared speak or write against anything the Fascists did. Mussolini's program was also extremely expensive. Both the big industrialists and the middle classes complained that they were being taxed out of existence for the benefit of the working classes. They began to ask what would become of the working classes themselves if the nation became bankrupt.

Meantime Mussolini began to build up and equip the Fascist army. There was endless drilling of the army and the youth groups. It appeared that the Fascists had decided on the next step.

Italy became an aggressor nation. Mussolini had determined to solve Italy's problem by force. In spite of her past record of liberalism and love of freedom, Mussolini made Italy an aggressor nation with the attack on Ethiopia in 1935.

Behind Italy's Ethiopian aggression lay a rather unhappy history of Italian colonization. In the 1880's, after other nations had claimed most of Africa, the Italians established colonies on the eastern coast of Africa in a small strip called Eritrea (ehr-ih-*tree*-uh). Then Italy tried to con-

MUSSOLINI. *Il Duce* the flamboyant leader, is shown here in a characteristic pose stating what his policies are to be for his people. Mussolini was captured by partisans and hanged upside down from a lamppost in Milan in 1945.

The Ethiopian War. Under cover of a tank, Italian infantrymen advance on an Ethiopian village. Although the Ethiopians fought bravely, they were no match for the mechanized equipment of the aggressor Italians.

quer Ethiopia to add to her colonial holdings, but the Ethiopian army defeated the Italians.

Early in the twentieth century, by clever diplomacy, Italy gained the approval of England and France for her claims to two Turkish provinces between Egypt and Tunisia. The Italians therefore made war on the Turks, took the provinces from them, and renamed the territory Libya. The Italians developed Libya, but its development cost more than it proved to be worth. About the only value of Italy's African colonies was the satisfaction of possessing them.

The Fascists brought disaster to Italy. After the experience in Africa, one might have thought that the Italians would abandon their desire for colonies. But the Fascists revived the old desires for an empire. They felt that new colonies would serve as markets for Italian manufactured goods and as sources of raw materials. Italy's economic condition at home was in such a state that a foreign war seemed almost a necessity. The Fascists hoped that foreign conquest would make the people forget their troubles at home. Furthermore, the Fascists, as part of their propaganda, had revived the memory of the old Roman Empire and had inspired the modern Italians with a desire to imitate its glories.

In 1935 Italy therefore picked a quarrel with Ethiopia and undertook an invasion of "punishment" against her. It was an act of sheer aggression, and Mussolini later boasted that he had planned it for some time. The League of Nations voted to punish Italy for her aggression by forbidding the other nations that belonged to the League to trade with her. Italy promptly withdrew from the League.

In the war with Italy, the Ethiopians were at a great disadvantage in men and equipment. The Italians used poison gas and planes against courageous men armed mostly with primitive weapons. The war soon ended in complete victory for the Italians. Italy had conquered a new colony.

Actually there could be little glory in a conquest by the modern Fascist army over the poorly equipped Ethiopian natives. Yet the conquest of Ethiopia was presented to the Italian people as an exploit worthy of their Roman ancestors.

To the rest of the world the Italian conquest of Ethiopia was one of the first acts of unchecked aggression which ushered in World War II. Nazi Germany, whose ideas about national unity and glory were similar to those of the Fascists, gave Italy support. Only a year after the invasion of Ethiopia, Italy returned this support by joining with Germany in the so-called Rome-Berlin Axis which was to plunge the world into the greatest war of history. You will read about World War II in Part 22.

PRESENT-DAY ITALY IS GUIDED BY A REPUBLICAN GOVERNMENT

The Italians established a republic after World War II. Mussolini's cooperation with Hitler brought suffering and defeat to the Italians. Since World War II they have rebuilt their devastated country. Part of this involved a major change in government. Because the monarchy had supported Fascism, the Italians voted in 1946 to make the country a republic. They drafted a new constitution which gave every Italian over twenty-one the right to vote for a parliament of two houses and outlawed the Fascist party.

Since World War II Italy has been governed by a coalition of moderate and liberal political groups including Christian Democrats, Social Democrats, and Socialists. The main force holding this coalition together has been their common opposition to political extremes on either side. To the far left are the Communists, who are the second largest party in Italy, and to the far right is the recently growing strength of Fascist-like groups.

Italy has rebuilt but faces new problems. After World War II Italy rebuilt with the help of food supplies, seeds, medicines, and machinery sent by the United States. American and Italian experts worked together to help solve some of the country's social and economic problems. Many great estates have been broken up by the government and sold or rented to poor farmers. To provide more land, swamps are being drained and dams built to prevent floods and to provide water for irrigation and hydroelectric power. Italian industry rebuilt and expanded so that by 1953 industrial production was 50 per cent higher than it had been before the war. Italy now has new exports like automobiles, typewriters, and computers, as well as her traditional ones like fine textiles and leather goods. The number of tourists who visit Italy each year, and a vibrant movie industry also aid the economy.

Italy has made much progress in winning back her place in world affairs. She is allied with Western European countries economically in the European Common Market and militarily in the North Atlantic Treaty Organization. But in recent years she has also promoted good relations

Italian Industry. Since World War II Italy has greatly increased her export of electrical machinery, automobiles, typewriters, and many other types of machine tools. Here new Fiat automobiles are given a final check as they roll off the assembly line.

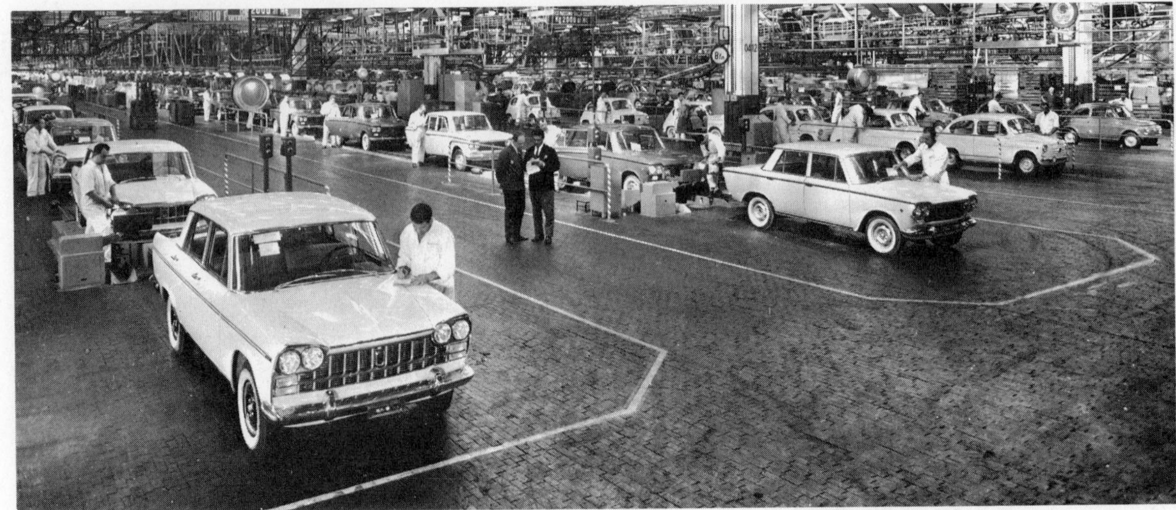

with Eastern European Communist countries. Italy has been a member of the United Nations since 1955.

But Italy's spectacular rebuilding and expansion since World War II is currently suffering from a slowdown, a demand for reforms, and the continuing poverty of the south as compared with the prosperity of the north. The present government is trying to keep production up by encouraging new investment and dealing with many strikes. It is pledged to reforms in housing, education, and taxes. It has also established a special fund to pump billions of dollars over several years into the poor and undeveloped southern part of the peninsula. But unless and until such programs succeed, discontent grows and the government's stability is threatened by the increasing strength of Communists at one extreme and neo-Fascists at the other.

Chapter Check-up

1. Into what three areas is Italy divided geographically?
2. What prevented Renaissance Italy from acting as a strong, national unit?
3. Why were Italian nationalists dissatisfied with the terms of the Congress of Vienna?
4. Who were the three great patriots who worked for the unification of Italy? What part did each play?
5. When was Italy finally unified, and what type of government did she establish?
6. What conditions in post-World War I Italy made Mussolini's rise to power possible?
7. Why did Mussolini invade Ethiopia?
8. Why was the League of Nations unsuccessful in stopping Mussolini?
9. What steps have been taken to rebuild and strengthen post-war Italy?
10. What problems face Italy today?

Chapter 46

Modern Science and Music Owe Much to Italy

ITALY HAS GIVEN MANY GREAT NAMES TO SCIENCE

From the Scientific Renaissance to the present day, Italy's scientists have continued to expand the horizons of man's knowledge about the world he lives in. Indeed, Italians have played a major role in a long series of discoveries and inventions, from the clock to the atomic bomb.

Galileo enlarged man's view of the world. One of the first modern scientists was Galileo, whom you met in Chapter 27 as an influential figure of the Scientific Renaissance. At eighteen, he made a discovery which led to the invention of the clock. The story is told that as he stood in the cathedral at Pisa, he saw a hanging lamp swinging rhythmically to and fro. He observed that since it took the same amount of time to complete each swing of the lamp, a swinging object, or pendulum, could be used to keep time. Galileo's discovery eventually became the basis for many precision instruments. Galileo also caused much discussion by his experiments with motion and force. His work helped to correct errors that had been believed for centuries. By dropping balls of various weights from the top of the Leaning Tower of Pisa, he proved that all objects, whether heavy or light, fall at the same speed.

Although Galileo was not the inventor of the telescope, he was the first to use it to study the heavens. He succeeded in observing the moons that revolve about Jupiter, and he discovered that the earth's moon was marked with valleys and mountains. Other observations confirmed the theory of Copernicus that the earth is one of the planets that move around the sun. Although these observations brought Galileo into conflict with the Church, his work helped reshape man's view of the universe.

One of Galileo's pupils, Torricelli (tor-ree-*chel*-lee), discovered the relationship between air pressure and the height of a column of mercury in a barometer. He constructed the first mercury barometer and used it to measure the heights of mountains. Today the same principle is used in the altimeter of an airplane, which tells the pilot how far above sea level he is flying.

Volta and Marconi experimented with electricity. In the nineteenth century, an Italian physicist named Volta made the first electric cell which could produce a constant electric current. Up to this time, scientists had been able to create only electric sparks that died immediately. Volta's new electric cell was used by Sir Humphrey Davy (see Chapter 34) in his experiments. It is the basis of modern electric cells such as the batteries in automobiles. Volta also invented an instrument which measures the force of an electric current. The unit of measure for that force is called a volt, after its inventor.

Guglielmo Marconi (mar-*ko*-nee) was the father of wireless telegraphy. While studying at the University of Bologna, he made experiments with sound. He believed that electrical impulses could be sent to distant places without wires. For years he experimented with electromagnetic waves. In 1895 he succeeded in sending a message to a station more than a mile away. In 1901 he sent a wireless message across the Atlantic Ocean. Marconi received a Nobel Prize for his contributions to science. From Marconi's work in wireless telegraphy have developed radio, radar, and television.

Cathedral and Leaning Tower of Pisa. In this beautiful Romanesque cathedral, Galileo is supposed to have begun to formulate the law of the pendulum as he watched a swinging chandelier. In the background is the bell tower, popularly known as the Leaning Tower.

Fermi helped develop the atom bomb. The great modern Italian physicist, Enrico Fermi (*fayr*-mee), is noted for his studies in nuclear physics and for his role in the creation of the atomic bomb. In 1938 he was awarded the Nobel Prize for his investigations of radioactive materials. Because he was bitterly opposed to the policies of Mussolini, Fermi came to the United States to live. During World War II he was a professor at Columbia University in New York and was also a leader of the American research team that developed the atomic bomb. Fermi discovered the element neptunium, which is radioactive. After World War II he served as an adviser to the U. S. Atomic Energy Commission.

MARCONI. The famous Italian inventor is shown in 1897 with his wireless apparatus, the forerunner of the radio.

ITALY HAS PRODUCED MEN OF MUSICAL GENIUS

In Chapter 26 you read about the marvelous painting and sculpture that was created by Italian artists during the Renaissance. Leonardo, Michelangelo, and Raphael established themselves among the greatest of the world's artists. With the decline of the city-states, Italian painting and sculpture lost importance. In the nineteenth century, however, Italy gained world renown as the homeland of famous composers and musicians.

Verdi's operas are world-famous. Italians have made glorious contributions in the field of opera. One of Italy's greatest operatic composers was Giuseppe Verdi (*vayr*-dee). As a small boy, he lived in a mountain village. One Sunday morning the church organist was absent. No one could be found to take his place. Someone suggested that young Giuseppe, who had taken a few music lessons, might replace him, so the boy was sent for. At the close of mass, the priest asked the organist whose music he had played. "Why," answered Giuseppe timidly, "I had no music—I played just as I felt."

So began the career of Verdi as a composer of music. His employer and various members of the church took an interest in helping him develop his talent. They found an excellent teacher. So rapid was his progress that they sent Verdi to Milan to finish his studies.

After he left the conservatory at Milan, Verdi began his serious work as a composer. He met heartaches and discouragement, but compared to the careers of some great composers, Verdi's rise to fame was rapid. At only twenty-nine he presented an opera which brought him recognition.

Although many of Verdi's early compositions were excellent, it was his later works that brought him enduring fame. In all, Verdi wrote more than thirty operas, three of which—*Rigoletto* (rig-oh-*let*-oh), *Il Trovatore* (troh-vah-*toh*-ray), and *Aïda* (ah-*ee*-dah)—are known the world over.

Other Italians have won fame as composers, singers, and orchestra conductors. Another of Italy's great operatic composers was Rossini (ros-*see*-nee), who wrote the dignified opera *William Tell* (see page 473) and the gay and lively *Barber of Seville.* Puccini (poo-*chee*-nee) is noted for his dramatic operas, with their haunting melodies and rich orchestral effects. His *La Bohème* and *La Tosca* are well known in the United States. *Madame Butterfly,* the story of a Japanese girl's love for an American naval officer, failed at first but became one of his most popular works.

VERDI. The composer of *Aïda* conducts the orchestra at a performance of his famous opera which was first performed at Cairo.

One of today's foremost operatic composers is Gian–Carlo Menotti (men-*aht*-tee). He was born in Italy but came to the United States when he was seventeen. Perhaps you have seen *Amahl and the Night Visitors,* the Christmas opera that he wrote in 1951. It was the first opera to be composed especially for television.

The Italian love of music has found outlets other than composition. The "golden-voiced" Enrico Caruso (kah-*roo*-zo) was called the world's greatest tenor because of the unusual power, quality, and range of his voice. He sang at the Metropolitan Opera in New York from 1903 to 1921.

The most famous orchestra conductor of the twentieth century was Arturo Toscanini (tos-kah-*nee*-nee), who directed opera at the famous La Scala Opera House in Milan and at the Metropolitan in New York. For ten years he led the New York Philharmonic Orchestra. Toscanini was remarkable for his fine sense of tempo and phrasing, his high standards of musicianship, his capacity for endless hard work, and his extraordinary memory. Throughout his life he conducted without a copy of the music before him. When Toscanini died in 1957, music lovers all over the world mourned the loss of his genius.

CARUSO. Dressed as the operatic clown Pagliacci, the great tenor is shown here in one of his most celebrated roles.

Chapter Check-up

1. What contributions to the field of science did Galileo make? Torricelli?
2. What did Volta contribute to modern science?
3. Whose work made possible the development of radio, radar, and television?
4. Italy's contributions in painting and sculpture came during what period of her history?
5. Italy has produced many men of musical genius. Name five and tell how each won his fame.

Italy: SYNOPSIS

The modern world owes much to Italy for her tremendous contributions to Western civilization. Italian artists and scholars were leaders of the Renaissance, which marked the change from medieval to modern times. In more recent years, Italy has gained a brilliant reputation for achievement in science and the musical arts. Men like Galileo, Volta, Marconi, and Fermi have expanded the horizons of scientific knowledge. Musicians like Verdi, Rossini, Puccini, Menotti, Caruso, and Toscanini have created pleasure for millions of people throughout the world.

Italy's cultural accomplishments have not always been matched, however, by similar achievements in government. Centuries of disunity left the Italians far behind other European peoples who were learning to overthrow absolute rulers and create democratic governments. Born late into the family of nations, Italy had just begun to gain experience in parliamentary government when Fascism and World War II stopped her progress.

Since the end of World War II, however, Italy has succeeded in overcoming many of the problems that had been created by the war and the Fascist dictatorship. As the Italian people have become more experienced in the workings of a democratic government, the Republic of Italy has grown more secure. Although the Italian Communist party is very large, its influence in the national government has been small. The relative economic prosperity and social stability enjoyed by Italians today is a good sign for the future.

Terms

Be sure that you understand clearly the meaning of each of the following:

barometer	Fascists	volt
Black shirts	opera	wireless
constitutional monarchy	Papal States	Young Italy

Important People

How has each of the following influenced the story of Italy?

Giuseppe Mazzini	Giuseppe Garibaldi	Guglielmo Marconi	Giuseppe Verdi
Camillo di Cavour	Galileo	Benito Mussolini	Gian-Carlo Menotti
Victor Emanuel II	Volta	Enrico Fermi	Arturo Toscanini

Questions for Discussion and Review

1. In what ways has Italy been handicapped by her geography?
2. How did the occupation by the French under Napoleon strengthen Italian nationalism and hasten the unification of Italy?
3. How did each of Italy's three great patriotic leaders hope to unify the country?
4. Why has real national unity been difficult for Italy to achieve?
5. What political and economic conditions seem to favor the rise and acceptance of a dictator?
6. Why was the failure of the League of Nations to halt Mussolini a step toward World War II?
7. Why is communism still a threat to Italian democracy?
8. In your opinion, what could be done in Italy to strengthen the government?
9. Why is Italy important to the future of Western Europe?
10. To which field do you think Italy has made her most important contribution? Why?

Interesting Things to Do

1. Make a map of Italy showing the surrounding lands and seas. Be sure to locate and label the important mountain ranges, rivers and cities. Use illustrations and colors.
2. Make a chart showing the achievements of modern Italy in science and music. Head your columns as follows: *Name of Person, Field of Work, Contributions or Achievements.*
3. Draw a series of sketches explaining one of the following: (a) wireless, (b) electric cell, (c) barometer, (d) pendulum.
4. Make a notebook of Italian recipes. Illustrate with magazine cut-outs wherever possible.
5. Arrange a recorded concert of Italian opera. Play selections from some of the well-known works of Verdi and Puccini, explaining something of the story of each.
6. Plan an Italian tour. Prepare a talk describing the places you would visit.
7. As an Italian reporter, write an editorial suggesting reforms to strengthen the government, to gain the support of the people, and to lessen the danger of communism.
8. Add to or begin your "Who's Who in World History" series by writing brief biographies of one or more of Italy's important leaders.

Interesting Reading about Italy

*Baker, Nina Brown, *Garibaldi*, Vanguard.

Coe, Douglas, *Marconi, Pioneer of Radio*, Messner.

Crow, John A., *Italy: A Journey through Time*, Harper & Row.

Durant, William, *The Renaissance: A History of Civilization in Italy, 1304–1576*, Simon and Schuster.

Hersey, John, *A Bell For Adano*, Knopf. The story of an American soldier who tries to help an Italian village during World War II.

Lampedusa, Giuseppe Di, *The Leopard*, Pantheon. A novel of nineteenth century Sicily.

McNeish, James, *Fire Under the Ashes*, Beacon. The life of Danilo Dolci.

Newman, Harold, *Newman's European Guide*, Holt, Rinehart and Winston.

Phillips, John, *The Italians—Face of a Nation*, McGraw-Hill.

Trease, Geoffrey, *The Italian Story*, Vanguard.

*Winwar, Frances, *Land of the Italian People*, Lippincott.

* Indicates easy reading

This young steel worker personifies the determination of the German people who have overcome the almost total destruction of World War II and made their country the workshop of Europe.

Part 14
GERMANY
STRUGGLE FOR UNITY AND MILITARY POWER

GERMANY AND SWITZERLAND

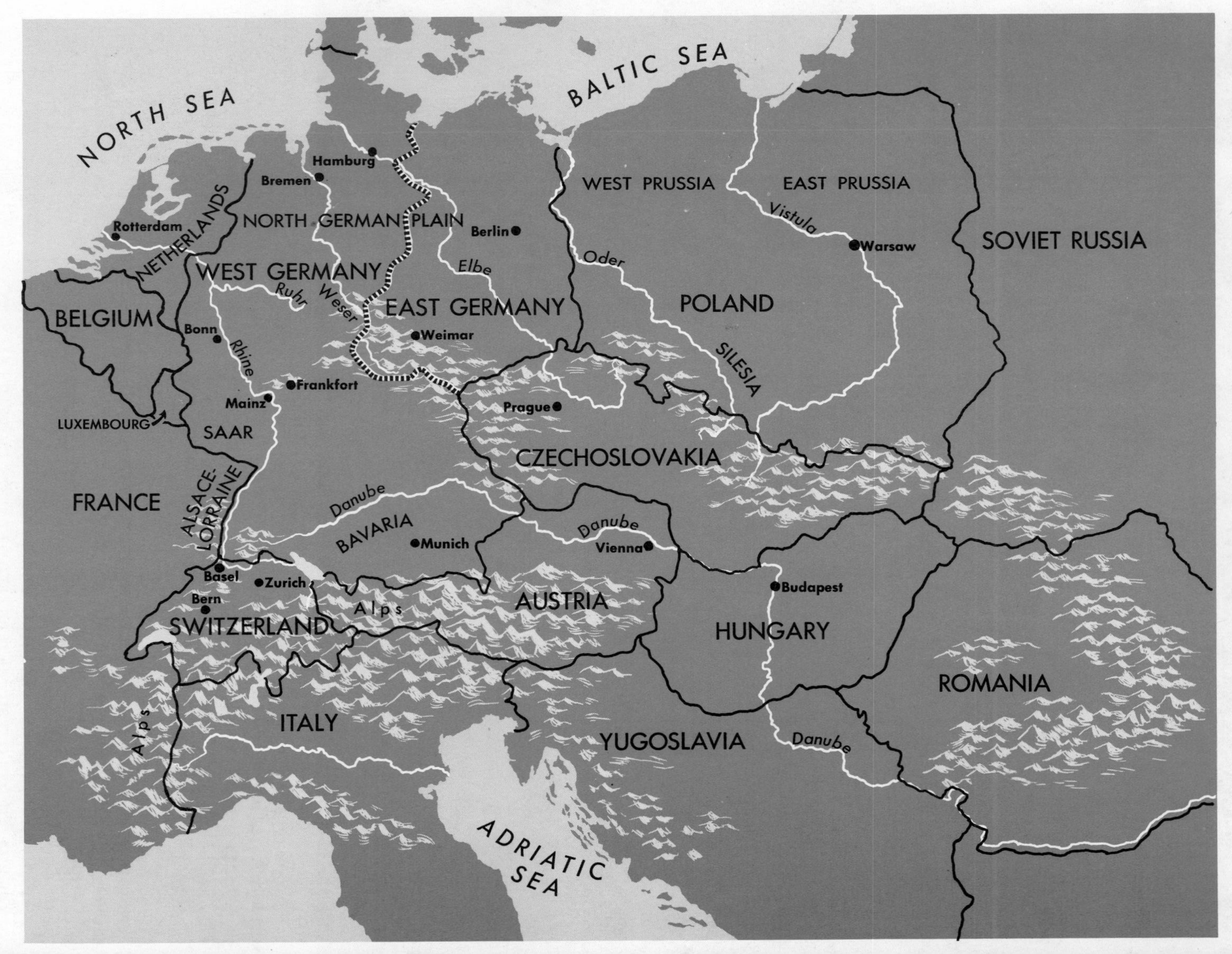

Germany: GEOGRAPHIC SETTING

Germany is a land with no natural boundaries except on the North Sea and the Baltic Sea. This fact, as you will see, has played an important part in the country's history. Geographically, Germany is divided into two sectors, north and south. Northern Germany is part of the vast plain that stretches across northern Europe, while southern Germany rises gradually through highlands and scattered mountain ranges until it merges with the Alps.

Politically, Germany is divided into east and west. In fact, since World War II there have been two German states. West Germany, which is now a free and independent democratic nation, is twice as large as East Germany and has three times the population. A highly industrialized state, West Germany has many mines and factories, especially in the Ruhr and Saar valleys. Here, rich coal and iron mines supply modern mills that turn out steel, pig iron, chemicals, and other industrial products. A network of deep navigable rivers makes it possible to ship these goods economically. Most of West Germany's important rivers, such as the Rhine, the Elbe, and the Weser, flow northward toward the sea. Natural resources, effective transportation, and a hard-working population make West Germany the most productive industrial nation in Europe.

East Germany, which is under the control of a Communist government supported by Russia, is still mainly agricultural. Recently the government has been trying to increase industrial productivity. East Germany, however, lacks both the great natural resources and the inspired labor force that have been the key to West Germany's amazing post-war development.

Germany: PERSPECTIVE

One June day in 1944, several hours before dawn, the greatest striking force man had ever organized began to move from England to the northern coast of France. Thousands of ships and thousands of planes carried the troops of the Allied nations across the English Channel, in hope of driving the German invaders out of France. Within a month, a million soldiers had landed; in two months, Paris was liberated; in three months, the Allies had fought their way into Germany itself. Within a year the Germans were defeated, and the war in Europe was over.

The problems created by Germany did not, however, vanish when she surrendered. In reading today's newspapers, you are almost certain to find some mention of Germany, because it is one of the most crucial areas in the post-war world. Divided between the democratic West and the communist East, it is the focal point of attention for those who hope to see the triumph of freedom over dictatorship.

This is not the first time Germany has been divided, nor the first time she has suffered the aftermath of war. Centuries ago, she was split into hundreds of tiny warring states, and twice in our own century she has been defeated in battle. What is the reason for Germany's instability? Why has she been involved in almost constant war? Does she pose a threat to world peace today? For the answers to these questions of the present, we must look deep into the past.

Chapter 47

Germany Was Divided into a Patchwork of Small States

GERMAN TRIBES INFLUENCED THE EARLY HISTORY OF EUROPE

Germanic tribes roamed over Europe. The earliest Germans seem to have taken possession of the land south of the Baltic Sea very long ago. Later, Caesar and other Roman writers reported that the "Teutons" (Germans) were strong and that they lived more by hunting and fishing than by cultivating the land. Each of their many warlike tribes had a strong chief, and the tribes often fought among themselves or attacked others.

When Caesar was governor of Gaul, the German tribes were a constant source of trouble, so Caesar tried to subdue them. He drove them back east to the Rhine, crossed the river, and fought them on their own lands. But he found the German fighters too powerful for him to conquer easily. So he drew back to the Rhine, set up forts along its banks, and tried to hem the barbarians in. Many rulers since Caesar have tried to keep the Germans east of the Rhine. When Roman power weakened in the fourth century, some German tribes swept over the Rhine into Gaul, and over the Alps into northern Italy.

You may recall that Clovis was the leader of a German tribe known as the Franks, who moved into the valley of the Seine River. They became the leading tribe in what is now northern France, and they laid the foundations of the French nation. The Frankish state under Clovis in the fifth century included much of what is now Germany. Several centuries later the empire of Charlemagne was actually more German than French. It reached north to the Baltic Sea and east to the Elbe River. Although they took part in the founding of France and England, when the German tribes tried to organize a nation of their own in Central Europe, they ran into trouble, as we shall see.

Charlemagne's grandsons divided the empire. In the latter half of the eighth century, under the firm rule of the great Frankish king Charlemagne, peace and order were restored in Western Europe. The Germans and their neighbors got along together fairly well. But, like many strong rulers, Charlemagne did not leave any successor who could carry on his work. His descendants were mostly weak, quarrelsome people.

Shortly after Charlemagne died, his grandsons fought over the division of his empire. Finally they made an agreement called the Treaty of Verdun, dividing the land into three parts. The eastern part went to one grandson, Louis the German. That was the beginning of Germany. The western part of the Empire went to Charles, another grandson. His domain was the foundation of the French nation.

The lands between the kingdoms of Louis and Charles went to a grandson of Charlemagne named Lothair. This territory came to be called Lothairingia, that is, "Lothair's kingdom." (From Lothairingia comes Lorraine, the modern name for this region. The southern part of Lorraine later was called Alsace, and the entire area is now often referred to as Alsace-Lorraine.) Lothair left his lands to his son, who died without an heir. His uncles divided Lorraine between them.

That was the beginning of a long series of difficulties. In the next two centuries the land passed back and forth from German to French control a half-dozen times. The same sort of thing was happening to most of the little states of Germany. But Lorraine was more important. It was a border state and it became a persistent cause of trouble between France and Germany as those nations were forming.

EARLY GERMAN HOMESTEAD. These German hunters of the first century have come home with a bear and other game. The bear's meat will provide food, its skin will be made into a rug, and its skull will decorate the house. Little is known of these hardy warriors and hunters until the Romans encountered them during military campaigns in the North.

THE HOLY ROMAN EMPIRE FAILED TO UNITE GERMANY

Many forces combined to weaken the authority of the Holy Roman Empire. A century and a half after Charlemagne died, Otto, the strong king of the German province of Saxony, tried to reunite the German tribes. He succeeded in getting the Pope to crown him "Emperor of Rome." Otto's realm did not include France, but it took in all the German states and northern Italy. Two centuries later, one of Otto's successors adopted the title Holy Roman emperor (see page 192), and his realm became known as the Holy Roman Empire. Although Charlemagne and Otto were not known in their lifetimes as Holy Roman emperors, they are often referred to by this title, because they laid the foundation for the empire.

You might expect that such an organized empire would help to unite the German people. But for several reasons the empire had almost the opposite effect. First, its emperor had no real power. He was elected for life by some of the more powerful princes, kings, dukes, and archbishops of Germany, called *electors*. The electors did not want to curb their own powers, so they usually picked a weak emperor. Second, there was no imperial army or tax system. The emperor could not even force the nobles to keep peace among themselves. All through the Middle Ages the German princes carried on private wars that kept the country in a state of turmoil.

Another reason for the weakness of the Holy Roman Empire grew out of its claim to northern Italy. The Italians resisted the claim, and emperors, one after the other, exhausted Germany by wars to hold or regain their Italian territories. Outside enemies also made almost continuous wars on the border states of Germany. The Poles, Bohemians, Hungarians, and Turks on the east, and the Danes and Swedes on the north were always a problem.

Still another cause of weakness was the German custom of dividing territory among all the sons of a ruler. This meant that the German states became smaller and weaker. At one time there were as many as 350 independent states in Germany, each resisting any attempt of the emperor to unify or strengthen Germany.

Finally, during the Middle Ages, the emperors frequently became involved in quarrels with the Pope (see Chapter 23). The Church claimed supreme power over all the Christian world and did not want an emperor to become strong enough to challenge its position. The Popes, therefore, used their influence and riches to help the nobles

The Emperor and Electors. In 1356 the number of electors was fixed at seven. Three were spiritual leaders—the bishops of Trier, Cologne, and Mainz. Four were secular leaders—the king of Bohemia, the palatine of the Rhine, the duke of Saxony, and the margrave of Brandenburg. Here they flank the emperor on left and right.

in Germany fight the emperor's attempts to strengthen his authority.

German cities became virtually independent. In the story of the Middle Ages you read of the growth of towns in the eleventh and twelfth centuries. Many towns and cities developed in Germany during that time, principally along her navigable rivers. Because of the weakness of the Empire and the everlasting fighting between the rulers of the small states, German towns became almost independent. They had to protect themselves, since the rulers were generally so weak. Many towns joined to help protect each other and to increase their trade.

One such union of cities, known as the Hanseatic League, became so powerful during the thirteenth and fourteenth centuries that it was able to ignore the emperor; it even made its own treaties with foreign countries. Such unions encouraged trade and helped keep peace. The leagues were good for business but they were no help in building any national feeling. The Germans in the towns were loyal to their own little section or group of cities. They paid little attention to the rest of the country, and they had no interest in a strong, united Germany.

The Hapsburgs built up Austria and took over the Holy Roman Empire. Two ruling families had a great deal to do with the story of the German people. They were the Hohenzollerns (ho-en-*tsol*-urnz), whom you will read about in the next chapter, and the Hapsburgs. For centuries the Hapsburgs ruled Austria, the Holy Roman Empire, and much of Europe. They started out as small landowners in the early Middle Ages. Through a series of carefully arranged marriages, their landholdings were greatly increased. This went on for several generations until the Hapsburgs controlled a huge area.

By the thirteenth century the family held title to all of Austria. Because Austria bordered the lands held by Hungarians, Bohemians, and later the Turks, its early rulers had a hard time trying to keep invaders out. When the Hapsburg gained control of Austria, they continued the struggle. They gained large territories besides their German lands and became one of the strongest ruling families in Germany. Their capital, Vienna, was a great center of learning and European politics. The romantic Danube, which flows through the heart of Austria, was an important trade route to the East. Profits from this trade helped Austria prosper sooner and progress faster than the other German states did.

During the thirteenth and fourteenth centuries several Hapsburgs became emperors of the Holy Roman Empire. In the fifteenth century the electors decided that the title of Holy Roman emperor should be hereditary in the Hapsburg family. We might reasonably expect such a powerful family to unify Germany in the same way the powerful Duke of Paris united France. But this did not prove to be the case. The Hapsburgs became more interested in bringing the peoples of southeastern Europe under their domination than in unifying Germany. Furthermore, they opposed unification by any other power because they thought it might endanger Austria.

Religious wars retarded the progress of Germany. The Reformation started in Germany in 1517, when Luther led the revolt against the medieval Catholic Church. As you read in the story of the Reformation, most of the northern part of Germany became Protestant, while the southern part of the country, including Austria, remained Catholic. The differences led to years of conflict. The Hapsburg emperors tried to stamp out Protestantism. The Lutheran princes fought just as hard to keep their religious faith. In 1555 the Austrian ruler, Charles V, made peace with the Protestants because the Turks were threatening his eastern border. He needed the help of the Protestants to protect his lands.

For over a half-century there was comparative peace. Then, early in the seventeenth century, fighting broke out between Protestant nobles of Bohemia and the Austrian Hapsburgs. This was the beginning of a new war, which became known as the Thirty Years' War because of its duration. The war, which began as a religious conflict, became a power struggle that involved all of the German states, Austria, and their neighbors.

In the beginning, the conflict was primarily a rebellion against the increasing power of the Hapsburgs in the loose federation of states known as the Holy Roman Empire. Later, however, Sweden, Denmark, France, and England entered the war because they feared the rise of a powerful and unified Holy Roman Empire under Hapsburg domination. This foreign intervention further complicated the war as anti-Hapsburg German nobles, both Protestant and Catholic, joined to recapture German lands that had been seized by Sweden and Denmark. In the final years of the war, the fighting spread to all the nations of Western Europe.

When peace finally came in 1648, Germany lay in ruins. Almost a third of the people had been killed or had starved to death. Cities were destroyed. Trade and commerce were at a standstill. Fields lay uncultivated. The German people were unable to protect themselves against tyrants at home or robber kings from abroad. At the close of the war France seized Alsace-Lorraine.

The Thirty Years' War. The suffering of the German people during the Thirty Years' War is reflected in this scene, which shows a procession of the crippled and the blind trying to escape the destruction that has swept over their country. How did the war affect the future of the German state?

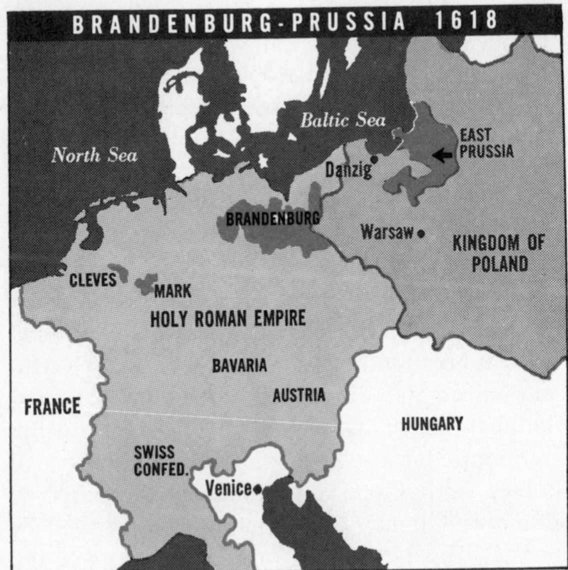

This act was the first of a long series of disputes over the territory.

Germany did not recover from the Thirty Years' War for over a hundred years. While other nations were becoming united and establishing colonial empires, the German nation remained divided and weak. The deep scars of the Thirty Years' War made unity between the Austrians and the people of northern Germany impossible. Instead, the job of welding together the German states was accomplished by a new power, as we shall see presently.

Chapter Check-up

1. Into what two states is Germany divided today?
2. Which ancient tribes were the ancestors of the Germans?
3. Why has it been so difficult for Germany to establish her eastern and western borders?
4. What is the historical connection between Germany and the empire of Charlemagne?
5. What was the purpose of the Hanseatic League?
6. How did the leagues retard the development of a unified Germany?
7. Why was Charles V forced to come to terms with the Protestants?
8. In what sense was the Thirty Years' War a power struggle rather than a religious conflict?
9. What were the political and economic effects of the Thirty Years' War on Germany?
10. Who were the Hapsburgs, and why did they fail to unify Germany?

CHAPTER 48

Prussia United the German States

A SERIES OF ABLE RULERS BUILT A STRONG PRUSSIA

The Hohenzollerns became rulers of Brandenburg-Prussia. In the last chapter we saw how the Hapsburg family gained lands and became the rulers of Austria and the Holy Roman Empire. Now we turn to the story of the Hohenzollern family, who built the state of Prussia and finally succeeded in uniting the German people into a modern nation. For many years the family ruled several tiny lands in central and western Germany. Then, early in the fifteenth century, Frederick Hohenzollern became a close friend and supporter of the ruler of Luxembourg. Frederick helped his friend become elected emperor and was rewarded by being given a northern German state known as Brandenburg. This possession made Frederick one of the electors who chose the Holy

Roman emperor. Thus the Hohenzollerns acquired the hereditary right to rule Brandenburg.

During the next century, the family strengthened Brandenburg, added to their territory, and set up their capital in Berlin. One member of the family decided that the Brandenburg lands should not be divided among many heirs as other German states were. He gave an order that Brandenburg should always go to the eldest son. His action had much to do with making the Hohenzollerns the strong rulers they became.

At the time of the Reformation the Hohenzollerns became Protestants. Early in the seventeenth century they acquired the land of East Prussia, a little state on the Baltic Sea, north of Poland. East Prussia was separated from Brandenburg by a narrow strip of Polish territory. Together the lands were known as *Brandenburg-Prussia*. Under a series of able rulers, Brandenburg-Prussia grew to become one of the most powerful German states.

Frederick William, the "Great Elector," fashioned Brandenburg-Prussia into a strong state. After they took over East Prussia, the Hohenzollerns were ready to go on conquering more land. But their ambitions suffered a setback because of the Thirty Years' War. The war damaged the land of the Hohenzollerns as it did

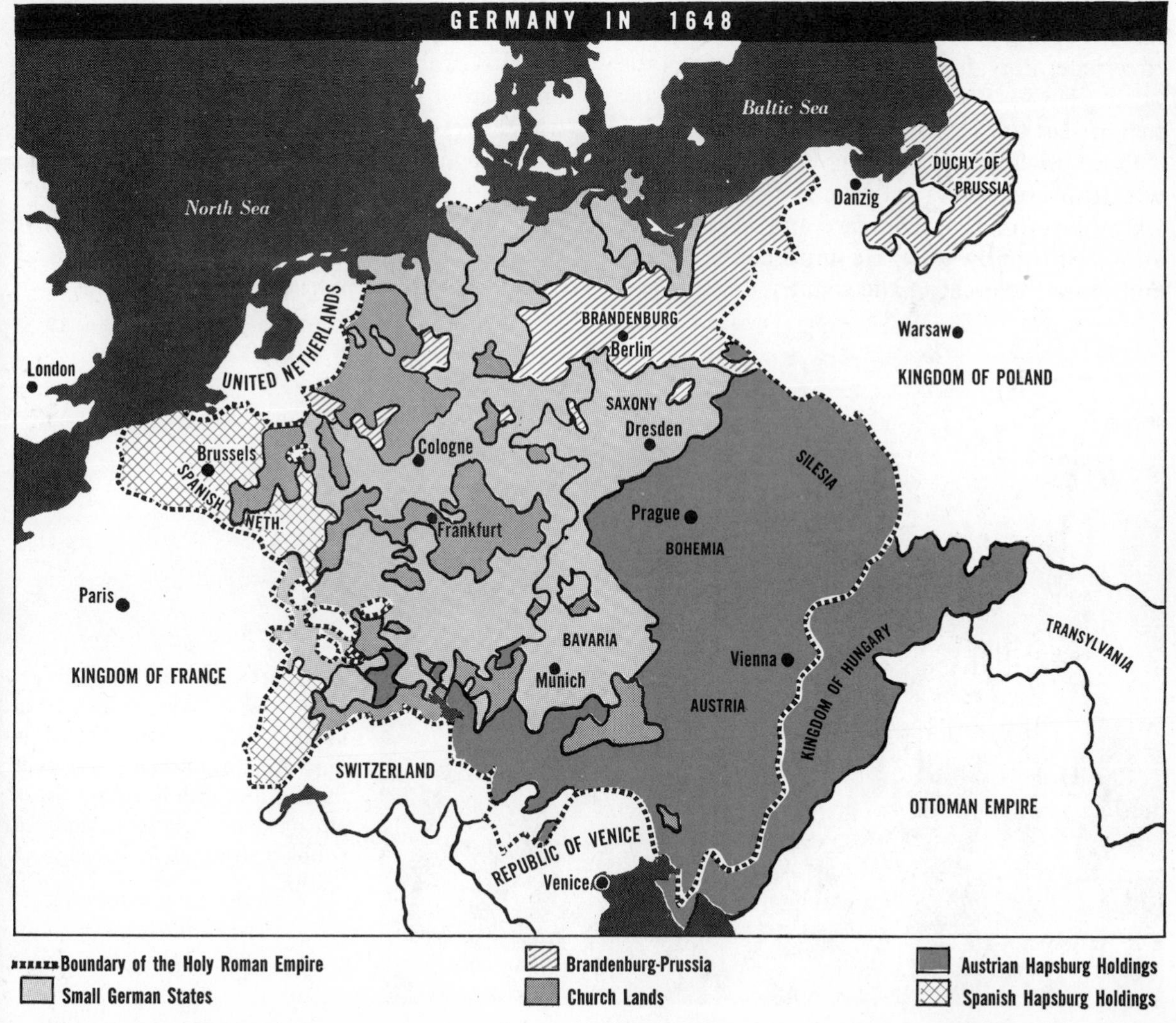

the rest of Germany. In the midst of the war, in 1640, an ambitious young man, Frederick William, became ruler of Brandenburg-Prussia. He found his lands devastated. More than half his subjects had died because of the war. Foreign armies and local outlaw nobles held much of his territory. He had no dependable troops and no money.

By making friends and using diplomacy, the young elector arranged an armistice within a year. That ended the damage of the war. He began to build a strong army. He got the towns and the nobles to agree to taxes to help build up defenses for the country. Gradually he subdued the outlaw nobles and increased his own power.

Frederick William did not hesitate to go to war to gain more land. He took advantage of quarrels between his neighbors, Sweden and Poland, to seize territory, first from one and then from the other. He was a good general, and he knew how to move fast to win victories.

Once, when he was fighting the French in the west, the Swedes invaded from the east. Frederick William did an about-face and marched his army swiftly to the east. He surprised the Swedes and drove them out of the country. After that, his subjects began to call him the "Great Elector."

Frederick William proved to be an able ruler. As a young man he had studied in Holland and learned how the government was run in that more advanced country. He built roads and canals. He improved agriculture, schools, and courts of law. Since there was a shortage of fruit trees, he ruled that no man could marry until he had first planted six new trees.

Perhaps the most lasting of the Great Elector's contributions was starting a permanent General Staff Corps for his army. Before his time, rulers raised armies by getting soldiers from their underlords or by hiring them when needed. The king and his nobles acted as officers. They might or they might not know anything about warfare. Usually they did not.

The Great Elector's General Staff Corps was made up of professional officers who spent their whole lives studying war. They learned all they could about warfare and taught it to those who were to follow them. From Frederick William's time until Hitler's, the Prussian General Staff Corps kept planning wars and building some of the greatest armies in history. Other nations have

A German Town. Not all German towns have grown into modern cities. Some, like this one, remain much as they were during the Middle Ages. Here an ox team clatters along a cobbled street under the sign of an inn.

Frederick the Great. Although Frederick was ruthless in his dealings with other nations, he was considerate of the welfare of his own subjects. He proclaimed religious toleration, abolished torture as a means of punishment, and made reforms in the administration of justice. Frederick is an excellent example of an "enlightened despot"—a ruler who uses his power benevolently.

copied the idea and have set up their own general staff corps. The Great Elector thus played an important part in starting modern militarism.

Frederick the Great proved a ruthless but able ruler. When the Great Elector's son came to power (his name was also Frederick) he was not satisfied with the title of elector. He also wanted to be known as king. He enlarged the army and took some more land nearby. Because he supplied the emperor with troops for a war against France, the emperor let him assume the title "King in Prussia." Thus all the Hohenzollern lands, with Brandenburg as the core, gradually came to be known as the Kingdom of Prussia.

A great-grandson of the Great Elector became for a time the most powerful leader in Europe. He earned the title Frederick the Great. As a youth, he was not interested in the business of kings or in war. He wanted to be a scholar and a writer. He played the flute and wrote French verses. But his father (known in history as Frederick William I) was determined to train him for kingship. They had bitter quarrels. At one time the son ran away. He was thrown into prison and was nearly shot as a deserter. Finally young Frederick agreed to follow his father's wishes. First he had to work long hours as a clerk. Later he went into the army, where he served as a private and then as an officer. When he came to the throne in 1740, just a hundred years after the Great Elector, he had had ten years of the strictest military discipline.

The young king showed a genius for war. The Prussian army had been made stronger by each succeeding king, and the General Staff Corps was doing its job. But this alone was not enough to account for Frederick's victories: he was a brilliant general. When Maria Theresa, a young Austrian archduchess, inherited the Austrian throne, Frederick saw his chance. He made a surprise attack on Austria and quickly forced her to give up the province of Silesia, which lies south of Brandenburg along the Oder River. Silesia was a rich prize, for it has some of the best coal deposits in Europe. Maria Theresa, with the help of France, tried for many years to regain Silesia. Again and again Frederick outfought or outmaneuvered his enemies. In 1763, at the end of the Seven Years' War, Frederick was still in possession of Silesia.

A few years later, Frederick joined Russia and Austria in dividing up Poland. He gained the vital province of West Prussia, which gave Prussia a long, solid strip of land along the Baltic Sea. It was hard on Poland, but few people cared. Poland was weak and at the mercy of her neighbors. (In Part 16 you will learn more about the ruthless carving up of Poland.) Frederick the Great did not worry about the justness of his claims. (See map on next page.) His comment was, "I take what I want; there will always be plenty of professors to justify what I do."

Frederick the Great was an enlightened despot. Although Frederick the Great made Prussia important in Europe by the use of ruthless military force, he liked to think of himself as a builder and a man of peace. He made improvements in farming, trade, and industry. To encourage industry at home he kept foreign goods out of the country. He traveled all over the kingdom to observe the needs of the people and to be sure that everything was done as he wished. Frederick's attitude toward the people was like that of a stern parent.

Frederick the Great was what historians call an "enlightened despot." He had complete power but he did not claim that he ruled by divine right. He said he held power because he was the one most capable of ruling. "Chief servant of the State," Frederick called himself. He claimed always to be guided by the welfare of the country as a whole. He was doubtless a much better ruler than the French kings of his time. When Frederick died he bequeathed most of his wealth to the national treasury.

During his long reign of forty-six years, Frederick the Great had made Prussia larger, stronger, and more important than it had ever been. Unfortunately, the rulers who followed him were less capable, and less well advised. In the next few years Prussia fell prey to Napoleon, and much of Frederick's work was undone.

NATIONALISTIC SPIRIT AROUSED THE GERMAN PEOPLE BUT FAILED TO UNITE THEM

Napoleon's conquests encouraged German nationalism. You learned in the story of France that the French Revolution in 1789 affected most of Europe. The people of Prussia and the other German states did not understand the uprisings in France and were not interested. The masses of the people in Germany were still serfs; there was virtually no middle class.

KINGDOM OF PRUSSIA 1795

Prussia before 1795
The Third Partition of Poland (1795)
To Prussia
To Austria
To Russia

At the end of the eighteenth century, when Napoleon seized power in France, Prussia's ruler was a weak descendant of Frederick the Great. Other nations fought Napoleon, but for more than ten years Prussia just looked on. Napoleon conquered a large part of Western Europe, including other parts of Germany. He combined the western states of Germany into the "Confederation of the Rhine" and brought them under his control. Then he finally forced the king of Prussia into a war. The Prussian army was quickly defeated, and the country had to give up parts of its territory. The proud Prussians did not forget the defeat or the shame. They waited for the chance to get even with France.

Unwittingly, Napoleon helped prepare the Germans for national unification. He reduced the nearly three hundred independent states to thirty-eight, thereby imposing partial unification. His easy victory made the Germans realize the weakness of their governments and their need to unite. As Queen Louise of Prussia said at that time, "We have fallen asleep on the laurels of Frederick the Great, the creator of the new era . . ."

So, Prussia, then at its lowest ebb as a European military and political power, became the scene of an internal reform movement which signalled the beginnings of a modern, progressive nation. This reform program was carried out by such able ministers of state as Karl vom Stein and Karl von Hardenberg. Under their leadership and the influence of Queen Louise, serfdom was abolished, the excessive privileges of the nobility were curbed, and, along with other social and economic reforms, a system of universal education was undertaken.

The reform movement affected even the army, the most conservative of Prussian institutions. The Prussian general Gerhard von Scharnhorst headed a commission to reorganize the army. He introduced a system of national conscription under which each male citizen was required to serve a short training period. Physical punishment became unlawful, and commoners were admitted for the first time to the officers' corps. Scharnhorst's reforms were so successful that thousands of Prussians volunteered for service when Prussia finally decided to throw off the yoke of France. In 1815, an awakened Prussia joined with other European nations to help defeat Napoleon at Waterloo.

Metternich opposed German unification. While the Hohenzollerns were making Prussia a leading power, the Hapsburgs of Austria were watching jealously. They kept disputing Prussia's attempts to expand. But Austria was too often fighting with the Turks or at war with the French to give enough attention to Prussia.

After the downfall of Napoleon, however, Austria had more to say. The ministers of Britain, Austria, Russia, and Prussia met in Vienna in 1814 to draw up the terms of peace (see Chapter 37). The Congress of Vienna was dominated by the Austrian representative, Prince Metternich (*met*-er-nik), who was the power behind the Austrian throne. Metternich recognized that Austria was in no position to unite the German states, and he was determined that no one else should do it. By clever diplomacy, he convinced the other representatives that Germany should be kept weak and divided. To this end, the German Confederation was established. (See map on page 448.) Each of the 39 member states was to adopt its own constitution and send a representative to a central diet, which could take no action without the unanimous consent of its members. Such an arrangement was intended to make each of the smaller states jealous of its constitution and identity and to allow Austria, as a member, to block any legislative attempt at German unification. As

Humiliation of Prussia. After entering Berlin in triumph in 1807, Napoleon greets the defeated Prussian monarchs, Queen Louise and Frederick William III. A short time later, Napoleon forced Frederick William to sign the Treaty of Tilsit, which gave France half of Prussia and made the Prussian king Napoleon's vassal. Prussia did not regain her sovereignty until 1813.

we shall see, Metternich's plan disregarded the rising spirit of German nationalism.

At the Congress of Vienna Austria also regained the lands and power she had lost to Napoleon, although the Holy Roman Empire was not restored. Prussia was given a section of land along the Rhine to compensate for the loss of some of her eastern land to Russia.

Metternich was afraid of the liberal ideas of liberty, self-government, and nationalism being spread by the French army. Such ideas might influence the peoples of Germany or the Austrian Empire to revolt. Therefore, he made every effort to make the princes of the German states absolute. He won their consent to clamp a tight censorship on all newspaper and book publishers in order to silence any dangerous new ideas. Metternich was determined to prevent political change because such change could destroy Austria.

The Revolution of 1848 was a failure. In spite of Metternich's precautions, the new liberal ideas could not be crushed. The year 1848 was marked by a series of uprisings in many of the countries of Europe, as the common people began to rebel against their harsh, autocratic rulers. Riots in Vienna forced Metternich to flee from Austria. Riots in Berlin forced the king of Prussia to promise a liberal constitution. A group of German nationalists, without asking the consent of the princes, gathered in Frankfurt, a city near

Congress of Vienna. In 1814–15, representatives of Europe's great powers met to settle the boundaries of Europe after the downfall of Napoleon. The meeting was a brilliant social gathering that was attended by the most famous statesmen of the time. Among them were Prince Metternich of Austria, the Duc de Talleyrand of France, and the Duke of Wellington from England.

REVOLUTION OF 1848. Behind barricades in Berlin, even women and children assisted the revolutionary forces by casting bullets. The woman at the right is removing the leading from a window, while the boys are melting lead and pouring it into molds. Although revolutionary riots broke out all over Germany, they failed to accomplish their purpose because the revolutionists could not agree on the best method for achieving national unity.

the Rhine. These middle-class lawyers and professors, who formed the *Frankfurt Assembly*, wrote a constitution designed to unite Germany under a king whose powers would be limited by law. After deciding that the new Germany should not include Austria, they hopefully offered the crown to the king of Prussia. He was too proud to accept a crown from the people, to "pick up a crown from the gutter" as he put it, so he refused. More riots broke out, and the king of Prussia, the emperor of Austria, and the German princes turned their armies on the people. The members of the Frankfurt Assembly had neither military backing nor support from the masses, as the leaders of the French Revolution had had. The Assembly was finally forced to disband, and the revolution quickly collapsed.

The failure of the Revolution of 1848 in Germany caused an important change in German thinking. Many Germans saw that the ideas of the Frankfurt Assembly, although they were sound and just in themselves, had accomplished nothing. Military power, not reason and justice, had won the day. Many Germans who still believed in freedom and self-government left for America. Those who remained decided that force, not ideas, changed history. They took the view, based on their experience, that might makes right.

BISMARCK UNITED GERMANY UNDER THE LEADERSHIP OF PRUSSIA

Bismarck adopted a "blood and iron" policy. The revolutions of 1848 resulted in one liberal improvement for Prussia: a parliament. Although Parliament was under the control of the upper class, it succeeded in limiting somewhat the absolute rule of the Prussian king, William. The parliament and the king did not get along. William wanted the members to vote a tax so that he could enlarge the army. The members, who felt that the army was already too strong, refused. At this crisis, in 1862, William chose a Prussian noble named Otto von Bismarck to be prime minister.

The new prime minister was no friend of parliament or democracy. He opposed liberal ideas about individual liberty and self-government. His background and training made him believe in the old Prussian military ideals of duty, obedience, and service to the state. His duty was to lead; the duty of the people was to follow. Accordingly, Bismarck collected the taxes without Parliament's consent. The Prussians, who, unlike the English, were accustomed to obeying royal officials, paid without protest. When Parliament complained that Bismarck had acted in violation of the constitution, he calmly replied that the welfare of the state was more important than the constitution. He reminded the Prussians that force had decided matters in 1848. He declared, "The great questions of our day will not be decided by speeches and majority votes . . . but by blood and iron."

Bismarck was too wise to ignore the greatest question of the day, the unification of Germany. He personally disliked the idea of unification because he did not want Prussia to be swallowed up in a larger German state. But the desire for unity had become so strong among the German people that it would probably have taken place in spite of him. Therefore, Bismarck felt that because he could not prevent unification, he should unify Germany himself. Then he could subject the other German states to Prussian rule.

Bismarck fought three wars to unite Germany. Two powerful opponents stood in the way of Bismarck's plans. They were France and Austria. Neither country was likely to stand by peacefully while a strong Germany developed on its borders. Bismarck did not let them or any other obstacle distract him from his goal. Like Cavour, he was prepared to use any means necessary to achieve his goal, even war. To prevent Austria and France from uniting against him, he kept his plans secret until he could defeat each country separately.

Bismarck's first move was to ask Austria's help in invading two provinces that Denmark claimed. After the Danish War (1864), he encouraged a quarrel with Austria over control of the new territories. Bismarck waited until Austria was preoccupied with a conflict in Italy, and then attacked. In the war that followed, the Seven Weeks' War (1866), the efficient Prussian army made short work of the once-proud Hapsburg forces. It was now evident to the German states that Prussia had become the leading power in Central Europe. Austria was expelled from the German Confederation. Bismarck proceeded to annex several north German states; the others were members of the Prussian-dominated North German Federation.

Bismarck's third move was to maneuver France into a war. He realized that he could never persuade the south German states to support Prussia, whom they regarded as an aggressor, unless he could unite them against a common enemy. (Bavaria, Württemberg, and Baden, for instance, had sided with Austria in the Seven Weeks' War.) In 1870 he saw his chance. The French ambassador had asked the Prussian king to make certain promises, which the king politely refused to do. Bismarck deliberately altered the wording of a telegram which referred to the incident, and then publicly released it. Both the French and the Germans were furious because the telegram, known in history as the *Ems Dispatch*, made it seem as though each side had insulted the other. Humiliated, the French emperor, Napoleon III, was forced to declare war on Prussia.

Bismarck was not, however, entirely responsible for the outbreak of the war. In France, too, a strong faction believed that war with Germany would bring advantages. Many Frenchmen feared the growth of a united Germany on the French border, and Napoleon III thought that a war with Germany, if successful, would increase his waning popularity. Thus, in neither country was there a genuine effort to keep peace.

As Bismarck had hoped, the south German states rallied to the support of Prussia. As you learned in the story of France, the Franco-Prussian War (1870) proved disastrous to Napoleon III and the French nation. France lost Alsace-Lorraine and was forced to pay her conqueror a huge sum of money. To add insult to the French plight, Bismarck arranged for the coronation of the new German emperor (or *kaiser*) in the famous palace of the French kings at Versailles. On January 18, 1871, German princes crowded the historic building to watch the king of Prussia proclaimed William I, Emperor of Germany. Bismarck, by the cold and calculated use of force,

BISMARCK. This portrait of the Iron Chancellor was made just before he reached his eightieth birthday. What does the portrait reveal about Bismarck's character?

had at last created a united German nation. Let us see what kind of a nation it was.

Bismarck's success marked the triumph of Prussian tradition. The new German Empire appeared to be a liberal democracy, but in reality the old Prussian form of government had not changed at all. Although there was a parliament whose lower house, the Reichstag (*rikes*-tahk), was elected by universal manhood suffrage, it did not choose or control the prime minister, or *chancellor*. Instead, the chancellor was appointed by the king. As you might have guessed, Bismarck held this office for many years. He contemptuously let the Reichstag debate German affairs, but with William's consent he proceeded to make all the major decisions himself.

The traditional Prussian idea of government had not changed, either. In the tradition of Frederick the Great, Bismarck felt that the government should look after the people in the manner of a stern father. It was not for them to tell the government what to do. The German Socialist party, which was Bismarck's leading opponent, urged the people to fight in Parliament for what they wanted. But Bismarck shrewdly provided the workers with sickness and accident insurance, pensions, and other social legislation so that the people would not have to win these benefits for themselves.

Bismarck's success in war and in government firmly crushed the liberal ideals of 1848. The Germans accepted the old idea that they were not capable of ruling themselves. They believed it their duty to obey the state, and they were sure that force, if it served the state, was right.

Germany struggled for a place in the sun. After 1870, the Germans turned their attention to making their country the greatest industrial nation in Europe. German science and technology became the most advanced in the world. Experts prepared nitrates to enable Germany's soil, which was poorer than that of France, to produce better crops than French lands could. German factories became leading producers of chemicals, drugs, and dyes. They also manufactured excellent cameras, microscopes, and telescopes. Soon the trademark "Made in Germany" became known throughout the world as a sign of superior workmanship. Germany rapidly became one of the world's leading industrial nations.

In 1888, the young emperor, William II, came to the throne. He had great respect for Bismarck but thought that the old empire-maker was a little out of date. What William really meant was that he wanted to rule Germany himself. In 1890, he commanded Bismarck to resign.

William proceeded to carry Bismarck's policy of "blood and iron" much further than the former

GERMANY UNITED. King William is proclaimed emperor of a united Germany in the Hall of Mirrors at Versailles after the defeat of the French in 1871. Bismarck stands in the center foreground.

DROPPING THE PILOT. A famous cartoon, which appeared in the English humor magazine *Punch,* shows King William left to pilot the ship of state himself upon Prince Bismarck's retirement.

chancellor had intended. Once Bismarck had achieved a strong, united Germany, he took care not to anger the rest of Europe. But William was not satisfied with Bismarck's policy of gaining equality with the great states of Europe. He wanted Germany to become a dominant power. He entered the race for colonies in Africa and China, and he built a navy to rival that of Britain. Soon German gunboats were prowling waters once considered the exclusive province of other European nations. You will remember that in the sixteenth and seventeenth centuries, Spain, France, England, and the Netherlands laid the foundation for their great colonial empires. At that time the disunited states of Germany were being ruined by disastrous wars. The German people always felt they were cheated in the race for colonies. This feeling was one of the underlying causes for their eagerness to build up their military power. Germany insisted that any new colonial agreements made must take into account Germany's right to a "place in the sun." Behind all this self-assertion lay a veiled suggestion that if Germany's demands were not satisfied, she would not hesitate to resort to war. You will read later how Germany's actions were one of the chief causes of World War I.

When World War I started, the German people thought that their army could not be conquered—that they could win a quick and final victory. Instead, defeat came in 1918, and Germany and Austria both lost much of their territory. (See maps on pages 452 and 453.) You will read about these events in more detail when you come to the story of World War I in Part 22.

Chapter Check-up

1. What family is most closely associated with the rise of Prussia?
2. How did Frederick William, the Great Elector, strengthen Brandenburg-Prussia?
3. How did Frederick the Great enlarge Prussia?
4. How did Napoleon unintentionally prepare the Germans for national unification?
5. Why and how was Metternich determined to prevent unification of Germany?
6. What were Bismarck's beliefs about the government and the individual?
7. How did Bismarck unite Germany?
8. What ideas of government did the Germans learn to accept and come to believe?
9. In what direction did Germany turn her efforts after 1870?
10. How did the policies of William II differ from Bismarck's?

CHAPTER 49

Hitler Brought the German People Under Nazi Control and Led Them to Disaster

A TROUBLED GERMANY ACCEPTED DICTATORSHIP

After World War I Germany became a republic. By the autumn of 1918, Germany had been at war for four years. She was nearly exhausted from the effort of holding off the combined attack of Britain, France, and the United States, and she was slowly being starved by the Allied blockade of her seaports. As the Allies drove toward Germany, a revolution took place in the country. When the people saw defeat coming, they turned against the leaders whom they believed were responsible for the war. William II, the same emperor who had dismissed Bismarck, fled to Holland. The new government became a republic. It was called the Weimar (*vie*-mahr) Republic because the constitution was drawn up in the city of Weimar. The Allies negotiated the terms of peace with the new government at the close of World War I.

The constitution of the Weimar Republic was one of the most democratic in the world. It declared that political authority is derived from the people. All citizens, men and women alike, had equal rights. No titles of nobility were to be granted. The people elected the president of the republic, but the president did not take a great part in politics. The chief responsibility of government rested on a chancellor, or prime minister, and on the Reichstag, the parliament elected by the people.

Many Germans opposed the Weimar Republic. The new German ship of state was launched on a rough sea. In the first place, the republic was identified with the idea of defeat and humiliation. It was the Weimar government that made peace settlements after World War I. The leaders had to agree to bitter terms. Under the Versailles Treaty Germany had to give Alsace-Lorraine back to France and surrender certain other territories to Belgium, Denmark, Poland, and Lithuania. The Germans were forced to disband their army and navy and agree to pay a huge bill for reparations, or war damages. Although the Germans never paid the huge sum

At A Glance

Important Periods and People in German History

Early German Rulers (800–973)
- Charlemagne
- Louis the German
- Otto of Saxony

Rise of Prussia (1640–1871)
- Frederick William, the Great Elector
- Frederick the Great
- Queen Louise
- William I
- Otto von Bismarck

German Empire (1871–1918)
- William I
- William II

Weimar Republic (1918–1934)
- Frederick Ebert
- Paul von Hindenburg

Third Reich (1934–1945)
- Adolf Hitler

Divided Germany (1945–Present)
- West German Federal Republic
  - Konrad Adenauer
- East German Democratic Republic

(35 billion dollars), the charges caused great bitterness among the German people. As a final blow, the Versailles Treaty stripped Germany of all her colonies.

German soldiers returned home to find that there was no work for them. Industries were disorganized and foreign trade was destroyed. The people did not get back the money they had loaned the government to carry on the war. A shortage of goods caused prices to rise rapidly, and the country was faced with ruinous inflation. In desperation the government printed more and more paper money, until German money became worthless. Before the war, four German marks

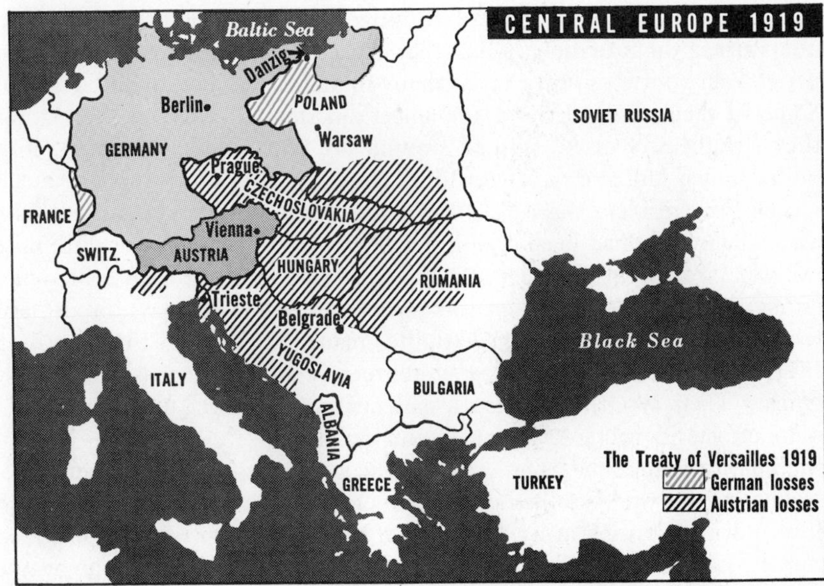

POSTWAR INFLATION. From 1920 to 1923, inflation in Germany was so severe that bank notes had only a fraction of their former value. Here large baskets of paper money are being loaded on a truck for delivery to banks. As the inflation increased, printing presses were kept running steadily to turn out new bills. Shoppers needed handfuls of money to make even the smallest purchase.

had equaled one American dollar, but at one time in 1923 an American dollar would buy more than four trillion marks!

The leaders of the new republic were honest men with good intentions. But they lacked experience in politics, so they made many mistakes. Some of them were so timid and uncertain that they let themselves be pushed around by the military men and the old-time ruling class.

The first president was a Socialist named Frederick Ebert. He had been a saddle maker before the war. People liked him, but he failed to take strong action against the men who were plotting to destroy the republic. Furthermore, many of the pre-war officials were allowed to remain in office. Their sympathies were usually with the old, autocratic ruling class of Germany rather than with the republic.

The Treaty of Versailles prevented Germany from having a strong army. Fearful of workers' revolts, the government hired bands of former soldiers to stamp out riots and uprisings. But the soldier-adventurers themselves turned out to be the worst enemies of the state. They wanted to overthrow the republic. They were bitter because of Germany's defeat and, in many cases, because they had lost their careers in the army. They organized, half secretly, on a large scale and called themselves the Free Corps. They hid guns which were supposed to be handed over to the Allies. They were guilty of secret political murders. Some of their victims were men in high government positions.

Adolf Hitler became the leader of the Nazis. The confusion and trouble of post-war Germany set the stage for the rise of a ruthless and determined Austrian named Adolf Hitler. Hitler's father had been a minor official in the Austrian government. At seventeen, when his father died, Hitler went to Vienna to study art. He was refused admission to art school and could find no steady job. Poor, friendless, and uneducated, he scraped along by tinting postcards and selling them. By day he passed in the street many people who had gained wealth and importance in the professions, in business, or in government. Among them were many Jews. By night he met, in the dingy public dormitories where he lived, the poor and miserable from all over the Austrian Empire. These circumstances aroused in Hitler and others like him an intense resentment toward the prosperous Jews. In time, his hatred for the Jews became an obsession.

From Vienna, Hitler moved to Munich (*myoo-nik*), a city in southern Germany. When World War I broke out, he joined the German army. War seemed to him thrilling and ennobling after his life of dull, miserable poverty. Hitler did not rise above the rank of corporal, but he took special satisfaction in serving the German Fatherland. After the war, he felt let down. His glamorous life was over. He was forced to join the ranks of the unemployed in Munich.

Post-war Munich swarmed with dissatisfied groups of men who bitterly opposed the Weimar Republic. Hitler joined one of these groups. His gifts as a speaker soon attracted many followers. His German was not very good, but his tense, emotional voice and his self-confident manner thrilled his audiences. In fiery speeches he told them that Germany must unite under a strong leader and take her rightful place as the dominant nation of the world.

By 1920 Hitler had become head of a political party which he called the National Socialist German Workers' party. Its members became known as Nazis (*naht*-sees). The Nazis adopted a red flag with a black swastika, an ancient symbol of good luck. They maintained a private armed band of soldier-adventurers called "storm troopers." The storm troopers broke up the meetings of other political parties and attacked their leaders. Some Germans were frightened by this violence. Others were impressed.

In 1923 Hitler, copying Mussolini's methods, tried to seize control of Germany by force. He fired a revolver in a Munich beer hall and declared that the republic was at an end. The police appeared, however, and Hitler was sentenced to jail for five years. The Weimar government believed in freedom of speech, and Hitler had not done much more than talk; so he was released a year later. During his prison term, he wrote *Mein Kampf*, which means "my battle." It is a confused account of his early life, his beliefs about the superiority of Germans, and his plans for making Germany a powerful nation again.

Hitler blamed the Depression on the Jews and used it to increase Nazi power. In 1924 the German economy began to revive. The Allies reduced the amount of reparations demanded from Germany, and many American businessmen began to invest in German industry. The government organized a stable money system, and factories reopened. Foreign trade increased. The Weimar Republic began to win the support of the workers and the middle class. Hitler, on the other hand, lost most of his following. He might have disappeared from history forever had not a new blow struck the young republic—the Great Depression of the 1930's.

The Great Depression (see Chapter 76) was felt on both sides of the Atlantic. When American investments in Germany stopped, the German factories closed. Soon six million men were without work. Bankruptcy and unemployment became widespread. The middle class and the workers lost their new-found faith in the Weimar Republic. Many workers turned to communism. The middle and upper classes, frightened by the increased strength of the Communists in the Reichstag, looked desperately about for someone to save them.

Hitler seized this new opportunity. The Nazis plastered walls with huge red and black posters. They arranged parades, torch-light processions, and mass ceremonies. Storm troopers and Communists fought gun battles in the streets. Hitler made violent speeches in which he blamed everyone except the Germans for Germany's troubles. He bitterly denounced the Allies for imposing unjust and harsh terms in the Versailles Treaty. He said that the Allies had stripped Germany of land

HITLER. This photo of the fiery orator shows him making one of the many speeches he made to the German people. His leadership led Germany to disaster.

and money and refused to allow her to rearm in order to keep the nation weak forever.

Hitler made his most violent attack on the Jews. He revived the popular myth that the army had not been defeated in 1918 but had been "stabbed in the back" by traitors at home who revolted against the emperor. Hitler declared that these traitors were the Jews and that all of Germany's troubles were the fault of the Jews. Although there was not a word of truth in the charges, they provided a glib explanation for Germany's troubles and thus were often given a sympathetic hearing. Again, as he had in 1920, Hitler proclaimed Germany's need for a strong leader who would rescue her from traitors and enemies.

Many Germans, disappointed in the failure of their government to keep order or bring the country out of the depression, voted for the Nazi party. By 1933, it was the largest party in the Reichstag. A group of industrialists and army officers, hoping that they could use Hitler as a tool against the Communists, persuaded the president to appoint him chancellor. Thus Hitler became head of the German government.

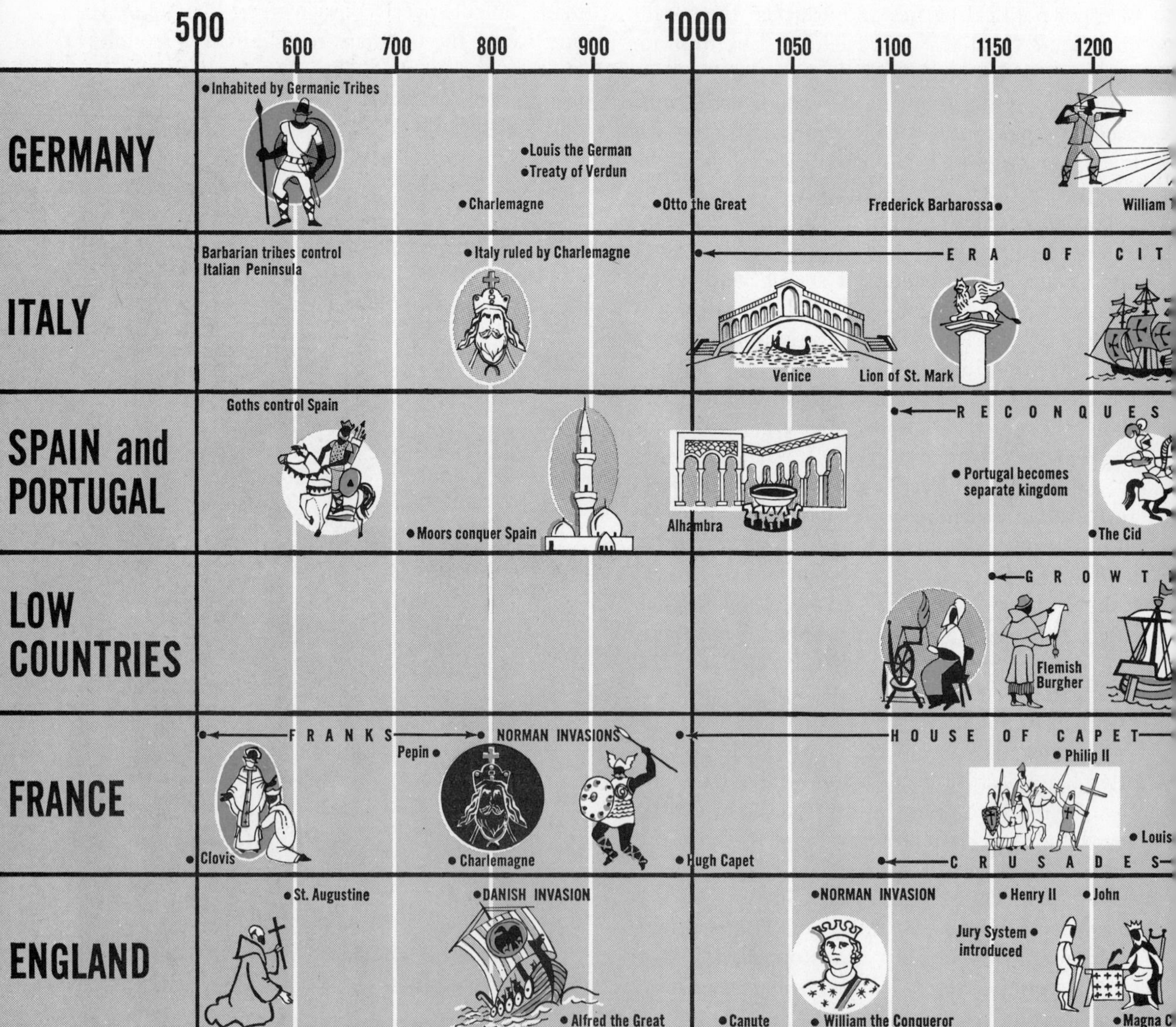

THE NAZIS MADE GERMANY A TOTALITARIAN STATE AND SET OUT TO CONQUER THE WORLD

Hitler obtained unlimited power. As he built up his party through more than ten years, Hitler had had some experience in the art of seizing power. But no one ever dreamed the new chancellor would make himself the absolute ruler of Germany within a few weeks. He used a number of devices to make his power complete.

One strong group in the Reichstag, the Communist party, still opposed Hitler. In February, 1933, the Reichstag building burned. No one is completely certain of all the facts behind the fire. The Nazis may well have started it themselves. However, they were quick to insist it was the work of the Communists, and Hitler used it as an excuse to bar Communist delegates from the parliament. Frightened, the other members voted to give Hitler dictatorial powers. When President von Hindenburg died in 1934, Hitler abolished

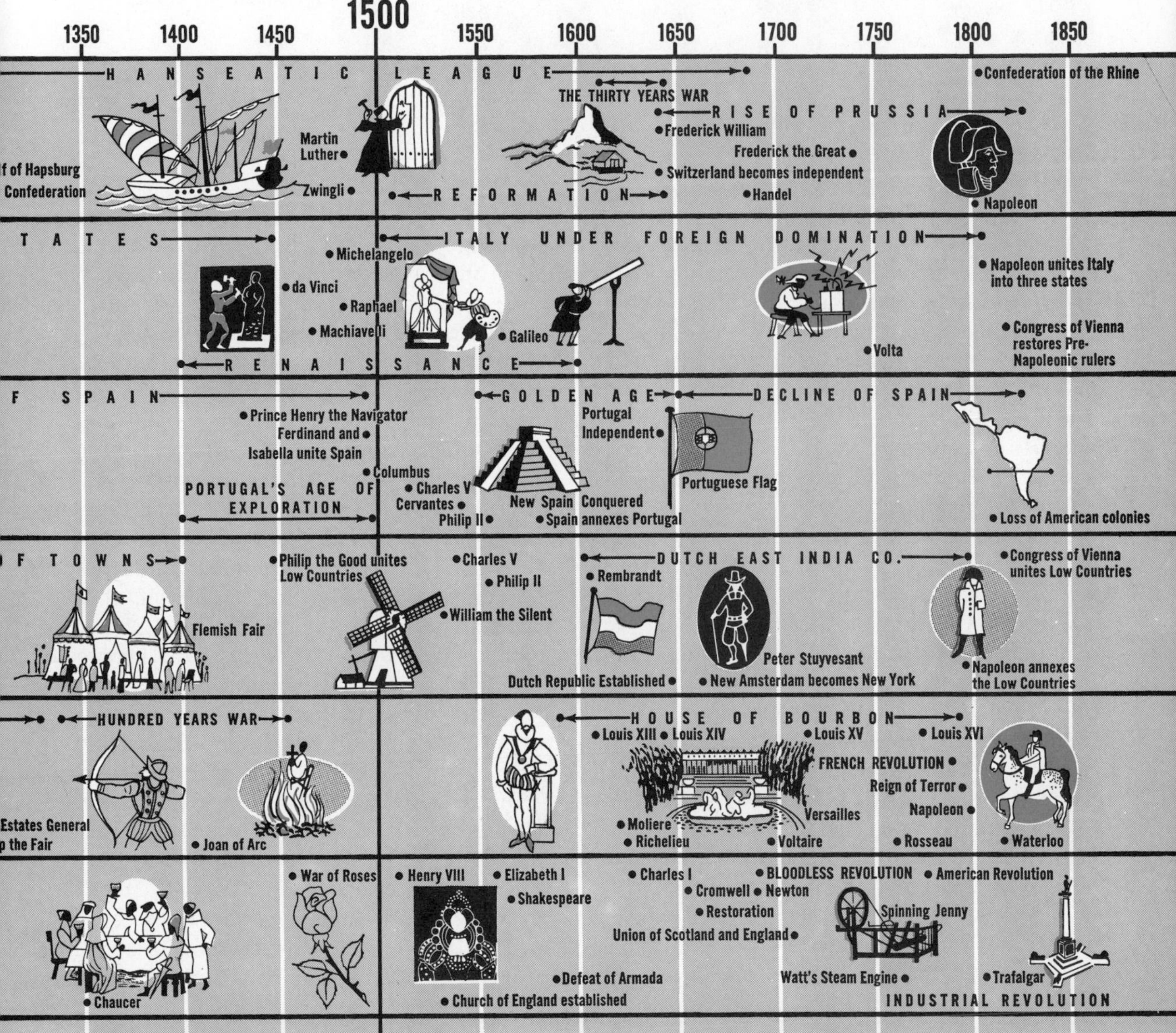

JEWS UNDER HITLER. Dragged from their homes by Nazi soldiers, these Jews await shipment to a concentration camp. Hitler blamed Germany's troubles on the Jewish people, and during World War II he ruthlessly ordered millions of them imprisoned or killed.

the office of president. There was no longer even a shadow of any other power in government. Hitler continued as chancellor, but was now called the Fuehrer (*fyoo*-rer), or leader of the nation.

Under the "Third Reich" (as Hitler called his new government) it became the sole duty of the individual to serve the state. Loyalty to the Fuehrer and the Fatherland allowed no room for individual opinion. Protestant and Catholic clergymen were forbidden to criticize the government. All political parties, except the National Socialist party, were outlawed. The labor unions were forbidden to strike. A secret police force, the Gestapo (ges-*tah*-po), saw to it that no one expressed any ideas critical of Hitler or the Nazi government. No one could offer to the public a book, magazine, newspaper, radio program, or movie without government approval. Germans were forbidden to read or listen to any communication from a foreign country. The Nazis burned German books written before 1933 if the ideas expressed in them were opposed to those of Hitler. Thus the Germans were sealed off from knowledge of the past and of the outside world.

The Nazis launched a cunning and efficient propaganda campaign to tell the people what the Nazis wanted them to know. The Nazis published newspapers and books and controlled all radio programs. Loudspeakers blared Hitler's ideas from street corners. Children were filled with Nazi ideas in school. They donned uniforms and learned more of the Nazi program when they joined the Hitler Youth Movement. After hearing nothing but Hitler's ideas endlessly repeated year after year, many people came to accept them and ultimately to believe them.

Hitler told the Germans that they were the "master race." To make sure that all Germans stood solidly behind the Fuehrer and the Fatherland, Hitler filled their minds with the idea that they were a "master race." He told them in endless streams of propaganda that Germans of "pure blood" were superior to any other people.

Hitler used the doctrine of racial superiority as an excuse to persecute the Jews. The Nazi government even pried into a suspected person's past to find out whether he had a Jewish ancestor. If he did, he had to pay heavy taxes and was driven out of business. Later, the storm troopers hunted down the Jews and imprisoned them in concentration camps. Many Jews fled from Germany, and many non-Jews who hated the Nazi policy also left. Germany lost some of her ablest scholars and scientists in this way. Hitler persecuted the Jews for a very practical reason; it took attention away from the serious problems that resulted from other Nazi policies.

The Nazis turned Germany into a war machine. Soon after coming to power, Hitler crushed all opposition. Those who disagreed with him quickly lost their posts of influence in schools, courts, and civil service. Next, Hitler made plans for war. Germany, he announced, needed more living space for her people. Germans living in neighboring countries should be reunited with the Fatherland, and Germany should take her rightful place as the leader of the world.

Accordingly, Germany withdrew from the League of Nations and, in defiance of the Versailles Treaty, began to rearm. Soldiers and young boys marched to the blare of trumpets and saluted the Nazi flag. They were trained to be strong, obedient, and ruthless. Anyone who valued ideas of peace, individual thought, or mercy was ridiculed as outdated and weak. German factories, controlled by the state even though privately owned, turned out guns and ammunition. Everyone was forced to work for the state. Anyone who opposed the Nazis was killed or thrown into a concentration camp. You will read in Part 22 how Hitler used his mighty war machine to conquer Germany's neighbors and plunge Europe into World War II.

What made Nazism possible in Germany? Why did the German people fall so easily under Hitler's spell? Let us review briefly some of the high points of the history of the German people. While it is true that the early German barbarians were warlike, so were the barbarians who invaded Gaul (France) and other parts of the Roman Em-

REVIEWING THE GERMAN TROOPS. Adolf Hitler reviews the troops that marched across Europe in the blitzkrieg ("lightning war") that he hoped would "divide and conquer" the world for the Third Reich.

GERMAN YOUTH. Central to Hitler's control of the people was the organization of youth groups. Fanatically devoted to their leader, these young boys, as shown here, formed an elite group that later served in Germany's armed forces. Many were to die for a worthless and brutal cause.

pire. The Northmen who settled in the British Isles and on the Continent were also a rough and warlike people. So early ancestors alone cannot explain the rise of the Nazis.

The Germans probably accepted many of the Nazi ideas because those ideas had their roots in German history. The Germans accepted Hitler as their leader because they had grown used to following orders. The tradition of Frederick the Great, Bismarck, and William II outweighed the fifteen short years of the Weimar Republic. Then too, the problems of inflation and depression that the Weimar government seemed unable to solve made the people value the jobs that Hitler created in rearming Germany. Prosperity seemed to return to the country. Businessmen made large profits in war goods, and German workers gained steady jobs.

Hitler's ideas of racial superiority were, of course, ridiculous. Scientists know that there is no such thing as a pure German "blood." Perhaps the Germans accepted Hitler's ideas because they were flattering to hear. Certainly he used every propaganda device at his disposal to drive them home. Once the Nazis had gained control over the minds of the German people, it was easy to control other aspects of their lives. Under Nazi domination, nothing could legally be thought, spoken, or done in Germany that was not approved by the government.

THERE ARE TWO POST-WAR GERMANIES

Germany was occupied by the Allies. Germany was defeated in World War II, and the Allies divided the country into four zones of occupation. The British held the northwest, the French the west, the Americans the south, and the Russians the east. Before long, the Western democracies and Russia began to quarrel over the future of Germany. Russia, without consulting the other Allies, took part of Poland and compensated Poland by giving her German territory east of the Oder River. The Russians made it clear that they would delay any final peace treaty that would allow Germany to become reunited. They had suffered so greatly from the German invasion during the war that they did not intend to allow a strong, united Germany to threaten Russia again. For this reason, the Russians allowed no political freedom in their occupation zone except to the German Communist party. Hopes of finding a common agreement among the Allies on the re-unification and future of Germany faded and disappeared.

The Western democracies established the West German Federal Republic. In 1947 Britain, France, and the United States decided to go ahead and unite their zone into an independent German state. The West German Federal Republic was established two years later. It has a democratic constitution which provides for nine states, each with its own legislature, and a central parliament with two houses. Most of the power of government is lodged in the lower house, the Bundestag (*boon*-des-tahk), which is elected by the German people every four years. The Bundestag elects the chancellor, who is the real head of the government, although there is a president elected by the people. Konrad Adenauer (*ah*-d'n-ow-er) was elected the first chancellor in 1949. His party, the Christian Demo-

EAST AND WEST MEET. West German Chancellor Willy Brandt (left) and East German Premier Willi Stoph are shown as they met in 1970 to bring about understanding between the democratic and communist areas of West and East Germany.

DIVIDED BERLIN. "Attention! You are now leaving West Berlin," reads the sign at the Brandenburg Gate. As is obvious from the barbed wire, however, the area is no thoroughfare. The wall, erected to prevent East Berliners from crossing to West Berlin, is patrolled on the other side by armed guards.

VIENNA. Once the gay capital of the Hapsburg Empire, Vienna has long been known as a great cultural center of Europe. Shown here is Schönbrunn royal palace, the residence of the eighteenth century Empress Maria Theresa. Schönbrunn somewhat copies the gardens of Versailles, yet it still remains one of the most beautiful of royal homes. It has been restored to its former magnificence after being damaged by the Russians in World War II.

cratic Union, has long been the largest party in the Bundestag. In 1963 Adenauer retired and was succeeded by Vice-Chancellor Ludwig Erhard, also a Christian Democrat. In 1966, however, Erhard was forced to resign and a coalition government was formed, dominated by the Christian Democrats and the Social Democrats. Kurt Georg Kiesinger, a Christian Democrat was elected Chancellor, and Willy Brandt, Mayor of West Berlin and a Social Democrat, became Vice-Chancellor.

West Germany has made an astonishing recovery from World War II. After twenty years of economic prosperity, the Federal Republic has become one of the richest nations in Europe.

Russia created the German Democratic Republic. In 1949 Russia proclaimed her occupation zone to be the German Democratic Republic. Its form of government is like that of West Germany, but it remains a Russian satellite. When German workers revolted in 1953, Russian troops put down the revolt. Nations of Western Europe and the Americas have not granted diplomatic recognition to the German Democratic Republic.

After the war the economy of East Germany was close to collapse. In the first years of occupation the Russians carried off a great deal of machinery, making industrial recovery more difficult. Drought and lack of fertilizer reduced East German agricultural output. The flight of skilled laborers to West Germany, and the worker uprising in 1953 were further proofs of the country's unstable economy. But East Germany's industry has now been integrated with that of the Soviet Union, and economic conditions have greatly improved.

Divided Berlin has already touched off two international crises. The first occurred in 1948 when the Russians closed the corridor leading into the western sector of the city (see page 766). The second crisis came in 1961 when the East German Communist government forbade its citizens to enter West Berlin and began erecting a wall to separate East and West Berlin. The Communist regime has suffered both embarrassment and economic loss from the flight of East Germans into West Germany. The Western powers have protested the Communist action and made it clear that they will not be forced out of Berlin.

The future of Germany is an international problem. All Germans wish to be reunited under one government, but reunification is unlikely to take place until Russia and the Western democracies can agree on the form of government and on guarantees that Germany will not become an aggressor nation again.

Austria gained her independence after the war. Hitler had made Austria a part of Germany in 1938, and after World War II the country was occupied by the allies. In 1945 Austria was reestablished as a republic. Disagreements between Great Britain, the United States, France, and Russia threatened to keep it permanently divided. In 1955 the Soviet Union finally agreed to withdraw from her occupied zone if Austria would make large payments of goods for the next ten years. (In 1964 Austria completed these payments delivering over 150 million dollars worth of goods to Russia.) The other allies also withdrew but without making any demands. This agreement of 1955 restored the Austrian frontiers of 1938 and gave back complete sovereignty to the country.

Austria has renounced possession of atomic weapons and declared its permanent neutrality. The republic has a president and two-house parliament. A chancellor and cabinet, appointed by the president, are responsible to parliament. Tourism, Austria's biggest industry, helps to balance her budget.

Chapter Check-up

1. How did the Treaty of Versailles, ending World War I, affect Germany?
2. For what reasons was the Weimar Republic opposed by many Germans?
3. What economic disaster spelled the end of the Weimar Republic?
4. On whom did Hitler place the blame for all of Germany's problems?
5. How did Hitler turn Germany into a completely totalitarian state?
6. How did the Third Reich control thought and public opinion?
7. What was the German belief about the "master race"?
8. Why are there two post-war Germanies?
9. What is the prospect for the eventual reunification of Germany?
10. What is the status of post-war Austria?

CHAPTER 50

The Germans Have Furthered Learning and the Arts

GERMAN WRITERS ARE KNOWN ALL OVER THE WORLD

Goethe wrote a great drama. The most famous of all German writers is Goethe (*ger*-teh). He lived during the latter part of the eighteenth and the first part of the nineteenth centuries. Goethe was a poet, novelist, and philosopher. His greatest work is *Faust* (fowst), a drama based on an old legend. The story is about a weary old scholar who sells himself to Mephistopheles (mef-ih-*stahf*-eh-leez), the devil, in order to taste the joys of youthful adventure. Many harrowing and sorrowful experiences are woven into the drama. Faust's wanderings over the earth in search of the pleasures of life are a symbol of the restless searchings of men in the nineteenth century. Faust at last finds peace in useful labor, and he triumphs over the power of darkness. An opera by the French composer Gounod (*goo*-no) is based on Goethe's dramatic poem.

Schiller and Heine believed in liberty. One of Goethe's close friends was Germany's greatest romantic playwright, Schiller (*shil*-ler). Schiller was one of the forerunners of the liberal, nationalist movement that caused the Revolutions of 1848. His passionate hatred of tyrannical rulers shows particularly in his best-known play, *William Tell.* Tell, as you will discover in the next chapter, was a Swiss hero who fought for Swiss independence from the Hapsburgs. *William Tell* has been made into a famous opera by the Italian composer Rossini.

GOETHE. As poet, novelist, dramatist, and scientist, Goethe left a lasting mark on his country's cultural history. His works have been translated into many languages and are popular in many countries outside Germany.

Heine (*hi*-neh), one of Germany's best romantic poets, shared Schiller's love of liberty and patriotism. Heine's lyrical poems encouraged young Germans to revolt and create a free, united Germany. His most famous poem, "The Lorelei," is taken from a German folk tale.

Other writers have enriched German literature. Two learned scholars, the brothers Grimm, also tried to encourage German patriotism. They gathered all the German fairy tales they could find in order to show the richness of Germany's traditions. Children all over the world have found delight in the stories of Hansel and Gretel, Snow White, Sleeping Beauty and other delightful characters in *Grimm's Fairy Tales*.

The most outstanding author of twentieth-century Germany is Thomas Mann. His novels, which contain excellent character studies, often show the struggle of the younger generation to be free of its parents and of the outworn conventions of nineteenth-century society. He expressed this theme in the well-known book, *The Magic Mountain*. Mann could not accept the controls of Nazi dictatorship. He left Germany for the United States where he made anti-Nazi radio broadcasts to the Germans. Mann used the legend of Faust as the theme for one of his most famous novels, *Dr. Faustus*.

GERMANS HAVE BEEN LEADERS IN SCIENCE AND EDUCATION

German scientists made possible Germany's rapid industrial development. The work of Germany's scientists is well known. Long ago her chemists discovered how to extract nitrogen from the air and how to use the chemical to make fertilizer. They turned waste gases from coal into dyes and medicines. Rudolph Diesel (*dee*-zel), an electrical engineer, invented a motor that could run on cheap crude oil. The diesel engine operates at such low cost that it caused a revolution in transportation. Today, diesel engines power the ocean liners, locomotives, and trucks of virtually every modern nation.

German universities attracted students from all over the world. They came to work under important doctors and under such physicists as Roentgen (*rurnt*-ghen), whose scientific studies led to the invention of the X-ray machine, and von Helmholtz (*helm*-holts), who worked in the field of thermodynamics (heat energy). Helmholtz formulated the law of the conservation of energy, which is one of the basic principles of modern physics. The law states that no energy in the physical universe is ever lost. For example, electrical energy may change its form and become heat energy (as it does in an electric light), but the amount of energy that exists in the universe remains the same.

EARLY X-RAY. This woodcut from 1900 shows an early X-ray machine, which was made possible by the studies of the scientist Roentgen. The man with the face mask is examining the hand of the other man.

Einstein developed the theory of relativity. One of the greatest scientists and mathematicians in history was Albert Einstein. He made many studies, such as those on the composition of light, but he is particularly famous for stating the "theory of relativity." This theory has made important changes in men's understanding of the motions of bodies in the universe. Einstein said that a rapidly moving object in the universe influences the relationship between time and space. The result is a universe of four dimensions instead of three dimensions, as was described by the Greek mathematician Euclid. Einstein believed that the gravitational force of the sun twists the motions of the planets slightly out of the orbits which Newton had described. Einstein's theory has made men wonder whether the universe is endless or whether it turns back on itself like a globe.

Einstein, influenced by Helmholtz's law, discovered that energy and matter are really the same but have different forms. His work in this field led scientists to realize that by smashing the atoms that make up matter, they could release enormous amounts of energy. Thus Einstein's ideas helped make possible the development of atomic energy.

Germans introduced new ideas in education. Friedrich Froebel, a nineteenth-century

HEIDELBERG. Overlooking the Neckar River in southwest Germany, this picturesque old town is the home of one of the country's great universities. In the nineteenth century, German universities were famous the world over and attracted students of every nationality.

EINSTEIN. This great German-born scientist came to this country in 1933 and became a citizen in 1940. For his achievements, which revolutionized the science of physics, he received a Nobel Prize in 1921.

German educator, thought children from four to six years old should learn to play and work together in pleasant surroundings. A *kindergarten* (the German word for "children's garden") is a school modeled on Froebel's ideas. Another educator named Herbart changed people's ideas about the education of older children. He thought that schools should teach students to live well-rounded lives instead of constantly cramming them full of facts to be memorized. Herbart, who was also noted as a philosopher, believed that students learn new facts most quickly when those facts are based on information that is already familiar. He also believed that moral instruction should be a part of education. Herbart's ideas helped bring about far-reaching changes in educational philosophy.

The Germans were the first to introduce health inspection in the schools and to build open-air schoolrooms. They also pioneered in establishing vocational schools for those boys and girls who did not want to go on to the university. American school systems have adopted many of the educational ideas developed in Germany.

GERMAN PHILOSOPHERS HAVE INFLUENCED WORLD HISTORY

Kant believed that every man had a moral duty to serve the state. One of Germany's many great philosophers was the eighteenth-century Prussian scholar Immanuel Kant (kahnt). Kant criticized the belief of the philosophers of the Enlightenment that reason could explain everything in the world, including religion. He said that reason could tell us the truth only about those things that men experienced through the senses. But, said Kant, men could also gain knowledge through faith and inner conviction. Thus man "knows" that God exists and that the universe is governed by a moral law, even if he can not demonstrate it scientifically.

Kant believed that man's highest moral duty was to serve God by serving the state. The Nazis adopted this part of Kant's philosophy, but they forgot about God and a universal moral law. They said that the state alone was useful to society; thus a German's duty was to obey the state.

Hegel believed that true freedom lay in serving the state. One of the few Germans who rejoiced when Napoleon conquered Prussia was a university professor named Hegel (*hay*-gel). Hegel believed that the history of the world was one long, inevitable process directed by God. Through that process, freedom became a reality for more and more men. Hegel thought that Napoleon, by inspiring the Germans to unite against him, was bringing that freedom closer to Prussia. Hegel believed that only a strong and unified state could protect its citizens from conquest by foreign invaders. Thus, their security and freedom depended ultimately on their nation's strength. He concluded that the state was more important than the individual, and that men achieved their highest purpose by serving the state. The Nazis used Hegel's idea to justify their demands for blind obedience to the state.

Marx was the father of communism. The ideas expressed by the German philosopher Karl Marx have become extremely important in the twentieth century. His theory of why men act in history has changed the history of the whole world. Marx adopted Hegel's idea that history is an inevitable process, but he said history is controlled by the economic needs of men rather than by God. Men do not act from religious, patriotic, or other spiritual motives. They act only because they want to make a living. Men cannot change history; their course of action is already decided. Historians have come to call this point of view *economic determinism.*

Marx declared that history is not the story of individual freedom but the story of a struggle between the classes. During the Middle Ages, he said, the nobles had used, or exploited, the peasants entirely for the nobles' benefit. From the peasants had emerged the bourgeoisie, who revolted against the nobles in the French Revolution. Then the bourgeoisie had exploited the poor, downtrodden industrial workers, the *proletariat* (pro-leh-*tair*-ih-at), as Marx called them. Now in the nineteenth century, it was the proletariat's turn to revolt against the bourgeoisie.

The goal of history, according to Marx, was the day when the proletariat would take control of the state. Then there would be no more class struggle. All wealth would be owned by the workers themselves, and men would live together in peace. The state (that is, the police, the law courts, and the army) would no longer be needed, and would "wither away." Such a perfect society would eventually come about, said Marx, but it would not be achieved peacefully. Violent revolution was necessary. This theory of proletarian ownership of all property brought about by revolution is called Marxian socialism and is the foundation for the doctrines of communism.

Freud tried to understand why people behave as they do. An Austrian doctor named Sigmund Freud (froyd) made important studies in the field of mental illness. He gave reasons for men's actions that were quite different from the reasons given by Marx. After careful study of many disturbed patients, Freud concluded that men are influenced by all sorts of unreasoning drives and forces, such as the desire to be important. Experiences in early childhood, said Freud, often twist or distort these forces and result in mental illness. Most people are unconscious of the forces and have forgotten the experiences. Freud found that by helping his patients to realize the existence of the forces and to recall the experiences, he could sometimes make their mental illness disappear. This process is called psychoanalysis. Freud's ideas have caused much controversy among psychologists, but today they are recognized as an important step forward in understanding human behavior.

KARL MARX. So radical were Marx's political and economic theories that he was forced to spend much of his life in exile. One of his most influential books, *Das Kapital*, was written while he lived in Britain. His writings have strongly influenced Communist thought.

GERMAN COMPOSERS ARE AMONG THE GREATEST IN THE WORLD

Bach wrote music to serve God. A German organist named Johann Sebastian Bach (bahk) is considered one of the greatest composers who ever lived. Bach had a large family to support and he was poorly paid, but he continued to create masterpieces of religious and secular music to show his devotion to God.

Bach's compositions, which fill fifty volumes, are constructed according to mathematical patterns. He achieved richness and depth in his music not by composing for a large orchestra but by arranging two or more melodies to be played simultaneously. His organ fugues require remarkable skill to perform. Bach's genius shows to best advantage in his choral works, which are written in the stately, classical style of the seventeenth century. *The Mass in B Minor* and *The St. Matthew Passion* have been sung and loved by Catholics and Protestants alike. Bach's classical perfection of form and his intensity of religious feeling have won him the name "master of masters."

BACH. As the great musical spokesman for the Protestant Reformation, Bach not only composed outstanding original works but also adapted for the church many melodies from folk tunes and popular ballads.

Handel created an inspiring oratorio. An attic bedroom late at night was the only place and time that the young George Frederick Handel (*han*-d'l) could find to practice his music. His father had forbidden the boy to study music so that he could devote all his efforts to becoming a lawyer. One night the father heard faint music. He rushed upstairs and found George playing a clavichord (an ancestor of the piano), which the boy had hidden in the attic. Convinced that his son was much too interested in music to become a lawyer, the father gave in to the boy's musical ambition. Later, Handel went to England to be court musician to George I.

In London, Handel became famous for writing operas in the Italian style. When the English lost interest in opera, Handel turned to a kind of religious opera called oratorio. His masterpiece, the *Messiah,* uses a chorus, soloists, and a small orchestra to tell how Jesus came to save the world. When the king heard one of the thrilling choruses, he stood up in his box at the theater to show his pleasure. The presentation of the *Messiah* has become a Christmastime institution in virtually all Christian countries, and audiences still observe the custom of standing for the inspiring "Hallelujah Chorus."

Mozart's genius was unrewarded in his own lifetime. The child prodigy, Wolfgang Mozart (*mo*-tsart), composed his own sonatas and minuets at the age of five. At six, he had mastered the violin and harpsichord. Soon he began to give public recitals. He played before the emperor and wrote an opera at his request. Although as a boy he was enthusiastically acclaimed, few appreciated

HANDEL. The composer and King George I sail down the Thames River listening to the famous "Water Music" being played by an orchestra on the barge in the background. As a youth Handel studied law, but when his father recognized the boy's great musical talent, he gave him permission to join an orchestra.

his genuis when he grew up. Publishers bought his work for a few pennies, and for many years his salary was a mere pittance. In spite of poverty and an unhappy marriage, Mozart composed over six hundred works. His symphonies and violin concertos are gay, graceful, and precise in the classical style of eighteenth-century music. His operas, *The Marriage of Figaro* and *Don Giovanni*, rank with the best ever written. His last composition, considered by many to be his greatest, was a *Requiem Mass*, a funeral mass in fifteen parts. He felt it to be his own requiem, and he was right. Before it could be rehearsed, he died of overwork and strain. Mozart died in Vienna and was buried there in an unmarked grave.

Beethoven combined the best of the classical and the romantic styles of music. Many music lovers consider Ludwig van Beethoven (*bay*-toe-ven) to be the greatest German composer. Beethoven wrote sonatas and symphonies in the classical, balanced form used by Mozart, but Beethoven was stirred and torn by strong emotions, just as the romantic poets in England and Germany were. He shared their love of liberty and concern for the common man. These emotions he poured into his music. For Beethoven and for thousands of men after him, music expressed the intense feelings and longings that they could not put into words. Among the frequently performed works of Beethoven are violin sonatas, piano concertos, string quartets, and his nine symphonies.

Beethoven became totally deaf when he was

BEETHOVEN. Although he began to lose his hearing at twenty-eight, Beethoven was such an accomplished musician that he composed some of his most brilliant works in his later years while totally deaf. He is shown here at work on his famous "Missa Solemnis."

about forty years old. Nevertheless, he understood music so well that he went on to compose some of his greatest works, although he could never hear them played.

Wagner created operas in a new style. Perhaps the most controversial genius in German music was Richard Wagner (*vahg*-ner). When he was the conductor of a small opera company, he developed some new ideas about opera. He believed that an opera, instead of emphasizing a famous singer, should combine the story, the music, the singing, and the scenery in one, united whole. Each character should have a particular melody to identify him whenever he appeared on stage. Because Wagner demanded a huge orchestra, expensive costumes and sets, and very difficult performances from his singers, he had trouble winning support for his ideas. Today audiences flock to hear his works played in the great opera houses of the world.

Wagner belongs wholly to the romantic school of music, with its love of folklore and emotional expression. In one set of four operas, *The Ring of the Nibelung,* he tells the story of the old Teutonic gods and the hero Siegfried. *Tristan and Isolde* is an old German legend about two ill-fated lovers. Hitler used Wagner's interest in the heroic German past as an excuse for making him one of the sources of the "master race" idea, but Wagner wrote for music lovers everywhere.

Chapter Check-up

1. Who is the most famous German writer, and for what work is he noted?
2. How did Diesel, Roentgen, and von Helmholtz each contribute to science?
3. What is the significance of Einstein's work?
4. How did Froebel and Herbart influence modern education?
5. What were the main ideas of Kant and Hegel? How did the Nazis make use of their ideas?
6. Who was Karl Marx and how has he changed world history?
7. Who was the father of psychoanalysis? What were his main ideas?
8. Name Germany's five most famous composers. Briefly describe the work of each.

CHAPTER 51

Switzerland Mastered the Arts of Democracy and Peace

THE SWISS ALPS HAVE SERVED AS A THOROUGHFARE AND A BARRIER

Modern Switzerland was once a German state, but geography has made her history quite different from that of Germany. The tiny Swiss nation is situated in the Alps and is surrounded by France, Germany, and Italy. A fourth of the land is covered by glaciers or snow-topped mountains. Three of Europe's most important rivers, the Rhine, the Rhone, and the Danube, have their source in or near the Alps. Each flows in a different direction to the sea. Thus the Alps are the watershed of the European continent. The rushing waters of these and smaller rivers have been harnessed to provide hydroelectric power, which is called the "white coal" of Switzerland.

The major passes over the Alps are in Switzerland. Hannibal (whom you met in the story of

THE ALPS. Below the snow-capped peaks of the Swiss Alps, a herd of cows grazes in a pasture. Switzerland, the most mountainous of all the countries of Europe, is noted for its dairy products.

Rome) crossed through the westernmost pass on his way to invade Italy. During the Middle Ages many monks and bishops crossed the Swiss Alps on their trips to Rome. Pack trains carried the riches of the east over the passes from Venice to the Rhine. In the eighteenth century, the French emperor Napoleon led his army over the Alps into Italy. Today tunnels and good roads make passage through the Alps much easier.

The mountainous terrain of their homeland has given the Swiss people a wonderfully effective natural protection. In case of invasion or attack, the Swiss can quickly block the Alpine passes and ambush any force that tries to push its way through. The formidable barrier created by the Alps is doubtless one reason why the Swiss have been left in peace.

For centuries the mountains have provided a means of livelihood for the Swiss. Many Swiss have become expert mountain climbers, guides, ski instructors, and hotel keepers. They serve the tourists who come to Switzerland to enjoy the marvelous scenery and the winter sports. In the high Alpine valleys, some Swiss still live in tiny wooden houses called chalets (sha-*lays*). They raise dairy cattle and goats just as their ancestors did for generations.

BERN. The capital of Switzerland was founded in the twelfth century as a military post. The clock was built into one of the original walls of the city and is a favorite attraction for tourists. At three minutes before each hour, a crowing rooster emerges from the doors above the clock face, and above in the spire small figures dance and strike the hour.

Only about a fifth of Switzerland's population actually lives in the Alps, however. Most of the inhabitants live on the high plains or in the valleys on the northern side of the Alps. In this section lie Zurich (*zoor*-ik), the most important Swiss city; Bern, the capital; and Basel (*bah*-zel), an old university town. The land yields wheat, potatoes, and sugar beets, but it is used mainly for cattle raising and dairy farming, the two major industries of the Swiss people.

Switzerland cannot produce enough food to support her population, so large supplies must be imported. To pay for these imports the Swiss have developed many small industries that require highly skilled workmanship but not much raw material. The Swiss are famous for their watches, clocks, precision instruments, drugs, chemicals, and fine embroidery. Their skill and hard work have made Switzerland a prosperous country in spite of its lack of natural resources.

THE SWISS WON POLITICAL AND RELIGIOUS FREEDOM

William Tell was the legendary hero of the Swiss struggle against the Hapsburgs. The area occupied by modern Switzerland was originally settled by Germanic tribes. Later, the land became part of Charlemagne's empire. There was no united Switzerland then, just as there was no united Germany. Instead, the area was divided into a number of tiny Swiss states called *cantons*. The three cantons of Uri, Unterwalden, and Schwyz around Lake Lucerne (loo-*sern*), known as the Forest Cantons, once belonged to the Hapburgs, whose family castle overlooked a river near Zurich. During the thirteenth century, the cantons had become independent of the Hapsburgs and were subject only to the Holy Roman emperor. When the Hapsburgs became emperors, they tried to make the cantons their personal property again.

The freedom-loving Swiss were loyal to the emperor, but they refused to be ruled directly by a Hapsburg archduke. In 1291 the Forest Cantons formed a league for common defense called the Swiss Confederation. The Swiss consider this alliance the beginning of their national history.

The struggle with the Hapsburgs went on for three centuries. Many of the Swiss national legends grew up in the early years of the conflict. One of the most famous is the legend of William Tell.

Early in the fourteenth century, according to the story, the Hapsburgs sent a cruel agent named Gessler to rule their Swiss lands. Gessler put a cap on a pole in the public square of Altdorf in the Canton of Uri, and ordered the Swiss to bow to it. The cap represented the Hapsburg overlordship.

William Tell. This monument to the Swiss hero is in Altdorf on Lake Lucerne. The great patriot is shown with his son and his famous crossbow.

William Tell, a mountaineer, famous for his marksmanship with crossbow and arrow, refused to bow to the cap. Tell's disobedience was considered treason. He and his six-year-old son, who was with him, were immediately arrested by one of Gessler's soldiers.

Gessler had heard of his prisoner's skill as a marksman, so the governor ordered an apple placed on the little boy's head and commanded the father to shoot the apple off. Tell's first arrow split the apple in half, but he told Gessler that in case of failure, a second arrow would have been for him. Gessler dragged Tell off to imprison him in another canton. While they were crossing Lake Lucerne, a storm arose and Tell escaped. Hidden above a mountain pass, he waited till Gessler had landed and was riding through. Then Tell's second arrow is said to have found its mark. News of the hated governor's death inspired patriots in the three cantons to join forces against the Hapsburgs.

In the next three hundred years, ten other cantons joined the Swiss Confederation. The Hapsburgs tried in vain to subdue the Confederation and by 1500 the Swiss were practically independent. At the close of the Thirty Years' War, the Swiss Confederation officially severed all ties with the Holy Roman Empire.

Zwingli and Calvin brought the Reformation to Switzerland. The Swiss played an important part in the Reformation. Ulrich Zwingli (*tsving*-lee), a priest at Zurich and a powerful preacher, led the Protestant movement in Switzerland as Luther led it in Germany. It was in the Swiss city of Geneva that John Calvin became one of the great leaders of Protestantism. He made Geneva a place of refuge for religious exiles, who fled there for protection. One of the refugees was John Knox, who later started the Scotch Protestant (or Presbyterian) Church.

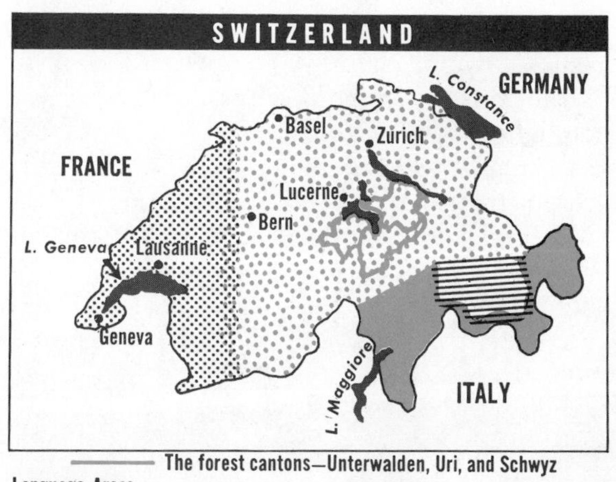

The religious conflicts that plagued Germany also caused serious trouble in Switzerland. Some cantons defended the Catholic faith, others became Protestant. For a century religious differences threatened to break up the Swiss Confederation. But by 1602 the cantons had accepted the idea of religious toleration. Switzerland thus avoided being drawn into the Thirty Year's War that proved so disastrous to Germany.

THE SWISS CANTONS BECAME A MODERN DEMOCRACY

The cantons adopted a liberal constitution. The Swiss cantons were divided by language and customs as well as by religion. In the north and east, the majority of the population is German in speech and traditions. Those who live in the west speak French. Those in the south speak Italian or Romansh, a Latin dialect. Yet these different peoples have learned to work together as a nation.

The French Revolution affected the Swiss, as it did all of Europe. The old confederation had left the matter of who should rule in each canton up to the local authorities. Many Swiss had no voice in the government. With French help the Swiss organized the Helvetian (hel-*vee*-shan) Republic. Later, Napoleon restored the confederation but kept the Swiss directly under his thumb. Thousands of Swiss soldiers had to give their lives in the service of Napoleon.

In the Congress of Vienna, after Napoleon's defeat, Switzerland added to her territory. At the

Lake Lucerne. The town of Lucerne in the foreground is one of many towns and villages that border this beautiful lake in the Alps. Lucerne is visited by many tourists who wish to enjoy Switzerland's breathtaking mountain scenery.

same time all the European powers guaranteed her permanent neutrality, which has never since been violated. There was a brief civil war in 1847 over the question of greater centralization of the government. The next year, when people all over Europe were demanding more voice in their governments, Switzerland adopted a liberal constitution modeled on that of the United States. The new constitution granted to all men the right to vote, and provided for a more closely bound union than had existed before. The same constitution is still in force.

Modern Switzerland serves the cause of peace. An Italian writer once said, "Happy is the nation without a history." Most of the history-making troubles of the last century and a half have left Switzerland alone. She managed to stay neutral in both world wars. Switzerland was a place of safety for people and treasure of both sides. Swiss officials cared for thousands of children made homeless or orphaned because of the war. Through Switzerland, Japan sent the first message to the United States asking for peace in the last war. The Red Cross, which helps people during the disasters of war or peace, was founded by the Swiss. Its symbol comes from the cross in the Swiss flag. The world headquarters of the International Red Cross are still in Switzerland.

The League of Nations set up its home in Geneva. The International Postal Union, which makes it possible for mail to go from one country to another, has its offices in the city of Bern.

Switzerland was also the site of the famous Geneva Convention of 1864, at which many nations agreed to give humane treatment to wounded enemy soldiers in time of war.

The Swiss have shown the world it is possible for people of differing languages, customs, and religions to co-operate intelligently and effectively. Switzerland's democratic constitution, provides for a workable federal government and strong local controls. It is a model of enlightened self-government to other nations of the world. Although not a member of the United Nations, Switzerland has joined many U.N. international agencies such as the World Health Organization (WHO), and the United Nations Educational, Scientific and Cultural Organization (UNESCO), that are devoted to raising the world's standard of living.

Chapter Check-up

1. How has geography influenced the history of Switzerland?
2. Where do the majority of the Swiss live?
3. What are some of the Swiss industries?
4. Why has Switzerland been able to maintain neutrality during European wars?
5. What event in 1291 marked the beginning of Swiss national history?
6. Who is the Swiss hero of the struggle with the Hapsburgs?
7. Who led the Reformation in Switzerland?
8. How did Switzerland settle the problem of religious differences?
9. How has modern Switzerland served the cause of world peace?
10. How is the democracy of Switzerland a lesson to the world?

WATCHMAKING. Swiss craftsmen are noted for the precision of their work. This watchmaker is checking a watch before it leaves the shop to be sold.

Germany: SYNOPSIS

Ever since the early nineteenth century, people have talked about a "German problem." At first they meant the problem of unifying Germany. Later, they meant the problem of preventing a war-minded Germany from dominating the world. Today, the problem is the creation of a unified, democratic Germany that will be a partner in preserving world peace.

The roots of the German problem lie far back of the nineteenth century. Throughout most of its history Germany was no more than the name of a geographic area. The hundreds of tiny states and free cities of the Holy Roman Empire remained disunited. In the seventeenth century, they fought one another bitterly during the disastrous Thirty Years' War. For the next 150 years, Western European nations thought of Germany as a backward, medieval land ruled by petty princes who seemed ridiculous because they gave themselves the airs of great kings. None of them, not even Frederick the Great, was strong enough to bring the others under his rule.

When the Napoleonic Wars aroused German nationalism, the states began to desire unification. They had been humiliated by the French and wanted to prove their power as a united people. The failure of the Frankfurt Assembly in 1848 made them willing to accept Bismarck's policy of "blood and iron." The tradition of blind obedience to the ruler, and acceptance of the calculated use of force which the Prussian rulers instilled in them made it easy for the Germans to follow William II into World War I. When the Weimar Republic failed, economic distress and those same traditions made the Germans obedient to Hitler. Twice Germany brought disaster to herself and to the world.

At the same time, the German people made outstanding achievements in such peaceful arts as literature, philosophy, science, and music. Writers like Goethe, Schiller, Heine, and Mann have enriched man's literature. Scientists like Diesel, Helmholtz, and Einstein have helped all nations by their work. Philosophers like Kant and Marx have influenced history (though not always to mankind's benefit). Composers like Bach, Mozart, and Beethoven have created some of the world's best-loved music. Today, men hope that Germany's political contributions will become as valuable as her cultural contributions have been.

Although it was once a German state, Switzerland has had a very different history from that of Germany. She achieved independence in the seventeenth century and adopted a liberal constitution in the nineteenth century. Traditionally a neutral nation, Switzerland has triumphed over differences of language and religion to create a successful and forward-looking democracy.

Important People

How has each of the following influenced the stories of Germany and Switzerland?

Louis the German
Frederick the Great
Prince Metternich
The Great Elector
Otto von Bismarck
William II
Otto of Saxony
Gerhard von Scharnhorst
Adolf Hitler
Frederick Ebert
Konrad Adenauer
Goethe
Thomas Mann
Immanuel Kant
Roentgen
Albert Einstein
Karl Marx
Richard Wagner
William Tell
Ulrich Zwingli
Sigmund Freud

Terms

Be sure that you understand clearly the meaning of each of the following:

communism
Hanseatic League
Hapsburgs
Hohenzollerns
"blood and iron" policy
Helvetian Republic
Revolution of 1848
Swiss Confederation
inflation
Nazis
propaganda
socialism
Reichstag
Frankfurt Assembly
economic determinism
proletariat
totalitarian
Weimar Republic
cantons
Thirty Years' War
Holy Roman emperor
Ems Dispatch
German Confederation
Bundestag

Questions for Discussion and Review

1. How did religious wars keep Germany poor and backward for over a century?
2. How and by whom was the unification of Germany finally accomplished?
3. How did their history condition the Germans to accept Nazi control and doctrine?
4. Why do dictators always need to control thought and public opinion?
5. What do scientists have to say about the ideas of "pure blood" and "master race"?
6. It is said that Hitler used the Jewish people as a "scapegoat" for Germany. Do you agree? (Consult a dictionary for the meaning of the term *scapegoat.*)
7. Do you accept the statement that Germany has made important contributions to civilization in most fields but politics? Explain why.
8. What, in your opinion, has been Germany's greatest contribution to civilization? Explain the reason for your choice.
9. How did Austria hope to use the "German Confederation" to keep the German states from uniting? Why did Metternich oppose German unification?
10. What problems faced the Weimar Republic at the end of World War I? Did the Allied powers share any of the responsibility for its failure? Explain your answer.
11. Why is the future of Germany considered an international problem?
12. In what ways have the Alps influenced political, economic, and military affairs in Switzerland? Is their influence as important today as it was in the nineteenth century?

Interesting Things to Do

1. Make a map of Central Europe showing (a) the present division of Germany (b) Austria (c) Switzerland (d) Alsace-Lorraine (e) the capitals of East and West Germany. Label the important rivers and mountain ranges. Color or illustrate your map to make it more interesting.
2. Prepare an historical atlas of Germany by making a series of maps, from the division of Charlemagne's Empire down to the division of East and West Germany.
3. Prepare a chart showing the contributions of the Germans to the fields of literature, philosophy, education, science, and music. Head your columns as follows: *Name of Person, Field of Work, Contributions or Achievements.*
4. Make a poster illustrating the achievements of the famous German scientists. Include in your poster: (a) Diesel (b) von Helmholtz (c) Roentgen and (d) Einstein. Be sure to show what contributions to modern science each of these men has made.
5. Prepare and present a program of recorded selections of the great German composers. Explain something about each selection before it is played.
6. Prepare and present a talk on "The Three B's of German Music," telling briefly of the lives and accomplishments of Bach, Beethoven, and Brahms.
7. Arrange and present an informal debate on the following topic: *Resolved,* That Germany should never again be allowed to become a strong and united nation.
8. Prepare a travel booklet, give a talk illustrated by pictures or slides, or write an imaginary travel journal about a trip down the historic Rhine River.
9. Read and prepare a book report on a novel, travel book, or biography dealing with Germany.
10. Add to or begin your "Who's Who in World History" series by writing brief biographies of one or more of the following men: (a) Frederick the Great (b) Otto von Bismarck (c) William Tell (d) Johann Bach (e) Karl Marx (f) Konrad Adenauer.

Interesting Reading about Germany and Switzerland

Bauer, M., and Peyser, E. R., *How Music Grew*, Putnam. History of music from the prehistoric to modern.

*Berner, Elsa, *Germany*, Holiday.

*Bragdon, Lillian J., *The Land of William Tell*, Lippincott. Geography, history, and customs of Switzerland.

Brandt, Willy, and Leo Lania, *My Road to Berlin*, Doubleday.

Carr, A. H. Z., *Men of Power*, Viking. Frederick the Great, pp. 73–91; Bismarck, pp. 149–75; Hitler, pp. 237–65.

Deutsch, Handel, *Our Changing German Problems*, Science Research Associates.

*Goss, Madeline, *Beethoven, Master Musician*, Holt, Rinehart and Winston.

Peel, Davis, *Inward Journey*, Houghton Mifflin. An American journalist describes young German Communists of the post-World War II period.

Snyder, Louis Leo, *Hitler and Nazism*, Watts.

Taylor, Alan J. P., *The Course of German History*, Coward-McCann.

Valentin, Veit, *The German People: Their History and Civilization from the Holy Roman Empire to the Third Reich*, Knopf.

Vogt, Hannah, *The Burden of Guilt*, Oxford. A history of modern Germany, 1914–1945.

Werstein, Irving, *The Franco-Prussian War*, Messner.

Wohlrabe, Raymond, and W. Krusch, *The Land and People of Germany*, Lippincott.

* Indicates easy reading

Modern descendents of the Vikings have built prosperous industrial nations. But many Scandinavians, like this Swedish fisherman, still seek a livelihood on the sea.

Part 15
SCANDINAVIA
FROM BOLD SEAFARERS TO SOCIAL PIONEERS

THE SCANDINAVIAN COUNTRIES

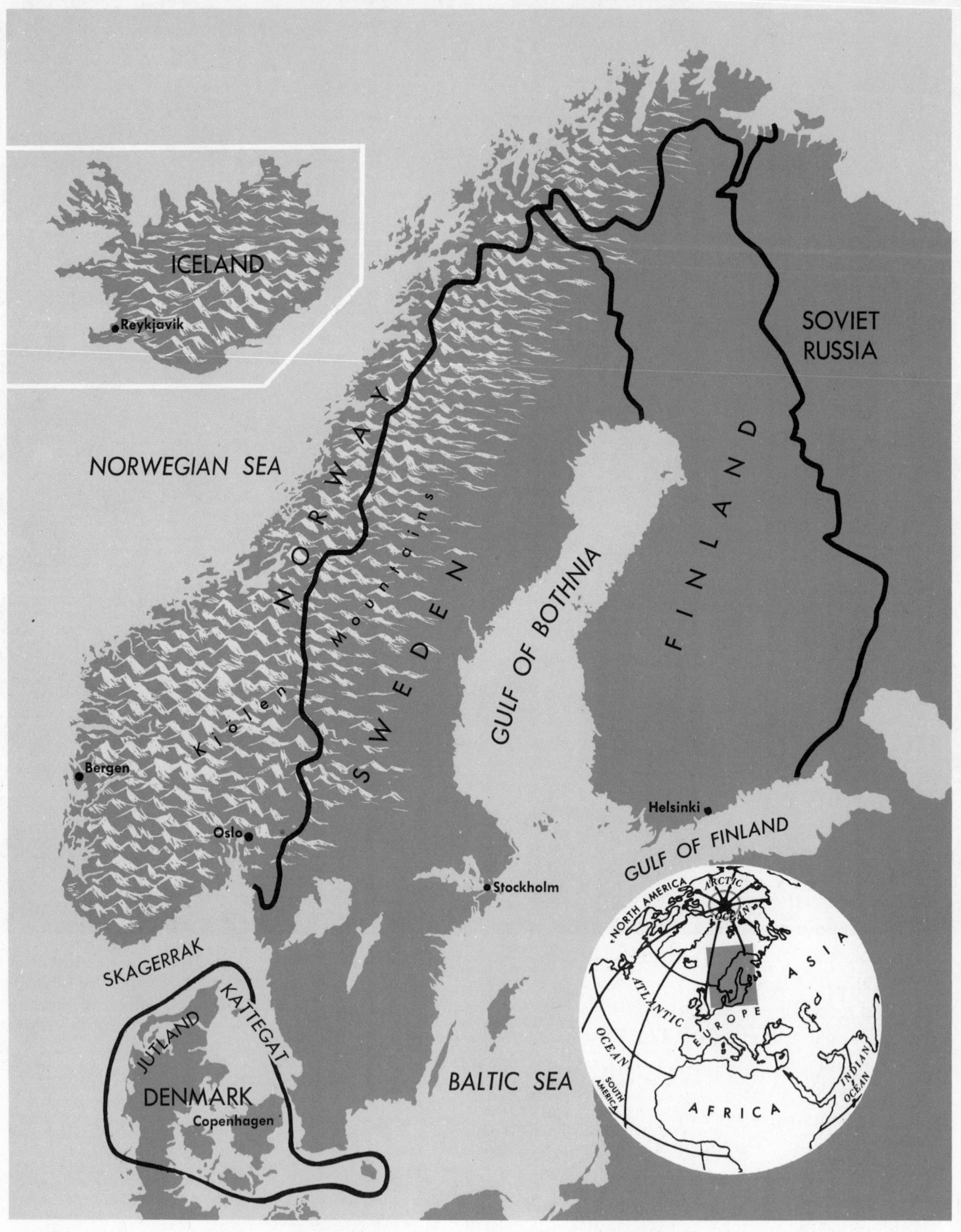
ICELAND
Reykjavik
NORWEGIAN SEA
NORWAY
SWEDEN
Kiölen Mountains
FINLAND
SOVIET RUSSIA
GULF OF BOTHNIA
Bergen
Oslo
Stockholm
Helsinki
GULF OF FINLAND
SKAGERRAK
KATTEGAT
JUTLAND
DENMARK
Copenhagen
BALTIC SEA
NORTH AMERICA
ARCTIC OCEAN
ASIA
ATLANTIC OCEAN
EUROPE
SOUTH AMERICA
AFRICA
INDIAN OCEAN

Scandinavia: GEOGRAPHIC SETTING

Scandinavia includes two peninsulas and neighboring islands in the northwestern part of Europe. Norway and Sweden jointly occupy the Scandinavian Peninsula which lies north of the Baltic Sea. Most of the peninsula is covered by the Kjölen (*chuh*-len) Mountains, a thickly forested range that rises to almost seven thousand feet. In Norway, the mountains start at the coast, leaving less than a third of the country fit for human habitation; in Sweden they slope more gently, forming a wide coastal plain. Here, cattle, sheep, and goats are grazed.

A third of the Scandinavian Peninsula is north of the Arctic Circle. For two months of the summer the people enjoy continuous daylight, but in the winter they have to endure two months of darkness. The climate is not as cold as you might expect, because the Gulf Stream flows north past Norway's shores. Little of the rugged Scandinavian Peninsula is suitable for farming, and the people have had to turn to other occupations. They make wood products from the dense forests, they mine rich ores from the mountains, and they fish for cod and herring in the surrounding waters.

Denmark is also a part of Scandinavia, although it does not occupy the same peninsula. It encompasses the Jutland Peninsula and five hundred neighboring islands. Although the land is flat, it is sandy and not very fertile. The Danes have therefore turned to dairying and livestock raising, and they have been remarkably successful at these occupations. Denmark exports more butter and pork products than any other nation of the world except the United States. The fishing grounds off the coast of Denmark are among the most profitable in all of Europe.

In Part 15 you will also learn about Finland, which is adjacent to both Sweden and Norway but is not, strictly speaking, a part of Scandinavia. The history of Finland has, however, been closely connected with that of the Scandinavian countries. Finland is a low, flat land that has a great number of lakes. There is some agriculture, but the Finns, like their neighbors on the peninsula, depend heavily on the forest and the sea for a living.

Scandinavia: PERSPECTIVE

Nearly five hundred years before Columbus' voyage to America other adventurers were roaming the shores of this continent. They were the Vikings, ancestors of today's Scandinavians. In small wooden galleys, they sailed the treacherous waters of the North Atlantic, skirting icebergs and weathering storms. They became so skillful at navigating their tiny vessels that in about 1000 A.D. a group reached Greenland and established a colony on its icy shores. Evidence indicates that a short time later they may have reached the New England coast.

The people of Scandinavia have often shown themselves to be ahead of their times. Just as the early Viking sailors worked together to make spectacular voyages, so their modern descendants have banded together to make spectacular progress as modern nations. The Scandinavian peoples are admired for the spirit of co-operation which has helped them develop standards of education and economic well-being that are among the highest in the world. They live under stable but forward-looking democratic governments. In Part 15 you will read how these bold seafarers became social pioneers.

Chapter 52

The Land of the Vikings Became Modern Norway, Denmark, and Sweden

SCANDINAVIA WAS INHABITED BY FIERCE WARRIORS

Scandinavia during the Viking Age was wild and primitive. About ten thousand years ago the ice sheets that covered northern Europe began to melt. As the land gradually warmed, the New Stone Age men of central Europe moved north into Scandinavia. Germanic tribes later followed them. At first they lived by hunting and fishing. Later they settled down to raise livestock and farm the land. By 200 B.C. they had learned to smelt iron ore from the mountains to make weapons and tools. Roman coins that have been discovered in Scandinavia show that these early peoples also carried on trade with Rome. They exchanged amber, furs, and iron for Roman jewelry, pottery, and glassware.

Even before the birth of Christ love of war and lack of food drove some of the Scandinavian tribes to explore central and southern Europe. Eventually they entered the Roman Empire and helped bring about its downfall (see Chapter 17). The Germanic tribes that remained in Scandinavia are known variously as Northmen, Norsemen, Danes, or Vikings. These names are used interchangeably to refer to the early Scandinavian tribesmen.

During the Middle Ages the Vikings continued to live in their primitive fashion long after the French, English, and Spanish had established great kingdoms. A number of Viking chieftains did form small kingdoms, but no one chieftain was able to unite all the tribes.

Yet, the Vikings developed a surprisingly advanced literature, and poetic skill was as highly prized as fighting ability. There were several kinds of poems, the best known of which are the *sagas*. These are long epic stories centering about either a legendary or an actual historical figure. The earliest poems were memorized and passed on orally, since the only alphabet was a limited one of characters called *runes,* used mainly for inscriptions on wood or stone. After a Romanized alphabet was introduced about 1100, the poems were preserved in writing.

The Northmen developed no feudal aristocracy. For several reasons, no class of feudal aristocrats grew up among the Northmen as it did in the other nations of Europe. The barren soil

Laplanders. Laplanders, who were the original inhabitants of the northernmost parts of Scandinavia, live mainly by tending herds of reindeer. Some of them are hunters or fishermen.

produced so little that conditions did not favor a system of feudal landholding like that in most of Europe. The Northmen divided their properties among their descendants, so that no large areas of land accumulated under one owner.

The soil of much of Scandinavia was not very productive. As the population increased, social and economic inequalities increased also. The head men of the tribes became more powerful. They tended to lay heavy taxes and otherwise tyrannize over the freemen.

Many Vikings, to escape tyranny, began to turn to the sea for their living. They were hardy, adventurous sailors, fishermen, pirates, and traders. Their excellent ships and their skill in navigation encouraged them to sail on longer and longer voyages. They ventured out into the North Atlantic. They sailed along the northern and western coasts of Europe and even into the Mediterranean. As the Northmen gained experience, they became bolder and more aggressive. They raided and plundered many towns and coasts, as you read in the stories of France, England, and the Low Countries. They even pushed eastward into Russia, sailing down the Dnieper (*nee*-per) River to the Black Sea. There they established trading states and for many years controlled commerce between Constantinople and the Baltic Sea.

In the ninth century the Vikings began to colonize Iceland, which had been discovered earlier by Irish monks. In about 1000 A.D. Eric the Red and his son Leif Ericson reached the shores of Greenland and Labrador. They had come across the open sea in tiny ocean-going crafts. Leif reported that the land they had reached was of no worth, being mostly rocks and ice. It is known that the Northmen touched the shores of North America nearly five hundred years before Columbus sailed west. They may have gone as far south as what is now Rhode Island, where today stands a strange stone tower, possibly of Viking origin. However, records are vague, and we cannot be sure.

THE VIKING VOYAGES AND SETTLEMENTS

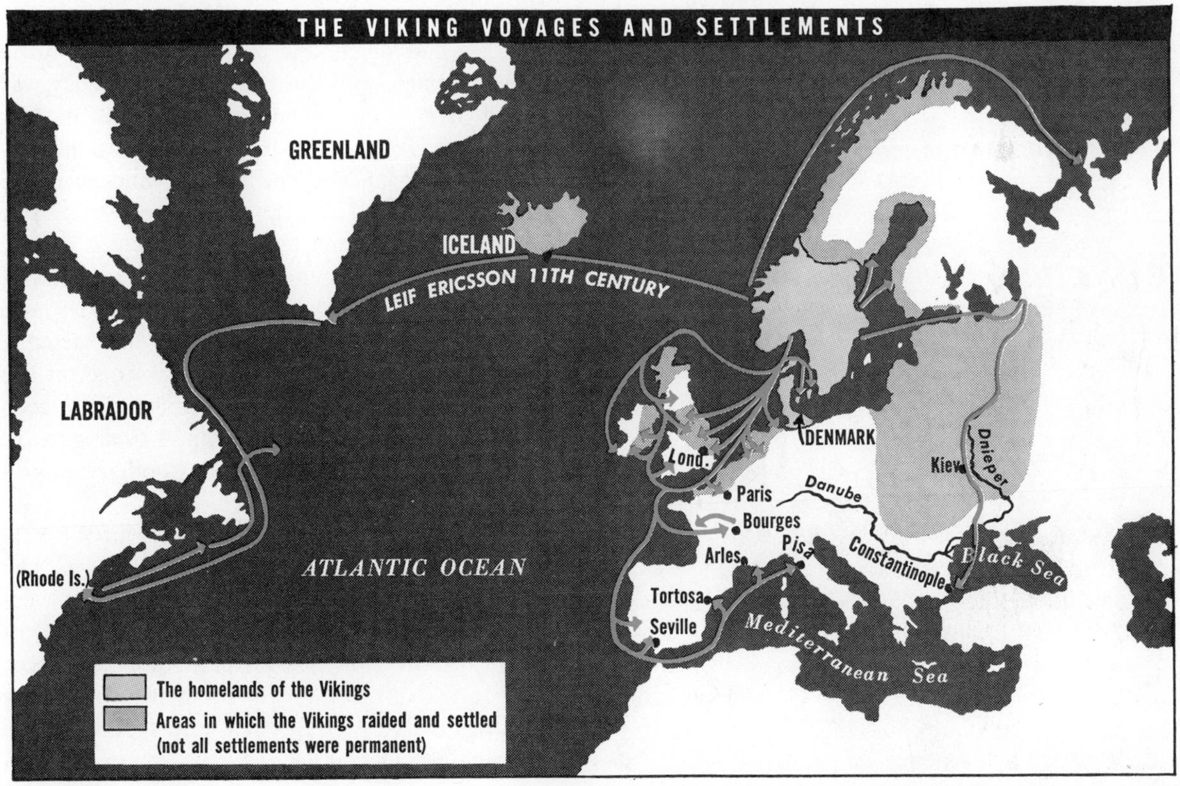

Viking raids developed into conquests. During the first half of the ninth century the voyages of the Vikings were summer expeditions. The raiders returned home with their booty in the autumn. However, when the Scandinavian countries became united under a few strong rulers, many tribal chiefs and petty rulers were too proud to accept their defeat. They looked to new lands for permanent homes.

Soon the Viking raids became expeditions in which men searched for land to settle. Thus, in the late ninth and tenth centuries, the Vikings began to establish permanent settlements in the lands that they had been plundering. Gradually, they intermarried with the earlier inhabitants and added their own skills to the civilizations that developed there.

VIKING SHIP. Sleek Viking ships like this one, which were mannned by crews of hardy oarsmen, struck terror in the hearts of coastal inhabitants a thousand years ago. The vessel shown here is in the Oslo Museum.

The voyages of the Vikings went on for more than three centuries. Inspired by a love of the sea, they developed sailing and navigation into a fine art. They knew how to tack (sail against the wind); they could chart their courses by the sun and the stars. Their sagas show what deep pride the Northmen took in their ships. They called them by such picturesque names as "Elk of the Fiords" and "Raven of the Sea." The ships, often assembled in fleets of more than a hundred, were capable of weathering severe storms despite their small size. The most common type of warship, the "long ship," often had as many as thirty oarsmen and sixty additional crewmen. The vessel was usually richly carved and decorated with rows of painted shields and brightly colored sails.

The Vikings became Christian. For centuries, the Vikings worshiped pagan gods like those of the Germanic tribes. These gods often represented the forces of nature. One-eyed Odin (*oh*-din) was king of the gods and patron of heroes. He had given one of his eyes for a drink from the magic well of wisdom. Wednesday was named after him (taken from *Woden,* another spelling of Odin). His wife, Frigga, was protectress of marriage and the home. She gave her name to Friday. The Vikings honored Odin's son Thor (Thursday) most of all. Thor was god of storm and war. His chariot wheels were believed to cause the thunder. He was armed with a magic hammer which always returned to him after it was cast. With his hammer Thor warded off the wicked giants, who were the enemies of the gods and men. The Vikings worshiped their gods in sacred groves, where they built wooden temples and burned animals in sacrifice.

Christian Europe knew nothing about the Vikings until the invasions of the ninth century. Devout Frankish, English, and Irish Christians were horrified to learn of the existence of thousands of pagans in the north. Brave missionaries went forth to convert them. By the eleventh century the kings of Norway, Sweden, and Denmark had become Christian. Olaf II (1016–28) of Norway, who was later made a saint, influenced his people to accept Christianity. Canute (1014–35) of Denmark, whom you met in the story of England, did the same for the Danes. The Swedish king spread the new faith in his country. In the late twelfth century, the Swedes went on a crusade to convert the Finns. As a result of missionary activities, Finland became a Swedish province and remained under Swedish control for over six hundred years.

DENMARK AND SWEDEN TOOK TURNS CONTROLLING SCANDINAVIA

Denmark brought Norway and Sweden into a Scandinavian union. From the eleventh to the fourteenth centuries there were no strong or lasting central governments in the Scandinavian countries. Each nation was torn by civil wars at one time or another. At times, by war or by intermarriage of royal families, a single nation might succeed in dominating or subduing one of the others. But such domination generally did not last long. In the late fourteenth century, when the kings of Norway and Sweden died, the nobles of these countries asked Margaret of Denmark (1387–1412) to be their queen. The "lady king," as she was called, was a very able ruler. She successfully governed a combined territory that stretched from Finland to Greenland and was the biggest empire in Europe at that time. She drew up a constitution for the union and joint defense of the three countries. Both Sweden and Norway were allowed to keep their own laws, but Denmark was the dominant force in the union.

Although the union lasted more than a century, Norway and Sweden grew dissatisfied with Danish control. In the early sixteenth century a Swedish nobleman led a revolt that won Sweden her independence. Norway, however, remained under Danish rule for more than three centuries. Denmark is the only Scandinavian country that has colonies today. Greenland, the world's largest island, is still a Danish possession.

STAVE CHURCH. Hundreds of wooden churches like this *stavkirke* in Norway were built in Scandinavia during the Middle Ages. Their unique architecture may have been inspired by the pagan temples that preceded them. Only a few are still in existence.

Under Gustavus Adolphus Sweden became a world power. During the sixteenth century, Scandinavian students who had been at German universities brought home the religious ideas of Martin Luther. The new ideas had a strong appeal among the Scandinavian peoples. The Reformation spread so fast that within a few years Lutheranism had become the state religion of all three Scandinavian countries. Young King Gustavus Adolphus (1611–32) of Sweden was an able ruler and a devout Lutheran. He was anxious to make his country one of the most powerful in Europe. When the Thirty Years' War broke out (see Chapter 47) Gustavus saw an opportunity to aid the Protestants and to gain land for Sweden.

Gustavus Adolphus was a brilliant general. His military campaigns against Russia, Poland and the German states won him new lands along the eastern and southern shores of the Baltic. He made the Baltic virtually a Swedish lake. At home, Gustavus Adolphus ruled firmly but justly. He granted a charter of rights to his nobles and improved the government and law courts. Shortly after his death in the Thirty Years' War, Sweden laid claim to a share of the New World by establishing a colony on the Delaware River. The Swedes eventually lost it to the Dutch, however.

At the beginning of the eighteenth century Denmark, Poland, and Russia formed a military alliance against Sweden to recover their lost territories. Sweden thus had to fight a long and costly war. The country was exhausted and finally defeated. In the treaty of peace after the war, all of Sweden's Baltic provinces except Finland fell to Russia.

A French general became king of Sweden. During the Napoleonic Wars, Russia seized the remaining Swedish province of Finland. The Swedes revolted against their king and forced him to abdicate. His successor left no heir, so the Swedish legislature elected one of Napoleon's most famous generals, Bernadotte, as their king. His descendants still occupy the Swedish throne.

Bernadotte soon showed that he placed the welfare of Sweden above his loyalty to Napoleon. When it seemed that Napoleon's policies were endangering Swedish freedom, Bernadotte led the Swedish army against his former commander. Denmark, however, remained an ally of the

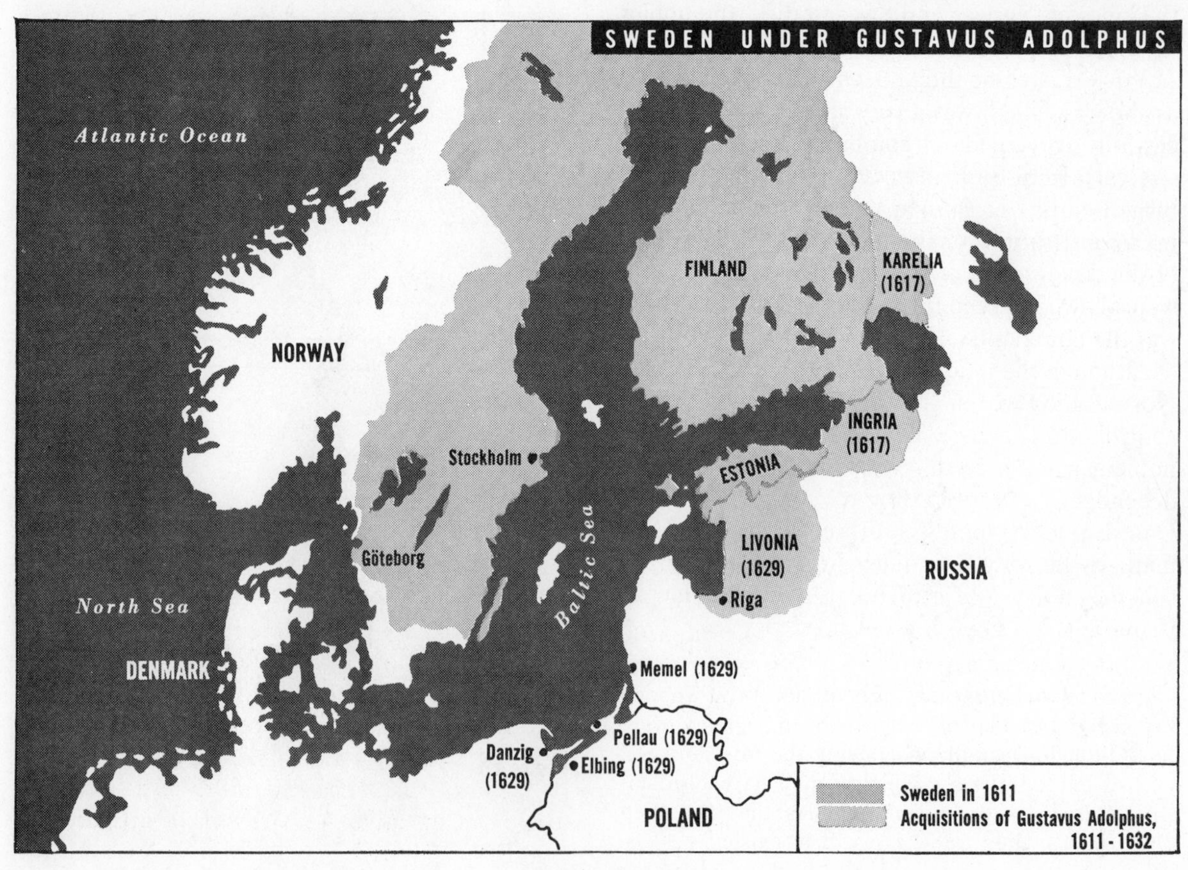

FINLAND. Finland is a country of many lakes. More than half of its area is water surface. Lakes are often used to transport lumber, one of the country's main resources.

French. When Napoleon was defeated, the victorious nations wanted to punish Denmark and compensate Sweden for her loss of Finland. They therefore took Norway away from Denmark and gave her to Sweden. The Norwegians, who had been part of Denmark for more than four hundred years, resented being handed over to Sweden without their consent. They were, after all, a high-spirited and independent people. Finally a compromise was reached. Norway was made a free and independent kingdom with a constitution and parliament of her own, but she agreed to accept the king of Sweden as the king of Norway also.

Scandinavia prospered in the late nineteenth century. The last half of the nineteenth century was a period of peace. The Industrial Revolution had brought machines, factories, and cheaper goods to all Scandinavia. The merchants and tradesmen grew into a prosperous middle class. Co-operative societies in Denmark and trade unions in Sweden came into being at this time. Trade with foreign lands began to increase rapidly.

The Norwegians developed a large merchant marine. The cargo ships of Norway sailed to ports all over the world. The descendants of the Vikings became modern merchant sailors. The Scandinavian nations also made great progress in government by keeping pace with the demands of changing times. Both Sweden and Denmark adopted new constitutions; they replaced their medieval assemblies with modern parliaments.

THREE INDEPENDENT SCANDINAVIAN STATES TOOK THEIR PLACE IN THE MODERN WORLD

Norway and Finland became independent nations. For many years the differences between Norwegian and Swedish customs, language, and traditions had been growing sharper. Finally, in 1905, the Norwegian parliament declared the union with Sweden to be at an end. Sweden recognized the strong national feeling of the Norwegians and agreed to a peaceful separation of the two countries. The Norwegians chose a Danish prince to be their king. He took the title of Haakon (*haw*-kon) VII. During World War I German troops invaded Finland and helped her gain her independence from Russia, which was busy with a revolution and civil war. Finland proclaimed herself an independent nation and, in 1920, established a republican government. In 1939 Russia demanded certain Finnish territories to aid her in building a network of military de-

DAG HAMMARSKJOELD. While serving as UN Secretary-General from 1953 to 1961, Hammarskjoeld gained fame as a globe-trotting peacemaker. He died in a plane crash while trying to negotiate a settlement among rival factions in the Congo.

fenses. When Finland refused, Russia seized the territories by military force.

In 1941, after World War II had begun, Finland and Russia clashed again. The war that developed between them placed the democratic nations, who at that time were fighting with the Russians against the Axis, in an awkward position. They had no reason to fight Finland. Finland claimed that she was not an Axis ally but was fighting a separate war with Russia. The Allies said that Finland was aiding the Axis, whatever her reasons were. The Germans, of course, wanted Finland to go on fighting the Russians. They sent troops into Finland. The Allies urged Finland to make peace with Russia, but Finland said that Russia's terms were not acceptable. Finally, the United States reluctantly broke off diplomatic relations with Finland. Early in the fall of 1944, however, Finland accepted Russia's peace terms. Russia gained the right to have a naval base in Finland and received some other ports for commercial use. Finland agreed to pay Russia three hundred million dollars in reparations.

Although Finland has retained her independence, she carefully avoids any ties with Western Europe or the United States for fear of angering her powerful neighbor, Russia.

Scandinavia has undergone an economic revolution and works for world peace. During World War II Denmark and Norway suffered from conquest and occupation by Germany, while Sweden was able to maintain an uneasy neutrality. Though these nations underwent a great economic drain, they did not have heavy manpower losses and were able to rebuild soon after the war.

This rebuilding of their economies included an economic revolution, for these nations which before the war had been mainly agricultural producers, became heavily industrialized, without neglecting farming. Sweden became a leading manufacturer of automobiles and Norwegian paper exports vastly expanded. But they have not forgotten their traditions, as the Viking spirit shows in Norway's world-ranging merchant fleet. The result has been a higher standard of living for the Scandinavians with both the comforts and the problems that an industrial society presents.

The governments of the Scandinavian nations, especially Sweden, have been pioneers in social welfare policies. They have spread the fruits of their prosperity to the whole population through such programs as national health insurance and high retirement pensions. But the cost of such programs is high taxes and here the Scandinavian governments are running into problems. Sweden, which has the highest standard of living in Europe and the most ambitious social welfare program, had widespread strikes in 1971 protesting high taxes and inflation.

In their new era the Scandinavian countries have not forgotten their close historical bonds and have built upon them. The inter-government Nordic Council manages a common labor market and consults on other areas of cooperation.

The Scandinavian nations also work for world-wide cooperation through the United Nations. The first Secretary-General of the UN was the Norwegian Trygve Lie (lee) and the second was Dag Hammarskjoeld (hahm-ahr-sheeld) of Sweden who lost his life in a plane crash in Africa while on a UN peace-keeping mission in 1961. In recent years Sweden has been a strong critic of United States involvement in Vietnam. Though Norway and Denmark are members of NATO, they do not allow foreign troops or nuclear weapons on their soil.

The challenge of the future for the Scandinavian nations is to continue as pioneers of balanced prosperity and social welfare without overtaxing their people as well as continuing as a force for world cooperation and peace. World cooperation was shown in 1972 when Sweden sponsored a world ecological conference.

ICELAND FOLLOWS AN INDEPENDENT COURSE

Iceland is an island nation lying just below the Arctic Circle, whose glaciers and volcanoes give it the name "the land of ice and fire." It was first settled by fearless independence-seekers from Norway. These people ruled themselves through an elected assembly called the Althing, which still exists and is regarded as the oldest parliament in the world. Though Iceland came under Danish rule in the fourteenth century, the Danes neglected their possession and the Icelanders maintained their own independent ways. When the Germans conquered and occupied Denmark during World War II, the Icelanders again proclaimed their independence and sided with the Western democracies.

These descendants of the Vikings also show their independent self-reliance by drawing a high living standard from the sea, since their country has few natural resources and little arable land. The Icelanders fierce defense of the fishing fields on which they depend was demonstrated in 1961 when they forced larger nations to ac-

ICELAND. In a harbor on the north coast of Iceland, herring are cleaned and salted. Fishing is the most important industry on the island, and herring and cod are the principal exports.

cept a prohibition on fishing within twelve miles of the island. In 1972 they plan to extend the limit to fifty miles in these rich waters.

Further evidence of Icelandic independent spirit is the republic's stance in East-West relations. When Cold-War tensions were high in the late 1940's, Iceland joined the North Atlantic Treaty Organization and provided a base for American troops, since she has no armed forces of her own. However, since these tensions have eased, the Icelandic government has announced the base will be phased out by 1975, though the republic will remain in NATO. Iceland itself was the scene of more peaceful East-West relations in 1972 when the American Bobby Fischer met the Russian Boris Spassky in a world championship chess match.

Chapter Check-up

1. What three countries are included in Scandinavia?
2. What do we call the Germanic tribes that settled in Scandinavia?
3. Where do we get our knowledge of the history of the Vikings?
4. What factors prevented the Northmen from developing a feudal aristocracy?
5. Who first unified the Scandinavian countries?
6. How did Gustavus Adolphus influence Swedish history?
7. How did a French general become Sweden's king?
8. Why has Finland had difficulty maintaining her independence?
9. What important United Nations statesmen have come from Scandinavia? What is each known for?

CHAPTER 53

The Scandinavians Have Made Important Achievements in Literature, Science, and Social Reform

SCANDINAVIAN LITERATURE AND MUSIC ARE KNOWN THROUGHOUT THE WORLD

Much of Scandinavian literature is based on folklore. For centuries, the Scandinavians spent the long winter evenings sitting around their firesides and telling the stories that had been handed down from their Viking ancestors. These stories were full of fairy people, such as trolls, gnomes, and elves, who were supposed to dwell in the mountains and who sometimes bewitched mortals. In the nineteenth century a Danish poet named Hans Christian Andersen wrote many wonderful stories based on the old legends. Two of his best known and most popular tales are "The Ugly Duckling" and "The Red Shoes."

Henrik Ibsen (*ib*-sen), the great Norwegian poet and dramatist, wove many of the old folk tales into fanciful stories. But Ibsen's literary fame rests chiefly on his great plays, in which he analyzed the social and economic problems of nineteenth-century Norway. He is considered one of the great figures in the history of modern drama. Two of his most widely admired plays are *Peer Gynt* and *A Doll's House*.

The Swedish novelist, Selma Lagerlöf (*lah*-ger-lerf), listened eagerly as a child to the tales of the past. When she became older she put them into literary form. Children love her account of *The*

SIBELIUS AND GRIEG. The two musicians, Sibelius (left) and Grieg (right), each used well-known folk melodies to capture the spirit of his country. Sibelius died in 1957 at the age of 92.

Wonderful Adventures of Nils, and older people enjoy *The Story of Gösta Berling.* Books by the Norwegian novelist, Sigrid Undset, who won a Nobel Prize for literature, are very popular in America. Girls especially enjoy her stories of *Kristin Lavransdatter,* the headstrong daughter of a kindly Norwegian nobleman.

Grieg and Sibelius expressed the spirit of their countrymen. The nineteenth-century composer Edvard Grieg (greeg) helped bring world attention to Norwegian music. Many of his compositions were based on the folk songs and traditions of Norway. When Grieg was thirty-one the Norwegian government agreed to support him for the rest of his life so he could devote all his time to composing. At Ibsen's request he wrote music for *Peer Gynt,* which has become one of his most popular works.

The Finnish composer Jan Sibelius (sih-*bay*-lih-us) has set many Finnish legends to music in the form of tone poems. These legends come particularly from a great epic poem, the *Kalevala,* which means "land of heroes." Sibelius has expressed the ruggedness, dependability, and patriotism of Finnish heroes in his tone poem *Finlandia.*

Scandinavia has also given the world many great singers. One hundred years ago the Swedish singer Jenny Lind thrilled thousands when P. T. Barnum, the founder of the circus, brought her to America. Her rich soprano voice won her the name of the "Swedish Nightingale." In recent times, radio, concert, and movie audiences throughout the world have enjoyed the voices of the great Scandinavian singers, Kirsten Flagstad and Lauritz Melchior (*mel*-kyahr). Both have made numerous appearances in this country.

HANS CHRISTIAN ANDERSEN. This gifted Danish storyteller wrote poems and novels before finally turning to the fairy tales that made his name famous. The statue above, depicting Andersen with the ugly duckling, is in Central Park, New York.

SCANDINAVIA IS THE HOME OF FAMOUS SCIENTISTS AND INVENTORS

One of the earliest great names in Scandinavian science is that of Linnaeus (lih-*nee*-us), an eighteenth-century Swedish botanist. He became world-famous for arranging plants into classes, orders, families, and species. The system of classification which he established is still used today.

Another well-known Scandinavian scientist was a Swedish chemist named Alfred Nobel (no-*bel*). He discovered how to make dynamite, smokeless powder, and many other new chemical compounds. Perhaps his knowledge of the destructiveness of the explosives he had developed led him to devote his great fortune to the cause of world peace. Nobel is best known throughout the world for the five prizes given annually in his name. There are Nobel prizes for outstanding achievement in physics, chemistry, medicine, literature, and world peace.

Nobel's vision of world citizenship is revealed in his statement: "I declare it to be my express desire that in the awarding of prizes no consideration whatever be paid to the nationality of candidates."

Another famous Swedish scientist is John Ericsson, the inventor of the marine propeller and the revolving gun turret. It was he who designed the revolving turret of the historic ship *Monitor*, which saved the Northern navy from destruction by the iron-clad *Merrimac* during our Civil War. Scandinavian scientists also invented the cream separator, the safety match, the non-sinkable lifeboat, and ball bearings.

THE NOBEL PRIZE MEDAL. This coveted medal, together with a $51,000 award, is given to five people every year. Alfred Nobel, who died in 1896, left $9,000,000 to provide the awards.

The Danish physicist Niels Bohr (bor) is said to have contributed as much as Einstein has to twentieth-century science. Bohr is called the "Father of Atomic Energy" because in 1913 he discovered the secret of atomic structure. He founded the Institute for Theoretical Physics at the University of Copenhagen, where physicists from many countries have studied. In 1957 he received the first "Atoms for Peace" award for his achievements in atomic research.

THE SCANDINAVIAN PEOPLES HAVE PIONEERED IN SOCIAL LEGISLATION

The Scandinavian governments provide housing and other economic benefits for workers. The Scandinavian countries are admired everywhere for their efforts to guarantee a better life for their citizens. They seem to have found solutions to the problems of poverty and unemployment. Scandinavian cities are virtually free of slums. The government of each country provides modern housing projects for families of low or middle income at prices each can afford. Electricity, from hydroelectric power, is so cheap that most housewives have electrical appliances.

Stockholm, the capital of Sweden, and other cities have set aside acres of ground in the suburbs which factory workers may rent for the summer at low cost. A man and his family work in early summer mornings and long evenings to raise flowers and vegetables for themselves. These garden projects, started during World War I, have been so successful that they are still carried on.

The Scandinavian countries have had few labor problems or clashes between factory and farm interests, largely because the governments have helped to raise the standard of living.

The establishment of Denmark's prosperous dairy industry provides an excellent example of such enlightened government assistance. Less than a century ago most farmers in Denmark produced only grain. Eventually the sandy soil became worn out, and Denmark was unable to meet the competition of cheap grain from the rich plains of the Americas and Russia. The government made a careful study of the agricultural situation and found that the Danish soil and climate were best suited to the dairy industry. Under government leadership an agricultural revolution was

DENMARK TODAY. In agriculture, industry, and trade, Denmark ranks among the most modern countries of the world. *Left:* An aerial view of Danish farmland shows well-tended fields surrounding neat dwellings. *Right:* A well-stocked co-operative store looks much like the huge supermarkets in the United States.

achieved. Experts were brought in to teach the farmers how to raise livestock and operate creameries and meat-packing plants.

Danish engineers drained the heather-covered wastelands to increase the amount of grazing land. The farmers were encouraged to grow only those crops which would feed livestock. Today the luxuriant Danish pastures support a greater number of animals per square mile of land than do the pastures of any other country in Europe.

To make industrial workers more secure, the Scandinavian governments have also sponsored unemployment insurance, public work projects, workman's sickness compensation, and old age pensions. Thus the Scandinavians have found an economic policy that is a middle way between unchecked private enterprise and complete government control of the economy. Their progressive measures for social improvement have helped them achieve a high standard of living.

The Danes learned that co-operation meant prosperity. The Scandinavian countries are noted for their spirit of practical co-operation. There is an old saying that if a Danish farmer has only one egg, he can export it and probably will —but not alone. In other words, the Danish farmers learned that groups of farmers working together were better off than hundreds of individual farmers working alone. The Danes formed associations called *co-operatives,* which handle both the buying of supplies and the selling of farm products. By buying in large quantities, co-operatives can get supplies at lower prices. They can also market farm products more profitably than each of the thousands of individual farmers could possibly do by himself.

The farmers have also joined together to hire experts to advise them about raising and feeding their cattle and hogs. Experts run their creameries, meat-packing plants, and butter and cheese factories. Under such excellent supervision, the co-operatives are sure of a quality product that will bring a good price in foreign markets. Britain normally buys most of Denmark's farm products.

The number of co-operatives has grown into the thousands. The idea was adopted by the other Scandinavian countries and has spread to other kinds of businesses. There are co-operative stores, banks, insurance firms, apartment houses, and even publishing houses, travel agencies, and film companies. With no middlemen between purchaser and producer, the members of co-operatives enjoy the profits in lower purchasing prices.

The Scandinavians are leaders in education. Denmark's system of adult education has excited educators in many countries. In the nineteenth

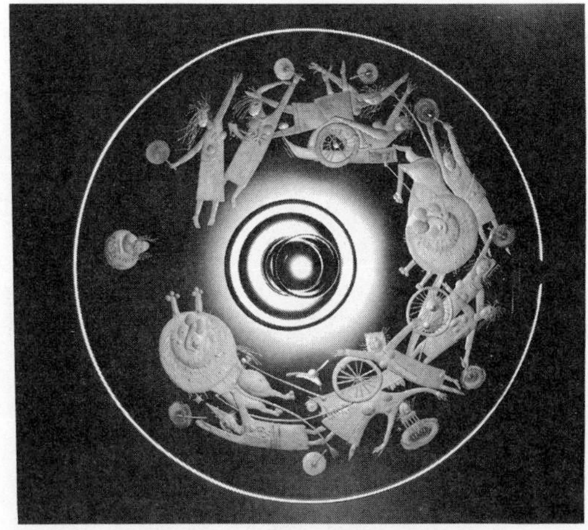

SWEDISH GLASSWORKER. Swedish artisans, like the one shown at the left, have created masterpieces in crystal. A beautiful example of their work is shown at the right.

century the Danes established rural vocational colleges for adults called the People's High Schools. Many farmers attend school for part of the winter when farm work is light. Young girls and farm wives study courses in domestic science. Sweden and Norway have set up similar plans of adult education. Today over 98 per cent of the people of Scandinavia can read and write.

American students are indebted to Sweden for the idea of manual training, or shop work, in the schools. Before the Industrial Revolution the Swedish people made cloth, pottery, and furniture in their homes. When they realized that factory-made goods were replacing handmade articles, they organized handicraft clubs for both men and women. The clubs revived interest in creative home crafts. Courses in handicrafts became part of the curriculum of the Swedish schools. Visiting educators from Europe and the United States were so favorably impressed that they introduced the new classes into their own schools.

The Scandinavians have not neglected the broader aims of education. They know that the books that boys and girls read in school have a great deal to do with the ideas they will have as adults. To encourage a point of view that will lead to world peace, the Scandinavian countries have recently appointed special commissions to examine school books. The commissions recommended new textbooks which have no trace of unfairness or national prejudice. The new textbooks are intended to give a factual report of events and a clear statement of different theories and opposing ideas.

DARING NORWEGIANS EXPLORED THE POLES

The mystery of the polar regions has been a challenge to the hardy explorers of many nations. Toward the end of the nineteenth century a Norwegian scholar and explorer named Nansen (*nahn*-sen) determined to solve some of the mysteries. He sailed north into the Arctic region until his ship became icebound. Leaving his ship, Nansen pushed forward on skis until he was within two hundred miles of the North Pole. This was far beyond any point earlier explorers had reached.

Another Norwegian explorer, Amundsen (*ah*-mun-sen), forced his little ship through the ice-

AMUNDSEN AND HEYERDAHL. In 1918 Roald Amundsen sailed to the North Pole. By 1971, Thor Heyerdahl had gone to the Pacific and to the Atlantic and made New World discoveries that questioned where native Americans came from.

choked waters of the famed Northwest Passage that led from the North Atlantic, through the Arctic Ocean to the North Pacific. He had realized the dreams of explorers who for centuries had hoped to sail over the top of the world.

A few years later, the daring Amundsen undertook a voyage to Antarctica. In 1911 he became the first man to reach the South Pole. After World War I Amundsen tried again to reach the North Pole. His expedition failed, but a short time later he arranged a successful dirigible flight over the Pole.

Thor Heyerdahl is an intrepid and dauntless explorer who in 1971 with a small crew sailed from Africa to Mexico in an open papyrus (pa-pie-rus) sail boat. The famed Norwegian archaeologist wanted to show how Africa and Latin America could have had cultural exchanges at a very early date in history. This theory is not accepted, however by many historians.

Chapter Check-up

1. What was Hans Christian Andersen's contribution to literature?
2. Who are the great Scandinavian singers?
3. What did Grieg and Sibelius contribute to the field of musical composition?
4. How did Linnaeus influence the science of botany?
5. What were Alfred Nobel's scientific contributions?
6. How did Nobel further the causes of science, literature, and world peace?
7. In what ways have the Scandinavians proved themselves capable of progressive, forward-looking government?
8. How did co-operatives help to guarantee Scandinavians a high standard of living?
9. What new educational ideas and practices have come from the Scandinavians?
10. How did Nansen and Amundsen help us to know our world better?

Scandinavia: SYNOPSIS

The land that we now know as Scandinavia was settled thousands of years ago, first by men of the New Stone Age and later by Germanic tribes. The early Northmen were skillful sailors who raided coastal towns and, long before Columbus' voyage, touched the shores of America. By the eleventh century the kings of Norway, Sweden, and Denmark had become Christians.

Under Gustavus Adolphus, Sweden became a world power in the seventeenth century, extending its territory along the Baltic Sea. After his death, Swedish power declined. During the period of peace in the last half of the nineteenth century, however, all Scandinavia prospered, largely as a result of the development of dairy farming and the coming of the Industrial Revolution. Although it suffered in World War II, the region has made a quick recovery.

The writings of such authors as Hans Christian Andersen and Ibsen have enriched the world's literature, just as the compositions of Grieg and Sibelius have increased the enjoyment of music lovers. Scientists like Linnaeus, Nobel, and Bohr have made major contributions to modern civilization. Perhaps the most noteworthy achievement of modern Scandinavia, however, is the social progress it has made. Thanks to a spirit of co-operation and enlightened government leadership, the Scandinavian peoples enjoy economic security, good housing, and an excellent educational system. In finding a middle way between complete government control and unchecked private enterprise, these social pioneers have maintained their freedom and achieved a high standard of living.

Important People

How has each of the following influenced the story of the Scandanavian countries?

Leif Ericson	Haakon VII	Jan Sibelius	Alfred Nobel
Margaret of Denmark	Dag Hammarskjoeld	Edvard Grieg	Niels Bohr
Gustavus Adolphus	Henrik Ibsen	Carolus Linnaeus	Roald Amundsen
Bernadotte	Trygve Lie	Count Folke Bernadotte	Hans Christian Andersen

Terms

Be sure that you understand clearly the meaning of each of the following:

co-operatives	People's High Schools	Thor
fiord	runes	Vikings
Nobel Prize	Scandinavia	sagas

Questions for Discussion and Review

1. How has each of the following geographic features influenced the progress of the Scandinavian countries: (a) nearness to the sea, (b) extensive and irregular coastlines, (c) northerly location, (d) type of soil, (e) mountain ranges, (f) remoteness from the rest of Europe.
2. How did economic and social conditions at home cause the medieval Vikings to become sailors and fighters?
3. Why did the people of other lands hate and fear the Vikings?
4. Why is Gustavus Adolphus a great hero to the Swedes?
5. How has the small nation of Denmark been able to maintain a stable economy and a high standard of living?
6. Why are Greenland and Iceland important to the United States?
7. What is the "middle way" by which the Scandinavian peoples have achieved a high standard of living?
8. In what two important ways have the Scandinavians contributed to world peace?
9. How has the United States been influenced by the progressive ideas of Scandinavia in education and government?
10. In your opinion, what has been the greatest contribution of the Scandinavians to the modern world? Why?

Interesting Things to Do

1. On a map of northern Europe show the Scandinavian countries and the surrounding lands and seas. Use colors and illustrations to make your map more interesting.
2. Make a summary information chart for Scandinavia. Arrange your chart to give the following information for each country: (a) capital city, (b) geographic features, (c) natural resources, (d) chief industries, (e) form of government, (f) outstanding people.
3. Build a model of a ship typical of those that carried the Vikings to all parts of Europe.
4. Make a notebook collection of pictures of geysers, fiords, forests, lakes, and other scenic wonders of Scandinavia.
5. Prepare and present an oral report on Nobel and the Nobel Prize.
6. Write a poem about a Viking ship, a Norwegian fiord, a Danish farm, or some other Scandinavian scene.
7. Write a newspaper account of the delicate position of Finland in modern international relations.
8. Add to or begin your "Who's Who in World History" series by writing brief biographies of one or more important Scandinavian leaders.

Interesting Reading about Scandinavia

Berry, Erick, *The Land and People of Finland*, Lippincott.

Childs, Marquis W., *Sweden, The Middle Way*, Yale.

Evans, Edwin B., *Scandinavia*, Holiday.

Innes, Hammond, and Editors of Life, *Scandinavia*, Time, Inc.

*McLean, Kathryn, *Mama's Bank Account*, Harcourt, Brace & World. True-to-life stories about a Norwegian family in old San Francisco.

Proctor, George, *The Young Traveler in Sweden*, Dutton. Everyday scenes in Sweden.

Rothery, Agnes, *Denmark: Kingdom of Reason*, Viking.

Strode, Hudson, *Sweden, Model for the World*, Harcourt, Brace & World.

*Thorne-Thomsen, G., *In Norway*, Viking.

Van Loon, Hendrik, *Gustavus Vasa: His Adventures and Escapades*, Dodd, Mead. Exciting account of Sweden's fight for independence from Denmark.

* Indicates easy reading

Communism loves a parade. But the dignity and strength of the Slavic peoples will aways reflect the love of homeland and a fierce pride in tradition.

Part 16
EASTERN EUROPE
REGION OF TURMOIL

EASTERN EUROPE

ESTONIA
Riga
LATVIA
BALTIC SEA
LITHUANIA
Danzig
Berlin
Poznań
Warsaw
Oder
POLAND
GERMANY
Kraków
Vistula
Prague
CZECHOSLOVAKIA
Danube
Vienna
Budapest
AUSTRIA
HUNGARY
RUMANIA
Trieste
Bucharest
Belgrade
Danube
YUGOSLAVIA
ADRIATIC SEA
Sofia
BULGARIA
ALBANIA
Istanbul
BOSPORUS
DARDANELLES
TURKEY
GREECE
Athens
SOVIET RUSSIA
BLACK SEA
NORTH AMERICA
ARCTIC OCEAN
ASIA
ATLANTIC OCEAN
EUROPE
SOUTH AMERICA
AFRICA
INDIAN OCEAN

Eastern Europe: GEOGRAPHIC SETTING

Hemmed in between powerful neighbors, the countries of Eastern Europe have often played the role of unwilling pawns in struggles for power and land. Their boundaries have shifted, they have been ravaged by invaders, and occasionally they have disappeared from the map altogether. Because of their strategic location between the democratic West and the communist East, they constitute one of the most critical areas in the world today.

There are twelve countries in Eastern Europe. They may be divided into three groups: the nations of the Balkan Peninsula, the inland countries, and those on the Baltic Sea. To the south are the six Balkan states: Yugoslavia, Albania, Greece, Rumania, Bulgaria, and European Turkey. Although not actually located on the Balkan Peninsula, Hungary has a history closely linked to that of her Balkan neighbors.

The mountainous character of the Balkan lands would seem to make them difficult to invade. Actually, however, there are several passes through the mountains which have for centuries permitted entry to wandering tribes, foreign armies, and peaceful merchants alike. (Notice that the Balkan Peninsula is separated from Asia only by two narrow straits, the Dardanelles and the Bosporus.) Although the mountains have not kept out invaders, they have prevented the Balkan peoples from uniting against them. As a result of disunity and frequent invasion, the people of the Balkans have fifteen different national backgrounds, speak a dozen different languages, and belong to six different religions.

North of the Balkan Peninsula, squeezed in between Russia and Germany, lie the countries of Poland and Czechoslovakia. Throughout much of their history, these two countries have been completely landlocked; that is, they had no access to the sea. Today, however, Poland's northern border provides her with a coast on the Baltic Sea.

Poland has had one of the unhappiest histories of any European country. Because of her open borders, she has been invaded and has fallen under foreign rule repeatedly. But in spite of their difficulties, the Polish people have managed to preserve their language and national traditions. Czechoslovakia is a mountainous land, but the mountains are low and do not prohibit entry or passage. One of the main routes between southeastern and northern Europe passes through Czechoslovakia. Thus its people have known frequent invasion and conquest.

To the north of Poland, on the Baltic Sea, lie the tiny lands of Estonia, Latvia, and Lithuania. Just before the outbreak of World War II, they were annexed by Soviet Russia. Although they are behind the Iron Curtain today, the United States has refused to recognize their seizure. We still consider them officially as separate nations rather than as part of Russia. The rest of the countries of Eastern Europe are under varying degrees of Soviet domination, but they have gradually been regaining their separate identities.

Eastern Europe: PERSPECTIVE

Once upon a time, a Balkan prince was told by his fairy godfather that he could receive for himself and his nation any one wish he cared to make. However, whatever he requested for himself and his people would be bestowed doubly upon his nation's neighbors. Without hesitation, the prince cried: "Oh, Fairy Godfather, then strike me and my people blind in one eye!"

Thus, in the Balkans and Eastern Europe exist peoples crippled by vicious hatreds and victimized by an unhappy geography. Rumanian oil, Polish coal, the heavy industry of Bohemia, the arable plains of Hungary, the very location of the

region as a gateway to the Near East or to Russia,—all this has proved an irresistible lure to the Great Powers! Small wonder that East Europeans have usually lived under the yoke of some foreign master,—Turkish or Russian, Austrian or German—and that whenever independence has come, it has been as essentially satellite peoples. "The Powder-keg of Europe" was the label fastened upon the Balkans for almost two centuries and, indeed, it was there in 1914 that the assassination of an Austrian archduke by a young Serb nationalist blew up into the outbreak of World War I.

Many times have the East Europeans demonstrated their courage. In World War II the outmanned Poles strove valiantly against the well-equipped Nazis. When, as a result of that war, Soviet domination of Eastern Europe replaced German control, the inhabitants had to accept Communist regimes. They have not, however, surrendered without a struggle. In 1948 the Yugoslavs, led by Marshal Tito, began their own brand of "national communism" and successfully broke away from Russian overlordship. The Hungarians in 1956 and the Czechs in 1968 tried essentially to imitate the Yugoslavs. They failed,—only because they were suppressed by Soviet tanks. Still it has been made clear to the rest of the world how desperately the forlorn East Europeans long for real independence.

CHAPTER 54

The Balkans Have Been the Powder Keg of Europe

INVADERS AND CONQUERORS HAVE LEFT THEIR MARK ON THE BALKANS

Waves of invaders pushed into the Balkans. The original inhabitants of the Balkans were probably the Illyrians, who lived in the mountains before the rise of Greek civilization. (Their descendants are the present-day Albanians.) In the second century A.D. the Roman emperor Trajan crossed the Danube and added to the Roman Empire the land which is now Rumania. Some historians believe that Rumanian people are descended from the Roman soldiers and settlers who came with Trajan. During the decline of Rome in the fourth and fifth centuries, the Balkans swarmed with invaders. The Huns swept in from central Asia, and the Germanic tribes poured down from the north.

From the sixth to the tenth centuries, the Balkans were invaded by a new group of tribes known as the Slavs. The Slavic peoples, who came from an area near the Vistula River in central Poland, included such tribes as the Serbs, the Croats (*kro*-ats), and the Slovenes (slow-*veenz*). They settled throughout the Balkan Peninsula and became dominant in the regions of Yugoslavia and Bulgaria. Toward the end of the ninth century, another Asiatic people, known as the Magyars, also moved into the Balkans and settled in the region of Hungary.

For many years after the fall of the Roman Empire in the west, the Eastern or Byzantine Empire maintained a rather flimsy rule over the Bal-

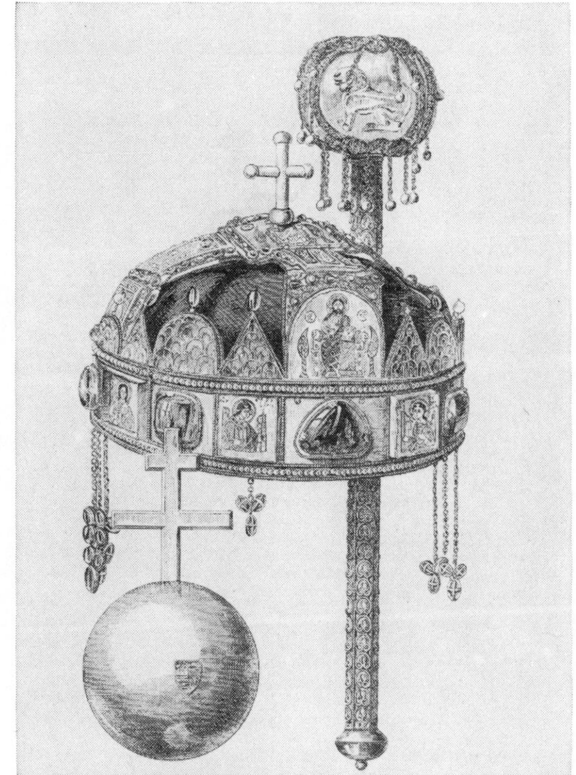

CROWN OF ST. STEPHEN. Because he converted the pagan Magyars to Roman Catholicism, Stephen received this crown from the Pope. On the left is the orb, symbolizing kingly power and justice; on the right the scepter, an emblem of authority.

kans. Ultimately, most of the Balkan peoples were converted to Christianity. When the religious split between Rome and Constantinople became final in 1054 (see page 155), most of the Balkan peoples remained loyal to Constantinople, and the Orthodox Eastern Church is still the main religious force in the Balkans. Some of the tribes, however, remained Roman Catholic. Thus religious differences became a further cause of division among the Balkan peoples.

St. Stephen united the Magyars into a Hungarian kingdom. During the early part of the eleventh century, in the region north of the Balkans, a strong kingdom was formed under a great Hungarian ruler, Stephen I. Stephen broke the power of the Magyar tribal chieftains and succeeded in uniting all the tribes. He encouraged agriculture and trade and built a strong system of defenses for his kingdom. The devout Stephen (later known as St. Stephen) converted the pagan Magyars to the Roman Catholic faith. He aided the establishment of monasteries by setting aside huge tracts of land for that purpose. For his services to the Church, the Pope sent Stephen a golden crown. It was later called the "Holy Crown of St. Stephen" and is enshrined in Budapest. (Possession of this crown is the reason why Hungary remained technically a kingdom until 1946, even during periods when there was no king in power.)

After Stephen's death, the Hungarian kings struggled to keep the kingdom united and independent. For over four hundred years they resisted the efforts of foreign emperors to annex their lands. In the fifteenth century, another great Hungarian king, Matthias Corvinus (kor-*veen*-us), came to the throne. Although he was only fifteen years old when he accepted the crown, he soon became an extremely able ruler. He built a strong army and set out to make Hungary the dominant force in central Europe. He encouraged learning, established a uniform code of laws, and greatly expanded his kingdom. Under his influence Renaissance learning and art spread throughout Hungary, and Budapest became a brilliant cultural center.

Balkan rulers were unable to build strong states. Long after St. Stephen had successfully established the kingdom of Hungary, the Balkan peoples remained divided. During the Middle Ages, tribal loyalties, the mountainous terrain, and religious differences tended to break them into small groups, each with its own ruler or tribal chieftain. Constant warfare made trade virtually impossible, and the people struggled desperately to make a living from the land. Several of the restless tribes revolted against Byzantine rule, but they were unsuccessful in maintaining their independence for long.

Then, in the early part of the fourteenth century, a strong Serbian ruler named Stephen Du-

shan appeared. He succeeded in uniting the Serbian tribes and building a powerful kingdom that was independent of Byzantine rule. After extending his kingdom to include nearly two-thirds of the Balkan Peninsula, Dushan proclaimed himself emperor of the Serbs, Greeks, Bulgars, and Albanians. He then established a code of laws to govern the tribes under his control.

Dushan died at the age of forty-six, just as he was beginning an ambitious campaign aimed at the conquest of Constantinople. But in the century following his death, Serbia, Hungary, and the whole of the Byzantine Empire were swallowed up by the warlike Turks.

The Turks conquered the Balkan Peninsula and threatened the rest of Europe. In the eleventh century a fierce tribe of warriors called Turks moved into Asia Minor from Central Asia. In the thirteenth century the Turks were welded into a powerful military force by a brilliant leader named Osman, or Ottoman. He laid the foundation for a great Turkish state, which became called the Ottoman Empire.

The Turks began a remarkable campaign of conquest with the capture of Constantinople in 1453. After the fall of that city, which they renamed Istanbul, the Turks overran much of Eastern Europe. Even the armies of the great Hungarian king Matthias Corvinus could not check the Turkish onslaught. The greatest of the Turkish sultans, Suleiman (syoo-lay-*mahn*) the Magnificent, led his armies to the gates of Vienna itself before he was finally stopped.

The Balkans remained under Turkish control until the nineteenth century. The Turks replaced the Christian nobles as the great landholders and warriors of the Balkans. The Christians were treated brutally, but they were allowed to keep their religion, principally because non-Moslems were subject to heavy taxes. For many years the Turkish government was supported chiefly by taxes on the Christian population.

In the middle of the seventeenth century the Turks launched a new offensive aimed at the conquest of the Holy Roman Empire. Again they besieged Vienna. This time the city and possibly all of Europe were saved from Turkish domination by the great Polish king, John Sobieski, about whom you will read in the next chapter. A few years later, under the leadership of the Hapsburg rulers, the Turks were driven out of Hungary, and it became a Hapsburg possession. The Balkan states, however, remained under Turkish control until late in the nineteenth century.

NATIONALISM IN THE BALKANS LED TO INDEPENDENCE AND WAR

The Eastern Question disturbed the great powers of Europe. In the early nineteenth century the wave of national sentiment that was sweeping through Europe reached the Balkans. Because most of the Balkan peoples were Christians, they were united in their desire to drive out the Turks. There Balkan unity stopped, however. All of the various Balkan tribes wanted to form their own independent states. Their struggles with the Turks and with one another made the Balkan Peninsula a scene of almost constant conflict.

The Balkans were not left to work out their future by themselves. The rivalries and fears of three great European powers made the "Eastern Question," as the situation in the Balkans was called, a threat to the peace of all Europe. The three powers were Austria, Russia, and Britain. Austria feared the Balkan movements for national independence because the many Slavic people within her empire would want to join the new states. She was also afraid that Russia would control the new states and endanger the Austrian frontier. You may recall that the Russian people were also of Slavic origin. This kinship enabled Russia to set herself up as protector and helper of all the Slavic peoples. Russia sent agents into the Balkan countries to help lead uprisings against Turkish rule. By playing the role of "big brother" to the Slavs, Russia hoped to extend her influence

THE OTTOMAN EMPIRE AND HAPSBURG LANDS 1763

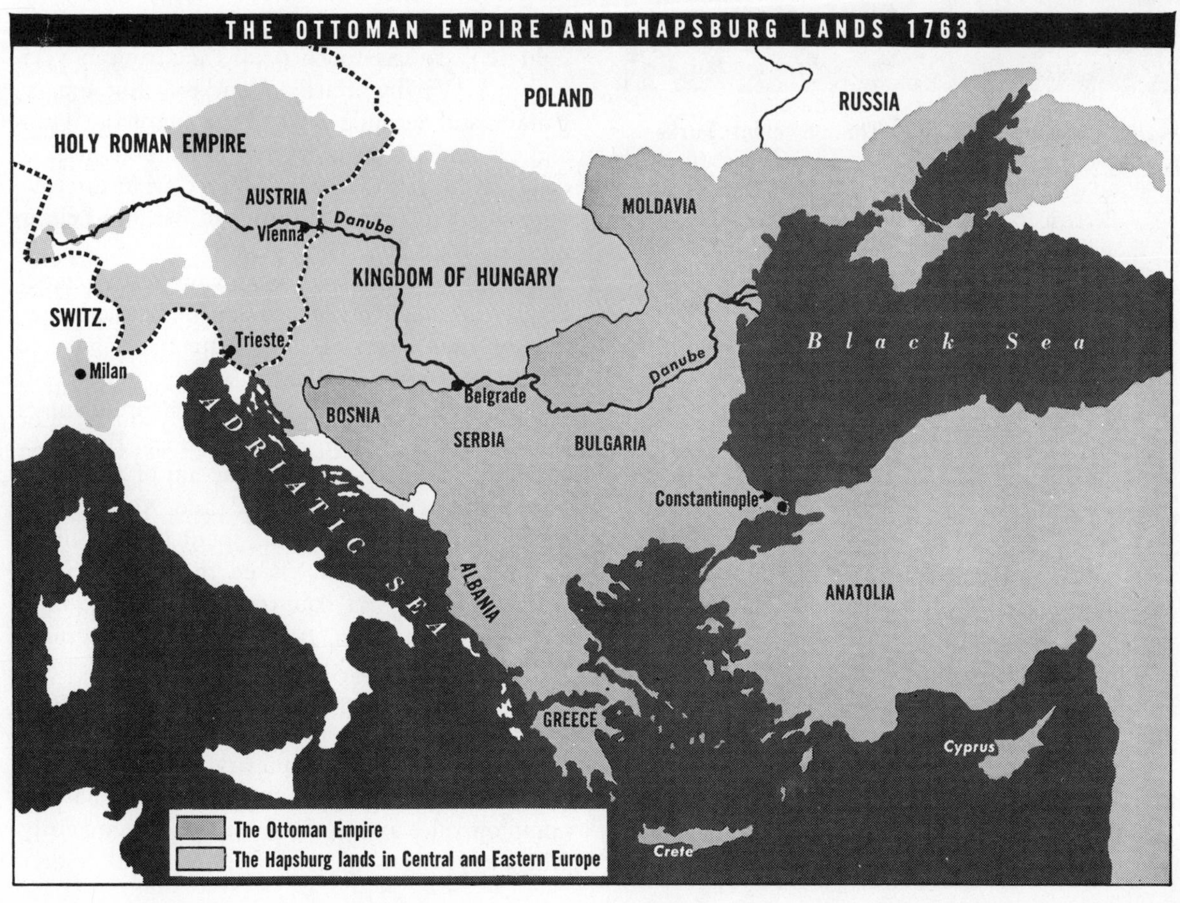

BATTLE OF LEPANTO. The powerful Turks suffered a major defeat in 1571 when their navy was destroyed off the coast of Greece by a fleet sent by the Christian powers. Although the battle did not diminish Turkish supremacy on land, it prevented the Turks from gaining control of the Mediterranean.

in the Balkans at the expense of the Ottoman Empire. Her chief goal was to gain control of the straits between the Black Sea and the Mediterranean, which Russia regarded as the "key to her back door."

Britain sympathized with Balkan nationalism, but she realized that the collapse of the Ottoman Empire would create a serious menace to her overseas possessions. If the Ottoman Empire were destroyed, Russia would become mistress of the straits and her warships could dominate the eastern Mediterranean, thereby threatening Britain's vital lifeline to the East. Thus Britain was determined to maintain Turkish power in the Balkans at any cost. As you can see, Balkan nationalism, when mixed with the conflicting interests of Austria, Russia, and Britain, created a potentially explosive situation.

The Eastern Question made a "powder keg" of southeastern Europe. During the nineteenth century the Balkan crisis erupted in a series of violent incidents. In 1804 the Serbs, encouraged by Russia, revolted against the Ottoman Empire. They were led by a fiery-tempered pork merchant named Karageorge. Although successful at first, Karageorge had an ill-fated career. He was eventually defeated by the Turks and murdered by a rival named Milosh Obrenovich (oh-*breh*-no-vitch). Milosh led another uprising, and in 1817 a small part of Serbia was granted self-government within the Ottoman Empire. A few years later the Greeks also revolted. After a bitter ten-year struggle, they gained their independence from Turkey. There were many other uprisings and incidents in the Balkans. Sometimes they led to wars which involved the great powers.

In 1853 Russia touched off the Crimean (kry-*mee*-un) War by attacking Turkey. But France, Britain, and Sardinia went to the aid of the Turks and checked Russian expansion. (You may recall that this was the war in which Cavour shrewdly offered aid to France in order to win her help in unifying Italy.)

Meantime, Hungary was growing restive under Hapsburg rule. In 1848, under the heroic leadership of Louis Kossuth, the Hungarians revolted against Austria. The uprising was temporarily successful, and Kossuth was chosen president of the independent Hungarian republic. But when the Czar of Russia came to the aid of the Hapsburgs, the republic collapsed and Kossuth was forced to flee Hungary. He spent the rest of his life in exile. He even visited the United States seeking help for his country.

Twenty years later, Austria's defeat by Prussia in the Seven Weeks' War left her too weak to resist Hungarian demands. Austria agreed to grant Hungary a measure of freedom, and the Dual Monarchy of Austria-Hungary was established. Under this arrangement the two states shared a common ruler and decided foreign policy jointly. But the Hungarians were allowed to have their own parliament and constitution, and they were free to control local affairs as they saw fit.

A few years after the formation of the Dual Monarchy, new uprisings in the Balkans led to another war between Russia and Turkey. This time the Turks were saved by the British fleet. As a result of the war, a conference of great nations in 1878 decided that Rumania and Serbia were to be completely independent of the Ottoman Empire, and Bulgaria was granted self-government within the Ottoman Empire.

The Young Turk revolution could not prevent more explosions in the Balkans. By the beginning of the twentieth century the Turks had been in Europe for five and a half centuries. Their rule had been despotic. They had repeatedly crushed liberal movements among the subject peoples. But, as we have seen, the Turks had begun to lose their grip in the Balkans. If other European powers had not interfered, Turkey would have been finished in Europe after her war with Russia in 1878.

During the next twenty years the Ottoman Empire continued to be plagued by revolts, and Turkey became known as the "sick man of Europe." Then, in 1908, Turkey began to show surprising signs of life. A group of Turkish reformers, called the Young Turks, decided that something should be done to give the empire a liberal, modern government that could keep the loyalty of its subjects. They led a revolt, seized control of the army, and forced the sultan to accept a constitution that provided for a parliamentary government. Bulgaria was given complete independence. The subjects

THE CRIMEAN WAR. During the Crimean War, Florence Nightingale cared for the wounded, introducing new methods of nursing. She is shown here in the hospital at Scutari, near Istanbul. Known as the Lady of the Lamp, Florence Nightingale was the first woman to receive the British Order of Merit.

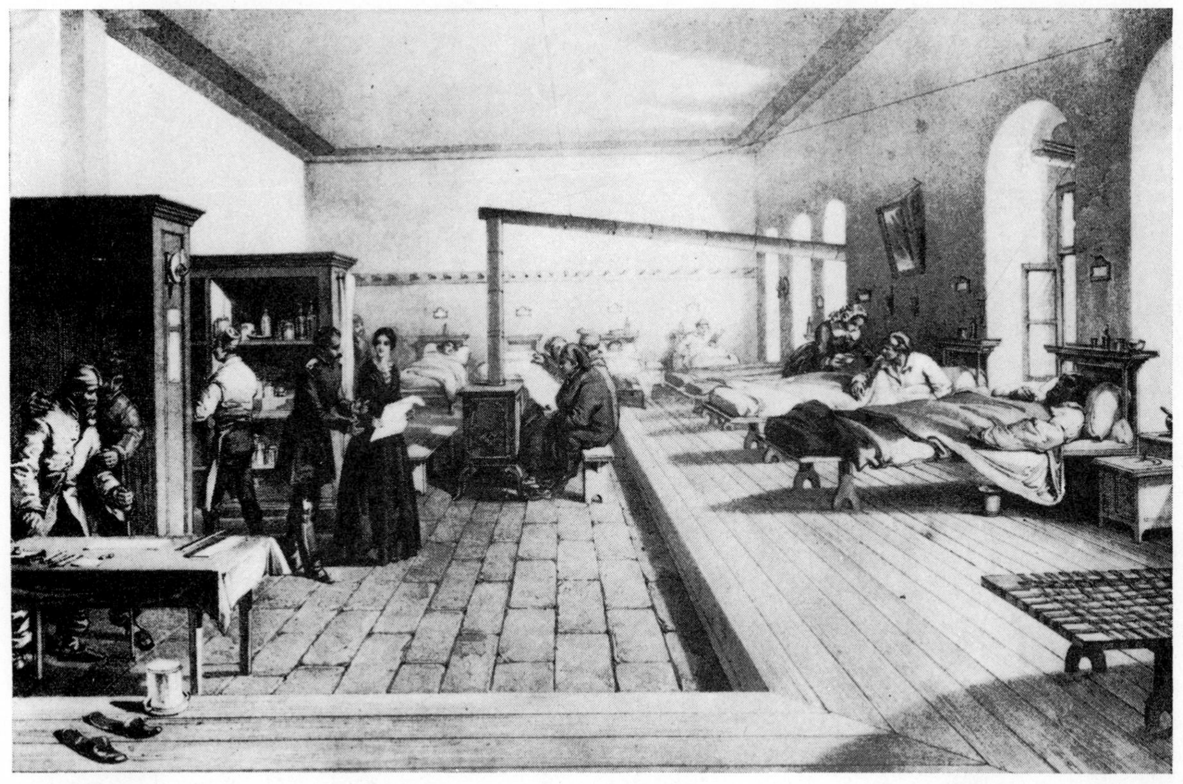

of the empire were delighted with what appeared to be the beginning of Turkish democracy. The experiment in democracy did not last long, however. There were many revolutions and counterrevolutions. The promised reforms did not appear. In 1912 Bulgaria, Serbia, and Greece attacked the Ottoman Empire in hope of gaining more land. The brief war that followed is known as the First Balkan War. Although the Balkan states were victorious, Bulgaria was not content with her share of the spoils. Serbia wanted an outlet on the Adriatic Sea. A series of disagreements led to a Second Balkan War in 1913. This time Greece, Serbia, and Rumania turned against Bulgaria and defeated her.

The Balkan wars had far-reaching effects on world history. For one thing, they brought the downfall of the Ottoman Empire. You will read later in *Story of Nations* how the Ottoman Empire was transformed into modern Turkey. You will also learn how the Balkan "powder keg" helped bring on World War I.

After World War I the Balkans were reorganized and fell into the hands of dictators. One of President Wilson's great desires was to change the map of Europe so that people who shared common backgrounds, languages, and traditions would rule themselves as independent states. The great powers, meeting in Paris after World War I, took several steps in an effort to achieve this goal. The Dual Monarchy of Austria-Hungary was broken up, and Hungary became an independent state. A portion of Austria's Balkan territory was taken away and combined with Serbia to create the new state of Yugoslavia, which means "land of the southern Slavs." The independence of Albania, Bulgaria, and Rumania was also confirmed.

Unfortunately, this arrangement did not solve the Balkan problem. Practically all of the new states wanted more land than they had been given. And the Balkan peoples were so thoroughly intermixed in some areas that it was impossible to draw boundaries based on nationalities. In the years

between the two world wars there were frequent boundary disputes. Both Hungary and Bulgaria strove to regain territory lost after World War I.

Another problem was the failure of the Balkan peoples to make democratic government work. All the Balkan states started out bravely to set up liberal, constitutional governments, but most of their citizens lacked political experience of any kind. The long years of oppressive Turkish rule had conditioned the subject peoples to the use of violence rather than compromise. Outlaws who had annoyed the Turks became Balkan heroes. Men who assassinated Turkish officers were considered great patriots. To the Balkan peasants, who made up most of the population, government meant only soldiers, tax collectors, and injustice. Thus the peasants learned to distrust all government, and the sudden gift of the right to vote could not wipe out centuries of tradition. By the time World War II broke out, dictatorships of one kind or another had been established in nearly all the Balkan countries.

THE BALKANS CAME UNDER COMMUNIST DOMINATION

Tito organized Communist resistance to Hitler and took over Yugoslavia. Hungary, Bulgaria, and Rumania joined forces with Hitler in World War II. Yugoslavia and Greece hoped to stay out of the war, but in the spring of 1941 they were overrun by the German armies. Although the Yugoslav army was defeated, many patriots took to the mountains. Under the leadership of a Serbian army officer, Draja Mikhailovitch (mee-*kie*-low-vich), an irregular army of patriots called the Chetniks fought a desperate guerilla war against the Germans.

At the same time, another Yugoslav guerilla leader, known as Tito (*tee*-toe), organized a second guerilla band. Tito had been a prisoner of war in Russia in World War I. There he became an enthusiastic Communist and later returned to Yugoslavia to organize metal workers into Communist groups. Arrested for his activities, he spent four years in prison. Then he left the country and lived for several years in Paris, still working for the Communists.

When Hitler invaded Yugoslavia, Tito managed to get back to his homeland. He formed an irregular army, called the Partisans, to fight the Nazis. His troops fought not only against Hitler's invaders, however, but also against Mikhailovitch's Chetniks. It is a question which enemy they fought harder. The point to remember is that Tito's whole effort was not directed at freeing Yugoslavia from Hitler. He also wanted to deliver Yugoslavia to the Communists.

MARSHAL TITO. Josip Broz, known as Marshal Tito, is President for life of the Socialist Federal Republic of Yugoslavia. He has become one of the world's most influential Communist leaders.

He succeeded in his efforts because Russian troops, after occupying Hungary, Bulgaria, and Rumania toward the end of the war, marched into Yugoslavia and proclaimed Tito the head of a Yugoslav Communist government. Tito captured Mikhailovitch, gave him a quick trial, and shot him as a traitor. Both the United States and Great Britain protested vigorously. They demanded the right to take part in the trial of Mikhailovitch, for the Chetniks had helped the Allies in many ways. But Tito and the Russians ignored the protests. The Communists took over Yugoslavia and dropped the Iron Curtain around it.

By 1946 all the Balkan states except Greece and Turkey were occupied by Russian troops. They were forced to adopt Communist governments and follow the dictates of the Soviet Union.

Tito refused to take orders from Russia. Tito quickly put his Communist program in effect in Yugoslavia. He brought Yugoslav industry and agriculture under government control, much as had been done in Soviet Russia. At first he followed the wishes of the Soviet Union and joined with the other Iron Curtain countries in treaties of mutual defense and trade.

Then, in 1948, Tito had the first of several serious quarrels with the Soviet dictator Stalin. Yugoslavia was expelled from the international Communist organization. The next year, when Tito refused to obey Stalin's wishes regarding a Yugoslav claim to certain Austrian territories, the Soviet Union renounced her treaty of friendship with Yugoslavia. Almost immediately the other Russian-dominated countries withdrew their friendship too.

Since Yugoslavia's whole economy was based on trade with those countries, she suffered severely for her defiance of Soviet Russia. Soon, however, Tito re-established friendly relations with the Western powers. They knew that he was still a Communist but they were happy to support him in his split with the Soviet Union. They loaned him money and furnished him with machinery, food, and other goods.

After Stalin's death in 1953 the Russians tried to win back Tito's friendship. Tito was willing to be

THE HUNGARIAN REVOLUTION. Russian tanks rumble through Budapest during the gallant Hungarian uprising in 1956. This newspaper photograph was made while the Russians were withdrawing on November 2—two days before the massive counterattack that crushed the Hungarian Freedom Fighters.

won provided he could remain master of Yugoslavia's domestic affairs. The Russians agreed. Since then, Tito has swung back and forth between neutralism and support of Soviet policy in world affairs, depending on which position gained him the most advantage.

The countries of Eastern Europe have become more independent. The other Balkan countries envied Yugoslavia's independence as they struggled under the Soviet yoke. The Hungarian revolt in 1956 provided a glimpse of the bitter resentment that had developed toward the Russians. Mercilessly crushed by overwhelming Soviet forces, it nevertheless taught the Soviet leaders a lesson. Their first reaction was to tighten their control. Then, gradually, they began to tread more softly in Eastern Europe. As in the Soviet Union itself, the suffering of the people was blamed on the Stalin regime.

In 1962, a "de-Stalinization" campaign was carried out in Eastern Europe, and many Stalinists were expelled from the governments of individual countries. At the same time, the leaders of these countries were given greater independence in internal affairs. Moreover, the need of the Soviet Union to keep their loyalty in its dispute with Red China (about which you will read in Part 19) gave them a lever with which to force some concessions from the Russians. Yet, despite these developments, oppression of the people themselves though lessened still continues.

Chapter Check-up

1. What are some of the many groups which invaded and settled the Balkans?
2. Why are most of the Balkan people members of the Orthodox Eastern Church?
3. Why were Balkan rulers unable to build strong states?
4. How did the Ottoman Turks treat the Balkan peoples?
5. What was the Crimean War?
6. Why did Russia and Britain take opposite sides on the Eastern Question?
7. How did the Balkan wars demonstrate the inability of the Balkan States to work together?
8. How were the Balkans reorganized after World War I?
9. Why did this reorganization fail to produce stable, unified states?
10. In what way is Tito different from most other Communist rulers?

CHAPTER 55

Poland and Czechoslovakia Became the Prey of Powerful Neighbors

POLAND HAS STRUGGLED UNSUCCESSFULLY TO MAINTAIN HER INDEPENDENCE

The Poles built a large kingdom in the Middle Ages. In the first century A.D. the land that was later called Poland lay far beyond the frontiers of the Mediterranean civilizations of Greece and Rome. The Slavs who lived there were wandering tribes of hunters who had never seen a city or even a plowed field. By the tenth century, however, six of the Slavic tribes had settled down and united under one ruler. This marked the beginning of the Polish nation. The Poles adopted Christianity and learned to write their language with the Latin alphabet.

Under her first king, Boleslav the Brave (992–1025), Poland became a large and important state. Successors to Boleslav defended and strengthened the kingdom. The city of Kraków (*krah*-koof) served as the early capital of Poland. Kraków was noted for its excellent university, and it became the cultural center of Eastern Europe.

Soon after Warsaw became the capital in the sixteenth century, Poland reached the height of her power and glory. Polish territory reached across Central Europe from the Carpathian Mountains to the Baltic Sea. The western boundary was only ninety miles from Berlin. Lithuania was then part of Poland.

The great Polish kingdom declined. Many things contributed to the decline of the once-powerful Polish nation. For one thing, the Polish Diet, or assembly, had an old-fashioned rule which required unanimous consent to any action which the government took. You can imagine how hard it would be for the United States to defend itself if every action taken by our Congress had to be agreed upon unanimously.

A POLISH NOBLEMAN. The seventeenth-century Dutch painter Rembrandt has expressed the sturdy character of the Polish people in his portrait of an unknown nobleman. During Poland's stormy history, the nobles never allowed the king to impose his will on theirs. Their dissension continually weakened Poland.

THE PARTITIONS OF POLAND

The Three Partitions of Poland—1772, 1793, 1795

To Russia To Austria To Prussia

Poland lacked a powerful middle class of merchants, businessmen, or tradesmen. Most of the people were poor peasants, held in miserable serfdom by a class of rich and powerful nobles. The nobles became more powerful than the king himself. They discouraged the rise of a middle class, which would have made Poland a stronger nation.

In the latter part of the seventeenth century the Turks pressed into central Europe, burning, killing, and pillaging. One of the best-known Polish kings, John Sobieski (so-*byes*-kee), or John III, was then reigning. He had to defend the nation with the Polish army, but the nobility gave him practically no help. John Sobieski was a great military leader. He became commander-in-chief of the Polish, Austrian, and other Christian armies which joined together to drive out the Turks. In 1683 Sobieski's armies saved the Austrian capital of Vienna, which the Turks had besieged for fifty-eight days.

In spite of his great military success and his popularity with the Polish people, John Sobieski could not curb the nobility. He failed to bring about needed reforms within Poland itself, and he died a disappointed man. There were no more great Polish leaders like Sobieski. The Austrians soon forgot their debt of gratitude to Poland. They were willing to take what they could from the weakening Polish kingdom.

Poland was partitioned three times by her neighbors. Poland's lack of central authority and her open borders made her easy prey for ambitious neighbors. Austria, Prussia, and Russia made their first partition of Poland in 1772 at the suggestion of Frederick the Great (see Chapter 48). Poland lost a third of her land. Sobered by this catastrophe, the Polish nobles attempted to strengthen the central power. In 1791 they wrote a new constitution which abolished the right of any one noble to veto legislation. But it was too late for such measures. Russia and Prussia, who were unwilling to see a strong Poland, each took another slice of the dwindling country in the Second Partition of Poland in 1793.

The next year, the Polish hero Thaddeus Kosciusko (kahs-ih-*us*-ko), who had helped Washington fight for American independence, led the Poles in a revolt against Russia. But Russian armies crushed the revolt, and in 1795 Prussia, Russia, and Austria shared in a Third Partition. This time Poland was wiped completely off the map. From 1795 until 1918 Poland existed only in the memories and hopes of patriots. Many Poles of intellect and learning fled to Paris.

The Polish nation was restored after World War I. The land of the Poles was a battleground during World War I and again during World War II, as you will learn in Part 22.

The Poles were determined to gain their freedom. They took World War I as a chance to fight for it. Unfortunately, they did not agree on which side they should join to gain Polish freedom. The result was that a Polish army fought under German command, not for love of the Germans, but to free Poland from Russia. Other Poles joined the Russian army and fought against the Germans—and their own brothers—to free Poland from Gemany. Still other Poles made their way to France and fought under French leadership.

The situation cleared up somewhat in 1917, when the United States came into the war. President Wilson said he favored the creation of an independent nation from all land occupied by "indisputably Polish" people. At the peace conference following the war Poland was restored as an independent nation. But many problems remained to be worked out.

For one thing, Poland needed a port on the Baltic Sea if she hoped to take her place among the European commercial powers. The Allies attempted to solve this problem by giving Poland a strip of land called the Polish Corridor. The Corridor cut across West Prussia from Poland to the seaport of Danzig (*dahn*-tsik). Danzig became a free city controlled by the League of Nations. Poland also gained a part of Upper Silesia.

The new Poland was dissatisfied with her borders, however. From 1920 on, she waged several small wars with Russia, Lithuania (which had also been restored after World War I), and Czechoslovakia (newly created after the war). From Russia she regained much of the territory she had held before the First Partition.

Poland adopted a democratic constitution based on that of France. Political rivalries and peasant uprisings caused so much disorder, however, that in 1926 a soldier, Marshal Pilsudski (peel-*soot*-skee), led a revolt and took over the government. He established a military dictatorship and suppressed all opposition. Even though he was a dictator, he gained recognition as one of the ablest diplomats in Europe. Pilsudski was one of the first European leaders to perceive the danger in Hitler's rise to power.

Germany's invasion of Poland started World War II. The German invasion of Poland in September, 1939, brought the beginning of World War II. The Polish Corridor was a thorn in the side of Nazi leaders because it separated Germany from East Prussia. Hitler demanded the cession of Danzig and the right to build a railroad and a highway across the Corridor. When Poland refused, German armies invaded the country and soon smashed the brave Polish resistance. The Russians at that time had a nonaggression treaty with Hitler. They demanded a part of Poland as their price for staying neutral. Thus the Soviet Union gained much of eastern Poland, which she still holds.

Perhaps no nation suffered more severely under German occupation than Poland. Warsaw, the capital city, was bombed. The Polish people, particularly those of Jewish birth, suffered terribly under German rule. Many thousands died of starvation and disease, and the Nazis ruthlessly murdered several million more.

At the end of World War II Poland found her land in ruins, with millions of her people killed or in Nazi labor camps. Russia liberated Poland's land and people from the Nazis but, in turn, enforced Soviet domination over Poland. They put a Communist government in control. The other Allies protested vainly. They wanted to let Poland's democratic government-in-exile take over Poland until the Polish people could have a chance to decide on their own government. Since Poland was occupied by the Soviet army, the Russians were able to enforce their will.

Poland has had to "walk a tight-rope." For years a Stalinist repression blanketed Poland. The "United Workers" was the only political party. Land was forcibly collectivized as the economy was fitted to Soviet needs. Russian troops garrisoned the country; a Soviet marshal became Poland's Minister of Defense.

THE BLITZKRIEG OF POLAND. The mechanized German army had little difficulty in rolling across Poland's flat plains in 1939. Attacked by the Germans in the west and the Russians in the east, Poland was forced to surrender six weeks after the invasion.

Russia retained the part of eastern Poland she had seized in 1939. Without West Germany's approval, Poland was compensated with a section of east Germany, including coal-rich Silesia (sigh-*leez*-yuh) and the port of Stettin (shteh-*teen*) on the Oder (*oh*-deh) River. This made Poland more dependent on the USSR's good will lest Russia agree to have this land restored to Germany.

Stalin's death weakened the Polish regime. In 1956 there were demonstrations in the city of Poznan (*poz*-nahn) against Soviet control. They were crushed but, fearing a Hungarian-type rebellion, Russian leaders agreed that reforms were needed in Poland.

Wladyslaw (*vlad*-iss-slav) Gomulka (go-*mul*-kuh), who had been expelled from the Communist Party for urging more freedom for Polish Marxists, was elevated to leadership. Controls were relaxed somewhat while Gomulka tried to appease Polish national pride without antagonizing the USSR. But within two years most restrictions were restored when the new regime became more sure of itself. In 1968 there were renewed campaigns against "revisionists" and troops were sent to Czechoslovakia to help subdue the uprising there.

In December, 1970 demonstrations against tough new wage policies caused Gomulka's fall. He was replaced by Edward Gierek (*gee*-rek) who introduced "softer" measures.

THE KINGDOM OF BOHEMIA BECAME THE REPUBLIC OF CZECHOSLOVAKIA

The ancient kingdom of Bohemia was conquered by the German emperor. By the sixth century A.D. certain Slavic tribes from north of the Carpathian Mountains had migrated south to Bohemia, where they formed three different groups: Czechs, Slovaks, and Moravians. In the ninth century the Czechs established the independent state of Bohemia (bo-*hee*-mee-uh) and adopted the Christian faith. One of the early Christian rulers of Bohemia was "good King Wenceslaus" (*wen*-ses-laws), whose name may be familiar to you from a famous Christmas carol. King Wenceslaus influenced the people of Bohemia to adopt the Christian faith, and eventually became the patron saint of his country.

The mountain-ringed forest land of Bohemia was considered a rich prize by her jealous neighbors. For many years the Bohemians were forced to resist the inroads of ambitious German rulers. In the tenth century Bohemia became a member of the Holy Roman Empire. You will remember that the empire was a loose union of Germanic states out of which came the Austro-Hungarian empire and modern Germany.

In the fourteenth century a king of Bohemia became emperor of the Holy Roman Empire. He was Charles IV, a capable ruler, who wanted to keep German influences out of his country. He founded the University of Prague (prahg), which became a famous seat of learning. His efforts to stimulate trade, industry, and cultural developments brought a Golden Age to Bohemia. Before the end of the fourteenth century, however, Emperor Rudolph of the Hapsburgs—the famous family which furnished many rulers of the Holy Roman Empire—reduced the size of Bohemia by taking away some of its land, partly because the king of Bohemia had opposed Rudolph's election as Holy Roman emperor.

CASTLE OF CHARLES IV. From the top of a wooded hill in Bohemia, the fourteenth-century emperor's castle looks down over the surrounding countryside. Charles, who became king of Bohemia after his father was killed in battle, was a skillful diplomat who was able to enlarge his territories and bring about peace among the peoples under his rule.

John Huss became a symbol of Bohemian national feeling. Bohemia and England had become friends through the marriage of King Richard II to a Bohemian princess in 1382. It was at this time that the English dissenter, John Wycliffe, was preaching the reformation of the Catholic Church in England. His writings impressed John Huss, a Bohemian priest at the University of Prague. Huss was a loyal Bohemian and a spirited advocate of Church reform. Huss secured a promise of safety from the German emperor to go to a Church council in Germany to make a bold plea for reform. Despite the emperor's promise of safety, Huss was arrested and burned at the stake as a heretic.

The tragedy of Huss' martyrdom deepened the hatred between the Czechs and Germans. Huss became a national hero. A series of conflicts, known as the Hussite Wars, broke out in Bohemia. In these wars Huss' supporters defended not only their religious views but also their national independence. The Hussite Wars lasted thirteen years, but the religious ideas of Huss and the goal of independence smoldered in Bohemia for a long time afterward. (These same quarrels helped touch off the Thirty Years' War which you read about in the story of Germany.) In the sixteenth century, Bohemia came under the control of the Hapsburg emperor, who was also the ruler of Austria. Later, Bohemia became part of the Austro-Hungarian Empire.

As a subject group in the Austro-Hungarian Empire the Czechs continued their remarkable industrial development and also kept on working and agitating for their independence.

The Czechs gained independence but soon lost their freedom. In the last months of World War I the Czechs declared their independence from the Austrian Empire. As created by the Paris Peace Conference, "Czechoslovakia" included the Czechs of Bohemia, the Slovaks to the east and some Ger-

MASARYK. Czechoslovakia's first president is shown here after opening an international farmers' congress in Vienna. Masaryk, who served as a university professor before becoming his country's leader, was respected as a great democratic statesman.

mans in "Sudetenland" on the west.

The first presidents, Thomas Masaryk (*mah*-sah-reek) and Eduard Benes (*ben*-esh), were able and sincere democrats. Czechoslovakia became the most advanced and prosperous land in Central Europe. But in 1938 Britain and France permitted Hitler to annex Sudetenland (see pages 729–730). In the next year Germany seized the rest of Czechoslovakia which remained under Nazi domination until liberated by Russian armies at the close of World War II.

There was a brief return to parliamentary democracy but in 1948, backed by the Soviet Army, the Czech Communists engineered a coup and made the country a docile satellite of the USSR.

Hope re-emerged in 1968 when the old Stalinist leadership was replaced and Alexander Dubček (*doob*-check) became Party First Secretary. He tried to establish "socialism with a human face." Censorship was lifted; a multi-party political system was promised. But in August, 1968, the reform regime was ousted by an invasion of Russian and East European troops. Dubček was soon expelled from the Communist Party, a more orthodox leader was installed, and Czechoslovakia became again a vassal to a foreign master.

POLAND AND CZECHOSLOVAKIA HAVE ENRICHED WESTERN CIVILIZATION

Although life in Poland and Czechoslovakia has frequently been disturbed by invasion and internal conflict, the people of these countries have nevertheless been able to retain their unique cultures and to make significant achievements in science and the arts.

In the story of France you have already read about the Polish scientist Marie Curie, who with her French husband discovered the element radium and thereby paved the way for later discoveries in the field of nuclear physics. Other Poles have been acclaimed for their achievements in music and literature.

The famous composer Frédéric Chopin (show-*pan*), although he died at thirty-nine, left a large number of works that are often performed today. He is noted for his *mazurkas* and *polonaises*, compositions that reflect his love of Poland in their imaginative use of native melodies. Another musician, Ignace Paderewski (pah-deh-*ref*-skee), was a world-famous pianist and composer who twice served as premier of Poland. A strong patriot, he worked for his country during World War I and represented Poland at Versailles after the war.

One of the world's great authors, Joseph Conrad (whose Polish name was Korzeniowski), became a British citizen and wrote his many novels in English. Conrad went to sea as a youth, and his varied experiences as a seaman are reflected in such widely read novels as *Lord Jim* and *Victory*.

Czechoslovakia has also produced outstanding composers. Anton Dvorak (*dvawr*-zhahk) based much of his work on the folk music of the Czechs, and his famous "Slavonic Dances" are filled with the spirit of his countrymen. From 1892 to 1894 he served as director of the National Conservatory in New York City, and an opera composed at that time, called "From the New World," suggests the melodies and rhythms of Negro folk music in the United States.

Another Czech composer, Bedrich Smetana (*smeh*-tah-nuh), also used his country's folk music as a basis for many of his works. He composed a symphony called "My Fatherland," in which he wove together fragments of Czechoslovakian songs and dances. One part of it presents a vivid tone picture of the Moldau River as it flows through dark forests and past the castles and fortresses of Bohemia.

Chapter Check-up

1. What weakness in her government helped cause Poland's decline?
2. How was Poland wiped off the map by partition?
3. How was the Republic of Poland created?
4. Where was Poland given access to the sea after World War I?
5. How did Poland fare under German occupation during World War II?
6. In what way did Poland obtain freedom from direct Soviet control in 1956?
7. How did John Huss become a martyr to the Bohemians?
8. When did the Czechs finally gain independence from the Austrian Empire?
9. How did Czechoslovakia become a Soviet satellite?
10. What leaders in the arts and sciences have come from Poland and Czechoslovakia?

Eastern Europe: SYNOPSIS

Eastern Europe's story is one of invasion, intense nationalism and age-old rivalry. In early times Hungary and the Balkans were invaded by the Slavs and Mongols. Later they fell to the Turks. In the nineteenth and early twentieth centuries nationalism, complicated by the ambitions of Russia, Austria and Britain, exploded into warfare. The Balkan area became known as the "powder keg of Europe." World War I was touched off by the violence there.

Meanwhile, Poland fought a constant battle against the Germans on the west and the Russians on the east. Both enemies took advantage of Poland's lack of natural boundaries and the absence of a strong central government. She disappeared from the map in 1795 when Prussia, Austria and Russia partitioned her for the third time.

Bohemia, too, struggled against powerful neighbors. Eventually, she became part of the Austro-Hungarian Empire. But at the end of World War I, Poland regained her independence and the new nation of Czechoslovakia was born. In the brief period between the two world wars, Czechoslovakia became a progressive, democratic country.

During World War II Eastern Europe was under Nazi control. Toward the war's end, the region was liberated by the Russians. Tragically, "liberation" meant simply one more change of masters. Backed by the Soviet army, local Communists turned their countries into Soviet satellites.

Under Marshal Tito, Yugoslavia was the first East European Communist state to be freed from Soviet domination. Tito's "national communism" has been less tyrannical than either Russian or Chinese Marxism. Yugoslavia has also carefully adhered to a neutralist role in the "Cold War."

The split which developed between the Soviet Union and Red China since Stalin's death has generally benefitted the East European Communist lands, for they have been able to wrest occasional concessions from Russia. Indeed, Albania has joined the Chinese camp entirely while Rumania has tried to maintain an independent stance between the two Red giants. To that extent, conditions have improved somewhat for the populations of the area. But, as the Hungarians learned in 1956 and the Czechs in 1968, they remain essentially satellites subservient to Russian interests.

Important People

How has each of the following influenced the story of Eastern Europe?

Stephen I	Suleiman	Tito	Wladyslaw Gomulka
Matthias Corvinus	Karageorge	Louis Kossuth	John Huss
Stephen Dushan	John Sobieski	Marshal Pilsudski	Thomas Masaryk

Terms

Be sure that you understand clearly the meaning of each of the following:

Balkans	Dual Monarchy	Polish Corridor
Bohemia	Eastern Orthodox Church	Russian satellite
Byzantine Empire	Hussite Wars	The Eastern Question
Chetniks	Ottoman Empire	Young Turks
Dardanelles	partition	Diet

Questions for Discussion and Review

1. What geographic features have made it easy to invade the Balkans and hard for the Balkan people to unite against invasion?
2. Why did Britain support Turkish control of the Balkans in the nineteenth century?
3. Who were the Young Turks and what did they hope to accomplish? How did they disappoint the Balkan peoples?
4. What were Woodrow Wilson's ideas for properly forming independent states in Eu-

rope following World War I? Were his proposals followed?

5. What lesson can we learn from the troubled story of Eastern Europe?
6. Which of the Eastern European states on the Balkan Peninsula have non-Communist governments?
7. Why are the Balkans known as the "powder keg" of Europe?
8. Do you think that the United States should aid Communist countries such as Yugoslavia and Poland? Why or why not?
9. Would you say that the present political organization of Eastern Europe is likely to be a lasting one? Why?
10. What achievements have the peoples of the Eastern European countries made in the fields of music, literature, and science?

Interesting Things to Do

1. Make a map of Europe showing the states of Eastern Europe and the surrounding lands and seas. Locate and label the important mountain ranges, rivers, and cities. Use colors and illustrations.
2. On an outline map of Europe use colors to show: (a) the Communist countries, (b) the non-Communist countries.
3. Make a chart of the Eastern European states. List all the countries in the first column. In the other columns list the capitals, the areas, the populations, the chief industries, the governments, and the present leaders.
4. Draw a political cartoon showing Tito's opposition to Soviet control of Yugoslavia.
5. Make a poster showing how the many different national backgrounds, languages, customs, and religions of the people of Eastern Europe have kept their countries weak.
6. Prepare a travel talk on the Danube River, describing the things you would see and the places you would visit in a trip along this historic waterway.
7. Arrange an informal debate on this question: *Resolved,* That the United States should not give aid to any Communist country, regardless of its degree of independence from the Soviet Union.
8. Choose one of the Eastern European states for special study. Prepare a booklet or a talk summarizing the information you gather.
9. Choose one or two of the Eastern European states and, for at least a week, cut out from current magazines and newspapers any articles that refer to the countries you have chosen. At the end of the week summarize the information that you have gathered in a written report.
10. Add to or begin your "Who's Who in World History" series by writing brief biographies of one or more of the important leaders of the Eastern European states.

Interesting Reading about Eastern Europe

Adamic, Louis, *Native's Return,* Harper & Row. An immigrant describes his return to his Yugoslavian homeland.

Blunden, Godfrey, and Editors of Life, *Eastern Europe,* Time, Inc. Czechoslovakia, Hungary, and Poland.

Ekrem, Selma, *Turkey, Old and New,* Scribner.

Halecki, Oscar, *History of Poland,* Roy.

*Kish, George, *Yugoslavia,* Holiday.

Stavrianos, Leftun, *Balkans Since 1453,* Holt, Rinehart and Winston.

Stillman, Edmund, and Editors of Life, *The Balkans,* Time, Inc. Yugoslavia, Albania, Roumania, Bulgaria.

Stransky, Jan, *East Wind Over Prague,* Random House.

Tornquist, David, *Look East, Look West,* Macmillan. Yugoslavia Under Tito.

* Indicates easy reading

This "medal lady" hawking her wares for a patriotic holiday in Red Square, is like her counterpart anywhere—proud of her country.

Part 17
RUSSIA
A NATION UNDER COMMUNISM

UNION OF SOVIET SOCIALIST REPUBLICS

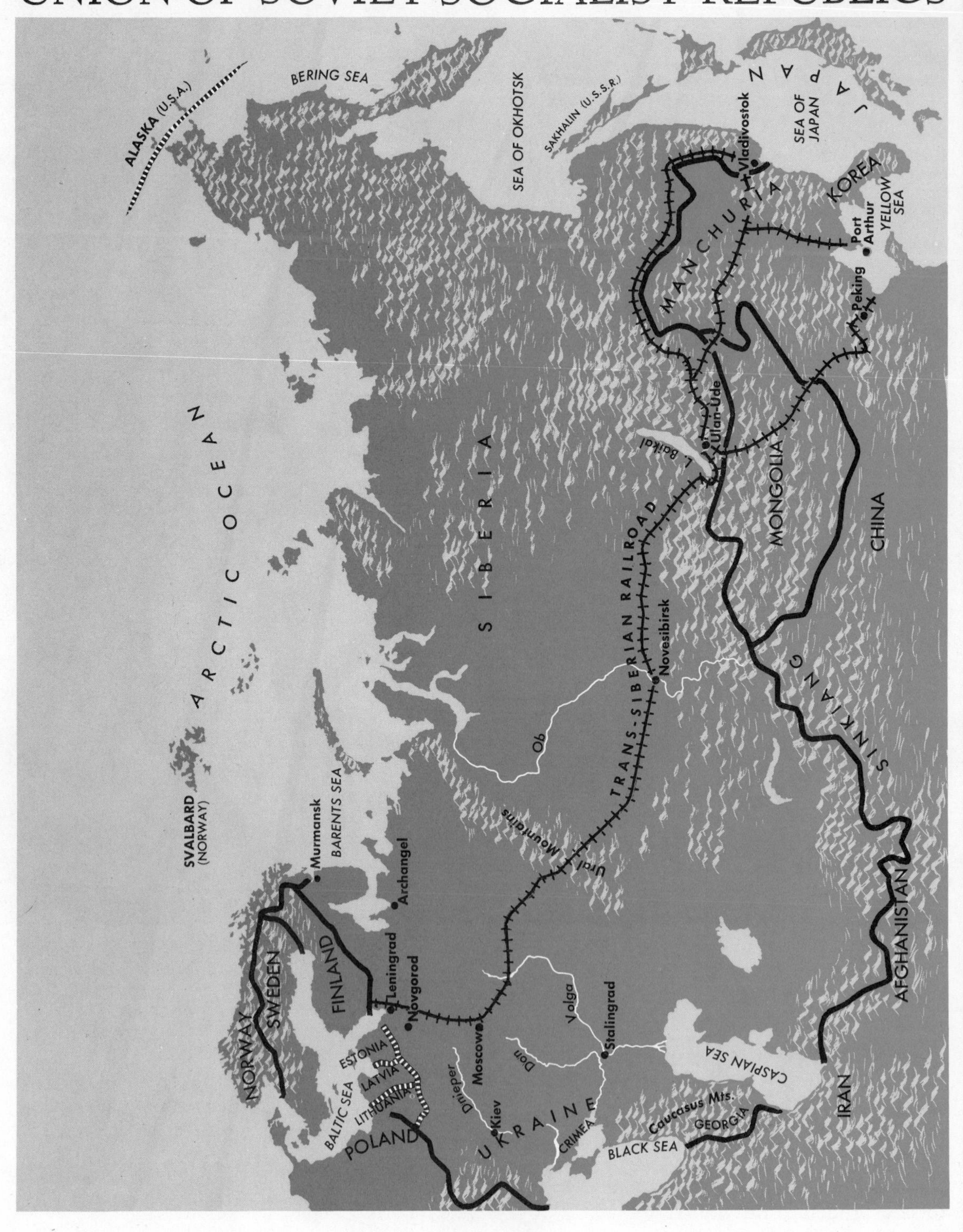

Russia: GEOGRAPHIC SETTING

The Union of Soviet Socialist Republics—Russia, as it is popularly called—is a vast land that covers a sixth of the globe and is nearly twice the size of the United States. Most of Russia is a great plain that consists of frozen marshland in the north and hot desert in the south. In between there are broad belts of dense forests and fertile grasslands. The mineral-rich Ural Mountains divide European Russia and Asian Russia.

Russia is more nearly self-sufficient than any other country in the world. Besides abundant food supplies, she has deposits of almost every known mineral. Her coal deposits are second only to those of the United States, and she has rich veins of iron ore. These two minerals are helping modern Russia to grow into a powerful industrial nation.

Russia's great size has made transportation a problem. From earliest times the country has depended on rivers for transportation. But because her rivers flow north and south, they have not helped much to unify the broad Russian plain. Today airlines and the Trans-Siberian Railway are the main links between European Russia and the eastern frontier at Vladivostok. Because of the great distance from east to west, however, most of Russia's industry and agriculture is still concentrated in the western part of the country.

Internal transportation problems have been matched by Russia's difficulty in exchanging goods with other countries. In her early history Russia was a completely landlocked state, but her rulers have worked unceasingly to extend her boundaries to the sea. Today she has major ports only on the Arctic Ocean and the Baltic, both of which are frozen much of the year, and on the Pacific, which is far from the main manufacturing centers. The lack of good seaports continues to be a problem.

Despite her lack of easy transportation and port facilities, Russia has made rapid strides since the nineteenth century, when she was chiefly an agricultural country. In recent years she has begun to develop her tremendously rich natural resources. Since World War II Russian industry has shown such startling growth that it is now second only to that of the United States.

Russia: PERSPECTIVE

Winston Churchill described Russia as "a riddle wrapped in a mystery inside an enigma." Because so very little is known with certainty about Russia, the rest of the world (even the "experts") have often been surprised by Soviet developments. Stalin's emergence as the most powerful Communist in the late 1920s, the behavior of the defendants in the "purge trials" of the 1930s, the performance of Soviet armies during World War II, the rise of Khrushchev after Stalin's death, Soviet success in space science,—these are just some of the more notable examples of this.

There are several reasons why it is hard to get at the "real truth" about the USSR. Much of it is due to the policy of the Soviet government. Dictatorships always control the news media and the Communist regime is especially skillful at this. Information from Soviet government sources is, therefore, of very limited reliability. Foreigners have generally not been permitted to travel freely through the USSR; they have usually seen just what the rulers have wished them to see. Added to this are the prejudices of observers reporting on the operations of a Marxist state. The Russian language itself has been mastered by relatively

few outsiders; this is another bar to getting at the "inside story" of what is transpiring within the USSR. So, while library shelves may be amply stocked with works on the Soviet Union, contained therein may be as much mis-information as verified fact.

In the history of pro-Communist Russia lie significant keys to understanding of Soviet developments. The gulf between Tsarist and Soviet times is not as wide or deep as Communists would like us to believe. "Police State," and "Iron Curtain,"—terms applied to the USSR, are conditions rooted deeply in the Tsarist past. Much of the thrust of Soviet foreign policy, especially in its aims towards the Middle East, India and China, is reminiscent of the Tsars' goals. "The Child is father of the Man," English poet William Wordsworth said. From the Tsarist "child" has sprung the Soviet "man."

CHAPTER 56

Despotism and the Russian Nation Developed Together

VIKING AND MONGOL INVADERS SHAPED EARLY RUSSIAN HISTORY

The Vikings became merchant-princes of Kiev. The origin of the Slavic peoples is obscure. Historians believe that sometime before the birth of Christ Slavic tribes settled on the great plain between the Vistula River and the Ural Mountains. Between the fifth and eighth centuries, while some of the tribes moved farther south and west (see Chapter 54), others moved eastward. These eastern Slavs became the ancestors of three-fourths of the peoples of modern Russia. The Slavs hunted, fished, farmed, and did a little trading. Unlike the Germanic tribes to the west, however, they were peaceful and poorly organized and were therefore easily conquered by Vikings who came from Sweden in the ninth century. The Finns called the Vikings *Rous,* which means "seafarers." Probably that term was the origin of the name *Russia.*

The Vikings took over the trading towns that the Slavs had established along the chief rivers of Western Russia. Viking merchants carried on a brisk trade with Constantinople. They exchanged furs and slaves (*Slav* originally meant "slave") for silks and other luxuries. These Viking merchants were also able warriors. They led the Slavs against invading Mongol tribes from Asia who were attracted by the rich black soil of the Russian *steppe,* a vast, treeless plain in the south. As their power increased, some of the Vikings became princes of small Slavic states centered around such important river towns as Novgorod (*nahv*-go-rahd) and Kiev (*kee*-yef). The princes of Kiev gradually made their city the commercial and cultural center of medieval Russia.

Vladimir the Saint converted the Russians to the Orthodox Eastern Church. In the late tenth century a ruthless Viking warrior fought his way to the throne of Kiev. Vladimir (*vlad*-ih-mihr) I hardly seems the sort of man who would bring Christianity to Russia, but that is just what he did. According to legend, some of Vladimir's nobles (known in Russia as *boyars*) advised him that Christianity would be a good thing for his realm. Vladimir sent trusted advisers to investi-

RUSSIAN NOBLEMEN. In this old print, sixteenth-century Russian noblemen, or boyars, are shown in battle dress as they prepare to wage war with the Golden Horde.

gate the religions of the peoples who were neighbors of the Russians. The adviser who visited the Moslems in the Middle East reported that none of the people ever seemed to smile. The one who went to Germany said that German churches lacked beauty. But the adviser who went to the Byzantine Empire said that the service of that church was filled with such beauty and grandeur that he could hardly describe it.

Whether or not the story is true, Vladimir accepted the Orthodox Eastern faith, and it became the official religion of Russia. Ever since then he has been known as Vladimir the Saint.

Vladimir's decision helped keep Western European ideas out of Russia for hundreds of years. Eastern Christianity established different traditions among the Russian people than the Roman faith established among the peoples of the West. The religious difference thus made it more difficult for the nations of Western Europe to understand Russia and to communicate effectively with her.

The Golden Horde conquered Russia. The Kingdom of Kiev reached great heights under Vladimir's son, Yaroslav the Wise (1019–54). He used the riches from trade to build fine churches, and he became known for his excellent collection of books. His children married into the great royal families of Europe. But succeeding princes of Kiev were not able to stem the invasion of the Mongols. In the twelfth century these fierce warriors pressed into Russia from the deserts of central Asia along Russia's great steppe. When they blocked the vital trade route to Constantinople, the Kingdom of Kiev declined.

By the early thirteenth century Kiev had collapsed, mainly from loss of population. At that time a group of Mongols called *Tartars* was united under the famous conqueror Genghiz Khan (*jeng-gis kahn*). His father, a chieftain, died when Genghiz was only thirteen, and the Tartars deserted the boy. But he soon fought his way to power and became the recognized leader, or *khan*. Under Genghiz Khan the Tartars conquered a huge area, including China and parts of India, Iran, and Russia. A Chinese author describes the Tartars as follows:

> "They are ignorant of writing and books . . . They respect nothing but strength and courage: . . . They move on horseback; . . . No place [can] resist them. After a siege the entire population is massacred without distinction of old or young, rich or poor, beautiful or ugly."

CHURCH OFFICIALS. Although Communist leaders have tried to suppress religious activity in Russia, they have not been entirely successful. Here, priests of the Orthodox Eastern Church are shown in the rich vestments in which they officiate. It was the beauty of this church's ritual that prompted Vladimir to adopt its faith for his country.

When Genghiz Khan died, his sons divided his vast lands. Batu, one of his grandsons, continued the conquest of Russia. Between 1237 and 1241 a huge band of Tartars, called the *Golden Horde* because of their richly decorated tents, laid waste Russia. They burned towns and massacred the inhabitants. According to one account, "Russian heads fell beneath the sword of the Tartars as grass beneath the scythes." Under Batu the Tartars penetrated as far west as the Danube River. Then in 1241 they withdrew to the region of Crimea, where they established a Tartar state known as the Khanate of the Golden Horde.

Although Europe was saved from the Tartars, the Russian people had to pay them heavy tribute for the next two and a half centuries. This period of Tartar domination made a lasting impression on Russia. She was completely cut off from contact with developments in Western Europe While English kings were learning the principles of representative government under pressure from the middle class, Russian princes were learning the principles of cruelty and despotism from their Tartar masters. After the Tartars were driven out the princes became all-powerful; crushing the boyars who dared to oppose them.

As we saw in the stories of England and France, it was the middle class which was instrumental in checking the power of autocratic rulers. In Russia no middle class developed. The peasants who toiled on the great estates had learned the meaning of fear at the hands of the Tartars, so it is not surprising that they obeyed the Russian princes without question. Ever since the Tartar conquest, Russian government has been characterized by despotic rulers and submissive citizens.

THE PRINCES OF MOSCOW BECAME CZARS OF RUSSIA

Ivan I made Moscow the chief state in Russia. During the early years of Russia's history most of the population centered along the Dnieper River in the state of Kiev. When Kiev fell in the thirteenth century, many people moved east in search of unoccupied land for farming. This shift of population made the town of Moscow not only the geographic center of Russia but also the center of its population.

Ivan I (1325–41), one of the early Grand Princes of Moscow, sought to extend Moscow's control over all the other states of Russia. Although he and the other Russian princes had to pay tribute to the Golden Horde, the Tartars let them rule their own states. Thus Ivan was free to carry out his ambitions. First, he persuaded the *metropolitan*, the highest church official in Russia, to move from Kiev to Moscow. This move made Moscow the spiritual center of Russia. Then Ivan began to hoard gold. He became known as Ivan "moneybags" because of his preoccupation with saving money. He used his wealth to gain favor with the Tartar khan. Impressed with Ivan's efficiency as a tax collector, the khan authorized him to collect the tribute from all of the other Russian princes. Thus Ivan served as an "overlord," and helped establish the supremacy of Moscow.

Ivan III made Moscow the third Rome. At the end of the fifteenth century, Ivan III, one of the ablest of the Grand Dukes, came to power. In time, he gained control over a vast area in Russia. Ivan strengthened his position by marrying the niece of the last Byzantine emperor. When the Turks conquered Constantinople Ivan's mar-

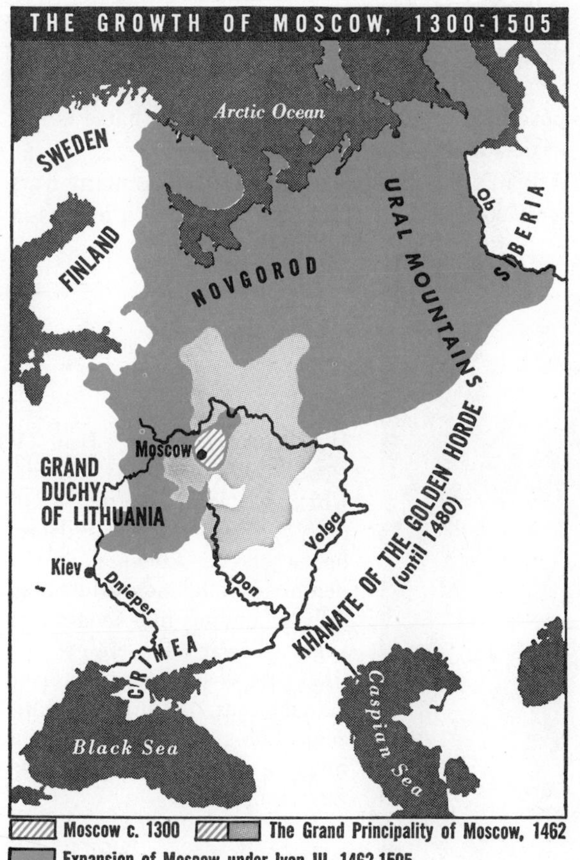

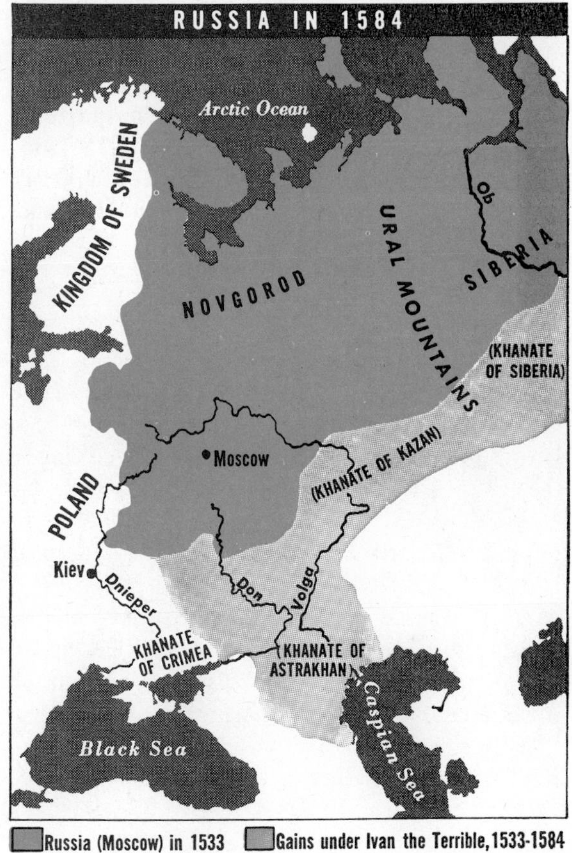

riage gave him an opportunity to claim heritage of the Byzantine Empire. The two-headed eagle used on the seal of Byzantium became the imperial symbol of Russia. The elaborate ceremonies of the Byzantine court added glory and prestige to the Russian ruler.

The Russian Orthodox Church considered Ivan to have inherited the Byzantine emperors' traditional duty of defending the "true faith." Ivan and the church looked upon Moscow as the third Rome. As a Russian expressed it in the early sixteenth century, "Moscow is the successor of the great world capitals: ancient Rome, and the second Rome—Constantinople: Moscow is the third Rome, and there will be no fourth." The belief that it was Russia's destiny to lead the world has influenced Russian rulers throughout her history.

During Ivan's reign the last of the Tartars was driven from Russia, and the country was free of Oriental domination at last. But the Orient left many influences. Indeed, the Russian court showed Oriental traces in dress and manners right up to its fall in 1917.

Ivan the Terrible strengthened the pattern of Russian despotism. When Ivan IV succeeded to the throne in 1533, he was crowned czar (zahr), or emperor, of Russia. Ivan III had called himself "czar," too, but his title was an unofficial one. (The word *czar* is the Slavic form of the name *Caesar.*) After Ivan IV, all Russian monarchs were known by this title.

Ivan IV, who was to go down in history as Ivan the Terrible, reformed and strengthened the army to keep out Tartar invasions. He waged a long war against Poland, Lithuania, and Sweden to break through to the Baltic Sea and was finally successful, although he could not hold his gains.

During Ivan's reign Russia began to expand into Asia. The vast northern part of Asia that we call Siberia was a thinly populated, unknown land in the sixteenth century. A Cossack adventurer led an expedition over the Ural Mountains and into western Siberia in 1581. That was the beginning of an eastward expansion that by 1637 extended Russian borders to the Pacific.

Ivan the Terrible not only enlarged Russia but also vigorously organized it. He broke the power of the lesser dukes and made them entirely subordinate to himself. He organized a powerful secret police force and executed anyone who opposed his orders. Ivan destroyed all that was left of personal liberty in Russia.

Ivan's elaborate government and his many wars were costly. The chief source of wealth in Russia

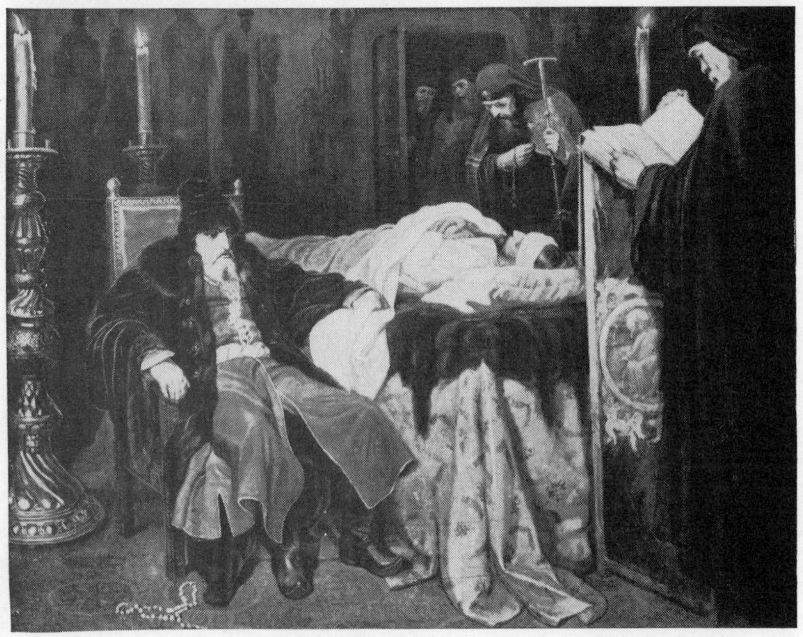

Ivan the Terrible. Ivan IV was a man of many moods, which varied from great kindness to terrible cruelty. Here, he is shown grieving at the deathbed of his son after mortally wounding him in a fit of rage. Toward the end of his life, Ivan lost all control over his emotions. At night the citizens of Moscow often heard him howling within the walls of the Kremlin.

St. Basil's. The great cathedral was built by order of Ivan the Terrible to commemorate Russia's victory over the Tartars. Typical of Russian architecture, it is a famous landmark in Moscow.

was land, most of which had been granted to nobles as fiefs in exchange for military service in the wars against the Tartars. The land was worked by peasants who lived in small villages and paid rent to the local landowner. When Ivan increased land taxes, the landlords raised the peasants' rent. Many peasants fled from the estates of central Russia and settled in unoccupied territory that had been taken from the Tartars. In time a shortage of labor developed on the estates, and the landlords could not pay their taxes. To solve this problem, many of the landlords tried to confine the peasants to the land. Finally, in 1649 serfdom was made legal in Russia. The peasants became property that could be bought and sold by their owners and absolute masters. Thus, just at the time when serfdom was dying out in Western Europe, it was becoming firmly established in Russia. Serfdom continued until the middle of the nineteenth century.

WESTERN INFLUENCE DID NOT WEAKEN THE CZAR'S DESPOTIC POWER

Peter the Great gave Russia a window on the west. In the early seventeenth century the line of czars that was descended from Ivan IV died out. Russia was torn by struggles for the throne and by wars with Sweden and Poland. Finally a national assembly elected a grandnephew of Ivan IV's wife as the new czar. The new czar, Michael Romanov (*ro*-muh-noff), was the first member of the family that ruled Russia until 1917.

The most famous of the Romanovs was Peter the Great (1689–1725). At the age of seventeen he gathered a group of soldiers and seized the throne from the regent. Peter possessed driving energy and the ambition to be absolute master of his realm. These qualities were just what he needed to awaken Russia, which had been a sluggish, backward state ever since the Tartar invasions four hundred years earlier. Peter was determined to make Russia a truly European country.

As a child Peter had studied all the books about shipbuilding that he could find. When he became czar he directed the building of a Russian navy. He fought a war with the Turks so he could get his fleet into the open waters of the Black Sea. Peter made a journey through Western Europe disguised as an unimportant member of a Russian embassy in order to work in Dutch and English shipyards. He was shocked to see how backward his country was, compared with the countries of Western Europe. He vowed to make Russia a modern nation.

Peter realized that in order to bring Russia into contact with the West he needed a seaport on the Baltic. To obtain one, he fought a long war with Sweden. Finally he gained a strip of land on the Baltic Coast which became Russia's "window on the west." At the mouth of the Neva (*nee*-vuh) River he began to build the city of St. Petersburg.

The location of St. Petersburg gave Russia greater contact with Western European civilization. However, Peter had chosen a very poor site for his city. The land was low, swampy, and easily flooded by the sea. Ruthlessly, Peter overcame these obstacles. He forced thousands of serfs to cut down trees and quarry stones to fill in the swamps. All the large buildings were supported on piles driven deep into the ground, and five hundred bridges were built over the canals and branches of the Neva. One historian described the scene as follows:

> "Like cattle the workmen were herded in these swamps to perish of cold, hunger, and scurvy. As fast as they were swallowed up, more serfs were driven in. They dug the soil with hands and sticks, carrying it off in caps and aprons. With thudding hammers, cracking whips, and groans of the dying, St. Petersburg rose . . . in the tears and anguish of the slaves."

The completed capital had broad avenues and splendid buildings. The architecture of the churches and palaces followed the classical style

PETER THE GREAT. A man of enormous strength, Peter stood nearly seven feet tall. He founded the city of St. Petersburg as a "window looking on Europe" and moved his capital there from Moscow in 1713.

of Western Europe, and contrasted sharply with the oriental "onion-dome" architecture of Moscow. To the west of the city Peter built a beautiful summer palace called the *Peterhof* that was modeled after the palace of the French kings at Versailles (see Chapter 36). Peter's new capital became a great center of Russian culture.

Peter forced Russia to adopt Western ideas. The construction of St. Petersburg was only one way in which Peter determined to westernize Russia. He built highways, introduced the study of science, and founded academies in which he invited European scholars to teach. Technicians from abroad were invited to Russia, and machinery was imported. As factories grew up around St. Petersburg, a class of highly specialized workers developed. Peter reformed the army according to Western standards and took great pains with the details of recruiting and supplying it. He reorganized the government and appointed a senate of ten men to carry out his orders. Peter insisted that every aristocrat serve the state either in the army or in the government.

His reforms extended also to dress and personal appearance. He ordered all men to stop wearing their long-skirted robes and to shave their beards as Europeans did. Peter even published a book of etiquette in an effort to improve the manners of his people. Although he did much to westernize Russia, Peter was not altogether successful. One writer of the period noted that:

> "Forty years have passed, yet only the summits have caught the Western light; the vast valleys still lie plunged in the shadow of the past."

Catherine the Great expanded Russian boundaries south and west. One of Peter's most outstanding successors was Catherine the Great (1762–96). This brilliant, energetic woman had been born an unimportant German princess and had married the heir to the Russian throne. Her incompetent (and probably insane) young husband still played with toy soldiers when he was in his twenties. A few months after he became czar, some soldiers who were loyal to Catherine imprisoned him and made Catherine empress of Russia. She set out, in the tradition of Peter the Great, to bring Russia into closer contact with the West. She fought two wars against the Ottoman Empire and annexed much territory in an attempt to gain control of the Black Sea and the straits leading to the Mediterranean. She took advantage of the weakness of Poland to ex-

WESTERNIZING RUSSIA. Following the orders of Peter the Great, officials cut the beards and shortened the coats of the Russian men. Although Peter tried earnestly to bring Western customs to his people, many of his reforms were of a superficial type.

tend Russia's boundaries westward. Catherine took part in each of the three partitions of Poland.

The gulf between the serfs and the aristocracy widened. Catherine greatly admired Western culture and was influenced by the writings of Voltaire. She tried to be an enlightened despot. She founded schools, hospitals, and libraries, and she drew up a code of laws to provide justice for the serfs.

Unfortunately, Catherine's position depended on the support of the aristocracy, which, after Peter's death, had cast off many of its obligations to the state. The aristocrats did not want any improvement in the lot of the serfs because they feared the loss of their own power. Catherine's law code therefore came to nothing. An angry Cossack soldier led millions of serfs in rebellion

CATHERINE THE GREAT. Although Catherine began her reign in a spirit of reform, she became more severe after the serfs rebelled against her policies. A ruler of great ability, she excelled in the handling of foreign affairs.

against heavy taxes and the injustice of their masters. Catherine became so frightened that she made the laws against the serfs more severe. She gave the landowners complete control over their serfs. An imperial decree provided that: "If any serf shall dare to petition against his master, he shall be punished with the knout [a kind of whip] and transported for life to the mines."

A serf was regarded as his owner's personal property. Russian landowners counted the "souls" on their estates as an important source of their wealth. This advertisement appeared in the Moscow Gazette in 1810:

> TO BE SOLD: two coachmen, well trained, and handsome, the one eighteen, and the other fifteen years of age, both of them good-looking and well acquainted with various kinds of handwork . . . In the same house are sold pianos and organs.

At a Glance

Important Rulers in Russian History

Early Rulers (980–1341)
- Vladimir the Saint
- Yaroslav the Wise
- Ivan I

Russia Under the Czars (1462–1917)
- Ivan III
- Ivan the Terrible

The Romanov Line (1613–1917)
- Michael
- Peter the Great
- Catherine the Great
- Alexander I
- Nicholas I
- Alexander II
- Alexander III
- Nicholas II

Provisional Government (March–November, 1917)

Russia Under the Communists (November, 1917-Present)
- Vladimir Lenin
- Joseph Stalin
- Georgi Malenkov
- Nikolai Bulganin
- Nikita Khrushchev

During Catherine's reign the gulf between the serfs, who made up 95 per cent of the population, and the landowning aristocracy became deeper than it was anywhere else in Europe. The two classes had nothing in common. Under the influence of Peter and Catherine, the nobles were encouraged to travel widely and to adopt the customs and manners of Western Europe. The serfs knew nothing of these Western influences. They were required by law to remain on the estate where they were born. No provision was made for their education and, as a group, they were almost totally illiterate. The nobles made no secret of their contempt for the ignorant serfs. In turn, the serfs hated the nobles for the cruelties and injustices they inflicted. Thus Russia became a land of master and slave, neither of whom understood the other.

Chapter Check-up

1. What ancient tribes are the ancestors of three-fourths of the people of modern Russia?
2. How did the Vikings affect Russia's history?
3. How did the Orthodox Eastern Church become the official church of Russia?
4. What was the Golden Horde? How did it influence the future of Russia?
5. What advantage was there for Ivan III in making Moscow "the Third Rome"?
6. Why is Ivan IV known as "the Terrible"?
7. How were Russia's borders extended by Ivan the Terrible?
8. Why was serfdom established in Russia just as it was dying out in Western Europe?
9. What steps were taken by Peter the Great to Westernize Russia?
10. Why did the gulf between the serfs and the aristocracy widen during Catherine's reign?

CHAPTER 57

Czarist Reforms Could Not Prevent the Russian Revolution

NINETEENTH-CENTURY CZARS BROUGHT WESTERN POLITICAL IDEAS TO RUSSIA

The liberalism of Alexander I did not last long. Czar Alexander I (1801–25) had been trained by his grandmother, Catherine the Great, to be an enlightened despot. He dreamed of creating a liberal Russia in which justice and freedom would prevail. Alexander encouraged the founding of universities and issued a decree that made it possible for landlords to free their serfs. He even discussed with his friends the possibility of giving Russia a constitution. Unfortunately, war with France interfered with Alexander's plans to make Russia a liberal nation.

You will remember reading in the story of France that Russia joined the other nations of Europe in the wars to defeat Napoleon Bonaparte. Napoleon and his Grand Army invaded Russia in the winter of 1812–13. He captured and burned the city of Moscow. But Napoleon learned the same lesson that Hitler learned later. It is difficult to conquer the distances and the climate of Russia. Napoleon's men were not prepared for the Russian winter. They ran out of food and supplies and were forced to retreat. Although a half-million men marched into Russia, only a handful returned to France. Napoleon's invasion and the burning of Moscow had important effects on the life of Alexander I and on the future of Russia.

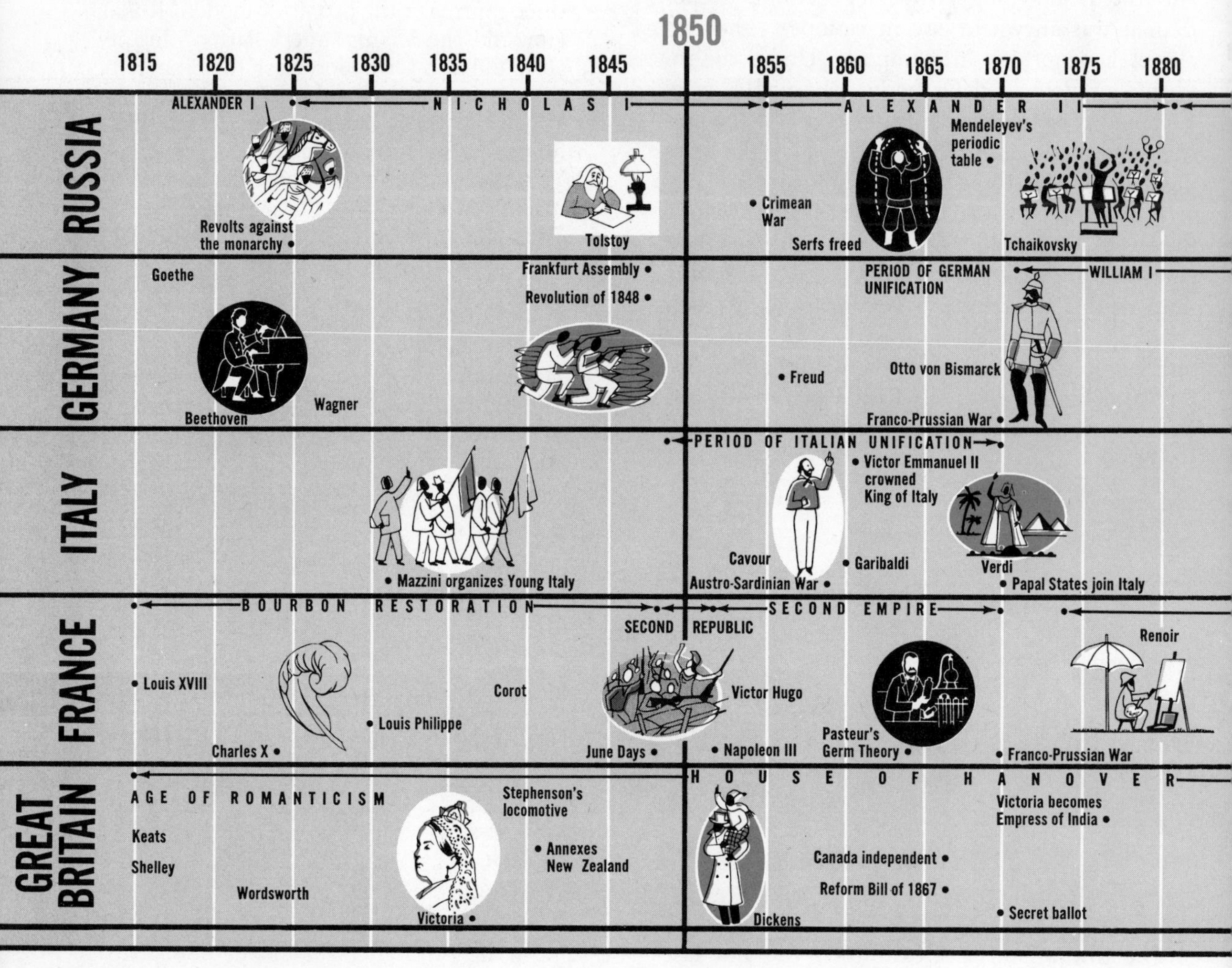

After defeating the French in Russia, Alexander I helped other European nations continue the war against Napoleon until he was finally defeated at Waterloo in 1815. Then the czar played an important part in the peace conference at Vienna. Alexander I had not altogether given up liberal ideas, but as a result of the French invasion he felt he had a divine mission to help keep order in Europe. He proposed the formation of a "Holy Alliance" of the allies who had defeated Napoleon, to help keep peace in Europe. The Austrian diplomat, Metternich, who controlled the Congress of Vienna, pretended to agree with Alexander. Actually, Metternich used Alexander's idea of the Holy Alliance to crush all attempts at liberal reforms in Europe.

But many young Russian noblemen who had served as officers in the czar's armies had been favorably impressed by the ideals expressed by the French revolutionists. They had seen Western representative assemblies in action and had read French writings about philosophy and politics. It may seem strange to us that the Russian officers should adopt the ideas of the people against

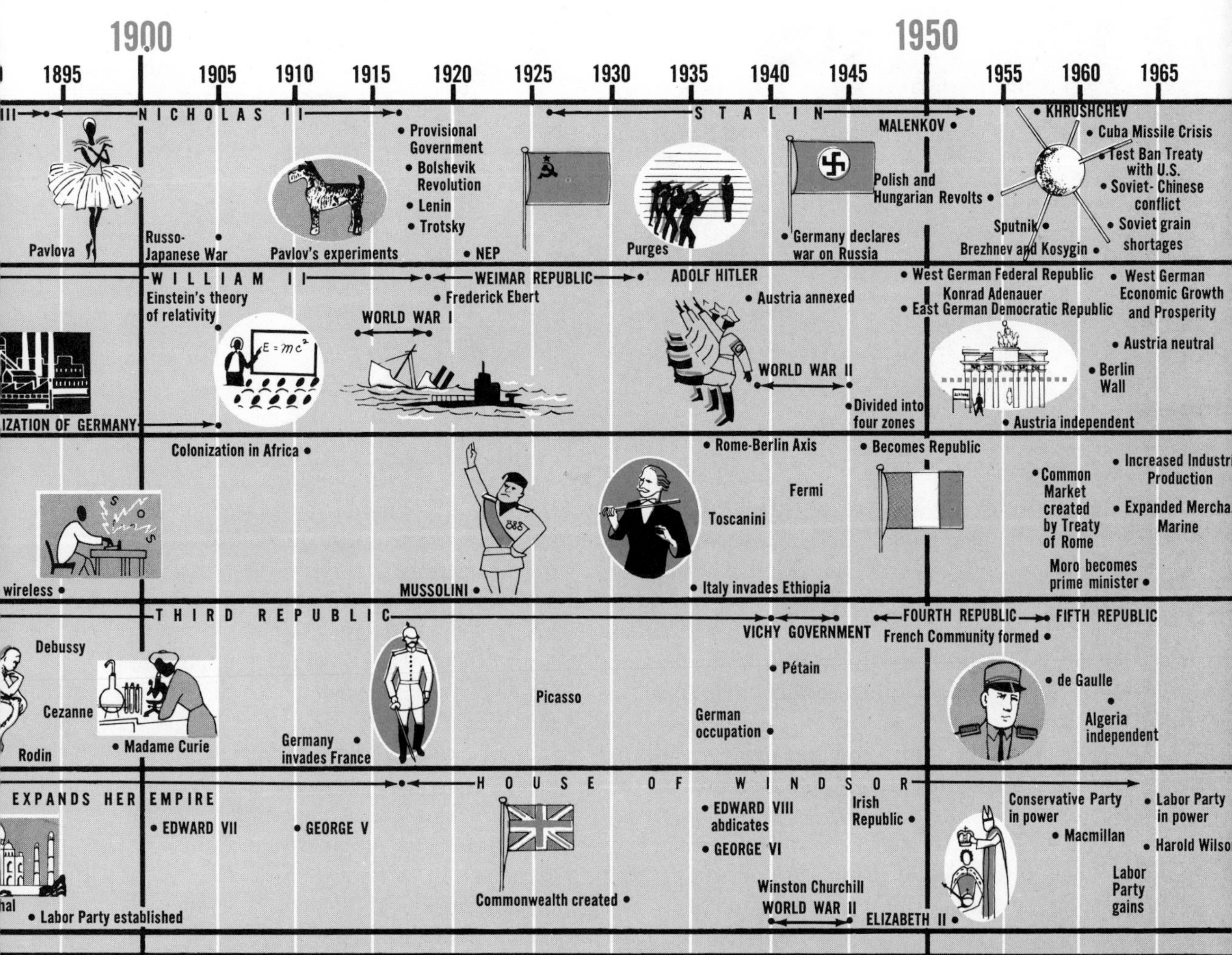

whom they had been fighting. Under absolute monarchs, however, the soldiers and even the officers often felt that wars were fought largely to satisfy the ambitions of their rulers. They themselves sometimes felt little interest in the quarrel beyond doing their professional duty.

The ideas of the French revolutionists lived on, even under Napoleon. The French people believed in liberty, equality, and fraternity; they were eager to pass their beliefs on to others. Thus the revolutionary ideas influenced many nations outside of France.

When the Russian soldiers and officers who had been affected by French ideas returned to Russia, they found fault with their own country. They did not like its autocratic and inefficient government, the conditions of the serfs, and the lack of public education. Many of them formed secret societies to work for reforms.

When Alexander died, these nobles led a revolt in the hope of establishing a constitutional monarchy. The new czar, Nicholas I (1825–55), put down the uprising and exiled the leaders to Siberia. Nicholas then ruled with the power of a

THE RETREAT FROM MOSCOW. Defeated by the Russian climate and the wily tactics of their opponent, the remnants of Napoleon's army straggled westward across Europe, suffering bitterly from cold and hunger.

traditional Russian despot. In spite of the strict censorship that he maintained, liberal ideas continued to bubble under the surface among the aristocracy. The serfs, of course, knew nothing of the French ideas, but their wretched condition drove them to make over five hundred serious outbreaks in the next thirty years. It became quite clear that something had to be done to reform Russia.

Alexander II freed the serfs and modernized the government. Nicholas I started the Crimean War (see page 506) as another step in Russia's effort to seize control of the Dardanelles. He died in the middle of the war and left his successor, Alexander II (1855–81), to carry on. Russia's defeat in the war made the new czar realize how inefficient his army had become. It seemed to prove that an army of serfs was no match for the free citizens who fought in the armies of the Western democracies. Obviously Russia would remain weak as long as her people remained serfs. Alexander remembered the constant uprisings of the serfs during Nicholas's reign. "Better to abolish serfdom from above," said Alexander, "than to wait till it begins to abolish itself from below." Alexander had no love for liberalism, but he was a practical man who was able to learn from history and his own experience. In 1861 he therefore issued his famous Emancipation Act. This one decree freed forty million serfs.

The life of a free peasant, however, proved not to be much different from that of a serf. The land that the peasant had worked did not become his own private property as the peasants' land had in France. It became the collective property of his village. The village then allotted land to the head of each family and was responsible for seeing that he paid the state for the land by installments over a period of forty-nine years. The state preferred to make these arrangements through the village because it was easier to collect money from a few villages than from a multitude of individual peasants. The peasants were not allowed to sell their land or move away from the village without the permission of the village council. Actually, the Emancipation Act bound them to the villages as firmly as they had been bound to the estates of their masters.

After freeing the peasants, Alexander set out to reform the Russian law courts. Under the old system, punishments imposed by the courts depended on whether the criminal were a serf or a nobleman. Trials were secret, and the accused had no lawyer. Alexander introduced a new system based on the English courts. All men became equal in the eyes of the law. Trials were made public, and the accused was permitted a jury trial and legal counsel.

Alexander also gave the people a degree of local self-government. The nobles had had complete control over their serfs. When the serfs were freed, local governments had to be reorganized. Alexander established town councils called *zemstvos* (*zemst*-voze) to which the people elected representatives. The zemstvos collected taxes to build schools, hospitals, and roads, and to make agricultural improvements. The zemstvos were important because they marked the first time that the Russian people had had any effective kind of local self-government.

Alexander encouraged industry. The government provided the capital to start new industries, build railroads, and establish a banking system. Gradually a middle class began to develop. Alexander was also interested in improving education. Before his reign, the only educated class was the nobility. Alexander established primary schools for peasants. Middle-class families sent their sons to secondary schools and universities to become doctors, lawyers, engineers, and writers. This growing class of professional people favored a more liberal government.

Dissatisfaction paved the way for Marxian socialism. Ironically, Alexander's efforts to modernize Russia only aroused more discontent. The nobles were angry about the loss of their serfs and the weakening of their power in local government. The peasants were unhappy with the terms under which they had to pay for the land they were given. The liberal intellectuals, who were mainly educated members of the middle class, felt that the reforms did not go nearly far enough. They

Return of an Exile. Justice under the czars was often harsh, especially for political opponents. Here, an exile returns to his village after many years of imprisonment. News of the French ideas of liberty, equality, and fraternity made many Russians intensely dissatisfied with their oppressive rulers.

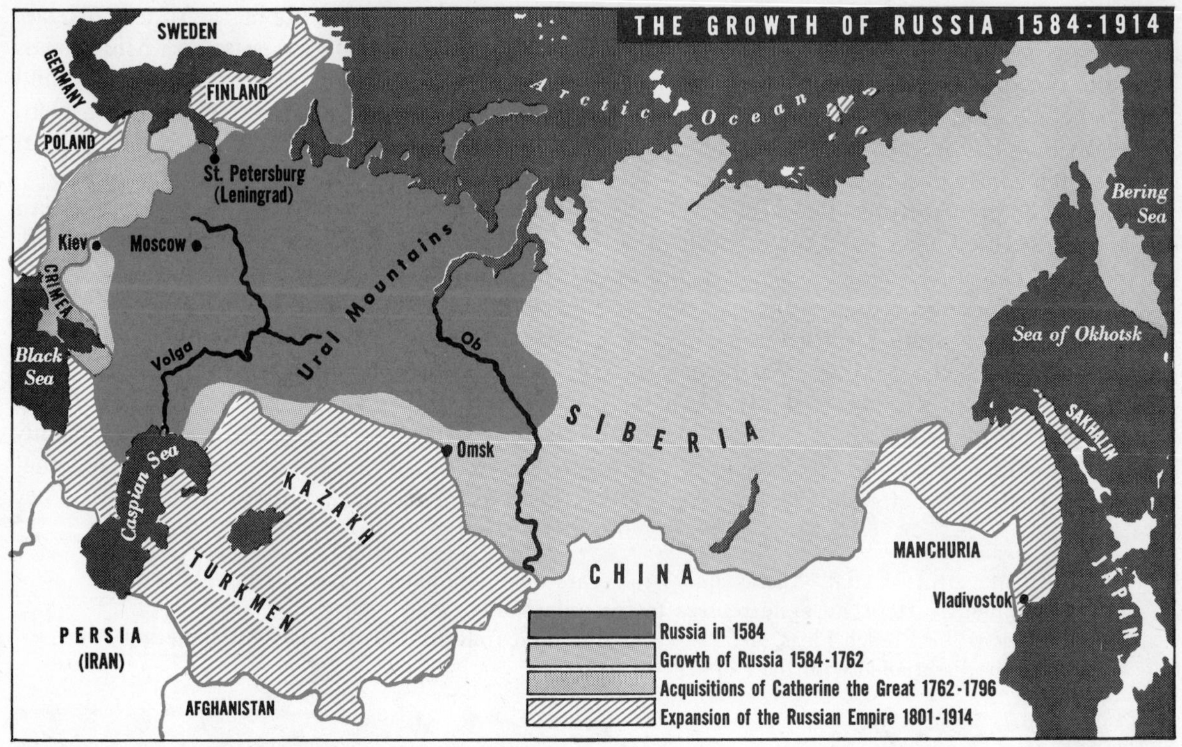

wanted to end the despotism of the czar and give the people a real voice in the government.

Because there was no parliament or national assembly through which reformers could work, many of them formed secret societies and plotted revolt or campaigns of terror against government officials. On the very day that Alexander had approved a plan for a more liberal government, members of one of these societies threw a bomb at his carriage and assassinated him.

Thoroughly frightened, the new czar, Alexander III (1881–94), was determined to suppress all liberal ideas. He rigidly controlled the universities and sharply restricted the power of the zemstvos. His secret police hunted men who were suspected of dangerous, revolutionary ideas and executed them or sent them to Siberia. Reformers dared not speak in public; they had to go "underground." Their experiences convinced them that the czar would never give up his power voluntarily. Many of them began to accept the ideas of the German political philosopher Karl Marx (see Chapter 50), who taught that violent overthrow of the government was the only way to gain reforms. This group, known as the Marxian Socialists, later provided the foundation for the Communist party.

The Russo-Japanese War forced the czar to give Russia a representative assembly. Nicholas II (1894–1917) shared the ideas of his father, Alexander III, that only the czar had the right to rule and that the duty of the people was to obey. Nicholas was a weak man who came under the influence of corrupt and misguided advisers. Discontent among the Russian people grew when the inefficiency and corruption of Nicholas' government came to light in the war with Japan.

During the sixteenth century Russia had annexed Siberia. Because the land was so far north, the Russian government now wanted to obtain for this area warm-water ports farther south in Chinese territory. The weak Chinese government allowed the Russians to extend the Trans-Siberian Railway through Manchuria and to build a branch to Port Arthur on the Yellow Sea (see map on page 523). Here the Russians came into conflict with the Japanese, who controlled Korea and also had designs on Port Arthur. In 1904 the Japanese launched a surprise attack against the Russians and won a series of victories.

Russia's humiliation at being defeated by a supposedly weak and backward nation stirred up the already smoldering political discontent. A band of workers in St. Petersburg joined in a march on the czar's palace to protest against conditions in Russia. They were fired on by the czar's soldiers. A few months later a general strike was conducted by Russian workingmen. The uprising received wide support among people of all classes in Russia. But the fighting accomplished little. The czar promised the people more power in the government. He permitted the formation of an elected assembly, the Duma (*doo*-mah), which he allowed very little actual power.

With the establishment of the Duma, Russia seemed to be making progress toward becoming a modern nation. The peasants were at last allowed to withdraw their land from village control. Government agricultural experts were sent to the villages to help improve farming methods. The government also encouraged industry. Mines and factories were opened and more railroads were built. Workers' wages rose, and health and accident insurance were established. Workers were allowed to form labor unions. Political parties, representing various interests, developed.

Given enough time, the Duma might have gained power in Russia, as Parliament had done in England. Unfortunately, before Russia could progress very far in this direction, the nation, although totally unprepared, was plunged into World War I.

THE RUSSIAN REVOLUTION CREATED A COMMUNIST DICTATORSHIP

Food riots flamed into revolution. The Russian people supported the war effort during the early part of World War I. But a series of crushing defeats at the hands of the Germans destroyed their morale. The Duma requested more power to direct the war. Nicholas refused and went off to lead the army himself. The army fared worse than ever. Labor shortages on the farms held back the production of food. The country's antiquated railroad system broke down. Soon famine swept through Russia.

At the outbreak of World War I, the city of St. Petersburg had been renamed Petrograd, which was considered a less "German sounding" name. (Ten years later it became Leningrad.) In March of 1917, crowds of starving, freezing workers rioted in Petrograd. The soldiers in Petrogad refused to fire on the hungry people. Instead, they joined them. The workers formed a council called a *soviet* to direct the rioting. Soon other soviets composed of workers, peasants, and soldiers sprang up all over Russia. This uprising was called the *March Revolution.*

When Nicholas II saw that he could not rely on the army to maintain his authority, he abdicated. The Duma declared Russia to be a republic and set up a provisional government to rule until an elected assembly could draw up a constitution. The provisional government proclaimed civil liberties and the equality of all Russians. It abolished the death penalty, released all political prisoners, and promised land to the peasants. But its decision to continue the war brought its downfall, for by this time the Russian people were thoroughly disillusioned with the conduct of the war. Many of the soldiers deserted and joined the soviets. When peasants did not receive the land they had expected, many of them seized it by force.

Lenin and Trotsky led the Bolshevik party. While the provisional government was struggling to keep order, a number of revolutionists who had been exiled from Russia hurried home. One of the most important of them was a brilliant but radical middle-class intellectual, Vladimir Lenin (*len*-in).

Nicholas II With His Family. The last czar of all the Russias was a weak man who was too easily influenced by those around him. Here he is shown with his family shortly before they were murdered in 1918. At the far right is the Grand Duchess Anastasia, whose death is disputed. In Germany there is a "Mrs. Anderson" who claims to be Anastasia.

Lenin's elder brother had been hanged for belonging to a secret revolutionary society that had tried to assassinate Alexander III. His brother's execution affected Lenin deeply. He became the leader of a radical group of Marxian socialists called *Bolsheviks* (*bole*-sheh-vix). He was arrested and exiled to Siberia. There he met other political prisoners and read and wrote about Marxian socialism. From 1900 to 1917 he lived in Western Europe, where he spent all his time plotting a Marxist revolution that would engulf not only Russia but also the rest of the world. When news of the czar's abdication reached Lenin in Switzerland, he persuaded the Germans to send him through their territory to Russia. The Germans agreed because they hoped he would stir up trouble in Russia and force her to withdraw from the war. Lenin arrived in Petrograd in April to find the revolution already in full swing.

Shortly after Lenin's arrival, another important Bolshevik leader, Leon Trotsky, appeared on the scene. Trotsky proved to be a fiery orator and a natural leader. He returned to Petrograd from exile in the United States and soon became second only to Lenin among the Bolsheviks. Trotsky was responsible for organizing the Red Army, so called because of the color of the Bolshevik flag.

The Bolsheviks led the November Revolution. Lenin was not content with the March Revolution because it had not gone far enough. He disliked the provisional government because it was dominated by middle-class liberals who wanted to carry out reforms in Russia by parliamentary methods. Lenin wanted a complete revolution in Russia that would inspire workers all over the world to revolt. He was determined to cause such a revolution.

Lenin laid careful plans. To win the support of the people, he preached a program that he knew would appeal to them—"Peace, Land, and Bread." He promised that he would stop the war, give all the land to the peasants (they already had three-fourths of it), and turn ownership of the factories and railroads over to the workers. He also promised that the new government would be under the complete control of the various soviets, or peoples' councils. This promise gained the support of many of the important soviets.

On the night of November 6, 1917, according to plan, soldiers and sailors attacked the Winter Palace at Petrograd, which housed the officials of the provisional government. At the same time workmen took over the railroad stations, telephone exchanges, and electric plants in the city.

STREET FIGHTING IN PETROGRAD. This picture was taken during a violent demonstration against the provisional government in July of 1917. A detachment of pro-Bolshevik sailors touched off the violence by firing on groups of well-dressed civilians, who they felt symbolized the provisional government.

By the afternoon of the next day the Bolsheviks held Petrograd and had driven out the provisional government. The second revolution had been accomplished with almost no bloodshed. It is important to note, however, that the Bolshevik leaders destroyed a government that was trying to reform Russia into a democracy. It is a mistake to think they rescued Russia from the czars.

The Communists fought hard to control the rest of Russia. A short time after the November Revolution, the Bolsheviks took the name *Communists,* and they later became known officially as the Communist party. Lenin immediately fulfilled his promise to withdraw Russia from the war, although the price was the loss of Poland (which Russia had captured), Finland, and other territory. Lenin accepted these unfavorable terms because he had to have peace at any cost if the Communists were to stay in power. Then too, if world revolution quickly followed, as he hoped, Russia's territorial losses to Germany would be immaterial.

Lenin then turned to face troubles at home. He found that the rest of Russia could not be as easily subdued as Petrograd had been. For over two years the Communists fought opponents of every kind. Czarist generals led uprisings in the Don Valley and Siberia. The Ukraine and various provinces near the Baltic tried to break away. The British and French landed troops in Archangel and Murmansk in hope of restoring the provisional government to power. Trotsky's Red Army fought fiercely to combat the many counter-revolutions and civil wars. Only the Baltic countries of Estonia, Latvia, and Lithuania succeeded in gaining independence from Russia.

TROTSKY. The organizer of the Red Army is shown here with his wife in Mexico, where he moved in 1937 as an exile from Russia. Trotsky, who believed that Stalin had betrayed the revolutionary cause, was for many years an outspoken opponent of Stalinism. He was finally murdered in 1940, by a man believed to be a Stalinist agent.

While these wars were going on, the Communists conducted a Red Terror, far worse than the Terror of the French Revolution, against all their political opponents. Under the pressure of the war they could not afford to have any opposition at home, so they ruthlessly executed anyone suspected of opposing the Communist government. They murdered the czar and his family and killed nearly all nobles and bourgeoisie who did not flee the country. They executed even peasants and workers who wanted to carry the revolution further than the Communist leaders felt was wise.

Lenin established a Communist dictatorship and the NEP. The Communist government established by Lenin was supposed to follow the Marxist pattern for a dictatorship of the proletariat (workers). In reality it quickly became a dictatorship by Lenin and the Communist party. The new constitution of 1918 made the local soviets the basis of the government. These soviets elected a national congress which appointed a cabinet headed by Lenin. But because the Communist party was the only party allowed, all candidates were Communists. Lenin, as head of the party and the government, was the dictator of Soviet Russia.

Under the Communists, the state took over the factories, banks, mines, and shops in the name of the people. In theory the workers controlled the factories, but they had to join government-dominated unions and were forbidden to strike. The state took over all the land in the name of the peasants, who were expected to give their surplus food to the state in exchange for the manufactured goods produced by the city workers. State officials collected the food by force when the peasants would not give it willingly.

After four years Lenin saw that this attempt at "pure" communism would not work. The peasants refused to co-operate because the government gave them so little in return for their crops. Unskilled workers, using antiquated machinery, produced goods of poor quality. Production was held back because neither farmers nor workers had any incentive to produce more efficiently. Lenin temporarily gave up pure communism and returned to many of the practices of capitalism. According to his New Economic Policy of 1921, (commonly called the "NEP"), peasants had to pay only a fixed share of their produce to the government. They could sell the rest on the open market for their own profit. Factory workers were offered higher wages as an incentive to increase their production of goods. In a few cases the government permitted factories and shops to be restored to private ownership.

Moscow Subway Station. The Russian people are proud of Moscow's excellent subway system, which was opened in 1935 and is one of the most beautiful in the world. Although few luxuries are available in Russia, the people have been promised more consumer goods in the future.

STALIN BECAME ABSOLUTE MASTER OF RUSSIA

Stalin replaced Lenin as dictator. Lenin's death in 1924 brought on a struggle for power. Most foreign observers thought the mantle of leadership would fall on Leon Trotsky. But a coalition of three Party leaders was formed to prevent this. Party Secretary Joseph Stalin (*stah*-lin) seemed the least important of this triumverate. "Stalin" ("Steel") was the alias adopted by this short mustached man with a deformed left arm who came from a poor family in Georgia, a province near the Black Sea. He was not regarded as a brilliant thinker; nor had he played a really important role in the 1917 revolution.

When Stalin became Party Secretary it was not realized how powerful that office could become. Since he kept all Party records, confirmed appointments and required a large staff, an unscrupulous Secretary could amass a huge personal following and exert enormous pressure upon his rivals. By the time the other Bolsheviks realized this it was too late to stop Stalin.

Besides a personal dislike, there were important political differences between Trotsky and Stalin. Stalin contended it was possible to "build socialism in one country" whereas Trotsky called for "permanent world revolution," using the USSR as a launching pad. Trotsky also demanded an end to the NEP and greater state control over agriculture and industry. When Trotsky pressed his ideas even after their rejection by the Party leadership, he was dismissed from his government and Party posts, then expelled from the Party and finally (in 1929) driven out of Russia. Hunted by the Soviet government, Trotsky was murdered by a Stalinist agent in Mexico in 1940.

Stalin then disposed of the other members of the triumverate and consolidated his power in the 1930s. In 1934 Sergei Kirov (*kir*-off), a popular Red leader, was assassinated. Charging that this signalized a plot to overthrow the government, Stalin had thousands arrested and scores of old Bolsheviks put on public trial. To the world's astonishment, most of them readily confessed to treasonable activities and begged for punishment. Almost all were executed. Historians now believe that Stalin himself ordered Kirov's murder and then used the crime as an excuse to get rid of other rivals! The public "confessions" were extorted chiefly through threats against the families of the men on trial. Between ten and twenty million people were sent to slave labor camps during the "Great Terror" of the 1930s. After Stalin's death several Communist leaders confirmed the fact that he had committed monstrous crimes.

LENIN AND STALIN. The revolutionary leader and his successor were photographed in 1922, just two years before Lenin's death. For a time the two men were joint editors of *Pravda*, which later became the official newspaper of the Communist party in the U. S. S. R.

The Soviet governmental system is not what it pretends to be. Defenders of the USSR have often denied that Russia's government is a dictatorship. They cite the Soviet Constitution as evidence that Russia is a democracy. This constitution, framed in 1936 under Stalin's guidance, is indeed remarkable. It guarantees to Soviet citizens such civil liberties as freedom of speech,

MARKET IN MOSCOW. At the Central Market in Moscow, fresh vegetables are sold. Most of the vegetables are grown on collective farms, although some private gardening for market is also permitted. Prices are fixed by the government, and the quantity that can be produced for market is carefully regulated.

press and assembly, protection from arbitrary arrest and the right to worship. There is to be no ethnic, racial or sex discrimination. Full employment and public assistance in old age are promised. Voting rights are granted to all citizens above age eighteen.

The Union of Soviet Socialist Republics (USSR) is a federal state of fifteen republics. The most important government body is supposedly the congress, called the "Supreme Soviet," of two houses, each elected for four years by popular vote. The Supreme Soviet selects a Presidium (pri-*sid*-ee-um) and a Council of Ministers. The Presidium convenes and dissolves the Supreme Soviet, appoints and relieves cabinet ministers and interprets the USSR's laws. The Chairman of the Presidium performs the ceremonial functions of the head of state while the Premier, as Chairman of the Council of Ministers, is the head of government. Similar arrangements exist for each Republic's government.

In its actual operation, the Soviet political system bears little resemblance to this constitutional portrait. The government has ignored the guarantees of civil liberties. Dissent is punished as treasonable. While labor unions exist, the right to strike is forbidden since this is an act against the state which is virtually the sole employer. Women's status is higher in Russia than in most countries. In particular, there are many Soviet women in professional occupations. But women have not attained top political posts in the USSR as they have in such places as Israel, India and Ceylon. Religious worship is under considerable handicap since atheism is a basic part of Communist belief and ambitious Russians are, of course, anxious for membership in the Communist Party. The Soviet government has long been accused of anti-Semitism; the eagerness of so many Russian Jews to emigrate lends substance to this charge.

Russian election procedures do not satisfy American concepts of democracy. There is only one candidate for each seat in the Supreme Soviet. Voting against the candidate can be done only by crossing out his name on the ballot with the pencil provided in a curtained voting booth. Voting is supposed to be secret but most voters deem it prudent to cast their ballots publicly (and, therefore, in favor of the candidate). The Supreme Soviet meets only a few days each year to approve, without debate, what has been done in its absence by the government. Not all delegates to the Supreme Soviet are Communist Party members but only Communists serve on the Presidium and Council of Ministers.

The Communist Party is the only party allowed. One cannot join through simple enrollment in the way an American becomes a Democrat or Republican. A candidate for Russian Communist membership undergoes an investigation of his beliefs and record. Communists are expected to submit unquestioningly to Party discipline and to work much harder than ordinary citizens. Consequently, only about a tenth of Russian adults are Party members. In theory, the millions of Communists elect their Party leaders. Actually, the real political and governmental power resides in the "Politburo" (political bureau) of about a dozen men. This includes the Party Secretary, who is usually the most powerful individual in Russia. Party Secretary Stalin did not trouble to have himself made Premier until 1941.

Stalin revolutionized Russia's economy. Stalin's greatest achievement was the rapid transformation of Russia into one of the world's most industrialized nations. Lenin's "New Economic Policy" had brought improvement to the shambles caused by World War I and the Bolshevik Revolution. But the NEP gave rise to profiteering businessmen (called "Nepmen") and richer peasants known as "kulaks" (*kool*-ahks). Both endangered Communist rule because their interests lay in the restoration of capitalism. Also, the USSR desperately needed greater industrialization in order to strengthen its military forces against its hostile neighbors. Accordingly, once Stalin had bested Trotsky in their power struggle, he adopted Trotsky's economic proposals and substituted for the NEP a program of intensive governmental economic planning.

Starting in 1928, a series of "Five Year Plans" was introduced which emphasized the production of "capital goods" (such as railways, steel mills, tractors and machine tools) instead of "consumer goods" (clothing, housing, household goods). All enterprises were government-operated. Wage rates were tied to production,—and production schedules were continually raised. Despite Communist theory, enormous gaps developed between the incomes received by managers and the most

RED SQUARE. Gathered around Lenin's tomb (left center), members of Communist youth organizations meet in Moscow's Red Square to celebrate the Bolshevik Revolution. November 1967 marked the fiftieth anniversary of this event.

Soviet Leaders. Foreign Minister Andrei Gromyko (left), President Nikolai Podgorny, Communist Party Leader Leonid Brezhnew, and Premier Alexei Kosygin, are shown together for the opening of Soviet American summit meeting in May, 1972.

skillful workers on the one hand, and the less adept on the other.

To man the new factories and feed the large numbers of new industrial workers, much more food had to be raised with less farm labor. The government tried to persuade the peasants to pool their individual lands, animals, and equipment into large "collective farms." Whatever profits were left to a collective farm after its expenses and taxes were met would be shared by its members. Most "kulaks" refused to enter collectives and some six million of them were sent to Siberian prisons. Embittered peasants took revenge by slaughtering millions of animals. There were years of dreadful famine.

Thus Russia's industrialization was achieved at a frightful cost. For years the masses were subjected to enormous strain and forced to accept a very low living standard. But, without the rapid industrialization of areas like Soviet Asia, the USSR could never have withstood the German invasion in World War II.

Agriculture, however, has remained the weak link in the Russian economy. Neither the collectives nor "state farms" (on which everything is government-owned and the farmers are salaried employees) have been able to satisfy Russia's food requirements. Since the mid-1930s, therefore, peasants on collective farms have been permitted to sell for personal profit produce raised on tiny privately-owned plots of land. Almost half of the food grown in the USSR comes from this source! Thus Russia's Communist rulers have had to revert to capitalistic techniques.

There were many shifts in Stalin's foreign policy. In the chaotic months following the end of World War I, Russia encouraged Communist uprising in such lands as Germany and Hungary and the Soviet army advanced westward to the gates of Warsaw, Poland. But by the early 1920s Communist influence in Europe had receded greatly and in 1927 the Chinese Communist Party suffered a smashing defeat from the Chinese Nationalists.

After this, Stalin's concern with domestic problems caused him to adopt a more cautious foreign policy. The USSR won recognition from several foreign governments and, in 1933, joined the League of Nations. Fearful of Fascist aggression, Russia made an alliance with France against Nazi Germany in 1935 and engaged in undeclared war with Japan along the Manchurian border in 1938. The Munich crisis of 1938 (see page 730) convinced the Soviet government that it could not rely upon France and Britain to oppose Hitler. So, in August of 1939, Stalin dumbfounded the world by concluding a "non-aggression" pact with Nazi Germany. Assured that he would not have to wage a two front war, Hitler began World War II less than a month later.

Until the summer of 1941 there was an uneasy collaboration between the USSR and Germany.

They partitioned Poland after its conquest in September, 1939. Russia shipped vital war materials to Germany but also annexed the Baltic states and part of Rumania in order to strengthen Soviet frontiers against a possible Nazi invasion. From December, 1939 through March, 1940, gigantic Russia warred on little Finland to obtain more defensive military bases. Nevertheless, Stalin was surprised when Hitler suddenly attacked the USSR on June 22, 1941. Faced with a powerful common enemy, Russia, Britain and the USA became allies for the remainder of World War II. (In Part 22 you can read more about Russia's role in the war.)

These twists in Soviet foreign policy appear to have been motivated less by Marxist zeal than by Russian national interests as interpreted by the ruling Communist clique. But, whatever its foreign policy, the USSR had the support of dedicated Communists all over the world who made the security of the Soviet Union their most important consideration. In 1919 Lenin established the "Third International" of Communist parties. In practice, all other members of this "Comintern" became vassals of the Russian party. For example, when France and Russia were allied, French Communists ceased their agitation against the French government but when the USSR was linked with Germany, French Communists tried to sabotage France's war effort against the Nazis. In addition, the USSR received valuable data from foreign Communists. Thus Communists in America, Canada, and Britain transmitted atomic secrets to Moscow which enabled the Russians to build nuclear weapons much sooner.

Of the three great allies, the USSR suffered most during World War II. Perhaps twenty million Russians were killed and much of the western part of the country lay in ruins. For this and for its contribution to victory, the Soviet Union won the sympathy of most Anglo-Americans. Yet, within two years of the close of the war, Stalin's alliance with Britain and the USA was shattered. Western historians disagree profoundly as to which government was most responsible. An important factor, surely, was the use of Soviet troops to set up Communist satellite governments in Eastern Europe. Americans interpreted this as Stalin's return to an aggressive foreign policy while Stalin insisted he was merely securing Russia's frontiers. Another factor was the cutting off of US financial aid to Russia soon after World War II's end despite the USSR's grave need. In any case, while Russia emerged from the war as one of the earth's two "super-powers," the last years (1946–1953) of Stalin's dictatorship were marked by the start of the "Cold War" and the formation of the "Iron Curtain." (See pages 761–8.)

STALIN'S SUCCESSORS HAVE MODIFIED HIS POLICIES

Russia has alternated between "collective" and "personal" rule. After World War II Stalin grew even more despotic. He was glorified as if he were a god. For example, the front page of the November 17, 1950 issue of the newspaper "Pravda" (*prahv*-duh) praised him 101 times! Suspicious of others almost to the point of madness, Stalin was preparing more purges when he suddenly died in 1953 at the age of 74.

Stalin's favorite, Georgi Malenkov (*mah*-lyenkof), was expected to be the new dictator. However, Malenkov reached for supreme power too quickly. He did become the new Premier but failed to secure the more important post of Party Secretary which went to the less-known Nikita Khrushchev (*kroosh*-chef). Russia, it was proclaimed, would be under "collective leadership" and in 1956 Khrushchev denounced Stalin's crimes and "cult of personality" to a stunned Communist Party Congress. But while this "de-Stalinization" campaign was proceeding, Khrushchev was building up his personal machine. In 1955 Malenkov was forced to resign and by 1958 Khrushchev was both Premier and Party Secretary. Unlike Stalin, however, Khrushchev did not kill or imprison defeated rivals but shunted them to obscure posts.

A quick-witted ex-coal miner, Khrushchev delighted the Russians with his salty language and frequent trips among them. But his extravagant boasts that Russian living standards would soon surpass America's and his eccentric behavior (as when, in 1960, he interrupted a UN session by angrily banging his shoe on a desk!) embarrassed his Politburo colleagues. Critical of his economic and foreign policy failures, they ousted him through a coup in 1964. Khrushchev died in pensioned retirement in 1971.

Again a "collective leadership" was promised,—this time under the joint control of Party Secretary Leonid Brezhnev (*brez*-nev) and Premier Aleksei Kosygin (koh-*see*-gun), both tough and colorless administrators in their sixties. By 1972, however, it had once more become evident that the Party Secretaryship was the key to Soviet power and that Brezhnev was the "strong man."

There has been some relaxation of controls. Post-Stalinist Russia remains a dictatorship with somewhat loosened political and economic controls. In the late 1950s many political prisoners were released and there have been no mass arrests. But the lot of the dissenter remains hard; writers are under censorship (see page 552) and persistent critics of the regime have been detained for "psychiatric treatment"!

The "Iron Curtain" has been relaxed considerably. Thousands of foreigners now visit the USSR each year and numbers of Russians are permitted to travel abroad. Consequently, Russians are far more aware of the deficiencies in their standard of living. From Malenkov on, Soviet rulers have had to make greater provision for "consumer goods" in their economic plans. Capitalist methods have been adopted to improve the quantity and quality of consumer goods. In particular, industry has been decentralized and local managers have been given much more power. The managerial and professional classes (of whom Kosygin is a representative) have become very influential. Agriculture, however, remains the economic "soft spot"; the failure of Khrushchev's attempt to extend grain cultivation into Siberia's arid sections was one of the reasons for his downfall.

Super-power Russia strives for world and Marxist leadership. In their foreign policy, Stalin's heirs have had both startling success and dismal failure. Soviet influence has been extended to new areas but Stalin's' undisputed command over international communism has not been maintained.

At the end of World War II, America's nuclear monopoly and superior navy more than offset the USSR's greater army. But the Soviets acquired an atom bomb in 1949, a hydrogen bomb in 1953 and their first inter-continental missile (before the USA) in 1957. By the 1960s Russia had become a formidable naval power. The launch of the first space ship, "Sputnik," in 1957 proved again that Soviet scientists were a match for the Americans. Victories by Soviet athletes in the Olympics further enhanced Russia's "superpower" image.

Since the mid-1950s, the Soviet Union has been able to infiltrate the Middle East,—an area Russians have been trying to control for over two centuries. Taking advantage of Arab resentment against American support of Israel, the USSR has supplied such massive economic and military help as to make most Arab states semi-protectorates. Russian influence in India has grown greatly since the early 1960s. The USSR gave notable diplomatic support to India in the latter's conflicts with China (1962) and Pakistan (1971–2).

Stalin's successors made a spectacular inroad into Latin America when Fidel Castro, turning Communist in 1960 after his seizure of power in Cuba, asked for Soviet protection. While Khrushchev suffered a diplomatic defeat in 1962 when President Kennedy compelled the withdrawal of Soviet missiles from Cuba, the USSR had still obtained an important outpost in the Western Hemisphere.

But there have been serious setbacks. Khrushchev's "de-Stalinization" campaign encouraged East European Communists to seek relaxation from Russian controls. In 1956 there were rebellions in Poland and Hungary, the latter so serious that Russian armed forces had to be used to suppress them. Similarly, in 1968 Soviet tanks were called in to put down a Czech uprising. So, although the East European states were linked militarily with the USSR through the "Warsaw Pact" of 1954, it was evident that the "satellites" were not reliable allies.

The greatest threat to Soviet leadership was from Communist China. Mao Tse-tung has resented "de-Stalinization" as undermining his own "cult of personality." Throughout the world, Maoist Communists accuse the Russians of retreating from Marxism by softening their attitude towards capitalism both at home and abroad. In turn, the Russians consider the Chinese dangerous "war-mongers" and impractical fanatics. By 1963 the Chinese challenge to Russia's Marxist leadership was in the open and in 1969 the split had flared into an undeclared war along the Sino-Russian border.

With the deterioration of Sino-Russian relations, the attitude of Soviet leaders towards the United States has grown friendlier. They have spoken often of the possibilities of "peaceful coexistence" between communism and Western capitalism. There were grave crises during the first two years of the Kennedy Administration provoked by the Communists' erection of the Berlin Wall in 1961 and the installation of Russian missiles in Cuba the following year. But this marked a turning point. The super-powers, faced with the prospect of nuclear war, drew back in horror and adopted measures to ease the tension between them. In 1963 a "hot line" communications system was created between the White House and the Kremlin to reduce the risk of conflict and a treaty was signed limiting nuclear testing. (By 1970 both powers had agreed to stop the spread of nuclear weapons.) Cultural and scientific exchange programs, initiated in 1958, have been expanded. While the two nations support opposing sides in the Vietnam War and the Arab-Israeli dispute, they have avoided hostile confrontations with each other and have probably tried to exert some moderating influence upon their client states.

This pacific trend was dramatically confirmed in May, 1972. Although President Nixon had just escalated the US bombing of North Vietnam (see page 582), he was welcomed on the first visit to Russia ever paid by an American President and signed a number of important pacts. The most significant of these was the freezing of both countries' offensive missile arsenals and the limitation of their defensive-missile systems to just two sites apiece. Therein both nations were admitting that each could destroy the other and both were relying upon this mutual deterrence to preserve the peace. Other accords included pledges of co-operation in scientific research and space exploration and hopes for increased trade. In July of 1972, American companies were negotiating commercial agreements with the Soviet government and a 1975 joint space venture for American astronauts and Russian cosmonauts was being arranged.

In August of 1972, as a sign of limiting defensive missiles, the United States approved the pact with the Soviet Union which would hopefully create an atmosphere of trust between the two giants of the nuclear age and forestall a holocaust which could result in mutual destruction. This agreement is considered to be the most important ever undertaken between the two countries.

Chapter Check-up

1. Why were Russian serfs not really freed by the Emancipation Act?
2. Why is the Duma of historical significance in Russia?
3. Why did the Russian people revolt against the czar in 1917?
4. What form of government was established after Nicholas II abdicated?
5. Why did Lenin and the Bolsheviks oppose the provisional government?
6. How was Stalin able to make himself master of Russia?
7. Why is the Soviet government not truly democratic?
8. Why did Stalin begin the Five Year Plans? Was he right or wrong in his aims and methods?
9. In what ways have Stalin's successors modified his policies?
10. What were the Moscow Accords of 1972?

CHAPTER 58

Russian Writers, Composers, and Scientists Created an Outstanding Culture

VIVID DESCRIPTION AND DEEP EMOTION CHARACTERIZE RUSSIAN LITERATURE

Many Americans have difficulty finding anything to admire in the political and economic institutions of Communist Russia. But we must not forget that Russian authors, musicians, and scientists have given the world fine books, important ideas, and beautiful music. In our public libraries there are volumes written by Russian poets and novelists. Over the radio we may hear deeply stirring music composed by Russian masters. There are so many evidences of Russian culture in the United States that we cannot be unaware of Russia's gifts to civilization. We can mention here only a few of the greatest men of literature, music, and science who represent the genius of their native land.

Pushkin laid the foundation for Russian literature. Russia's greatest poet, Alexander Pushkin (*poosh*-kin), played the same role in the Russian literature of the nineteenth century that Dante played in the Italian literature of the thirteenth century. Pushkin, like Dante, discovered a poetic beauty in the speech of the common people and laid the groundwork for a vernacular literature. He wrote many poems and stories about the history, manners, and legends of Russia. One of his best-known works, *Boris Godunov,* tells the tragic story of an early czar. Pushkin was inspired by the ideals of the French Revolution and had to live in exile because of his writings.

Russian authors gave a realistic picture of the evils of Russian life. Many nineteenth-century Russian writers boldly uncovered the political and social evils in the Russia of their day. Nikolai Gogol (*gaw*-gawl), the "father of the Russian novel," realistically described life on the great estates before the Emancipation Act. His most famous novel, *Dead Souls,* is a humorous but sarcastic attack on serfdom in Russia. Gogol also wrote a famous play called *The Inspector-General,* a satire on the corruption of the czar's officials, in which he intended "to drag into light all that was bad in Russia . . . and hold it up to ridicule."

One of Gogol's admirers was Ivan Turgenev (toor-*gay*-nyef). He described the hardships of the serfs so vividly in his book *A Sportsman's Sketches* that he helped pave the way for the Emancipation Act. His masterpiece, *Fathers and Sons,* deals with the disturbing effect of Western ideas on the younger generation.

The dramatist and short story writer Anton Chekov (*cheh*-kuf) was one of the most influential of the Russian writers of the late nineteenth century. He had a keen understanding of human nature. His plays, the most famous of which was *The Cherry Orchard,* portrayed the weakness and stagnation of Russian aristocratic society.

Another of Russia's novelists and playwrights, Maxim Gorki, was a fiery preacher of revolution. He was active in the Revolution of 1905, and had to flee Russia. When he returned in 1928, he was given a hero's welcome by the Communists. The town in which he was born has since been renamed for him.

Dostoevski delved deep into human emotions. One of Russia's greatest novelists, Feodor Dostoevski (dahs-tuh-*yev*-skee), began his career by joining one of Russia's outlawed secret societies. As a result, he was condemned to death by the czar. As he stood before a firing squad, however, a messenger arrived with the news that Dostoevski's sentence had been reduced to four years' hard labor in Siberia. His suffering during those years helped him to understand and pity the miserable and oppressed.

Dostoevski's powerful novels grew out of his misfortunes and his great compassion. With deep insight, he was able to describe the harsh, ugly details of daily life. In Russia his novels were recognized as the works of a great writer even during his lifetime. After his death in 1881 his reputation spread over the world, and today he is recognized everywhere as one of the world's great writers. Among his best works are *The Idiot, The Possessed,* and *The Brothers Karamazov.* His greatest novel, *Crime and Punishment,* tells the story of a rash, young university student who coldly commits a murder and successfully escapes detection. The young man's conscience finally drives him to confess his crime, and he is sent to Siberia as punishment. There, amid sufferings and hardships that are much like those Dostoevski himself endured, he atones for the murder by finding love and humility. The novel is remarkable for its insight into character and emotion.

Tolstoy believed in truth and the simple life. Perhaps Russia's most important writer was Count Leo Tolstoy (*tol*-stoy), who died in 1910 at the age of eighty-two. His experience in the Crimean War prepared him to write his masterpiece, *War and Peace.* This story of Napoleon's invasion of Russia shows the uselessness of war and reflects Tolstoy's belief that history is shaped by blind forces, not by the decisions of leaders. The characters of the novel are so strikingly drawn that their personalities are vivid and memorable.

Tolstoy's gay youth in St. Petersburg furnished the material for *Anna Karenina,* the tragic tale of a married woman who is driven to despair by her love for a young officer. Tolstoy describes her mental torment in a society that condemned anyone who tried to escape from an unhappy marriage through divorce.

Throughout all his writings, Tolstoy expressed deep sympathy for the common people of Russia. He tried unsuccessfully to free his own serfs and set up a school for them on his estate. But for all his criticism of society, Tolstoy did not advocate radical reforms or revolution. He had strong faith in the power of Christian love. He felt that a man should never use violence to protect himself or others, but should always do good to his enemies. Tolstoy believed that men are better off if they live a simple, natural existence. Although he himself belonged to the nobility, he gave up a life of ease and worked in the field beside the peasants. One night he horrified his family by telling them that he intended to divide his property among the poor. Only after hours of pleading was he persuaded to turn it over to his wife instead. From that night, Tolstoy made his living by mending shoes and writing. Never again did he touch a penny he himself had not earned.

TOLSTOY. The great writer, dressed as a *mujik,* or peasant, is shown on his family estate in 1901.

When Tolstoy died, he was mourned in many countries. Though people did not always agree

PASTERNAK. Virtually unknown in the Western world before 1958, Pasternak is now recognized as one of the great writers of the present day. He died in 1960.

with his ideas, they respected him for his honesty and his craftmanship as a writer. His works were translated into forty-five languages. In everything he wrote, Tolstoy was fearless in making plain the evils of his day. The government was afraid of his criticisms because his writings influenced many people. If he had not been a noble, he would probably have been punished.

Pasternak and Solzhenitsyn criticized conditions in Communist Russia. In 1958 and in 1970 Russian novelists were awarded the Nobel Prize for Literature. They were Boris Pasternak (*pass*-ter-nak) and Aleksandr Solzhenitsyn (sulz-*nyet*-sin) Usually a government is proud of citizens who receive such prestigious prizes. But the Soviet regime was displeased because both writers had become famous for novels which were highly critical of life in the USSR.

In 1958 Pasternak, a poet who had not been widely read outside Russia, had a novel called "Dr. Zhivago" published in twelve foreign languages, although it was rejected by Soviet publishers. It created a major sensation because it was a great work of art and very outspoken against the fanaticism of the Bolshevik revolution and the hypocrisy of Marxism. Pasternak was expelled from the Soviet Writers' Union and felt compelled to refuse the Prize. He spent the remainder of his days under a cloud of abuse, dying of natural causes in 1960 in his 70th year.

Solzhenitsyn has had a long record of dissent. In 1945 he was sentenced to eight years in a forced labor camp for describing Stalin unfavorably in a personal letter. His novel, "One Day in the Life of Ivan Denisovich" (1962), based on his prison experiences, was published in Russia during the "de-Stalinization" campaign. But Solzhenitsyn's later works, while acclaimed in the West, have been circulated in Russia only through the underground. Among them are "The Cancer Ward," about life in a prison hospital, and "The First Circle," dealing with a Stalinist scientific center. Although expelled from the Soviet Writers' Union so that his work will not be published in Russia, Selzhenitsyn has refused to reject the Nobel Prize or to go into exile.

RUSSIAN MUSIC FUSED WESTERN FORMS WITH RUSSIAN THEMES

Russian folk songs influenced nineteenth-century composers. Russian peasants had for centuries found delight in song and dance. Their music had both Slavic and Asiatic elements, but serious composers paid little attention to it until the nineteenth century. Nikolai Rimski-Korsakov (*rim*-skee kor-suh-*kawf*) used Western European forms, such as opera and symphony, to express Russian history and folk songs. His *Song of India* and *Scheherezade* show the Asiatic influences on Russian music.

Modest Mussorgsky (moo-*sawrg*-skee), a friend

of Rimski-Korsakov, wrote many songs and dances based on Russian folk music. His most famous opera, *Boris Godunov,* contains strong, appealing folk melodies.

Tchaikovsky brought Russian music to its height. Peter Tchaikovsky (chy-*kawf*-skee) is perhaps the greatest of all Russian composers and one of the most versatile who ever lived. His work ranges from simple waltzes and delightful suites, such as the gay *Nutcracker Suite,* to his great piano concertos and magnificent symphonies. The *Symphonie Pathétique* is the most famous of all his works. In this symphony the melancholy and tragic despair found in many of his finest compositions reaches its greatest intensity. One cannot listen to the strange, passionate melody without catching the composer's spirit.

Russia produced three outstanding modern composers. The work of Sergei Prokofiev (pruh-*kawf*-yef) is often satirical or humorous. He uses Russian themes in such pieces as the *Scythian Suite* and has written music for films and operas about Russian history. His music often tells a story. As a child you may have enjoyed *Peter and the Wolf,* the musical tale of an adventurous boy's encounter with a wolf.

Igor Stravinsky (struh-*vin*-skee), whose strange, wild music reflects the influence of his teacher, Rimski-Korsakov, has greatly influenced modern music. He wrote such famous ballets as *The Firebird* and *Petrouchka,* which caused a sensation when they were first heard because they achieved great beauty while seeming to lack harmony and melody. Today he lives in the United States.

Dmitri Shostakovich (shahs-tuh-*ko*-vich) had written six symphonies before the outbreak of World War II. The *Sixth Symphony* in particular was well known in America. Then, during the siege of Leningrad in 1941, he wrote the *Seventh Symphony,* which received great acclaim in America as well as in Russia. Shostakovich himself divided his time that year between working as a fire-fighter in defense of the city and composing this great work, which is, as he said, "an interpretation of the war." It meant a great deal to the Russian people that the composition of this work had gone on even while the enemy was at their gates. Shostakovich's *Eighth Symphony,* performed in 1943, was likewise based directly on Russia's part in the war.

Russians are considered masters of ballet. A ballet is a dance by one or more people which usually tells a story or expresses a mood. Ballet began in Renaissance Italy but reached its peak in nineteenth-century Russia. The czars supported a ballet school that the Communist government still subsidizes. During World War II ballet companies danced for Russian troops, sometimes just behind the lines. One of the first things Russians visiting Moscow do is to go to the ballet.

NIJINSKY AND PAVLOVA are considered to be the greatest ballet performers of all time. They thrilled audiences with their grace and incomparable technique. They were members of the Imperial Ballet which became the Bolshoi Ballet.

Folk Dancers. Each of the many nationalities in the Soviet Union has its own costumes, languages, and traditions. This dance of the Ukrainian Cossacks includes the spectacular leap which the dancer is executing here.

Two of the best dancers of the Russian Imperial School of Ballet were Anna Pavlova (*pah*-vluh-vah) and Vaslav Nijinsky (nih-*zhin*-skee). Pavlova won great acclaim for her perfect style and her lightness and grace. In her most famous ballet, *The Dying Swan*, she danced so beautifully that the idea of swan-like grace is still associated with her name. Nijinsky was especially noted for his great leaps in which he seemed to be in flight. Nijinsky's performance of *Petrouchka* and *Afternoon of a Faun* are world-famous. Both of these dancers were stars of the ballet company of Sergei Diaghilev (*dyah*-gih-lyef). He commissioned such masters as Stravinsky and Debussy to write music for his performers.

Russian ballets and the performances of Russian dancers are still outstanding. During the visits of the Bolshoi Theater Ballet to the United States, critics have been impressed by the grace and strength of the performers. Especially notable is the prima ballerina, Maya Plisetskaya. One former Bolshoi member, Rudolf Nureyev, has defected to the West and has become one of the main attractions of London's Royal Ballet.

RUSSIAN SCIENTISTS HAVE ADVANCED THE WORLD'S KNOWLEDGE

One of the most useful tools of modern chemists is the periodic table, in which all the elements are arranged according to their atomic weight and properties. A Russian scientist named Dmitri Mendeleev (myen-dyih-*lyay*-yef) was responsible for drawing up this table. By using it, he could predict the existence of some elements before they had been discovered. He could even predict what the characteristics of the unknown elements would be. Mendeleev investigated the effect of heat on liquids and gases and studied the nature of petroleum. His best-known book, *The Principles of Chemistry*, was translated into many languages.

Another great Russian scientist of the nineteenth century was the biologist Ilya Metchnikoff (*mech*-nih-kof). He was particularly interested in the nature and behavior of microbes. To learn more about them, he journeyed to Messina, then to Paris to study with Pasteur, the chemist you read about in the story of France.

Metchnikoff contributed to the discovery that certain types of white blood corpuscles constantly fight bacteria and devour them in the body. He wrote a famous book called *Immunity in Infectious Diseases*, which was translated into English. In recognition of his discoveries, Metchnikoff received the Nobel Prize for medicine in 1908.

Ivan Pavlov won the Nobel Prize in 1904 for his work in physiology. From his experiments with the behavior of dogs he learned how human beings as well as animals acquire habits without realizing it. His study of conditioned reflexes has enabled psychologists to gain a deeper understanding of human behavior.

SOVIET SCIENCE. The Russian contribution to scientific progress has been notable over the last fifty years and has attracted young earnest students. Shown here is a Soviet scholar superintending the installation of a vacuum device at the Catalysis Institute.

ART AND SCIENCE ARE UNDER THE STRICT CONTROL OF THE COMMUNISTS

Writers, composers and scientists, like everyone else in Soviet Russia, work for the government. According to Marx, art and science are products of economic conditions. At first, therefore, the Communist leaders allowed Russian artists and scientists a great deal of freedom. It was assumed that their work would naturally reflect the spirit of the Communist environment in which they lived. But Stalin decided to take no chances and began to enforce party discipline. He appointed a minister of culture to see that all art and science properly reflected Communist doctrine. Art, it was believed, is valueless unless it reveals the virtues of communism and the sins of capitalism.

Russian composers were told to avoid the influence of Western music, particularly American jazz. Russian music, however, was already so thoroughly flavored with Western forms that most Soviet composers have some freedom. They have tried to compose ballets about workers' lives but the results have been so poor that even Communist critics condemned them. Most Russian composers avoid writing new ballets lest the authorities read anti-Communist messages into them.

Science flourishes in Russia although only ideas in harmony with Communist doctrines may be taught. Russian achievements in mathematics, physics and chemistry are equal to the best work done anywhere. As of 1972, however, Soviet achievement in computer science was several years behind the United States. The Communists have encouraged scientific progress in many ways: scientists are offered good salaries, better living conditions, high prestige and the best equipment possible. Scientific progress, however, presents a serious dilemma for the Communist leadership. It is recognized that scientists must have as much intellectual freedom as possible in order to achieve their best results. Is it possible to prevent Soviet scientists from applying this freedom to thoughts in non-scientific areas? Increasingly, there is evidence that some Russian scientists have begun to speak out as dissenters on social and political issues.

Chapter Check-up

1. What important role did Pushkin play in the development of Russian literature?
2. What were the themes and purposes of the writing of Gogol, Turgenev, Chekhov, and Gorki?
3. Why is Dostoevski known as one of Russia's greatest novelists? Name four of his most important novels.
4. What is the significance of the work of Count Leo Tolstoy? Boris Pasternak?
5. Which Russian composers were most influenced by the folk music of the land? For what compositions is Tschaikovsky noted?
6. The names of Pavlova and Nijinsky remind us of Russian excellence in which of the arts?
7. How was mankind's scientific knowledge furthered by the work of Metchnikoff? Mendeleev? Pavlov?
8. How are the Russian arts and sciences influenced by the Soviet government?

Russia: SYNOPSIS

Russia is the world's largest nation and its abundant stores of raw materials make it almost self-sufficient. But throughout Russian history these advantages have been partially offset by two serious geographic handicaps. The first is the absence of natural frontiers. Russia's unprotected borders have repeatedly served as highways for invaders,—from the Tartars of the twelfth century to the two German attacks of this century.

The second handicap is that Russia is essentially landlocked. Accordingly, much of its history is the story of a search for good sea routes. Ivan the Terrible fought Sweden, Lithuania and Poland to gain a port on the Baltic. Peter the Great established a "window on the west." Catherine the Great took large sections of Poland to insure Russia's position in the west. Russia's desire to control the Dardanelles touched off the Crimean War.

World War I brought sweeping changes. Nicholas II's abdication was followed by a brief period of liberal constitutional government. That period ended with the Bolshevik revolution of November, 1917. The men who have ruled Russia since then have called themselves Communists. Yet the methods of government, the foreign policies and the ideas that guide the Russian state have really changed little since the Middle Ages. The leaders still seek outlets to the seas and are still trying to safeguard Russian borders. The despotism and police state of today are rooted firmly in the methods of the Czars.

What has changed is the weight of Russian influence in world affairs. The Soviet Union's rapid transformation from a basically agricultural country to one possessed with enormous heavy industry has made it one of the earth's two military super-powers. Nor is Russian influence the result of military and economic capability only. Since the inception of the Soviet state, Russia has had the devotion of thousands of foreign Communists who have been willing to further the USSR's interests even (in some cases) to the extent of betraying their own countries.

Although Communist ideology and the reaction to it has deepened world tension, other considerations apparently count more with Soviet leaders. Despite direct confrontations over Berlin and Cuba, Russia and the United States have been able to avoid a shooting war. In the 1970s Russian hostility seems directed more against

Communist China than capitalistic America. The USSR and the USA have a common interest in defusing their rivalry and in reducing their very costly weapons systems. Hopefully, their future rivalry can be confined to the realm of peaceful competition.

The creativity of Russian artists and scientists has been remarkable in view of the despotism under which they have lived. Tolstoy, Dostoevsky, Chekov and Pushkin are counted among the greatest writers of all time, while Pasternak and Solzhenitsyn have won recent Nobel prizes in literature. Similarly, several Russian composers and musicians have been ranked at or near first-rank in their fields while Russian scientists have made important contributions to the welfare of mankind.

Terms

Be sure that you understand clearly the meaning of each of the following:

boyars
"window on the west"
zemstvo
Golden Horde
Emancipation Act
Duma
Provisional Government
Politburo
Marxian socialism
November Revolution
Bolsheviks
March Revolution
Red Terror
NEP
Presidium
Five-Year Plan
collective farm
soviet
U.S.S.R.
Kremlin
Supreme Soviet
purge

Important People

How has each of the following influenced the story of Russia?

Vladimir the Saint
Batu
Ivan III
Ivan the Terrible
Peter the Great
Aleksandr Solzhenitsyn
Alexander II
Karl Marx
Nicholas II
Vladimir Lenin
Leon Trotsky
Aleksei Kosygin
Joseph Stalin
Nikita Khrushchev
Alexander Pushkin
Feodor Dostoevski
Leo Tolstoy
Georgi Malenkov
Boris Pasternak
Peter Tchaikovsky
Anna Pavlova
Dmitri Mendeleev
Ivan Pavlov
Leonid Brezhnev

Questions for Discussion and Review

1. What are some of Russia's geographic advantages and disadvantages?
2. What influence did the Mongol invasions have on the history of Russia?
3. What events led to the overthrow of Czar Nicholas II?
4. What is the meaning of the slogan of the Bolshevik Revolution, "Peace, Land, and Bread"?
5. In your opinion, were the common people of Russia better off under the czars than they are under the Communists?

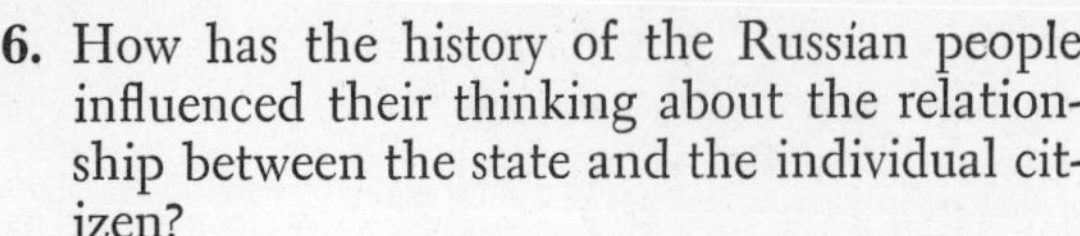

6. How has the history of the Russian people influenced their thinking about the relationship between the state and the individual citizen?
7. In which field do you think the Russians have made the greatest contributions to man's progress? Why?
8. What has been the effect of the Communist doctrine on the creative arts? Why?
9. Do you think the United States or the Soviet Union has a more efficient government and economy? Why?
10. Is "peaceful co-existence" between the USA and USSR possible?

Interesting Things to Do

1. Make a map of the U.S.S.R. and the surrounding lands and seas. Locate and label the important mountain ranges, rivers, cities, and industrial areas. Use colors or shading to show the four natural geographic belts into which Russia is divided.
2. On an outline map of the world, show in red the areas dominated by Russia and its Communist allies and satellites. Let another color indicate the land controlled by the Western powers. Use a third color to highlight the areas that are neutral or non-strategic. (See the opening map in Part 23.)
3. Make a summary chart of the contributions of the Russians to the fields of literature, music and science. Head your columns as follows: *Name of Person, Field of Work, Contributions or Achievements.*
4. Prepare a chart comparing the United States and the U.S.S.R. as to area, population, climate, natural resources, industrial and agricultural production, arts and sciences, education, government, and individual and civil rights.
5. Collect pictures from magazines and newspapers for a booklet entitled "The Men Who Rule Russia."
6. Make notebook charts showing the organization of (a) the Soviet government and (b) the Communist party.
7. Prepare a talk about Siberia to describe its present condition and future possibilities. Make your discussion a lively blend of history, geography, and description.
8. Prepare a written or oral report on "An American Visits Moscow," describing the things one might see and experience during a stay in the Russian capital.
9. Add to or begin your "Who's Who in World History" series by writing brief biographies of one or more important Russian leaders.

Interesting Reading about Russia

Abramov, Fyodor, *One Day in the "New Life,"* Praeger. A novel about life in a Soviet village today.

*Baker, Nina Brown, *Peter The Great,* Vanguard. A very interesting and readable biography of the eighteenth-century czar.

Fainsod, Merle, *How Russia is Ruled,* Harvard.

*Folsom, Franklin, *The Soviet Union,* Nelson.

Goldston, Robert, *The Russian Revolution,* Bobbs-Merrill. How it happened and why.

Habberton, Williams, *Russia: The Story of a Nation,* Houghton Mifflin.

Harper, Theodore, *Red Sky,* Viking. Life in Russia before the revolution of 1917.

Lamb, Harold, *The Mind of Muscovy; Ivan the Terrible and the Growth of the Russian Empire, 1400–1768,* Doubleday.

*Martin, John (editor), *Picture Story of Russia,* Crown.

*Nazaroff, A. I., *Land of the Russian Peoples,* Lippincott.

Seeger, Elizabeth, *Pageant of Russian History,* Longsmans Green.

Sinevirsky, Nicola, *Smersh,* Holt, Rinehart and Winston. Secret police organization of Russia.

Wolfe, Bertram D., *Three Men Who Made a Revolution,* Beacon.

* Indicates easy reading

Modern India, with its many cultures and centuries-old traditions, is trying to create a democratic state that will be a model to Southeast Asia and to the world.

Part 18
INDIA AND SOUTHEAST ASIA
FROM COLONIES TO INDEPENDENT NATIONS

INDIA AND SOUTHEAST ASIA

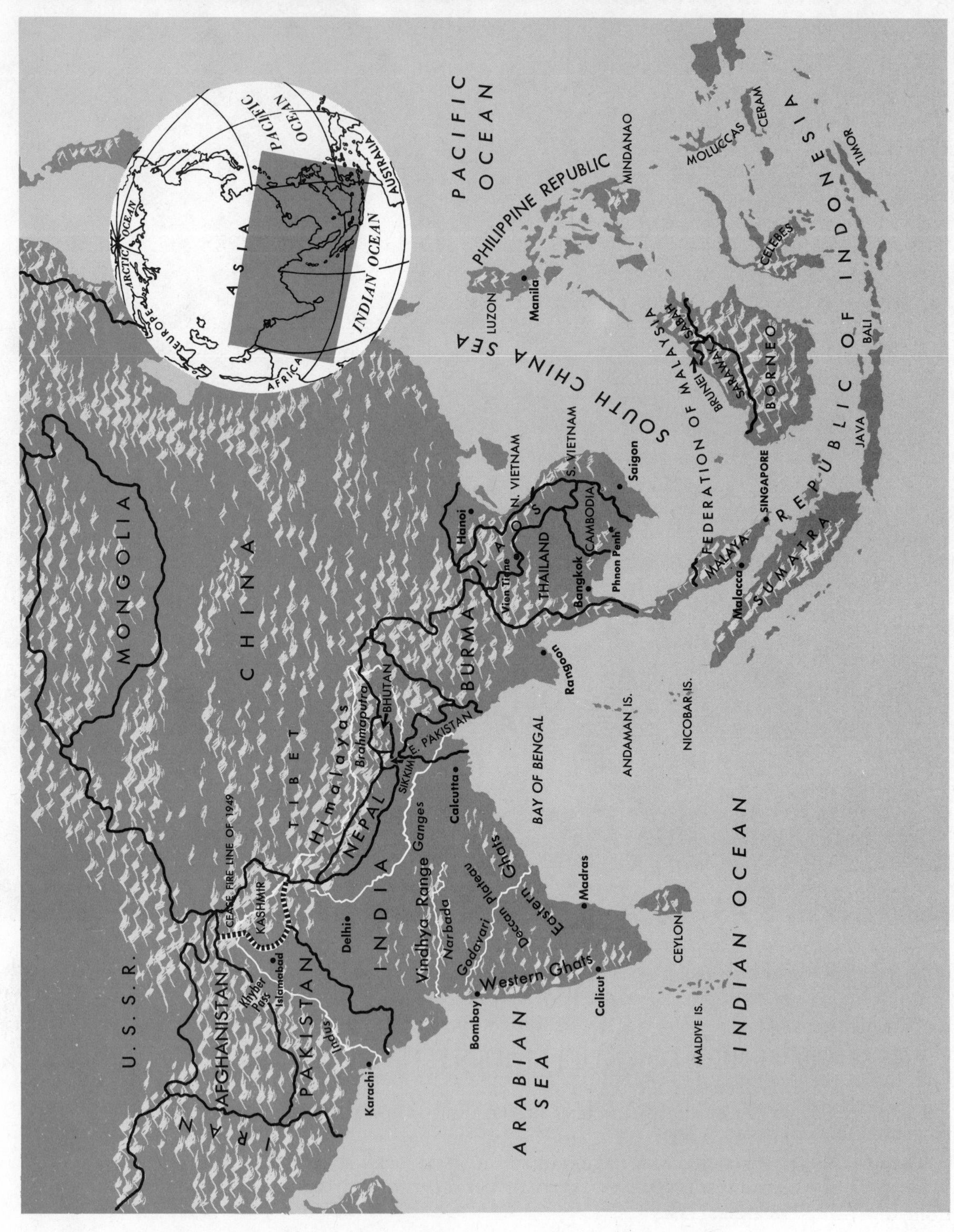

India and Southeast Asia: GEOGRAPHIC SETTING

India is a large, triangular peninsula projecting from southern Asia into the Indian Ocean. The Himalayas, the world's highest mountains, separate India from China. An extension of the Himalayas on the northwest isolates India from Afganistan and Persia, except at the Khyber Pass, the historic route of invaders.

Three great rivers, the Indus, the Ganges (*gan*-jeez), and the Brahmaputra (brah-muh-*poo*-truh), flow from the Himalayas across the vast plain of northern India. Although the plain is dry and barren at the western end, the eastern sector is a rich agricultural district that supports the largest part of India's population. South of the plain, the low Vindhaya (*vind*-h'yuh) Mountains separate northern India from the highlands that are called the Deccan (*dek*-un). Low hills rise along the coast and shut off the Deccan from the ocean. The narrow strip of plains between the hills and the coasts is fertile and thickly inhabited. Off the tip of India lies the green, mountainous island of Ceylon.

Southeast Asia includes the great Indochina Peninsula at the southeast corner of the continent, the narrow Malay Peninsula farther south, and a mass of islands to the southeast. Located on the Indochina Peninsula are: Burma, Thailand (*tie*-land), Cambodia (kam-*bo*-dee-uh), Laos (*lah*-oz), and North and South Vietnam (vee-*et*-*nahm*). Malaya (muh-*lay*-uh), now part of the new country of Malaysia (muh-*lay*-zhuh), occupies the Malay Peninsula. Malaysia also includes Singapore at the tip of the Peninsula and Sarawak and Sabah on the island of Borneo. Indonesia (in-do-*nee*-zhuh) encompasses a 3000-mile island chain, the main islands of which are Sumatra (soo-*mah*-truh), Java, and part of Borneo. Northeast of Indonesia is the Philippine Republic, covering an archipelago of over 7000 islands.

Much of Southeast Asia is mountainous or covered with jungle, but there are fertile river valleys and coastal plains. With a hot, humid, and rainy climate, rice growing especially is spectacularly successful in some of these areas.

India and Southeast Asia: PERSPECTIVE

Throughout 1962, reports of clashes between Indian and Red Chinese patrols came down to the capital of New Delhi from the Ladakh region in the Himalayan Mountains to the north. There, in the barren sweeps of the high mountain country, lies part of the disputed border between India and China. Exchanges of notes produced no results. Prime Minister Nehru refused to negotiate the dispute until Chinese troops were withdrawn from Indian territory, and China refused to withdraw the troops. Then, in the fall of the year, the Chinese attacked in force, both in Ladakh and in India's North East Frontier Agency near the little country of Bhutan. A state of national emergency was declared in India and the army was mobilized. Britain, the United States, and Canada were quick to supply India with military equipment. China received no support at all from the Soviet Union. Finally she decided to pull back, and the situation hung fire for the time being.

The border action in 1962 brought into direct conflict for the first time the two most populous countries in the world—India, a struggling democracy, and China, a Communist dictatorship. The Western nations were prompt in providing India with arms in 1962, and she has also been one of the main recipients of foreign aid from the United States. The West realizes that if India is unable to create a successful democracy, the struggle against communism in Asia will be lost.

Equally important to the free world is the vast region of Southeast Asia. Here the focus is on South Vietnam, whose Mekong Delta is one of the richest rice-producing areas in the world. The Geneva Conference of 1954 divided the former French colony of Vietnam into two countries—North Vietnam and South Vietnam. Free elections in 1956 were to determine the future of both states. But the communist-led government of North Vietnam immediately began a campaign of guerrilla warfare within non-Communist South Vietnam, and elections were never held. Instead, the Viet Cong, as the Communists are called in the south, were aided by the Soviet Union and China. The United States committed itself to help South Vietnam. This conflict has grown enormously, and all peace efforts have thus far failed. There are now almost 500,000 U.S. soldiers in Vietnam, and casualties continue to grow.

CHAPTER 59

India Has Known Ancient Glory, British Rule, and Modern Independence

HINDUISM AND BUDDHISM INFLUENCED INDIAN CIVILIZATION

Civilization developed early in the Indus River Valley. Archaeologists have found ruins of an ancient civilization that flourished in the Indus Valley about 2300 B.C. Apparently these early inhabitants of India had made considerable progress. They lived in walled cities and built three-story brick houses of unique design. A citizen of Harappa (hah-*rahp*-uh), one of the chief cities of ancient India, could rent an apartment with a kitchen, bathroom, and private stairway. Archaeologists have also unearthed fine pottery, carved seals like those used by the Sumerians, and sculpture of bronze and stone. This evidence suggests that these early peoples of India traded with Sumer, Egypt, and Crete.

Aryan invaders laid the foundation of Hinduism. By 1750 B.C. the Indus Valley civilization had declined. No one knows why—possibly the Indus River was blocked off from the sea, and the valley gradually flooded. At about that time, a group of fair-skinned tribes known as the Aryans (*air*-ee-unz) wandered out of the northern highlands and settled on India's fertile plain. The Persians later called this region *Hindustan,* which meant "land of the Hindus." The Aryans were simple herdsmen who worshiped nature gods, such as *Indra,* the god of storm, and *Agni,* the god of fire. These early gods have since been absorbed into Hinduism, which is the national religion of India today.

At first the father of each family conducted its religious worship. Later, priests called Brahmans (*brah*-munz) took over that function. The Brahmans also composed hymns and prayers in honor of the gods. Collections of these works, called the Vedas (*vay*-duz), give historians a picture of life among the Aryan tribes. They date from about 1000 B.C. and are the earliest sacred books of Hinduism.

The Aryan invaders considered themselves superior to the dark-skinned people called the Dravidians (druh-*vid*-ee-unz), whom they conquered or drove into the Deccan. To keep their dominant position, the Aryans permitted only their own people to become priests, warriors, or craftsmen. The Dravidians were forced to be laborers. This arrangement marked the beginning of the *caste* system which divided the people of India into rigid social classes. As the Aryan tribes developed the religion of Hinduism, the caste system became an important part of their faith.

The Hindus believe that a man's soul can be born again. Gradually, in the years between 1200 B.C. and 800 B.C., the Indo-Aryans pressed east into the Ganges Valley, where they formed small states. The hot climate of the valley, with its uncertain rainfall and the threat of famine, was more depressing than the climate of the northwestern part of the plain near the mountains. This change in the surroundings of the Aryan tribes had great influence on their religious beliefs. Previously they had been concerned mainly with earthly life, and their worship consisted of a kind of bargaining with the gods for certain favors. Gradually, as life on earth grew more difficult, they became more concerned with an after life.

The priests introduced new gods, the chief of which they called *Brahma*, the "One Spirit" or "World Soul" that filled the entire universe. The Hindus came to believe that the soul of each person was a part of the World Soul, and that every man was merely an expression of Brahma. They believed that man's greatest goal in life was to merge his soul with that of Brahma. Only then could he find complete happiness and absolute peace. These teachings were set forth in the *Upanishads* (uh-*pan*-ih-shads), a group of writings that date from about 500 B.C. Like the Vedas, they are among the most important works of Hinduism.

One of the most interesting of the Hindu beliefs is that of the *transmigration of souls*, or reincarnation—the passing of the soul, when the body dies, into another body. According to this belief, if a man lives a selfish, greedy, or wicked life, his soul is reborn in a body of lower status. He might become a dog, a pig, a snake, or even a stone. If he lived a good life, his soul would return in a person of higher status or caste. Eventually he might even become a Brahman. As the

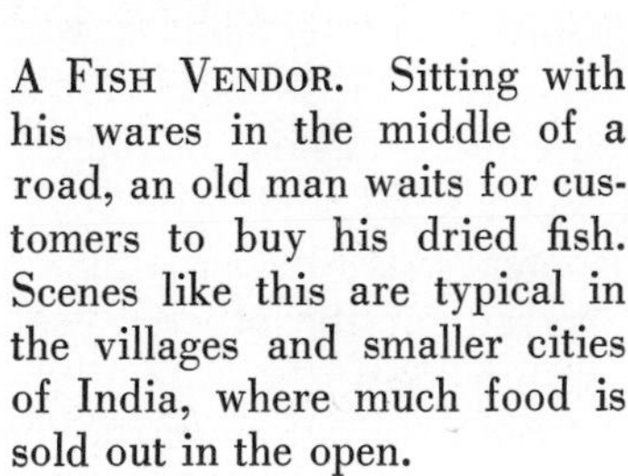

A FISH VENDOR. Sitting with his wares in the middle of a road, an old man waits for customers to buy his dried fish. Scenes like this are typical in the villages and smaller cities of India, where much food is sold out in the open.

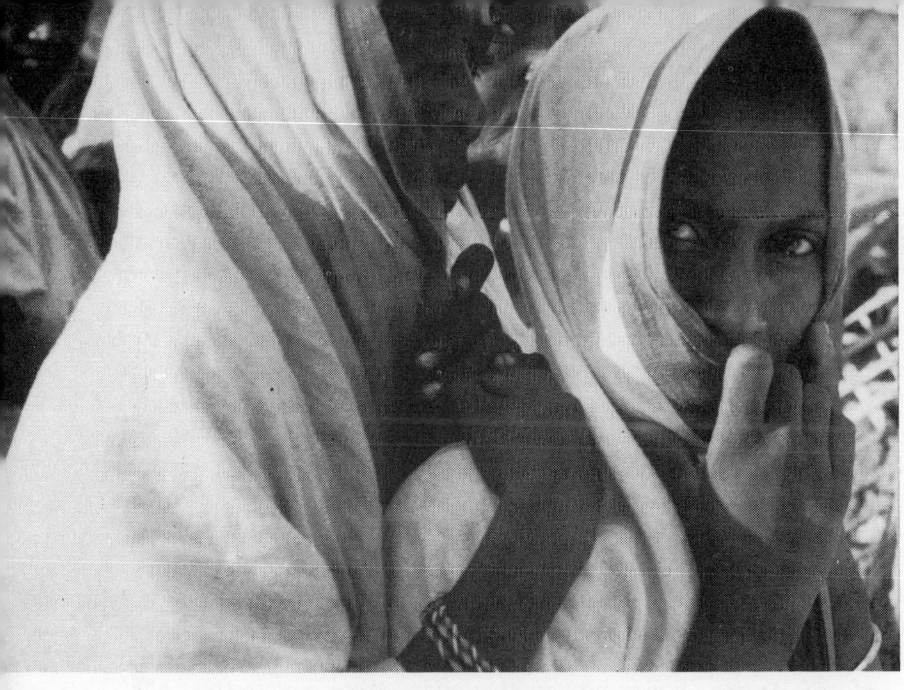

"Children of God." Formerly known as untouchables, these two girls are members of the group that for centuries was considered to be of the lowest rank in Indian society. Called "children of God" by the Indian leader Ghandhi, untouchables are no longer regarded by the government as worthless—but custom is dying hard.

Brahma. The three chief gods of Hinduism are represented in this rock carving in a cave near Bombay. The three faces symbolize Brahma the creator, Vishnu the preserver, and Siva the destroyer.

soul dwells in a long series of living creatures, it gradually gains the experience necessary to live a better and better life. If it finally learns to live the perfect life, the soul is rewarded by being absorbed into Brahma and gaining release from this cycle of rebirth and the miseries of earthly life.

The caste system is part of Hinduism. To maintain their dominant position in Indian society, the Brahmans divided people into classes. These were subdivided into occupational castes, which determined each man's rank in his class. The Brahmans, or teachers, formed the highest class. The second class was made up of warrior-kings, the Kshatriya (*kshat*-ree-yuh), whose duty was to protect society. The third class, which included farmers, craftsmen, and merchants, was called the Vaisya (*vi*-syuh). These three upper classes were permitted certain religious privileges, such as reading the Vedas. The fourth class, consisting of hired laborers, was called the Sudra (*sho*-druh). They worked for the other classes and did not share their privileges.

Below the Sudra, at the very bottom of the social order, were the wretched untouchables, the "outcasts" of society. These, the most primitive of the Dravidians, were considered unclean because they practiced disagreeable trades like hunting, scavenging, and sweeping refuse off the streets. Even the shadow of an untouchable falling on a man of caste might pollute him. The untouchables were forced to live outside the villages and were forbidden to enter the temples or use the village wells.

The Brahmans drew up strict rules to prevent mixing of the classes. A person from one class could not marry, eat with, or even talk to a person of another class. Sons had to follow the professions of their fathers. Thus the untouchables were doomed to lives of poverty, ignorance, and squalor. Neither the Sudra nor the untouchables objected to the system, however, because they knew no other and because it was necessary to their religion. Even an untouchable, if he kept the rules applying to his class, could look forward to being reborn into a better life. As the Hindus expressed it, "Just as he behaves, so he becomes." Thus, keeping the caste rules became one of the most important ways of improving one's status.

The belief that every man's rank in life was the reward or punishment for a previous life explains why no one tried to move out of his caste or envied those of higher rank. This belief also explains why Hindus stressed the duties rather than the rights of each caste. The caste system kept Indian society stable for hundreds of years and is still very strong. Today however, many Indian leaders are seeking to do away with it. The harsh rules against the untouchables have been declared unlawful by the Indian government.

Buddha saw "the way of life." During the sixth century B.C., in northern India near the sacred river Ganges, was born the founder of one of the world's great religions. His name was Gautama (*gow*-tuh-muh), but later he came to be known as "the Buddha." His father was a wealthy rajah who ruled one of the Indian states. Little is known of the Buddha's early life, but he probably lived in princely luxury like most nobles. When he was nineteen years old he married a beautiful princess.

As he neared the age of thirty, a great change came over the Buddha. According to legend, he was driving with his trusted servant Channa one day, when he saw an old man, bent and feeble. "Such is the way of life," said Channa. "To that we must all come." Soon afterward they came upon a man suffering from a terrible disease. Again Channa said, "Such is the way of life." While still pondering these things, they saw an unburied body. Once more Channa repeated, "Such is the way of life."

The Buddha felt as if his eyes had suddenly been opened to all the miseries of life. He was no longer content to live for mere pleasure, and he no longer felt at ease in his luxurious palace when so much poverty and unhappiness existed outside the palace walls.

THE TEACHING BUDDHA. This representation of the Buddha, created during the Gupta period of Indian history, portrays the religious leader as a teacher. Buddhists instantly recognize this "teaching pose" by the symbolic position of his hands and by the manner in which he is seated.

That night, accompanied by Channa, the Buddha fled into the darkness in search of someone or something to show him the deeper meaning of life. He paused in his flight to cut off his flowing hair and beard. He exchanged his silks and linens for the ragged clothing of a beggar whom he met on the road. He tore off his jewels and ornaments and gave them to Channa to return to his wife. But the Buddha himself did not turn back. He joined a group of hermits who lived in mountain caves. They sat under the trees talking of the mysteries of life.

One day the Buddha was seated beneath a giant tree. He resolved not to stir until he understood the meaning of life. After forty-nine days of meditation, the truth suddenly burst upon him. He felt he understood at last why men suffer and die. This revelation is called the Enlightenment (the name Buddha means "the enlightened one"). The Buddha spent the rest of his life wandering through India clad in a yellow robe and holding a begging bowl. Refusing the invitations of princes, he spent his time, as Jesus later did, with the poor and lowly.

Buddha taught men the four Noble Truths. The Buddha's Enlightenment explained the meaning of life by revealing the four "Noble Truths." The first truth is that man's life is filled with misery and suffering. The second explains that this suffering is caused by man's own selfish desires. The third says that man can end his suffering only by completely overcoming his desires and ridding himself of any trace of jealousy, greed, or selfishness. The soul of such a perfect man is not reborn but immediately attains the state of *Nirvana.* The Buddha never fully described Nirvana; he said only that it was like a great sea of silence and peace in which all desire ceases.

Those who faithfully believed in the first three Noble Truths were ready to follow the fourth, which told how to achieve Nirvana by overcoming one's selfish desires through "right living." Buddha emphasized gentleness, self-denial, and kindness to others. Because all men were brothers, they should not kill, lie, steal, or hate. Notice the similarities between the teachings of the Buddha and those of Jesus (see Chapter 19).

What the Buddha meant to do was to reform Hinduism; he did not intend to establish a new religion. He wanted to free religion from the control of the Brahmans and to offer hope to the lower castes. The Buddha accepted the Brahman teachings that life was essentially a miserable existence and that escape depended on man's own actions. He taught, however, that any man could win release in his own lifetime, that a perfect life did not depend on obedience to caste rules, and that man did not have to be reborn a Brahman before deserving release from worldly troubles. Instead, the Buddha stressed unselfishness and ethical living as a path by which any man could attain Nirvana. Thus the Buddha showed low-caste men and untouchables a direct way to salvation that did not depend on the Brahmans.

Buddhism spread all over eastern Asia. About a century and a half after the Buddha's death, a great king named Asoka (uh-*sho*-kuh) brought most of India under his control. Although Asoka had been a great warrior, he grew to hate war and regretted his bloodthirsty deeds. Gradually he adopted the teachings of the Buddha, and finally he made Buddhism his state religion. He ordered the principles of Buddhism taught to his officials. Throughout his empire he erected stone columns on which he carved Buddhist teachings in the language of the people.

As a result of Asoka's encouragement and Buddhism's appeal for ordinary men, the new faith began to take root in India. Thousands left their homes to enter monasteries. They took vows of poverty, chastity, and kindness to living things, as the Buddha recommended. Wearing yellow robes, they went begging in the streets every morning. The monks met in councils to write down the Buddhist scriptures. These works, called the *Tripitaka* ("Three Baskets"), included the Buddha's sayings, monastic rules, and philosophic discussions. At Asoka's command, many monks carried the Tripitaka to the Middle East, Ceylon, Burma, and China. In the last three areas they were especially successful in spreading the new faith among the people.

As Buddhism gained followers, many of its beliefs changed. Converts, especially in India and

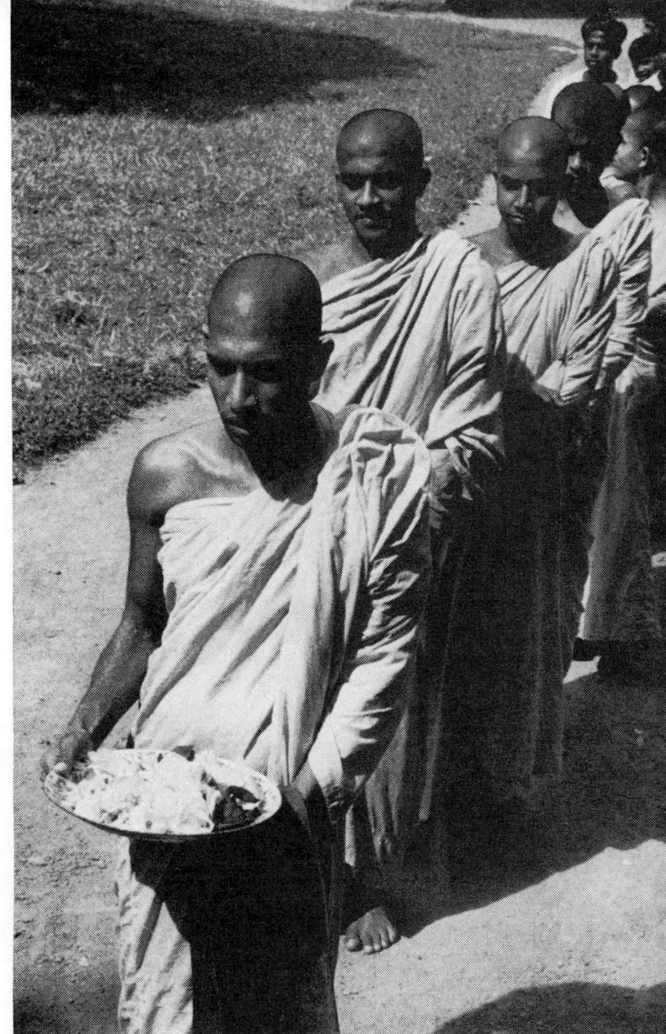

Buddhist Monks. Candidates for monkhood begin their training as children, attending special schools in which they are taught both religious and secular subjects. Here, monks and students proceed to the temple before school to offer flowers to the Buddha.

China, forgot that the Buddha had been a man and that he had disapproved of temples and ritual. Like the Egyptians, Greeks, and Romans, the Buddha's followers preferred to perform ceremonies rather than to live strict, ethical lives. Many Indians began to worship the Buddha as a god. They built temples and statues in his honor. They called local village gods buddhas and saints and worshiped them too. The Chinese followed the Indians' example. Buddhism tended to lose its moral emphasis and became a religion that was popular for its ritual, legends, and magic charms.

Buddhism influenced Hinduism. Indian Buddhism eventually became absorbed into Hinduism and disappeared after the seventh century A.D. But it strongly influenced the traditional Hindu faith. Brahman priests put more stress on meditation and the importance of leading an ethical life. They also introduced new gods, such as Siva (*shee*-vuh), Vishnu, and Krishna, who were expressions of the World Soul but were much closer to the people than was Brahma. The Brahmans preferred to worship the stern Siva, whom they called "the destroyer." Most lower-caste Hindus worshiped the kindly Vishnu, who they believed was reborn, or incarnated, several times because he wanted to help suffering mankind. They were especially fond of one of his incarnations as Krishna, the handsome cowherd. Krishna is an important figure in the great epic poem, the *Mahabharata* (muh-*hah*-bah-ruh-tuh), which was composed between 200 B.C. and 200 A.D. The Mahabharata became a kind of encyclopedia of the legendary history of India. It is still very popular today.

The Gupta period was India's Golden Age. From the fourth to the sixth century A.D., India came under the rule of a series of able emperors known as the Gupta (*goup*-tuh) Dynasty. The Gupta rulers founded what were probably the first universities in the world. The best-known, the University of Nalanda, offered courses in religion, philosophy, art, and archaeology, and it even included a school of agriculture with a model farm. The Indian universities attracted scholars from all over India and Southeast Asia. The Gupta emperors, who were Hindus, encouraged these scholars to write down caste rules and Hindu philosophy. They also wrote works of poetry and literature. Hindu mathematicians made important contributions. They introduced the use of the decimal, the zero, and the minus sign. They also invented "Arabic numerals," which they later passed to the Arabs.

Under the Gupta rulers, India prospered. It was at this time that some of India's most famous

SIVA. The god Siva is shown here standing atop a dwarf who symbolizes ignorance. The dance he is performing is part of his role as Nataraja, or dance-king. In this dance, he destroys and recreates the world.

temples were built (see Chapter 61). The Gupta era is often called India's Golden Age.

The wealth to support this brilliant culture came from the people, most of whom were peasant-farmers living in small villages. In many of the villages there were skillful craftsmen who wove fine cloth and rugs and worked in wood, ivory, gold, and bronze. Some fashioned steel armor and weapons long before such instruments of warfare were known in Western Europe. The craftsmen were organized into small castes within the Vaisya class.

Each village had a Brahman family, the head of which conducted prayers and ceremonies for the whole village. The village elders met to decide local affairs, although the emperor's word was law in all matters that affected the country as a whole.

The taxes imposed by the emperor were a heavy burden on the peasants. Matters were made worse by the custom of dividing a man's land holdings among all his sons when he died. Thus the farms grew smaller and smaller with each generation. A farmer could not, of course, leave his caste to find some other kind of work. He was expected to live and work on his family's land. This restriction kept the peasants from improving their lot. But village life, which was closely tied with family and religious traditions, gave them a measure of security. Today three-fourths of India's population lives in such villages. Only gradually is this age-old way of life beginning to change.

Moslems ruled India for many centuries. In the sixth century A.D. the Gupta Empire was broken up by Mongol invaders (relatives of the Huns who were raiding the Roman Empire at about the same time). These invaders settled in northern India, intermarried with Indian nobles, and established the warrior state of Rajputana

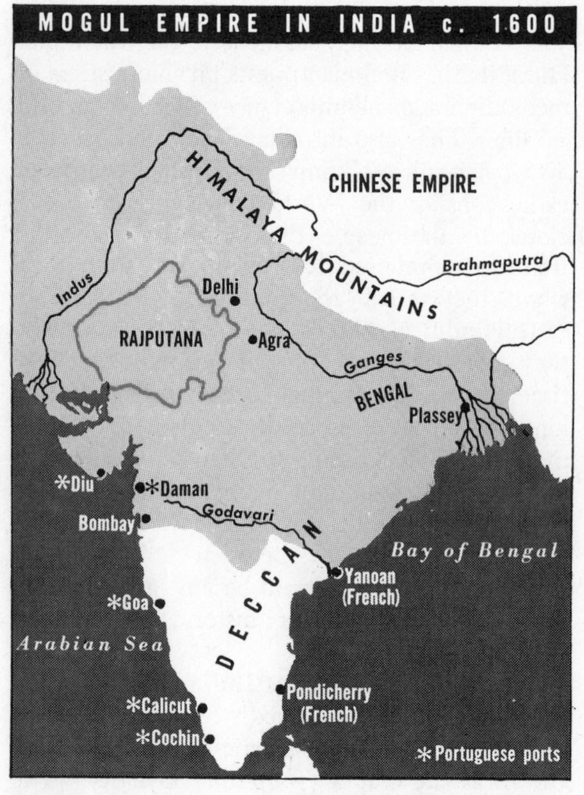

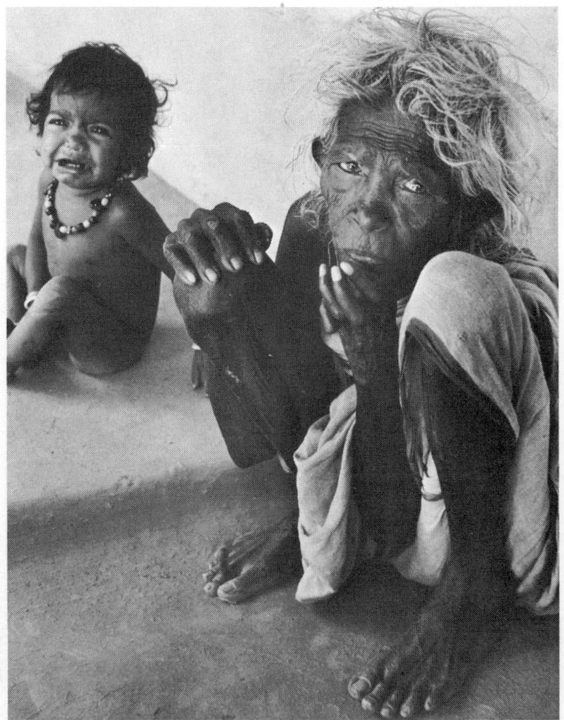

MISERY. The anguish and despair of the elderly Indian grandmother and child are all to frequent sights in the sub-continent.

(rahj-poo-*tah*-nuh). Several centuries later, the Arabs began their great expansion of the Moslem Empire. They conquered Rajputana and eventually brought most of India under their control. The Arabs established a Moslem state in India, and made Delhi their capital. They taxed the Hindus heavily and looted many of their temples.

Moslem power in India reached its height with the creation of the great Mogul Empire in the sixteenth century. The Moguls were a Mongol tribe which had been converted to Islam. The most capable Mogul ruler, Akbar the Great, brought nearly all of India under Moslem control. Akbar proved to be a wise ruler. He knew that he needed the support of the Hindus as well as that of the Moslems. He abolished the tax formerly collected from non-Moslems and chose many Hindus as officials in his government. He married a Hindu princess and tried to establish a single religion that would please both groups.

Akbar failed to achieve religious unity, but he did create an efficient government. He paid his officials in money so they would be loyal, and he rotated governors of provinces so that they would not have time to plot revolt. He kept a paid army, and he devised a fair, efficient tax system. These measures held the empire together even when Akbar's weak successors spent more time pursuing pleasure than attending to affairs of state.

The Persian culture which the Moguls brought with them merged gradually with the ancient Indian culture. Thus many Persian influences can be seen in Hindu architecture and painting. High-caste Hindus adopted the Moslem custom of secluding their women in harems. Many low-caste Hindus and untouchables became Moslems, because Islam had no caste system. Hinduism remained the chief religion of India, however, and the strict laws of the caste system prevented any substantial mixing of the two faiths.

INDIA BECAME PART OF THE BRITISH EMPIRE

The British East India Company gained control of India. For many centuries Arab merchants had acted as middle men in the sale of silk, jewelry, and Indian spices to Western nations. Vasco da Gama's discovery of a new water route to India in the late fifteenth century (see Chapter 27) put Europe in direct contact with Indian trade for the first time. A few years later the Portuguese established the first permanent European trading post at Goa, near Bombay. English and French trading companies secured trading rights in the seventeenth century.

At first the Mogul emperors paid little attention to the Europeans, except to exact tribute from them. As the Mogul Empire declined, India came more and more under the control of local princes. Because there was no strong central government to keep order, the Europeans built forts and imported soldiers. They wanted not to conquer India but to protect their trade. Sometimes force seemed the only way to deal with local princes.

By the eighteenth century the British and French were bitter rivals for Indian trade. During the Seven Years' War (see Chapter 35) Robert Clive, an official of the British East India Company, commanded a British army that defeated the French at the battle of Plassey, a village north of Calcutta. His victory cleared the way for British control of India.

The British government did not interfere in the affairs of the East India Company. The company made alliances with friendly princes and supported them by training native soldiers, or *sepoys.* In exchange, the company received the right to collect taxes from the princes. The company's European-trained troops were more than a match for the weak Mogul emperor and the rival princes. As the East India Company increased its intervention in Indian affairs, more and more rulers came under company control. This political power enabled the company to make vast profits on Indian trade. The company controlled the export of such popular items of trade as spices, tea, calico cloth (from Calicut), cashmere (from the province of Kashmir), and Madras embroidery (from Madras).

India became a British colony. Many Indians bitterly resented the control of their country by the British East India Company. This resent-

THE SEPOY REBELLION. The cavalry of the East India Company attacks the sepoy rebels in this scene depicting the mutiny of 1857. The British were able to repress the rebellion with the help of other Indian soldiers who remained loyal.

ment was increased by the impact of the Industrial Revolution in the eighteenth century. Indian tradesmen, who once prospered from the sale of textiles to Britain, were suddenly put out of business by the power-driven machinery used in British mills. Mass-produced English textiles undersold Indian goods even in India itself.

At the same time, the East India Company, in order to prevent competition with British goods, forbade Indians to build factories of their own and imposed a heavy duty on British machinery. Indian industries collapsed, and millions of Indians were thrown out of work. The company expected them to become farmers and to raise raw cotton, jute, and tea for the British, but there was not enough land for them. The standard of living fell lower and lower. India was ripe for revolt.

In 1857 a great mutiny took place among the sepoys in the British army. Rumors spread to the Moslem sepoys, whose religion forbade them to touch pork, that their new gun cartridges had been greased with pork fat. At the same time rumors were spread to the Hindu sepoys, to whom the cow was sacred, that their cartridges were greased with beef fat. A bloody uprising followed. The rebellion spread through northern India and cost the lives of thousands before it was put down by the British. After suppressing the uprising, the British abolished the East India Company and made India a British colony under direct control of the crown. In 1877 Queen Victoria was proclaimed Empress of India.

A RAJAH. Under British rule, the territories of India were governed by local rulers known as rajahs. The British introduced reforms in an attempt to keep the Indians satisfied, but nationalist sentiment continued to grow.

The benefits of British rule did not prevent the rise of nationalism. When India became a British colony the event marked a turning point in her history. The British government tried to rule wisely. Some of the provinces were ruled directly; others were ruled through native princes, called *rajahs*. A British viceroy, or governor, was appointed by the crown to supervise the states ruled by the rajahs. He also directed the Indian Civil Service, which administered the provinces that were ruled directly by the crown. Most of the civil servants were British and were almost always well trained, honest, and efficient. They built roads, railways, dams, and canals. They traveled from village to village, trying to introduce new farming methods, to provide for better sanitation, and to prevent famine and disease. They also established schools and universities for the Indian people. The British army kept peace on the borders and prevented trouble among the various states.

The British did a great deal for India from their point of view, but Indian resentment remained strong. Wealthy Indians often went to English universities, where they absorbed liberal ideas of freedom and national independence. They returned home instilled with these Western ideas only to find that the British would not give them responsible jobs in the civil service or in the army. They could not enter British homes or clubs.

They paid taxes but had little to say about how the money was spent. Denied almost all chance to co-operate with the British, the Indian intellectuals began to form their own political parties.

In 1885 Hindu leaders founded the Indian National Congress party, which began to work for political equality with the British. Almost at once, the party split into two groups, the moderates wanting parliamentary government under British supervision, the radicals wanting complete independence. In 1906 Moslem leaders, fearing that the Hindus would become too powerful if India were independent, formed the All-Indian Moslem League to safeguard Moslem interests. The British claimed that this division among the Indians proved that they were not yet ready for self-rule. To suppress the radicals, the British passed laws under which Indians could be exiled or jailed without trial. These harsh measures were so bitterly resented that they spoiled the effects of other laws that gave the Indians more power in the government.

INDIA WON HER INDEPENDENCE

Mahatma Gandhi was the father of Indian independence. During World War I the Indians loyally aided the British war effort. Gratefully the British promised that India would be given gradual self-government after the war. When the promise was not kept, riots broke out. At this point, the great Indian patriot, Mohandas K. Gandhi, later known as Mahatma ("great soul"), became the leader of India's struggle for independence.

The deeply religious Gandhi believed that only good actions could bring good results. He thought that love, patience, and truth could overcome the injustice of British rule better than violence could. Therefore, instead of inciting the Indians to riot, he urged them to disobey laws they considered unjust but to offer no active resistance when arrested. Instead of telling them to burn warehouses filled with British cotton goods, he encouraged them to spin and weave

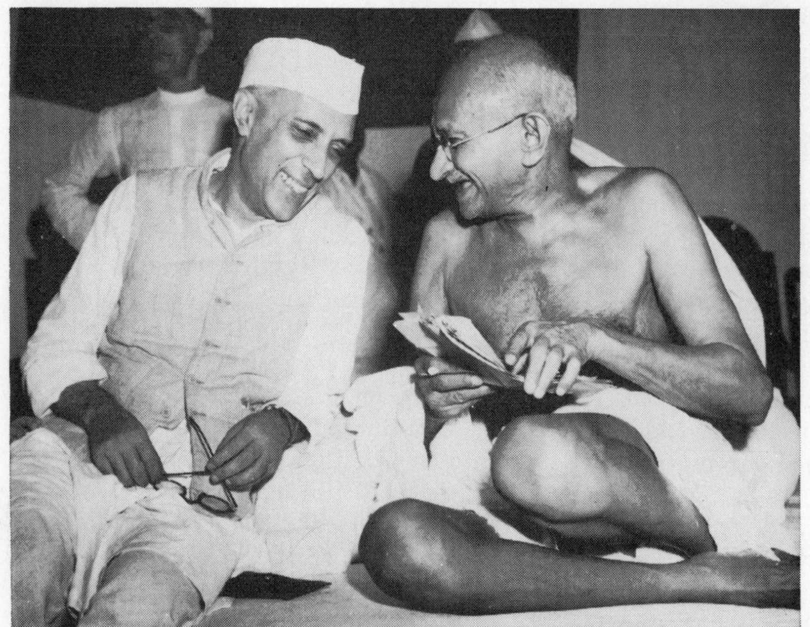

Nehru and Gandhi. India's first Prime Minister, Jawaharal Nehru died in 1964. He is shown here with Mahatma Gandhi, the leader of India's long struggle for independence. Gandhi achieved his political goals by nonviolence and passive resistance. On many occasions he won concessions by going on a hunger strike.

The Misery of War. When West Pakistan decided in 1971 to bring rebellious East Pakistan, now recognized as Bengla Desh, back to the central government, thousands had to flee. The result for many people of Bengla Desh were these concrete homes. Squalor and misery are their home companions.

their own clothing. He himself was often seen spinning cloth. Gandhi's policy of non-violent opposition to British rule won the support of the Indian masses, and he became their spokesman.

When the British found Gandhi's policies troublesome, they put the beloved Indian leader in jail. But they found it hard to explain the arrest of a man who preached love and non-violence. When in jail, Gandhi usually went on a hunger strike to dramatize his cause. Younger men rallied round him, including Jawaharlal Nehru (*nay*-roo), an equally sincere nationalist. He became the leader of the radical group in the Indian National Congress party.

Gradually, the British extended voting rights among the Indians and gave them a larger voice in Indian government. But the Indian nationalists were still dissatisfied. When World War II broke out, the Congress party demanded complete independence as the price of co-operation in the war effort. The British made generous proposals, all of which the Congress party rejected because they fell short of complete independence. The Moslem League also rejected the British offers because they did not provide for a separate Moslem state. New riots broke out, and Gandhi and the other leaders were jailed.

After the war the Labor government came to power in England and released the imprisoned Indian leaders. After much discussion, the British finally agreed to withdraw from India. Accordingly, on August 15, 1947, the British colony was replaced by two nations, the Hindu Dominion of India and the Moslem Dominion of Pakistan.

Independence has brought strife between India and Pakistan. The new states' boundaries were drawn chiefly on religious grounds. Thus, the northwest and northeast corners of the subcontinent, where the Moslems were concentrated, became the two parts of Pakistan, separated by almost a thousand miles. But some 15 million Hindus were left in Pakistan and 35 million Moslems in India. With British rule ending, religious tensions exploded. Hundreds of thousands were killed as millions of Hindus rushed to India and millions of Moslems to Pakistan.

Gandhi, who was trying to bring an end to this horror, was assassinated in 1948 by a Hindu fanatic objecting to the Mahatma's tolerant attitude towards Moslems. Indians of all faiths mourned his death and the violence subsided.

But in the quarter-century since independence, India-Pakistan hostility has deepened. Both lands have poured into armies great sums which might otherwise have been used to improve living conditions. Wars have erupted on four occasions: in 1947–8, twice in 1965 and in 1971.

Two conflicts were over possession of Kashmir, a province lying between India and Pakistan. At the time of partition, the Hindu ruler of Kashmir

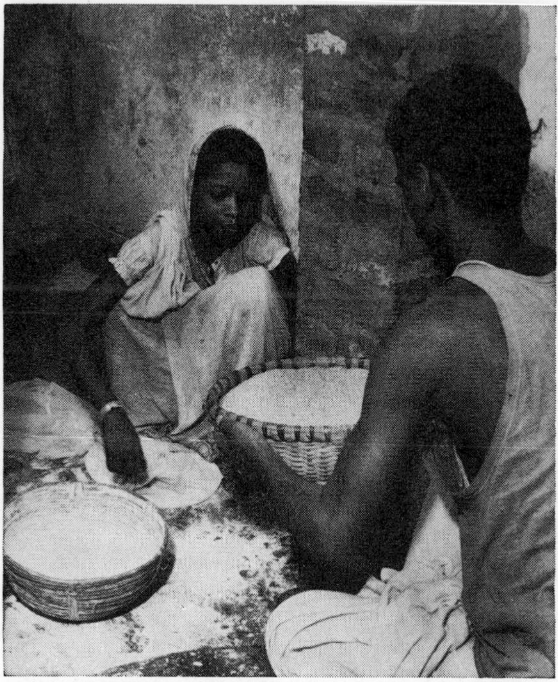

BUYING RICE. In time-honored fashion, a woman bargains over the price of rice. The food problem is serious in India, and many staples must be imported to feed her people.

chose to join India. Pakistan objected because the Kashmiri population is largely Moslem and whoever governs Kashmir controls the rivers which flow into West Pakistan. In 1948 the United Nations ordered an election to let the Kashmiris decide which country they preferred. India has not permitted such elections and has annexed much of Kashmir.

The disputes in 1965 over Kashmir and the boundary at the Rann of Kutch (in 1965) ended in inconclusive truces since both sides quickly exhausted their military resources. But the fourteen day struggle of December, 1971 resulted in Pakistan's defeat and dismemberment.

Over the years each combatant, in its desire to vanquish the other, has altered its foreign commitments drastically. India abandoned its neutral policy to become greatly dependent on Russia, with whom it signed a treaty of friendship in 1971. Pakistani policy went through several phases until, in the early 1970s, it was virtually an ally of Communist China.

Despite enormous problems, India has remained a democracy. Even without troubled relations with Pakistan, it would be extremely hard to govern India, for its domestic difficulties are so complex. The heart of those difficulties lies in the characteristics of India's population. In a third of the area of continental United States live over 500 million Indians whose numbers grow by 15 millions a year! There are over 1600 different languages and dialects with 15 recognized as national tongues. Although the caste system is supposedly outlawed, the former "untouchables" still suffer discrimination. Seventy per cent of the Indians are illiterate. Eighty per cent are peasants toiling on farms of just a few acres each. In the teeming cities, thousands live on the streets and millions are unemployed. Americans' average life expectancy is 70 years and our annual per capita income is over $3500; the statistics for Indians are 52 years and under $100!

Amid such poverty it is remarkable that India, unlike so many other new nations, has not turned to dictatorship. The devotion to democracy of India's leaders accounts for much of this. Prime Minister Nehru provided responsible democratic guidance until his death in 1964. His daughter, Mrs. Indira Gandhi, who became Prime Minister in 1966, has proved herself an adroit politician, establishing firm direction over the governing Congress Party.

The competition between India and China is not merely for the leadership of Asia but provides an indication of whether democracy or dictatorship is the better system for developing nations of Asia and Africa. When Chinese troops mauled India's army in a 1962 frontier war, democracy also took a beating. But India's prospects have since improved,—in some ways far beyond expectations.

Helped financially by the United States and Russia, India has combined a mild form of socialism with democracy. Heavy industry is being developed under a series of Five Year Plans. Government-sponsored family planning programs have been started, but with just fair success since

Hindu culture up until now has encouraged high birth rates. The great phenomenon has been the "Green Revolution," commencing in the late 1960s, whereby, through the use of better fertilizer and seed and more modern tools, India has begun to supply almost all of her own food requirements.

Pakistan has become a "disaster area." In many ways, Pakistan's problems have been even worse than India's. Pakistan has less industry and fewer natural resources. Moslems were less experienced than Hindus in self-government. There were enormous differences between West and East Pakistan. The West, inhabited chiefly by Punjabis speaking the Urdu language, had some industry, was less crowded and more prosperous and dominated the government. In the East, where Bengali is the chief language, the population density is among the world's highest. There is almost no industry, and jute (the main export product) brings in less and less income. In effect, no national party existed to bring the two sections together.

Almost from the first, Pakistan strayed from democracy with the army exerting control. The anti-Indian focus of Pakistan's foreign policy led it into a virtual alliance with Communist China after the Sino-Indian border war of 1962.

In 1971 Pakistan came apart. The Awami League, representing East Pakistan, had captured a majority of the National Assembly seats in the election of December, 1970. Some Bengali extremists began to call for the creation of a new East Pakistan nation, to be called Bangla Desh (*bahng*-luh-desh). In March, 1971 the Pakistani government postponed the National Assembly's meeting. Civil War followed. The West Pakistani army soon occupied East Pakistan, imprisoning Sheik Mujib (*moo*-jib), head of the Awami League. Ten million Bengalis fled to neighboring India to escape persecution.

Swamped with refugees and eager to assist in the dismemberment of Pakistan, India came to Bangla Desh's rescue in December, 1971. The two week war, during which China and the United States supported Pakistan while Russia backed India, resulted in Pakistan's defeat. Sheik Mujib was freed and became head of Bangla Desh, now the world's eighth most populous land and with

TEMPLE OF THE TOOTH. According to legend, when Asoka sent missionaries to convert the inhabitants of Ceylon to Buddhism, he sent with them a tooth of the Buddha, a replica of which is shown at the left. The Temple of the Tooth, located in the city of Kandy, was named after the relic and is the most famous temple in Ceylon. The base of the sacred tooth is the lotus blossom, which symbolizes the Buddha.

MOHAMMED ALI JINNAH. Champion of the movement for the creation of a Moslem state, Mohammed Ali Jinnah was president of the Moslem League and later the first governor of the Dominion of Pakistan. Like Gandhi in India, he died soon after the realization of his lifelong aims.

a per capita annual income of $40! The world's hopes were raised by a conference in July, 1972 between Mrs. Gandhi and the new Pakistani President, Zulfikar Ali Bhutto (*boot*-oh), at which the two countries pledged to settle their differences peacefully.

Chapter Check-up

1. What great mountain range separates India from China?
2. What are the basic religious beliefs of the Hindus?
3. What are the divisions of the Hindu caste system?
4. What are the four "noble truths" of Buddhism?
5. Why was Buddhism readily accepted by many lower-caste Hindus?
6. What were some of the achievements during India's Golden Age?
7. How did India come under the control of the British East India Company?
8. In what manner did Gandhi urge the Indians to oppose British rule?
9. How did independence for India bring about division and religious strife?
10. What were the causes for the dismemberment of Pakistan?

CHAPTER 60

Imperialism and Nationalism Shape Modern Southeast Asia

EUROPEAN NATIONS DOMINATED SOUTHEAST ASIA

Southeast Asia has absorbed many cultures. As early as 100 A.D. Indian merchants crossed the Indian Ocean to trade and settle in Southeast Asia. They introduced their language and religion to the people of this region. Eventually the Hindu religion and culture was adopted by the people of Burma, Siam, Cambodia, and Laos. In some areas, such as Indonesia and Malaya, Moslem missionaries succeeded in converting the natives to Islam. The people of Vietnam, which was once part of the Chinese Empire, have absorbed Chinese religion and culture, while many people in the Philippines were converted to Christianity by Spanish and U.S. missionaries. Thus the many nations of Southeast Asia have a variety of cultural backgrounds.

Europeans carved out colonies in Southeast Asia. During the Middle Ages, Arab and European merchants were attracted to Southeast Asia. After they conquered India, the Arabs took over the Indian merchants' thriving spice trade and acted as middle men in the sale of spices to European merchants. In the sixteenth century, Europeans started trading directly with Southeast Asia and gradually began to gain political control of the area.

The first part of Southeast Asia controlled by Europeans was the East Indies, or "Spice Islands" (today called Indonesia). The Portuguese arrived there in the early sixteenth century and were followed by the Spanish, Dutch, and English. It was the Dutch, however, who won control of the islands. Eventually the East Indies became the richest colony in the Dutch Empire.

The Philippines were the next to fall. Magellan discovered these islands in 1521 and claimed them for Spain. The Spanish did not make permanent settlements there until 1569, when they sent out an expedition from New Spain (Mexico) and named the islands in honor of Philip II. Gradually the islands came under Spanish rule, and the Filipinos became Christians and among the most Westernized of all the Asian peoples. During the Spanish-American War the United States captured the Philippines, put down a Filipino revolution for independence, and governed there until 1946.

Malaya came under European influence in the sixteenth century, when the Portuguese set up a trading post at Malacca. It was the British, however, who eventually gained control of Malaya. In 1819 the British bought the island of Singapore, just off the tip of the peninsula, from a Malay ruler. As the British Empire grew, Singapore became a key port on Britain's lifeline to the East. In the last quarter of the nineteenth century, when British imperialism was strong, the British brought most of the Malay Peninsula under their control. At the same time, they added Burma to the British Indian Empire.

Vietnam, Laos, and Cambodia came under the rule of France. Together they were known as French Indochina. The French government first became interested in Indochina as the result of an effort to protect French missionaries who had settled there.

By the end of the nineteenth century, Siam (Thailand) was the only independent country

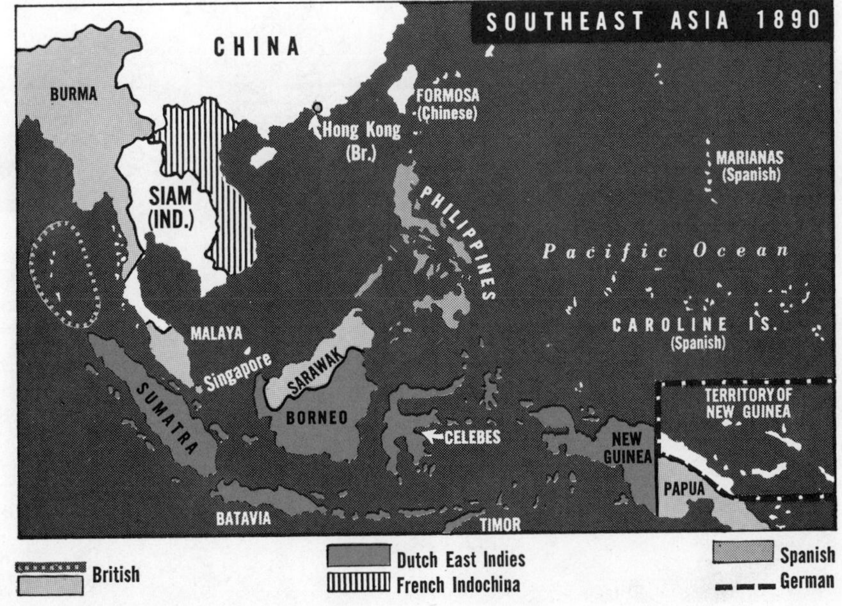

left in Southeast Asia. Siam owed her freedom partly to her able kings and partly to the fact that neither the British nor the French wanted the other to control her. One of Siam's most capable kings, Rama IV (1851–68), realized the need of modernizing his country to protect her from European conquest. He signed trade agreements with Britain and other Western powers and brought in teachers and advisers from several countries to prevent any single country from becoming dominant. Rama's son carried on the reforms by abolishing feudalism and slavery and by modernizing the government. In spite of these improvements, however, France forced Siam to give up Laos and other territories on the Indochinese border.

Europeans exploited their colonies. Thousands of Europeans settled in the Southeast Asian colonies. Some came in the name of humanity. Some to convert these Asian peoples to Christianity. Many, however, came simply to make money. Because factory owners were eager for the raw materials of the East, Europeans ruthlessly exploited the mineral and agricultural wealth of the colonies. In the East Indies the Dutch established sugar, tea, and rubber plantations and developed rich tin mines and oil fields. The islands also produced large quantities of quinine, spices, kapok, coffee, tobacco, and tropical fruits and vegetables. Dutch ships carried these products to markets all over the world.

Malaya's tin and rubber were very profitable to the British. Because the Malayan jungles were sparsely populated and Malayans were unwilling to work for the British, Indian and Chinese laborers were brought in. By 1940 the Chinese con-

ANGKOR WAT. One of the great architectural monuments of Southeast Asia, this temple was built nearly a thousand years ago near the capital of the Cambodian Empire. Within the gate is the shrine of Vishnu. The central tower is nearly 200 feet high.

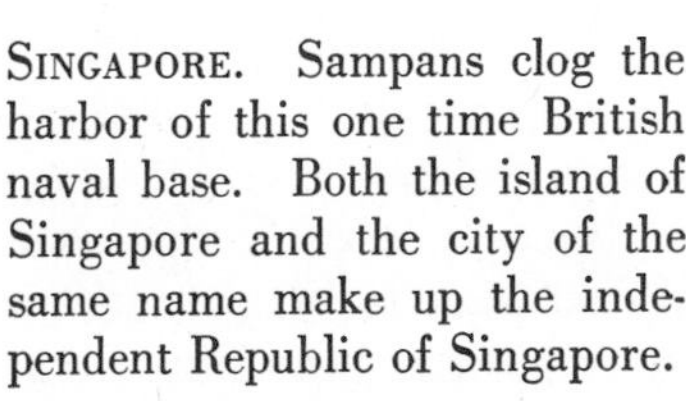

Singapore. Sampans clog the harbor of this one time British naval base. Both the island of Singapore and the city of the same name make up the independent Republic of Singapore.

stituted almost 40 per cent of Malaya's population. Burma also furnished the British with valuable supplies of oil, teak, tungsten, silver, and lead. French Indochina had rich deposits of coal but was otherwise the poorest country of Southeast Asia.

Southeast Asia was left almost totally undeveloped industrially because the colonies were regarded as producers of raw materials for the factories of the mother countries. The profits that resulted from exporting these raw materials went to the Europeans, who had the capital and skill to develop them. They controlled trade and administered colonial governments with the purpose of taking as much wealth out of the colonies as possible. The Europeans formed the highest level of society. Below them was a small middle class made up of Indian and Chinese immigrants who owned the retail shops and were moneylenders. They charged very high rates of interest on loans made to the indigenous people.

Southeast Asians, who made up the bulk of the population, formed the lowest class. They did not share in the wealth produced by their land. The peasant-farmers usually received low prices for their products. If they left their farms to become laborers on European-owned plantations or in mines, they were paid meager wages.

Uneducated Southeast Asians were unable to improve their position. They made few objections to their exploitation because they scarcely realized what was happening to them. They had no understanding of money, banking, and the other intricate tools of modern business. The Europeans purposely did not educate the natives because they feared the loss of their dominant position. They were there to make money, not to educate the people.

The people of the Dutch East Indies were still 93 per cent illiterate after three centuries of Dutch rule. Although each colony had a university and a few schools of agriculture and forestry, the number of Asian students was small. A few hundred Southeast Asians studied in Europe each year. These were the men who usually became the leaders of nationalist movements because, just as in India, they were allowed no important posts in the government.

SOUTHEAST ASIA HAS BECOME A WORLD TROUBLE SPOT

Nationalism and Communism have dominated recent Southeast Asian history. During World War II Japan's invasion of Southeast Asia ended European domination of the region. Using the slogan "Asia for the Asians," the Japanese set up puppet governments. When the war was over the newly-armed Asians resisted the Europeans efforts to regain their colonies.

Of the European powers Britain adjusted most readily to the changed situation. In 1948 the British withdrew from Burma, which became an independent republic. While Burma has followed a neutralist foreign policy, the Burmese have not had much internal peace. There have been several civil wars and sectionalist uprisings to plague the dictatorship imposed since 1962 by General Ne Win (nee win).

The Malay peninsula states were unified by Britain and, in 1957, made a self-governing monarchy within the British Commonwealth. Hostility between the Malays and the Chinese ethnic minority was deepened by the presence of a Chinese-supported Communist guerrilla movement between 1948 and 1960. An expanded federation of Malaysia was formed in 1962 but so great was the Malays' fear of the Chinese that Singapore (the most concentrated area of the Chinese) seceded from the federation in 1965.

Indonesia's population of over 120 million and its vast oil, tin, and rubber resources make it Southeast Asia's most important country. In 1949, after four years of struggle, the Indonesians won their freedom from Holland and Achmed Sukarno (soo-*kahr*-noh), hero of the independence movement, became President.

In time, Sukarno had himself made "president for life" and began an authoritarian system he termed "guided democracy." To bring more national unity to the 3,000 island republic, Sukarno embarked on an aggressive foreign policy which included attacks on Malaysian territory (1963–5), withdrawal from the United Nations (1965) and close ties to Communist China.

In September, 1965 the Indonesian Communists tried to seize the government. In the purge that followed their unsuccessful coup, some 300,000 Communists were killed. Sukarno was suspected of involvement in the Red plot and he was stripped of power by General Suharto (soo-*hahr*-toh), commander of the army. After Suharto became President in 1967, Indonesia resumed her U.N. membership and followed a pro-Western and anti-Chinese foreign policy.

Indochina became Southeast Asia's chief battleground. After World War II France made a determined effort to repossess Indochina. The Vietminh (vyet-*min*), a nationalist movement led by long-time Communist, Ho Chi Minh (ho-chee-min), successfully opposed this. With the French and their Indochinese allies receiving equipment from the United States and the Vietminh getting support from Russia and the Chinese Reds, the fighting continued from 1945 to 1954 when the Vietminh captured the French fort of Dienbienphux (*d'yen*-b'yen'foo).

At the Geneva Conference of 1954, in which Britain, the United States, Russia and Red China participated along with France and the Indochinese, Indochina was freed and split into segments: Laos and Cambodia became neutral states; North and South Vietnam were divided at the 17th parallel and elections were to be held in 1956 to create a single all-Vietnam government. Neither the U.S. nor South Vietnam signed this agreement and, due to their opposition, the promised 1956 election was not held.

Under Ho Chi Minh, North Vietnam became a typical Communist state. In South Vietnam, a new President, Ngo Dinh Diem (z'*yem*) provided a strong anti-Communist regime. However, within a few years the policies of Diem, a Catholic, irritated the Buddhist majority. As the 1960s began, Communists in South Vietnam, who were called "Viet Cong" (vyet-kong) by their enemies, started guerrilla warfare against the Diem government. Dissatisfaction with Diem culminated in his overthrow in October, 1963 by anti-Communist officers. South Vietnam then suffered a series of political crises until General Nguyen Van Thieu (thoo) was elected President in 1967.

INDONESIAN DEMONSTRATORS. Seeking union with the new Republic of Indonesia, students march in a 1950 demonstration against the Dutch-sponsored East Indonesian state. The banner above the procession reads, "Dissolve East Indonesia—Make It a Republic."

Thieu's undemocratic practices and rigged elections were criticized by many Americans but he did bring greater political stability.

As the Viet Cong menace grew so did American involvement. In 1954 the United States and seven other lands founded the Southeast Asian Treaty Organization (SEATO) which pledged aid to area victims of Communist aggression. The Eisenhower Administration sent financial help and several hundred military advisers to South Vietnam. By 1963 President Kennedy had raised this force to some 20,000 troops. When Communists began to attack U.S. soldiers, bases, and ships and as the conviction grew that the South Vietnamese regime would collapse without massive American support, the Johnson Administration escalated the U.S. commitment. By 1968, there were about 530,000 U.S. troops in Vietnam and air bombing of North Vietnam exceeded the World War II strikes over Germany. The United States was spending 30 billion dollars a year on a venture which had already cost some 40,000 American lives.

The Vietnam War became a crucial issue in U.S. presidential elections between 1964 and cited the "domino theory"–that Communist victory in Vietnam would lead to Marxist takeovers in Southeast Asia, to the injury of American interests. They also contended that the war was

FIGHTING MALARIA. Like many of the Southeast Asian states, Thailand needs improved health facilities. Here a Thai doctor, using a table borrowed from a nearby temple, examines a group of children to detect early symptoms of malaria. With UN help, malaria has been nearly eliminated in Thailand.

basically an attempt by North Vietnam to annex territory against the wishes of the South Vietnamese. Critics charged that the U.S. had no right to intervene in what they believed was essentially a civil war of no vital concern to Americans. The criticism had become so widespread by early 1968 that President Johnson announced he would not seek re-election, suspended bombings of most of North Vietnam and called for peace negotiations. Later in the year peace talks began in Paris among representatives of North and South Vietnam, the Viet Cong and the United States. As of mid-1972, however, the talks had gone on for almost four years without real accomplishment.

How much the Nixon Administration has reversed the Johnson policies is disputable. On the one hand, President Nixon planned for "Vietnamization" of the conflict, whereby the South Vietnamese would do all of the ground fighting. The number of U.S. troops in Vietnam was steadily reduced until there were fewer than 40,000 in September, 1972. On the other hand, Nixon repeatedly assured the Thieu regime of his support and contended that a U.S. defeat in Vietnam would be a catastrophic blow to American prestige. The war was widened in 1970 when U.S. forces were ordered briefly into Cambodia to destroy North Vietnamese supply depots there. American air attacks on North Vietnam were stepped up greatly to counter a full-scale North Vietnamese drive which began in April, 1972. In May, the United States mined the North Vietnamese chief port of Haiphong (high-*fong*) for the first time. This posed a threat to Russian and Chinese ships there but American relations with the two Communist powers were not worsened and the North Vietnamese drive against hard-pressed South Vietnam was slowed.

Chapter Check-up

1. What are the major countries of Southeast Asia?
2. What two Asiatic cultures influenced the countries of Southeast Asia?
3. Which European countries have played leading roles in Southeast Asia?
4. What resources and products made the colonies of Southeast Asia valuable to European nations?
5. How were the Asian colonies exploited by their European owners?
6. Why did World War II result in the end of European imperialism in Southeast Asia?
7. What are the arguments for and against American involvement in the Vietnam War?

Chapter 61

Religious Influence Is Dominant in the Culture of India and Southeast Asia

The people of India and Pakistan have two classical languages and well over seven hundred modern languages and dialects. The classical language of educated Indians, *Sanskrit,* was used for literature and philosophy, much as medieval Europeans used Latin. *Persian* was the classical language of the Moguls. The common people spoke hundreds of local languages and dialects, of which *Hindi,* developed from Sanskrit, was most widespread. An attempt to make Hindi the national language of India failed because people speaking other languages protested. Urdu, a

Krishna and the Serpent. The thousands of exploits of Krishna, as related in the *Mahabharata,* were favorite subjects of Indian artists of the Mogul period. Here we see Krishna subduing the serpent Kaliya, while Kaliya's wives plead for his life.

mixture of Sanskrit, Persian, and Turkish, is the official language of Pakistan.

The Hindu gods are very important in Indian literature, particularly in the two great epic poems written in Sanskrit between 200 and 300 A.D. The *Mahabharata* (see page 567) tells of the struggles of five heroic Pandava brothers to win the throne from their wicked cousins. The god Krishna helps the Pandavas overcome them in battle. The *Ramayana* (rah-*mah*-yuh-nuh) is the story of Prince Rama (*rah*-muh), an incarnation of the Hindu god Vishnu. He and his faithful wife Sita (*see*-tuh) are banished by his father to the forest for fourteen years. One day Sita is carried off by the demon king of Ceylon. Rama and his brother, helped by an army of monkeys, build a bridge of steppingstones to Ceylon, defeat the king, and rescue Sita. The story of Rama and Sita is one of India's most popular legends.

Tulsi Das (*toul*-see *dahs*), one of the greatest of the Hindi poets, lived during the time of Akbar and was devoted to the worship of Rama. He described the adventures of Rama in Hindi poetry, which became as well known to Indians as the Bible was to Englishmen. Storytellers carried the legends of Rama to the villages, where people could not read. Today moving pictures do the same job. India has one of the largest film industries in the world. The films are shown not only in big cities but also in the smallest villages. In recent years, a number of Indian films have been acclaimed for their excellence. The legends of Rama provide the themes for many of the moving pictures.

One of India's most famous playwrights was Kalidasa (kah-lee-*dah*-sah), sometimes called "the Shakespeare of India." He is also widely admired for his poetry. His best-known play, *Sakuntala* (suh-*koon*-tuh-lah), is named for its heroine, a beautiful maiden whose husband is bewitched so that he forgets her. But like nearly all Indian dramas, it has a happy ending. The spell is broken when the husband finds Sakuntala's ring in the body of a fish. The theme of *Sakuntala* is typical of the Indian interest in legend and fairy tales.

INDIAN DANCE AND MUSIC HAVE RELIGIOUS MEANING

Indian plays are well known for their unique music and dancing. The dancers use certain formal movements of the head and hands to tell their story. Their eyes show emotion, and their feet, jingling with hundreds of bells tied at the ankles, move in constant rhythm. Rajahs kept troupes of dancers for their amusement. Other troupes were commissioned to dance at temples in honor of the gods. Hindus believe that the gods themselves enjoy dancing. The temples in India are covered with carvings of dancing figures, and in statuary the gods are often depicted performing a dance.

Dancing girls in India belong to a special caste and begin their training when they are seven years old. By the time they are twelve they are ready to appear in public. They wear a short, tight blouse, a long, full skirt embroidered with gold

INDIAN DANCERS. The beautiful symbolic dances of India are quite unlike the dances of the Western world. Their subtle rhythms and gestures often portray religious tales and legends, such as those in the *Mahabharata*.

and silver, and heavy bracelets and earrings. Sometimes they also wear the *sari*, a long, brilliantly colored silk scarf that is draped around the body and over the head. A simpler version of this costume is the usual dress of most Indian women.

The traditions of Indian dancing spread to Southeast Asia and were influenced by Buddhism. The Buddhist dancers of Siam and the island of Bali are famous for their gilt headresses and vivid sarongs. American audiences enthusiastically acclaimed a Balinese troupe that appeared in New York City in 1957. In the Moslem adaptation of Indian dancing, human dancers are replaced by flat paper dolls that are made to act out dances and stories somewhat in the manner of marionettes.

Indian music is extremely intricate and beautiful. It has a scale of twenty-two notes instead of the twelve customary in Western music. Some of the notes are so much alike that an untrained ear can scarcely detect the difference between them. The music is divided into special patterns of melody and rhythm that express certain emotions, such as love, terror, anger, or surprise. In this way the music helps the dancer establish the mood she is seeking to create.

INDIAN ARCHITECTURE AND SCULPTURE HONORED THE GODS

The art and architecture of India, like that of medieval Europe, were inspired mainly by religion and reflect the reverence of the Indians for their gods. Even when poverty forced the people to live in simple mud huts, they created great temples to honor their deities. Among the best examples of Indian architecture are the shrines and temples of the Gupta period. These are mainly heavy, flat-roofed buildings that are decorated with carved animals, flowers, and figures of the gods. By the thirteenth century, however, architecture had become more complex. Buildings were constructed to much greater heights and were more elaborately decorated with marvelous carvings and sculpture.

The Moslems destroyed many Hindu temples when they conquered India. In their place they built beautiful mosques decorated with domes, minarets, and pointed arches. One of the most beautiful examples of this type of architecture is the Taj Mahal (tahj muh-*hahl*), which was created by a Moslem emperor as a tomb for his wife. It took 20,000 men eleven years to construct the tomb. The Moslems also introduced Persian painting, which looks much like that in medieval illuminated manuscripts.

Indian sculpture usually represented the gods. Much of it was carved on temple walls. Statues of the Buddha in bronze or stone showed a graceful, meditating figure seated cross-legged. His calm expression was supposed to instill peace in the worshiper. Statues of Siva often showed him dancing with joy. His many heads and arms expressed his divine power. (See the examples of such sculpture on pages 564, 565, and 568.)

These styles of Indian architecture and sculpture spread to Southeast Asia where, because of Moslem destruction in India, the best-preserved examples of Indian architecture are to be found today. Angkor Thom (*ang*-kor *tahm*), capital of the Cambodian kings, was built in the tenth century, deserted in the fourteenth, and then overgrown by jungle. French archaeologists discovered it in the nineteenth century. Angkor Thom was surrounded by a moat that was crossed by five causeways leading through five elaborate gates to a great terrace. Here the palace and temples were located. The main temple has tall, square towers, each of which bears the four faces of a Buddhist saint.

In Java, the Dutch discovered a lost temple which had been a center for Buddhist pilgrims in the eighth and ninth centuries. Today the traveler can still inspect the scenes from Indian mythology carved on the fifteen hundred panels of the lower terraces. The upper terraces contain no decoration because they represent the higher world of abstract ideas. On the roof of the temple rest seventy-two bell-shaped domes. Each dome is pierced by a hole through which the visitor can observe a statue of Buddha meditating in the darkness within.

Chapter Check-up

1. What is Sanskrit and how has it influenced the development of languages in India and Pakistan?
2. What are the two great epic poems of Indian literature?
3. Who was the most famous Indian playwright and for what is he known?
4. How are Indian music and dancing influenced by religion?
5. How does Indian music differ from Western music?
6. What is the most important influence in Indian art and architecture?
7. What is the Taj Mahal? Is it typical of Indian architecture?
8. Why are the best-preserved examples of Indian architecture and sculpture found in Southeast Asia rather than India itself?

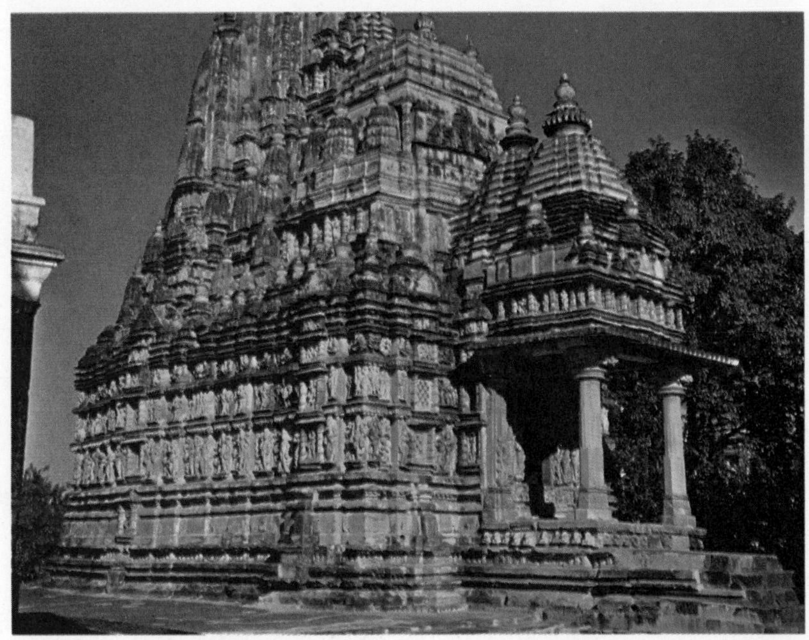

HINDU TEMPLE. Of the many Hindu temples found at Khajraho, a village in central India, this is the best known. Its intricate carvings and design are typical of Indian architecture.

India and Southeast Asia: SYNOPSIS

The foundations of Indian society were laid about 2000 B.C. when Aryan invaders introduced the caste system, a division of people into rigid classes. This was especially supported by the Brahmans, or priestly caste. Indian Brahamanism eventually became the Hinduism of today. From the fourth to the sixth centuries A.D. India had its Golden Age under the Gupta emperors. Their empire fell before Moslem invaders, Moslem power reaching its height in the fifteenth and sixteenth centuries. Bitter hatred has existed between Moslems and Hindus because their customs and beliefs are so different.

In the eighteenth century the British gained control over India after defeating the French at the Battle of Plassey. India became the "brightest jewel" in the imperial British Crown but Indians followed the pacifist Gandhi in demanding freedom. Independence was finally achieved in 1947 but under terms which created two states,—the Moslem nation of Pakistan being separated from India. Many difficulties have since afflicted India and Pakistan, for both suffer acutely from poverty, illiteracy and overpopulation. Moreover, the constant hostility between the two nations has flared into three brief wars. The most recent conflict occurred in 1971 when India quickly defeated Pakistan, making it possible for what had been "East Pakistan" to form the new country of Bangladesh.

Southeast Asia began to fall under European control in the sixteenth century. During World War II the British, French and Dutch were driven from the region by the Japanese. When these Europeans tried to recover their colonial possessions after the war, they met with strong resistance from the native peoples. In 1948–9 the British withdrew from Burma, the Dutch were forced out of Indonesia and the French were engaged in a bitter conflict in Indochina which ended in 1954 with the creation of the independent states of Laos, Cambodia and North and South Vietnam. The United States became heavily involved in military support of anti-Communist regimes against what the American government has felt were Communist aggressions under chiefly North Vietnamese direction. This undeclared, frustrating American war in Vietnam has resulted in enormous dissension among Americans.

The religions of Hindu India and mainly Buddhist Southeast Asia have been the chief influence in shaping the area's culture. Some of the finest examples of Indian sculpture and architecture may be found in parts of Southeast Asia which Hindus also penetrated.

Important People

How have each of the following influenced the story of India or Southeast Asia?

Buddha	Jawaharlal Nehru	Bao Dai	Ne Win
Asoka	Mohammed Ali Jinnah	Ho Chi-Minh	Tulsi Das
Akbar the Great	Rama IV	Achmed Sukarno	Kalidasa
Mahatma Gandhi	Mohammed Ayub Khan	Indira Gandhi.	Nguyen Van Thieu

Terms

Be sure that you understand clearly the meaning of each of the following:

Brahman	monsoon	Spice Islands
caste system	exploitation	Hinduism
untouchables	Moguls	Sanskrit
Buddhism	Gupta period	Hindi
four Noble Truths	non-violent opposition	Taj Mahal
Domino Theory	Green Revolution	Bengali

Questions for Discussion and Review

1. In what way does his religion encourage the Hindu to lead a good life?
2. How did the caste system give stability to Indian culture on the one hand, and retard the development of a modern civilization on the other?
3. How did British rule benefit India? In what ways was it harmful?
4. Why did the Europeans fail to hold their Southeast Asian colonies?
5. Why does a period of strong nationalism usually follow a period of strong imperialism?
6. How do you feel about the idea behind the slogan "Asia for the Asians"? Why?
7. How would you suggest that India might meet her pressing educational, social, economic, and political problems?
8. In your opinion, was it wise or unwise to partition India in 1948?
9. To what extent should the United States become involved in the affairs of South East Asia?
10. How has religion influenced Indian art, music, and literature?

Interesting Things to Do

1. Make a map of Asia showing India and the countries of Southeast Asia. Label the important mountain ranges, rivers, and cities.
2. Make a chart of the countries of Southeast Asia. List the names of all the countries in the first column. For each country list the capital, the area, the population, the resources, the products, the type of government, and the leaders of today.
3. Prepare a poster to help teach respect for different religions.
4. Make a graph or pie chart showing the relative number of followers of each of the world's great religions. Use an encyclopedia or an almanac as your reference book.
5. Prepare a travel poster or booklet describing and illustrating the sights one might see on a trip through India or Southeast Asia.
6. Explain the story and play for the class some selections from the musical comedy "The King and I."
7. Prepare and present to the class an oral report on some of the rituals and beliefs of Hinduism or Buddhism.
8. Organize and present an informal debate. *Resolved*, That British occupation and control was beneficial to India's development.
9. Imagine that you were an Indian reporter and a follower of Gandhi. Write an editorial describing this great leader, his philosophy, and his ideas on achieving independence for India.
10. Add to or begin your "Who's Who in World History" series by writing brief biographies of one or more of the important leaders of India and Southeast Asia.

Interesting Reading about India and Southeast Asia

*Bothwell, Jean, *Cobras, Cows, and Courage*, Coward-McCann. Depicts the life of a peasant in northern India.

Bro. Marguerite, *Indonesia: Land of Challenge*, Harper & Row.

*Bryce, L. Winifred, *India Land of Rivers*, Nelson.

Burling, Robbins, *Hill Farms and Padi Fields: Life in Mainland Southeast Asia*, Prentice-Hall.

Cranston, Ruth, *World Faith: The Story of the Religions of the United Nations*, Harper & Row.

*Eaton, Jeanette, *Gandhi, Fighter Without a Sword*, Morrow.

*Feldman, Herbert, *The Land and People of Pakistan*, Macmillan.

Fersh, Seymour, *India and South Asia*, Macmillan.

Hammer, Ellen, *Vietnam: Yesterday and Today*, Holt, Rinehart and Winston. Its history, peoples, current dilemma.

*Modak, Manorama, *Land and The People of India*, Lippincott.

Rama Rau, Santha, *This Is India*, Harper & Row.

*Rankin, L. S., *Daughter of the Mountains*, Viking. Adventure story with a Tibetan heroine and setting.

Romulo, Carlos P., *Crusade in Asia: Philippine Victory*, Day. Description of a country's fight against communism.

Schultz, George F., *Vietnamese Legends*, Tuttle.

*Trease, Geoffrey, *Young Traveler in India and Pakistan*, Dutton. A travel account of modern India and Pakistan.

Trumbull, Robert, *The Scrutable East: Southeast Asia Today*, McKay.

Wiser, William and Charlotte, *Behind Mud Walls, 1930–1960*, University of California. A sympathetic account of Indian village life.

Zinkin, Taya, *India*, Walker.

———, *The Story of Gandhi*, Criterion.

* Indicates easy reading

The Far East has many faces, but none more significant than these two ladies pausing on a winter's day in Japan. Dignity and decorum are reflected both in the parasols they hold and the gesture of their bodies as they pass the time.

Part 19
THE FAR EAST
ANCIENT CIVILIZATIONS, MODERN PROBLEMS

THE FAR EAST

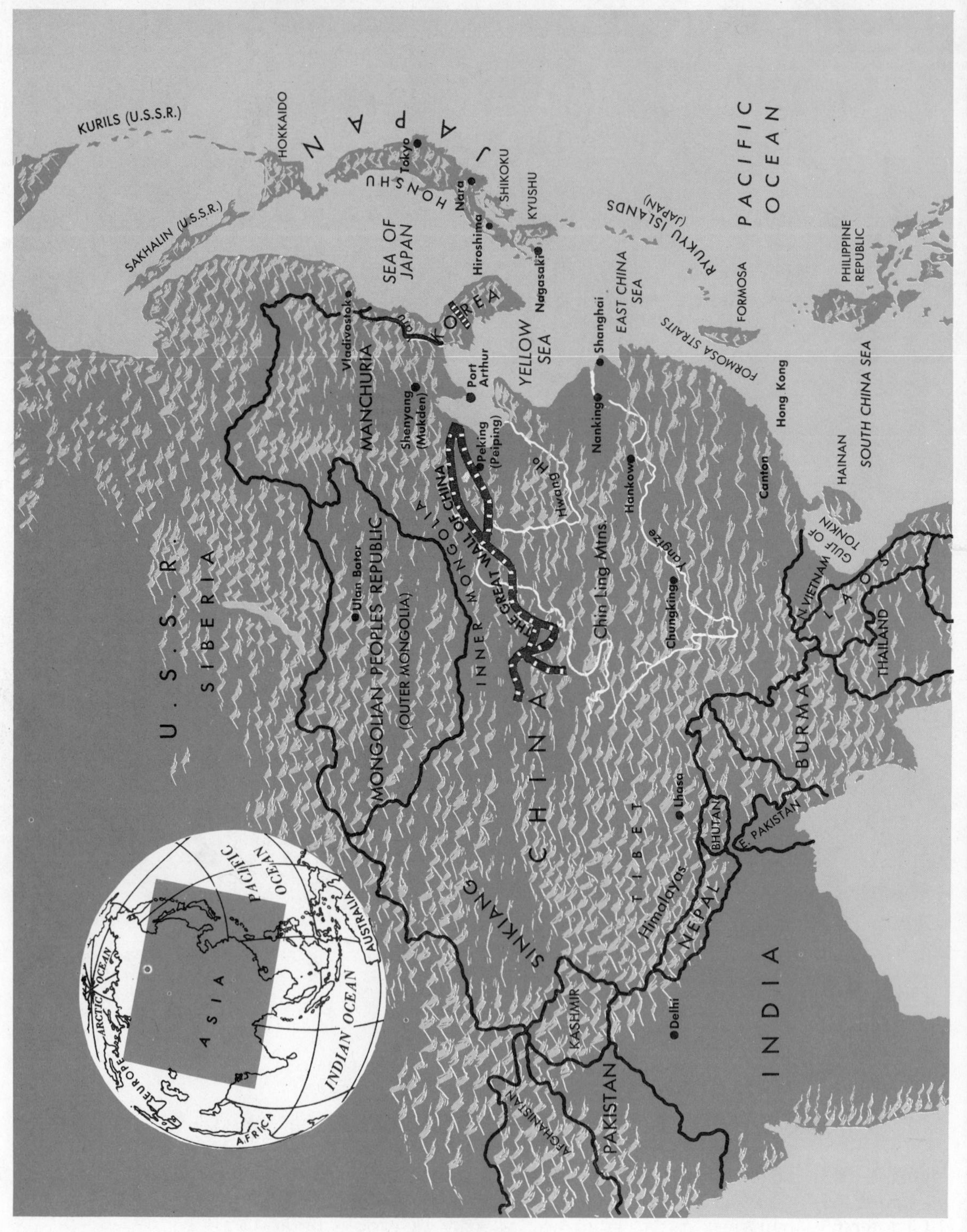

KURILS (U.S.S.R.)
HOKKAIDO
JAPAN
Tokyo
HONSHU
Nara
SHIKOKU
KYUSHU
Hiroshima
Nagasaki
SAKHALIN (U.S.S.R.)
SEA OF JAPAN
KOREA
Vladivostok
MANCHURIA
Port Arthur
Shenyang (Mukden)
Peking (Peiping)
YELLOW SEA
Shanghai
EAST CHINA SEA
RYUKYU ISLANDS (JAPAN)
PACIFIC OCEAN
FORMOSA
FORMOSA STRAITS
PHILIPPINE REPUBLIC
Nanking
Hankow
Hong Kong
SOUTH CHINA SEA
HAINAN
Canton
Hwang Ho
Yangtze
GULF OF TONKIN
N. VIETNAM
LAOS
THAILAND
BURMA
Chungking
Chin Ling Mtns.
THE GREAT WALL OF CHINA
INNER MONGOLIA
CHINA
U. S. S. R.
SIBERIA
Ulan Bator
MONGOLIAN PEOPLES REPUBLIC
(OUTER MONGOLIA)
TIBET
Lhasa
BHUTAN
E. PAKISTAN
Himalayas
NEPAL
SINKIANG
INDIA
Delhi
KASHMIR
PAKISTAN
AFGHANISTAN
ARCTIC OCEAN
EUROPE
ASIA
AFRICA
INDIAN OCEAN
PACIFIC OCEAN
AUSTRALIA

The Far East: GEOGRAPHIC SETTING

China is the heartland of the Far East, covering about one-fourth of the continent of Asia. It includes the provinces of Manchuria, Inner Mongolia, and Sinkiang. Tibet is also commonly considered part of China.

In land area, China is approximately the size of the United States, but its population is over three times as large. The vast majority of the Chinese people are crowded into the lowland areas along the east coast, especially in the river valleys. Several regions number more than a thousand inhabitants per square mile. Yet even in these densely populated areas, most of the people make a living by farming.

The Hwang-Ho (Yellow) River made north China an early cradle of civilization, and it is still a rich agricultural land and the home of millions of farmers. More important today, however, is the region farther south, along the fertile basin of the Yangtze River. This area is one of the world's great "rice bowls," and recently it has become important industrially, too. Some of China's most important cities, such as Hankow, Nanking, and Shanghai, are located on the Yangtze.

West China is a region that has remained isolated from the rest of the country because of its extensive mountains. While the mountains have for generations been a hindrance to progress, they proved a blessing during World War II when Japanese invaders began to move westward along the Yangtze. The Chinese government moved to Chungking, and millions of refugees came into the protected region.

Southeast of Manchuria is the five-hundred-mile-long peninsula of Korea. The Yalu River forms a large part of Korea's land border with China. Three-fourths of the country is mountainous and there is little space for farming. Wild, forested mountains with snowy peaks cover the northeast. But fertile coastal plains slope down the southwest side of the peninsula to the Yellow Sea. This comparatively small coastal section is the main agricultural region of Korea.

To the east of Korea lies the island chain of Japan. It consists of more than three thousand islands, but most of the population lives on the four largest, Hokkaido (hah-*ky*-doe), Honshu, Shikoku (shih-*ko*-koo), and Kyushu (*kyoo*-shoo). The islands are covered with steep mountains and volcanoes, a number of which still erupt occasionally. Earthquakes are frequent, and in the spring and early autumn severe windstorms sweep northward from the China Sea. Aside from the severity of these natural phenomena, however, the climate of Japan is similar to that of our own Atlantic Coast. The northern islands are chilly like Maine, while the southern islands are sub-tropical like Florida.

There are many mountain ranges, which give Japan its famous dramatic beauty. The mountains take up so much room that only about one-seventh of the land is fit for farming. Japan is no larger than California, but it has more than half as many people as the whole United States. Arable land is very scarce and is farmed intensively, as is true throughout most of the Far East.

The Far East: PERSPECTIVE

Until the sixteenth century the existence of Japan remained unknown to Europeans. Then, one day in 1542, a Portuguese ship was sailing across the China Sea when a severe storm blew up from the south. The vessel, swept off course by high winds, was driven northward. Soon the Portuguese sailors found themselves on a strange island that proved to be one of the Japanese islands south of Kyushu. The discovery opened up new markets for European traders, who began to make

regular voyages to Japan. In the same century China was opened to the first European traders (although it had been open to Arab and Indian merchants much earlier). In the late nineteenth century Korea, which had become known as the "hermit kingdom" finally permitted foreigners within her borders.

In the years since the various Far Eastern countries first came into contact with the Western world, their importance in international affairs has increased enormously. Within the last two generations, American troops have been in conflict with Japanese, Chinese and Koreans. For three years, in the 1950s, little Korea was the focus of world attention. Mainland China has become an atomic power and Japan one of the three greatest industrial nations on earth.

Why have China, Korea and Japan become, almost overnight, countries that play a crucial role in world affairs? Part of the answer, of course, lies in improved communications and in the ships and airplanes that can circle the globe in a few days or hours. Because of the speed of modern travel, the Far East is no longer the remote region it once was. The rest of the answer lies in the historical forces that have brought these countries into the limelight of present-day events. In Part 19 you will learn about some of those forces and why they have created modern problems for three ancient civilizations.

CHAPTER 62

China Struggles to Become a Modern Nation and Breaks with Ancient Traditions

THE TEACHINGS OF CONFUCIUS AND LAO-TSU ARE THE FOUNDATION OF CHINESE CIVILIZATION

China's civilization is very old. The story of China begins shortly after the stories of Egypt and Mesopotamia. The civilizations that flourished along the Nile and the Tigris-Euphrates have long since vanished. Until very recently, however, the civilization of the Chinese farmers who settled in the valley of the Hwang Ho had seen little change in over three thousand years.

Archaeologists have concluded that by 1400 B.C. the Chinese had developed a written language, an organized government, and a religion which involved a kind of ancestor worship. One after another, various dynasties (families of rulers) rose to power. From the tenth to the third century B.C., the emperors of the Chou (jo) dynasty ruled the Hwang Ho Valley. They fought hostile Mongols, including Tartars and Huns, who swept down from their arid plains to invade the fertile river valley. Often the princes of border states fought one another or the emperor.

During this period there lived in China two great philosophers whose ideas helped shape the lives of generations of Chinese. Their names were Confucius and Lao-tsu (low-*dzuh*). Although they lived at the same time, their teachings were very different. But the ideas of each strongly influenced Chinese religion, government, education, and family life.

Confucius upheld the traditional Chinese respect for the family. Confucius was a scholarly aristocrat who lived in the fifth century B.C. As a young man, he diligently studied all the books of Chinese poetry, history, and philosophy that he could find. Then he began to lecture on these subjects. When Confucius was in his early twenties, he was already an extremely popular teacher. His pupils were not children, but young men who wished to learn about standards of conduct, government, and their great ancestors.

One of the most important of the traditions which Confucius taught was respect for the family. The Chinese were a practical people to whom the family was very important. A Chinese family then, as now, usually included a grandfather or grandmother, all their sons, the sons' wives, and all their children. The practical advantage of this arrangement was that the larger the family, the more hands there were to work the soil or look after the family business. The land, wages, or profits of each member belonged to the whole family. Rich members considered it their duty to take care of their poor relations. The Chinese view of family responsibilities was "Contribute all you can, take only what you must."

Another advantage in having a large family under one roof was that there were more members to worship the family ancestors. The men thought of themselves as links in an endless chain that bound all generations together. A man obeyed his father while he was alive and honored his grave when he died. His own sons then gave him the same obedience and honor. If a man had no sons, he often adopted a poor relation to keep the family line unbroken. A woman was not considered equal to a man; she lived with her husband's family and taught her sons to respect their father's ancestors rather than hers.

The presence of so many people under one roof made order and authority necessary. Confucius provided that order by establishing a complex set of rules that told how each member of the family should behave. The sons obeyed the father, the wives obeyed their husbands, children obeyed their parents, the younger always obeyed the older. As a sign of respect, wives bowed to their husbands and fathers-in-law, and children bowed to their elders. Everyone was expected to behave with justice and consideration. Confucius instructed men "Never to do to others what you would not like them to do to you," a teaching that closely resembles the Golden Rule.

CONFUCIUS. An old print shows the great teacher who is remembered for his lasting influence on Chinese life and for his wise maxims. A man of profound wisdom, Confucius once said: "Learning, undigested by thought, is labor lost; thought, unassisted by learning, is perilous."

The principles laid down by Confucius regulated a wide variety of social customs. They were designed not only to keep peace and order but also to maintain everyone's dignity, that is, to save "face." Public shame was considered one of the

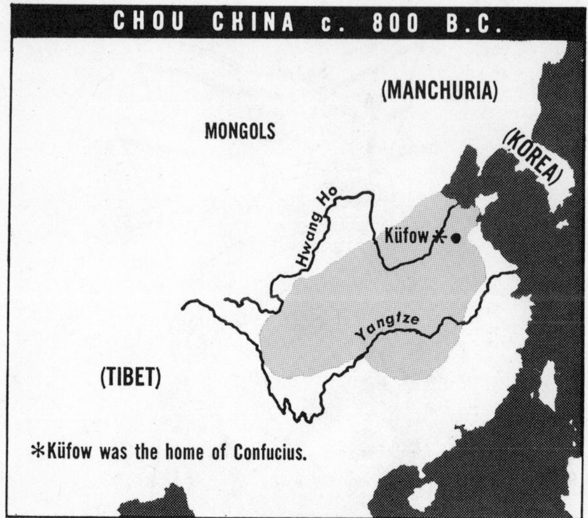

worst evils that could befall a man. Teachers were cautioned never to criticize a pupil before others for fear the pupil would lose face. It became the custom that if a government official had to be removed from office, he was not fired but was given a "vacation." He took the hint and did not return.

Confucius cautioned his followers to present at all times a calm, pleasant appearance to the world, no matter what their emotions might be. Any show of violent anger, strong affection, or deep sorrow involved a loss of dignity because it showed that a man had lost control of himself. The dignity of the family was even more important than that of the individual. Confucian rules insist that the family stand by all its members in public. Likewise, no individual must do anything to tarnish the family name.

Confucius encouraged the Chinese to respect the emperor. Confucius believed that peace and harmony would prevail throughout China if all Chinese looked upon themselves as members of one family. The nation would then prosper if each person behaved according to his position in the "family." The emperor was the father who should treat his children, the people, with justice and kindness. If he set a good example, they in turn would become obedient, respectful, model subjects.

The ruler of the state of Lu, impressed by these teachings, made Confucius the minister of crime. According to legend, Confucius ended crime in Lu and inspired virtue in all its citizens. Unfortunately, the lord of a neighboring state feared that virtue would make Lu so strong that it would become a threat to his own province. He sent a troupe of dancing girls, musicians, and fine horses to the ruler of Lu to distract his attention from Confucius. Their performances resembled those of a modern circus. The ruse succeeded. Confucius began to lose his power and influence, and he eventually was forced to give up his post. For the next thirteen years he wandered from state to state offering his services to various princes, but no one had a place for him. He died believing that he was a failure, but his disciples

CEREMONIAL VESSEL. Fashioned in the twelfth century B.C., this bronze vessel was used in the ritual of ancestor worship. It is believed to have contained the wine used in the ceremony.

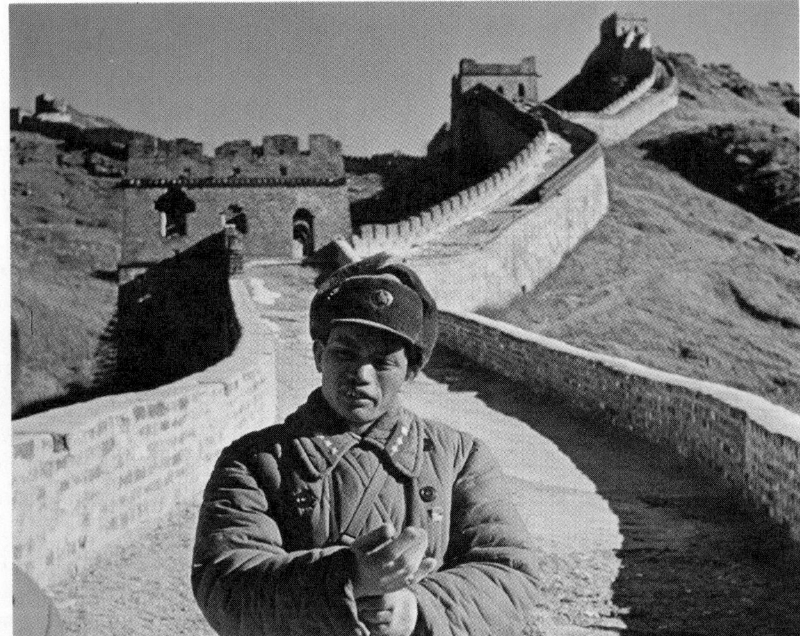

GREAT WALL OF CHINA. The great wall, built in the third century B.C. by the First Emperor of China, extended for 1,500 miles. Although it was twenty-five feet high and had watchtowers at regular intervals, it proved to be of only slight military value.

wrote down all his teachings. The Confucian classics were widely read and taught. Gradually Confucian teachings became the foundation of Chinese life. Men built temples in the philosopher's honor and worshiped him as if he were a god.

Knowledge of the Confucian classics was the path to success. About two hundred years after Confucius' death, the ruler of the warlike state of *Ch'in,* from which the name China comes, rose to power. He founded the Ch'in dynasty and called himself the First Emperor of China. He confiscated the weapons of the nobles and made them move to his capital where he could watch them. He taxed the peasants heavily and forced thousands of them to build the Great Wall across the northwestern border to protect China from the Mongols. It was said that each stone of the wall represented a man who had died of whipping or hunger.

When Confucian scholars protested against such cruel treatment, the First Emperor beheaded them and burned all the books that were influenced by Confucian ideas. For a time it seemed that the work of Confucius might be blotted out of Chinese history. But when the First Emperor died, civil war broke out. A farm boy led a peasant army and finally gained control of the country. He became the first emperor of the Han (hahn) dynasty (206 B.C.–220 A.D.).

During the Han dynasty the principles of Confucius triumphed. The Han emperors claimed that because they had won the war, they had heaven's favor (they called themselves "sons of heaven"). Although the Han emperors ruled as despots, they used their power to serve the people. They established government bureaus to take charge of the two functions in which the people needed help most, flood control and military defense. Officials were appointed to run the bureaus and to represent the imperial government in the provinces. These officials drafted peasants to build dams and dikes and to dig irrigation canals. They also gave seed to the peasants to encourage agricultural production. To protect their land, the emperor sent imperial armies on campaigns against invading Mongols and Tibetans.

The Han emperors wisely allowed the provincial officials freedom to follow local customs whenever possible, instead of continuing the rigid control that had been the policy of the First Emperor. However, the Han emperors sent out inspectors (as Charlemagne and Henry II later did) to see that no official became too powerful. Thus the emperors, like the good father in Confucian tradition, looked after their people.

The Han emperors realized that they needed competent men to serve as their officials. They devised a system for determining the "worth" of applicants for government posts. Confucius had taught the qualities that made a man worthy: virtue, wisdom, dignity, and self-discipline. The emperors decided that candidates for government office should pass an examination on the teachings of Confucius.

A young scholar was required to master all the Confucian classics. Often he had to memorize long passages. After years of hard study he could take the annual examination that was held in each district. If he passed, he rose in status and was allowed to wear a blue gown instead of the short coat and trousers worn by the peasants. After more study, he could take an examination held in each province every three years. If he passed that, he would be ready for a fairly important post. If he passed a final, even more difficult examination, given every five years in the capital, he was presented to the emperor himself for questioning. Few candidates got that far, but if they did, they received a high government post and great honor. This method of choosing officials by examination was much like the American civil service system. On the whole it worked well and was used in China until 1911.

Tilling Rice Fields. For centuries the Chinese peasant has planted and gathered rice in the same manner. The backbreaking labor is done by a coolie who is often aided by all the members of his family.

Lao-tsu offered solace to China's masses. Another great philosopher, Lao-tsu, lived in China at the same time as Confucius. He was also a famous scholar and teacher, and his ideas have had great influence on Chinese thought. Lao-tsu, whose name may be translated "Old Scholar," is said to have been court librarian in the province of Chou. According to tradition, the young reformer, Confucius, met Lao-tsu when he was sent to deposit some books in the royal library. Confucius was surprised to learn that Lao-tsu refused to support his suggested reforms of certain laws. In fact, Lao-tsu rebuked Confucius for his efforts to reform society, which he said would introduce "disorder into the nature of man." Lao-tsu has often been criticized for shunning reforms and withdrawing into "convenient irresponsibility."

The ideal of life, said Lao-tsu, is inactivity and passivity. These, he said, can be learned by contemplation of nature. Water is strong by being weak; the soft overcomes the hard, the weak the strong. For a man even to defend himself from injury was against the principles taught by Lao-tsu. "To them that are good, I am good; to them that are not good, I am also good," he declared. Thus, over five hundred years before the time of Jesus, a Chinese philosopher told the world that it is best to return good for evil.

Humility was also a virtue strongly emphasized by Lao-tsu. "He who overcomes others is strong; he who overcomes himself is mighty." Only as one learns to claim no credit and to exert no authority can one accomplish great things: "Keep behind and thou shalt inevitably be kept in front."

Lao-tsu also taught the value of frugality, or being thrifty. He believed that as strength comes from weakness and prominence comes from humility, so liberality comes from frugality. Lao-tsu said, "The wise man does not accumulate. The

THE FORBIDDEN CITY. Peking consists of two parts, the Outer or Chinese City and the Tartar City, each of which is surrounded by a wall. This view shows the part of the Tartar City known as the Forbidden City, because at one time only the emperor and his family were allowed within its walls. A city has existed on the site of Peking since the eighth century B.C. The present city was established in the thirteenth century as Kublai Khan's capital.

more he expends for others, the more doth he possess of his own; the more he giveth to others, the more hath he for himself."

Taoism became an established religion. Lao-tsu made no attempt to found a religion. Indeed, he did not believe in temples, ritual, and priests. He advised his followers to achieve harmony with Tao (dow), the law of the universe. To Lao-tsu, Tao was the supreme power and governing principle of the universe, not a personal being or God.

Lao-tsu practiced his beliefs. He spent the rest of his life following Tao. Then one day he disappeared into the mountains of the West and was never heard of again. According to legend, before he passed the last outpost of the empire, the gatekeeper asked him to write down his wisdom so that it would not be lost. Lao-tsu did so, and his book became the Bible of his millions of followers, who are called *Taoists*. His teachings appealed especially to the poorer people because the precepts he laid down seemed to make wealth, power, and position unimportant.

Gradually Taoism changed from a noble philosophy to a religion of ritual, superstition, and magic. Men began to look upon Lao-tsu not as a human teacher of ethics but as a god who would give them eternal life. They built temples to him and to lesser gods of nature. Many men found it difficult to live according to Lao-tsu's teachings, so instead they tried to follow Tao by buying charms and magic potions (such as powdered dragon's teeth). For centuries, Taoism consoled millions of Chinese for failure in worldly affairs and gave them hope for a better future life.

Scholars were the most respected of China's four classes of society. Gradually the people of China became divided into four traditional classes. Because they honored scholarship so highly and made it the path to government office and wealth, they considered scholars to be the first class. Even an impoverished scholar was of higher rank than a rich but uneducated man.

The second class of society was made up of landholders, both nobles and peasants. Instead of spending their time fighting and hunting as the nobles of medieval Europe did, Chinese nobles often became scholars, poets, painters, and philosophers. Because usually only nobles had the leisure to study, they were the candidates for government office. The peasants often rented their land from the nobles. They were free men, but it was their hard work that supported the comfortable life and supplied the luxuries enjoyed by the officials and the emperor.

The third class in Chinese society was composed of craftsmen, hired farmhands, and servants. Many craftsmen, such as carpenters, cooks, and stone masons, belonged to district guilds like the guilds of medieval Europe.

The fourth and lowest class were the merchants. Although many merchants were able men who amassed considerable wealth, they were barred from taking the examinations for government office. According to Confucian teachings, gentlemen were to think of virtue, not money-making.

Confucianism has helped keep Chinese society stable. After the collapse of the Han dynasty in the third century A.D., China became divided into three kingdoms. At this time Huns and Mongols invaded the land, and there was almost constant warfare. Disorder and chaos continued for four hundred years. During this troubled time many Chinese turned to the teachings of Buddha, which had been introduced into their land by missionaries from India. (You will recall that Buddha had taught that man could escape earthly miseries by overcoming his desires and selfish impulses.) Buddhism became very popular in China. It did not, however, replace Confucianism or Taoism. Most converts to Buddhism simply added the new teachings to their list of religious beliefs.

Of the three sets of beliefs, those of Confucius have probably been most influential in the lives of the Chinese people. The respect for tradition and authority which he stressed has tended to keep China's society stable throughout her long history. Confucian emphasis on the importance of the family has had a similar effect. China has seen rulers come and go, but the outlook of the Chinese people and the basic pattern of their lives remained virtually unchanged right up to the twentieth century.

CHINA CAME INTO CONTACT WITH THE WEST

Medieval China produced a brilliant culture. In the seventh century A.D. order was restored in China by a strong new emperor who began the T'ang (tahng) dynasty. Under the T'ang emperors China became the most civilized state in the world. (It was at this time that Europe was experiencing the Dark Ages.) The emperors restored the government and based it on the Confucian principles that had been developed during the Han dynasty. They rebuilt dikes and canals and encouraged improvements in agriculture and handicrafts. Chinese crafts-

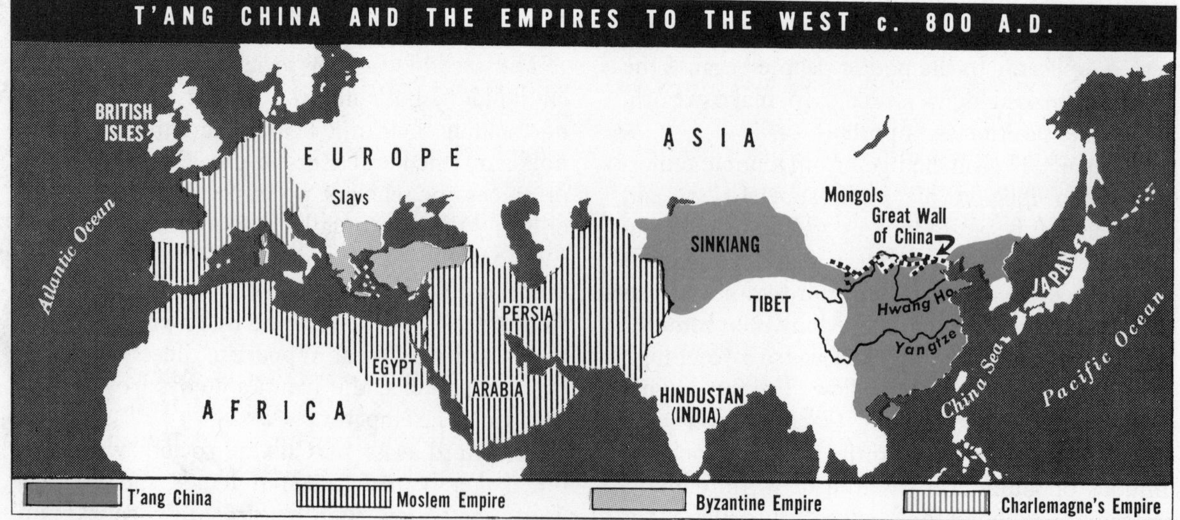

men wove beautiful garments of silk and made fine pottery and porcelain. During the T'ang dynasty, the Chinese invented gunpowder and introduced a method of printing from carved wood blocks. The earliest printed books known were produced in China during the T'ang dynasty. Scholars wrote the history of China and poets produced outstanding lyrics that have lasted over a thousand years. The T'ang emperors expanded their empire to include Korea, Tibet, and northern India. Conquered peoples sent yearly tribute to the Chinese capital.

During the Sung (soong) dynasty (960–1279), rich cities grew up along the Yangtze Valley. Merchants exchanged the tea of South China for the horses of the Mongols. Skillful craftsmen made chests, screens, and bowls that were intricately decorated with red and gold lacquers. Chinese artists produced landscape paintings unequaled in beauty anywhere else in the world.

China's brilliant medieval civilization came to an end in the thirteenth century when the Mongols, led by the famous Genghiz Khan and his grandson, Kublai Khan, swept through China. Kublai Khan built a great empire in the Far East and established his capital at the city of Cambaluc, which is the site of modern Peking (see the map above). The court created by Kublai Khan at the capital was world renowned for its brilliance, and attracted many visitors. (You may recall that Marco Polo was for a time in the employ of Kublai Khan).

The Mongol rulers were known as the Yüan (yew-*ahn*) dynasty. In the fourteenth century they were overthrown and the power of the native Chinese emperors was restored. The emperors of the new Ming dynasty (1368–1644) did their best to eradicate all traces of Mongol influence in China. The Ming dynasty is known for its very delicate and beautiful porcelain ware.

The Manchus established China's last great dynasty. Northeast of the Great Wall of China is the area known as Manchuria. Here a group of tribes, called Manchus, had been steadily gaining strength. In the middle of the seventeenth century they defeated the last of the Ming emperors and seized control of China. The Manchus established the last great line of Chinese emperors, the Ch'ing dynasty (1644–1912).

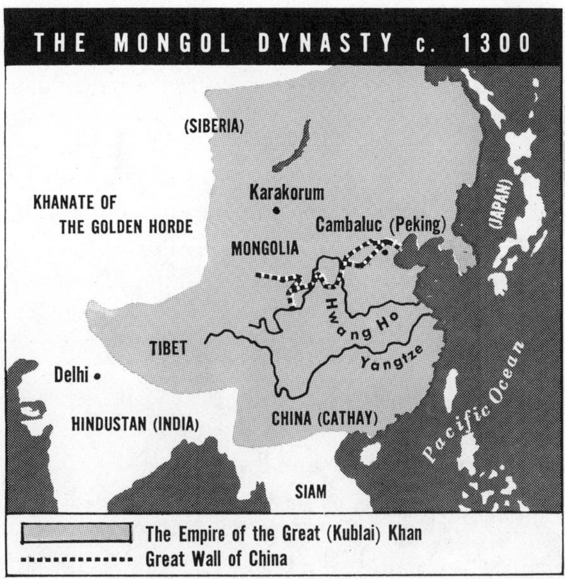

The Manchus made little change in the Chinese pattern of government, and they always remained separate from the people they ruled. They had their own laws and special privileges. Naturally, the Manchu government was not popular with the people. By the middle of the nineteenth century it had grown dishonest and indifferent. There were numerous revolts against it. In the greatest of these, the Taiping (ty-*ping*) Rebellion, millions of people on both sides of the conflict were killed by violence and butchery.

The Western world and Japan made demands on China. Until modern times the Chinese had little contact with the Western world except through Dutch, Spanish, and Portuguese seamen, who had first gone to China to trade in the sixteenth century. Then, in the nineteenth century, when China was going through disturbances at home, great Western powers demanded territory or greater trading privileges. Twice in the last half of the nineteenth century China found herself at war with Great Britain over trading rights. In both the wars China had to yield.

Other nations did not wish to be left behind in the race to secure trading advantages in the Far East. The French established an empire in Indo-

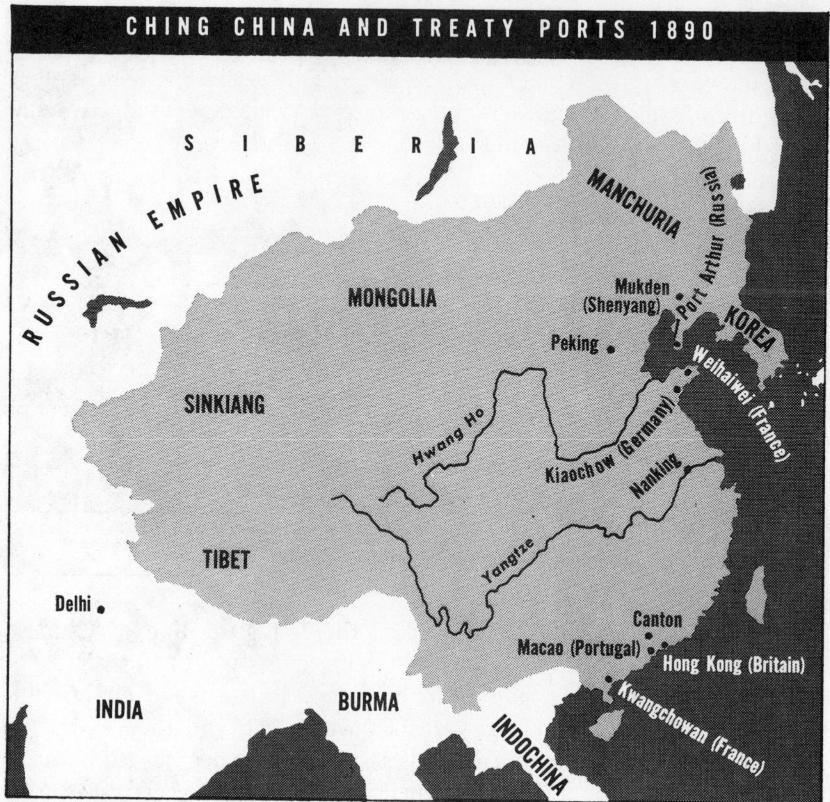

china. Russia seized part of Manchuria. China was forced to grant to Russia, France, Germany, and the United States, the right to trade in certain ports called "treaty ports." China itself began to be divided into "spheres of influence." One of the great powers, such as France, Britain, or Germany, would gain control of all the railroads, mines, and other commercial assets in a province. They would then make special arrangements to benefit their own merchants and exclude those of foreign nations.

In the last half of the nineteenth century, China's government was in the hands of the dowager empress Tz'u Hsi (tsoo *shee*). This highly educated, strong-minded woman had entered the palace to serve the emperor. Soon she became his favorite wife. Her son inherited the throne at the age of five, and she ruled as regent until his mysterious death. Then she managed to obtain the throne, illegally, for her three-year-old nephew so that she could remain the real ruler of China.

Tz'u Hsi hated the foreign nations because of the humiliating treaties they had forced on China. Yet she refused to adopt modern ways. Although China was in desperate need of a fleet of modern warships, Tz'u Hsi decided that it would be too expensive. Instead she spent the money to rebuild the Summer Palace. The Chinese promptly named it "the Chinese Navy."

The Sino-Japanese War (1894) showed that Tz'u Hsi had made a serious mistake. Japan's modern navy made short work of the old-fashioned Chinese war junks. As a result of the war, China lost Korea and Formosa to Japan. In desperation the dowager empress reluctantly accepted loans from Britain, France, and Germany to build up Chinese transportation and industry. As security on the loans, she gave them the right to collect all Chinese customs for themselves.

China's resentment of foreign nations led to the Boxer Rebellion. Tz'u Hsi's nephew, the emperor, wanted to put a stop to China's decline.

His advisers, who had been educated in the West, convinced him that China should be modernized so that she could hold her own with foreign nations. The emperor began the Hundred Days of Reform. Because the reforms would have meant less power and money for the Manchu officials, however, Tz'u Hsi seized the emperor and imprisoned him. Then she beheaded several of his officials and canceled the reforms. The Chinese government became more conservative than ever.

The United States wanted to prevent further carving up of China. Our government insisted that, except for privileges already given, all foreign nations from then on should receive the same treatment in China. Partly because the great powers could not come to any other agreement with one another about their different claims in China, they said they would follow the policy of the United States, which was called the Open Door Policy.

The Open Door Policy did little to restore China's dignity or make foreigners in China more popular. Tz'u Hsi encouraged a secret society called the *Boxers* to riot against all foreigners and Chinese Christians. During the Boxer Rebellion in 1900, mobs killed foreign missionaries and attacked the foreign legations in Peking. The combined forces of the Western nations finally put down the revolt. Tz'u Hsi was forced to grant more concessions. She finally began to make a few reforms in China's government before her death in 1908. Unfortunately her liberal-thinking nephew also died, and his successor proved even more conservative than Tz'u Hsi had been. It seemed that China was doomed to remain a backward nation.

Boxer Prisoners. Boxer prisoners await prosecution after their capture by seamen of the Western powers. The Boxers, who were members of a secret society known as the "Righteous Harmonious Fists," were for the most part peasants from the north.

THE CHINESE BEGAN TO BUILD A MODERN NATION

Sun Yat-sen became the beloved leader of the Chinese Republic. During the last years of Tz'u Hsi's rule, the corrupt, crumbling Manchu regime was being undermined by the plots of a young revolutionary named Sun Yat-sen. Sun came from a poor peasant family near Canton and was educated in mission schools in Hawaii, where his brother was working. Sun later became the first graduate of the new medical school at the British University of Hong Kong. His knowledge of Western ideas and his concern for China's great poverty made him, like many other educated Chinese, burn with a desire to reform the government. When Manchu officials ignored his suggestions, he began to plot revolution against the government.

He soon had to flee the country. Sun Yat-sen spent years in the United States, Japan, and Europe. He worked constantly to persuade the Chinese in foreign countries to give money for a revolution. Many times he barely escaped being killed by the emperor's spies, who followed him all over the world. In 1911 some soldiers in northern China mutinied. Many cities immediately declared themselves against the Manchu government. The chieftains in Outer Mongolia declared their independence. At last the revolution had come! Sun hurried home from England to take part.

A revolutionary assembly met at Nanking in the south and elected Sun president of the United Provinces of China. Unfortunately, Sun Yat-sen was a thinker and a dreamer. He lacked practical experience and soon was in trouble with the politicians and rival leaders. Twice he was driven out of the government. Once he had to flee to Japan. The republic he headed collapsed in about a year. But Sun Yat-sen continued to write and lecture. The young people revered him, and his influence spread throughout China, even after his death. His "Three Principles of the People" mean as much to the Chinese as the Declaration of Independence does to us. The three principles are: (1) China must be free from foreign rule, (2) China must have a democratic government, (3) everybody must have economic security, or freedom from want.

Sun Yat-sen's wife was a member of the famous Soong family, many of whose members achieved prominence in China. One of her sisters is Madame Chiang Kai-shek, wife of the general who later took over the political party Sun Yat-sen had founded.

At A Glance

Important Periods, People, Events in Chinese History

Chou Dynasty (*c.* 1027 B.C.–256 B.C.)
- Confucius
- Lao-tsu

Ch'in Dynasty (221 B.C.–206 B.C.)
- Great Wall of China built

Han Dynasty (206 B.C.–220 A.D.)
- "Civil service" introduced

T'ang Dynasty (618–907)
- Chinese Empire expanded
- Gunpowder, wood block printing invented

Sung Dynasty (907–1279)
- Prosperous trade developed
- Excellent paintings, handicrafts produced

Yüan Dynasty (1279–1368)
- Mongols dominate China

Ming Dynasty (1368–1644)
- Outstanding ceramics created

Ch'ing Dynasty (1644–1912)
- Manchus dominate China
- China divided into "spheres of influence"
- Boxer Rebellion

Chinese Republic (1912–1949)
- Sun Yat-sen
- Chiang Kai-shek

Contemporary China (1949–Present)
- Communists control Chinese mainland
  - Mao Tse-tung
- Nationalist government moves to Formosa

CHIANG KAI-SHEK AND SUN YAT-SEN. The leader of the movement to create a Chinese republic died two years before his dream came true in 1927. Chiang Kai-shek succeeded Sun and during World War II led his people against the Japanese. He now heads the Nationalist government from Taiwan.

Japan interfered in China's government. For about fifteen years after the collapse of the republican government, China was ruled by war lords, men who kept their own private armies and fought with each other for more power. Although the world was not aware of it at the time, the Japanese had long been planning to gain complete control of China. Agents of the Japanese government gave financial support to the war lords and kept them supplied with arms. The Japanese leaders wanted China to remain weak and disorganized.

In 1915, while Europe was busy fighting World War I, Japan saw an opportunity to carry out her plan for seizing China. She believed that the great powers would not dare risk further trouble by interfering with her. So she presented to the Chinese government a list of "Twenty-One Demands." Acceptance of the demands would have given Japan complete control of China's finances, customs service, and foreign policy. The huge country of China would have become a mere colony of Japan. The United States and Great Britain brought pressure on Japan, and the Japanese withdrew some of their demands. But Japan continued to plot and wait for a favorable opportunity to seize control of China.

The People's Party set up the Nationalist government. Sun Yat-sen had organized the first genuine political party in China, the *Kuomintang* (*kwo*-min-*dahng*) or People's Party. In 1923 the party established a government in Canton. It was in control of several southern provinces, while various war lords controlled different sections of the north and west. The chief aim of the Kuomintang was to unify the country under one Chinese government.

Sun Yat-sen, the founder of the Nationalist movement, died in 1925, and the leadership passed to Generalissimo Chiang Kai-shek. Chiang's power was based partly on the army, but he managed to hold together for a considerable period many different types of people in support of the Nationalist government. He started an ambitious program for the economic development of China. He began to build highways, railways, and bridges, and to improve the waterways.

During the Manchu rule, government officials had frequently stolen or misused public funds. Later the war lords had done the same thing. The new government had to struggle with problems that had been piling up for generations. If conditions in the world had been favorable, they might have succeeded. But luck was not with the Nationalists or the Chinese people. The world-wide depression of the 1930's made their Japanese neighbors desperate. Foreign trade, on which Japan depended, kept shrinking. The Japanese had to have foreign markets and cheap raw materials or go bankrupt. They thought the answer was to seize China and make it a colony. They were sure the United States and the other Western powers were too busy with their own troubles to interfere.

The Japanese needed an excuse to attack China. They found it in the so-called "Mukden Incident" of 1931, which many historians believe was deliberately manufactured by Japan. A section of the Japanese controlled railroad which passed through the city of Mukden, Manchuria, was mysteriously demolished. The Japanese blamed Chinese "Bandits," and proceeded with a well-planned invasion of Manchuria.

In the following months, the conflict between Japan and China spread to other parts of China, although the Japanese continued to insist the invasion was just an "incident." The United States gave China money and supplies because we felt she was the victim of a lawless attack. At the same time, however, we continued to sell scrap iron and war materials to Japan, because if we had cut off our trade with Japan, it would have been an unfriendly act. We still hoped we could influence Japan to halt her aggression.

China fought alone until 1941, when the Pearl Harbor attack brought the United States into the

Mao Tse-Tung. Chairman Mao Tse-Tung, the leader of the Chinese Communist Party (first from the right) is shown with other Party leaders at the celebration of the seventeenth anniversary of the founding of the Chinese People's Republic.

THE RUINS OF WAR. In this famous photograph, a Chinese child cries helplessly amid the ruins of a railroad station in Shanghai, which was bombed by the Japanese in 1937 during their undeclared war on China.

war. One of the important reasons the Japanese attacked Pearl Harbor was to stop American aid to China. Even after Pearl Harbor the Chinese did not receive as much help as they expected, for the United States had to concentrate its forces against Germany. Many Chinese became unfriendly toward the United States because we could not give them all the material they needed.

The Communists came to power in China. As the war continued, the Nationalist government grew unpopular. Chiang Kai-shek was blamed for China's defeats. Officials were linked to landlords and bankers who were exploiting the peasants. To pay its debts, the government printed almost worthless paper money. Prices soared; within a two year period (1946-8), prices doubled 67 times! China's middle class was ruined. Government personnel became repressive, antagonizing all who favored democracy. Thus many Chinese began to listen sympathetically to the Communists.

The Communists had been active in China since the early 1920s when they cooperated with the Kuomintang to rid China of its war lords. But a split occurred in 1927 and Chiang Kai-shek mounted several military campaigns against the Reds. The Communists were badly mauled but not destroyed. After a 6,000 mile "Long March" from southern China in the early 1930s, they established a Soviet-type republic at Yenan (*yen-ahn*) in the northwest. In 1937 the Reds and Chiang made a truce so both might fight against Japan.

The truce was very beneficial to the Communists. In 1937 they had controlled only 30,000 square miles of territory, with just 2 million inhabitants; by 1945 they possessed 300,000 square miles containing 95 million people. Nevertheless, when civil war resumed in 1947, Chiang Kai-shek seemed to have the advantage. His well-equipped forces were twice as large as the Red armies. The Kuomintang received two billion dollars worth of American aid—far more help than the USSR gave the Communists. Yet so incompetent was the Nationalist leadership that by 1949 all of mainland China had been lost and Chiang's forces had been driven to the island of Taiwan (formerly called Formosa), a hundred miles away.

Protected by the U.S. Seventh Fleet and the recipient of much American financial aid, the Taiwanese have one of Asia's highest living standards. Chiang has made the economic reforms in Taiwan that he neglectel to institute in China. But the native Taiwanese (four-fifths of the island's 14 million people) resent the rule of the emigres from the mainland and don't share Chiang's dream for the reconquest of China. As Chiang neared his 85th birthday in 1972, fewer and fewer nations continued to recognize him as the legal government of China.

The Communists made tremendous changes in China. The architect of the Communist victory is Party Chairman Mao Tse-tung (*mow-zuh-dung*). As leader of the Communists since 1931, Mao revised Leninist teachings by relying chiefly upon the peasants rather than the urban working class. It was against Stalin's advice that Mao resumed his struggle against the supposedly superior Nationalists after World War II. Mao believes it is not possible for Marxist states to co-exist peacefully with capitalist nations. His philosophy and theories of how to wage guerrilla war have been studied by radicals in many lands. In China itself Mao has been elevated into semi-divine status.

The government of the "People's Republic of China" (Red China's formal title), ended the inflation, greatly expanded China's industrial plant and, through its military and scientific exploits, enhanced national pride. But critics charged that the regime has imprisoned or executed millions of opponents while failing to observe the freedoms promised in its constitution of 1954. Much has been done to undermine traditional institutions and beliefs,—the family, Taoism and Confucianism—which might compete with the Party and the State.

When struggling for power, the Communists had promised that every peasant would own the land he farmed. But there isn't enough arable land in China to accomplish this and private ownership of land is not in accord with Communist principles. Therefore, the redistribution of lands to peasants was halted within a few years of Mao's accession to power. Instead, peasants were "encouraged" to share land and equipment in cooperatives.

SCHOOL FOR WORKERS. A Discussion Group such as shown here is a common occurance in China. After hours workers gather to discuss political situations and Maoist theories. Indoctrination of youth is especially practised.

In 1958 Mao began a "Great Leap Forward" program. Every peasant was "persuaded" to join a "commune." Each commune covered thousands of acres and included villages, factories and thousands of people. All land was collectivized. Labor schedules were set at a feverish pace. Men, women and children were segregated in huge communal barracks. Very little personal property was allowed. The result was catastrophic. Bad weather combined with lack of incentive caused such a drop in food production that China had to import grain. "Steps backward" were necessary: communes and work projects were made less ambitious; some communal features were abandoned; peasants were allotted small private plots in order to spur crop production.

The failure of the "Great Leap Forward" was a severe defeat for Mao. He lost power to a faction led by President Liu Shao-chi (*lee-show-chee*). In this group were most of the Party officials and economic managers. They felt the time had come to slow down the pace of change. Regarding them as "revisionists" who had lost their Marxist zeal, the 73 year old Mao tried to purge them in 1966. Mao's "Cultural Revolution" enlisted the support of China's youth who, as "Red Guards," terrorized the cities and the countryside. In the resultant upheaval, Liu's group was vanquished but the economy was so disrupted that within three years the army had intervened to restore order. As of 1972, most observers believed China's economy was recovering but the army had taken much power from the Party and Premier Chou En-lai (*Joe-in-lie*), who had not participated in the upheaval, may have become China's most important figure.

China has pursued an aggressive foreign policy. Despite domestic crises, China has been bold in its international relations. In 1950 Tibet, semi-independent since 1904, was recaptured by Chinese forces. China defied the United Nations during the Korean War (see page 609) and supported the Vietnamese Reds in their struggles in Indochina. Indian troops were badly beaten in the frontier war of 1962. Becoming Asia's first nuclear power in 1964, China has persistently refused to participate in atomic-test agreements.

Poor as China is, it has extended economic aid to several Afro-Asian lands and Albania, in Europe, became a Chinese satellite in the 1960s. But it is in their relations with the super-powers, Russia and the United States, that the Chinese have displayed particular daring.

In 1950 China contracted a thirty year alliance with Russia, receiving substantial economic aid. Chinese political and economic measures were patterned after Soviet models. But after Stalin's death in 1953, China was no longer content with a "junior partnership." Mao resented taking direction from Stalin's successors. While the Russians derided Mao's "Great Leap Forward" as foolish fanaticism, the Chinese accused the Soviets of refusing to share nuclear secrets and of retreating from Marxist doctrine. By 1963 there were open bitter exchanges and in 1969 came reports of armed conflict along the vast Sino-Russian border.

Because of its staunch support of the Nationalists, the United States was for years the nation most hated by Maoists. During the Korean War Chinese and American troops were locked in combat. Few Americans were permitted to visit China. Although Richard Nixon had long been a noted anti-Communist, it was during his Administration that a thaw in the Sino-American "cold war" occurred. The Chinese made the first big move, motivated possibly by fears of trouble with Russia. In April, 1971 an American table tennis team was suddenly invited to tour China. This "ping pong diplomacy" was soon followed by an invitation to President Nixon. In October, Red China took Taiwan's place in the United Nations, as the United States dropped its long-standing opposition to China's entry. The highly publicized Nixon trip to China in February, 1972 renewed hopes of increased cultural and economic relations between the two countries.

Chapter Check-up

1. In what region of China do most of the inhabitants live? Why?
2. Briefly summarize the teachings of Confucius. How did they influence family life in China?
3. In what way was knowledge of the Confucian classics a path to success?
4. What is Taoism? Why did it hold special appeal for the poor?
5. Into what four traditional classes were the Chinese divided?
6. What important events or achievements are associated with (a) the Han dynasty (b) the T'ang dynasty (c) the Sung dynasty?
7. How did the Western powers take advantage of China? Why was this possible?
8. What factors brought about the downfall of Chiang Kai-shek's government?
9. What was the "Mukden Incident"?
10. What good and bad things have the Communists done to China?

Chapter 63

Korea Sought for Independence and Peace

"THE LAND OF THE MORNING CALM" HAS BEEN TORN BY WARS AND INVASIONS

Korea is a small country that is only about two hundred miles wide and five hundred miles long. Its location is a strategic one, however, and it is sometimes called the gateway to the Asian continent. The Chinese emperors used it as an outpost to protect China's eastern frontier from the Huns. For most of its history Korea has been under the rule of China, but at the end of the nineteenth century it came under the domination of Japan.

Not much is known about prehistoric Korea. Archaeologists have had very little opportunity to work in the country because of its remoteness and the policy of isolation that its rulers followed for many centuries. Most of our present knowledge comes from the written records left by Chinese scholars during the Han Dynasty, when Korea was first conquered by China. Historians believe that the ancient Koreans were related to the Mongols in Manchuria and Siberia. They called their land Ch'ao Hsein (cho-sen), "the Land of Morning Calm."

Although Koreans became independent of China during the early Middle Ages, they continued to absorb Chinese civilization, including the teachings of Buddha and Confucius. They also adopted the Chinese language and copied many of the Chinese arts. Korean civilization is basically Chinese in the same way that American civilization is basically European.

Between the thirteenth and the seventeenth centuries Korea suffered attacks from three foreign invaders, the Mongols, the Japanese, and the Manchus. Each of these invasions brought great misery to the Korean people. The Japanese invasion, led by the ambitious General Hideyoshi (hee-day-*oh*-shee), about whom you will read in the next chapter, was particularly devastating. Tens of thousands on both sides were killed, and cities and villages were destroyed. Although the Japanese invasion was repulsed, Korea was so weakened that it fell an easy prey to the Manchus who swept over the Orient in the middle of the seventeenth century.

From this time on, Korea chose isolation as the answer to its problems. It withdrew as much as possible from contact with either the Western world or the rest of Asia, and it thereafter became known as the "hermit kingdom." But Korea was unable to remain completely isolated from the rest of the world. Her strategic position (Japan considered Korea a "dagger pointed straight at the heart of Japan"), and her mineral resources made Korea an attractive prize. Toward the end of the nineteenth century, China, Russia, and Japan contested for control of the land. Japan, by defeating China in 1895 and Russia in 1905, won the contest. In 1910 Japan made Korea (renamed Chosen) part of the Japanese Empire. A Korean patriot, Dr. Syngman Rhee (ree), led a rebellion against the Japanese in the same year, but it was put down.

Japan needed Korean markets and raw materials to support her industry. She therefore built railroads, factories, and hydroelectric power plants in Korea. Farming and lumbering were also improved. The Koreans thus gained a modern economy, but the new industries were owned by the Japanese, and the wealth they produced went to Japan. The great mass of Korean people remained in poverty.

SEOUL. This portion of South Korea's capital was reduced to rubble during the fighting that ravaged the country in 1950. This picture shows the city as it appeared before the conflict. The building in the foreground is called the Temple of Heaven.

KOREA WAS DIVIDED AND BECAME A "COLD WAR" BATTLEGROUND

As World War II ended, Allied armies liberated Korea. Russian forces swept over the area north of the thirty-eighth parallel of latitude while Americans occupied the territory south of that line. When the two Powers failed to agree on the form of government to be created, a United Nations Commission was appointed to supervise an election. The USSR refused to admit the U.N. into her zone but in the American zone elections were held. On August 15, 1948 the Republic of Korea was proclaimed, with Syngman Rhee as its president. Three weeks later Russia set up the Korean People's Democratic Republic in North Korea. This was a Communist state headed by Kim Il Sung (Kim Il *Soong*), a young Moscow-trained military leader. After furnishing their client republics with arms, Russia and the United States withdrew their occupation forces.

From time to time came reports of border incidents. On Sunday, June 25, 1950, North Korean troops crossed the frontier in a massive surprise attack, apparently hoping to unify the country before anyone could stop them. After vainly ordering the North Koreans to withdraw, the United Nations Security Council voted to send military aid to South Korea. This decision was taken only because the USSR happened to be boycotting the Security Council's meetings at the time (over a matter concerning Nationalist China) and therefore could not use its veto.

General Douglas MacArthur, the American Supreme Commander in the Far East, was assigned to lead a force under the U.N. flag. Most of his troops were American but sixteen other countries of the United Nations joined the "police action."

At first the Communists captured most of the Korean peninsula but a brilliantly executed U.N. counter-attack sent them reeling back over the thirty-eighth parallel. The U.N. army then invaded North Korea, approaching the Yalu River on the Korean-Manchurian border, where many of Red China's power stations were. Although China never officially entered the war, hundreds of thousands of Chinese "volunteers" came into action, causing the surprised United Nations troops to retreat. The conflict soon developed into a stalemated war north of latitude thirty-eight.

SYNGMAN RHEE. A former Methodist missionary, Dr. Rhee fought for Korean independence for more than fifty years. He led the Korean government-in-exile, and served as president of Korea from 1948 to 1960. He died in 1965.

Truce talks began in July, 1951 but dragged on for two years before agreement was reached. Under the accord, South Korea gained an additional fifteen hundred square miles of territory and prisoners of war were permitted to pick the country to which they would be sent.

North Korea's aggression had been stopped and temporarily the United Nations prestige received a much-needed lift. But thirty-three thousand American soldiers had been killed and billions more of American dollars were required to bring about the recovery of devastated South Korea.

THE KOREAN WAR. South Korean infantrymen defend a position in the rugged countryside near the 38th parallel in the early days of the Korean War. Because of Korea's mountainous terrain, the use of mechanized equipment and modern weapons of war was limited. Advances were extremely difficult and casualties were heavy.

With such American aid, South Korea has made enormous economic progress. Political stability has also been achieved under the leadership of General Chung Park. Staunchly pro-American and anti-Communist, Park sent thousands of troops to South Vietnam during the 1960s in support of the U.S. forces there.

Still under Kim II Sung's rule, North Korea has remained one of the most rabid members of the Communist bloc. In 1968 North Korean warships seized the U.S. naval vessel "Pueblo." To secure the American crew's release eleven months later, the U.S. government was compelled to say that the "Pueblo" had been on an illegal mission. Although South Korea, with twice the population of North Korea has one of the largest military establishments in the non-Communist world, a supporting American garrison of fifty thousand men has been stationed there since the close of the Korean War.

Chapter Check-up

1. Why is Korea considered a strategic area?
2. Which countries have principally influenced Korean civilization?
3. Why was Korea once known as the "hermit kingdom"?
4. What happened to Korea at the close of World War II?
5. What part did Syngman Rhee play in the history of modern Korea?
6. Of what significance is the thirty-eighth parallel?
7. How were the U.N., USSR, USA, China each involved in Korea's history after World War II?
8. Who are the present leaders of North and South Korea?
9. Why must it be said that Korea is still a battleground in the "Cold War"?

CHAPTER 64

Japan Became the First Industrial Nation in the Far East

THE EARLY INHABITANTS OF JAPAN DEVELOPED A NATIONAL RELIGION AND ADOPTED CHINESE CULTURE

The Japanese believed that their emperor was descended from the sun-goddess. Historians have no written records of early Japan because the Japanese had no written language until the fourth century A.D. Archaeologists think that the earliest inhabitants of the land were an Indo-European people known as *Ainus* (*i*-nooz). Later, Mongols from the mainland and Malayans from the south invaded the islands and brought some of the culture of early China with them.

These ancient Japanese, like most primitive peoples, worshiped the sun. Because they lived where the morning sun rose out of the sea to light Asia, the sun seemed to have a special meaning for them. They identified the sun with their country, which they called *Nippon* (nih-*pahn*), "the place where the sun rises." The red circle on the Japanese flag represents the rising sun.

The Japanese invented many myths about the sun-goddess and other nature gods. These myths gradually became incorporated into a primitive, patriotic religion called *Shinto,* the "way of the gods." According to one myth, a god dipped his jeweled spear into the ocean. The drops of water that fell from the spear when he withdrew it formed the islands of Japan. Another myth told how Jimmu, who became the first emperor of Japan in 660 B.C., was descended from the sun-goddess. Each year the Japanese celebrate February 11 as the traditional day on which Jimmu ascended the throne and established the Japanese Empire. Because of his divine ancestry, the Japanese called their emperor the "son of heaven." Until after World War II, they considered him a living god who ruled both heaven and earth.

Whatever the legends about the emperor, his-

AINUS. Believed to have been the earliest inhabitants of Japan, the Ainus have a unique language and culture. Here a group of them celebrates one of the ancient festivals. Over the years, invaders forced the Ainus to retreat northward, and today only a few of them remain in Hokkaido, Sakhalin, and some of the Kurile Islands.

THE GOLDEN PAVILION. The gold leaf with which it is gilded gives this historic shrine at Kyoto its name. The pavilion shown here is a replica of the original building, which was destroyed by fire in 1950. The original structure was built for a shogun near the end of the fourteenth century.

torians know that the early Japanese were organized into families, or clans. Each clan gained control of a certain area. Between the first and fourth centuries A.D., the Yamato clan had taken over the most important islands. The emperors of Japan have always belonged to this clan. Thus their line is the oldest in the modern world.

Buddhist missionaries brought Chinese civilization to Japan. During the sixth century a Korean king dispatched Buddhist missionaries to Japan. He also sent books containing Buddhist and Confucian teachings and a splendid statue of Buddha as a gift to the Japanese emperor. The emperor was doubtful about the new faith, but he agreed to let one of the clans adopt Buddhism as an experiment. The new faith grew very popular and quickly spread throughout Japan. There was little conflict with Shinto because the Buddhist monks allowed the Japanese to follow their traditional religion as another aspect of Buddhism. The Japanese eagerly absorbed the Buddhist scriptures and the Confucian classics. The first important result was that they learned the Chinese language. Once they had mastered the Chinese characters, they adapted them to their own spoken words. These books gave the Japanese wider knowledge of the advanced Chinese civilization.

Prince Shotoku (sho-to-koo), who controlled the government for nearly thirty years (593–621), made Chinese civilization an important part of Japanese life. He drew up the *Seventeen Article Constitution,* which simplified the moral principles of the Buddha and Confucius so that they could be more easily understood. Shotoku established rules of court etiquette based on the teachings of Confucius, and he founded many Buddhist monasteries and temples.

The Japanese also copied the architecture, painting, and literature of China. In 720 the Japanese established a permanent capital at Nara. The city was laid out in the same pattern as an earlier capital of China. During the Nara period (the eighth century) Japanese scholars studied in China, brought back new ideas in Chinese art and literature, and introduced new Buddhist sects. The emperor built Buddhist monasteries modeled on those of China, and Japanese nobles wrote poems in Chinese.

A rigid class system developed in Japan. During the Nara period the Japanese settled into a class structure that remained almost unchanged for over a thousand years. At the top were the wealthy and powerful clans. Their members held all the government offices and all the land, although they were supposed to govern in the name of the emperor. The Japanese nobles, like their Chinese counterparts, spent much of their time painting, writing poetry, and taking part in elaborate court ceremonies.

Beneath the clans were workers organized into guilds. The vast majority of people were serfs on the estates of the nobles. It was almost impossible for a man to rise from his class. He often died in the same peasant hut in which he was born, and his children and grandchildren lived there after him.

WARRIOR LORDS CONTROLLED MEDIEVAL JAPAN

Warlike nobles rose to power. The great clans were not content for long to be loyal subjects of the emperor. They wanted to be the power behind the throne. Between the eighth and twelfth centuries a feudal baron frequently took the real power away from the emperor, forcing him into the background. Near the end of the twelfth century the emperor who was then on the throne accepted the changed situation. He appointed a powerful lord to be his military dictator, or *shogun* (*sho*-goon), which means "barbarian-subduing great general." After that, the shoguns, rather than the emperors, were the real rulers of the nation. The shoguns continued to rule in Japan for nearly seven hundred years. Several generations of shoguns from the same clan would rule uninterruptedly for years. Then they would lose power to another clan as the result of civil war. None of the shoguns ever tried to become emperor. It was more convenient for them to keep the emperor under their control and rule Japan in his name.

FEUDAL FAMILIES AT WAR. This detail from a fourteenth-century scroll depicts a battle between two great feudal families. Here the disguised emperor is seen fleeing from his palace with some of his warriors. The palace, which the rival family has set afire, is seen in another section of the scroll.

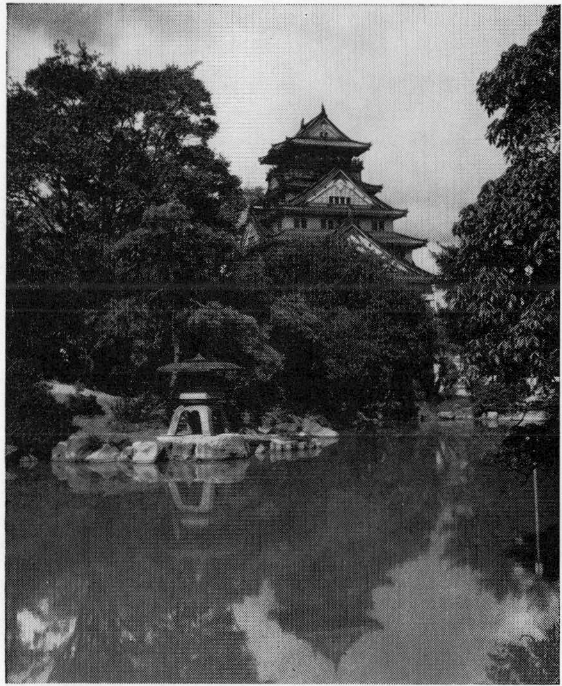

FEUDAL CASTLE. A modern restoration of an old feudal stronghold known as Osaka Castle is reflected in the calm waters of the adjoining lake. It was once the family home of one of the great ruling clans.

The actual position of the emperor changed greatly from time to time. Some shoguns provided for the emperors very generously and even consulted with them on governmental affairs. At other times the emperor was completely ignored and was not well provided for. One of the emperors was so poor that to supplement his meager income he sold his autograph at the palace gate.

Japan became a country of warriors. Under the rule of the shoguns the Chinese traditions that had been so important during the Nara period were disregarded. Japan became a military state. Gradually the clans lost their importance, and warriors became the new aristocracy. The most important of these warriors were the *daimio* (*dy*-myo), who controlled large areas of land and ruled over the lesser warriors, who were called *samurai* (*sam*-oo-ry). The samurai served the daimio in much the same way that vassals served feudal lords in medieval Europe. The daimios supported the shogun in his efforts to repel the Mongol forces of Kublai Khan, which invaded Japan twice in the thirteenth century. Two centuries later, however, the daimios rebelled against the shogun and set up independent feudal states. For over a century Japan was torn by feudal wars.

The new warrior aristocracy developed a military code of conduct which was like the European knights' code of chivalry. The Japanese code, however, was much sterner. It prescribed a rigorous life of exercise and training to make the samurai an effective, ruthless, fighting man. The code also taught that a samurai must be ready to sacrifice his family and his life if his daimio asked it.

The most famous of the Japanese warriors was the peasant general Hideyoshi, whom you read about on page 608. Near the end of the sixteenth century he helped one of the great daimios conquer the rival lords, thus putting an end to Japan's feudal warfare. When the daimio was killed, Hideyoshi made himself master of Japan. He never received the title of shogun, however, because of his low birth. With great confidence, Hideyoshi announced his intention of conquering the whole world. First he tried to enlist the aid of the king of Korea in an attack on China. When the Korean king indignantly refused, Hideyoshi invaded Korea. Although he killed thousands and destroyed many cities, he did not conquer the country, nor did his soldiers ever set foot on the soil of China. The Japanese troops finally withdrew from Korea in 1600, bringing back with them thousands of slaves.

Japanese boys, until after World War II, were taught to remember the "dream of Hideyoshi"—to conquer the whole world and make all nations subject to Japan. It was such teaching that led Japan to disaster in World War II.

Japan sealed itself against the outside world. The ruling classes of Japan—the shogun, the daimios, and their samurai—hated and feared foreigners and looked on them as barbarians. They were afraid of new religions and political ideas and dreaded the thought of other nations getting a foothold in their country.

A little less than a half-century after Magellan's trip around the world, the great Spanish missionary St. Francis Xavier arrived in Japan with a few other Jesuit priests. There they made some converts to Christianity. As time went by there was a strong reaction against the priests and other foreigners. Hideyoshi felt that they were trying to gain political power, so he began to persecute them. Early in the seventeenth century all foreign priests were forced to leave Japan. Some years later many of the Christian converts were massacred. Japanese Christians continued to meet secretly, however, and when missionaries were allowed to return many years later, they found a surprising number of Christians living in Japan.

In 1637 the ruling shogun issued an order that barred all foreigners from Japan. The only exceptions were some Dutch traders who were allowed to send one trading ship a year to a small port on a lesser island. It was even made a crime for the Japanese to leave their own land or to send letters abroad. When other nations tried to deal with the Japanese, they replied curtly, "Speak to the Dutch. They will carry any message it is necessary for us to know." The policy of isolation continued for more than two hundred years.

Commodore Perry delivered a letter. The closed-door policy of Japan did not please other nations. They wanted to trade with the Japanese and they did not see why their ships should not be allowed to enter Japan's ports—at least for supplies. The American government became aroused by reports of the inhuman and cruel treatment suffered by sailors who were shipwrecked on the Japanese coast.

President Fillmore of the United States was determined to make a treaty with Japan. He wrote a letter to the emperor and asked Commodore Perry to deliver it. Perry, with four ships of the Navy, arrived in the Bay of Tokyo in July, 1853.

The Japanese were very much disturbed when they saw the four strange warships in the bay just ten miles from their capital. They gazed in curiosity and anger at the powerful-looking fleet of "foreign barbarians." Never having seen a steamship, they could not understand how a ship could move without sails. They sent messengers to persuade Perry to leave, but he insisted that his letter must go to the emperor.

At last the Japanese agreed to deliver the letter. They received Perry on the beach, where he landed with three hundred soldiers and sailors. When they had accepted the President's letter, the Japanese handed Perry a note which read, "The letter being received, you will leave." Perry informed them that he would return in a few months for an answer to the letter.

The people of Japan were excited by Perry's visit. The ruling shogun considered whether he

Samurai Warrior. The soldiers of feudal Japan garbed themselves in clothing like that worn by the Japanese actor shown here. A samurai was governed by the rigid code of Bushido, which demanded that he surrender his life if his daimio requested it.

JAPANESE ARCHITECTURE

Asia, especially East Asia, has an architectural style that is noticeably different from the Western World. The Pagodas, Lamaseries and exotic temples are strange, occult, and most deceptive to the Western culture.

Japanese architecture today is as modern as the United Nations buildings in New York, but fear of earthquakes has kept the buildings in a fairly low profile. But we don't think or want to think of Japan as Western. We want to see temples and people in kimonos. Japan won't quite fit the mold because it is as modern as it is old. Just remember that Japan has a subway system that is more crowded than New York's, and that modern, teeming Tokyo is the largest city in population in the world.

But still the myth and reality exist. Here are shown an exquisite temple in Kyoto, a lakeside shrine, and the immaculate exterior and interior of a home. All reflect beauty, simplicity and cleanliness of design.

ought to make a treaty with foreigners. He sent copies of the President's message to all the daimios and asked for their advice. The daimios protested. The Japanese began to arm themselves for the return visit. They made bells into cannons and built mud forts. They drilled the samurai in the use of guns.

In February, 1854, Commodore Perry returned with a fleet of seven ships and two thousand men. He brought the Japanese a number of presents, including a telegraph line with a mile of wire and a model steam railroad, complete with engine, car, and circular track. There were also rifles, clocks and a sewing machine. Perry had the gifts set up on the beach, where he demonstrated them to the people. The Japanese saw that they could never hope to resist the foreigners until they, too, had learned to handle Western machines. It was clear that the West had much to teach them.

Japan agreed to a treaty of navigation with the United States, giving us the privilege of calling at certain ports for fuel and water and promising humane treatment for shipwrecked sailors. The American consul-general, after great effort, made a trade treaty. The medieval nation of Japan suddenly opened its eyes to a modern world of steam and humming factories.

Japan became a modern industrial nation. Some of the daimios and samurai rebelled when the shogun signed a trade treaty with the United States. The dissatisfied groups started a movement to restore the power of the emperors. In time they forced the shoguns out of office. The last shogun resigned in 1868, at the same time that a new emperor, Mutsuhito (*moot*-soo-hee-to), came to the throne.

PERRY IN JAPAN. Commodore Perry is escorted ashore with some of his men to deliver the historic letter that ultimately led to Japan's introduction to modern civilization.

THE NEW AND THE OLD. Although Japan has become a modern industrial nation, her people retain their love of the simple arts. *Left:* huge transformers of a hydroelectric project; *right:* two girls practicing the art of *ikebana,* or flower arranging, which has also become popular in the United States.

The restoration of the emperors caused a new wave of patriotism and unity. Some daimios gave up their powers and land of their own free will, and others were forced out. The samurai class was abolished at the same time. But in most cases the daimios received land, and the samurai were granted government pensions.

The new emperor was anxious to see his nation advance. All groups united behind him, and Japan began to make itself over according to Western standards. A delegation of Japanese traveled around the world to learn of any new ideas that might be used to advantage at home. Unusually capable students were sent to foreign universities to study.

The Japanese started a public school system modeled on that of the United States. In 1889 Japan even adopted a constitution. The principal purpose of the constitution, however, was to uphold the supreme authority of the ruling group. It contained no bill of rights for the people. A *diet,* or legislature, with a house of peers and a house of representatives was set up. New titles for the nobles, such as prince, count, and baron, were borrowed from Europe. The titles helped to console some of the former samurai, who had lost all of their earlier honors. The vote was granted to a small number of men, depending on their tax payments. The women could not vote at all. In the meantime, a modern navy was built and the army was reorganized on the model of the French army, with German officers to drill it.

Japanese industry also made rapid progress after Perry's visit. Factories and railroads were built, and foreign trade grew. Unfortunately, the common people did not benefit very much from all the progress. A few powerful families controlled business. The "Big Families," as they were called, soon tried to get control of the government also. But there they ran into opposition from the army and navy.

The Japanese military leaders thought they ought to run the country. They could count on the unquestioning obedience of thousands of common soldiers in the new Japanese army. The rich landowners usually supported the military men, so

GATHERING TEA LEAVES. Because their country is small and mountainous and their population large, the Japanese have learned to make the most of every inch of arable soil. Here women work diligently to gather tea leaves.

the government of Japan became a kind of tug-of-war between different groups.

Japan became a world power. Japan's population increased along with her trade and industry. By the late nineteenth century there were more people than the tiny islands could support. Because mountains made so much of the land unsuitable for agriculture, the Japanese cultivated every inch of available soil. They raised tea on carefully terraced mountainsides that American farmers would consider hopeless for growing crops. They irrigated the fields in the south so that they could raise two rice crops each year. They planted mulberry trees on the ridges between the fields to provide food for silkworms. The Japanese could not afford to eat meat because there was no room to raise cattle. Instead they sent fishing boats over half the globe—from the crab and salmon grounds in the North Pacific to the tuna grounds in the South Pacific and the Indian Ocean. For good reason the Japanese were called "farmers of the sea." In spite of their efforts, however, the Japanese could not feed their population without importing food from abroad.

Besides food imports, the Japanese needed raw materials, such as cotton, coal, iron ore, and oil. They also needed markets in which to sell their finished products. Believing that a large colonial empire could furnish all these things, the Japanese looked toward the rich Chinese mainland. Before long the combined force of military ambition and the economic needs of the small, highly industrialized island kingdom drove her into war.

First Japan defeated China in the Sino-Japanese War of 1894. As a result of the conflict she gained control of Formosa and dominant influence in Korea, although she did not actually annex Korea until 1910. Second, Japan's newly modernized navy defeated the Russian fleet in the Russo-Japanese War (1904–5). As a result of this war, Japan received Port Arthur and Russia's rail and mining rights in Manchuria. At last Japan had a foothold on the mainland. The Western nations began to realize that Japan was no longer a quaint, backward country but a serious rival.

In the meantime Japan and Britain had made an alliance (1902) because they both feared Russia's expansion in the Far East. In 1914 Japan used this alliance as an excuse to enter World War I against Germany. Her purpose was to gain control of German territories in the Far East. Under the terms of the peace treaty at the conclusion of the war, Japan was given control over the Pacific islands that had once belonged to the German Empire. These islands were important Japanese naval bases during World War II.

Japan also took advantage of World War I to capture markets for her finished products. During the war European nations were too busy fighting to maintain their foreign trade. After the war Japan's lower labor costs allowed her to undersell many European countries. Thus she became an important commercial rival of the Western nations.

Japan tried to control Asia by means of war. During the 1920's Japan's Big Families controlled her government. They were bankers, industrialists, and merchants, and they favored peaceful trade. Japan's foreign policy was therefore more cautious. But she was soon to return to a policy of aggression. The depression that began in 1929 struck a heavy blow to this peaceful element. Trade fell off and Japan faced bankruptcy. Worse still, China began to shut out Japanese goods in order to give Chinese industry a chance to grow. In 1931 the Japanese suddenly seized Manchuria (see the account of the Mukden Incident on page 604) in an effort to keep their trading rights there. At this point, Japan's military faction seized control of the government. The army leaders had been trained to believe in Hideyoshi's dream. They were convinced that Japan's path to glory lay in conquest. Specifically, they wanted to create, by force if necessary, a *Greater East Asia Co-Prosperity Sphere* under Japanese control. They murdered or otherwise disposed of their peace-minded opponents. Under their leadership, Japan grew more aggressive.

Japan did not have the wealth or natural resources to support a large army and navy. Her one asset was her millions of skilled workers who would toil for long hours and were accustomed to low pay. Japanese factories began to turn out war materials instead of consumer goods. The schools taught Shinto beliefs in order to stimulate militant patriotism in the children. They were taught to believe in Japanese superiority, the divinity of the emperor, and the glory of dying in battle. Boys learned military drill and played war games.

After seizing Manchuria, Japan stepped up the tempo of her undeclared war against China. By 1939 Japan had captured most of China. At this

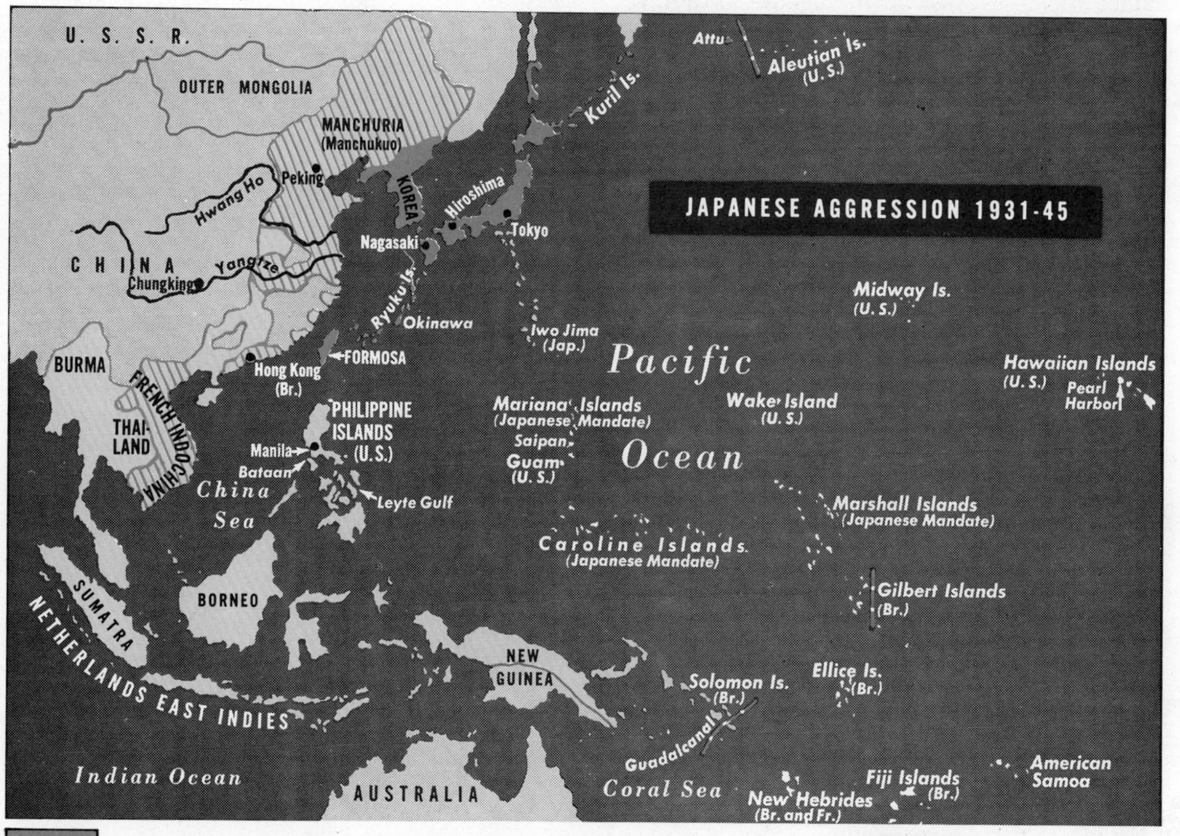

crucial moment, the British, French, and Russians withdrew their forces in the Orient to fight World War II in Europe. The sole remaining power in the Pacific was the United States, which had bases in the Philippines, Guam, and Hawaii. The United States, unwilling to provoke war, continued to send Japan scrap iron. When the Japanese seized French Indochina, the United States finally stopped all exports to her. Then on December 7, 1941, while her envoys were negotiating for peace in Washington, Japan launched a surprise attack against the United States' fleet at Pearl Harbor, in what is now the State of Hawaii. The United States promptly declared war.

In the next few months, the well-trained and fully prepared Japanese army took over the Philippines, the Dutch East Indies, and Burma. The United States, caught off guard, painfully regained island after island by bloody, costly invasion. By the summer of 1945 the Japanese had been driven back to their home islands. Instead of invading, the Americans dropped atomic bombs on Hiroshima and Nagasaki. A short time later, Russia declared war on Japan. Thoroughly crushed, Japan surrendered unconditionally. The Japanese signed formal papers of surrender on September 2, 1945 aboard the American battleship "Missouri."

American occupation forces tried to teach democracy to Japan. American troops led by General Douglas MacArthur, who had directed the war in the Pacific, immediately occupied Japan. He held more power over the conquered country than any Japanese ruler had possessed. It was clear that Emperor Hirohito was a harmless figurehead who had had no real part in causing the war. The Americans made him renounce all claim to divine ancestry, but they allowed him to remain as an imperial symbol because they believed that his co-operation would make it easier for them to govern Japan.

After four years of bitter fighting, the two former enemies settled down to work for a common cause, the rebuilding of the defeated country. Most Japanese welcomed the occupying American forces when they found that the Americans were willing to help Japan recover. The Americans tried as criminals many of the military leaders who had helped cause the war. Seven of them were executed and others were imprisoned. There was also an attempt to break up the holdings of the Big Families. Most Japanese factories had been bombed, but the Americans helped Japanese industry to recover. Today Tokyo looks much like any big city in the Western world.

The United States set out to teach the Japanese people democracy. Under American encouragement, the school system was reorganized and a modern, democratic constitution was adopted. The office of emperor was preserved, but all power was given to the Japanese Diet (parliament). For the first time women were allowed to vote and received equal rights before the law. The new constitution outlawed war.

MT. FUJIYAMA. Rising majestically above the clouds, Fujiyama symbolizes Japan to the world just as Mt. Olympus did to the ancient Greeks. Incidentally, it is not always capped in snow.

The Japanese Surrender. Aboard the battleship "Missouri," the Japanese formally surrendered to General Douglas MacArthur on September 2, 1945, bringing to an end World War II and Japan's dream of a Pacific empire.

Japan signed a peace treaty with the United States and most of her other former opponents in 1951. Russia and her satellites refused to sign because the Western powers would not recognize Communist China. Japan lost all of her empire by the terms of the treaty. The United States made a defensive alliance with her, withdrew the occupation troops, and restored her right of self-defense. Japan is once more self-governing. Russia finally signed a peace treaty with Japan in 1956, and a short time later Japan joined the United Nations.

Democracy has proved a success in Japan. The hatreds aroused during the war gradually disappeared. Today, the Japanese are among America's best friends in the Far East. However, the economic needs that helped make Japan an aggressor nation have never been satisfied. Japan must still import food to feed her steadily increasing population, and she must still obtain raw materials and find markets for her manufactured goods. Unfortunately, her nearest neighbors and natural markets include China, North Korea, and Russia, all of which are under Communist control. Most of her trade with these nations has stopped since the end of World War II. But many Japanese leaders feel that their country must come to some kind of agreement with Communist China if Japan is to survive. Since Japan needs both the continued support of the United States and trade with her neighbors, she hopes for an early end of the "cold war" between the Communist nations and the West.

Chapter Check-up

1. How were the early Japanese influenced by Chinese culture?
2. Why did her rulers seal Japan off from the rest of the world?
3. How did Commodore Perry influence the history of Japan?
4. How were the Japanese able to modernize and industrialize their country in a relatively short time?
5. Why did Japan become an aggressor nation in the 1930's?
6. What part did the atom bomb play in ending the war between the United States and Japan?
7. How did the United States help to rebuild Japan after World War II? What changes were made in Japan's government?
8. What is present-day Japan's most urgent problem?
9. Identify the following: (a) shogun (b) Shinto (c) "dream of Hideyoshi."

CHAPTER 65

Oriental Artists Followed Ancient Traditions of Beauty

CHINESE AND JAPANESE PAINTERS SOUGHT HARMONY WITH NATURE

Painting is one of the most widely admired arts in China and Japan. China and Japan have long ranked among the world's most accomplished nations in the fine arts. In the Orient a gentleman's training in painting is considered as important as his training in reading and writing. Most painting is not done for a commercial purpose, but simply to satisfy the desire of the artist for creative recreation.

For the most part, oriental artists prefer to depict nature as a whole rather than to center their works on man, as has been common in the Western world since the Renaissance. The Chinese and Japanese believe that nature provides many subjects just as interesting as men. Instead of painting portraits or representing saints and gods in human form, they concentrated chiefly on painting landscapes or studies of trees and flowers. The chief objects in a landscape are usually a range of mountains and a brook or waterfall. Indeed, the Chinese word for landscape means "mountains and water." There is occasionally a tiny figure of a man on a boat or on a bridge, but he is not more emphasized than the mountains or a nearby rock. The purpose of such painting is to show that man is only a small part of nature and should seek to achieve harmony with it. This idea underlies both the Taoist and Buddhist philosophies.

AN ALBUM LEAF. This early Chinese masterpiece conveys a mood of repose that is intended to lead the viewer's mind into contemplation. It is the work of Ma Yüan, one of China's great landscape painters. Round paintings like this one are known as album leaves.

Oriental artists are less concerned with creating life-like reproductions of their subjects than they are with instilling a particular mood in the viewer. Often their paintings represent seemingly unimportant things, but they give hints of deep meaning. A drawing of a bird or a tree may consist of only a few lines, but it will show loving observation and understanding of nature. The artist includes as few details as possible in order to leave room for the viewer to use his imagination.

Chinese and Japanese painters use unique brush strokes to achieve the desired mood or quality. Each artist develops his own particular style. For example, Wu Tao-tzu (woo tow-*tsoo*), one of the greatest Chinese painters, had a very powerful stroke that made his figures look like sculpture. Different kinds of brush strokes were considered appropriate to different objects or moods, such as the "silk stroke" or the "running water stroke."

A Japanese Woodblock Print. A child diverts his mother's attention from her spinning. Woodblock prints usually depict scenes from everyday life. They are called *U-kiyoye,* "the passing scene."

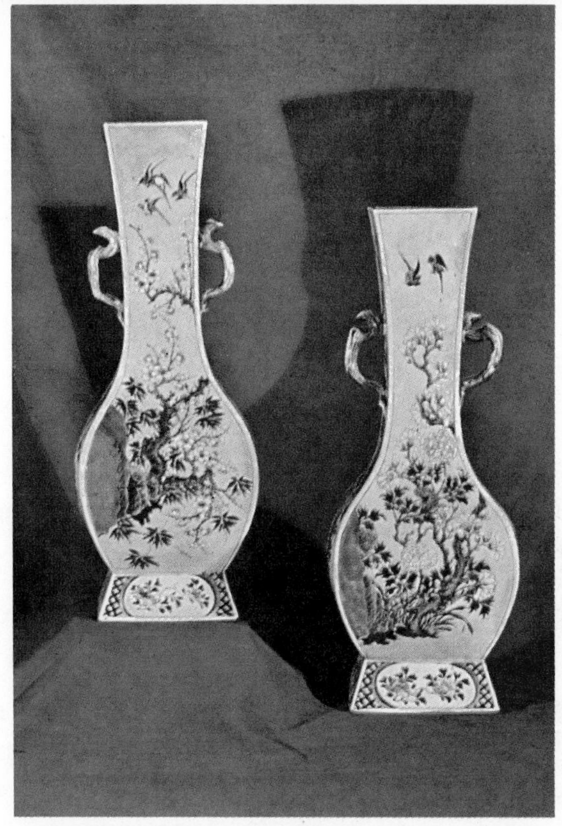

Chinese Vases. These two painted enamel vases were made early in the Ch'ing dynasty. Such vases are classified by "family." These belong to the *famille jaune,* or "yellow family," because of the color of their backgrounds.

A Wedding Robe. The ceremonial splendor of life among the nobility of eighteenth century Japan is evident in this lavish wedding robe from that period. The over-all design represents a flowering Paulownia tree with Ho-o birds in its branches. Both are symbols of good fortune. The scene on the screen at the left depicts a step in the training of an entertainer, or *geisha.*

Most paintings are done on silk cloth in black ink or water color. Once a brush stroke is made, it cannot be erased or repainted as can a brush stroke in ordinary oil paints. Therefore the painter has to visualize the whole picture in his mind before he picks up his brush. Years of careful observation of nature and constant practice lie behind one simple brush stroke on silk.

Chinese writing was like Chinese painting. In early China, formal writing was considered as much an art as painting and was practiced with the same materials. Scholars prided themselves on the beautiful brush strokes which they employed in writing. Several strokes made up a single *character*. A Chinese character, like an Egyptian hieroglyph, represents an object or idea rather than a letter or syllable. Thus the character resembles a painting because it is used only to suggest a meaning rather than to state it clearly and exactly. This usage makes the Chinese language much more difficult to read than to speak. For many years only trained scholars could read the great Chinese classics that contained the ideas of Confucius, the Buddha, and Lao-tsu.

THE CHINESE INVENTED PRINTING

You may recall that the ancient Sumerians used seals impressed in wax on soft clay to sign important documents. From a Chinese modification of this custom may have developed the art of printing. The Chinese learned that by inking the seal, it could be reproduced when pressed on cloth or on a sheet of paper. (The Chinese had begun to manufacture paper by the second century A.D.) The idea of the inked seal was expanded to permit the printing of a whole page of writing. The text was carved in reverse on a slab of fruitwood, then inked and pressed on paper. The earliest printed books were religious works—Buddhist and Taoist scriptures—just as the earliest printed books in Europe were Bibles.

The Chinese made illustrations for their books by carving designs on the surface of a wooden block. The carved block was known as a *woodcut*. When the woodcut was inked, its design could be reproduced on paper just as a block of type could. By the mid-fifteenth century the Chinese were able to print woodcuts in several colors.

Later this art was adapted by the Japanese, who became masters of color printing. Skilled Japanese craftsmen turned out beautiful colored woodblock prints so cheaply that even the poorest Japanese families could afford them. Many of the prints were handbills advertising Japanese plays. They were discovered by Europeans in the nineteenth century and influenced the work of such famous European artists as Degas, Van Gogh, and Toulouse-Lautrec.

THE CHINESE AND JAPANESE WERE EXPERT CRAFTSMEN

Oriental painting was done chiefly by the nobility or men of leisure. Other arts, including sculpture and architecture, were considered crafts and were practiced by professional craftsmen. Most of the early sculpture was religious. In the Ch'in and Han dynasties, sculptors made small clay representations of men, which the Chinese put in tombs as the Egyptians did. They also sculptured animal figures out of stone and bronze. Later, Buddhas and Buddhist saints became popular subjects. The sculptors made their works symbolic rather than realistic. They did not attempt to represent the details of physical features.

Chinese craftsmen became skilled in many other fields beside sculpture. They are noted for the beautiful bells which they cast in bronze. They also fashioned delicate statuettes, vases, and fragile cups out of a hard, polished green mineral

BUDDHA OF KAMAKURA. This enormous Buddha, cast in bronze over 700 years ago, is situated at the seaside resort of Kamakura, on the island of Honshu. Buddhism is a strong force in Japanese life today.

called jade. The Chinese invented the process of applying layers of resin solution, or lacquer, to wood to give it a hard, glossy finish in red, black, or gold. Both the Chinese and Japanese raised silkworms and wove all kinds of fabrics, from thin summer silk to heavy, patterned material suitable for an emperor's robe. Often the fabrics were elaborately embroidered with bright flowers, birds, and butterflies.

Perhaps the best known craft of the Chinese is that of making porcelain, or "china." Porcelain is pottery made of special clay which is baked at such high temperatures that it becomes hard, brittle, and translucent. The Chinese molded the wet clay into graceful cups, bowls, and vases, baked it, and colored it with glaze. Then the article was baked again. The emperors encouraged porcelain factories to make dishes for the court. In the eighteenth century the Chinese exported much porcelain to Europe and the United States, but Western craftsmen soon learned to make porcelain, or "china," for themselves.

ORIENTAL ARCHITECTURE FOLLOWED ANCIENT TRADITIONS

Chinese architecture begins with a wall. Many of China's cities are surrounded by walls. In fact, the same Chinese word is used for "city" and "city wall." In some cities, as in Peking, there are walls within walls. Sometimes these walls are mere mounds of dried mud built about a small village. Sometimes they are massive structures that tower far above the single-story Chinese houses which they shelter. Ornamental gates allow passage into the city at well-guarded points.

The most famous structure in all China is the Great Wall, which was built to keep out invading Mongols from the north. The Great Wall is like a continuous massive fort about seventeen hundred miles in length. Straightened out, it would reach from Washington, D. C., to Denver, Colorado.

The wall is from twenty to thirty feet high in most places and wide enough to allow for a roadway along its top. It is really two walls made of huge bricks, filled in with earth and broken stones and paved with bricks. Every few hundred yards a tall, square tower rises. On the top, signal fires were once kept ready. Soldiers stationed in the towers would pass on an alarm from one tower to another and defend the wall when attacked.

Most Chinese buildings are one storied structures of wood and brick. The most striking feature is the high, overhanging roof. It is supported by tall wooden pillars near the center of the main room and lower ones near the walls so that the roof slopes sharply. Often the sides of the roof curve upward. This characteristic is believed to have been inspired by the shape of the tents in which the early Chinese tribes lived.

One of the world's most interesting types of building is the *pagoda*, a tower-like temple which is built in tiers with a number of overhanging roofs (see the picture on page 603). A pagoda is either six-or-eight sided and always has an odd number of stories. There are many pagodas in both China and Japan.

Most buildings in China are less than a century old because wood and clay decay quickly, but builders continue to copy the old style of architecture. In Japan, famous buildings are taken apart every twenty years, new pieces of wood are cut to replace the rotted parts, and the buildings are reassembled. Thus, by looking at the temples of Nara which have been preserved in this way, modern men can know what Japanese architecture was like in the eighth century.

Japanese houses show simplicity and love of nature. The Japanese adapted Chinese architecture to suit themselves, much as the Romans adapted Greek styles. The Japanese used wood more freely than the Chinese because it is plentiful in Japan. The palaces and tombs of the shoguns were marvelously ornate and often brightly lacquered in red and gold. Private homes, however, are much more subdued. They show the influence of the Buddhist principles of simplicity, withdrawal, and love of nature. The Japanese home is usually built in a garden, so that the occupants can occasionally withdraw from the world for meditation. Large, paper-covered windows are provided to admit light into the home. Instead of solid walls, sliding paper screens are used to separate one room from another. Thick straw mats cover the floor. Often the main room has a recess to hold a painting or a graceful arrangement of flowers. The overall atmosphere is one of quiet and peace. In recent years Japanese home design has begun to influence architectural styles in the United States.

THE CHINESE AND JAPANESE FOUND MUCH PLEASURE IN POETRY AND DRAMA

Chinese and Japanese poetry was closely linked to painting. Often a poem was chosen as a subject for a painting and was written on the painting itself. The poet, like the painter, suggested a mood rather than giving an exact description. Poems were often very short, and one poetic form had only three lines. The poet tried to create a mood or idea with a single word. Thus for him each word became the "leaf of an idea," and suggested much more than the word itself. Many of China's famous poets were scholarly noblemen who lived during the T'ang dynasty and helped make it the golden age of Chinese literature.

The Chinese did not consider drama or the novel to be true literature. There is no Chinese equivalent of Shakespeare or Tolstoy. The Chinese did, however, have traditional dances and music for religious festivals. During the Mongol period, these developed into a kind of popular drama which, like opera, used music, song, and dance to tell the story. The stories were usually familiar tales in which a hero was torn between loyalty to his family and loyalty to the emperor.

Jay on a Branch. Using only a few deft brush strokes, the artist has created a vivid ink drawing of a bird poised on a branch. Although early Japanese painters took their inspiration from Chinese works, they introduced unique qualities of their own. The seal stamped on the drawing below the bird's tail is the owner's signature.

The actors were all men, some of whom played women's parts. They wore elaborate masks but appeared in very simple settings. For instance, a small screen might represent a castle or four soldiers might stand for an army. One of the plays had 240 acts and took two years to perform. The spectators wandered in and out of the theater whenever they were so inclined.

The Japanese have developed a very distinctive kind of drama called the *no* play. (The word *no* means "ability.") The main characters represent Buddhist and Shinto gods or ghosts of famous warriors. The actors wear masks to indicate the roles they are playing. The stage is a roofed platform open to the audience on three sides. A painting of a pine tree is placed near the actors' entrance to show that the plays were once performed outdoors at shrines. Musicians furnish background music with drums and flutes. Much of the play is told through pantomime rather than spoken lines. The *no* plays were very popular, and they were often performed before the emperor and his court.

Chapter Check-up

1. How does Oriental painting differ from that of the Western world?
2. Why is formal Chinese writing considered an art?
3. How did printing begin in China? What is a woodcut?
4. In what crafts have the Chinese and Japanese excelled?
5. What are the most important characteristics of Oriental architecture?
6. What forms of drama developed in China and Japan?

The Far East: SYNOPSIS

China's civilization reflects the influence of two great philosophers: Confucius and Lao-tsu. Confucius taught respect for the family and the emperor, and established rules for upright living. Lao-tsu stressed the virtues of humility and unselfishness and offered comfort to China's masses. In the Middle Ages, China produced a series of brilliant civilizations under the Han, T'ang and Sung emperors. But in the seventeenth century China came under the rule of the Manchus. During their harsh and often corrupt regime China fell far behind the nations of the West.

The Chinese long resisted Westernization, but the Sino-Japanese War of 1894 showed them that this was an error, for through that war China lost Korea and Taiwan to the more advanced Japanese. Meanwhile China was being divided into "spheres of influence" by the European powers. Chinese resentment against this led to the Boxer Rebellion.

By the early twentieth century China was striving to modernize under Sun Yat-sen, who was succeeded in 1925 by Chiang Kai-shek. Chiang's government became increasingly unpopular and ineffective during World War II. The Communists, led by Mao Tse-tung, took power in 1949 after a civil war which drove Chiang to the island of Taiwan. Mao created a totalitarian government on the mainland. Under his direction, Red China became an atomic power, fought the United States to a stand-still in the Korean War, vied with the USSR for leadership of the Communist world and in 1972 joined the United Nations on virtually its own terms.

Korea became known as the "hermit kingdom" because it had for generations deliberately isolated itself from world affairs. In 1910, however, she was forced to become part of the Japanese Empire and did not regain her freedom until the end of World War II. Trouble soon developed between Communist North Korea, which had been occupied by Russia, and South Korea, a client state of the United States and the United Nations. The Korean War, in which the United Nations opposed North Korea's aggression, resulted in a stalemate. Today there is an uneasy truce between the still-separated sections of the country.

Although there are many important Chinese ingredients in Japan's civilization, many differences exist between the two countries. While China was under the influence of peaceful philosophers, a military aristocracy arose in Japan. In the seventeenth century Japan was closed to foreigners but it was re-opened in 1854 by Commodore Perry. The Japanese were soon persuaded to Westernize. By the start of the twentieth century, Japan had become a world power. Spurred by a sense of divine mission as proclaimed in the teachings of Shinto, Japan became an aggressor nation until defeated in World War II. Since that war, with massive American assistance, a new peaceful and democratic Japan has emerged to become one of the world's industrial leaders.

The Oriental love of nature is much reflected in Chinese and Japanese art. The work of Oriental sculptors, architects and writers is also greatly admired throughout the world.

Terms

Be sure that you understand clearly the meaning of each of the following:

dynasty	Confucianism	pagoda
Great Wall	Open Door Policy	samurai
ancestor worship	"hermit kingdom"	Shinto
Taiping Rebellion	Boxer Rebellion	shogun
Taoism	Twenty-One Demands	commune
Kuomintang	"spheres of influence"	Mukden Incident
"Cultural Revolution"	Liu Shao-chi	Kim Il Sung
"Long March"	Chou En-lai	Douglas MacArthur

Important People

How has each of the following influenced the story of the Far East?

Confucius	Mao Tse-tung	Tz'u Hsi	Toyotomi Hideyoshi
Lao-tsu	Syngman Rhee	Prince Shotoku	Wu Tao-tzu
Chiang Kai-shek	Sun Yat-sen	Chung Hee Park	

Questions for Discussion and Review

1. How did the social classes of medieval China compare with those of Japan?
2. How did the influence of Confucius benefit China? How did it serve to slow progress and reform?
3. What conditions in China helped the Communists to gain control?
4. Do you think the United States should recognize the Communist government of mainland China? Why?
5. Why is Manchuria more important than the other outlying provinces of China?
6. Who do you suppose the Chinese regard as their greater enemy today—the United States or the Soviet Union? Explain.
7. Do you think that the Korean "police action" was justified? Why?
8. How has Japan's geography influenced her economy and her history?
9. How was Shinto used to support the militarism of Japan in World War II?
10. Do you feel that the United States can rely on the support of Japan in the Far East? Why?

Interesting Things to Do

1. Make a map of Asia showing China, Korea, and Japan. Locate and label the important seas, provinces, rivers, mountains, and cities. Use color and illustrations to make your map more interesting and meaningful.
2. Make a chart comparing Communist China and Nationalist China with respect to area, population, economy, government, leaders, international relations and military strength.
3. Make a series of drawings for travel posters of China and Japan. Include such things as a Chinese pagoda, a dragon, a Chinese junk, a

statue of the Buddha, and Mount Fujiyama.

4. Prepare a poster with drawings, cut-outs, or samples illustrating the imports and exports between the United States and Japan.

5. Collect and display such objects of oriental culture as silk, china, lacquer ware, carved jade, and fans. Include brief explanatory labels with each article in your exhibit.

6. Write a report on the contributions of Chinese and Japanese-Americans to life in the United States.

7. Prepare and present a talk on the subject, "Life in China under the Communists." Consult newspapers and newsmagazines for your information.

8. Read John Hershey's *Hiroshima* and prepare a book report on this memorable account of the destruction of a Japanese city.

9. Write a newspaper editorial entitled "Japan Faces the Future." Discuss the problems and handicaps that the Japanese must overcome.

10. Add to or begin your "Who's Who in World History" series by writing brief biographies of one or more of the important leaders of China and Japan.

Interesting Reading about China and Japan

*Baker, Nina Brown, *Sun Yat-sen,* Vanguard. Biography of the leader of the Chinese Revolution.

Battistini, L. H., *Japan and America,* Day. A study of Japanese-American foreign relations from the days of Perry to the twentieth century.

Behn, Harry, *Cricket Songs: Japanese Haiku,* Harcourt, Brace, & World.

Kirk, Ruth, *Japan Crossroads of East and West,* Nelson.

Langer, Paul F., *Japan: Yesterday and Today,* Holt, Rinehart and Winston.

McCune, Shannon, *Korea's Heritage, a Regional and Social Survey,* Tuttle.

Pak, Chong Yong, *Korean Boy,* Lothrop, Lee and Shepard. Personal experiences of a young Korean during the Korean conflict.

Riboud, Mark, *Three Banners of China,* Macmillan. Remarkable photographs of Mao's China.

Seeger, Elizabeth, *The Pageant of Chinese History,* McKay.

Storry, Richard, *Japan,* Oxford.

Stuart, J. L., *Fifty Years in China,* Random House. Memoirs of an American ambassador in pre-Communist China.

Tung, Chi-ping, and Humphrey Evans, *The Thought Revolution,* Coward-McCann. Student life in China under Communism.

*Vaughn, Josephine Budd, *Land and People of Japan,* Lippincott.

Wong, Jade Snow, *Fifth Chinese Daughter,* Harper & Row. Autobiography of an American-born girl of Chinese parentage and her childhood days in San Francisco.

* Indicates easy reading

Africa is bursting with energy and youth, but many of the old traditions still have a place in the life of the people. The Emir of Zaria. Nigeria is a proud representative of the old ways.

Part 20
AFRICA
CONTINENT OF TOMORROW

AFRICA

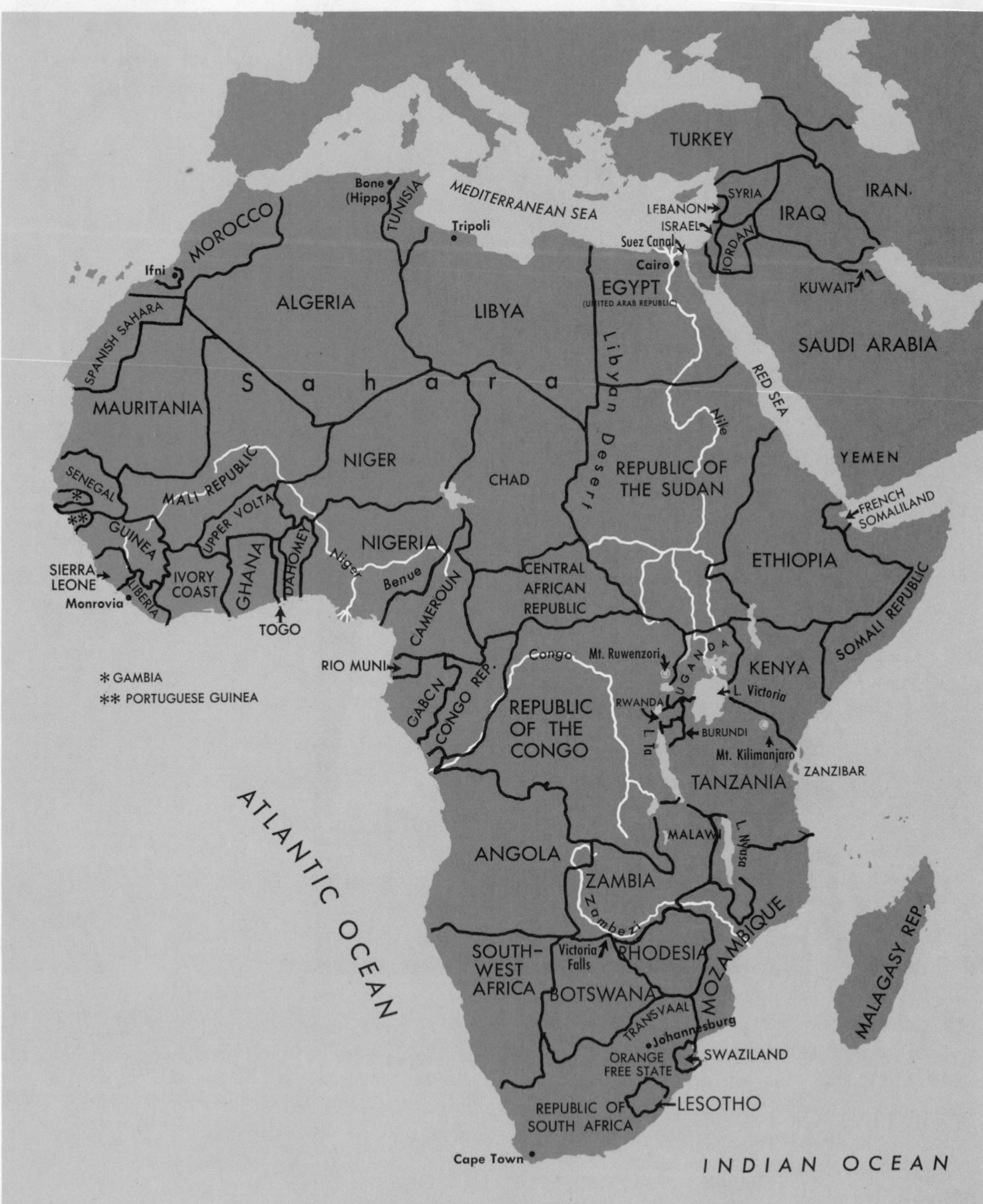

TURKEY
IRAN
SYRIA
LEBANON
ISRAEL
IRAQ
JORDAN
KUWAIT
SAUDI ARABIA
YEMEN
MEDITERRANEAN SEA
Bone (Hippo)
TUNISIA
Tripoli
MOROCCO
Ifni
ALGERIA
LIBYA
Suez Canal
Cairo
EGYPT
(UNITED ARAB REPUBLIC)
SPANISH SAHARA
S a h a r a
Libyan Desert
RED SEA
MAURITANIA
NIGER
Nile
REPUBLIC OF THE SUDAN
CHAD
SENEGAL
MALI REPUBLIC
FRENCH SOMALILAND
GUINEA
UPPER VOLTA
DAHOMEY
NIGERIA
Niger
ETHIOPIA
SIERRA LEONE
LIBERIA
IVORY COAST
GHANA
Benue
CENTRAL AFRICAN REPUBLIC
SOMALI REPUBLIC
Monrovia
TOGO
CAMEROUN
RIO MUNI
Congo
Mt. Ruwenzori
UGANDA
KENYA
* GAMBIA
** PORTUGUESE GUINEA
GABON
CONGO REP.
REPUBLIC OF THE CONGO
RWANDA
L. Victoria
BURUNDI
L. Ta
Mt. Kilimanjaro
ZANZIBAR
TANZANIA
ATLANTIC OCEAN
MALAWI
L. Nyasa
ANGOLA
ZAMBIA
Zambezi
MOZAMBIQUE
MALAGASY REP.
SOUTH-WEST AFRICA
Victoria Falls
RHODESIA
BOTSWANA
TRANSVAAL
Johannesburg
SWAZILAND
ORANGE FREE STATE
LESOTHO
REPUBLIC OF SOUTH AFRICA
Cape Town
INDIAN OCEAN

Africa: GEOGRAPHIC SETTING

Africa, a continent more than three times the size of the United States, is a land of extremes—a region of rich farmland and arid deserts, of flat plateaus and towering mountains, of intense heat and icy cold. Across the northern part of Africa lie the vast Sahara and Libyan deserts, but in the southern portion the fertile land produces grains, coffee, and other crops. Most of the continent is a plateau, but Mount Kilimanjaro (kil-ih-mun-*jah*-ro) rises out of the highlands of the east to a height of nearly four miles. About three-quarters of Africa is in the tropics, yet many of her mountains are capped with snow.

Africa was long known as the "dark continent." Her smooth, regular coastline and lack of inlets and harbors prevented explorers from docking their ships, and the few foreigners who did land had difficulty penetrating the inland jungles and deserts. Even today, much of Africa is unknown territory; population and geographical boundaries can only be estimated.

Africa is potentially a very rich continent. It has long been called the "land of gold and diamonds." More recently it has become one of the world's leading producers of uranium, and vast oil reserves have been discovered in the Sahara Desert. Great rivers like the Nile, the Congo, the Niger, and the Zambezi (zam-*bee*-zee) are now being harnessed to produce hydroelectric power. On the other hand, geographic factors also create serious problems. One of the most important of these factors is rainfall. In the vast deserts of Africa years sometimes pass without any rain. But in certain jungle regions near the equator, over a hundred inches of rain falls annually. Torrents frequently drench the land, ruining crops and damaging villages.

There are really two Africas. North Africa, linked with Europe by the easily navigable Mediterranean Sea, is the part whose history has been closely connected with that of Europe. In the south, beyond the vast expanses of the Sahara and Libyan deserts, is another part that has risen to prominence only in recent years. These two Africas, and the states included in them, are the subjects of Part 20.

Africa: PERSPECTIVE

"We prefer poverty in liberty to riches in slavery." Those proud words were spoken one day in 1958 by Sékou Touré, leader of the tiny West African state of Guinea, during a visit by Charles de Gaulle of France. De Gaulle had just offered the French territories in Africa a choice between self-government within the French Community or complete independence. After Touré's attack on French "colonialism" the split between France and Guinea was complete. In a referendum a few weeks later, 95 per cent of Guinea's voters chose independence.

Guinea's choice sharply dramatized the enthusiasm for freedom that began to sweep over Africa after World War II. In the years since, many more African states have gained independence and have been admitted to the United Nations. Today Africa is composed chiefly of politically independent states rather than European colonies or territories. Nearly one-third of the members of the United Nations are African. These emerging nations have learned quickly how to use their votes in UN assemblies to gain common objectives. In 1963 some thirty African states formed the Organization of African Unity to promote common

cultural, political, scientific and economic policies. The OAU's headquarters is in Addis Abada, Ethiopia.

As former colonies, most of the newly created states have had virtually no experience in self-government. Frequently, their inhabitants have little sense of nationality or patriotism, for they are still devoted to tribal loyalties. Few Africans have acquired the managerial skills or technical "know-how" to supervise economic or political functions or to operate essential services competently. Racial and ethnic antagonisms,—between blacks and whites, between Arabs and Negroes—further complicate the problem. As can be expected under such circumstances, disorders and civil wars have often occurred with dictatorship supplanting democratic government. While some African leaders may speak glibly of creating a "United States of Africa," it is more likely that Africans will have to pass through many of the phases of national development with which Westerners are familiar, before continental federation becomes truly feasible.

CHAPTER 66

Sub-Saharan Africa Enters the Modern World

THE SAHARA DESERT HAS DIVIDED AFRICA INTO TWO PARTS, NORTH AND SOUTH

The great belt of the Sahara Desert divides African history as much as it cuts the great continent into two sections. The story of the northern half of Africa is as old as that of Egypt, but Africa south of the Sahara has only recently come into the full light of history.

We have already touched on the history of North Africa in earlier parts of *Story of Nations*. In the Nile Valley the Egyptians built one of the first great civilizations. Along the northwestern coast Phoenicians founded colonies, the greatest of which was Carthage. Rome conquered Egypt and Carthage and made the coastal fringes of Africa part of her empire. Even today the well-preserved remains of many splendid Roman cities dot the coast, among them Hippo (modern Bone in Algeria), the city where the great Christian writer St. Augustine was bishop. In the fifth century A.D. one of the Germanic tribes, the Vandals, crossed from Spain and brought North Africa under its rule.

In the seventh century all of North Africa fell into the hands of the Moslems. The Arabs converted the tough Berber tribesmen to the Moslem faith. (It was the Moslem Berbers who conquered Spain and helped extend Islam deep into Europe.) A few centuries later the Arabs also gained control of the eastern coast of Africa. There they established coastal settlements and traded with the natives for ivory, gold, and slaves.

Small areas remained where Christianity persisted, most notably in the mountainous country of Ethiopia which escaped conquest by the Arabs. The rest of North Africa, however, has since re-

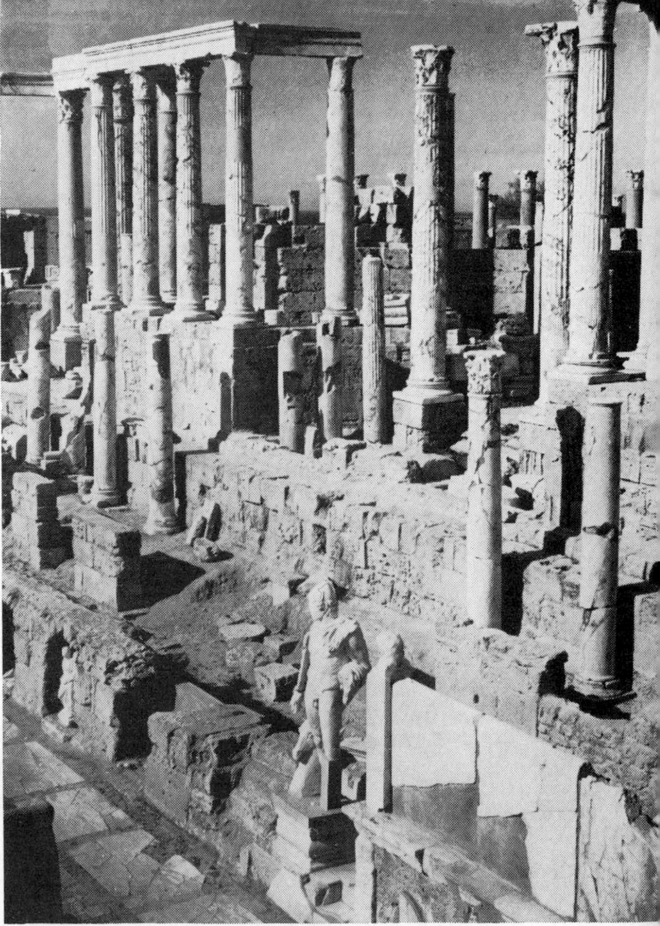

LEPTIS MAGNA. Located about eighty miles east of Tripoli in Libya, Leptis Magna is one of the oldest cities on the northern coast of Africa. It was founded by the Phoenicians and later taken over by the Romans. Septimius Severus was born there, and after becoming emperor of Rome in 193 A.D., he had the city rebuilt in the Roman style. The ruins pictured here are the remains of the forum.

mained Moslem, and its later history is related to that of the other Moslem peoples.

After the twelfth century North African civilization declined. A succession of civil wars and uprisings left the prosperous farms and villages in ruin. Much of North Africa became grazing land, supporting primitive nomad tribes instead of settled farmers. The cities lay deserted. The most prosperous period of North African history was already past.

We know very little about African history south of the Sahara before the tenth century, when a Negro empire, the kingdom of Ghana, arose in West Africa. The kingdom was composed of a federation of tribes that occupied a territory reaching from the Atlantic coast to the Niger River. All of the tribes paid tribute to a native king who resided at the capital city of ancient Ghana, a center of trade and industry. Ghana developed an effective government and adopted a code of laws that dealt sternly but justly with any who disturbed the peace and order of the kingdom. An Arab writer who visited the city reveals that Moslem influence was very strong. The official language was Arabic and many of the royal ministers were Moslems. The Arab visitor was impressed by the size of the city, the magnificence of its buildings, the luxurious living of the inhabitants, and the high level of learning and the arts. In the eleventh century the Moslems of North Africa conquered Ghana. But new Negro empires arose in the same area in the fourteenth and sixteenth centuries. It was these empires that first became known to Europeans.

EUROPEAN NATIONS "DISCOVERED" AFRICA, THEN PARTITIONED IT

Europeans began to settle on the African coasts. Unlike the Arabs, most Europeans knew nothing about Africa south of the Sahara. Its coastal waters, they believed, were inhabited by sea monsters, serpents, and other fearsome creatures. Then, in the fifteenth century, Europeans suddenly became eager to find better routes to India and China. The Portuguese were the first to sail down the west coast of Africa. In 1497 Vasco da Gama sailed around Africa to India. The Portuguese built a chain of forts along both the west and east coasts of Africa. That was the begin-

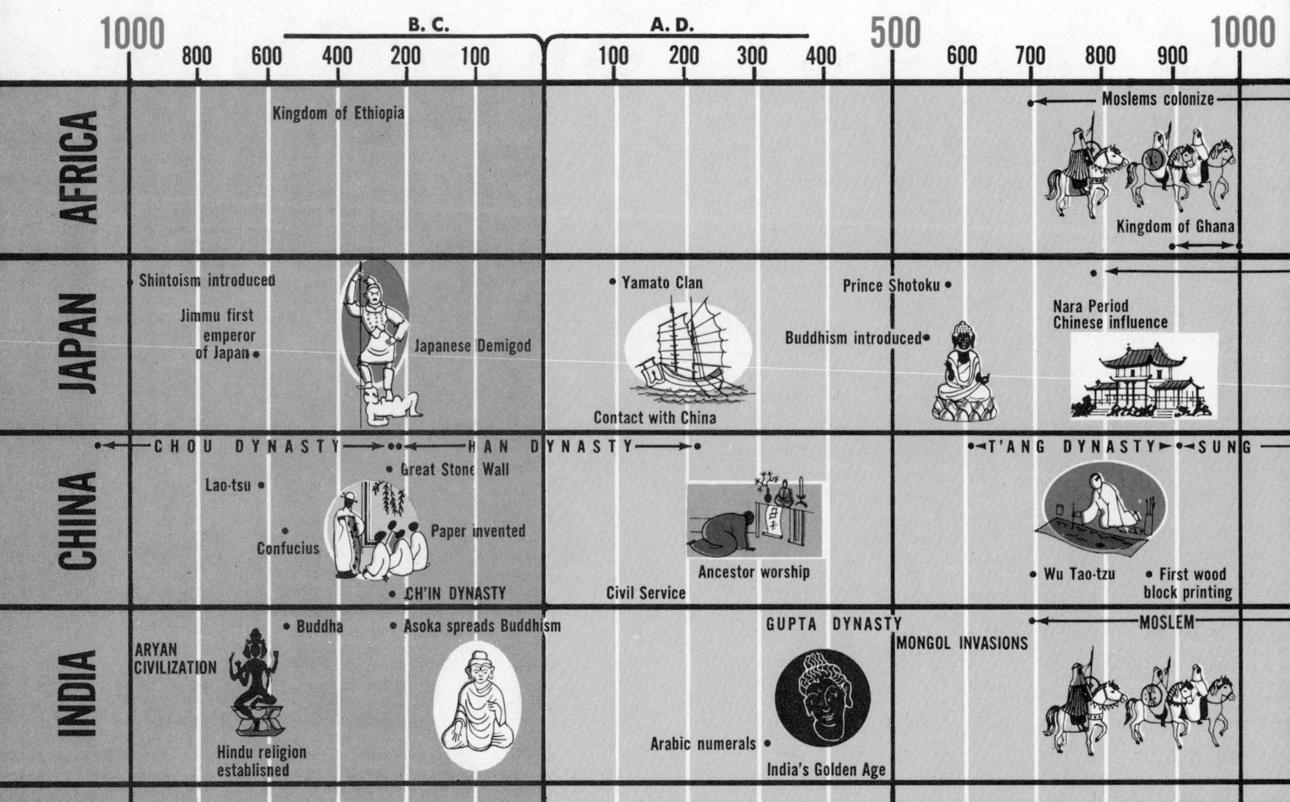

ning of Portugal's African empire, much of which she still holds.

A little later the French, Dutch, and British arrived and built more trading posts on Africa's west coast. They were chiefly interested in the gold, ivory, and slaves brought from the interior by Arab merchants and native kings. Slavery had long flourished in Africa itself, and the African chiefs willingly sold prisoners, taken in wars against neighboring tribes, to the captains of slave ships. Thus began the cruel slave trade that eventually brought millions of Africans to North and South America.

After several centuries, men of conscience began to protest the inhumanity of the slave trade. By the beginning of the nineteenth century nearly all European countries had agreed to outlaw slavery and put a stop to the slave trade. European settlements on the African coasts were used to intercept the slave traders, particularly the Arabs.

Europeans began to see Africa as a potential source of raw materials and a market for the sale of their manufactured goods. Missionaries suddenly became aware that millions of Africans were still pagans who had never been taught Christian beliefs. By the middle of the nineteenth century, explorers and missionaries began an ambitious effort to learn all about the interior of the "dark continent." British, French, and German explorers, laboriously making their way into the interior, found their efforts well rewarded. Some of them had the thrill of discovering and naming beautiful lakes and waterfalls, and of tracing the

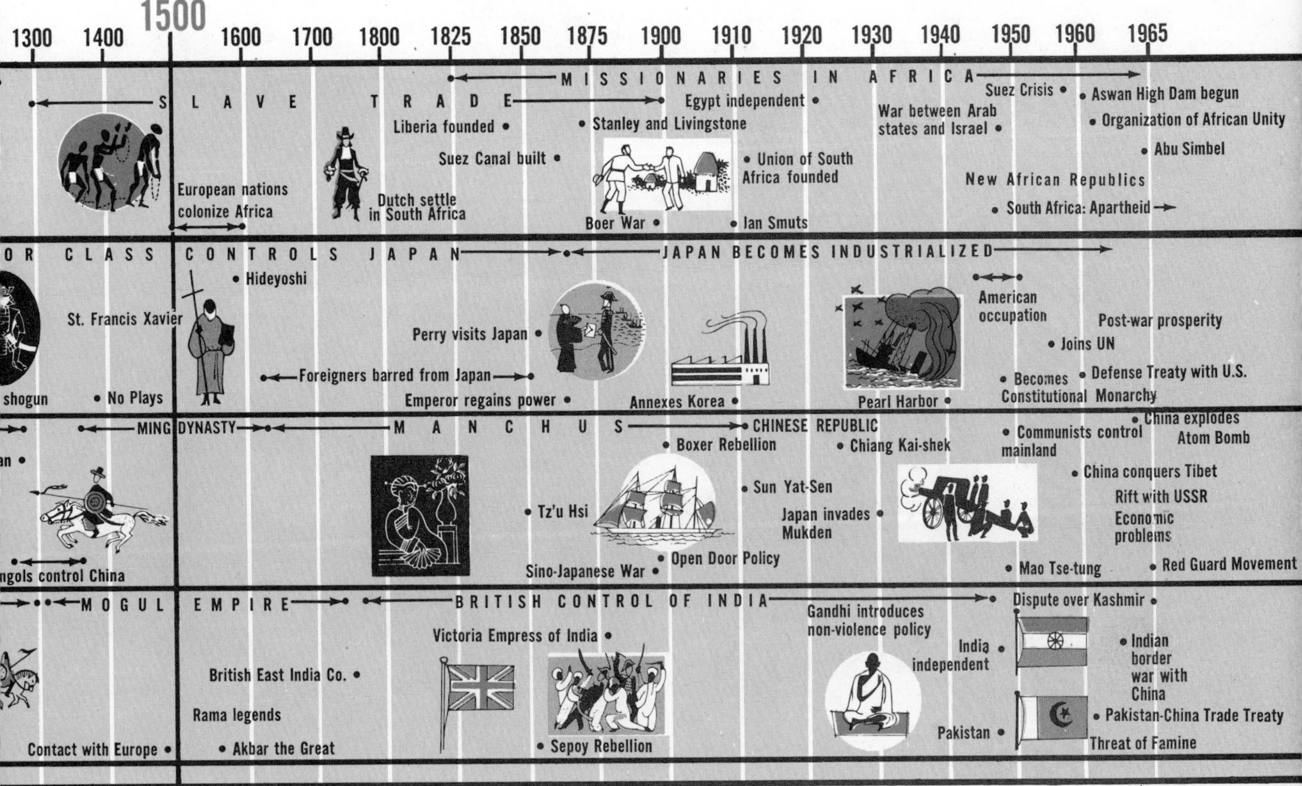

African rivers to their sources. Others found gold and diamond deposits and many raw materials that were in demand in Europe.

Livingstone and Stanley helped explore Africa. Probably the most famous English explorers in Africa were David Livingstone and Henry Morton Stanley. Livingstone, a Scottish missionary, studied medicine so that he could help raise health standards among the natives. As soon as he had his medical degree he went to South Africa. Soon he realized how little was known of Africa, and he became fascinated by the idea of exploring the vast continent. Livingstone discovered several lakes and the great Zambezi River. He traced the Zambezi's course from the Indian Ocean to its source not far from Africa's west coast, and he was the first European to see the magnificent Victoria Falls. On a later trip he explored the Lake Nayasa region and helped establish a mission there. His careful records and accurate maps proved very valuable to later explorers and missionaries.

No explorer had been able to find the source of Africa's most famous river, the Nile. Here was a challenge David Livingstone could not resist. In 1866 he organized an expedition and set out. He traveled into the Lake Tanganyika (tan-gun-*yee*-kuh) region. Then all reports stopped. Livingstone disappeared. Years went by, but the silence continued.

Newspapers and magazines carried stories about the mysterious disappearance of Dr. Livingstone. Other explorers went searching for him but found no clues. Was he really dead? An editor of an

STANLEY AND LIVINGSTONE. The historic meeting between Henry Stanley and David Livingstone took place in November of 1871 after an eight-month journey by Stanley into the interior of Africa. Together the two men explored the northern shores of Lake Tanganyika before Stanley left in March of 1872. He took Livingstone's journals to England, where he was received with gifts and thanks by Queen Victoria.

American newspaper, the *New York Herald*, realized the fascinating story that would result if Livingstone were found. He called in a reporter named Henry Stanley and said, "Find Livingstone."

Henry Stanley knew nothing about Africa, but he was an able reporter ready to overcome any obstacle for a story. Stanley, who had been born in Wales, had shipped as a cabin boy to New Orleans when he was eighteen. He arrived in America just in time to fight in the Civil War. After the war he became a reporter.

Stanley left immediately for Africa. Pushing into the continent from the eastern side, he reached the magnificent grasslands. Although months of searching brought terrible hardships, Africa began to fascinate him. Natives told him vague stories of a lone white man somewhere to the west. Finally, on the shores of Lake Tanganyika he reached a camp where he had been told a white doctor lived. A bearded, obviously ill man stepped slowly from a hut to greet the reporter.

"Dr. Livingstone, I presume?" asked the young reporter brightly.

Stanley tried to persuade the aging, sickly explorer to come home, but Livingstone wanted to continue his explorations. Stanley gave him supplies and returned to the coast. His reports of the meeting made him world famous.

A year later came news of Livingstone's death in Africa. Stanley decided to give up reporting and return to Africa to carry on the work Livingstone had been unable to finish. Neither Stanley nor Livingstone ever found the source of the Nile. It was an English explorer, John Speke, who discovered Lake Victoria and made the journey down the great river to the Mediterranean. But Stanley discovered the fabled "Mountains of the Moon," the Ruwenzori (roo-wen-*zo*-ree) Mountains just above the equator, and made a long, dangerous journey down the Congo River to the Atlantic coast.

Always a good newspaper man, Stanley saw to it that his discoveries were fully reported in both European and American newspapers. He realized the possibilities of bringing Africa's riches to Europe as well as making Africa a market for manufactured goods. He tried unsuccessfully to interest British officials in developing the Congo region. It was King Leopold II of Belgium who finally heeded Stanley. As a result, Belgium gained control of the incredibly rich Congo, a region eighty times as large as Belgium itself.

VICTORIA FALLS. Situated on the Zambezi River between Northern and Southern Rhodesia, these falls are 343 feet high, twice the height of Niagara Falls. They were discovered by David Livingstone in November of 1855 and named for Queen Victoria.

EUROPEAN NATIONS PARTITIONED AFRICA

France obtained the largest area, England and Belgium the most valuable. In 1876, when Stanley first sailed down the Congo River, only 10 per cent of Africa was claimed by Europeans. The French had colonies in North Africa, and the Spanish and Portuguese had some forts and trading posts on the coast. There was also a Dutch settlement at Cape Town near the southern tip of Africa that the British had taken over after the Napoleonic Wars. Thirty-six years later nearly all of Africa had been brought under the control of European nations. Only Liberia and Ethiopia managed to remain free.

The race for African lands by Western European nations after 1870 resulted from several causes. Each of the large nations feared that one of the others might gain a monopoly of African trade and close Africa's markets to competing nations. They sought to protect their trading privileges by establishing their own colonies in Africa. To some degree, however, the scramble for colonies reflected a sincere desire by Europeans to help the African natives. Not understanding the native traditions, they felt that the "savage" needed to learn European ways, to become Christian, and to experience the blessings of European medical knowledge and higher standards of living. At this time, a wave of nationalism was sweeping through Europe. Each of the European nations believed its culture was the most advanced, and each therefore felt it was best fitted to help the natives.

In the scramble for Africa, France won the most territory (but much of it in the Sahara), and Great Britain and Belgium got the most valuable areas. Portugal and Spain managed to hang on

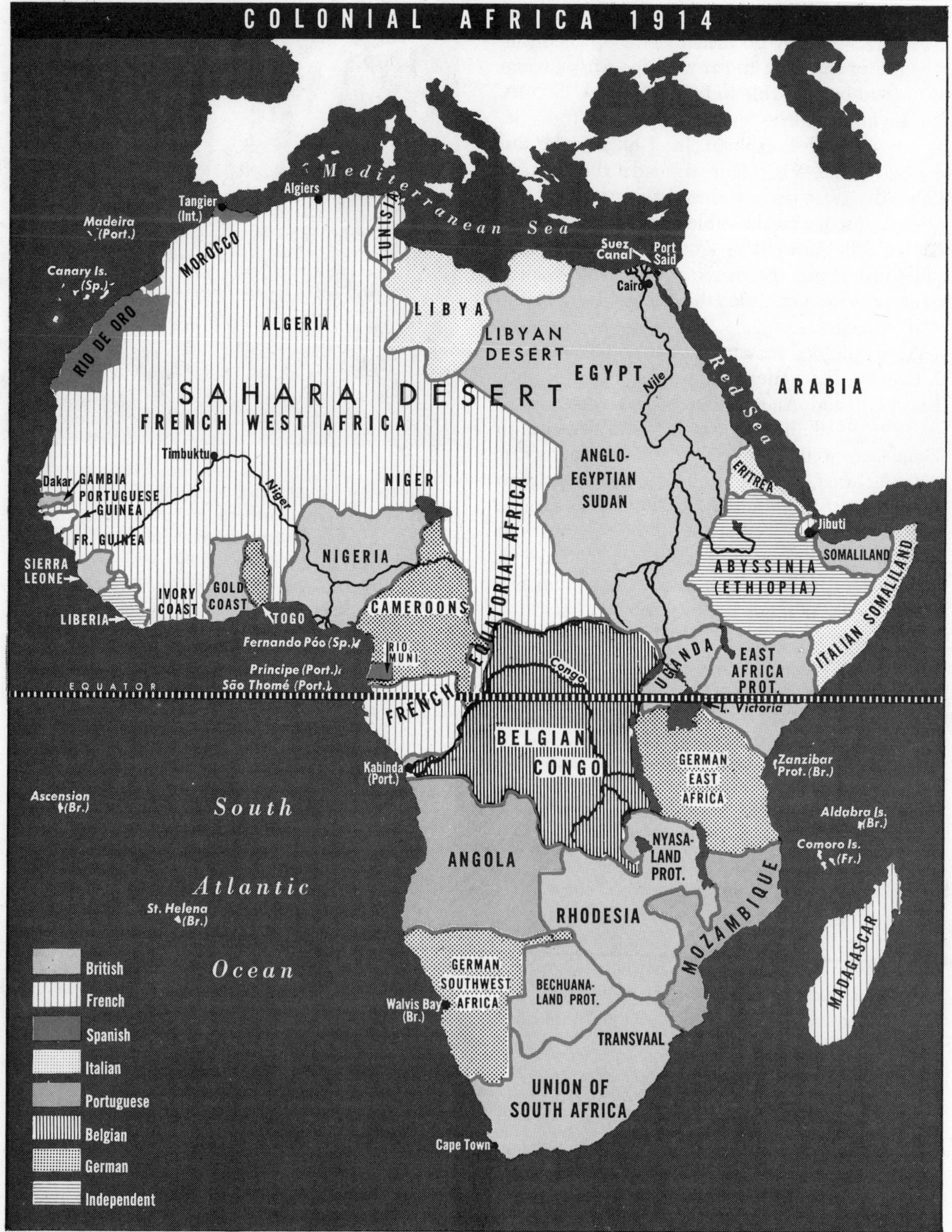
COLONIAL AFRICA 1914
Mediterranean Sea
Tangier (Int.)
Algiers
Madeira (Port.)
Canary Is. (Sp.)
MOROCCO
TUNISIA
Suez Canal
Port Said
Cairo
RIO DE ORO
ALGERIA
LIBYA
LIBYAN DESERT
EGYPT
Nile
Red Sea
ARABIA
SAHARA DESERT
FRENCH WEST AFRICA
Timbuktu
ANGLO-EGYPTIAN SUDAN
ERITREA
Dakar
GAMBIA
PORTUGUESE GUINEA
Niger
NIGER
FR. GUINEA
Jibuti
SOMALILAND
SIERRA LEONE
NIGERIA
EQUATORIAL AFRICA
ABYSSINIA (ETHIOPIA)
IVORY COAST
GOLD COAST
LIBERIA
TOGO
CAMEROONS
ITALIAN SOMALILAND
Fernando Póo (Sp.)
RIO MUNI
Congo
UGANDA
EAST AFRICA PROT.
Principe (Port.)
São Thomé (Port.)
EQUATOR
FRENCH
L. Victoria
BELGIAN CONGO
GERMAN EAST AFRICA
Kabinda (Port.)
Zanzibar Prot. (Br.)
Ascension (Br.)
South
Aldabra Is. (Br.)
NYASA-LAND PROT.
ANGOLA
Comoro Is. (Fr.)
Atlantic
St. Helena (Br.)
RHODESIA
MOZAMBIQUE
MADAGASCAR
GERMAN SOUTHWEST AFRICA
BECHUANA-LAND PROT.
Ocean
Walvis Bay (Br.)
TRANSVAAL
UNION OF SOUTH AFRICA
Cape Town
British
French
Spanish
Italian
Portuguese
Belgian
German
Independent

Traditional Africa. An African chieftain sits surrounded by his family and members of his tribe. Although the majority of Africans still live in tribal cultures, tribal traditions are rapidly breaking down.

to the colonies they had won centuries earlier. Italy and Germany, which appeared late on the scene, had to take what was left.

African nationalism grew strong after World War II. Between 1900 and 1914 spectacular changes took place in Africa. Roads, railroads, telegraph lines, plantations, and factories that were built by the colonial powers transformed the landscape. Christian missionaries reached every part of Africa, bringing new ideas and Western culture. More and more Africans drifted into towns or came to work on European plantations and in mines. Gradually the old tribal customs and laws that had once governed African society broke down and gave way before the half-understood ideas and values of the white man.

Africa played a vital role in World War II. In 1941 the Germans invaded North Africa and almost captured Egypt and the Suez Canal. A little later American and British troops landed in North Africa and used it as a steppingstone for the invasion of Europe. The Allied nations built many airfields and highways in northern and western Africa. Many natives were given more responsible jobs than they had ever held before. Native soldiers served overseas, and many of them saw for the first time how peoples in other countries lived. The Africans heard their European rulers proclaim again and again that they were fighting for freedom and democratic ideals. The Africans realized now that they were given none of these advantages. African resentment of foreign rule steadily increased. At the end of the war riots and disorder broke out in many of the French and British colonies.

Since 1946 great changes have taken place in Africa. Most African territories have won inde-

Johannesburg. This modern city was originally a gold-rush camp in the late nineteenth century. The people here, as elsewhere in South Africa, have begun to realize that apartheid is hurting themselves as well as the natives.

AFRICAN GRASSLANDS. Vast areas of tropical grassland lie both above and below the equatorial rain forest region of Africa. At one time large herds of wild game, such as these zebras, roamed the grasslands, but now the herds have been so greatly reduced by hunters and trappers that some kinds of game are in danger of becoming extinct.

pendence or the right to govern themselves. The European powers that still have African possessions are trying desperately to maintain the remnants of their empires. They are by no means agreed on how best to do this, however. In Chapter 67 you will read about the changes taking place in Africa, and you will see how the various nations are adjusting to them.

Chapter Check-up

1. How has the Sahara Desert influenced Africa's history?
2. What religion has dominated North Africa since the seventh century?
3. Has North or South Africa been more important historically? Why?
4. Why did Europeans first sail south along the coast of Africa?
5. How did Livingstone and Stanley influence the development of Africa?
6. For what reasons did European countries partition almost all of Africa?
7. Which European countries gained the most valuable areas of Africa in the late nineteenth century?
8. Why did African nationalism increase after World War II?

CHAPTER 67

Independent States Began to Emerge in Africa

NORTH AFRICA IS CHIEFLY INHABITED BY MOSLEM ARABS

All of North Africa's six states have gained their independence. Africa is so big and so diversified that it would take many books to discuss each of its more than forty countries and colonies. In this and the following chapter we will visit some of the most important regions on the continent. (As you read these chapters you will find it helpful to refer frequently to the maps on pages 634 and 642.)

North Africa today includes six independent states: Morocco, Tunisia, Libya, Egypt, the Sudan, and Algeria. All six of these North African countries have a long history and share common traditions. In all of these lands Arabic is the common language, and Islam, the religion taught by Mohammed, is the common faith. Because these countries were so close to Europe, they were always more highly developed than the rest of Africa, and, except for Algeria, they were the first to achieve independence from their colonial rulers. Domination by the Europeans did not cause these people to change their ways. Instead, they clung more fiercely to their own religious and cultural traditions. By the end of World War II an exhausted Western Europe found it could no longer retain control over the area. All the North African states but Algeria won their freedom. In 1962, Algeria, too, became independent.

Egypt has become the leader of the Arab states. Egypt, the oldest country in Africa, has known many conquerors since the great days of the ancient Egyptian Empire. Greeks, Romans, Arabs, and Turks have ruled Egypt. In the nineteenth century the weakness of the Turkish rulers gave the French and British a chance to gain influence in Egyptian affairs. A French company completed the Suez Canal in 1869, but a few years later the British managed to buy enough shares in the company to get control of this important waterway to their colonial possessions in India. A few years later Britain became "protector of Egypt," although Turkey still claimed to rule the country. When Turkey sided with Germany in World War I, the British rushed troops to the Nile and virtually took over all Egypt in order to protect the Suez Canal. After the war Egypt was allowed to proclaim her independence, but British soldiers remained in the country and British warships guarded the coast and the canal.

After 1922 Egyptian internal affairs were controlled by the Egyptians themselves. A parliamentary government similar to Britain's was established and Egypt became a constitutional monarchy. But it was a hopelessly corrupt government. The upper classes used the government to make themselves rich, and nothing was done to help the poverty-stricken masses. Vast slum areas developed in great cities like Cairo. The peasantry suffered from poor food, poor housing, and a lack of medical care. Egypt's kings were notorious for their lives of pleasure and luxury. To keep the people from rising against the government, the politicians and the king convinced them that their troubles were caused by the British occupation. Resentment against Britain mounted steadily.

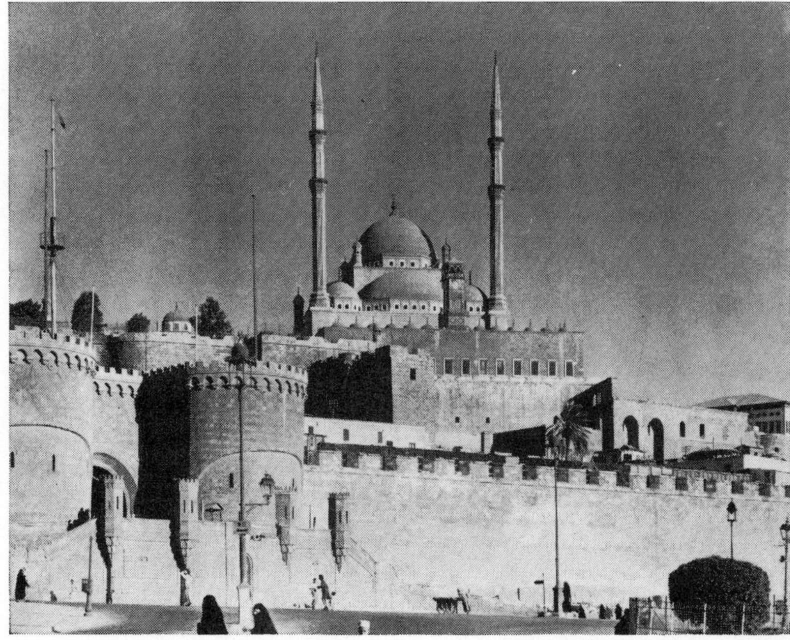

EGYPTIAN MOSQUE. Islam, the religion taught by Mohammed, was established in Egypt through force by the Arabs in the last part of the seventh century. Today Islam is the principal religion throughout North Africa. Millions of people worship every day at mosques like the one shown here.

Tunisian Street Scene. People go about their business outside the ninth-century walls of Sousse, in northeastern Tunisia. The young man on his bicycle and the children in simple frocks contrast with the donkey cart and the woman in traditional dress. This scene typifies the mingling of old and new that is found in North Africa.

After World War II, Britain retained only the Suez Canal zone. Heading an eight-nation Arab League, Egypt led an attack on the new state of Israel in 1948. But the out-numbered Israelis repelled the invaders and forced the Arabs to accept a truce.

Blaming their corrupt government for Egypt's defeat, a "Free Officers" group staged a coup in 1952. Two years later Colonel Gamel Abdel Nasser (*nass*-er) emerged as president of the newly proclaimed republic.

Important reforms were introduced. Individual landholdings were restricted to a hundred acres. A million peasants received up to five acres each. Agricultural co-operatives and industrialization were encouraged. All but the smallest businesses came under state control.

This "Arab socialism" was, however, only partly successful. Changes were made too quickly. With Egypt's population growth rate so high and desert covering over ninety-five per cent of the country, there was just not enough farm land for effective agricultural reform.

Hoping to irrigate a million acres of desert and make more water power available, Nasser planned the construction of a "high dam" at Aswan (*ass*-won), six hundred miles up the Nile. With Russian financial and technical aid, the dam was completed after eleven years in 1971 but it served to dramatize how much Egypt had been absorbed into the Soviet Union's orbit.

For this Nasser's desire to become the Arab world's leader was largely responsible. He fanned the flames of Arab nationalism against Israel, the still-hated British and Arab rulers who would not accept his direction. When the Western democracies, fearing another Egyptian attack on Israel, refused to supply arms to Nasser he began to purchase them in 1958 from Communist lands. This caused the United States to cancel its aid for the construction of the Aswan Dam and Nasser responded by seizing the Suez Canal in 1956 to obtain additional revenue. His action touched off an Anglo-French-Israeli invasion. Just as Nasser's regime seemed about to topple, joint Russo-American pressure forced the invaders to withdraw. Nasser's military disaster was transformed into a political triumph and he was the hero of Arabs everywhere.

Nasser was not nearly so lucky in 1967 when, after provoking another crisis with Israel, he saw his Soviet-equipped forces routed in the "Six Day War." Even then, however, he retained the affections of Egypt's masses who would not let him resign from office.

Nor were Nasser's efforts to unify the Arabs

truly successful. He presided briefly (1958–1961) over a "United Arab Republic" of Egypt and Syria until the Syrians seceded. His intervention in a civil war in Yemen (1962–7) was costly and fruitless.

Nasser died from a sudden heart attack in 1970. His successor, Anwar Sadat (sah-*dot*), has continued his policies. Sadat has threatened renewed war with Israel, signed a fifteen year "friendship" pact with Russia and placed Egypt (now called the "Arab Republic of Egypt") into a new federation with Syria and Libya.

Conflict has ravaged the Sudan. Lying just south of Egypt is the Sudan. Its unhappy history is due largely to geographic and cultural factors. The Egyptians realize that an unfriendly Sudan could, by controlling the Nile, turn Egypt into a desert. Accordingly, since ancient times, Egypt has tried to dominate its Southern neighbor.

In 1956 the Sudanese were finally able to free themselves from joint Anglo-Egyptian rule. But freedom has brought terrible problems since the northern and southern regions of the country have so little in common. The areas have about the same numbers of people but the South is inhabited by Negro pagans while the more advanced North is the home of Arab Moslems. Even before full Sudanese independence was achieved, Southerners began a bloody secession movement. The conflict has dragged on into the 1970s and is said to have resulted in a million casualties. In March, 1972 there were indications that hostilities might soon end.

Even at peace the Sudan will have much difficulty. Only a bit of this largest of Africa's countries is habitable or productive. The one important commercial crop,—long-staple cotton—is raised in a relatively small region around the capital city of Khartoum (kar-*toom*). Seeking a Marxist solution to the Sudan's economic problems, Communist and Socialist military cliques have been vying for power.

Pp. 647-8

Morocco and Tunisia: "twins with a difference." There are important similarities between Tunisia and Morocco. Both are chiefly Arabic but with large Berber minorities. Both have absorbed much French culture. Both possess big reserves of phosphates, used in making fertilizer and munitions. Both became World War II battlefields and demanded independence from France when the war ended. After riots and rebellions, both received freedom in 1956, with Spain also renouncing her part of Morocco. Tunisia became a republic and Morocco a monarchy but both have remained essentially pro-Western in their political outlook.

Habib Bourguiba (ha-*beeb* boor-*gee*-bah), leader of Tunisia's freedom fight, has been president since 1957. He is noted for progressive reforms, particularly in behalf of women's rights. Improvements in the economy, health and education have been impressive. Tunisia is the only Arab state to remain on consistently good terms with Israel; for this Bourguiba has been much

NASSER AND KHRUSHCHEV. In 1964 the two leaders joined hands after setting off an explosion to divert the Nile and allow completion of the Aswan Dam, built with Soviet aid.

criticised by other Arabs. Tunisians' greatest anxiety is about the frail health of their aging president.

Morocco has had a much stormier history due to an enormous population growth rate, high unemployment and illiteracy. Hasan II (ha-*san*), who ascended the throne in 1961, violated the constitution by ruling autocratically from 1965 to 1970. In 1971 he barely survived an attempted military coup.

Algeria's "bark" has been worse than its "bite." In 1962, after a long struggle with France, Algeria won independence, (see pages 348–9). The new country's leaders made ambitious pledges: Algeria was to be second only to Egypt as an Arab power; Algerians would lead the struggle for "socialism" and "Arab nationalism" against "Western imperialism."

These pledges have often proved to be empty boasts. Algeria's condition has not permitted the fulfillment of grand designs. The million Europeans who had provided most of the essential services fled to France when Algeria became free. Such a blow was dealt to the economy that for a while seventy per cent of the Algerian work force was unemployed! Even in better times unemployment has been around twenty-five per cent.

While there has been some socialization of lands and industries, Algeria has welcomed financial and technical aid from Western as well as Marxist countries. Similarly, Algeria has vehemently denounced Israel's existence but has never sent forces to battle the Israelis. Houari Boumedienne (boo-made-*yen*), president since 1963, has threatened much but acted much less.

Libya has risen from "rags" to "riches." Libya, lying between Egypt and Tunisia, was taken by Italy after a war with Turkey in 1912. Following World War II it was under Anglo-French control until granted its freedom by the United Nations in 1952.

Then Libya was one of the world's poorest nations. Dry farming and live-stock grazing were about the only occupations for the two million residents of this desert land. In return for financial aid, Libya welcomed the installation of British and American military bases.

In 1959 large oil deposits were discovered and the situation changed. Newly-rich Libya now became much sought-after. In 1969 the aged, pro-Western king was overthrown by army officers who set up a left-wing republic. A year later, the government seized the large US air-base. Westerners were encouraged to depart, being replaced chiefly by Egyptians. In 1971 Libya, Syria, and Egypt formed a "Federation of Arab Republics."

ETHIOPIA AND LIBERIA WERE THE FIRST INDEPENDENT NATIONS OF CENTRAL AFRICA

Ethiopia has long been a "one man show." Ethiopia's name comes from two Greek words meaning "sun-burned faces," referring to the dark skins of the inhabitants. About 1100 B.C. Ethiopia won her freedom from Egypt and was able to keep that freedom despite the Arab conquest of North Africa in the seventh century A.D. The Ethiopians have also rejected the advances of Moslem missionaries and have remained faithful to the Coptic version of Christianity.

Italy tried to conquer Ethiopia in 1896 but her army was destroyed by the Ethiopians. In 1936, under Mussolini, the Italians invaded again. Haile Selassie (*high*-lee seh-*lass*-ee), who ruled Ethiopia as regent or Emperor since 1916, appealed to the League of Nations. The League condemned Italy but applied ineffective sanctions. Italy merely left the League and made Ethiopia her colony. During World War II Ethiopia was liberated with Haile Selassie returning in triumph. The former Italian colony of Eritrea was incorporated into Ethiopia to give the country a seacoast.

The Emperor has tried valiantly to modernize Ethiopia. New industries and water power projects have been developed. There is free public education. Broad avenues and high-rise

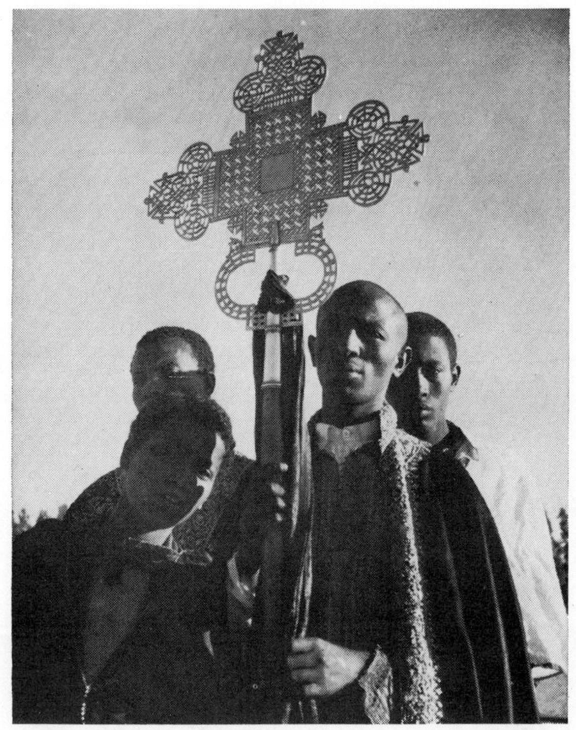

COPTIC PRIESTS. The Coptic religion is one of the oldest of Christian sects. It is especially strong in Ethiopia. The priests in this picture are taking part in ceremonies celebrating the Feast of the Timkat, or Epiphany, in Addis Ababa, the capital city of Ethiopia.

buildings adorn the capital, Addis Ababa (*ad*-iss *aba*-buh), making it a suitable headquarters for the Organization of African Unity. A constitution provides for a popularly elected lower house.

But there are enormous obstacles to progress. Ethiopians have been conditioned to scorn hard labor. Peasants use the most primitive farming methods. The illiteracy rate is ninety per cent and the Coptic Church, which controls education, teaches that the earth is flat. Land reform is urgent, for nine-tenths of the population is composed of tenant farmers owing their first allegiance to their feudal lords. But such reform is, of course, opposed by the nobles and Church who are the regime's most important props.

With all important power still in the Emperor's aging hands, uprisings have occurred, notably a rebellion in Eritrea in 1971, supported by some of Ethiopia's Moslem neighbors. What will happen when Haile Selassie finally leaves the political scene, no one can prophesy.

Liberia is America's "poor relations." On the opposite side of Africa lies Liberia, the continent's oldest independent republic. Hot, moist, and primitive, Liberia is of special interest to Americans. Its constitution and flag follow American models. Its capital, Monrovia, is named for President James Monroe. Two-thirds of its trade is with the United States and its currency is the American dollar.

This has happened because Liberia was founded in 1847 by freed Negro slaves from the United States. Their return to Africa some years before had been aided by white Americans who felt this was a method of coping with America's racial problems. The fifteen thousand "Americo-Liberians" soon dominated the million and a half inhabitants of the interior.

Liberia, then, may be considered a "child" of the United States but Liberia's condition cannot make Americans proud of the relationship. Liberia has under twenty miles of paved road, fewer than a half dozen native doctors, a less than fifteen per cent rate of literacy. Elections and government are corrupt and undemocratic: William Tubman was president from 1943 until his death in 1971. Most shameful was the revelation in 1931, in a League of Nations report, that high Liberian officials (themselves descendants of slaves) were selling countrymen as slaves to other regions!

Liberia's natural resources could provide a brighter future. Since the 1920s the Firestone Company has invested heavily in rubber plantations. The iron ore reserves are of particularly good quality and have attracted much foreign capital in the last fifteen years. The forests could yield considerable amounts of valuable timber. But America's "poor relation" still requires considerable help.

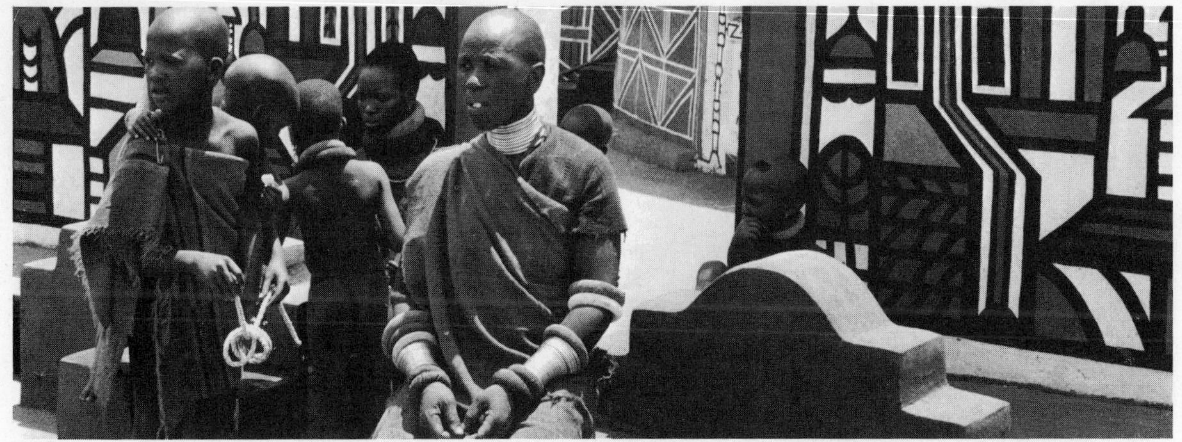

SOUTH AFRICAN VILLAGE. A mother and her children congregate before the entrance to the strikingly decorative village of Mapoch near Pretoria in the Republic of South Africa. Such compounds, though culturally attractive, only emphasize the abhorrent apartheid condition that still exists in South Africa, and which continues to keep both black and white apart.

DESCENDANTS OF DUTCH SETTLERS RULE THE REPUBLIC OF SOUTH AFRICA

The Dutch were conquered by the British. At the southern tip of Africa lies a nation entirely unlike Liberia, for the Republic of South Africa is a country in which the Negro population has no voice in the government. White men alone rule. Of a population of about sixteen million, about 20 per cent are of European descent, 10 per cent (called *Coloureds*) are of mixed European and African descent, and somewhat less than three per cent are Asiatics, mostly from India. The remaining eleven million are Africans, mostly Bantu Negroes.

The Dutch settlement in South Africa had declared itself a republic as early as 1795, but only a few months later the republic was conquered by the British, and many Englishmen came to settle in the new British colony. The British and the South Africans of Dutch descent, called Boers (boorz), did not mix well, because their feelings about the Negroes differed greatly. When the British abolished slavery in all British territories early in the nineteenth century, the Boers became very angry. They believed that the Bible taught that Negroes had been created to be slaves to white men. In order to get away from British rule, five thousand Boers moved north into wild territory. They established two independent republics called the Transvaal and the Orange Free State. Unfortunately for the Boers and their hopes, gold was discovered in the Transvaal and diamonds in the Orange Free State. Hundreds of prospectors, mostly British, came hurrying into the Boer republics. Again there was trouble. This time the Boers knew that they could not move away. They stayed and fought the British. Surprisingly, it took Great Britain three years, from 1899 to 1902, to defeat the Boers and take over their states.

The British were anxious to end the bitterness caused by the war, and they tried to win the Boers' support by allowing them a large amount of self-government. It was through the efforts of a

Dutch farmer and former Boer general, Jan Christian Smuts, that the settlers of Dutch descent came to accept British rule. After the war Smuts made every effort to bring peace between the Boers and Great Britain. He gained the confidence of both sides. In 1910 Great Britain gave up control of South Africa and united the four provinces of Cape Colony, Natal, Transvaal, and the Orange Free State into the Union of South Africa. The Union became a self-governing member of the British Commonwealth of Nations, and Smuts became a minister in the first cabinet of the new government.

Although the form of government was modeled on that of Britain, the Union of South Africa did not become a true democracy. Political control remained in the hands of the British and the South Africans of Dutch descent, the latter forming the Nationalist-Afrikaner Party. Afrikaans (af-rih-*kahns*) is a Dutch dialect, and the South Africans of Dutch descent are called Afrikaners.

CAPETOWN. This view of the Cape Peninsula shows the beautiful city of Capetown nestling at the foot of Table Mountain. The city is one of the leading cultural centers of South Africa and is also famous as a resort area. Its Mediterranean climate is similar to that of the Riviera and southern California.

The Afrikaners have imposed "apartheid" on South Africa. Whites in South Africa have long enjoyed Africa's highest living standard. Their prosperity is based largely on South Africa's rich gold and diamond mines. By the hundreds of thousands Bantus have come from other lands to work in those mines. They come because their wages, though low by Western standards, give them a greater income than they could have at home. After working in the mines, most Bantus have grown so accustomed to a money economy that they migrate to South Africa's cities rather than return to their own villages.

While this Bantu labor is welcomed, the greatly outnumbered whites fear loss of their own power. In 1948 the Nationalist Party, composed mainly of Afrikaners, won control of the parliament. It has governed the country ever since, largely by denying voting rights to non-whites.

The Nationalists began "Apartheid" (Uh *part* ate), which is a policy of racial segregation ex-

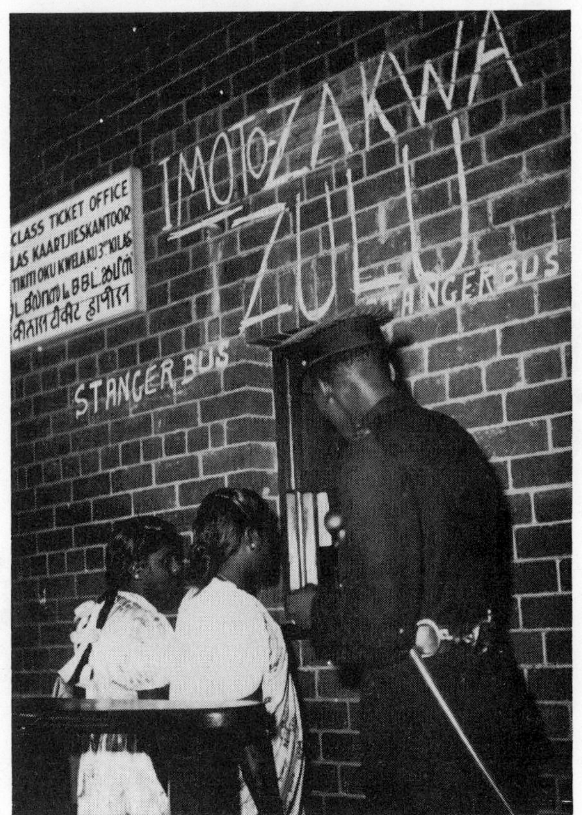

APARTHEID. In South Africa, the official policy of separating whites and non-whites makes it necessary for these two girls to buy their railroad tickets at the special third-class ticket window reserved for non-whites.

tremely unfavorable to non-whites. Bantus may reside only in ghettos, are subject to curfew rules and must carry complicated passports. Their educational and vocational opportunities are limited and wage scales are based on race.

"Apartheid" was condemned by the UN General Assembly and the British Commonwealth of Nations. In anger, South Africa withdrew from the Commonwealth in 1961, becoming an independent republic. The Nationalist government has made some concessions. Since 1963 a few "Bantustans" (partially self-governing Bantu "homelands") have been created. In the early 1970s certain foreign black dignitaries and athletes have been permitted to visit South Africa and there were friendlier relations with a few black African governments. But the condition of most non-whites has remained deplorable and most African nations are still hostile to the Nationalist regime.

Chapter Check-up

1. Which of North Africa's six states was the last to gain its independence?
2. What do all the North African states have in common?
3. What crisis was touched off by Egypt's seizure of the Suez Canal? What was the eventual result?
4. What was the purpose of the United Arab Republic? In what year did the country of Syria withdraw?
5. Why is Egypt interested in Sudan?
6. When did Morocco and Tunisia become independent? Describe their present relationship to France.
7. Which were the first independent nations in Central Africa? Which is the oldest country?
8. How did Britain gain control of South Africa?
9. Who are the Afrikaners? What policy have they introduced in South Africa? What have been some results of this policy?

CHAPTER 68

Former European Colonies Are Now Independent

GREAT BRITAIN PREPARED HER COLONIES FOR SELF-GOVERNMENT

Africa is no longer governed largely by European nations. Only Great Britain and Portugal still rule sizable territories in Africa, and Great Britain has been rapidly giving her territories independence. (Spain has several colonies along the sandy west coast of Africa, but they are small both in size and importance.)

The conditions under which the African colonies have gained their independence have varied. In the former Belgian colony of the Congo, independence resulted in chaos, civil strife, and the loss of many lives. The French and British colonies, however, became independent in a peaceful manner.

Ghana was one of the first British colonies in Africa to gain independence. The British colony of the Gold Coast became the independent state of Ghana in March, 1957. Preparations had begun in 1951 when Britain granted her colony a new constitution and its own parliament. With independence, the leader of the freedom movement, Kwame Nkrumah (en-*kroo*-mah), became prime minister. In 1960 Ghana became a Republic, and Nkrumah became president.

Accra. The capital city of Ghana reflects both the old British control when the country was known as the Gold Coast and the new era when the people are breaking into a period of certainty and expansion.

Despite Ghana's praliamentary form of government, however, Nkrumah was gradually able to turn his country into a one-party socialist state. In 1961 he assumed absolute control of his Convention People's Party. The press and radio were subjected to government censorship. Political opponents were harassed and jailed. In 1962 the Ghanaian Parliament voted to make Nkrumah president for life. And in 1964 he was given dictatorial power.

Many of Ghana's people were not happy with these developments. Plots, bombings, and attempted assassinations showed the country's unrest. Nevertheless, Nkrumah continued his policies. Communist Chinese and East German technicians appeared in Ghana. The Convention People's Party took over supervision of the army, police, universities, and many other social institutions.

Nkrumah also tried to establish himself as the dominant figure in Africa. He was one of the leaders in the Pan-African movement that resulted in the formation of the Organization for African Unity. Nkrumah's aim was the creation of a United States of Africa under the leadership of Ghana.

Domestic unrest continued in Ghana. In 1966 while Nkrumah was visiting China a group of army officers formed a National Liberation Council and took over the government. They freed over 400 political prisoners, and jailed many officials of the Nkrumah regime. The Council promised free elections, and a new constitution. Communist teachers and technicians were expelled. Nkrumah, forced into exile, found shelter in the country of Guinea.

Ghana has had economic as well as political troubles. Nkrumah's policies had pushed the country deeply into debt. The new government is trying to restore Ghana's credit. That the country has vast mineral resources is suggested by her colonial name of the Gold Coast. Ghana has large deposits of gold, diamonds and manganese ore. Her chief export, however, is cacao, the plant from which chocolate is made. Ghana produces more than a third of the world's supply. A huge hydroelectric project on the Volta River, completed in 1965, will permit industrial expansion.

Nigeria seeks unity. When formed in 1960, the prospects for the Federal Republic of Nigeria appeared very bright. Its 55 million inhabitants make Nigeria Africa's largest nation in an area greater than every European country except Russia. The economy is well-rounded with several products (including petroleum and peanuts) bringing good income. Under British guidance,

RUSH-HOUR TRAFFIC. This picture was taken during the rush hour on Carter Bridge, between the city of Lagos and the residential community of Apapa in Western Nigeria. Lagos is the federal capital.

Nigerians had had a decade of experience in self-rule before achieving independence.

But these prospects depend on Nigerian unity and there has been little of that. There are over 250 tribal and language groups. Moslems dominate the north and east while Christians and pagans live in the south and west. Bitter rivalries exist. The Ibos (ee-*bohs*), an extremely ambitious tribe, are particularly resented by the others.

Two military coups in 1966 were followed by a massacre of thousands of Ibos. General Yakubu Gowon (go-*wan*), the new head of government, began to reform the federal structure. Still dissatisfied, the Ibos converted the eastern region into a "Republic of Biafra" (bee-*af*-ruh) and tried to secede. There were thirty months of bitter civil war. Reduced to semi-starvation, the Biafrans surrendered in January, 1970.

Under Gowon's extremely strong regime, Nigeria's economy has recovered remarkably well since the civil war. But the country is under military dictatorship and it is questionable if Gowon's pledge to restore democracy in 1975 will be carried out.

Serious problems beset East Africa. Many are the difficulties of the new East African states: the usual tribal rivalries have been aggravated by racial problems caused by the presence of sizable European and Asian minorities. In addition, some of the new heads of government have exhibited dictatorial tendencies or have experimented carelessly with self-style "African socialism."

In the 1950s the British colony of Kenya was a particular trouble spot. The "Mau Mau" (*mow-mow*), a secret tribal society, waged terrorist war against the Europeans who had monopolized Kenya's best lands. Although the terror was finally quashed, the movement for independence was so sharpened that the Mau Mau's alleged leader, Jomo Kenyatta (ken-*yah*-tuh) became Prime Minister when Kenya became independent in 1963.

The elderly Kenyatta has proved to be a clever political leader. Under his "Africanization" program, natives have taken over the best lands from the Europeans and the businesses of thousands of Asians who have been pressured to emigrate. Kenyatta's "Kenya African Union" (KANU) has become virtually the only political party.

One of the most respected African statesmen is Julius Nyerere (nye-ray-ray), who led Tanganyika to peaceful independence from Britain in 1961. Three years later he became the president of Tanzania,—the name given to the union between Tanganyika and the nearby island of Zanzibar.

Land Reform in Kenya. African farmers are shown as they choose their own plots of land by lot from slips of paper mixed together in a basket. The plots were carved out of large farms formerly owned by Europeans. Land ownership has been a major problem in Kenya.

Marxists have controlled that island ever since they overthrew the Arab rulers just prior to Zanzibar's merger with Tanganyika. On the mainland Nyerere has nationalized private business, established communal farming and has urged his people to practice "self-reliance" rather than depend upon foreign assistance.

Racism has been an especially keen issue in Rhodesia where the whites, though only five per cent of the population, hold all the political power. In 1964 Britain granted freedom to Malawi and Zambia, Rhodesia's northern neighbors, but refused to do likewise for Rhodesia until a more representative type of government was established. In 1965 Rhodesian Prime Minister Ian Smith unilaterally proclaimed Rhodesia's independence. Both Britain and the United Nations have advocated an economic boycott of Rhodesia. But this had not been effective; due to the considerable help of South Africa, Rhodesia has remained quite prosperous.

The new nations of Malawi, Zambia, and Rhodesia. In 1953 Britain formed three of her territories, Northern Rhodesia, Southern Rhodesia, and Nyasaland, into a federation. Northern Rhodesia and Nyasaland whose governments had African majorities, objected to federation with the white-dominated government of Southern Rhodesia whose racial views were similar to those of South Africa (see page 651). The union was dissolved in January, 1964.

On July 6, 1964 Nyasaland became the independent Republic of Malawi, and Northern Rhodesia became the Republic of Zambia on October 24, 1964. Britain refused to grant Rhodesia (formerly Southern Rhodesia) independence until the white-dominated government broadened the voting rights of the African majority. Rhodesia unilaterally declared her independence on November 11, 1965. The UN backed Britain's call for economic sanctions against Rhodesia.

Julius Nyerere. President Nyerere of Tanzania has worked hard to make his country democratic.

FRANCE HAS ECONOMIC AND CULTURAL TIES WITH HER FORMER COLONIES

France adopted a policy of assimilation. At one time, France's colonial possessions covered nearly all of northwestern Africa. Most of the territory was desert, however. These colonies included Algeria, French West Africa, and French Equatorial Africa (see map on page 642). France also controlled the island of Madagascar in the Indian Ocean, and a small colony at the mouth of the Red Sea, French Somaliland. Today almost all of these colonies are independent.

Until 1958, France's policy toward her African colonies was much less liberal than that of Britain. Instead of preparing their colonies for self-government, the French adopted a policy of *assimilation*, by which they hoped to turn the Africans into Frenchmen. French leaders hoped that someday all of her colonial subjects would regard themselves as living in "Greater France," and would look toward Paris as their own cultural center and capital.

West and Equatorial Africa are now made up of independent states. French West Africa used to be called "Cinderella" by some Frenchmen because, like the fairy tale heroine, it was neglected for so long. Then, after World War II, the French began to invest large sums of money in both West Africa and Equatorial Africa. Railroad mileage was extended and roads built, opening up such productive sources of wealth as manganese mines and oil fields. The output of coffee, cacao, peanuts, and cotton increased. A multi-million dollar development program the French began in Equatorial Africa during the 1950's included new dams, new factories, and better facilities at the seaport of Pointe-Noire, now in the Congo Republic.

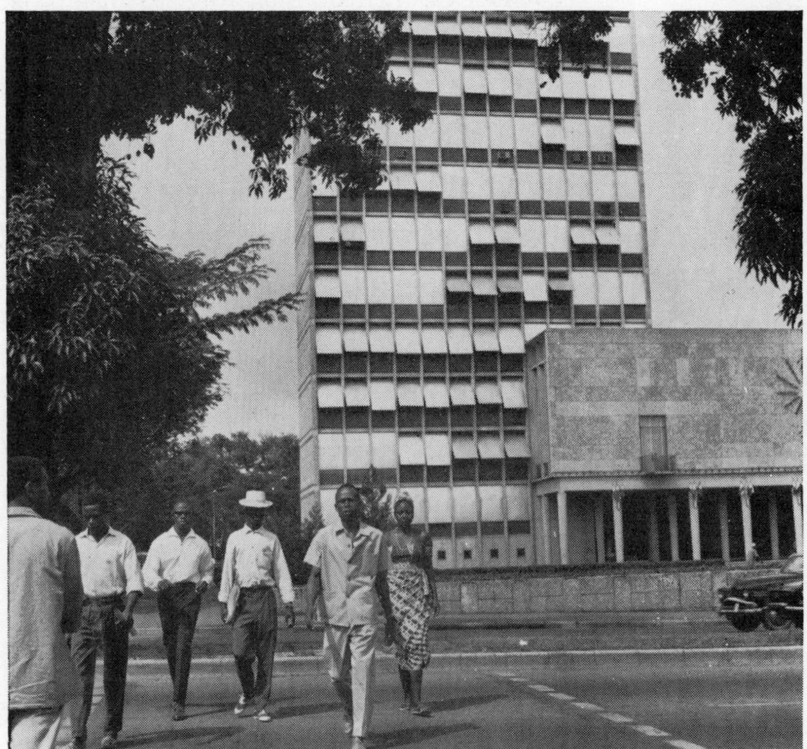

Abidjan City Hall. Abidjan is the capital of the Ivory Coast, one of the most well-developed of the states in what was formerly French West Africa. The Ivory Coast has an economic alliance with Niger, Dahomey, and Upper Volta called the Council of the Entente. Also, though outside the French Community, it still has close trade ties with France.

The new interest of France in her lands below the Sahara was most obvious in Dakar, now the capital of Senegal. Dakar is the closest point to the Americas on the Africa mainland. It lies just sixteen hundred miles east of the coast of Brazil. During World War II it became an important Allied base. After the war the French improved its harbor facilities, and it continued to grow. Today it handles over three and one-half million tons of cargo a year, more than is handled by most ports in France itself.

France's efforts to develop her colonies and her policy of assimilation were not enough to overcome African desire for self-government. When France adopted the new constitution of 1958 (see page 349), she also established a French Community, that included France, her Overseas Departments and Trusts, and twelve independent Republics that were created out of her former African colonies. Six of these twelve Republics: the Republic of Senegal, the Central African Republic, Gabon Republic, the Republic of Chad, the Republic of the Congo, and the Malagasy Republic have remained within the Community. The six others: the Islamic Republic of Mauritania, the Republic of Dahomey, the Republic of the Ivory Coast, the Republic of the Niger, the Republic of Mali, and the Republic of the Upper Volta have kept economic and cultural ties with France outside the French Community.

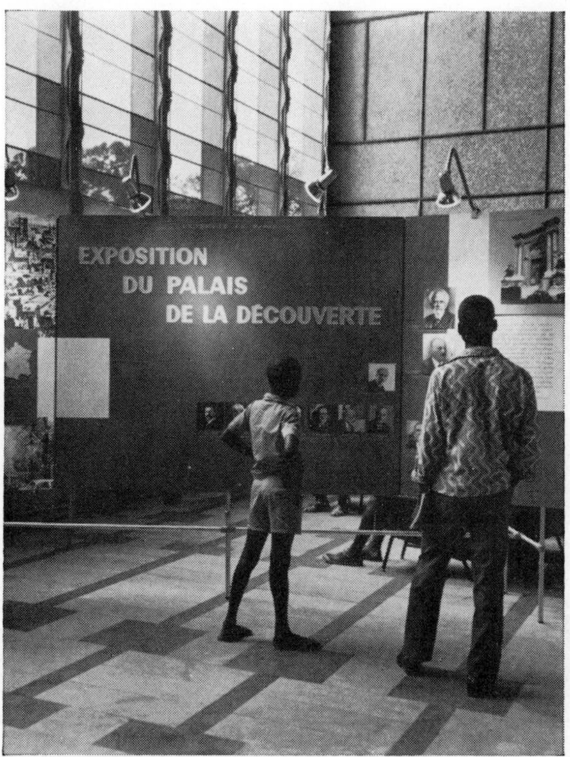

FRENCH SCIENCE EXHIBIT. This "Exposition of the Palace of Discovery" in the city of Abidjan is an example of the strong cultural influence still exercised by France in her former African colonies. Many Africans continue to be educated in France.

OTHER AFRICAN COLONIES HAVE BEEN MARKED BY UNREST

The Belgian Congo received its independence. Four times the size of Texas, the Congo is a rich country in the heart of the continent. In spite of its hot, tropical climate, it is economically well-developed. It is one of the world's leading producers of uranium, cobalt, copper, and diamonds. Belgian colonial policy in the Congo improved the economic conditions of the African Congolese natives but did not give them political rights. No political activity was allowed, either by the Africans or the European settlers. The thirteen million African Congolese were not allowed to vote and were denied any participation in their government. Belgian leaders wrongly felt that as long as the government was working for the economic and social betterment of the Congolese people they would consent to remain under Belgian colonial rule.

In 1959 however, political unrest began to develop. As it increased the Belgians decided to grant the Congo independence. In June of 1960 the Democratic Republic of the Congo was established. For a short time conditions were orderly. Then they became chaotic. Congolese soldiers revolted against the Belgian officers who had remained to lead them, and Belgian residents

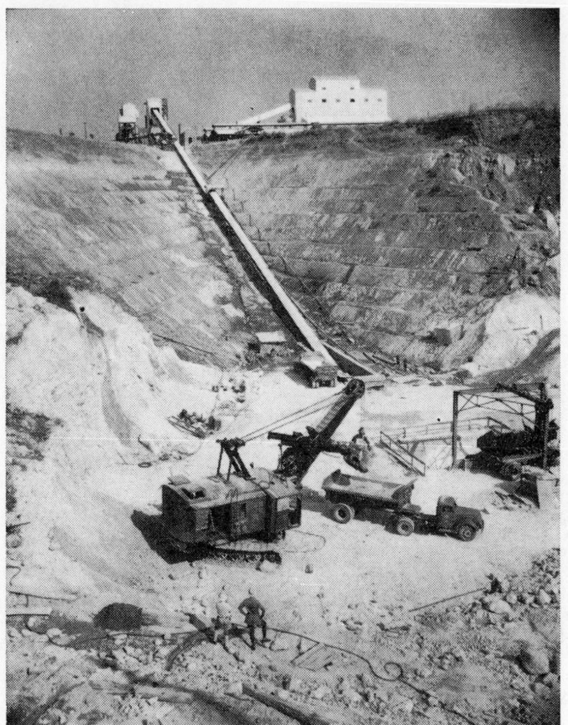

Open-pit Mining. The Katanga area in the Congo, where this mine is located, is noted for its rich copper deposits. However, in digging for copper, mining engineers have often discovered other valuable minerals as well. This tin mine was opened in 1950 and produces 10,000 tons of tin a year.

fled. Services and communications broke down. The mining and industrial province of Katanga seceded from the central government, and tribal warfare erupted.

Responding to appeals from the Congo, a United Nations force arrived to restore order and compel Katanga to end its secession. In 1964–5 white mercenaries were employed to suppress a leftist uprising around Stanleyville. But the tide turned for the better in late 1965 when army commander Joseph Mobutu (moh-*boo*-too) named himself president. He strengthened the central government and encouraged foreign investment while reducing Belgian influence. In 1970, as the only candidate, Mobutu was "re-elected" to the presidency for a seven year term.

Portugal holds on to the remnants of an empire. Portugal's main holdings in Africa are Angola (an-*gole*-uh) on the southwest coast and Mozambique (mo-zum-*beek*) in the southeast. Both were acquired centuries ago; both have overwhelmingly black populations; both are over ten times larger than Portugal. In both, agriculture is important and Angola has considerable mineral wealth.

In 1951 Portugal converted its colonies to "Overseas Portugal,"—regions equal to the mother country. There is no official racial discrimination. Any native may attain full Portuguese status by proving he has fully adopted European culture. But few natives can achieve the educational requirements or live in the European manner. Moreover, virtually all African men are compelled to do forced labor six months each year.

African Miners. These laborers are leaving the head of a mine pit at the end of a day's work. Many Africans are migrating from the backward sections of the continent to the more highly developed mining areas, where they can receive higher wages.

Guerrillas have been fighting for Angola's and Mozambique's independence since the early 1960s. In 1962 the UN General Assembly condemned Portugal's colonial rule. Using troops and encouraging white colonization, Portugal appears determined to hold on grimly to its possessions.

Spain has lost most of her African empire. At one time Spain held important possessions in Africa, but most of them have been lost. The remaining Spanish colonies are patches of land along the continent's west coast. They include tiny Ifni (*if*-nee) and the Spanish Sahara in the northwest corner of Africa and Rio Muni (*ree*-oh moon-ee) near the equator. (Find these on the map on page 634.) The Spanish philosopher, Jose Ortega y Gasset (orr-*tay*-guh ee gas-*set*) has called Spain's African colonies "specks of the dust of history," leftovers from the days of her empire.

Chapter Check-up

1. Which territories in Africa are still under the control of European nations?
2. What was Britain's policy concerning self-government for her African colonies?
3. In which of her colonies were Britain's policies most effective? In which were they least effective?
4. What was the basic issue involved in the Mau Mau uprisings?
5. How did the colonial policies of the French and British in Africa differ?
6. Why has Britain refused to accept Rhodesia's unilateral declaration of independence?
7. How successful was the French colonial policy of assimilation?
8. What major mistake did Belgium make in her colonial policy in the Congo?
9. Which of Portugal's African possessions has caused her the most trouble?

Chapter 69

Africans Have Developed Their Own Music, Art, and Literature

African music has influenced American music. Although the Africans have lagged behind the modern world in political and economic development, they have created outstanding art and music. African music is especially noteworthy. Its distinctive rhythms have greatly influenced modern music all over the world. Negro slaves brought African music to the Americas, where it became a major force in the development of new musical forms. North American jazz and "swing" music, the Calypso tunes of the Caribbean region, the lively dance music of Latin America—all these owe much to rhythms that crossed the Atlantic on slave ships. Negro spirituals, such as "Swing Low, Sweet Chariot," also show evidence of African influence. In fact, some writers claim that the only truly American music is Negro music, for all the rest is based on European compositions.

Music is the most universal art among African tribes. "The drum is Africa's heartbeat," a recent visitor declared. "It beats for Africans' dances and for their funerals, for their meetings and for their ceremonies, and it brings them the news." According to an African folk tale, "In the beginning the Creator created the drummer, the hunter, and the smith." It is significant that the drummer comes first. The next time you hear jazz, listen carefully and you will probably be able to distinguish a drum-beat rhythm born in Africa.

JAZZ BAND. Trummy Young, Louis Armstrong, Edmund Hall, and Arvell Shaw in this jazz combo are playing music descended directly from African rhythms. Jazz was originated by Negro musicians in New Orleans during the last part of the nineteenth century.

European settlers in Africa have also been inspired to create music of their own. Perhaps you have heard some of the "Songs of the Veld," the stirring ballads sung by Dutch settlers in South Africa.

Modern dance also shows the influence of Africa. There is an old saying that "When the sun goes down, all Africa dances." Like the American Indians, African tribesmen developed dances for many occasions and purposes. Many of their dances had religious meaning. Like African music, African dances have traveled to many other lands and have greatly influenced modern dancing, particularly in the Americas. First the Cake-Walk, later the Charleston, and in recent times the Conga, Samba, and Mambo have set Americans dancing to ancient African patterns.

African art is strange and impressive. African sculpture and handicrafts were much slower than music in becoming known abroad, but today African art is very highly regarded. Museums in Britain, France, and the United States compete vigorously to obtain examples of African art. Modern artists have studied African art forms carefully and have found much to admire in them.

Sculpture and painting have a long history in Africa. Caves in many parts of the continent contain paintings thousands of years old. The African "rock paintings" resemble closely the prehistoric cave paintings found in France and Spain (see page 9). The inspiration for African art seems to have been chiefly religious. Mohammed's teachings forbade representation of the human figure, so the Moslem countries have produced little in the way of sculpture and painting. This type of art has flourished in other areas, however. Ethiopia, a Christian country since the fourth century A.D., has produced many frescoes that tell biblical stories.

Most of the African tribesmen are still pagan; that is, they believe in many gods and spirits. The apparent purpose of their sculpture was to frighten away evil spirits and to please friendly ones. Among the most prized examples of African art are the bronze and ivory work from the Benin section of Nigeria in West Africa. On page 633, the title page to this Part, you will find one of the most famous of these examples reproduced. It is a beautifully detailed mask, carved in ivory with iron and copper inlays. Such masks were often worn as pendants, or good luck charms. On page 662 you will find a picture of a primitive African sculpture.

Africans have also produced beautiful designs on fabrics. Almost four centuries ago a representative sent to the Congo by the Pope reported:

"I must mention the marvelous art of the Congolese people and the neighboring ones in the matter of weaving. They manufacture different kinds of stuffs, velvet, taffeta, brocade, damask, and others. But these are not made of silk—The threads they employ are taken from the leaves of the palm trees; with them they weave all kinds of material, adorned with flowers and leaves, so as to liken them to velvet."

Where did the Africans learn to make such beautiful objects? Perhaps from ancient Egyptian travelers; perhaps from the Arabs; perhaps they discovered their own methods. For reasons still unknown, African art reached its peak in the sixteenth and seventeenth centuries.

Unfortunately, European domination brought on a decline in African culture. The native art produced since the seventeenth century seems to have lost much of the freshness and inspiration that won it high critical acclaim.

African folk tales are wise and humorous. Have you read any of the stories of Uncle Remus? Did you know that B'rer Rabbit and Tar Baby are immigrants? Long ago they came from Africa to the American South. The stories Joel Chandler Harris heard as a child and later wrote down for other children are merely one version of ancient African legends. For generations the people of West Africa told the stories to one another. When they moved from one place to another they took their legends and fables with them. In that way, the stories came to the United States and, in slightly different versions, to the West Indies and South America.

In recent years a modern African literature has begun to develop. South Africa has produced a growing number of writers who rank with the best in any land. Many of their works deal

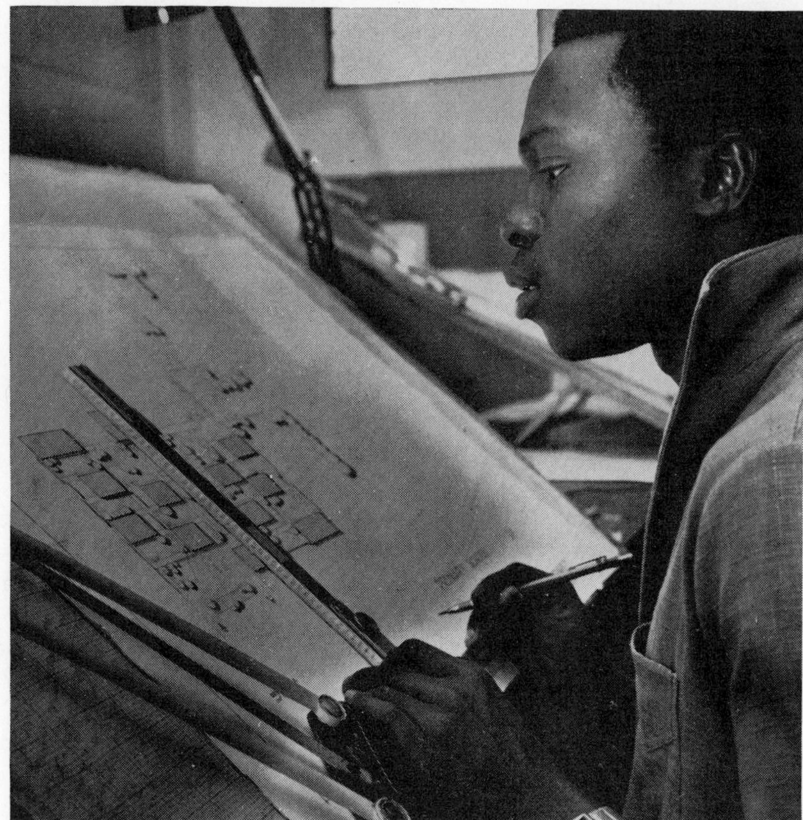

Architecture Student. Artists in the modern African nations are now branching out in new directions. Traditional carved masks, for example, have given way to bas-reliefs decorating the sides of modern buildings created by young architects such as the student shown here. He is at work on a project at Ahmadu Bello University in Northern Nigeria, whose school of architecture is one of its most important departments.

AFRICAN SCULPTURE. This nineteenth-century wood carving is thought to represent a demon, or evil spirit. African art declined as European colonialism intruded on the pattern of native life. This example comes from the Guinea Coast of West Africa.

with modern South Africa's racial troubles. Perhaps the best known South African writer is Alan Paton. His most famous work, *Cry, The Beloved Country*, is the sad story of a senseless murder that destroyed the happiness of both an English and a native African family.

The literature of the newer countries is just beginning to be read in the United States, and several paperback collections are now available. One writer who is almost always represented is Amos Tutuola from Nigeria. Like many new African writers, he is strongly influenced by the continent's vast oral literature. His delightful fantasies, such as *My Life in the Bush of Ghosts*, are a substantial addition to African literature.

Chapter Check-up

1. How has African music influenced that of the Americas?
2. What instrument is most important in African music?
3. What has been the chief inspiration for African art?
4. Why have the Moslem countries produced little of note in painting and sculpture?
5. How have African folk tales and legends influenced American literature?
6. What literary contributions have come from the countries of Africa?

Africa: SYNOPSIS

Of the two big regions of Africa, the northern part has been most closely linked with Europe. Centuries ago the northern coast was part of the Roman empire and the remains of Roman cities may still be seen there. In the seventh century the Moslems overran all of North Africa.

Not till the fifteenth century did Europeans first begin to penetrate into the southern half of the continent. First came the Portuguese, closely followed by the French, Dutch and English. By the late nineteenth century most of Africa was under European domination. After World War II, however, a strong wave of nationalism began to sweep over Africa.

As the trend toward self-government became obvious, Britain sought to prepare the native populations of her colonies for eventual independence. In some colonies, tribal leaders were permitted to govern under British supervision. Since then British colonies have been granted freedom as quickly as they could form responsible regimes. The French also were obliged to grant their African colonies independence and have been able to retain the friendship of most. Portugal, on the other hand, has tried desperately to hold on to her possessions even when this has required the use of repressive force.

A number of the new nations have encountered serious difficulties. There have been bloody civil wars and frequent overturns of popularly elected governments by military cliques. The racist policies of white-controlled South Africa and Rhodesia have aroused bitter resentment in the rest of the continent. Both sides in the Cold War have, of course, been interested in African developments. Some of the new states have dabbled in "African Socialism" but most have tried to maintain a "neutralist" posture, accepting as much aid as they can get from both Communist and anti-Communist sources.

Africa's unique culture is admired for its primitive beauty. African stories, dances and songs were brought to the United States by Negro slaves. Africa sculpture, handicrafts and painting can be seen in museums throughout the world. Recently, too, African literature has been gaining wide recognition.

Terms

Make sure you understand clearly the meaning of each of the following:

Afrikaners	Mau Mau	Berbers
Apartheid	United Arab Republic	National Colonization Society
assimilation	Suez Canal	Coloureds
Boers	"dark continent"	rock paintings

Important People

How have each of the following influenced the story of Africa?

David Livingstone	Gamal Abdul Nasser	Jan Christian Smuts	Amos Tutuola
Henry Stanley	Haile Selassie	Alan Paton	Sékou Touré
King Leopold II	Kwame Nkrumah	Jomo Kenyatta	Julius K. Nyerere

Questions for Discussion and Review

1. What part did Livingstone and Stanley play in opening Africa to European colonization?
2. Compare the African colonial policies of Britain, France, and Belgium. What do you think were the strong and weak points of each? Which do you feel was the most effective? Why?
3. In your opinion, what will be the outcome of the situation in Ghana?
4. Why have Tunisia and Morocco been having

difficulty resisting pressure by Egypt's president, Gamal Nasser?

5. What do you think is the future of the Pan-African movement? Why?
6. What could be done to reduce tension in the Republic of South Africa?
7. During what period did the artistic achievement of native Africans seem to reach its highest point? What do you think may have caused it to decline later?
8. In your opinion, what is Africa's greatest contribution to civilization? Why?

Interesting Things to Do

1. Make a map of Africa showing the surrounding lands and seas. Label carefully the various countries, states, and colonies. Color your map according to a key, using a different color for those lands that are independent and those that are associated with Britain, Portugal, or Spain.
2. Using drawings, labels, cut-outs, or samples, make a map of Africa to show the principal products of the various regions.
3. Make a chart of Africa, showing for each of its major countries the area, population, capital, important cities, type of government, leaders, geographical features, imports, exports, and interesting features.
4. Prepare and display for the class a series of magazine pictures or photographs showing various aspects of Africa.
5. Imagine that you are planning a trip to Africa. Prepare a written itinerary of the places you will visit and the things you will see and do.
6. Play for the class a record of the "Songs of the South African Veld," as sung by Josef and Miranda Marais.
7. Prepare a report on "Africa, 1970." Consult newspapers and newsmagazines for your information.
8. Present a talk on "What American Music Owes to Africa."
9. Present an informal debate: *Resolved,* African nations are better off under one-party systems until they gain political maturity.
10. Add to or begin your "Who's Who in World History" series by writing brief biographies of one or more important African leaders.

Interesting Reading about Africa

Bernheim, Marc, and Evelyn Bernheim, *From Bush to City,* Harcourt, Brace & World. Emerging Africa.

Busoni, Rafaello, *Stanley's Africa,* Viking. Combines a biography of Stanley, the African explorer, with late nineteenth-century African history.

*Gatti, Attilio, *Here is the Veld,* Scribner.

Gatti, Ellen and Attilio, *Here is Africa,* Scribner. The lives and customs of the African peoples.

Gunther, John, *Inside Africa,* Harper & Row. Describes the past, present, and probable future of Africa.

Hapgood, David, Africa: *From Independence to Tomorrow,* Atheneum.

Lengyel, Emil, *Africa in Ferment,* Oxford. A well organized and up-to-date report.

Morehead, Alan, *The White Nile,* Dell. A fascinating account of the search for the source of the Nile.

Ogrizek, Dore, *North Africa,* McGraw-Hill.

Quinn, Vernon, *Picture Map Geography of Africa,* Lippincott.

Savage, Katherine, *The Story of Africa South of the Sahara,* Walck.

Shinnie, Margaret, *Ancient African Kingdoms,* St. Martin's Press.

Turnbull, Colin M., *The Lonely African,* Doubleday. Life sketches of contemporary Africans.

Waldeck, Theodore, *On Safari,* Viking.

* Indicates easy reading

Concerned people the world over recognize the need to protect the original inhabitants of all lands. This Amahuaca native in Brazil may soon be extinct.

Part 21
LATIN AMERICA

STRIVING TOWARD POLITICAL MATURITY

LATIN AMERICA

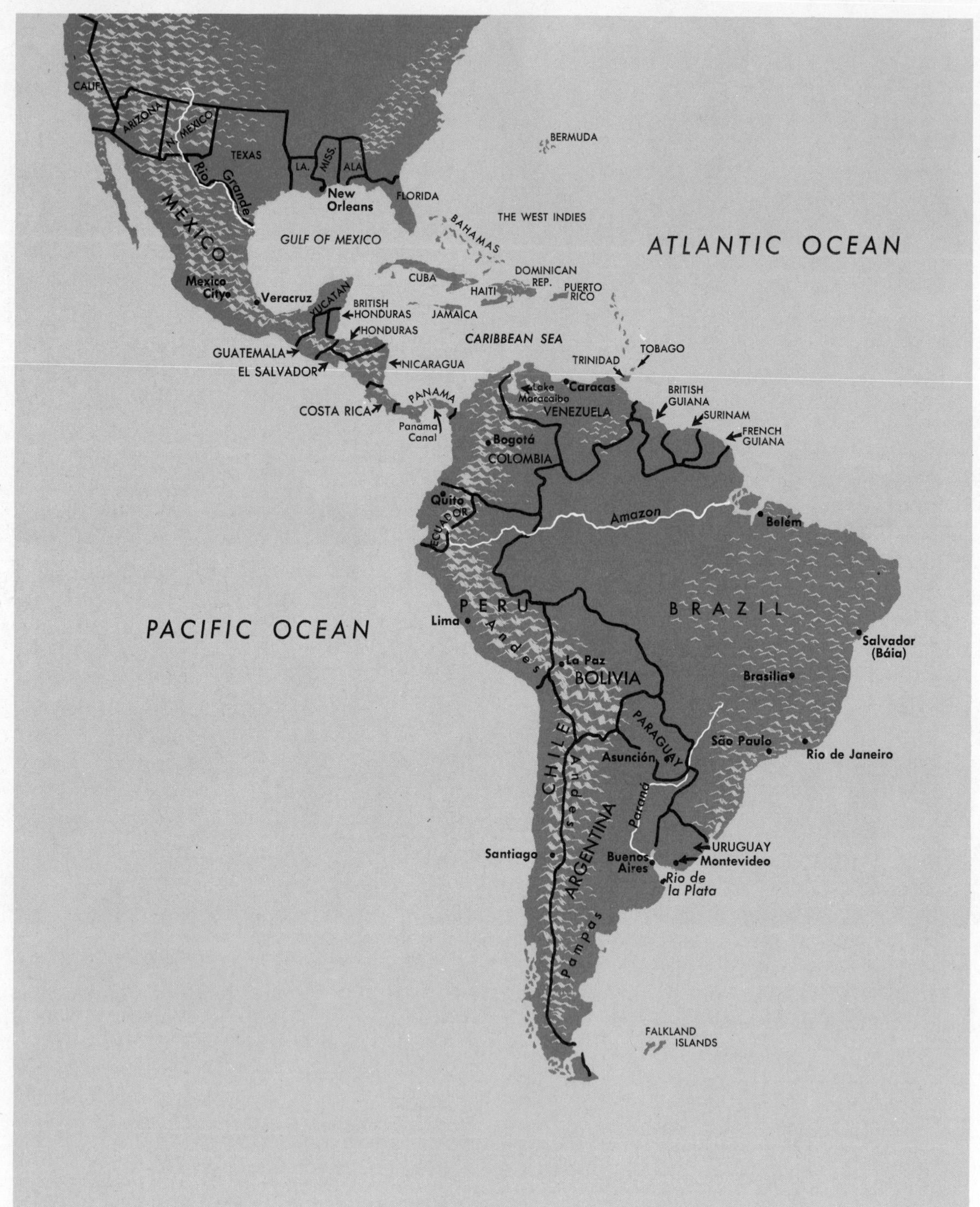
CALIF.
ARIZONA
N. MEXICO
TEXAS
LA.
MISS.
ALA.
Rio Grande
MEXICO
New Orleans
FLORIDA
BERMUDA
BAHAMAS
THE WEST INDIES
GULF OF MEXICO
ATLANTIC OCEAN
Mexico City
Veracruz
YUCATAN
BRITISH HONDURAS
CUBA
HAITI
DOMINICAN REP.
PUERTO RICO
JAMAICA
HONDURAS
CARIBBEAN SEA
GUATEMALA
EL SALVADOR
NICARAGUA
TRINIDAD
TOBAGO
Lake Maracaibo
Caracas
VENEZUELA
BRITISH GUIANA
SURINAM
FRENCH GUIANA
COSTA RICA
PANAMA
Panama Canal
Bogotá
COLOMBIA
Quito
ECUADOR
Amazon
Belém
PERU
Lima
Andes
PACIFIC OCEAN
BRAZIL
Salvador (Báia)
La Paz
BOLIVIA
Brasilia
PARAGUAY
São Paulo
Rio de Janeiro
Asunción
CHILE
Paraná
ARGENTINA
URUGUAY
Santiago
Buenos Aires
Montevideo
Rio de la Plata
Pampas
FALKLAND ISLANDS

Latin America: GEOGRAPHIC SETTING

Latin America consists of Mexico, the West Indies, Central America, and South America. The combined area is three times as large as the United States but contains fewer people. The term *Latin America* is applied to these lands because they were settled by Spain and Portugal, two of the "Latin" nations of Europe.

Mexico, the United States' closest neighbor to the south, lies just across the Rio Grande River, bordering on Texas, New Mexico, Arizona, and California. Less than a hundred miles off the tip of Florida are the West Indies, an island chain in the Caribbean Sea.

Central America is the bridge that links North America with South America. It includes Guatemala, British Honduras, Honduras, El Salvador, Nicaragua, Costa Rica, and Panama. Although Central America is hundreds of miles wide at some points, it narrows in Panama to a mere forty miles. This is the site of the Panama Canal, the main shipping route between the Atlantic and Pacific.

Farther to the south lies South America, a continent of towering mountains, steaming jungles, and lofty plateaus. It ranges in climate from the sultry heat of Ecuador, which sits astride the Equator, to the temperate weather of southern Chile and Argentina, about four thousand miles southward. The most important geographical feature of South America is the Andes Mountain chain, whose snow-capped peaks stretch along the west coast from the Caribbean to the southernmost tip of the continent. Ranging in width from one hundred to four hundred miles, the Andes form a barrier that divides South America into two parts. The western slope, as it dips toward the Pacific, becomes a narrow coastal plain. To the east of the Andes are the great plateaus of Brazil and the vast, treeless plains, or pampas (*pam*-puz), of Argentina.

Flowing northeastward into the Atlantic Ocean is the Amazon, the world's largest river. Fed by many smaller rivers that rush down from the Andes onto the broad Brazilian plateau, the river winds through dark jungles that few humans have ever explored. South America's population lives mainly along the coastal plain to the west of the Andes, in the cool highlands of the many mountains, or along the Atlantic Coast.

Latin America: PERSPECTIVE

Latin America is a region of contrasts, where old and new, primitive and modern exist side by side. In the mountains of Ecuador and in the upper Amazon basin live uncivilized Indians who hunt with blowpipes and poisoned arrows. Explorers report that such savages are almost totally unaware of the world that exists outside their jungle homes.

Meanwhile, across the broad tablelands of Brazil is the city of Rio de Janeiro with a modern metropolitan area of over seven million people. Factories, skyscrapers and apartment buildings give "Rio" a skyline much like that of large American cities.

Such contrasts make Latin America a wonderfully interesting place for tourists but they also suggest some of the problems that still face the inhabitants.

Significant changes have been occurring, but with very mixed results. Traditionally, Latin American economies have been based on one or two agricultural or mineral products,—coffee, sugar, bananas, cattle or wheat; copper, tin or petroleum. In several lands there has been a trend towards rapid industrialization

in order to build a better economic balance. The middle class has grown larger. Living standards for many have improved. However, these sudden changes have brought "galloping inflation" and intensified tensions between rich and poor. Military dictatorships have replaced several democratic governments. Communist and other extremist movements have become increasingly influential. The properties of foreign investors have been seized by a number of governments. Thus, as it enters the decade of the 1970s, Latin America's immediate future is very uncertain.

CHAPTER 70

Latin America Struggled for Political Independence

LATIN AMERICAN TRIBES ESTABLISHED BRILLIANT CIVILIZATIONS BUT WERE CONQUERED BY THE SPANISH

The first men to inhabit America were apparently Stone Age hunters from Siberia who crossed the Bering Strait to Alaska thousands of years ago and drifted down into Central and South America. Other tribes followed them. Perhaps people from the South Sea islands came in their long canoes to the Pacific Coast. Stories of curly-headed tribes in Brazil before the Spanish conquest have led some historians to believe that even people from Africa may have immigrated there. Wherever the natives came from, it has been estimated that when Columbus reached the West Indies there were from ten to fifteen million of them living in Central and South America. When Columbus discovered America, he thought he had found the Indies, so he called all of America's inhabitants Indians. These people were not all the same, however. The Central and South American tribes were more numerous and much more civilized than the North American tribes.

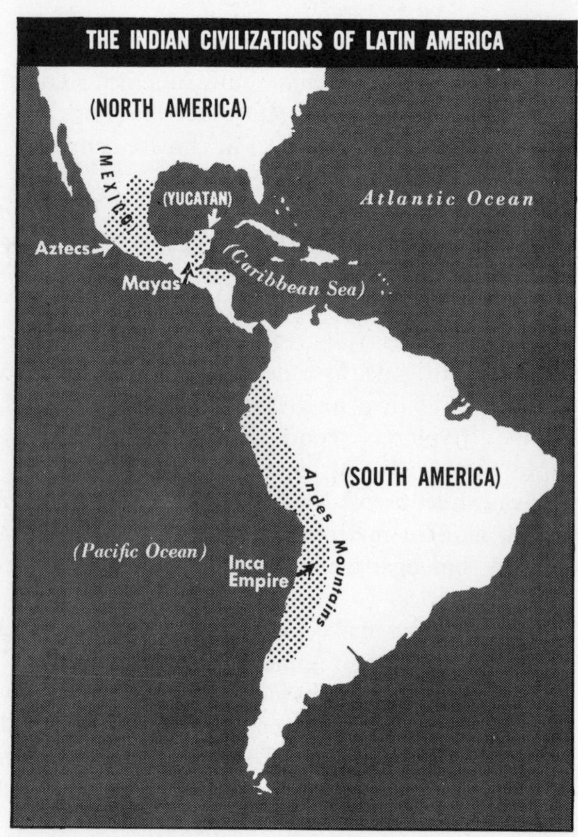

The Indians established three great civilizations. Shortly after the birth of Christ, the gifted *Mayas* were living in the region that now comprises Guatemala, British Honduras, and the Yucatán Peninsula of Mexico. There they

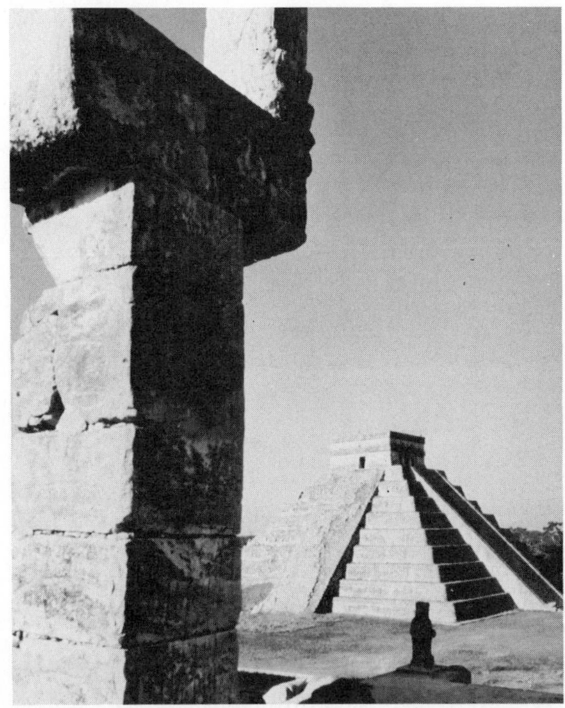

Mayan Ruins. The city of Chichén Itzá on the Yucatan Peninsula is almost fifteen hundred years old, and its history spanned two great periods of Mayan civilization. It was abandoned sometime after 1194. The temple shown here is typical of Mayan architectural style.

built a civilization that may have been as advanced as that of ancient Egypt. The Mayas were a religious people who worshipped the sun-god and other nature deities. They lived in city-states and were ruled by priest-kings. In the center of each city were great flat-topped pyramids on which temples were built. The priests used the temples as observatories. They studied the heavens and succeeded in creating an accurate calendar. They also developed a complicated system of hieroglyphic writing. Both the calendar and writing were used mainly for religious purposes.

The majority of the Mayas were farmers who grew corn in fields around the city. Because their system of farming was wasteful, however, the soil was ruined after a few generations and the farmers had to find new land. Sometime after 1200 A.D. the Mayan civilization declined for reasons that we do not yet know.

The calendar and other discoveries of the Mayas were appropriated by the warlike *Aztecs*, who built a new civilization in central Mexico. The Aztecs are sometimes called "the Romans of the New World." Like the Romans, the Aztecs were skillful rulers, excellent builders, and fine sculptors. Many traces of Aztec civilization can be seen in modern Mexico. Aztec craftsmen learned to make jewelry of gold, silver, and copper, and to weave fine cotton cloth. They were also accomplished artists and sculptors. Their religious ceremonies, however, often involved the use of human sacrifices.

Early in the twelfth century the *Incas* of Peru established another great Indian civilization. Their empire was one of the most extensive in history. It included Peru, Ecuador, Chile, and parts of Bolivia and Argentina. The Incas, who were better farmers than the Mayas, terraced their land and used fish for fertilizer. They built fortresses and palaces of beautifully cut stone. Since they had not discovered the principle of the wheel, they used the llama to transport heavy loads. The llama was the only beast of burden known in America prior to the arrival of the Spanish.

All the Indian civilizations of Latin America were organized in rigid caste systems. The Incas probably had one of the most absolute governments in all history. Every worker was provided for; the government gave him his clothes and enough to eat. But he could not leave his village without permission, and he was constantly spied upon. He had to remain at his assigned job until his death. The ruler of the Incas was considered to be a divine descendant of the sun-god. The centralization of authority made it easy for the Spaniards to conquer the Incas and Aztecs. When the rulers were captured, the people were helpless to make decisions.

Despite their undemocratic governments, the Mayas, Aztecs, and Incas made a number of discoveries that were not known in Europe or Asia until the Spaniards came to Latin America. One was the manufacture and use of rubber. In addition, such food crops as corn, cacao, and potatoes were first cultivated by the Indians.

The conquistadors robbed and subjugated the native Indians. The Spaniards who explored the Americas after Columbus are called the *conquistadors* (kahn-*kwis*-tah-dorz), or conquerors. They were probably the most daring adventurers in all history. Although they were a mere handful of men, they ransacked Central and South America almost at will. The unfortunate Indians fell easy victims to the Spanish conquerors, who were equipped with firearms and rode horseback. The cruel conquistadors enslaved the Indian peoples and virtually wiped out their proud civilizations.

With only six hundred men and sixteen horses, Hernando Cortez, the greatest of the conquistadors, invaded Mexico in 1519 and overthrew its emperor, Montezuma (mahn-teh-*zoo*-muh), who had hundreds of thousands of warriors. Landing in desolate Yucatán, Cortez burned his ships to prevent his men from turning back. They fought their way through hundreds of miles ot jungle to the capital of the Aztec empire, which was on the site of modern Mexico City. Montezuma and his Aztecs received them courteously and offered them gifts. In return, Cortez destroyed the city, starved the people, and tortured Montezuma to death. Under his harsh rule, Mexico became Spain's wealthiest colony.

Festivals are a part of everyone's culture. Shown here are O'ero Indians at the O'eylloi Rite celebration in Peru.

In Peru, the pattern of conquest was much the same. There, Francisco Pizarro (pih-*zar*-o) took millions of dollars in gold from the Incas. He captured the Inca emperor by inviting him to the Spanish camp, then held him for a ransom of a roomful of gold. When the Indians had delivered the gold, Pizarro treacherously executed their emperor. There were also lesser conquistadors, like Pedro de Valdivia (vahl-*dee*-vyah) in Peru, but the story was always the same: a policy of deceit, cruelty, and destruction that robbed and enslaved the Indians.

In the century after the voyages of Columbus, much of Central and South America was explored. Spanish explorers extended Spain's holdings until they included all of Central and South America except Brazil. There, Portugal established a claim and developed a colony.

The Spanish established a huge colonial empire in America. The period of colonization in Latin America began earlier and lasted longer than in North America. The Spaniards established beautiful cities long before the Pilgrims left England, and the Latin American lands remained under Spanish and Portuguese rule for forty years after the United States became independent. Since Spain kept her colonies tied to her so closely and so long, Spanish culture continues to influence Latin America in many ways.

Most of the early Spanish settlers were nobles or soldiers who had no inclination for farming. They established large estates called haciendas (hah-see-*en*-duz). Because the Mayas, Aztecs, and Incas had already learned how to farm, the Spaniards and Portuguese were able to use them as laborers. The Indians suffered but survived, and there are still many people of pure Indian blood living in Latin America. Because few European women came to Latin America, the Span-

SPANISH CONQUISTADORS. After the Tlaxcalan Indians were defeated by Cortez in the battle pictured here, they became his allies in fighting the Aztecs. At one point in the campaign, Cortez was able to use the Tlaxcalans' main city as a stronghold from which to attack the Aztec capital.

ish and Portuguese settlers intermarried with the Indians and produced many people of mixed blood, called *mestizos* (mes-*tee*-zoze). They are the most common type in most of Latin America today. The importation of Negro slaves into Brazil and the Caribbean area resulted in further mixture of the races. In more recent times, numerous Japanese and Chinese have come to Latin America to trade and to establish small businesses. All of the races apparently work well together, and there is little conflict between them.

The owners of the haciendas ruled their estates and handed them on to their sons, just as European lords had done in the Middle Ages. Very often the owner left the care of his estate to a manager, while he and his family went to live in a city. There his standard of living was high. He could enjoy good food, music, and art. His children were often sent to Europe to be educated.

His life was in the greatest contrast to that of the Indians, who lived in small, isolated communities in ignorance and poverty. Such was the dark picture that formed the background for the brilliant aristocratic society of the cities.

Since Spain and Portugal were devoutly Catholic countries, Catholic missionaries came to con-

vert the Indians in the colonies. They founded new settlements around their mission churches. At each settlement they brought together the Indians from many small, scattered communities and established them on the land as farmers, teaching new agricultural techniques and importing new crops. They also instructed the Indians in weaving and other arts. Some of the missionaries founded universities in the cities. These schools became famous for the excellent training which they offered in such fields as law and philosophy.

Spain kept a jealous watch over her vast lands in America. All aspects of colonial life were supervised by the Spanish king and his special advisors. Their main concern was how best to exploit their colonies in Latin America for the benefit of Spain. The colonies were forbidden to trade with each other or with any nation except Spain. People born in the colonies—even those of pure Spanish blood—were looked down upon in Spain and were not permitted to hold any high offices. The Spanish government demanded more and more taxes and gave little in return except censorship and petty interference. In spite of their close cultural ties with Spain, the people in Latin America began to dream of political independence.

THE PEOPLE OF LATIN AMERICA FOUGHT FOR THEIR FREEDOM

The idea of becoming independent began to appeal to the colonists. News of the American Revolution probably reached few people in Latin America, where censorship and geographic isolation prevented the spread of information. But the events of 1776 set one young man to dreaming. He was Francisco Miranda, a native of Venezuela who served with the French in our War for Independence. After his service in the United States, Miranda went back to South America. There, he began to plan for South American independence. But his plot was discovered and he had to flee. While in exile in France and Great Britain, he planned and conspired with others who wanted to free South America from Spain. Britons and Americans gave him encouragement and financial support. (A free and independent Latin America, open to trade with all the world, was an attractive prospect for merchants.)

The French Revolution inspired other young Latin Americans to work for freedom. Their op-

Bolívar Meets San Martín at Guayaquil. After this meeting in 1822, San Martín retired from the field, leaving Bolívar to go on to become the most powerful man in South America. Both men died poor and in exile.

Incan Wall. The ancient Incas built walls and roads that rival Roman achievements. This market scene in Peru attests to the remarkable durability of Incan engineering.

portunity came when Spain, like the rest of Europe, was drawn into the long Napoleonic Wars. Napoleon easily conquered the weak Spanish government and made his brother king of Spain. Many of the Latin American colonies refused to recognize the new king and so enjoyed a few years of freedom from European interference. When the old king returned to the throne in 1814 after the defeat of Napoleon, the colonial officials rebelled against him and thus started the Latin American wars for independence.

The Latin American struggle for independence was a much harder and longer effort than the American Revolution. It was waged over most of South America as well as in Mexico. The fighting in the mountains and jungles went on for over fifteen years.

José de San Martín and Simón Bolívar liberated South America. Probably the ablest general in South America was José de San Martín (sahn mar-*teen*) of Argentina. He had served as an officer in the Spanish army and had fought Napoleon in Europe. After the Napoleonic Wars he returned to Argentina, where he led a patriot army in a successful revolution against the Spanish government. Then, in spite of terrible hardships, he marched his army across the snow-covered Andes Mountains to conquer both Chile and Peru.

Another of South America's great patriots was Simón Bolívar (bo-*lee*-var), who has been called "the George Washington of South America." Bolívar was born in Venezuela, the son of an aristocratic family. He devoted his life and fortune to the cause of freedom. He began by overthrowing the government in Venezuela. Then he marched south to meet San Martín in Ecuador. San Martín gave up his command to Bolívar because he thought the ambitious young man was more popular and better fitted for uniting an independent South America. Bolívar failed, however, to create one great Latin American republic as he had hoped to do. Old feuds and suspicions caused South and Central America to break up into many unfriendly nations. Bolívar died in exile, disappointed at his failure.

Cuba and Puerto Rico remained under Spanish control until 1899 but the other Spanish colonies had won their independence by 1825. Britain, France and the Netherlands have also had colonies, chiefly in the Caribbean. In the 1960s the most important British colonies received freedom while the Dutch and French possessions have been treated as equal partners by their respective "mother countries."

That the Latin American nations finally gained independence was probably as much the result of world events that weakened Spain's grasp as it was the consequence of their own efforts. Only about a third of the population had taken an active part in the struggle. The rest were too poor and ignorant to care. Could such backward and oppressed peoples master the art of self-government?

The answer has been about as varied as the number of countries involved. Some like little Uruguay and tinier Costa Rica, have been fairly stable middle class democracies. In Chile political democracy endured despite the great gap between rich and poor. Argentina and Colombia are examples of places where dictatorships have often replaced elected governments. Haiti, Bolivia and Paraguay are among the unfortunate states with almost unrelieved records of poverty and tyranny.

Happily, there have been fewer wars within Latin America than in most continents. More boundary disputes have been arbitrated peacefully in this region than in any other part of the world.

Chapter Check-up

1. Why do we use the term *Latin America* to describe the lands south of the United States?
2. What areas are included in Latin America?
3. Locate South America's (a) longest river (b) most important mountain range (c) main centers of population.
4. Describe briefly each of the three great Indian civilizations of early Latin America.
5. Who were the conquistadors? How were they able to subjugate the Indians?
6. What part did each of the following play in winning Latin American independence: (a) Francisco Miranda (b) José de San Martín (c) Simón Bolívar?

Chapter 71

Mexico and Central America Have Made Progress in the Face of Many Handicaps

In Chapter 70 we surveyed the whole vast area of Latin America, and read about the ancient civilizations that existed there. We saw many similarities in the historical development of the countries and their inhabitants. However, geography, climate, and racial composition have had varying effects on each of the nations of Latin America. Costa Rica and Nicaragua are neighbors but, except for their common language, they differ greatly. Argentina and Brazil are as different from each other as Massachusetts is from Louisiana.

Since we cannot study all twenty-two republics in detail, let us imagine we are taking a tour of Latin America, pausing briefly in some of the countries. Mexico deserves our attention first because it is our nearest southern neighbor. After we have visited Mexico, we will move on to the countries of Central America and the Caribbean region. Then, in Chapter 72, we shall read about the nations of South America.

THE MEXICANS TRAVELED A ROCKY ROAD TO INDEPENDENCE

A small class of Spaniards owned all of Mexico's land. Almost as soon as you cross the border into Mexico you begin to feel that here is a land of poverty and hardship. Ever since the Spanish conquest, the Indian people of Mexico have been struggling against the burden of large estates and foreign control. Mexico is one-fourth as large as the United States, but not more than 8 per cent of the land can be used for raising crops. Because she has the second largest population in Latin America, it is no wonder that the people of Mexico have had difficulty in raising their living standards.

After Cortez and his soldiers overcame Montezuma, the country became a colony in which a small class of wealthy Spaniards owned most of the land and dominated a large class of poverty-stricken Indians. The Indians worked on huge estates, as serfs had done in medieval Europe.

The Church, too, was wealthy and owned large areas of land. Many poor priests devoted their lives to trying to help and educate the Indians, but the Church leaders tended to side with the wealthy ruling class. This turned many Mexicans against the Church and began a long, bitter religious controversy that still divides Mexico.

Mexico won her independence but suffered under dictatorships. It was one of the humble priests, Miguel Hidalgo, who in 1810 led the first movement for Mexican independence. Crying "Death to bad government," Hidalgo led his Indian followers in a temporarily successful uprising. A year later, however, Hidalgo was captured and executed by the Spanish. But finally the aristocrats also grew tired of Spanish interference. They led a rebellion in 1822 that separated Mexico from Spain. A long period of dictatorship and political misrule followed.

While the United States was growing stronger and expanding westward, Mexico floundered in debt and disorder. In 1836 Texas won its independence from Mexico. A few years later, Mexico suffered a crushing defeat in a disastrous war with the United States. She was forced to cede California and parts of the southwest.

Juárez defeated the French puppet emperor, Maximilian. Santa Anna and other dictators borrowed large sums at high interest from France and other European nations. The money was wasted, and Mexico could not or would not repay the loans. When the United States was busy fighting the War Between the States, the French Emperor Napoleon III (a nephew of the great Napoleon) tried to make Mexico a French satellite state. He persuaded the young Austrian Archduke Maximilian that it was his duty to restore order and financial responsibility to Mexico.

French soldiers established Maximilian and his wife, Carlota, as rulers in Mexico City. Maximilian and Carlota earnestly tried to give Mexico a stable, honest government. The Mexicans, like most people, preferred their own government, good or bad, to foreign rule.

The American secretary of state protested vigorously against the French action. Our government gave encouragement to Benito Juárez

Death of Maximilian. Although well-meaning, Maximilian had no real understanding of Mexico. He managed to make enemies of both the conservatives and the revolutionaries. He was captured and shot by Juárez in 1867.

Pancho Villa. From 1910 until he was assassinated in 1923, Pancho Villa was a force in Mexican politics. He aided in the overthrow of Porfiro Díaz in 1911, and plagued the regime of President Carranza with bandit activities in northern Mexico. Villa finally made peace with the Mexican government in 1920 when Carranza was succeeded by Adolfo de la Huerta.

(*hwah*-rays), who led the Mexicans against the French invaders. Juárez, a full-blooded Indian who is called "the Mexican Lincoln," finally captured Maximilian. All Europe shuddered when a prince of the Hapsburg family fell before a firing squad of Mexican peasants. Juárez, who had risen from poverty, wanted to break up the estates of the large landholders and distribute the land to the peasants. But he died before he was able to accomplish much.

After Juárez, one of his lieutenants, Porfiro Díaz (*dee*-ahs), established a dictatorship that lasted thirty years. He had administrative ability and brought peace and prosperity to Mexico, but he managed to accomplish this only by reversing the policies of Juárez and forcing the Indian masses into virtual slavery. At the end of his reign only 1 per cent of the population owned 85 per cent of the land. Haciendas of a million acres or more were not uncommon. Díaz also allowed foreign companies to exploit the land and resources of Mexico. Although the Díaz dictatorship ended in 1911, Mexicans are still struggling to correct the uneven distribution of the country's wealth.

Disagreements between the United States and Mexico were bad for both countries. History shows that disorder and revolutions almost always follow a long period of dictatorship. That pattern held true in Mexico after Díaz. Presidents were assassinated in the struggle to get power, bandits roamed the land, and Mexico lost her credit standing. The United States became impatient and intervened in Mexican affairs more than once.

On one occasion Pancho Villa (*vee*-yah), one of the bandit leaders, raided an American border town and killed seventeen people. Then he shot another sixteen Americans in Mexico to show what he thought of American meddling. The Mexican government could not or would not arrest Villa, who was regarded as a Robin Hood by the Mexican peasants. The United States sent General Pershing and an army of American soldiers into northern Mexico, where for months they tried unsuccessfully to capture Villa. The Mexicans resented the presence of American troops in their territory, and they also resented the shelling of Veracruz (*ver*-uh-*krooz*) by United States warships.

At just this time, World War I was starting in Europe. The Germans hoped to win Mexico to their side. They promised to give back to Mexico the territory she had lost to the United States. When America learned of this offer, we began to realize the importance of good relations

THE LIBRARY OF THE UNIVERSITY OF MEXICO. This modern university is part of the new Mexico, rising from its past of dictatorships and revolutions to become a stable, dynamic country. The striking murals were done by the famous Mexican artist Diego de Rivera.

with Mexico. However, Mexico remained neutral in World War I.

In the 1920's the United States angrily protested the seizure of the properties of American oil companies and landowners in Mexico. Relations between the two countries remained bad until President Coolidge happened to choose a college friend, Dwight Morrow, as ambassador to Mexico. The Mexicans received Morrow, whom they considered a rich "gringo capitalist," with suspicion.

To the surprise of everyone, however, Dwight Morrow soon became one of the most popular men in Mexico. He arranged compromise settlements for many disputes. He persuaded Mexicans to relax their anti-Church program, which had shocked Catholics all over the world. President Franklin Roosevelt continued the work that Dwight Morrow had begun. Instead of being a critic and meddler, the United States has tried to become a good neighbor. Relations between the two countries have improved markedly.

Mexican progress has been spectacular but uneven. In Mexico occurred this century's first real social revolution. Dating from Diaz's overthrow, the revolution has been generally peaceful.

The Constitution of 1917 promised vast reforms but these remained largely unfulfilled until the presidency of Lazaro Cardenas (kar-than-ahs) from 1934 to 1940. Then millions of acres of farmland from private estates were given to poor villagers. Railways and oil properties were nationalized. To the end of his life in 1970 Cardenas retained the deep affection of Mexico's masses.

The revolution slowed considerably after Cardenas' administration but Mexico has made some

MEXICAN STREET SCENE. The Indian peon with his blanket (called a *serape*) and his burro is a common sight throughout Mexico. Although many of these Indians are still miserably poor, their lot is steadily improving in Mexico.

impressive gains. Industrialization has been rapid and freed of foreign control. The middle class is among Latin America's largest. The 1968 Olympics in Mexico City brought great international prestige. Clearly, Mexico is one of the most prosperous of the developing nations.

Nevertheless, there are still serious problems. Mexico's population growth rate is one of the world's highest and there is grave overcrowding. Perhaps half the people live wretchedly. Finally, it is questionable how democratic the political system is.

True, the Church and the military possess little political power in Mexico. Nor has there been lasting personal dictatorship because the Presidents have all been limited to six years in office. But, since 1929, power has been monopolized by the "Institutional Revolutionary Party" ("P.R.I."). Capturing almost ninety percent of the vote, it has elected every President and virtually every Governor and Senator. Although "P.R.I." is a broad coalition of business, labor and peasant groups, there are complaints that it has grown unconcerned with the masses. Student riots on the eve of the 1968 Olympics revealed the discontent of many Mexicans. It may be that Mexico faces a crucial cross-roads in the 1970's.

THE PANAMA CANAL DOMINATES CENTRAL AMERICA

Southeast of Mexico, in an area smaller than Texas, are the six republics of Central America. The most northerly is the Republic of Guatemala, with its lost Mayan cities hidden in the jungle. El Salvador, the smallest of the six republics, is the only one without an Atlantic seacoast. Honduras, Nicaragua, and Costa Rica, which border on both the Atlantic and the Pacific Oceans, are often called "banana republics." Bananas and other tropical fruits are their chief exports.

In 1912 the United States sent marines to Nicaragua to protect American commercial interests and to preserve order. They remained twenty years. This American policy of interfering in the internal affairs of Central American and Caribbean countries, to promote or protect American interests, has been called "dollar diplomacy." Today however, through the Organization of American States, and through the UN, the United States tries to be a good neighbor to all the countries of Central and South America.

The southernmost republic of Central America is the Republic of Panama, which includes the Panama Canal. The canal, so important to world trade and to the defense of the Americas, is also the chief reason why Panama became independent.

AN IRRIGATED BANANA PLANTATION. Bananas are native to southeastern Asia but are now grown throughout the tropics. They are one of the main sources of income for Costa Rica, Nicaragua, and Honduras. Many of the plantations are owned by American companies.

PANAMA CANAL. Small electric cars on the tracks at the sides draw the ship through the lock. The canal is about fifty miles long between channel entrances, and the passage takes from seven to eight hours.

As early as the sixteenth century the Spanish conquerors of Latin America talked of a canal across the Isthmus of Panama, but the actual construction of one only began in the late nineteenth century. In 1879 a private French company began digging a canal. Ferdinand de Lesseps, who had built the Suez Canal, was chief engineer. The French company, however, had badly underestimated the cost and the physical difficulties. After ten years the company went bankrupt with less than half the work completed.

For a long time the United States was not much interested in a canal project. After the Mexican War, however, California and Texas had become parts of the United States, and the need for a shorter sea route between the nation's Atlantic and Pacific coasts became more obvious. At that time Panama was a province of Colombia, and the United States began trying to acquire canal-building rights from Colombia. The Colombian officials proved difficult to deal with. It appeared they were trying to obtain an exorbitant price and negotiations stalled.

The Spanish American War again demonstrated the usefulness of a canal. In 1903 the Panamanian people revolted, and declared their independence from Colombia. President Theodore Roosevelt took advantage of this revolt to recognize Panama as an independent republic. (The revolt had begun on November 3, 1903; we recognized the new government on November 6.) The Colombian people did not like our action but could do nothing. When Colombia tried to put down the rebellion, American warships prevented the Colombian troops from landing. A few days after becoming independent, the Republic of Panama signed a treaty with the United States creating a Canal Zone under American control.

The Panama Canal is an American engineering triumph. The main work of building the locks and dams was completed by 1914 but a landslide closed the canal in 1915–16. President Wilson officially opened the canal on July 12, 1920.

The treaty establishing the Canal Zone made Panama virtually an American colony. Employment and social practices in the "Zone" discriminated against Panamanians. Only reluctantly did Panama grant more land for U.S. air bases during World War II. In 1964 occurred a violent Panamanian riot against U.S. control of the Canal Zone. Suggested new treaties would give Panama far greater supervision over the Canal but no treaty has yet been ratified. The present Canal's narrowness will soon make it obsolete so the possibility of other waterways through Central America is being explored.

Chapter Check-up

1. What factors have hindered the people of Mexico in overcoming poverty?
2. How did the Church become involved in the strife between the Indians and the aristocracy of Mexico?
3. What did Benito Juárez, "the Mexican Lincoln," hope to do for his people?
4. How did the long rule of Porfiro Díaz retard the progress of the common man in Mexico?
5. How has the system of landholding changed in Mexico since Díaz?
6. How has illiteracy been reduced in Mexico?
7. Which are the "banana republics" of Latin America?
8. Why is the Panama Canal important?
9. How did the United States acquire canal-building rights in Panama?

CHAPTER 72

South America Faces Challenging Problems

ARGENTINA, LAND OF THE PAMPAS, GREW RICH

Buenos Aires was founded twice. Early in the sixteenth century the first large Spanish expedition sailed to the Río de la Plata, the estuary into which some of Argentina's major rivers flow, and established a settlement on the southern bank. The first settlers noted how fine the air was, so the colony became known as the city of "good air," or Buenos Aires (*bway*-nus *air*-eez).

There were not many Indians living in Argentina before the Spanish arrived, but the few who were there soon showed themselves to be independent and warlike. They attacked the settlers again and again. Soon famine and pestilence appeared, and in a few years most of the inhabitants died. The remainder sailed up the river and founded the city of Asunción (ah-soon-*syawn*) in Paraguay. Paraguay progressed rapidly, and many colonists there gradually moved back down the river. In 1580, nearly forty years after Buenos Aires had been deserted, they built their new capital on the ashes of the old city.

ARGENTINE PATAGONIA. Although this semi-arid region in southern Argentina makes up more than one-third of the country, it contains only one per cent of the country's population. The main activity in Patagonia is sheep raising.

In the meantime, something had been happening that affected the entire history of the country. When the weary colonists left Buenos Aires, they abandoned many horses and cattle. These animals escaped to the open pampas, where they became the ancestors of herds of wild horses and cattle. They became the wealth of the new Argentina.

In colonial days Buenos Aires was a wide-awake commercial center, full of merchants, cowmen, and smugglers. The colonial policy of Spain did not permit ships to enter the harbor of Buenos Aires; all imported goods were supposed to come by way of Panama and Peru. Prices were exorbitant. A yard of imported cloth cost twenty-five dollars, and a quart of imported olive oil sold for thirty dollars. The colonists did not propose to endure such a situation long. Whether the central government liked it or not, they smuggled many items directly from Europe.

The Gaucho was Argentina's frontiersman and pioneer. The wild cattle and horses on the pampas continued to increase. Many of the colonists made their living by rounding them up. At the time, the animals were valuable chiefly for their hides. In some years nearly a million and a half hides went to Spain. But the life of the hide traders was not easy. Indian warfare had never ceased; until the last quarter of the nineteenth century, the central parts of Argentina were still dangerous for the white man. The frontier was like a no-man's land, with only a series of small forts as protection against Indian raids. The territory around these forts was occupied by Gauchos (*gow*-choze).

The Gaucho has been called the Argentine cowboy, but he was more than that. He was a frontiersman, pioneer, and border soldier. His father as a rule was white, his mother Indian, and the Gaucho always identified himself with his father's race. His horse was his pride and the saddle was his castle, for he dwelt in no home very long. For his wife and family he constructed a simple hut on the pampas and lived by killing wild cattle and selling the hides to traders from the coast. He followed the herds from place to place. He was both a protection against the Indians of the interior and a racial link with them.

LORDS OF THE PAMPAS. The owner of an *estancia* and his second in command, both dressed in gaucho style, ride off for the daily inspection tour of the ranch.

Argentina became an independent nation. Gradually the Argentine landowner extended his fences over the pampas and made the wild cattle herds his own. He took over the Gauchos, organized them into bands of horsemen who served either as cowboys or private armies, depending upon the will of the landowner. With his Gaucho soldiers he participated in the struggle against the Spanish-born officials who were still trying to rule the country. When Argentina declared her independence in 1816, there were several large fortunes in the country, all derived from the raising of cattle. Buenos Aires was then a small city of perhaps twenty-five thousand, and the entire nation's population was only half a million.

But the basis of a vigorous and wealthy independent nation had already been established. The people fought hard to build their country. Now they were ready to try to govern it themselves. There was one serious obstacle to unity, however. Each district was jealous of the others, and all were unwilling to submit to a central authority that would have meant the dominance of Buenos Aires. The situation was much like that in our country when the constitution was adopted, but the people of Argentina chose a different course from that of the writers of our constitution. They made the states more powerful than the national government. Civil war broke out on a large scale. One petty tyrant clashed with another, and all of them clashed with Buenos Aires.

Unification was achieved only through the rule of a dictator. Juan Manuel de Rosas, the governor of Buenos Aires, gained control over the whole country and ruled Argentina with an iron hand from 1829 to 1852.

Modern Argentina was born in the mid-nineteenth century. After Rosas, Argentina adopted a constitution modeled on that of the United States. The constitution united the Argentine states into a federal system. Several honest and capable presidents restored democratic methods. The greatest of them, Domingo Sarmiento (sar-*myen*-to), served from 1868 to 1874 and was one of the best friends the United States has had in Latin America. Sarmiento admired the United States and did everything in his power to make Argentina develop along the same general lines. New cities were built, commerce was encouraged, and new railroads and roads were constructed. Sarmiento, a close friend of Horace

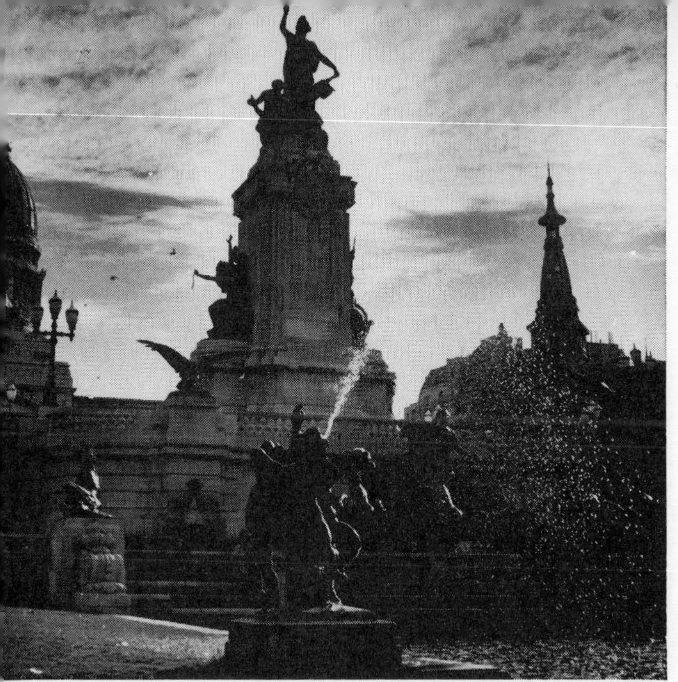

Buenos Aires. The busy capital of Argentina is dotted with many monuments and statues, such as this memorial to Argentine independence in 1816. With a population of almost three million, Buenos Aires is one of the great cities of the world.

Mann, the founder of our public school system, arranged to have sixty-three school teachers from America come to Argentina to found a national school system.

The stability and progressiveness of Argentina attracted European immigrants in increasing numbers. Several million Italians and Spaniards became fine citizens and workers. There were also many English and Irish immigrants and nearly a hundred thousand Germans. Today, 97 per cent of the population of Argentina is of European descent. Unlike many of the other Latin American countries, Argentina has very few mestizos, Indians, or Negroes.

These immigrants brought with them European traditions in art, literature, education, and philosophy. The artists, writers, and educated people of Argentina even today look to Paris, Rome, and Madrid for inspiration.

Before these settlers came, most Argentines were ranchers, but the new peoples settled down on farms and planted crops on the rich soil of the pampas. Soon wheat farming was of major importance in Argentina, and wheat overtook meat as the major export.

Buenos Aires became a giant among cities. As more railroads linked the interior with Buenos Aires, the city expanded. The wealth of Argentina flowed through Buenos Aires as liquids flow through a funnel. In forty-five years (1895–1940) the population of the city grew to more than three million. It is now the largest city in Latin America. Nearly a fourth of Argentina's population lives there.

Argentina became industrialized. For a long time, Great Britain was Argentina's best customer. Britain bought most of Argentina's wheat and beef. She supplied money to build Argentina's railroads. She sent manufactured goods and coal to Argentina. Indeed, it was sometimes said that Argentina was unofficially a part of the British Empire.

During the two world wars, however, Argentina was cut off from Britain and other sources of supply. Argentina decided to develop her own industries. She began to turn her raw materials into flour, leather shoes, woolen cloth, furniture, rubber goods, and many other commodities for her own people. But her new industries did not make Argentina independent of overseas markets as her leaders had hoped. Her dependence on foreign trade results from the fact that Argentina's mineral resources are not large. She does have some oil and iron deposits, but at least half of the coal needed to run her factories must be imported. During World War II, for instance, when her coal imports were reduced, Argentina had to keep her trains and machines running by burning wood and even grain. In times of financial or political trouble in the world, Argentina suffers, but in good times she prospers.

Argentina resents the influence of the United States. Argentina must sell her agricultural products to pay for the coal, machinery, and other imports she must have. She has grown to dislike the United States because for a number of years we have severely limited the amount of Argentine beef and wheat that enters our country

Eva Perón. The wife of Juan Perón was enormously popular in Argentina. After her death, she was, and still is, worshiped by many of the people as a saint. She is shown here making a world broadcast in 1948.

in competition with our own. At the same time, our business leaders have exported large quantities of automobiles, machinery, and other products to Argentina, and have gained ownership of important Argentine industries.

In 1946, after several military coups, Colonel Juan Peron (pay-*rawn*) emerged as "strong man." Peron's was a new sort of dictatorship for Argentina. Relying not merely on the support of the army, he appealed to the urban poor (called the "shirtless ones"). Handsome and charming, Peron had the valuable aid of his glamorous actress-wife, Eva, who became extremely popular through charitable work with funds extorted from the wealthy. The civil service was expanded. Labor unions received governmental favors. Nationalists applauded the dictator's denunciations of U.S. "Yankee imperialism." Argentina became a "police state" as the free press was detroyed, anti-Semitism flourished, elections were rigged and organized mobs were used to quell opposition.

But Peron ruined the economy by milking the grain and cattle interests for money to nationalize railroads and build heavy industry. Inflation set in. Beef shortages followed and meat-rationing was introduced. After Eva Peron's death from cancer in 1952, rumors of the regime's immorality and corruption grew. The Church was antagonized by attempts to reduce its control over education and by the legalization of divorce. In 1955, after several efforts, Peron was overthrown by the military and sought refuge in Spain.

The problems raised by Peron also remain. The cost of living has been climbing by a staggering twenty to thirty percent a year. Meat shortages have continued. Discension has split most political parties and factionalized the armed forces. There have been three coups between 1968 and 1972, with generals succeeding each other in the presidency.

BRAZIL FOUND PEACEFUL SOLUTIONS TO MANY PROBLEMS

The Portuguese settled Brazil. In 1500 the Portuguese took possession of the land we know as Brazil. The Portuguese got their prize partly as the result of a lucky accident in which the explorer Pedro Cabral (kah-*brahl*) was blown away from Africa over to the Brazilian coast. Because there were no legends about rich deposits of gold, the king of Portugal had difficulty persuading colonists to settle there. His government sent criminals and large numbers of persecuted Jews to the new colony. Soon the colonists had the good fortune to meet shipwrecked Portuguese sailors who had already been living among the natives for many years. These sailors and their friends helped the new settlers adjust themselves to their strange surroundings.

The principal product in those days came from a native tree that produced a much-prized red dye known as *brazil*. This dye gave its name to both the tree and to the land in which it grew.

Northern Brazil grew rich on sugar cane. Fifty years passed before Portugal undertook the colonization of Brazil on a large scale. By that time conditions had become so bad among the settlers, who were fighting the Indians and each other, that a governor was sent to restore order. In 1549 he established a large colony at Baía (bah-*ee*-ah) in northern Brazil.

In the second half of the sixteenth century there was a spectacular demand in Europe for a new product, sugar made from cane. The colonists in northern Brazil found the climate suitable for growing sugar cane, and soon Baía became the center of a prosperous sugar-growing region.

The use of Indian slaves on the sugar plantations was not successful. The supply was inadequate, and those who had been forced into slave labor were not good workers. Negro slavery seemed to the plantation owners the only solution. Thousands of Negroes came in chains to Brazil in the seventeenth and eighteenth centuries.

The sugar plantations of northern Brazil were similar to those of the old South in our country. There was the "great house" with its thick walls, its dozens of rooms, its school, its hospital, and its rich furnishings. There were the slave quarters, crowded buildings where the Negroes lived. Many of the slaves were well-educated Mohammedan Negroes who knew how to read and write Arabic. It was not long before there was considerable intermarriage between the two groups. A large mulatto class grew up in Brazil.

The bandeirantes looked for gold, diamonds, and slaves. The settlers in southern Brazil at São Paulo (soun *pow*-loo) did not share in the wealth of their northern neighbors. Many of them organized expeditions that journeyed into the interior in search of the gold that was rumored to abound there. These men were called *bandeirantes* (bahn-day-*rahn*-tays) or "followers of the banner," because they marched in groups of thousands behind a banner.

The bandeirantes were pioneers. They explored the whole Amazon basin, and they are responsible for pushing the borders of Brazil far to the south and west. They tramped through the jungle for years, taking time out to raise food. At first they did not find any gold, but they found many Indians whom they carried off into slavery. The Jesuits who had missions in the interiors tried to protect the Indians when they could, but the slave traders were relentless.

Finally, in about 1700, gold and diamonds were discovered in the southwestern part of the country. There was a great rush toward the gold

PLANTATION LIFE IN BRAZIL. This lithograph shows Negroes in Brazil preparing manioc, the root of the cassava plant. Cassava is native to Brazil and is still one of the staples of the diet there. In the United States it is known mainly in the form of tapioca. Most of the work necessary to prepare it was done by women slaves, since the men were more valuable in the cane fields.

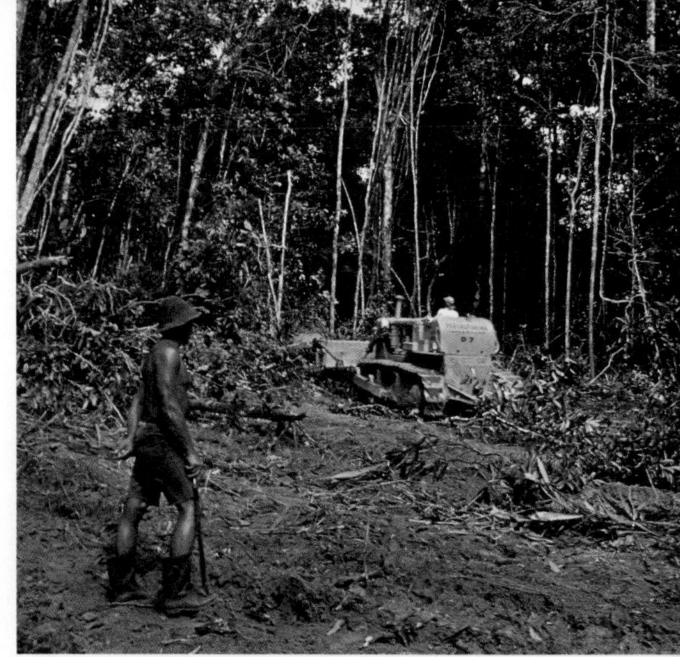

TRANS-AMAZON ROAD. Attempting to open up the impenetrable interior, Brazil is building a highway which will give access to the vast resources of the jungle. Ecologists, however, are fearful of its effect upon wildlife and the native population.

and diamond regions. Prices of food, clothing, and shelter went sky-high, as they did in California during the gold rush of 1849.

The discovery of the mines changed Brazilian life almost overnight, for the huge plantations were neglected while the hunt for gold was on. Brazil has suffered many such sudden changes in her economic life, each of which seemed to promise great wealth at the beginning but proved a deception in the end. First it was brazilwood, then sugar cane, and next gold and diamonds. Around 1900 wild rubber brought fabulous prices, and now coffee is the backbone of the economy.

As a result of these changes, Brazil has always been largely a one-crop country. She has never produced a variety of products. Reliance on a single crop has not only kept her much poorer than she would otherwise have been, but it has meant that her extremes of poverty and wealth were intense and almost constant.

Brazil became an empire in her own right. In 1807, when Napoleon advanced on Lisbon, the Portuguese king fled to Brazil. His fleet carried hundreds of the wealthiest families of Portugal to Rio de Janeiro. They brought along all their possessions, art treasures, and books. Rio de Janeiro became a cosmopolitan city. A few years later, in 1821, after Napoleon had been defeated, the Portuguese king went back to his old country, but he left his twenty-two-year-old son, Pedro, to rule Brazil. A few years later, when Brazil declared itself independent of Portugal, Pedro became the first king of Brazil.

When Pedro II, the grandson, came to the throne, he made an excellent emperor. One Latin American historian wrote that the greatest democracy in South America during the past century was the empire of Pedro II. He was liberal-minded, progressive, and a great patron of the arts. His rule was one of the longest in history. Thousands of European settlers arrived, and Brazil became a modern nation. In 1888 Brazilian slaves were freed by decree.

Brazil became a republic. In spite of the enlightened rule of their emperor, the Brazilians began to feel that their empire was out of date. The landowners were angry about the freeing of the slaves. The young, progressive people wanted a republic. The army officers were upset because the emperor would not let the generals interfere in politics. In 1889 Pedro II was finally asked to leave the country. He did so, and the nation became a republic without violent conflict. The new constitution that was adopted a few years later was excellent and helped to maintain an orderly government. The stable and peaceful conditions in Brazil allowed the new republic to prosper and marked the beginning of the country's modern development. Millions of dollars were spent on ports and railways and on sanitation projects that practically wiped out yellow fever, bubonic plague, and smallpox.

Brazil found new wealth in her "black gold." Rubber was known to the Mayans and the Aztecs but it did not reach Europe until the nineteenth century. When the automobile was invented, a great demand for rubber for tires suddenly developed. When the price of the new commodity rose to over three dollars a pound,

Brazilians abandoned their easy life in the cities to seek their fortunes in the jungles. For a time, Brazil had a virtual monopoly on rubber. But a few years later some shoots of rubber trees were smuggled out and planted in the Dutch East Indies. Production there, on carefully supervised plantations, produced high-quality rubber that soon displaced Brazil's "black gold." The price went down to about twenty cents a pound. Another of Brazil's economic bubbles had burst.

Brazil's coffee found a world market. In 1754 a Franciscan monk planted coffee seeds in the garden of his monastery near Rio de Janeiro. This was the beginning of an immense new coffee industry. The plant throve easily in the mild climate, and before long Brazil's production surpassed that of Arabia, the home of the coffee plant. Brazil is now the single greatest supplier of coffee in the world. At present, the general market for coffee is good, but in the past there have been disastrous slumps. During the 1930's the Brazilian government burned half a billion dollars' worth of coffee in order to check production and keep prices up. Colombia and other coffee-growing countries seized the chance to grab part of the world market. As a result, Brazil's plan to limit the supply was a costly failure.

The United States purchases a major portion of Brazil's coffee. This is one reason for the close relationship between the two countries during the past several decades. Another reason is that Brazil is the only Portuguese-speaking country in Latin America. Feeling different from the Spanish-speaking nations around her, she has sought friendship in the great democracy to the north. In World War I Brazil was the only South American country to join the Allies. In World War II Brazilian troops fought in Italy beside British and American forces.

Brazil is held back by economic and political problems. Brazil is an immense country with rich resources, and even today it is sparsely inhabited. The narrow strip along the coast is the only highly developed region. In this coastal territory are Brazil's major industries and cities, including Rio de Janeiro, the country's main city. Many travelers have called this city the most beautiful in the world.

About three hundred miles south of it stands

BRASILIA. These pictures show two views of the "Palace of the Dawn," which is the residence of the President of Brazil in the country's new capital.

RIO DE JANEIRO. Considered by many to be the most beautiful harbor in the world, Rio de Janeiro was visited by Portugese explorers in January, 1502, thus the name: River of January. Shown here is the crescent sweep of Copacabana beach ending at famed Sugar Loaf.

the city of São Paulo, where most of the factories of Brazil are situated. The state of São Paulo produces half the entire industrial output of the country and pays more than half the federal taxes. The city of São Paulo has nearly four million people and seems to enjoy a constant building boom. Everything is new and bustling in São Paulo. Great rivalry exists between industrious São Paulo and easy-moving Rio de Janeiro.

South of São Paulo is a great agricultural and cattle region. About half a million German immigrants and their descendants live here. Perhaps three times that number of Italians have also settled in this fertile southern region, which has a climate much like that of the southern United States. It is the most promising section of the country.

Conditions in Brazil are favorable for industrial development. Her area and population are approximately equal to that of the other nine South American nations combined. Continued immigration is likely to increase her wealth and population. There are mountains of high-grade iron ore and great reserves of manganese, a metal used in making steel. Like the rest of Latin America, however, Brazil lacks good coal, but she hopes to develop water power as a substitute.

Capital is needed to develop Brazil's resources, but in the early 1960's, it was not forthcoming. Instead, each year there were dangerously large deficits in the national budgets. As a result, inflation decreased the buying power of the currency. Hand in hand with these economic problems went political instability. A drawn-out series of government crises led finally to a military takeover in 1964. With her great wealth, Brazil should be able to look forward to a bright future. But first she must achieve economic and political stability.

COFFEE. Shown here is a coffee picker plucking the ripe red berries for processing. Though Brazil has moved into many other productive areas, coffee still remains the most important economic product.

NATURAL RESOURCES AND SELF-RELIANCE MADE MODERN CHILE

Progressive Chile developed along the Pacific Coast. As geographers point out, there are really three Chiles, each completely different from the others. In the north is a great desert that is rich in nitrate and copper deposits. Middle Chile is a fertile valley where most of the Chileans live. In the south is the "Chilean Switzerland," a vacation land of mountain peaks, clear lakes, and forests. Here we find sheep and cattle ranches as well as coal and iron deposits.

Chile begins at the southern border of Peru and extends southward for nearly three thousand miles. At its broadest point the country is only about two hundred miles wide. It is twice as large as California, but its population is much smaller. The geography of Chile, together with the hardy and warlike Indians who lived there when the Spaniards arrived, combined to make the Chilean people alert and forward-looking.

BERNARDO O'HIGGINS. After helping San Martín free Chile from Spain, O'Higgins proclaimed Chilean independence in 1818 and became the new country's first president. His reforms aroused much opposition among the wealthy classes, and he was forced to resign in 1823.

Chileans today enjoy more personal freedom than do the citizens of almost any other Latin American nation.

When Pedro de Valdivia and his Spaniards began the conquest of Chile, it took them a year to travel across the forbidding northern desert of Chile, where no green thing grows. When the Spaniards finally entered the central valley, they founded the first Chilean city, Santiago (san-tih-*ah*-go), in 1541. There was little gold in this wild land, and the scattered Indian tribes could never be met in a single great battle and defeated.

After nearly half a century of constant warfare, the Spaniards managed to push the natives down into the southern part of the country. Then, along the banks of a river, the colonists established forts and garrisons on a frontier that had to be defended for nearly two hundred and fifty years. It was not until 1882 that a final peace treaty was signed with the southern Indians.

Few Spanish soldiers brought wives or families to live with them in this dangerous territory, but many of them married Indian women. From these families, most modern Chileans are descended.

O'Higgins became the Chilean hero. Everywhere in modern Chile one sees the name O'Higgins on parks, streets, and hotels. Since Chile is a Spanish-speaking land, this puzzles Americans who have never heard of the Irishman who freed Chile from Spain. Ambrosio O'Higgins was a traveling salesman who made a fortune in Chile. He sent his son, Bernardo, to school in England. When Bernardo had trouble understanding mathematics, he arranged to have special tutoring. The tutor was a Venezuelan refugee named Francisco Miranda. You have already heard of him as one of the leaders in Latin America's wars for independence. Instead of mathematics, Miranda taught the boy the dream of freedom for South America.

O'Higgins was back in Chile when the aristocrats refused to recognize the new king of Spain,

CHILEAN TOWN. This muddy street in a small town in Aconcagua Province, is in stark contrast to the gleaming stone and steel of Santiago, the capital city. Chile, the longest country in the world, is itself a land of great contrasts with deserts in the north and semi-polar lands in the extreme south.

Napoleon's brother. It was easy for young O'Higgins to head a rebellion. At first, things went badly. After a humiliating defeat, he had to flee to Argentina. There he helped the great liberator, San Martín, train an army. Together they led their troops over the Andes to Chile and defeated the surprised Spaniards.

O'Higgins became the first president of Chile, but it was not long before his enemies complained that he was opposed to the Church and that he was never willing to compromise. O'Higgins, seeing that his leadership was no longer effective, resigned. Like San Martín and Bolívar, he died in exile, almost forgotten by the people he had led to freedom.

Left without a leader, Chile suffered for years before order returned and a stable government emerged. Gradually, Chile became one of the most democratic countries in Latin America. There have been revolutions, but Chileans respect and maintain the political rights granted to the people by their constitution.

Chile has had great problems. For years Chile enjoyed great prosperity from its monopoly of the natural nitrates so essential to the preparation of fertilizer and explosives. Income from nitrates paid for most government expenses. Ironically, World War I, which expanded the demand for explosives, proved a boomerang for Chile. Cut off from South America, the Germans learned how to make nitrates artificially and other nations followed suit. Unable to rely on revenues from nitrate exports, Chile's government had to raise taxes and, consequently, tensions increased between the rich and poor.

Periods of national prosperity have scarcely affected the poor. In the north, miners toiled miserably for foreign copper companies. Semi-feudalism has prevailed in the Central Valley where wheat fields, vineyards and cattle are tended by peasants and tenants on huge estates or fundos (*foon* dos).

Happily, political democracy has been fairly sturdy. Although bitterly waged, elections have been generally honest. There are so many parties that coalitions are usually necessary but there have been relatively few uprisings.

In 1964 Christian Democrat Eduardo Frei (fry) became President in a "revolution by ballot." Backed by the United States, Frei began a pro-

STONE MILL. This millstone was once drawn by horses, but the mill is now abandoned since the farmer has recently been able to buy a new machine to do the work.

gram of land reform and "Chileanization" of the copper industry, promising fair payment to the ousted owners.

Chile's constitution prohibited Frei from seeking re-election in 1970. Winning a three-man contest by a small plurality, Socialist Salvador Allende (ahl *yenda*) was the first Marxist to gain national power through democratic means. In its first year, his administration accelerated the break-up of fundos, froze prices and raised wages, seized American copper mines and telephone companies. How long Allende can retain power democratically in the face of rising opposition only time can tell.

SOUTH AMERICA'S SMALLER COUNTRIES FACE SERIOUS PROBLEMS

The eight smaller republics of South America have had checkered histories. Some have known periods of prosperity. But at present all have such grave difficulties that none can be called truly successful in satisfying the economic and political needs of its common people.

Guyana is South America's newest Republic. The youngest of South America's independent lands lies on the northeast coast of the continent between the Dutch colony of Surinam and Venezuela. It is the only South American country in which English is the official language. Originally territory inhabited by the fierce Carib Indians, it was the scene of competition between Britain and Holland. The victorious British created the colony of British Guiana in 1831. In 1966 the colony, now called Guyana, became an independent state within the British Commonwealth and proclaimed itself a republic in 1970.

Internal conditions have been far from tranquil. Since the Caribs were unsuited for work on the sugar plantations, the British imported African Negroes and East Indians. The two groups have not gotten along well. The Negroes generally absorbed British culture while the East Indians have clung to their Hindu or Moslem ways. The two chief political parties are based on racial divisions with the East Indians' "People's Progressive Party" having a definite Marxist tinge. As the 1970s began the Negro-supported "People's National Congress," led by Prime Minister Forbes Burnham, was in control.

Uruguay has become a "paradise lost." Uruguay is a grassy plateau well suited for wheat and cattle. In 1828 this smallest South American republic was created as a buffer between Brazil and Argentina. For years her political situation was chaotic. Both neighbors tried to dominate her while such bitterness existed between the two major parties,—the liberal "Colorados" and the conservative "Blancos"—that from 1830 to 1903 there were forty revolts and twenty-five different governments.

The election of "Colorado" leader Pose Batlle

Women Miners. In the Andean countries, women have often done the work of men. They do not work underground in the mines, however, but do surface digging.

(*Baht* yay) to the presidency in 1903 was the turning point. Batlle established a firm democracy and one of the world's first welfare states.

By the 1930s Uruguay was being hailed as a "Utopia" and "the Switzerland of South America." Her almost entirely European and middle class population had the lowest growth rate and about the highest literacy rate in Latin America. Although the "Colorados" ruled for over ninety years, democracy was preserved. The economy, based largely on wool exports and tourism, was prosperous and the currency was stable.

But serious weaknesses were exposed from the late 1950s on. Control of land and industry was in too few hands, for there had been no attempt at land reform. Uruguayan agriculture had grown too inefficient to compete successfully in the world's markets. Welfare state programs had been so expanded that every phase of life received protection. With over half of the population at least fifty years old, some 350,000 pensioners were being supported by fewer than a million workers. A huge bureaucracy was needed to operate this system: forty per cent of all workers were government employees. The government was forced to borrow heavily from foreign sources and galloping inflation developed. Between 1955 and 1970 Uruguay suffered a 9000 per cent rise in the cost of living!

Sheep in Uruguay. Although wheat and corn are raised on Uruguay's plains, the country is still dependent on sheep and cattle for much of its income.

Paraguay has had a tragic history. Modern Paraguay has grown out of the wreckage of one of history's most disastrous wars. This landlocked region, inhabited chiefly by mestizos and Indians, was part of Argentina until 1811. Some fifty years later, Francisco Lopez (*low*-pes), a tyrant with Napoleonic ambitions, made war simultaneously against Brazil, Argentina and Uruguay. Outnumbered by ten to one, the Paraguayans fought for five years, surrendering only after Lopez's death in 1870 and their male population had been reduced to only 28,000.

From 1932 to 1935 Paraguay was again in a bloody conflict. This time it was against Bolivia over control of the Gran Chaco (*grahn chah*-ko),

LAKE TITICACA. Located at an altitude of 12,500 feet in the Andes between Bolivia and Peru, Lake Titicaca is the highest large lake in the world. It is an important avenue of transportation between the two countries and has regular steamer service. These unique canoes made from reeds and used by the Indians along its shores.

a huge jungle thought to contain oil. Although Paraguay defeated her better-equipped enemy, it was at the cost of 40,000 Paraguayan lives and a ruined economy.

The most recent of Paraguay's many dictators has been President Alfredo Stroessner (*stress*-ner), who seized power in 1954 and has been periodically "re-elected." The currency has remained comparatively stable; a token opposition has been permitted in the congress. But Paraguay continues to be Argentina's puppet. One per cent of the landholders still own three-quarters of the farmland. Workers' wages average a dollar per day and at least a fourth of the population is illiterate. Thousands of youths have emigrated seeking better pay while there are perhaps a half-million political exiles from this unhappy police state.

Bolivia has been "a beggar sitting on a pile of gold." Most of the five million Bolivians are Indians and mestizos living in dreadful poverty on one of the world's highest plateaus within reach of rich tin and silver resources. The plateau's soil is too thin for good farming. Lung diseases shorten the miners' lives. Little wonder that most Bolivians chew cocaine to forget.

There have been some 175 "revolutions" since Bolivia won independence in the 1820s. Most have been coups instead of attempts at real social change. The Bolivian upper classes have given little thought to the plight of the poor. This is true even of the few who have themselves risen from humble origins, like Simon Patino (puh-*teen*-yo) who obtained control of half of Bolivia's tin mines. Patino contributed very little of his fortune to Bolivia, spending most of it abroad.

Bolivia's foreign wars have been disastrous. She yielded her seacoast to Chile in the War of the Pacific (1879–1884) and lost the Chaco War

(1932–5) to Paraguay. But in the latter conflict, Bolivia's peasants and miners emerged from their isolation to gain some sense of nationalism and some realization of their problems.

Thereafter, Bolivian politicians have had to promise reforms. A left-wing "National Revolution," backed by the powerful miners' union and led by Victor Paz (pas) began in 1952. Paz granted voting rights to all adults, confirmed the break-up of large estates and nationalized the tin mines of the Patino and other interests.

Because this was a revolution without aggressive designs on other nations, it was supported by the United States. But the "National Revolution" ended in 1964. Allowing power to "go to his head," Paz made many enemies and was finally ousted by the army. Since then men have vied for power with the military in real control.

Peru is a land of minerals, Indians—and generals. Peru is mainly a high tableland ridged by towering branches of the Andes. The country is a treasure-house of minerals (copper, gold, silver, lead). Railroads built through the Andes by American financier Henry Meiggs (megs) in the late nineteenth century have made most of these minerals accessible.

Peru's feudal-type social structure has been dominated by the so-called "forty families." The middle class is small, although Lima (*lee*-muh) has almost two million people. But Lima's beauty is marred by the horrible slums in its outskirts. The rural Indians, it is said, are more likely to know "who they belong to" than "where they live."

Peruvian history has been a dreary record of political feuds and dictatorships. But in APRA (American Popular Revolutionary Alliance), Peru had the first mass movement for the poor in South America. APRA's founder, Victor Haya (*eye*-ya), has been the national storm center since 1930. Often he and APRA have been denied the fruits of election victories by the aristocracy and the generals. For five years (1949–1954), Haya was forced to hide in the Colombian Embassy in Lima while government troops surrounded the building! However, Haya has become more conservative of late and has allied APRA with some of its former enemies.

In 1968 still another military junta seized power. With the Church's support, these generals promised reforms while rejecting both communism and capitalism. Foreign mineral and industrial properties have been confiscated and

Transportation in the Andes. For many years, the Andes were an almost insurmountable barrier to transportation in western South America. Recent engineering developments, such as this road in Peru between Lima and Cerro de Pasco, are helping to overcome the problem. The truck in this picture has just delivered a load of oil products.

SALT MINING. The worker shown here is refining salt in a mine north of Bogotá where Colombia's major salt works are located.

some redistribution of the land has begun.

Ecuador's human woes have dwarfed her natural advantages. "Ecuador" means "equator" in Spanish, for this little country does straddle the earth's center. A visit to Ecuador's equator, however, can be a chilling experience because of the snow-capped mountains in the country! Those mountains contain many minerals, including gold, silver, copper, iron and coal while timber products, bananas and cacao (used to make chocolate) are found in the forested lowlands.

But since breaking away from Greater Colombia in 1830, Ecuador's social and political ills have kept her among the world's poorest nations. The ten per cent of the population which is of European ancestry owns the bulk of the good land and dominates the Indians, mestizos and Negroes who form the Ecuadorean majority. There has always been bitter rivalry between the two largest cities, —Quito (*Kee* tow), the conservative, clean highland capital and Guayaqil (Gwa yah *kee*), the turbulent lowland port. Politics have been so chaotic that President Velasco Ibarra (Vel *ass* ko Ee *bar* ruh), who became dictator in 1970, has been able to serve out his full term only once in four previous times as President! With her poverty, limited population and domestic troubles, it is hardly surprising that Ecuador has lost three-quarters of her original territory to her neighbors, —Peru, Brazil and Colombia.

Ecuador needs badly to be industrialized but this has been opposed by the landowners whose income depends on their banana and cacao crops.

Colombia is a product of its geography. More than most lands, Colombia owes its strengths and weaknesses to its geography. Three ranges of the Andes dominate the country, forming a rugged terrain. It is on the plateaus of those ranges that most Colombians live since, in equatorial regions, one must reside in high altitudes to be comfortable. The mountains contain valuable minerals and Colombia is called "coffee on the rocks," for it is upon the coffee raised on the uplands that the national prosperity chiefly depends.

But from the mountains have also come handicaps. In the 1820s a "Greater Colombia," formed with Ecuador and Venezuela, soon broke up because of the mountain barriers between the regions. Colombia itself has been virtually a land of city-states with little sense of national unity. One of the long-standing political issues has been the Conservatives' emphasis on centralization as opposed to federalism supported by the Liberals.

Colombia's loss of her province of Panama in 1903 was due partly to geographic factors. (See page 679 for the full account.) The dense jungle separating Panama from Colombia made communication between the two regions difficult and made it easier for the Panamanians to think of secession. For several years after the loss of Panama, Colombia was understandably angry at the United States. By the outbreak of World War II, however, Colombia had become friendly again and was among the first Latin American nations to join the conflict against the Axis.

Colombians are a people of interesting contrasts. They like to regard themselves as the intellectuals of South America and do speak the purest Spanish on the continent. Yet Bogota (boh-goh-

tah), the capital, has been one of the world's most unsafe cities, largely because of bitter political feuds between Conservatives and Liberals. The assassination in 1948 of a popular Liberal leader gave rise to a bloody twenty year period costing at least 200,000 lives. This "La Violencia" ("Violence") led to a brutal dictatorship. Upon its overthrow in 1957, Conservative and Liberal leaders worked out an arrangement under which the two parties would alternate in governing Colombia. For years the compromise worked well but in the 1970s there have been splits in this coalition so that new political troubles may lie ahead.

Venezuela has been a mis-managed treasure-house. Few countries have as rich resources as Venezuela ("Little Venice"). Lake Maracaibo (mar-a-*kigh*-bo), an arm of the Caribbean Sea, contains the "black coal" that makes Venezuela the world's third largest oil producer. There are also mountains of barely touched iron ore and ample reserves of other minerals.

Strangely, the early Spanish settlers did not regard Venezuela as valuable. When Simon Bolivar led the struggle for freedom, so many Venezuelans followed him to other lands that in twenty years Venezuela lost a quarter of its people!

Not until the dictatorship of Juan Gomez (*go*-mes), between 1909 and 1935, were Venezuela's oil reserves really tapped. Foreign companies were given concessions, paying royalties which accounted for over two-thirds of government revenues. The capital, Caracas (ka-*rak*-us) was modernized but wealth remained in just a few hands. Industry and agriculture were so neglected and Venezuelans relied so much on imports for their needs that Caracas became one of the world's costliest cities to live in. Many of these trends continued after Gomez's death, particularly under the brutal tyranny of Marcos Perez Jiménez (puh-*res* he-*may*-nes) who fled in 1958 with over two hundred million dollars.

The election of Romulo Betancourt (betan-*cour*) followed Perez Jiménez's downfall and marked the start of reform. Industrialization was encouraged and there was some re-distribution of land. Steering a moderate, democratic course which won the applause of the United States, Betancourt faced bitter opposition from the aristocrats on the one hand, and from Cuban-backed Communists, on the other. Surviving uprisings and assassination attempts, he became Venezuela's first president to serve out his full term constitutionally. His successors have been continuing his policies and in 1971 steps were taken to ensure the nationalization of all oil properties within a decade.

But the elections of 1968 indicated that Venezuelan democracy is still very fragile. There were so many candidates that the president-elect received under thirty per cent of the votes and Perez Jiménez, back in the country, won a Senatorial seat by a huge margin!

Caracas. The Venezuelan capital is a thriving city whose modern appearance belies its deep set problems of poverty and the population explosion.

DEMOCRACY VIES WITH DICTATORSHIP IN LATIN AMERICA

Despite constitutions modeled after that of the United States, many Latin American nations are still unaccustomed to self-government. Since 1900 there have been over eighty successful revolutions in the region.

There are several reasons why democracy has had a difficult time. The people have been used to autocracy under both Indian and Spanish rule. Impoverished and hungry masses are tempted to follow "strong men" and demagogues who promise to improve their conditions. Accordingly, few Latin American lands have been able to follow truly democratic procedures for long periods.

Most Latin American dictatorships have been military-based regimes aiming chiefly at self-enrichment or self-gratification. Streossner in Paraguay and Duvalier in Haiti head such governments. Some dictators have attracted mass allegiance with pledges of social and economic reforms. Peron's success in Argentina was due largely to this. The rise to power of Marxists has added a new element. Marxist government in Chile has not yet (as of mid-1972) brought dictatorship but the experience of Cuba under Fidel Castro (fee-*dell kas*-tro) shows what can happen to liberty when militant Marxists gain control.

Cuba became the western hemisphere's first Communist state. Cuba achieved independence in 1898 as a result of the Spanish-American War but until 1934 had to concede the United States' right to intervene in Cuban affairs. Sugar cane production dominated the island's economy with the Cubans becoming extremely dependent upon American markets, products and financial aid. In the 1950s Cuba's middle class was one of the largest and best off in Latin America. But the condition of the peasants was terrible and President Fulgencio Batista's (bah-*teesta*) ruthless dictatorship had apparently the full backing of the United States.

In 1956 Fidel Castro, son of a wealthy planter, began a guerrilla campaign against Batista. Castro's bands never reached the status of an army. But so hateful had Batista's tyranny become that the dictator's support melted away and he fled in 1959.

Upon coming to power, Castro pledged to enforce the liberal constitution that Batista had ignored and to hold democratic elections soon. The elections never took place. Opponents, including some of Castro's now-disillusioned followers, were imprisoned or exiled. Spurning the Eisenhower Administration's offers of financial help, Castro confiscated American-owned plantations and oil refineries. In 1960 he admitted he was a Communist and sought economic and political links with Russia.

In 1961 the United States broke diplomatic relations with Cuba and President Kennedy gave military aid to an ill-fated invasion of the "Bay of Pigs" by a thousand anti-Castro Cuban exiles. The Russo-American "Cuban missile crisis," about which you may read on page 769, occurred in 1962. Since then Cuba has felt the serious effects of the USA's general economic boycott.

How Cubans have fared under Premier Castro is a subject of much controversy. Attempts to diversify the economy have failed while sugar cane production has fallen steadily. There are great shortages in consumers' goods, so the communalization of land and industry cannot be called successful. Cuba has become Russia's economic vassal. Thousands of middle class Cubans have chosen exile. However, Castro probably remains very popular with the poorest classes, for his regime has provided them with better housing, more education and work than they have ever had before.

Of vital concern are Castro's attempts to extend his influence throughout Latin America. "Fidelistas" have inspired guerrilla movements in Bolivia, Uruguay and Pero and efforts to assassinate high officials in Venezuela and the Dominican Republic.

OUTDATED FARM METHODS IN LATIN AMERICA. In spite of the fact that modern farm equipment is being used more and more in Latin America, older methods still persist. The farm hand is using oxen to plow a field, and the woman is grinding corn by a method similar to that used by the Indians.

The United States has opposed the spread of communism in several ways. American agents helped to overthrow a Marxist regime in Guatemala in 1954. In 1965 President Johnson sent troops to the Dominican Republic to prevent a possible Communist takeover. Often the USA has supported anti-Communist dictators. But encouragement has also been given to non-Communist social reform movements, such as Betancourt's in Venezuela and Paz's in Bolivia. Under the "Alliance for Progress" begun by President Kennedy in 1961, the United States has contributed over ten billion dollars in a decade to help finance land, educational, taxation and health reforms in Latin America. But the "Alliance" has had just moderate success because of the reluctance of upper class Latin Americans to enact real changes. Although this is frustrating, the United States knows it can no longer dictate to Latin Americans. Following Franklin Roosevelt's "Good Neighbor Policy" of the 1930s and the formation of the "Organization of American States" in 1948, the emphasis is now placed on co-operation and partnership.

Chapter Check-up

1. What is the importance in Argentine history of the following: (a) the pampas (b) the Gaucho (c) Domingo Sarmiento (d) Juan Perón?
2. Why have relations between Argentina and the United States sometimes been unfriendly?
3. How did Brazil come under the control of Portugal?
4. Name 5 of the crops or minerals that showed promise of bringing great wealth to Brazil.
5. What is the outlook for Brazil's economic future?
6. Describe the three distinct regions found in Chile.
7. What part did Bernardo O'Higgins play in Chilean history?
8. Why can Uruguay be termed a "Paradise Lost"?
9. What factors have hindered Paraguay's development?
10. What important resources are found in: (a) Bolivia? (b) Peru? (c) Colombia? (d) Venezuela?
11. In what ways has the United States tried to prevent the extension of communism in Latin America?

Chapter 73

The Culture of Latin America Shows Native and European Influences

The people of Latin America have a long history of achievement in culture and the arts. In prehistoric times, sculptors in the Andes Mountains fashioned statues and monuments of stone. When Europeans first began to explore Central and South America in the sixteenth century, they found advanced civilizations that were creating jewelry of gold and silver, brilliantly colored textiles, and exquisite pottery. The native crafts of South America were so firmly rooted that even during the centuries of domination by the Spaniards and Portuguese the people continued to create their traditional works of art.

For generations the artists of Latin America, isolated from the rest of the world, produced work that was not influenced by the great art of Europe. But the European settlers who came to Latin America in the seventeenth and eighteenth centuries introduced many changes. Latin Americans became aware of civilizations in other areas of the world. They absorbed some of the culture of the Spanish, the Portuguese, and the other settlers who came to South America. For this reason, Latin American culture today is a mixture of that of various peoples, chiefly the Spanish, Portuguese, and Indian. Latin American achievement has been particularly noteworthy in handicrafts, literature, music and dancing, and painting.

Native handicrafts reflect the past. In the Spanish colonies of the seventeenth and eighteenth centuries, silver was so abundant that many great families had their own silversmiths who kept busy making jewelry, silverware, and kitchen utensils. Silver was available in such vast quantities that even common utensils like plates and dippers were made of it. Today many of these beautiful objects may be seen in museums.

The handicrafts and folk art of Latin America are especially popular with tourists. While machine-made goods are slowly replacing hand-made objects, many craftsmen continue to make fine pottery, furniture, silverware, and tinware, just as their ancestors did hundreds of years ago. Latin America is also noted for brilliantly colored textiles that are woven by the natives on hand looms.

Literature is popular in Latin America. The literature of Latin America during the colonial period was widely influenced by that of the Spanish and Portuguese settlers. In the seventeenth and eighteenth centuries, however, as Latin Americans were beginning to grow restless under foreign domination, authors turned for their inspiration to the writers of other nations, particularly to those who supported the French and the American revolutions. These writers helped stimulate the people of Latin America in their struggles to achieve independence.

For many years Latin-American authors based their work on the writings of Europe but toward the end of the nineteenth century a new movement, called modernista, marked the start of a truly Latin American literature. The originator of this movement was a Nicaraguan poet, Ruben Dario (dah-*ree*-oh). He created a style that was unique rather than an imitation of European models. Dario's "Songs of Life and Hope" (1905) is considered most representative of his best work.

That Latin American literary achievement is now receiving world attention is shown in the fact that two Chilean poets have won the prestigious Nobel Prize for Literature. Gabriela Mistral (mee-*strahl*), author of "Desolatio" (1922) received the Prize in 1945. Noted Marxist and diplomat Pablo Neruda (neh-*roodah*), who wrote "Spain In My Heart" (1937), took the coveted 1971 award.

Another popular form of literary expression in Latin America is newspaper writing. While newspaper readers in the United States read the daily paper mainly for news and entertainment, Latin American readers are eager to learn the opinions of the writers. Newspapers print many political articles as well as philosophical and literary essays. These are read and discussed with great interest.

LA ARGENTINA. This great dancer was born in Buenos Aires. Her performances throughout the United States in 1928 won her fame and brought about a revival of interest in the classical dances of Spain.

Music and dancing are important in Latin American life. From the earliest times, the people of Latin America have considered music and dancing a necessary part of life. Gay songs and dances are a part of every social gathering, and they often serve a religious purpose as well. In the rural regions of South America, the Indians consider their colorful dances an important part of fiestas and other celebrations.

Modern Latin American music and dancing are well known in the United States. The rumba, tango, and samba are played frequently by dance bands in this country, and classical works by Latin American composers are known to concert-goers all over the world. Perhaps the most musical people of Latin America are the Brazilians, who have created numerous compositions of great richness and variety. One of the first modern works to show strong Latin American influences was *Il Guarany*, an opera by the nineteenth-century Brazilian composer Carlos Gomes. His opera, which employed Indian characters and music, achieved world-wide fame. The best-known Brazilian composer today is Heitor Villa-Lobos (*vee*-lah *law*-baws), who like Gomes is also famous for his use of Indian musical themes.

Painting is an ancient art in Latin America. When European conquerors first arrived in Latin America, they found skilled artists among the natives, and the artistic tradition continues to flourish in the works of modern painters. Probably the best known of contemporary Latin American artists are two Mexicans, Diego Rivera (ree-*vay*-ruh) and José Orozco (oh-*rose*-ko). Rivera and Orozco carefully studied the work of the Aztecs and Mayas, and used many Indian designs in their own paintings. They revived the old art of murals, or wall paintings. Art lovers from all over the world have come to Mexico to admire their extraordinary murals.

Rivera was so poor he could study painting only in night classes. His work shows deep feeling for the Mexican peasants. He has covered the walls of many buildings with huge paintings showing the suffering of the downtrodden. The colors of his finished murals are wonderfully brilliant. (See the picture at the top of page 677.)

Mural by Orozco. Like Rivera, Orozco was often inspired by social themes. His work is usually simple and sometimes stark. This mural is in Guadalajara, Mexico. A famous Orozco mural may be seen at Dartmouth College in New Hampshire.

Orozco lost his left hand in an accident when he was a child, but he never let his handicap interfere with his career. When he was in the first grade he had to pass a printing shop on his way to and from school. He always stopped to watch a cartoonist who sat in the shop window making drawings for the printer. It was not long before the boy himself dared to pick up a pencil and began to draw too. Orozco's family was able to give him a good education at the National University and the Academy of Fine Arts in Mexico City.

Orozco came to the United States several times, not as a tourist, but to work. He painted murals at Pomona College in California and in New York City. One of his most famous murals is at Dartmouth College in New Hampshire. Like many of his murals, it shows the strength and achievements of the Mexican Indians. Artists from all over the world have imitated the style and methods of the Mexican mural painters.

Chapter Check-up

1. What have been the chief influences on Latin American culture?
2. How did native writers influence the history of Latin America in the seventeenth and eighteenth centuries?
3. Who originated the *modernista* movement and what was his effect on Latin American literature?
4. What Brazilian composer is well known today?
5. Who are the two most famous Latin American painters? How have ancient civilizations influenced their works?

Latin America: SYNOPSIS

Before the sixteenth century, Latin America was the home of the Mayas, Aztecs and Incas. These Indians, who developed remarkable civilizations, had never seen Europeans. But within a century after the voyages of Columbus, Spain held all of Central and South America except Brazil, which became a Portuguese territory.

Until the nineteenth century the countries of Latin America remained firmly under foreign rule, but the revolutions in the United States and France awakened revolutionary leaders to the possibility of independence for the Spanish and Portuguese colonies. Led by such men as Miranda, San Martin, and Bolivar, the Latin Americans successfully fought for their freedom.

However, social, economic and political problems have continued to plague most Latin American states. Only in a few places has enough of a middle class emerged to bridge the wide gap between the small, rich, European upper class and the impoverished Indian, mestizo or Negro masses. While there is a growing trend to industrialization, the economy of most countries still relies too heavily upon one or two crops or minerals. Moreover, attempts to make economic changes rapidly has often led to inflation, worsening the misery of the poor. Few nations have been able to preserve democratic institutions for long periods. Military dictatorships have been frequent and in recent times Marxist movements have posed a serious challenge to liberalism. As the 1970s began, Marxists had come to power in Cuba and Chile and were responsible for guerrilla or terroristic activity in several other regions.

The culture of Latin America reflects the influences of the various peoples who have lived there, especially the Spanish, Portuguese and Indians. Latin Americans have won world recognition for their handicrafts, literature, music, dancing and painting.

Terms

Make sure you understand clearly the meaning of each of the following:

conquistadors	Mayas	Organization of American States
Aztecs	*mestizos*	"Yankee imperialism"
Gaucho	pampas	bandeirantes
hacienda	Pan American Union	Incas
Latin America	Fidel Castro	*modernista*

Important People

How has each of the following influenced the story of Latin America?

Benito Juárez	Porfiro Díaz	Pedro II	Rómulo Betancourt
Simon Bolívar	Lázaro Cárdenas	Bernardo O'Higgins	Rubén Darío
Francisco Miranda	Juan Perón	Francisco López	Diego Rivera
Jose San Martín	Fidel Castro	Juan Gómez	Heitor Villa-Lobos

Questions for Discussion and Review

1. What were the contributions of the great Indian civilizations of Latin America?
2. Why was the Latin American struggle for independence longer and harder than the American Revolution?
3. What part did religion play in the development of Latin America?
4. How has geography prevented the development of a Latin American federation?
5. What problems stand in the way of the com-

plete industrialization of Latin America?

6. Why has "government by revolution" been typical of the Latin American republics?
7. Explain how the United States acquired the site for the Panama Canal.
8. In what ways have the Cuban people been affected by Fidel Castro's regime?
9. In what ways are Latin America and the United States dependent upon each other today?
10. In your opinion, what reforms are most needed in Latin America to bring about economic prosperity? What can be done to establish political stability?

Interesting Things to Do

1. Make a map showing the Latin American countries. Outline and label countries, oceans, seas, important cities, mountains, and rivers. Add any other features that will make your map more meaningful and interesting.
2. With labels, drawings, cut-outs, or samples make a map of Latin America, showing the products that are exported to the United States and to Europe.
3. Make a chart of the Latin American countries, showing for each the area, population, capital, chief cities, natural resources, agricultural and industrial products, type of government, leaders, and current problems.
4. Prepare a classroom display of pictures showing the great civilizations of the Mayas, Aztecs, and Incas.
5. Prepare and present a series of color slides on "Mexico, Our Neighbor to the South." If possible, use slides taken by members of the class or their parents, showing the places they have been and the things they have seen.
6. Arrange and present an informal debate on the topic: *Resolved*, That formation of a Latin American Federation is the answer to the social, economic, and political problems of the republics.
7. Present to the class an oral report on "The Rise and Fall of a Latin American Dictator, Juan Perón."
8. Prepare a special report on one of the Latin American countries. Include maps, charts, and pictures as well as a written report to describe the geography, history, economy, government, and problems of that country.
9. Write a poem about the conquest of Mexico or San Martín's march over the Andes.
10. Add to or begin your "Who's Who in World History" series by writing one or more brief biographies of Latin American leaders.

Interesting Reading about Latin America

Blake, W. T., *From Sea to Sea in South America*, McBride. An English journalist recalls his South American travel adventures.

Brown, Rose, *The Land and People of Brazil*, Lippincott.

Bruce, J., *Those Perplexing Argentines*, Longmans Green. The Argentines and their customs.

Chase, S. and Tyler, M., *Mexico*, Macmillan.

Crow, John A., *The Epic of Latin America*, Doubleday.

Faraday, Margaret, *The Young Traveler in South America*, Dutton.

*Goetz, Delia, *Let's Read About South America*, Fideler.

Howarth, David, *Panama*, McGraw-Hill.

Peck, Anne Merriam, *Pageant of South American History*, Longmans Green. An historical survey from ancient to modern times.

Szulc, Tad, *Latin America*, Atheneum.

Wendt, Herbert, *The Red, White and Black Continent*, Doubleday.

Worchester, Donald E., *The Three Worlds of Latin America*, Dutton. Mexico, Central and South America.

The tragedy and futility of war and the enduring fact of human compassion is dramatized once again in a Sicilian Village in World War II.

Part 22
TWO WORLD WARS
TRAGEDIES OF THE TWENTIETH CENTURY

EUROPE TODAY

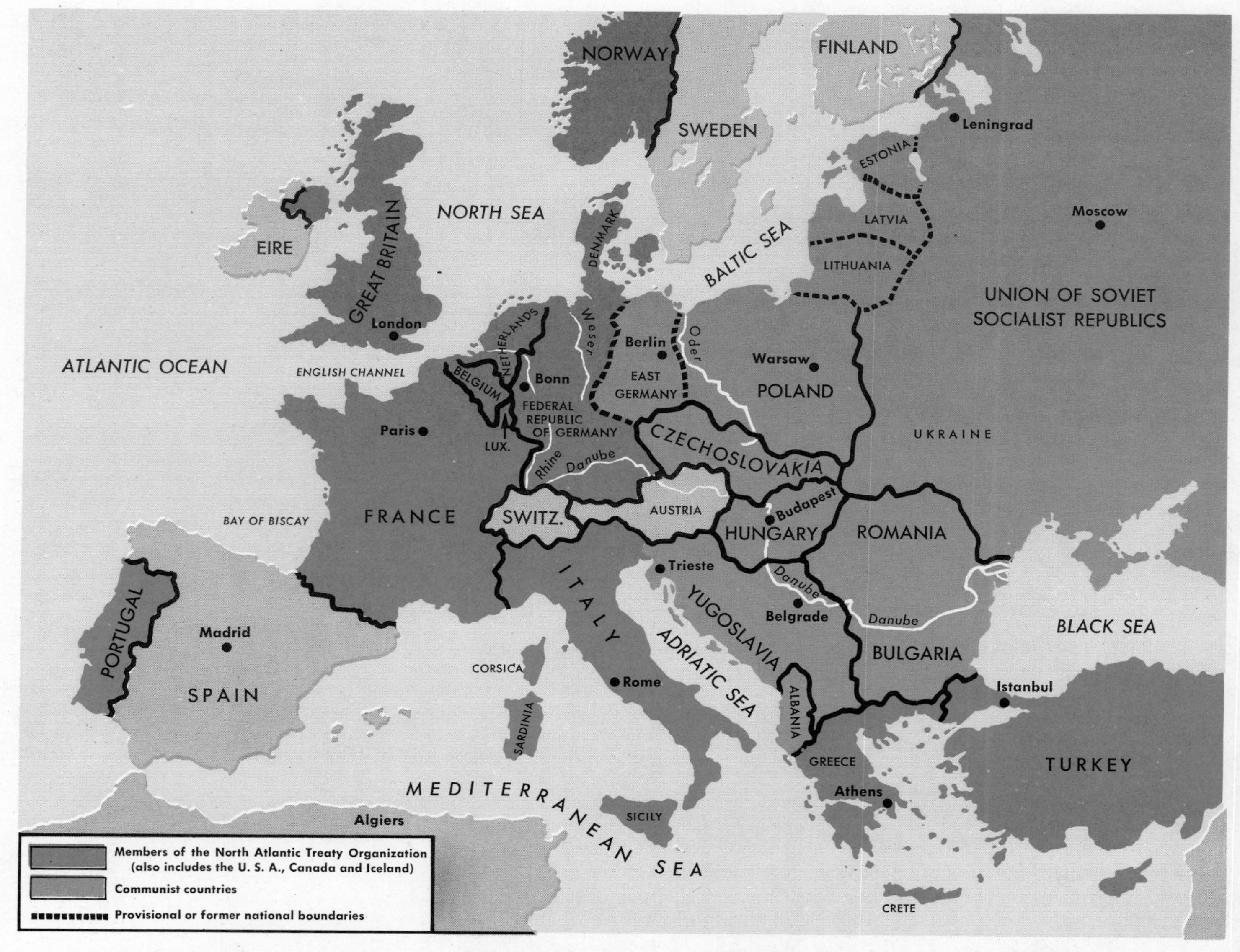

Two World Wars: PERSPECTIVE

One summer morning in 1945 a B-29 Superfortress appeared over the hilly green terrain of southern Japan. It was carrying an atomic bomb, the most destructive weapon ever known. Approaching Hiroshima, a seaport and the site of a Japanese army base, the airplane's crew made a final check of the bomb. Then, just after nine o'clock, it was dropped on the city. A few seconds later Hiroshima was a flaming shambles of wreckage, and some 150,000 people lay dead or wounded under the towering mushroom cloud that rose into the sky. Three days later another atomic bomb, more powerful than the first, was released over Nagasaki, and the tragedy was repeated.

The two atomic bombs were the terrible climax of World War II, a conflict that lasted six years and cost the lives of about fifteen million combatants and at least as many civilians. Waged in nearly every part of the world, it left few people untouched by its horrors. When finally the war ended, one fact had become glaringly clear: in modern warfare there are no real victors.

Mankind has witnessed two major wars in the twentieth century, as well as innumerable "minor" conflicts. Since World War II there has been really *no* peace in the world. Starting in 1950 with the Korean conflict, fighting has erupted in the Middle East, Hungary, Latin America, Southeast Asia, Pakistan, Northern Ireland, and the rest of the world waits nervously to see if tension will ease. By looking at the origins of World War I and World War II perhaps we can see some hope for averting a possible third World War. Perhaps we can ask ourselves, what price war, what price glory and certainly, what price peace!

CHAPTER 74

Nationalism, Imperialism, and Militarism Resulted in World Conflict

THE TENSIONS BETWEEN EUROPEAN NATIONS INCREASED IN THE TWENTIETH CENTURY

As we have followed the story of mankind from the days of the cave men to the twentieth century, we have seen how wars have again and again destroyed great nations and mighty empires. In spite of all the discoveries and advances of mankind, the world continued to experience the destruction and devastation of war. Today the world is again divided into armed camps.

Why has man, with all his technical and cultural progress, failed to find a way to live in peace with his neighbors? What are the obstacles to such a widely desired goal? There is no single or universally accepted answer to these questions. To begin to understand the underlying causes of modern war, we must go back several hundred years in European history.

The growth of democracy did not make Europe more peaceful. In the eighteenth century many men believed that wars occurred because rulers and the upper classes, ambitious to increase their power and wealth, built armies to conquer and pillage their neighbors. In 1792 the American Revolutionary leader Thomas Paine wrote that when all governments had become democratic there would be an end to wars. Ordinary men, he believed, marched off to the battlefield only to satisfy their rulers' ambitions. "What inducement has the farmer," asked Paine, "while following the plough to lay aside his peaceful pursuits and go to war with the farmer of another country?" Whether the ruler won or lost, Paine said, the farmer's life was sure to become more miserable because taxes would have to be raised to pay for the war.

In *Story of Nations* we have seen how democracy grew after the eighteenth century. By the beginning of the twentieth century, Great Britain, France, and Italy all had democratic governments. Even German rulers had to take into consideration the desires of their people before making decisions. In Russia, too, the czar bowed to popular demands and allowed a representative assembly, the Duma, to be formed in 1905.

In spite of democracy's great advances, however, the first half of the twentieth century has seen two of the worst wars in history. Things have not turned out as Thomas Paine predicted they would. Why has the increasing influence of the "common man" in his government failed to make the world more peaceful? The answer is that other powerful forces have influenced the course of history in recent years. In this chapter you will read about three of the most significant of those forces.

Nationalism has become a potentially dangerous force. We have already studied the development of nationalism in France, England, and other countries. Nationalism is the feeling that all people of a country are one family and that they should work for their own interests. Usually the people speak the same language. They have, or think they have, the same history and a common set of traditions and customs. Often they believe in the same religion. They therefore feel that they are like each other, that they ought to be united under one government and that

BATTLE OF ROCROI. Here, during the Thirty Years' War, a French aristocrat leads his men against the Spanish. Such aristocrats, claimed Thomas Paine, were the cause of wars. Paine felt that once nations became democratic, there would be no more wars.

HUNGARIAN DANCERS. This Hungarian troupe is performing a traditional national dance. Differences in costumes, languages, and traditions among the various European countries help stimulate and perpetuate nationalism.

they must be loyal to their nation above everything else. They often regard other people as strangers who cannot be trusted, and they feel they must "stick together" in opposing them.

Nationalism is related to patriotism, or love of one's country. Patriotism usually has good results. It makes men willing to suffer hardship to protect themselves, their families, and their neighbors from those who try to enslave them or destroy the things they value. Nationalism, however, is an extreme form of patriotism that can be dangerous to world peace. Extreme nationalists believe that any action, no matter how wicked, is right if it helps their nation grow stronger at the expense of other nations. This attitude amost inevitably leads to war. Extreme nationalism influenced the actions of Cavour and Bismarck in uniting the Italian and German nations. As we shall see, this same fervor infected the Balkan peoples in the early part of the twentieth century. Bitterness and hatred grew intense within the Austro-Hungarian Empire. But Austria steadfastly refused to let her Slavic subjects become independent or even follow their own traditions and use their own languages.

Nationalism often implies the notion that the people of one nation are superior to all other peoples. In this case war is believed to be not only justifiable but also desirable, because by war the "superior" nation will bring all other nations under the leadership of the people best fitted to rule. It was nationalism of this kind that led the Germans to accept Hitler's dictatorial rule.

Nationalism can lead to imperialism. Imperialism, which comes from the word *empire*, means the rule of one people over another. Back at the dawn of civilization, Egyptian Pharaohs conquered Syria and other neighboring lands. Later the Romans and then the Arabs created huge empires. During the sixteenth and seventeenth centuries Spain, France, and Britain also built empires. Up to this point imperialism was considered primarily a means by which a country could increase its wealth and power. It was related to a country's prosperity, but not necessarily to its survival.

Modern imperialism, on the other hand, developed from fear. At the same time that the nations of Europe became increasingly distrustful of each other, they discovered that they were also becoming increasingly dependent upon each other. The Industrial Revolution had wrought an enormous change in European economic relations. Until the middle of the eighteenth century each country grew the food it needed for itself, while trade consisted primarily of luxury goods like silks and spices or easily transported goods like cloth. The Industrial Revolution improved transportation and lowered the cost of producing manufactured goods. Advances in shipbuilding and railroad construction and the introduction of refrigeration in the middle of the nineteenth century made possible the shipment of grain, meat, dairy products, raw materials, and industrial goods to

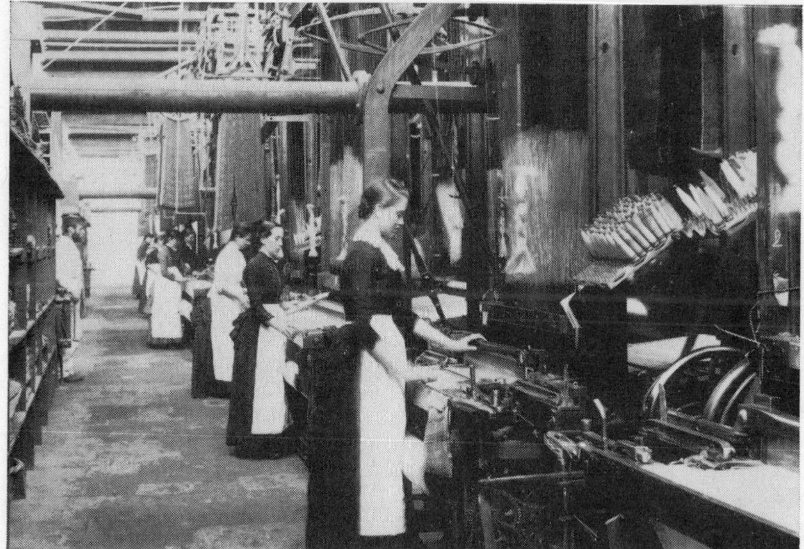

FACTORY WORKERS. These nineteenth-century linen weavers are shown at work in a factory in Belfast, Northern Ireland. The development of industry, with its great need for manpower, took many workers, both men and women, away from the fields; so that food production became a serious problem in Great Britain.

all parts of the world. European countries began to develop industries and to import food and raw materials. Some countries, particularly Great Britain, had to import much of their food by the end of the nineteenth century because the majority of their population worked in factories. Everyone in Britain depended upon food from abroad and upon the sale of British manufactures in foreign markets.

This dependence on the rest of the world for raw materials, food, and markets began to alarm Europeans, who feared that in wartime they could be starved into submission if their supply lines failed or if unfriendly nations closed their ports to trade. They therefore became imperialists and began to look everywhere in the world for lands and people whom they could bring under their control. After 1870, European nations began a feverish race for colonies. It was then that Africa and much of Asia came under the control of European nations. Possession of colonies seemed to promise the mother country security against any warlike intent on the part of her neighbors.

Imperialism led to militarism. The race for colonies increased hatred and suspicion among European powers. The result was a greatly increased emphasis on military power. Germany, for example, wanted colonies, but she was late getting into the race. Her leaders decided that she must have what they called "a place in the sun," where Germany could buy raw materials and sell the finished products of her rapidly growing industries. German leaders believed that only armed might would force Britain and France to grant her demands. She frightened France by keeping her army strong; she threatened Great Britain by building a modern navy. Britain, whose security depended on control of sea routes, felt impelled to increase her own naval strength.

Thus nationalism and imperialism created a third cause of modern wars: *militarism,* or the building of huge armies and navies. International militarism is extremely expensive, but nations were able to finance it because the Industrial Revolution had made Europe much richer. Instead of putting the increased wealth to peaceful uses, nations spent millions on armaments.

Increasing their nation's military power did not make people feel safe, however, because they knew their neighbors were doing the same thing. The nations therefore began to join together in groups, or *alliances.* Each alliance was designed to protect its members at the expense of other nations. The European nations thus became divided into two armed camps before both World War I and World War II.

The systems of alliances divided Europe. World War I did not break out until 1914, but the roots of the trouble go back at least fifty years, to the establishment of a united Germany. By 1871, as a result of three wars, Bismarck had united Germany (see Chapter 48). But he feared that France, who did not want a strong power along her borders on the Rhine, would try to undo his work and reduce Germany to a collection of petty states again. He set to work to prevent the formation of any anti-German coalition.

Bismarck was determined to protect Germany by keeping France weak and isolated from her neighbors. He began by making alliances with those nations that were most apt to be friendly with France. First he made an alliance with Germany's neighbor to the south, Austria-Hungary. Later he brought Italy into the agreement, thus creating the *Triple Alliance.* Bismarck also kept on friendly terms with Russia. Although he doubted that czarist Russia would have any interest in democratic France, where revolutions had unseated three kings since 1789, Bismarck took no chances. He knew that if France and Russia ever became allies, Germany would have enemies on both her western and eastern frontiers. By means of another secret treaty, Bismarck assured Germany of Russia's friendship.

Conditions changed, however, when young Emperor William II of Germany dismissed Bismarck

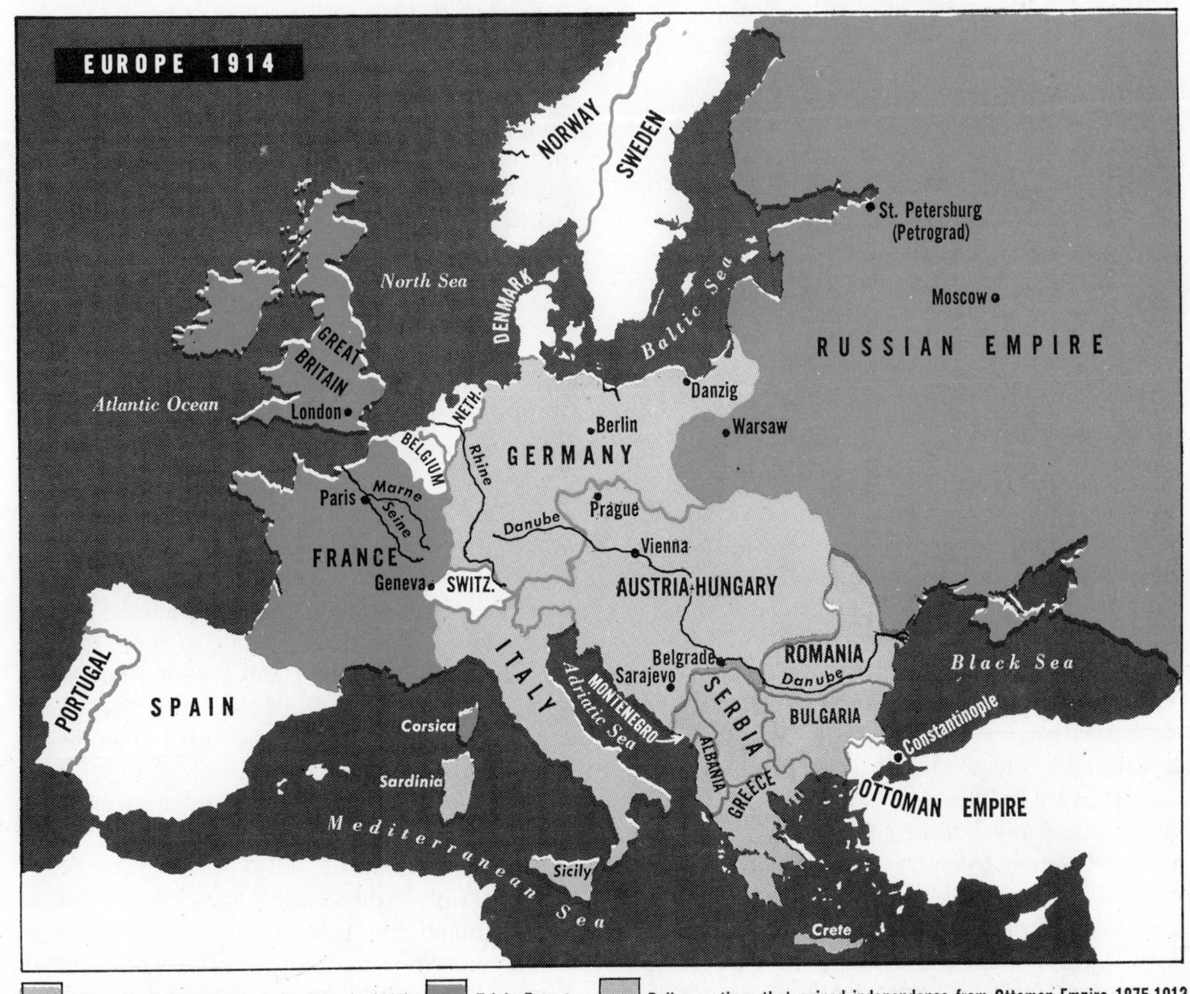

Triple Alliance (Italy joined the Allies in 1915) | Triple Entente | Balkan nations that gained independence from Ottoman Empire 1875-1913

ANTI-GERMAN CARTOON. The Entente Cordiale was a friendly understanding between England and France, out of which developed the Triple Entente of England, France, and Russia. This cartoon shows the German kaiser stubbing his toe against the rock of the Entente Cordiale.

in 1890 and took charge of affairs himself. William considered Germany's treaty with Russia an unfriendly action against Austria-Hungary. Russia and Austria-Hungary both had ambitions in the Balkans, and William saw that quarrels between them could lead to war. William realized that Germany could not live up to the terms of both treaties if Austria and Russia went to war against each other. He did not see that Bismarck had intended to force Austria-Hungary and Russia to negotiate any Balkan conflicts by threatening to use German troops against whichever nation provoked an unjustified war. William considered this kind of diplomacy immoral. He therefore kept the agreement with Austria-Hungary but did not renew Germany's treaty with Russia.

Russia tried to get Emperor William to reconsider his position. The czar still did not like the French and their ideas of "liberty, equality, and fraternity." But France worked hard to gain Russian friendship and finally succeeded. In 1894 France and Russia made an alliance.

For a long time Great Britain stayed outside the system of alliances. It had been Britain's policy never to make alliances until one nation tended to become too strong in Europe. Then she would join the weaker side and restore the "balance of power." Such alliances lasted only as long as there was an emergency. Britain looked upon herself as a nation that could not tie herself to a permanent alliance system.

The growing power of Germany changed the minds of the British, however. German factories were turning out a huge volume of high-quality goods, such as scientific instruments, machines, and chemicals. The Germans sold their products in many places where British merchants had once been the only traders. The British were worried about German competition. When the Germans, who had the strongest army in Europe, began to build a navy, Britain became alarmed.

Britain reluctantly sought new security agreements. She tried to come to terms with Germany, but the German demands were too high. Britain turned also to Japan and made an alliance with her in 1902 to protect British interests in the Far East. But this alliance did not help Britain in Europe.

The British did not really want to team up with France and Russia. France had been Britain's traditional enemy for centuries, and the British always distrusted Russia. They feared Russia's ambitions in Persia and India. But the British had become more afraid of Germany than of any other country. When the British leaders finally decided to join France and Russia, the event Bismarck most dreaded had finally occurred. France was united with Britain and Russia in the *Triple Entente* (ahn-*tahnt*).

The Triple Alliance and the Triple Entente split Europe into two hostile groups and thus made every dispute a threat to the peace of all Europe. Austria-Hungary, certain now of Germany's support, was ready to resist Russia more vigorously. France was no longer afraid to talk back to Germany because she knew she could depend on help from Russia and Britain. In the early years of the twentieth century there were several disputes and crises that almost led to the war. Each time one side or the other gave way—until the fateful quarrel between Austria-Hungary and Serbia.

Balkan troubles ended in war. There were two countries in Eastern Europe whose population did not consist mainly of one kind of people. These were Austria-Hungary and Turkey. Both were empires that included many nationalities. Nationalism among the Slavs had already reduced Turkish power in the late nineteenth century, and the new nations of Greece, Romania, Bulgaria, Albania, and Serbia had been formed. Slavic nationalism gradually began to be felt in Austria-Hungary, where the Germans of Austria and the Magyars of Hungary held tight control of the government. Throughout the nineteenth century Slavic peoples in Austria-Hungary demanded the right to have their own languages and histories taught in their own schools and to have a voice in the government. When these rights were denied, the Austrian government found it more and more difficult to keep order in the areas that were overwhelmingly Slavic.

Austria-Hungary's problem was made more difficult by the existence of the new Slavic state of Serbia on her borders. Most of southern Austria-Hungary was inhabited by Serbs who wanted to unite with their fellows in Serbia. Serbia was equally anxious to incorporate these areas. Russia encouraged Serbia, believing that any loss by Austria-Hungary would increase Russian influence in the Balkans. The Serbs and Russians spread anti-Austrian propaganda and kept the Slavs in Austria-Hungary stirred up. Gradually Austrian leaders decided that the only way to solve the problem was to conquer and annex Serbia.

The heir to the Austrian throne, Archduke Francis Ferdinand, made a tour of the southeastern provinces of Austria-Hungary. The Austrians hoped his visit would please the Slavs and make them more willing to accept Austrian rule. But the archduke's trip cost him his life, for when he appeared in Sarajevo a young Serb fanatic assassinated him and his wife.

The Austrians blamed the Serbs for the tragedy. (There is some evidence that the Serbian officials

THE ARREST OF PRINCIP. A young student fanatic, Gavrilo Princip, fired the shot that killed Archduke Francis Ferdinand of Austria and started World War I. Here he is shown as police seized him after the shooting. He was imprisoned during the war and released at its end. He died shortly afterward.

TAXI ARMY. Within a month after the outbreak of World War I, German troops had fought their way to the outskirts of Paris, where they were stopped by heroic Allied resistance in the first battle of the Marne. Some of the troops were rushed to the front in taxicabs requisitioned off the streets of Paris.

had known of a plot to kill the archduke and had done nothing to stop it.) The angry Austrian government handed Serbia a long list of humiliating demands. The Austrians knew Serbia would not accept these demands, and they hoped to conquer and annex her by a quick war. The Serbs, sure of Russian support, agreed to only part of Austria's demands. They mobilized their troops before sending an answer. As expected, Austria-Hungary declared war on Serbia.

Germany was not anxious to become involved in the quarrel between Austria-Hungary and Serbia, but she had promised to support her ally. She became concerned when she saw Austria's list of demands, and she tried to restrain Austria-Hungary from taking such a rash step. Then Russia began mobilizing her troops. Germany warned Russia to halt the mobilization and demanded assurances of neutrality from France in the event of a war between Germany and Russia. When neither demand was met, Germany declared war on both countries. She hoped to crush France before the Russian army could begin an attack on the eastern frontier.

As a member of the Triple Entente, Great Britain was committed to come to the aid of Russia and France, but she delayed action momentarily. Then Germany sent troops through Belgium to attack France. That was the only way the Germans could get into France without fighting long, bloody battles. Belgium was a neutral country, and the nations of Europe had solemnly promised never to attack her. Great Britain, shocked and angered, declared war on Germany.

Italy remained neutral for a year, although she had an alliance with Germany and Austria. Italy's long coastline made her fear the British navy. She had nothing to gain by joining Germany and Austria-Hungary, but there were lands in Austria-Hungary along Italy's northern borders that she did want. By a secret treaty, Britain and France promised to give certain colonies and a slice of Austrian territory to Italy. In 1915 Italy therefore declared war on her former partners. Japan also entered the war on the side of the Triple Entente but played no part in the war in Europe. She contented herself with occupying German colonies in the Far East.

Germany and Austria-Hungary found themselves fighting the combined forces of the major nations of the world. Although they persuaded Turkey and Bulgaria to join them, they did not get much help from these allies.

Chapter Check-up

1. How does nationalism differ from patriotism? When may nationalism become a dangerous force?

2. What is imperialism? How did the imperialism of the twentieth century differ from that of the sixteenth century?

3. Why does militarism often result from nationalism and imperialism?

4. Why did the nations of Europe form international alliances? Which nations composed the Triple Alliance? The Triple Entente?

5. Why was Serbia important to both Russia and Austria-Hungary?

6. Describe the chain of events which led to the outbreak of World War I.

7. How did the alliance system create a world war out of a local conflict?

CHAPTER 75

The Allied Nations Won World War I

AMERICA ENTERED THE WAR AND TIPPED THE BALANCE OF POWER IN FAVOR OF THE ALLIES

Germany was strong on land, but the Allies controlled the seas. When World War I began in July, 1914, people on both sides expected it to last only a few months. Few guessed that fighting would continue for more than four years. Germany was far better prepared for war than were her opponents. The Germans expected to subdue France before the Russian czar's forces could move against Germany's back door on the east. Once France was defeated, Germany's leaders thought they could easily dispose of England's small army.

The plan called for speed to catch the Allies unprepared and paralyze them before they could strike back. So German troops struck into Belgium. The little Belgian army, by heroic resistance, set back Germany's schedule. The delay gave England time to send help to France, and it allowed Russia to attack East Prussia. But the Germans fought their way into France, where they were finally halted in the first Battle of the Marne, only thirty-five miles from Paris.

The war on the Western Front then settled down to four exhausting years of trench warfare. The Allies in the west seemed able to do little more than hold the Germans at bay. But while the Allies were unable to break the German lines on the Western Front, they did much to weaken the German war machine. The British, French, Italian, and later the United States navies kept the Central Powers (as Germany and her allies were called) from importing raw materials and other goods. Germany's fleet was bottled up in the North Sea most of the time. However, German submarines, or U-boats, sank ship after ship. They almost cut off England's supply of food and ammunition.

On the Eastern Front the Germans were able to defeat the large, poorly equipped armies of the Russian czar. As you read in Chapter 57, the Communists seized control of Russia in 1917 and made a separate peace with Germany. The end of war with Russia helped the Germans greatly; now they had to fight on only one front. They transferred their eastern armies to France and renewed their efforts to defeat the Allies in the west.

The United States entered the war against Germany. At the beginning of the war the Germans did not worry much about America. They thought it unlikely that the United States would join the Allies. But that supposition turned out to be a fatal mistake. Early in 1917 the United States declared war on Germany. America's armed might and her great industries, added to those of the Allies, proved to be more than the Germans could match.

GERMAN U-BOAT. It was Germany's unrestricted submarine warfare that caused the United States to enter World War I in April of 1917.

Why did the United States enter the war? There were many reasons. The immediate cause was the savage, unrestricted submarine warfare that Germany waged against our ships. Over a hundred American lives were lost in the U-boat attacks. When our government protested, Germany promised to respect our rights as neutrals. But the promise was not kept. The Germans wanted to stop us from shipping food, war materials, and other supplies to Britain. We claimed we had the right as neutrals to send our ships where we pleased. We had always believed in neutrality and freedom of the seas.

The well-planned propaganda of the Allies also had an influence. Many Americans became convinced that Germany was responsible for the war.

War Bond Poster. Posters such as this one were used in the government's campaign to raise money and arouse patriotic spirit for the war effort. Americans responded with characteristic enthusiasm.

They regarded Germany as an aggressor which should be halted and punished. Furthermore, England and France were democracies. Americans naturally tended to sympathize with them against the undemocratic, militaristic government of the German emperor.

President Wilson expressed our ideals in his address to Congress asking for a declaration of war on Germany. He said that we must fight because:

> "The world must be made safe for democracy. Its peace must be planted upon the tested foundations of political liberty. We have no selfish ends to serve. We desire no conquest, no dominions. We seek no indemnities for ourselves, no compensation for the sacrifices we shall freely make. We are but one of the champions of the rights of mankind. We shall be satisfied when those rights have been made as secure as the faith and freedom of nations can make them."

When Congress declared war on Germany in 1917, the people of the United States wholeheartedly supported the declaration. Our factories worked overtime to produce ammunition, clothing, shoes, and other supplies for the French and British armies as well as for our own. Our farmers raised wheat, corn, and livestock to feed our Allies, whose normal food supplies had been greatly reduced.

When we entered the war, we had only a small army. Although military experts said it would take two years to raise and train an army of a million men, the United States had two million men in training within a year. By the fall of 1918 there were about two million "Yanks" in France, many of them on the firing lines.

The Allies tried but failed to drive the Germans back from a long line of trenches that extended from the borders of Switzerland, northward through France and Belgium, to the North Sea. Bitter, costly attacks, in which troops went over the top at zero hour after the artillery barrages were lifted, often accomplished little more than to straighten out a portion of the line here and there.

AN ALLIED ADVANCE. Much of World War I consisted of battles between armies dug into opposing lines of trenches. The area between the trenches was a shell-pocked "no man's land." Here, Allied soldiers are advancing over "no man's land" toward the enemy trenches. The soldiers are wearing gas masks, as poison gas was used in World War I.

Early in 1918 the Germans opened a powerful drive that nearly won the war for them. It was evident that a united command was necessary to defeat Germany. Accordingly, Marshal Ferdinand Foch (fawsh) of the French army was selected in the spring of 1918 to weld the armies of the Allies, including the American forces, into a single war machine. Marshal Foch was noted for his bulldog stubbornness and his courage. On one occasion he said, "My right has been rolled up, my left has been driven back, my center has been smashed. I have ordered an advance from all directions." As a result of this kind of courage, Foch is known as one of the greatest heroes of French military history.

American armies helped turn the tide in 1918. In the late spring of 1918 the American forces began to play a part in the Allied offensive. Then, in September, 1918, General John J. Pershing's American troops were ready for action on a large scale. They took over the southern part of the front, while French, British, and Canadian forces farther north prepared for the final drives.

The repeated blows of the unified Allied armies under Marshal Foch were too much for the Germans. In the fall of 1918 the military machine of the Central Powers showed signs of breaking. High German military leaders warned the German government that there was no hope of victory. Then Austria asked for an armistice.

Everywhere German armies were meeting disaster. The soldiers were discontented; revolution broke out among the people. The German emperor, William II, fled to Holland. A new republican government was chosen which immediately asked for peace. The armistice was signed on November 11, 1918. It is important to remember, however, that Germany did not surrender unconditionally. Her armies still occupied Belgium and parts of France. The Germans expected generous peace terms from President Wilson. When they were disappointed, they felt that they had been betrayed. That feeling is one reason that they later followed Hitler, who promised them revenge.

THE VICTORIOUS ALLIES FAILED TO ACHIEVE A LASTING PEACE

The Treaty of Versailles disregarded most of Wilson's Fourteen Points. As you know from what you have read earlier in *Story of Nations,* a war often breeds the hate and fear that gives rise to later wars. President Wilson was determined that it should not happen after the "war to end war." In a message to Congress in January, 1918, he set forth his famous *Fourteen Points.* They were the basis upon which he believed a just and lasting peace could be built. It was upon the Fourteen Points that Germany had relied when she asked for an armistice.

The Fourteen Points dealt with three main topics: (1) world-wide problems, (2) special national problems, and (3) the need for an international peace organization.

Because the secret alliances had clearly contributed to the war, Wilson demanded an end to secret treaties (Point One).

Because submarine attacks on our ships had involved the United States in the war, Wilson asked for freedom of the seas (Point Two), or the right of neutral nations to send their ships across the ocean without interference.

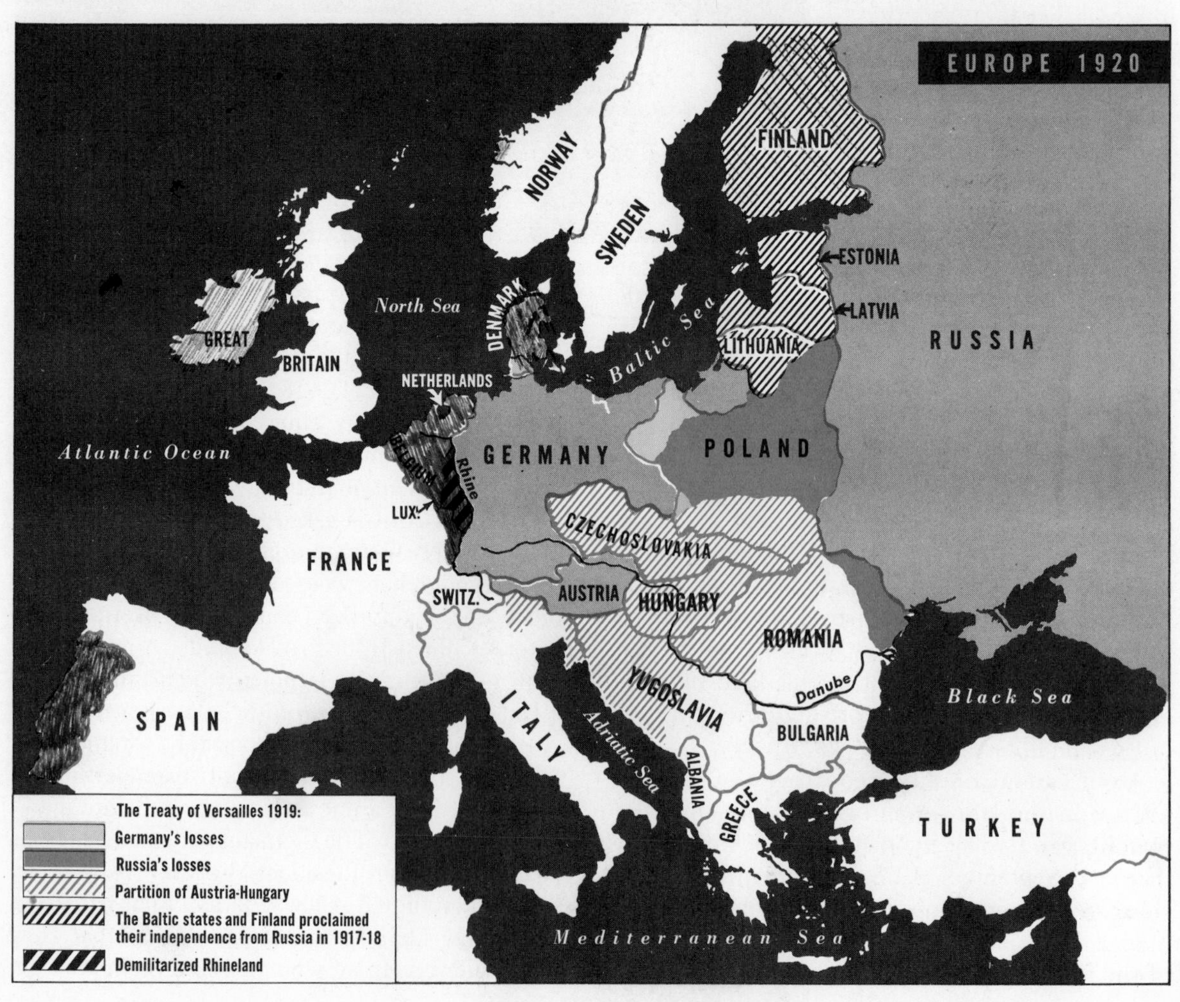

THE BIG FOUR. Meeting at the Paris Peace Conference were, from left to right, Orlando of Italy, Lloyd George of England, Clemenceau of France, and Wilson of the United States. Out of this meeting came the Treaty of Versailles.

Since high tariffs hindered the free exchange of goods and often created bad feeling between nations, Point Three called for removal of tariffs.

Wilson realized the dangers of militarism, so he demanded a reduction in the size of armies and navies (Point Four).

Wilson also recognized imperialism as a cause of war, and he therefore called for an end to colonial rivalry (Point Five). He said the interests of the people in the colonies should be considered first in making any changes in the status of the various colonies.

Points Six through Thirteen dealt with different trouble spots in Europe. The new revolutionary government in Russia should be allowed to go its own way without interference (Point Six). Belgium deserved help (Point Seven). France should regain Alsace-Lorraine (Point Eight). Italy should receive Austrian territory inhabited by Italians (Point Nine). The various discontented nationalities in the Austro-Hungarian Empire and in Turkey were entitled to freedom, or the right of *self-determination* (Points Ten and Twelve). Serbia and Romania should receive certain Slavic provinces of Austria-Hungary (Point Eleven). There should be an independent Poland with an outlet to the sea (Point Thirteen).

Wilson regarded his fourteenth point as unquestionably the most important. It called for the creation of a world organization, or "league of nations," in which differences between countries could be settled peacefully. He believed that such an organization could abolish forever the threat of war.

A few weeks after the armistice was signed, delegates of the Allied powers met at Versailles, a few miles outside of Paris, to make a treaty of peace. Germany was not allowed to send any representatives. The world waited breathlessly to see the terms of the treaty. Many people believed that the wartime unity and idealism displayed by the Allies would surely result in such a fair and just peace treaty that future wars would be prevented. But the results were deeply disappointing.

The Treaty of Versailles and the various other agreements made at the same time were supposed to be based on the Fourteen Points. At the peace conference Wilson fought hard, but he failed to get many of his principles included in the peace treaty. Extreme nationalism and the old, persistent rivalries and jealousies among the nations defeated him. Let us take a closer look at the provisions that were set forth in the Treaty of Versailles.

Secret diplomacy was not abolished. The nations promised to make all their treaties public, but many failed to keep the promise. Freedom of the seas was soon almost forgotten, even in America. Tariffs and trade barriers increased rapidly in the post-war period. As we shall see, there were sincere attempts to reduce armies and navies, but they did not accomplish much. The nations continued to be imperialistic. France, Great Britain, and Japan seized all of Germany's colonies. The new League of Nations was supposed to supervise the former German colonies under a plan called the "mandate system," but that also met with little success.

Wilson's plans for dealing with specific trouble spots were somewhat more successful. Belgium regained her independence. Alsace-Lorraine again became French territory. Italy gained much Austrian territory, including some areas inhabited by Austrians and Slavs. The cession of those areas created bad feeling between Italians and Slavs that continues to this day. Czechoslovakia, Austria, and Hungary were carved out of the old country of Austria-Hungary. Romania and Serbia gained much land. Serbia became the center around which the new state of Yugoslavia was created. The Turkish Empire also lost territory; some new Arab states were formed in the old Fertile Crescent under the administration of Britain and France.

Another new state was Poland. It was made up of various provinces taken from Germany, Austria-Hungary, and Russia. To give Poland a seaport, the Treaty of Versailles cut a "corridor" through Germany to the free city of Danzig (see Chapter 55). As we shall see, the Polish Corridor caused bitter resentment among the Germans.

The treaty, which also required Germany to pay reparations, declared that Germany alone was responsible for causing the war. The Germans knew they were not the only guilty ones, but the other nations felt they had to pin war guilt on Germany to force her to pay damages.

Wilson objected to certain terms of the treaty, which he believed was too severe. The Germans sent a written protest, and the German Cabinet resigned rather than submit to such an unfair settlement. But Germany was still blockaded by the

Woodrow Wilson. Both during his term as governor of New Jersey and during his first term as President of the United States, Wilson achieved a reputation as a reformer. However, when he tried to extend his reforms to the international scene after World War I, he received disillusioning setbacks. Here, he is shown riding with President Poincaré of France.

CHRISTMAS IN BERLIN, 1923. A major depression hit Germany as a result of World War I and the Treaty of Versailles. Municipal kitchens were set up to help feed the jobless. The warm meal being eaten by the people in this picture probably provided them with their only source of heat as well as nourishment.

British navy. German children were hungry because food could not get into the country. So Germany was forced to sign the Treaty of Versailles. Many Germans felt more angry and bitter about the treaty than they did about their defeat.

But Wilson did get a world peace organization, the League of Nations. That, he thought, made up for everything. He believed that the League would sooner or later be able to correct the injustices and mistakes of the peace treaties. As we shall see, the League proved a tragic failure.

Why were Wilson's ideas not adopted at the Paris Conference? Wilson had high ideals of "a peace without victory" but he met disappointment at every turn. Part of the trouble was Wilson himself. He was probably the most scholarly and best educated president America ever had, but he did not always handle people skillfully. Members of the Congress complained that they were not properly informed or consulted regarding his plans for a peace treaty.

Before becoming President, Wilson had taught in several colleges and then became president of Princeton University in New Jersey. Wilson believed deeply in democracy and fought for it. At Princeton, for example, he tried to get rid of many customs and organizations that he thought were snobbish and undemocratic. The people of New Jersey thought of him as a fighter for democracy. Wilson became governor of the state and then President of the United States.

When the war was over, Wilson announced that he would go to Paris himself to help make peace. Many people felt he should have stayed at home and sent someone to represent him, as other presidents had done. But Wilson believed in doing things himself. Leaders of the Republican party felt that Wilson (who was a Democrat) had completely ignored their interests in America's post-war plans.

At Paris he had to deal with European leaders who had seen their nations destroyed by four years of war. Paris was filled with anger and bitterness toward the Germans; hatred could not be forgotten overnight. Allied leaders had promised their people that they would make Germany pay for all the destruction of the war. As victors, they saw no reason why the losers should not pay in goods and money. All the Allies, but particularly the French, were convinced that Wilson did not understand their problems or realize the high cost they had borne. America, it was pointed out, made enormous profits by supplying arms to the Allies. How were the Allies to pay back American loans if Germany did not pay reparations?

Who were the other leaders of the Paris Peace Conference with whom Wilson argued and fought? The British Empire was represented by Prime Minister David Lloyd George, a fiery Welshman, who probably had the greatest sympathy with Wilson's ideas. Premier Georges Clemenceau (klem-en-*so*), the "Tiger of France," had been a bitter enemy of Germany all his life and was determined to bring Germany to its knees. Clemenceau remembered how Germans had entered Paris in triumph in 1871, and he looked now with renewed bitterness on France's devastated lands. He was convinced that only by crushing Germany could France be spared future disasters. Premier Vittorio Orlando, representing Italy, demanded that the British and French abide by all the terms of the secret treaty that led Italy to declare war. The three European leaders forced Wilson to give way on many of his Fourteen Points. Wilson gave in because they promised to back his proposal for the League of Nations. He felt sure the League would repair the weak spots and correct the injustices of the Treaty of Versailles.

The Great Powers created a League of Nations. The basic plan, or constitution, of the League of Nations was called the *Covenant*. The Covenant provided for a League composed of two branches, the Assembly and the Council. There was also a Secretariat, or permanent body of officers, to keep records, publish information, and run the various international bureaus. The League's headquarters was in Geneva, Switzerland.

Another body provided for in the Covenant of the League, although independent of it, was the World Court. Its duty was to settle international legal problems, which were to be voluntarily sub-

League of Nations Palace. This picture shows the League's Council Chamber. In the central pit and on the sides near the camera are the Secretariat and Diplomatic sections. The seats in the rear were for the press and those up in the gallery for the public. The door at the left of the picture leads to a private council chamber used for meetings in which the press and the public were not allowed.

mitted by nations in disagreement. There was no way of forcing nations to submit their disputes to the World Court. Nevertheless, the decisions of the court helped strengthen international law.

Ironically, although President Wilson had taken a leading part in setting up the League of Nations, the United States never became a member. For many reasons, the American people were against the League. Perhaps the chief reason was their fear of being drawn into European troubles. Many people believed that America had gained nothing—indeed, that it had lost a great deal—by entering World War I. They felt that by joining the League of Nations the United States would constantly be involved in disputes that did not concern us. Many citizens favored the old policy of remaining isolated from the affairs of European nations.

Unfortunately, the League also became a political issue. One group of United States senators resented the way Wilson had handled affairs at the Peace Conference. They were determined to defeat anything the President favored. When Wilson urged that the United States enter the League of Nations, the Senate therefore refused to follow his recommendation.

The fight to bring America into the World Court lasted for years. Every American President from Wilson to Franklin D. Roosevelt urged the United States to join the World Court, with certain reservations to protect her interests. But their efforts were no more successful than Wilson's attempt to make the United States a member of the League of Nations.

The League of Nations lacked power and firm support. The League was founded for the promotion of international good will and co-operation. During its early days it seemed to grow in power and influence. It provided a chance for the representatives of many nations to talk over their difficulties and arrive at acceptable agreements. It helped several countries, especially Austria and Hungary, to recover from World War I. It was even successful in settling disputes between small nations. But the League failed, as we shall see in the next chapter, to settle disputes between the larger ones.

There were many reasons for the failure of the League of Nations. Nationalism was the major cause. The powerful members of the League would not co-operate. They refused to give any real power to the League. France, which had practically no faith in the League, built up an alliance system with other European nations to protect herself against Germany. Britain felt that the League was suitable only as a place for discussion. Nobody was willing to give to the League any rights that would prevent a nation from doing exactly as it pleased. The refusal of one of the world's greatest powers, the United States, to join the League weakened its effectiveness still more.

The League of Nations was not a complete failure, however. It awakened its members to the danger of the international traffic in drugs and encouraged them to co-operate in order to control it. It discussed many other humanitarian problems, such as child labor. By dealing successfully with many minor problems it proved that an international organization can help men of good will solve their problems.

Chapter Check-up

1. When did World War I begin and end?
2. How did Germany plan to win World War I? What upset her plans?
3. Why did the United States enter the war against Germany? How did our entry affect the outcome? Could Germany have been defeated if we had not entered?
4. Briefly summarize Wilson's Fourteen Points. Which was the most important? Why? Were any of them unrealistic?
5. Who were the leaders of the Paris Peace Conference? What were the principal points of view represented by each of these leaders?
6. In what respects did the Treaty of Versailles fail to include the principles expressed in the Fourteen Points? Why did the Germans agree to the treaty? Why did Wilson agree?
7. Describe the organization of the League of Nations. Why did the United States refuse to join?
8. In what areas was the League of Nations a success? In what areas could it be considered a failure?

CHAPTER 76

Between Wars, Nations Tried to Find Security

THE GREAT NATIONS CO-OPERATED IN EFFORTS TO EASE INTERNATIONAL TENSIONS

In the 1920's people wanted to forget the war. During the 1920's Great Britain and the United States did their best to forget the war. Ideas of peace, prosperity, and security occupied the minds of their people. The United States turned to a policy of *isolation,* or keeping out of Europe's political affairs. We never signed the treaty of peace and never joined the League of Nations. We insisted on bringing our soldiers home from Europe immediately. "Get the boys out of the trenches and home by Christmas," people demanded as soon as the armistice was signed. The soldiers came home, and soon the great American military force was a thing of the past.

Even in England, so close to the main stream of affairs in Europe, and in Canada, Australia, and other parts of the British Empire, the same spirit was apparent. "Let's have it over, let's get on together" was the common feeling. Armed forces were demobilized. People became preoccupied with their own affairs. They wanted to make up for things they had missed during the war.

GERMAN DESTRUCTION. The town of Louvain in Belgium is shown after German bombardment in 1914. Scenes like this made people want to forget the war as soon as possible.

Neither France nor Germany forgot the war so easily, however. France insisted that Germany pay its reparations promptly. When Germany failed to make payments in 1922, France sent troops into the Ruhr Valley. The German government urged "passive resistance," and all workers in the factories were to stay away from their jobs. The government supported the idle factory workers by printing paper money for them to use. Inflation swept disastrously over Germany as prices soared because of the addition of this great amount of paper money. The inflation wiped out the savings and destroyed the hopes of the middle class. The Germans felt desperate. Americans paid little attention. It was none of our business, or so we thought. The United States was busy and prosperous. In the 1920's almost everybody had a good job. People bought new cars and speculated on the stock market. The boom of the Twenties was on!

There was peace and co-operation in the 1920's. In the decade after World War I a few statesmen tried hard to win agreements to keep the peace.

The Washington Conference is a good example of the spirit of international co-operation of the 1920's. Soon after World War I ended, a race started between Britain, the United States, and Japan to see which could build the most warships. President Harding and his Secretary of State, Charles Evans Hughes, decided that such a race was a foolish waste of money. They called a conference at Washington. There, in 1922, repre-

Ticker Tape Parade. The parade for Charles Lindbergh after his solo flight across the Atlantic in 1927 was typical of the carefree spirit with which people in the Twenties threw themselves into celebrations. The nation was prosperous and World War I a thing of the past.

sentatives of most of the leading nations signed agreements that stopped the naval race for several years. They agreed to build no warships except those needed to replace old ones that had to be scrapped. The statesmen also signed another treaty, promising to respect the rights of China. Years later, in the 1930's, Japan tried to take over China and the Far East, and the Washington treaties came to a futile end. But in the 1920's they seemed to promise peace.

The Locarno (lo-*kahr*-no) Agreement was an even greater step forward. In 1925 Aristide Briand (bree-*ahnd*), the French foreign minister, thought the time had come to try to have better relations with Germany. Gustav Stresemann (*shtray*-zeh-mahn), who was in charge of foreign affairs in Germany, agreed with Briand. The two men became good friends. They arranged a conference of several nations at Locarno, in Switzerland. There France, Germany, and Belgium agreed never to invade one another's territories or go to war to settle a dispute. Great Britain and Italy also took part in the Locarno Conference. They promised to back up the agreement with all their power.

The "spirit of Locarno" was something new in Europe's long, bloody history. It seemed to mean the end of the troubles between France and Germany. Germany was admitted to the League of Nations and became a member of the Security Council. Briand and Stresemann used to sit beside each other in meetings, whispering together like two school chums. Their friendship was a striking symbol of the new spirit of friendship existing in Europe.

Briand was also anxious to have the United States co-operate in efforts for peace. He felt that France was weak and needed many friends to protect her. In 1928 he persuaded the American Secretary of State, Frank Kellogg, to join with him in sponsoring an agreement to outlaw war. It was called the Kellogg-Briand Pact. Most of the nations signed it. They promised they would never go to war to settle a dispute. Unfortunately, there was no way to make them keep their promise.

WORLD-WIDE ECONOMIC DEPRESSION BROUGHT A NEW CRISIS

The great depression began in 1929 and plunged the world into uncertainty and confusion. In the Thirties the nations again began to play the dangerous game of power politics. The flames of nationalism and imperialism burned fiercely again. The armaments race started anew, and the world plunged into the depths of a world-wide business depression. The Thirties were a time of fear and insecurity. For those few who could read the signs, they pointed directly to another great war.

The period of despair began in the fall of 1929, when a stock market crash occurred in Wall Street, New York, the financial center of the United States. The panic soon became world-wide. It led to the great depression and the breakdown of the machinery of business, trade, and finance throughout the world. The depression had many causes. In the period of optimism in the 1920's there had been much overexpansion and inflation. Too many factories were built, and too many goods were produced to sell for prices that were too high. A world exhausted by war could not pay for or use up all the goods. Manufacturers had overestimated the amount of goods people could buy at the high boom-time prices.

There was also the problem of sound money. Because most of the business of the world is done on credit, the money used in the various nations has to have a known and stable value. No one wants to sell goods to the people of a foreign country if he cannot be sure of the value of their money. The Treaty of Versailles required such heavy payments for damages done by Germany and Austria that the financial systems of the two countries were badly affected. In some instances they suffered a complete breakdown. The defeated nations were often quite willing to help the process along by their own acts. They hated the Treaty of Versailles and were glad enough to drag down the victorious nations with them.

In Germany, paper money became almost worthless. In order to stave off trouble, the Allied nations and the United States several times ar-

The Crash of 1929. The optimistic boom of the Twenties ended in panic when the stock market crashed in October of 1929. Many banks failed as a result of this crash, and many people lost all of their savings. Today, savings deposits are insured by the Federal Deposit Insurance Corporation.

The Depression. A bread line is shown in New York City's Times Square. These unemployed men are receiving sandwiches and coffee from a truck stationed near Forty-third Street. Such bread lines were the only source of food for many people during the depression years, and they are remembered today as one of the main symbols of that period.

ranged new terms for settling debts with the Germans. But their efforts were of no use; the business life of Western Europe continued to grow worse. The Germans blamed everything on the harsh terms of the Treaty of Versailles.

Government powers increased during the depression. The world-wide depression had many other causes that we cannot relate here. It is important to note how some of the nations faced the problem of economic breakdown. During the war the governments of all the fighting nations had taken over control of production in agriculture and manufacturing. In many cases governments placed controls on the everyday lives of their people. There was strict regulation of war contracts, communication, business, and labor relations. Everybody was surprised at the way industrial power increased under government control. Thus, when the great depression came, the natural result was for the people to turn to the government for help. The slogan became, "Let's fight the depression just as we fought the war."

This was true in the United States in 1933 when Franklin Roosevelt and the Democratic Party started the New Deal. It was true in England where Socialist ideas steadily gained popularity, and it was also the trend in other parts of the British Empire. People in many nations granted dictatorial powers to their rulers in an effort to solve the problems of the depression.

Insecurity and pessimism marked the 1930's. With the coming of the depression, confidence and prosperity disappeared. People in all nations suffered. Some lost more than others, but everybody felt the pinch. Farmers suffered; manufacturers had to shut down their factories; men lost their jobs; merchants failed; and statesmen became confused and discouraged.

If your father had made a trip around the world in the early 1930's he would have seen idle dock hands and rusting ships in once-busy harbors, closed mills, bread lines, and a generation of young people that had never had jobs. He could have told of the feverish drilling of armies and the hurried building up of navies and air forces. He would have noticed the deep distrust of neighboring countries. He would have seen propaganda exciting people to frenzies of patriotic fervor. He could have told of governments taken over by dictators who disregarded the rights of citizens, of bandits who became respected war lords, and of politicians who got ahead by deceit and dishonesty. He would have described the terrible overcrowding in many countries that was causing rulers to look greedily at neighboring lands and territories.

TOTALITARIAN GOVERNMENT AND INTENSE ECONOMIC RIVALRY CHARACTERIZED THE 1930'S

The growth of many "isms" endangered peace and security. World War I was hard on the world's royal families. Russia, Germany, Austria, and other smaller countries got rid of their rulers. The deposed kings, czars, emperors, kaisers—no matter what they were called—all had symbolized authority and leadership to their subjects. The people in many countries felt lost without the firm leadership of their traditional rulers.

Some of the nations of Europe that had no democratic traditions were willing to abandon democracy and let a strong man or strong party take over the government. Communism, fascism, national socialism, and other "isms" became popular. Totalitarian governments were established in Europe and other parts of the world.

During the depression many people were discouraged and frightened. They lost faith in their ability to solve their problems by democratic methods. Arguments of the various political parties confused them. Not accustomed to making decisions, they wanted someone to decide for them and to tell them what to do. They found it

HITLER VISITS MUSSOLINI. Both of these men came to power as a result of economic depressions. Mussolini fell under Hitler's influence, and the two totalitarian leaders joined forces, even though their countries had been bitter enemies in World War I.

Rearmament. This cartoon in the New York *Herald Tribune* pointed up the danger of the armaments race. While the nations conspire about weapons, the ghost of World War I stands in the background over the crosses of war dead.

convenient to choose strong, self-confident leaders who would tell them how to get out of their difficulties.

This is what happened in Italy in 1922. The people were suffering because of an economic depression after World War I, and the parliamentary leaders seemed to have no idea how to improve conditions. The Italians let Benito Mussolini and his Black Shirts (see Chapter 45) set up a Fascist dictatorship.

Much the same thing happened in Germany in 1933. The Germans had lost their savings in the terrible post-war inflation of the early 1920's. Then, just as they were beginning to prosper again, the depression closed down their industries and left millions unemployed. Germans blamed their new democracy, the Weimar Republic, and began looking for a leader. Because Adolf Hitler and the Nazis seemed to promise them security and glory, the Germans let Hitler take over the government. Hitler destroyed the democratic government and replaced it with a dictatorship.

Russia's totalitarian government was older than the governments of Italy and Germany. It had appeared at the end of World War I, when Lenin led the Communists in a successful revolution. After Lenin's death Joseph Stalin made himself supreme ruler of Russia. Japan also had a totalitarian government. Although there was no single leader as in Germany and Russia, a group of army and navy leaders and rich manufacturers held tight control over the country.

Economic rivalry increased tensions in the 1930's. The rulers in the totalitarian countries told the people that their nations had been treated unfairly. They argued that it was not fair for Germany, Italy, and Japan to have so few natural resources while Great Britain, France, and the United States had rich sources of iron and coal and many colonies. Germany, of course, had some of the richest coal mines in the world, but Hitler insisted that Germany was a "have-not" nation because she had no colonies. As a "have-not" nation, he argued, Germany had a right to increase her holdings and recover the Asian and African colonies she had lost after World War I. Suspicions grew among the nations, particularly because the dictators glorified war and taught their people that only by war could they take from the "have" nations what they required.

Another cause of trouble arose from the efforts of different nations to interfere with world trade. As the depression went on year after year, trade between nations fell off sharply. The less trade there was, the harder each nation tried to get what was left. They used all sorts of schemes to gain commercial advantages. The decrease in trade made the depression worse and increased the bad feeling between the "haves" and the "have-nots."

In the 1930's each nation was trying to look out for itself and keep other nations from getting any of its wealth and trade. We call such selfishness among nations *economic nationalism.* It is much the same thing as the old-fashioned doctrine of mercantilism (see Chapter 35). More than a hundred years ago Great Britain and other countries discovered that mercantilism does not pay. But it is one of the tragedies of history that nations so often repeat the mistakes of the past. Under the stress of the depression, many nations revived the old idea of regulating foreign trade for the benefit of themselves.

Fear led to increased armaments and alliances. As the nations tried to make themselves more secure economically, they also began to strengthen their armies and navies. Tensions and fears between the "have" and the "have-not" nations became greater. In Chapter 75 we saw how these same forces helped bring on World War I. That is why some historians claim that World War I and World War II were really just one war, with a long armistice in between.

The history of Europe in the 1930's is a record of repeated war scares and crises. In 1936 Italy attacked and conquered Ethiopia, in defiance of the League of Nations. Ethiopia was a backward, peaceful country in the mountains of northeast Africa. Mussolini thought a foreign war would make the Italians forget how bad things were at home. So he picked a fight with Ethiopia. Soon Ethiopia was an Italian colony.

In 1937 Japan began a new invasion of China. A year later, Hitler's Nazis marched into Austria. The last remnant of the great Hapsburg empire became just a province of Germany. Thus the rising tide of dictatorships during the 1930's drowned the rights and interests of other nations. Why were the aggressor nations not checked before they plunged the world into global war? Let us see how the dictators set about obtaining their demands.

THE POLICY OF APPEASEMENT FAILED TO PREVENT WORLD WAR II

The techniques of aggressor nations led to World War II. The dictators increased nationalism in their countries by campaigns of propaganda in the press, over the air, and in the schools —all of which were under their control. The dictators also armed their nations heavily, sacrificing bread and butter for swords and submarines. They staged grand military and naval reviews and gave their people a new sense of power. At the same time, they ridiculed the democracies for being reluctant to sacrifice democratic ideals for military power. The "have-not" nations built up their military power until they thought they could take what they wanted.

The aggressors found a method for achieving their goals. The first step was to disregard any treaty or international agreement that stood in their way. Hitler defied the Versailles Treaty. When Italy decided upon her conquest of Ethiopia, she withdrew from the League and defied the member nations to stop her. Japan, as you know, ignored her treaties concerning China and also took steps to build up fortifications on the Pacific islands.

Once the aggressor nations renounced an international agreement or twisted its meaning, they were ready for the next step. This was to bluff concessions from the "have" nations. The plan was to make loud demands for a new piece of territory, for favored treatment, or some other concession—accompanied by threats of war. The scheme worked for a time, because Great Britain and France believed that it was better to give in than to have war.

The United States remained aloof. Our attitude was that Europe and the Far East were of little concern to us. We were still following a policy of isolationism by simply minding our own business in the United States. The attempt to recover from the great depression seemed to give us enough to do at home. England and France adopted a policy of *appeasement*, or giving in on certain points. Thus none of the great democracies did anything to check the aggressors.

MUNICH PEACE PACT. At the famous Munich Conference, Hitler in effect was given part of Czechoslovakia as a token of appeasement. Here British Prime Minister Neville Chamberlain shakes hands with Mussolini. German Field Marshal Herman Goering stands grinning at the left of the picture, and Hitler (partly concealed) is behind him.

Unfortunately, the dictators were in a position to make very strong threats. In the late 1930's Hitler had the world's most powerful air force. British and French statesmen dared not refuse his demands because they realized London and Paris could easily be bombed. The dictator nations were therefore able to enlarge their territories at the expense of other nations.

The policy of appeasement let Hitler grab Czechoslovakia. Hitler wanted the land of his neighbor, Czechoslovakia, because it stood between him and his plan for eastward expansion. Hitler began by demanding that Czechoslovakia turn over to Germany a part of the country known as the Sudetenland (soo-*day*-t'n-land), in which many Germans lived. Czechoslovakia refused the demand but agreed to guarantee the safety and rights of the Germans who lived there. Hitler was not satisfied. German agents in Czechoslovakia trumped up stories of atrocities, and Hitler's propaganda machine went to work. Such agents came to be known as "fifth columnists." Their use be-

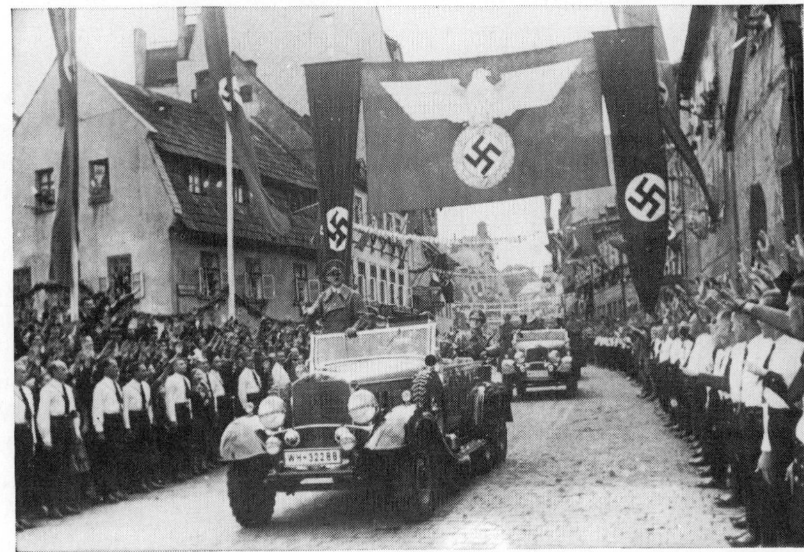

HITLER OCCUPIES SUDETENLAND. After the Munich Conference, Hitler drove in triumph through his newly acquired territory. Prime Minister Chamberlain meanwhile promised that the Conference would bring "peace in our time." This statement became one of the great ironies of the twentieth century.

came a standard practice by dictator nations. British and French statesmen feared that war between Nazi Germany and Czechoslovakia would begin, so they persuaded Czechoslovakia to give Hitler some of its land.

Hitler was still not satisfied. He said he would send his armies into the little country by October 1, 1938. His threat worked. Three days before his deadline, Hitler, Mussolini, and the leaders of the British and French governments met at a conference in Munich. Czechoslovakia was carved up to suit the Nazi leader. But the policy of appeasement did not end Hitler's demands. A few months later, in the spring of 1939, Hitler took over what was left of Czechoslovakia. Then he began to make demands upon Poland.

Meanwhile, the nations that wanted peace built up their armaments in the hope that adequate defense would increase their ability to bargain with the dictatorships. The showdown came when Hitler tried to seize territory in Poland, as we shall see in the next chapter.

Chapter Check-up

1. In what ways did the United States follow a policy of isolationism after World War I?
2. What pacts, agreements, and conferences symbolized the desire for international peace and co-operation in the 1920's?
3. Describe the economic crisis that began in 1929. What caused it?
4. How did the depression help dictators to gain power in the 1930's.
5. What is economic nationalism?
6. What technique was used by the dictators to force concessions from the democracies?
7. How did Hitler gain control of Czechoslovakia?

Chapter 77

In World War II the Dictators Brought Horror and Suffering to Millions

WORLD WAR II BECAME A WAR FOR SURVIVAL

World War II was a global war. In chapters 74 and 75 you read of the complex developments that made twentieth century Europe the setting for two great wars. As you will see, the two great conflicts are similar in many respects. In fact some historians think of them as a single conflict interrupted by a twenty-year truce.

Of the two tragic wars, the second is more properly labeled a "world" war. In that war the fighting was not confined to Western Europe and the Atlantic. In World War I, as you have learned, the Central Powers of Europe were pitted against the Allies and the United States. In World War II, it was Italy, Germany, and Japan (called the Rome-Berlin-Tokyo Axis) against the Allies: Great Britain, France, China, the United States, and many small nations. (During World War II the Allies became known as the *United Nations.*) World War II was waged in Europe, Africa, and Asia, and on the Atlantic and the Pacific. There were few places on the earth that did not suffer the effects of World War II. It was truly a global war.

World War II was an all-out war. World War I seems almost a gentleman's war when we compare it with World War II. In previous conflicts nations followed generally accepted rules of warfare. It was the men in the armed forces who did the fighting—the soldiers, sailors, and marines—and not the civilians. Sometimes the rules of war were violated, as they were by the use of poison gas in World War I. But if civilians were likely to be involved in the sinking of ships or the attack on a city, they were usually warned by the enemy to stay off the seas or to flee from their homes. Most nations had agreed to the Geneva Convention of the International Red Cross, by which nations agreed to practice humane treatment of war prisoners and the sick and wounded. These standards of conduct were generally respected in World War I.

World War II was different. From the beginning, Germany and her Axis partners waged all-out war against armed forces and the civilian population alike. The unarmed civilian was as likely to suffer attack as the soldier in uniform. The civilian population suffered as many casualties from bombs, epidemics, starvation, and planned massacre as the armed forces did from battle.

When the troops of the German army caught up with a fleeing population, the Nazis captured thousands of men and women and sent them to concentration camps. Often they sent their civilian captives to Germany as slave laborers to keep their farms and factories producing. By the end of the war, some ten million persons had been moved from their homes. The *displaced persons*, or DP's as they came to be called, were

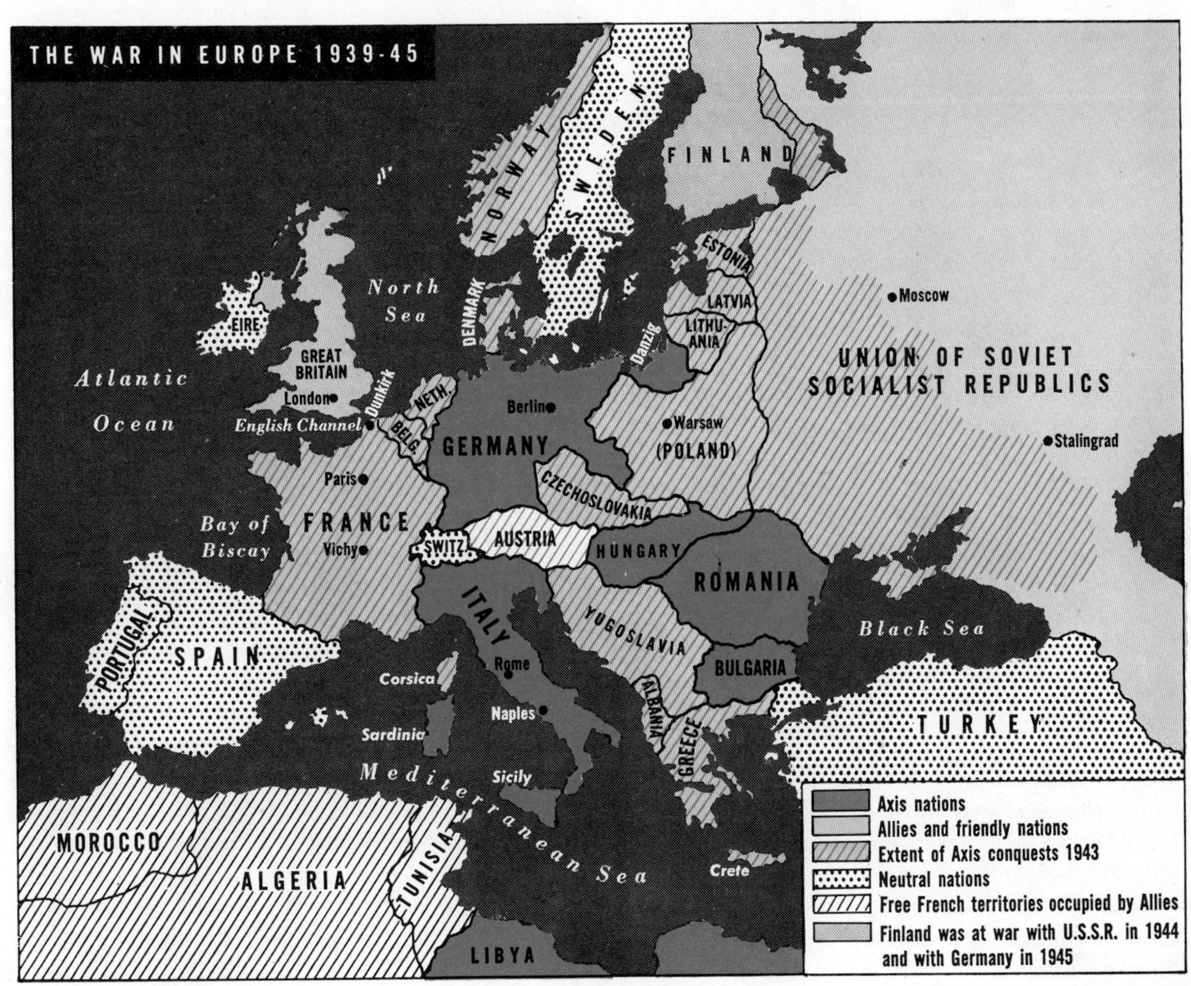

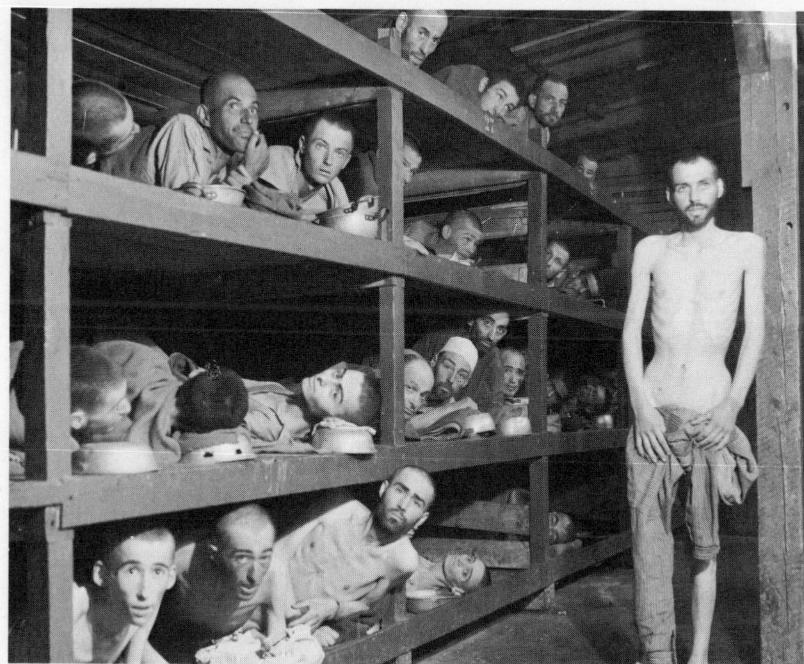

CAMP DACHAU. Prisoners at the notorious concentration camp are shown here in a barracks after being liberated in 1945. The lackluster stares and the chilling emaciation of their bodies are grim reminders of the Nazi brutality to the Jews in World War II.

broken, homeless, jobless persons, without a country of their own. They presented a very serious problem at the end of the war.

In other and more horrible ways the Nazi war leaders went all-out in their uncivilized practices. They put to death people in Germany and the conquered territories whom they considered political enemies. You will recall that Hitler blamed all of Germany's misfortunes on the Jews. After the war we learned that Hitler and his followers had killed some six million Jews—men, women, and even children. The evidence is clear; unfortunately, it is no propaganda story. American troops arrived in time to save some prisoners in the death camps. Proof of the atrocities is in the records of the war-guilt trials held at Nuremberg, Germany, after the war. Photographers took pictures of thousands of corpses. It is a sickening story that shows how the Nazi leaders planned from first to last to dominate the earth. President Franklin D. Roosevelt correctly called World War II "the war for survival."

World War II was increasingly a war of machines, science, and psychology. The German General Staff remembered the three-year stalemate of trench warfare on the Western Front in World War I. They understood that modern war must be more efficient if other nations were to be conquered quickly and with the least possible loss. In the 1930's, therefore, the Germans learned to put war on wheels. Proudly they boasted of their "lightning war," or *blitzkrieg* (*blits*-kreeg). They used low-flying planes to "strafe" troops and the countryside. Their bombers blasted fortifications and flattened cities. Then their mechanized troops, called *Panzer* (German for "armored") divisions, moved into action.

When the Panzer divisions invaded a country, German photographers recorded the speed and the striking power of the troops and the terror of the people in their path. The films were then rushed to countries next on the list in order to "soften them up" for quick conquest. Psychological warfare, though not new, was increasingly used in World War II as an effective way to break down the civilian and military morale of an enemy.

World War II saw the use of new and improved weapons, machines, explosives, healing sulfa drugs, insect repellents (DDT), and canned rations. The mechanically efficient Germans developed rapid-fire light artillery and heavy tanks, which were highly effective weapons. The British developed "spitfire" fighter planes and learned how to use radar. Other new fighting tools, such as the bombsight, the automatic pilot, and the proximity fuse, were the result of American inventiveness. The United States had the industrial "know-how" to supply the United Nations with thousands of jeeps, trucks, ships, airplanes, bombs, and other weapons to defeat the Germans.

In the air, on the land, and in the sea, men on both sides in World War II brought destruction to a new peak of efficiency. German submarines cruised under the sea. German torpedoes automatically traced the whirring propellers of our ships. Near the close of the war, their V-2 bombs brought devastation to the cities of England.

Over Hitler's Europe swept clouds of American bombers—the B-17 and B-24. They dropped British "block-busters" and other high explosives on the cities and railroads and on the Atlantic Wall fortifications which the Germans thought would prevent an invasion of northern Europe. American and British airplanes dropped over two million tons of bombs on Nazi Europe. Then, near the end of the war in Japan, came the greatest destructive force the mind of man had yet conceived, the atomic bomb.

American, British, and Canadian scientists learned how to derive vast amounts of energy from the basic unit of the universe, the atom. American money and the power of American industry produced the atom bomb. Here was a single weapon with twenty thousand times the destructive power of a ton of TNT, the most powerful explosive known before the atom bomb. World War II was a total war in which new weapons brought modern civilization to the brink of self-destruction.

THE AXIS POWERS WERE VICTORIOUS IN THE EARLY YEARS OF THE WAR

Hitler's march on Poland started World War II. Some authorities say that World War II began long before Germany's attack on Poland in September, 1939. They claim that the war began when Japan invaded Manchuria in 1931 and exploited its iron and coal to build up the Japanese war machine. Others claim that the war began when Mussolini's war machine crushed Ethiopia in 1935, or when Japan invaded China in 1937. Many agree with Winston Churchill that World War II began at Munich, Germany, in 1938, when Hitler bluffed France and Great Britain into allowing him to take the Sudetenland from Czechoslovakia. But as far as the official records are concerned, World War II began when Hitler's armies launched their unprovoked offensive against Poland. This action at last forced England and France to abandon their policy of appeasement. They dared not stand aside and watch Poland crushed as they had done in the case of Czechoslovakia only a short time before.

Why did Hitler attack Poland and so begin the war that destroyed Germany as a great power? Part of the trouble dated back to the Treaty of Versailles. You will recall that under the terms of the treaty, Germany had to give up certain territory to the new Polish nation. The Allies created the Polish Corridor, which separated East Prussia from the rest of Germany. The port of Danzig, where many Germans lived, became a "Free City" under control of the League of Nations. The whole arrangement was awkward and inconvenient. It irritated the Germans constantly. Hitler was determined to regain the Polish Corridor as well as the city of Danzig. The Nazi Party in Danzig got control of the local government. That was Hitler's first step.

France and Great Britain were friendly with Poland. They agreed to come to her aid if Germany attacked her. But Hitler did not think the democracies, which had so far remained peaceful, would fight. He was sure his air force and

GERMAN-RUSSIAN UNITY. In this picture, the Russian dictator, Joseph Stalin, is shown with Germany's von Ribbentrop. At this 1939 meeting in Moscow, Poland was split up between Germany and Russia.

armored divisions could crush any opposition. The only thing he seemed to fear was that Russia and the Western democracies might join forces against him. The German generals remembered how they had had to fight on both the eastern and western borders in World War I, and they did not want another two-front war. Hitler therefore decided to make a deal with Russia. It was a decision that amazed the world.

For years the Nazis had been shouting that Russia was their worst enemy and that they were going to save the world from communism. But in August, 1939, Germany made a nonaggression treaty with her eastern neighbor. The treaty stated that for ten years neither nation would attack the other. This meant that, for a while at least, Hitler would not have to fear an attack at Germany's back door. The agreement with Russia left Germany free to attack Poland and to defy France and Great Britain.

Why were the Russians willing to sign such an agreement with their old enemy? Stalin knew he could not trust Hitler, but he was willing to do almost anything to buy time in which Russia could strengthen her forces. Russia was not ready for war in 1939 and Stalin knew it. Stalin also saw a chance to grab parts of Poland and Finland in order to gain a frontier that could be defended more easily.

The new agreement was a great shock to Communists outside Russia. Never did the party line (the carefully regulated policy of Communists in all nations) make such an abrupt about-face. Hitler had been the Communists' most bitter foe. Now, suddenly, he became their ally, and the hated Nazis were their comrades! It was too much for some Communists. They left the party. But most of them obediently accepted the policy reversal and adopted the new party line.

Late in August, 1939, Hitler made new threats and demands on Poland. The British and French representatives tried to persuade him to modify his demands and to delay action. But Hitler would not listen. He claimed that the Poles were persecuting the Germans in Poland and that it was no use trying to deal with them peacefully. At dawn on September 1, 1939, the Nazi war machine rolled into Poland. Great Britain demanded that the invasion be halted, but Hitler paid no attention. As a result, Britain declared war on Germany on September 3, 1939, and France followed. Italy did not declare war on France and Great Britain until almost a year later. Japan did not join her Axis partners until December, 1941.

The German blitzkrieg disposed of Poland in a few weeks. Meantime, Russian troops also invaded Poland and occupied its eastern frontier. After the Polish campaign, there was a period known as the *Sitzkrieg* (*sits*-kreeg), or "sit-down war," when there was little actual fighting. British and French soldiers watched the Germans from a string of fortifications called the Maginot (*mazh*-ih-no) line. Some people called it a "phony" war and said neither side meant to fight.

The phony war turned into a real war. The Russians, however, were not idle. After seizing eastern Poland, they made demands on Finland.

When the plucky Finns resisted, Russia declared war on them. By the spring of 1940, Russia had added a part of Finland and a section of Romania to her conquests. Then, by political and military pressure, Russia forced Lithuania, Latvia, and Estonia to join the U.S.S.R.

In the spring of 1940 the Germans struck with such fury on their Western front that the world was left gasping. Overnight Germany occupied Denmark and Norway. The Norwegian minister of defense, Vidkun Quisling (*kwiz*-ling), helped the Nazis take over his country. (Today the word *quisling* means "traitor.")

The next month (May, 1940), the Germans turned west, rolling their war machine over the flat, defenseless lands of Holland and Belgium. Within four days Holland had to surrender. Belgium managed to hold out until the end of the month. Even before that, the Nazis had found a weak spot in the Maginot line and were smashing into France. The British army, trapped by the unexpected surrender of the Belgians and the collapse of the French armies to the south, retreated to the seacoast. The Germans actually pushed them into the sea. But British sailors and civilians —even schoolboys and girls—came to rescue their men in every sort of boat they could find.

On the long, flat beaches near Dunkirk, a French city on the English Channel, there occurred a miraculous evacuation. Some eight hundred and fifty ships of all sizes and kinds were rounded up in the British Isles. Tugboats, steamers, river boats, fishing craft, small power boats, many that had never been out in the open sea, came across the English Channel. Long lines of men waded out to small boats that ferried them to the larger ships. The fighter pilots of the R.A.F. furnished protection against German planes.

The "Mosquito Armada" did its work. More than 338,000 soldiers were landed in England in early June, 1940. The British saved their army, but they lost practically all of their tanks, guns, and supplies. It was then that Prime Minister Churchill rose in the House of Commons and declared:

> ". . . we shall defend our island, whatever the cost may be, we shall fight on the beaches, we shall fight on the landing grounds, we shall fight in the fields and in the streets, we shall fight in the hills; we shall never surrender . . ."

Winston Churchill gave the British inspired leadership. Many historians consider Winston Churchill the greatest of Britain's modern leaders. His background of family, education, and long experience is unusual. He is the direct

The Miracle of Dunkirk. This painting depicts the heroic evacuation of the British army at Dunkirk. The evacuation lasted from May 26 until June 4 of 1940. The Germans entered Dunkirk immediately afterward and held the city until the end of the war in 1945.

descendant of the Duke of Marlborough, one of the greatest generals in English history. His father was a British lord and a high official in the government. Churchill's mother was an American. Famed for her beauty, she was the daughter of a wealthy lawyer who was co-editor of the *New York Times.*

As a youngster in school, Churchill seemed to be a very ordinary boy. He showed no great ability as a student. Later in life he told how he had stayed in the lowest grades "three times longer than anyone else."

After a long political career, Churchill became Prime Minister of Great Britain early in World War II. Through his inspiring speeches he gave courage to the British people, who had every reason to fear an immediate and powerful invasion by Hitler's troops. Over the radio he told his countrymen:

> "What is our policy? . . . It is to wage war by sea, land, and air . . . with all the strength that God can give us. . . . What is our aim? . . . Victory . . . for without victory there is no survival."

WINSTON CHURCHILL. A strong opponent of Chamberlain's policy of appeasement, Churchill became prime minister after Chamberlain was forced to resign. Here, Churchill is shown giving his famous V-for-victory sign.

Then again, in Britain's most critical hour, Churchill closed an important speech with an expression that will never be forgotten in the history of English-speaking people:

> "The whole fury and might of the enemy must very soon be turned on us. Hitler knows that he will have to break us in this island or lose the war. If we can stand up to him, all Europe may be free and the life of the world may move forward into broad, sunlit uplands. But if we fail, the whole world, including the United States, including all that we have known and cared for, will sink into the abyss of a new Dark Age . . . Let us therefore brace ourselves, that, if the British Empire and its Commonwealth last for a thousand years, men will still say, 'This was their finest hour.' "

The United States became the arsenal of democracy. Shocked by the realization that Hitler was about to bring all of Europe under his control, the United States abandoned its policy of isolationism. While we still remained technically neutral, President Roosevelt, on his own responsibility, sent the British all the reserve weapons of our army: hundreds of field guns, thousands of machine guns and rifles, and millions of rounds of ammunition. Later events proved that Roosevelt had had the vision to see that the British were fighting the battle for our way of life; if Britain fell, the United States would be next.

In September, 1940, the President exchanged fifty American destroyers with the British in return for leases on bases from Newfoundland to Trinidad. The bases could help, if necessary, to protect our Atlantic waters. Within a year (on March 11, 1941) our Congress passed the Lend-Lease Act after bitter debate. The law gave the President power to sell, lend, or lease weapons, ships, and munitions to any nation whose defense he thought was "vital to the defense of the United States."

Though we had not yet entered the war, lend-lease was really the end of our neutrality. Before the war was over the remarkable productive power

THE BATTLE OF BRITAIN. A searchlight scans the skies for German bombers. From June 22, 1940, when France surrendered, until June 22, 1941, when Germany attacked Russia, Britain stood alone.

of American industry and agriculture supplied over fifty billion dollars worth of lend-lease goods. Of the amount, over thirty-one billion went to the British Empire and over eleven billion to Soviet Russia. As President Roosevelt said, our country became the "arsenal of democracy."

Hitler built his Atlantic Wall. The occupation of Norway and Denmark, the conquest of Holland and Belgium, and the occupation of France seemed to point to a complete victory for Germany. Mussolini thought it was time to climb on the band wagon. In June, 1940, Italy declared war on France and Great Britain.

From the North Cape to the Bay of Biscay, the Germans controlled the west coast of Europe. They heavily fortified it for both offensive and defensive purposes. They built submarine "pens" from which came the U-boats to attack Allied ships in the Battle of the Atlantic. They installed platforms from which to launch their deadly rocket bombs. It was the tough Atlantic Wall of fortifications that General Dwight D. Eisenhower, commander-in-chief of the Allied forces, had to penetrate when D-day came on the beaches of Normandy on June 6, 1944.

The first years of the war definitely favored the Axis powers. An alliance with Germany and Italy gave Japan a free hand in Asia. In the Battle of Britain that followed the evacuation of Dunkirk, Hitler tried to soften and conquer Britain with massive aerial bombings. The young men of the British R.A.F., with the help of radar, fought off the attack with their superior Spitfire fighter planes.

Hitler took a gamble and lost. Because of the valiant resistance of the British, Hitler was forced to postpone his plans for an invasion of Britain. Without warning, in June, 1941, Hitler suddenly turned on Russia. Less than two years after Germany made her nonaggression treaty with Moscow, German motorized armies rolled across Russian Poland and penetrated deep into Russia. But Hitler's Panzer troops met stiff resistance. Wherever the Russians retreated; they burned crops and blew up factories in order to leave nothing the Germans could use. The struggle was along a two-thousand-mile front between the two largest armies in the world. Now the Germans were fighting a two-front war.

The attack on Russia was a gamble that did not pay off. Russian mud and the Russian winter defeated Hitler just as they had defeated Napoleon more than a hundred years before. Why did the Germans make such a disastrous move? Apparently they thought the Russians would not put up much of a fight. The Germans thought they could grab farm lands and oil wells to provide the food and fuel they needed desperately. Hitler expected results with his blitzkrieg methods. But the Russians stopped him.

The stand the Russians made at Stalingrad in the winter of 1942–43, was, like the evacuation of Dunkirk, an epic of courage and determination. In months of hand-to-hand street fighting, they saved their shattered city and captured what was left of a large German army. They showed the world that the Germans could be stopped. Stalingrad undermined the faith of the German generals and common soldiers in their Führer, Hitler. Thousands and thousands of German "supermen" froze to death in Russia or became prisoners of war.

ROOSEVELT AND CHURCHILL. The two leaders met several times during the war. Out of these meetings came such important joint agreements as the *Atlantic Charter* and the "unconditional surrender" statement.

The Atlantic Charter stated the war aims of the democracies. Although the United States had abandoned its policy of isolationism, we remained officially neutral. Actually, of course, we had made our sympathies clear by giving all possible aid to Britain and Russia. In the summer of 1941, several months before the United States entered the shooting war, Prime Minister Churchill of Great Britain and President Roosevelt held an historic meeting on an American battleship off the coast of Newfoundland. Their purpose was to restate and make clear the war aims of nations that believed in the democratic way of life. The list of policies they drew up came to be known as the *Atlantic Charter*.

In many ways the ideas expressed in the Charter resembled Woodrow Wilson's Fourteen Points. The Atlantic Charter influenced the thinking of the people of many nations about war, peace, and the probable post-war problems. It marked another step by the United States toward active participation in the war. Here is a summary of the points in the Atlantic Charter:

1. No territorial or other gains should result from the war.
2. No territorial changes should be made without "the freely expressed wishes of the people concerned."
3. All people should have the right to choose the form of government under which they will live, and self-government should be restored to those deprived of it.
4. All nations should have "access on equal terms, to the trade and to the raw materials of the world . . ."

BATTLE OF STALINGRAD. The bitter fighting at Stalingrad in 1942–43 marked the turning point of the war in Russia. After the Germans were defeated in this battle, the Russians began a westward offensive that did not stop until the end of the war. Stalingrad has been rebuilt and is now one of the major industrial cities of Russia.

5. The nations should co-operate to provide improved labor conditions, economic advancement, and social security.

6. The Nazi tyranny should be destroyed so that a peace may be established, permitting peoples and nations to live in safety and freedom from want and fear.

7. The men of all nations should be free to "traverse the high seas and oceans without hindrance."

8. Aggressor nations should be disarmed, and provisions made for the organization of a wider, more permanent system of general security.

THE UNITED STATES ENTERED WORLD WAR II

An arrogant and overconfident Japan attacked the United States. While Hitler and Mussolini were expanding their conquests in Europe in 1939, 1940, and 1941, Japan was having things pretty much her own way in Asia. The United States was the only power able to interfere with Japan's ambitions. We sent supplies and gave encouragement to the Chinese in their struggle against Japan. Japan resented our interference. The Japanese leaders decided to try to cripple the United States Navy with a single daring blow. Then they would be free to expand their empire from the North Pacific to the South Seas without America's interference.

On Sunday morning, December 7, 1941, without any warning, planes from Japanese aircraft carriers swept down on Pearl Harbor, our important naval base in Hawaii. Small Japanese submarines also took part in the raid. The Japanese sank or damaged five American battleships and three destroyers. One hundred fifty American planes were wrecked, most of them on the ground. Over two thousand of our men were killed. Japanese losses were light. The next day President Roosevelt solemnly addressed Congress:

> "Yesterday, December 7, 1941—a date which will live in infamy—the United States of America was suddenly and deliberately attacked by naval and air forces of the Empire of Japan . . . I ask that the Congress declare that since the unprovoked and dastardly attack by Japan, on Sunday, December Seventh, a state of war has existed between the United States and the Japanese Empire."

Two and a half hours after the attack on Pearl Harbor, Japan declared war on the United States and Great Britain. Germany and Italy also declared war on us. A few days later the United States declared war on the Axis and became a member of the Allies. The war had now become a global one.

The American people were quick to recognize their danger. Our forces in the Pacific were crippled and out of action. We had no large and well-equipped standing army, even though Congress had passed America's first peacetime draft bill in 1940. For the first time in our history we were faced with a two-front war.

The President and his advisers had to make a very difficult decision about American strategy. Would it be better to strike back at the Japanese immediately or put our first efforts into winning the war in Europe? President Roosevelt knew that the popular demand in the country was to deal with the Japanese. He also knew that our power in the Pacific was woefully weak. Within six months after Pearl Harbor, Japan had seized our mid-Pacific possessions as well as the Philippine Islands.

Stories of the surrender at Corregidor and the "Death March" from Bataan angered our people. But Roosevelt and the military and naval leaders knew that to withdraw aid from Britain and Russia might be fatal. To remove our ships from the battle of the Atlantic would cut the pipeline of supplies to our Allies and might let Germany win the European phase of the war.

American strategists realized that it would take months to build up our power in the Pacific. We

PEARL HARBOR. The battleship *Arizona* of the United States Navy is shown sinking after the Japanese attack. A bomb was dropped down her smokestack. Today, the bridge of the *Arizona,* which remained above water, contains a memorial plaque commemorating the men who went down with the ship.

had to win bases beyond Hawaii and build all kinds of ships and landing craft. Fuel and supplies would have to be carried across the great distances of the Pacific. So in the months of 1941 and 1942 we did not strike back in the Pacific. We fought a holding operation and devoted our major effort to Europe.

Tojo was the symbol of Japanese aggression. During World War II, General Hideki Tojo stood as the symbol of Japanese militarism and aggression. He was the key man in the little group that ruled Japan.

Tojo was a member of an old samurai family, the warrior class you read about in the story of Japan. In 1940 Tojo, as minister of war, persuaded Japan to join the Rome-Berlin Axis. Tojo's group of Japanese imperialists built up their power and seized complete control of the government in October, 1941. The emperor, of course, was just a puppet of the Tojo group. He ruled in name only. In November, 1941, Tojo sent a special representative to the United States, saying that Japan wished peace with our country. But Tojo wanted no peace; all he wanted was to throw us off our guard and thereby gain enough time to plan and carry out the attack on our fleet at Pearl Harbor.

Tojo was not a personal dictator as Hitler and Mussolini were. Rather, he acted as spokesman for a group of army and navy officers and powerful industrialists who dictated the affairs of Japan. As leader, however, Tojo became the symbol of Japanese aggression.

The war in the West shifted to the Mediterranean Theater. In 1942, while we were desperately trying to hang on in the Pacific area, the war in the West shifted to a new front. For nearly two years the Allies had been on the defensive. Then at last came the first major offensive action—the invasion of North Africa.

The invasion was largely an American action commanded by General Eisenhower. Some of the invasion forces sailed directly from America, the rest from the British Isles. Nearly three hundred thousand men, with thousands of tons of equipment and supplies, landed in North Africa. The time was November 8, 1942—eleven months and one day after Pearl Harbor. North Africa was important to the defense of both the Americas and the British Empire. The port of Dakar is just sixteen hundred miles from the Brazilian coast. If the Nazis had captured Dakar, they could have used it as a base to launch an invasion of South America. The eastern end of North Africa contained the vital Suez Canal, Britain's lifeline to India and Australia.

The North African campaign gave us a foothold from which we later invaded Italy and other parts of southern Europe. It also proved to be excellent training for D-day and the invasion of Europe a year and a half later. In North Africa, the Allied troops had to fight the best of the German army, the Africa Corps, under one of Hitler's ablest generals, Erwin Rommel, "the Desert Fox." The Allied forces suffered many setbacks and heavy losses. Finally, however, the Germans were defeated in North Africa, and their army of two hundred thousand men was captured.

Then the shores of North Africa became the springboard for the invasion of Sicily and southern Italy. Mussolini fled to his German masters in the north. The Italian campaign was long and bitter. Our army suffered high casualties. Slowly the Germans retreated northward, making the Allied forces pay in blood for every step of the way. When the German troops reached northern Italy, they "dug in," and did not surrender until Germany herself was crushed.

The Allied action in the Mediterranean Theater during 1942 and 1943 entirely changed the war picture in Western Europe. It helped to relieve the terrific pressure on the Russians. It cleared the Mediterranean shipping lanes and made them safe against attack by submarine or airplane. The oil of the Near East, vitally needed for ships and machines, was safe. Equipment and

WILLIE AND JOE. Both the humor and the tragedy of the war became symbolized for many Americans by the two Bill Mauldin cartoon characters, Willie and Joe. Cartoons like the two shown here helped remind us of the human side of the war.

"Tell him to look at th' bright side o' things, Willie. His trees is pruned, his ground is plowed up, an' his house is air-conditioned."

"Spring is here."

supplies flowed to Great Britain through the Suez from the Far East. American lend-lease supplies could now reach China by way of the Indian Ocean.

And now the titanic Battle of Europe was next, bringing the liberation of France and the invasion of Germany.

The Battle of Europe was fought in the air, on the sea, and on the land. The Battle of Europe opened with D-day, popularly called "deliverance day," June 6, 1944, and closed with V-E day, or victory in Europe, May 8, 1945.

Months before the invasion of Europe, it was necessary to stockpile in the British Isles millions of tons of supplies and munitions. Landing craft, trucks, tanks, and all the other weapons of mechanized warfare had to be on the spot. The Americans had to train millions of men, place weapons in their hands, and have them ready on the British beaches of the English Channel.

Our troops played important parts in the tank battles in Normandy. While American tanks were racing across the French countryside, American armies made a second speedy invasion in southern France. Soon the Americans in the south pushed up and met the Allied forces in northern France.

THE FLEET. The war in the Pacific was to a large extent a naval war. These battleships of our Seventh Fleet are moving toward the Philippines to shell the island of Luzon before the troops land. This action was part of the long road back to Japan.

American soldiers showed their courage in the Bastogne (bahs-*tawn*-yuh) Bulge, where Hitler made a last desperate effort to stop the Allied invasion of Germany. Eight Panzer divisions surrounded American troops. When they sent a message demanding surrender, the American commander, General McAuliffe, replied with one word: "Nuts!" It was such a typically American expression that it delighted our men and gave them new courage to fight on to victory.

In the months following the Normandy invasion, the German forces were caught in a gigantic pincer. Within a year the Germans were completely crushed by the great drive of the Russians from the east and the drive of the American, British, Canadian, and Free French armies from the west. The two forces met at the Elbe River. By May, 1945, the war in Europe was over.

The end of the Axis leaders is a grim story. In the closing days of the war in Europe. Hitler committed suicide in his private bomb shelter in Berlin. A number of the top Nazi officials followed the example of their fanatical leader. While attempting to escape to Switzerland, Mussolini was captured and shot by some of his own countrymen. His body was hung by the heels in front of a garage in Milan. The people he had betrayed spat upon his corpse.

The road back to Japan was long and difficult. The end of the war in Europe allowed the United States to concentrate all its efforts on defeating Japan. As we have seen, the war in the Pacific-Asiatic Theater during the first two years was a holding operation. Our aim was to keep the Japanese from attacking Australia and India and from expanding in China. Otherwise, the Japanese had little difficulty in the Far East. They took Indochina, Thailand, Hong Kong, Singapore, the East Indies, much of Northern China, and the American island possessions of Guam, Wake, and the Philippines. They also landed on some of the Aleutian Islands off Alaska.

Even while our fleet was recovering from the

The Wounded

The Troops

The Prisoners

The Victims

The Dead

The Victors

WORLD WAR II

An essay in pictures

Iwo Jima. Marines raise Old Glory over Mt. Suribachi, Iwo Jima. This island had an important air base and was taken by United States forces in March of 1945 at a tremendous cost in lives.

blow at Pearl Harbor, we managed to keep the lines open to Australia. There was heroic action at Guadalcanal in the Solomons, and in the desperate Battle of the Coral Sea. At the Battle of Midway we destroyed a strong Japanese invasion fleet headed for Hawaii. All these actions took place in 1942, while the Battle of Britain and the Battle of Russia were in progress. If the British and Russians held out, we knew that we would have time to arm and take the offensive in the Pacific.

From 1943 until the final victory, the story was different. The Americans, the Australians, and the New Zealanders took the offensive. The Pacific was no longer a Japanese lake. But the road back was long and difficult. As the British Isles were the United Nations base for the Battle of Europe, so Australia was our base in the Pacific. There were many battle fronts spread over thousands of miles of land and sea.

In the Pacific our troops had to learn jungle fighting. Dank weather rotted equipment and plagued our men. Jungle insects carried the ever-present danger of malarial fever and other crippling diseases. The lack of roads and firm ground for airfields made the operation of the war machines extremely difficult.

The Battle of China was a part of the road back. The Allied forces were determined to open a new front in China. The Japanese had closed the Burma Road, over which supplies had gone to China. The Americans, under General Stilwell, built a new route that bypassed the Japanese-held area. This was the Stilwell Road. To aid China, the United States Army Air Transport Command also flew thousands of tons of supplies, men, and munitions over the Himalaya Mountains each month. The operation was known as "flying the Hump."

The strategy was hop, skip, and jump to Japan. The Allies followed an island-hopping strategy in the Pacific area, bypassing isolated groups of the enemy, and planning the final strike at Japan from Okinawa. General Douglas MacArthur, who had been ordered by the President to leave the Philippines before the surrender, was in charge of operations in the South Pacific. Admiral Nimitz commanded the advance across the Central Pacific. From New Guinea and Guadalcanal, MacArthur's forces made their difficult way. Ships of our fleet bombarded islands, aircraft from the carriers dropped their bombs, and landing craft put marines and soldiers ashore.

Meanwhile, Admiral Nimitz was crossing the Pacific from one island group to another. In October, 1944, the vise closed on the Philippines. A great invasion force landed in Leyte (*lay*-tee) Gulf on the east side of the islands on October 19 and 20. The naval forces were under the command of Admiral Halsey. General Douglas MacArthur stepped ashore, thus making good his promise to the people of the Philippines that he would return. Though the fighting on Luzon Island continued until the end of the war, the Philippines had been liberated. The lifelines of

The Atomic Bomb. This gigantic column over Nagasaki convinced the Japanese they should surrender, while the stunned world gasped at the power which had been released.

the Japanese Empire to the rich resources of the South Seas were cut.

Japan was next on the Pacific-Asiatic timetable. By the beginning of 1945 the defeat of Japan was certain. The large island of Okinawa, just south and west of the Japanese chain of islands, was the last major objective before Japan itself. It was heavily defended. Japanese suicide planes—the *kamikaze* (kahm-ih-*kah*-zee)—repeatedly attacked American ships. In the span of a few weeks, thirty-three ships were sunk, forty-five were damaged, and ten thousand sailors were killed, but we took Okinawa. Japan was now cut off completely and subject to constant air attacks from the islands of Saipan, Tinian, and Okinawa.

Japan surrendered. In the summer of 1945 President Truman called upon the Japanese to surrender or be destroyed. (President Roosevelt had died a few months earlier.) Japan hesitated, so our forces prepared for the invasion. British and American battleships shelled the Japanese islands. B-29 Superfortresses averaged twelve hundred attacks a week over Japan. Still the Japanese held out.

About that time, a trial atomic bomb was detonated on the desert sands of New Mexico. President Roosevelt had risked two billion dollars to develop it. On August 6, 1945, an atom bomb was dropped on Hiroshima. It completely destroyed the city. President Truman again called on Japan to surrender. When the demand was not answered, another atom bomb was dropped on Nagasaki on August 9, 1945. The mushroom cloud rose miles in the air and could be seen nearly two hundred miles away. The proud city of Nagasaki was a mass of rubble. The Japanese, who had had enough, surrendered unconditionally. The signing of the formal surrender papers took place aboard the battleship "Missouri" on September 2, 1945.

All three Axis partners had been defeated. The war was over, and the world hoped peace had come to stay. But the end of World War II brought many new problems, as you will learn in Part 23.

Hiroshima. This was what was left of Hiroshima's main business and industrial section after the first atomic bomb was dropped. Out of the city's population of over 300,000 people, some 150,000 were killed or injured, and 60,000 buildings were destroyed.

Chapter Check-up

1. Why do we refer to World War II as a global war?
2. Which countries comprised the Axis powers and which comprised the Allied powers in World War II?
3. In what ways was World War II more of an all-out war than World War I?
4. How did World War II begin?
5. In what sense did the United States become the "arsenal of democracy?"
6. What events brought the United States into active participation in World War II?
7. Who were the three important Axis leaders?
8. What were the steps by which the Allied nations conquered the Axis powers in Europe?
9. What was the Allies' strategy in winning the war in the Pacific?
10. What new weapon helped to bring the war with Japan to a close?

Two World Wars: SYNOPSIS

The growth of three powerful forces in Europe set the stage for the disastrous wars of the twentieth century. The first was nationalism, an extreme form of patriotism that unites the people of a nation but sometimes leads them to overlook the rights of other nations. The second was imperialism, or a desire to rule over other peoples in order to gain trading advantages and sources of supply. The third and most dangerous force, militarism, grew out of the first two. It placed emphasis on military power rather than peaceful diplomacy as a means of settling international differences.

These three forces were at work in pre-World War I Europe, when the major powers made two secret alliances: the Triple Alliance, which linked Germany, Austria-Hungary, and Italy; and the Triple Entente, which included France, Russia, and Great Britain. When the heir to the Austrian throne, Archduke Francis Ferdinand, was assassinated in 1914, these pacts dragged all of Europe into the ensuing war. After three years of fighting, America entered the conflict and tipped the balance in favor of the Allies, who finally achieved victory in 1918.

In an effort to prevent future wars, President Wilson of the United States drew up his famous Fourteen Points, which outlined what he considered to be the basis for a lasting peace. But the Treaty of Versailles largely ignored Wilson's proposals. He did, however, meet with success in one proposal that he considered of major importance: the formation of the League of Nations. Ironically, the United States never joined the League, and the organization was unable to accomplish most of its aims.

After a period of peace that lasted into the 1920's, a world-wide depression made the nations of Europe ripe for dictatorships. Mussolini came to power in Italy, and Hitler destroyed Germany's democratic government and replaced it with a dictatorship. As the nations of the world struggled for economic security during the depression, tensions between the "have" and the "have-not" nations increased. As a result, the 1930's was a period of repeated war scares and crises.

The tensions erupted into war when Hitler invaded Poland in 1939, and before long the conflict was being waged in nearly every part of the world. By 1941, when the United States entered the war after Japan's surprise attack on Pearl

Harbor, the world had split into two powerful camps, the Allies and the Rome-Berlin-Tokyo Axis. While fighting a holding operation in the Pacific, the Allies concentrated on defeating their opponents in Europe. The turning point came on D-day, when a massive invasion force landed at Normandy in France. Less than a year later, the Allies had won that phase of the war and were free to turn their attention to the Pacific Theater. After a bitter series of campaigns on the islands of the Pacific, President Truman warned the Japanese to surrender or be destroyed. When Japan hesitated, the British and Americans began to bombard the Japanese islands themselves. The Japanese were finally crushed when atomic bombs were dropped on the cities of Hiroshima and Nagasaki. The Japanese surrendered immediately, and World War II was at an end.

Important People

How has each of the following influenced the story of the two world wars?

Bismarck
William II
Francis Ferdinand
Woodrow Wilson
Ferdinand Foch
John J. Pershing
David Lloyd George
Georges Clemenceau
Vittorio Orlando
Douglas MacArthur
Aristide Briand
Gustav Stresemann
Adolf Hitler
Benito Mussolini
Harry Truman
Vidkun Quisling
Dwight D. Eisenhower
Winston Churchill
Hideki Tojo
Franklin D. Roosevelt

Terms

Be sure that you understand clearly the meaning of each of the following:

nationalism
imperialism
militarism
Triple Alliance
Triple Entente
Western Front
Eastern Front
Central Powers
Fourteen Points
Treaty of Versailles
League of Nations
Polish Corridor
World Court
isolation policy
Washington Conference
Locarno Agreement
Kellogg-Briand Pact
totalitarianism
economic nationalism
appeasement
Geneva Convention
D-Day
Lend-Lease Act
Atlantic Charter

Questions for Discussion and Review

1. How did nationalism, imperialism, and militarism lead us into two world wars?
2. What conditions contributed to the failure of the League of Nations?
3. Do you believe that the United States acted wisely in staying out of the League of Nations? Why?
4. How did the great depression of the 1930's help to bring on World War II?
5. Why do some historians say that the two

world wars were really parts of the same conflict?

6. Why does war often bring much technical and scientific progress?
7. Why have the policies of isolationism and appeasement proved to be ineffective in dealing with modern international problems?
8. How has our foreign policy changed as a result of two world wars?
9. Do you feel that the United States was justified in using the atom bomb against Japan? Why?
10. Do you think that international war is inevitable? Why?

Interesting Things to Do

1. Make two outline maps of the world. On the first, use one color to show the Central Powers and another to show the Allied nations in World War I. Show on the second map the Axis powers and the Allied powers of World War II. Mount the two maps side by side for comparison.
2. Using photographs, magazine cut-outs, or drawings, make a poster showing some of the medical, technical, and scientific achievements that resulted from World War II.
3. Make a poster showing some of the famous quotations from history about war. With each quotation, include the name of its author, his nationality, and the period of history in which he lived.
4. Prepare a talk on the Treaty of Versailles, pointing out what it attempted to accomplish and what it actually did accomplish.
5. Arrange and present an informal debate on the topic: *Resolved,* That the League of Nations would have succeeded with the support of the United States.
6. Write an analysis of the various methods or techniques employed by the dictators to gain absolute power.
7. Prepare a chart showing some of the important issues that have come before the United Nations, listing for each issue what action the UN took.
8. Add to or begin your "Who's Who in World History" series by writing brief biographies of one or more important leaders of the nations involved in the two world wars.

Interesting Reading about the Two World Wars

Blond, G., *Death of Hitler's Germany,* Macmillan. Account of the end of the Nazi dictatorship.

Bradley, Omar N., *A Soldier's Story,* Holt, Rinehart and Winston. World War II seen through the eyes of a military leader.

Brogan, D. W., *The Era of Franklin D. Roosevelt,* Yale. Our wartime President's impact on his nation and the world.

Churchill, Winston L. S., *Gathering Storm,* Houghton Mifflin.

———, *Their Finest Hour,* Houghton Mifflin.

———, *Grand Alliance,* Houghton Mifflin.

———, *Closing the Ring,* Houghton Mifflin.

———, *Hinge of Fate,* Houghton Mifflin.

———, *Triumph and Tragedy,* Houghton Mifflin.

Commager, Henry S., *Story of the Second World War,* Little, Brown.

Eisenhower, Dwight D., *Crusade in Europe,* Doubleday.

Hershey, John, *Hiroshima,* Knopf. The atom bomb's effect on individuals in a Japanese city.

*Lawson, Don, *United States in World War I,* Abelard-Schuman.

*———, *United States In World War II,* Abelard-Schuman.

*Life, *Life's Picture History of World War II,* Simon and Schuster.

Slosson, Preston W., *Great Crusade and After, 1914–1928,* Macmillan.

* Indicates easy reading

On August 15, 1963, a camera caught this East German soldier jumping over a barbed wire barricade into West Berlin. His leap for freedom dramatizes one of the problems of our divided world.

Part 23
TOWARD WORLD UNDERSTANDING
MAN'S SEARCH FOR LASTING PEACE

THE WORLD TODAY

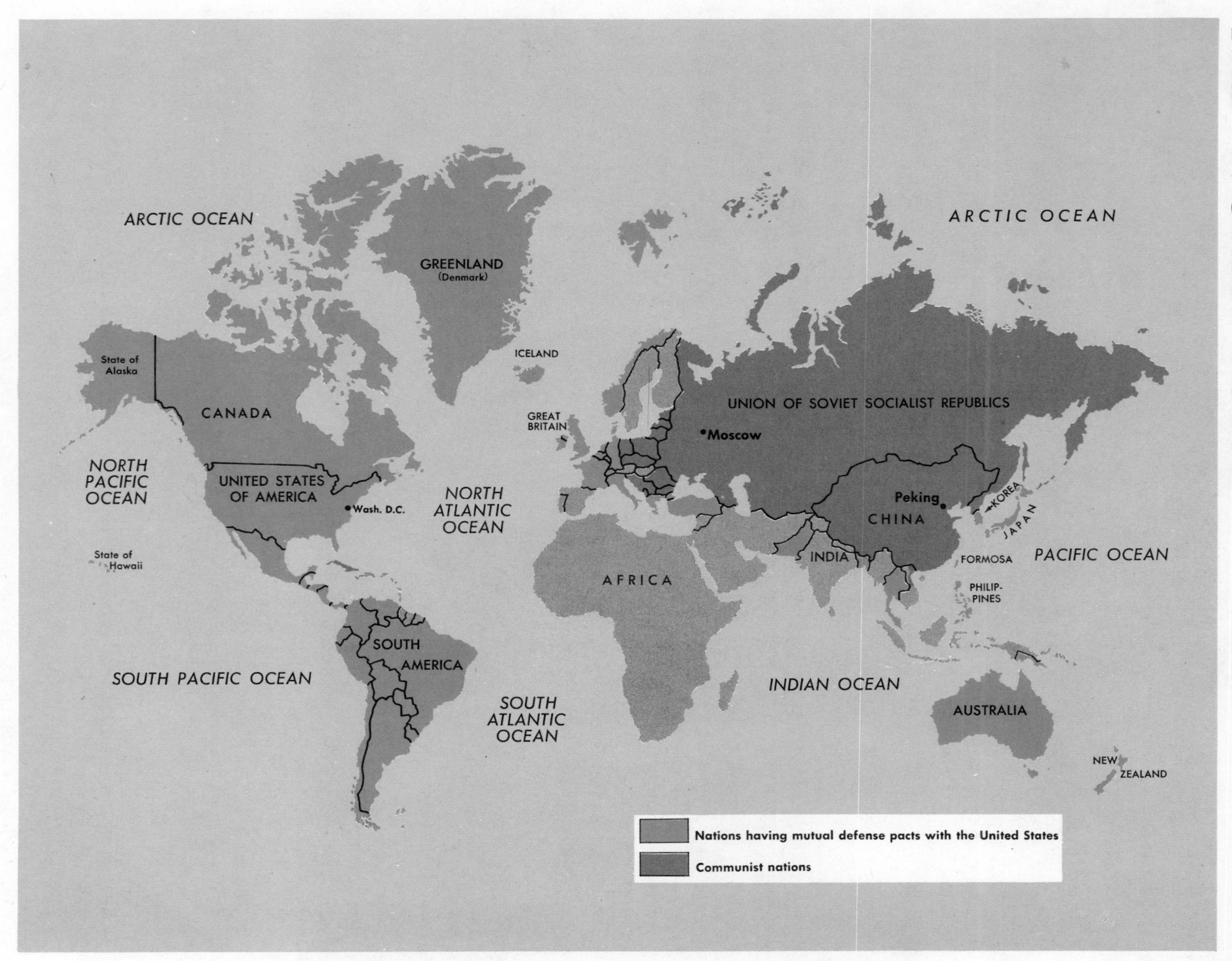

Toward World Understanding: PERSPECTIVE

When the horror and bloodshed of World War II came to an end in 1945, the peoples of the world looked forward hopefully to a lasting peace. After six years of global warfare, they were anxious to repair the scars of conflict and resume peaceful occupations. But they were soon to be disappointed. The fighting had scarcely stopped when a new kind of struggle began—a kind of "cold war"—between the Communist nations and the democracies.

Signs of this cold war began to appear soon after the United Nations was organized. While the delegates of most of the countries represented in the UN tried to lay a stable foundation for peace, the Soviet Union as leader of the Communist bloc, used its veto power to test the resolve of the democratic nations and to further the expansion of world Communism. Soon the cold war entered even more dangerous phases as the Soviet Union supported open conflict in Korea and created crises in Berlin and elsewhere. It quickly became apparent to all nations that the problems of keeping peace could be just as difficult as those of waging war.

When Nikita Khrushchev emerged as leader of the Soviet Union in the late 1950's, it seemed that tensions might ease. Khrushchev agreed to an Austrian peace treaty and spoke of "peaceful co-existence" between the Communist and non-Communist worlds. The United States and the Soviet Union arranged for cultural exchanges. In 1959, Premier Khrushchev visited the United States and the United Nations.

But this relaxation of tension between East and West proved to be short-lived. The Soviet Union became more belligerent. A new crisis erupted over Berlin and East Germany began erecting a wall across the divided city. This phase of the cold war reached a climax in 1962 when the Soviet Union began to install missiles in Cuba. The United States reacted vigorously and the missiles were removed.

In October of 1964 Premier Khrushchev was removed by the Russian Communist Party. Aleksei N. Kosygin became premier and Leonid I. Brezhnev took over party leadership. The new Soviet leaders rejected a bid from the Communist Party in China to condemn ex-Premier Khrushchev's doctrine of "peaceful co-existence" as a betrayal of the revolutionary principles of Marx and Lenin. Instead the rift between China and the Soviet Union deepened. Both nations began to compete openly for the leadership of the Communist world. And in October of 1964 China successfully exploded its first atomic device and became an atomic power.

In 1971 Communist China was admitted to the U.N. and Nationalist China was unseated. Whether this will lead to better relations between the East and the West, especially U.S. and China remains to be seen.

In space there is time and distance. The United States landed the first man on the moon in 1969 and overcame both, yet there is still space between man and man, nation and nation here on earth. From his dim past, to his chaotic present man continues to achieve and to fail. While searching for the stars, his grasp here on earth has not been too secure. War, poverty, racism, over-population, still are not solved and plague his existence and cause concern for his future. Will man learn from the past? Will he make a break through into understanding and love? Will he begin to live with his fellow man? Shall we tune in next century and find out?

Chapter 78

The Victorious Allies Organized the UN to Keep Peace in the World

THE UN HAS IMPORTANT BUT LIMITED POWERS

Modern wars create more problems than they solve. An American general once said that there is no such thing as a good war or a bad peace. The Indian statesman Nehru said, "Bad means can never make good ends." The whole history of the twentieth century proves the wisdom of both remarks. You have just read in Part 22 the tragic story of two terrible world wars. You saw how the high hopes that President Wilson expressed at the end of World War I came to nothing. New and more serious problems brought on a second and more horrible world war. The post-World War II period, in turn, produced new tensions. These events showed that the end of a war does not automatically bring peace. It seems to create new problems that threaten to bring on a new war.

What are the new problems that threaten to cause a third world war, and what are the nations of the world trying to do about them? In this Part we shall learn something about what is going on in the world today. You will see that the situation is serious but not hopeless. War is hateful to all people and everyone must try to prevent any future conflict. War, solves no purpose. You have already read about some of the work of the United Nations. In this chapter we shall see why it was organized and what it has done so far in an effort to keep peace in the world.

The United Nations decided to organize for peace. One of the chief hopes for peace in the world lies in the work of the UN (as we call the United Nations Organization). Though it has not so far been completely successful, it has done much useful work. It is one of the few places and perhaps the only real forum for the exchange of ideas and differences between the Communist world and the democracies of the free world. Let us see how the UN came into being and some of the things it has done and is doing to ward off a third world war.

Four months before the Japanese attack on Pearl Harbor, President Roosevelt met with Prime Minister Churchill on a British warship off the coast of Newfoundland. Together they drew up a declaration that has become known as the Atlantic Charter (see page 738), in which they presented the war aims and the peace aims of the United States and Great Britain. The sixth article of the Charter provides the inspiration for the UN:

> "After the final destruction of Nazi tyranny, they hope to see established a peace which will afford to all nations the means of dwelling in safety within their own borders, and which will afford assurance that all the men in all lands may live out their lives in freedom from fear and want."

The attack on Pearl Harbor drew us into the war. President Roosevelt felt that all nations that were then fighting against the Axis powers should declare their united purpose. On January 1, 1942, twenty-six nations signed the United Nations Declaration. They all agreed, among other things, to support the principles which had been set down in the Atlantic Charter in 1941 (see page 738).

In the next year, Britain, Russia, and the United States joined in declaring "the necessity of establishing . . . a general international organization . . . for maintenance of international peace and security."

THE UNITED NATIONS. Rising above New York City's East River, the United Nations Building stands as a symbol of the world's hope for peace. The skyscraper contains the Secretariat's offices; the low building along the edge of the river houses the council chambers and conference rooms; and the domed building in the center contains the General Assembly.

You will remember that the League of Nations, established at the end of World War I, had been an international organization. It had failed to establish peace and security in the world. Many people believed that one of the chief reasons the League of Nations failed was that the United States had never joined it. The question in the minds of many people was "Will the Senate agree to our joining another world association of nations?" The question was answered in the fall of 1943 when both the Senate and the House of Representatives adopted resolutions expressing the desire of the United States to take part in an international peace organization.

The organizational meeting was held in San Francisco in the spring of 1945. There the UN Charter was written and agreed to. It is a people's charter. Unlike the League of Nations Covenant (agreement), which began, "We, the high contracting Parties . . . ," the Preamble of the United Nations Charter reads:

"We the people of the United Nations

"Determined to save succeeding generations from the scourge of war, which twice in our lifetime has brought untold sorrow to mankind, and

"To reaffirm faith in fundamental human rights, in the dignity and worth of the human person, in the equal right of men and of nations, large and small, and

"To establish conditions under which justice and respect for the obligations arising from treaties and other sources of international law can be maintained, and

"To promote social progress and better standards of life in larger freedom, and for these ends

"To practice tolerance and life together in peace with one another as good neighbors, and

"To unite our strength to maintain international peace and security,

"To insure, by the acceptance of principles and the institution of methods, that armed force shall not be used, save in the common interest, and

"To employ international machinery for the promotion of the economic and social advancement of all people . . .

". . . do hereby establish an international organization to be known as the United Nations."

Often in *Story of Nations* you have seen that the roots of the present are deep in the past. So it was when the UN Charter was adopted. The delegates at San Francisco borrowed ideas from past experience—experience gained in disarmament conferences, in the League of Nations and the World Court, and in the many conferences held during World War II.

On October 24, 1945, enough nations agreed to the Charter to establish the UN officially. Early the next year, representatives of all the member nations met in London. They com-

San Francisco Conference. Dean Virginia Gildersleeve, United States delegate to the San Francisco Conference, receives a handshake from President Truman after signing the United Nations Charter. Fifty-one nations participated in the founding of the world organization.

pleted the organization and elected Trygve Lie (see Chapter 53) the first secretary-general. As chairman of the committee that wrote the UN Charter, he had won the respect and trust of the delegates at San Francisco. Thus they elected him to the UN's most important position.

How does the UN work? It is necessary to understand the structure of the UN to see what it can and cannot do. You must know, for instance, that the UN is not a world government. It cannot force its member nations to do anything. Some people think this is a serious weakness. But in the present state of the world, most leaders understand that very few nations would give up any of their sovereign powers to a world organization.

The UN, therefore, is designed mainly for discussion. The representatives may reach a majority decision and try to use the pressure of public opinion to influence nations to do what the UN decides. We shall see, however, that although the UN has helped keep the peace in some instances, it has not been successful in others.

The work of the UN is carried out by: (1) six major organs, (2) several commissions, and (3) a variety of specialized agencies. The six major organs are:

1. General Assembly
2. Security Council
3. Economic and Social Council
4. Trusteeship Council
5. International Court of Justice
6. Secretariat

The General Assembly is the legislative body of the UN. All member nations are represented, and each member has one vote. It is here that general discussion takes place. It might be called the "town meeting of nations." In the General Assembly, representatives try to settle problems that might otherwise lead to war.

The Security Council was designed to be the chief agency in keeping world peace. It has eleven members, five of whom are permanent and represent Britain, France, Nationalist China, Soviet Russia, and the United States. The General Assembly elects six other nations to be members for terms of two years. The men who drew up the UN Charter were realistic. They knew that unless the most powerful nations kept the peace and supported the UN, it would fail, just as the League of Nations did. They provided, therefore, that the negative vote of one of the five permanent members of the Security Council would defeat any action of the Security Council. Such a negative vote is called a *veto*.

DESPITE HANDICAPS, THE UN HAS MADE GREAT CONTRIBUTIONS TO HUMAN WELFARE

Differences among the great powers have reduced the effectiveness of the Security Council. Rivalry between Russia and her former allies began as soon as the UN was organized. Russia soon discovered that on most issues the other four permanent members usually united against her. For this reason, Russia has used the veto power far more than has any other member.

Russia has used the veto power so often that the Security Council has not always been able to work effectively. Some observers have urged that the veto power be abolished. We should note, however, that the United States as well as Russia insisted on the veto. It is probable that the Senate and the people of our country would have rejected the UN Charter if the United States did not have the right to veto the decisions of the Security Council.

Two major problems that must be solved to insure world peace have not been resolved by the Security Council, in part because Russia has used the veto, but mainly because distrust between Communist and non-Communist nations has grown stronger since the war. One of these problems is control of atomic weapons; the other is the organization of an international police force.

The UN set up a commission to study the control of atomic weapons and atomic power. The commission recommended methods of control. Its plan included international inspection of all atomic plants and installations. Russia has refused to let anyone inspect Russian atomic installations. Two reasons, both of which stem from the nature of the Soviet Union and its totalitarian government, help to explain this refusal.

First, the Russian people live in a controlled state, a closed society. Communist officials apparently fear that allowing UN inspection teams to roam at will through the Soviet Union could

Seating of Red China. George Bush (left), U.S. Ambassador to the UN, Sir Colin Crowe of the United Kingdom, and Yakov Malik of the Soviet Union confer during the seating of Red China to the Security Council of the UN in 1972.

FIGHTING DISEASE. Dusting teams, supplied by UNICEF with DDT powder, are giving the inhabitants of a remote village in Peru a thorough spraying. Thanks to the work of the UN teams, typhus was virtually eliminated in the village.

undermine their control. Second, the Russian leaders have always stressed secrecy and have long been suspicious of the West. They are not anxious to let potential adversaries, the non-Communist world, know anything about their nuclear capabilities. In an open society such as the United States with its free press it is difficult to conceal governmental activities from the world. On the other hand, we know only what the Soviet leaders wish us to know about most of the activities within the Soviet Union.

Russia has also frustrated the UN's attempts to form a permanent international police force. The Charter provides for the establishment of a UN military staff and an army large enough to keep peace in trouble spots of the world. However, the Russians have vetoed all attempts to organize such a force.

The UN has accomplished much. Despite the stalemates and difficulties caused by Russia's repeated use of the veto, the UN has compiled an impressive record of achievement since it was organized in 1945. Even before its formal organization, the UN was at work providing relief for the people of war-torn areas. The UN Relief and Rehabilitation Administration, or UNRRA, was set up in 1943 and did valuable work for several years before other permanent agencies of the UN took over parts of its work.

Another important agency is the International Refugee Organization which was established after World War II to find homes for displaced persons. The homes of many displaced persons were in countries occupied by Soviet troops. In the post-war period these countries became Russian satellites behind the Iron Curtain. Many of the refugees did not want to go back and live under a Communist dictatorship.

The World Health Organization (WHO) is trying to stamp out disease in parts of the world where medical care has previously been almost unknown. There are UN organizations to study food problems, labor problems, transportation, and communication. All are laying a valuable groundwork for peace. To learn how such specialized agencies work, let us look a little more closely at one of the most important.

UNESCO attempts to instill the ideas of peace in the minds of men. The Constitution of UNESCO (the United Nations Educational, Scientific, and Cultural Organization), adopted in Paris in 1945, states that ". . . since wars begin in the minds of men, it is in the minds of men that the defenses of peace must be constructed." There, in a few words, is the purpose of UNESCO —promoting international understanding.

Julian Huxley, the British biologist who served two years as the first director-general of UNESCO, said the aim of UNESCO is ". . . to help strengthen the peace and to help raise human welfare through science, education, and culture." To dissolve the prejudices of people, to build the ideas of peace and international understanding, will clearly take a long time. Thus UNESCO is a long-range program.

In its organization, UNESCO follows the general pattern of the UN Charter. There is a director-general and an international staff of some seven hundred clerks, research workers, and others. The headquarters are at UNESCO House, a former hotel near the Arch of Triumph in Paris. Each year the member nations meet to decide the policies and programs of work. UNESCO now has over one hundred members and associate members, including several Communist countries. It has sponsored educational projects in many countries. It maintains offices in Africa, Asia, and Latin America that are centers of scientific and technical information for peoples of underdeveloped areas. The new African nations, especially, have taken useful advantage of UNESCO's facilities. UNESCO has also encouraged the exchange of teachers and students among various nations in order to foster international understanding.

UNESCO is only one of the UN's specialized agencies. Another important one is the International Children's Emergency Fund, or UNICEF. It has cared for and treated millions of sick, starving, and homeless children in some ninety countries.

The UN helped to establish the nation of Israel. Besides teaching peace and preventing war, the UN tries to stop wars that break out anywhere in the world. Let us see what the UN did to stop a serious war in Palestine. We shall have to go back to the early years of the present century to understand the situation in the ancient

MARINE BIOLOGY COURSE. As part of the UNESCO program, an international course in Marine Biology was held in Bombay, India, in 1958. In this picture, the Director of the Institute of Science in Bombay is describing the characteristics of local marine animals to Bombay's Deputy Minister for Education.

Holy Land that caused so much trouble after the end of World War II.

As you read in Chapter 18, the Jews lost their homeland centuries ago and became scattered about the world. They suffered persecution and were a minority group in many different countries. At the beginning of the twentieth century a number of prominent Jews founded the Zionist (*zy*-un-ist) movement. (Zion is a Hebrew name for Jerusalem.) The Zionists wanted to establish a homeland for Jews. Naturally, they hoped to go back to their ancient home in Palestine. The Turkish Empire had controlled Palestine for centuries. So the Zionists got permission from the Turks to buy some land and make a few Jewish settlements in their ancient homeland.

By the outbreak of World War I, several thousand Jews had established themselves in Palestine. During the war, Turkey fought on the side of the Germans, and the British conquered Palestine.

SHOES FOR GREEK CHILDREN. New shoes made from leather supplied by UNICEF are being tried on with much pleasure by children in a day nursery in Athens, Greece.

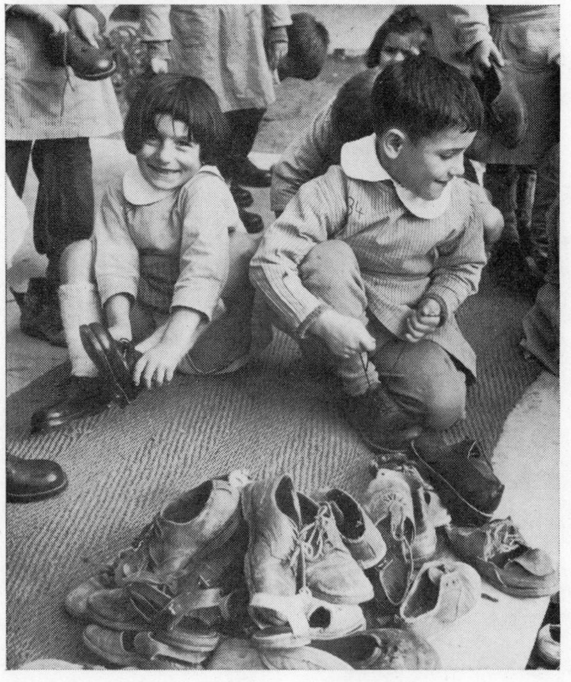

In the peace treaty the British received a mandate over the territory. While the war was still going on, Lord Balfour, the British Minister of Foreign Affairs, had written in an official letter that:

> ". . . [the British government favors] the establishment in Palestine of a national home for the Jewish people and will use their best endeavors to facilitate the achievement of that object; it being clearly understood that nothing shall be done which may prejudice the civil and religious rights of existing non-Jewish communities in Palestine."

The statement became known as the *Balfour Declaration.* When the British took over control of Palestine, they began to carry out the policy. In the next twenty years thousands of Jews settled in Palestine. They made great progress in agriculture and manufacturing, set up schools, built irrigation projects, and generally improved the country.

As the Jewish communities developed, however, the Arabs began to fear that they would be outnumbered and would lose control of their own land. There was some ill feeling and trouble before World War II. After the war, it became more serious. The Jews, who had been horribly persecuted in Nazi-held territory, thought of Palestine as their promised land. Most of those who lived through the Nazi horrors wanted to go to the Jewish homeland.

The British were in a difficult position. They wanted to follow the Balfour Declaration and also to keep the Moslem world's friendship. All the Moslem states were opposed to any more Jewish immigration. Thousands of Jews had no place else to go. The Jews in Palestine were determined to bring in all who wanted to come. They also wanted to become independent of the Arab states surrounding their homeland. Warfare broke out, and the British suppressed it, but they could not solve the difficulties.

Finally the British announced that they would turn the Palestine problem over to the UN and that they would get out of Palestine on May 15, 1948. The UN adopted a resolution calling for

FORTIFYING THE GAZA STRIP. Major General Moshe Dayan, Chief of Staff of Israel's army, is shown digging in after Israel occupied this coastal area during the 1956 Suez crisis. A UN task force now patrols it.

the partition of Palestine and the establishment of a new, independent Jewish state. Neither side liked the decision. The Jews believed they were entitled to more territory than the UN proposed for the new state. The Arab states were determined that there should be no Jewish state at all.

On May 14, 1948, the day before the British finally withdrew from Palestine, the Jews proclaimed the state of Israel as a new and independent nation. The Arab states at once went to war with the new state. The UN urged the armies of both sides to cease fire, but neither obeyed. The UN sent a mediation committee headed by Count Folke Bernadotte of Sweden to arrange an armistice. In September, Bernadotte was assassinated in Jerusalem. The achievement of peace seemed an impossible task. Fanatics on both sides refused to listen to reason. The assassination of Count Bernadotte put the burden on the shoulders of Bernadotte's assistant, an American named Ralph J. Bunche.

Dr. Bunche, who was born in Detroit, Michigan, is the grandson of a slave. He was graduated from the University of California at Los Angeles and became a teacher. He was particularly interested in the problems of colonial government. In his study of colonial peoples and their problems, he decided he needed to know more about the backgrounds of the people themselves. So he worked to become an expert in anthropology, or the study of man. Bunche became an adviser to the

BUNCHE AND BEN GURION. Dr. Ralph Bunche (*right*), United Nations Mediator for Palestine, is pictured in Tel Aviv conferring with Israeli Prime Minister David Ben-Gurion. The armistice Dr. Bunche negotiated was an important victory for the United Nations, as well as a personal victory for Dr. Bunche.

The Suez Canal is a point of separation, but also a point of contention between Israel and Egypt. The UN observers are part of the maintainence force in the canal zone and will help clear the waterway of sunken ships.

State Department. He joined the UN when the organization was setting up its Trusteeship Council to handle the problems of colonial peoples. The UN sent him as an assistant to the mediator in Palestine. On Bernadotte's death, Bunche became acting mediator.

He worked with tact and persistence. The Israeli army proved to be stronger than the armies of the Arab states, and finally Bunche was able to convince the Arab states that they should give up. He got both sides together, arranged an armistice, and started the work of drawing up permanent peace treaties. For his work in Palestine, Dr. Bunche received the Nobel Peace Prize in 1950.

Dr. Bunche became an honored man throughout the world. He continued to seek peaceful solutions to world problems wherever they arose. The world lost a great statesman when he died in 1971 after a prolonged illness.

The first president of Israel was Dr. Chaim Weizmann, a research chemist and a leader in the Zionist movement. The constitution under which he served contains a bill of rights much like that in our Constitution. It provides for a parliamentary government like that of the British. Schools and a university were established. In 1949 the United States loaned Israel a hundred million dollars to help develop agricultural production. Despite the problems of increasing immigration and clashes with the Moslems, Israel is a firmly established republic. In 1949 she became the fifty-ninth member of the UN.

The UN continues to work for peace. Besides its establishment of Israel as a nation, the UN has also achieved other successes since its organization. It has been particularly effective in settling international disputes that might otherwise have erupted into serious crises. Although its charter limits its powers, the more than 100 members of the UN have on numerous occasions been able to use the force of public opinion to reduce tension in trouble spots.

Among the major actions of the UN have been: obtaining the withdrawal of Russian occupation troops from Iran (1946); assisting in free elections in South Korea and the establishment of the Republic of South Korea (1947); arranging a truce between India and Pakistan over the control of Kashmir (1949); organizing a military force to halt Communist aggression in Korea (1950); condemning Russia for "depriving Hungary of its liberty and independence" (1956); using UN troops to keep peace in Suez (1956); collecting money to aid Hungarian refugees (1957), and reducing tension in the Congo (1963).

In 1971 the Peoples Republic of China (Communist China) was voted into the UN and Nationalist China (Formosa) was forced out of the Security Council and the Assembly. Some felt that Communist China would obstruct the cause of peace and pursue its own interests. Most, however, considered the Peoples Republic's place in the UN a definite advantage, because the forum of the UN would serve as a common meeting ground where differences could be aired and problems solved.

Chapter Check-up

1. What chain of events led to the organization of the UN?
2. What important purposes of the UN are stated in the Preamble of the United Nations Charter?
3. What part does the General Assembly play in the work of the UN?
4. What is the main function of the Security Council?
5. Which five nations are permanently represented in the Security Council?
6. What is the veto power? How has Russia used it to her advantage?
7. Why has the UN been unable to reach agreement on the international control of atomic weapons?
8. Do you think Communist China's admission to the UN has helped the cause of peace? Explain your answer.

CHAPTER 79

The Cold War Between Communism and Democracy Has Made Peace Uncertain

THE UNITED STATES AND RUSSIA COMPETED FOR WORLD LEADERSHIP

World War II caused a shift in the balance of power among nations. We saw in the last chapter how the Allies established the UN, basing their hopes for peace on the co-operation of the five great powers. They felt that the strong nations could keep peace if they came to an agreement on world problems by discussing them in the Security Council. The plan looked like a good one, but there were several serious obstacles.

In the first place, at the end of the war there were not five equally strong nations, each one powerful enough to influence the actions of the others. Instead there were only two great world powers: the United States and the Soviet Union. Every world issue became a tug of war between the two. What happened to Britain, France, and China? Let us look briefly at each.

After the defeat of the Spanish Armada in 1588, Britain began to grow as a world power. The British built a vast empire, and their mighty navy ruled the seas. With their sea power and their policy of preserving the balance of power, they did much to keep the world at peace during the century before World War I. But the frightful cost of two world wars left Britain bankrupt at the end of World War II. All foreign investments had been sold to pay for the wars. The interest payments from these investments had made the difference between poverty and prosperity, and the disappearance of that source of revenue severely crippled Britain's economy.

Following World War II the British people had to live under an "austerity" program to keep down the cost of imports. Since much of their food had

THE TROOPS RETURN. Within six months after the end of the war, the bulk of American forces had been withdrawn from Europe. Later, our diplomats regretted our too rapid demobilization.

to be imported, food was strictly rationed. The government worked desperately to sell more goods abroad than were imported. The loss of some of Britain's colonies (particularly India) eliminated many profitable British markets and made the government's task extremely difficult.

Trouble in Northern Ireland still plagued the British, but in 1972 admission to the European Common Market seemed to indicate a new and stronger economic future. Resilience and determination made Britain great in the past, and these qualities will help her in the future, but she no longer ruled as Brittania once did.

France was overrun by the Nazis and, as you read in Chapter 38, was devastated by the war. The French, who had been divided and weakened by the Nazi occupation, were in no position to make their influence felt in the immediate post-war period.

China was torn by civil war, as you learned in Chapter 62, and fell to the Communists. The Nationalist government, headed by Chiang Kai-shek, lost the mainland of China and was forced to retreat to the island of Formosa. The Nationalist government had a permanent seat in the UN Security Council but Communist China is now in their place. The China mainland is Communist, and Formosa's influence is small.

The United States became the leader of the Western democracies. You may recall that after World War I the American people had demanded the immediate demobilization of American armed forces. The same demand was made after World War II. Most Americans thought that we should reduce our large wartime army and navy to a small standby force. There seemed little risk in this act. We had faith in the ability of our wartime allies to make the UN an effective agency for preserving peace. In addition, our industrial, scientific, and technological advantage over all other nations made us feel secure. Until 1949 the United States alone possessed the secret of the atomic bomb.

Our aims, in war and in peace, were clear. We wanted no conquests. We rejected the idea that to the victors belong the spoils. We still wanted to "make the world safe for democracy." Most Americans had given up their belief in isolationism, which had been very strong in our country after World War I. This time we appeared ready to accept the responsibility of leadership of the Western democracies. We helped feed, clothe, and rebuild war-ravaged countries.

We hoped to work in peace and harmony with Soviet Russia. We were willing to compromise, as the Russians said they were. But we soon found that the Communists' idea of compromise meant doing everything Russia wanted.

The Soviet Union became the leader of the Communist nations. The shift in the position and power of nations as a result of World War II benefited Russia. The Soviet Union became the most powerful nation in Asia and Europe.

After the defeat of the Germans, the Russians no longer feared invasion across the level plains on their western border. The decline of British power meant that the Russians did not have to worry about the balance of power in Europe. Russia knew the British could no longer juggle the balance, siding first with one nation and then with another to block Russian ambitions. With France in a weakened condition, there was no nation in Europe which alone could oppose the ambitions of the Soviet Union.

Stalin and other Communist leaders believed that the Soviet Union could become as great a world power as the United States. They sought to extend Russian influence by any means. At the end of the war, when the United States quickly reduced her armed forces, Russia kept hers at wartime strength. Today the Soviet Union has about three and a half million men under arms and many more in reserve.

It soon became clear that Russia planned to get control of all the territory she could without fighting for it. Her army was used mainly as a threat. Stalin feared that outright military aggression on the part of Russia would give the United States a reason to unleash an atomic attack. He tried to increase Russia's power by setting up puppet governments in the countries under Russia's control, and by spreading communist propaganda in an effort to win other countries over to the communist camp.

Russia dropped the Iron Curtain between the East and West. Before the end of the war, Russia occupied most of the Eastern European states, as you read in Part 16. At the Yalta Conference in 1945 and at the Potsdam Conference after the defeat of Germany, the United States and Britain insisted that as soon as possible the people of the occupied Eastern European states should freely elect their own governments. At first Russia agreed. Later, however, she broke her promise and set up Communist governments in all the occupied states.

COMMUNIST LEADERS. In January, 1965, leaders of Communist nations met in Warsaw for a meeting of the Warsaw Treaty Organization (Warsaw Pact), a mutual defense alliance set up by the USSR in opposition to NATO. Pictured here at a reception are, from left to right, A. N. Kosygin, USSR, W. Gomulka, Poland, W. Ulbricht, East Germany, G. Dej and I. G. Maurer, Romania, and L. I. Brezhnev, USSR.

Poland in particular became a problem. Russia, you will remember, took a large piece of territory from Poland early in the war. At that time Russia had an agreement with Hitler, and a piece of Poland was the price Stalin asked for his neutrality in the war. At the end of the war, Russia proposed to keep her Polish territory. She offered Poland a section of German territory to make up for the Polish land Russia held.

Britain and the United States would not agree to such an arrangement. They could do little about it then, but they insisted that in the German peace treaty the whole question of Polish borders would have to be worked out. Russia agreed but has never allowed the matter to be settled.

In the months after the war, the Western democracies tried to settle issues by compromising. Always the Russians did as they pleased. We were getting nowhere, but we still hoped for some sign of co-operation.

In March, 1946, Winston Churchill came to the United States. Although he was not at that time head of the British government, his words carried great weight in the world. He was invited to speak at a college in Missouri. President Truman went to Fulton with Churchill and sat on the platform as the British statesman spoke. In his speech, Churchill openly denounced Russia. He pointed out that the Communists were trying to expand their power at the expense of the democracies. He said that Russia had created an "Iron Curtain" between the communist world and the democratic world. It was the first use of a term that has since come into general use. Churchill further called on America and Britain to join in a "fraternal association" to defeat Russia's aggressive ambitions.

His frank speech shocked many people, particularly the leaders of Soviet Russia. The fact that the President of the United States was on the platform with Churchill gave even more force to what was said. Churchill's forthright words did not change the fundamental policy of the Russian leaders, but it did force the people of the democ-

Yalta Conference. Churchill, Roosevelt, and Stalin smile broadly as they sit in the patio of Livadia Palace at Yalta. During this eight-day conference, the "big three" made agreements about what would take place after the defeat of Germany. Many of these agreements were later broken by the Soviet Union.

racies to face the facts. At this point Americans began to realize there was a real war going on, even though it was not a shooting war. We came to understand slowly that we had to do something in the struggle with world communism.

Certain extremists became so disturbed by the Russian threat that they became convinced that the United States should wage a "preventive war." They meant by this that we should make war on Russia while we were still the only nation that possessed atomic weapons. Otherwise, they argued, Russia might become strong enough to defeat us. But the idea of a "preventive war" was unthinkable to Americans, regardless of the threat from Russia. Such a war would be contrary to every moral and ethical principle that the United States stood for. Any thought of a preventive war as a means of stemming Russian power was immediately rejected. Instead we adopted a vigorous and farsighted program which included the Truman Doctrine, the Marshall Plan, and the North Atlantic Treaty Organization.

THE COLD WAR BEGAN

Communist aggression in Greece was answered by the Truman Doctrine. The one Balkan country that the Russians did not occupy at the end of the war was Greece. There the British army had helped drive the Nazis out. Britain favored the return of the Greek king, and in 1946 the Greek people voted to restore the monarchy.

The Greek people had suffered terribly in the war. Hunger, disorganization, and ineffective government made the peasants easy prey for communism. Supported by the Communist-dominated countries on the Greek borders, guerrilla bands kept up a civil war in Greece. In 1946 the UN sent a commission to find out what was going on. It was clear that the continuing unrest was an attempt by Russia to drop the Iron Curtain around still another country.

The British found in 1947 that they could not give the Greek government the men and money necessary to hold off the communist threat. President Truman asked Congress to appropriate enough money for the United States to come to the assistance of Greece. He pointed out that we urgently needed to keep communism from spreading and to contain it within its present borders. His policy of "containing" communism became known as the *Truman Doctrine.*

After Congress voted the money, we sent men, arms, and supplies to the Greek government and thus began to actively meet the challenge of Soviet Russia. We decided we would face the threat of communism and try to defeat it wherever we met it.

The Marshall Plan helped stop the spread of communism in Europe. General George C. Marshall, then United States Secretary of State, made a short but extremely important speech at Harvard University on June 5, 1947. Here is a quotation from his speech:

> "Our policy is not directed against any country or doctrine, but against hunger, poverty, desperation, and chaos. Its purpose should be the revival of a working economy in the world so as to permit the emergence of political and social conditions in which free institutions can exist."

He did not name Russia in his speech, but everybody knew to whom his remarks were directed when he said:

> "Any government which maneuvers to block recovery of other countries cannot expect help from us. Furthermore, governments, political parties, or groups which seek to perpetuate human misery in order to profit therefrom politically or otherwise will encounter the opposition of the United States."

Marshall's speech was received with enthusiasm by the European democracies. They organized the European Recovery Program, which came to be known as the *Marshall Plan.* Russia and the countries she controlled refused to join.

The Marshall Plan was a method of co-operation between the United States and all the European countries that joined. We served as the banker and advanced the money necessary to help Europe rebuild and "get on its feet." The loans we provided were used for industrial machinery, farm machinery, hand tools, seed, cattle, and other things that would help the people of Europe to help themselves.

Western Europe achieved its present prosperity, however, not only through American aid, but by organizing economic alliances. The most important were Benelux (about which you read in Part 11); the Schuman Plan, or European Coal and Steel Community; and the European Economic Community, or Common Market.

The Schuman Plan, established by treaty in 1951, pooled Western Europe's coal and steel resources under a single authority. The Common Market, established in 1957, was an even more important step toward unity. The Treaty of Rome, which created the Common Market, was signed by six nations: France, West Germany, Italy, Belgium, the Netherlands, and Luxembourg. The treaty provided for merging the six countries into a single economic unit with a common tariff. This would be accomplished in three stages over a period of fifteen years. Already, the Common Market has helped raise Europeans' standard of living to a level far higher than before the war. In 1972, Britain, Norway, Denmark, and Ireland were let in to the Common Market.

Berlin became the center of the cold war in the West. Disagreement between Russia and the Western democracies was sharpest over the future of Germany. In 1947 a meeting of the four major powers reached no agreement, and the United States, Britain, and France decided to unite their respective zones and allow a return of self-government. The Soviet government denounced this action. When Soviet criticism failed to stop the other three governments from going ahead with their plan, the Russians attempted to force them out of Berlin.

You will recall that Berlin was located entirely within the Russian zone of Germany (see the map below). At the conclusion of World War II, it had been agreed that the four powers would each control a sector of Berlin. Russia agreed to allow the Western powers access to their sectors of Berlin through a narrow corridor. In June of 1948 Soviet troops closed the corridor on the excuse that some bridges along the access route needed to be repaired.

The Western Allies responded to this act by organizing what was known as the "Berlin airlift." For more than a year, through the stormy winter of 1948–49, American and British planes carried more than two million tons of food and fuel. They made over 270,000 flights into West Berlin. Simultaneously, all shipments to the Russian zone of Germany from western Germany were cut off. By the fall of 1949 Russia admitted defeat. The Soviet government agreed to reopen the corridor if the West would stop its blockade.

The problem of Berlin is still not settled. A new crisis was touched off in the summer of 1961 when the Soviet puppet government in East Germany forbade all East German citizens from entering West Berlin. The Communists erected

Berlin Air Lift. A group of Berliners are standing on a rubble pile to watch the constant stream of planes coming into Templehof Airport with food and fuel for the western sector of Berlin.

a wall in the city to help stem the tide of refugees fleeing from Communist East Germany.

The Western democracies joined in NATO. The Charter of the United Nations recognized the right of nations to join in mutual agreements for defense. The Berlin crisis convinced the United States that economic reconstruction of Europe was not enough. The Western democracies needed greater military unity. The Pan-American nations had pledged themselves to come to each other's aid in case of attack. Next, the nations of the North Atlantic area agreed in 1949 to join forces, rearm, and fight together in case any member nation was attacked.

Again, it was the United States that led in the formation of the North Atlantic Treaty Organization. We were the best prepared, and it was from the factories of America that many of the new machines of war had to come. General Dwight D. Eisenhower became commander-in-chief of the NATO forces. Eisenhower gave the morale of all Western Europe a great lift when he arrived in Paris to organize his forces early in 1951.

Communist victory in China created new problems in the cold war. While the democracies were gaining ground or holding their own in Europe, communism was gathering adherents in Asia. You read in the story of China how the Chinese Communists defeated the Nationalist government and took over all of China except the island of Formosa. The Russians demanded that the Communist government of China take over China's seat in the Security Council of the United Nations. The United States refused to give in to the demand. The democracies, however, did not agree among themselves on the China issue. Britain and India recognized the Communist government of China, while we refused to do so.

We should note that even in the United States there was a great difference of opinion over our China policy. The United States had at first aided Chiang Kai-shek's government with money and weapons. But we stopped much of our aid because many Americans believed that Chiang could not win. His government, they thought, was too corrupt and had lost the support of most Chinese. Other Americans, who saw how effective our aid to Europe was, maintained that stopping aid to Chiang was exactly what the Communists wanted.

Russia kept demanding that the Nationalist China representative in the UN be unseated and a representative of Communist China be substituted. In January, 1950, Russia finally walked out of the Security Council and refused to take part in any UN activity at which a Chinese delegate was present.

The Soviet boycott of the UN—particularly of the Security Council—seemed to be a serious problem at first. Could the UN accomplish anything if Russia refused to discuss matters with the democratic nations? As it turned out, the boycott was Russia's big mistake. When the North Korean Communists invaded the Republic of Korea (South Korea) in June, 1950, Russia was not in the Security Council. That made it possible for the other members of the United Nations to

SIGNING OF THE NUCLEAR TEST BAN TREATY. Signing the treaty from left to right are American Secretary of State Dean Rusk, Soviet Foreign Minister Andrei Gromyko, and British Foreign Secretary Lord Home (later Prime Minister).

take positive action against North Korea, as you saw in Chapter 63. The action, which marked the first time troops had ever gone into battle at the request of an international organization, demonstrated the determination of the United Nations not to be bullied in the cold war.

The cold war has followed an uneven path. On the surface the cold war appears to be a clash of interests between the United States and the Communist nations, but it is actually far more than that. The cold war is a struggle rooted deeply in the minds of men. It is a conflict between the democratic way of life and the Communist pattern, a conflict between those who want to defend the rights of man and those who would destroy individual liberty.

The tension generated by this conflict has varied in intensity during the last fifteen years. From 1950 to 1953, the two blocs fought an undeclared shooting war in Korea (see page 609). Then, after Stalin's death in 1953, international tensions eased somewhat. An Austrian peace treaty was concluded and both Allied and Russian troops were withdrawn from Austria. Soviet Premier Khrushchev re-established friendly relations between Russia and Yugoslavia. Poland was allowed to develop a kind of national communism which allowed the Poles some freedom from Soviet control. However, any illusions that the West may have had about a permanent change of heart on the part of Soviet leaders were soon shattered by the Hungarian revolution of 1956 (see page 511).

In the 1956–57 period the Hungarian incident, along with the Suez crisis in the Middle East (see page 646) and the launching of Russia's first space satellite (see page 780), heightened tensions between the Soviet Union and the Western nations. However, armed conflict was avoided and by 1959 the cold war entered another brief period of thaw. The Soviet Union and the United States each held well-attended exhibits in the other's country. In September of 1959, Premier Khrushchev himself visited the United States to tour the country and confer with President Eisenhower.

This period of improved relations was temporary. In May of 1960, Khrushchev angrily charged the United States with "aggression" because of the flight of an American U-2 aircraft over Russia. He used the incident as an excuse to break up a scheduled summit meeting in Paris. A short time later, he demanded that UN headquarters be moved out of the United States. In the summer of 1961, Khrushchev created a new crisis over Berlin by threatening to sign a separate peace treaty with the East German Communist regime. This action would have imperiled American access rights to West Berlin. The threat was underscored when the East German regime erected a wall in Berlin to prevent the flight of Germans living within the Communist zone. Then, to the dismay of an outraged world, the Soviet Union abandoned the moratorium on testing of nuclear weapons that had existed since 1959. Within two months, Russia exploded over thirty nuclear bombs, adding enormous quantities of deadly radioactive matter to the earth's atmosphere. President Kennedy, faced with the need to protect the security of the United States, reluctantly ordered the resumption of American testing in 1962. The Russians countered with another round of their own tests.

The climax to this dangerous chain of events came in October of 1962. American reconnaissance planes had taken pictures proving that the Soviet Union was building missile bases in Cuba. The range of the missiles would cover most of North America and much of South America. President Kennedy's response was to use the United States Navy to "quarantine" Cuba so no additional missiles could be shipped to the island. Soviet ships bound for Cuba were stopped and inspected. Kennedy also demanded that the missile bases be dismantled and the missiles themselves removed. This demand was backed by an immediate build-up of American military power in the Caribbean area. After several tense days, the Soviet Union agreed to dismantle the bases and remove the missiles.

Another thaw in the cold war followed the Cuban missile crisis. For not only had the crisis showed plainly the dangers of the cold war, but the Soviet Union was having economic troubles at home. An especially serious problem was the failure of Russian farms to produce enough food. By the end of 1963, the Soviet Union was forced to follow in China's footsteps and buy grain from the West. Then there was the Soviet-Chinese rift, about which you read in Part 19. The image of the Communist world as a monolith, or "single stone," was shattered as Communist parties throughout the world split into pro-Soviet and pro-Chinese factions. At the same time that the Communist movement was being weakened,

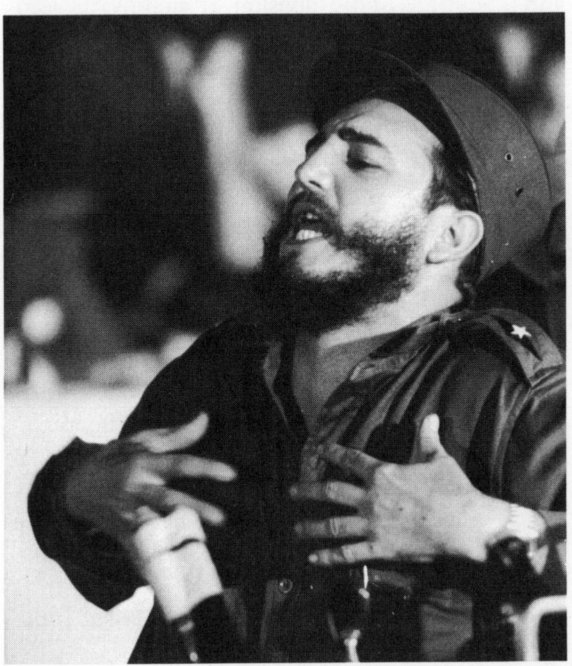

FIDEL CASTRO. The flamboyant Cuban leader is shown here in a characteristic pose. Cuba is still burdened by its one crop economy: sugar.

the military and economic strength of the West were greater than ever. Confronted with this situation the Soviet Union became less aggressive.

One of the most important results of the new cold-war thaw was the limited nuclear test ban treaty negotiated in the summer of 1963 by the United States, Britain, and the Soviet Union. All tests in the air and underwater were banned. In 1967, President Johnson and Premier Kosygin met in Glassboro, N.J., in an attempt to ease differences. In 1972, President Nixon visited the Soviet Union in the hope that further understandings between the two countries would be achieved. Tension seemed to be lessened by disarmament pacts, but suspicion is still great in the United States over Soviet world policy.

THE PROBLEMS OF THE LESS DEVELOPED NATIONS HAVE CAUSED INCREASING CONCERN

The world is divided between North and South as well as between East and West. Because most of the world's Communist nations are east of Western Europe, we often label them the "East." This East-West division, as we have seen, is primarily one of ideas. It is a division between those who advocate a totalitarian society with emphasis upon the power of the state, and those who advocate a democratic society with emphasis on individual rights. However, the world can be divided another way—between "North" and "South." This division is mainly an economic one. It is between the advanced, highly industrialized countries, most of whom are in the northern half of the world, and the economically underdeveloped countries, most of whom are in the southern part. (Communist China is the notable exception.)

The majority of the underdeveloped nations are in Africa, Asia, and Latin America. From your study of these regions in *Story of Nations*, you know that they comprise a variety of cultures and political systems. Some areas, like the Indus Valley and the Nile Valley, were ancient cradles of civilization. Others have entered the mainstream of history comparatively recently. In India and Southeast Asia, the people are largely Hindu and Buddhist in their religion. In the Middle East and North Africa, Islam is the dominant religion, and in Latin America, it is Christianity. Some of the Nations, like India and Ghana are democratic republics. Others, like Nigeria and Paraguay are dictatorships.

But the underdeveloped nations have two important characteristics in common. First, with only a few exceptions, all were at one time either colonized outright or dominated politically and economically by European powers or the United States. Thus there are bitter memories and a lingering resentment toward the West among the people of the underdeveloped countries. Second, the great majority of these countries, being underdeveloped, are poor. The average individual income for all the countries of Africa, Asia, and Latin America taken together is about $100 a year. In the United States it is about $3,900 a year.

Geography and population factors work against the underdeveloped countries. The continents of Asia, Africa, and South America contain vast natural resources, including iron ore and other important minerals. But there are some crucial gaps. For example, both Africa and South America are deficient in the most important source of cheap power—coal. You will remember that when the industrial revolution began in Britain, there were ample quantities of both iron and coal. In Western Europe, too, large iron and coal deposits are found close together, as they are in the western part of the Soviet Union and in the Midwestern United States.

Hydroelectric power can be developed as a substitute for coal—as, in fact, is being done on a large scale in Brazil and West Africa. But dams

THE PEACE CORPS. Through agencies such as the Peace Corps, the United States helps other countries of the world solve problems of the lack of education and economic underdevelopment. Here a volunteer Peace Corps worker chats with children in Borel, a slum on the outskirts of Rio de Janeiro, Brazil.

and other installations require great amounts of initial capital, which if not available in the countries themselves, must be obtained through foreign aid or private investments from abroad. Political instability and other factors often impede the flow of capital.

Even in agriculture, geography has not always favored the underdeveloped nations. The Middle East and North Africa, for example, are largely made up of arid and semi-arid land that can support few people. For those countries that lie in the tropics, the long growing season is offset by poor soils that tend to be quickly worn out when cultivated.

The single greatest problem of the underdeveloped countries, however, is too many people. High birth rates added to declining death rates have given Asia, Latin America, and parts of Africa the highest rates of population increase in the world. The population of Latin America, for example, is increasing at an annual rate of about 2.5 per cent. This means that the population will *double* every twenty-seven and a half years. Confronted with such an increase, many of the poorer countries are having trouble keeping living standards from going down, let alone improving them. Several countries have taken measures to control the rate of population increase, but so far without success except in a few areas.

The underdeveloped nations need help to make progress. Problems of geography and overpopulation are not the only difficulties. Cultural and educational handicaps exist as well. In many parts of Africa and Asia, progress must be made despite resistance from a traditional culture which views progress as something alien and to be feared. India, with its caste system, is an example (see page 574). Modern education is the answer to this problem, but teachers are so scarce in most of the countries that educational progress is slow. This is one reason Peace Corps volunteers from the United States, the majority of whom are teachers, are so much in demand.

The Peace Corps is one means by which the United States helps the underdeveloped nations. Foreign aid is another. Western European countries also send aid to their former colonies. The emphasis today, however, is on trade. The colonial powers, influenced by the theory of mercantilism (see page 302), used their colonies mainly as sources of raw materials. Those colonies now comprise the majority of the underdeveloped nations. As a result of colonial policy, many of these nations have been left dependent on exporting one or two basic commodities, such as rubber, coffee, and cacao. Low prices for these commodities mean less income for the exporter.

But the exporting countries do receive help. Thus the marketing of some products (coffee, for example) is regulated by international agreement to keep prices from falling too low. Also, the countries in the British Commonwealth get lower tariffs and other trade benefits from Britain, as do the countries in the French Community from France and the Common Market nations. In 1964, the United States offered to cut tariffs on imports from underdeveloped countries without asking cuts in tariffs on its own exports.

The problems of the underdeveloped nations endanger world peace. About two-thirds of the world's people live in economically underdeveloped countries. So great a segment of mankind, living a life of increasing frustration amid sub-standard conditions, is an obvious threat to peace. The pressure from such a situation can mount until finally it erupts in violence.

Moreover, many of these nations achieved independence at a time when a new doctrine was being preached and practiced—communism. The Soviet Union and Red China both have the advantage of not having been colonial powers. Thus Communist propagandists have tried to convince the people of the underdeveloped nations that Western Europe and the United States are imperialistic states trying to dominate the small or backward states for their own benefit. Furthermore, communism has seemed to some leaders in the underdeveloped nations a quick way for them to achieve the industrial strength they desperately want. The future of these nations, as a result, has become closely linked with the cold war.

Chapter Check-up

1. How did World War II upset the balance of power among nations?
2. How did Soviet Russia gain control of Eastern Europe?
3. What are the meanings of the terms *Iron Curtain* and *cold war?*
4. What was the Truman Doctrine and what effect did it have on the cold war?
5. How did the Marshall Plan help to rebuild Europe after World War II?
6. How did NATO strengthen the West?
7. Why has the representation of China posed a problem for the UN?
8. What difference of opinion developed over American policy toward China after World War II?
9. What are some of the problems of the underdeveloped nations? How has the West helped these nations?

CHAPTER 80

The Middle East Is One of the World's Problem Areas

THE OTTOMAN EMPIRE BECAME MODERN TURKEY

The Middle East is the crossroads of three continents. The term *Middle East* has long been applied to a vast area that includes parts of western Asia, northeastern Africa, and southeastern Europe. Largely an underdeveloped area, it has been the scene of some of the most serious threats to world peace in the past ten years.

In many ways conditions in the Middle East resemble those in the Balkan Peninsula during the nineteenth and early twentieth centuries. We saw in Chapter 75 how the conflicting ambitions of the great powers and the nationalist as-

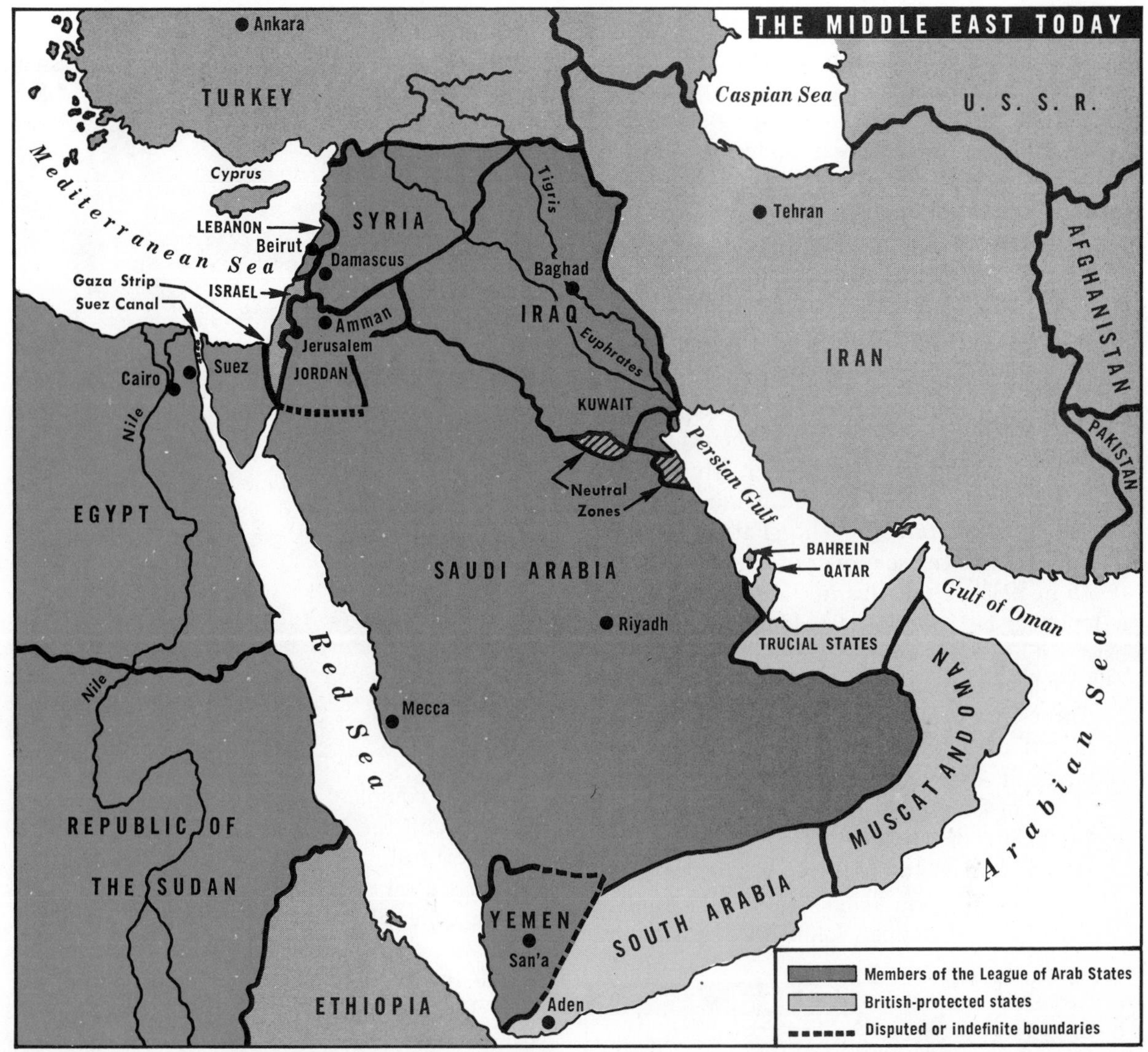

pirations of the Balkan peoples led to World War I in 1914. Many people fear that a similar clash of interests in the Middle East could provide the spark for another and far more terrible war.

Fifty years ago not many Americans were particularly concerned about the Middle East. Most of this huge but generally poor area was part of the old Byzantine Empire that had been taken over by the Ottoman Turks in the fifteenth and sixteenth centuries. As the Ottoman Empire declined in the eighteenth and nineteenth centuries, the nations of Europe saw their chance to take away some of the Turkish territory or to help Balkan nations shake off their centuries-old yoke. In the upheaval caused by World War I, in which Turkey sided with Germany and Austria-Hungary, she lost her lands along the eastern Mediterranean.

Turkey was reborn as a small but vigorous nation. Strangely enough, although most of her territories had been taken from her, Turkey revived after centuries of decay. Today she is stronger than at any time since the seventeenth

KEMAL ATATÜRK. Born Mustafa Kemal, Atatürk changed his name in 1934. Kemal means "the Perfect," and Atatürk "the father of the Turks." He was elected president in 1923, 1927, 1931, and 1935.

century. You read in Chapter 54 how the "young Turks" overthrew the Sultan of Turkey in a revolution in 1908 and tried to introduce representative government and Western educational methods. But the defeats that Turkey suffered in the Balkan conflicts and in World War I led to dictatorship instead of democracy.

A military hero of World War I, Mustafa Kemal (keh-*mahl*), who took the name of Kemal Atatürk (ah-tah-*turk*), "The Father of the Turks," became the sole ruler of Turkey until his death in 1938. Under his rule Turkey was called a republic, but political freedom did not truly exist. Opponents were sometimes summarily executed, and revolts were ruthlessly suppressed. Nevertheless, Atatürk used his dictatorial power to help Turkey become a modern, Westernized country. The capital was moved from the ancient city of Istanbul to Ankara, which was closer to the center of Turkey.

Atatürk worked to end the conservative influence of the Moslem religion and to stimulate Turkish national feeling. Church and State were separated, complete religious tolerance was proclaimed, and the schools were removed from religious control. The old code of law, which had been based on the Koran, was replaced by modern law codes like those in Switzerland, Italy, and Germany. The Latin alphabet replaced the Arabic, the Western calendar was introduced, and even the Christian day of rest, Sunday, was substituted for Friday, the day of rest fixed by Mohammed. Ancient Turkish customs were replaced by those of the West. Equal opportunities for education were offered to all. Health conditions were improved, and malaria and other diseases were nearly stamped out. Efforts were made to introduce industry. The new state developed coal mines, railroads, textile mills, and sugar refineries. Advances were made in communications, and large naval bases were built.

Twelve years after Atatürk's death free parliamentary elections were held, and the opposition party won a sweeping victory. A peaceful change of rule took place. This was probably because both parties accepted and promised to follow

Atatürk's policies regarding modernizing Turkey.

The new president, Celal Bayar (by-*ar*) came to office in 1950. He appointed an energetic and resourceful lawyer, Adnan Menderes (men-deh-*res*) as prime minister. Menderes worked hard to try to make Turkey a modern industrial nation, but he sometimes used his powers in a highhanded way. He suppressed all who criticized his rule. In 1960 the Bayar-Menderes government was overthrown by a group of army officers who ruled Turkey for over a year. In 1961 a new government was elected and General Cemal Gursel was chosen president. Tension with Greece over the Republic of Cyprus has engaged the Turkish government since 1964 when heavy fighting broke out between Greek and Turk partisans on that island. And war between the two nations was averted in 1967 by the mediation of the United States. Strained relations, however, still exist between Turkey and Greece. In 1971 Turkey agreed to ban the opium poppy, principal source of heroin, which had become a cause of friction between the United States and Turkey. Turkey is however, a staunch ally of the West, and a full fledged member of NATO.

THE ARAB STATES SEEK INDEPENDENCE AND ECONOMIC STABILITY

The other states of the Middle East have not done as well as Turkey. Few observers supposed fifty years ago that Turkey, the "sick man of Europe," would transform itself into a modern, Westernized nation. People were much more hopeful about the future of the Arab states that were breaking away from Turkish control. The histories of these states—Egypt, Lebanon, Syria, Jordan, and Iraq—show that they have not lived up to those hopes. Since their liberation from Turkey in 1918, they have been the scene of oppression, political corruption, poverty, and internal division.

After the breakup of the old Ottoman Empire at the end of World War I, most Arabs expected that they would be allowed independence. They

KING HUSSEIN. King Hussein of Jordan is shown here during a press conference in Amman, the capital. He has established a reputation as a courageous ruler, not totally shared by Israel which borders his country.

had long dreamed of shaking off Turkish rule and of reviving the great empire that once stretched from Gibraltar to the borders of India. In 1920 King Faisal I (*fy*-sal), an Arabian prince descended from the family of Mohammed, established himself as the head of an Arab state and set up his capital at Damascus. But the British and French had made a secret agreement in 1916 to divide the Asian parts of the old Turkish empire. After the war this plan received the approval of the League of Nations. France was given a mandate (the right to administer a territory) over Syria and Lebanon, and the British received mandates over Palestine and Iraq. French troops drove Faisal out of Damascus. This destruction of Arab hopes at the end of World War I caused bitter anti-Western feelings among the Arab peoples.

The state of Jordan was created by the British. You have already read about the establishment of the nation of Israel out of part of Palestine. The rest of Palestine, called Jordan, was set up as a separate kingdom in 1923. Abdullah ibn Hussein (hoo-*sine*), the older brother of King Faisal, became Jordan's first king, and the present King Hussein is his grandson.

The creation of this new state was not accomplished in answer to the wishes of its inhabitants, but as part of British policy to preserve the stability of the Middle East and to protect British interests in that area. British money financed the new state, and British officers trained a Jordanian army. King Abdullah was loyal to Britain, and his army was the best in the Middle East. But the people of Jordan never developed a strong feeling of national unity, and many thought Jordan should become part of Syria.

In 1948 Jordan's population was doubled by an influx of Palestinian refugees, most of whom were Arabs from the new state of Israel. These Arabs are strongly anti-British and anti-American because they blame England and the United States for the successful creation of Israel.

King Abdullah was assassinated in 1951. King Hussein took over at age 16. Ever since 1967 when Israel defeated the Jordanians and the United Arab Republic in the "Six Day War", Jordan has been badgered by its own people and by Palestinian guerrillas, Trying to recognize Israel and defend his nation, Hussein recently came to the U.S. for aid and assistance; maintaining himself in office while trying to make peace with Israel. This kind of politics usually doesn't last —at least in the Arab world.

Iraq is a question mark in Middle Eastern affairs. The Arab leader Faisal became king of Iraq in 1921, shortly after the French forced him to abdicate the throne of Syria. In 1925 rich deposits of oil were discovered in Iraq and developed by British, French, Dutch, and American companies. Five years later Britain ended her mandate over Iraq, and in 1932 Iraq became the first of the new Arab states to be admitted to the League of Nations. Faisal II, the grandson of Faisal I, became king in 1939.

Political conditions in Iraq were relatively stable for nearly twenty years. Under a Western-sponsored government Iraq enjoyed comparative prosperity based on huge revenues from oil. Iraq's prospects for development as a strong ally of the West looked bright. In 1958, however, Faisal's monarchy was overthrown by a nationalist group led by Abdul Karim Kassem. Faisal and the crown prince were killed and their bullet ridden bodies were displayed throughout Bagdhad.

After the successful rebellion, Kassem was proclaimed head of the government, which immediately received diplomatic recognition from the United Arab Republic.

But Kassem didn't last. He was executed in 1963 and a succession of leaders ruled until 1968 when Hassan al-Baks became president.

Iraq has maintained a generally isolated position with the rest of the world but the Kurdish problem (the Kurds are a strong non-Arab minority) has kept the country in a continual anxious position with Iran to the northeast. It is a land where justice, if it exists at all is swift and brutal, and in the 1970's Iraq is a real question mark among the civilized nations of the world.

The United States intervened in Lebanon. Lebanon, a mountainous state smaller than Con-

PRESIDENT ANWAR AL-SADAT. President Sadat of Egypt greets President Podgorny of USSR at the inauguration of the Egyptian Aswan High Dam in 1971.

necticut, lies on the Mediterranean coast between Israel and Syria. Although her population is Arab, half her people are Christian and the remainder are Moslem. In 1920 the French carved Lebanon out of Syrian territory in order to create a Christian state that would be friendly to France. Lebanon became a republic under French control in 1926, but during World War II Lebanon became completely independent. To prevent friction between Moslems and Christians the Lebanese decided that the president of the Republic must always be Christian and the prime minister Moslem.

The rebellion in Iraq in July, 1958, sent waves of political unrest through several countries in the Middle East, including Lebanon. The day after the rebellion, President Eisenhower delivered a special message to Congress in which he announced that he had ordered United States Marines into Lebanon at the request of the Lebanese president, Camille Chamoun (shuh-*moon*). The President said that Chamoun had asked for aid in putting down a Moslem rebellion supported by the United Arab Republic. The next day, the first of over fourteen thousand Marines landed in Lebanon and stood by to prevent possible trouble from the rebels. No shots were fired, however. Because Chamoun's term as president was scheduled to expire in September, the two factions in Lebanon—those favoring the West and those on the side of the United Arab Republic—agreed on a compromise candidate to succeed him. They selected General Fuad Chehab (shuh-*hob*), head of the Lebanese army.

A few days later, when all danger of an armed revolt had passed, the United States Marines were withdrawn. The intervention of American troops in Lebanon indicated United States determination to prevent pro-Western nations in the Middle East from coming under possible Communist domination. In 1964 President Charles Helou was elected to succeed President Chehab.

Syria has long been a country of turmoil. As you will remember, King Faisal established his capital at Damascus after World War I. Thus Syria expected to become the center of a powerful new Arab state. Syrian hopes were crushed, however, when the French drove King Faisal out of Damascus in 1920. The states of Lebanon and Jordan were then created out of lands which Syria claimed as her own. Since Syria is a relatively poor country without oil or industries and with large stretches of forbidding desert, her people angrily protested the loss of these territories.

The embittered Syrians stubbornly resisted French rule. Rebellions and uprisings were common. In 1925 the French had to undertake

Saudi Arabia. This Bedouin in Saudi Arabia is employed by the Aramco Oil Company as a watchman. However, he and his family continue to live in a tent on the desert near the Aramco camp.

large-scale military operations and resort to air attacks on Damascus to maintain control of Syria. In 1930 the French were finally forced to declare Syria a republic. The new constitution, however, left the French with a great measure of control. Finally, during World War II, the Syrians gained their independence. In 1946 the last French troops were withdrawn from Syria.

In 1957, a pro-Communist group gained control of Syria's government. The following year Syria merged with Egypt to form the United Arab Republic. However, Syria was dominated to a large degree by Egypt in the union, and in 1961 the Syrians withdrew from the UAR. Since then Syria has turned to the USSR for aid and has discarded all connections with the West.

Saudi Arabia is still a medieval state. The only part of the Arab world that was left free at the end of World War I was the Arabian Peninsula itself, the original homeland of the Arabs. Arabia was one of the poorest countries in the Middle East until 1933, when oil was found under its desert sands. Today Saudi Arabia produces more oil than any country in the Middle East. A thousand-mile pipeline carries the oil across the desert to the Mediterranean. Ibn Saud, who became king in 1926, enjoyed a yearly income of $160,000,000 until his death in 1953.

Saudi Arabia today is a strange mixture of old and new. The rich oil revenues provide air-conditioned automobiles and sumptuous palaces for royal officials. New schools, hospitals, hotels, and office buildings of concrete and stucco rise out of the desert. But the average Saudi still lives in a miserable hut or goatskin tent. More than three-fourths of the population is illiterate, and disease is common.

Saudi Arabia is governed by a royal prince according to the laws of the Koran. The drastic punishments meted out for criminal offenses are the same as those in force in the time of Mohammed centuries ago. For theft, the culprit's hand is amputated; a murderer is publicly beheaded with a sword. There are no labor unions, and strikes are forbidden by royal decree. Non-Moslems are not welcome in Saudi Arabia unless they are useful for some specific reason. Engineers, salesmen, traders, or others connected with the oil industry, for example, are permitted to enter the country. No Jews are ever allowed in Saudi Arabia.

The British still control rich oil lands in the Arabian Peninsula. Besides these larger Arab states, there are a few smaller ones. Among them is Yemen, governed until 1962 by a king called the Imam. In 1962, with Egyptian support, the Yemeni army overthrew the Imam and set up a republic. Forces loyal to the Imam resisted. Civil war broke out and has continued. Saudi Arabia has aided the Imam's supporters. A cease-fire was arranged in 1965, but collapsed.

Bordering Yemen on the south are a number of small Arab states known as the Aden Protectorate of Britain. The tiny port of Aden is a British feuling station and military base. Yemen lays claim to the whole of this region and frequently launches frontier raids. The British also have a number of protectorates along the northern and western shores of the Persian Gulf. The oil fields in this region, together with those of Iran, contain an estimated two-thirds of the world's known oil reserves.

Oil-rich Iran is trying to modernize. Iran (called Persia before 1935) is usually included as a nation of the Middle East. Its population is not Arab, but its people are Moslems. Iran has usually been friendly to the Western countries because it fears the Russians, who for years have dreamed of direct access to the Persian Gulf.

After World War I Britain tried to make all Iran a protectorate, but General Riza Pahlavi (pah-lah-*vee*) seized the government and was subsequently elected *shah*, or king. A constitutional monarchy, independent of foreign influence, was set up. The new shah did much to modernize the country. However, Iran, like many other countries in the Middle East, is hampered by an age-old landholding system. The majority of Iran's twenty-nine million people are tenant farmers and not much better off than serfs were in the Middle Ages. Much of the land is held by relatively few land owners.

Pahlavi's son, who became shah in 1941, has tried to reduce the difference between rich and poor. He has given away his personal lands to the farmers who worked on them, and through a land-reform law passed in 1962, he has put pressure on other landlords to divide up their lands. In 1948 a Seven-Year Plan was organized to put the rich oil revenues (over two hundred million dollars in 1962) to work in the interests of the people of Iran. The United States sent technicians to help carry out the ambitious reforms that were planned. In 1971 the United States and Great Britain extended $1 billion to Iran in anticipation of British withdrawal from her protectorate along the Persian Gulf.

TENSIONS IN THE MIDDLE EAST SHOW NO SIGNS OF EASING

The nations of the Middle East are weak and divided. You can see that the Middle East is divided into a number of troubled nations that differ greatly in wealth, religion, and people. There are Christian Arabs in Lebanon, while Israel is predominately Jewish. Islam, the major religion of the Middle East, has broken into a number of sects, as Christianity did during the Reformation. The Moslem faith of Turkey and Iran is unlike that of Saudi Arabia. Neither Turks nor Iranians, moreover, are Arabs.

Another line of division is between the "haves" and the "have-nots." Four Middle Eastern countries—Iran, Iraq, Kuwait, and Saudi Arabia—have incredibly rich oil reserves. Some of the have-not nations, led by Egypt, have been saying, "This is Arab oil, and its benefits should be shared by all Arabs." But the Arab states that have oil do not like the share-the-wealth plan.

Within each nation of the Middle East there are further divisions. There are those who want to continue the traditions of the past and those who want to introduce economic and political changes and Western ways. The conservatives are mainly the upper classes and great landowners, who have no interest in the poverty-stricken masses, and the strict Moslems, who want to follow the Koran to the letter. On the other side are the radicals, who want to make rapid changes or to create a new Arab Empire. To most of the poor, the promises of the radicals are more appealing. The many sharp differences among the peoples of the Middle East have intensified the discontent and instability in that region.

Arab leaders dream of building a united Arab nation. Arab people are scattered from the Atlantic shores of Morocco to the frontiers of Iran and Turkey. Although they have intermarried with native peoples, they all consider themselves Arabs because they speak Arabic and share Moslem culture and history.

Although the Arab nations frequently quarrel among themselves, they unite if an outside power tries to interfere with any one of them. The attack by Britain, France, and Israel on Egypt in 1956 was an example. To show their sympathy with Egypt, Syrians cut the oil pipelines that ran through their country. In nearly every Arab state there were demonstrations against the British and French.

The factor that binds the Arabs most closely together is hatred of Israel. Arabs consider the creation of Israel a great injustice. They look upon Israel as an alien state that was imposed on the Middle East by the Western powers. Having failed to defeat Israel on the battlefield, all the Arab countries maintain a relentless blockade and boycott of Israel. Egypt has closed the Suez Canal to Israeli ships. In 1967 Israel waged a lightning "Six Day War" against Egypt and Jordan and expanded its territory. Mediation has been accomplished, as both the Arab world and Israel continue to maintain hostile positions. The Arab world has turned more to the USSR for military assistance while Israel has sought and received aid from the West, especially the United States.

Chapter Check-up

1. Why is there so much bitterness toward the British and the French in the Middle East?
2. What areas are included in the Middle East?
3. Why does Turkey's location make her friendship important to the United States?
4. Describe the changes made in Turkey by Kemal Atatürk.
5. What are some of the problems and differences which divide the Middle East?
6. How is Israel a focal point for Arab unity?

CHAPTER 81

The Beginning of the Space Age Challenges Twentieth-Century Man

The Space Age began in 1957. One of man's greatest scientific adventures began on July 1, 1957, with the opening of the *International Geophysical Year*. Ten thousand scientists from sixty-seven nations agreed to co-operate in order to learn as much as possible about the earth and the space through which it moves. Of the many new scientific advances made during this International Geophysical Year, the most sensational was the launching, on October 4, 1957, of the first earth satellite, the Russian Sputnik. In 1955 both the United States and the Soviet Union had announced plans for sending aloft artificial "moons" to explore space and survey the earth. With the

APOLLO 15. In 1969, Apollo 11 landed man on the moon. In July, 1971 Apollo 15 landed. With technology more distant planets are possible to man. The moon was the first step, but man will always seek more distant worlds.

Russian achievement, the world suddenly entered a new era, the space age. Once fantastic dreams of travel to the moon and planets now appeared to be within the reach of twentieth-century man. Even more surprising, perhaps, was the fact that the Soviet Union, which had been badly crippled by World War II, had taken the lead in this technological and scientific breakthrough.

American scientists challenged the Russians in the space race. Less than four months after Sputnik was launched, on January 31, 1958, the first American satellite went into orbit from a missile testing site at Cape Canaveral, Florida (now called Cape Kennedy in honor of the late president). Called Explorer I, the satellite weighed slightly over thirty pounds and carried a payload of instruments for measuring cosmic rays and other phenomena of space.

Since 1957 both the United States and the Soviet Union have continued to send up many additional space satellites. American satellites have usually been smaller than their Soviet counterparts, because the Russian launching rockets have been much more powerful engines. But the more complicated technical equipment carried by the American satellites has probably made them more useful scientific instruments.

Satellites in an earth orbit have greatly increased man's knowledge of the planet and of space. Weather satellites, such as the United States TIROS, have provided new data about storms and opened a new era in weather forecasting. Communications satellites have made it possible to relay live television programs between different parts of the globe. Scientific satellites and space probes have been launched by both the USSR and the U.S. Both nations have sent satellites into orbit around the moon and relayed back to earth pictures of the moon's surface. And both nations have achieved controlled instrument-landings on the moon's surface. A Russian space probe reached Venus and a United States vehicle photographed Mars and sent pictures back to earth. Military satellites can detect missile firings and help defend against possible aggression.

The Soviet Union achieved another first in space on April 12, 1961 when Yuri A. Gagarin became the first man in space, and the first to orbit the earth. In the same year another Russian, Gherman Titov, made a seventeen-orbit flight around the earth. Russia's powerful rockets have also enabled her to launch the first group flights. In 1964 the USSR sent up a spacecraft with three men on board.

American astronauts prepare to go to the moon. The United States program for manned space flights, under the direction of a National Aeronautics and Space Administration (NASA), began with Project Mercury. It has continued with Projects Gemini and Project Apollo, which has succeeded in landing the first men on the moon.

The first American astronaut to orbit the earth was Colonel John H. Glenn. In February of 1962, his Mercury capsule made three orbits. This was followed by another three-orbit flight by M. Scott Carpenter in May, and a six-orbit flight by Walter M. Schirra in October. In May of 1963, Gordon Cooper made a twenty-two orbit flight. Since that time, the United States has also sent up pairs of astronauts (in the Gemini program), and successfully carried out docking maneuvers in space. Both the Soviet Union and the United States have also sent men on space walks outside their orbiting capsules.

The Apollo project, which is to end in 1972, achieved the ultimate in manned space flights. In July of 1969 Apollo Eleven succeeded in landing Neil Armstrong and Edwin Aldrin as the first men on the moon. It was as Armstrong said when he alighted on the moon's surface: "One small step for man, one giant step for mankind." The great cost of continuing these and other projects however argues well for international cooperation, for man will continue to seek the stars.

Scientific achievements have become part of the cold war. Both the United States and Russia are trying to attain much the same goals in space technology, but their methods and purposes are different. The U.S. program is under civilian control, and its successes and failures have been well-publicized. The Soviet program continues to be conducted in great secrecy and, seemingly, under military control. However, on the same day that the tragic space accident occurred in the United States, sixty-two nations, including the U.S. and the USSR signed an historic treaty to limit military activities in outer space. Mistrust and suspicion exist between the Soviet Union and the United States, and unfortunate emphasis is placed upon prestige and a "space race." The real goals of all space programs are expansion of knowledge and exploration of the universe.

New scientific gains can make the world a better place in which to live. If military might were the only goal of the United States and the Soviet Union, the future would be grim indeed. An arms race between the two countries to invent still more deadly weapons would bring no blessings to the peoples of the earth. But hopefully, men will apply new scientific knowledge for the benefit of all mankind.

The atomic power that destroyed Hiroshima and Nagasaki in World War II, offers a promise of a virtually inexhaustible source of energy. Throughout *Story of Nations* you have read how each nation's industrial development has been helped or hindered by its natural resources. The use of atomic power offers men everywhere—especially in the emerging and underdeveloped nations—a tremendous opportunity to acquire the benefits of technology and raise their standard of living.

In the industrialized countries of Western Europe that lack oil, atomic plants are being built rapidly. In 1956 Britain put into operation the world's first nuclear power station, and she plans to have over twenty generating plants by 1970. The six Common Market nations—France, Germany, Italy, Belgium, Luxembourg, and the Netherlands—have created an organization called *Euratom* to build atomic plants. Within twenty-five years Western Europe hopes to get most of its electricity from atomic power.

No one can deny the great achievements made by man in his efforts to conquer space. In terms of technical accomplishment and human adventure and talent, all else seems insignificant, But the problems of man on earth still defy solution. War, poverty, racism, disease, pollution of the atmosphere and the water, the population explosion, are still very real.

Chapter Check-up

1. What was the purpose of the International Geophysical Year?
2. What was the highlight of the IGY?
3. Should the "race for space" be only a Russian or U.S. concern? Explain your answer.
4. Is science and technology the answer to man's problems? Explain your answer.
5. Can man learn from history? Explain your answer.

Space Photos of the Earth and the Moon. In August and November 1966, the United States placed two satellites, called Lunar Orbiters I and II, in orbit around the moon. Both were equipped with cameras that took pictures on photographic film and processed them automatically. The high quality photographs were then relayed to earth by television. The picture on the top was taken by the Lunar Orbiter II. It shows the floor of the crater Copernicus which is visible from the earth with a good pair of binoculars. Lunar Orbiter II was twenty-eight miles above the moon's surface when this picture was taken. Copernicus is sixty miles in diameter and two miles deep. The distance from the lunar horizon to the base of the photograph is about one hundred eighty miles. The picture at the bottom was taken by Lunar Orbiter I and shows the first view of the earth taken from a spacecraft in orbit around the moon. In the foreground is the surface of the moon.

Toward World Understanding: SYNOPSIS

The story of the contemporary world is a mixed one—a story of progress and turmoil, of hope and fear. The years since World War II have been filled with international crises, tensions between East and West, and a cold war that has made the future uncertain. Although Russia had been an ally of the United States during World War II, it became apparent soon afterward that she was unwilling to co-operate in establishing peace. As the home of communism, she was bent on spreading her doctrines throughout the world. But the Western democracies replied to the Soviet challenge by such counter-measures as the Truman Doctrine, the Marshall Plan, and NATO. Recently, there have been the beginnings of a genuine search for lasting peace, as both East and West have come to realize that no one would be the winner in a third world war.

Even before the end of World War II, the Allied powers had begun to make plans for the formation of the United Nations, an organization whose purpose was to be the "maintenance of international peace and security." The UN was founded in 1945. Today it has a solid record of accomplishment. Through its various branches, it has helped reduce suffering in the world. It was a major force in establishing the nation of Israel and, by the use of UN troops, in preventing the spread of communism in Korea.

In 1957, the first Russian earth satellite was launched, an achievement that demonstrated the great technical skill of Soviet scientists. Although Soviet rockets had much greater firing power, American scientists were also able to place satellites in orbit.

In 1969, America became the first nation on the moon. Science and technology had proven itself, but man on earth was still trying to solve problems of his own doing: War, poverty, disease, racism, pollution and over-population. As the world came towards the mid-seventies man began to realize that understanding and love for fellow man were the only real means of achieving peace.

Terms

Be sure that you understand clearly the meaning of each of the following:

Atlantic Charter
United Nations
General Assembly
Security Council
Formosa
WHO
Peoples Republic
UNICEF
Moratorium
Saturn

Balfour Declaration
Iron Curtain
"preventive war"
cold war
Truman Doctrine
Marshall Plan
Berlin Airlift
Common Market
underdeveloped nations
TIROS

NATO
Treaty of Rome
International Geophysical Year
Sputnik
Explorer I
Pollution
astronauts
nuclear test ban treaty
Project Mercury
Apollo

Important People

How has each of the following influenced the story of the modern world?

Trygve Lie	President Truman	King Faisal II	Fuad Chehab
President Eisenhower	George C. Marshall	Abdul Karim el-Kassem	Riza Pahlavi
Count Folke Bernadotte	Kemal Atatürk	Camille Chamoun	Gamal Abdul Nasser
Ralph J. Bunche	Adnan Menderes	Abdullah ibn Hussein	Abdel Sarim Arif
Dr. Chaim Weizmann	King Faisal I	John H. Glenn	Gordon Cooper

Questions for Discussion and Review

1. Do you feel that the UN will be successful in preventing a third world war? Why?
2. Why is the Security Council of the United Nations more powerful than the General Assembly?
3. Why has the UN been unable to establish an effective plan for the control of atomic weapons?
4. What have been some of the accomplishments of the UN?
5. What solution would you offer to the problem of Arab antagonism toward Israel?
6. Do you think the United States should strive continually to surpass Russia in science, education, and armaments?
7. Do you agree with the statement "There is no such thing as a good war or a bad peace"? Why or why not?
8. Why is world peace especially important today?

Interesting Things to Do

1. On an outline map of the world, show the Communist and Communist-dominated nations in red and the free nations in blue. Use another color for those countries that have tried not to take sides.
2. Make a map of the Middle East. Carefully label the countries, oceans, and seas and indicate which of the countries have oil. Use colors to indicate which nations are pro-Western, which are anti-Western, and which are neutral.
3. Make a chart showing the organization of the United Nations and its agencies.
4. Prepare a UN bulletin board for your classroom. Include the Preamble to the Charter, a chart of the UN organization, and other materials illustrating the work and accomplishments of the UN and its agencies. See the books listed in the bibliography below for source materials.
5. Arrange and present an informal debate on the topic: *Resolved,* That a world government should be formed to replace the United Nations.
6. Re-enact a session of the Security Council, letting members of your class represent different countries. Let the representatives try to solve some critical question, such as the plan for atomic disarmament.
7. Present an oral report to the class on the purpose and achievements of the International Geophysical Year.
8. Compile a notebook concerning current events in the nations of the Middle East. At the end of a week, summarize for the class the happenings in this important area.
9. Write a radio script for Voice of America to be broadcast to the Middle East, setting forth the advantages of democracy and the dangers of communism.
10. Complete your "Who's Who in World History" series by writing brief biographies of one or more of today's important world leaders.

Interesting Reading about Space and the Search for Peace

Bingham, June, *U Thant*, Knopf.

Caidin, Martin, *The Greatest Challenge*, Dutton.

Clarke, Arthur C., and Editors of Life, *Man and Space*, Time, Inc.

Dean, G. E., *Report on the Atom*, Knopf. A former chairman of the United States Atomic Energy Commission presents a history of atomic development.

Eichelburger, Clark M., *UN: The First Twenty Years*, Harper & Row.

Gallant, Roy A., *Man's Reach into Space*, Doubleday.

*Galt, T. F., *Story of Peace and War*, Crowell Collier. The United Nations' and the world's attempt to find peace.

Howard, William E., and James Baar, *Spacecraft and Missiles of the World;* Harcourt, Brace & World.

Roosevelt, Eleanor, and Ferris, Helen, *Partners: the United Nations and Youth*, Doubleday. An account of what the United Nations has done for children throughout the world.

UNESCO, *UNESCO: a World Programme*, Columbia Press pamphlet.

United Nations Department of Public Information, Columbia Press. Various UN publications.

Wade, W. W., *UN Today*, Wilson.

Wadsworth, James J., *The Glass House*, Praeger. The UN in action.

* Indicates easy reading

Acknowledgements

For the black and white and color photographs on the following pages, we gratefully credit:

Acme Photo (UPI) 718
Alinari 75 top, 79 bot, 81, 87 bot, 91, 95, 98, 99, 103, 114 bot, 117, 130, 146, 148, 151, 204, 222, 226 top, 227, 394, 419
Allen Memorial Art Museum, Oberlin College, Oberlin, Ohio 295 top
Alpha Photo Associates 367
Courtesy of the American Museum of Natural History 6 both, 7 bot, 9
Anderson (Alinari) 86, 122, 123, 144 top, 149, 154, 155, 219, 393
Jean Anderson 89 both
Arab Information Center 157, 637
Roloff Beny 73
Bettmann Archive 83, 192, 196, 198, 199, 203 top, 210, 243, 263, 274, 276, 278, 292 left, 293, 334 top, 340, 355, 371, 383 bot, 396, 420, 421, 429, 437, 438, 447, 450, 465, 469 both, 503, 507, 517, 672, 684, 710
Bibliotheque Nationale, Paris 230
Black Star 24 (Tor Eigeland), 298 (D. McCoy), 299 (Brian Seed), 310 (Tom Picton), 375, 406, 454, 458, 459 (Dever), 460 (Douglas Slacombe), 526, 541 bot, 552, 564, 609, 617 both (John Launois), 651 bot, 660 (Lebeck), 745 bot
British Information Service 258, 273, 284 top, 640, 658 bot
Trustees of the British Museum 49, 63, 79, 118, 170, 397
Brown Brothers 65, 132, 195
Busch-Reisinger Museum, Harvard University 240

Culver Pictures 74, 77 top, 114, 115 bot, 119, 173, 175, 185, 193, 254, 260, 262, 268, 270, 271, 272, 286 top, 288, 300, 301, 304, 325, 337, 359 r, 368, 370 top, 372, 399, 408, 410, 411, 420 l&r, 430 both, 445, 466, 467, 468, 472, 491 both, 493 r, 536, 540, 541 top, 570, 593, 601, 603 r, 618, 671, 675, 676, 699, 706, 708, 711, 712, 713, 719

Richard Davis 677 top, 682, 686 both

Courtesy, Mrs. J. Dent-Brocklehurst (Royal Academy Photo) 266

Russell Dian 343

Dublin, Department of External Affairs 252

Eastfoto 604, 707, 763

Edinburgh University Library 142 ctr

European Art Color Slides Company 101, 112, 373 top

Ewing Galloway 30, 73, 77 bot, 90, 201, 208 both, 220, 251, 279, 297, 321, 324, 428, 474, 489, 516, 551, 571, 575 l, 580 (Deane Dickson), 596, 615, 619 l, 658, 679

Fototeca 125

Freelance Photographers Guild (Kurt Lubinski) 363

Freer Gallery of Art, Smithsonian Institution, Washington, D.C. 594

French Embassy Press & Information Division 334, 359

French Government Tourist Office 209

The Frick Collection 153

Philip D. Gendreau (Bettmann Archive) 110, 223, 691

German Information Center (Ted Russell) 433

Giraudon, 361, 107, 131, 238, 328, 336 top, 339, 343, 344

Andre Held 92

Hirmer Fotoarchiv 41, 69, 142

Henry E. Huntington Library and Art Gallery, San Marino, California 295 bot

Imperial War Museum, London 735

Government of India Tourist Office 564, 565, 568

Information Service of India 584

IBM 225 bot

Italian Government Travel Office 426

Japan National Tourist Organization 611, 614, 619 r, 627

Louvre, Paris 36 top

Magnum 7 (Ian Berry), 9 (Elliott Erwitt), 15 (Erich Lessing, 20 (Elliott Erwitt), 32 (René Burri), 39 (Elliott Erwitt), 97 (Erich Lessing), 141 (Erich Lessing), 165 (Bruno Barbey), 169 (Bruno Barbey), 177 (Erich Hartmann), 179 (Bruno Barbey), 256 (Erich Lessing), 317 (Marc Riboud), 387 (David Seymour), 391 (Elliott Erwitt), 405 (Robert Capa), 415 (Ernst Haas), 498 (Bruno Barbey), 520 (Burt Glinn), 529 (Bruno Barbey), 559 (Marilyn Silverstone) 569 (Marilyn Silverstone), 573 (Bruno Barbey), 578 (Marc Riboud), 579 (René Burri), 589 (Burt Glinn), 595 (Marc Riboud), 595 (Marc Riboud), 603 l (George Rodger), 606 (Marc Riboud), 622 (Burt Glinn), 633 (Marilyn Silverstone), 641 (Marilyn Silverstone), 650 (Inge Morath), 653 (Marc Riboud), 665 (Cornell Capa), 669 (René Burri), 670 (Sergio Larrain), 673 (René Burri), 687 top (René Burri), 689 (Sergio Larrain), 743 top l, bot ctr, bot (Robert Capa), 769 (Bob Henriques), 775 (Bruno Barbey), 777 (Bruno Barbey)

Reproduced by courtesy of Bill Mauldin. Drawings copyrighted © 1944 by United Features Syndicate, Inc.; Copyright © 1945 Bill Mauldin's *Army* 741

Francis G. Mayer 29, 32, 179, 186, 187, 351, 354, 380, 381, 625

Metropolitan Museum of Art 19, 22, 23, 27, 31, 35, 51 bot, 84, 87 top, 127, 142, 152, 161, 181, 215, 235 ctr, 267, 283, 331, 345, 353 bot, 411, 412, 583

Monkmeyer Press Photo 485, 673, 680, 681, 692, 694, 737, 742, 743 top r

Mt. Wilson and Palomar Observatories 3

Courtesy Museum of Fine Arts, Boston 613

Collection, Museum of Modern Art, New York 353 top, 382 both

Museum of Primitive Art 662

NASA 781, 783 both

The National Gallery, London 231 bot, 378

National Gallery of Art, Washington, D.C. 225 top, 379, 512

National Portrait Gallery, London 287 both

Netherlands Information Service 383

New York Herald Tribune (F. Strothmann) 727

New York Public Library 94, 150, 171, 189, 211, 224, 231 top, 233, 235 l&r, 237, 241, 242, 255, 261, 277, 280, 286 bot, 292 r, 304 top, 322 bot, 333, 335, 336 bot, 341, 420 l, 439, 443, 449, 451, 464, 525, 528, 530, 531, 532, 537

Orient and Occident 446

Oriental Institute 66

AB Orrefors Glasbruk, Sweden 495

Pan American Airlines 28, 462

Peabody Museum (Dordogne Project), Harvard University 1

Peace Corps 646, 771 (Paul Conklin)

Photo Researchers, Inc. 4, 160 (Fritz Henle), 203 bot, 247 (Tom Hollyman), 487 (Fritz Henle)

Pix, Inc. 40, 40 l ctr, 40 l bot (Günther Reitz), 348 (Leon Herschritt), 544

Rapho-Guillumette Pictures 356, 403 (Bernard B. Silberstein), 461 bot, 482 bot (Davis Pratt), 563

(Bradley Smith), 567, 574 (Bradley Smith), 575, 643 top, 644, 677, 700
Royal Danish Ministry Press Department 494 both
Scala New York/Florence 24, 33, 75, 126, 128, 129, 147, 182, 226 both, 227, 228, 269, 298, 342, 465, 616 (Minoru Warashina, Orion Press)
Rev. Raymond V. Schoder, S.J. 80
Shostal Associates 303 r (R. V. Johnson), 306 (Robert Leahey), 350 (Ray Manley), 376 top (Emily Bush), 376 bot (Robert E. Gerlach), 612, 620 (Dave Forbert)
Information Service of South Africa 651
South Africa Railways 643 bot
Sovfoto 542, 543, 545, 738 bot, 743 ctr
Spanish National Tourist Office 391 bot
Standard Oil Company (N.J.) 690, 691 top, 693, 697, 778
Stedelijk Museum, Amsterdam 373 bot
Swedish Information Service 493 both
Swiss National Tourist Office 471 both, 475
Three Lions 24, 115, 172, 303 l (Nocella), 424, 462, 555 (Almasy), 585 (Harrington), 695, 732
Trans World Airlines 19, 188, 395, 442, 645
Trinity College Dublin Library 190
United Nations 488 (Karsh, Ottawa), 581 bot, 643, 649, 753, 756, 757, 758, 759 bot
United Press International 605, 643 bot r
United States Army 703
University Museum, Philadelphia 51 top, 53
University Prints 352
Tony Vaccarro 40 top
Wadsworth Atheneum 82
Wide World Photos 290, 308, 346, 404, 406, 425, 455, 461 top, 496 left, 511, 515, 546, 572, 576, 581 top, 608, 610, 623, 647, 683, 717, 719, 720, 723, 724, 725, 726, 729 both, 734, 736, 740, 744, 754, 755, 759, 760, 762, 764, 767, 768
Herbert D. Willians 52
Woodfin Camp & Associates 329 (Adam Woolfitt), 342 (Adam Woolfitt), 643, 654, 655 top & bot, 656, 657, 661 (all by Marc & Evelyne Bernheim), 685 (Toby Molenaar), 687 (Loren MacIntyre)

Index